WileyPLUS

W9-BIU-387

WileyPLUS gives you the freedom and flexibility to tailor curated content and easily manage your course to keep students engaged and on track.

When course materials are presented in an organized way, students are more likely to stay focused, develop mastery, and participate in class. WileyPLUS gives students a clear path through the course material.

Starting with Wiley's quality curated content, you can customize your course by hiding or rearranging learning objectives, setting the pacing of content, and even integrating videos, files, or links to relevant material. The easy-to-use, intuitive interface saves you time getting started, managing day-to-day class activities, and helping individual students stay on track.

Customized Content
Using the content editor, you can add videos, documents, pages, or relevant links to keep students motivated.

Interactive eTextbook
Students can easily search content, highlight and take notes, access instructor's notes and highlights, and read offline.

Drag-and-Drop Customization
Quick reordering of learning objectives and modules lets you match content to your needs.

Linear Design and Organization
Customizable modules organized by learning objective include eTextbook content, videos, animations, interactives, and practice questions.

Calendar
The drag-and-drop calendar syncs with other features in WileyPLUS—like assignments, syllabus, and grades—so that one change on the calendar shows up in all places.

Instructor App
You can modify due dates, monitor assignment submissions, change grades, and communicate with your students all from your phone.

www.wileyplus.com/instructors

WILEY

Business Statistics

Third Canadian Edition

Business Statistics

For Contemporary Decision-Making

Third Canadian Edition

KEN BLACK
University of Houston—Clear Lake

TIFFANY BAYLEY
University of Western Ontario

IGNACIO CASTILLO
Wilfrid Laurier University

WILEY

DIRECTOR, BUSINESS, ACCOUNTING, AND FINANCE	Michael McDonald
EDITOR	Alden Farrar
EDITORIAL ASSISTANT	Cecilia Morales
ASSOCIATE INSTRUCTIONAL DESIGNER	Daleara Hirjikaka
PRODUCT DESIGN MANAGER	Karen Staudinger
MARKETING MANAGER	Jenny Geiler
SENIOR CONTENT MANAGER	Dorothy Sinclair
SENIOR COURSE PRODUCTION OPERATIONS SPECIALIST	Meaghan MacDonald
DESIGN	Wiley
COVER DESIGN	Joanna Vieira/Wiley

COVER PHOTOGRAPHS: Light trails © John Lund, Getty Images
(*top, left to right*)
Stock market composite © Photographer is my life, Getty Images
Financial charts on tablet © Towfiqu Photography, Getty Images
Using smartphone/laptop for business © Busakorn Pongparnit, Getty Images
Business meeting top view © andresr, Getty Images

This book was set in 9.5/12 STIXTwoText by Lumina Datamatics, Ltd. Printed and bound by Quad Graphics.

Founded in 1807, John Wiley & Sons, Inc. has been a valued source of knowledge and understanding for more than 200 years, helping people around the world meet their needs and fulfill their aspirations. Our company is built on a foundation of principles that include responsibility to the communities we serve and where we live and work. In 2008, we launched a Corporate Citizenship Initiative, a global effort to address the environmental, social, economic, and ethical challenges we face in our business. Among the issues we are addressing are carbon impact, paper specifications and procurement, ethical conduct within our business and among our vendors, and community and charitable support. For more information, please visit our website: www.wiley.com/go/citizenship.

Copyright © 2020 John Wiley & Sons Canada, Ltd.

All rights reserved. No part of this work covered by the copyrights herein may be reproduced, transmitted, or used in any form or by any means—graphic, electronic, or mechanical—without the prior written permission of the publisher.

Any request for photocopying, recording, taping, or inclusion in information storage and retrieval systems of any part of this book shall be directed to The Canadian Copyright Licensing Agency (Access Copyright). For an Access Copyright Licence, visit www.access-copyright.ca or call toll-free, 1-800-893-5777.

Care has been taken to trace ownership of copyright material contained in this text. The publishers will gladly receive any information that will enable them to rectify any erroneous reference or credit line in subsequent editions.

Evaluation copies are provided to qualified academics and professionals for review purposes only, for use in their courses during the next academic year. These copies are licensed and may not be sold or transferred to a third party. Upon completion of the review period, please return the evaluation copy to Wiley. Return instructions and a free-of-charge return shipping label are available at www.wiley.com/go/return label. If you have chosen to adopt this textbook for use in your course, please accept this book as your complimentary desk copy. Outside of the United States, please contact your local representative.

ISBN (e-PUB) 978-1-119-57758-4

The inside back cover will contain printing identification and country of origin if omitted from this page. In addition, if the ISBN on the cover differs from the ISBN on this page, the one on the cover is correct.

Printed and bound in the United States.

V422915_031020

WILEY

90 Eglinton Avenue East, Suite 300
Toronto, Ontario, M4P 2Y3 Canada
Visit our website at: www.wiley.ca

The third Canadian edition of *Business Statistics for Contemporary Decision-Making* continues the tradition of using clear, complete, and student-friendly pedagogy to present and explain business statistics topics. The vast ancillary resources available through *WileyPLUS* complement the text in helping instructors effectively deliver this subject matter and assisting students in their learning.

In the third edition, all the features of the second edition have been updated and changed as needed to reflect today's business world. A new field of business methodology and quantitative investigation, business analytics, has arisen to meet the challenges, opportunities, and potentialities presented to business decision-makers through the advent of big data. Realizing the potential of this new approach, we have infused the third edition with the language of business analytics along with its definitions, approaches, and explanations to help students understand business analytics and the role that business statistics plays in it. To facilitate this, there have been a number of important changes and additions to the third edition.

The title of Chapter 1 has been changed to "Introduction to Statistics and Business Analytics," with new sections on big data and its four dimensions, on the three categories of business analytics, and on data mining and data visualization.

One of the key areas of business analytics is data visualization, a quick and often simple way to obtain an overview of data that has the potential to communicate information to a broader audience. With that in mind, the title of Chapter 2 has been changed to "Visualizing Data with Charts and Graphs." Because business analytics sometimes uses historical data—measures taken over time—to predict what might happen in the future, there is a new section in Chapter 2 entitled "Visualizing Time-Series Data."

The other major changes in the text related to business analytics involve databases. Because business analytics has developed in response to the rise of big data, more emphasis has been placed in the third edition on analyzing databases, with a broader selection of larger databases. In particular, a new feature has been created for the third edition called Big Data Case, which appears at the end of each chapter. The Big Data Case focuses on one large database throughout the text. The American Hospital Association (AHA) database contains data on 12 variables from over 2,000 U.S. hospitals drawn from the AHA's compilation of information from over 6,000 U.S. hospitals in a recent year. In this feature, the student is asked to perform several tasks related to the material introduced in the chapter, using variables, samples, and data from this large database. As students progress through the text, they will become more familiar with the AHA database and will obtain a better understanding of the hospitals under study.

This book is written and designed for a two-semester introductory undergraduate business statistics course or an MBA-level introductory course. In addition, with 19 chapters, this text lends itself nicely to adaptation for a one-semester introductory business statistics course. The text is written with the assumption that the student has a mathematical background in university algebra. No calculus is used in the presentation of material in the text. An underlying philosophical approach to the text is that every statistical tool presented in the book has some business application. While the text contains statistical rigour, it is written so the student can readily see that the proper application of statistics in the business world goes hand in hand with good decision-making. In this edition, statistics are presented as a means for converting data into useful information that can be used to assist business decision-makers as they make more thoughtful, information-based decisions. Thus, the text presents business statistics as "value-added" tools in the process of converting data into useful information.

Changes for the Third Edition

Chapters

In the third edition, the chapter organization remains the same as in the second edition—there are 19 chapters organized into five units. The purpose of the unit organization is to locate chapters with similar topics together, thereby increasing the likelihood that students will grasp the bigger picture of statistics.

Unit I, Introduction, contains the first four chapters of the text. In this unit, students are given some important foundational tools for understanding topics presented in the rest of the course. The titles of two of the chapters in this unit have changed to highlight the new emphasis on business analytics. The Chapter 1 title has changed from "Introduction to Statistics" to "Introduction to Statistics and Business Analytics." The Chapter 2 title has changed from "Charts and Graphs" to "Visualizing Data with Charts and Graphs." In Unit II, Distributions and Sampling, consisting of Chapters 5 through 7, students are presented with six population distributions and two sampling distributions. In Unit III, Making Inferences about Population Parameters, which includes Chapters 8 through 11, students learn about estimating and testing population parameters. Unit IV, Chapters 12 through 15, is called Regression Analysis and Forecasting. In this unit, students explore relationships between variables, including developing models to predict a variable by other variables and developing models to forecast. Unit V, Special Topics, includes nonparametric statistics and quality, which are covered in Chapters 16 through 18. In these chapters, students are presented with a series of well-known nonparametric techniques along with a number of quality-improvement concepts and techniques. This unit also includes Chapter 19 on decision analysis.

Topical Changes

In the third edition, some section and topical changes were made to reflect contemporary usage and the additional inclusion of business analytics. Specifically, new sections have been added to Chapter 1, "Introduction to Business Analytics," that address such topics as big data, business analytics, data mining, and data visualization. Chapter 2 has a new section entitled "Visualizing Time-Series Data." In Chapter 3, a section titled "Descriptive Statistics on the Computer" has been replaced by "Business Analytics Using Descriptive Statistics." Presented in this section are data on unemployment rates in Canada over the past 60 years, which are analyzed using the techniques introduced in the chapter.

In addition, also in Chapter 3, a section "Measures of Central Tendency and Variability: Grouped Data" has been deleted. In the past, this particular section focused on methodologies for the hand calculation of statistics on grouped data that few statisticians, researchers, and analysts still do. However, the concepts of grouped data and the construction of frequency distributions are still presented in Chapter 2. In Chapter 18, "Statistical Quality Control," three of the more current quality topics—value-stream mapping, Kaizen Event, and quality and business analytics—have replaced two of the older quality topics—failure mode and effects analysis (FMEA) and quality circles and Six Sigma teams.

Decision Dilemma and Decision Dilemma Solved

The Decision Dilemmas are real-life business vignettes that open each chapter. They set the tone for the chapter by presenting a business dilemma and asking a number of managerial or statistical questions, the solutions to which require the use of techniques presented in the chapter. The Decision Dilemma Solved feature discusses and answers the managerial and statistical questions posed in the Decision Dilemma, using techniques from the chapter, thus bringing closure to the chapter. All Decision Dilemmas from the second edition have been revised and updated. Solutions given in the Decision Dilemma Solved features have been revised for new data and for new versions of computer output. In addition, in Chapter 6, we present a new Decision Dilemma on CSX Corporation, a leading rail transportation company, and in Chapter 8, we present a Decision Dilemma on the average life of batteries and bulbs.

Thinking Critically About Statistics in Business Today

The third edition includes one or two Thinking Critically About Statistics in Business Today features in every chapter.

This feature (previously entitled *Statistics in Business Today*) presents a real-life example of how the statistics presented in that chapter apply in the business world today. Several of these features have been revised and in some cases replaced with more relevant issues, including "Recycling Statistics," "Newspaper Readership of Canadians," "Risk Taking by Ad Agencies," and "Are Facial Characteristics Correlated with CEO Traits."

Chapter Cases

Every chapter in this text contains a unique business case. All cases in the third edition have been updated for today's market. These business cases are more than just long problems, and in the discussion that follows the business scenario, several issues and questions are posed that can be addressed using techniques presented in the chapter. Some new cases have been added to the third edition, including ones on WestJet airlines, 3M, A&W Restaurants, and Caterpillar Inc.

Problems

Problems and demonstration problems are presented throughout each chapter to give students a chance to apply their new-found knowledge before moving on to other sections. We examined the problems from the second edition for timeliness, appropriateness, and logic before we included them in the third edition. Those that fell short were replaced or rewritten. While the total number of problems in the text is 956, a concerted effort has been made to include only problems that make a significant contribution to the learning process.

All demonstration problems and example problems were thoroughly reviewed and edited for effectiveness. A demonstration problem is an extra example containing both a problem and its solution and is used as an additional pedagogical tool to supplement explanations and examples in the chapters. Virtually all example and demonstration problems in this edition are business oriented and contain the most current data available to us.

Problems are located at the end of most sections in the chapters. A significant number of additional problems are provided at the end of each chapter in the Supplementary Problems. The Supplementary Problems are "scrambled"—problems using various techniques introduced in the chapter are presented in no particular order—so that students can test themselves on their ability to discriminate and differentiate ideas and concepts, and select the appropriate technique to solve each problem.

Databases

Available with the third edition are six databases that provide additional opportunities for students to apply the statistics presented in the text. These six databases represent a variety of business areas: the stock market, international labour, finance, energy, agri-business, and, new to this edition, registered retirement savings plan (RRSP) contributions. The data are gathered from such reliable sources as Statistics Canada, the Toronto Stock Exchange, the Bureau of Labor Statistics of the U.S. Department of Labor, and the Global Environment Outlook (GEO) Data Portal. In the spirit of business analytics and big data, in the third edition, the feature Analyzing the Databases has been renamed Exploring the Databases with Business Analytics.

Student Video Support

With the advent of online business statistics courses, increasingly large class sizes, and the number of commuter students who have very limited access to educational resources on business statistics, it is often difficult for students to get the learning assistance that they need to bridge the gap between theory and application on their own. Two innovative features of the *WileyPLUS* package that address this issue are:

Video Tutorials by Ken Black

An exciting feature of the *WileyPLUS* package that will enhance the effectiveness of student learning in business statistics and significantly enhance the presentation of course material is the series of video tutorials by Ken Black.

There are 21 video tutorial sessions on key difficult topics in business statistics, delivered by Ken Black. The tutorials are:

1. Chapter 1: Levels of Data Measurement
2. Chapter 2: Stem-and-Leaf Plot
3. Chapter 3: Computing Variance and Standard Deviation
4. Chapter 3: Understanding and Using the Empirical Rule
5. Chapter 4: Constructing and Solving Probability Matrices
6. Chapter 4: Solving Probability Word Problems
7. Chapter 5: Solving Binomial Distribution Problems, Part I
8. Chapter 5: Solving Binomial Distribution Problems, Part II
9. Chapter 6: Solving Problems Using the Normal Curve
10. Chapter 7: Solving for Probabilities of Sample Means Using the z Statistic
11. Chapter 8: Confidence Intervals
12. Chapter 8: Determining which Inferential Technique to Use: Confidence Intervals
13. Chapter 9: Hypothesis Testing Using the z Statistic
14. Chapter 9: Establishing Hypotheses
15. Chapter 9: Understanding p Values
16. Chapter 9: Type I and Type II Errors
17. Chapter 9: Two-Tailed Tests
18. Chapter 10: Hypothesis Tests of the Difference in Means of Two Independent Populations Using the t Statistic
19. Chapter 11: Computing and Interpreting a One-Way ANOVA
20. Chapter 12: Testing the Regression Model I—Predicted Values, Residuals, and Sum of Squares of Error
21. Chapter 12: Testing the Regression Model II—Standard Error of the Estimate and r^2

Office Hours Videos by Ignacio Castillo

The third edition includes additions to the library of Office Hours Videos, problem-solving video tutorials based on chapter problems prepared by Canadian author Ignacio Castillo. Word marks in the text indicate problems that are accompanied by online Office Hours Videos.

The videos by Ken Black and Ignacio Castillo are available for adopters on *WileyPLUS* and can easily be uploaded for classroom use to augment lectures and enrich classroom presentations. Each video is around 10 minutes in length.

Features and Benefits

Hallmark Features

Each chapter of the book contains sections called Learning Objectives, Decision Dilemma, Demonstration Problems, Concept Checks, Section Problems, Thinking Critically About Statistics in Business Today, Decision Dilemma Solved, Key Considerations, Why Statistics Is Relevant, Summary of Learning Objectives, Key Terms, Formulas, Supplementary Problems, Exploring the Databases with Business Analytics, Case and Big Data Case, and Using the Computer.

- **Learning Objectives.** Each chapter begins with a statement concerning the chapter's main learning objectives. This statement gives the reader a list of key topics that will be discussed and the goals to be achieved by studying the chapter.
- **Decision Dilemma.** At the beginning of each chapter, a short case describes a real company or business situation in which managerial and statistical questions are raised. In most Decision Dilemmas, actual data are given and the student is asked to consider how the data can be analyzed to answer the questions.

- **Demonstration Problems.** Virtually every section of every chapter in the book contains demonstration problems. A demonstration problem contains both an example problem and its solution, and is used as an additional pedagogical tool to supplement explanations and examples.

- **Concept Checks.** Concept checks are conceptual questions aimed to reinforce the conceptual understanding of the material presented. They are presented following each main section of the chapter. These questions do not require students to use calculations.

- **Section Problems.** Problems for practice are found at the end of almost every section of the text. Most problems use real data gathered from a plethora of sources.

- **Thinking Critically About Statistics in Business Today.** Every chapter in the book contains at least one Thinking Critically feature. These focus boxes contain an interesting application of how techniques from that particular chapter are used in the business world today. They are usually based on real companies, surveys, or published research.

- **Decision Dilemma Solved.** Situated at the start of each End-of-Chapter Review, the Decision Dilemma Solved feature addresses the managerial and statistical questions raised in the Decision Dilemma. Data given in the Decision Dilemma are analyzed computationally and by computer using techniques presented in the chapter. Answers to the managerial and statistical questions raised in the Decision Dilemma are arrived at by applying chapter concepts, thus bringing closure to the chapter.

- **Key Considerations.** With the abundance of statistical data and analysis, there is also considerable potential for the misuse of statistics in business dealings. Each chapter contains an important Key Considerations feature that underscores this potential misuse by discussing such topics as lying with statistics, failing to meet statistical assumptions, and failing to include pertinent information for decision-makers. Many users of statistics are unaware of the traps that await the unwary, and through the Key Considerations feature, instructors can begin to integrate the topic of ethics with applications of business statistics.

- **Why Statistics Is Relevant.** This section in each chapter discusses how the material discussed in the chapter is related to real-life decision-making.

- **Summary of Learning Objectives.** Each chapter concludes with a summary of the important concepts, ideas, and techniques introduced in the chapter. This feature can serve as a preview of the chapter as well as a chapter review.

- **Key Terms.** Important terms appear in colour, and their definitions, where possible, are italicized throughout the text as they are discussed. At the end of the chapter, a list of the key terms from the chapter is presented. In addition, these terms appear with their definitions in the end-of-book Glossary.

- **Formulas.** Important formulas are highlighted in the text to make it easy for students to locate them. In several chapters, formulas are numbered for ease of reference

and clarity if they are referred to more than once. At the end of each chapter, most of the chapter's formulas are listed together as a handy reference.

- **Supplementary Problems.** At the end of each chapter is an extensive set of additional problems. The Supplementary Problems are divided into three groups: Calculating the Statistics, which are strictly computational problems; Testing Your Understanding, which are problems for application and understanding; and Interpreting the Output, which are problems that require the interpretation and analysis of software output.

- **Exploring the Databases with Business Analytics.** There are six major databases located on the student companion website that accompanies the book. The end-of-chapter Exploring the Databases section contains several questions/problems that require the application of techniques from the chapter to data in the variables of the databases. It is assumed that most of these questions/problems will be solved using a computer.

- **Case and Big Data Case.** End-of-chapter cases are based on real companies, many featuring Canadian businesses. These cases give the student an opportunity to use statistical concepts and techniques presented in the chapter to solve a business dilemma. Some cases feature very large companies, while others pertain to smaller businesses that have overcome obstacles to survive and thrive. Most cases include raw data (often large) for analysis, and questions that encourage the student to use several of the techniques presented in the chapter. In many cases, the student must analyze software output in order to reach conclusions or make decisions.

- **Using the Computer.** The Using the Computer section contains directions for producing the Excel for Office 365 software output presented in the chapter. It is assumed that students have a general understanding of a Microsoft environment. Directions include specifics about menu bars, drop-down menus, and dialogue boxes. Each dialogue box is not discussed in detail; the intent is to provide enough information for students to produce the same statistical output analyzed and discussed in the chapter.

Tree Diagram of Inferential Techniques

To assist the student in sorting out the plethora of confidence intervals and hypothesis testing techniques presented in the text, tree diagrams are presented at the beginning of Chapters 8 through 11 and 17, and also comprehensively in Appendix B. The tree diagram in Appendix B displays virtually all of the inferential techniques presented in Chapters 8–11 so that the student can construct a view of the "forest for the trees" and determine how each technique plugs in to the whole. The additional tree diagram at the beginning of each of these four chapters is presented to display the branch of the tree that applies to techniques in that particular chapter. Chapter 17 includes a tree diagram for just the nonparametric statistics presented in that chapter.

In determining which technique to use, there are several key questions that a student should consider. Listed here are some of the key questions (displayed in a list in Appendix B) that delineate what students should ask themselves to determine the appropriate inferential technique for a particular analysis: Does the problem call for estimation (using a confidence interval) or testing (using a hypothesis test)? How many samples are being analyzed? Are you analyzing means, proportions, or variances? If means are being analyzed, is (are) the variance(s) known or not? If means from two samples are being analyzed, are the samples independent or related? If three or more samples are being analyzed, are there one or two independent variables and is there a blocking variable?

Digital Resources for Students and Instructors

Business Statistics, Third Canadian Edition, is completely integrated with *WileyPLUS,* featuring a suite of teaching and learning resources. *WileyPLUS* allows students to create a personalized study plan, assess their progress along the way, and access the content and resources needed to master the material. *WileyPLUS* provides immediate insight into students' strengths and problem areas with visual reports that highlight what's most important for both the instructor and student. Many dynamic resources are integrated into the course to help students build knowledge and understanding, stay motivated, and prepare for decision-making in a real-world context. *WileyPLUS* also includes integrated adaptive practice that helps students build proficiency and use study time most effectively. Additional features of the *WileyPLUS* course include resources for students and instructors.

Resources for Students

- **eBook.**   The complete Vitalsource eBook is available on *WileyPLUS* with highlighting, search, and notetaking capabilities.

- **Lecture Videos.**   There are 21 videos of Ken Black explaining concepts and demonstrating how to work problems for some of the more difficult topics.
- **Office Hours Videos.**   These are worked video examples of selected problems from the text prepared by Canadian author Ignacio Castillo.
- **Data Sets.**   Several problems in the text, along with the case problems and the databases, are available to students in Excel. New for the third edition is the American Hospital Association database for the Big Data Case that is included in each chapter.
- **Student Study Manual.**   Complete solutions to all odd-numbered questions.

Resources for Instructors

- **Data Analytics & Decision-Making Module.**   With the emergence of data analytics transforming the business environment, Wiley has partnered with business leaders in the Business-Higher Education Forum (BHEF) to identify the competencies graduates need to be successful in their careers. As a result, *WileyPLUS* includes a new data analytics module with industry-validated content that prepares operations management students for a changing workforce.
- **Real-World Video Activities.**   A new feature in *WileyPLUS* offers chapter-level graded analysis activities on cutting-edge business video content from Bloomberg.
- **Adaptive Practice.**   This adaptive, personalized learning experience delivers easy-to-use analytics so you can see exactly where your students excel and where they need help.

Other resources include instructors' manuals, solutions manuals, test banks, and clicker questions.

A selection of the ancillary teaching and learning materials is also available on the student and instructor companion site: www.wiley.com/go/blackcanada

---

Acknowledgements

John Wiley & Sons Canada, Ltd., and the authors would like to thank the reviewers who cared enough and took the time to provide us with their excellent insights and advice, which were used to shape and mould the various iterations of the Canadian edition of this text. Our appreciation goes to:

Fouzia Baki, McMaster University
Sylvie Bequet, Bishop's University

Andrew Flostrand, Simon Fraser University
Paramjit Gill, University of British Columbia, Okanagan
Wayne Horn, Carleton University
Muhammad Hossain, MacEwan University
Tracy Jenkin, Queen's University
Denis Keroack, The Northern Alberta Institute of Technology
Ehsan Latif, Thompson Rivers University
Samie Li Shang Ly, Concordia University

Mohammad Mahbobi, Thompson Rivers University
Stan Miles, Thompson Rivers University
Peggy Ng, York University
Cecilia Rodriguez, The Northern Alberta Institute of Technology
Keith Rogers, Queen's University
Brian Smith, McGill University
Don St. Jean, George Brown College
Augustine Wong, York University
Morty Yalovsky, McGill University

Special thanks to our contributors for preparing the various supplements accompanying the text:

Rohit Jindal, Grant MacEwan University
Denis Keroack, The Northern Alberta Institute of Technology
Mark Morpurgo, The Northern Alberta Institute of Technology
Gabriela Schneider
Seema Sehgal, The Northern Alberta Institute of Technology
Wendy Tarrel, Nova Scotia Community College
Emmanuel Wiredu, The Northern Alberta Institute of Technology

There are several people working at or with John Wiley & Sons to bring this edition to fruition whom we would like to thank for their invaluable assistance on the project. Special thanks go to Alden Farrar, Daleara Hirjikaka, Joanna Vieira, Meaghan MacDonald, Deanna Durnford, Audrey McClellan, and Neha Bhargava.

—TIFFANY BAYLEY
—IGNACIO CASTILLO
JANUARY 29, 2020

FOR MATT, DEAN, AND JOAN

THANK YOU FOR THE JOY AND BALANCE YOU BRING ME EVERY DAY. LOVE YOU ALWAYS.
—TIFFANY

FOR MERCY, GARY, AND WALDO THANK YOU FOR YOUR LOVE.
—IGNACIO

About the Authors

KEN BLACK is currently professor of quantitative management in the College of Business at the University of Houston–Clear Lake. Born in Cambridge, Massachusetts, and raised in Missouri, he earned a bachelor's degree in mathematics from Graceland University, a master's degree in math education from the University of Texas at El Paso, a Ph.D. in business administration (management science), and a Ph.D. in educational research from the University of North Texas.

Since joining the faculty of UHCL in 1979, Professor Black has taught all levels of statistics courses, business analytics, forecasting, management science, market research, and production/operations management. He received the 2014 Outstanding Professor Alumni Award from UHCL. In 2005, he was awarded the President's Distinguished Teaching Award for the university. He has published over 20 journal articles and 20 professional papers, as well as two textbooks: *Business Statistics: An Introductory Course* and *Business Statistics for Contemporary Decision-Making*. Dr. Black has consulted for many different companies, including Aetna, the city of Houston, NYLCare, AT&T, Johnson Space Center, Southwest Information Resources, UTMB, and Doctors Hospital at Renaissance. Dr. Black is active in the quality movement and is a certified Master Black Belt in Lean Six Sigma.

Ken Black and his wife, Carolyn, have two daughters, Caycee and Wendi, and a grandson, Antoine. His hobbies include playing the guitar, reading, and travelling.

Courtesy of the University of Houston–Clear Lake

TIFFANY BAYLEY is an assistant professor of management science at the Ivey Business School, University of Western Ontario. She holds a Ph.D. and M.A.Sc in applied operations research from the University of Waterloo, and a B.A.Sc in industrial and manufacturing systems engineering from the University of Windsor. Her research and teaching interests include business analytics; optimization and decomposition approaches for production planning, health care, and supply chain management problems; and experiential learning design for operations management and business analytics pedagogy. Dr. Bayley received the Natural Sciences and Engineering Research Council of Canada (NSERC) Alexander Graham Bell Canada Graduate Scholarship and the NSERC Postgraduate Doctoral Scholarship. She is a member of the Canadian Operational Research Society and the Institute for Operations Research and the Management Sciences.

Courtesy of Tiffany Bayley

IGNACIO CASTILLO is a professor of operations and decision sciences at the Lazaridis School of Business & Economics, Wilfrid Laurier University. He holds a Ph.D. in industrial engineering from Texas A&M University, an M.S.E. in industrial engineering from Arizona State University, and a B.S. (magna cum laude) in applied sciences from Universidad San Francisco de Quito, Ecuador. His research and teaching interests include business statistics, facility location, facility layout and material handling systems, manufacturing and service operations and logistics, and sustainable and closed-loop supply chain management. Dr. Castillo is a former LASPAU Scholar and Glenn Carroll Teaching Fellow, has served as adjunct faculty at the University of Alberta and the University of Waterloo, and is a member of the Alpha Pi Mu Industrial Engineering Honor Society, the Honor Society of Phi Kappa Phi, and Pinnacle Honor Society.

Courtesy of Wilfrid Laurier University

Brief Contents

Contents

17 Nonparametric Statistics 17-1

18 Statistical Quality Control 18-1

19 Decision Analysis 19-1

CHAPTER 1

Introduction to Statistics and Business Analytics

LEARNING OBJECTIVES

The primary objective of Chapter 1 is to introduce you to the world of statistics and analytics thereby enabling you to:

1.1 Define important statistical terms, including population, sample, and parameter, as they relate to descriptive and inferential statistics.

1.2 Explain the difference between variables, measurement, and data, and compare the four different levels of data: nominal, ordinal, interval, and ratio.

1.3 Explain the differences between the four dimensions of big data.

1.4 Compare and contrast the three categories of business analytics.

1.5 Describe the data mining and data visualization processes.

Decision Dilemma

Statistics Describe the State of Business in India's Countryside

India is the second-most-populous country in the world, with more than 1.25-billion people. Nearly 70% of the people live in rural areas, scattered about the countryside in 600,000 villages. In fact, it may be said that more than one in every ten people in the world live in rural India. While it has a per capita income of less than US$1 per day, rural India, which has been described in the past as poor and semi-literate, now contributes about one-half of the country's gross national product (GNP). However, rural India still has the most households in the world without electricity, with the number of such households exceeding 300,000.

Despite its poverty and economic disadvantages, there are compelling reasons for companies to market their goods and services to rural India. This market has been growing at five times the rate of the urban Indian market. There is increasing agricultural productivity, leading to growth in disposable income, and there is a reduction in the gap between the tastes of urban and rural customers. The literacy level is increasing, and people are becoming more conscious of their lifestyles and of opportunities for a better life. Around 60% of all middle-income

iStock.com/Kailash soni

households in India are in rural areas, and more than one-third of all rural households now have a main source of income other than farming. Virtually every home has a radio, almost one-third have a television, and more than one-half of rural households benefit from banking services. Forty-two percent of the people living in India's villages and small towns use toothpaste, and that proportion is increasing as rural incomes rise and as there is greater awareness of oral hygiene.

Consumers are gaining more disposable income due to the movement of manufacturing jobs to rural areas. It is estimated that nearly 75% of the factories that opened in India in the past decade were built in rural areas. Products that are selling well to people in rural India include televisions, fans, bicycles, bath soap, two- or three-wheelers, and cars. According to MART, a New Delhi–based research organization, rural India buys 46% of all soft drinks and 49% of motorcycles sold in India. Because of such factors, many global and Indian firms, such as Microsoft, General Electric, Kellogg's, Colgate-Palmolive, Hindustan-Unilever, Godrej, Nirma, Novartis, Dabur, Tata Motors, and Vodafone India, have entered the rural Indian market with enthusiasm. Marketing to rural customers often involves persuading them to try products that they may not have used before. Rural India is a huge, relatively untapped market for businesses. However, entering such a market is not without risks and obstacles. The dilemma facing companies is whether to enter this marketplace and, if so, to what extent and how.

Managerial, Statistical, and Analytical Questions

1. Are the statistics presented in this report exact figures or estimates?

2. How and where could the business analysts have gathered such data?

3. In measuring the potential of the rural Indian marketplace, what other statistics could have been gathered?

4. What levels of data measurement are represented by data on rural India?

5. How can managers use these and other statistics to make better decisions about entering this marketplace?

6. What big data might be available on rural India?

Sources: Adapted from "Marketing to Rural India: Making the Ends Meet," *India Knowledge@Wharton*, March 8, 2007, knowledge.wharton. upenn.edu/india/article.cfm?articleid=4172; "Rural Segment Quickly Catching Up," India Brand Equity Foundation (IBEF), September 2015, www.ibef.org/industry/indian-rural-market.aspx; Mamta Kapur, Sanjay Dawar, and Vineet R. Ahuja, "Unlocking the Wealth in Rural Markets," *Harvard Business Review*, June 2014, hbr.org/2014/06/unlocking-the-wealth-in-rural-markets; Nancy Joseph, "Much of Rural India Still Waits for Electricity," *Perspectives Newsletter*, University of Washington, October 2013, artsci.washington.edu/news/2013-10/much-rural-india-still-waits-electricity.

Introduction

Every minute of the working day, decisions are made by businesses around the world that determine whether companies will be profitable and grow or whether they will stagnate and die. Most of these decisions are made with the assistance of information gathered about the marketplace, the economic and financial environment, the workforce, the competition, and other factors. Such information usually comes in the form of data or is accompanied by data. Business statistics and business analytics provide the tools by which such data are collected, analyzed, summarized, and presented to facilitate the decision-making process, and both business statistics and business analytics play an important role in the ongoing saga of decision-making within the dynamic world of business.

There is a wide variety of uses and applications of statistics in business. Several examples follow.

- A survey of 1,465 workers by Hotjobs found that 55% of workers believe that the quality of their work is perceived the same when they work remotely as when they are physically in the office.

- In a survey of 477 executives by the Association of Executive Search Consultants, 48% of men and 67% of women said they were more likely to negotiate for less business travel compared with five years earlier.

- A survey of 1,007 adults by RBC Capital Markets showed that 37% of adults would be willing to drive 8 to 15 km to save 5 cents on a litre of gas.

- A Deloitte Retail "Green" survey of 1,080 adults revealed that 54% agreed that plastic, non-compostable shopping bags should be banned.

- A survey by Statistics Canada determined that in 2017, the average annual household net expenditure in Canada was $86,070 and that households spent an average of $3,986 annually on recreation.[1] In addition, employment rates and wages increased more in Canada than in the United States between 2000 and 2017.[2]

---

[1] Statistics Canada, "Household Spending by Household Type," Table 11-10-0222-01, December 12, 2018, www150.statcan.gc.ca/t1/tbl1/en/tv.action?pid=1110022401.

[2] André Bernard and René Morissette, Statistics Canada, "Economic Insights: Employment Rates and Wages of Core-Aged Workers in Canada and the United States, 2000 to 2017," June 4, 2018, www150.statcan.gc.ca/n1/pub/11-626-x/11-626-x2018082-eng.htm.

- In a 2014 survey of 17 countries conducted by GlobeScan for the National Geographic Society, Canada ranked 16th out of 17 when it came to environmental and climate footprint. This was due mostly to Canadian preferences for bigger houses and an established culture of using privately owned cars as opposed to transit.[3]

Note that, in most of these examples, business analysts have conducted a study and provided rich and interesting information that can be used in business decision-making.

In this text, we will examine several types of graphs for visualizing data as we study ways to arrange or structure data into forms that are both meaningful and useful to decision-makers. We will learn about techniques for sampling from a population that allow studies of the business world to be conducted in a less expensive and more timely manner. We will explore various ways to forecast future values and we will examine techniques for predicting trends. This text also includes many statistical and analytics tools for testing hypotheses and for estimating population values. These and many other exciting statistics and statistical techniques await us on this journey through business statistics and analytics. Let us begin.

1.1 | Basic Statistical Concepts

LEARNING OBJECTIVE 1.1

Define important statistical terms, including population, sample, and parameter, as they relate to descriptive and inferential statistics.

Business statistics, like many areas of study, has its own language. It is important to begin our study with an introduction of some basic concepts in order to understand and communicate about the subject. We begin with a discussion of the word *statistics*. This word has many different meanings in our culture. *Webster's Third New International Dictionary* gives a comprehensive definition of **statistics** as *a science dealing with the collection, analysis, interpretation, and presentation of numerical data*. Viewed from this perspective, statistics includes all the topics presented in this text. **Figure 1.1** captures the key elements of business statistics.

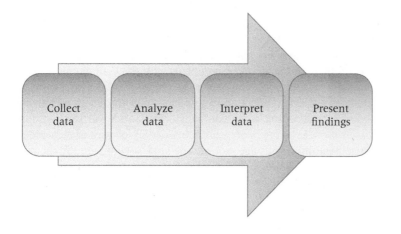

FIGURE 1.1 The Key Elements of Statistics

The study of statistics can be organized in a variety of ways. One of the main ways is to subdivide statistics into two branches: descriptive statistics and inferential statistics. To understand the difference between descriptive and inferential statistics, definitions of *population*

---

[3] GlobeScan, "Environmental Behaviour of Canadians: Mining National Geographic's and GlobeScan's Greendex Research," November 3, 2016, globescan.com/wp-content/uploads/2017/07/GlobeScan_PCO_Greendex_CAN_Report.pdf.

and *sample* are helpful. *Webster's Third New International Dictionary* defines **population** as *a collection of persons, objects, or items of interest.* The population can be a widely defined category, such as "all automobiles," or it can be narrowly defined, such as "all Ford Escape crossover vehicles produced from Year 1 to Year 2." A population can be a group of people, such as "all workers employed by Microsoft," or it can be a set of objects, such as "all Toyota RAV4s produced in February of Year 1 by Toyota Canada at the Woodstock, Ontario, plant." The analyst defines the population to be whatever he or she is studying. When analysts *gather data from the whole population for a given measurement of interest,* they call it a **census**. Most people are familiar with the Canadian Census. Every five years, the government attempts to measure all persons living in this country. As another example, if an analyst is interested in ascertaining the grade point average for all students at the University of Toronto, one way to do so is to conduct a census of all students currently enrolled there.

A **sample** is *a portion of the whole* and, if properly taken, is representative of the whole. For various reasons (explained in Chapter 7), analysts often prefer to work with a sample of the population instead of the entire population. For example, in conducting quality control experiments to determine the average life of light bulbs, a light bulb manufacturer might randomly sample only 75 light bulbs during a production run. Because of time and money limitations, a human resources manager might take a random sample of 40 employees instead of using a census to measure company morale.

If a business analyst is *using data gathered on a group to describe or reach conclusions about that same group,* the statistics are called **descriptive statistics**. For example, if an instructor produces statistics to summarize a class's examination results and uses those statistics to reach conclusions about that class only, the statistics are descriptive. The instructor can use these statistics to discuss class average, talk about the range of class scores, or present any other data measurements for the class based on the test.

Most athletic statistics, such as batting averages, save percentages, and first downs, are descriptive statistics because they are used to describe an individual or team effort. Many of the statistical data generated by businesses are descriptive. They might include number of employees on vacation during June, average salary at the Edmonton office, corporate sales for the current fiscal year, average managerial satisfaction score on a company-wide census of employee attitudes, and average return on investment for Lululemon for the first ten years of operations.

Another type of statistics is called **inferential statistics**. If an analyst *gathers data from a sample and uses the statistics generated to reach conclusions about the population from which the sample was taken,* the statistics are inferential statistics. The data gathered from the sample are used to infer something about a larger group. Inferential statistics are sometimes referred to as *inductive statistics.* The use and importance of inferential statistics continue to grow.

One application of inferential statistics is in pharmaceutical research. Some new drugs are expensive to produce, and therefore tests must be limited to small samples of patients. Utilizing inferential statistics, analysts can design experiments with small, randomly selected samples of patients and attempt to reach conclusions and make inferences about the population.

Market analysts use inferential statistics to study the impact of advertising on various market segments. Suppose a soft drink company creates an advertisement depicting a dispensing machine that talks to the buyer, and market analysts want to measure the impact of the new advertisement on various age groups. The analyst could stratify the population into age categories ranging from young to old, randomly sample each stratum, and use inferential statistics to determine the effectiveness of the advertisement for the various age groups in the population. The advantage of using inferential statistics is that they enable the analyst to effectively study a wide range of phenomena without having to conduct a census. Most of the topics discussed in this text pertain to inferential statistics.

A *descriptive measure of the population* is called a **parameter**. Parameters are usually denoted by Greek letters. Examples of parameters are population mean (μ), population variance (σ^2), and population standard deviation (σ). A *descriptive measure of a sample* is called a **statistic**. Statistics are usually denoted by Roman letters. Examples of statistics are sample mean ($\bar{x}$), sample variance (s^2), and sample standard deviation (s).

Differentiation between the terms *parameter* and *statistic* is important only in the use of inferential statistics. A business analyst often wants to estimate the value of a parameter or conduct tests about the parameter. However, the calculation of parameters is usually either impossible or infeasible because of the amount of time and money required to take a census. In such cases, the business analyst can take a random sample of the population, calculate a statistic on the sample, and infer by estimation the value of the parameter. The basis for inferential statistics, then, is the ability to make decisions about parameters without having to complete a census of the population.

For example, a manufacturer of washing machines would probably want to determine the average number of loads that a new machine can wash before it needs repairs. The parameter is the population mean or average number of washes per machine before repair. A company analyst takes a sample of machines, computes the number of washes before repair for each machine, averages the numbers, and estimates the population value or parameter by using the statistic, which in this case is the sample average. **Figure 1.2** demonstrates the inferential process.

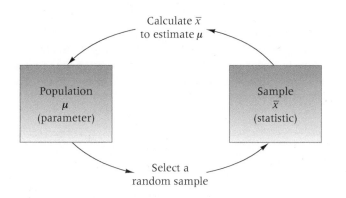

Inferences about parameters are made under uncertainty. Unless parameters are computed directly from the population, the statistician never knows with certainty whether the estimates or inferences made from samples are true. In an effort to estimate the level of confidence in the result of the process, statisticians use probability statements. For this and other reasons, part of this text is devoted to probability (Chapter 4).

Concept Check

Fill in the blanks.

1. Descriptive statistics can be used to _____ the data to describe a data sample either numerically or graphically.
2. Statistical inference is inference about a _____ from a random data _____ drawn from it.

1.2 | Variables, Data, and Data Measurement

LEARNING OBJECTIVE 1.2

Explain the difference between variables, measurement, and data, and compare the four different levels of data: nominal, ordinal, interval, and ratio.

Business statistics is about measuring phenomena in the business world and organizing, analyzing, and presenting the resulting numerical information in such a way that better, more informed business decisions can be made. Most business statistics studies contain variables, measurements, and data.

In business statistics, a **variable** is *a characteristic of any entity being studied that is capable of taking on different values.* Some examples of variables in business might include return on investment, advertising dollars, labour productivity, stock price, historic cost, total sales, market share, age of worker, earnings per share, kilometres driven to work, time spent in store shopping, and many, many others. In business statistics studies, most variables produce a measurement that can be used for analysis. A **measurement** occurs *when a standard process is used to assign numbers to particular attributes or characteristics of a variable.* Many measurements are obvious, such as the time a customer spends shopping in a store, the age of the worker, or the number of kilometres driven to work. However, some measurements, such as labour productivity, customer satisfaction, and return on investment, have to be defined by the business analyst or by experts within the field. Once such measurements are recorded and stored, they can be denoted as "data." It can be said that **data** are *recorded measurements.* The processes of measuring and data gathering are basic to all that we do in business statistics and analytics. It is data that are analyzed by business statisticians and analysts in order to learn more about the variables being studied. Sometimes, sets of data are organized into databases as a way to store data or as a means for more conveniently analyzing data or comparing variables. Valid data are the lifeblood of business statistics and business analytics, and it is important that the business analyst pay thoughtful attention to the creation of meaningful, valid data before embarking on analysis and reaching conclusions (see Thinking Critically About Statistics in Business Today 1.1).

Thinking Critically About Statistics in Business Today 1.1

Cellular Phone Use in Japan

The Communications and Information Network Association of Japan conducts an annual study of cellular phone use in Japan. A recent survey was taken as part of this study using a sample of 1,200 cellphone users split evenly between men and women and almost equally distributed over six age brackets. The survey was administered in the greater Tokyo and Osaka metropolitan areas. The study produced several interesting findings.

Of the respondents, 90.7% said that their main-use terminal was a smartphone, while 9.2% said it was a feature phone. Of the smartphone users, 41.5% reported that their second device was a tablet (with telecom subscription), compared to the response the previous year, where 35.9% said that a tablet was their second device. Smartphone users in the survey reported that the two decisive factors in purchasing a new smartphone were purchase price (87.7%) and monthly payment cost (87.6%). Feature phone users also indicated purchase price and monthly cost as decisive factors in purchasing their next feature phone, with rates of 80.8% and 78.8%, respectively. In terms of usage of smartphone features and services, the most popular use was voice communication (96.3%) followed by SNS message (92.1%) and email (91.8%).

Things to Ponder

1. In what way was this study an example of inferential statistics?
2. What is the population of this study?
3. What are some of the variables being studied?
4. How might a study such as this yield information that is useful to business decision-makers?

Source: Adapted from "CIAJ Releases Report on the Study of Mobile Phone Use," Communications and Information Network Association of Japan (CIAJ), July 26, 2017, www.ciaj.or.jp/en/news/news2017/451.html.

Immense volumes of numerical data are gathered by businesses every day, representing myriad items. For example, numbers represent dollar costs of items produced, geographical locations of retail outlets, masses of shipments, and rankings of employees at yearly reviews. Not all such data should be analyzed in the same way statistically because the entities represented by the numbers are different. For this reason, the business analyst needs to know the *level of data measurement* represented by the numbers being analyzed.

The disparate use of numbers can be illustrated by the numbers 40 and 80, which could represent the masses of two objects being shipped, the ratings received on a consumer test by two different products, or the hockey jersey numbers of a centre and a winger. Although 80 kg is twice as much as 40 kg, the winger is probably not twice as big as the centre! Averaging the two masses seems reasonable but averaging the hockey jersey numbers makes no sense. The appropriateness of the data analysis depends on the level of measurement of the data gathered. The phenomenon represented by the numbers determines the level of data measurement. Four common levels of data measurement are:

Highest level of data measurement

1. Nominal
2. Ordinal
3. Interval
4. Ratio

Nominal is the lowest level of data measurement, followed by ordinal, interval, and ratio. Ratio is the highest level of data, as shown in **Figure 1.3**.

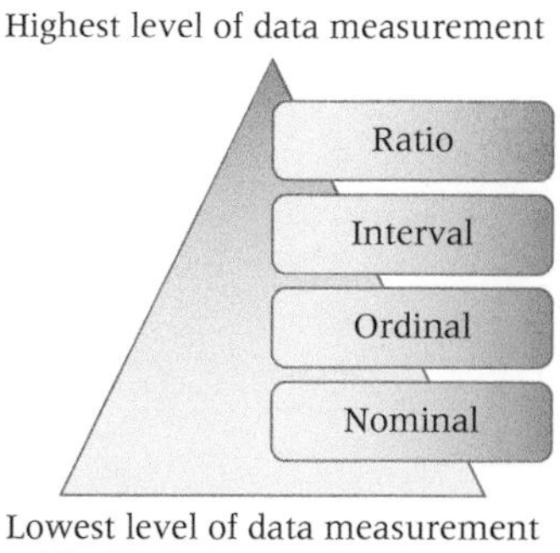

Lowest level of data measurement

FIGURE 1.3 **Hierarchy of Levels of Data**

Nominal Level

The *lowest level of data measurement* is the nominal level. Numbers representing **nominal-level data** (the word *level* is often omitted) can be *used only to classify or categorize.* Employee identification numbers are an example of nominal data. The numbers are used only to differentiate employees and not to make a value statement about them. Many demographic questions in surveys result in data that are nominal because the questions are used for classification only. The following is an example of a question that would result in nominal data:

Which of the following employment classifications best describes your area of work?

a. Educator
b. Construction worker
c. Manufacturing worker
d. Lawyer
e. Doctor
f. Other

Suppose that, for computing purposes, an educator is assigned a 1, a construction worker is assigned a 2, a manufacturing worker is assigned a 3, and so on. These numbers should be used only to classify respondents. The number 1 does not denote the top classification. It is used only to differentiate an educator (1) from a lawyer (4) or any other occupation.

Other types of variables that often produce nominal-level data are sex, religion, ethnicity, geographic location, and place of birth. Social insurance numbers, telephone numbers, and employee ID numbers are further examples of nominal data. Statistical techniques that are appropriate for analyzing nominal data are limited. However, some of the more widely used statistics, such as the chi-square statistic, can be applied to nominal data, often producing useful information.

Ordinal Level

Ordinal-level data measurement is higher than nominal level. In addition to having the nominal-level capabilities, ordinal-level measurement can be used to rank or order objects. For example, using ordinal data, a supervisor can evaluate three employees by ranking their productivity with the numbers 1 through 3. The supervisor could identify one employee as the most productive, one as the least productive, and one as somewhere in between by using ordinal data. However, the supervisor could not use ordinal data to establish that the intervals between the employees ranked 1 and 2 and between the employees ranked 2 and 3 are equal; that is, the supervisor could not say that the differences in the amount of productivity between the workers ranked 1, 2, and 3 are necessarily the same. With ordinal data, the distances between consecutive numbers are not always equal.

Some Likert-type scales on questionnaires are considered by many analysts to be ordinal in level. The following is an example of such a scale:

This computer tutorial is

not helpful	somewhat helpful	moderately helpful	very helpful	extremely helpful
1	2	3	4	5

When this survey question is coded for the computer, only the numbers 1 through 5 will remain, not the descriptions. Virtually everyone would agree that a 5 is higher than a 4 on this scale and that it is possible to rank responses. However, most respondents would not consider the differences between not helpful, somewhat helpful, moderately helpful, very helpful, and extremely helpful to be equal.

Mutual funds are sometimes rated in terms of investment risk by using measures of default risk, currency risk, and interest rate risk. These three measures are applied to investments by rating them as high, medium, or low risk. Suppose high risk is assigned a 3, medium risk a 2, and low risk a 1. If a fund is awarded a 3 rather than a 2, it carries more risk, and so on. However, the differences in risk between categories 1, 2, and 3 are not necessarily equal. Thus, these measurements of risk are only ordinal-level measurements. Another example of the use of ordinal numbers in business is the ranking of the 50 best employers in Canada in *Report on Business* magazine. The numbers ranking the companies are only ordinal in measurement. Certain statistical techniques are specifically suited to ordinal data, but many other techniques are not appropriate for use on ordinal data.

Because nominal and ordinal data are often derived from imprecise measurements such as demographic questions, the categorization of people or objects, or the ranking of items, *nominal and ordinal data* are **nonmetric data** and are sometimes referred to as *qualitative data*.

Interval Level

Interval-level data measurement is the *next to the highest level of data, in which the distances between consecutive numbers have meaning and the data are always numerical.* The distances represented by the differences between consecutive numbers are equal; that is, interval data have equal intervals. An example of interval measurement is Celsius temperature. With Celsius temperature numbers, the temperatures can be ranked, and the amounts of heat between consecutive readings, such as 20°, 21°, and 22°, are the same.

In addition, with interval-level data, the zero point is a matter of convention or convenience and not a natural or fixed zero point. Zero is just another point on the scale and does not mean the absence of the phenomenon. For example, zero degrees Celsius is not the lowest possible temperature. Some other examples of interval-level data are the percentage change in employment, the percentage return on a stock, and the dollar change in share price.

Ratio Level

Ratio-level data measurement is *the highest level of data measurement.* Ratio data *have the same properties as interval data,* but ratio data have an *absolute zero* and *the ratio of two numbers is meaningful.* The notion of absolute zero means that zero is fixed, and *the zero value in the data represents the absence of the characteristic being studied.* The value of zero cannot be arbitrarily assigned because it represents a fixed point. This definition enables the statistician to create *ratios* with the data.

Examples of ratio data are height, mass, time, volume, and Kelvin temperature. With ratio data, an analyst can state that 180 kg of mass is twice as much as 90 kg or, in other words, make a ratio of 180:90. Many of the data gathered by machines in industry are ratio data.

Other examples in the business world that are ratio level in measurement are production cycle time, work measurement time, passenger distance, number of trucks sold, complaints per 10,000 flyers, and number of employees. With ratio-level data, no b factor is required in converting units from one measurement to another, that is, $y = ax$. As an example, in converting height from metres to feet, 1 m = 3.28 ft.

Because interval- and ratio-level data are usually gathered by precise instruments often used in production and engineering processes, in standardized testing, or in standardized accounting procedures, they are called **metric data** and are sometimes referred to as *quantitative* data.

Comparison of the Four Levels of Data

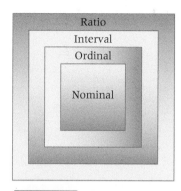

FIGURE 1.4 **Usage Potential of Various Levels of Data**

Figure 1.4 shows the relationships of the usage potential among the four levels of data measurement. The concentric squares denote that each higher level of data can be analyzed by any of the techniques used on lower levels of data but, in addition, can be used in other statistical techniques. Therefore, ratio data can be analyzed by any statistical technique applicable to the other three levels of data plus some others.

Nominal data are the most limited data in terms of the types of statistical analysis that can be used with them. Ordinal data allow the statistician to perform any analysis that can be done with nominal data and some additional ones. With ratio data, a statistician can make ratio comparisons and appropriately do any analysis that can be performed on nominal, ordinal, or interval data. Some statistical techniques require ratio data and cannot be used to analyze other levels of data.

Statistical techniques can be separated into two categories: parametric statistics and nonparametric statistics. **Parametric statistics** require that data be interval or ratio. If the data are nominal or ordinal, **nonparametric statistics** must be used. Nonparametric statistics can also be used to analyze interval or ratio data. This text focuses largely on parametric statistics, with the exception of Chapter 16 and Chapter 17, which contain nonparametric techniques. Thus, much of the material in this text requires interval or ratio data. **Figure 1.5** contains a summary of metric data and nonmetric data.

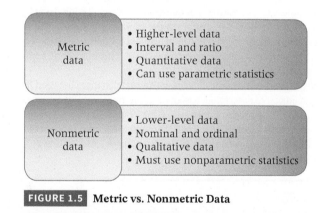

FIGURE 1.5 **Metric vs. Nonmetric Data**

Concept Check

Match the level with the correct measurement.

1. Nominal   **a.** Measures with a fixed zero that means "no quantity"; a constant interval (distance on the scale)

2. Ordinal   **b.** Measures require a fixed distance, but the zero point is arbitrary

3. Interval   **c.** Measures classified by shared attributes (characteristics)

4. Ratio   **d.** Measures by orderings (ranks)

DEMONSTRATION PROBLEM 1.1

Many changes continue to occur in the health-care system. Because of the increasing pressure to deliver a high level of service at increasingly low costs and the need to determine how providers can better serve their patients, hospital administrators sometimes administer a quality satisfaction survey to their patients after release from hospital. The following types of questions are sometimes asked on such a survey. These questions will result in what level of data measurement?

1. How long ago were you released from the hospital?

2. Which type of unit were you in for most of your stay?

   ___Coronary care unit

   ___Intensive care unit

   ___Maternity care unit

   ___Medical unit

   ___Pediatric/children's unit

   ___Surgical unit

3. How serious was your condition when you were first admitted to the hospital?

   __Critical   __Serious   __Moderate   __Minor

4. Rate the skill of your doctor:

   __Excellent   __Very Good   __Good   __Fair   __Poor

5. On the following scale from one to seven, rate the nursing care:

   Poor   1   2   3   4   5   6   7   Excellent

Solution   Question 1 is a time measurement with an absolute zero and is therefore a ratio-level measurement. A person who has been out of the hospital for two weeks has been out twice as long as someone who has been out of the hospital for one week.

Question 2 yields nominal data because the patient is asked only to categorize the type of unit he or she was in. This question does not require a hierarchy or ranking of the type of unit. Questions 3 and 4 are likely to result in ordinal-level data. Suppose a number is assigned to each descriptor in each of these two questions. For question 3, "critical" might be assigned a 4, "serious" a 3, "moderate" a 2, and "minor" a 1. Certainly, the higher the number, the more serious is the patient's condition. Thus, these responses can be ranked by selection. However, the increases in importance from 1 to 2 to 3 to 4 are not necessarily equal. This same logic applies to the numeric values assigned in question 4.

Question 5 displays seven numeric choices with equal distances between the numbers shown on the scale and no adjective descriptors assigned to the numbers. Many analysts would declare this to be interval-level measurement because of the equal distance between numbers and the absence of a true zero on this scale. Other analysts might argue that because of the imprecision of the scale and the vagueness of selecting values between "poor" and "excellent," the measurement is only ordinal in level.

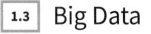

1.3 | Big Data

LEARNING OBJECTIVE 1.3

Explain the differences between the four dimensions of big data.

In the current world of business, there is exponential growth in the data available to decision-makers to help them produce better business outcomes. Growing sources of data are available from the Internet, social media, governments, transportation systems, health care, environmental organizations, and a plethora of business data sources, among others. Business data include, but are not limited to, consumer information, labour statistics, financials, product and resource tracking information, supply chain information, operations information, and human resource information. According to vCloud, 2.5-quintillion bytes of data are created every day. As a business example, from its millions of products and hundreds of millions of customers, Walmart alone collects multi-terabytes of new data every day, which are then added to its petabytes of historical data.[4]

The advent of such growth in the amount and types of data available to analysts, data scientists, and business decision-makers has resulted in a new term, "Big Data." **Big data** has been defined as *a collection of large and complex datasets from different sources that are difficult to process using traditional data management and processing applications.*[5] In addition, big data can be seen as *a large amount of either organized or unorganized data that is analyzed to make an informed decision or evaluation.*[6] All data are not created in the same way, nor do they represent the same things. Thus, analysts recognize that there are at least four characteristics or dimensions associated with big data.[7] These are:

1. Variety
2. Velocity
3. Veracity
4. Volume

Variety refers to *the many different forms of data based on data sources.* A wide variety of data is available from such sources as mobile phones, videos, text, retail scanners, Internet searches, government documents, multimedia, empirical research, and many others. Data can be structured (such as databases or Excel sheets) or unstructured (such as writing and photographs). **Velocity** refers to *the speed at which the data is available and can be processed.* The velocity characteristic of data is important in ensuring that data is current and updated in real time.[8] **Veracity** of data *has to do with data quality, correctness, and accuracy.*[9] Data lacking veracity may be imprecise, unrepresentative, inferior, and untrustworthy. In using such data to better understand business decisions, it might be said that the result is "Garbage In, Garbage Out." Veracity indicates reliability, authenticity, legitimacy, and validity in the data. **Volume** *has to do with the ever-increasing size of the data and databases.* Big data produces vast amounts of data, as exemplified by the Walmart example mentioned above. A fifth characteristic or dimension of data that is sometimes considered is *Value.* Analysis of data that does not generate value makes no contribution to an organization.[10]

Along with this unparalleled explosion of data, major advances have been made in computing performance, network functioning, data handling, device mobility, and other areas. When businesses capitalize on these developments, new opportunities become available for discovering greater and deeper insights that could produce significant improvements in the way businesses operate and function. So how do businesses go about capitalizing on this potential?

---

[4] "How Walmart Makes Data Work for Its Customers," SAS.com, 2016, at www.sas.com/en_us/insights/articles/ analytics/how-walmart-makes-data-work-for-its-customers.html.

[5] Shih-Chia Huang, Suzanne McIntosh, Stanislav Sobolevsky, and Patrick C. K. Hung, "Big Data Analytics and Business Intelligence in Industry," *Information Systems Frontiers* 19 (2017): 1229–32.

[6] Ibid.

[7] Hans W. Ittmann, "The Impact of Big Data and Business Analytics on Supply Chain Management," *Journal of Transport and Supply Chain Management* 9, no. 1 (2015).

[8] Huang et al., "Big Data Analytics and Business Intelligence in Industry."

[9] Ittmann, "The Impact of Big Data and Business Analytics on Supply Chain Management."

[10] Roger H. L. Chiang, Varun Grover, Ting-Peng Lian, and Zhang Dongsong, "Special Issue: Strategic Value of Big Data and Business Analytics," *Journal of Management Information Systems* 35, no. 2: 383–87.

1.4 Business Analytics

LEARNING OBJECTIVE 1.4

Compare and contrast the three categories of business analytics.

To benefit from the challenges, opportunities, and potentialities presented to business decision-makers by big data, the new field of "business analytics" has emerged. There are different definitions of business analytics in the literature. However, one that most accurately describes the intent of the approach here is that **business analytics** *is the application of processes and techniques that transform raw data into meaningful information to improve decision-making.*[11] Because big data sources are so large and complex, new questions have arisen that cannot always be effectively answered with traditional methods of analysis.[12] In light of this, new methodologies and processing techniques have been developed, giving birth to a new era in decision-making referred to as the "business analytics period."[13] Other names sometimes used to refer to business analytics are business intelligence, data science, data analytics, analytics, and even big data, but the goal in all cases is to convert data into actionable insight for more timely and accurate decision-making.[14] For example, when applied to the business environment, data analytics becomes synonymous with business analytics.[15]

Business analytics provides added value to data, resulting in deeper and broader business insights that can be used to improve decision-makers' insights and understanding in all aspects of business, as shown in **Figure 1.6**.

 **FIGURE 1.6** **Business Analytics Add Value to Data**

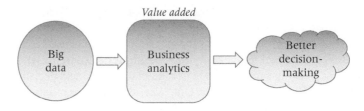

Value added

Big data → Business analytics → Better decision-making

There are many new opportunities for employment in business analytics, yet there is presently a shortage of available talent in the field. In fact, an IBM survey of 900 business and information technology executives cited the lack of business analytics skills as a top business challenge.[16] Today's executives say that they are seeking data-driven leaders. They are looking for people who can work comfortably with both data and people—managers who can build useful models from data and also lead the team that will put it into practice.[17] A paper on "Canada's Big Data Talent Gap" estimated that this country will face a shortage of "between 10,500 and 19,000 professionals with deep data and analytical skills, such as those required

[11] Coleen R. Wilder and Ceyhun O. Ozgur, "Business Analytics Curriculum for Undergraduate Majors," *Informs* 15, no. 2 (January 2015): 180–87, doi.org/10.1287/ited.2014.0134.

[12] Dursun Delen and Hamed M. Zolbanin, "The Analytics Paradigm in Business Research," *Journal of Business Research* 90 (2018): 186–95.

[13] M. J. Mortenson, N. F. Doherty, and S. Robinson, "Operational Research from Taylorism to Terabytes: A Research Agenda for the Analytic Sage," *European Journal of Operational Research* 241, no. 3 (2015): 583–95.

[14] R. Sharda, D. Delen, and E. Turban, *Business Intelligence Analytics and Data Science: A Managerial Perspective* (Upper Saddle River, NJ: Pearson, 2017).

[15] C. Aasheim, S. Williams, P. Rutner, and A. Gardner, "Data Analytics vs. Data Science: A Study of Similarities and Differences in Undergraduate Programs Based on Course Descriptions," *Journal of Information Systems Education* 26, no. 2 (2015): 103–15.

[16] G. Finch, C. Reese, R. Shockley, and R. Balboni, "Analytics: A Blueprint for Value: Converting Big Data and Analytics Insights into Results," IBM Institute for Business Value, 2013, www-935.ibm.com/services/us/gbs/thoughtleadership/ninelevers/.

[17] Dan LeClair, "Integrating Business Analytics in the Marketing Curriculum: Eight Recommendations," *Marketing Education Review* 28, no. 1 (2018): 6–13.

for roles like Chief Data Officer, Data Scientist, and Data Solutions Architect." An additional 150,000 professionals with solid data and analytical skills will be needed to fill managerial positions such as Business Manager and Business Analyst.[18]

Categories of Business Analytics

It might be said that the mission of business analytics is to apply processes and techniques to transform raw data into meaningful information. There is a plethora of such techniques available, drawing from such areas as statistics, operations research, mathematical modelling, data mining, and artificial intelligence, to name a few. The various techniques and approaches provide different information to decision-makers. Accordingly, the business analytics community has organized and classified business analytic tools into three main categories: Descriptive Analytics, Predictive Analytics, and Prescriptive Analytics.

Descriptive Analytics   The simplest and perhaps the most commonly used of the three categories of business analytics is *descriptive analytics*. Often the first step in the analytics process, **descriptive analytics** *takes traditional data and describes what has happened or is happening in a business*. It can be used to condense big data into smaller, more useful data.[19] Also referred to as reporting analytics, descriptive analytics can be used to discover hidden relationships in the data and identify undiscovered patterns.[20] Descriptive analytics drills down in the data to uncover useful and important details, and mines data for trends.[21] At this step, visualization can be a key technique for presenting information.

Much of what is taught in a traditional introductory statistics course could be classified as descriptive analytics, including descriptive statistics, frequency distributions, discrete distributions, continuous distributions, sampling distributions, and statistical inference.[22] We could probably add correlation and various clustering techniques to the mix, along with data mining and data visualization techniques.

Predictive Analytics   The next step in data reduction is **predictive analytics**, *which finds relationships in the data that are not readily apparent with descriptive analytics*.[23] With predictive analytics, patterns or relationships are extrapolated forward in time, and the past is used to make predictions about the future.[24] Predictive analytics also provides answers that move beyond using the historical data as the principal basis for decisions.[25] It builds and assesses algorithmic models that are intended to make empirical rather than theoretical predictions, and are designed to predict future observations.[26] Predictive analytics can help managers develop likely scenarios.[27]

Topics in predictive analytics can include regression, time-series, forecasting, simulation, data mining (see Section 1.5), statistical modelling, machine-learning techniques, and others. They can also include classifying techniques, such as decision-tree models and neural networks.[28]

---

[18] "Closing Canada's Big Data Talent Gap," report by Canada's Big Data Consortium, October 2015.

[19] Jeff Bertolucci, "Big Data Analytics: Descriptive vs. Predictive vs. Prescriptive," *Information Week*, December 31, 2018, www.informationweek.com/big-data/big-data.

[20] C. K. Praseeda and B. L. Shivakumar, "A Review of Trends and Technologies in Business Analytics," *International Journal of Advanced Research in Computer Science* 5, no. 8 (November-December 2014): 225–29.

[21] Watson ioT, "Descriptive, Predictive, Prescriptive: Transforming Asset and Facilities Management with Analytics," IBM paper, 2017, www-01.ibm.com/common/ssi/cgi-bin/ssialias?infotype=SA&subtype=WH&htmlfid=TIW14162USEN.

[22] Wilder and Ozgur, "Business Analytics Curriculum for Undergraduate Majors."

[23] B. Daniel, "Big Data and Analytics in Higher Education: Opportunities and Challenges," *British Journal of Educational Technology* 46, no. 5 (2015): 904–920, onlinelibrary.wiley.com/doi/abs/10.1111/bjet.12230.

[24] Praseeda and Shivakumar, "A Review of Trends and Technologies in Business Analytics."

[25] Ibid.

[26] Delen and Zolbanin, "The Analytics Paradigm in Business Research."

[27] Watson ioT, "Descriptive, Predictive, Prescriptive."

[28] Sharda, Delen, and Turban, *Business Intelligence Analytics and Data Science*.

Prescriptive Analytics The final stage of business analytics is **prescriptive analytics**, which is still in its early stages of development.[29] Prescriptive analytics follows descriptive and predictive analytics in an attempt to find the best course of action under certain circumstances.[30] The goal is to examine current trends and likely forecasts and use that information to make better decisions.[31] Prescriptive analytics *takes uncertainty into account, recommends ways to mitigate risks, and tries to see what the effect of future decisions will be in order to adjust the decisions before they are actually made.*[32] It does this by exploring a set of possible actions based on descriptive and predictive analyses of complex data, and then suggesting courses of action.[33] Prescriptive analytics evaluates data and determines new ways to operate while balancing all constraints,[34] at the same time continually and automatically processing new data to improve recommendations and provide better decision options.[35] It not only foresees what will happen and when, but also suggests why it will happen and recommends how to act in order to take advantage of the predictions.[36] Predictive analytics uses a set of mathematical techniques that computationally determine an optimal action or decision given a complex set of objectives, requirements, and constraints.[37]

Topics in prescriptive analytics come from the fields of management science or operations research and are generally aimed at optimizing the performance of a system, using tools such as mathematical programming, simulation, network analysis, and others.[38]

1.5 | Data Mining and Data Visualization

LEARNING OBJECTIVE 1.5

Describe the data mining and data visualization processes.

The dawning of the big data era has given rise to new and promising prospects for improving business decisions and outcomes. Two main components in the process of transforming the mountains of data now available into useful business information are data mining and data visualization.

Data Mining

In the field of business, **data mining** is *the process of collecting, exploring, and analyzing large volumes of data in an effort to uncover hidden patterns and/or relationships that can be used to enhance business decision-making.* In short, data mining is a process used by companies to turn raw data into meaningful information that can potentially lead to some business advantage. Data mining allows business people to discover and interpret useful information

---

[29] Praseeda and Shivakumar, "A Review of Trends and Technologies in Business Analytics."

[30] Delen and Zolbanin, "The Analytics Paradigm in Business Research."

[31] Sharda, Delen, and Turban, *Business Intelligence Analytics and Data Science.*

[32] Praseeda and Shivakumar, "A Review of Trends and Technologies in Business Analytics."

[33] Watson ioT, "Descriptive, Predictive, Prescriptive."

[34] Daniel, "Big Data and Analytics in Higher Education."

[35] A. Basu, "Five Pillars of Prescriptive Analytics Success," *Analytics* (March/April 2013), pp. 8–12, analytics-magazine.org/executive-edge-five-pillars-of-prescriptive-analytics-success/.

[36] Praseeda and Shivakumar, "A Review of Trends and Technologies in Business Analytics."

[37] I. Lusting, B. Dietrich, C. Johnson, and C. Dziekan, "The Analytics Journey," *Analytics Magazine* 3, no. 6 (2010): 11–13.

[38] Sharda, Delen, and Turban, *Business Intelligence Analytics and Data Science.*

that will help them make more knowledgeable decisions and better serve their customers and clients.

Figure 1.7 displays the process of data mining, which involves finding the data, converting the data into useful forms, loading the data into a holding or storage location, managing the data, and making the data accessible to business analytics' users. Data scientists often refer to the first three steps of this process as ETL (extract, transform, and load). Extracting involves locating the data by asking the question "Where can it be found?" Countless pieces of data are unearthed the world over in a great variety of forms and from multiple disparate sources. Because of this, extracting data can be the most time-consuming step.[39] After a set of data has been located and extracted, it must be transformed or converted into a usable form. Included in this transformation may be a sorting process that determines which data are useful and which are not. In addition, data are typically "cleaned" by removing corrupt or incorrect records and identifying incomplete, incorrect, or irrelevant parts of the data.[40] Often the data are sorted into columns and rows to improve usability and searchability.[41] After the set of data is extracted and transformed, it is loaded into an end target, which is often a database. Data are often managed through a database management system, which is a software system that enables users to define, create, maintain, and control access to the database.[42] Lastly, the ultimate goal of the process of data mining is to make the data accessible and usable to the business analyst.

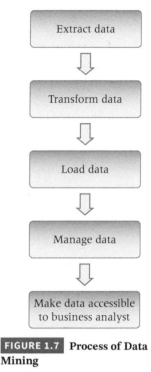

FIGURE 1.7 **Process of Data Mining**

Data Visualization

As business organizations amass large reservoirs of data, one swift and easy way to obtain an overview of the data is through data visualization, which has been described as perhaps the most useful component of business analytics, and the element that makes it truly unique.[43] So what is data visualization? Generally, data visualization is any attempt made by data analysts to help individuals better understand data by putting it in a visual context. Specifically, **data visualization** *is the study of the visual representation of data and is employed to convey data or information by imparting it as visual objects displayed in graphics.*

Interpretation of data is vital to unlocking the potential value it holds and to making the most informed decisions.[44] Using visual techniques to convey information hidden in data allows for a broader audience with a wider range of backgrounds to view and understand its meaning. Data visualization tools help make data-driven insights accessible to people at all levels throughout an organization and can reveal surprising patterns and connections, resulting in improved decision-making. To communicate information clearly and efficiently, data visualization uses statistical graphics, plots, information graphics, and other tools. Numerical data may be encoded, using dots, lines, or bars, to visually communicate a quantitative message, thereby making complex data more accessible, understandable, and usable.[45]

---

[39] Shirley Zhao, "What Is ETL? (Extract, Transform, Load)," paper from Experian Data Quality, October 20, 2017, www.edq.com/blog/what-is-etl-extract-transform-load/.

[40] S. Wu, "A Review on Coarse Warranty Data and Analysis," *Reliability Engineering and System Safety* 114 (2013): 1–11, doi.org/10.1016/j.ress.2012.12.021.

[41] Zhao, "What Is ETL?"

[42] Thomas M. Connolly and Carolyn E. Begg, *Database Systems: A Practical Approach to Design Implementation and Management*, 6th ed. (Harlow, UK: Pearson, 2014), 64.

[43] James R. Evans. *Business Analytics: Methods, Models, and Decisions*, 2nd ed. (Boston: Pearson, 2016), 7.

[44] R. Roberts, R. Laramee, P. Brookes, G.A. Smith, T. D'Cruze, and M.J. Roach, "A Tale of Two Visions—Exploring the Dichotomy of Interest between Academia and Industry in Visualisation," in *Proceedings of the 13th International Joint Conference on Computer Vision, Imaging and Computer Graphics Theory and Applications*, vol. 3 (Setúbal, Portugal: SciTePress, 2018), 319–26.

[45] Stephen Few, "Eenie, Meenie, Minie, Moe: Selecting the Right Graph for Your Message," paper from Perceptual Edge, 2004, www.perceptualedge.com/articles/ie/the_right_graph.pdf.

Visualization Example As an example of data visualization, consider the top five organizations in the manufacturing industry to receive Canadian government funding and their respective amount funded (in dollars) in a recent year, displayed in **Table 1.1**.[46]

TABLE 1.1	Top Five Manufacturing Firms to Receive Canadian Government Funding	
Company Name		**Dollars Funded**
FCA Canada Inc. (Chrysler)		$85,800,000
Bombardier Inc.		$54,150,000
Produits Kruger		$39,500,000
Sonaca Montréal Inc.		$23,250,000
Hanwha L&C Canada Inc.		$15,000,000

One of the leading companies to develop data visualization software is Tableau©. **Figure 1.8** is a bubble chart of the Table 1.1 data, developed using Tableau©. One of the advantages of using visualization to display data is the variety of types of graph or charts. **Figure 1.9** contains a Tableau©-produced bar chart of the same information to give the user a different perspective.

FIGURE 1.8 Bubble Chart of the Top Five Manufacturing Firms to Receive Canadian Government Funding

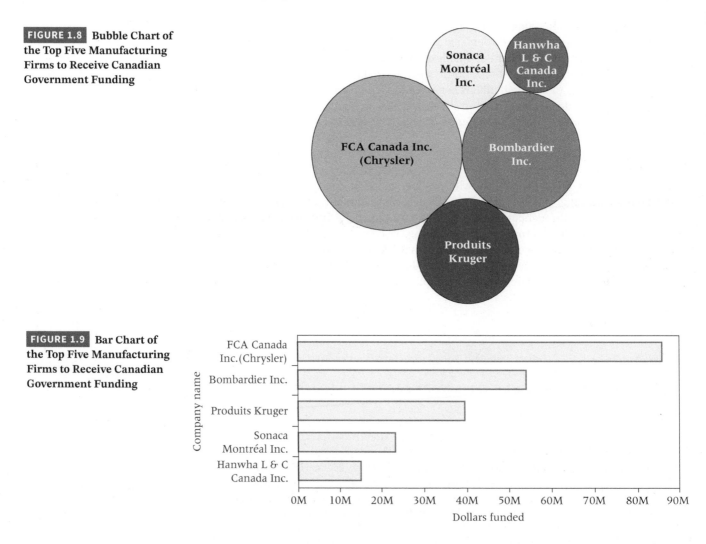

FIGURE 1.9 Bar Chart of the Top Five Manufacturing Firms to Receive Canadian Government Funding

[46] "Top 50 Companies That Received Canadian Government Funding," *The Globe and Mail*, July 19, 2017, www.theglobeandmail.com/report-on-business/top-50-report-on-business-the-funding-portal/article19192109/.

End-of-Chapter Review

Decision Dilemma Solved

Statistics Describe the State of Business in India's Countryside

Several statistics were reported in the Decision Dilemma about rural India. The authors of the sources from which the Decision Dilemma was drawn never stated whether the reported statistics were based on actual data drawn from a census of rural India households or on estimates taken from a sample of rural households. If the data came from a census, then the totals, averages, and percentages presented in the Decision Dilemma are parameters. If, on the other hand, the data were gathered from samples, then they are statistics. Although governments do conduct censuses and at least some of the reported numbers could be parameters, more often than not such data are gathered from samples of people or items. For example, in rural India, the government, academicians, or business analysts could have taken random samples of households, gathering consumer statistics that are then used to estimate population parameters, such as percentage of households with televisions, and so forth.

In conducting research on a topic like consumer consumption in rural India, a wide variety of statistics can be gathered that represent several levels of data. For example, ratio-level measurements on items such as income, number of children, age of household heads, number of heads of livestock, and grams of toothpaste consumed per year might be obtained. On the other hand, if analysts use a Likert-type scale (1-to-5 measurements) to gather responses about the interests, likes, and preferences of rural Indian consumers, an ordinal-level measurement would be obtained, as with the ranking of products or brands in market research studies. Other variables, such as geographic location, sex, occupation, or religion, are usually measured with nominal data.

The decision to enter the rural India market is not just a marketing decision. It involves production and operations capacity, scheduling issues, transportation challenges, financial commitments, managerial growth or reassignment issues, accounting issues (accounting for rural India may differ from techniques used in urban markets), information systems, and other related areas. With so much on the line, company decision-makers need as much relevant information available as possible. In this Decision Dilemma, it is obvious to the decision-maker that rural India is still quite poor and illiterate. Its capacity as a market is great. The statistics on the increasing sales of a few personal-care products look promising. What are the future forecasts for the earning power of people in rural India? Will major cultural issues block the adoption of the types of products that companies want to sell there? The answers to these and many other interesting and useful questions can be obtained by the appropriate use of statistics. The approximately 800-million people living in rural India certainly make it a market segment worth studying further.

Key Considerations

With the abundance and proliferation of statistical data, potential misuse of statistics in business dealings is a concern. It is, in effect, unethical business behaviour to use statistics out of context. Unethical business people might use only selective data from studies to underscore their point, omitting statistics from the same studies that argue against their case. The results of statistical studies can be misstated or overstated to gain favour.

This chapter noted that, if data are nominal or ordinal, then only nonparametric statistics are appropriate for analysis. The use of parametric statistics to analyze nominal and/or ordinal data is wrong and could be considered under some circumstances to be unethical.

In this text, each chapter contains a section on ethics that discusses how businesses can misuse the techniques presented in the chapter in an unethical manner. As both users and producers, business students need to be aware of the potential ethical pitfalls that can occur with statistics.

Why Statistics Is Relevant

In the contemporary business world, good decisions are driven by data. In all areas of business, amazing amounts of diverse data are available for interpretation and quantitative insight. Business managers and professionals are increasingly required to justify decisions on the basis of data analysis. Thus, the ability to extract useful information from data is one of the most important, and marketable, skills business managers and professionals can acquire. This text is an introduction to the theory and, more importantly, the methods used to intelligently collect, analyze, and interpret data relevant to business decision-making.

Summary of Learning Objectives

LEARNING OBJECTIVE 1.1   Define important statistical terms, including population, sample, and parameter, as they relate to descriptive and inferential statistics.

Statistics is an important decision-making tool in business and is used in virtually every area of business. In this text, the word *statistics* is defined as the science of gathering, analyzing, interpreting, and presenting data.

The study of statistics can be subdivided into two main areas: *descriptive statistics* and *inferential statistics*. Descriptive statistics result from gathering data from a body, group, or population and reaching conclusions only about that group. Inferential statistics are generated from the process of gathering sample data from a group, body, or population and reaching conclusions about the larger group from which the sample was drawn.

LEARNING OBJECTIVE 1.2   Explain the difference between variables, measurement, and data, and compare the four different levels of data: nominal, ordinal, interval, and ratio.

Most business statistics studies contain variables, measurements, and data. A variable is a characteristic of any entity being studied that is capable of taking on different values. Examples of variables might include monthly household food spending, time between arrivals at a restaurant, and patient satisfaction rating. A *measurement* is when a standard process is used to assign numbers to particular attributes or characteristics of a variable. Measurements of monthly household food spending might be taken in dollars, time between arrivals might be measured in minutes, and patient satisfaction might be measured using a 5-point scale. *Data* are recorded measurements. It is data that are analyzed by business statisticians in order to learn more about the variables being studied.

The appropriate type of statistical analysis depends on the level of data measurement, which can be (1) nominal, (2) ordinal, (3) interval, or (4) ratio. Nominal is the lowest level, representing the classification of only data, such as geographic location, sex, or social insurance number. The next level is ordinal, which provides rank ordering measurements in which the intervals between consecutive numbers do not necessarily represent equal distances. Interval is the next highest level of data measurement, in which the distances represented by consecutive numbers are equal. The highest level of data measurement is ratio. This has all the qualities of interval measurement, but ratio data contain an absolute zero, and ratios between numbers are meaningful. Interval and ratio data are sometimes called *metric* or *quantitative* data. Nominal and ordinal data are sometimes called *nonmetric* or *qualitative* data.

Two major types of inferential statistics are (1) *parametric statistics* and (2) *nonparametric statistics*. Use of parametric statistics requires interval or ratio data and certain assumptions about the distribution of the data. The techniques presented in this text are largely parametric. If data are only nominal or ordinal in level, nonparametric statistics must be used.

LEARNING OBJECTIVE 1.3   Explain the differences between the four dimensions of big data.

The emergence of exponential growth in the number and type of data existing has resulted in a new term, big data, which is *a collection of large and complex datasets from different sources that are difficult to process using traditional data management and process applications*. There are four dimensions of big data: (1) variety, (2) velocity, (3) veracity, and (4) volume. Variety refers to the many different forms of data, velocity refers to the speed at which the data are available and can be processed, veracity has to do with data quality and accuracy, and volume has to do with the ever-increasing size of data.

LEARNING OBJECTIVE 1.4   Compare and contrast the three categories of business analytics.

Business analytics is a relatively new field of business dealing with the challenges, opportunities, and potentialities available to business analysts through big data. Business analytics is *the application of processes and techniques that transform raw data into meaningful information to improve decision-making*. There are three categories of business analytics: (1) descriptive analytics, (2) predictive analytics, and (3) prescriptive analytics.

LEARNING OBJECTIVE 1.5   Describe the data mining and data visualization processes.

Two main components in the process of transforming the mountains of data now available are data mining and data visualization. Data mining is the process of collecting, exploring, and analyzing large volumes of data in an effort to uncover hidden patterns and/or relationships that can be used to enhance business decision-making. One effective way of communicating data to a broader audience of people is data visualization. Data visualization is any attempt made by data analysts to help individuals better understand data by putting it in a visual context. Specifically, data visualization is the study of the visual representation of data and is employed to convey data or information by imparting it as visual objects displayed in graphics.

Key Terms

big data   1-11
business analytics   1-12
census   1-4
data   1-6
data mining   1-14
data visualization   1-15
descriptive analytics   1-13
descriptive statistics   1-4
inferential statistics   1-4
interval-level data   1-8

measurement   1-6
metric data   1-9
nominal-level data   1-7
nonmetric data   1-8
nonparametric statistics   1-9
ordinal-level data   1-7
parameter   1-4
parametric statistics   1-9
population   1-4
predictive analytics   1-13

prescriptive analytics   1-14
ratio-level data   1-8
sample   1-4
statistic   1-4
statistics   1-3
variable   1-6
variety   1-11
velocity   1-11
veracity   1-11
volume   1-11

Supplementary Problems

1.1 Give a specific example of data that might be gathered from each of the following business disciplines: accounting, finance, human resources, marketing, operations and supply chain management, information systems, production, and management. An example in the marketing area might be "number of sales per month by each salesperson."

1.2 State examples of data that can be gathered for decision-making purposes from each of the following industries: manufacturing, insurance, travel, retailing, communications, computing, agriculture, banking, and health care. An example in the travel industry might be the cost of business travel per day in various European cities.

1.3 Give an example of *descriptive* statistics in the recorded music industry. Give an example of how *inferential* statistics could be used in the recorded music industry. Compare the two examples. What makes them different?

1.4 Suppose you are an operations manager for a plant that manufactures batteries. Give an example of how you could use *descriptive* statistics to make better managerial decisions. Give an example of how you could use *inferential* statistics to make better managerial decisions.

1.5 There are many types of information that might help the manager of a large department store run the business more efficiently and better understand how to improve sales. Think about this in such areas as sales, customers, human resources, inventory, suppliers, and so on. List five variables that might produce information that could aid the manager in his or her job. Write a sentence or two describing each variable, and briefly discuss some numerical observations that might be generated for each variable.

1.6 Suppose you are the owner of a medium-sized restaurant in a small city. What are some variables associated with different aspects of the business that might be helpful to you in making business decisions about the restaurant? Name four of these variables. For each variable, briefly describe a numerical observation that might be the result of measuring the variable.

1.7 **Video** Classify each of the following as nominal, ordinal, interval, or ratio data.

    a. The time required to produce each tire on an assembly line

    b. The number of litres of milk a family drinks in a month

    c. The ranking of four machines in your plant after they have been designated as excellent, good, satisfactory, and poor

    d. The telephone area code of clients in Canada

    e. The age of each of your employees

    f. The dollar sales at the local pizza house each month

    g. An employee's identification number

    h. The response time of an emergency unit

1.8 Classify each of the following as nominal, ordinal, interval, or ratio data.

    a. The ranking of a company by *Report on Business* magazine's Top 1000

    b. The number of tickets sold at a movie theatre on any given night

    c. The identification number on a questionnaire

    d. Per capita income

    e. The trade balance in dollars

    f. Profit/loss in dollars

    g. A company's tax identification number

    h. The Standard & Poor's bond ratings of cities based on the following scales:

Rating	Grade
Highest quality	AAA
High quality	AA
Upper medium quality	A
Medium quality	BBB
Somewhat speculative	BB
Low quality, speculative	B
Low grade, default possible	CCC
Low grade, partial recovery possible	CC
Default, recovery unlikely	C

1.9 **Video** The Mapletech Manufacturing Company makes electric wiring, which it sells to contractors in the construction industry. Approximately 900 electrical contractors purchase wire from Mapletech annually. Mapletech's director of marketing wants to determine electrical contractors' satisfaction with Mapletech's wire. She develops a questionnaire that yields a satisfaction score of between 10 and 50 for participant responses. A random sample of 35 of the 900 contractors is asked to complete a satisfaction survey. The satisfaction scores for the 35 participants are averaged to produce a mean satisfaction score.

    a. What is the population for this study?

    b. What is the sample for this study?

    c. What is the statistic for this study?

    d. What would be a parameter for this study?

Exploring the Databases with Business Analytics   *see* the databases on the Student Website and in *WileyPLUS*

Six major databases constructed for this text can be used to apply the business analytics and statistical techniques presented in this course. These databases are located in *WileyPLUS*, and each one is available in a few electronic formats for your convenience. These six databases represent a wide variety of business areas: the stock market, international labour, finance, energy, and agri-business. The data are gathered from such reliable sources as Statistics Canada, the Toronto Stock Exchange, *Yahoo Finance,* the Fraser Institute, and the Global Environment Outlook (GEO) Data Portal. Four of the six databases contain time-series data that can be especially useful in forecasting and regression analysis. Here is a description of each database, along with information that may help you to interpret outcomes.

Canadian Stock Market Database

The stock market database contains seven variables on the Toronto Stock Exchange. Weekly observations for a period of five years yield a total of 257 observations per variable. The variables are Composite Index, Energy Index, Financial Index, Health Index, Utility Index, I.T. Index, and Gold Index. These data were obtained directly from TMX Inc.

Canadian RRSP Contribution Database

The registered retirement savings plan database contains five variables: Number of Tax Filers, Total RRSP Contributors, Average Age of RRSP Contributors, Total RRSP Contributions ($ × 1,000), and Median RRSP Contributions ($). There are 156 entries for each variable in this database, representing 10 years of data for each of 10 provinces and 3 territories in Canada. The data in this database were obtained from Statistics Canada.

International Labour Database

This time-series database contains the civilian unemployment rates in percent from seven countries (G7) presented yearly over a 30-year period. The data are published by the Bureau of Labor Statistics of the U.S. Department of Labor. The countries are Canada, France, Germany, Italy, Japan, the United Kingdom, and the United States.

Financial Database

The financial database contains observations on 12 variables for 100 companies. The variables are Industry Group, Type of Industry, Total Revenues, Price, Average Yield, Dividend Growth, Average Price/Earnings (P/E) Ratio, Dividends per Share, Total Debt/Total Equity, Price/Cash Flow, Price/Book, and One-Year Total Return. The data were gathered from the Toronto Stock Exchange. The companies represent seven different types of industries. The variable "Type" displays a company's industry type as follows:

1 = Real Estate

2 = Financial Institutes

3 = Chemicals

4 = Mining, Electric, Oil & Gas, Pipelines

5 = Telecommunications, Retail, Commercial Services, Auto Parts & Equipment, Transportation

6 = Insurance

7 = Food, Pharmaceuticals, Electronics, Media, Aerospace/Defence, Hand/Machine Tools, Agriculture, Iron/Steel, Holding Companies, Engineering and Construction, Machinery—Diversified, Forest Products and Paper

Energy Resource Database

The energy resource database consists of data for North America and Europe on nine variables related to energy supply and emission of carbon dioxide over a period of 35 years. The database is adapted from the Global Environment Outlook (GEO) Data Portal. The nine variables are the seven total primary energy supplies of Solar, Wind, Tide, and Wave; Nuclear; Natural Gas; Coal and Coal Products; Crude Oil; Hydro; and Petroleum Products, plus the two sources of emissions of CO_2: Manufacturing Industries and Construction, and Transportation.

Agri-Business Canada Database

The agri-business time-series database contains the monthly weight (in thousands of pounds) of seven different grains over an eight-year period. Each of the seven variables represents 94 months of data. The seven grains are Wheat; Wheat, Excluding Durum; Durum Wheat; Oats; Barley; Flaxseed; and Canola. The data are published by Statistics Canada under Agri-business.

Use the databases to answer the following question.

1. In the Financial Database, what is the level of data for each of the following variables?

   a. Type of Industry
   b. Average Price
   c. Price/Cash Flow

Case

Canadian Farmers Dealing with Stress

Farming is an extremely demanding job whose success depends largely on the dedication of the farmers. In order to tackle the rigorous tasks of the trade, farmers must be in good physical and mental condition. The University of Guelph conducted a study in 2017/18 which showed that Canadian farmers experienced higher levels of anxiety and depression and displayed lower levels of help-seeking behaviour compared to the general Canadian populace. The study indicated that Canadian farmers were at a heightened risk of suicide compared to the rest of the population. The Canadian Agricultural Safety Association (CASA) also recently sponsored research on the stress level of Canadian farmers.

Western Opinion Research Inc. conducted the research study, which was completed by 1,100 farmers across Canada. The survey asked farmers to rate their stress level, ranging from "stressed" to "somewhat stressed" to "very stressed." The results varied and revealed the following: two-thirds of farmers indicated feeling "stressed," 45% indicated feeling "somewhat stressed," and one in five indicated

feeling "very stressed." The results of the survey also revealed that the major causes of stress among farmers were (a) financial concerns related to prices of commodities, (b) diseases affecting livestock, and (c) finances regarding general farm expenses. The results also revealed that a large percentage of farmers (35%) were interested in having access to more stress-related resources in order to help alleviate their stress level.

This study allowed CASA to realize that stress within the farming industry is a major issue, therefore making it imperative to take action and offer stress counselling resources to farmers. These resources include (a) confidential meeting with a health care professional, (b) over-the-phone consultation with a health care professional, and (c) attending workshops such as retreats that focus on relaxation techniques and role playing with other farmers.

Over the last few years, CASA has made great progress to help reduce the stress level of Canadian farmers. For example, successful counselling services that deal with farmers and their problems were established using phone, email, and online chat help lines. These include the Manitoba Farm, Rural & Northern Support Services and the Saskatchewan Farm Stress Line. These services are well recognized and are having great success in helping farmers, mainly because they are staffed by paid professional counsellors who all have farming backgrounds, making the farmers feel more comfortable because they are connecting with someone who understands their work-related issues.

Discussion

Think of the market research that was conducted by CASA.

1. What are some of the populations that CASA might have been interested in measuring for these studies? Did CASA attempt to contact entire populations? What samples were taken? In light of these two questions, how was the inferential process used by CASA in its market research? Can you think of any descriptive statistics that might have been used by CASA in its decision-making process?

2. In the various market research efforts made by CASA to determine stress experienced by farmers, some of the possible measurements appear in the following list. Categorize these by level of data. Think of some other measurements that CASA analysts might have taken to help them in this research effort and categorize them by level of data.

   a. Ranking of the level of stress on a stress test
   b. Number of farmers that ask for professional help
   c. Number of farmers that are aware of professional help resources
   d. Number of farmers that try to manage stress on their own
   e. Number of farmers that are interested in having access to more stress-related resources
   f. Number of farmers that are close to being out of business
   g. Number of farmers that would prefer dealing with stress on their own
   h. Number of farmers that would prefer dealing with stress with a professional over the telephone
   i. Number of farmers that would prefer dealing with stress with a professional in person
   j. Age of survey respondent
   k. Gender of survey respondent
   l. Geographical region of survey respondent
   m. Amount of time farmers spend dealing with their stress
   n. Rating of the most stress-related factors on a scale from 1 to 10, where 1 is the least stress-related factor and 10 is the most stress-related factor
   o. Rating of the reasons why farmers do not seek more help for stress on a scale from 1 to 10, where 1 is the least important reason and 10 is the most important reason

Sources: Klinic Community Health, "Annual Report 2017/18," klinic. mb.ca/wp-content/uploads/2018/06/AnnualReport1718.pdf; Manitoba Farm and Rural Stress Line, "Annual Report," 2008, 2010, www. ruralsupport.ca/index.php?pageid=22; Saskatchewan Farm Stress Line, www.mobilecrisis.ca/farm-stress-line-rural-sask; Canadian Agricultural Safety Association, "National Stress and Mental Survey of Canadian Farmers," February 11, 2005, www.casa-acsa.ca/en/safetyshop-library/ national-stress-and-mental-survey-of-canadian-farmers/.

Big Data Case

Virtually every chapter in this text will end with a big data case. Unlike the chapter cases, which feature a wide variety of companies and business scenarios, the big data case will be based on data from a single industry, U.S hospitals. Drawing from the American Hospital Association database of over 2,000 hospitals, we will use business analytics to mine data on these hospitals in different ways for each chapter based on analytics presented in that chapter.

The hospital database features data on twelve variables, thereby offering over 24,000 observations to analyze. Hospital data for each of the 50 states are contained in the database with qualitative data representing state, region of the country, type of ownership, and type of hospital. Quantitative measures include Number of Beds, Number of Admissions, Census, Number of Outpatients, Number of Births, Total Expenditures, Payroll Expenditures, and Personnel.

Using the Computer

Statistical Analysis Using Excel

The advent of the modern computer opened many new opportunities for statistical analysis. The computer allows for storage, retrieval, and transfer of large data sets. Furthermore, computer software has been developed to analyze data by means of sophisticated statistical techniques. Some widely used statistical techniques, such as multiple regression, are so tedious and cumbersome to compute manually that they were of little practical use to analysts before computers were developed. In this textbook, the end-of-chapter "Using the Computer" feature will show you how you can use software to apply the statistical techniques you learn in each chapter.

- Business statisticians use many popular statistical software packages, including MINITAB, SAS, and SPSS. Many computer spreadsheet software packages can also analyze data statistically. In this text, when it is appropriate to use a computer, we will use Microsoft Excel for data analysis.

- Excel is by far the most commonly used spreadsheet for PCs, making it the obvious choice for basic statistical analysis. Excel can perform a variety of calculations and includes a large collection of statistical functions. The Data Analysis ToolPak provides a further suite of statistical macro-functions.

- We note, however, that although Excel is a fine spreadsheet, it is not a professional statistical data analysis package: there are some important limitations. Key limitations to keep in mind include the following: missing values in Excel are difficult to handle when performing data analysis; data organization differs according to analysis, sometimes forcing you to reorganize your data; some output and charts produced by Excel are of poor quality from a statistical point of view and are sometimes inadequately labelled; and there is no record of how an analysis was done if the Data Analysis ToolPak is used.

- Despite these limitations, Excel is the most commonly used package in the business environment and is the package you are most likely to use in your professional life.

- It is important to remember that a statistical software package is not a replacement for a thorough understanding of correct statistical methods. The business analyst is responsible for determining the most appropriate statistical methods for a given business problem. Simply relying on convenient software tools that may be at hand without thinking through the most appropriate approach can lead to errors, oversights, and poor decisions. One of the goals of this text is to show you when and how to use statistical methods to provide information that can be used in business decisions.

Visualizing Data with Charts and Graphs

LEARNING OBJECTIVES

The overall objective of Chapter 2 is for you to master several techniques for summarizing and visualizing data, thereby enabling you to:

2.1 Explain the difference between grouped and ungrouped data and construct a frequency distribution from a set of data. Explain what the distribution represents.

2.2 Describe and construct different types of quantitative data graphs, including histograms, frequency polygons, ogives, and stem-and-leaf plots. Explain when these graphs should be used.

2.3 Describe and construct different types of qualitative data graphs, including pie charts, bar charts, and Pareto charts. Explain when these graphs should be used.

2.4 Display and analyze two variables simultaneously using cross tabulation and scatter plots.

2.5 Describe and construct a time-series graph. Visually identify any trends in the data.

Decision Dilemma

Energy Consumption Around the World

As most people suspect, the United States is the number one consumer of oil in the world, followed by China, India, Japan, Saudi Arabia, and the Russian Federation. (Canada ranks tenth, with a consumption that is below that of Germany and above that of Mexico.) China, however, is the world's largest consumer of coal, with India coming in at number two, followed by the United States, Japan, and the Russian Federation. (Canada ranks 18th, below Malaysia and above Thailand.) The annual oil and coal consumption figures for six of the top total energy-consuming nations in the world, according to figures released by the BP Statistical Review of World Energy for a recent year, are as follows.

iStock.com/instamatics

Country	Oil Consumption (thousands of barrels)	Coal Consumption (million tonnes oil equivalent)
U.S.	19,880	332.1
China	12,799	1,892.6
India	4,690	424.0
Japan	3,988	120.5
Russian Federation	3,224	92.3
Brazil	3,017	16.5

Source: *BP Statistical Review of World Energy*, June 2018. www.bp.com/content/dam/bp/en/corporate/pdf/energy-economics/statistical-review/bp-stats-review-2018-full-report.pdf.

Managerial, Statistical, and Analytical Questions

Suppose you are an energy industry analyst and you are asked to prepare a brief report showing the leading energy-consumption countries in both oil and coal.

1. What is the best way to display the data on energy consumption in a report? Are the raw data enough? Can you effectively display the data graphically?

2. Is there a way to graphically display oil and coal figures together so that readers can visually compare countries on their consumptions of the two different energy sources?

Introduction

In this era of seemingly boundless big data, the application of business analytics has great potential to unearth business knowledge and intelligence that can substantially improve business decision-making. A key objective of business analytics is to convert data into deeper and broader actionable insights and understandings for all aspects of business. One of the first steps is to visualize the data through graphs and charts, thereby providing business analysts with an overview of the data and a glimpse into any underlying relationships.

In this chapter, we will study how to visually represent data in order to convey information that can unlock potentialities for making better business decisions. Remember, using visuals to convey information hidden in the data allows for a broader audience with a wide range of backgrounds to understand its meaning. Data visualization tools can reveal surprising patterns and connections, making data-driven insights accessible to people at all levels of an organization. Graphical depictions of data are often much more effective communication tools than tables of numbers in business meetings. In addition, key characteristics of graphs often suggest appropriate choices among potential numerical methods (discussed in later chapters) for analyzing data.

A first step in exploring and analyzing data is to reduce important and sometimes expansive data to a graphic picture that is clear, concise, and consistent with the message of the original data. Converting data to graphics can be creative and artful. This chapter focuses on graphical tools for summarizing and presenting data. Charts and graphs discussed in detail in Chapter 2 include histograms, frequency polygons, ogives, dot plots, stem-and-leaf plots, bar charts, pie charts, and Pareto charts for one-variable data, and cross-tabulation tables and scatter plots for two-variable numerical data. In addition, there is a section on time-series graphs for displaying data gathered over time. Box-and-whisker plots are discussed in Chapter 3.

A non-inclusive list of other graphical tools includes the line plot, area plot, bubble chart, treemap, map chart, Gantt chart, bullet chart, doughnut chart, circle view, highlight table, matrix plot, marginal plot, probability distribution plot, individual value plot, and contour plot.

Recall the four levels of data measurement discussed in Chapter 1: nominal, ordinal, interval, and ratio. The lowest levels of data, nominal and ordinal, are referred to as qualitative data, while the highest levels of data, interval and ratio, are referred to as quantitative data. In this chapter, Section 2.2 will present quantitative data graphs and Section 2.3 will present qualitative data graphs. Note that the data visualization software Tableau© divides data variables into measures and dimensions based on whether data are qualitative or quantitative.

2.1 | Frequency Distributions

LEARNING OBJECTIVE 2.1

Explain the difference between grouped and ungrouped data and construct a frequency distribution from a set of data. Explain what the distribution represents.

Raw data, or data that have not been summarized in any way, are sometimes referred to as **ungrouped data**. As an example, **Table 2.1** contains raw data showing 60 years of unemployment rates for Canada. *Data that have been organized into a frequency distribution* are called **grouped data**. **Table 2.2** presents a frequency distribution for the data displayed in Table 2.1. The distinction between ungrouped and grouped data is important because statistics are calculated differently for each type of data. Several of the charts and graphs presented in this chapter are constructed from grouped data.

TABLE 2.1   Unemployment Rates for Canada over 60 Years (Ungrouped Data)

6.0	6.4	12.0	9.5	6.0
7.0	6.3	11.3	9.6	6.1
7.1	5.6	10.5	9.1	8.3
5.9	5.4	9.6	8.3	8.1
5.5	7.1	8.8	7.6	7.5
4.7	7.1	7.8	6.8	7.3
3.9	8.0	7.5	7.2	7.1
3.6	8.4	8.1	7.7	6.9
4.1	7.5	10.3	7.6	6.9
4.8	7.5	11.2	7.2	7.0
4.7	7.6	11.4	6.8	6.3
5.9	11.0	10.4	6.3	5.8

TABLE 2.2   Frequency Distribution of 60 Years of Unemployment Data for Canada (Grouped Data)

Class Interval	Frequency
2–under 4	2
4–under 6	10
6–under 8	29
8–under 10	11
10–under 12	7
12–under 14	1

One particularly useful tool for grouping data is the **frequency distribution**, which is *a summary of data presented in the form of class intervals and frequencies.* How is a frequency distribution constructed from raw data? That is, how are frequency distributions like the one displayed in Table 2.2 constructed from raw data like those presented in Table 2.1? Frequency distributions are relatively easy to construct. Although some guidelines help in their construction, frequency distributions vary in final shape and design, even when the original raw data are identical. In a sense, frequency distributions are constructed according to individual business analysts' tastes.

When constructing a frequency distribution, the business analyst should first determine the range of the raw data. The **range** is often defined as *the difference between the largest and smallest numbers*. The range for the data in Table 2.1 is 8.4 (12.0 − 3.6).

The second step in constructing a frequency distribution is to determine how many classes it will contain. One guideline is to select between *5 and 15 classes*. If the frequency distribution contains too few classes, the data summary may be too general to be useful. Too many classes may result in a frequency distribution that does not aggregate the data enough to be helpful. The final number of classes is arbitrary. The business analyst arrives at a number by examining the range and determining a number of classes that will span the range adequately and be meaningful to the user. The data in Table 2.1 were grouped into six classes for Table 2.2.

After selecting the number of classes, the business analyst must determine the width of the class interval. An approximation of the class width can be calculated by dividing the range by the number of classes. For the data in Table 2.1, this approximation is 8.4/6, or 1.4. Normally, the number is rounded up to the next whole number, which in this case is 2. The frequency distribution must start at a value equal to or lower than the lowest number of the ungrouped data and end at a value equal to or higher than the highest number. The lowest unemployment rate is 3.6 and the highest is 12.0, so the business analyst starts the frequency distribution at 2 and ends it at 14. Table 2.2 contains the completed frequency distribution for the data in Table 2.1. Class endpoints are selected so that no value of the data can fit into more than one class. The class interval expression "under" in the distribution of Table 2.2 avoids this problem.

Class Midpoint

The *midpoint of each class interval* is called the **class midpoint** and is sometimes referred to as the **class mark**. It is *the value halfway across the class interval* and can be calculated as *the average of the two class endpoints*. For example, in the distribution of Table 2.2, the midpoint of the class interval 4–under 6 is 5, or (4 + 6)/2.

$$\text{Class Beginning Point} = 4$$
$$\text{Class Width} = 2$$
$$\text{Class Midpoint} = 4 + \frac{1}{2}(2) = 5$$

The class midpoint is important because it becomes the representative value for each class in most group statistics calculations. The third column in **Table 2.3** contains the class midpoints for all classes of the data from Table 2.2.

TABLE 2.3	Class Midpoints, Relative Frequencies, and Cumulative Frequencies for Unemployment Data			
Interval	Frequency	Class Midpoint	Relative Frequency	Cumulative Frequency
2–under 4	2	3	0.0333	2
4–under 6	10	5	0.1667	12
6–under 8	29	7	0.4833	41
8–under 10	11	9	0.1833	52
10–under 12	7	11	0.1167	59
12–under 14	1	13	0.0167	60
Totals	60		1.0000	

Relative Frequency

Relative frequency is *the proportion of the total frequency that is in any given class interval in a frequency distribution*. Relative frequency is the individual class frequency divided by the total frequency. For example, from Table 2.3, the relative frequency for the class interval

6–under 8 is 29/60 = 0.4833. We consider the relative frequency here to prepare for the study of probability in Chapter 4. Indeed, if values are selected randomly from the data in Table 2.1, the probability of drawing a number that is 6–under 8 is 0.4833, the relative frequency for that class interval. The fourth column of Table 2.3 lists the relative frequencies for the frequency distribution of Table 2.2.

Cumulative Frequency

The **cumulative frequency** is *a running total of frequencies through the classes of a frequency distribution*. The cumulative frequency for each class interval is the frequency for that class interval added to the preceding cumulative total. In Table 2.3, the cumulative frequency for the first class is the same as the class frequency: 2. The cumulative frequency for the second class interval is the frequency of that interval (10) plus the frequency of the first interval (2), which yields a new cumulative frequency of 12. This process continues through the last interval, at which point the cumulative total equals the sum of the frequencies (60). The concept of cumulative frequency is used in many areas, including sales cumulated over a fiscal year, sports scores during a contest (cumulated points), years of service, points earned in a course, and costs of doing business over a period of time. Table 2.3 gives cumulative frequencies for the data in Table 2.2.

DEMONSTRATION PROBLEM 2.1

The following data are the average weekly interest rates for a 60-week period.

7.29	7.03	7.14	6.77	6.35	7.16	6.78	6.79	7.07	7.03
6.69	7.02	7.40	7.16	6.96	6.87	6.80	7.10	7.13	6.95
6.98	7.56	6.75	6.87	7.11	7.08	7.24	7.34	7.47	7.31
7.39	7.28	6.97	6.90	6.57	6.96	6.70	6.57	6.88	6.84
7.11	6.95	7.23	7.31	7.00	7.02	7.40	7.12	7.16	7.16
7.30	7.17	6.96	6.78	7.30	6.99	6.94	7.29	7.05	6.84

Construct a frequency distribution for these data. Calculate and display the class midpoints, relative frequencies, and cumulative frequencies for this frequency distribution.

Solution How many classes should this frequency distribution contain? The range of the data is 1.21 (7.56 − 6.35). If seven classes are used, each class width is approximately:

$$\text{Class Width} = \frac{\text{Range}}{\text{Number of Classes}} = \frac{1.21}{7} = 0.173$$

If a class width of 0.20 is used, a frequency distribution can be constructed with endpoints that are more uniform looking and allow presentation of the information in categories more familiar to interest rate users.

The first class endpoint must be 6.35 or lower to include the smallest value; the last endpoint must be 7.56 or higher to include the largest value. In this case, the frequency distribution begins at 6.30 and ends at 7.70. The resulting frequency distribution, class midpoints, relative frequencies, and cumulative frequencies are listed in the following table.

Class Interval	Frequency	Class Midpoint	Relative Frequency	Cumulative Frequency
6.30–under 6.50	1	6.40	0.0167	1
6.50–under 6.70	3	6.60	0.0500	4
6.70–under 6.90	12	6.80	0.2000	16
6.90–under 7.10	18	7.00	0.3000	34
7.10–under 7.30	16	7.20	0.2666	50
7.30–under 7.50	9	7.40	0.1500	59
7.50–under 7.70	1	7.60	0.0167	60
Totals	60		1.0000	

The frequencies and relative frequencies of these data reveal the interest rate classes that are likely to occur during the period. Most of the interest rates (55 of the 60) are in the classes starting with (6.70–under 6.90) and going through (7.30–under 7.50). The rates with the greatest frequency, 18, are in the 6.90–under 7.10 class.

Concept Check

Fill in the blanks.

The value halfway across the class interval (calculated as the average of the two class endpoints) is called the class _____. For each class, the individual class frequency divided by the total frequency is called the _____ frequency. Moreover, a running total of frequencies through the classes of a frequency distribution is called the _____ frequency.

2.1 Problems

2.1 The following data represent the afternoon high temperatures for 50 construction days during a year in Toronto.

6	21	18	8	19	21	23	3	9	–4
13	29	–12	–4	7	–1	17	8	17	29
–9	4	27	–9	2	–8	4	2	7	–8
3	26	2	2	–5	18	24	12	–1	16
–1	3	11	–9	27	–11	16	6	–1	1

a. Construct a frequency distribution for the data using five class intervals.

b. Construct a frequency distribution for the data using 10 class intervals.

c. Examine the results of (a) and (b) and comment on the usefulness of the frequency distribution in terms of temperature summarization capability.

2.2 A packaging process is supposed to fill small boxes of raisins with approximately 50 raisins so that each box will have the same mass. However, the number of raisins in each box will vary. Suppose 100 boxes of raisins are randomly sampled, the raisins counted, and the following data are obtained.

57	51	53	52	50	60	51	51	52	52
44	53	45	57	39	53	58	47	51	48
49	49	44	54	46	52	55	54	47	53
49	52	49	54	57	52	52	53	49	47
51	48	55	53	55	47	53	43	48	46
54	46	51	48	53	56	48	47	49	57
55	53	50	47	57	49	43	58	52	44
46	59	57	47	61	60	49	53	41	48
59	53	45	45	56	40	46	49	50	57
47	52	48	50	45	56	47	47	48	46

Construct a frequency distribution for these data. What does the frequency distribution reveal about the box fills?

2.3 The owner of a fast-food restaurant ascertains the ages of a sample of customers. From these data, the owner constructs the frequency distribution shown. For each class interval of the frequency distribution, determine the class midpoint, the relative frequency, and the cumulative frequency.

Class Interval	Frequency
0–under 5	6
5–under 10	8
10–under 15	17
15–under 20	23
20–under 25	18
25–under 30	10
30–under 35	4

What does the relative frequency tell the fast-food restaurant owner about customer ages?

2.4 The human resources manager for a large company commissions a study in which the employment records of 500 company employees are examined for absenteeism during the past year. The business analyst conducting the study organizes the data into a frequency distribution to assist the human resources manager in analyzing the data. The frequency distribution is shown. For each class of the frequency distribution, determine the class midpoint, the relative frequency, and the cumulative frequency.

Class Interval	Frequency
0–under 2	218
2–under 4	207
4–under 6	56
6–under 8	11
8–under 10	8

2.5 List three specific uses of cumulative frequencies in business.

2.2 Quantitative Data Graphs

LEARNING OBJECTIVE 2.2

Describe and construct different types of quantitative data graphs, including histograms, frequency polygons, ogives, and stem-and-leaf plots. Explain when these graphs should be used.

Data graphs can generally be classified as quantitative or qualitative. Quantitative data graphs are plotted along a numerical scale, and qualitative graphs are plotted using non-numerical categories. In this section, we will examine four types of quantitative data graphs: (1) histogram, (2) frequency polygon, (3) ogive, and (4) stem-and-leaf plot.

Histograms

One of the more widely used types of graphs for quantitative data is the **histogram**. A histogram is *a series of contiguous rectangles that represents the frequency of data in given class intervals*. If the class intervals used along the horizontal axis are equal, then the heights of the rectangles represent the frequency of values in a given class interval. If the class intervals are unequal, then the areas of the rectangles can be used for relative comparisons of class frequencies. Construction of a histogram involves labelling the *x*-axis with the class endpoints and the *y*-axis with the frequencies, drawing a horizontal line segment from class endpoint to class endpoint at each frequency value, and connecting each line segment vertically from the frequency value to the *x*-axis to form a series of rectangles. **Figure 2.1** is a histogram of the frequency distribution in Table 2.2.

A histogram is a useful tool for differentiating the frequencies of class intervals. A quick glance at a histogram reveals which class intervals produce the highest frequency totals. Figure 2.1 clearly shows that the class interval 6–under 8 yields by far the highest frequency count (29). Examination of the histogram reveals where large increases or decreases occur between classes, such as from the 2–under 4 class to the 4–under 6 class, an increase of 8, and from the 6–under 8 class to the 8–under 10 class, a decrease of 18.

Note that the scales used along the *x* and *y* axes for the histogram in Figure 2.1 are almost identical. However, because ranges of meaningful numbers for the two variables being graphed often differ considerably, the histogram may have different scales on the two axes. **Figure 2.2** shows what the histogram of unemployment rates would look like if the scale on

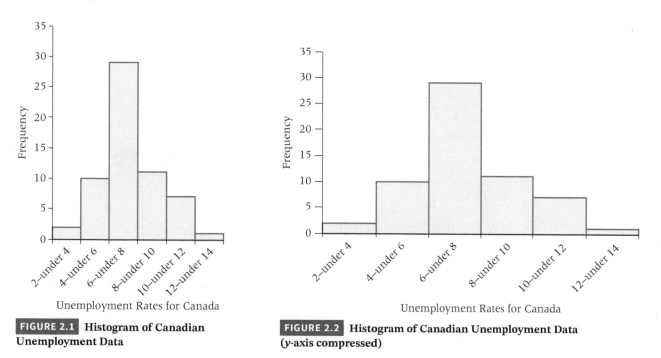

FIGURE 2.1 **Histogram of Canadian Unemployment Data**

FIGURE 2.2 **Histogram of Canadian Unemployment Data (*y*-axis compressed)**

the *y*-axis were more compressed than that on the *x*-axis. Notice that less difference in the height of the rectangles appears to represent the frequencies in Figure 2.2. It is important that the user of the graph clearly understand the scales used for the axes of a histogram. Otherwise, a graph's creator can lie with statistics by stretching or compressing a graph to make a point.[1]

Using Histograms to Get an Initial Overview of the Data   Because of the widespread availability of computers and statistical software packages to business decision-makers, the histogram continues to grow in importance for yielding information about the shape of the distribution of a large database, the variability of the data, the central location of the data, and outlier data. Although most of these concepts are presented in Chapter 3, the notion of the histogram as an initial tool to access these data characteristics is presented here.

For example, suppose a financial decision-maker wants to use data to reach some conclusions about the stock market. **Figure 2.3** shows a histogram of 324 stock volume observations. What can we learn from this histogram? Virtually all stock market volumes fall between 78-million and 1-billion shares. The distribution takes on a shape that is high on the left end and tapered to the right. In Chapter 3, we will learn that the shape of this distribution is skewed toward the right end. In statistics, it is often useful to determine whether data are approximately normally distributed (bell-shaped curve), as shown in **Figure 2.4**. We can see by examining the histogram in Figure 2.3 that the stock market volume data are not normally distributed. Although the centre of the histogram is located near 500-million shares, a large portion of stock volume observations falls in the lower end of the data, somewhere between 100-million and 400-million shares. In addition, the histogram shows some outliers in the upper end of the distribution. Outliers are data points that appear outside the main body of observations and may represent phenomena that differ from those represented by other data points. By looking closely at the histogram, we notice a few data observations near 1 billion. One could conclude that on a few stock market days an unusually large volume of shares are traded. These and other insights can be gleaned by examining the histogram and show that histograms play an important role in the initial analysis of data.

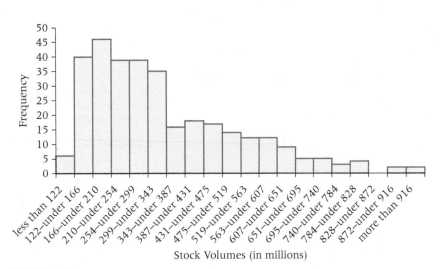

FIGURE 2.3   **Histogram of Stock Volumes**

FIGURE 2.4   **Normal Distribution**

Frequency Polygons

A **frequency polygon**, like the histogram, is *a graphical display of class frequencies*. However, instead of using rectangles like a histogram, in a frequency polygon each class frequency is plotted as a dot at the class midpoint, and the dots are connected by a series of line segments.

---

[1] It should be pointed out that Excel uses the term *histogram* to refer to a frequency distribution. However, if you check Chart Output in the Excel histogram dialogue box, a graphical histogram is also created.

Pie Charts

A **pie chart** is *a circular depiction of data where the area of the whole pie represents 100% of the data and slices represent a percentage breakdown of the sublevels.* Pie charts show the relative magnitudes of parts to a whole. They are widely used in business, particularly to depict such things as budget categories, market share, and time and resource allocations. However, the use of pie charts is minimized in the sciences and technology because they can lead to less accurate judgments than are possible with other types of graphs.[2] Generally, it is more difficult for the viewer to interpret the relative size of angles in a pie chart than to judge the length of rectangles in a histogram or the relative distance of a frequency polygon dot from the *x*-axis. In the feature Thinking Critically About Statistics in Business Today 2.1, "Where Are Soft Drinks Sold?," graphical depictions of the percentage of sales by place were displayed by both a pie chart and a vertical bar chart.

Thinking Critically About Statistics in Business Today 2.1

Where Are Soft Drinks Sold?

Beverages that contain more than 1% by weight of flavours are considered to be soft drinks, including flavoured bottled water, soda water, seltzer water, and tonic water. Based on data from Statista, the value of Canadian domestic retail sales for flavoured soft drinks in 2018 contributed around $1.67 billion to the country's gross domestic product. Aside from Pepsi and Coca Cola, popular soft drinks in Canada include Canada Dry, Crush, Big 8, and Clearly Canadian.

Where are soft drinks sold? The following data from Bernstein Research indicate that the four leading places for soft drink sales in the U.S. are supermarkets, soda fountains or snack bars, convenience stores/gas stations, and vending machines.

Place of Sales	Percentage
Supermarkets	44
Soda fountains	24
Convenience stores/gas stations	16
Vending machines	11
Mass merchandisers	3
Drugstores	2

These data can be displayed graphically in several ways. Displayed here are a pie chart and a bar chart of the data. Some statisticians prefer the histogram or the bar chart over the pie chart because they believe it is easier to compare categories that are similar in size with the histogram or the bar chart rather than the pie chart.

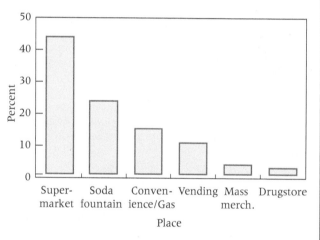

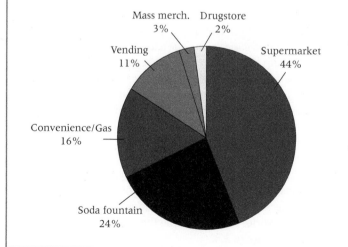

Things to Ponder

1. How might this information be useful to large soft drink companies?

2. How might the packaging of soft drinks differ according to the top four places where soft drinks are sold?

3. How might the distribution of soft drinks differ between the various places where soft drinks are sold?

---

[2]William S. Cleveland, *The Elements of Graphing Data* (Monterey, CA: Wadsworth Advanced Books and Software, 1985).

Construction of the pie chart is done by determining the proportion of the subunit to the whole. **Table 2.6** contains annual sales for the top petroleum-refining companies in the U.S. in a recent year. To construct a pie chart from these data, convert the raw sales figures to proportions by dividing each sales figure by the total sales figure. This proportion is analogous to the relative frequency computed for frequency distributions. The pie chart in **Figure 2.7** depicts the data from Table 2.6.

TABLE 2.6 Leading U.S. Petroleum-Refining Companies

Company	Annual Sales (US$ millions)	Proportion
ExxonMobil	270,772	0.4232
Chevron Texaco	147,967	0.2313
ConocoPhillips	121,663	0.1902
Valero Energy	53,919	0.0843
Marathon Petroleum	45,444	0.0710
Totals	639,765	1.0000

FIGURE 2.7 Pie Chart of Petroleum-Refining Sales by Brand

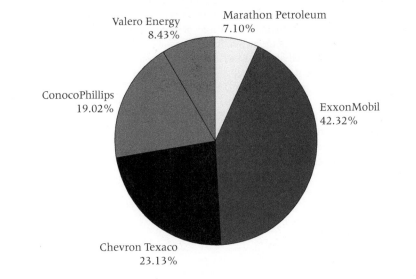

Bar Charts

Another widely used qualitative data graphing technique is the **bar chart** or **bar graph**. A bar graph or chart contains *two or more categories along one axis and a series of bars, one for each category, along the other axis.* Typically, the length of the bar represents the magnitude of the measure (amount, frequency, money, percentage, etc.) for each category. The bar chart is qualitative because the categories are non-numerical, and it may be either horizontal or vertical. A bar chart generally is constructed from the same type of data that are used to produce a pie chart. However, an advantage of using a bar chart over a pie chart for a given set of data is that for categories that are close in value, it is considered easier to see the difference in the bars of bar charts than to discriminate between pie slices.

As an example, consider the data in **Table 2.7** regarding how much the average university student spends on back-to-school items. Constructing a bar chart from these data, the categories are electronics, clothing and accessories, residence furnishings, school supplies, and miscellaneous. Bars for each of these categories are made using the dollar figures given in the table. The resulting bar chart is shown in **Figure 2.8**.

TABLE 2.7 Back-to-School Spending by the Average University Student

Category	Amount Spent ($)
Electronics	211.89
Clothing and accessories	134.40
Residence furnishings	90.90
School supplies	68.47
Miscellaneous	93.72

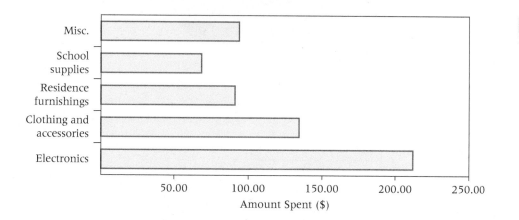

FIGURE 2.8 Bar Chart of Back-to-School Spending

DEMONSTRATION PROBLEM 2.3

According to the National Retail Federation and Center for Retailing Education at the University of Florida, the four main sources of inventory shrinkage are employee theft, shoplifting, administrative error, and vendor fraud. The estimated annual dollar amount in shrinkage (in US$ millions) associated with each of these sources is shown below.

Construct a pie chart to depict these data.

Employee theft	$17,918.6
Shoplifting	15,191.9
Administrative error	7,617.6
Vendor fraud	2,553.6
Total	$43,281.7

Solution Convert each raw dollar amount to a proportion by dividing each individual amount by the total.

Employee theft	17,918.6/43,281.7	=	0.414
Shoplifting	15,191.9/43,281.7	=	0.351
Administrative error	7,617.6/43,281.7	=	0.176
Vendor fraud	2,553.6/43,281.7	=	0.059
Total			1.000

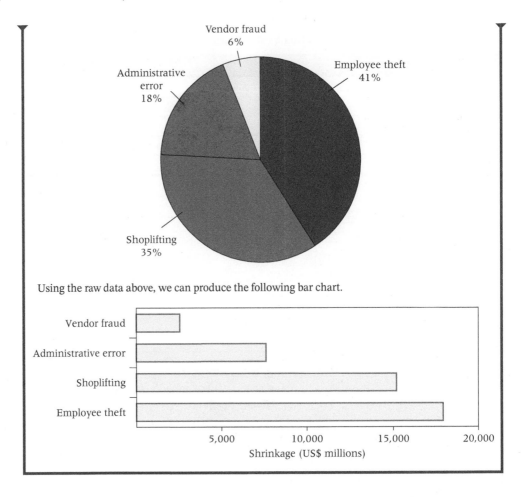

Using the raw data above, we can produce the following bar chart.

Pareto Charts

A third type of qualitative data graph is a Pareto chart, which could be viewed as a particular application of the bar chart. One of the important aspects of the quality movement in business is the constant search for causes of problems in products and processes. A graphical technique for displaying problem causes is Pareto analysis. Pareto analysis is a quantitative tallying of the number and types of defects that occur with a product or service. Analysts use this tally to produce *a vertical bar chart that displays the most common types of defects, ranked in order of occurrence from left to right.* The bar chart is called a **Pareto chart.**

Pareto charts were named after an Italian economist, Vilfredo Pareto, who observed more than 100 years ago that most of Italy's wealth was controlled by a few families who were the major drivers behind the Italian economy. Quality expert J. M. Juran applied this notion to the quality field by observing that poor quality can often be addressed by attacking a few major causes that result in most of the problems. A Pareto chart enables decision-makers responsible for quality management to separate the most important defects from trivial defects, which helps them set priorities for needed quality improvement work.

Suppose the number of electric motors being rejected by inspectors for a company has been increasing. Company officials examine the records of several hundred motors in which at least one defect was found, to determine which defects occurred more frequently. They find that 40% of the defects involved poor wiring, 30% involved a short in the coil, 25% involved a defective plug, and 5% involved seizing of bearings. **Figure 2.9** is a Pareto chart constructed from this information. It shows that the three main problems with defective motors—poor wiring, a short in the coil, and a defective plug—account for 95% of the problems. From the Pareto chart, decision-makers can formulate a logical plan for reducing the number of defects.

Company officials and workers would probably begin to improve quality by examining the segments of the production process that involve the wiring. Next, they would study the construction of the coil, then examine the plugs used and the plug-supplier process.

Figure 2.10 is a different rendering of this Pareto chart. In addition to the bar chart analysis (primary axis), the Pareto analysis contains a cumulative percentage line graph

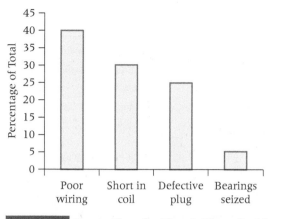

FIGURE 2.9 Pareto Chart for Electric Motor Problems

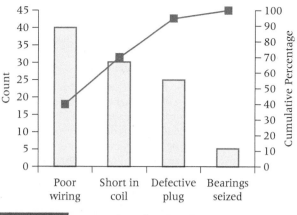
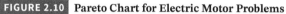

FIGURE 2.10 Pareto Chart for Electric Motor Problems

(secondary axis). Observe the slopes on the line graph. The steepest slopes represent the more frequently occurring problems. As the slopes level off, the problems occur less frequently. The line graph gives the decision-maker another tool for determining which problems to solve first.

Concept Check

1. True or false?

   Pie charts are an effective way of displaying data if the intent is to compare the size of a slice with the whole pie, rather than comparing the slices among themselves.

2. What type of chart do you think could be used to help answer the following questions?

   a. What are the main issues that our business is facing?

   b. What 20% of sources are causing 80% of our quality control problems?

   c. Where should we focus our efforts to achieve the largest improvement?

3. What is the key difference between histograms and bar charts?

2.3 Problems

2.13 The top seven airlines in the world by passengers carried in a recent year were Delta Airlines with 164.6 million, United Airlines with 140.4 million, Southwest Airlines with 134.0 million, American Airlines with 107.9 million, China Southern Airlines with 86.5 million, Ryanair with 79.6 million, and Lufthansa with 74.7 million. Construct a pie chart and a bar chart to depict this information.

2.14 The following is a list of the six largest pharmaceutical and biotech companies in the world ranked by health-care revenue (in US$ millions). Use this information to construct a pie chart and a bar chart to represent these six companies and their revenues.

Pharmaceutical Firm	Revenue (US$ millions)
Pfizer	67,809
Novartis	53,324
Merck & Co.	45,987
Bayer	44,200
GlaxoSmithKline	42,813
Johnson and Johnson	37,020

2.15 Initial public offerings (IPOs) can be a risky investment; thus, in an IPO, the issuer may obtain the assistance of an underwriting firm. Shown here is a list of the top five Canadian underwriting firms with the amount of money they raised in a recent year. Construct a bar chart to display these data. Construct a pie chart to represent these data and label the slices with the appropriate percentages. Comment on the effectiveness of using a pie chart to display the total amount raised by these top underwriting firms.

Underwriting Firm	Total Amount ($ millions)
RBC Capital Markets	29,172
TD Securities	25,193
CIBC World Markets	19,875
National Bank Financial	17,653
BMO Capital Markets	16,958

Source: Barry Critchley, "'Out of Sync' Canadian Markets Dampen Dealmaking in First Half," *Financial Post*, August 2, 2018. Material reprinted with the express permission of National Post, a division of Postmedia Network Inc.

2.16 The Canada Beef Export Federation reports that the top six destinations for Canadian beef in a recent year were the U.S. with $1,697 million, Mexico with $269 million, Japan with $171 million, South Korea with $28 million, Taiwan with $16 million, and China with $4 million. Construct a pie chart to depict this information.

2.17 An airline uses a call centre to take reservations. It has been receiving an unusually high number of customer complaints about its reservation system. The company conducted a survey of customers, asking them whether they had encountered any of the following problems in making reservations: busy signal, disconnection, poor connection, too long a wait to talk to someone, could not get through to an agent, or transferred to the wrong person. Suppose a survey of 744 complaining customers resulted in the following frequency tally.

Number of Complaints	Complaint
184	Too long a wait
10	Transferred to the wrong person
85	Could not get through to an agent
37	Got disconnected
420	Busy signal
8	Poor connection

Construct a Pareto chart from this information to display the various problems encountered in making reservations.

2.4 | Charts and Graphs for Two Variables

LEARNING OBJECTIVE 2.4

Display and analyze two variables simultaneously using cross tabulation and scatter plots.

It is very common in business statistics to want to analyze two variables simultaneously in an effort to gain insight into a possible relationship between them. For example, business analysts might be interested in the relationship between years of experience and amount of productivity in a manufacturing facility or in the relationship between a person's technology usage and their age. Business analysts have many techniques for exploring such relationships. Two of the more elementary tools for observing the relationships between two variables are cross tabulation and scatter plot.

Cross Tabulation

Cross tabulation is *a process for producing a two-dimensional table that displays the frequency counts for two variables simultaneously*. As an example, suppose a job satisfaction survey of a randomly selected sample of 177 bankers is taken in the banking industry. The bankers are asked how satisfied they are with their job using a 1 to 5 scale where 1 denotes very dissatisfied, 2 denotes dissatisfied, 3 denotes neither satisfied nor dissatisfied, 4 denotes satisfied, and 5 denotes very satisfied. In addition, each banker is asked to report his or her age by using one of three categories: under 30 years, 30 to 50 years, and over 50 years. **Table 2.8** displays how some of the data might look as they are gathered. Note that age and level of job satisfaction are recorded for each banker. By tallying the frequency of responses for each combination of categories between the two variables, the data are cross tabulated according to the two variables. For instance, in this example there is a tally of how many bankers rated their level of satisfaction as 1 and were under 30 years of age, there is a tally of how many bankers rated their level of satisfaction as 2 and were under 30 years of age, and so on until frequency tallies are determined for each possible combination of the two variables. **Table 2.9** shows the completed cross-tabulation table for the banker survey. A cross-tabulation table is sometimes referred to as a contingency table, and Excel calls such a table a PivotTable.

TABLE 2.8   Banker Data Observations by Job Satisfaction and Age

Banker	Level of Job Satisfaction	Age
1	4	53
2	3	37
3	1	24
4	2	28
5	4	46
6	5	62
7	3	41
8	3	32
9	4	29
.	.	.
.	.	.
.	.	.
177	3	51

TABLE 2.9   Cross-Tabulation Table of Banker Data

		Age Category			Total
		Under 30	30–50	Over 50	
	1	7	3	0	10
Level of Job Satisfaction	2	19	14	3	36
	3	28	17	12	57
	4	11	22	16	49
	5	2	9	14	25
Total		67	65	45	177

Scatter Plot

A **scatter plot** is a two-dimensional graph plot of pairs of points from two numerical variables. The scatter plot is a graphical tool that is often used to examine possible relationships between two variables.

As an example of two numerical variables, consider the data in **Table 2.10**. Displayed are the base salary and total compensation (cash bonuses, stock-based bonuses, options-based bonuses, pension value, and any other payments aside from base salary) for the 25 highest-paid Canadian CEOs in a recent year. Do these two numerical variables exhibit any relationship? It might seem logical that when the base salary is high, the total CEO compensation would be high as well. However, the scatter plot of these data, displayed in **Figure 2.11**, shows somewhat mixed results. The apparent tendency is that total CEO compensations occur mostly in the range between $10,000 and $30,000 (in $ thousands) for the entire range of base salaries, with a single exception that takes the highest total CEO compensation for a rather average base salary.

TABLE 2.10	Total Compensation and Base Salary for the 25 Highest-Paid Canadian CEOs
Total Compensation ($ thousands)	**Base Salary ($ thousands)**
83,131	1,300
28,614	431
24,603	1,030
21,427	267
18,830	2,905
17,777	2,110
17,592	1,371
17,370	1,314
15,872	887
15,855	1,284
15,381	1,803
14,641	618
14,193	86
12,905	1,375
12,752	525
12,578	1,381
12,245	1,467
12,132	1,193
11,998	446
11,894	0 ($1.00)
11,822	1,373
11,816	1,373
11,764	1,000
11,580	1,457
11,522	1,496

Source: Adapted from Canadian Business staff, "Canada's Top 100 Highest-Paid CEOs," *Canadian Business*, January 2, 2018. www.canadianbusiness.com/lists-and-rankings/richest-people/canada-100-highest-paid-ceos/.

FIGURE 2.11 Scatter Plot of Total Compensation and Base Salary for the 25 Highest-Paid Canadian CEOs

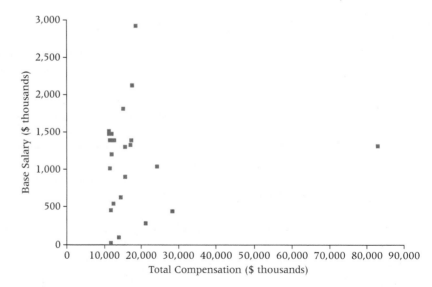

Concept Check

1. Draw the outline of a scatter plot for each of the following sets of two numerical variables.

   a. The mass and height of 30 people selected at random

   b. The mass and IQ of 30 people selected at random

   c. The number of advertising dollars spent by a company and the total sales revenue

2.4   Problems

2.18 The U.S. National Oceanic and Atmospheric Administration, National Marine Fisheries Service, publishes data on the quantity and value of domestic fishing in the U.S. The quantity (in millions of kilograms) of fish caught and used for human food and for industrial products (oil, bait, animal food, etc.) over a decade follows. Is a relationship evident between the quantity used for human food and the quantity used for industrial products for a given year? Construct a scatter plot of the data. Examine the plot and discuss the strength of the relationship of the two variables.

Human Food	Industrial Product
1,661	1,285
1,612	1,105
1,493	1,401
1,472	1,455
1,509	1,417
1,497	1,347
1,542	1,199
1,794	1,341
2,085	1,184
2,820	1,027

2.19 Are the advertising dollars spent by a company related to total sales revenue? The following data represent the advertising dollars and the sales revenues for various companies in a given industry during a recent year. Construct a scatter plot of the data from the two variables and discuss the relationship between the two variables.

Advertising ($ millions)	Sales ($ millions)
4.2	155.7
1.6	87.3
6.3	135.6
2.7	99.0
10.4	168.2
7.1	136.9
5.5	101.4
8.3	158.2

2.20 It seems logical that the number of days per year that an employee is late for work is at least somewhat related to the employee's job satisfaction. Suppose 10 employees are asked to record how satisfied they are with their job on a scale from 0 to 10, with 0 denoting completely unsatisfied and 10 denoting completely satisfied. Suppose also that through human resource records, it is determined how many days each of these employees was tardy last year. The scatter plot below graphs the job satisfaction scores of each employee against the number of days he or she was tardy. What information can you glean from the scatter plot? Does there appear to be any relationship between job satisfaction and tardiness? If so, how might they appear to be related?

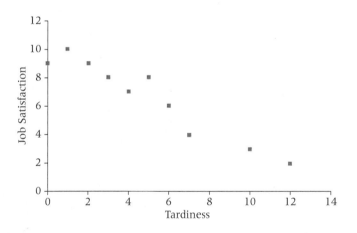

2.21 The human resources manager of a large chemical plant was interested in determining what factors might be related to the number of non-vacation days that workers were absent during the past year. One of the factors the manager considered was the distance the worker commutes to work. She wondered if longer commutes result in stress and whether increases in the likelihood of transportation failure might result in more worker absences. The manager studied company records, randomly selected 532 plant workers, and recorded the number of non-vacation days the workers were absent the previous year and how far their place of residence was from the plant. She then recoded the raw data in categories and created the cross-tabulation table shown below. Study the table and comment on any relationship that may exist between distance to the plant and number of absences.

		One-Way Commute Distance (in km)		
		0–3	4–10	More than 10
Number of Annual Non-Vacation-Day Absences	0–2	95	184	117
	3–5	21	40	53
	More than 5	3	7	12

2.22 A customer relations expert for a retail tire company is interested in determining if there is any relationship between a customer's level of education and his or her rating of the quality of the tire company's service. The tire company administers a very brief survey to each customer who buys tires and has them installed at the store. The customer is asked to describe the quality of the service rendered as either "acceptable" or "unacceptable." In addition, each respondent is asked the level of education attained from the categories of "high school only" or "university degree." These data are gathered on 25 customers and are given at right. Use this information to construct a cross-tabulation table. Comment on any relationships that may exist in the table.

Customer	Level of Education	Rating of Service
1	high school only	acceptable
2	university degree	unacceptable
3	university degree	acceptable
4	high school only	acceptable
5	university degree	unacceptable
6	high school only	acceptable
7	high school only	unacceptable
8	university degree	acceptable
9	university degree	unacceptable
10	university degree	unacceptable
11	high school only	acceptable
12	university degree	acceptable
13	university degree	unacceptable
14	high school only	acceptable
15	university degree	acceptable
16	high school only	acceptable
17	high school only	acceptable
18	high school only	unacceptable
19	university degree	unacceptable
20	university degree	acceptable
21	university degree	unacceptable
22	high school only	acceptable
23	university degree	acceptable
24	high school only	acceptable
25	university degree	unacceptable

2.5 Visualizing Time-Series Data

LEARNING OBJECTIVE 2.5

Describe and construct a time-series graph. Visually identify any trends in the data.

As part of big data and the business analytics process, business analysts sometimes use historical data—measures taken over time—to estimate what might happen in the future. One type of data that is often used in such analysis is **time-series data**, defined as *data gathered on a particular characteristic over a period of time at regular intervals.* Such a time period might be hours, days, weeks, months, quarters, years, or some other unit. To be useful to analysts, time-series data need to be "cleaned," such that measurements are taken at regular time intervals and arranged according to time of occurrence. Some examples of time-series data are five years of monthly retail trade data, weekly Treasury bill rates over a two-year period, and one year of daily household consumption data.

As an example, **Table 2.11** shows time-series data for motor vehicles produced from 1999 through 2018 for both Canada and Japan.

TABLE 2.11	Motor Vehicles Produced from 1999 through 2018 for both Canada and Japan	
Year	Motor Vehicles Produced in Canada (thousands)	Motor Vehicles Produced in Japan (thousands)
1999	3,059	9,895
2000	2,962	10,141
2001	2,533	9,777
2002	2,629	10,257
2003	2,553	10,286
2004	2,712	10,512
2005	2,688	10,800
2006	2,572	11,484
2007	2,579	11,596
2008	2,082	11,576
2009	1,490	7,934
2010	2,068	9,629
2011	2,135	8,399
2012	2,463	9,943
2013	2,380	9,630
2014	2,394	9,775
2015	2,283	9,278
2016	2,370	9,205
2017	2,200	9,694
2018	2,021	9,729

By visualizing these time-series data using a line chart, a business analyst can make it easier for a broader audience to see any trends or directions in the data. **Figure 2.12** is an Excel-produced line graph of the data. Looking at this graph, the business analyst can see that motor vehicle production in Canada began a downward slide in 2008 that has continued until 2018.

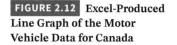

FIGURE 2.12   Excel-Produced Line Graph of the Motor Vehicle Data for Canada

Suppose we want to compare motor vehicle production for Canada to that of Japan during this same period of time. **Figure 2.13** is an Excel-produced line graph showing the data in Table 2.11. By looking at the visualization (graph) rather than just the raw data, it is easier to see that both countries had a dip in production in the middle years. In contrast to Canada, Japan has recently reached levels close to those in the early 2000s.

FIGURE 2.13 Excel-Produced Line Graph of the Motor Vehicle Data for both Canada and Japan

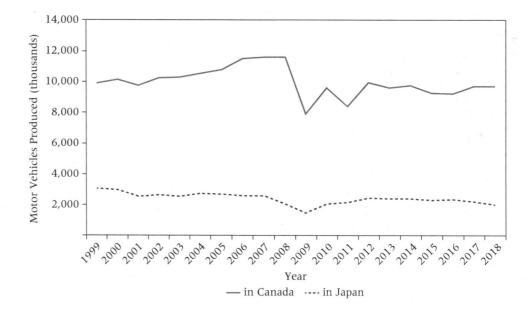

DEMONSTRATION PROBLEM 2.4

Consider the time-series data given below displaying the number of passengers per year for the major airport of each of seven cities over a period of seven years. How could a business analyst display the data in a visual way that would add interest to the data and help decision-makers more readily see trends for each city and differences between cities?

Number of Passengers per Airport of Seven Cities Over a Seven-Year Period (millions)

Year	Atlanta	Beijing	Dubai	London	Shanghai	Bangkok	Madrid
1	92.389	78.675	50.978	69.434	41.448	47.911	49.653
2	94.957	81.929	57.685	70.037	44.88	53.002	45.176
3	94.431	83.712	66.432	72.368	47.19	51.364	39.729
4	96.179	86.128	70.476	73.409	51.688	46.423	41.823
5	101.491	89.939	78.015	74.99	60.053	52.808	46.78
6	104.172	94.394	83.654	75.716	66.002	55.892	50.398
7	103.903	95.786	88.242	78.015	70.001	60.861	53.386

Solution   Make a time-series graph of the data using multiple lines. The resulting graph is:

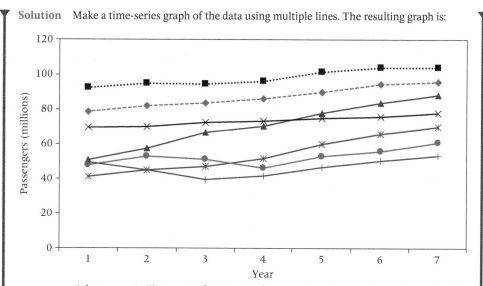

Studying this visual, we can see that the Atlanta airport was the largest, followed by Beijing, for the entire seven-year period. We can also see that while London remained fairly constant, the Dubai airport continually increased at a near constant rate, resulting in it becoming the number-three airport in passengers by year 7. Meanwhile, Shanghai maintained a steady growth, but Madrid's airport was down and up, as was the Bangkok airport.

While most visualizations are considered to be descriptive business analytics, in Chapter 15 we will explore ways to use time-series data such as these as predictive business analytics, to develop future forecasts.

Concept Check

Time-series data represent data gathered for a particular characteristic over a period of time at regular intervals. Draw the outline of a time-series graph for each of the following variables.

a. Canada's yearly CO_2 emissions for a period of 20 consecutive years

b. USD/CAD daily average exchange rate for a period of 30 consecutive days (Exchange rates are expressed as 1 unit of the foreign currency converted into Canadian dollars.)

c. Live births by month in Canada for a period of 12 consecutive months

2.5 Problems

2.23 Shown here are the sales data (in $ millions) for furniture and home furnishing stores over a recent period of five years. Using this data:

a. Construct a time-series graph for one year of the data. Looking at your graph, what are some of your insights and conclusions regarding this industry in that year?

b. Construct one graph that displays the data from each of the five years separately but in the same graph so that you can compare the five years. What insights and/or conclusions might you reach about this industry now that you can see the five years in one graph?

c. Place the data together in order (perhaps one long column) and construct one graph (similar to part a) with all the data. Seeing one graph with all 60 data points lined up, what insights and understanding can you gain that perhaps you didn't see in part b?

Month	Year 1	2	3	4	5
January	6,866	7,296	7,203	7,974	8,166
February	7,169	7,088	7,227	7,537	8,363
March	7,787	7,873	8,105	8,647	9,233
April	6,872	7,312	7,791	8,298	8,632
May	7,682	7,831	8,385	8,934	8,964
June	7,378	7,556	7,881	8,613	9,067
July	7,551	7,979	8,403	9,147	9,124
August	8,065	8,463	8,735	9,174	9,513
September	7,438	7,851	8,371	8,983	9,483
October	7,260	8,060	8,440	9,110	9,031
November	8,259	8,843	8,949	9,471	9,967
December	9,215	9,197	10,228	10,891	10,966

2.24 The table below shows the quarterly exports (in $ millions) from eight fictional towns in North America over a two-year period.

City	Year 1				Year 2			
	1	2	3	4	1	2	3	4
Coolsville	2,174	2,287	2,170	2,162	2,194	2,280	2,227	2,276
Genius Grove	9,968	11,004	10,758	10,469	11,100	11,834	11,216	11,373
Highland	6,389	6,848	6,578	6,677	6,350	6,626	6,164	6,714
Inner City	2,730	2,626	2,306	2,752	2,235	2,366	3,247	2,882
Metro City	5,994	5,604	7,818	9,737	8,006	6,611	7,840	9,279
New New York	2,014	1,932	1,780	2,212	2,281	2,351	2,205	2,477
Orbit City	4,092	4,516	4,756	4,706	4,272	4,603	4,897	4,849
Springfield	4,543	5,336	5,706	6,106	5,009	5,190	5,587	5,680

a. Construct a time-series graph for one of the cities. Looking at your graph, what are some of your insights and conclusions regarding this city's exports over the two years?

b. Construct one graph that displays the eight quarters of data for each city separately but in the same graph so that you can compare the eight cities. What insights and/or conclusions about the exports of these cities do you have now that you can see all five in one graph?

End-of-Chapter Review

Decision Dilemma Solved

Energy Consumption Around the World

Sometimes it is difficult for the reader to discern the relative sizes of pie slices that are close in magnitude. For that reason, a bar chart might be a better way to display the data. Shown below is a bar chart of the oil consumption data. It is easy to see that the U.S. dominates world oil consumption, and if the percentage figures were not there in the pie chart, it would be easier to see in the histogram than in the pie chart that Japan uses more oil than the Russian Federation.

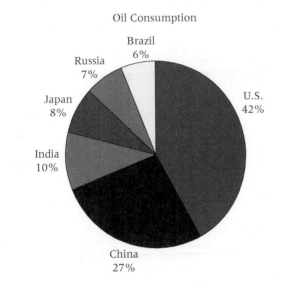

Oil Consumption

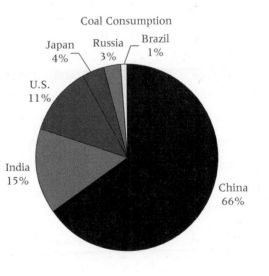

Coal Consumption

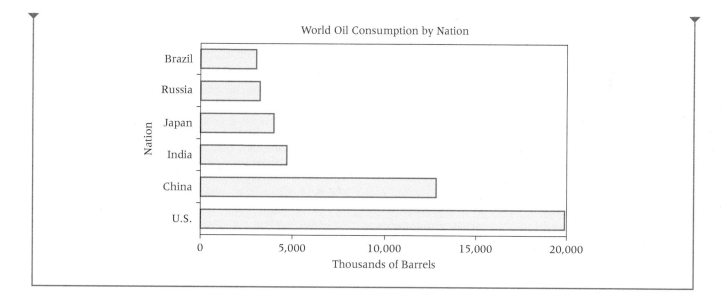

Key Considerations

Ethical considerations for the techniques learned in Chapter 2 begin with the data chosen for representation. With the abundance of available data in business, the person constructing the data summary must be selective when choosing the reported variables. The potential is great for the analyst to select variables or even data within variables that are favourable to his or her own situation or that are perceived to be well received by the audience.

In Section 2.1, we noted that the number of classes and the size of the intervals in frequency distributions are usually selected by the analyst. The analyst should be careful to select values and

sizes that will give an honest, accurate reflection of the situation and not a biased over- or understated case.

In Sections 2.2 to 2.5, we discussed the construction of charts and graphs. We pointed out that in many instances it makes sense to use unequal scales on the axes. However, doing so opens the possibility of cheating with statistics by stretching or compressing the axes to underscore the analyst's point. It is imperative that frequency distributions and charts and graphs be constructed in a manner that best reflects actual data and not merely the analyst's own agenda.

Why Statistics Is Relevant

The old cliché "a picture is worth a thousand words" is put to the test in this chapter. Charts and graphs are effective visual tools: they present information quickly and easily. Charts and graphs are powerful in business because the human mind takes the quickest route to understand reality, and visual statistics are often the answer to understanding managerial problems. It is certainly not surprising that charts and graphs are heavily used by print and electronic media.

Summary of Learning Objectives

LEARNING OBJECTIVE 2.1 Explain the difference between grouped and ungrouped data and construct a frequency distribution from a set of data. Explain what the distribution represents.

The two types of data are grouped and ungrouped. Grouped data are data organized into a frequency distribution. Differentiating between

grouped and ungrouped data is important, because statistical operations on the two types are computed differently.

Constructing a frequency distribution involves several steps. The first step is to determine the range of the data, which is the difference between the largest value and the smallest value. Next, the number of classes is determined, which is an arbitrary choice of the analyst. However, too few classes overaggregate the data into meaningless categories, and too many classes do not summarize the data enough to be useful. The third step in constructing the frequency distribution is to determine the width of the class interval. Dividing the range of values by the number of classes yields the approximate width of the class interval.

The class midpoint is the midpoint of a class interval. It is the average of the class endpoints and represents the halfway point of the class interval. Relative frequency is computed by dividing an individual frequency by the sum of the frequencies. Relative frequency represents the proportion of total values in a given class interval. The cumulative frequency is a running total frequency tally that starts with the first frequency value and adds each ensuing frequency to the total.

LEARNING OBJECTIVE 2.2 Describe and construct different types of quantitative data graphs, including histograms, frequency polygons, ogives, and stem-and-leaf plots. Explain when these graphs should be used.

Two types of graphical depictions are quantitative data graphs and qualitative data graphs. Quantitative data graphs presented in this chapter are histograms, frequency polygons, ogives, and stem-and-leaf plots. A histogram is a vertical bar chart in which a line segment connects class endpoints at the value of the frequency. Two vertical lines connect this line segment down to the *x*-axis, forming a rectangle. A frequency polygon is constructed by plotting a dot at the midpoint of each class interval for the value of each frequency and then connecting the dots. Ogives are cumulative frequency polygons. Points on an ogive are plotted at the class endpoints. Stem-and-leaf plots are another way to organize data. The numbers are divided into two parts, a stem and a leaf. The stems are the leftmost digits of the numbers and the leaves are the rightmost digits. The stems are listed individually, with all leaf values corresponding to each stem displayed beside that stem.

LEARNING OBJECTIVE 2.3 Describe and construct different types of qualitative data graphs, including pie charts, bar charts, and Pareto charts. Explain when these graphs should be used.

Qualitative data graphs presented in this chapter are pie charts, bar charts, and Pareto charts. A pie chart is a circular depiction of data. The amount of each category is represented as a slice of the pie proportionate to the total. The analyst is cautioned in using pie charts because it is sometimes difficult to differentiate the relative sizes of the slices. The bar chart or bar graph uses bars to represent the frequencies of various qualitative categories. The bar chart can be displayed horizontally or vertically. A Pareto chart is a vertical bar chart that is used in the quality movement in business to graphically display the causes of problems. The Pareto chart presents problem causes in descending order to help the decision-maker determine which problems to solve first.

LEARNING OBJECTIVE 2.4 Display and analyze two variables simultaneously using cross tabulation and scatter plots.

Cross tabulation is a process for producing a two-dimensional table that displays the frequency counts for two variables simultaneously. The scatter plot is a two-dimensional plot of pairs of points from two numerical variables. It is used to graphically determine whether any apparent relationship exists between the two variables.

LEARNING OBJECTIVE 2.5 Describe and construct a time-series graph. Visually identify any trends in the data.

Time-series data are defined as data gathered on a particular characteristic over a period of time at regular intervals. Time-series data plots can give the business analyst insights into various trends over time.

Key Terms

bar chart or graph 2-14	grouped data 2-3	relative frequency 2-4
class midpoint or mark 2-4	histogram 2-7	scatter plot 2-19
cross tabulation 2-18	ogive 2-9	stem-and-leaf plot 2-10
cumulative frequency 2-5	Pareto chart 2-16	time-series data 2-22
frequency distribution 2-3	pie chart 2-13	ungrouped data 2-3
frequency polygon 2-8	range 2-4	

Supplementary Problems

Calculating the Statistics

2.25 **Video** For the following data, construct a frequency distribution with six classes.

57	23	35	18	21
26	51	47	29	21
46	43	29	23	39
50	41	19	36	28
31	42	52	29	18
28	46	33	28	20

2.26 For each class interval of the frequency distribution given, determine the class midpoint, the relative frequency, and the cumulative frequency.

Class Interval	Frequency
20–under 25	17
25–under 30	20
30–under 35	16
35–under 40	15
40–under 45	8
45–under 50	6

Descriptive Statistics

LEARNING OBJECTIVES

The focus of Chapter 3 is the use of statistical techniques to describe data, thereby enabling you to:

3.1 Apply various measures of central tendency—including the mean, median, and mode—to a set of data.

3.2 Apply various measures of variability—including the range, interquartile range, mean absolute deviation, variance, and standard deviation (using the empirical rule and Chebyshev's theorem)—to a set of data.

3.3 Describe a data distribution statistically and graphically using skewness, kurtosis, and box-and-whisker plots.

3.4 Use descriptive statistics as a business analytics tool to better understand meanings and relationships in data so as to aid business people in making better decisions.

Decision Dilemma

Laundry Statistics

According to Euromonitor's recent Laundry Care in Canada Report, Canadians spent $1.4 billion on laundry detergent in a recent year. Statistics show that Canadians wash almost four billion loads each year: that works out to about two loads per person per week, and 500 loads per year for a family of five. According to Procter & Gamble, 35-billion loads of laundry are run in the U.S. each year. Every second, 1,100 loads are started. Statistics show that one person in the U.S. generates about a quarter of a tonne of dirty clothing each year.

Designers and producers of laundry machinery are interested in manufacturing more efficient washing machines, and environmentalists are concerned about reducing water consumption. In Canada and the U.S., new energy-efficient washing machines are considered to have excellent water usage if they use approximately 62 L of water. In Europe, the figure is about 15 L. The average wash cycle of a Canadian or an American wash is about 35 minutes compared to 90 minutes in Europe.

Canadians and Americans have traditionally preferred top-loading washing machines because they are less expensive, they have a longer life expectancy, and the user does not have to bend over to load and unload. However, the percentage of North Americans using front loaders is increasing. Europeans, on the other hand, prefer front loaders because they use less water, are stackable, and use less space. Around 90% of Europeans prefer front loaders. Europeans use the smaller front-loading machines because of smaller living spaces.

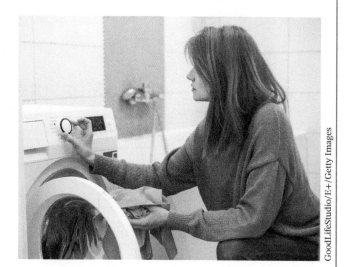

GoodLifeStudio/E+/Getty Images

Managerial, Statistical, and Analytical Questions

Virtually all of the statistics cited here are gleaned from studies or surveys.

1. Suppose a study of laundry usage is done in 50 Canadian households that contain washers and dryers. Water measurements are taken for the number of litres of water used by

each washing machine in completing a cycle. The following data are the number of litres used by each washing machine during the washing cycle. Summarize the data to describe washing machine water usage so that business people and environmentalists can more clearly understand the efficiency of washing machines in using water resources.

58	65	62	58	62	65	69	58	54	58
62	62	65	62	58	58	65	54	58	62
62	65	54	58	46	58	62	54	54	62
58	50	62	65	65	58	62	62	62	54
65	62	65	54	62	50	62	58	62	58

2. Is the amount of laundry done by a household each year related in some way to the household income? Suppose eight households of two adults and two children are randomly chosen for a study. Over a year, a record is kept of the mass of clothing washed by each household, and the annual household income is ascertained. From the following study data, determine whether a relationship exists between a household's income and the mass of laundry done.

Mass of Laundry (in kilograms)	Household Income ($ thousands)
549	42
397	31
857	60
658	68
925	110
603	45
299	56
676	72
885	93

Sources: Adapted from "Washing Machines," Consumer Reports, www.consumerreports.org/cro/washing-machines.htm; "Residential Clothes Washer Introduction," www.allianceforwaterefficiency.org; "The Eco-Impact of Laundry Detergent in Canada," March 27, 2013, mydizolve.com/2013/03/27/the-eco-impact-of-laundry-detergent-incanada/; "'Laundry Care in Canada' Now Available at Fast Market Research," SBWire, August 27, 2012.

Introduction

Chapter 2 presented graphical techniques for organizing and displaying data. Even though these graphs allow the analyst to make some general observations about the shape and spread of the data, a more complete understanding of the data can be attained by summarizing the data using statistics. This chapter presents such statistical measures, including measures of central tendency, measures of variability, and measures of shape.

3.1 | Measures of Central Tendency

LEARNING OBJECTIVE 3.1

Apply various measures of central tendency—including the mean, median, and mode—to a set of data.

One type of measure that is used to describe a set of data is the **measure of central tendency**. Measures of central tendency *yield information about the centre, or middle part, of a group of numbers*. Table 3.1 displays P/E ratio (price-to-earnings ratio, rounded to the nearest whole number) for 20 large Canadian companies in a recent year. For these data, measures of central tendency can yield such information as the average P/E ratio, the middle P/E ratio, and the most frequently occurring P/E ratio. Measures of central tendency do not focus on the span of the data set or how far values are from the middle numbers. The measures of central tendency presented here are the mean, the median, the mode, percentiles, and quartiles.

Mean

The **arithmetic mean** is *the average of a group of numbers* and is computed by summing all numbers and dividing by the number of numbers. Because the arithmetic mean is so widely used, most statisticians refer to it simply as the *mean*.

The population mean is represented by the Greek letter mu (μ). The sample mean is represented by $\bar{x}$. The formulas for computing the population mean and the sample mean are given in the boxes that follow.

Population Mean

$$\mu = \frac{\Sigma x_i}{N} = \frac{x_1 + x_2 + x_3 + \ldots + x_N}{N} \qquad (3.1)$$

Sample Mean

$$\bar{x} = \frac{\Sigma x_i}{n} = \frac{x_1 + x_2 + x_3 + \ldots + x_n}{n} \qquad (3.2)$$

The capital Greek letter sigma (Σ) is commonly used in mathematics to represent a summation of all the numbers in a grouping.[1] Also, N is the number of terms in the population, and n is the number of terms in the sample. The algorithm for computing a mean is to sum all the numbers in the population or sample and divide by the number of terms. It is inappropriate to use the mean to analyze data that are not at least interval level in measurement.

Suppose a company has five departments with 24, 13, 19, 26, and 11 workers each. The *population mean* number of workers in each department is 18.6 workers. The computations follow:

$$\Sigma x_i = 24 + 13 + 19 + 26 + 11 = 93$$

and

$$\mu = \frac{\Sigma x_i}{N} = \frac{93}{5} = 18.6$$

The calculation of a sample mean uses the same algorithm as for a population mean and will produce the same answer if computed on the same data. However, it is inappropriate to compute a sample mean for a population or a population mean for a sample. Because both populations and samples are important in statistics, a separate symbol is necessary for the population mean and for the sample mean.

Consider the P/E ratio data in **Table 3.1**. The mean P/E ratio for the list of 20 large Canadian companies given in Table 3.1 is 19.2.

TABLE 3.1	P/E Ratios (rounded to the nearest whole number) for 20 Large Canadian Companies in a Recent Year			
	12	11	8	17
	31	10	17	15
	11	14	61	40
	12	14	25	20
	18	10	17	20

---

[1] The mathematics of summations is not discussed here. A more detailed explanation is given in *WileyPLUS*, Chapter 3.

The mean is affected by each and every value, which is an advantage. The mean uses all the data, and each data item influences the mean. It is also a disadvantage because extremely large or small values can cause the mean to be pulled toward the extreme value.

The mean is the most commonly used measure of central tendency because it uses each data item in its computation, it is a familiar measure, and it has mathematical properties that make it attractive to use in inferential statistics analysis.

Median

The **median** is *the middle value in an ordered array of numbers*. For an array with an odd number of terms, the median is the middle number. For an array with an even number of terms, the median is the average of the two middle numbers. The following steps are used to determine the median.

1. Arrange the observations in an ordered data array (an ordering of the numbers from smallest to largest).
2. For an odd number of terms, find the middle term of the ordered array. It is the median.
3. For an even number of terms, find the average of the middle two terms. This average is the median.

Suppose a business analyst wants to determine the median for the following numbers.

15   11   14   3   21   17   22   16   19   16   5   7   19   8   9   20   4

The analyst arranges the numbers in an ordered array.

3   4   5   7   8   9   11   14   15   16   16   17   19   19   20   21   22

Because the array contains 17 terms (an odd number of terms), the median is the middle number, or 15.

If the number 22 is eliminated from the list, the array contains only 16 terms.

3   4   5   7   8   9   11   14   15   16   16   17   19   19   20   21

Now, for an even number of terms, the analyst determines the median by averaging the two middle values, 14 and 15. The resulting median value is 14.5.

Another way to locate the median is by finding the $[(n + 1)/2]$th term in an ordered array. For example, if a data set contains 77 terms, the median is the 39th term. That is,

$$\frac{n + 1}{2} = \frac{77 + 1}{2} = \frac{78}{2} = 39\text{th term}$$

This formula is helpful when a large number of terms must be manipulated.

Consider the P/E ratio data in Table 3.1. Because this data set contains 20 values, or $n = 20$, the median for these data is located at the $[(20 + 1)/2]$th term, or the 10.5th term. This result indicates that the median is located halfway between the 10th and 11th terms or the average of 15 and 17. Thus, the median P/E ratio for the list of 20 large Canadian companies given in Table 3.1 is 16.0.

The median is unaffected by the magnitude of extreme values. This characteristic is an advantage, because large and small values do not inordinately influence the median. For this reason, the median is often the best measure of location to use in the analysis of variables such as house costs, income, and age. Suppose, for example, that a real estate broker wants to determine the median selling price of 10 houses listed at the following prices.

$67,000	$105,000	$148,000	$5,250,000
91,000	116,000	167,000	
95,000	122,000	189,000	

The median is the average of the two middle terms, $116,000 and $122,000, or $119,000. This price is a reasonable representation of the prices of the 10 houses. Note that the house priced at $5,250,000 did not enter into the analysis other than to count as one of the 10 houses. If the price of the 10th house were $200,000, the results would be the same. However, if all the house prices were averaged, the resulting mean of the original 10 houses would be $635,000, higher than 9 of the 10 individual prices because the $5,250,000 house is included in the calculation.

A disadvantage of the median is that not all the information from the numbers is used. For example, information about the specific asking price of the most expensive house does not really enter into the computation of the median. The level of data measurement must be at least ordinal for a median to be meaningful.

Mode

The **mode** is *the most frequently occurring value in a set of data.* For the data in Table 3.1, the mode is 17 because the P/E ratio that occurs the most times (3) is 17. Organizing the data into an ordered array helps to locate the mode. The following is an ordered array of the values from Table 3.1.

8	10	10	11	11	12	12	14	14	15
17	17	17	18	20	20	25	31	40	61

This grouping makes it easier to see that 17 is the most frequently occurring number.

In the case of a tie for the most frequently occurring value, *two modes are listed.* Then the data are said to be **bimodal**. If a set of data is not exactly bimodal but contains two values that are more dominant than others, some analysts take the liberty of referring to the data set as bimodal even without an exact tie for the mode. *Data sets with more than two modes are* referred to as **multimodal**.

In the world of business, the concept of mode is often used in determining sizes. For example, shoe manufacturers might produce inexpensive shoes in three widths only: small, medium, and large. Each width represents a modal width of feet. By reducing the number of sizes to a few modal sizes, companies can reduce total product costs by limiting machine setup costs. Similarly, the garment industry produces shirts, dresses, suits, and many other clothing products in modal sizes. For example, all size M men's shirts in a given lot are produced in the same size. This size is the modal size for medium-sized men.

The mode is an appropriate measure of central tendency for nominal-level data. The mode can be used to determine which category occurs most frequently.

DEMONSTRATION PROBLEM 3.1

Shown below is a list of various motor vehicle producers and the number of cars (rounded to the nearest million) that each produced in a recent year according to the OICA (International Organization of Motor Vehicle Manufacturers).

Auto Manufacturer	Production (millions)
Volkswagen	8
General Motors	7
Toyota	7
Hyundai	6
Nissan	4
PSA Peugeot Citroën	3
Honda	3
Ford	3
Renault	2
Suzuki	2
Fiat	2

Compute the sample mean, the median, and the mode.

Solution

Mean: The total number of vehicles produced by these 11 companies is $47 = \Sigma x_i$.

$$\bar{x} = \frac{\Sigma x_i}{n} = \frac{47}{11} = 4.3$$

Median: With 11 different companies in this sample, $n = 11$. The median is located at the $(11 + 1)/2 = $ 6th position. Because the data are already ordered, the 6th term is 3 (million), which is the median.

Mode: There are three companies that produce 3 (million) and also three companies that produce 2 (million); therefore, this sample is bimodal.

Source: "World Motor Vehicle Production: OICA Correspondents Survey," OICA, 2011, www.oica.net/wp-content/uploads/ranking-without-china-30-nov-12.pdf.

Percentiles

Percentiles are *measures of central tendency that divide a group of data into 100 parts.* There are 99 percentiles because it takes 99 dividers to separate a group of data into 100 parts. The *n*th percentile is the value such that at least *n* percent of the data are below that value and at most $(100 - n)$ percent are above that value. Specifically, the 87th percentile is a value such that at least 87% of the data are below the value and no more than 13% are above the value. Percentiles are "stair-step" values, as shown in **Figure 3.1**, because the 87th percentile and the 88th percentile have no percentile between them. If a plant operator takes a safety examination and 87.6% of the safety exam scores are below that person's score, he or she still scores at only the 87th percentile, even though more than 87% of the scores are lower.

FIGURE 3.1 **Stair-Step Percentiles**

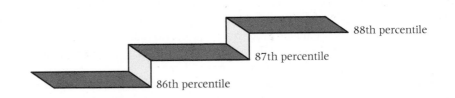

88th percentile

87th percentile

86th percentile

Percentiles are widely used in reporting test results. Almost all students have taken provincial achievement tests in elementary and secondary education. In most cases, the results for these examinations are reported in percentile form and also as raw scores. Shown next is a summary of the steps used in determining the location of a percentile.

Steps in Determining the Location of a Percentile

1. Organize the numbers into an ascending-order array.
2. Calculate the percentile location (*i*) by:

$$i = \frac{P}{100}(n)$$

where
$\quad P = $ the percentile of interest
$\quad i = $ percentile location
$\quad n = $ number in the data set

3. Determine the location by either (a) or (b).

    a. If *i* is a whole number, the *P*th percentile is the average of the value at the *i*th location and the value at the $(i + 1)$th location.

    b. If *i* is not a whole number, the *P*th percentile value is located at the whole-number part of $i + 1$.

For example, suppose you want to determine the 80th percentile of 1,240 numbers. P is 80 and n is 1,240. First, order the numbers from least to greatest. Next, calculate the location of the 80th percentile.

$$i = \frac{80}{100}(1,240) = 992$$

Because $i = 992$ is a whole number, follow the directions in step 3(a). The 80th percentile is the average of the 992nd number and the 993rd number.

$$P_{80} = \frac{992\text{nd number} + 993\text{rd number}}{2}$$

DEMONSTRATION PROBLEM 3.2

Determine the 30th percentile of the following eight numbers: 14, 12, 19, 23, 5, 13, 28, 17.

Solution   For these eight numbers, we want to find the value of the 30th percentile, so $n = 8$ and $P = 30$.

First, organize the data into an ascending-order array.

5	12	13	14	17	19	23	28

Next, compute the value of i.

$$i = \frac{30}{100}(8) = 2.4$$

Because i is not a whole number, use step 3(b). The value of $i + 1$ is 2.4 + 1, or 3.4. The whole-number part of 3.4 is 3. The 30th percentile is located at the third value. The third value is 13, so 13 is the 30th percentile. Note that a percentile may or may not be one of the data values, as in P_{25}, below.

Quartiles

Quartiles are *measures of central tendency that divide a group of data into four subgroups or parts.* The three quartiles are denoted as Q_1, Q_2, and Q_3. The first quartile, Q_1, separates the first, or lowest, one fourth of the data from the upper three fourths and is equal to the 25th percentile. The second quartile, Q_2, separates the second fourth of the data from the third fourth. Q_2 is located at the 50th percentile and equals the median of the data. The third quartile, Q_3, divides the first three fourths of the data from the last fourth and is equal to the value of the 75th percentile. These three quartiles are shown in **Figure 3.2**.

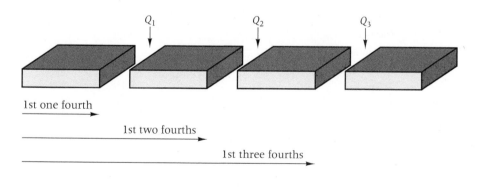

FIGURE 3.2 **Quartiles**

Suppose we want to determine the values of Q_1, Q_2, and Q_3 for the following numbers.

106	109	114	116	121	122	125	129

For this set of data, $n = 8$. The value of Q_1 is found at the 25th percentile, P_{25}, by:

$$i = \frac{25}{100}(8) = 2$$

Because i is a whole number, P_{25} is the average of the second and third numbers.

$$P_{25} = \frac{109 + 114}{2} = 111.5$$

The value of Q_1 is $P_{25} = 111.5$. Notice that one fourth, or two, of the values (106 and 109) are less than 111.5.

The value of Q_2 is equal to the median. Because the array contains an even number of terms, the median is the average of the two middle terms.

$$Q_2 = \text{median} = \frac{116 + 121}{2} = 118.5$$

Notice that exactly half of the terms are less than Q_2 and half are greater than Q_2.

The value of Q_3 is determined by P_{75} as follows:

$$i = \frac{75}{100}(8) = 6$$

Because i is a whole number, P_{75} is the average of the sixth and the seventh numbers.

$$P_{75} = \frac{122 + 125}{2} = 123.5$$

The value of Q_3 is $P_{75} = 123.5$. Notice that three fourths, or six, of the values are less than 123.5 and two of the values are greater than 123.5.

DEMONSTRATION PROBLEM 3.3

The following shows the top 16 global marketing categories for advertising spending for a recent year according to Advertising Age. Determine the first, the second, and the third quartiles for these data.

Category	Ad Spending (US$ millions)
Automotive	22,195
Personal care	19,526
Entertainment and media	9,538
Food	7,793
Drugs	7,707
Electronics	4,023
Soft drinks	3,916
Retail	3,576
Cleaners	3,571
Restaurants	3,553
Computers	3,247
Telephone	2,488
Financial	2,433
Beer, wine, and liquor	2,050
Candy	1,137
Toys	699

Solution For 16 categories, $n = 16$. $Q_1 = P_{25}$ is found by:

$$i = \frac{25}{100}(16) = 4$$

Because i is a whole number, Q_1 is found to be the average of the fourth and fifth values from the bottom:

$$Q_1 = \frac{2433 + 2488}{2} = 2460.5$$

$Q_2 = P_{50}$ = median; with 16 terms, the median is the average of the eighth and ninth terms:

$$Q_2 = \frac{3571 + 3576}{2} = 3573.5$$

$Q_3 = P_{75}$ is solved by:

$$i = \frac{75}{100}(16) = 12$$

Q_3 is found by averaging the 12th and 13th terms:

$$Q_3 = \frac{7707 + 7793}{2} = 7750$$

Concept Check

1. Match the measure of central tendency with its correct definition.

   a. Quartiles
   b. Arithmetic mean
   c. Mode
   d. Percentiles
   e. Median

   i. The middle value in an ordered array of numbers
   ii. Measures of central tendency that divide a group of data into 100 parts
   iii. The average of a group of numbers
   iv. The most frequently occurring value in a set of data
   v. Measures of central tendency that divide a group of data into four subgroups or parts

2. What are the differences between the mean, median, and mode? What are the advantages and disadvantages of each measure?

3. Is the arithmetic mean greatly affected by any extreme value or values? Explain.

4. Can you contrive a small set of data with no mode?

3.1 Problems

3.1 Compute the mean for the following numbers.

   17.3   44.5   31.6   40.0   52.8   38.8   30.1   78.5

3.2 Compute the mean for the following numbers.

   7   -2   5   9   0   -3   -6   -7   -4   -5   2   -8

3.3 Determine the median for the numbers in Problem 3.1.

3.4 Determine the median for the following numbers.

   213   345   609   73   167   243   444   524   199   682

3.5 Determine the median and the mode for the following numbers.

   2   4   8   4   6   2   7   8   4   3   8   9   4   3   5

3.6 Compute the 35th percentile, the 55th percentile, Q_1, Q_2, and Q_3 for the following data.

   16   28   29   13   17   20   11   34   32   27   25   30   19   18   33

3.7 Compute P_{20}, P_{47}, P_{83}, Q_1, Q_2, and Q_3 for the following data.

120	138	97	118	172	144
138	107	94	119	139	145
162	127	112	150	143	80
105	116	142	128	116	171

3.8 The following list shows the 15 largest banks in the world by assets according to Standard and Poor's. Compute the median and the mean assets from this group. Which of these two measures do you think is most appropriate for summarizing these data, and why? What is the value of Q_2? Determine the 63rd percentile for the data. Determine the 29th percentile for the data. How could such information on percentiles potentially help banking decision-makers?

Bank	Assets (US$ millions)
Industrial & Commercial Bank of China (ICBC)	4,009
China Construction Bank Corp.	3,400
Agricultural Bank of China	3,236
Bank of China	2,992
Mitsubishi UFJ Financial Group	2,785
JPMorgan Chase & Co.	2,534
HSBC Holdings	2,522
BNP Paribas	2,357
Bank of America	2,281
Credit Agricole	2,117
Wells Fargo & Co.	1,952
Japan Post Bank	1,874
Citigroup Inc.	1,842
Sumitomo Mitsui Financial Group	1,175
Deutsche Bank	1,166

3.9 The following lists 12 large automakers and the number of cars produced by each in a recent year. Compute the median, Q_3, P_{20}, P_{60}, P_{80}, and P_{93} for these data.

Auto Manufacturer	Production
Volkswagen	8,157,058
General Motors	6,867,465
Toyota	6,793,714
Hyundai	6,118,221
Nissan	3,581,445
PSA Peugeot Citroën	3,161,955
Honda	2,886,343
Ford	2,639,735
Renault	2,443,040

Auto Manufacturer	Production
Suzuki	2,337,237
Fiat	1,804,523
B.M.W.	1,738,160

Source: "World Motor Vehicle Production: OICA Correspondents Survey," OICA, 2011, www.oica.net/wp-content/uploads/ranking-without-china-30-nov-12.pdf.

3.10 The following lists the number of fatal accidents by scheduled commercial airlines over a 17-year period according to the Air Transport Association of America. Using these data, compute the mean, median, and mode. What is the value of the third quartile? Determine P_{11}, P_{35}, P_{58}, and P_{67}.

4 4 4 1 4 2 4 3 8 6 4 4 1 4 2 3 3

3.2   Measures of Variability

LEARNING OBJECTIVE 3.2

Apply various measures of variability—including the range, interquartile range, mean absolute deviation, variance, and standard deviation (using the empirical rule and Chebyshev's theorem)—to a set of data.

Measures of central tendency yield information about particular points of a data set. However, business analysts can use another group of analytic tools, **measures of variability**, to *describe the spread or the dispersion of a set of data*. Using measures of variability in conjunction with measures of central tendency makes possible a more complete numerical description of the data.

For example, a company has 25 salespeople in the field, and the median annual sales figure for these people is $1.2 million. Are the salespeople successful as a group or not? The median provides information about the sales of the person in the middle, but what about the other salespeople? Are all of them selling $1.2 million annually, or do the sales figures vary widely, with one person selling $5 million annually and another selling only $150,000 annually? Measures of variability provide the additional information necessary to answer that question (see Thinking Critically About Statistics in Business Today 3.1).

Figure 3.3 shows three distributions in which the mean of each distribution is the same ($\mu = 50$) but the variabilities differ. Observation of these distributions shows that a measure of variability is necessary to complement the mean value in describing the data. This section focuses on seven measures of variability: range, interquartile range, mean absolute deviation, variance, standard deviation, z scores, and coefficient of variation.

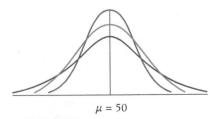

$\mu = 50$

FIGURE 3.3 **Three Distributions with the Same Mean but Different Dispersions**

Thinking Critically About Statistics in Business Today 3.1

Recycling Statistics

There are many interesting statistics with regard to recycling. Each ton of recycled paper saves about 17 trees, over 1,700 litres of oil, over 2 cubic metres of landfill space, 4,000 kilowatts of energy, and close to 32,000 litres of water. The energy saved by recycling one glass bottle can run a 100-watt light bulb for four hours. Recycling one aluminum can saves enough energy, the equivalent of 2 litres of gasoline, to run a television for three hours. In general, Canadians have done a good job at recycling containers: approximately 75% of aluminum cans, 80% of non-refillable glass, and 60% of PET plastic beverage bottles are collected for recycling. On average, one Canadian recycles 132 kg of waste per year. The United States is number one in the world in producing trash, with an average of 730 kg per person per year.

Things to Ponder

1. On average, one Canadian recycles 132 kg of waste per year. What different information might a median yield on these data, and how might it help decision-makers?

2. Canada produces trash at an average of 282 kg per person per year. What additional information could be gleaned by also knowing a measure of variability on these data?

Sources: Adapted from National Recycling Coalition, nrcrecycles.org; Environmental Protection Agency, www.epa.gov; "Recycling Facts," Recycling Revolution, www.recycling-revolution.com/recycling-facts.html; Earth 911, earth911.com; "Solid Waste Diversion and Disposal," Environment and Natural Resources Canada, www.canada.ca/en/environment-climate-change/services/environmental-indicators/solid-waste-diversion-disposal.html; Giroux Environmental Consulting, *State of Waste Management in Canada*, report prepared for Canadian Council of Ministers of Environment, www.ccme.ca/files/Resources/waste/wst_mgmt/State_Waste_Mgmt_in_Canada%20April%202015%20revised.pdf.

Range

The **range** is *the difference between the largest value of a data set and the smallest value of the set.* Although it is usually a single numeric value, some business analysts define the range of data as the ordered pair of smallest and largest numbers (smallest, largest). It is a crude measure of variability, describing the distance to the outer bounds of the data set. It reflects those extreme values because it is constructed from them. An advantage of the range is its ease of computation. One important use of the range is in quality assurance, where the range is used to construct control charts. A disadvantage of the range is that, because it is computed with the values that are on the extremes of the data, it is affected by extreme values, and its application as a measure of variability is limited.

The data in Table 3.1 represent the P/E ratios (rounded to the nearest whole number) for 20 large Canadian companies in a recent year. The lowest P/E ratio was 8 and the highest P/E ratio was 61. The range of the P/E ratios can be computed as the difference of the highest and lowest values:

$$\text{Range} = \text{Highest} - \text{Lowest} = 61 - 8 = 53$$

Interquartile Range

Another measure of variability is the **interquartile range**. The interquartile range (IQR) is *the range of values between the first and third quartiles.* Essentially, it is the range of the middle 50% of the data and is determined by computing the value of $Q_3 - Q_1$. The interquartile range is especially useful in situations where data users are more interested in values toward the middle and less interested in extremes. In describing a real estate housing market, real estate brokers might use the interquartile range as a measure of housing prices when describing the middle half of the market for buyers who are interested in houses in the midrange. In addition, the interquartile range is used in the construction of box-and-whisker plots.

Interquartile Range

$$\text{IQR} = Q_3 - Q_1 \qquad\qquad (3.3)$$

The following data indicate the top 10 trading partners of Canada based on Canadian exports to the country in a recent year according to Industry Canada.

Country	Exports ($ billions)
United States	438.3
China	27.7
United Kingdom	16.3
Japan	13.0
Mexico	8.2
South Korea	5.9
Germany	4.8
Netherlands	4.7
India	4.3
Hong Kong	3.9

What is the interquartile range for these data? The process begins by computing the first and third quartiles as follows.

Solving for $Q_1 = P_{25}$ when $n = 10$:

$$i = \frac{25}{100}(10) = 2.5$$

P_{25} is found as the third value from the bottom:

$$Q_1 = P_{25} = 4.7$$

Solving for $Q_3 = P_{75}$:

$$i = \frac{75}{100}(10) = 7.5$$

P_{75} is found as the eighth value from the bottom.

$$Q_3 = P_{75} = 16.3$$

The interquartile range is:

$$Q_3 - Q_1 = 16.3 - 4.7 = 11.6$$

The middle 50% of the exports for the top 10 Canadian trading partners spans a range of 11.6 ($ billions).

Mean Absolute Deviation, Variance, and Standard Deviation

Three other measures of variability are the variance, the standard deviation, and the mean absolute deviation. They are obtained through similar processes and are, therefore, presented together. These measures are not meaningful unless the data are at least interval-level data. The variance and standard deviation are widely used in statistics. Although the standard deviation has some stand-alone potential, the importance of the variance and standard deviation lies mainly in their role as tools used in conjunction with other statistical devices.

Suppose a small company started a production line to build computers. During the first five weeks of production, the output was 5, 9, 16, 17, and 18 computers, respectively. Which descriptive statistics could the owner use to measure the early progress of production? In an attempt to summarize these figures, the owner could compute a mean.

$$\Sigma x_i = 5 + 9 + 16 + 17 + 18 = 65 \quad \mu = \frac{\Sigma x_i}{N} = \frac{65}{5} = 13$$

What is the variability in these five weeks of data? One way for the owner to begin to look at the spread of the data is to subtract the mean from each data value. *Subtracting the mean from each data value* yields the **deviation from the mean** $(x_i - \mu)$. **Table 3.2** shows

TABLE 3.2 **Deviations from the Mean for Computer Production**

Number (x)	Deviations from the Mean ($x - \mu$)
5	$5 - 13 = -8$
9	$9 - 13 = -4$
16	$16 - 13 = +3$
17	$17 - 13 = +4$
18	$18 - 13 = +5$
$\Sigma x_i = 65$	$\Sigma(x_i - \mu) = 0$

these deviations for the computer company production. Note that some deviations from the mean are positive and some are negative. **Figure 3.4** shows that, geometrically, the negative deviations represent values that are below (to the left of) the mean and positive deviations represent values that are above (to the right of) the mean.

An examination of deviations from the mean can reveal information about the variability of data. However, the deviations are used mostly as a tool to compute other measures of variability. Note that in both Table 3.2 and Figure 3.4 these deviations total zero. This phenomenon applies to all cases. For a given set of data, the sum of all deviations from the arithmetic mean is always zero. This property requires considering alternative ways to obtain measures of variability.

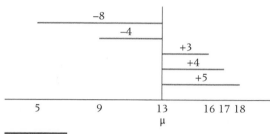

FIGURE 3.4 **Geometric Distances from the Mean (from Table 3.2)**

Sum of Deviations from the Arithmetic Mean Is Always Zero

$$\Sigma(x_i - \mu) = 0$$

One obvious way to force the sum of deviations to have a nonzero total is to take the absolute value of each deviation around the mean. Utilizing the absolute value of the deviations about the mean makes solving for the mean absolute deviation possible.

Mean Absolute Deviation

The **mean absolute deviation (MAD)** is *the average of the absolute values of the deviations around the mean for a set of numbers.*

Mean Absolute Deviation

$$\text{MAD} = \frac{\Sigma|x_i - \mu|}{N} \tag{3.4}$$

Using the data from Table 3.2, the computer company owner can compute a mean absolute deviation by taking the absolute values of the deviations and averaging them, as shown in **Table 3.3**. The mean absolute deviation for the computer production data is 4.8.

Because it is computed by using absolute values, the mean absolute deviation is less useful in statistics than other measures of dispersion. However, in the field of forecasting, it is used occasionally as a measure of error.

TABLE 3.3   **Mean Absolute Deviation for Computer Production Data**

x	$x - \mu$	$\lvert x - \mu \rvert$
5	−8	+8
9	−4	+4
16	+3	+3
17	+4	+4
18	+5	+5
$\Sigma x_i = 65$	$\Sigma(x_i - \mu) = 0$	$\Sigma \lvert x_i - \mu \rvert = 24$

$$\text{MAD} = \frac{\Sigma \lvert x_i - \mu \rvert}{N} = \frac{24}{5} = 4.8$$

Variance

Because absolute values are not conducive to easy manipulation, mathematicians developed an alternative mechanism for overcoming the zero-sum property of deviations from the mean. This approach utilizes the square of the deviations from the mean. The result is the variance, an important measure of variability.

The **variance** is *the average of the squared deviations about the arithmetic mean for a set of numbers.* The population variance is denoted by σ^2.

Population Variance

$$\sigma^2 = \frac{\Sigma(x_i - \mu)^2}{N} \tag{3.5}$$

Table 3.4 shows the original production numbers for the computer company, the deviations from the mean, and the squared deviations from the mean.

TABLE 3.4   **Computing a Variance and a Standard Deviation from the Computer Production Data**

x	$x - \mu$	$(x - \mu)^2$
5	−8	64
9	−4	16
16	+3	9
17	+4	16
18	+5	25
$\Sigma x_i = 65$	$\Sigma(x_i - \mu) = 0$	$\Sigma(x_i - \mu)^2 = 130$

$$SS_x = \Sigma(x_i - \mu)^2 = 130$$

$$\text{Variance} = \sigma^2 = \frac{SS_x}{N} = \frac{\Sigma(x_i - \mu)^2}{N} = \frac{130}{5} = 26.0$$

$$\text{Standard Deviation} = \sigma = \sqrt{\frac{\Sigma(x_i - \mu)^2}{N}} = \sqrt{\frac{130}{5}} = 5.1$$

The sum of the squared deviations around the mean of a set of values—called the **sum of squares of x** and sometimes abbreviated as SS_x—is used throughout statistics. For the computer company, this value is 130. Dividing it by the number of data values (5 weeks) yields the variance for computer production:

$$\sigma^2 = \frac{130}{5} = 26.0$$

Because the variance is computed from squared deviations, the final result is expressed in terms of squared units of measurement. Statistics measured in squared units are problematic to interpret. Consider, for example, Mattel Toys attempting to interpret production costs in terms of squared dollars or BlackBerry Limited (formerly Research in Motion) measuring production output variation in terms of squared BlackBerrys. Therefore, when used as a descriptive measure, variance can be considered as an intermediate calculation in the process of obtaining the sample standard deviation.

Standard Deviation

The standard deviation is a popular measure of variability. It is used both as a separate entity and as a part of other analyses, such as computing confidence intervals and in hypothesis testing (see Chapters 8, 9, and 10).

Population Standard Deviation

$$\sigma = \sqrt{\frac{\Sigma(x_i - \mu)^2}{N}}$$

(3.6)

The **standard deviation** is *the square root of the variance.* The population standard deviation is denoted by σ.

Like the variance, the standard deviation utilizes the sum of the squared deviations around the mean (SS_x). It is computed by averaging these squared deviations (SS_x/N) and taking the square root of that average. One feature of the standard deviation that distinguishes it from a variance is that the standard deviation is expressed in the same units as the raw data, whereas the variance is expressed in those units squared. Table 3.4 shows the standard deviation for the computer production company: $\sqrt{26}$ or 5.1.

What does a standard deviation of 5.1 mean? The meaning of standard deviation is more readily understood from its use, which is explored in the next section. Although the standard deviation and the variance are closely related and can be computed from each other, differentiating between them is important, because both are widely used in statistics.

Meaning of Standard Deviation   What is a standard deviation? What does it do, and what does it mean? The most precise way to define standard deviation is by reciting the formula used to compute it. However, insight into the concept of standard deviation can be gleaned by viewing the manner in which it is applied. Two ways of applying the standard deviation are the empirical rule and Chebyshev's theorem.

Empirical Rule   The **empirical rule** is an important guideline that *is used to state the approximate percentage of values that lie within a given number of standard deviations from the mean of a set of data if the data are normally distributed.*

The empirical rule is used only for three numbers of standard deviations: 1σ, 2σ, and 3σ. More detailed analysis of other numbers of σ values is presented in Chapter 6. Also discussed in further detail in Chapter 6 is the normal distribution, a unimodal, symmetrical distribution that is bell (or mound) shaped. The requirement that the data be normally distributed contains some tolerance, and the empirical rule generally applies as long as the data are approximately mound shaped.

Empirical Rule*

Distance from the Mean	Values within Distance
$\mu \pm 1\sigma$	68%
$\mu \pm 2\sigma$	95%
$\mu \pm 3\sigma$	99.7%

*Based on the assumption that the data are approximately normally distributed.

If a set of data is normally distributed, or bell-shaped, approximately 68% of the data values are within one standard deviation of the mean, 95% are within two standard deviations, and almost 100% are within three standard deviations.

Suppose a recent report states that for Ontario, the average province-wide price of a litre of regular unleaded gasoline is $1.26. Suppose regular unleaded gasoline prices vary across the province with a standard deviation of $0.02 and are normally distributed. According to the empirical rule, approximately 68% of the prices should fall within $\mu \pm 1\sigma$, or $1.26 \pm 1(\$0.02)$. Approximately 68% of the prices should be between $1.24 and $1.28, as shown in **Figure 3.5 A**. Approximately 95% should fall within $\mu \pm 2\sigma$ or $1.26 \pm 2(\$0.02) = \$1.26 \pm \$0.04$, or between $1.22 and $1.30, as shown in **Figure 3.5 B**. Nearly all regular gasoline prices (99.7%) should fall between $1.20 and $1.32 ($\mu \pm 3\sigma$).

FIGURES 3.5 A and B
Empirical Rule for One and Two Standard Deviations of Gasoline Prices

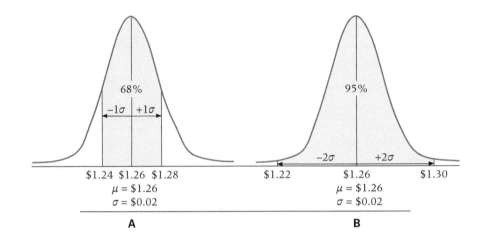

Note that with 68% of the gasoline prices falling within one standard deviation of the mean, approximately 32% are outside this range. Because the normal distribution is symmetrical, the 32% can be split in half such that 16% lie in each tail of the distribution. Thus, approximately 16% of the gasoline prices should be less than $1.24 and approximately 16% of the prices should be greater than $1.28.

Many phenomena are distributed approximately in a bell shape, including most human characteristics, such as height and mass; therefore, the empirical rule applies in many situations and is widely used.

DEMONSTRATION PROBLEM 3.4

A company produces a lightweight valve that is specified to have a mass of 1,365 g. Unfortunately, because of imperfections in the manufacturing process not all of the valves produced have a mass of exactly 1,365 g. In fact, the masses of the valves produced are normally distributed with a mean mass of 1,365 g and a standard deviation of 294 g. Within what range of masses would approximately 95% of the valve masses fall? Approximately 16% of the masses would be more than what value? Approximately 0.15% of the masses would be less than what value?

Solution Because the valve masses are normally distributed, the empirical rule applies. According to the empirical rule, approximately 95% of the masses should fall within $\mu \pm 2\sigma = 1,365 \pm 2(294) = 1,365 \pm 588$. Thus, approximately 95% should fall between 777 and 1,953. Approximately 68% of the masses should fall within $\mu \pm 1\sigma$ and 32% should fall outside this interval. Because the normal distribution is symmetrical, approximately 16% should lie above $\mu + 1\sigma = 1,365 + 294 = 1,659$. Approximately 99.7% of the masses should fall within $\mu \pm 3\sigma$ and 0.3% should fall outside this interval. Half of these or 0.15% should lie below $\mu - 3\sigma = 1,365 - 3(294) = 1,365 - 882 = 483$.

Chebyshev's Theorem The empirical rule applies only when data are known to be approximately normally distributed. What do analysts use when data are not normally distributed or when the shape of the distribution is unknown? Chebyshev's theorem applies to all distributions regardless of their shape and thus can be used whenever the data distribution shape is unknown or is nonnormal. Even though Chebyshev's theorem can in theory be applied to data that are normally distributed, the empirical rule is more widely known and is preferred whenever appropriate. Chebyshev's theorem is not a guideline, as the empirical rule is; rather, it is presented in formula format and therefore can be more widely applied. **Chebyshev's theorem** states that *at least* $1 - 1/k^2$ *values will fall within* $\pm k$ *standard deviations of the mean regardless of the shape of the distribution.*

Chebyshev's Theorem

Within k standard deviations of the mean, $\mu \pm k\sigma$, lie at least

$$1 - \frac{1}{k^2} \qquad (3.7)$$

proportion of the values.

Assumption: $k > 1$

Specifically, Chebyshev's theorem says that at least 75% of all values are within $\pm 2\sigma$ of the mean regardless of the shape of a distribution because if $k = 2$, then $1 - 1/k^2 = 1 - 1/2^2 = 3/4 = 0.75$. **Figure 3.6** provides a graphic illustration. In contrast, the empirical rule states that if the data are normally distributed, 95% of all values are within $\mu \pm 2\sigma$. According to Chebyshev's theorem, the percentage of values within three standard deviations of the mean is at least 89%, in contrast to 99.7% for the empirical rule. Because a formula is used to compute proportions with Chebyshev's theorem, any value of k greater than 1 ($k > 1$) can be used. For example, if $k = 2.5$, at least 0.84 of all values are within $\mu \pm 2.5\sigma$, because $1 - 1/k^2 = 1 - 1/(2.5)^2 = 0.84$.

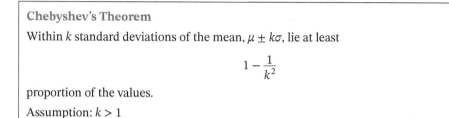

FIGURE 3.6 Application of Chebyshev's Theorem for Two Standard Deviations

DEMONSTRATION PROBLEM 3.5

In the computing industry, the average age of professional employees tends to be younger than in many other business professions. Suppose the average age of a professional employed by a particular computer firm is 28 with a standard deviation of 5 years. A histogram of professional employee ages with this firm reveals that the data are not normally distributed but rather are amassed in the 20s with few workers over 40. Apply Chebyshev's theorem to determine within what range of ages at least 85% of the workers' ages would fall.

Solution   Because the ages are not normally distributed, it is not appropriate to apply the empirical rule; therefore, Chebyshev's theorem must be applied to answer the question.

Chebyshev's theorem states that at least $1 - 1/k^2$ proportion of the values are within $\mu \pm k\sigma$. Because 85% of the values are within this range, let

$$1 - \frac{1}{k^2} = 0.85$$

Solving for k yields

$$0.15 = \frac{1}{k^2}$$
$$k^2 = 6.667$$
$$k = 2.58$$

Chebyshev's theorem says that at least 0.85 of the values are within $\pm 2.58\sigma$ of the mean. For $\mu = 28$ and $\sigma = 5$, at least 0.85, or 85%, of the values are within $28 \pm 2.58(5) = 28 \pm 12.9$ years of age or between 15.1 and 40.9 years old.

Population Versus Sample Variance and Standard Deviation The sample variance is denoted by s^2 and the sample standard deviation by s. The main use for sample variances and standard deviations is as estimators of population variances and standard deviations. Because of this, computation of the sample variance and standard deviation differs slightly from computation of the population variance and standard deviation. Both the sample variance and sample standard deviation use $n - 1$ in the denominator instead of n because using n in the denominator of a sample variance results in a statistic that tends to underestimate the population variance. While discussion of the properties of *good estimators* is beyond the scope of this text, one of the properties of a good estimator is being *unbiased*. Whereas using n in the denominator of the sample variance makes it a *biased* estimator, using $n - 1$ allows it to be an *unbiased* estimator, which is a desirable property in inferential statistics.

Sample Variance

$$s^2 = \frac{\Sigma(x_i - \bar{x})^2}{n - 1}$$

(3.8)

Sample Standard Deviation

$$s = \sqrt{\frac{\Sigma(x_i - \bar{x})^2}{n - 1}}$$

(3.9)

Shown here is a sample of six of the largest accounting firms in Canada and their revenue for a recent year as reported by The Bottom Line: Annual Top 30 Survey of Accounting Firms.

Firm	Revenue ($ millions)
Deloitte	2,088
KPMG	1,324
PwC	1,290
Ernst & Young	1,111
Grant Thornton Canada	597
MNP	597

The sample variance is 308,190.17 and the sample standard deviation is 555.15.

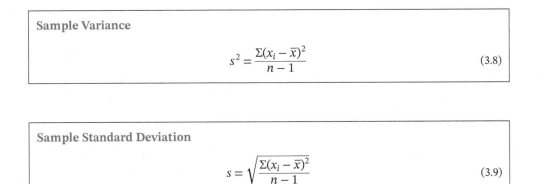

x_i	$(x_i - \bar{x})^2$
2,088	846,706.69
1,324	24,388.03
1,290	14,924.69
1,111	3,230.03
597	325,850.69
597	325,850.69

$$\Sigma x_i = 7{,}007.00 \qquad \Sigma(x_i - \bar{x})^2 = 1{,}540{,}950.83$$

$$\bar{x} = \frac{7{,}007.00}{6} = 1{,}167.83$$

$$s^2 = \frac{1{,}540{,}950.83}{5} = 308{,}190.17$$

$$s = \sqrt{308{,}190.17} = 555.15$$

Computational Formulas for Variance and Standard Deviation

An alternative method of computing variance and standard deviation, sometimes referred to as the computational method or shortcut method, is available. Algebraically,

$$\Sigma(x_i - \mu)^2 = \Sigma x_i^2 - \frac{(\Sigma x_i)^2}{N}$$

and

$$\Sigma(x_i - \overline{x})^2 = \Sigma x_i^2 - \frac{(\Sigma x_i)^2}{n}$$

Substituting these equivalent expressions into the original formulas for variance and standard deviation yields the following computational formulas.

Computational Formulas for Population Variance and Standard Deviation

$$\sigma^2 = \frac{\Sigma x_i^2 - \dfrac{(\Sigma x_i)^2}{N}}{N}$$

$$\sigma = \sqrt{\sigma^2}$$

Computational Formulas for Sample Variance and Standard Deviation

$$s^2 = \frac{\Sigma x_i^2 - \dfrac{(\Sigma x_i)^2}{n}}{n - 1}$$

$$s = \sqrt{s^2}$$

These computational formulas utilize the sum of the x values and the sum of the x^2 values instead of the difference between the mean and each value and computed deviations. In the pre-calculator/computer era, this method was usually faster and easier than using the original formulas.

For situations in which the mean is already computed or is given, alternative forms of these formulas are

$$\sigma^2 = \frac{\Sigma x_i^2 - N\mu^2}{N}$$

$$s^2 = \frac{\Sigma x_i^2 - n(\overline{x})^2}{n - 1}$$

Using the computational method, the owner of the start-up computer production company can compute a population variance and standard deviation for the production data, as shown in Table 3.5. (Compare these results with those in Table 3.4.)

TABLE 3.5 Computational Formula Calculations of Variance and Standard Deviation for Computer Production Data

x_i	x_i^2
5	25
9	81
16	256
17	289
18	324
$\Sigma x_i = 65$	$\Sigma x_i^2 = 975$

$$\sigma^2 = \frac{975 - \dfrac{65^2}{5}}{5} = \frac{975 - 845}{5} = \frac{130}{5} = 26$$

$$\sigma = \sqrt{26} = 5.1$$

DEMONSTRATION PROBLEM 3.6

The effectiveness of prosecution lawyers can be measured by several variables, including the number of convictions per month, the number of cases handled per month, and the total number of years of conviction per month. An analyst uses a sample of five prosecution lawyers in a city and determines the total number of years of conviction that each lawyer won against defendants during the past month, as reported in the first column in the following tabulations. Compute the mean absolute deviation, the variance, and the standard deviation for these figures.

Solution The analyst computes the mean absolute deviation, the variance, and the standard deviation for these data in the following manner.

x_i	$|x_i - \bar{x}|$	$(x_i - \bar{x})^2$
55	41	1,681
100	4	16
125	29	841
140	44	1,936
60	36	1,296
$\Sigma x_i = 480$	$\Sigma|x_i - \bar{x}| = 154$	$\Sigma(x_i - \bar{x})^2 = 5,770$

$$\bar{x} = \frac{\Sigma x_i}{n} = \frac{480}{5} = 96$$

$$\text{MAD} = \frac{154}{5} = 30.8$$

$$s^2 = \frac{5,770}{4} = 1,442.5$$

$$s = \sqrt{s^2} = 37.98$$

She then uses computational formulas to solve for s^2 and s and compares the results.

x_i	x_i^2
55	3,025
100	10,000
125	15,625
140	19,600
60	3,600
$\Sigma x_i = 480$	$\Sigma x_i^2 = 51,850$

$$s^2 = \frac{51,850 - \frac{480^2}{5}}{4} = \frac{51,850 - 46,080}{4} = \frac{5,770}{4} = 1,442.5$$

$$s = \sqrt{1,442.5} = 37.98$$

The results are the same. The sample standard deviation obtained by both methods is 37.98, or 38, years.

z Scores

A **z score** represents *the number of standard deviations a value (x) is above or below the mean of a set of numbers when the data are normally distributed.* Using z scores allows a value's raw distance from the mean to be translated into units of standard deviations.

---

z Score

$$z = \frac{x_i - \mu}{\sigma} \tag{3.10}$$

For samples,

$$z = \frac{x_i - \bar{x}}{s}$$

If a z score is negative, the raw value (x) is below the mean. If the z score is positive, the raw value (x) is above the mean.

For example, for a data set that is normally distributed with a mean of 50 and a standard deviation of 10, suppose a statistician wants to determine the z score for a value of 70. This value ($x = 70$) is 20 units above the mean, so the z value is

$$z = \frac{70 - 50}{10} = +2.00$$

This z score signifies that the raw score of 70 is two standard deviations above the mean. How is this z score interpreted? The empirical rule states that 95% of all values are within two standard deviations of the mean if the data are approximately normally distributed. **Figure 3.7** shows that because the value of 70 is two standard deviations above the mean ($z = +2.00$), 95% of the values are between 70 and the value ($x = 30$) that is two standard deviations below the mean, or $z = (30 - 50)/10 = -2.00$. Because 5% of the values are outside the range of two standard deviations from the mean and the normal distribution is symmetrical, 2.5% (half of the 5%) are below the value of 30. Thus 97.5% of the values are below the value of 70. Because a z score is the number of standard deviations an individual data value is from the mean, the empirical rule can be restated in terms of z scores.

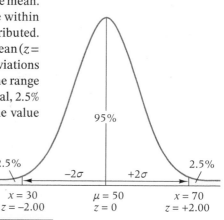

Between $z = -1.00$ and $z = +1.00$ are approximately 68% of the values.

Between $z = -2.00$ and $z = +2.00$ are approximately 95% of the values.

Between $z = -3.00$ and $z = +3.00$ are approximately 99.7% of the values.

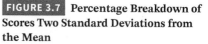

FIGURE 3.7   **Percentage Breakdown of Scores Two Standard Deviations from the Mean**

The topic of z scores is discussed more extensively in Chapter 6.

Coefficient of Variation

The **coefficient of variation** is a statistic that is *the ratio of the standard deviation to the mean expressed in percentage* and is denoted CV.

Coefficient of Variation

$$CV = \frac{\sigma}{\mu}(100) \tag{3.11}$$

The coefficient of variation is essentially a relative comparison of a standard deviation to its mean. The coefficient of variation can be useful in comparing standard deviations that have been computed from data with different means.

Suppose five weeks of average prices for stock A are 57, 68, 64, 71, and 62. To compute a coefficient of variation for these prices, first determine the mean and standard deviation: $\mu = 64.40$ and $\sigma = 4.84$. The coefficient of variation is:

$$CV_A = \frac{\sigma_A}{\mu_A}(100) = \frac{4.84}{64.40}(100) = 0.075 = 7.5\%$$

The standard deviation is 7.5% of the mean.

Sometimes financial investors use the coefficient of variation or the standard deviation or both as measures of risk. Imagine a stock with a price that never changes. An investor bears no risk of losing money from the price going down because no variability occurs in the price. Suppose, in contrast, that the price of the stock fluctuates wildly. An investor who buys at a low price and sells for a high price can make a nice profit. However, if the price drops below what the investor buys it for, the stock owner is subject to a potential loss. The greater the variability is, the more the potential for loss. Hence, investors use measures of variability such as standard deviation or coefficient of variation to determine the risk of a stock. What does the coefficient of variation tell us about the risk of a stock that the standard deviation does not?

Suppose the average prices for a second stock, B, over these same five weeks are 12, 17, 8, 15, and 13. The mean for stock B is 13.00 with a standard deviation of 3.03. The coefficient of variation can be computed for stock B as:

$$CV_B = \frac{\sigma_B}{\mu_B}(100) = \frac{3.03}{13}(100) = 0.233 = 23.3\%$$

The standard deviation for stock B is 23.3% of the mean.

With the standard deviation as the measure of risk, stock A is more risky over this period of time because it has a larger standard deviation. However, the average price of stock A is almost five times as much as that of stock B. Relative to the amount invested in stock A, the standard deviation of $4.84 may not represent as much risk as the standard deviation of $3.03 for stock B, which has an average price of only $13.00. The coefficient of variation reveals the risk of a stock in terms of the size of the standard deviation relative to the size of the mean (in percentage). Stock B has a coefficient of variation that is nearly three times as much as the coefficient of variation for stock A. Using the coefficient of variation as a measure of risk indicates that stock B is riskier.

The choice of whether to use a coefficient of variation or raw standard deviations to compare multiple standard deviations is a matter of preference. The coefficient of variation also provides an optional method of interpreting the value of a standard deviation (see Thinking Critically About Statistics in Business Today 3.2).

Thinking Critically About Statistics in Business Today 3.2

Business Travel

Findings from the National Travel Survey reveal that Canadian residents made over 72-million trips in Canada and abroad in a recent year, spending over $17 billion. Of these trips, close to 9 million (about 12%) were trips abroad: either to the United States or overseas. Concentrating on business-related trips, just over 1 in 10 trips to the United States made by Canadians were for business-related purposes, while only about 7% of the overseas trips were business-related. It has been reported that the per diem cost of business travel to New York City is about US$523, to Beijing is about US$346, to Moscow is about US$463, and to Paris is about US$580.

Things to Ponder

1. It is reported here that just over 1 in 10 trips to the United States made by Canadians were for business-related purposes, while about 7% of the overseas trips were business-related.

What do you think will happen if we have enough data to calculate the overall mean business-related distance traveled? How do the 3000+ km overseas trips impact the mean?

2. It is reported here that the per diem cost of business travel to New York City is about US$523. Would the median or even the mode be more representative for the per diem cost? How might a measure of variability add insight?

Sources: Adapted from Statistics Canada, "National Travel Survey, Fourth Quarter 2018 and Annual 2018," *The Daily*, May 28, 2019, www150.statcan.gc.ca/n1/daily-quotidien/190528/dq190528c-eng.htm; Office of Allowances, US Department of State, aoprals.state.gov/content.asp?content_id=184&menu_id=78.

Concept Check

1. The more dispersed the data are, the larger the range, the interquartile range, the variance, and the standard deviation will be. True or false? Explain.

2. If a set of data contains observations that are all the same, the range, the interquartile range, the variance, and the standard deviation will all be 0. True or false? Explain.

3. Can the values for the range, the interquartile range, the variance, and the standard deviation ever be negative? Explain.

4. What measure of variability can be used to compare variables when they have different units of measurement?

3.2 Problems

3.11 A data set contains the following seven values.

6   2   4   9   1   3   5

a. Find the range.

b. Find the mean absolute deviation.

c. Find the population variance.

d. Find the population standard deviation.

e. Find the interquartile range.

f. Find the z score for each value.

3.12 A data set contains the following eight values.

4   3   0   5   2   9   4   5

a. Find the range.

b. Find the mean absolute deviation.

c. Find the sample variance.

d. Find the sample standard deviation.

e. Find the interquartile range.

3.13 A data set contains the following six values.

12   23   19   26   24   23

a. Find the population standard deviation using the formula containing the mean (the original formula).

b. Find the population standard deviation using the computational formula.

c. Compare the results. Which formula was faster to use? Which formula do you prefer? Why do you think the computational formula is sometimes referred to as the "shortcut" formula?

3.14 Use a calculator or a computer to find the sample variance and sample standard deviation for the following data.

57	88	68	43	93
63	51	37	77	83
66	60	38	52	28
34	52	60	57	29
92	37	38	17	67

3.15 Use a calculator or a computer to find the population variance and population standard deviation for the following data.

123	90	546	378
392	280	179	601
572	953	749	75
303	468	531	646

3.16 Determine the interquartile range for the following data.

44	18	39	40	59
46	59	37	15	73
23	19	90	58	35
82	14	38	27	24
71	25	39	84	70

3.17 According to Chebyshev's theorem, at least what proportion of the data will be within $\mu \pm k\sigma$ for each value of k?

a. $k = 2$

b. $k = 2.5$

c. $k = 1.6$

d. $k = 3.2$

3.18 Compare the variability of the following two sets of data by using both the population standard deviation and the population coefficient of variation.

Data Set 1	Data Set 2
49	159
82	121
77	138
54	152

3.19 A sample of 12 small accounting firms reveals the following numbers of professionals per office.

7	10	9	14	11	8
5	12	8	3	13	6

a. Determine the mean absolute deviation.

b. Determine the variance.

c. Determine the standard deviation.

d. Determine the interquartile range.

e. What is the z score for the firm that has six professionals?

f. What is the coefficient of variation for this sample?

3.20 The following is a list of the companies with the most new products in a recent year.

Company	Number of New Products
Avon Products	768
L'Oreal	429
Unilever U.S.	323
Revlon	306
Garden Botanika	286
Philip Morris	262
Procter & Gamble	215
Nestlé	172
Paradiso	162
Tsumura International	148
Grand Metropolitan	145

a. Find the range.

b. Find the mean absolute deviation.

c. Find the population variance.

d. Find the population standard deviation.

e. Find the interquartile range.

f. Find the z score for Nestlé.

g. Find the coefficient of variation.

3.21 A distribution of numbers is approximately bell-shaped. If the mean of the numbers is 125 and the standard deviation is 12, between what two numbers would approximately 68% of the values fall?

Between what two numbers would 95% of the values fall? Between what two values would 99.7% of the values fall?

3.22 Some numbers are not normally distributed. If the mean of the numbers is 38 and the standard deviation is 6, what proportion of values would fall between 26 and 50? What proportion of values would fall between 14 and 62? Between what two values would 89% of the values fall?

3.23 According to Chebyshev's theorem, how many standard deviations from the mean would include at least 80% of the values?

3.24 The time needed to assemble a particular piece of furniture with experience is normally distributed with a mean time of 43 minutes. If 68% of the assembly times are between 40 and 46 minutes, what is the value of the standard deviation? Suppose 99.7% of the assembly times are between 35 and 51 minutes and the mean is still 43 minutes. What is the value of the standard deviation now? Suppose the time needed to assemble another piece of furniture is not normally distributed and that the mean assembly time is 28 minutes. What is the value of the standard deviation if at least 77% of the assembly times are between 24 and 32 minutes?

3.25 Environmentalists are concerned about emissions of sulphur dioxide into the air. The average number of days per year in which sulphur dioxide levels exceed 150 mg/m^3 in Milan, Italy, is 29. The number of days per year in which emission limits are exceeded is normally distributed with a standard deviation of 4.0 days. What percentage of the years would average between 21 and 37 days of excess emissions of sulphur dioxide? What percentage of the years would exceed 37 days? What percentage of the years would exceed 41 days? In what percentage of the years would there be fewer than 25 days with excess sulphur dioxide emissions?

3.26 Shown below are the maximum per diem rates for 11 international cities provided by the U.S. Department of State. The per diem rates include hotel, car, and food expenses. Use this list to calculate the z scores for Lagos, Riyadh, and Bangkok. Treat the list as a sample.

City	Per diem expense (US$)
London	482
Mexico City	362
Tokyo	485
Bangalore	493
Bangkok	241
Riyadh	485
Lagos	446
Cape Town	315
Zurich	546
Paris	608
Guatemala City	240

3.3 | Measures of Shape

LEARNING OBJECTIVE 3.3

Describe a data distribution statistically and graphically using skewness, kurtosis, and box-and-whisker plots.

Measures of shape are *tools that can be used to describe the shape of a distribution of data.* In this section, we examine two measures of shape, skewness and kurtosis. We also look at box-and-whisker plots.

Skewness

A distribution of data in which the right half is a mirror image of the left half is said to be *symmetrical.* One example of a symmetrical distribution is the normal distribution, or bell curve, which is presented in more detail in Chapter 6.

Skewness is when *a distribution is asymmetrical or lacks symmetry.* The distribution in **Figure 3.8** has no skewness because it is symmetric. **Figure 3.9** shows a distribution that is skewed left, or negatively skewed, and **Figure 3.10** shows a distribution that is skewed right, or positively skewed.

The skewed portion is the long, thin part of the curve. Many analysts use skewed distribution to denote that the data are sparse at one end of the distribution and piled up at the other end. Instructors sometimes refer to a grade distribution as skewed, meaning that few students scored at one end of the grading scale, and many students scored at the other end.

Concept Check

1. Describe what is meant by "inferential statistics."
2. Which branch of statistics is supported by probability theory?
3. What are the three methods of assigning probabilities?
4. What's the difference between the classical and relative frequency methods?
5. How is subjective probability different from the other two methods?

4.2 Structure of Probability

LEARNING OBJECTIVE 4.2

Deconstruct the elements of probability by defining experiments, sample spaces, and events; classifying events as mutually exclusive, collectively exhaustive, complementary, or independent; and counting possibilities.

In the study of probability, developing a language of terms and symbols is helpful. The structure of probability provides a common framework within which the topics of probability can be explored.

Experiment

As previously stated, an **experiment** is *a process that produces outcomes.* The following are examples of business-oriented experiments with outcomes that can be statistically analyzed:

- Interviewing 20 randomly selected consumers and asking them which brand of appliance they prefer
- Sampling every 200th bottle of ketchup from an assembly line and weighing the contents
- Testing new pharmaceutical drugs on samples of cancer patients and measuring the patients' improvement
- Auditing every 10th account to detect any errors
- Recording the Toronto Stock Exchange average on the first Monday of every month for 10 years

Event

Because an **event** is *an outcome of an experiment,* the experiment defines the possibilities of the event. If the experiment is to sample five bottles coming off a production line, an event could be to get one defective and four good bottles. In an experiment to roll a die, one event could be to roll an even number and another event could be to roll a number greater than two. Events are denoted by uppercase letters: italic capital letters (e.g., A and $E_1, E_2, \ldots$) represent the general or abstract case, and Roman capital letters (e.g., H and T for heads and tails) denote specific things and people.

Elementary Events

Events that cannot be decomposed or broken down into other events are called **elementary events**. Elementary events are denoted by lowercase letters (e.g., $e_1, e_2, e_3, \ldots$). Suppose the experiment is to roll a die. The elementary events for this experiment are to roll a 1 or roll a

2 or roll a 3, and so on. Rolling an even number is an event, but it is not an elementary event because the even number can be broken down further into events 2, 4, and 6.

In the experiment of rolling a die, there are six elementary events {1, 2, 3, 4, 5, 6}. Rolling a pair of dice results in 36 possible elementary events (outcomes). For each of the six elementary events possible on the roll of one die, there are six possible elementary events on the roll of the second die, as depicted in the tree diagram in **Figure 4.2**. **Table 4.1** contains a list of these 36 outcomes.

FIGURE 4.2 **Possible Outcomes for the Roll of a Pair of Dice**

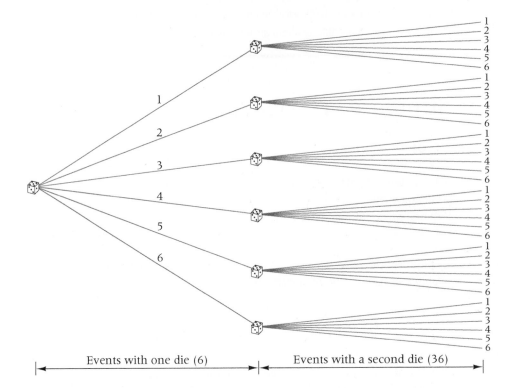

Events with one die (6)   Events with a second die (36)

TABLE 4.1	**All Possible Elementary Events in the Roll of a Pair of Dice (Sample Space)**				
(1,1)	(2,1)	(3,1)	(4,1)	(5,1)	(6,1)
(1,2)	(2,2)	(3,2)	(4,2)	(5,2)	(6,2)
(1,3)	(2,3)	(3,3)	(4,3)	(5,3)	(6,3)
(1,4)	(2,4)	(3,4)	(4,4)	(5,4)	(6,4)
(1,5)	(2,5)	(3,5)	(4,5)	(5,5)	(6,5)
(1,6)	(2,6)	(3,6)	(4,6)	(5,6)	(6,6)

In the experiment of rolling a pair of dice, other events could include outcomes such as two even numbers, a sum of 10, a sum greater than five, and others. However, none of these events is an elementary event because each can be broken down into several of the elementary events displayed in Table 4.1.

Sample Space

A **sample space** is *a complete roster or listing of all elementary events for an experiment.* Table 4.1 is the sample space for the roll of a pair of dice. The sample space for the roll of a single die is {1, 2, 3, 4, 5, 6}.

Sample space can aid in finding probabilities. Suppose an experiment is to roll a pair of dice. What is the probability that the dice will sum to 7? An examination of the sample space shown in Table 4.1 reveals that there are six outcomes in which the dice sum to 7—{(1, 6), (2, 5), (3, 4), (4, 3), (5, 2), (6, 1)}—in the 36 total possible elementary events in the sample space. Using this information, we can conclude that the probability of rolling a pair of dice that sum to 7 is 6/36, or 0.1667. However, using the sample space to determine probabilities is unwieldy and cumbersome when the sample space is large. Hence, business analysts usually use other more effective methods of determining probability.

Unions and Intersections

Set notation, the use of braces to group numbers, is used as *a symbolic tool for unions and intersections* in this chapter. The **union** of X, Y is *formed by combining elements from both sets* and is denoted $X \cup Y$. An element qualifies for the union of X, Y if it is in either X or Y or both X and Y. The union expression $X \cup Y$ can be translated to "X or Y." For example, if

$$X = \{1, 4, 7, 9\} \text{ and } Y = \{2, 3, 4, 5, 6\}$$
$$X \cup Y = \{1, 2, 3, 4, 5, 6, 7, 9\}$$

Note that all the values of X and all the values of Y qualify for the union. However, none of the values is listed more than once in the union. In **Figure 4.3**, the shaded region of the Venn diagram denotes the union.

An intersection is denoted $X \cap Y$. To qualify for intersection, an element must be in both X and Y. The **intersection** *contains the elements common to both sets*. Thus, the intersection symbol, $\cap$, is often read as *and*. The intersection of X, Y is referred to as X and Y. For example, if

$$X = \{1, 4, 7, 9\} \text{ and } Y = \{2, 3, 4, 5, 6\}$$
$$X \cap Y = \{4\}$$

Note that only the value 4 is common to both sets X and Y. The intersection is more exclusive than and hence equal to or (usually) smaller than the union. Elements must be characteristic of both X and Y to qualify. In **Figure 4.4**, the shaded region denotes the intersection.

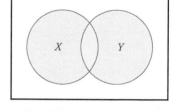

FIGURE 4.3 A Union

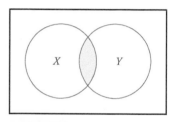

FIGURE 4.4 An Intersection

Mutually Exclusive Events

Two or more events are **mutually exclusive events** if *the occurrence of one event precludes the occurrence of the other event(s)*. This characteristic means that mutually exclusive events cannot occur simultaneously and therefore can have no intersection.

A manufactured part is either defective or acceptable. The part cannot be both acceptable and defective at the same time because "acceptable" and "defective" are mutually exclusive categories. In a sample of the manufactured products, the event of selecting a defective part is mutually exclusive with the event of selecting a nondefective part. Suppose an office building is for sale and two different potential buyers have placed bids on the building. It is not possible for both buyers to purchase the building; therefore, the event of buyer A purchasing the building is mutually exclusive with the event of buyer B purchasing the building. In the toss of a single coin, heads and tails are mutually exclusive events. The person tossing the coin gets either a head or a tail but never both.

The probability of two mutually exclusive events occurring at the same time is zero. **Figure 4.5** shows a Venn diagram of mutually exclusive events.

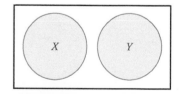

FIGURE 4.5 **Mutually Exclusive Events** X **and** Y

Mutually Exclusive Events X and Y	
$P(X \cap Y) = 0$	(4.2)

Independent Events

Two or more events are **independent events** if *the occurrence or non-occurrence of one of the events does not affect the occurrence or non-occurrence of the other event(s)*. Certain experiments, such as rolling dice, yield independent events; each die is independent of the other. Whether a 6 is rolled on the first die has no influence on whether a 6 is rolled on the second die. Coin tosses are always independent of each other. The event of getting a head on the first toss of a coin is independent of getting a head on the second toss. It is generally believed that certain human characteristics are independent of other events. For example, left-handedness is probably independent of the possession of a credit card. Whether a person wears glasses or not is probably independent of the brand of milk preferred.

Many experiments using random selection can produce either independent or non-independent events. In these experiments, the outcomes are independent if sampling is done with replacement; that is, after each item is selected and the outcome is determined, the item is restored to the population and the population is shuffled. This way, each draw becomes independent of the previous draw. Suppose an inspector is randomly selecting bolts from a bin that contains 5% defects. If the inspector samples a defective bolt and returns it to the bin, on the second draw there are still 5% defects in the bin regardless of the fact that the first outcome was a defect. If the inspector does not replace the first draw, the second draw is not independent of the first; in this case, fewer than 5% defects remain in the population. Thus, the probability of the second outcome is dependent on the first outcome.

If X and Y are independent, the following symbolic notation is used.

Independent Events X and Y

$$P(X|Y) = P(X) \qquad \text{and} \qquad P(Y|X) = P(Y) \qquad (4.3)$$

$P(X|Y)$ denotes the probability of X occurring given that Y has occurred. If X and Y are independent, then the probability of X occurring given that Y has occurred is just the probability of X occurring. Knowledge that Y has occurred does not affect the probability of X occurring because X and Y are independent. For example, P(prefers Pepsi|person is right-handed) $= P$(prefers Pepsi) because a person's handedness is independent of brand preference.

Collectively Exhaustive Events

A list of **collectively exhaustive events** contains *all possible elementary events for an experiment.* Thus, all sample spaces are collectively exhaustive lists. The list of possible outcomes for tossing a pair of dice contained in Table 4.1 is a collectively exhaustive list. The sample space for an experiment can be described as a list of events that are mutually exclusive and collectively exhaustive. Sample space events do not overlap or intersect, and the list is complete.

Complementary Events

The **complement of an event**, A, is denoted A', pronounced "not A." All *the elementary events of an experiment not in A make up its complement.* For example, if, in rolling one die, event A is getting an even number, the complement of A is getting an odd number. If event A is getting a 5 on the roll of a die, the complement of A is getting a 1, 2, 3, 4, or 6. The complement of event A contains whatever portion of the sample space event A does not contain, as the Venn diagram in **Figure 4.6** shows.

Using the complement of an event can sometimes be helpful in solving for probabilities because of the following rule.

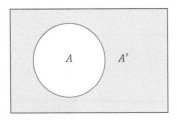

FIGURE 4.6 **The Complement of Event A is A'**

Probability of the Complement of A

$$P(A') = 1 - P(A) \qquad (4.4)$$

Suppose 32% of the employees of a company have a university degree. If an employee is randomly selected from the company, the probability that the person does not have a university degree is $1 - 0.32 = 0.68$. Suppose 42% of all parts produced in a plant are moulded by machine A and 31% are moulded by machine B. If a part is randomly selected, the probability that it was moulded by neither machine A nor machine B is $1 - 0.73 = 0.27$. (Assume that a part is only moulded on one machine.)

Counting the Possibilities

In statistics, a collection of techniques and rules for counting the number of outcomes that can occur for a particular experiment can be used. Some of these rules and techniques can delineate the size of the sample space. Presented here are three of these counting methods.

The *mn* Counting Rule Suppose a customer decides to buy a certain brand of new car. Options for the car are two different engines, five different paint colours, and three interior packages. If each of these options is available with each of the others, how many different cars can the customer choose from? To determine this number, we can use the *mn* counting rule. For an operation that can be done *m* ways and a second operation that can be done *n* ways, the two operations can then occur, in order, *mn* ways. This rule can be extended to cases with three or more operations.

---

mn Counting Rule

$$mn \tag{4.5}$$

where

   m = number of ways the first operation can be performed

   n = number of ways the second operation can be performed

Using the *mn* counting rule, we can determine that the automobile customer has $(2)(5)(3) = 30$ different car combinations of engines, paint colours, and interiors available.

Suppose an analyst wants to set up a research design to study the effects of sex (M, F), marital status (never married, divorced, married), and economic class (lower, middle, and upper) on the frequency of airline ticket purchases per year. The analyst would set up a design in which 18 different samples are taken to represent all possible groups generated from these customer characteristics.

$$\text{Number of Groups} = (\text{Sex})(\text{Marital Status})(\text{Economic Class})$$
$$= (2)(3)(3) = 18 \text{ Groups}$$

Sampling from a Population with Replacement In the second counting method, sampling *n* items from a population of size *N with replacement* provides

---

Sampling with Replacement

$$N^n \text{ possibilities} \tag{4.6}$$

where

   N = population size

   n = sample size

For example, each time a die, which has six sides, is rolled, the outcome is independent (with replacement) of the previous roll. If a die is rolled three times in succession, how many different outcomes can occur? That is, what is the size of the sample space for this experiment? The size of the population, N, is 6, the six sides of the die. We are sampling three dice rolls, $n = 3$. The sample space is

$$N^n = 6^3 = 216$$

Suppose in a lottery six numbers are drawn from the digits 0 through 9, with replacement (digits can be reused). How many different groupings of six numbers can be drawn? N is the population of 10 numbers (0 through 9) and n is the sample size, six numbers.

$$N^n = 10^6 = 1,000,000$$

That is, a million six-digit numbers are available!

Combinations: Sampling from a Population without Replacement

The third counting method uses **combinations** or *sampling without replacement*. Sampling n items from a population of size N without replacement provides the following number of possibilities:

Sampling without Replacement (Combinations)

$$_NC_n = \binom{N}{n} = \frac{N!}{n!(N-n)!}$$

(4.7)

where

N = population size

n = sample size

For example, suppose a small law firm has 16 employees and three are to be selected randomly to represent the company at the annual meeting of the Ontario Bar Association. How many different combinations of lawyers could be sent to the meeting? This situation does not allow sampling with replacement because three *different* lawyers will be selected to go. This problem is solved by using combinations. $N = 16$ and $n = 3$, so

$$_NC_n = {}_{16}C_3 = \frac{16!}{3!13!} = 560$$

A total of 560 combinations of three lawyers could be chosen to represent the firm.

Counting the Possible Sequences

In the above example each combination consisted of a set of three lawyers. Suppose one such set is {Amy, Bob, and Bill}. This set is no different from {Bob, Bill, and Amy} or {Bob, Amy, and Bill} or any other sequence. But sometimes the sequences can also be important. Suppose the annual meeting is followed by a conference. The firm may decide that the first person chosen would attend the meeting and the second person would attend the conference and the third person both. Here we need to consider which three are chosen (who gets to represent the firm) and in what order (what sessions they would attend). The *number of sequences in a set* are called **permutations**. When we use all members of a set in every sequence, the number of permutations for a given combination equals $n!$.

$$_nP_n = n!$$

In our example, each set consisted of three lawyers. Therefore the number of possible sequences or permutations is $3! = (3)(2)(1) = 6$. The sequences are 1. {Amy, Bill, Bob}, 2. {Amy, Bob, Bill}, 3. {Bill, Amy, Bob}, 4. {Bill, Bob, Amy}, 5. {Bob, Amy, Bill}, and 6. {Bob, Bill, Amy}.

This would indicate, for example, that while Amy's probability of representing the company is 105/560, her chances of attending both the meeting and the conference are 2/6 or 1/3, *if* she is chosen to represent the company. Therefore, Amy's probability of representing the company by attending both the meeting and the conference is

$$(105/560)(1/3) = 0.0625$$

We may want to use only a part of the set. For example, when the firm chooses a set of three as potential candidates, it may, at a later date, choose only two out of the three to actually attend the meeting. Now the problem is how many sequences of two there are in a set of three. This is given by the *generalized formula*

Permutation

$$_nP_r = \frac{n!}{(n-r)!}$$

(4.8)

where

n = the number of elements in the set

r = the number of elements to be selected from the set

In this example, the set consists of 3 and we need to select 2 out of this.

$$_nP_r = \frac{n!}{(n-r)!} = \frac{3!}{(3-2)!} = 6$$

This shows that if we take two elements from a set of three, we can order them in six different ways (coincidentally the same as taking three elements from a set of three).

Concept Check

1. Briefly explain the following terms: experiment, elementary events, sample space.

2. How would you draw a diagram to represent (a) the intersection and (b) the union of two events?

3. What is the difference between mutually exclusive events and independent events?

4. If two events can never occur together, are they mutually exclusive or independent?

5. What are collectively exhaustive events?

6. How would you describe the complement of an event A?

7. What is the *mn* counting rule?

8. What is meant by "combinations"?

4.2 Problems

4.1 A supplier shipped a lot of six parts to a company. The lot contained three defective parts. Suppose the customer decided to randomly select two parts and test them for defects. How large a sample space is the customer potentially working with? List the sample space. Using the sample space list, determine the probability that the customer will select a sample with exactly one defect.

4.2 Given $X = \{1, 3, 5, 7, 8, 9\}$, $Y = \{2, 4, 7, 9\}$, and $Z = \{1, 2, 3, 4, 7\}$, solve the following.

    a. $X \cup Z = $ _____
           f. $(X \cup Y) \cap Z = $ _____

    b. $X \cap Y = $ _____
           g. $(Y \cap Z) \cup (X \cap Y) = $ _____

    c. $X \cap Z = $ _____
           h. X or Y = _____

    d. $X \cup Y \cup Z = $ _____
       i. Y and Z = _____

    e. $X \cap Y \cap Z = $ _____

4.3 If a population consists of the positive even numbers through 30 and if $A = \{2, 6, 12, 24\}$, what is A'?

4.4 A company's customer service toll-free telephone system is set up so that the caller has six options. Each of these six options leads to a menu with four options. For each of these four options, three more options are available. For each of these three options, another three options are presented. If a person calls the toll-free number for assistance, how many total options are possible?

4.5 A bin contains six parts. Two of the parts are defective and four are acceptable. If three of the six parts are selected from the bin, how large is the sample space? Which counting rule did you use and why? For this sample space, what is the probability that exactly one of the three sampled parts is defective?

4.6 A company places a seven-digit serial number on each part that is made. Each digit of the serial number can be any number from 0 through 9. Digits can be repeated in the serial number. How many different serial numbers are possible?

4.7 A small company has 20 employees. Six of these employees will be selected randomly to be interviewed as part of an employee satisfaction program.

    a. How many different groups of six can be selected?

    b. In how many different sequences can the six employees be selected?

4.3 | Marginal, Union, Joint, and Conditional Probabilities

LEARNING OBJECTIVE 4.3

Compare marginal, union, joint, and conditional probabilities by defining each one.

Four particular types of probability are presented in this chapter. The first type is **marginal probability**. Marginal probability is denoted $P(E)$, where E is some event. A marginal probability is usually *computed by dividing some subtotal by the whole*. An example of marginal probability is the probability that a person owns a Ford car. This probability is computed by dividing the number of Ford owners by the total number of car owners. The probability of a person wearing glasses is also a marginal probability. This probability is computed by dividing the number of people wearing glasses by the total number of people.

A second type of probability is *the union of two events*. **Union probability** is denoted $P(E_1 \cup E_2)$, where E_1 and E_2 are two events. $P(E_1 \cup E_2)$ is the probability that E_1 will occur or that E_2 will occur or that both E_1 and E_2 will occur. An example of union probability is the probability that a person owns a Ford or a Chevrolet. To qualify for the union, the person only has to have at least one of these cars. Another example is the probability of a person wearing glasses or having red hair. All people wearing glasses are included in the union, along with all redheads and all redheads who wear glasses. In a company, the probability that a person is male or a clerical worker is a union probability. A person qualifies for the union by being male or by being a clerical worker or by being both (a male clerical worker).

A third type of probability is *the intersection of two events*, or **joint probability**. The joint probability of events E_1 and E_2 occurring is denoted $P(E_1 \cap E_2)$. Sometimes $P(E_1 \cap E_2)$ is read as the probability of E_1 and E_2. To qualify for the intersection, both events must occur. An example of joint probability is the probability of a person owning both a Ford and a Chevrolet. Owning one type of car is not sufficient. A second example of joint probability is the probability that a person is a redhead and wears glasses.

The fourth type is **conditional probability**. Conditional probability is denoted $P(E_1|E_2)$. This expression is read as *the probability that E_1 will occur given that E_2 is known to have occurred*. Conditional probabilities involve knowledge of some prior information. The information that is known or given is written to the right of the vertical line in the probability statement. An example of conditional probability is the probability that a person owns a Chevrolet given that she owns a Ford. This conditional probability is only a measure of the proportion of Ford owners who have a Chevrolet—not the proportion of total car owners who own a Chevrolet. Conditional probabilities are computed by determining the number of items that have a specific outcome out of some subtotal of the population. In the car owner example, the possibilities are reduced to Ford owners, and then the number of Chevrolet owners out of those Ford owners is determined. Another example of a conditional probability is the probability that a worker in a company is a professional given that he is male. Of the four probability types, only conditional probability does not have the population total as its denominator. Conditional probabilities have a population subtotal in the denominator. **Figure 4.7** summarizes these four types of probability.

FIGURE 4.7 **Marginal, Union, Joint, and Conditional Probabilities**

Marginal	Union	Joint	Conditional
$P(X)$	$P(X \cup Y)$	$P(X \cap Y)$	$P(X \mid Y)$
The probability of X occurring	The probability of X or Y occurring	The probability of X and Y occurring	The probability of X occurring given that Y has occurred
Uses total possible outcomes in denominator	Uses total possible outcomes in denominator	Uses total possible outcomes in denominator	Uses subtotal of the possible outcomes in denominator

Concept Check

1. How is union probability different from joint probability?
2. Can joint probability ever be greater than union probability? Explain.
3. How is marginal probability different from conditional probability?
4. Can conditional probability ever be greater than marginal probability? Explain.

4.4 | Addition Laws

LEARNING OBJECTIVE 4.4

Calculate probabilities using the general law of addition, along with a joint probability table, the complement of a union, or the special law of addition if necessary.

Several tools are available for use in solving probability problems. These tools include sample space, tree diagrams, the laws of probability, probability matrices, and insight. Because of the individuality and variety of probability problems, some techniques apply more readily in certain situations than in others. No best method is available for solving all probability problems. In some instances, the probability matrix lays out a problem in a readily solvable manner. In other cases, setting up the probability matrix is more difficult than solving the problem in another way. The probability laws can almost always be used to solve probability problems.

Four laws of probability are presented in this chapter: the addition laws, conditional probability, the multiplication laws, and Bayes' rule. The addition laws and the multiplication laws each have a general law and a special law.

The general law of addition is used to find the probability of the union of two events, $P(X \cup Y)$. The expression $P(X \cup Y)$ denotes the probability of X occurring or Y occurring or both X and Y occurring.

General Law of Addition

$$P(X \cup Y) = P(X) + P(Y) - P(X \cap Y) \tag{4.9}$$

where X, Y are events and $(X \cap Y)$ is the intersection of X and Y.

Yankelovich Partners conducted a survey in which workers were asked which changes in office design would increase productivity. Respondents were allowed to select more than one type of design change. The number one change, selected by 70% of the workers, was reducing noise. In second place was more storage/filing space, selected by 67%. If one of the survey respondents was randomly selected and asked which office design changes would increase worker productivity, what is the probability that this person would select reducing noise *or* more storage/filing space?

Let N represent the event "reducing noise." Let S represent the event "more storage/filing space." The probability of a person responding with N *or* S can be symbolized statistically as a union probability by using the law of addition.

$$P(N \cup S)$$

Recall that N ∪ S means either N or S or both. To successfully satisfy the search for a person who responds with reducing noise *or* more storage/filing space, we need only find someone who wants *at least one* of those two events. Because 70% of the surveyed people responded that reducing noise would create more productivity, $P(N) = 0.70$. In addition, because 67% responded that increased storage space would improve productivity, $P(S) = 0.67$. Either of these would satisfy the requirement of the union. Thus, the solution to the problem seems to be

$$P(N \cup S) = P(N) + P(S) = 0.70 + 0.67 = 1.37$$

However, we have already established that probabilities cannot be more than 1.00. What is the problem here? Notice that all people who responded that *both* reducing noise *and* increasing storage space would improve productivity are included in *each* of the marginal probabilities $P(N)$ and $P(S)$. Certainly a respondent who recommends both of these improvements should be included as favouring at least one. However, because they are included in $P(N)$ *and* $P(S)$, the people who recommended both improvements are *double counted*. For that reason, the general law of addition subtracts the intersection probability, $P(N \cap S)$.

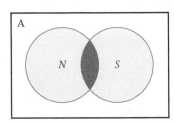

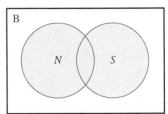

FIGURE 4.8 Solving for the Union in the Office Productivity Problem

In **Figure 4.8**, Venn diagrams illustrate this discussion. Notice that the intersection area of N and S is double shaded in diagram A, indicating that it has been counted twice. In diagram B, the shading is consistent throughout N and S because the intersection area has been subtracted out. Thus, diagram B illustrates the proper application of the general law of addition.

So what is the answer to the union probability question? Suppose 56% of all respondents to the survey had said that *both* noise reduction *and* increased storage/filing space would improve productivity: $P(N \cap S) = 0.56$. Then we could use the general law of addition to solve for the probability that a person responds that *either* noise reduction *or* increased storage space would improve productivity.

$$P(N \cup S) = P(N) + P(S) - P(N \cap S) = 0.70 + 0.67 - 0.56 = 0.81$$

Hence, 81% of the workers surveyed responded that *either* noise reduction *or* increased storage space would improve productivity.

Probability Matrices

In addition to the formulas, another useful tool in solving probability problems is a probability matrix. A **probability matrix** *displays the marginal probabilities and the intersection (joint) probabilities of a given problem.* Union probabilities and conditional probabilities are not directly displayed in the matrix but can be computed from the matrix. Generally, a probability matrix is constructed as a two-dimensional table with one variable on each side of the table. For example, in the office design problem, noise reduction would be on one side of the table and increased storage space on the other. In this problem, a Yes row and a No row would be created for one variable and a Yes column and a No column would be created for the other variable, as shown in **Table 4.2**.

Once the matrix is created, we can enter the marginal probabilities. $P(N) = 0.70$ is the marginal probability that a person responds yes to noise reduction. This value is placed in the "margin" in the row of Yes to noise reduction, as shown in **Table 4.3**. If $P(N) = 0.70$, then 30% of the people surveyed did not think that noise reduction would increase productivity. Thus, $P(\text{not } N) = 1 - 0.70 = 0.30$. This value, also a marginal probability, goes in the row indicated by No under noise reduction. In the column under Yes for increased storage space, the marginal probability $P(S) = 0.67$ is recorded. Finally, the marginal probability of No for increased storage space, $P(\text{not } S) = 1 - 0.67 = 0.33$, is placed in the No column. In this probability matrix, all four marginal probabilities are given or can be computed simply by using the probability of a complement rule, $P(\text{not } A) = 1 - P(A)$.

The intersection of noise reduction and increased storage space is given as $P(N \cap S) = 0.56$. This value is entered into the probability matrix in the cell under Yes Yes, as shown in Table 4.3. The rest of the matrix can be determined by subtracting the cell values from the marginal probabilities. For example, subtracting 0.56 from 0.70 and getting 0.14 yields the value for the cell under Yes for noise reduction and No for increased storage space. In other words, 14% of all respondents said that noise reduction would improve productivity but increased

TABLE 4.2 Probability Matrix for the Office Design Problem

		Increased Storage Space	
		Yes	No
Noise Reduction	Yes		
	No		

TABLE 4.3 Completed Probability Matrix for the Office Design Problem

		Increased Storage Space		
		Yes	No	
Noise Reduction	Yes	0.56	0.14	0.70
	No	0.11	0.19	0.30
		0.67	0.33	1.00

Implementing the special law of addition gives

$$P(M \cup I) = P(M) + P(I) = 0.18 + 0.08 = 0.26$$

DEMONSTRATION PROBLEM 4.3

If a student is randomly selected from among the graduates described in Demonstration Problem 4.1, what is the probability that the graduate would have obtained a master's or a doctoral degree that year? What is the probability that the student is either a basic graduate or has a master's degree?

Solution Examine the raw values matrix of the data shown in Demonstration Problem 4.1. In many raw value and probability matrices like this one, the rows are non-overlapping or mutually exclusive, as are the columns. In this matrix, a graduate can be classified as having obtained only one type of degree that year and as either male or female but not both. Thus, the categories of type of degree are mutually exclusive, as are the categories of gender, and the special law of addition can be applied to the education data to determine the union probabilities.

Let B denote (basic) undergraduate, MD denote master's, and DD denote doctoral. The probability that a student has either a master's or a doctoral degree is

$$P(MD \cup DD) = P(MD) + P(DD) = (48,258/227,772) + (5,718/227,772)$$
$$= 53,976/227,772 = 0.237$$

The probability that a student has either a basic undergraduate or a master's degree is

$$P(B \cup MD) = P(B) + P(MD) = (173,796/227,772) + (48,258/227,772)$$
$$= 222,054/227,772 = 0.9749$$

DEMONSTRATION PROBLEM 4.4

Use the data from the matrices in Demonstration Problem 4.2. What is the probability that a randomly selected respondent is from Calgary or Montreal?

$$P(E \cup G) = ?$$

Solution Because geographic location is mutually exclusive (the work location is either in Calgary or in Montreal but not in both),

$$P(E \cup G) = P(E) + P(G) = 0.17 + 0.21 = 0.38$$

Concept Check

1. Under what condition can you use the special law of addition instead of the general law?
2. If you apply the general law of addition where the special law may be used, would your calculations be wrong? Explain why.
3. Give two examples of cases where you can use the special law of addition instead of the general law.
4. What is a probability matrix?
5. What is meant by the "complement of a union"?

4.4 Problems

4.8 Given $P(A) = 0.10$, $P(B) = 0.12$, $P(C) = 0.21$, $P(A \cap C) = 0.05$, and $P(B \cap C) = 0.03$, solve the following.

a. $P(A \cup C) = $ ____

b. $P(B \cup C) = $ ____

c. If A and B are mutually exclusive, $P(A \cup B) = $ ____

4.9 Use the values in the matrix to solve the equations given.

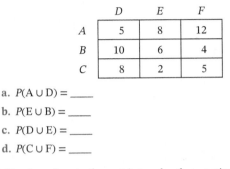

	D	E	F
A	5	8	12
B	10	6	4
C	8	2	5

a. $P(A \cup D) = $ ____

b. $P(E \cup B) = $ ____

c. $P(D \cup E) = $ ____

d. $P(C \cup F) = $ ____

4.10 Use the values in the matrix to solve the equations given.

	E	F
A	0.10	0.03
B	0.04	0.12
C	0.27	0.06
D	0.31	0.07

a. $P(A \cup F) = $ ____

b. $P(E \cup B) = $ ____

c. $P(B \cup C) = $ ____

d. $P(E \cup F) = $ ____

4.11 Suppose that 47% of all Canadians have flown in an airplane at least once and that 28% of all Canadians have ridden on a train at least once. What is the probability that a randomly selected Canadian has either ridden on a train or flown in an airplane? Can this problem be solved? Under what conditions can it be solved? If the problem cannot be solved, what information is needed to make it solvable?

4.12 Suppose that currently 75% of women 25 through 49 years of age are participating in the labour force. Suppose that 78% of the women in that age group are married. Suppose also that 61% of all women 25 through 49 years of age are married and are participating in the labour force.

a. What is the probability that a randomly selected woman in that age group is married or is participating in the labour force?

b. What is the probability that a randomly selected woman in that age group is married or is participating in the labour force but not both?

c. What is the probability that a randomly selected woman in that age group is neither married nor participating in the labour force?

4.13 A survey estimated that 67% of all households with television subscribe to a digital streaming service. Seventy-four percent of all households with television have two or more TV sets. Suppose 55% of all households with television subscribe to a digital streaming service and have two or more TV sets. A household with television is randomly selected.

a. What is the probability that the household subscribes to a streaming service or has two or more TV sets?

b. What is the probability that the household subscribes to a streaming service or has two or more TV sets but not both?

c. What is the probability that the household neither subscribes to a streaming service nor has two or more TV sets?

d. Why does the special law of addition not apply to this problem?

4.14 A survey in the U.S. asked companies about the procedures they use in hiring. Only 54% of the responding companies review the applicant's university results as part of the hiring process, and only 44% consider faculty references. Assume that these percentages are also true for the population of companies in Canada and that 35% of all companies use both the applicant's university results and faculty references.

a. What is the probability that a randomly selected company uses either faculty references or university results as part of the hiring process?

b. What is the probability that a randomly selected company uses either faculty references or university results but not both as part of the hiring process?

c. What is the probability that a randomly selected company uses neither faculty references nor university results as part of the hiring process?

d. Construct a probability matrix for this problem and indicate the locations of your answers for parts (a), (b), and (c) on the matrix.

4.5 Multiplication Laws

LEARNING OBJECTIVE 4.5

Calculate joint probabilities of both independent and dependent events using the general and special laws of multiplication.

General Law of Multiplication

As stated in Section 4.3, the probability of the intersection of two events $(X \cap Y)$ is called the joint probability. The general law of multiplication is used to find the joint probability.

General Law of Multiplication

$$P(X \cap Y) = P(X) \cdot P(Y|X) = P(Y) \cdot P(X|Y) \qquad (4.11)$$

The notation $X \cap Y$ means that both X *and* Y must happen. The general law of multiplication gives the probability that *both* event X and event Y will occur at the same time.

According to Statistics Canada, in the year 2018, 47% of the Canadian labour force was female.[1] If 27% of the women in the labour force work part-time, what is the probability that a randomly selected member of the Canadian labour force is a woman *and* works part-time? This question is one of joint probability, and the general law of multiplication can be applied to answer it.

Let W denote the event that the member of the labour force is a woman. Let T denote the event that the member is a part-time worker. The question is:

$$P(W \cap T) = ?$$

According to the general law of multiplication, this problem can be solved by

$$P(W \cap T) = P(W) \cdot P(T|W)$$

Since 47% of the labour force is female, $P(W) = 0.47$. $P(T|W)$ is a conditional probability that can be stated as the probability that a worker is a part-time worker given that the worker is a woman. This condition is what was given in the statement that 27% *of the women in the labour force* work part-time. Hence, $P(T|W) = 0.27$. From there it follows that

$$P(W \cap T) = P(W) \cdot P(T|W) = (0.47)(0.27) = 0.1269$$

It can be stated that 12.7% of the Canadian labour force are women *and* work part-time. The Venn diagram in **Figure 4.11** shows these relationships and the joint probability.

Determining joint probabilities from raw value or probability matrices is easy because every cell of these matrices is a joint probability. In fact, some statisticians refer to a probability matrix as a *joint probability table*.

For example, suppose the raw values matrix of the data from Demonstration Problem 4.1 and the Decision Dilemma is converted to a probability matrix by dividing by the total number of graduates ($N = 227{,}772$), resulting in **Table 4.5**. Each value in the cell of Table 4.5 is an intersection, and the table contains all possible intersections (joint probabilities) for the events of gender and type of degree. For example, the probability that a randomly selected student is male *and* has a master's degree, $P(M \cap MD)$, is 0.085. The probability that a randomly selected worker is female *and* has a doctorate, $P(F \cap DD)$, is 0.013. Once a probability matrix is constructed for a problem, usually the easiest way to solve for the joint probability is to find the appropriate cell in the matrix and select the answer. However, sometimes because of what is given in a problem, using the formula is easier than constructing the matrix.

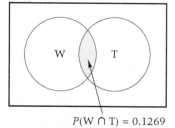

$$P(W \cap T) = 0.1269$$

FIGURE 4.11 **Joint Probability That a Woman Is in the Labour Force and Is a Part-Time Worker**

TABLE 4.5   **Probability Matrix of Gender of Graduates**

	Males	Females	Total
Basic	0.300	0.463	0.763
Master's	0.085	0.127	0.212
Doctoral	0.013	0.013	0.025
Total	0.398	0.603	1.000 (rounded)

---

[1] Statistics Canada, Table 14-10-0327-01 "Labour Force Characteristics by Sex and Detailed Age Group, Annual," doi.org/10.25318/1410032701-eng.

DEMONSTRATION PROBLEM 4.5

A company has 140 employees, of whom 30 are supervisors. Eighty of the employees are married, and 20% of the married employees are supervisors. If a company employee is randomly selected, what is the probability that the employee is married and is a supervisor?

Solution Let M denote married and S denote supervisor. The question is:

$$P(M \cap S) = ?$$

First, calculate the marginal probability:

$$P(M) = \frac{80}{140} = 0.5714$$

Then, note that 20% of the married employees are supervisors, which is the conditional probability $P(S|M) = 0.20$. Finally, applying the general law of multiplication gives

$$P(M \cap S) = P(M) \cdot P(S|M) = (0.5714)(0.20) = 0.1143$$

Hence, 11.43% of the 140 employees are married and are supervisors.

DEMONSTRATION PROBLEM 4.6

From the data obtained from the interviews of 200 executives in Demonstration Problem 4.2, find:
a. $P(B \cap E)$

b. $P(G \cap A)$

c. $P(B \cap C)$

Probability Matrix

Industry Type		Toronto D	Calgary E	Vancouver F	Montreal G	
	Finance A	0.12	0.05	0.04	0.07	0.28
	Manufacturing B	0.15	0.03	0.11	0.06	0.35
	Communications C	0.14	0.09	0.06	0.08	0.37
		0.41	0.17	0.21	0.21	1.00

(Geographic Location spans Toronto, Calgary, Vancouver, Montreal)

Solution

a. From the cell of the probability matrix, $P(B \cap E) = 0.03$. To solve by the formula, $P(B \cap E) = P(B) \cdot P(E|B)$, first find $P(B)$:

$$P(B) = 0.35$$

The probability of E occurring given that B has occurred, $P(E|B)$, can be determined from the probability matrix as $P(E|B) = 0.03/0.35$. Therefore,

$$P(B \cap E) = P(B) \cdot P(E|B) = (0.35)\left(\frac{0.03}{0.35}\right) = 0.03$$

Although the formula works, finding the joint probability in the cell of the probability matrix is faster than using the formula.

An alternative formula is $P(B \cap E) = P(E) \cdot P(B|E)$, and, from the table, $P(E) = 0.17$. Then, $P(B|E)$ means the probability of B if E is given. There are 0.17 Es in the probability matrix and 0.03 Bs in these Es. Hence,

$$P(B|E) = \frac{0.03}{0.17} \text{ and } P(B \cap E) = P(E) \cdot P(B|E) = (0.17)\left(\frac{0.03}{0.17}\right) = 0.03$$

b. To obtain $P(G \cap A)$, find the intersecting cell of G and A in the probability matrix, 0.07, or use one of the following formulas:

$$P(G \cap A) = P(G) \cdot P(A|G) = (0.21)\left(\frac{0.07}{0.21}\right) = 0.07$$

or

$$P(G \cap A) = P(A) \cdot P(G|A) = (0.28)\left(\frac{0.07}{0.28}\right) = 0.07$$

c. The probability $P(B \cap C)$ means that one respondent would have to work both in the manufacturing industry and the communications industry. The survey used to gather data from the 200 executives, however, requested that each respondent specify only one industry type for his or her company. The matrix shows no intersection for these two events. Thus, B and C are mutually exclusive. None of the respondents is in both manufacturing and communications. Hence,

$$P(B \cap C) = 0.0$$

Special Law of Multiplication

If events X and Y are independent, a special law of multiplication can be used to find the intersection of X and Y. This special law utilizes the fact that when two events X, Y are independent, $P(X|Y) = P(X)$ and $P(Y|X) = P(Y)$. Thus, the general law of multiplication, $P(X \cap Y) = P(X) \cdot P(Y|X)$, becomes $P(X \cap Y) = P(X) \cdot P(Y)$ when X and Y are independent.

Special Law of Multiplication

$$\text{If } X, Y \text{ are independent, } P(X \cap Y) = P(X) \cdot P(Y) \qquad (4.12)$$

According to a study published by *Canadian Grocer,* 32% of all Canadian grocery chains have an automated banking machine and 19% have pharmacies. Is having an automated banking machine independent of the chain having a pharmacy? If they are independent, what is the probability of a randomly selected grocery chain having an automated banking machine and a pharmacy? Let A denote an automated banking machine and P denote a pharmacy.

$$P(A) = 0.32$$
$$P(P) = 0.19$$
$$P(A \cap P) = P(A) \cdot P(P) = (0.32)(0.19) = 0.061$$

Therefore, 6% of all grocery chains in Canada have both an automated banking machine *and* a pharmacy. (It is important to understand the implications of our calculation here. We are assuming that having a pharmacy and having an automated banking machine are not related to each other. This may not necessarily be true. For example, if larger outlets tended to have pharmacies *and* automated banking machines, they are not independent of each other and therefore the calculations are not valid.)

DEMONSTRATION PROBLEM 4.7

A manufacturing firm produces pads of bound paper. Three percent of all paper pads produced are improperly bound. An inspector randomly samples two pads of paper, one at a time. Because a large number of pads are being produced during the inspection, the sampling being done, in essence, is with replacement. What is the probability that the two pads selected are both improperly bound?

TABLE 4.6

Contingency Table of Data from Independent Events

	D	E	
A	8	12	20
B	20	30	50
C	6	9	15
	34	51	85

Solution Let I denote improperly bound. The problem is to determine

$$P(I_1 \cap I_2) = ?$$

The probability of I = 0.03, or 3% are improperly bound. Because the sampling is done with replacement, the two events are independent. Hence,

$$P(I_1 \cap I_2) = P(I_1) \cdot P(I_2) = (0.03)(0.03) = 0.0009$$

Most probability matrices contain variables that are not independent. If a probability matrix contains independent events, the special law of multiplication can be applied. If not, the special law cannot be used. In Section 4.6, we explore a technique for determining whether events are independent. Table 4.6 contains data from independent events.

DEMONSTRATION PROBLEM 4.8

Use the data from Table 4.6 and the special law of multiplication to find $P(B \cap D)$.

Solution

$$P(B \cap D) = P(B) \cdot P(D) = \frac{50}{85} \cdot \frac{34}{85} = 0.2353$$

This approach works *only* for contingency tables and probability matrices in which the variable along one side of the matrix is *independent* of the variable along the other side of the matrix. Note that the answer obtained by using the formula is the same as the answer obtained by using the cell information from Table 4.6.

$$P(B \cap D) = \frac{20}{85} = 0.2353$$

Concept Check

1. Under what condition can you use the special law of multiplication instead of the general law?
2. Under what conditions are the general law and the special law interchangeable?

4.5 Problems

4.15 Use the values in the contingency table to solve the equations given.

	C	D	E	F
A	5	11	16	8
B	2	3	5	7

a. $P(A \cap E) = \underline{\hspace{1cm}}$
b. $P(D \cap B) = \underline{\hspace{1cm}}$
c. $P(D \cap E) = \underline{\hspace{1cm}}$
d. $P(A \cap B) = \underline{\hspace{1cm}}$

4.16 Use the values in the probability matrix to solve the equations given.

	D	E	F
A	0.12	0.13	0.08
B	0.18	0.09	0.04
C	0.06	0.24	0.06

a. $P(E \cap B) = \underline{\hspace{1cm}}$
b. $P(C \cap F) = \underline{\hspace{1cm}}$
c. $P(E \cap D) = \underline{\hspace{1cm}}$

4.17 a. A batch of 50 parts contains six defects. If two parts are drawn randomly one at a time without replacement, what is the probability that both parts are defective?

b. If this experiment is repeated, with replacement, what is the probability that both parts are defective?

4.18 Eighty-three percent of the Canadian population now live in urban areas.[2] Assume that about 15% of all Canadian adults care for ill relatives and that 11% of adults living in urban areas care for ill relatives.

a. Use the general law of multiplication to determine the probability of randomly selecting an adult from the Canadian population who lives in an urban area and is caring for an ill relative.

b. What is the probability of randomly selecting an adult from the Canadian population who lives in an urban area and does not care for an ill relative?

c. Construct a probability matrix and show where the answers to this problem lie in the matrix.

d. From the probability matrix, determine the probability that an adult lives in a nonurban area and cares for an ill relative.

4.19 According to the Canadian Tourism Human Resource Council, 11% of all Canadians in the labour force are employed in the tourism industry.[3] Fifty-one percent of those who work in this sector are under 35 years of age. Assume that of those in the Canadian labour force not employed in the tourism industry, only 44% are under 35.[4] Suppose you choose someone randomly from the Canadian labour force.

a. What is the probability that this person is not employed by the tourism industry?

b. What is the probability that this person is employed by the tourism industry and is under 35 years of age?

c. What is the probability that this person is employed by the tourism industry and is over 35 years of age?

d. What is the probability that this person is not employed by the tourism industry and is under 35 years of age?

e. What is the probability that this person is not employed by the tourism industry and is over 35 years of age?

f. What is the probability that this person is neither employed by the tourism industry nor over 35 years of age?

g. What is the probability that this person is neither employed by the tourism industry nor under 35 years of age?

4.20 According to Statistics Canada (for 2017), 60% of all Canadian households have an air conditioner and 81% have trees on their property.[5] Suppose 91% of all Canadian households with an air conditioner have trees on their property. A Canadian household is randomly selected.

a. What is the probability that the household has an air conditioner and trees on the property?

b. What is the probability that the household has an air conditioner or trees on the property?

c. What is the probability that the household has an air conditioner and does not have any trees on the property?

d. What is the probability that the household has neither an air conditioner nor trees on the property?

e. What is the probability that the household does not have an air conditioner and does have trees on the property?

4.21 A recent study found that 30% of the travelling public said that their flight selections are influenced by perceptions of airline safety. Thirty-nine percent of the travelling public want to know the age of the aircraft. Suppose 87% of the travelling public who say that their flight selections are influenced by perceptions of airline safety want to know the age of the aircraft.

a. What is the probability of randomly selecting a member of the travelling public and finding out that she says that flight selection is influenced by perceptions of airline safety and she does not want to know the age of the aircraft?

b. What is the probability of randomly selecting a member of the travelling public and finding out that he says that flight selection is not influenced by perceptions of airline safety and he does not want to know the age of the aircraft?

c. What is the probability of randomly selecting a member of the travelling public and finding out that she says that flight selection is not influenced by perceptions of airline safety but she wants to know the age of the aircraft?

4.22 Statistics Canada states that 90% of all Canadian households have energy-saving lights. In addition, 40% of all Canadian households have a truck, van, or sport utility vehicle (SUV).[6] Suppose 38% of all Canadian households have both energy-saving lights and a truck/van/SUV. A Canadian household is randomly selected.

a. What is the probability that the household has energy-saving lights or a truck/van/SUV?

b. What is the probability that the household has neither energy-saving lights nor a truck/van/SUV?

c. What is the probability that the household does not have energy-saving lights and does have a truck/van/SUV?

d. What is the probability that the household does have energy-saving lights and does not have a truck/van/SUV?

---

[2] Statistics Canada, "2016 Census: 150 Years of Urbanization in Canada," www.statcan.gc.ca/eng/sc/video/2016census_150yearsurbanization.

[3] Tourism HR Canada, "Labour Market Information: Tourism Facts," tourismhr.ca/labour-market-information/tourism-facts/.

[4] Tourism HR Canada, "Census Data: Who Works in Tourism?" tourismhr.ca/labour-market-information/tourism-census-data/.

[5] Statistics Canada, Table 38-10-0019-01 "Air Conditioners," www150.statcan.gc.ca/t1/tbl1/en/tv.action?pid=3810001901, and Statistics Canada, Table 38-10-0273-01 "Trees, Bushes and Hedges on Property," www150.statcan.gc.ca/t1/tbl1/en/tv.action?pid=3810027301.

[6] Statistics Canada, Table: 38-10-0048-01 "Use of Energy-Saving Lights, Canada and Provinces," www150.statcan.gc.ca/t1/tbl1/en/tv.action?pid=3810004801, and Statistics Canada, "Estimates of Number of Vehicles in Scope for Canada—By Type of Vehicle and Vehicle Body Type," www150.statcan.gc.ca/n1/pub/53-223-x/2009000/t010-eng.htm.

4.6 | # Conditional Probability

LEARNING OBJECTIVE 4.6

Calculate conditional probabilities with various forms of the law of conditional probability, and use them to determine if two events are independent.

Conditional probabilities are computed based on the prior knowledge that a business analyst has about one of the two events being studied. If X, Y are two events, the conditional probability of X occurring given that Y is known or has occurred is expressed as $P(X|Y)$ and is given in the *law of conditional probability*.

Law of Conditional Probability

$$P(X|Y) = \frac{P(X \cap Y)}{P(Y)} = \frac{P(X) \cdot P(Y|X)}{P(Y)}$$

(4.13)

The conditional probability of $(X|Y)$ is the probability that X will occur given Y. The formula for conditional probability is derived by dividing both sides of the general law of multiplication by $P(Y)$.

In the study by Yankelovich Partners to determine what changes in office design would improve productivity, 70% of the respondents believed noise reduction would improve productivity and 67% said increased storage space would improve productivity. In addition, suppose 56% of the respondents believed both noise reduction and increased storage space would improve productivity. A worker is selected randomly and asked about changes in office design. This worker believes that noise reduction would improve productivity. What is the probability that this worker also believes increased storage space would improve productivity? That is, what is the probability that a randomly selected person believes storage space would improve productivity *given that* he or she believes noise reduction improves productivity? In symbols, the question is:

$$P(S|N) = ?$$

Note that the given part of the information is listed to the right of the vertical line in the conditional probability. The formula solution is

$$P(S|N) = \frac{P(S \cap N)}{P(N)}$$

We know that

$$P(N) = 0.70 \text{ and } P(S \cap N) = 0.56$$

so

$$P(S|N) = \frac{P(S \cap N)}{P(N)} = \frac{0.56}{0.70} = 0.80$$

Eighty percent of workers who believe noise reduction would improve productivity also believe increased storage space would improve productivity.

Note in **Figure 4.12** that the area for N in the Venn diagram is completely shaded because it is given that the worker believes noise reduction will improve productivity. Also notice that the intersection of N and S is more heavily shaded. This portion of noise reduction includes increased storage space. It is the only part of increased storage space that is in noise reduction, and because the person is known to favour noise reduction, it is the only area of interest that includes increased storage space.

Examine the probability matrix in **Table 4.7** for the office design problem. None of the probabilities given in the matrix are conditional probabilities. To reiterate what has been previously stated, a probability matrix contains only two types of probabilities, marginal and joint. The cell values are all joint probabilities and the subtotals in the margins are marginal probabilities. How are conditional probabilities determined from a probability matrix? The law of conditional probabilities shows that a conditional probability is computed by dividing the joint probability by the marginal probability. Thus, the probability matrix has all the necessary information to solve for a conditional probability.

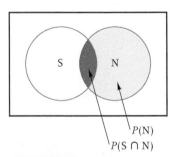

FIGURE 4.12 **Conditional Probability of Increased Storage Space Given Noise Reduction**

TABLE 4.7	Office Design Problem Probability Matrix

		Increased Storage Space		
		Yes	No	
Noise Reduction	Yes	0.56	0.14	0.70
	No	0.11	0.19	0.30
		0.67	0.33	1.00

What is the probability that a randomly selected worker believes noise reduction would not improve productivity given that the worker does believe increased storage space would improve productivity? That is,

$$P(\text{not N}|S) = ?$$

The law of conditional probability states that

$$P(\text{not N}|S) = \frac{P(\text{not N} \cap S)}{P(S)}$$

Notice that because S is given, we are interested only in the column that is shaded in Table 4.7, which is the Yes column for increased storage space. The marginal probability, $P(S)$, is the total of this column and is found in the margin at the bottom of the table as 0.67. $P(\text{not N} \cap S)$ is found as the intersection of No for noise and Yes for storage. This value is 0.11. Hence, $P(\text{not N} \cap S)$ is 0.11. Therefore,

$$P(\text{not N}|S) = \frac{P(\text{not N} \cap S)}{P(S)} = \frac{0.11}{0.67} = 0.164$$

The second version of the conditional probability law formula is:

$$P(X|Y) = \frac{P(X) \cdot P(Y|X)}{P(Y)}$$

This version is more complex than the first version, $P(X \cap Y)/P(Y)$. However, sometimes the second version must be used because of the information given in the problem—for example, when solving for $P(X|Y)$ but $P(Y|X)$ is given. The second version of the formula is obtained from the first version by substituting the formula for $P(X \cap Y) = P(X) \cdot P(Y|X)$ into the first version.

In general, this second version of the law of conditional probabilities is likely to be used for solving $P(X|Y)$ when $P(X \cap Y)$ is unknown but $P(X|Y)$ is known. (See Thinking Critically About Statistics in Business Today 4.1.)

Thinking Critically About Statistics in Business Today 4.1

Newspaper Readership of Canadians

A national survey by Totum Research for News Media Canada reveals some interesting statistics about newspaper readership among Canadians. Eighty-eight percent of Canadians read newspapers each week, in either print or digital formats. This percentage is higher for baby boomers (90%) than millennials (88%), and business decision-makers are considered "news junkies," with 93% of them engaging in weekly readership. Baby boomers read news on all platforms, with 56% reading news in print and 59% accessing news on their phone. The younger generation has stronger preferences, with 78% of millennials reading news on their phone and only 43% in print. Time of day also impacts readership: both millennials and boomers tend to consume news more in the early morning (55% and 50%, respectively) and after dinner (51% and 49%, respectively) than at other times of the day. Readership for both groups dips during lunch, but less so for millennials (44%) than boomers (26%). Canadians living in Ontario lead the country in terms of news readership by phone (79%), in contrast to those living in Atlantic Canada (65%), Western Canada (64%), and Quebec (59%).

These facts can be converted to probabilities: the marginal probability that a Canadian reads news each week is 0.88. Many of the other statistics represent conditional probabilities. For example, the probability that a Canadian reading the news is a baby boomer is 0.90; the probability that a Canadian reading the news on their phone is a millennial is 0.78. About 7% of the Canadian population resides in Atlantic Canada. From this, and from the conditional probability that a Canadian living in Atlantic Canada reads the news on their phone (0.65), one can compute the joint probability that a randomly selected Canadian reads the news on their phone and lives in Atlantic Canada: $(0.07)(0.65) = 0.0455$. That is, 4.55% of all Canadians live in Atlantic Canada and read news on their phone.

Things to Ponder

1. It is clear from the information given here that many Canadians enjoy reading news on their phones. If you are a business owner in Canada, what implications might this have for any marketing campaigns you pursue?

2. What factors do you think might contribute to the fact that 20% more Canadians living in Ontario use their phones to read the news than Canadians in Quebec?

Sources: Data from News Media Canada, "Newspapers 24/7," nmc-mic.ca/ad-resources/newspapers-247/; Statistics Canada, "Population and Dwelling Count Highlight Tables, 2016 Census," Statistics Canada Catalogue no. 98-402-X2016001 (Ottawa: Statistics Canada, February 8, 2017), www12.statcan.gc.ca/census-recensement/2016/dp-pd/hlt-fst/pd-pl/Table.cfm?Lang=Eng&T=101&S=50&O=A.

As an example, in Section 4.5, data relating to women in the Canadian labour force were presented. Included in this information was the fact that 47% of the Canadian labour force is female and the assumption that 27% of the females in the Canadian labour force work part-time. If we further assume that 19.6% of all Canadian labourers are part-time workers, what is the probability that a randomly selected Canadian worker is a woman if that person is known to be a part-time worker? Let W denote the event of selecting a woman and T denote the event of selecting a part-time worker. In symbols, the question to be answered is:

$$P(W|T) = ?$$

The first form of the law of conditional probabilities is

$$P(W|T) = \frac{P(W \cap T)}{P(T)}$$

Note that this version of the law of conditional probabilities requires knowledge of the joint probability, $P(W \cap T)$, which is not given here. We therefore try the second version of the law of conditional probabilities, which is

$$P(W|T) = \frac{P(W) \cdot P(T|W)}{P(T)}$$

For this version of the formula, everything is given in the problem.

$$P(W) = 0.47$$
$$P(T) = 0.196$$
$$P(T|W) = 0.27$$

The probability of a worker being a woman given that the person works part-time can now be computed.

$$P(W|T) = \frac{P(W) \cdot P(T|W)}{P(T)} = \frac{(0.47)(0.27)}{(0.196)} = 0.647$$

Hence, 64.7% of part-time workers are women.

DEMONSTRATION PROBLEM 4.9

The data from the executive interviews given in Demonstration Problem 4.2 are repeated here. Use these data to find:

a. $P(B|F)$

b. $P(G|C)$

c. $P(D|F)$

Probability Matrix

		Toronto D	Calgary E	Vancouver F	Montreal G	
	Finance A	0.12	0.05	0.04	0.07	0.28
Industry Type	Manufacturing B	0.15	0.03	0.11	0.06	0.35
	Communications C	0.14	0.09	0.06	0.08	0.37
		0.41	0.17	0.21	0.21	1.00

Geographic Location

Solution

a.
$$P(B|F) = \frac{P(B \cap F)}{P(F)} = \frac{0.11}{0.21} = 0.524$$

Determining conditional probabilities from a probability matrix by using the formula is a relatively painless process. In this case, the joint probability, $P(B \cap F)$, appears in a cell of the matrix (0.11); the marginal probability, $P(F)$, appears in a margin (0.21). Bringing these two probabilities together by the formula produces the answer, $0.11/0.21 = 0.524$. This answer means that 52.4% of the Vancouver executives (the F values) are in manufacturing (the B values).

b.
$$P(G|C) = \frac{P(G \cap C)}{P(C)} = \frac{0.08}{0.37} = 0.216$$

This result means that 21.6% of the responding communications industry executives (C) are from Montreal (G).

c.
$$P(D|F) = \frac{P(D \cap F)}{P(F)} = \frac{0.00}{0.21} = 0.00$$

Because D and F are mutually exclusive, $P(D \cap F)$ is zero and so is $P(D|F)$. The rationale behind $P(D|F) = 0$ is that, if F is given (the respondent is known to be located in Vancouver), the respondent could not be located in D (Toronto).

Independent Events

If X and Y are independent events, the following must be true:

$$P(X|Y) = P(X) \qquad \text{and} \qquad P(Y|X) = P(Y)$$

In each equation, it does not matter that X or Y is given because X and Y are *independent*. When X and Y are independent, the conditional probability is solved as a marginal probability.

Sometimes it is important to test a contingency table of raw data to determine whether events are independent. If *any* combination of two events from the different sides of the matrix fails the test $P(X|Y) = P(X)$, the matrix does not contain independent events.

DEMONSTRATION PROBLEM 4.10

Test the matrix for the 200 executive responses to determine whether industry type is independent of geographic location.

Raw Values Matrix

		Geographic Location				
		Toronto D	Calgary E	Vancouver F	Montreal G	
	Finance A	24	10	8	14	56
Industry Type	Manufacturing B	30	6	22	12	70
	Communications C	28	18	12	16	74
		82	34	42	42	200

Solution   Select one industry and one geographic location (say, A—Finance and G—Montreal). Does $P(A|G) = P(A)$?

$$P(A|G) = \frac{14}{42} \text{ and } P(A) = \frac{56}{200}$$

Does $14/42 = 56/200$? No, $0.33 \neq 0.28$. Industry and geographic location are not independent because at least one exception to the test is present.

DEMONSTRATION PROBLEM 4.11

Determine whether the contingency table shown as Table 4.6 and repeated here contains independent events.

	D	E	
A	8	12	20
B	20	30	50
C	6	9	15
	34	51	85

Solution Check the first cell in the matrix to find whether $P(A|D) = P(A)$.

$$P(A|D) = \frac{8}{34} = 0.2353$$
$$P(A) = \frac{20}{85} = 0.2353$$

The checking process must continue until all the events are determined to be independent. In this matrix, all the possibilities check out. Thus, Table 4.6 contains independent events.

Concept Check

1. Using an example, explain the difference between unconditional probability and conditional probability.
2. What is the relationship between conditional probability and independent events?

4.6 Problems

4.23 Use the values in the contingency table to solve the equations given.

	E	F	G
A	15	12	8
B	11	17	19
C	21	32	27
D	18	13	12

a. $P(G|A) =$ _____
b. $P(B|F) =$ _____
c. $P(C|E) =$ _____
d. $P(E|G) =$ _____

4.24 Use the values in the probability matrix to solve the equations given.

	C	D
A	0.36	0.44
B	0.11	0.09

a. $P(C|A) =$ _____
b. $P(B|D) =$ _____
c. $P(A|B) =$ _____

4.25 The results of a survey asking, "Do you have a calculator and/or a computer in your home?" follow.

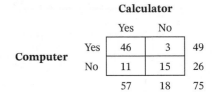

		Calculator		
		Yes	No	
Computer	Yes	46	3	49
	No	11	15	26
		57	18	75

Is the variable "calculator" independent of the variable "computer"? Why or why not?

4.26 In Years 1 and 2 combined, 3,337,380 motor vehicles were sold in Canada. Year 2 accounted for 1,716,803 of these vehicles. Suppose that those manufactured overseas (outside North America) accounted for 444,070 of the vehicles sold in Year 2. Suppose 325,421 vehicles built overseas were sold in Year 1. A vehicle is randomly selected from this list of motor vehicles.

a. What is the probability that the vehicle was manufactured overseas?

b. What is the probability that the vehicle was sold in Year 2 or manufactured overseas?

c. What is the probability that the vehicle was sold in Year 2 if it is known that the vehicle was manufactured overseas?

d. What is the probability that the vehicle was manufactured overseas if it is known that the vehicle was sold in Year 2?

e. What is the probability that the vehicle was not manufactured overseas if it is known that the vehicle was not sold in Year 2?

f. Given that the vehicle was sold in Year 2, what is the probability that the vehicle was not manufactured overseas?

4.27 A survey of U.S. small-business owners was conducted to determine the challenges for growth for their businesses. The top challenge, selected by 46% of the small-business owners, was the economy. A close second was finding qualified workers (37%). Suppose 15% of the small-business owners selected both the economy and finding qualified workers as challenges for growth. A small-business owner is randomly selected.

a. What is the probability that the owner believes the economy is a challenge for growth if the owner believes that finding qualified workers is a challenge for growth?

b. What is the probability that the owner believes that finding qualified workers is a challenge for growth if the owner believes that the economy is a challenge for growth?

c. Given that the owner does not select the economy as a challenge for growth, what is the probability that the owner believes that finding qualified workers is a challenge for growth?

d. What is the probability that the owner believes neither that the economy is a challenge for growth nor that finding qualified workers is a challenge for growth?

4.28 With the advent of online ordering, shipping has become more important to consumers. One survey showed that 80% of online consumers want same-day shipping. Another study showed that 24% of online consumers are shopping lovers who enjoy buying and purchase often. Suppose that 61% of online consumers who are shopping lovers want same-day shipping. If an online consumer is randomly selected, determine the following probabilities:

a. The consumer wants same-day shipping and is a shopping lover.

b. The consumer does not want same-day shipping but is a shopping lover.

c. The consumer is not a shopping lover but does want same-day shipping.

d. The consumer does not want same-day shipping and is not a shopping lover.

4.29 According to a survey of restaurant owners in the United States by Must-Have Menus, 77% of restaurant owners believe that they need to use social media as a marketing tool. A different survey by national restaurant owners revealed that 80% of restaurant owners started their careers at entry-level positions. Suppose that 83% of restaurant owners who started their careers at entry-level positions believe that they need to use social media as a marketing tool. Assuming that these percentages apply to all restaurant owners, if a restaurant owner is randomly selected, determine the following probabilities:

a. The owner believes that he/she needs to use social media as a marketing tool and started his/her career at an entry-level position.

b. The owner either believes that he/she needs to use social media as a marketing tool or he/she started his/her career at an entry-level position.

c. The owner does not believe that he/she needs to use social media as a marketing tool, given that he/she started his/her career at an entry-level position.

d. The owner believes that he/she needs to use social media as a marketing tool, given that he/she did not start his/her career at an entry-level position.

e. The owner did not start his/her career at an entry-level position, given that he/she does not believe he/she needs to use social media as a marketing tool.

4.30 In a study undertaken by Catalyst, 43% of women senior executives agreed or strongly agreed that a lack of role models was a barrier to their career development. In addition, 46% agreed or strongly agreed that gender-based stereotypes were barriers to their career advancement. Suppose 77% of those who agreed or strongly agreed that gender-based stereotypes were barriers to their career advancement agreed or strongly agreed that the lack of role models was a barrier to their career development. If one of these female senior executives is randomly selected, determine the following probabilities:

a. What is the probability that the senior executive does not agree or strongly agree that a lack of role models was a barrier to her career development given that she does agree or strongly agree that gender-based stereotypes were barriers to her career development?

b. What is the probability that the senior executive does not agree or strongly agree that gender-based stereotypes were barriers to her career development given that she does agree or strongly agree that the lack of role models was a barrier to her career development?

c. If it is known that the senior executive does not agree or strongly agree that gender-based stereotypes were barriers to her career development, what is the probability that she does not agree or strongly agree that the lack of role models was a barrier to her career development?

4.7 Revision of Probabilities: Bayes' Rule

LEARNING OBJECTIVE 4.7

Calculate conditional probabilities using Bayes' rule.

An extension to the conditional law of probabilities is Bayes' rule, which was developed by and named for Thomas Bayes (1702–1761). **Bayes' rule** is *a formula that extends the use of the law of conditional probabilities to allow revision of original probabilities with new information.*

Bayes' Rule

$$P(X_i|Y) = \frac{P(X_i) \cdot P(Y|X_i)}{P(X_1) \cdot P(Y|X_1) + P(X_2) \cdot P(Y|X_2) + \cdots + P(X_n) \cdot P(Y|X_n)} \qquad (4.14)$$

Recall that the law of conditional probability for

$$P(X_i|Y)$$

is

$$P(X_i|Y) = \frac{P(X_i) \cdot P(Y|X_i)}{P(Y)}$$

Compare Bayes' rule to this law of conditional probability. The numerators of Bayes' rule and the law of conditional probability are the same, the intersection of X_i and Y shown in the form of the general rule of multiplication. The new feature that Bayes' rule uses is found in the denominator of the rule:

$$P(X_1) \cdot P(Y|X_1) + P(X_2) \cdot P(Y|X_2) + \cdots + P(X_n) \cdot P(Y|X_n)$$

The denominator of Bayes' rule includes a product expression (intersection) for every partition in the sample space Y, including the event (X_i) itself. The denominator is thus a collectively exhaustive listing of mutually exclusive outcomes of Y. This denominator is sometimes referred to as the "total probability formula." It represents a weighted average of the conditional probabilities, with the weights being the prior probabilities of the corresponding event.

By expressing the law of conditional probabilities in this new way, Bayes' rule enables the statistician to make new and different applications using conditional probabilities. In particular, statisticians use Bayes' rule to "revise" probabilities in light of new information.

A particular formulation of an over-the-counter drug is produced by only two companies, Prairie Pharmaceuticals and Badlands Generics. Suppose Prairie produces 65% of the drug and Badlands produces 35%. Eight percent of the users of the drug produced by Prairie show some side effects and 12% of the Badlands users show similar side effects. A customer randomly picks up one of these drugs at the pharmacy. What is the probability that Prairie produced the drug? What is the probability that Badlands produced the drug? The customer uses the product and develops side effects. Now what is the probability that Prairie produced the drug? That Badlands produced the drug?

The probability was 0.65 that the drug came from Prairie and 0.35 that it came from Badlands. These are called prior probabilities because they are based on the original information.

The new information that the drug produced side effects changes the probabilities because one company's drug causes a higher incidence of side effects than the other company's drug does. How can this information be used to update or revise the original probabilities? Bayes' rule allows such updating. One way to lay out a revision-of-probabilities problem is to use a table. Table 4.8 shows the analysis for the over-the-counter drug problem.

TABLE 4.8 Bayesian Table for Revision of Over-the-Counter Drug Problem Probabilities

Event	Prior Probability $P(E_i)$	Conditional Probability $P(d|E_i)$	Joint Probability $P(E_i \cap d)$	Posterior or Revised Probability
Prairie	0.65	0.08	0.052	$\frac{0.052}{0.094} = 0.553$
Badlands	0.35	0.12	0.042	$\frac{0.042}{0.094} = 0.447$
			$P(\text{side effects}) = 0.094$	

The process begins with the prior probabilities: 0.65 for Prairie and 0.35 for Badlands. These prior probabilities appear in the second column of Table 4.8. Because the product is found to have side effects, the conditional probabilities, P(side effects|Prairie) and P(side effects|Badlands) should be used. Eight percent of the Prairie users experience side effects: P(side effects|Prairie) = 0.08. Twelve percent of the Badlands users experience side effects: P(side effects|Badlands) = 0.12. These two conditional probabilities appear in the third column. Eight percent of Prairie's 65% of the customers develop side effects: (0.08)(0.65) = 0.052, or 5.2% of the total. This figure appears in the fourth column of Table 4.8; it is the joint probability of getting the product that was made by Prairie and developing side effects. Because the user experienced side effects, these are the only Prairie users that are of interest. Twelve percent of Badlands' 35% of the users develop side effects. Multiplying these two percentages yields the joint probability of getting a Badlands drug leading to side effects. This figure also appears in the fourth column of Table 4.8: (0.12)(0.35) = 0.042; that is, 4.2% of the total. It is the joint probability of getting the product that was made by Badlands and developing side effects. This percentage includes the only Badlands customers of interest because the customer experienced side effects.

Column 4 is totalled to get 0.094, indicating that 9.4% of all users developed side effects (Prairie and side effects = 0.052 + Badlands and side effects = 0.042). The other 90.6% of the users are not of interest because they did not develop any side effects. To compute the fifth column, the posterior or revised probabilities, involves dividing each value in column 4 by the total of column 4. For Prairie, 0.052 of the total users used Prairie *and* experienced side effects out of the total of 0.094 who experienced side effects. Dividing 0.052 by 0.094 yields 0.553 as a revised probability that the purchased product was made by Prairie. This probability is lower than the prior or original probability of 0.65 because fewer of Prairie's users (as a percentage) experienced side effects compared with Badlands users. The product that caused side effects is now less likely to have come from Prairie than before the knowledge of the occurrence of side effects. Badlands' probability is revised by dividing the 0.042 joint probability of the product being made by Badlands *and* causing side effects by the total probability of the product causing side effects (0.094). The result is 0.042/0.094 = 0.447. The probability that side effects are caused by the Badlands drug has increased because a higher percentage of Badlands users develop side effects.

Tree diagrams are another common way to solve Bayes' rule problems. **Figure 4.13** shows the solution for the over-the-counter drug problem. Note that the tree diagram contains all possibilities, including both side effect and no side effect proportions. When new information is given, only the pertinent proportions are selected and used. The joint probability values at the ends of the appropriate branches are used to revise and compute the posterior possibilities. Using the total number of users with side effects, 0.052 + 0.042 = 0.094, the calculation is as follows:

$$\text{Revised Probability: Prairie} = \frac{0.052}{0.094} = 0.553$$
$$\text{Revised Probability: Badlands} = \frac{0.042}{0.094} = 0.447$$

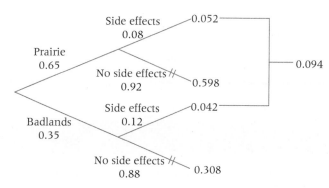

FIGURE 4.13 **Tree Diagram for Over-the-Counter Drug Problem Probabilities**

DEMONSTRATION PROBLEM 4.12

Machines A, B, and C all produce the same two parts, X and Y. Of all the parts produced, machine A produces 60%, machine B produces 30%, and machine C produces 10%. In addition,

40% of the parts made by machine A are part X.
50% of the parts made by machine B are part X.
70% of the parts made by machine C are part X.

A part produced by this company is randomly sampled and is determined to be an X part. With the knowledge that it is an X part, revise the probabilities that the part came from machine A, B, or C.

Solution The prior probability of the part coming from machine A is 0.60, because machine A produces 60% of all parts. The prior probability is 0.30 that the part came from B and 0.10 that it came from C. These prior probabilities are more pertinent if nothing is known about the part. However, the part is known to be an X part. The conditional probabilities show that different machines produce different proportions of X parts. For example, 0.40 of the parts made by machine A are X parts, but 0.50 of the parts made by machine B and 0.70 of the parts made by machine C are X parts. It makes sense that the probability of the part coming from machine C would increase and that the probability that the part was made on machine A would decrease because the part is an X part.

The following table shows how the prior probabilities; conditional probabilities; joint probabilities; and marginal probability, $P(X)$, can be used to revise the prior probabilities to obtain posterior probabilities.

Event	Prior $P(E_i)$	Conditional $P(X|E_i)$	Joint $P(X \cap E_i)$	Posterior
A	0.60	0.40	$(0.60)(0.40) = 0.24$	$\frac{0.24}{0.46} = 0.52$
B	0.30	0.50	$(0.30)(0.50) = 0.15$	$\frac{0.15}{0.46} = 0.33$
C	0.10	0.70	$(0.10)(0.70) = 0.07$ $P(X) = 0.46$	$\frac{0.07}{0.46} = 0.15$

After the probabilities are revised, it is apparent that the probability of the part being made at machine A decreased and that the probabilities that the part was made at machines B and C increased. A tree diagram presents another view of this problem.

Revised probabilities: Machine A: $\frac{0.24}{0.46} = 0.52$

Machine B: $\frac{0.15}{0.46} = 0.33$

Machine C: $\frac{0.07}{0.46} = 0.15$

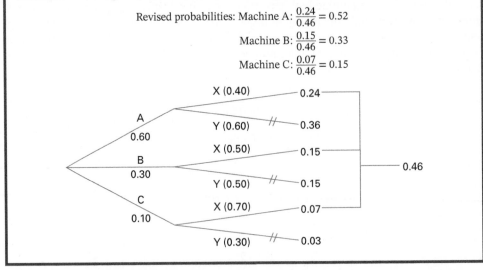

Concept Check

1. Both conditional probability and Bayes' rule incorporate in their calculations what we already know. In what way are they different?

4.7 Problems

4.31 In a manufacturing plant, machine A produces 10% of a certain product, machine B produces 40% of this product, and machine C produces 50% of this product. Five percent of machine A products are defective, 12% of machine B products are defective, and 8% of machine C products are defective. The company inspector has just sampled a product from this plant and has found it to be defective. Determine the revised probabilities that the sampled product was produced by machine A, machine B, or machine C.

4.32 Alex, Natasha, and Juan fill orders in a fast-food restaurant. Alex incorrectly fills 20% of the orders he takes. Natasha incorrectly fills 12% of the orders she takes. Juan incorrectly fills 5% of the orders he takes. Alex fills 30% of all orders, Natasha fills 45% of all orders, and Juan fills 25% of all orders. An order has just been filled.

   a. What is the probability that Natasha filled the order?

   b. If the order was filled by Juan, what is the probability that it was filled correctly?

   c. Who filled the order is unknown, but the order was filled incorrectly. What are the revised probabilities that Alex, Natasha, or Juan filled the order?

   d. Who filled the order is unknown, but the order was filled correctly. What are the revised probabilities that Alex, Natasha, or Juan filled the order?

4.33 In a small town, two lawn companies fertilize lawns during the summer. Maritime Lawn Service has 72% of the market. Thirty percent of the lawns fertilized by Maritime could be rated as very healthy one month after service. Greenchem has the other 28% of the market. Twenty percent of the lawns fertilized by Greenchem could be rated as very healthy one month after service. A lawn that has been treated with fertilizer by one of these companies within the last month is selected randomly. If the lawn is rated as very healthy, what are the revised probabilities that Maritime or Greenchem treated the lawn?

4.34 Suppose 70% of all companies are classified as small companies and the rest as large companies. Suppose further that 82% of large companies provide training to employees, but only 18% of small companies provide training. A company is randomly selected without knowing if it is a large or small company; however, it is determined that the company provides training to employees. What are the prior probabilities that the company is a large company or a small company? What are the revised probabilities that the company is large or small? Based on your analysis, what is the overall percentage of companies that offer training?

End-of-Chapter Review

Decision Dilemma Solved

Education, Gender, and Employment

The graduate data given in the Decision Dilemma are displayed in a raw values matrix. Using the techniques presented in this chapter, it is possible to statistically answer the managerial questions.

- If an employer randomly selects a person from the pool of graduates, the probability that the graduate is female, $P(F)$, is 137,235/227,772 or 0.603. This marginal probability indicates that roughly 60.3% of all graduates are female. Given that the graduate has a master's degree, the probability that the graduate is female, $P(F|MD)$, is 28,836/48,258 or 0.598.

- The proportion of basic graduates who are female is 0.607. This means that there is a 60.7% chance that a randomly picked basic graduate is female. Therefore, if a randomly picked basic graduate is a woman, it does not exhibit any bias against men.

- Suppose an employer wants a graduate and picks a graduate at random. The probability that the person has a doctoral degree is 0.025 or 2.5%, derived by dividing all doctoral graduates by the total number of graduates (5,718/227,772).

- To identify the probability of picking a female with a doctoral degree, we must identify $P(F \cap DD)$. Since there are 2,850 graduates who are females with doctoral degrees, the probability of choosing a graduate who is a female with a doctoral degree is 2,850/227,772 = 0.013 or 1.3%.

The probability that a randomly chosen graduate is male with a master's degree is given by

$$P(M \cap MD) = 19,422/227,772 = 0.085$$

The probability that a randomly chosen graduate is *not* male with a master's degree is a complementary event to the above. Therefore, the probability is

$$P(M \cap MD)' = 1 - 0.085 = 0.915$$

If the chosen person is male, the probability of his having a basic undergraduate degree is given by the conditional probability

$$P(B|M) = 68,247/90,537 = 0.754$$

Many other questions about education and employment can be answered using probabilities.

The probability approach to hiring is a factual, numerical approach to people selection taken without regard to individual talents, skills, and worth to the company. Of course, in most instances, many other considerations go into the hiring, promoting, and rewarding of workers besides the random drawing of their name. However, company management should be aware that attacks on hiring, promotion, and reward practices are sometimes made using statistical analyses such as those presented here. It is not being argued here that management should base decisions merely on the probabilities within particular categories. Nevertheless, by being aware of the probabilities, management can proceed to support their decisions with documented evidence of worker productivity and worth to the organization.

Key Considerations

One of the potential misuses of probability occurs when subjective probabilities are used. Most subjective probabilities are based on a person's feelings, intuition, or experience. Almost everyone has an opinion on something and is willing to share it. As professional people, it is important that we do not give our best-guess probability of an occurrence if we are not relatively confident of what will happen. Optimistic people will tend to give higher probabilities of the likelihood of a company or client attaining some goal. Pessimistic people may tend to dampen the probability of such a goal being attained. Although such probabilities are not strictly unethical to report, they can be misleading and disastrous to other decision-makers. We should be cautious in offering our subjective probabilities in decision-making situations where our opinion is highly valued. In addition, subjective probabilities leave the door open for unscrupulous people to overemphasize their point of view by manipulating the probability. Psychological studies have shown that the human mind is typically weak at intuitive probability assessments.

Relative frequency of occurrence probabilities are basically computed on historical figures. It is important that such historical information be accurate and valid. "Padding" the figures from the past can lead to incorrect and misleading probabilities.

The decision-maker should remember that the laws and rules of probability are for the long run. If a coin is tossed, even though the probability of getting a head is 0.5, the result will be either a head or a tail. It isn't possible to get a half head. The probability of getting a head (0.5) will probably work out in the long run, but in the short run an experiment might produce 10 tails in a row. Suppose the probability of striking oil on a geological formation is 0.10. This probability means that, in the long run, if the company drills enough holes on this type of formation, it should strike oil in about 10% of the holes. However, if the company has only enough money to drill one hole, it will either strike oil or have a dry hole. The probability figure of 0.10 may mean something different to the company that can afford to drill only one hole than to the company that can drill many hundreds. Classical probabilities could be used unethically to lure a company or client into a potential short-run investment with the expectation of getting at least something in return, when in actuality the investor will either win or lose. The oil company that drills only one hole will not get 10% back from the hole. It will either win or lose on the hole. Thus, classical probabilities open the door for unsubstantiated expectations, particularly in the short run.

Why Statistics Is Relevant

Many business and personal decisions need to be made under conditions of uncertainty. For example, an organization needs to market a product without any guarantee that it will succeed in the market. A factory needs to invest in machinery without any guarantee that the factory will recuperate the costs through sales. A marketer needs to supply goods to all stores with no guarantee that they will be sold. A judge has to make a decision on the guilt or innocence of the person on evidence that is necessarily incomplete. A university has to admit students without knowing whether the students will pass or fail.

In all such conditions, probability calculations provide a means of increasing the ratio of success to failure. Probability does not eliminate risk, but it provides a numerical estimate of it. As more information becomes available, probability methods offer a way to incorporate the new information, thereby reducing the chance of making incorrect decisions.

Decisions based on probability models may not always be right. But, if used properly, probability models will ensure an increase in the proportion of right decisions, potentially saving millions of dollars for the company.

Summary of Learning Objectives

LEARNING OBJECTIVE 4.1 Describe what probability is, when one would use it, and how to differentiate among the three methods of assigning probabilities.

The study of probability addresses ways of assigning probabilities, types of probabilities, and laws of probabilities. Probabilities support the notion of inferential statistics. Using sample data to estimate and test hypotheses about population parameters is done with uncertainty.

If samples are taken at random, probabilities can be assigned to outcomes of the inferential process.

Three methods of assigning probabilities are (a) the classical method, (b) the relative frequency of occurrence method, and (c) subjective probabilities. The classical method can assign probabilities a priori, or before the experiment takes place. It relies on the laws and rules of probability. The relative frequency of occurrence method assigns probabilities based on historical data or empirically derived data. Because of the speed with which new data arrive and are processed, the importance of the relative frequency of occurrence method in determining and updating probabilities has increased in recent times. Subjective probabilities are based on the feelings, knowledge, and experience of the person determining the probability.

LEARNING OBJECTIVE 4.2   Deconstruct the elements of probability by defining experiments, sample spaces, and events; classifying events as mutually exclusive, collectively exhaustive, complementary, or independent; and counting possibilities.

Certain special types of events necessitate amendments to some of the laws of probability: mutually exclusive events and independent events. Mutually exclusive events are events that cannot occur at the same time, so the probability of their intersection is zero. In determining the union of two mutually exclusive events, the law of addition is amended by the deletion of the intersection. With independent events, the occurrence of one has no impact or influence on the occurrence of the other. Certain experiments, such as those involving coins or dice, naturally produce independent events. Other experiments produce independent events when the experiment is conducted with replacement. If events are independent, the joint probability is computed by multiplying the individual probabilities, which is a special case of the law of multiplication.

Three techniques for counting the possibilities in an experiment are the mn counting rule, the N^n possibilities, and combinations. The mn counting rule is used to determine in how many total possible ways an experiment can occur in a series of sequential operations. The N^n formula is applied when sampling is being done with replacement or events are independent. Combinations are used to determine the possibilities when sampling is being done without replacement.

LEARNING OBJECTIVE 4.3   Compare marginal, union, joint, and conditional probabilities by defining each one.

Four types of probability are marginal probability, conditional probability, joint probability, and union probability.

LEARNING OBJECTIVE 4.4   Calculate probabilities using the general law of addition, along with a joint probability table, the complement of a union, or the special law of addition if necessary.

The general law of addition is used to compute the probability of a union.

LEARNING OBJECTIVE 4.5   Calculate joint probabilities of both independent and dependent events using the general and special laws of multiplication.

The general law of multiplication is used to compute joint probabilities.

LEARNING OBJECTIVE 4.6   Calculate conditional probabilities with various forms of the law of conditional probability, and use them to determine if two events are independent.

The conditional law is used to compute conditional probabilities. Conditional probabilities are used when we want to incorporate prior knowledge one may have regarding the two events studied.

LEARNING OBJECTIVE 4.7   Calculate conditional probabilities using Bayes' rule.

Bayes' rule is a method that can be used to revise probabilities when new information becomes available; it is a variation of the conditional law. Bayes' rule takes prior probabilities of events occurring and adjusts or revises those probabilities on the basis of information about what subsequently occurs.

Key Terms

a priori 4-3
Bayes' rule 4-31
classical method 4-3
collectively exhaustive events 4-8
combinations 4-10
complement of a union 4-17
complement of an event 4-8
conditional probability 4-12
elementary events 4-5

event 4-5
experiment 4-5
independent events 4-7
intersection 4-7
joint probability 4-12
marginal probability 4-11
mn counting rule 4-9
mutually exclusive events 4-7
permutations 4-10

probability matrix 4-14
relative frequency of
   occurrence method 4-4
sample space 4-6
set notation 4-7
subjective method 4-4
union 4-7
union probability 4-12

Formulas

(4.1) Classical method of assigning probabilities
$$P(E) = \frac{n_e}{N}$$

(4.2) Mutually exclusive events X and Y
$$P(X \cap Y) = 0$$

(4.3) Independent events X and Y
$$P(X|Y) = P(X) \text{ and } P(Y|X) = P(Y)$$

(4.4) Probability of the complement of A
$$P(A') = 1 - P(A)$$

(4.5) Counting rule
$$mn$$

(4.6) Sampling with replacement
$$N^n$$

(4.7) Sampling without replacement (Combination)
$$_NC_n = \binom{N}{n} = \frac{N!}{n!(N-n)!}$$

(4.8) Permutation
$$_nP_r = \frac{n!}{(n-r)!}$$

(4.9) General law of addition
$$P(X \cup Y) = P(X) + P(Y) - P(X \cap Y)$$

(4.10) Special law of addition
$$P(X \cup Y) = P(X) + P(Y)$$

(4.11) General law of multiplication
$$P(X \cap Y) = P(X) \cdot P(Y|X) = P(Y) \cdot P(X|Y)$$

(4.12) Special law of multiplication
$$P(X \cap Y) = P(X) \cdot P(Y)$$

(4.13) Law of conditional probability
$$P(X|Y) = \frac{P(X \cap Y)}{P(Y)} = \frac{P(X) \cdot P(Y|X)}{P(Y)}$$

(4.14) Bayes' rule
$$P(X_i|Y) = \frac{P(X_i) \cdot P(Y|X_i)}{P(X_1) \cdot P(Y|X_1) + P(X_2) \cdot P(Y|X_2) + \cdots + P(X_n) \cdot P(Y|X_n)}$$

Supplementary Problems

Calculating the Statistics

4.35 **Video** Use the values in the contingency table to solve the equations given.

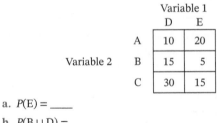

		Variable 1 D	Variable 1 E
	A	10	20
Variable 2	B	15	5
	C	30	15

   a. $P(E) = \underline{\quad}$

   b. $P(B \cup D) = \underline{\quad}$

   c. $P(A \cap E) = \underline{\quad}$

   d. $P(B|E) = \underline{\quad}$

   e. $P(A \cup B) = \underline{\quad}$

   f. $P(B \cap C) = \underline{\quad}$

   g. $P(D|C) = \underline{\quad}$

   h. $P(A|B) = \underline{\quad}$

4.36 Are variables 1 and 2 in Question 4.35 independent? Why or why not?

4.37 **Video** Use the values in the contingency table to solve the equations given.

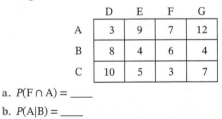

	D	E	F	G
A	3	9	7	12
B	8	4	6	4
C	10	5	3	7

   a. $P(F \cap A) = \underline{\quad}$

   b. $P(A|B) = \underline{\quad}$

   c. $P(B) = \underline{\quad}$

   d. $P(E \cap F) = \underline{\quad}$

   e. $P(D|B) = \underline{\quad}$

   f. $P(B|D) = \underline{\quad}$

   g. $P(D \cup C) = \underline{\quad}$

   h. $P(F) = \underline{\quad}$

4.38 The following probability matrix contains a breakdown on the age and gender of physicians in a large city in a recent year.

PHYSICIANS IN A LARGE CITY

		Age (Years) <35	35–44	45–54	55–64	≥65	
Gender	Male	0.11	0.20	0.19	0.12	0.16	0.78
	Female	0.07	0.08	0.04	0.02	0.01	0.22
		0.18	0.28	0.23	0.14	0.17	1.00

a. What is the probability that one randomly selected physician is 35–44 years old?

b. What is the probability that one randomly selected physician is both female and 45–54 years old?

c. What is the probability that one randomly selected physician is male or is 35–44 years old?

d. What is the probability that one randomly selected physician is less than 35 years old or 55–64 years old?

e. What is the probability that one randomly selected physician is female if the physician is 45–54 years old?

f. What is the probability that a randomly selected physician is neither female nor 55–64 years old?

For example, suppose 10% of the population of the world is left-handed and that a sample of 20 people is selected randomly from the world's population. If the first person selected is left-handed—and the sampling is conducted without replacement—the value of $p = 0.10$ is virtually unaffected because the population of the world is so large. In addition, with many experiments the population is continually being replenished even as the sampling is being done. This condition is often the case with quality control sampling of products from large production runs. Some examples of binomial distribution problems follow.

1. Suppose a machine producing computer chips has a 6% defective rate. If a company purchases 30 of these chips, what is the probability that none is defective?

2. One ethics study suggested that 84% of Canadian companies have an ethics code. From a random sample of 15 companies, what is the probability that at least 10 have an ethics code?

3. A survey found that nearly 67% of company buyers stated that their company had programs for preferred buyers. If a random sample of 50 company buyers is taken, what is the probability that 40 or more have companies with programs for preferred buyers?

Solving a Binomial Problem

A survey of relocation administrators by Runzheimer International revealed several reasons why workers reject relocation offers. Included in the list were family considerations, financial reasons, and others. Four percent of the respondents said they rejected relocation offers because they received too little relocation help. Suppose five workers who just rejected relocation offers are randomly selected and interviewed. Assuming the 4% figure holds for all workers being offered relocation, what is the probability that the first worker interviewed rejected the offer because of too little relocation help and the next four workers rejected the offer for other reasons?

Let T represent too little relocation help and R represent other reasons. The sequence of interviews for this problem is as follows:

$$T_1, R_2, R_3, R_4, R_5$$

The probability of getting this sequence of workers is calculated by using the special rule of multiplication for independent events (assuming the workers are independently selected from a large population of workers). If 4% of the workers rejecting relocation offers do so for too little relocation help, the probability of one person being randomly selected from workers rejecting relocation offers who does so for that reason is 0.04, which is the value of p. The other 96% of the workers who reject relocation offers do so for other reasons. Thus, the probability of randomly selecting a worker from those who reject relocation offers who does so for other reasons is $1 - 0.04 = 0.96$, which is the value for q. The probability of obtaining this sequence of five workers who have rejected relocation offers is

$$P(T_1 \cap R_2 \cap R_3 \cap R_4 \cap R_5) = (0.04)(0.96)(0.96)(0.96)(0.96) = 0.03397$$

Obviously, in the random selection of workers who rejected relocation offers, the worker who did so because of too little relocation help could have been the second worker or the third or the fourth or the fifth. All the possible sequences of getting one worker who rejected relocation because of too little help and four workers who did so for other reasons follow.

$$T_1, R_2, R_3, R_4, R_5$$
$$R_1, T_2, R_3, R_4, R_5$$
$$R_1, R_2, T_3, R_4, R_5$$
$$R_1, R_2, R_3, T_4, R_5$$
$$R_1, R_2, R_3, R_4, T_5$$

The probability of each of these sequences occurring is calculated as follows.

$$(0.04)(0.96)(0.96)(0.96)(0.96) = 0.03397$$
$$(0.96)(0.04)(0.96)(0.96)(0.96) = 0.03397$$
$$(0.96)(0.96)(0.04)(0.96)(0.96) = 0.03397$$
$$(0.96)(0.96)(0.96)(0.04)(0.96) = 0.03397$$
$$(0.96)(0.96)(0.96)(0.96)(0.04) = 0.03397$$

Note that in each case the final probability is the same. Each of the five sequences contains the product of 0.04 and four 0.96s. The commutative property of multiplication allows for the re-ordering of the five individual probabilities in any one sequence. The probabilities in each of the five sequences may be reordered and summarized as $(0.04)^1(0.96)^4$. Each sequence contains the same five probabilities, which makes recomputing the probability of each sequence unnecessary. What *is* important is to determine in how many different ways the sequences can be formed and multiply that figure by the probability of one sequence occurring. For the five sequences of this problem, the total probability of getting exactly one worker who rejected relocation because of too little relocation help in a random sample of five workers who rejected relocation offers is

$$5(0.04)^1(0.96)^4 = 0.16985$$

An easier way to determine the number of sequences than by listing all possibilities is to use *combinations* to calculate them. (The concept of combinations was introduced in Chapter 4.) Five workers are being sampled, so $n = 5$, and the problem is to get one worker who rejected a relocation offer because of too little relocation help, $x = 1$. Hence $_nC_x$ will yield the number of possible ways to get x successes in n trials. For this problem, $_5C_1$ tells the number of sequences of possibilities.

$$_5C_1 = \frac{5!}{1!(5-1)!} = 5$$

Weighting the probability of one sequence with the combination yields

$$_5C_1(0.04)^1(0.96)^4 = 0.16985$$

Using combinations simplifies the determination of how many sequences are possible for a given value of x in a binomial distribution.

Now suppose 70% of all Canadians believe cleaning up the environment is an important issue. What is the probability of randomly sampling four Canadians and having exactly two of them say that they believe cleaning up the environment is an important issue? Let E represent the success of getting a person who believes cleaning up the environment is an important issue. For this example, $p = 0.70$. Let N represent the failure of not getting a person who believes cleaning up is an important issue (N denotes not important). The probability of getting one of these people is $q = 0.30$.

The various sequences of getting two Es in a sample of four follow.

$$E_1, E_2, N_3, N_4$$
$$E_1, N_2, E_3, N_4$$
$$E_1, N_2, N_3, E_4$$
$$N_1, E_2, E_3, N_4$$
$$N_1, E_2, N_3, E_4$$
$$N_1, N_2, E_3, E_4$$

Two successes in a sample of four can occur in six ways. Using combinations, the number of sequences is

$$_4C_2 = 6 \text{ ways}$$

The probability of selecting any individual sequence is

$$(0.70)^2(0.30)^2 = 0.0441$$

Thus, the overall probability of getting exactly two people who believe cleaning up the environment is important out of four randomly selected people, when 70% of Canadians believe cleaning up the environment is important, is

$$_4C_2(0.70)^2(0.30)^2 = 0.2646$$

Generalizing from these two examples yields the binomial formula, which can be used to solve binomial problems.

Binomial Formula

$$P(x) = {}_nC_x \cdot p^x \cdot q^{n-x} = \frac{n!}{x!(n-x)!} \cdot p^x \cdot q^{n-x} \qquad (5.4)$$

where

n = the number of trials (or the number being sampled)

x = the number of successes desired

p = the probability of getting a success in one trial

$q = 1 - p$ = the probability of getting a failure in one trial

---

The binomial formula summarizes the steps presented so far to solve binomial problems. The formula allows the solution of these problems quickly and efficiently. (See Thinking Critically About Statistics in Business Today 5.1.)

Thinking Critically About Statistics in Business Today 5.1

Plastic Bags vs. Bringing Your Own

In a move to protect and improve the environment, governments and companies around the world are making an effort to reduce the use of plastic bags by shoppers for transporting purchased food and goods. Two of the most prevalent approaches for phasing out lightweight plastic bags are charges and bans. In 2002, Bangladesh became the first country to impose a total ban on lightweight plastic bags. More recently, such bans have been introduced in 54 countries, with varying degrees of enforcement, and 32 other countries have imposed a charge per bag.

Under the Revised Containers and Packaging Recycling Law, which came into force in April 2007, Japan has been making efforts to raise awareness among consumers by promoting waste reduction and encouraging retailers to charge for plastic packages and containers, as well as distributing reusable shopping bags to customers. Specifically, in Yamagata City in northern Japan, the city concluded an agreement with seven local food supermarket chains to reduce plastic bag use by having them agree to charge for the use of such bags. Before the agreement, the average percentage of shoppers bringing their own shopping bags was about 35%. Within a few months, the percentage had risen to almost 46%. Later that year, when 39 stores of nine supermarket chains (two other chains had joined the agreement) were charging for the use of plastic bags, the percentage rose to nearly 90%.

Working with governments and businesses across Canada, the Government of Canada plans to ban harmful single-use plastics (such as plastic bags, straws, cutlery, plates, and stir sticks) as early as 2021. It will introduce standards and targets for companies that manufacture plastic products or sell items with plastic packaging so they become responsible for their plastic waste.

Things to Ponder

1. While some private businesses in Canada have banned plastics bags, many businesses still provide plastic bags for free. Do you think that Canadian consumers would reduce their use of plastic bags if they were always charged for them? Why or why not?

2. Do you think that the Canadian initiatives will be as effective as the Japanese initiatives? Why or why not? Do you believe that a country's cultural value systems have anything to do with the success of such programs? That is, do you believe that it is the extra money that consumers have to spend to purchase the plastic bags that drives the decrease in usage, or are there other factors in addition to the added cost?

Sources: Adapted from Japan for Sustainability website, www.japanfs.org/en/; Lisa Skumatz and Dana D'Souza, "Bag Ban Basics," *Plastics Recycling Update* (November 2016), resource-recycling.com/plastics/2016/12/08/bag-ban-basics/; Jane Onyanga-Omara, "Plastic Bag Backlash Gains Momentum," BBC News, September 14, 2013, www.bbc.com/news/uk-24090603; "Canada to Ban Harmful Single-Use Plastics and Hold Companies Responsible for Plastic Waste," news release from Office of the Prime Minister, June 10, 2019, pm.gc.ca/eng/news/2019/06/10/canada-ban-harmful-single-use-plastics-and-hold-companies-responsible-plastic-waste.

DEMONSTRATION PROBLEM 5.2

A Gallup survey found that 65% of all financial consumers were very satisfied with their primary financial institution. Suppose that 25 financial consumers are sampled. If the Gallup survey result still holds true today, what is the probability that exactly 19 are very satisfied with their primary financial institution?

Solution   The value of p is 0.65 (very satisfied), the value of $q = 1 - p = 1 - 0.65 = 0.35$ (not very satisfied), $n = 25$, and $x = 19$. The binomial formula yields the final answer:

$$_{25}C_{19}(0.65)^{19}(0.35)^6 = (177,100)(0.00027884)(0.00183827) = 0.0908$$

If 65% of all financial consumers are very satisfied, about 9.08% of the time the analyst would get exactly 19 out of 25 financial consumers who are very satisfied with their financial institution. How many very satisfied consumers would one expect to get in 25 randomly selected financial consumers? If 65% of the financial consumers are very satisfied with their primary financial institution, one would expect to get about 65% of 25 or $(0.65)(25) = 16.25$ very satisfied financial consumers. While in any individual sample of 25 the number of financial consumers who are very satisfied cannot be 16.25, business analysts understand the x values near 16.25 are the most likely occurrences.

DEMONSTRATION PROBLEM 5.3

Statistics Canada reported recently that approximately 7% of all workers in Canada are unemployed. In conducting a random telephone survey, what is the probability of getting two or fewer unemployed Canadian workers in a sample of 20?

Solution   This problem must be worked as the union of three problems: (1) zero unemployed, $x = 0$; (2) one unemployed, $x = 1$; and (3) two unemployed, $x = 2$. In each problem, $p = 0.07$, $q = 0.93$, and $n = 20$. The binomial formula gives the following result:

$x = 0$		$x = 1$		$x = 2$	
$_{20}C_0(0.07)^0(0.93)^{20}$	$+$	$_{20}C_1(0.07)^1(0.93)^{19}$	$+$	$_{20}C_2(0.07)^2(0.93)^{18}$	$=$
0.2342	$+$	0.3526	$+$	0.2521	$=$ 0.8390

If 7% of the workers in Canada are unemployed, the telephone surveyor would get zero, one, or two unemployed workers 83.9% of the time in a random sample of 20 workers. The requirement of getting two or fewer is satisfied by getting zero, one, or two unemployed workers. Thus, this problem is the union of three probabilities. Whenever the binomial formula is used to solve for cumulative success (not an exact number), the probability of each x value must be solved and the probabilities summed. If an actual survey produced such a result, it would serve to validate the Statistics Canada figures.

Using the Binomial Table

Anyone who works enough binomial problems will begin to recognize that the probability of getting $x = 5$ successes from a sample size of $n = 18$ when $p = 0.10$ is the same no matter whether the five successes are left-handed people, defective parts, brand X purchasers, or any other variable. Whether the sample involves people, parts, or products does not matter in terms of the final probabilities. The essence of the problem is the same: $n = 18$, $x = 5$, and $p = 0.10$. Recognizing this fact, we have constructed a set of binomial tables containing presolved probabilities.

Two parameters, n and p, describe or characterize a binomial distribution. Binomial distributions are actually a family of distributions. Every different value of n and/or every different value of p gives a different binomial distribution, and tables are available for various combinations of n and p values. Because of space limitations, the binomial tables presented in this text are limited. Table A.2 in Appendix A contains binomial tables. Each table is headed by a value of n. Nine values of p are presented in each table of size n. In the column below each value of p is the binomial distribution for that combination of n and p. **Table 5.5** contains a segment of Table A.2 with the binomial probabilities for $n = 20$.

TABLE 5.5   **Excerpt from Table A.2, Appendix A**

$n = 20$	Probability								
x	0.1	0.2	0.3	0.4	0.5	0.6	0.7	0.8	0.9
0	0.122	0.012	0.001	0.000	0.000	0.000	0.000	0.000	0.000
1	0.270	0.058	0.007	0.000	0.000	0.000	0.000	0.000	0.000
2	0.285	0.137	0.028	0.003	0.000	0.000	0.000	0.000	0.000
3	0.190	0.205	0.072	0.012	0.001	0.000	0.000	0.000	0.000
4	0.090	0.218	0.130	0.035	0.005	0.000	0.000	0.000	0.000
5	0.032	0.175	0.179	0.075	0.015	0.001	0.000	0.000	0.000
6	0.009	0.109	0.192	0.124	0.037	0.005	0.000	0.000	0.000
7	0.002	0.055	0.164	0.166	0.074	0.015	0.001	0.000	0.000
8	0.000	0.022	0.114	0.180	0.120	0.035	0.004	0.000	0.000
9	0.000	0.007	0.065	0.160	0.160	0.071	0.012	0.000	0.000
10	0.000	0.002	0.031	0.117	0.176	0.117	0.031	0.002	0.000
11	0.000	0.000	0.012	0.071	0.160	0.160	0.065	0.007	0.000
12	0.000	0.000	0.004	0.035	0.120	0.180	0.114	0.022	0.000
13	0.000	0.000	0.001	0.015	0.074	0.166	0.164	0.055	0.002
14	0.000	0.000	0.000	0.005	0.037	0.124	0.192	0.109	0.009
15	0.000	0.000	0.000	0.001	0.015	0.075	0.179	0.175	0.032
16	0.000	0.000	0.000	0.000	0.005	0.035	0.130	0.218	0.090
17	0.000	0.000	0.000	0.000	0.001	0.012	0.072	0.205	0.190
18	0.000	0.000	0.000	0.000	0.000	0.003	0.028	0.137	0.285
19	0.000	0.000	0.000	0.000	0.000	0.000	0.007	0.058	0.270
20	0.000	0.000	0.000	0.000	0.000	0.000	0.001	0.012	0.122

DEMONSTRATION PROBLEM 5.4

Solve the binomial probability for $n = 20$, $p = 0.40$, and $x = 10$ by using Table A.2, Appendix A.

Solution   To use Table A.2, first locate the value of n. Because $n = 20$ for this problem, the portion of the binomial tables containing values for $n = 20$ presented in Table 5.5 can be used. After locating the value of n, search horizontally across the top of the table for the appropriate value of p. In this problem, $p = 0.40$. The column under 0.40 contains the probabilities for the binomial distribution of $n = 20$ and $p = 0.40$. To get the probability of $x = 10$, find the value of x in the leftmost column and locate the probability in the table at the intersection of $p = 0.40$ and $x = 10$. The answer is 0.117. Working this problem by the binomial formula yields the same result:

$$_{20}C_{10}(0.40)^{10}(0.60)^{10} = 0.1171$$

DEMONSTRATION PROBLEM 5.5

According to Information Resources, which publishes data on market share for various products, Oreos control about 10% of the market for cookie brands. Suppose 20 purchasers of cookies are selected randomly from the population. What is the probability that fewer than four purchasers choose Oreos?

Solution   For this problem, $n = 20$, $p = 0.10$, and $x < 4$. Because $n = 20$, the portion of the binomial tables presented in Table 5.5 can be used to work this problem. Search along the row of p values for 0.10. Determining the probability of getting $x < 4$ involves summing the probabilities for $x = 0, 1, 2$, and 3. The values appear in the x column at the intersection of each x value and $p = 0.10$.

x Value	Probability
0	0.122
1	0.270
2	0.285
3	0.190
$(x < 4) =$	0.867

If 10% of all cookie purchasers prefer Oreos and 20 cookie purchasers are randomly selected, about 86.7% of the time fewer than four of the 20 will select Oreos.

Using the Computer to Produce a Binomial Distribution

Excel can be used to produce the probabilities for virtually any binomial distribution, thus offering yet another option for solving binomial problems besides using the binomial formula or the binomial tables. The advantages of using a software package for this purpose are convenience (if the binomial tables are not readily available and a computer is) and the potential for generating tables for many more values than those printed in the binomial tables.

For example, a study of bank customers stated that 64% of all financial consumers believe banks are more competitive today than they were five years ago. Suppose 23 financial consumers are selected randomly and we want to determine the probabilities of various x values occurring. Table A.2 in Appendix A could not be used because only nine different p values are included and $p = 0.64$ is not one of those values. In addition, $n = 23$ is not included in the table. Without the computer, we are left with the binomial formula as the only option for solving binomial problems for $n = 23$ and $p = 0.64$. Particularly if cumulative probability questions are asked (for example, $x \leq 10$), the binomial formula can be a tedious way to solve the problem.

Shown in **Table 5.6** is the Excel output for the binomial distribution of $n = 23$ and $p = 0.64$. With this computer output, a business analyst could obtain or calculate the probability of any occurrence within the binomial distribution of $n = 23$ and $p = 0.64$. **Table 5.7**

TABLE 5.6	Excel Output for the Binomial Distribution of $n = 23$, $p = 0.64$		
x Value	**Probability**	**x Value**	**Probability**
0	0.000000	12	0.084041
1	0.000000	13	0.126420
2	0.000000	14	0.160533
3	0.000001	15	0.171236
4	0.000006	16	0.152209
5	0.000037	17	0.111421
6	0.000199	18	0.066027
7	0.000858	19	0.030890
8	0.003051	20	0.010983
9	0.009040	21	0.002789
10	0.022500	22	0.000451
11	0.047273	23	0.000035

TABLE 5.7	Excel Output for the Binomial Problem, $P(x \leq 10)$, with $n = 23$, and $p = 0.64$	
	x Value	**$P(x \leq 10)$**
	10	0.035692

TABLE 5.8	Output for Demonstration Problem 5.3 and the Binomial Distribution of $n = 20$, $p = 0.07$

x Value	Probability
0	0.234239
1	0.352618
2	0.252141
3	0.113870
4	0.036426
5	0.008774
6	0.001651
7	0.000249
8	0.000030
9	0.000003
10	0.000000
$P(x \leq 2 | n = 20$ and $p = 0.07) = 0.838997$	

contains the output for the particular binomial problem, $P(x \leq 10)$ when $n = 23$ and $p = 0.64$, solved by using Excel's cumulative probability capability.

Shown in **Table 5.8** is Excel output for all values of x that have probabilities greater than 0.000001 for the binomial distribution discussed in Demonstration Problem 5.3 ($n = 20$, $p = 0.07$) and the solution to the question posed in Demonstration Problem 5.3. Note that the final answer shown (0.838997) in Table 5.8 is obtained directly from Excel. Due to rounding of the values in Table 5.8, there is a slight discrepancy in this summation.

Mean and Standard Deviation of a Binomial Distribution

A binomial distribution has an expected value or a long-run average, which is denoted by μ. The value of μ is determined by $n \cdot p$. For example, if $n = 10$ and $p = 0.4$, then $\mu = n \cdot p = (10)(0.4) = 4$. The long-run average or expected value means that, if n items are sampled over and over for a long time and if p is the probability of getting a success on one trial, the average number of successes per sample is expected to be $n \cdot p$. If 40% of all graduate business students at a large university are women and if random samples of 10 graduate business students are selected many times, the expectation is that, on average, 4 of the 10 students would be women.

Mean and Standard Deviation of a Binomial Distribution

$$\mu = n \cdot p \quad (5.5)$$
$$\sigma = \sqrt{n \cdot p \cdot q} \quad (5.6)$$

Examining the mean of a binomial distribution gives an intuitive feeling about the likelihood of a given outcome.

As mentioned above, 64% of all financial consumers believe banks are more competitive today than they were five years ago. If 23 financial consumers are selected randomly, what is the expected number who believe banks are more competitive today than they were five years ago? This problem can be described by the binomial distribution of $n = 23$ and $p = 0.64$ given in Table 5.6. The mean of this binomial distribution yields the expected value for this problem.

$$\mu = n \cdot p = 23(0.64) = 14.72$$

In the long run, if 23 financial consumers are selected randomly over and over and if indeed 64% of all financial consumers believe banks are more competitive today, then the experiment should average 14.72 financial consumers out of 23 who believe banks are more competitive today. Realize that because the binomial distribution is a discrete distribution you will never actually get 14.72 people out of 23 who believe banks are more competitive today. The mean of the distribution does reveal the relative likelihood of any individual occurrence. Examine Table 5.6. Notice that the highest probabilities are those near $x = 14.72$: $P(x = 15) = 0.1712$, $P(x = 14) = 0.1605$, and $P(x = 16) = 0.1522$. All other probabilities for this distribution are less than these probabilities.

The standard deviation of a binomial distribution is denoted σ and is equal to $\sqrt{n \cdot p \cdot q}$. The standard deviation for the financial consumer problem described by the binomial distribution in Table 5.6 is

TABLE 5.9	Probabilities for Three Binomial Distributions with $n = 8$		
	Probabilities for		
x	$p = 0.20$	$p = 0.50$	$p = 0.80$
0	0.1678	0.0039	0.0000
1	0.3355	0.0312	0.0001
2	0.2936	0.1094	0.0011
3	0.1468	0.2187	0.0092
4	0.0459	0.2734	0.0459
5	0.0092	0.2187	0.1468
6	0.0011	0.1094	0.2936
7	0.0001	0.0312	0.3355
8	0.0000	0.0039	0.1678

$$\sigma = \sqrt{n \cdot p \cdot q} = \sqrt{(23)(0.64)(0.36)} = 2.30$$

Chapter 6 shows that some binomial distributions are nearly bell-shaped and can be approximated by using the normal curve. The mean and standard deviation of a binomial distribution are the tools used to convert these binomial problems to normal curve problems.

Graphing Binomial Distributions

The graph of a binomial distribution can be constructed by using all the possible x values of a distribution and their associated probabilities. The x values are usually graphed along the horizontal axis and the probabilities are graphed along the vertical axis.

Table 5.9 lists the probabilities for three different binomial distributions: $n = 8$ and $p = 0.20$, $n = 8$ and $p = 0.50$, and $n = 8$ and $p = 0.80$. Figure 5.2 displays Excel graphs for each of these three binomial

FIGURE 5.2 Excel Graphs of Three Binomial Distributions with $n = 8$

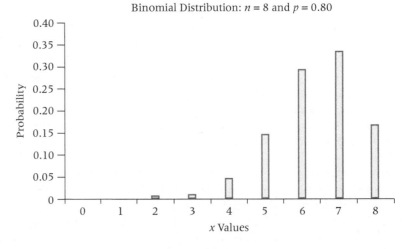

distributions. Observe how the shape of the distribution changes as the value of p increases. For $p = 0.50$, the distribution is symmetrical. For $p = 0.20$, the distribution is skewed right, and for $p = 0.80$, the distribution is skewed left. This pattern makes sense because the mean of the binomial distribution $n = 8$ and $p = 0.50$ is 4, which is in the middle of the distribution. The mean of the distribution $n = 8$ and $p = 0.20$ is 1.6, which results in the highest probabilities being near $x = 2$ and $x = 1$. This graph peaks early and stretches toward the higher values of x. The mean of the distribution $n = 8$ and $p = 0.80$ is 6.4, which results in the highest probabilities being near $x = 6$ and $x = 7$. Thus, the peak of the distribution is nearer to 8 than to 0 and the distribution stretches back toward $x = 0$.

In any binomial distribution, the largest x value that can occur is n and the smallest value is zero. Thus, the graph of any binomial distribution is constrained by zero and n. If the p value of the distribution is not 0.50, this constraint will result in the graph "piling up" at one end and being skewed at the other end.

DEMONSTRATION PROBLEM 5.6

A manufacturing company produces 10,000 plastic mugs per week. This company supplies mugs to another company, which packages the mugs as part of picnic sets. The second company randomly samples 10 mugs sent from the supplier. If two or fewer of the sampled mugs are defective, the second company accepts the lot. What is the probability that the lot will be accepted if the mug manufacturing company is actually producing mugs that are 10% defective? 20% defective? 30% defective? 40% defective?

Solution   In this series of binomial problems, $n = 10$, $x \leq 2$, and p ranges from 0.10 to 0.40. From Table A.2—and cumulating the values—we have the following probability of $x \leq 2$ for each p value and the expected value ($\mu = n \cdot p$).

p	Lot Accepted $P(x \leq 2)$	Expected Number of Defects (μ)
0.10	0.930	1.0
0.20	0.677	2.0
0.30	0.382	3.0
0.40	0.167	4.0

These values indicate that if the manufacturing company is producing 10% defective mugs, the probability is relatively high (0.930) that the lot will be accepted by chance. For higher values of p, the probability of lot acceptance by chance decreases. In addition, as p increases, the expected value moves away from the acceptable values, $x \leq 2$. This move reduces the chances of lot acceptance.

Concept Check

1. List the key characteristics of a binomial experiment.
2. Give an example of a binomial random variable. What do the values of the variable represent? How are the values of the variable defined?

5.3 Problems

5.5 Solve the following problems by using the binomial formula.

a. If $n = 4$ and $p = 0.10$, find $P(x = 3)$.

b. If $n = 7$ and $p = 0.80$, find $P(x = 4)$.

c. If $n = 10$ and $p = 0.60$, find $P(x \geq 7)$.

d. If $n = 12$ and $p = 0.45$, find $P(5 \leq x \leq 7)$.

5.6 Solve the following problems by using the binomial tables (Table A.2).

a. If $n = 20$ and $p = 0.50$, find $P(x = 12)$.

b. If $n = 20$ and $p = 0.30$, find $P(x > 8)$.

c. If $n = 20$ and $p = 0.70$, find $P(x < 12)$.

d. If $n = 20$ and $p = 0.90$, find $P(x \leq 16)$.

e. If $n = 15$ and $p = 0.40$, find $P(4 \leq x \leq 9)$.

f. If $n = 10$ and $p = 0.60$, find $P(x \geq 7)$.

5.7 Solve for the mean and standard deviation of the following binomial distributions.

a. $n = 20$ and $p = 0.70$

b. $n = 70$ and $p = 0.35$

c. $n = 100$ and $p = 0.50$

5.8 Use the binomial probability tables in Table A.2 and sketch the graph of each of the following binomial distributions. Note on the graph where the mean of the distribution falls.

a. $n = 6$ and $p = 0.70$

b. $n = 20$ and $p = 0.50$

c. $n = 8$ and $p = 0.80$

5.9 In a recent survey, buyers were asked a series of questions with regard to Internet usage. One question asked was how they would use the Internet if security and other issues could be resolved. Suppose that 78% said they would use it for pricing information, 75% said they would use it to send purchase orders, and 70% said they would use it for purchase order acknowledgments. Assume that these percentages hold true for all buyers. A business analyst randomly samples 20 buyers and asks them how they would use the Internet if security and other issues could be resolved.

a. What is the probability that exactly 14 of these buyers would use the Internet for pricing information?

b. What is the probability that all of the buyers would use the Internet to send purchase orders?

c. What is the probability that fewer than 12 would use the Internet for purchase order acknowledgments?

5.10 *The Wall Street Journal* reported some interesting statistics on the job market. One statistic is that 40% of all workers say they would change jobs for "slightly higher pay." In addition, 88% of companies say that there is a shortage of qualified job candidates. Suppose 16 workers are randomly selected and asked if they would change jobs for slightly higher pay. What is the probability that nine or more say yes? What is the probability that three, four, five, or six say yes? If 13 companies are contacted, what is the probability that exactly 10 say there is a shortage of qualified job candidates? What is the probability that all of the companies say there is a shortage of qualified job candidates? What is the expected number of companies that would say there is a shortage of qualified job candidates?

5.11 An increasing number of consumers believe they have to look out for themselves in the marketplace. According to a survey conducted by the Yankelovich Partners for *USA WEEKEND* magazine, 60% of all consumers have called an information line for a product. Suppose a random sample of 25 consumers is contacted and interviewed about their buying habits.

a. What is the probability that 15 or more of these consumers have called an information line for a product?

b. What is the probability that more than 20 of these consumers have called an information line for a product?

c. What is the probability that fewer than 10 of these consumers have called an information line for a product?

5.12 Assume that a study has shown that about half of all Canadian workers who change jobs cash out their pension plans rather than leaving the money in the account to grow. The percentage is much higher for workers with small pension plan balances. In fact, 87% of workers with pension plan accounts less than $5,000 opt to take their balance rather than roll it over into other retirement accounts when they change jobs. Assuming that 50% of all workers who change jobs cash out their pension plans, if 16 workers who have recently changed jobs that had pension plans are randomly sampled, what is the probability that more than 10 of them cashed out their pension plan? If 10 workers who have recently changed jobs and had pension plans with accounts less than $5,000 are randomly sampled, what is the probability that exactly 6 of them cashed out?

5.13 In the past few years, outsourcing overseas has become more frequently used than ever before by Canadian and U.S. companies. However, outsourcing is not without problems, and so consultants are frequently used. Suppose that 20% of the companies that outsource overseas use a consultant. Suppose 15 companies that outsource overseas are randomly selected.

a. What is the probability that exactly five companies that outsource overseas use a consultant?

b. What is the probability that more than nine companies that outsource overseas use a consultant?

c. What is the probability that none of the companies that outsource overseas use a consultant?

d. What is the probability that between four and seven (inclusive) companies that outsource overseas use a consultant?

e. Construct a graph for this binomial distribution. In light of the graph and the expected value, explain why the probability results from parts (a) through (d) were obtained.

5.14 According to the Financial Planners Standards Council, 22% of certified financial planners (CFPs) earn between $100,000 and $149,999 per year. Thirty-two percent earn $150,000 or more. Suppose a complete list of all CFPs is available and 18 are randomly selected from that list.

a. What is the expected number of CFPs who earn between $100,000 and $149,999 per year? What is the expected number who earn $150,000 or more per year?

b. What is the probability that at least eight CFPs earn between $100,000 and $149,999 per year?

c. What is the probability that two, three, or four CFPs earn more than $150,000 per year?

d. What is the probability that none of the CFPs earn between $100,000 and $149,999 per year? What is the probability that none earn $150,000 or more per year? Which probability is higher and why?

5.4 | Poisson Distribution

LEARNING OBJECTIVE 5.4

Solve problems involving the Poisson distribution using the Poisson formula and the Poisson table.

The Poisson distribution is another discrete distribution. It is named after Siméon Denis Poisson (1781–1840), a French mathematician, who published its essentials in a paper in 1837. The Poisson distribution and the binomial distribution have some similarities but also several differences. The binomial distribution describes a distribution of two possible outcomes designated as success and failure from a given number of trials. The **Poisson distribution** *focuses only on the number of discrete occurrences over some interval or continuum.* A Poisson experiment does not have a given number of trials (*n*) as a binomial experiment does. For example, whereas a binomial experiment might be used to determine how many cars assembled in Canada are in a random sample of 20 cars, a Poisson experiment might focus on the number of cars randomly arriving at an automobile repair facility during a 10-minute interval.

The Poisson distribution describes the occurrence of *rare events*. In fact, the Poisson formula has been referred to as the *law of improbable events.* For example, serious accidents at a chemical plant are rare, and the number per month might be described by the Poisson distribution. The Poisson distribution is often used to describe the number of random arrivals per some time interval. If the number of arrivals per interval is too frequent, the time interval can be reduced enough so that a rare number of occurrences is expected. Another example of a Poisson distribution is the number of random customer arrivals per five-minute interval at a small boutique on weekday mornings.

The Poisson distribution can also be applied in the field of management science. The models used in queuing theory (theory of waiting lines) are usually based on the assumption that the Poisson distribution is the proper distribution to describe random arrival rates over a period of time.

The Poisson distribution has the following characteristics:

- It is a discrete distribution.
- It describes rare events.
- Each occurrence is independent of the other occurrences.
- It describes discrete occurrences over a continuum or interval.
- The occurrences in each interval can range from zero to infinity.
- The expected number of occurrences must hold constant throughout the experiment.

The following are examples of Poisson-type situations:

1. Number of telephone calls per minute at a small business
2. Number of hazardous waste sites per province in Canada
3. Number of major oil spills in the oil sands of Alberta per month
4. Number of cars entering the 407 Express Toll Route in Ontario coming from Highway 427 per minute between 3 A.M. and 4 A.M. in January
5. Number of times a one-year-old personal computer printer breaks down per quarter (three months)
6. Number of sewing flaws per pair of jeans during production
7. Number of times a tire blows on a commercial airplane per week
8. Number of paint spots per new automobile
9. Number of flaws per bolt of cloth
10. Number of cases of a rare blood disease per 100,000 people

Each of these examples represents a rare occurrence of events for some interval. Note that, although time is a more common interval for the Poisson distribution, *intervals* can range from a province in Canada to a pair of jeans. Some of the intervals in these examples might have zero occurrences. Moreover, the average occurrence per interval for many of these examples is probably in the single digits (1–9). (See Thinking Critically About Statistics in Business Today 5.2.)

Thinking Critically About Statistics in Business Today 5.2

Air Passengers' Complaints

Recently, airline passengers in Canada and the United States have expressed more dissatisfaction with airline service than ever before. A recent news report suggests that U.S. regulations are far more consumer-friendly than Canadian ones. For instance, passengers who have been stuck on a grounded U.S. flight for more than 30 minutes after their scheduled departure have the option of getting off. There is no equivalent regulation in Canada. In fact, a Sunwing Airlines flight that was grounded during a snowstorm at Toronto's Pearson International Airport left 200 passengers trapped on the plane for 13 and a half hours!

Typical complaints include flight delays, lost baggage, long runway delays with little or no onboard service, overbooked flights, cramped space due to fuller flights, cancelled flights, and grumpy airline employees. A majority of dissatisfied flyers merely grin and bear it. However, the average number of complaints per 100,000 passengers boarded in the United States has recently reached 0.88.

Because these average numbers are relatively small, it appears that the actual number of complaints per 100,000 is low and may follow a Poisson distribution. In this case, λ represents the average number of complaints and the interval is 100,000 passengers. For example, using $\lambda = 0.88$ complaints (average for

all airlines), if 100,000 boarded passengers were contacted, the probability that exactly three of them logged a complaint could be computed as

$$\frac{(0.88)^3 e^{-0.88}}{3!} = 0.0471$$

That is, if 100,000 boarded passengers were contacted over and over, 4.71% of the time exactly three would have logged complaints.

Things to Ponder

1. Based on the figures given in this feature, can you reach any conclusions about the rate of passenger complaints in general?

2. Passenger complaints appear to be rare occurrences. Can you suggest some reasons why this is the case?

Sources: Adapted from Kathryn Weatherly, "Canada 'Procrastinating' on Improving Air Passenger Rights," CBC News online, February 19, 2013, www.cbc.ca/news/canada/story/2013/02/14/f-air-passenger-rights.html; "Air Travel Consumer Report," U.S. Department of Transportation, www.transportation.gov/airconsumer/air-travel-consumer-reports-2018 John Spears, "Vacation Flight Sits on Tarmac at Pearson Airport All Day," *Toronto Star*, February 9, 2013.

If a Poisson-distributed phenomenon is studied over a long period of time, a *long-run average* can be determined. This average is denoted **lambda** (λ). Each Poisson problem contains a λ value from which the probabilities of particular occurrences are determined. Note that n and p are required to describe a binomial distribution; however, a Poisson distribution can be described by λ alone. The Poisson formula is used to compute the probability of occurrences over an interval for a given λ value.

Poisson Formula

$$P(x) = \frac{\lambda^x e^{-\lambda}}{x!} \tag{5.7}$$

where

$x = 0, 1, 2, 3, \ldots$

λ = long-run average

$e = 2.718281 \ldots$

Here, x is the number of occurrences per interval for which the probability is being computed, λ is the long-run average, and $e = 2.718281. . .$ is the base of natural logarithms.

A word of caution about using the Poisson distribution to study various phenomena is necessary. The λ value must hold constant throughout a Poisson experiment. The analyst must be careful not to apply a given λ to intervals for which λ changes. For example, the average number of customers arriving at a large department store during a one-minute interval will vary from hour to hour, day to day, and month to month. Different times of the day or week might produce different λ values. The number of flaws per pair of jeans might vary from Monday to Friday. The analyst should be specific in describing the interval for which λ is being used.

Working Poisson Problems by Formula

Suppose bank customers arrive randomly on weekday afternoons at an average of 3.2 customers every 4 minutes. What is the probability of exactly five customers arriving in a 4-minute interval on a weekday afternoon? The λ for this problem is 3.2 customers per 4 minutes. The value of x is five customers per 4 minutes. The probability of five customers randomly arriving during a 4-minute interval when the long-run average has been 3.2 customers per 4-minute interval is

$$\frac{(3.2^5)(e^{-3.2})}{5!} = \frac{(335.54)(0.0408)}{120} = 0.1141$$

If a bank averages 3.2 customers every 4 minutes, the probability of five customers arriving during any one 4-minute interval is 0.1141.

DEMONSTRATION PROBLEM 5.7

Bank customers arrive randomly on weekday afternoons at an average of 3.2 customers every 4 minutes. What is the probability of having more than seven customers in a 4-minute interval on a weekday afternoon?

Solution

$$\lambda = 3.2 \text{ customers/4 minutes}$$
$$x > 7 \text{ customers/4 minutes}$$

In theory, the solution requires obtaining the values of $x = 8, 9, 10, 11, 12, 13, 14, \ldots, \infty$. In actuality, each x value is determined until the values are so far away from $\lambda = 3.2$ that the probabilities approach zero. The probabilities are then summed to find $P(x > 7)$.

$$P(x = 8 \mid \lambda = 3.2) = \frac{(3.2^8)(e^{-3.2})}{8!} = 0.0111$$

$$P(x = 9 \mid \lambda = 3.2) = \frac{(3.2^9)(e^{-3.2})}{9!} = 0.0040$$

$$P(x = 10 \mid \lambda = 3.2) = \frac{(3.2^{10})(e^{-3.2})}{10!} = 0.0013$$

$$P(x = 11 \mid \lambda = 3.2) = \frac{(3.2^{11})(e^{-3.2})}{11!} = 0.0004$$

$$P(x = 12 \mid \lambda = 3.2) = \frac{(3.2^{12})(e^{-3.2})}{12!} = 0.0001$$

$$P(x = 13 \mid \lambda = 3.2) = \frac{(3.2^{13})(e^{-3.2})}{13!} = 0.0000$$

$$P(x > 7) = P(x \geq 8) = 0.0169$$

If the bank has been averaging 3.2 customers every 4 minutes on weekday afternoons, it is unlikely that more than seven people would randomly arrive in any one 4-minute period. This answer indicates that more than seven people would randomly arrive in a 4-minute period only 1.69% of the time. Bank officers could use these results to help them make staffing decisions.

DEMONSTRATION PROBLEM 5.8

A bank has an average random arrival rate of 3.2 customers every 4 minutes. What is the probability of getting exactly 10 customers during an 8-minute interval?

Solution

$$\lambda = 3.2 \text{ customers}/4 \text{ minutes}$$
$$x = 10 \text{ customers}/8 \text{ minutes}$$

This example is different from the first two Poisson examples in that the intervals for λ and the sample are different. The intervals must be the same in order to use λ and x together in the probability formula. The right way to approach this dilemma is to adjust the interval for λ so that it and x have the same interval. The interval for x is 8 minutes, so λ should be adjusted to an 8-minute interval. Logically, if the bank averages 3.2 customers every 4 minutes, it should average twice as many, or 6.4 customers, every 8 minutes. If x were for a 2-minute interval, the value of λ would be halved from 3.2 to 1.6 customers per 2-minute interval. The wrong approach to this dilemma is to equalize the intervals by changing the x value. Never adjust or change x in a problem. Just because 10 customers arrive in one 8-minute interval does not mean that there would necessarily have been five customers in a 4-minute interval. There is no guarantee how the 10 customers are spread over the 8-minute interval. Always adjust the λ value. After λ has been adjusted for an 8-minute interval, the solution is

$$\lambda = 6.4 \text{ customers}/8 \text{ minutes}$$
$$x = 10 \text{ customers}/8 \text{ minutes}$$

$$\frac{(6.4)^{10} e^{-6.4}}{10!} = 0.0528$$

Using the Poisson Tables

Every value of λ determines a different Poisson distribution. Regardless of the nature of the interval associated with a λ, the Poisson distribution for a particular λ is the same. Table A.3, Appendix A, contains the Poisson distributions for selected values of λ. Probabilities are displayed in the table for each x value associated with a given λ if the probability has a nonzero value to four decimal places. **Table 5.10** presents a portion of Table A.3 that contains the probabilities of $x \le 9$ if $\lambda = 1.6$.

TABLE 5.10

Poisson Table for $\lambda = 1.6$

x Value	Probability
0	0.2019
1	0.3230
2	0.2584
3	0.1378
4	0.0551
5	0.0176
6	0.0047
7	0.0011
8	0.0002
9	0.0000

DEMONSTRATION PROBLEM 5.9

If a real estate office sells 1.6 houses on an average weekday and sales of houses on weekdays are Poisson distributed, what is the probability of selling exactly four houses in one day? What is the probability of selling no houses in one day? What is the probability of selling more than five houses in a day? What is the probability of selling 10 or more houses in a day? What is the probability of selling exactly four houses in two days?

Solution

$$\lambda = 1.6 \text{ houses}/\text{day}$$
$$P(x = 4|\lambda = 1.6) = ?$$

Table 5.10 gives the probabilities for $\lambda = 1.6$. The left column contains the x values. The line $x = 4$ yields the probability 0.0551. If a real estate firm has been averaging 1.6 houses sold per day, only on 5.51% of the days would it sell exactly four houses and still maintain the λ value. Line 1 of Table 5.10 shows the probability of selling no houses in a day (0.2019). That is, on 20.19% of the days, the firm would sell no houses if sales are Poisson distributed with $\lambda = 1.6$ houses per day. Table 5.10 is not cumulative. To determine $P(x > 5)$, more than five houses, find the probabilities of $x = 6, x = 7, x = 8, x = 9, \ldots, x = ?$. At $x = 9$, the probability to four decimal places is zero, and Table 5.10 stops when an x value zeros out at four decimal places. The answer for $x > 5$ follows.

x Value	Probability
6	0.0047
7	0.0011
8	0.0002
9	0.0000
	$x > 5 = 0.0060$

What is the probability of selling 10 or more houses in one day? As the table zeros out at $x = 9$, the probability of $x \geq 10$ is essentially 0.0000—that is, if the real estate office has been averaging only 1.6 houses sold per day, it is virtually impossible to sell 10 or more houses in a day. What is the probability of selling exactly four houses in two days? In this case, the interval has been changed from one day to two days. Lambda is for one day, so an adjustment must be made: A λ of 1.6 for one day converts to a λ of 3.2 for two days. Table 5.10 no longer applies, so Table A.3 must be used to solve this problem. The answer is found by looking up $\lambda = 3.2$ and $x = 4$ in Table A.3: the probability is 0.1781.

Mean and Standard Deviation of a Poisson Distribution

The mean or expected value of a Poisson distribution is λ. It is the long-run average of occurrences for an interval if many random samples are taken. λ is usually not a whole number, so most of the time actually observing λ occurrences in an interval is impossible.

For example, suppose $\lambda = 6.5$/interval for some Poisson-distributed phenomenon. The resulting numbers of x occurrences in 20 different random samples from a Poisson distribution with $\lambda = 6.5$ might be as follows.

6   9   7   4   8   7   6   6   10   6   5   5   8   4   5   8   5   4   9   10

Computing the mean number of occurrences from this group of 20 intervals gives 6.6. In theory, for infinite sampling the long-run average is 6.5. Note from the samples that, when λ is 6.5, several 5s and 6s occur. Rarely would sample occurrences of 1, 2, 3, 11, 12, 13, . . . occur when $\lambda = 6.5$. Understanding the mean of a Poisson distribution gives a feel for the actual occurrences that are likely to happen.

The variance of a Poisson distribution is also λ. The standard deviation is $\sqrt{\lambda}$. Combining the standard deviation with Chebyshev's theorem indicates the spread or dispersion of a Poisson distribution. For example, if $\lambda = 6.5$, the variance is also 6.5, and the standard deviation is 2.55. Chebyshev's theorem states that at least $1 - 1/k^2$ values are within k standard deviations of the mean. The interval $\mu \pm 2\sigma$ contains at least $1 - (1/2^2) = 0.75$ of the values. For $\mu = \lambda = 6.5$ and $\sigma = 2.55$, 75% of the values should be within the $6.5 \pm 2(2.55) = 6.5 \pm 5.1$ range. That is, the range from 1.4 to 11.6 should include at least 75% of all the values. An examination of the 20 values randomly generated for a Poisson distribution with $\lambda = 6.5$ shows that actually 100% of the values are within this range.

Graphing Poisson Distributions

The values in Table A.3, Appendix A, can be used to graph a Poisson distribution. The x values are on the x-axis and the probabilities are on the y-axis. **Figure 5.3** is a graph for the distribution of values for $\lambda = 1.6$.

The graph reveals a Poisson distribution skewed to the right. With a mean of 1.6 and a possible range of x from zero to infinity, the values will obviously "pile up" at 0 and 1. Consider, however, the graph of the Poisson distribution for $\lambda = 6.5$ in **Figure 5.4**. Note that with

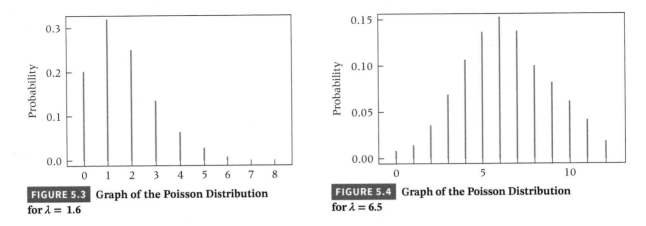

FIGURE 5.3 **Graph of the Poisson Distribution for $\lambda = 1.6$**

FIGURE 5.4 **Graph of the Poisson Distribution for $\lambda = 6.5$**

$\lambda = 6.5$, the probabilities are greatest for the values of 5, 6, 7, and 8. The graph has less skewness, because the probability of occurrence of values near zero is small, as are the probabilities of large values of x.

Using the Computer to Generate Poisson Distributions

Using the Poisson formula to compute probabilities can be tedious when one is working problems with cumulative probabilities. The Poisson tables in Table A.3, Appendix A, are faster to use than the Poisson formula. However, Poisson tables are limited by the amount of space available, and Table A.3 only includes probability values for Poisson distributions with λ values to the tenth place in most cases. For analysts who want to use λ values with more precision or who feel that the computer is more convenient than textbook tables, some statistical computer software packages are an attractive option.

Excel will produce a Poisson distribution for virtually any value of λ. For example, one study by the National Center for Health Statistics claims that, on average, an American has 1.9 acute illnesses or injuries per year. If these cases are Poisson distributed, λ is 1.9 per year. What does the Poisson probability distribution for this λ look like? **Table 5.11** contains the Excel computer output for this distribution. **Table 5.12** displays the probabilities produced by Excel for the real estate problem from Demonstration Problem 5.9 using a λ of 1.6.

TABLE 5.11	**Excel Output for the Poisson Distribution $\lambda = 1.9$**
x Value	**Probability**
0	0.149569
1	0.284180
2	0.269971
3	0.170982
4	0.081216
5	0.030862
6	0.009773
7	0.002653
8	0.000630
9	0.000133
10	0.000025

TABLE 5.12	**Excel Output for the Poisson Distribution $\lambda = 1.6$**
x Value	**Probability**
0	0.201897
1	0.323034
2	0.258428
3	0.137828
4	0.055131
5	0.017642
6	0.004705
7	0.001075
8	0.000215
9	0.000038

Approximating Binomial Problems
by the Poisson Distribution

Using the Poisson distribution can approximate certain types of binomial distribution problems. Binomial problems with large sample sizes and small values of p, which then generate rare events, are potential candidates for use of the Poisson distribution. As a guideline, if $n > 20$ and $n \cdot p \leq 7$, the approximation is close enough to use the Poisson distribution for binomial problems.

If these conditions are met and the binomial problem is a candidate for this process, the procedure begins with computation of the mean of the binomial distribution, $\mu = n \cdot p$. Because μ is the expected value of the binomial, it translates to the expected value, λ, of the Poisson distribution. Using μ as the λ value and using the x value of the binomial problem allows approximation of the probability from a Poisson table or by the Poisson formula.

Large values of n and small values of p are usually not included in binomial distribution tables, thereby precluding the use of binomial computational techniques. Using the Poisson distribution as an approximation to such a binomial problem in such cases is an attractive alternative; indeed, when a computer is not available, it can be the only alternative.

As an example, the following binomial distribution problem can be worked by using the Poisson distribution: $n = 50$ and $p = 0.03$. What is the probability that $x = 4$? That is, $P(x = 4 | n = 50 \text{ and } p = 0.03) = ?$

To solve this equation, first determine λ:

$$\lambda = \mu = n \cdot p = (50)(0.03) = 1.5$$

As $n > 20$ and $n \cdot p \leq 7$, this problem is a candidate for the Poisson approximation. For $x = 4$, Table A.3 yields a probability of 0.0471 for the Poisson approximation. For comparison, working the problem using the binomial formula yields the following results:

$$_{50}C_4 (0.03)^4 (0.97)^{46} = 0.0459$$

The Poisson approximation is 0.0012 different from the result obtained by using the binomial formula to work the problem.

A graph of this binomial distribution follows.

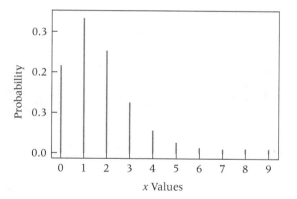

With $\lambda = 1.5$, the Poisson distribution can be generated. A graph of this Poisson distribution follows.

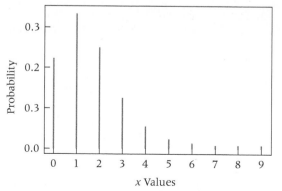

From the graphs, it is difficult to tell the difference between the binomial distribution and the Poisson distribution because the approximation of the binomial distribution by the Poisson distribution is close.

DEMONSTRATION PROBLEM 5.10

Suppose the probability of a bank making a mistake in processing a deposit is 0.0003. If 10,000 deposits (n) are audited, what is the probability that more than six mistakes were made in processing deposits?

Solution

$$\lambda = \mu = n \cdot p = (10,000)(0.0003) = 3.0$$

Because $n > 20$ and $n \cdot p \leq 7$, the Poisson approximation is close enough to analyze $x > 6$. Table A.3 yields the following probabilities for $\lambda = 3.0$ and $x \geq 7$.

	$\lambda = 3.0$
x	**Probability**
7	0.0216
8	0.0081
9	0.0027
10	0.0008
11	0.0002
12	0.0001
	$x > 6 = 0.0335$

To work this problem using the binomial formula requires starting with $x = 7$:

$$_{10,000}C_7(0.0003)^7(0.9997)^{9993}$$

This process would continue for x values of 8, 9, 10, 11, . . . , until the probabilities approach zero. Obviously, this process is impractical, making the Poisson approximation an attractive alternative.

Concept Check

1. What are the key characteristics of the Poisson distribution?
2. Assume that $x = 0, 1, 2, 3, . . .$ is a random variable that follows a Poisson distribution. What do the values of x represent?

5.4 Problems

5.15 Find the following values by using the Poisson formula.

a. $P(x = 5 | \lambda = 2.3)$

b. $P(x = 2 | \lambda = 3.9)$

c. $P(x \leq 3 | \lambda = 4.1)$

d. $P(x = 0 | \lambda = 2.7)$

e. $P(x = 1 | \lambda = 5.4)$

f. $P(4 < x < 8 | \lambda = 4.4)$

5.16 Find the following values by using the Poisson tables in Appendix A.

a. $P(x = 6 | \lambda = 3.8)$

b. $P(x > 7 | \lambda = 2.9)$

c. $P(3 \leq x \leq 9 | \lambda = 4.2)$

d. $P(x = 0 | \lambda = 1.9)$

e. $P(x \leq 6 | \lambda = 2.9)$

f. $P(5 < x \leq 8 | \lambda = 5.7)$

5.17 Sketch the graphs of the following Poisson distributions. Compute the mean and standard deviation for each distribution. Locate the mean on the graph. Note how the probabilities are graphed around the mean.

    a. $\lambda = 6.3$

    b. $\lambda = 1.3$

    c. $\lambda = 8.9$

    d. $\lambda = 0.6$

5.18 On Monday mornings, a CIBC branch has only one teller window open for deposits and withdrawals. Experience has shown that the average number of arriving customers in a 4-minute interval on Monday mornings is 2.8, and each teller can serve more than that number efficiently. The random arrivals at this bank on Monday mornings are Poisson distributed.

    a. What is the probability that on a Monday morning exactly six customers will arrive in a 4-minute interval?

    b. What is the probability that no one will arrive at the bank to make a deposit or withdrawal during a 4-minute interval?

    c. Suppose the teller can serve no more than four customers in any 4-minute interval at this window on a Monday morning. What is the probability that, during any given 4-minute interval, the teller will be unable to meet the demand? What is the probability that the teller will be able to meet the demand? When demand cannot be met during any given interval, a second window is opened. What percentage of the time will a second window have to be opened?

    d. What is the probability that exactly three people will arrive at the bank during a 2-minute period on Monday mornings to make a deposit or a withdrawal? What is the probability that five or more customers will arrive during an 8-minute period?

5.19 A restaurant manager is interested in taking a more statistical approach to predicting customer load. She begins the process by gathering data. One of the restaurant hosts or hostesses is assigned to count customers every 5 minutes from 7 P.M. until 8 P.M. every Saturday night for three weeks. The data are shown here. After the data are gathered, the manager computes λ using the data from all three weeks as one data set as a basis for probability analysis. What value of λ did she find? Assume that these customers randomly arrive and that the arrivals are Poisson distributed. Use the value of λ computed by the manager and help the manager calculate the probabilities in parts (a) through (e) for any given 5-minute interval between 7 P.M. and 8 P.M. on Saturday night.

Number of Arrivals

Week 1	Week 2	Week 3
3	1	5
6	2	3
4	4	5
6	0	3
2	2	5
3	6	4
1	5	7
5	4	3
1	2	4
0	5	8
3	3	1
3	4	3

    a. What is the probability that no customers arrive during any given 5-minute interval?

    b. What is the probability that six or more customers arrive during any given 5-minute interval?

    c. What is the probability that during a 10-minute interval fewer than four customers arrive?

    d. What is the probability that between three and six (inclusive) customers arrive in any 10-minute interval?

    e. What is the probability that exactly eight customers arrive in any 15-minute interval?

5.20 According to the United Nations Environment Programme and the World Health Organization, in Mumbai, India, air pollution standards for particulate matter are exceeded an average of 5.6 days in every three-week period. Assume that the number of days exceeding the standards per three-week period is Poisson distributed.

    a. What is the probability that the standard is not exceeded on any day during a three-week period?

    b. What is the probability that the standard is exceeded on exactly six days of a three-week period?

    c. What is the probability that the standard is exceeded on 15 or more days during a three-week period? If this outcome actually occurred, what might you conclude?

5.21 Suppose the average number of annual trips per family to amusement parks in Canada is Poisson distributed, with a mean of 0.6 trips per year. What is the probability of randomly selecting a Canadian family and finding the following?

    a. The family did not make a trip to an amusement park last year.

    b. The family took exactly one trip to an amusement park last year.

    c. The family took two or more trips to amusement parks last year.

    d. The family took three or fewer trips to amusement parks over a three-year period.

    e. The family took exactly four trips to amusement parks during a six-year period.

5.22 Ship collisions in the Vancouver harbour are rare. Suppose the number of collisions is Poisson distributed, with a mean of 1.2 collisions every four months.

    a. What is the probability of having no collisions occur over a four-month period?

    b. What is the probability of having exactly two collisions in a two-month period?

    c. What is the probability of having one or fewer collisions in a six-month period? If this outcome occurred, what might you conclude about harbour conditions during this period? What might you conclude about harbour safety awareness during this period? What might you conclude about weather conditions during this period? What might you conclude about λ?

5.23 A pen company averages 1.2 defective pens per carton produced (200 pens). The number of defects per carton is Poisson distributed.

    a. What is the probability of selecting a carton and finding no defective pens?

    b. What is the probability of finding eight or more defective pens in a carton?

    c. Suppose a purchaser of these pens will stop buying from the company if a carton contains more than three defective pens. What is the probability that a carton contains more than three defective pens?

5.24 A medical researcher estimates that 0.00004 of the population has a rare blood disorder. If the researcher randomly selects 100,000 people from the population, what is the probability that seven or more people will have the rare blood disorder? What is the probability that more than 10 people will have the rare blood disorder? Suppose the researcher gets more than 10 people who have the rare blood disorder in the sample of 100,000, but the sample was taken from a particular geographic region. What might the researcher conclude from the results?

5.25 A data firm records a large amount of data. Historically, 0.9% of the pages of data recorded by the firm contain errors. If 200 pages of data are randomly selected,

    a. what is the probability that six or more pages contain errors?

    b. what is the probability that more than 10 pages contain errors?

    c. what is the probability that none of the pages contain errors?

    d. what is the probability that fewer than five pages contain errors?

5.26 A high percentage of people who fracture or dislocate a bone see a doctor for that condition. Suppose the percentage is 99%. Consider a sample in which 300 people who have fractured or dislocated a bone are randomly selected.

    a. What is the probability that exactly five of them did not see a doctor?

    b. What is the probability that fewer than four of them did not see a doctor?

    c. What is the expected number of people who would not see a doctor?

5.5 | Hypergeometric Distribution

LEARNING OBJECTIVE 5.5

Solve problems involving the hypergeometric distribution using the hypergeometric formula.

Another discrete statistical distribution is the hypergeometric distribution. Statisticians often use the **hypergeometric distribution** to complement the types of analyses that can be made by using the binomial distribution. Recall that the binomial distribution applies, in theory, only to experiments in which the trials are done with replacement (independent events). The hypergeometric distribution applies only to experiments in which the trials are done without replacement.

The hypergeometric distribution, like the binomial distribution, consists of two possible outcomes: success and failure. However, the user must know the size of the population and the proportion of successes and failures in the population to apply the hypergeometric distribution. In other words, because the hypergeometric distribution is used when sampling is done without replacement, information about population makeup must be known in order to redetermine the probability of a success in each successive trial as the probability changes.

The hypergeometric distribution has the following characteristics:

- It is a discrete distribution.
- Each outcome consists of either a success or a failure.
- Sampling is done without replacement.
- The population, N, is finite and known.
- The number of successes in the population, A, is known.

Hypergeometric Formula

$$P(x) = \frac{{}_A C_x \cdot {}_{N-A} C_{n-x}}{{}_N C_n} \tag{5.8}$$

where

    N = size of the population

    n = sample size

    A = number of successes in the population

    x = number of successes in the sample; sampling is done *without* replacement

---

5.5 Problems

5.27 Compute the following probabilities by using the hypergeometric formula.

    a. The probability of $x = 3$ if $N = 11$, $A = 8$, and $n = 4$

    b. The probability of $x < 2$ if $N = 15$, $A = 5$, and $n = 6$

    c. The probability of $x = 0$ if $N = 9$, $A = 2$, and $n = 3$

    d. The probability of $x > 4$ if $N = 20$, $A = 5$, and $n = 7$

5.28 Shown here are 19 oil-refining companies. Some of the companies are privately owned and others are state owned. Suppose six companies are randomly selected.

    a. What is the probability that exactly one company is privately owned?

    b. What is the probability that exactly four companies are privately owned?

    c. What is the probability that all six companies are privately owned?

    d. What is the probability that none of the companies are privately owned?

Company	Ownership Status
ExxonMobil	Private
Royal Dutch Shell	Private
BP	Private
Total S.A.	Private
PDVSA	State
Sinopec Limited	Private
Saudi Aramco	State
China Petrochemical	State
Petrobras	State
Pemex	State
National Iranian Oil Company	State
Texaco	Private
Chevron Corporation	Private
Repsol S.A.	Private
Kuwait Petroleum Corporation	State
Agip	Private
JXTG Nippon Oil & Energy	Private
Marathon Petroleum	Private
Pertamina	State

5.29 The *Report on Business* Top 1,000 ranks 1,000 Canadian companies using various criteria. Of the top 20 companies by number of employees, 4 are banks. Suppose four companies are randomly selected.

    a. What is the probability that none of the companies are banks?

    b. What is the probability that all four companies are banks?

    c. What is the probability that exactly two are banks?

5.30 W. Edwards Deming in his red bead experiment had a box of 4,000 beads, of which 800 were red and 3,200 were white.[1] Suppose a researcher conducts a modified version of the red bead experiment. In her experiment, she has a bag of 20 beads, of which 4 are red and 16 are white. This experiment requires a participant to reach into the bag and randomly select five beads without replacement.

    a. What is the probability that the participant will select exactly four white beads?

    b. What is the probability that the participant will select exactly four red beads?

    c. What is the probability that the participant will select all red beads?

5.31 Shown here are the 10 Canadian provinces ranked by operating revenue for the hotels, motor hotels, and motels industry as compiled by Statistics Canada for a recent year.

Rank	Province	Operating Revenue ($ millions)
1	Ontario	3,824.0
2	British Columbia	2,636.6
3	Alberta	2,628.2
4	Quebec	2,169.3
5	Manitoba	778.0
6	Saskatchewan	603.2
7	Nova Scotia	309.2
8	New Brunswick	219.4
9	Newfoundland and Labrador	212.0
10	Prince Edward Island	65.2

Source: Adapted from *Traveller Accommodation Services 2012*, service bulletin, Statistics Canada catalogue no. 63-253-X, www150.statcan.gc.ca/n1/pub/63-253-x/2014001/t004-eng.htm.

Suppose four of these provinces are selected randomly.

    a. What is the probability that exactly two provinces are west of Ontario?

    b. What is the probability that none of the provinces are Atlantic provinces?

    c. What is the probability that exactly three of the provinces are ones with more than $1,000 million of operating revenue?

5.32 A company produces and ships 16 personal computers knowing that 4 of them have defective wiring. The company that purchased the computers will thoroughly test three of the computers. The purchasing company can detect the defective wiring. What is the probability that the purchasing company will find the following?

    a. No defective computers

    b. Exactly three defective computers

    c. Two or more defective computers

    d. One or fewer defective computers

[1] Mary Walton, "Deming's Parable of Red Beads," *Across the Board* (February 1987): 43–48.

5.33 A western city has 18 police officers eligible for promotion. Eleven of the 18 are men. Suppose only five of the police officers are chosen for promotion and that one is a man. If the officers chosen for promotion had been selected by chance alone, what is the probability that one or fewer of the five promoted officers would have been men? What might this result indicate?

End-of-Chapter Review

Decision Dilemma Solved

Life with a Cellphone

The study says that 32.5% of Canadian households consider their cellphone as their primary phone number. If 20 households are randomly selected, what is the probability that more than three consider the cellphone as their primary phone number? Converting the 32.5% to a proportion, the value of p is 0.325, and this is a classic binomial distribution problem with $n = 20$ and $x > 3$. Because the binomial distribution probability tables (Appendix A, Table A.2) do not include $p = 0.325$, the problem will have to be solved using the binomial formula for each of $x = 4, 5, 6, 7, \ldots, 20$.

For $x = 4$: $\quad _{20}C_4(0.325)^4(0.675)^{16} = 0.1004$

Solving for $x = 5, 6, \ldots 15$ in a similar manner results in probabilities of 0.1547, 0.1862, ..., 0.0001, respectively. Since the probabilities zero out at $x = 15$, we need not proceed on to $x = 16, 17, \ldots, 20$. Summing these probabilities ($x = 4, 5, 6, \ldots, 15$) results in a total probability of 0.9299 as the answer to the posed question. To further understand these probabilities, we calculate the expected value of this distribution as

$$\mu = n \cdot p = 20(0.325) = 6.5$$

In the long run, one would expect to average about 6.5 Canadian households out of every 20 that consider their cellphone as their primary phone number. In light of this, there is a considerably high probability (0.9299) that more than three households would do so.

The study also stated that 8 out of 10 cell users encounter others using their phones while driving. If you randomly select 25 cellphone users, what is the probability that fewer than 20 will report that they see others using their phones while driving? Converting this to $p = 0.80$ and using $n = 25$ and $x < 20$, this, too, is a binomial problem, but it can be solved by using the binomial tables, obtaining the values shown below:

x	Probability
19	0.163
18	0.111
17	0.062
16	0.029
15	0.012
14	0.004
13	0.001
12	0.000

The total of these probabilities is 0.383. Probabilities for all other values ($x \leq 12$) are displayed as 0.000 in the binomial probability table and are not included here. If 80% of all cellphone users encounter others using their phones while driving, the probability is considerable (0.383) that out of 25 randomly selected cellphone users, fewer than 20 encounter others using their phones while driving. The expected number in any random sample of 25 is (25) (0.80) = 20.

Suppose, on average, cellphone users receive 3.6 calls per day. Given that information, what is the probability that a cellphone user receives no calls per day? Since random telephone calls are generally thought to be Poisson distributed, this problem can be solved by using either the Poisson probability formula or the Poisson table (Table A.3, Appendix A). In this problem, $\lambda = 3.6$ and $x = 0$, and the probability associated with this is

$$\frac{\lambda^x e^{-\lambda}}{x!} = \frac{(3.6)^0 e^{-3.6}}{0!} = 0.0273$$

What is the probability that a cellphone user receives five or more calls in a day? Since this is a cumulative probability question ($x > 5$), the best option is to use the Poisson probability table (Table A.3, Appendix A) to obtain:

x	Probability
5	0.1377
6	0.0826
7	0.0425
8	0.0191
9	0.0076
10	0.0028
11	0.0009
12	0.0003
13	0.0001
14	0.0000
Total	0.2936

There is a 29.36% chance that a cellphone user will receive five or more calls per day if, on average, such a cellphone user averages 3.6 calls per day.

Key Considerations

Several points must be emphasized about the use of discrete distributions to analyze data. The independence and/or size assumptions must be met to use the binomial distribution in situations where sampling is done without replacement. Size and λ assumptions must be satisfied to use the Poisson distribution to approximate binomial problems. In either case, failure to meet such assumptions can result in spurious conclusions.

As n increases, the use of binomial distributions to study exact x-value probabilities becomes questionable in decision-making. Although the probabilities are mathematically correct, as n becomes larger, the probability of any particular x value becomes lower because there are more values among which to split the probabilities. For example, if $n = 100$ and $p = 0.50$, the probability of $x = 50$ is 0.0796. This probability of occurrence appears quite low, even though $x = 50$ is the expected value of this distribution and is also the value most likely to occur. It is more useful to decision-makers and, in a sense, probably more ethical to present cumulative values for larger sizes of n. In this example, it is probably more useful to examine $P(x > 50)$ than $P(x = 50)$.

The reader is warned in the chapter that the value of λ is assumed to be constant in a Poisson distribution experiment. Analysts may produce spurious results because the λ value changes during a study. For example, suppose the value of λ is obtained for the number of customer arrivals at a toy store between 7 P.M. and 9 P.M. in the month of December. Because December is an active month in terms of traffic volume through a toy store, the use of such a λ to analyze arrivals at the same store between noon and 2 P.M. in February is inappropriate.

It is important that statisticians and analysts adhere to assumptions and appropriate applications of these techniques. The inability or unwillingness to do so opens the way for inappropriate (and perhaps unethical) decision-making.

Why Statistics Is Relevant

Distributions (both discrete and continuous) are important because most of the analyses done in business statistics are based on the characteristics of a particular distribution. Unlike data, statistical distributions are formal models that describe the likelihood of a random variable taking on a value or a range of values. Thus, statistical distributions are not only found in business statistics; they are part of the general vocabulary for communicating basic ideas. Understanding the differences between a data distribution (a histogram, for example) and a statistical distribution is one of the most profound insights an analyst can have. Being able to interpret a statistical distribution and make formal, well-reasoned statements about a random variable by studying its distribution is a very important analytical skill.

Summary of Learning Objectives

LEARNING OBJECTIVE 5.1   Define a random variable in order to differentiate between a discrete distribution and a continuous distribution.

Probability experiments produce random outcomes. A variable that contains the outcomes of a random experiment is called a random variable. Random variables for which the set of all possible values is at most a finite or countably infinite number of possible values are called discrete random variables. Random variables that take on values at all points over a given interval are called continuous random variables. Discrete distributions are constructed from discrete random variables. Continuous distributions are constructed from continuous random variables.

LEARNING OBJECTIVE 5.2   Determine the mean, variance, and standard deviation of a discrete distribution.

The measures of central tendency and measures of variability discussed in Chapter 3 can be applied to discrete distributions to compute a mean, a variance, and a standard deviation. Important examples of discrete distributions are the binomial distribution, the Poisson distribution, and the hypergeometric distribution.

LEARNING OBJECTIVE 5.3   Solve problems involving the binomial distribution using the binomial formula and the binomial table.

The binomial distribution fits experiments when only two mutually exclusive outcomes are possible. In theory, each trial in a binomial experiment must be independent of the other trials. However, if the population size is large enough in relation to the sample size ($n < 5\%N$), the binomial distribution can be used where applicable in cases where the trials are not independent. The probability of getting a desired outcome on any one trial is denoted as p, which is the probability of getting a success. The binomial distribution can be used to analyze discrete studies involving such things as heads/tails, defective/good, and employed/unemployed. The binomial formula is used to determine the probability of obtaining x outcomes in n trials. Binomial distribution problems can be solved more rapidly with the use of binomial tables than by formula. A binomial table can be constructed for every different pair of n and *p* values. Table A.2 of Appendix A contains binomial tables for selected values of *n* and *p*.

LEARNING OBJECTIVE 5.4 Solve problems involving the Poisson distribution using the Poisson formula and the Poisson table.

The Poisson distribution is usually used to analyze phenomena that produce rare occurrences. The only information required to generate a Poisson distribution is the long-run average, which is denoted by lambda (λ). The Poisson distribution pertains to occurrences over some interval. The assumptions are that each occurrence is independent of other occurrences and that the value of λ remains constant throughout the experiment. Examples of Poisson-type experiments are number of flaws per page of paper and number of

calls per minute to a switchboard. Poisson probabilities can be determined by either the Poisson formula or the Poisson tables in Table A.3 of Appendix A. The Poisson distribution can be used to approximate binomial distribution problems when *n* is large ($n > 20$), *p* is small, and $n \cdot p \leq 7$.

LEARNING OBJECTIVE 5.5 Solve problems involving the hypergeometric distribution using the hypergeometric formula.

The hypergeometric distribution is a discrete distribution that is usually used for binomial-type experiments when the population is small and finite and sampling is done without replacement. Because using the hypergeometric distribution is a tedious process, using the binomial distribution whenever possible is generally more advantageous.

Key Terms

binomial distribution 5-8
continuous distribution 5-3
continuous random variable 5-3
expected value 5-5

discrete distribution 5-3
discrete random variable 5-3
hypergeometric distribution 5-28
lambda (λ) 5-20

mean value 5-5
Poisson distribution 5-19
random variable 5-2

Formulas

(5.1) Mean value or expected value of a discrete distribution

$$\mu = E(x) = \Sigma[x_i \cdot P(x_i)]$$

(5.2) Variance of a discrete distribution

$$\sigma^2 = \Sigma[(x_i - \mu)^2 \cdot P(x_i)]$$

(5.3) Standard deviation of a discrete distribution

$$\sigma = \sqrt{\Sigma[(x_i - \mu)^2 \cdot P(x_i)]}$$

(5.4) Binomial formula

$$P(x) = {}_nC_x \cdot p^x \cdot q^{n-x} = \frac{n!}{x!(n-x)!} \cdot p^x \cdot q^{n-x}$$

(5.5) Mean of a binomial distribution

$$\mu = n \cdot p$$

(5.6) Standard deviation of a binomial distribution

$$\sigma = \sqrt{n \cdot p \cdot q}$$

(5.7) Poisson formula

$$P(x) = \frac{\lambda^x e^{-\lambda}}{x!}$$

(5.8) Hypergeometric formula

$$P(x) = \frac{{}_AC_x \cdot {}_{N-A}C_{n-x}}{{}_NC_n}$$

Supplementary Problems

Calculating the Statistics

5.34 Solve for the probabilities of the following binomial distribution problems by using the binomial formula.

    a. If $n = 11$ and $p = 0.23$, what is the probability that $x = 4$?

    b. If $n = 6$ and $p = 0.50$, what is the probability that $x \geq 1$?

    c. If $n = 9$ and $p = 0.85$, what is the probability that $x > 7$?

    d. If $n = 14$ and $p = 0.70$, what is the probability that $x \leq 3$?

5.35 **Video** Use Table A.2, Appendix A, to find the values of the following binomial distribution problems.

    a. $P(x = 14 | n = 20$ and $p = 0.60)$

    b. $P(x < 5 | n = 10$ and $p = 0.30)$

    c. $P(x \geq 12 | n = 15$ and $p = 0.60)$

    d. $P(x > 20 | n = 25$ and $p = 0.40)$

5.36 Use the Poisson formula to solve for the probabilities of the following Poisson distribution problems.

    a. If $\lambda = 1.25$, what is the probability that $x = 4$?

    b. If $\lambda = 6.37$, what is the probability that $x \leq 1$?

    c. If $\lambda = 2.4$, what is the probability that $x > 5$?

5.37 **Video** Use Table A.3, Appendix A, to find the following Poisson distribution values.

  a. $P(x = 3 | \lambda = 1.8)$

  b. $P(x < 5 | \lambda = 3.3)$

  c. $P(x \geq 3 | \lambda = 2.1)$

  d. $P(2 < x \leq 5 | \lambda = 4.2)$

5.38 Solve the following problems by using the hypergeometric formula.

  a. If $N = 6$, $n = 4$, and $A = 5$, what is the probability that $x = 3$?

  b. If $N = 10$, $n = 3$, and $A = 5$, what is the probability that $x \leq 1$?

  c. If $N = 13$, $n = 5$, and $A = 3$, what is the probability that $x \geq 2$?

Testing Your Understanding

5.39 In a study by Peter D. Hart Research Associates for the Nasdaq Stock Market, it was determined that 20% of all stock investors are retired people. In addition, 40% of all adults invest in mutual funds. Suppose a random sample of 25 stock investors is taken. What is the probability that exactly seven are retired people? What is the probability that 10 or more are retired people? How many retired people would you expect to find in a random sample of 25 stock investors? Suppose a random sample of 20 adults is taken. What is the probability that exactly eight adults invested in mutual funds? What is the probability that fewer than six adults invested in mutual funds? What is the probability that none of the adults invested in mutual funds? What is the probability that 12 or more adults invested in mutual funds? For which exact number of adults is the probability the highest? How does this figure compare with the expected number?

5.40 A service station has a pump that distributes diesel fuel to automobiles. The station owner estimates that only about 3.2 cars use the diesel pump every two hours. Assume the arrivals of diesel pump users are Poisson distributed.

  a. What is the probability that three cars will arrive to use the diesel pump during a one-hour period?

  b. Suppose the owner needs to shut down the diesel pump for half an hour to make repairs. However, the owner hates to lose any business. What is the probability that no cars will arrive to use the diesel pump during a half-hour period?

  c. What is the probability of five or more cars arriving during a one-hour period to use the diesel pump? If this outcome actually occurred, what might you conclude?

5.41 **Video** In a particular manufacturing plant, two machines (A and B) produce a particular part. One machine (B) is newer and faster. In one five-minute period, a lot consisting of 32 parts is produced. Twenty-two are produced by machine B and the rest by machine A. Suppose an inspector randomly samples a dozen of the parts from this lot.

  a. What is the probability that exactly three parts were produced by machine A?

  b. What is the probability that half of the parts were produced by each machine?

  c. What is the probability that all of the parts were produced by machine B?

  d. What is the probability that seven, eight, or nine parts were produced by machine B?

5.42 Suppose that, for every lot of 100 computer chips a company produces, an average of 1.4 are defective. Another company buys many lots of these chips at a time, from which one lot is selected randomly and tested for defects. If the tested lot contains more than three defects, the buyer will reject all the lots sent in that batch. What is the probability that the buyer will accept the lots? Assume that the defects per lot are Poisson distributed.

5.43 According to the Heart and Stroke Foundation of Canada, in a recent year 17.6% of Canadians between the ages of 65 and 79 report having heart disease or stroke. Suppose you live in a province where the environment is conducive to good health and low stress and you believe these conditions promote healthy hearts. To investigate this theory, you conduct a random telephone survey of 20 persons 65 to 79 years of age in your province.

  a. On the basis of the figure from the Heart and Stroke Foundation, what is the expected number of people 65 to 79 years of age in your survey who have heart disease or stroke?

  b. Suppose only one person in your survey has heart disease or stroke. What is the probability of getting one or fewer people with heart disease or stroke in a sample of 20 if 17.6% of the population in this age bracket has this health problem? What do you conclude about your province from the sample data?

5.44 Suppose a survey reveals that 69% of Canadian workers say job stress causes frequent health problems. One in four said they expected to burn out on the job in the near future. Thirty-two percent said they thought seriously about quitting their job last year because of workplace stress. Forty-nine percent said they were required to work more than 40 hours a week very often or somewhat often.

  a. Suppose a random sample of 10 Canadian workers is selected. What is the probability that more than seven of them say job stress caused frequent health problems? What is the expected number of workers who say job stress caused frequent health problems?

  b. Suppose a random sample of 15 Canadian workers is selected. What is the expected number of these sampled workers who say they will burn out in the near future? What is the probability that none of the workers say they will burn out in the near future?

  c. Suppose a sample of seven workers is selected randomly. What is the probability that all seven say they are asked very often or somewhat often to work more than 40 hours a week? If this outcome actually happened, what might you conclude?

5.45 According to Padgett Business Services, 20% of all small-business owners say the most important advice for starting a business is to prepare for long hours and hard work; 25% say the most important advice is to have good financing ready; 19% say having a good plan is the most important advice; 18% say studying the industry is the most important advice; and 18% list other advice. Suppose 12 small-business owners are contacted, and assume that the percentages hold for all small-business owners.

  a. What is the probability that none of the owners would say preparing for long hours and hard work is the most important advice?

  b. What is the probability that six or more owners would say preparing for long hours and hard work is the most important advice?

  c. What is the probability that exactly five owners would say having good financing ready is the most important advice?

  d. What is the expected number of owners who would say having a good plan is the most important advice?

5.46 Suppose that the probability that a passenger files a complaint with the Canadian Transportation Agency about a particular airline is 0.000014. Suppose 100,000 passengers who flew with this particular airline are randomly contacted.

a. What is the probability that exactly five passengers filed complaints?

b. What is the probability that none of the passengers filed complaints?

c. What is the probability that more than six passengers filed complaints?

5.47 A hairstylist has been in business for one year. Sixty percent of his customers are walk-in business. If he randomly samples eight of the people from last week's list of customers, what is the probability that three or fewer were walk-ins? If this outcome actually occurred, what would some of the reasons be?

5.48 According to a recent census, about 63% of Manitoba residents live in cities with a population of 10,000 or more people. A catalogue sales company in Ontario just purchased a list of Manitoba consumers. Its market analyst randomly selects 25 people from this list.

a. What is the probability that exactly 15 people live in metropolitan areas?

b. What is the probability that the analyst would get more than 20 people in this sample who live in metropolitan areas?

c. Suppose the analyst got more than 20 people who live in metropolitan areas from the group of 25. What might she conclude about the company's list of Manitoba consumers? What might she conclude about the census figure?

5.49 **Video** Suppose that, for every family vacation trip by car of more than 2,000 km, an average of 0.60 flat tires occurs. Suppose also that the distribution of the number of flat tires per trip of more than 2,000 km is Poisson. What is the probability that a family will take a trip of more than 2,000 km and have no flat tires? What is the probability that the family will have three or more flat tires on such a trip? Suppose trips are independent and the value of λ holds for all trips of more than 2,000 km. If a family takes two trips of more than 2,000 km during a summer, what is the probability that the family will have no flat tires on either trip?

5.50 The Canadian Newspaper Association releases figures on the top newspapers in Canada. Shown here are the top 20 daily newspapers in Canada ranked according to circulation.

Rank	Newspaper
1	The Globe and Mail, Toronto
2	Toronto Star, Toronto
3	Le Journal de Montréal, Montreal
4	National Post, Toronto
5	Le Journal de Québec, Quebec City
6	Vancouver Sun, Vancouver
7	Toronto Sun, Toronto
8	The Province, Vancouver
9	The Hamilton Spectator, Hamilton
10	Calgary Herald, Calgary
11	Winnipeg Free Press, Winnipeg
12	Edmonton Journal, Edmonton
13	Ottawa Citizen, Ottawa
14	The Chronicle Herald, Halifax
15	Montreal Gazette, Montreal
16	Le Soleil, Quebec City
17	The London Free Press, London
18	Times Colonist, Victoria
19	Waterloo Region Record, Kitchener
20	Windsor Star, Windsor

Suppose a business analyst wants to sample a portion of these newspapers and compare the sizes of the business sections of the Saturday papers. She randomly samples eight of these newspapers.

a. What is the probability that the sample contains exactly one newspaper located in Ontario?

b. What is the probability that half of the newspapers are ranked in the top 10 by circulation?

c. What is the probability that none of the newspapers are located in British Columbia?

d. What is the probability that exactly three of the newspapers are located in provinces that begin with the letter N?

5.51 An office in Calgary, Alberta, has 24 workers including management. Eight of the workers commute to work from Airdrie. Suppose six of the office workers are randomly selected.

a. What is the probability that all six workers commute from Airdrie?

b. What is the probability that none of the workers commute from Airdrie?

c. Which probability from parts (a) and (b) was greater? Why do you think this is?

d. What is the probability that half of the workers do not commute from Airdrie?

5.52 According to Statistics Canada, 16% of the workers in Calgary use public transportation. If 25 Calgary workers are randomly selected, what is the expected number to use public transportation? Graph the binomial distribution for this sample. What are the mean and the standard deviation for this distribution? What is the probability that more than eight of the selected workers use public transportation? Explain conceptually and from the graph why you would get this probability. Suppose you randomly sample 25 Calgary workers and actually get 10 who use public transportation. Is this outcome likely? How might you explain this result?

5.53 **Video** One of the earliest applications of the Poisson distribution was in analyzing incoming calls to a telephone switchboard. Analysts generally believe that random phone calls are Poisson distributed. Suppose phone calls to a switchboard arrive at an average rate of 2.4 calls per minute.

a. Suppose an operator wants to take a one-minute break. What is the probability that there will be no calls during a one-minute interval?

b. If an operator can handle at most five calls per minute, what is the probability that the operator will be unable to handle the calls in any one-minute period?

c. What is the probability that exactly three calls will arrive in a two-minute interval?

d. What is the probability that one or fewer calls will arrive in a 15-second interval?

5.54 According to a study, the proportion of Canadian households relying solely on a cellphone for telephone service is about 13%. A marketing analyst randomly selects 50 Canadian households.

a. How many households would the analyst expect to rely solely on a cellphone?

b. What is the probability that eight or more households rely solely on a cellphone?

c. What is the probability that between two and six households (inclusive) rely solely on a cellphone?

5.55 According to the Canadian Medical Association, about 55% of all Canadian physicians under the age of 35 are women. Your company has just hired eight physicians under the age of 35 and only two are women. If a group of women physicians under the age of 35 want to sue your company for discriminatory hiring practices, would they have a strong case based on these numbers? Use the binomial distribution to determine the probability of the company's hiring result occurring randomly and comment on the potential justification for a lawsuit.

5.56 The following table lists the 28 largest Canadian universities according to full-time undergraduate enrolment figures. The province of location is given in parentheses.

University	Enrolment
University of Toronto (ON)	60,660
York University (ON)	46,640
University of British Columbia (BC)	41,700
Université de Montréal (QC)	41,055
Athabasca University (AB)	36,240
Ryerson University (ON)	36,200
University of Ottawa (ON)	36,042
Université du Québec à Montréal (QC)	33,100
Concordia University (QC)	32,347
University of Alberta (AB)	31,904
University of Waterloo (ON)	30,000
Simon Fraser University (BC)	29,697
University of Western Ontario (ON)	29,500
Université Laval (QC)	27,530
Mount Royal University (AB)	24,768
McGill University (QC)	23,758
University of Manitoba (MB)	23,640
University of Calgary (AB)	23,320
McMaster University (ON)	22,940
Carleton University (ON)	20,950
University of Guelph (ON)	19,800
MacEwan University (AB)	18,897
University of Victoria (BC)	18,863
Wilfrid Laurier University (ON)	18,500
Kwantlen Polytechnic University (BC)	16,811
Queen's University (ON)	16,700
University of Saskatchewan (SK)	16,430
Brock University (ON)	15,747

Source: Wikipedia, s.v. "List of Universities in Canada," last updated July 16, 2019, en.wikipedia.org/wiki/List_of_universities_in_Canada.

a. If five different universities are selected randomly from the list, what is the probability that three of them have enrolments of 18,000 or more?

b. If eight different universities are selected randomly from the list, what is the probability that two or fewer are universities in Quebec?

c. Suppose universities are being selected randomly from this list with replacement. If five universities are sampled, what is the probability that the sample will contain exactly two universities in British Columbia?

5.57 In one western city, the government has 14 repossessed houses, which are evaluated to be worth about the same. Ten of the houses are on the north side of town and the rest are on the west side. A local contractor submitted a bid to purchase four of the houses. Which houses the contractor will get is subject to a random draw.

a. What is the probability that all four houses selected for the contractor will be on the north side of town?

b. What is the probability that all four houses selected for the contractor will be on the west side of town?

c. What is the probability that half of the houses selected for the contractor will be on the west side and half on the north side of town?

5.58 Public Citizen's Health Research Group studied the serious disciplinary actions that were taken during a recent year against nonfederal medical doctors in the U.S. The American average was 3.05 serious actions per 1,000 doctors. Assume that the Canadian average is the same; moreover, assume that the numbers of serious actions per 1,000 doctors is Poisson distributed.

a. What is the probability of randomly selecting 1,000 Canadian doctors and finding no serious actions taken?

b. What is the probability of randomly selecting 2,000 Canadian doctors and finding six serious actions taken?

c. Assume that British Columbia has an average of 1.6 serious actions per 1,000 doctors. What is the probability of randomly selecting 3,000 British Columbia doctors and finding fewer than seven serious actions taken?

Interpreting the Output

5.59 Study the following output. Discuss the type of distribution, the mean, the standard deviation, and why the probabilities fall as they do.

Probability Density Function	
Binomial with $n = 15$ and $p = 0.36$	
x Value	Probability
0	0.001238
1	0.010445
2	0.041128
3	0.100249
4	0.169170
5	0.209347
6	0.196263
7	0.141940
8	0.079841
9	0.034931
10	0.011789
11	0.003014
12	0.000565
13	0.000073
14	0.000006
15	0.000000

5.60 Study the following output. Explain the distribution in terms of shape and mean. Are these probabilities what you would expect? Why or why not?

	A	B
1	x Values	Poisson Probabilities: $\lambda = 2.78$
2	0	0.0620
3	1	0.1725
4	2	0.2397
5	3	0.2221
6	4	0.1544
7	5	0.0858
8	6	0.0398
9	7	0.0158
10	8	0.0055
11	9	0.0017
12	10	0.0005
13	11	0.0001

5.61 Study the following graphical output. Describe the distribution and explain why the graph takes the shape it does.

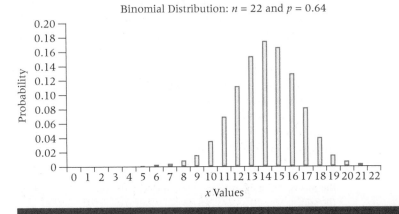

Binomial Distribution: $n = 22$ and $p = 0.64$

5.62 Study the following graph. Discuss the distribution, including type, shape, and probability outcomes.

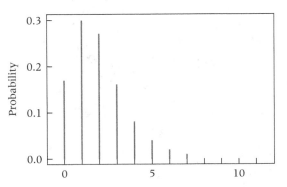

Poisson Distribution: $\lambda = 1.784$

Exploring the Databases with Business Analytics *see* the databases on the Student Website and in *WileyPLUS*

1. Use the Canadian RRSP Contribution Database. What proportion of tax filers come from British Columbia, Alberta, and Saskatchewan? Use this as the value of *p* in a binomial distribution. What is the expected number of tax filers from British Columbia, Alberta, and Saskatchewan? And what is the standard deviation?

If you were to randomly select 20 tax filers, what is the probability that

a. fewer than three tax filers are from British Columbia, Alberta, and Saskatchewan?

b. at least three tax filers are from British Columbia, Alberta, and Saskatchewan?

c. no more than 15 tax filers are *not* tax filers from British Columbia, Alberta, and Saskatchewan?

2. Use the Financial Institutes (Type 2) variable in the Financial Database. If five of these companies are selected randomly, what is the probability that exactly three have Total Debt/Total Equity of 30% or more? What is the probability of randomly selecting eight Mining, Electric, Oil & Gas, Pipelines (Type 4) companies and getting exactly four of them with Average Yield of less than 1%?

Case

Whole Foods Market Grows Through Mergers and Acquisitions

Over three decades ago, four businesspeople who had experience in retailing natural foods through food stores believed that there was a demand for a supermarket for natural foods.

As a result, in 1980 in Austin, Texas, they founded the first Whole Foods Market store in a building that had around 900 square metres and with a staff of 19. This store was quite large compared with health food stores at the time. By 1984, the company was successful enough

to expand to Houston and Dallas. In 1988, they purchased the Whole Food Company in New Orleans and expanded there. The next year, they moved into the U.S. west coast with a store in Palo Alto, California. Even though the company has built a number of its own stores, much of the company growth has come through mergers and acquisitions, many of which came in the 1990s in such states as North Carolina, Massachusetts, Rhode Island, California, and Michigan. After the turn of the century, Whole Foods Market established a presence in New York City, followed by a move into Canada and later into the United Kingdom.

Presently, Whole Foods Market has 433 stores in the United States, Canada, and the United Kingdom. There are fourteen stores in Canada, in British Columbia and Ontario. There are over 91,000 team members, many of whom are full-time employees. Existing stores now average 43,000 square feet in size, over four times as large as the original "supermarket." Whole Foods Market is the fifth-largest food and drug store in the United States, with over $15 billion in sales in 2016, when it ranked 176th on the list of Fortune 500 companies.

Whole Foods Market is the largest retailer of natural and organic foods and prides itself on doing the research necessary to assure customers that its products are free of artificial flavours, colours, sweeteners, preservatives, or hydrogenated fats. The company attempts to customize each store by stocking it with products that are most in demand in any given community. Whole Foods Market management cares about their employees, and the company has been named by *Fortune* magazine as one of the "100 Best Companies to Work For" in the United States every year since the list was first compiled in 1998. The company attempts to be a good community citizen, and it gives back at least 5% of after-tax profits to the communities in which the stores operate. In January 2008, Whole Foods Market was the first U.S. supermarket to commit to completely eliminating disposable plastic bags.

In June 2017, Amazon bought Whole Foods for $13.7 billion. Before the purchase, Whole Foods was struggling, with some expansion plans on hold in Canada, and the closure of nine stores in the United States. A year later, revenues were up slightly, and Amazon was offering discounts to Amazon Prime members who shopped at Whole Foods. Amazon was also trying to relax Whole Foods' standards so the stores could sell products with artificial sweeteners and flavours. In early 2019 there were also rumours that Whole Foods might be moving into locations formerly occupied by Sears and Kmart, expanding the grocers' reach.

Discussion

1. Whole Foods Market has shown steady growth at a time when traditional supermarkets have been flat. This could be attributed to a growing awareness of and demand for more natural foods. According to a study by Mintel in 2006, 30% of consumers have a high level of concern about the safety of the food they eat. Suppose we want to test this figure to determine if consumers have changed since then.

Assuming that the 30% figure still holds, what is the probability of randomly sampling 25 consumers and having 12 or more respond that they have a high level of concern about the safety of the food they eat? What would the expected number be? If an analyst actually got 12 or more out of 25 to respond that they have a high level of concern about the safety of the food they eat, what might this mean?

2. Suppose that, on average, in a Whole Foods Market in Vancouver, 3.4 customers want to check out every minute. Based on this figure, store management wants to staff checkout lines such that demand for checkout cannot be met less than 1% of the time. In this case, store management would have to staff for what number of customers? Based on the 3.4 customer average per minute, what percentage of the time would the store have 12 or more customers who want to check out in any two-minute period?

3. Suppose a survey is taken of 30 managers of Whole Foods Market stores and it is determined that 17 are at least 40 years old. If another analyst randomly selects 10 of these 30 managers to interview, what is the probability that 3 or fewer are at least 40 years old? Suppose 9 of the 30 surveyed managers are female. What is the probability of randomly selecting 10 managers from the 30 and finding out that 7 of the 10 are female?

Source: Information found at Whole Foods Market website, www.wholefoodsmarket.com; William A. Knudson, "The Organic Food Market," a working paper from the Strategic Marketing Institute, Michigan State University, 2007; "Fortune 100 Best Companies to Work For: 2013," money.cnn.com/magazines/fortune/best-companies/2013/list/?iid=bc_sp_full; Caroline Banton, "The World's Largest Grocery Store Chains," The Balance: Small Business website, updated July 23, 2019, www.thebalancesmb.com/largest-us-based-grocery-chains-3862932; Jeff Wells, "A Year Later, How Has Amazon Changed Whole Foods?" Food Dive, August 23, 2018, www.fooddive.com/news/a-year-later-how-has-amazon-changed-whole-foods/530791/; Dan Healing, "Whole Foods' Canadian Expansion Plans Slow," *Toronto Star*, January 9, 2017, www.thestar.com/business/2017/01/09/whole-foods-canadian-expansion-plans-slow.html; Nathaniel Meyersohn, "Hundreds of Old Sears Stores Are Empty. Amazon and Whole Foods Might Move In," CNN Business, April 11, 2019, www.cnn.com/2019/04/11/business/whole-foods-amazon-sears-kmart-stores-lidl/index.html.

Big Data Case

Using the American Hospital Association database, determine the number of hospitals in this database that are investor-owned for-profit. (*Hint:* In Control, 5 = investor-owned for-profit.) From this number, calculate p, the proportion of hospitals that are for-profit. Using this value of p and the binomial distribution, determine the probability of randomly selecting 15 hospitals from this database and getting more than 6 that are for-profit. If this actually occurred, what might it mean to analysts studying the database?

Suppose that at a large hospital, the average arrival rate of patients to the emergency room is 5.9 patients per hour during evening hours (7 P.M. to midnight). Based on that, what percentage of the time would fewer than 4 patients arrive in one hour? In what way might this impact staffing for the emergency room? What percentage of the time would more than 8 patients arrive in one hour? In what way might this impact staffing for the emergency room? Given these two pieces of information, what might you tell hospital administrators about staffing for the emergency room?

Using the Computer

- Excel can be used to compute exact or cumulative probabilities for particular values of discrete distributions including the binomial, Poisson, and hypergeometric distributions.
- Calculation of probabilities from each of these distributions begins with the **Insert Function (fx)**. To access the **Insert Function**, go to the **Formulas** tab on an Excel worksheet. The **Insert Function** is on the far left of the ribbon. In the **Insert Function** dialogue box at the top, there is a pull-down menu labelled **Or select a category**. From the pull-down menu associated with this command, select **Statistical**.

- To compute probabilities from a binomial distribution, select **BINOM.DIST** from the **Insert Function's Statistical** menu. In the **BINOM.DIST** dialogue box, there are four lines to which you must respond. On the first line, **Number_s**, enter the value of x, the number of successes. On the second line, **Trials**, enter the number of trials (sample size, n). On the third line, **Probability_s**, enter the value of p. The fourth line, **Cumulative**, requires a logical response of either TRUE or FALSE. Place TRUE in the slot to get the cumulative probabilities for all values from 0 to x. Place FALSE in the slot to get the exact probability of getting x successes in n trials.

- To compute probabilities from a Poisson distribution, select **POISSON.DIST** from the **Insert Function's Statistical** menu. In the **POISSON.DIST** dialogue box, there are three lines to which you must respond. On the first line, **X**, enter the value of x, the number of events. On the second line, **Mean**, enter the expected number, λ. The third line, **Cumulative**, requires a logical response of either TRUE or FALSE. Place TRUE in the slot to get the cumulative probabilities for all values from 0 to x. Place FALSE in the slot to get the exact probability of getting x successes when λ is the expected number.

- To compute probabilities from a hypergeometric distribution, select **HYPGEOM.DIST** from the **Insert Function's Statistical** menu. In the **HYPGEOM.DIST** dialogue box, there are five lines to which you must respond. On the first line, **Sample_s**, enter the value of x, the number of successes in the sample. On the second line, **Number_sample**, enter the size of the sample, n. On the third line, **Population_s**, enter the number of successes in the population. On the fourth line, **Number_pop**, enter the size of the population, N. The fifth line, **Cumulative**, requires a logical response of either TRUE or FALSE. Place TRUE in the slot to get the cumulative probabilities for all values from 0 to x. Place FALSE in the slot to get the exact probability of getting x successes in n trials.

Continuous Distributions

LEARNING OBJECTIVES

The primary learning objective of Chapter 6 is to help you understand continuous distributions, thereby enabling you to:

6.1 Solve for probabilities in a continuous uniform distribution.

6.2 Solve for probabilities in a normal distribution using z scores, and for the mean, the standard deviation, or a value of x in a normal distribution when given information about the area under the normal curve.

6.3 Solve problems from the discrete binomial distribution using the continuous normal distribution and correcting for continuity.

6.4 Solve for probabilities in an exponential distribution and contrast the exponential distribution with the discrete Poisson distribution.

Decision Dilemma

CSX Corporation

The CSX Corporation is a leading rail transportation company in the United States, moving cargo via traditional rail service and shipping goods using intermodal containers and trailers. Based in Jacksonville, Florida, the CSX Transportation network has 33,800 kilometres of track spread across the eastern half of the United States and the Canadian provinces of Ontario and Quebec.

Founded in 1827, when America's first common carrier railroad, the Baltimore & Ohio, was founded, CSX presently has over 24,000 employees, US$37 billion in total assets, and an annual revenue of over $12 billion. CSX has access to over 70 water terminals in the United States and Canada and moves a broad range of products across its service area. In its intermodal shipping, CSX uses special containers so that goods and products can be transferred from ship to rail to truck without having to be repacked.

Since 1999, CSX and five other North American freight railroads have voluntarily reported three weekly performance measures—Cars On Line, Train Speed, and Terminal Dwell—to the Railroad Performance Measures website in an effort to improve communications with their customers. In addition, CSX keeps data on such variables as Network Velocity, % On-Time Arrivals, % On-Time Originations, Average Daily Trains Holding for Power, and Train Crew Delay Hours by Week.

Managerial, Statistical, and Analytical Questions

1. Suppose the average rail freight line-haul speed in any given year is 38 km per hour (km/h). If rail freight line-haul speeds are uniformly distributed in a year with a minimum of

Ken MacKay/Alamy Stock Photo

34 km/h and a maximum of 42.5 km/h, what percentage of line-hauls would have speeds between 35.5 and 38.5 km/h? What percentage of line-hauls would have speeds of more than 40 km/h?

2. Terminal dwell time, typically measured in hours, is the time a rail car resides in a rail terminal on the same train (excluding cars on run-through trains). Suppose terminal dwell time is normally distributed for rail cars in the United States with a mean of 27.5 hours and a standard deviation of 2.6 hours. Based on these statistics, what is the probability that a randomly selected rail car has a terminal dwell

time of more than 32.4 hours? What is the probability that a randomly selected rail car has a terminal dwell time of less than 26 hours?

3. Suppose that 45% of all freight trains arrive on time. If this is true, what is the probability of randomly selecting 120 trains and finding out that more than 65 were on time?

4. Suppose that at a relatively small railroad, on average, 1.7 employees call in sick per day. What is the probability that at least two days go by with no worker calling in sick?

Sources: Compiled using information from www.csx.com; U.S. Department of Transportation, Research and Innovative Technology Administration, Bureau of Transportation Statistics; and www.railroadpm.org/.

Introduction

Whereas Chapter 5 focused on the characteristics and applications of discrete distributions, Chapter 6 concentrates on information about continuous distributions. Continuous distributions are constructed from continuous random variables in which values are taken on for every point over a given interval and are usually generated from experiments in which things are "measured" as opposed to "counted." With continuous distributions, probabilities of outcomes occurring between particular points are determined by calculating the area under the curve between those points. In addition, the entire area under the whole curve is equal to one. In business analytics, it is important to determine the underlying distribution of an array of data so that business decision-makers can visualize the data and so that statisticians can determine the proper analysis of the data. Like the discrete distributions in Chapter 5, continuous distributions have their own unique attributes that make possible particular statistical inquiries. The many continuous distributions in statistics include the uniform distribution, the normal distribution, the exponential distribution, the t distribution, the chi-square distribution, and the F distribution. This chapter presents the uniform distribution, the normal distribution, and the exponential distribution.

6.1 | Uniform Distribution

LEARNING OBJECTIVE 6.1

Solve for probabilities in a continuous uniform distribution.

The **uniform distribution**, sometimes referred to as the **rectangular distribution**, is *a relatively simple continuous distribution in which the same height, or* f(x), *is obtained over a range of values.* The following probability density function defines a uniform distribution.

Probability Density Function of a Uniform Distribution

$$f(x) = \begin{cases} \dfrac{1}{b-a} & \text{for } a \leq x \leq b \\ 0 & \text{for all other values} \end{cases}$$

(6.1)

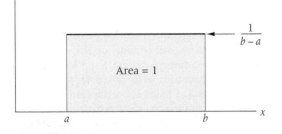

FIGURE 6.1 **Uniform Distribution**

Figure 6.1 is an example of a uniform distribution. In a uniform, or rectangular, distribution, the total area under the curve is equal to the product of the length and the width of the rectangle and equals one. By definition, the distribution lies between the x values of a and b, so the length of the rectangle is $b - a$. Combining this area calculation with the fact that the area equals one, the height of the rectangle can be solved as follows.

Area of Rectangle = (Length)(Height) = 1

But

$$\text{Length} = b - a$$

Therefore,

$$(b - a)(\text{Height}) = 1$$

and

$$\text{Height} = \frac{1}{b - a}$$

These calculations show why, between the x values of a and b, the distribution has a constant height of $1/(b - a)$.

The formulas to determine mean and standard deviation of a uniform distribution are as follows:

Mean and Standard Deviation of a Uniform Distribution

$$\mu = \frac{a + b}{2}$$ (6.2)

$$\sigma = \frac{b - a}{\sqrt{12}}$$

Many possible situations arise in which data might be uniformly distributed. As an example, suppose a production line is set up to manufacture machine braces in lots of five per minute during a shift. When the lots are weighed, variation among the masses is detected, with lot masses ranging from 41 g to 47 g in a uniform distribution. The height of this distribution is

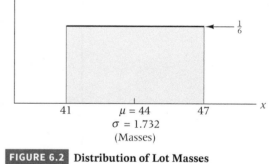

$$f(x) = \text{Height} = \frac{1}{b - a} = \frac{1}{47 - 41} = \frac{1}{6}$$

The mean and standard deviation of this distribution are

$$\text{Mean} \quad = \frac{a + b}{2} = \frac{41 + 47}{2} = \frac{88}{2} = 44$$

$$\text{Standard Deviation} = \frac{b - a}{\sqrt{12}} = \frac{47 - 41}{\sqrt{12}} = \frac{6}{3.464} = 1.732$$

Figure 6.2 provides the uniform distribution for this example, with its mean, standard deviation, and the height of the distribution.

FIGURE 6.2 **Distribution of Lot Masses**

Determining Probabilities in a Uniform Distribution

With discrete distributions, the probability function yields the value of the probability. For continuous distributions, probabilities are calculated by determining the area over an interval of the function. With continuous distributions, there is no area under the curve for a single point. The following equation is used to determine the probabilities of x for a uniform distribution between a and b:

Probabilities in a Uniform Distribution

$$P(x) = \frac{x_2 - x_1}{b - a}$$ (6.3)

where

$$a \leq x_1 \leq x_2 \leq b$$

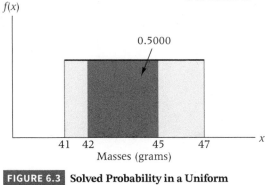

FIGURE 6.3   **Solved Probability in a Uniform Distribution**

Remember that the area between a and b is equal to one. The probability for any interval that includes a and b is 1. The probability of $x \geq b$ or of $x \leq a$ is 0 because there is no area above b or below a.

Suppose that on the machine braces problem we want to determine the probability that a lot has a mass of between 42 g and 45 g. This probability is computed as follows:

$$P(x) = \frac{x_2 - x_1}{b - a} = \frac{45 - 42}{47 - 41} = \frac{3}{6} = 0.5000$$

Figure 6.3 displays this solution.

The probability that a lot has a mass of more than 48 g is zero, because $x = 48$ is greater than the upper value, $x = 47$, of the uniform distribution. A similar argument gives the probability of a lot having a mass of less than 40 g. Because 40 is less than the lowest value of the uniform distribution range, 41, the probability is zero.

DEMONSTRATION PROBLEM 6.1

Suppose the amount of time it takes to assemble a plastic module ranges from 27 to 39 seconds and that assembly times are uniformly distributed. Describe the distribution. What is the probability that a given assembly will take between 30 and 35 seconds? Less than 30 seconds?

Solution

$$f(x) = \frac{1}{39 - 27} = \frac{1}{12}$$

$$\mu = \frac{a + b}{2} = \frac{27 + 39}{2} = 33$$

$$\sigma = \frac{b - a}{\sqrt{12}} = \frac{39 - 27}{\sqrt{12}} = \frac{12}{\sqrt{12}} = 3.464$$

The height of the distribution is 1/12. The mean time is 33 seconds with a standard deviation of 3.464 seconds.

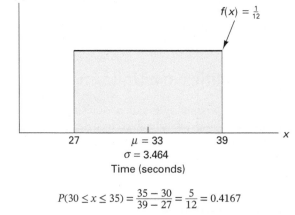

$$P(30 \leq x \leq 35) = \frac{35 - 30}{39 - 27} = \frac{5}{12} = 0.4167$$

There is a 0.4167 probability that it will take between 30 and 35 seconds to assemble the module.

$$P(x < 30) = \frac{30 - 27}{39 - 27} = \frac{3}{12} = 0.2500$$

There is a 0.2500 probability that it will take less than 30 seconds to assemble the module. Because there is no area less than 27 seconds, $P(x < 30)$ is determined by using only the interval $27 \leq x < 30$. In a continuous distribution, there is no area at any one point (only over an interval). Thus, the probability of $x < 30$ is the same as the probability of $x \leq 30$.

DEMONSTRATION PROBLEM 6.2

According to the Insurance Bureau of Canada, the average annual cost for automobile insurance in Canada in a recent year was $945. Suppose automobile insurance costs are uniformly distributed in Canada with a range of from $275 to $1,615. What is the standard deviation of this uniform distribution? What is the height of the distribution? What is the probability that a person's annual cost for automobile insurance in Canada is between $410 and $825?

Solution   The mean is given as $945. The value of a is $275 and the value of b is $1,615.

$$\sigma = \frac{b-a}{\sqrt{12}} = \frac{1,615 - 275}{\sqrt{12}} = 386.8$$

The height of the distribution is $\frac{1}{1,615 - 275} = 0.0007$. Using $x_1 = 410$ and $x_2 = 825$, we have

$$P(410 \leq x \leq 825) = \frac{825 - 410}{1,615 - 275} = \frac{415}{1,340} = 0.3097$$

The probability that a randomly selected person pays between $410 and $825 annually for automobile insurance in Canada is 0.3097. That is, about 30.97% of all people in Canada pay in that range.

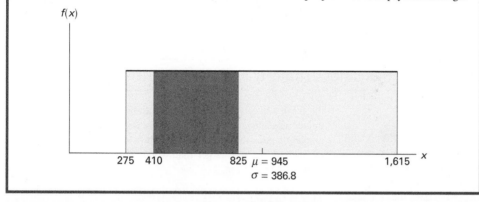

Concept Check

1. List two important properties of the uniform distribution.

2. Describe a situation (in business or otherwise) in which the use of the uniform distribution would be appropriate. Clearly define the random variable.

6.1 Problems

6.1 Values are uniformly distributed between 200 and 240.

a. What is the value of $f(x)$ for this distribution?

b. Determine the mean and standard deviation of this distribution.

c. Probability of $(x > 230) = ?$

d. Probability of $(205 < x < 220) = ?$

e. Probability of $(x < 225) = ?$

6.2 x is uniformly distributed over a range of values from 8 to 21.

a. What is the value of $f(x)$ for this distribution?

b. Determine the mean and standard deviation of this distribution.

c. Probability of $(10 < x < 17) = ?$

d. Probability of $(x < 22) = ?$

e. Probability of $(x > 7) = ?$

6.3 The retail price of a medium-sized box of a well-known brand of cornflakes ranges from $2.80 to $3.14. Assume these prices are uniformly distributed. What are the average price and standard deviation of prices in this distribution? If a price is randomly selected from this list, what is the probability that it will be between $3.00 and $3.10?

6.4 The average fill volume of a regular can of soft drink is 355.0 mL. Suppose the fill volume of these cans ranges from 354.0 mL to 355.8 mL and is uniformly distributed. What is the height of this distribution? What is the probability that a randomly selected can contains more than 355.2 mL of fluid? What is the probability that the fill volume is between 354.3 mL and 355.2 mL?

6.5 Suppose the average Canadian household spends $2,100 a year on all types of insurance. Suppose the figures are uniformly distributed between the values of $400 and $3,800. What are the standard deviation and the height of this distribution? What proportion of households spends more than $3,000 a year on insurance? More than $4,000? Between $700 and $1,500?

Normal Distribution

LEARNING OBJECTIVE 6.2

Solve for probabilities in a normal distribution using *z* scores, and for the mean, the standard deviation, or a value of *x* in a normal distribution when given information about the area under the normal curve.

Probably the most widely known and used of all distributions is the **normal distribution**. It fits many human characteristics, such as height, mass, length, speed, IQ, scholastic achievement, and years of life expectancy. Like their human counterparts, living things in nature, such as trees, animals, and others, have many characteristics that are normally distributed.

Many variables in business and industry are also normally distributed. Some examples of variables that could produce normally distributed measurements are the annual cost of household insurance, the cost per square foot of renting warehouse space, and managers' satisfaction with support from ownership on a five-point scale. In addition, most items produced or filled by machines are normally distributed. (See Thinking Critically About Statistics in Business Today 6.1.)

Thinking Critically About Statistics in Business Today 6.1

Warehousing

Tompkins International, whose client list includes BlackBerry and the Canada Revenue Agency, conducted a study of warehousing in the U.S. The study revealed many interesting facts. Warehousing is a labour-intensive industry that presents considerable opportunity for improvement in productivity. What does the "average" warehouse look like? The construction of new warehouses is constrained by expense. Perhaps for that reason, the average age of a warehouse is 19 years. Warehouses vary in size, but the average size is about 4,600 m². To visualize such an "average" warehouse, picture one that is square with about 65 m on each side or a rectangle that is 100 m by 46 m. The average clear height of a warehouse in the U.S. is about 6.7 m.

Suppose the ages of warehouses, the sizes of warehouses, and the clear heights of warehouses are normally distributed. Using the mean values already given and the standard deviations, techniques presented in this section could be used to determine, for example, the probability that a randomly selected warehouse is less than 15 years old, is larger than 5,500 m², or has a clear height between 6 m and 7 m.

Things to Ponder

1. The feature states that "warehousing is a labour-intensive industry that presents considerable opportunity for improvement in productivity." How might there be opportunities for improvement in productivity of warehousing?

2. What are some reasons why new warehouses might be prohibitively expensive?

3. With current technology, what are some ways that warehousing may be changing?

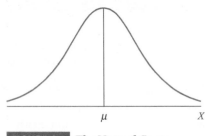

FIGURE 6.4 **The Normal Curve**

Because of its many applications, the normal distribution is extremely important. Aside from the many variables mentioned above that are normally distributed, the normal distribution and its associated probabilities are an integral part of statistical process control (see Chapter 18). When large enough sample sizes are taken, many statistics are normally distributed regardless of the shape of the underlying distribution from which they are drawn (as discussed in Chapter 7). **Figure 6.4** is the graphic representation of the normal distribution: the normal curve.

History of the Normal Distribution

The discovery of the normal curve of errors is generally credited to mathematician and astronomer Karl Gauss (1777–1855), who recognized that the errors of repeated measurement of objects are often normally distributed.[1] Thus, the normal distribution is sometimes referred to as the *Gaussian distribution* or *the normal curve of error*. A modern-day analogy of Gauss's

---

[1] John A. Ingram and Joseph G. Monks, *Statistics for Business and Economics* (San Diego: Harcourt Brace Jovanovich, Publishers, 1989).

work might be the distribution of measurements of machine-produced parts, which often yield a normal curve of error around a mean specification.

To a lesser extent, some credit has been given to Pierre-Simon de Laplace (1749–1827) for the normal distribution. However, many people now believe that Abraham de Moivre (1667–1754), a French mathematician, first understood the normal distribution. De Moivre determined that the binomial distribution approached the normal distribution as a limit. De Moivre worked with remarkable accuracy. His published table values for the normal curve are only a few ten-thousandths off the values of currently published tables.[2]

The normal distribution exhibits the following characteristics:

- It is a continuous distribution.
- It is a symmetrical distribution about its mean.
- It is asymptotic to the horizontal axis.
- It is unimodal.
- It is a family of curves.
- The area under the curve is 1.

The normal distribution is symmetrical. Each half of the distribution is a mirror image of the other half. Many normal distribution tables contain probability values for only one side of the distribution because probability values for the other side of the distribution are identical due to symmetry.

In theory, the normal distribution is *asymptotic* to the horizontal axis. That is, it does not touch the x-axis, and it goes forever in each direction to both $-\infty$ and $+\infty$. The reality is that most applications of the normal curve are experiments that have finite limits of potential outcomes. For example, even though standardized test scores are analyzed by the normal distribution, the range of scores in a standardized test may be, for instance, from 200 to 800.

The normal curve is sometimes referred to as the *bell-shaped curve*. It is unimodal in that values *mound up* in only one portion of the graph—the centre of the curve. The normal distribution is actually a family of curves. Every unique value of the mean and every unique value of the standard deviation result in a different normal curve. In addition, *the total area under any normal distribution is 1.* The area under the curve yields the probabilities, so the total of all probabilities for a normal distribution is 1. Because the distribution is symmetric, the area of the distribution on each side of the mean is 0.5.

Probability Density Function of the Normal Distribution

The normal distribution is described or characterized by two parameters: the mean, μ, and the standard deviation, σ. The values of μ and σ produce a normal distribution.

Probability density function of the normal distribution

$$f(x) = \frac{1}{\sigma\sqrt{2\pi}}e^{-1/2[(x-\mu)/\sigma]^2} \tag{6.4}$$

where

μ = mean of x

σ = standard deviation of x

π = 3.14159. . .

e = 2.71828. . .

Using integral calculus to determine areas under the normal curve from this function is difficult and time-consuming; therefore, virtually all analysts use computers or table values to analyze normal distribution problems rather than this formula.

---

[2] Roger E. Kirk, *Statistical Issues: A Reader for the Behavioral Sciences* (Monterey, CA: Brooks/Cole Publishing Co., 1972).

Standardized Normal Distribution

Every unique pair of μ and σ values defines a different normal distribution. **Figure 6.5** shows graphs of normal distributions for the following three pairs of parameters.

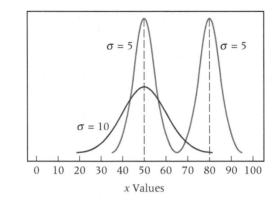

FIGURE 6.5 Normal Curves for Three Different Combinations of Means and Standard Deviations

1. $\mu = 50$ and $\sigma = 5$
2. $\mu = 80$ and $\sigma = 5$
3. $\mu = 50$ and $\sigma = 10$

Note that every change in a parameter (μ or σ) determines a different normal distribution. This characteristic of the normal curve (a family of curves) could make analysis by the normal distribution tedious. Fortunately, a mechanism was developed by which all normal distributions can be converted into a single distribution: the z distribution. This process yields the **standardized normal distribution** (or curve). The conversion formula for any x value of a given normal distribution follows.

---

z Formula

$$z = \frac{x - \mu}{\sigma}, \sigma \neq 0 \tag{6.5}$$

A **z score** is *the number of standard deviations that a value, x, is above or below the mean.* If the value of x is less than the mean, the z score is negative; if the value of x is more than the mean, the z score is positive; and if the value of x equals the mean, the associated z score is 0. This formula allows conversion of the distance of any x value from its mean into standard deviation units. A standard z score table can be used to find probabilities for any normal curve problem that has been converted to z scores. The **z distribution** is *a normal distribution with a mean of 0 and a standard deviation of 1.* Any value of x at the mean of a normal curve is 0 standard deviations from the mean. Any value of x that is one standard deviation above the mean has a z value of 1. The empirical rule, introduced in Chapter 3, is based on the normal distribution in which about 68% of all values are within one standard deviation of the mean regardless of the values of μ and σ. In a z distribution, about 68% of the z values are between $z = -1$ and $z = +1$.

The z distribution probability values are given in Table A.5. For discussion purposes, a list of z distribution values is presented in **Table 6.1**.

Table A.5 gives the total area under the z curve between 0 and any point on the positive z axis. Since the curve is symmetric, the area under the curve between z and 0 is the same whether z is positive or negative. (The sign on the z value designates whether the z score is above or below the mean.) The table areas or probabilities are always positive.

6.19 Where appropriate, work the following binomial distribution problems using the normal curve. Also, use Table A.2 to find the answers by using the binomial distribution and compare the answers obtained by the two methods.

  a. $P(x = 8 | n = 25 \text{ and } p = 0.40) = ?$

  b. $P(x \geq 13 | n = 20 \text{ and } p = 0.60) = ?$

  c. $P(x = 7 | n = 15 \text{ and } p = 0.50) = ?$

  d. $P(x < 3 | n = 10 \text{ and } p = 0.70) = ?$

6.20 The Zimmerman Agency conducted a study for Residence Inn by Marriott of business travellers who take trips of five nights or more. According to this study, 37% of these travellers enjoy sightseeing more than any other activity that they do not get to do as much at home. Suppose 120 randomly selected business travellers who take trips of five nights or more are contacted. What is the probability that fewer than 40 enjoy sightseeing more than any other activity that they do not get to do as much at home?

6.21 One study on managers' satisfaction with management tools reveals that 59% of all managers use self-directed work teams as a management tool. Suppose 70 managers selected randomly in Canada are interviewed. What is the probability that fewer than 35 use self-directed work teams as a management tool?

6.22 According to The Yankee Group, 53% of all cable households rate cable companies as good or excellent in quality transmission. Sixty percent of all cable households rate cable companies as good or excellent in having professional personnel. Suppose 300 cable households are randomly contacted.

  a. What is the probability that more than 175 cable households rate cable companies as good or excellent in quality transmission?

  b. What is the probability that between 165 and 170 (inclusive) cable households rate cable companies as good or excellent in quality transmission?

  c. What is the probability that between 155 and 170 (inclusive) cable households rate cable companies as good or excellent in having professional personnel?

  d. What is the probability that fewer than 200 cable households rate cable companies as good or excellent in having professional personnel?

6.23 Recent market research reported that HP controlled 23% of the PC market in Canada. Suppose a business analyst randomly selects 130 recent purchasers of PCs in Canada.

  a. What is the probability that more than 35 PC purchasers bought an HP computer?

  b. What is the probability that between 24 and 34 PC purchasers (inclusive) bought an HP computer?

  c. What is the probability that fewer than 19 PC purchasers bought an HP computer?

  d. What is the probability that exactly 29 PC purchasers bought an HP computer?

6.24 A study about strategies for competing in the global marketplace states that 52% of the respondents agreed that companies need to make direct investments in foreign countries. It also states that about 70% of those responding agree that it is attractive to have a joint venture to increase global competitiveness. Suppose CEOs of 95 manufacturing companies are randomly contacted about global strategies.

  a. What is the probability that between 44 and 52 (inclusive) CEOs agree that companies should make direct investments in foreign countries?

  b. What is the probability that more than 56 CEOs agree with that assertion?

  c. What is the probability that fewer than 60 CEOs agree that it is attractive to have a joint venture to increase global competitiveness?

  d. What is the probability that between 55 and 62 (inclusive) CEOs agree with that assertion?

6.4 | Exponential Distribution

LEARNING OBJECTIVE 6.4

Solve for probabilities in an exponential distribution and contrast the exponential distribution with the discrete Poisson distribution.

Another useful continuous distribution is the exponential distribution. It is closely related to the Poisson distribution. Whereas the Poisson distribution is discrete and describes random occurrences over some interval, the **exponential distribution** is *continuous and describes a probability distribution of the times between random occurrences.* The following are the characteristics of the exponential distribution.

- It is a continuous distribution.
- It is a family of distributions.
- It is skewed to the right.
- The x values range from zero to infinity.
- Its apex is always at $x = 0$.
- The curve steadily decreases as x gets larger.

The exponential probability distribution is determined by the following formula.

Exponential Probability Density Function

$$f(x) = \lambda e^{-\lambda x} \qquad\qquad (6.7)$$

where

$x \geq 0$

$\lambda > 0$

and $e = 2.71828\ldots$

An exponential distribution can be characterized by the single parameter λ. Each unique value of λ determines a different exponential distribution, resulting in a family of exponential distributions. **Figure 6.15** shows graphs of exponential distributions for four values of λ. The points on the graph are determined by using λ and various values of x in the probability density formula. The mean of an exponential distribution is $\mu = 1/\lambda$, and the standard deviation of an exponential distribution is $\sigma = 1/\lambda$.

FIGURE 6.15 **Graphs of Some Exponential Distributions**

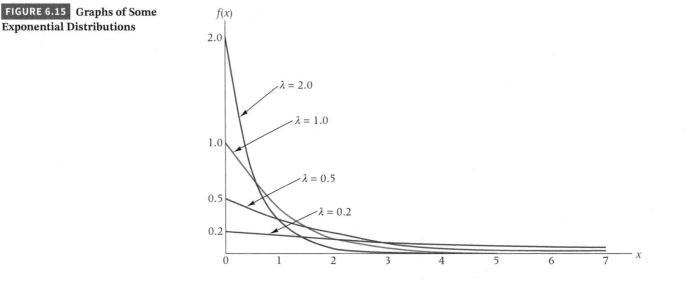

Probabilities of the Exponential Distribution

Probabilities are computed for the exponential distribution by determining the area under the curve between two points. Applying calculus to the exponential probability density function produces a formula that can be used to calculate the probabilities of an exponential distribution.

Probabilities of the Right Tail of the Exponential Distribution

$$P(x \geq x_0) = e^{-\lambda x_0} \qquad\qquad (6.8)$$

where

$x_0 \geq 0$

To use this formula requires finding values of e^{-x}. These values can be computed on most calculators or obtained from Table A.4, which contains the values of e^{-x} for selected values of x.

is determined from a probability density function that contains equal values along some interval between the points *a* and *b*. Basically, the height of the curve is the same everywhere between these two points. Probabilities are determined by calculating the portion of the rectangle between the two points *a* and *b* that is being considered.

LEARNING OBJECTIVE 6.2 Solve for probabilities in a normal distribution using *z* scores, and for the mean, the standard deviation, or a value of *x* in a normal distribution when given information about the area under the normal curve.

The most widely used of all distributions is the normal distribution. Many phenomena are normally distributed, including characteristics of most machine-produced parts; many measurements of the biological and natural environment; and many human characteristics such as height, mass, IQ, and achievement test scores. The normal curve is continuous, symmetrical, unimodal, and asymptotic to the axis; actually, it is a family of curves. The parameters necessary to describe a normal distribution are the mean and the standard deviation. For convenience, data being analyzed by the normal curve should be standardized by using the mean and the standard deviation to compute *z* scores. A *z* score is the distance that an *x* value is from the mean, μ, in units of standard deviation. With the *z* score of an *x* value, the probability of that value occurring by chance from a given normal distribution can be determined by using a table of *z* scores and their associated probabilities.

LEARNING OBJECTIVE 6.3 Solve problems from the discrete binomial distribution using the continuous normal distribution and correcting for continuity.

The normal distribution can be used to work certain types of binomial distribution problems. Doing so requires converting the *n* and *p* values of the binomial distribution to μ and σ of the normal distribution. When worked by using the normal distribution, the binomial distribution solution is only an approximation. If the values of $\mu \pm 3\sigma$ are within a range from 0 to *n*, the approximation is reasonably accurate. Adjusting for the fact that a discrete distribution problem is being worked using a continuous distribution requires a correction for continuity. The correction for continuity involves adding 0.50 to or subtracting 0.50 from the *x* value being analyzed. This correction usually improves the normal curve approximation.

LEARNING OBJECTIVE 6.4 Solve for probabilities in an exponential distribution and contrast the exponential distribution with the discrete Poisson distribution.

Another continuous distribution is the exponential distribution. It complements the discrete Poisson distribution. The exponential distribution is used to compute the probabilities of times between random occurrences. The exponential distribution is a family of distributions described by the single parameter λ. The distribution is skewed to the right and always has its highest value at $x = 0$.

Key Terms

Formulas

(6.1) Probability density function of a uniform distribution

$$f(x) = \begin{cases} \dfrac{1}{b-a} & \text{for } a \le x \le b \\ 0 & \text{for all other values} \end{cases}$$

(6.2) Mean and standard deviation of a uniform distribution

$$\mu = \frac{a+b}{2}$$
$$\sigma = \frac{b-a}{\sqrt{12}}$$

(6.3) Probabilities in a uniform distribution

$$P(x) = \frac{x_2 - x_1}{b-a}$$

(6.4) Probability density function of the normal distribution

$$f(x) = \frac{1}{\sigma\sqrt{2\pi}} e^{-(1/2)[(x-\mu)/\sigma]^2}$$

(6.5) *z* formula

$$z = \frac{x-\mu}{\sigma}$$

(6.6) Conversion of a binomial problem to the normal curve

$$\mu = n \cdot p \quad \text{and} \quad \sigma = \sqrt{n \cdot p \cdot q}$$

(6.7) Exponential probability density function

$$f(x) = \lambda e^{-\lambda x}$$

(6.8) Probabilities of the right tail of the exponential distribution

$$P(x \ge x_0) = e^{-\lambda x_0}$$

Supplementary Problems

Calculating the Statistics

6.34 Data are uniformly distributed between the values of 6 and 14. Determine the value of $f(x)$. What are the mean and standard deviation of this distribution? What is the probability of randomly selecting a value greater than 11? What is the probability of randomly selecting a value between 7 and 12?

6.35 **Video** Assume a normal distribution and find the following probabilities.

a. $P(x < 21 | \mu = 25 \text{ and } \sigma = 4)$

b. $P(x \geq 77 | \mu = 50 \text{ and } \sigma = 9)$

c. $P(x > 47 | \mu = 50 \text{ and } \sigma = 6)$

d. $P(13 < x < 29 | \mu = 23 \text{ and } \sigma = 4)$

e. $P(x \geq 105 | \mu = 90 \text{ and } \sigma = 2.86)$

6.36 Work the following binomial distribution problems using the normal distribution. Check your answers by using Table A.2 to solve for the probabilities.

a. $P(x = 12 | n = 25 \text{ and } p = 0.60)$

b. $P(x > 5 | n = 15 \text{ and } p = 0.50)$

c. $P(x \leq 3 | n = 10 \text{ and } p = 0.50)$

d. $P(x \geq 8 | n = 15 \text{ and } p = 0.40)$

6.37 **Video** Find the probabilities for the following exponential distribution problems.

a. $P(x \geq 3 | \lambda = 1.3)$

b. $P(x < 2 | \lambda = 2.0)$

c. $P(1 \leq x \leq 3 | \lambda = 1.65)$

d. $P(x > 2 | \lambda = 0.405)$

Testing Your Understanding

6.38 Statistics Canada reports that of people who usually work full-time, the average number of hours worked per week is 42.2. Assume that the number of hours worked per week for those who usually work full-time is normally distributed. Suppose 12% of these workers work more than 48 hours. Based on this percentage, what is the standard deviation of number of hours worked per week for these workers?

6.39 Statistics Canada reports that one in four people 15 years of age or older volunteers some of his or her time. If this figure holds for the entire population and if a random sample of 150 people 15 years of age or older is taken, what is the probability that more than 50 of those sampled do volunteer work?

6.40 An entrepreneur opened a small hardware store in a strip mall. During the first few weeks, business was slow, with the store averaging only one customer every 20 minutes in the morning. Assume that the random arrival of customers is Poisson distributed.

a. What is the probability that at least 1 hour would elapse between customers?

b. What is the probability that 10 to 30 minutes would elapse between customers?

c. What is the probability that less than 5 minutes would elapse between customers?

6.41 According to an NRF survey conducted by BIGresearch, the average family spends about $237 on electronics (computers, cell-phones, etc.) in post-secondary back-to-school spending per student. Suppose this family spending on electronics is normally distributed with a standard deviation of $54. If a family of a returning post-secondary student is randomly selected, what is the probability that:

a. They spend less than $150 on back-to-school electronics?

b. They spend more than $400 on back-to-school electronics?

c. They spend between $120 and $185 on back-to-school electronics?

6.42 According to Alberta Egg Producers, Alberta egg farmers produce millions of eggs every year. Suppose egg production per year in Alberta is normally distributed, with a standard deviation of 83-million eggs. If during only 3% of the years Alberta egg farmers produce more than 2,655-million eggs, what is the mean egg production by Alberta farmers?

6.43 The U.S. Bureau of Labor Statistics releases figures on the number of full-time wage and salary workers with flexible schedules. The numbers of full-time wage and salary workers in each age category are almost uniformly distributed by age, with ages ranging from 18 to 65 years. If a worker with a flexible schedule is randomly drawn from the U.S. workforce, what is the probability that he or she will be between 25 and 50 years of age? What is the mean value for this distribution? What is the height of the distribution?

6.44 A business convention holds its registration on Wednesday morning from 9 A.M. until 12 noon. History has shown that registrant arrivals follow a Poisson distribution at an average rate of 1.8 every 15 seconds. Fortunately, several facilities are available to register convention members.

a. What is the average number of seconds between arrivals to the registration area for this convention based on past results?

b. What is the probability that 25 seconds or more would pass between registration arrivals?

c. What is the probability that less than 5 seconds will elapse between arrivals?

d. Suppose the registration computers went down for a 1-minute period. Would this condition pose a problem? What is the probability that at least 1 minute will elapse between arrivals?

6.45 The Canada Mortgage and Housing Corporation lists average monthly apartment rents for many cities in Canada. According to its report, the average cost of renting a two-bedroom apartment in Halifax is $833. Suppose that the standard deviation of the cost of renting a two-bedroom apartment in Halifax is $84 and that two-bedroom apartment rents in Halifax are normally distributed. If a Halifax two-bedroom apartment is randomly selected, what is the probability that the price is:

a. $900 or more?

b. Between $800 and $1,000?

c. Between $725 and $825?

d. Less than $600?

6.46 According to *The Wirthlin Report*, 24% of all workers say that their job is very stressful. If 60 workers are randomly selected, what is the probability that 17 or more say that their job is very stressful?

What is the probability that more than 22 say that their job is very stressful? What is the probability that between 8 and 12 (inclusive) say that their job is very stressful?

6.47 Statistics Canada reports that the average annual family income in Regina is $81,832. Suppose annual family income in Regina is normally distributed, with a standard deviation of $7,712. A Regina family is randomly selected.

a. What is the probability that the family's income is more than $90,700?

b. What is the probability that the family's income is less than $72,500?

c. What is the probability that the family's income is more than $63,500?

d. What is the probability that the family's income is between $70,800 and $85,600?

6.48 Suppose interarrival times at a hospital emergency room during a weekday are exponentially distributed, with an average interarrival time of 9 minutes. If the arrivals are Poisson distributed, what is the average number of arrivals per hour? What is the probability that less than 5 minutes will elapse between any two arrivals?

6.49 **Video** Suppose the average speeds of passenger trains travelling from Winnipeg to Churchill in Manitoba are normally distributed, with a mean average speed of 142 km/h and a standard deviation of 10.3 km/h.

a. What is the probability that a train will average less than 110 km/h?

b. What is the probability that a train will average more than 130 km/h?

c. What is the probability that a train will average between 145 km/h and 160 km/h?

6.50 The Conference Board published information on why companies expect to increase the number of part-time jobs and reduce full-time positions. Eighty-one percent of the companies said the reason was to get a flexible workforce. Suppose 200 companies that expect to increase the number of part-time jobs and reduce full-time positions are identified and contacted. What is the expected number of these companies that would agree that the reason is to get a flexible workforce? What is the probability that between 150 and 155 (not including the 150 or the 155) would give that reason? What is the probability that more than 158 would give that reason? What is the probability that fewer than 144 would give that reason?

6.51 According to Statistics Canada, about 71% of commuters in Canada drive to work. Suppose 150 Canadian commuters are randomly sampled.

a. What is the probability that fewer than 105 commuters drive to work?

b. What is the probability that between 110 and 120 (inclusive) commuters drive to work?

c. What is the probability that more than 95 commuters drive to work?

6.52 It has been reported that the mean western Canadian production of wheat and durum over a 10-year period was 22.45-million tonnes. Assume that the Canadian production of wheat over this period has been approximately uniformly distributed. If the height of this distribution is 8.94-million tonnes, what are the values of *a* and *b* for this distribution?

6.53 The U.S. Federal Reserve System publishes data on family income based on its Survey of Consumer Finances. When the head of the household has a university degree, the mean pre-tax family income is US $85,200. Suppose that 60% of the pre-tax family incomes when the head of the household has a university degree are between US $75,600 and US $94,800 and that these incomes are normally distributed. What is the standard deviation of pre-tax family incomes when the head of the household has a university degree?

6.54 According to The Polk Company, a survey of households using the Internet to buy or lease cars reported that 81% were seeking information about prices. In addition, 44% were seeking information about products offered. Suppose 75 randomly selected households that are using the Internet to buy or lease cars are contacted.

a. What is the expected number of households that are seeking price information?

b. What is the expected number of households that are seeking information about products offered?

c. What is the probability that 67 or more households are seeking information about prices?

d. What is the probability that fewer than 23 households are seeking information about products offered?

6.55 **Video** Coastal businesses in the Atlantic provinces worry about the threat of hurricanes during the season from June through October. Suppose the arrival of hurricanes during this season is Poisson distributed, with an average of three hurricanes threatening Atlantic Canada during the 5-month season. If a hurricane has just threatened the Atlantic provinces, what is the probability that at least 1 month will pass before this happens again? What is the probability that another hurricane will threaten in 2 weeks or less? What is the average amount of time between hurricanes threatening Atlantic Canada?

6.56 With the growing emphasis on technology and the changing business environment, many workers are discovering that training such as re-education, skill development, and personal growth is of great assistance in the job marketplace. A recent Gallup survey found that 80% of Generation Xers considered the availability of company-sponsored training as a factor to weigh in taking a job. If 50 Generation Xers are randomly sampled, what is the probability that fewer than 35 consider the availability of company-sponsored training as a factor to weigh in taking a job? What is the expected number? What is the probability that between 42 and 47 (inclusive) consider the availability of company-sponsored training as a factor to weigh in taking a job?

6.57 **Video** It has been reported that the average operating cost of an MD-80 jet airliner is $2,087 per hour. Suppose the operating costs of an MD-80 jet airliner are normally distributed with a standard deviation of $175 per hour. What cost would 20% of the operating costs be less than? What cost would 65% of the operating costs be more than? What cost would be more than 85% of operating costs?

6.58 Supermarkets usually become busy at about 5 P.M. on weekdays, because many workers stop by on the way home to shop. Suppose at that time arrivals at a supermarket's express checkout station are Poisson distributed, with an average of 0.8 people/minute. If the clerk has just checked out the last person in line, what is the probability that at least 1 minute will elapse before the next customer arrives? Suppose the clerk wants to go to the manager's office to ask a quick question and needs 2.5 minutes to do so. What is the probability that the clerk will get back before the next customer arrives?

6.59 According to the Canadian Newspaper Association, the average daily circulation of *The Globe and Mail* based on recent figures is 302,190. Suppose the standard deviation is 7,308. Assume the paper's daily circulation is normally distributed. On what percentage of days would it surpass a circulation of 315,000? Suppose the paper cannot support the fixed expenses of a full-production setup if the circulation drops below 286,000. If the probability of this event occurring is low, the production manager might try to keep the full crew in place and not disrupt operations. How often will this event happen, based on the historical information?

6.60 Incoming phone calls are generally thought to be Poisson distributed. If an operator averages 2.2 phone calls every 30 seconds, what is the expected (average) amount of time between calls? What is the probability that a minute or more would elapse between incoming calls? Two minutes?

Interpreting the Output

6.61 Use the output shown here and suppose the data represent the number of sales associates who are working in a department store on any given retail day. Describe the distribution, including the mean and standard deviation. Interpret the shape of the distribution and the mean in light of the data being studied. What do the probability statements mean?

Cumulative Distribution Function

Continuous uniform distribution on 11 to 32

x	$P(X \le x)$
28	0.80952
34	1.00000
16	0.23810
21	0.47619

6.62 A manufacturing company produces a metal rod. Use the Excel output shown here to describe the mass of the rod. Interpret the probability values in terms of the manufacturing process.

	A	B
1	Normal Distribution	
2		
3	Mean	227 mg
4	Standard Deviation	2.30 mg
5		
6	x Value	Probability $\le x$ Value
7	220	0.0012
8	225	0.1923
9	227	0.5000
10	231	0.9590
11	238	1.0000

6.63 Suppose the output shown here represents the analysis of the length in minutes of home-use cellphone calls. Describe the distribution of cellphone call lengths and interpret the meaning of the probability statements.

Cumulative Distribution Function

Normal distribution with mean = 2.35 and standard deviation = 0.11

x	$P(X \le x)$
2.60	0.988479
2.45	0.818349
2.30	0.324718
2.00	0.000732

6.64 A restaurant averages 4.51 customers per 10 minutes during the summer in the late afternoon. Shown here is the Excel output for this restaurant. Discuss the type of distribution used to analyze the data and the meaning of the probabilities.

	A	B
1	x Value	Probability < x Value
2	0.1	0.3630
3	0.2	0.5942
4	0.5	0.8951
5	1.0	0.9890
6	2.4	1.0000

Exploring the Databases with Business Analytics   *see* the databases on the Student Website and in *WileyPLUS*

1. Select the Agri-Business Canada time-series database. The data represent the monthly weight (in tonnes) of each grain. Compute the mean, median, and standard deviation for the variable Barley and the variable Oats. By comparing the mean to the respective median (differences are small), the distributions are approximately normally distributed. If a month were randomly selected from the Barley distribution, what is the probability that the weight would be more than 500,000 pounds? What is the probability that the weight would be between 250,000 and 350,000 pounds? If a month were randomly selected from the Oats distribution, what is the probability that the weight would be more than 400,000 pounds? What is the probability that the weight would be between 135,000 and 170,000 pounds?

2. Use the Energy Resource Database. The emission of CO_2 from Manufacturing Industries and Construction in the American data is nearly uniformly distributed in this database, with values from 600 to 1,200. What is the height of this distribution? What is the probability of randomly selecting an emission from 800 to 1,000 if the distribution is uniform? (Use the uniform distribution theory to work this problem, not the actual number from the database.)

3. Select the Canadian RRSP Contribution Database. Compute the population mean and standard deviation for the annual median RRSP contribution. Now take a random sample of 32 years of median RRSP contributions. Compute the sample mean.

   Using techniques presented in this chapter, determine the probability of getting a sample mean that is less than the calculated sample mean. Work this problem both with and without the finite correction factor and compare the results by discussing the differences in answers.

The term *census* refers to a study of all units of the population of interest. The term *sample* refers to a study of only a portion of that population. Suppose a women's clothing manufacturer is interested in knowing how much money adult women in Montreal spend per month on clothes. An analyst who chooses to interview *all* adult women in Montreal is carrying out a census. An analyst who chooses to interview a few hundred adult women in Montreal (a far more likely scenario) to achieve the same purpose is using a sample.

Reasons for Sampling

Taking a sample instead of conducting a census offers several advantages.

1. The sample can save money.
2. The sample can save time.
3. For given resources, the sample can broaden the scope of the study.
4. Because the research process is sometimes destructive, the sample can save product.
5. If accessing the population is impossible, the sample is the only option.

A sample can be cheaper to obtain than a census for a given magnitude of questions. For example, if an 8-minute telephone interview is being undertaken, conducting the interviews with a sample of 100 customers rather than with a population of 100,000 customers is obviously less expensive. In addition to the cost savings, the significantly smaller number of interviews usually requires less total time. Thus, if obtaining the results is a matter of urgency, sampling can provide them more quickly. With the volatility of some markets and the constant barrage of new competition and new ideas, sampling has a strong advantage over a census in terms of research turnaround time, particularly now in the era of big data and business analytics.

Businesses do not have unlimited resources. For example, a business cannot realistically be expected to survey *all* consumers (there may be millions) or a toothpaste manufacturer cannot be expected to test *every* tube of toothpaste manufactured (it may cost more than the manufacturer's profit margin). In fact, when the population of interest is large, as in the examples above, conducting a census is not practical. Since statistical principles allow us to assess the accuracy of our results, our resources may be better spent on a well-selected sample. One organization budgeted $100,000 for a study and opted to take a census instead of a sample by using a mail survey. The analysts mass-mailed thousands of copies of a 20-question survey in which each question could be answered with a Yes or No response. One of the questions was "Are you satisfied with the service that you received at the XYZ store?" For the same amount of money, the company could have taken a random sample from the population, held interactive one-on-one sessions with highly trained interviewers, and gathered detailed information about customer opinions and attitudes about products, service, layout, availability, and more. For a given amount of resources, business analysts can "drill down" deeper on fewer individuals or items, thereby potentially unearthing more valuable information.

Some research processes are destructive to the product or item being studied. For example, if light bulbs are being tested to determine how long they burn or if chocolate bars are being taste-tested to determine whether the taste is acceptable, the product is destroyed. By using a sample in destructive testing, only a portion of the population is ruined.

Sometimes a population is virtually impossible to access for research. For example, some people refuse to answer sensitive questions, and some telephone numbers are unlisted. Some items of interest (such as a 1957 Chevrolet) are so scattered that locating all of them would be extremely difficult. When the population is inaccessible for these or other reasons, sampling is the only option.

Reasons for Taking a Census

Sometimes it is preferable to conduct a census of the entire population rather than taking a sample. A business analyst may opt to take a census rather than a sample for at least three reasons, providing there is adequate time and money available to conduct such a study: (1) to eliminate the possibility that by chance a randomly selected sample may not be representative of the population, (2) for the safety of the consumer, and (3) to benchmark data for future studies.

Even when proper sampling techniques are implemented in a study, it is possible that a sample could be selected by chance that does not represent the population. For example, if the population of interest is all truck owners in Alberta, a random sample of truck owners could yield mostly ranchers when, in fact, many of the truck owners in Alberta are urban dwellers. If the analyst or study sponsor cannot tolerate such a possibility, then taking a census may be the only option.

Sometimes a census is taken to protect the safety of the consumer. For example, there are some products, such as airplanes and heart defibrillators, whose performance is so critical to the consumer that 100% of the products are tested, and sampling is not a reasonable option. In addition, companies often want to establish performance baselines in areas like cost, time, and quality by taking a census at least one time. With such a baseline, future managers can compare their results with past baselines to determine how well their processes are performing.

Frame

Every research study has a target population that consists of the individuals, institutions, or entities that are the object of investigation. When a sample is drawn from a population, it is actually selected from a *list, map, directory, or some other source that represents the population*. This list, map, or directory is called the **frame**. Because the sample is drawn from the frame, the frame is sometimes referred to as the *working population*. Examples of frames can include a phone directory, trade association list, or even a list sold by a list broker. Ideally, a one-to-one correspondence exists between the frame units and the population units. In reality, the frame and the target population are often different, as shown in **Figure 7.1**. In such cases, a frame can be *over-registered* in that it contains units that are not in the target population; and it can be *under-registered* because it does not contain some of the units that are in the target population. In theory, the target population and the frame are the same. In reality, a business analyst's goal is to minimize the differences between the frame and the target population.

For example, suppose the target population is all families living in Montreal. A feasible frame would be the residential pages of the Montreal telephone book. How would the frame differ from the target population? Some families may have only a cellphone but no land line. Other families have unlisted numbers. Still other families might have moved and/or changed numbers since the directory was printed. Some families even have multiple listings under different names.

FIGURE 7.1 **The Frame and the Target Population**

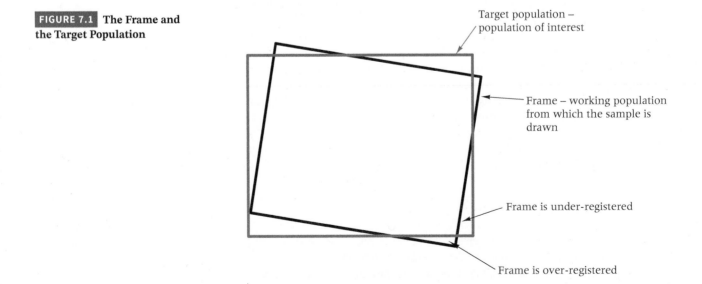

Target population – population of interest

Frame – working population from which the sample is drawn

Frame is under-registered

Frame is over-registered

Random versus Nonrandom Sampling

The two main types of sampling are random and nonrandom. In **random sampling**, *every unit of the population has the same probability of being selected into the sample.* Random sampling implies that chance enters into the process of selection. For example, most people would like to believe that winners of nationwide magazine sweepstakes or numbers selected as lottery winners are selected by some random draw of numbers.

In **nonrandom sampling**, *each unit of the population has an unknown probability of being included in the sample.* Members of nonrandom samples are not selected by chance. For example, they might be selected because they are at the right place at the right time or because they know the people conducting the research.

Sometimes random sampling is called *probability sampling* and nonrandom sampling is called *nonprobability sampling.* Because every unit of the population is not equally likely to be selected, assigning a probability of occurrence in nonrandom sampling is impossible. The statistical methods presented and discussed in this text are based on the assumption that the data come from random samples. *Nonrandom sampling methods are not appropriate techniques for gathering data to be analyzed by most of the statistical methods presented in this text.* However, several nonrandom sampling techniques are described in this section, primarily to alert you to their characteristics and limitations.

Random Sampling Techniques

The four basic random sampling techniques are simple random sampling, stratified random sampling, systematic random sampling, and cluster (or area) random sampling. Each technique offers advantages and disadvantages. Some techniques are simpler to use, some are less costly, and others show greater potential for reducing sampling error.

Simple Random Sampling   The most elementary random sampling technique is **simple random sampling**. A simple random sample is defined as *one that gives each member of the sampling frame an equal chance of being selected and each possible sample of a given size an equal chance of being selected.* Simple random sampling can be viewed as the basis for the other random sampling techniques. Random numbers are a sequence of numbers that lack any pattern. Each number has an equal opportunity to be included in a sample. With simple random sampling, each unit of the frame is numbered from 1 to N (where N is the size of the population). Next, a table of random numbers or a random number generator is used to select n items into the sample. A random number generator is usually a computer program that allows computer-calculated output to yield random numbers.

Table 7.1 contains a brief table of random numbers. Table A.1 in Appendix A contains a full table of random numbers. These numbers are random in all directions. The spaces in the table are there only for ease of reading the values. For each number, any of the 10 digits (0–9) is equally likely, so getting the same digit twice or more in a row is possible.

TABLE 7.1   **A Brief Table of Random Numbers**

91567	42595	27958	30134	04024	86385	29880	99730
46503	18584	18845	49618	02304	51038	20655	58727
34914	63974	88720	82765	34476	17032	87589	40836
57491	16703	23167	49323	45021	33132	12544	41035
30405	83946	23792	14422	15059	45799	22716	19792
09983	74353	68668	30429	70735	25499	16631	35006
85900	07119	97336	71048	08178	77233	13916	47564

As an example, from the population frame of companies listed in Table 7.2, we will use simple random sampling to select a sample of six companies. First, we number every member of the population. We select as many digits for each unit sampled as there are in the largest number in the population. For example, if a population has 2,000 members, we select four-digit numbers. Because the population in Table 7.2 contains 30 members, only two digits need be selected for each number. The population is numbered from 01 to 30, as shown in Table 7.3.

TABLE 7.2	A Population Frame of 30 Companies	
Acceleware Corp.	Filemobile Inc.	PrecisionERP Inc.
Apption Software (Apption Corp.)	Hutton Forest Products Inc.	Scalar Decisions Inc.
	KMA Contracting Inc.	Siamons International Inc.
Auctionwire Inc.	League Assets Corp.	Simcoe Canada Land Development Inc.
Audability Inc.	Lettuce Eatery (Freshii Inc.)	
b5media Inc.	LOGiQ3 Inc.	Stiris Research Inc.
Bond Consulting Group Inc.	MedicLINK Systems Ltd.	Sweetspot.ca Inc.
Cadre Staffing Inc.	Mortgagebrokers.com Holdings Inc.	TAG Recruitment Group Inc.
Direct Sales Force Inc.		Unity Telecom Corp.
Diversified Brands 2005 Inc.	Rapido Trains Inc.	Vortex Mobile (Vortxt Interactive Inc.)
Eagle Wake Ltd./Ticket Gold	Pacesetter Directional and Performance Drilling Ltd.	
EFT Canada Inc.		

TABLE 7.3	Numbered Population of 30 Companies	
01 Acceleware Corp.	11 EFT Canada Inc.	21 Pacesetter Directional and Performance Drilling Ltd.
02 Apption Software (Apption Corp.)	12 Filemobile Inc.	
	13 Hutton Forest Products Inc.	22 PrecisionERP Inc.
03 Auctionwire Inc.		23 Scalar Decisions Inc.
04 Audability Inc.	14 KMA Contracting Inc.	24 Siamons International Inc.
05 b5media Inc.	15 League Assets Corp.	25 Simcoe Canada Land Development Inc.
06 Bond Consulting Group Inc.	16 Lettuce Eatery (Freshii Inc.)	
		26 Stiris Research Inc.
07 Cadre Staffing Inc.	17 LOGiQ3 Inc.	27 Sweetspot.ca Inc.
08 Direct Sales Force Inc.	18 MedicLINK Systems Ltd.	28 TAG Recruitment Group Inc.
09 Diversified Brands 2005 Inc.	19 Mortgagebrokers.com Holdings Inc.	29 Unity Telecom Corp.
10 Eagle Wake Ltd./ Ticket Gold	20 Rapido Trains Inc.	30 Vortex Mobile (Vortxt Interactive Inc.)

The object is to sample six companies, so six different two-digit numbers must be selected from the table of random numbers. Because this population contains only 30 companies, all numbers greater than 30 (31–99) must be ignored. If, for example, the number 67 is selected, the process is continued until a value between 1 and 30 is obtained. If the same number occurs more than once, we proceed to another number. For ease of understanding, we start with the first pair of digits in Table 7.1 and proceed across the first row until $n = 6$ different values between 01 and 30 are selected. If additional numbers are needed, we proceed across the second row, and so on. Often an analyst will start at some randomly selected location in the table and proceed in a predetermined direction to select numbers.

In the first row of digits in Table 7.1, the first number is 91. This number is out of range so it is cast out. The next two digits are 56. Next is 74, followed by 25, which is the first usable number. From Table 7.3, we see that 25 is the number associated with Simcoe Canada Land Development Inc., so this is the first company selected into the sample. The next number is 95, unusable, followed by 27, which is usable. Twenty-seven is the number for Sweetspot.ca Inc., so this company is selected. Continuing the process, we pass over the numbers 95 and 83. The next usable number is 01, which is the value for Acceleware Corp. Thirty-four is next, followed by 04 and 02, both of which are usable. These numbers are associated with Audability

Inc. and Apption Software (Apption Corp.), respectively. Continuing along the first row, the next usable number is 29, which is associated with Unity Telecom Corp. Because this selection is the sixth, the sample is complete. The following companies constitute the final sample.

Simcoe Canada Land Development Inc.
Sweetspot.ca Inc.
Acceleware Corp.
Audability Inc.
Apption Software (Apption Corp.)
Unity Telecom Corp.

Excel's RANDBETWEEN function offers a very simple alternative to using the table of random numbers. In our example, there are 30 companies, numbered from 1 to 30. The function RANDBETWEEN(1,30) in Excel will return a random number between 1 and 30. As with random number tables, Excel will also produce duplicates. For this reason, if an analyst has 30 items, he may want to generate many more than 30 random numbers, for example, some 150 random numbers. As with random number tables, an analyst can start at some randomly selected location in the table and proceed in a predetermined direction to select numbers. **Table 7.4** shows

TABLE 7.4 Random Numbers between 1 and 30, Generated by Excel

12	9	26	14	9
14	26	11	10	10
10	14	8	3	28
2	18	26	10	1
28	16	27	10	26
4	22	17	8	7
1	8	6	17	5
5	18	11	17	7
29	19	21	30	26
29	22	18	28	19
8	7	20	30	29
10	3	23	4	30
29	8	23	11	23
23	26	24	23	7
24	24	16	27	23
25	12	30	27	19
10	17	1	26	5
9	23	22	16	1
29	23	6	2	30
4	8	13	5	30
21	1	6	11	1
6	16	20	12	8
8	19	25	15	23
12	8	25	17	14
7	5	28	25	11
2	30	12	12	29
9	15	10	2	4
17	23	14	29	27
11	11	21	16	5
6	4	24	5	29

a random number table generated by Excel. Using Excel to generate random numbers has two advantages: it is easily accessible and you can control the range of numbers that will be included in the table, so you have fewer unproductive numbers.

Simple random sampling is easier to perform on small populations than on large ones. The process of numbering all the members of the population and selecting items is cumbersome for large populations.

Stratified Random Sampling

Stratified Random Sampling A second type of random sampling is **stratified random sampling**, in which *the population is divided into nonoverlapping subpopulations called strata*. The analyst then extracts a simple random sample from each of the subpopulations. There are many reasons for using stratified random samples. For example, stratified random samples allow the analyst to study each stratum individually by making sure that even a small stratum of interest is properly represented, and they have the potential to reduce sampling error, which occurs when, by chance, the sample does not represent the population. However, stratified random sampling can involve additional work because each unit of the population must be assigned to a stratum before the random selection process begins.

Strata selection is usually based on available information. Such information may have been gleaned from previous censuses or surveys. Stratification benefits increase as the strata differ more. Internally, a stratum should be relatively homogeneous; externally, strata should contrast with each other. Stratification is often done by using demographic variables, such as gender, socio-economic class, geographic region, religion, and ethnicity. For example, if a national election poll is to be conducted by a market research firm, what important variables should be stratified? The gender of the respondent might make a difference because a gender gap in voter preference has been noted in past elections; that is, men and women tended to vote differently in national elections. Geographic region also provides an important variable in national elections because voters are influenced by local cultural values that differ from region to region. Voters in Alberta may prefer conservative candidates, while voters in the Atlantic provinces may prefer a more liberal candidate.

In cable television markets, age of viewer is an important determinant of the type of programming offered by a station. **Figure 7.2** contains a stratification by age with three strata, based on the assumption that age makes a difference in preference of programming. This stratification implies that viewers 20 to 29 years of age tend to prefer the same type of programming, which is different from that preferred by viewers 30 to 39 and 40 to 49 years of age. Within each age subgroup (stratum), *homogeneity* or alikeness is present; between each pair of subgroups, a difference, or *heterogeneity,* is present.

FIGURE 7.2 **Stratified Random Sampling of Cable Television Viewers**

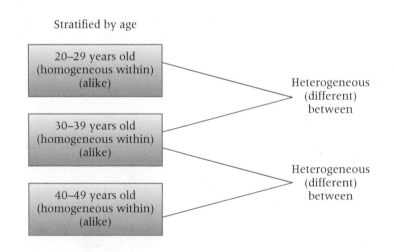

Stratified by age

20–29 years old (homogeneous within) (alike)

30–39 years old (homogeneous within) (alike)

40–49 years old (homogeneous within) (alike)

Heterogeneous (different) between

Heterogeneous (different) between

Stratified random sampling can be either proportionate or disproportionate. **Proportionate stratified random sampling** occurs *when the percentage of the sample taken from each stratum is proportionate to the percentage that each stratum is within the whole population.* For example, suppose voters are being surveyed in Toronto and the sample is being stratified by ethnicity. If 53% of the Toronto population is English/Irish/Scottish and if a sample of

1,000 voters is taken, the sample would require inclusion of 53% English/Irish/Scottish people to achieve proportionate stratification. Any other number of English/Irish/Scottish would be disproportionate stratification. The sample proportion of other ethnicities, such as South Asian/Indo-Caribbean (12%), Chinese (11%), black African-Caribbean (8%), and so on, would also have to follow population percentages (as given in parentheses). Or consider the metropolitan area of Montreal, Quebec, where the population is approximately 65% French. If an analyst is conducting a metropolitan area poll in Montreal and if stratification is by language, a proportionate stratified random sample should contain 65% French speakers. *Whenever the proportions of the strata in the sample are different from the proportions of the strata in the population,* **disproportionate stratified random sampling** occurs. (See Thinking Critically About Statistics in Business Today 7.1.)

Thinking Critically About Statistics in Business Today 7.1

Sampling Canadian Manufacturers

Statistics Canada, Canada's national statistical agency, administers the Monthly Survey of Manufacturing (MSM), which includes information on such variables as sales of goods manufactured, inventories, and orders. The MSM data are used as indicators of the economic condition of manufacturing industries in Canada along with inputs for Canada's gross domestic product, economic studies, and econometric models. The sampling frame for the MSM is the Business Register of Statistics Canada. The target population consists of all establishments on the business register that are classified as in the manufacturing sector. The frame is further reduced by eliminating the smallest units of the survey population. As a result, there are 27,000 establishments in the sampling frame, of which approximately 6,500 are in the final sample. Before the sample is taken, the sampling frame is stratified by both industry and province. Further stratification is then made within each cell by company size so that companies of similar size are grouped together. Selected establishments are required to respond to the survey, and data are collected directly from the survey respondents and extracted from administrative files. Sampled companies are contacted by either mail or telephone, whichever they prefer.

Things to Ponder

1. According to the information presented, the MSM sample is stratified by province, industry, and size. Do you think that these strata make sense? If so, why? Can you think of other strata that might be used in this survey?

2. Sampled companies are contacted either by mail or telephone. Do you think that survey responses might differ depending on whether they were obtained by mail or telephone? Explain why or why not.

Source: Based on information from Statistics Canada, "Monthly Survey of Manufacturing," www23.statcan.gc.ca/imdb/p2SV.pl?Function=getSurvey&SDDS=2101.

Systematic Sampling   Systematic sampling is a third random sampling technique. Unlike stratified random sampling, systematic sampling is not done in an attempt to reduce sampling error. Rather, systematic sampling is used because of its convenience and relative ease of administration. With **systematic sampling**, *every kth item is selected to produce a sample of size* n *from a population of size* N. The value of k, sometimes called the sampling cycle, can be determined by the following formula. If k is not an integer value, the whole-number value should be used.

Determining the Value of k

$$k = \frac{N}{n} \qquad\qquad (7.1)$$

where

n = sample size

N = population size

k = size of interval for selection

As an example of systematic sampling, a management information systems analyst wanted to sample the manufacturers in Canada. She had enough financial support to sample 1,000 companies (*n*). *Scott's National Manufacturers of Canada Directory* lists approximately 190,000 total manufacturers in Canada (N) in alphabetical order. The value of k was 190 (190,000/1,000) and the analyst selected every 190th company in the directory for her sample.

Did the analyst begin with the first company listed or the 190th or one somewhere in between? In selecting every kth value, a simple random number table should be used to select a value between 1 and k inclusive as a starting point. The second element for the sample is the starting point plus k. In the example, $k = 190$, so the analyst would have gone to a table of random numbers to determine a starting point between 1 and 190. Suppose she selected the number 5. She would have started with the 5th company, then selected the 195th (5 + 190), and then the 385th, and so on.

Besides convenience, systematic sampling has other advantages. Because systematic sampling is evenly distributed across the frame, a knowledgeable person can easily determine whether a sampling plan has been followed in a study. However, a problem can occur with systematic sampling if the data are subject to any periodicity and the sampling interval is in syncopation with it. In such a case, the sampling would be nonrandom. For example, if a list of 150 university students is actually a merged list of five classes with 30 students in each class, and if each of the lists of the five classes has been ordered with the names of top students first and bottom students last, then systematic sampling of every 30th student could cause selection of all top students, all bottom students, or all mediocre students; that is, the original list is subject to a cyclical or periodic organization. Systematic sampling methodology is based on the assumption that the source of population elements is random.

Cluster (or Area) Sampling

Cluster (or area) sampling is a fourth type of random sampling. **Cluster (or area) sampling** involves *dividing the population into nonoverlapping areas or clusters*. However, in contrast to stratified random sampling, where strata are homogeneous within, cluster sampling identifies clusters that tend to be internally heterogeneous. In theory, each cluster contains a wide variety of elements, and the cluster is a miniature, or microcosm, of the population. Examples of clusters are towns, companies, homes, universities, areas of a city, and geographic regions. Often clusters are naturally occurring groups of the population and are already identified, such as provinces or cities. Although area sampling usually refers to clusters that are areas of the population, such as geographic regions and cities, the terms *cluster sampling* and *area sampling* are used interchangeably in this text.

After randomly selecting clusters from the population, the business analyst either selects all elements of the chosen clusters or randomly selects individual elements into the sample from the clusters. One example of business research that makes use of clustering is test marketing of new products. Often in test marketing, Canada is divided into clusters of test market cities, and individual consumers within the test market cities are surveyed. (A test market is a geographical area used to test potential sales or viability of a typically new product. Such test markets are typically assumed to represent the larger market.)

Sometimes the clusters are too large, and *a second set of clusters is taken from each original cluster*. This technique is called **two-stage sampling**. For example, an analyst could divide Canada into clusters of cities. She could then divide the cities into clusters of blocks and randomly select individual houses from the block clusters. The first stage is selecting the test cities and the second stage is selecting the blocks.

Cluster or area sampling offers several advantages. Two of the foremost advantages are convenience and cost. Clusters are usually convenient to obtain, and the cost of sampling from the entire population is reduced because the scope of the study is reduced to the clusters. The cost per element is usually lower in cluster or area sampling than in stratified sampling because of lower element listing or locating costs. The time and cost of contacting elements of the population can be reduced, especially if travel is involved, because clustering reduces the distance to the sampled elements. In addition, administration of the sample survey can be simplified. Sometimes cluster or area sampling is the only feasible approach because the sampling frames of the individual elements of the population are unavailable and therefore other random sampling techniques cannot be used.

Cluster or area sampling also has several disadvantages. If the elements of a cluster are similar, cluster sampling may be statistically less efficient than simple random sampling.

In an extreme case—when the elements of a cluster are the same—sampling from the cluster may be no better than sampling a single unit from the cluster. Moreover, the costs and problems of statistical analysis are greater with cluster or area sampling than with simple random sampling.

Nonrandom Sampling

Sampling techniques used to select elements from the population by any mechanism that does not involve a random selection process are called **nonrandom sampling techniques**. Because chance is not used to select items from the samples, these techniques are non-probability techniques and are not desirable for use in gathering data to be analyzed by the methods of inferential statistics presented in this text. Sampling error cannot be determined objectively for these sampling techniques. Four nonrandom sampling techniques are presented here: convenience sampling, judgment sampling, quota sampling, and snowball sampling.

Convenience Sampling

In **convenience sampling**, *elements for the sample are selected for the convenience of the analyst.* The analyst typically chooses elements that are readily available, nearby, or willing to participate. The sample tends to be less variable than the population because in many environments the extreme elements of the population are not readily available. The analyst will select more elements from the middle of the population. For example, a convenience sample of homes for door-to-door interviews might include houses where people are at home, houses with no dogs, houses near the street, first-floor apartments, and houses with friendly people. In contrast, a random sample would require the analyst to gather data only from houses and apartments that have been selected randomly, no matter how inconvenient or unfriendly the location. If a research firm is located in a mall, a convenience sample might be selected by interviewing only shoppers who pass the shop and look friendly.

Judgment Sampling

Judgment sampling occurs when *elements selected for the sample are chosen by the judgment of the analyst.* Analysts often believe they can obtain a representative sample by using sound judgment, which will result in saving time and money. Ethical, professional analysts might sometimes believe they can select a more representative sample than the random process will provide. They might be right! However, some studies show that random sampling methods outperform judgment sampling in estimating the population mean even when the analyst who is administering the judgment sampling is trying to put together a representative sample. When sampling is done by judgment, calculating the probability that an element is going to be selected into the sample is not possible. The sampling error cannot be determined objectively because probabilities are based on *nonrandom* selection.

Other problems are associated with judgment sampling. The analyst tends to make errors of judgment in one direction. These systematic errors lead to what are called *biases*. The analyst is also unlikely to include extreme elements. Judgment sampling provides no objective method for determining whether one person's judgment is better than another's.

Quota Sampling

A third nonrandom sampling technique is **quota sampling**, which appears to be similar to stratified random sampling. *Certain population subclasses, such as age group, gender, and geographic region, are used as strata.* However, instead of randomly sampling from each stratum, the analyst uses a nonrandom sampling method to gather data from one stratum until the desired quota of samples is filled. Quotas are described by quota controls, which set the sizes of the samples to be obtained from the subgroups. Generally, a quota is based on the proportions of the subclasses in the population. In this case, the quota concept is similar to that of proportional stratified sampling.

Quotas are often filled by using available, recent, or applicable elements. For example, instead of randomly interviewing people to obtain a quota of Italian Canadians, the analyst would go to the Italian area of the city and interview there until enough responses are obtained to fill the quota. In quota sampling, an interviewer begins by asking a few filter questions; if the respondent represents a subclass whose quota has been filled, the interviewer terminates the interview. Note that quotas are filled by using convenience sampling, and the result, while appearing to be scientific, is actually nonrandom sampling.

Quota sampling can be useful if no frame is available for the population. For example, suppose an analyst wants to stratify the population into owners of different types of cars but fails to find any lists of Toyota van owners. Through quota sampling, the analyst would proceed by interviewing all car owners and casting out non–Toyota van owners until the quota of Toyota van owners is filled.

Quota sampling is less expensive than most random sampling techniques because it is essentially a technique of convenience. However, cost may not be meaningful because the quality of nonrandom and random sampling techniques cannot be compared. Another advantage of quota sampling is the speed of data gathering. The analyst does not have to call back or send out a second questionnaire if he does not receive a response; he just moves on to the next element. Also, preparatory work for quota sampling is minimal.

The main problem with quota sampling is that, when all is said and done, it is still only a *nonrandom* sampling technique. Some analysts believe that if the quota is filled by *randomly* selecting elements and discarding those not from a stratum, quota sampling is essentially a version of stratified random sampling. However, most quota sampling is carried out by the analyst going where the quota can be filled quickly. The object is to gain the benefits of stratification without the high field costs of stratification. Ultimately, it remains a nonprobability sampling method.

Snowball Sampling Another nonrandom sampling technique is **snowball sampling**, in which *survey subjects are selected based on referral from other survey respondents*. The analyst identifies a person who fits the profile of subjects wanted for the study. The analyst then asks this person for the names and locations of others who would also fit the profile of subjects wanted for the study. Through these referrals, survey subjects can be identified cheaply and efficiently, which is particularly useful when survey subjects are difficult to locate. This is the main advantage of snowball sampling; its main disadvantage is that it is nonrandom.

Sampling Error

Sampling error is *the difference between the estimate obtained from the sample and the population parameters as a result of the sample being only a subset of the population*. Since all samples are by definition subsets of the relevant population, sampling errors can never be completely eliminated. Whenever we take a sample, regardless of the method, it is subject to sampling errors. The statistic computed on the sample may often deviate from the estimate of the population parameter because of sampling error. However, with random samples, sampling error can be computed and analyzed.

Nonsampling Errors

All errors other than sampling errors are **nonsampling errors**. Nonsampling errors can introduce biases. Nonsampling errors arise for many reasons, such as missing data, recording errors, input processing errors, and analysis errors. In some surveys (such as mail surveys), the respondent can choose to respond or not much more easily than in a telephone interview. This results in respondent self-selection, which introduces what is known as the selection bias. Nonsampling errors can also result from the measurement instrument, such as errors of unclear definitions, defective questionnaires, and poorly conceived concepts. Improper definition of the frame is a nonsampling error. In many cases, finding a frame that perfectly fits the population is impossible. Insofar as it does not fit, a nonsampling error can arise.

Response errors are also nonsampling errors. They occur when people do not know, will not say, or overstate. Virtually no statistical method is available to measure or control for nonsampling errors. The statistical techniques presented in this text are based on the assumption that none of these nonsampling errors were committed. The analyst should try to eliminate these errors by carefully planning and executing the research study. In many surveys, sampling error is the only part of the total survey error that is measurable. Nonsampling errors, on the other hand, can be not only numerous but also, for the most part, very difficult to measure and, in some cases, to identify. Therefore, one should assume that the reported error includes all possible survey errors.

Concept Check

1. What is the basic difference between a random and a nonrandom sample?
2. Suppose there are 100 students in your class. You are asked to pick four students at random. You look around and pick four students in a specific order. Is this a true random sample?
3. What is the only reason for sampling errors?
4. Why do nonsampling errors occur?

7.1 Problems

7.1 Develop a frame for the population of each of the following research projects.

   a. Measuring the job satisfaction of all union employees in a company

   b. Conducting a telephone survey in Edmonton, Alberta, to determine the level of interest in opening a new hunting and fishing specialty store in the West Edmonton Mall

   c. Interviewing passengers of a major airline about its food service

   d. Studying the quality control programs of boat manufacturers

   e. Attempting to measure the corporate culture of cable television companies

7.2 Make a list of 20 people you know. Include men and women, various ages, various educational levels, and so on. Number the list and then use the random number list in Table 7.1 to select six people randomly from your list. How representative of the population is the sample? Find the proportion of men in your population and in your sample. How do the proportions compare? Find the proportion of 20-year-olds in your sample and the proportion in the population. How do they compare?

7.3 Use the random numbers in Table A.1 of Appendix A to select 10 of the companies from the 30 companies listed in Table 7.2. Compare the types of companies in your sample with the types in the population. How representative of the population is your sample?

7.4 For each of the following research projects, list three variables for stratification of the sample.

   a. A nationwide study of motels and hotels is being conducted. An attempt will be made to determine the extent of the availability of online links for customers. A sample of motels and hotels will be taken.

   b. A consumer panel is to be formed by sampling people in Manitoba. Members of the panel will be interviewed periodically in an effort to understand current consumer attitudes and behaviours.

   c. A large soft drink company wants to study the characteristics of the Canadian bottlers of its products, but the company does not want to conduct a census.

   d. The business research bureau of a large university is conducting a project in which the bureau will sample paper-manufacturing companies.

7.5 In each of the following cases, the variable represents one way that a sample can be stratified in a study. For each variable, list some strata into which the variable can be divided.

   a. Age of respondent (person)

   b. Size of company (sales volume)

   c. Size of retail outlet (square feet)

   d. Geographic location

   e. Occupation of respondent (person)

   f. Type of business (company)

7.6 A city's telephone book lists 100,000 people. If the telephone book is the frame for a study, how large would the sample size be if systematic sampling were done on every 200th person?

7.7 If every 11th item is systematically sampled to produce a sample size of 75 items, approximately how large is the population?

7.8 If a company employs 3,500 people and if a random sample of 175 of these employees has been taken by systematic sampling, what is the value of k? The analyst would start the sample selection between which two values? Where could the analyst obtain a frame for this study?

7.9 For each of the following research projects, list at least one area or cluster that could be used in obtaining the sample.

   a. A study of road conditions in the province of Nova Scotia

   b. A study of Canadian offshore oil wells

   c. A study of the environmental effects of petrochemical plants west of the St. Lawrence River

7.10 Give an example of how judgment sampling could be used in a study to determine how prosecutors feel about lawyers advertising on television.

7.11 Give an example of how convenience sampling could be used in a study of *Report on Business Magazine's* Top 1,000 executives to measure corporate attitude toward paternity leave for employees.

7.12 Give an example of how quota sampling could be used to conduct sampling by a company test-marketing a new personal computer.

7.2 | Sampling Distribution of $\bar{x}$

LEARNING OBJECTIVE 7.2

Describe the distribution of a sample's mean using the central limit theorem, correcting for a finite population if necessary.

In the inferential statistics process, a business analyst selects a random sample from the population, computes a statistic on the sample, and reaches conclusions about the population parameter from the statistic. In attempting to analyze the sample statistic, it is essential to know the distribution of the statistic. So far we have studied several distributions, including the binomial distribution, the Poisson distribution, the hypergeometric distribution, the uniform distribution, the normal distribution, and the exponential distribution.

In this section, we explore the sample mean, $\bar{x}$, as the statistic. The sample mean is one of the more common statistics used in the inferential process. To compute and assign the probability of occurrence of a particular value of a sample mean, the analyst must know the distribution of the sample means. One way to examine the distribution possibilities is to take a population with a particular distribution, randomly select samples of a given size, compute the sample means, and attempt to determine how the means are distributed.

Suppose a small finite population consists of only $N = 8$ numbers:

54   55   59   63   64   68   69   70

Using an Excel-produced histogram, we can see the shape of the distribution of this population of data.

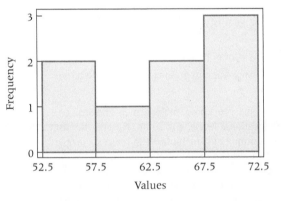

Suppose we take all possible samples of size $n = 2$ from this population with replacement. The result is the following pairs of data.

(54, 54)	(55, 54)	(59, 54)	(63, 54)
(54, 55)	(55, 55)	(59, 55)	(63, 55)
(54, 59)	(55, 59)	(59, 59)	(63, 59)
(54, 63)	(55, 63)	(59, 63)	(63, 63)
(54, 64)	(55, 64)	(59, 64)	(63, 64)
(54, 68)	(55, 68)	(59, 68)	(63, 68)
(54, 69)	(55, 69)	(59, 69)	(63, 69)
(54, 70)	(55, 70)	(59, 70)	(63, 70)
(64, 54)	(68, 54)	(69, 54)	(70, 54)
(64, 55)	(68, 55)	(69, 55)	(70, 55)
(64, 59)	(68, 59)	(69, 59)	(70, 59)
(64, 63)	(68, 63)	(69, 63)	(70, 63)
(64, 64)	(68, 64)	(69, 64)	(70, 64)
(64, 68)	(68, 68)	(69, 68)	(70, 68)
(64, 69)	(68, 69)	(69, 69)	(70, 69)
(64, 70)	(68, 70)	(69, 70)	(70, 70)

The means of all of these samples follow.

54	54.5	56.5	58.5	59	61	61.5	62
54.5	55	57	59	59.5	61.5	62	62.5
56.5	57	59	61	61.5	63.5	64	64.5
58.5	59	61	63	63.5	65.5	66	66.5
59	59.5	61.5	63.5	64	66	66.5	67
60	61.5	63.5	65.5	66	68	68.5	69
61.5	62	64	66	66.5	68.5	69	69.5
62	62.5	64.5	66.5	67	69	69.5	70

Again using an Excel-produced histogram, we can see the shape of the distribution of these sample means.

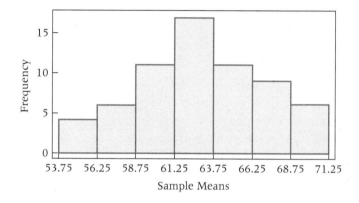

Notice that the shape of the histogram for sample means is quite unlike the shape of the histogram for the population. The sample means appear to "pile up" toward the middle of the distribution and "tail off" toward the extremes.

Figure 7.3 is a histogram of the data from a Poisson distribution of values with a population mean of 1.25. Note that the histogram is skewed to the right. Suppose 90 samples of size $n = 30$ are taken randomly from a Poisson distribution with $\lambda = 1.25$ and the means are computed on each sample. The resulting distribution of sample means is displayed in **Figure 7.4**. Notice that although the samples were drawn from a Poisson distribution, which is skewed to the right, the sample means form a distribution that approaches a symmetrical, nearly normal-curve-type distribution.

Suppose a population is uniformly distributed. If samples are selected randomly from a population with a uniform distribution, how are the sample means distributed? **Figure 7.5** displays the histogram distributions of sample means from five different sample sizes. Each of these histograms represents the distribution of sample means from 90 samples generated

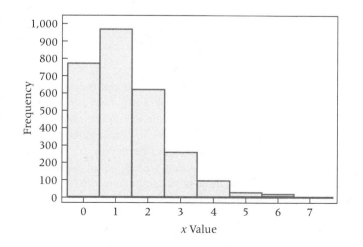

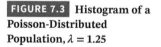

FIGURE 7.3 **Histogram of a Poisson-Distributed Population, $\lambda = 1.25$**

FIGURE 7.4 Histogram of Sample Means for the Data Shown in Figure 7.3

FIGURE 7.5 Sample Means from 90 Samples Ranging in Size from $n = 2$ to $n = 30$ from a Uniformly Distributed Population with $a = 10$ and $b = 30$

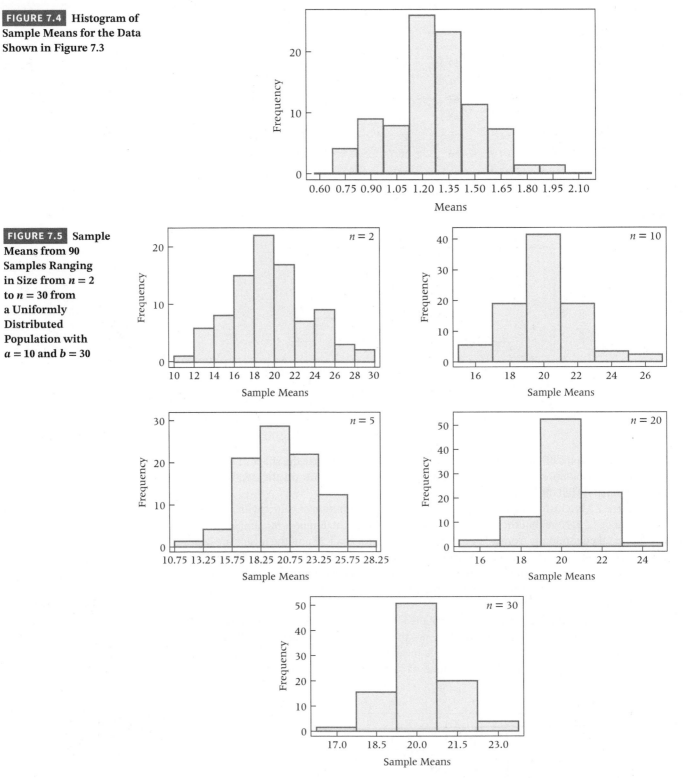

randomly from a uniform distribution in which $a = 10$ and $b = 30$. Observe the shape of the distributions. Notice that even for small sample sizes, the distributions of sample means for samples taken from the uniformly distributed population begin to pile up in the middle. As sample sizes become much larger, the sample mean distributions begin to approach a normal distribution and the variation among the means decreases.

So far, we have examined three populations with different distributions. However, the sample means for samples taken from these populations appear to be approximately normally distributed, especially as the sample sizes become larger. What would happen to the distribution of sample means if we studied populations with differently shaped distributions? The answer to that question is given in the **central limit theorem**.

Central Limit Theorem

If samples of size n are drawn randomly from a population that has a mean of μ and a standard deviation of σ, the sample means, $\bar{x}$, are approximately normally distributed for sufficiently large sample sizes ($n \geq 30$) regardless of the shape of the population distribution.[1] If the population is normally distributed, the sample means are normally distributed for any size sample.

From mathematical expectation,[2] it can be shown that the mean of the sample means is the population mean:

$$\mu_{\bar{x}} = \mu$$

and the standard deviation of the sample means (called the standard error of the mean) is the standard deviation of the population divided by the square root of the sample size:

$$\sigma_{\bar{x}} = \frac{\sigma}{\sqrt{n}}$$

The central limit theorem creates the potential for applying the normal distribution to many problems when sample size is sufficiently large. Sample means that have been computed for random samples drawn from normally distributed populations are normally distributed. However, the real advantage of the central limit theorem comes when sample data drawn from populations not normally distributed or from populations of unknown shape can also be analyzed by using the normal distribution because the sample means are normally distributed for sufficiently large sample sizes.[3] Column 1 of **Figure 7.6** shows four different population distributions. Each succeeding column displays the shape of the

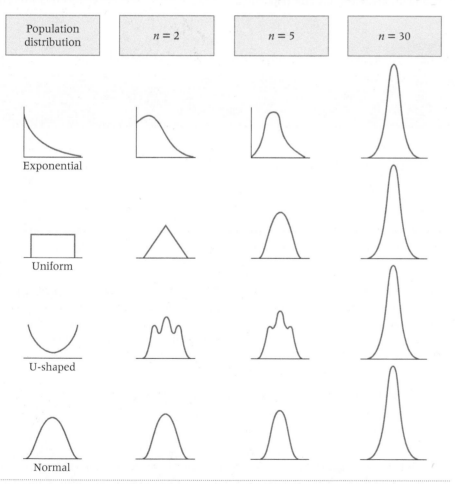

FIGURE 7.6 **Shapes of the Distributions of Sample Means for Three Sample Sizes Drawn from Four Different Population Distributions**

[1] Note that the central limit theorem itself does not specify what a "large sample size" is. As a guideline, it is assumed to be 30 or more, although this does not follow from the central limit theorem itself.
[2] The derivations are beyond the scope of this text and are not shown.
[3] The actual form of the central limit theorem is a limit function of calculus. As the sample size increases to infinity, the distribution of sample means literally becomes normal in shape.

distribution of the sample means for a particular sample size. Note in the bottom row for the normally distributed population that the sample means are normally distributed even for $n = 2$. Note also that with the other population distributions, the distribution of the sample means begins to approximate the normal curve as n becomes larger. For all four distributions, the distribution of sample means is approximately normal for $n = 30$.

How large must a sample be for the central limit theorem to apply? The sample size necessary varies according to the shape of the population. However, in this text (as in many others), a sample size of *30 or larger* will suffice. Recall that if the population is normally distributed, the sample means are normally distributed for sample sizes as small as $n = 1$.

The shapes displayed in Figure 7.6 coincide with the results obtained empirically from the random sampling shown in Figures 7.4 and 7.5. As shown in Figure 7.6, and as indicated in Figure 7.5, as sample size increases, the distribution narrows, or becomes more leptokurtic. This trend makes sense because the standard deviation of the mean is $\sigma/\sqrt{n}$. This value will become smaller as the size of n increases.

In **Table 7.5**, the means and standard deviations of the means are displayed for random samples of various sizes ($n = 2$ through $n = 30$) drawn from the uniform distribution of $a = 10$ and $b = 30$ shown in Figure 7.5. The population mean is 20, and the standard deviation of the population is 5.774. Note that the mean of the sample means for each sample size is approximately 20 and that the standard deviation of the sample means for each set of 90 samples is approximately equal to $\sigma/\sqrt{n}$. A small discrepancy occurs between the standard deviation of the sample means and $\sigma/\sqrt{n}$, because not all possible samples of a given size were taken from the population (only 90). In theory, if all possible samples for a given sample size are taken exactly once, the mean of the sample means will equal the population mean and the standard deviation of the sample means will equal the population standard deviation divided by the square root of n.

TABLE 7.5 $\mu_{\bar{x}}$ and $\sigma_{\bar{x}}$ of 90 Random Samples for Five Different Sizes*

Sample Size	Mean of Sample Means	Standard Deviation of Sample Means	μ	$\dfrac{\sigma}{\sqrt{n}}$
$n = 2$	19.92	3.87	20	4.08
$n = 5$	20.17	2.65	20	2.58
$n = 10$	20.04	1.96	20	1.83
$n = 20$	20.20	1.37	20	1.29
$n = 30$	20.25	0.99	20	1.05

*Randomly generated by Excel using a uniform distribution with $a = 10$ and $b = 30$.

The central limit theorem states that sample means are normally distributed regardless of the shape of the population for large samples and for any sample size with normally distributed populations. Thus, sample means can be analyzed by using z scores. Recall from Chapters 3 and 6 the formula to determine z scores for individual values from a normal distribution:

$$z = \frac{x - \mu}{\sigma}$$

If sample means are normally distributed, the z score formula applied to sample means is:

$$z = \frac{\bar{x} - \mu_{\bar{x}}}{\sigma_{\bar{x}}}$$

This result follows the general pattern of z scores: the difference between the statistic and its mean divided by the statistic's standard deviation. In this formula, the mean of the statistic of interest is $\mu_{\bar{x}}$, and *the standard deviation of the statistic of interest is $\sigma_{\bar{x}}$*, sometimes referred to as the **standard error of the mean**. To determine $\mu_{\bar{x}}$, the analyst randomly draws out all possible samples of the given size from the population, computes the sample means, and averages them. This task is virtually impossible to accomplish in any realistic period of time. Fortunately, $\mu_{\bar{x}}$ equals the population mean, μ, which is easier to access. Likewise, to determine directly the value of $\sigma_{\bar{x}}$, the analyst takes all possible samples of a given size from a population, computes the sample means, and determines the standard deviation of sample means. This task is also practically impossible. Fortunately, $\sigma_{\bar{x}}$ can be computed by using the population standard deviation divided by the square root of the sample size.

As sample size increases, the standard deviation of the sample means becomes smaller and smaller because the population standard deviation is being divided by larger and larger values of the square root of n. The ultimate benefit of the central limit theorem is a practical, useful version of the z formula for sample means.

---

z Formula for Sample Means

$$z = \frac{\bar{x} - \mu}{\dfrac{\sigma}{\sqrt{n}}}$$

(7.2)

When the population is normally distributed and the sample size is 1, this formula for sample means becomes the z formula for individual values that we used in Chapter 6. The reason is that the mean of one value is that value, and when $n = 1$ the value of $\sigma/\sqrt{n} = \sigma$.

Suppose, for example, that the mean expenditure per customer at a grocery store is \$85.00, with a standard deviation of \$9.00. If a random sample of 40 customers is taken, what is the probability that the sample average expenditure per customer for this sample will be \$87.00 or more? Because the sample size is greater than 30, the central limit theorem can be used, and the sample means are normally distributed. With $\mu = \$85.00$, $\sigma = \$9.00$, and the z formula for sample means, z is computed as:

$$z = \frac{\bar{x} - \mu}{\dfrac{\sigma}{\sqrt{n}}} = \frac{\$87.00 - \$85.00}{\dfrac{\$9.00}{\sqrt{40}}} = \frac{\$2.00}{\$1.42} = 1.41$$

From the z distribution (Table A.5), $z = 1.41$ produces a probability of 0.4207. This number is the probability of getting a sample mean between \$87.00 and \$85.00 (the population mean). Solving for the tail of the distribution yields:

$$0.5000 - 0.4207 = 0.0793$$

which is the probability of $\bar{x} > \$87.00$. That is, 7.93% of the time, a random sample of 40 customers from this population will yield a sample mean expenditure of \$87.00 or more. **Figure 7.7** shows the problem and its solution.

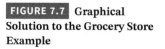

FIGURE 7.7 Graphical Solution to the Grocery Store Example

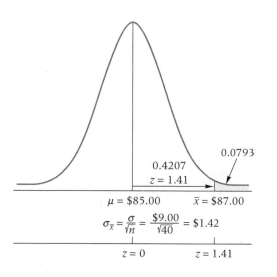

DEMONSTRATION PROBLEM 7.1

Suppose that during any hour in a large department store, the average number of shoppers is 448, with a standard deviation of 21 shoppers. What is the probability that a random sample of 49 different shopping hours will yield a sample mean between 441 and 446 shoppers?

Solution For this problem, $\mu = 448$, $\sigma = 21$, and $n = 49$. The problem is to determine $P(441 \leq \bar{x} \leq 446)$. The following diagram depicts the problem.

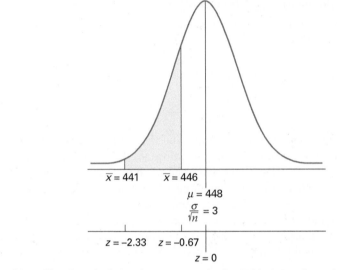

Solve this problem by calculating the z scores and using Table A.5 to determine the probabilities.

$$z = \frac{441 - 448}{\frac{21}{\sqrt{49}}} = \frac{-7}{3} = -2.33$$

and

$$z = \frac{446 - 448}{\frac{21}{\sqrt{49}}} = \frac{-2}{3} = -0.67$$

z Value	Probability
−2.33	0.4901
−0.67	−0.2486
	0.2415

The probability of a z value being between $z = -2.33$ and $z = -0.67$ is 0.2415; that is, there is a 24.15% chance of randomly selecting 49 hourly periods for which the sample mean is between 441 and 446 shoppers.

Sampling from a Finite Population

The examples shown so far in this section and in Demonstration Problem 7.1 were based on the assumption that the population was infinitely or extremely large. In cases of a finite population, *a statistical adjustment can be made to the z formula for sample means.* The adjustment is called the **finite correction factor**: $\sqrt{(N-n)/(N-1)}$. It operates on the standard deviation of sample means, $\sigma_{\bar{x}}$. Following is the z formula for sample means when samples are drawn from finite populations.

---

z Formula for Sample Means of a Finite Population

$$z = \frac{\bar{x} - \mu}{\frac{\sigma}{\sqrt{n}} \sqrt{\frac{N-n}{N-1}}} \qquad (7.3)$$

If a random sample of size 35 were taken from a finite population of only 500, the sample mean would be less likely to deviate from the population mean than would be the case if a sample of size 35 were taken from an infinite population. For a sample of 35 taken from a finite population of size 500, the finite correction factor is

$$\sqrt{\frac{500-35}{500-1}} = \sqrt{\frac{465}{499}} = 0.965$$

Thus, the standard error of the mean is adjusted downward by using 0.965. As the size of the finite population becomes larger in relation to sample size, the finite correction factor approaches 1. In theory, whenever analysts are working with a finite population, they can use the finite correction factor. A rough guideline for many analysts is that if the sample size is less than 5% of the finite population size or $n/N < 0.05$, the finite correction factor does not significantly modify the solution. **Table 7.6** contains some illustrative finite correction factors.

TABLE 7.6 Finite Correction Factor for Some Sample Sizes

Population Size	Sample Size	Value of Correction Factor
2,000	30 (<5%N)	0.993
2,000	500	0.866
500	30	0.971
500	200	0.775
200	30	0.924
200	75	0.793

DEMONSTRATION PROBLEM 7.2

A production company's 350 hourly employees average 37.6 years of age, with a standard deviation of 8.3 years. If a random sample of 45 hourly employees is taken, what is the probability that the sample will have an average age of less than 40 years?

Solution   The population mean is 37.6, with a population standard deviation of 8.3; that is, $\mu = 37.6$ and $\sigma = 8.3$. The sample size is 45, but it is being drawn from a finite population of 350; that is, $n = 45$ and $N = 350$. The sample mean under consideration is 40, or $\bar{x} = 40$. The following diagram depicts the problem on a normal curve.

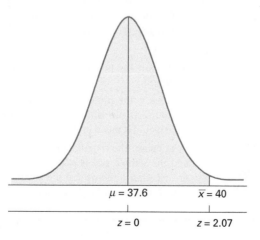

$\mu = 37.6 \qquad \bar{x} = 40$

$z = 0 \qquad z = 2.07$

Using the z formula with the finite correction factor gives

$$z = \frac{40 - 37.6}{\frac{8.3}{\sqrt{45}}\sqrt{\frac{350-45}{350-1}}} = \frac{2.4}{1.157} = 2.07$$

> This z value yields a probability (Table A.5) of 0.4808. Therefore, the probability of getting a sample average age of less than 40 years is $0.4808 + 0.5000 = 0.9808$. Had the finite correction factor not been used, the z value would have been 1.94, and the final answer would have been 0.9738.

Concept Check

1. What do you understand by the central limit theorem and why is it relevant?
2. What happens to the sample mean as you increase the sample size?
3. What is a finite population? What is the finite population correction factor?

7.2 Problems

7.13 A population has a mean of 50 and a standard deviation of 10. If a random sample of 64 is taken, what is the probability that the sample mean is each of the following?

   a. Greater than 52

   b. Less than 51

   c. Less than 47

   d. Between 48.5 and 52.4

   e. Between 50.6 and 51.3

7.14 A population is normally distributed, with a mean of 23.45 and a standard deviation of 3.8. What is the probability of each of the following?

   a. Taking a sample of size 10 and obtaining a sample mean of 22 or more

   b. Taking a sample of size 4 and getting a sample mean of more than 26

7.15 Suppose a random sample of size 36 is drawn from a population with a mean of 278. If 86% of the time the sample mean is less than 280, what is the population standard deviation?

7.16 A random sample of size 81 is drawn from a population with a standard deviation of 12. If only 18% of the time a sample mean greater than 300 is obtained, what is the mean of the population?

7.17 Find the probability in each case.

   a. $N = 1{,}000$, $n = 60$, $\mu = 75$, and $\sigma = 6$; $P(\bar{x} < 76.5) = ?$

   b. $N = 90$, $n = 36$, $\mu = 108$, and $\sigma = 3.46$; $P(107 < \bar{x} < 107.7) = ?$

   c. $N = 250$, $n = 100$, $\mu = 35.6$, and $\sigma = 4.89$; $P(\bar{x} \geq 36) = ?$

   d. $N = 5{,}000$, $n = 60$, $\mu = 125$, and $\sigma = 13.4$; $P(\bar{x} < 123) = ?$

7.18 Let's assume that the average annual consumption of fresh fruit per person in a recent year is 77.8 kg. Suppose the standard deviation of fresh fruit consumption is about 20 kg. Suppose an analyst took a random sample of 38 people and had them keep a record of the fresh fruit they ate for one year.

   a. What is the probability that the sample average would be less than 76 kg?

   b. What is the probability that the sample average would be between 77 kg and 82 kg?

   c. What is the probability that the sample average would be less than 85 kg?

   d. What is the probability that the sample average would be between 75 kg and 76 kg?

7.19 Suppose a small town in British Columbia contains 1,500 houses. A sample of 100 houses is selected randomly and evaluated by an appraiser. If the mean appraised value of a house in this town for all houses is $277,000, with a standard deviation of $10,500, what is the probability that the sample average is greater than $285,000?

7.20 Suppose the average checkout tab at a large supermarket is $65.12, with a standard deviation of $21.45. Twenty-three percent of the time when a random sample of 45 customer tabs is examined, the sample average should exceed what value?

7.21 According to Canadian Radio-television and Telecommunications Commission, the average number of hours of TV viewing among adults is 27 hours per week.[4] Suppose the standard deviation is 6.7 hours and a random sample of 42 Canadian households is taken.

   a. What is the probability that the sample average is more than 29 hours?

   b. What is the probability that the sample average is less than 23 hours?

   c. What is the probability that the sample average is less than 20 hours? If the sample average actually is less than 20 hours, what would it mean in this context?

   d. Suppose the population standard deviation is unknown and the sample size is still 42. If 71% of all sample means are greater than 26 hours and the population mean is still 27 hours, what is the value of the population standard deviation?

---

[4]"Figure 9.4 Average Number of Hours Canadians 18+ Watched Traditional Television and Internet-Based Television Each Week," in "Television Sector: Sector Overview" of CRTC, *Communications Monitoring Report 2018* (Ottawa: Canadian Radio-Television and Telecommunications Commission, 2019), crtc.gc.ca/eng/publications/reports/policymonitoring/2018/cmr4c.htm#f904.

7.3 | Sampling Distribution of $\hat{p}$

LEARNING OBJECTIVE 7.3

Describe the distribution of a sample's proportion using the z formula for sample proportions.

Sometimes in analyzing a sample, a business analyst will choose to use the sample proportion, denoted $\hat{p}$. If research produces *measurable* data such as mass, distance, time, and income, the sample mean is often the statistic of choice. However, if research results in *countable* items such as how many people in a sample choose Dr. Pepper as their favourite soft drink or how many people in a sample have a flexible work schedule, the sample proportion is often the statistic of choice. Whereas the mean is computed by averaging a set of values, the **sample proportion** is *computed by dividing the frequency with which a given characteristic occurs in a sample by the number of items in the sample.*

Sample Proportion

$$\hat{p} = \frac{x}{n} \qquad (7.4)$$

where

   x = number of items in a sample that have the characteristic

   n = number of items in the sample

For example, in a sample of 100 factory workers, 30 workers might belong to a union. The value of $\hat{p}$ for this characteristic, union membership, is $30/100 = 0.30$. In a sample of 500 businesses in suburban malls, if 10 are shoe stores, then the sample proportion of shoe stores is $10/500 = 0.02$. The sample proportion is a widely used statistic and is usually computed on questions involving Yes or No answers. For example, do you have at least a high school education? Are you predominantly right-handed? Are you female? Do you belong to the student accounting association?

How does a business analyst use the sample proportion in analysis? The central limit theorem applies to sample proportions in that the normal distribution approximates the shape of the distribution of sample proportions as the sample size gets larger, regardless of the shape of the population distribution. This convergence is achieved better when $n \cdot p > 5$ and $n \cdot q > 5$ (p is the population proportion and $q = 1 - p$). The mean of sample proportions for all samples of size n randomly drawn from a population is p (the population proportion) and the standard deviation of sample proportions is $\sqrt{p \cdot q / n}$, which is sometimes referred to as the **standard error of the proportion**. Sample proportions also have a z formula.

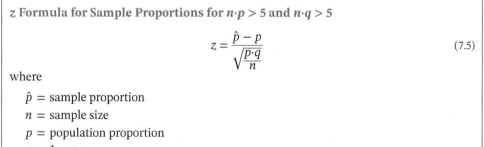

z Formula for Sample Proportions for $n \cdot p > 5$ and $n \cdot q > 5$

$$z = \frac{\hat{p} - p}{\sqrt{\dfrac{p \cdot q}{n}}} \qquad (7.5)$$

where

   $\hat{p}$ = sample proportion

   n = sample size

   p = population proportion

   $q = 1 - p$

Suppose 60% of the electrical contractors in a region use a particular brand of wire. What is the probability of taking a random sample of size 120 from these electrical contractors and finding that 0.50 or less use that brand of wire? For this problem,

$$p = 0.60 \quad \hat{p} = 0.50 \quad n = 120$$

The z formula yields

$$z = \frac{0.50 - 0.60}{\sqrt{\frac{(0.60)(0.40)}{120}}} = \frac{-0.10}{0.0447} = -2.24$$

From Table A.5, the probability corresponding to $z = -2.24$ is 0.4875. For $z < -2.24$ (the tail of the distribution), the answer is $0.5000 - 0.4875 = 0.0125$. **Figure 7.8** shows the problem and solution graphically.

FIGURE 7.8 Graphical Solution to the Electrical Contractor Example

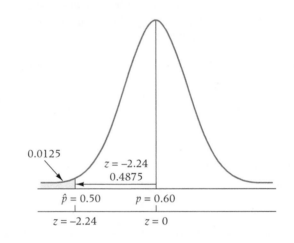

This answer indicates that a business analyst would have difficulty (probability of 0.0125) finding that 50% or less of a sample of 120 contractors use a given brand of wire if indeed the population market share for that wire is 0.60. This sample result may actually occur for one of the following reasons: it is a rare chance result, the 0.60 proportion does not hold for this population, or the sampling method was not random.

DEMONSTRATION PROBLEM 7.3

If 10% of a population of parts is defective, what is the probability of randomly selecting 80 parts and finding that 12 or more parts are defective?

Solution   Here, $p = 0.10$, $\hat{p} = 12/80 = 0.15$, and $n = 80$. Entering these values in the z formula yields:

$$z = \frac{0.15 - 0.10}{\sqrt{\frac{(0.10)(0.90)}{80}}} = \frac{0.05}{0.0335} = 1.49$$

Table A.5 gives a probability of 0.4319 for a z value of 1.49, which is the area between the sample proportion, 0.15, and the population proportion, 0.10. The answer to the question is:

$$P(\hat{p} \geq 0.15) = 0.5000 - 0.4319 = 0.0681$$

Thus, about 6.81% of the time, 12 or more defective parts would appear in a random sample of 80 parts when the population proportion is 0.10. If this result actually occurred, the 10% proportion for population defects would be open to question. The diagram shows the problem graphically.

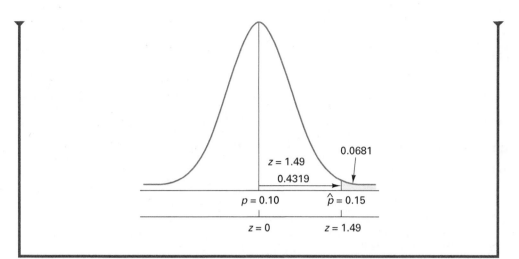

Concept Check

1. For what kind of data would you use the sampling distribution of proportions?

7.3 Problems

7.22 A given population proportion is 0.25. For the given value of n, what is the probability of getting each of the following sample proportions?

   a. $n = 110$ and $\hat{p} \leq 0.21$

   b. $n = 33$ and $\hat{p} > 0.24$

   c. $n = 59$ and $0.24 \leq \hat{p} \leq 0.27$

   d. $n = 80$ and $\hat{p} > 0.30$

   e. $n = 800$ and $\hat{p} > 0.30$

7.23 A population proportion is 0.58. Suppose a random sample of 660 items is sampled randomly from this population.

   a. What is the probability that the sample proportion is greater than 0.60?

   b. What is the probability that the sample proportion is between 0.55 and 0.65?

   c. What is the probability that the sample proportion is greater than 0.57?

   d. What is the probability that the sample proportion is between 0.53 and 0.56?

   e. What is the probability that the sample proportion is less than 0.48?

7.24 Suppose a population proportion is 0.40, and 80% of the time when you draw a random sample from this population you get a sample proportion of 0.35 or more. How large a sample were you taking?

7.25 If a population proportion is 0.28 and if the sample size is 140, 30% of the time the sample proportion will be less than which value if you are taking random samples?

7.26 According to a study by Ipsos-Reid, 40% of Canadians rely on doctors for drug information. Suppose a random sample of 600 Canadians is taken. What is the probability that more than 150 of them rely on doctors for drug information?

7.27 The same study mentioned above found that 36% of Canadians rely on pharmacists for drug information. Suppose 200 Canadians are randomly surveyed.

   a. What is the probability that fewer than 90 of the Canadians rely on pharmacists for drug information?

   b. What is the probability that more than 100 of the Canadians rely on pharmacists for drug information?

   c. What is the probability that more than 80 of the Canadians rely on pharmacists for drug information?

7.28 The Travel Weekly International Air Transport Association survey asked business travellers about the purpose of their most recent business trip. Nineteen percent responded that it was for an internal company visit. Suppose 950 business travellers were randomly selected.

   a. What is the probability that more than 25% of the business travellers said that the reason for their most recent business trip was an internal company visit?

   b. What is the probability that between 15% and 20% of the business travellers said that the reason for their most recent business trip was an internal company visit?

   c. What is the probability that between 133 and 171 of the business travellers said that the reason for their most recent business trip was an internal company visit?

End-of-Chapter Review

Decision Dilemma Solved

What Is the Attitude of Maquiladora Workers?

Because of limited resources, limited time, and a large population of workers, most work attitude and cultural studies of maquiladora workers are accomplished through the use of random sampling. To ensure the inclusion of certain groups and in an effort to reduce sampling error, a proportionate stratified sampling technique might be selected. Such a sampling plan could include as strata such things as geographic location of the plant in Mexico, type of industry, size of the plant, number of maquiladora workers at that facility, age of the worker, gender of the worker, and level of responsibility of the worker.

Lists of maquiladora companies and plants can be obtained for use as a company frame for the study. Each company is likely to have a complete list of all workers. These lists could serve as a frame for the sampling of workers. If granted permission to use the lists, the analyst could then identify strata within the lists and randomly sample workers from these lists.

Attitude and culture questions are not easy to formulate in a way that produces valid data. Experts on the measurement of such things should be consulted. However, if questions are asked in a way that produces numerical responses that can be averaged, sample means can be computed. If sample sizes are large enough, the central limit theorem can be invoked, enabling the business analyst to analyze mean sample responses as though they came from normally distributed populations.

Some of the questions asked might require only a Yes or No response. For example, the question "Are working conditions in a maquiladora plant owned by a Canadian company considerably different from those in a plant owned by an equivalent Mexican company?" requires only a Yes or No response. These responses, when tallied, can be used to compute sample proportions. If the sample sizes are large enough, the business analyst can assume from the central limit theorem that sample proportions come from a normal distribution, which can provide the basis for analysis.

Key Considerations

Considerable research is reported under the guise of random sampling when, in fact, nonrandom sampling is used. Remember, if nonrandom sampling is used, probability statements about sampling error are not appropriate. Some analysts purport to be using stratified random sampling when they are actually using quota sampling. Others claim to be using systematic random sampling when they are actually using convenience or judgment sampling.

In the process of inferential statistics, business analysts use sample results to make conclusions about a population. These conclusions are disseminated to the interested public. The public often assumes that sample results truly reflect the state of the population. If the sample does not reflect the population because questionable sampling practices were used, it could be argued that unethical research behaviour occurred. Valid representative sampling is not an easy task. Analysts and statisticians should exercise extreme caution in taking samples to be sure the results obtained reflect the conditions in the population as nearly as possible.

The central limit theorem is based on large samples unless the population is normally distributed. In analyzing small-sample data, we cannot assume a sample mean is from a normal distribution unless the population can be shown with some confidence to be normally distributed. Using the normal distribution to analyze sample proportions can also be problematic if sample sizes are smaller than those recommended by the experts.

Why Statistics Is Relevant

Modern businesses, political institutions, and social institutions constantly require information that is reliable and can be gathered quickly. Is there a market for the new product that a firm is considering? Are our customers satisfied with our service? What issues are important to voters? Have the issues changed since we surveyed them last month? How many people live below the poverty line? How long will a computer last if it is used 24/7? How many beds should a maternity ward in a hospital have? We cannot collect information on, for example, every voter, every consumer, or every computer to answer these questions. Collecting information on everyone or every object can be expensive, time-consuming, and in many cases not physically feasible. This necessarily means that we need to confine our information collection to a sample. The problem then is how do we know if the sample represents the population? This is where statistics comes in and provides us with a means of obtaining reliable results from just a sample, which can be a small proportion of the population. Without statistics, many business decisions (as well as decisions in many other fields) would be mostly guesswork.

Summary of Learning Objectives

LEARNING OBJECTIVE 7.1   Contrast sampling to census and differentiate methods of sampling, which include simple, stratified, systematic, and cluster random sampling; and convenience, judgment, quota, and snowball nonrandom sampling, by assessing the advantages associated with each.

For much business analysis, successfully conducting a census is virtually impossible, and the sample is a feasible alternative. Other reasons for sampling are cost reduction, potential for broadening the scope of the study, and loss reduction when the testing process destroys the product. To take a sample, a population must be identified. Often the analyst cannot obtain an exact roster or list of the population and so must find some way to identify the population as closely as possible. The final list or directory used to represent the population and from which the sample is drawn is called the frame.

The two main types of sampling are random and nonrandom. Random sampling occurs when each unit of the population has the same probability of being selected for the sample. Nonrandom sampling is any sampling that is not random.

The four main types of random sampling are simple random sampling, stratified sampling, systematic sampling, and cluster or area sampling. In *simple random sampling*, every unit of the population is numbered. A table of random numbers or a random number generator is used to select *n* units from the population for the sample. *Stratified random sampling* uses the analyst's prior knowledge of the population to stratify the population into subgroups. Each subgroup is internally homogeneous but different from the others. Stratified random sampling is an attempt to reduce sampling error and ensure that at least some items of each of the subgroups appear in the sample. After the strata are identified, units can be sampled randomly from each stratum. If the proportions of units selected from each subgroup for the sample are the same as the proportions of the subgroups in the population, the process is called proportionate stratified sampling. If not, it is called disproportionate stratified sampling. With *systematic sampling*, every *k*th item of the population is sampled until *n* units have been selected. Systematic sampling is used because of its convenience and ease of administration. *Cluster or area sampling* involves subdividing the population into non-overlapping clusters or areas. Each cluster or area is a microcosm of the population and is usually heterogeneous within. Individual units are then selected randomly from the clusters or areas to get the final sample. Cluster or area sampling is usually done to reduce costs. If a second set of clusters or areas is selected from the first set, the method is called two-stage sampling.

There are four major types of nonrandom sampling: convenience, judgment, quota, and snowball. In *convenience sampling*, the analyst selects units from the population to be in the sample for convenience. In *judgment sampling*, units are selected according to the judgment of the analyst. *Quota sampling* is similar to stratified sampling, with the analyst identifying subclasses or strata. However, the analyst selects units from each stratum by some nonrandom technique until a specified quota from each stratum is filled. With *snowball sampling*, the analyst obtains additional sample members by asking current sample members for referral information.

Sampling error occurs because we select only a proportion (sample) from a larger population. Random sampling methods allow us to estimate the size of the sampling error. Nonsampling errors are all other research and analysis errors that occur in a study. They include recording errors, input errors, missing data, and incorrect definition of the frame.

LEARNING OBJECTIVE 7.2   Describe the distribution of a sample's mean using the central limit theorem, correcting for a finite population if necessary.

If a population is normally distributed, the sample means for samples taken from that population are also normally distributed regardless of sample size. The central limit theorem says that if the sample sizes are large ($n \geq 30$), the sample mean is approximately normally distributed regardless of the distribution shape of the population. This theorem is extremely useful because it enables analysts to analyze sample data by using the normal distribution for virtually any type of study in which means are an appropriate statistic, as long as the sample size is large enough.

LEARNING OBJECTIVE 7.3   Describe the distribution of a sample's proportion using the *z* formula for sample proportions.

The central limit theorem states that sample proportions are normally distributed for large sample sizes.

Key Terms

central limit theorem   7-16
cluster (or area) sampling   7-10
convenience sampling   7-11
disproportionate stratified
  random sampling   7-9
finite correction factor   7-20
frame   7-4
judgment sampling   7-11

nonrandom sampling   7-5
nonrandom sampling techniques   7-11
nonsampling errors   7-12
proportionate stratified
  random sampling   7-8
quota sampling   7-11
random sampling   7-5
sample proportion   7-23

sampling error   7-12
simple random sampling   7-5
snowball sampling   7-12
standard error of the mean   7-18
standard error of the proportion   7-23
stratified random sampling   7-8
systematic sampling   7-9
two-stage sampling   7-10

Formulas

(7.1) Determining the value of k

$$k = \frac{N}{n}$$

(7.2) z formula for sample means

$$z = \frac{\bar{x} - \mu}{\frac{\sigma}{\sqrt{n}}}$$

(7.3) z formula for sample means of a finite population

$$z = \frac{\bar{x} - \mu}{\frac{\sigma}{\sqrt{n}} \sqrt{\frac{N-n}{N-1}}}$$

(7.4) Sample proportion

$$\hat{p} = \frac{x}{n}$$

(7.5) z formula for sample proportions

$$z = \frac{\hat{p} - p}{\sqrt{\frac{p \cdot q}{n}}}$$

Supplementary Problems

Calculating the Statistics

7.29 **Video** The mean of a population is 76 and the standard deviation is 14. The shape of the population is unknown. Determine the probability of each of the following occurring from this population.

a. A random sample of size 35 yielding a sample mean of 79 or more

b. A random sample of size 140 yielding a sample mean of between 74 and 77

c. A random sample of size 219 yielding a sample mean of less than 76.5

7.30 Forty-six percent of a population possesses a particular characteristic. Random samples are taken from this population. Determine the probability of each of the following occurrences.

a. The sample size is 60 and the sample proportion is between 0.41 and 0.53.

b. The sample size is 458 and the sample proportion is less than 0.40.

c. The sample size is 1,350 and the sample proportion is greater than 0.49.

Testing Your Understanding

7.31 Suppose the age distribution in a city is as follows.

Under 18	22%
18–25	18%
26–50	36%
51–65	10%
Over 65	14%

An analyst is conducting proportionate stratified random sampling with a sample size of 250. Approximately how many people should he sample from each stratum?

7.32 Candidate Liu believes he will receive 0.55 of the total votes cast in his riding. However, in an attempt to validate this figure, his pollster contacts a random sample of 600 registered voters in the riding. The poll results show that 298 of the voters say they are committed to voting for him. If he actually has 0.55 of the total vote, what is the probability of getting a sample proportion this small or smaller? Do you think he actually has 55% of the vote? Why or why not?

7.33 Determine a possible frame for conducting random sampling in each of the following studies.

a. The average amount of overtime per week for production workers in a plastics company in Manitoba

b. The average number of employees in all Safeway supermarkets in British Columbia

c. A survey of commercial lobster catchers in Newfoundland

7.34 A particular automobile costs an average of $21,755 in British Columbia. The standard deviation of prices is $650. Suppose a random sample of 30 dealerships in Vancouver and Victoria is taken, and their managers are asked what they charge for this automobile. What is the probability of getting a sample average cost of less than $21,500? Assume that only 120 dealerships in all of British Columbia sell this automobile.

7.35 A company has 1,250 employees, and you want to take a simple random sample of $n = 60$ employees. Explain how you would go about selecting this sample by using the table of random numbers. Are there numbers that you cannot use? Explain.

7.36 Suppose the average client charge per hour for out-of-court work by lawyers in Saskatchewan is $125. Suppose further that a random telephone sample of 32 lawyers in Saskatchewan is taken and that the sample average charge per hour for out-of-court work is $110. If the population variance is $525, what is the probability of getting a sample mean of $110 or larger? What is the probability of getting a sample mean larger than $135 per hour? What is the probability of getting a sample mean of between $120 and $130 per hour?

7.37 **Video** A survey of 2,645 consumers by DDB Needham Worldwide showed that how a company handles a crisis when at fault is one of the top influences in consumer buying decisions, with 73% claiming it is an influence. Quality of product was the number one influence, with 96% of consumers stating that quality influences their buying decisions. How a company handles complaints was number two, with 85% of consumers reporting it as an influence in their buying decisions. Suppose a random sample of 1,100 consumers is taken and each is asked which of these three factors influences their buying decisions.

a. What is the probability that more than 810 consumers claim that how a company handles a crisis when at fault is an influence in their buying decisions?

b. What is the probability that fewer than 1,030 consumers claim that quality of product is an influence in their buying decisions?

c. What is the probability that between 82% and 84% of consumers claim that how a company handles complaints is an influence in their buying decisions?

7.38 Suppose you are sending out questionnaires to a randomly selected sample of 100 managers. The frame for this study is the membership list of the Board of Trade. The questionnaire contains demographic questions about the company and its top manager. In addition, it asks questions about the manager's leadership style. Research assistants are to score and enter the responses into the computer as soon as they are received. You are to conduct a statistical analysis of the data. Name and describe four nonsampling errors that could occur in this study.

7.39 A business analyst is conducting a study of Loblaw supermarkets across the country. How can she use cluster or area sampling to take a random sample of employees of this firm?

7.40 A directory of personal computer retail outlets in Canada contains 12,080 alphabetized entries. Explain how systematic sampling could be used to select a sample of 300 outlets.

7.41 In an effort to cut costs and improve profits, many companies have been turning to outsourcing. In fact, according to *Purchasing* magazine, 54% of companies surveyed outsourced some part of their manufacturing process in the past two to three years. Suppose 565 of these companies are contacted.

a. What is the probability that 339 or more companies outsourced some part of their manufacturing process in the past two to three years?

b. What is the probability that 288 or more companies outsourced some part of their manufacturing process in the past two to three years?

c. What is the probability that 50% or less of these companies outsourced some part of their manufacturing process in the past two to three years?

7.42 The average rent of a one-bedroom apartment in a town is $850 per month. What is the probability of randomly selecting a sample of 50 one-bedroom apartments in this town and getting a sample mean of less than $830 if the population standard deviation is $100?

7.43 According to the International Atomic Energy Agency, electricity per-capita consumption in Canada was 16,621 kWh in 2016.[5] A random sample of 51 households was monitored for one year to determine electricity usage. If the population standard deviation of annual usage is 3,500 kWh, what is the probability that the sample mean will be each of the following?

a. More than 18,000 kWh

b. More than 17,500 kWh

c. Between 17,000 kWh and 18,000 kWh

d. Less than 16,000 kWh

e. Less than 15,000 kWh

7.44 Use Table A.1 to select 20 three-digit random numbers. Did any of the numbers occur more than once? How is it possible for a number to occur more than once? Make a stem and leaf plot of the numbers with the stem being the left digit. Do the numbers seem to be equally distributed, or are they bunched together?

7.45 Marketing companies are turning to mobile media for new opportunities. A recent study by IBM showed that 46% of all marketers conduct transactions on mobile websites. Suppose a random sample of 300 marketing companies is taken.

a. What is the probability that between 114 and 153 (inclusive) marketing companies are using a mobile website?

b. What is the probability that 51% or more of marketing companies are using a mobile website?

c. Suppose a random sample of 800 marketing companies is taken. Now what is the probability that 51% or more are using a mobile website? How does this answer differ from the answer in part (b)? Why do the answers differ?

7.46 Suppose that 20% of all people 16 years of age or older do volunteer work. Further suppose that women volunteer slightly more than men, with 22% of women volunteering and 19% of men volunteering. What is the probability of randomly sampling 140 women 16 years of age or older and getting 35 or more who do volunteer work? What is the probability of getting 21 or fewer from this group? Suppose a sample of 300 men and women 16 years of age or older is selected randomly from the population. What is the probability that the sample proportion of those who do volunteer work is between 18% and 25%?

7.47 Suppose you work for a large firm that has 20,000 employees. The CEO calls you in and asks you to determine employee attitudes toward the company. She is willing to commit $100,000 to this project. What are the advantages of taking a sample versus conducting a census? What are the tradeoffs?

7.48 In a particular area in the Prairies, an estimated 75% of the homes use heating oil as the principal heating fuel during the winter. A random telephone survey of 150 homes is taken in an attempt to determine whether this figure is correct. Suppose 120 of the 150 homes surveyed use heating oil as the principal heating fuel. What is the probability of getting a sample proportion this large or larger if the population estimate is true?

7.49 According to Statistics Canada, the average hourly wages in the manufacturing sector are as follows: Alberta: $26.50, Ontario: $24.69, British Columbia: $26.47.[6] Suppose 40 workers are selected randomly from across Alberta and asked what their hourly wage is. What is the probability that the sample average will be between $25 and $26? Suppose 35 manufacturing workers are selected randomly from across Ontario. What is the probability that the sample average will exceed $27? Suppose 50 manufacturing workers are selected randomly from across British Columbia. What is the probability that the sample average will be less than $24.90? Assume that in all three provinces, the standard deviation of hourly wages is $3.

7.50 Give a variable that could be used to stratify the population for each of the following studies. List at least four subcategories for each variable.

a. A political party wants to conduct a poll prior to an election for the premier of New Brunswick

---

[5]International Atomic Energy Agency, "Country Nuclear Power Profiles: Canada," updated 2018, cnpp.iaea.org/countryprofiles/Canada/Canada.htm.

[6]Statistics Canada, Table 14-10-0206-01 "Average Hourly Earnings for Employees Paid by the Hour, by Industry, Annual," www150.statcan.gc.ca/t1/tbl1/en/tv.action?pid=1410020601.

b. A soft drink company wants to take a sample of soft drink purchases in an effort to estimate market share

c. A retail outlet wants to interview customers over a one-week period

d. An eyeglasses manufacturer and retailer wants to determine the demand for prescription eyeglasses in its marketing region

7.51 **Video** A survey shows that a typical business traveller spends an average of $280 per day in Toronto. This cost includes hotel, meals, car rental, and incidentals. A survey of 60 randomly selected business travellers who have been to Toronto on business recently is taken. For the population mean of $280 per day, what is the probability of getting a sample average of more than $270 per day if the population standard deviation is $50?

Exploring the Databases with Business Analytics   *see* the databases on the Student Website and in *WileyPLUS*

1. Consider the Canadian RRSP Contribution Database. Compute the population mean and standard deviation for the annual median RRSP contribution. Now take a random sample of 32 years of median RRSP contributions. Compute the sample mean.

Using techniques presented in this chapter, determine the probability of getting a sample mean that is less than the calculated sample mean. Work this problem both with and without the finite correction factor and compare the results by discussing the differences in answers.

Case

3M

The 3M company is a global innovation company with over 100,000 patents, $31.7 billion in sales, and 91,000 employees. 3M has 27 business units organized under five business groups: consumer, electronics and energy, health care, industrial, and safety and graphics. It has 46 technology platforms, including adhesives, abrasives, electronics and software, light management, microreplication, nanotechnology, nonwoven materials, and surface modification. Related to this, 3M has 8,500 analysts worldwide, and its products are sold in nearly 200 countries. Included in 3M's more widely known products are Scotch® Tape, Post-it® Notes, and Ace™ bandages.

3M was born as a small-scale mining company in 1902 when the five founders invested in harvesting a mineral known as corundum from a mine in Minnesota on the shores of Lake Superior. The mine ultimately did not produce much corundum, but the company used a spirit of innovation, collaboration, and technology to discover other materials and products that could be of use to consumers and companies. In 1910, the company, then known as Minnesota Mining and Manufacturing (3M), moved its headquarters to St. Paul, where it is today. In the early 1920s, 3M created the world's first waterproof sandpaper, which helped open up opportunities for the company in the automotive industry. In 1925, a young lab assistant invented masking tape, thereby helping to diversify the company's offering. Over the next few decades, many of the "Scotch™" products were developed and marketed, including Scotch® Tape, Scotchlite™, and Scotchgard™. In the 1960s, 3M introduced dry-silver microfilm, photographic products, carbonless papers, overhead projection systems, and numerous health-care and dental products. In 1980, 3M introduced Post-it® Notes, creating a new category in the marketplace. By the year 2000, there were new products such as Post-it® Super Sticky Notes, Scotch® Transparent Duct Tape, optical films for LCD televisions, and a family of new Scotch-Brite™ Cleaning Products. In 2009, 3M introduced a new line of stethoscopes in health care, and introduced new products in the grinding industry. In later years, 3M developed 3M® Solar Mirror Film 1100 for concentrated solar power.

Today, one-third of 3M's sales come from products invented within the past 5 years, during which time over $8 billion has been invested in R&D and related expenditures. According to company information sources, the global 3M team is committed to creating the technology and products that advance every company, enhance every home, and improve every life.

Discussion

1. 3M has developed the 3M™ Value Index Score, which provides a standard metric to assess accountable value in health care. This index score is a composite measure based on six critical primary care domains derived from 16 measures of key processes and outcomes that effect value in health care. According to 3M, this Value Index Score can increase the understanding of provider and system performance, thereby prioritizing the areas where improvement is needed and accelerating that improvement. This measure can be used by both providers and payers to help improve patient outcomes and to control costs. Suppose you were asked to develop a sampling plan for a study to determine the value of the index, usage rates of the index, and general attitudes toward the index. What sampling plan would you use? What is the target population (or are there multiple target populations)? What might you use for the frame(s)? Which of the four types of random sampling discussed in the chapter would you use and why? If you were to use stratified random sampling, what would be your strata?

2. In 2009, the Global Strategy Group conducted an online survey, commissioned by Scotch® Tape, in which they asked adults in the United States about their personal gift-wrapping behaviours and trends. One finding was that the average number of presents wrapped by adults in a typical December holiday season is 15.3. In addition, the study found that women wrap more presents than men, with women averaging 20.3 and men averaging 9.9. Suppose that the figures obtained from the sample are true for the entire Canadian population, and that the standard deviation for all adults, women and men, is 4.5. If a random sample of 35 Canadian adults is taken, what is the probability that the sample mean number of presents wrapped in a typical December holiday season is more than 16? If a random sample of 60 Canadian men is taken, what is the probability that the sample mean number of presents wrapped by a man in a typical December holiday season is more than 9? If a random sample of 43 Canadian women is taken, what is the

probability that the sample mean number of presents wrapped by a woman in a typical December holiday season is between 20 and 22?

3. In 2015, 3M commissioned a survey conducted by Wakefield Research regarding colour quality in electronic devices (phones, tablets, notebook PCs, and LCD TVs). Among the results of the survey are that 62% of device owners wish there was better colour quality on their display devices, 29% want more realistic colours, 18% want bolder colours, and 14% want richer dark colours. Assume these figures are true for the general population of device owners. If a random sample of 450 device owners is taken, what is the probability that more than 65% wish there was better colour quality on their display devices? If a random sample of 270 device owners is taken, what is the probability that 25% or fewer want more realistic colours? If a random sample of 950 device owners is taken, what is the probability that between 152 and 200 want bolder colours?

Source: Adapted from information at the 3M website, www.3m.com/3M/en_US/company-us/all-3m-products.

Big Data Case

In Chapter 7, we want to research the American Hospital Association (AHA) database using the sampling distributions of both the sample mean and the sample proportion. Do this by exploring the following:

1. Calculate the mean number of Personnel in the database. Letting this mean represent the population mean for all hospitals, and using a population standard deviation of 500, what is the probability of randomly selecting 40 hospitals and the sample mean number of personnel being between 700 and 900?

2. Determine the proportion of hospitals that are under the control of non-governmental not-for-profit organizations (category 4). Assume that this proportion represents the entire population of all hospitals. If you randomly selected 500 hospitals from across the United States, what is the probability that 17% or more are under the control of non-governmental not-for-profit organizations? If you randomly selected 100 hospitals, what is the probability that less than 11% are under the control of non-governmental not-for-profit organizations?

Using the Computer

- Random numbers can be generated from Excel for several different distributions, including the binomial distribution, the Poisson distribution, the uniform distribution, and the normal distribution. To generate random numbers from a particular distribution, begin by selecting the **Data** tab on the Excel worksheet. From the **Analyze** panel at the right top of the **Data** tab worksheet, click on **Data Analysis**. If your Excel worksheet does not show the **Data Analysis** option, then you can load it as an add-in following the directions given in Chapter 2. From the **Data Analysis** dialogue box, select **Random Number Generation**.

- In the **Random Number Generation** dialogue box, enter the number of columns of values you want to produce into **Number of Variables**.

- Next, enter the number of data points to be generated in each column into **Number of Random Numbers**.

- The third line of the dialogue box, **Distribution**, contains the choices of distributions. Select from which of the following distributions you want to generate random data: **discrete**, **uniform**, **normal**, **Bernoulli**, **binomial**, **Poisson**, and **patterned**.

- The options and required responses in the **Random Number Generation** dialogue box will change with the chosen distribution.

CHAPTER 8

Statistical Inference: Estimation for Single Populations

LEARNING OBJECTIVES

The overall learning objective of Chapter 8 is to understand estimating parameters of single populations, thereby enabling you to:

8.1 Estimate the population mean with a known population standard deviation with the z statistic, correcting for a finite population if necessary.

8.2 Estimate the population mean with an unknown population standard deviation using the t statistic and properties of the t distribution.

8.3 Estimate a population proportion using the z statistic.

8.4 Use the chi-square distribution to estimate the population variance given the sample variance.

8.5 Determine the sample size needed in order to estimate the population mean and population proportion.

Decision Dilemma

Batteries and Bulbs: How Long Do They Last?

What is the average life of a battery? As you can imagine, the answer depends on the type of battery, what it is used for, and how it is used. Car batteries are different from iPhone batteries, which are different from flashlight batteries. Nevertheless, a few statistics are available on the life of batteries.

For example, according to Apple, an iPhone 7 Plus has up to 16 days of life if kept in standby, without making any calls or running any applications. In one study, several smartphones were tested to determine battery life. In the test, the phones continually surfed the net until they died. The average battery life without recharge for the brand with the top battery life was 15 hours 35 minutes, with other brands varying from 11 hours 26 minutes to 15 hours 19 minutes. According to another study, the average battery life of a laptop computer is 10.44 hours, and a laptop computer battery should last through around 500 charges. The typical AA battery, used in such things as flashlights, digital cameras, etc., will last 4.3 hours in constant use. According to a source at

DBURKE/Alamy Stock Photo

the Canadian Automobile Association in Ontario, Canada's cold winters can be a factor in the average life expectancy of a car battery. The typical life span is three to five years, but extreme cold, or extreme heat, can shorten that. According to BatteryStuff.com, only 30% of car batteries make it to age four before dying.

The life of a light bulb varies with the type of bulb. For example, the typical incandescent bulb lasts between 1,000 and 2,000 hours. One source says that the average life of an incandescent 60-watt bulb is 1.4 years based on a 3-hours-per-day usage (1,533 hours). The estimated yearly energy cost of such a bulb is $7.79. Another source says that the average lifespan of a compact fluorescent light (CFL) is about 8,000 hours, and light-emitting diodes (LEDs) have a lifespan of approximately 25,000 hours. In terms of switching over from traditional light bulbs to LEDs, 70% of Socket Survey respondents said they have purchased at least one LED bulb for their home. However, many of these respondents use a variety of types of bulbs including incandescent light bulbs.

Managerial, Statistical, and Analytical Questions

1. According to a study mentioned here, the average battery life of a laptop computer is 10.44 hours. Undoubtedly, this figure was obtained by testing a sample of laptops. Suppose the 10.44-hour average was obtained by sampling 60 tablet computers. If a second sample of 60 tablet computers was selected, do you think that the average battery life would also be 10.44 hours? How could this figure be used to estimate the average battery life of all laptop computers?

2. One source says that the average life of an incandescent 60-watt bulb is 1.4 years based on a 3-hours-per-day usage (1,533 hours). Do you think that the 1,533 hours figure was obtained from a sample or from the population of all incandescent 60-watt bulbs? What are the reasons for your answer? Suppose the 1,533-hour figure was computed from a sample of 41 light bulbs. How could it be used to estimate the average number of hours of burn for all 60-watt bulbs?

3. According to BatteryStuff.com, only 30% of car batteries make it to age four before dying. If this figure was obtained by studying 280 car batteries over a four-year period, how could these results be used to estimate the percentage of all car batteries that make it to age four before dying?

4. According to Socket Survey, 70% of respondents said that they use LED light bulbs in their home. Suppose there were 900 respondents in this survey; how could the results be used to estimate the percentage for all homes?

Sources: Philip Michaels, "Smartphones with the Longest Battery Life," Tom's Guide, July 26, 2019, www.tomsguide.com/us/ smartphones-best-battery-life,review-2857.html; Dan Ackerman, "The 35 Best Battery Life Laptops for 2019," CNET, May 24, 2019, www.cnet. com/news/best-battery-life-laptops-for-2019/; Tyler Lacoma, "How to Care for Your Laptop's Battery and Extend Its Life," Digital Trends, March 25, 2019, www.digitaltrends.com/computing/how-to-care-for-your-laptops-battery/; Jennifer Warnick and Shawn Maclauchlan, "Which Batteries Last Longest?" WWBT NBC 12, June 27, 2012, www.nbc12.com/story/18276282/which-batteries-last-longest/; "Winter Driving Tips: Is That Battery About to Die?" CBC News, January 2, 2014, www.cbc.ca/amp/1.2481968; 3 Signs That You Need a New Car Battery," Canada Drives, November 14, 2016, www.canadadrives. ca/blog/maintenance-tips/3-signs-that-you-need-a-new-car-battery; "Battery Basics: A Layman's Guide to Batteries," BatteryStuff.com, www.batterystuff.com/kb/articles/battery-articles/battery-basics.html; Eric A. Taub, "How Long Did You Say That Bulb Would Last?," *New York Times*, February 11, 2009, bits.blogs.nytimes.com/2009/02/11/ how-long-did-you-say-that-bulb-will-last/; "Electricity Usage of an Incandescent Light Bulb," Energy Use Calculator, energyusecalculator. com/electricity_incandescent.htm; Holly Johnson, "Light Bulb Showdown: LED vs. CFL vs. Incandescent," The Simple Dollar, December 13, 2017, www.thesimpledollar.com/the-light-bulb-showdown-leds-vs-cfls-vs-incandescent-bulbs-whats-the-best-deal-now-and-in-the-future/; "SYLVANIA Socket Survey Shows Rise of Smart Lighting," Sylvania website, July 12, 2016, www.sylvania.com/en-us/ newsroom/press-releases/Pages/2016-Socket-Survey.aspx.

Introduction

In this text, Chapters 8 to 11 present, discuss, and apply various statistical techniques for making inferential estimations and hypothesis tests to enhance decision-making in business. Figure B.1 in Appendix B displays a tree diagram taxonomy of these techniques, organizing them by usage, sample size, and level of data. Chapter 8 contains the portion of these techniques that can be used for estimating a mean, a proportion, or a variance for a population with a single sample. Displayed in **Figure 8.1** is the leftmost branch of the tree diagram taxonomy in Figure B.1. This branch of the tree contains all statistical techniques for constructing confidence intervals from one-sample data presented in this text. Note that at the bottom of each tree branch in Figure 8.1, the title of the statistical technique along with its respective section number is given for ease of identification and use.

In Chapter 8, techniques are presented that allow a business analyst to estimate a population mean, proportion, or variance by taking a sample from the population, analyzing the data from the sample, and projecting the resulting statistics back onto the population. Because it is often extremely difficult to obtain and analyze population data for a variety of reasons (mentioned in Chapter 7), the importance of the ability to estimate population parameters from sample statistics cannot be underestimated. **Figure 8.2** depicts this process. If a business analyst is estimating a population mean and the population standard deviation is known, he will use the z confidence interval for μ contained in Section 8.1. If the population standard deviation is unknown, and the analyst is using the sample standard deviation, the

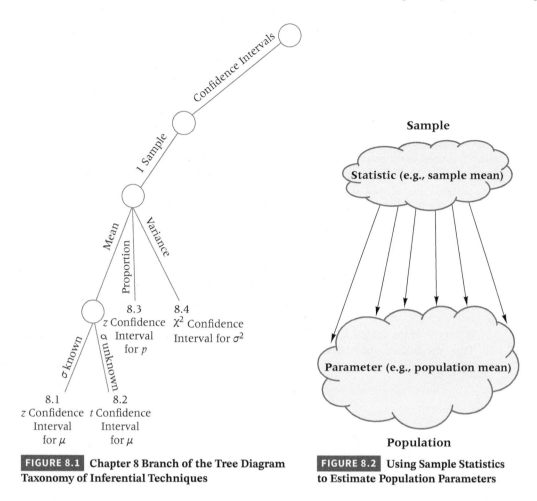

FIGURE 8.1 Chapter 8 Branch of the Tree Diagram Taxonomy of Inferential Techniques

FIGURE 8.2 Using Sample Statistics to Estimate Population Parameters

appropriate technique is the *t* confidence interval for μ contained in Section 8.2. If another business analyst is estimating a population proportion, she will use the *z* confidence interval for *p* presented in Section 8.3. If the analyst wants to estimate a population variance with a single sample, she will use the χ^2 confidence interval for σ^2 presented in Section 8.4. Section 8.5 contains techniques for determining how large a sample to take in order to ensure a given level of confidence within a targeted level of error.

8.1 | Estimating the Population Mean Using the *z* Statistic (σ Known)

LEARNING OBJECTIVE 8.1

Estimate the population mean with a known population standard deviation with the *z* statistic, correcting for a finite population if necessary.

On many occasions, estimating the population mean is useful in business research. For example, the manager of human resources in a company might want to estimate the average number of days of work an employee misses per year because of illness. If the firm has thousands of employees, direct calculation of a population mean such as this may be practically impossible. Instead, a random sample of employees can be taken, and the sample mean number of sick days can be used to estimate the population mean. Suppose another company develops a new process for prolonging the shelf life of a loaf of bread. The company wants to be able to date each loaf for freshness, but company officials do not know exactly how long the bread will stay fresh. By taking a random sample and determining the sample mean shelf life, they can estimate the average shelf life for the population of bread.

As the mobile phone industry has grown and matured, it is apparent that the use of texting has increased dramatically. Suppose that a large mobile phone company wishing to meet the needs of its users hires a business research company to estimate the average number of text messages used per month by Canadians in the 35-to-54-year age bracket. The research company studies the phone records of 85 randomly sampled Canadians in the 35-to-54-years-of-age category and computes a sample monthly mean of 1,300 texts. This mean, which is a statistic, is used to estimate the population mean, which is a parameter. If the mobile phone company uses the sample mean of 1,300 texts as an estimate for the population mean, the same sample mean is used as a point estimate.

A **point estimate** is *a statistic taken from a sample that is used to estimate a population parameter*. Note that a point estimate is only as good as the representativeness of its sample. If other random samples are taken from the population, the point estimates derived from those samples are likely to vary. Because of variation in sample statistics, estimating a population parameter with an interval estimate is often preferable to using a point estimate. An **interval estimate (confidence interval)** is *a range of values within which the analyst can declare, with some confidence, that the population parameter lies*. How are confidence intervals constructed?

As a result of the central limit theorem, the following z formula for sample means can be used if the population standard deviation is known when sample sizes are large, regardless of the shape of the population distribution, or for smaller sizes if the population is normally distributed:

$$z = \frac{\bar{x} - \mu}{\frac{\sigma}{\sqrt{n}}}$$

Rearranging this formula algebraically to solve for μ gives

$$\mu = \bar{x} - z\frac{\sigma}{\sqrt{n}}$$

Because a sample mean can be greater than or less than the population mean, z can be positive or negative. Thus, the preceding expression takes the following form:

$$\bar{x} \pm z\frac{\sigma}{\sqrt{n}}$$

Rewriting this expression yields the confidence interval formula for estimating μ with large sample sizes if the population standard deviation is known.

$100(1 - \alpha)\%$ Confidence Interval to Estimate μ: σ Known

$$\bar{x} \pm z_{\alpha/2}\frac{\sigma}{\sqrt{n}} \qquad (8.1)$$

or

$$\bar{x} - z_{\alpha/2}\frac{\sigma}{\sqrt{n}} \leq \mu \leq \bar{x} + z_{\alpha/2}\frac{\sigma}{\sqrt{n}}$$

where

α = the area under the normal curve outside the confidence interval area
$\alpha/2$ = the area in one end (tail) of the distribution outside the confidence interval

---

Alpha (α) is the area under the normal curve in the tails of the distribution outside the area defined by the confidence interval. We will focus more on α in Chapter 9. Here we use α to locate the z value in constructing the confidence interval, as shown in **Figure 8.3**. Because the standard normal table is based on areas between a z of 0 and $z_{\alpha/2}$, the table z value is found by locating the area of $0.5000 - \alpha/2$, which is the part of the normal curve between the middle of the curve and one of the tails. Another way to locate this z value is to change the confidence level from percentage to proportion, divide it in half, and go to the table with this value. The results are the same.

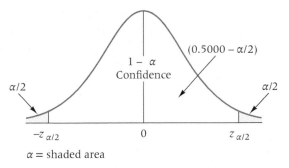

FIGURE 8.3 *z* Scores for Confidence Intervals in Relation to *α*

The confidence interval formula yields a range (interval) within which we feel with some confidence the population mean is located. It is not certain that the population mean is in the interval unless we have a 100% confidence interval that is infinitely wide. If we want to construct a 95% confidence interval, the level of confidence is 95% or 0.95. If 100 such intervals are constructed by taking random samples from the population, it is likely that 95 of the intervals would include the population mean and 5 would not.

As an example, in the mobile phone company's effort to estimate the population monthly mean number of texts in the 35-to-54-year-old age category, from a sample of 85 bills it is determined that the sample mean is 1,300 texts. Using this sample mean, a confidence interval can be calculated within which the analyst is relatively confident that the actual population mean is located. To make this calculation using the formula, the value of the population standard deviation and the value of *z* (in addition to the sample mean, 1,300, and the sample size, 85) must be known. Suppose that history and similar studies indicate that the population standard deviation is about 160.

The value of *z* is driven by the level of confidence. An interval with 100% confidence is so wide that it is meaningless. Some of the more common levels of confidence used by business analysts are 90%, 95%, 98%, and 99%. Why would a business analyst not just select the highest confidence and always use that level? The reason is that tradeoffs between sample size, interval width, and level of confidence must be considered. For example, as the level of confidence is increased, the interval gets wider, provided the sample size and standard deviation remain constant.

For the cellphone problem, suppose the business analyst decided on a 95% confidence interval for the results. **Figure 8.4** shows a normal distribution of sample means about the population mean. When using a 95% level of confidence, the analyst selects an interval centred on μ within which 95% of all sample mean values will fall and then uses the width of that interval to create an interval around the *sample mean* within which he has some confidence the population mean will fall.

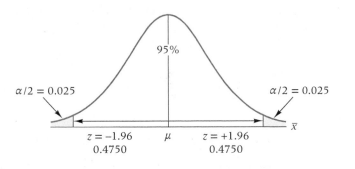

FIGURE 8.4 Distribution of Sample Means for 95% Confidence

For 95% confidence, $\alpha = 0.05$ and $\alpha/2 = 0.025$. The value of $z_{\alpha/2}$ or $z_{0.025}$ is found by looking in the standard normal table (Table A.5) under $0.5000 - 0.0250 = 0.4750$. This area in the table is associated with a *z* value of 1.96. The table *z* value can be located in another way. Because the distribution is symmetric and the intervals are equal on each side of the population mean, ½(95%), or 0.4750, of the area is on each side of the mean. Table A.5 yields a *z* value of

1.96 for this portion of the normal curve. Thus, the z value for a 95% confidence interval is always 1.96. In other words, of all the possible $\bar{x}$ values along the horizontal axis of the diagram, 95% of them should be within a z score of 1.96 on either side of the population mean.

The business analyst can now complete the mobile phone problem. To determine a 95% confidence interval for $\bar{x} = 1,300$, $\sigma = 160$, $n = 85$, and $z = 1.96$, the analyst estimates the average monthly number of texts by including the value of z in the confidence interval formula:

$$1300 - 1.96 \frac{160}{\sqrt{85}} \leq \mu \leq 1300 + 1.96 \frac{160}{\sqrt{85}}$$

$$1300 - 34.01 \leq \mu \leq 1300 + 34.01$$

$$1265.99 \leq \mu \leq 1334.01$$

From this interval, the research company can conclude with 95% confidence that the population mean number of texts per month in the 35-to-54-year-old age category is between 1,265.99 texts and 1,334.01 texts. Note that actually the confidence interval is constructed from two values, the point estimate (1,300), and another value (34.01) that is added to and subtracted from the point estimate. This value, 34.01, or $\pm 1.96 \frac{160}{\sqrt{85}}$, is the **margin of error of the interval** and is *the distance between the statistic computed to estimate a parameter and the parameter.* The margin of error takes into account the desired level of confidence, sample size, and standard deviation. When *the margin of error is added to the point estimate, the result* is the **upper bound of the confidence interval**. When *the margin of error is subtracted from the point estimate, the result* is the **lower bound of the confidence interval**.

All confidence intervals presented in this text are constructed from the point estimate plus and minus the margin of error as shown in **Figure 8.5**.

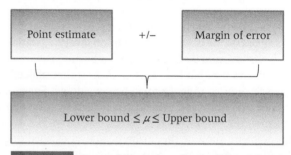

FIGURE 8.5 **General Structure of a Confidence Interval**

What does being 95% confident that the population mean is in an interval actually indicate? It indicates that, if the company analyst were to randomly select 100 samples of 85 bills and use the results of each sample to construct a 95% confidence interval, approximately 95 of the 100 intervals would contain the population mean. It also indicates that 5% of the intervals would not contain the population mean. The company analyst is likely to take only a single sample and compute the confidence interval from that sample information. That interval either contains the population mean or it does not. **Figure 8.6** depicts the meaning of a 95% confidence interval for the mean. Note that if 20 random samples are taken from the population, 19 of the 20 are likely to contain the population mean if a 95% confidence interval is used (19/20 = 95%). If a 90% confidence interval is constructed, only 18 of the 20 intervals are likely to contain the population mean.

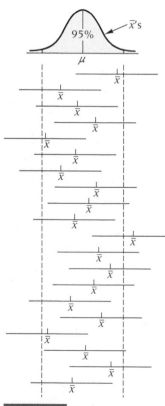

FIGURE 8.6 **Twenty 95% Confidence Intervals of μ**

DEMONSTRATION PROBLEM 8.1

A survey was taken of companies that do business with firms in India. One of the questions on the survey was "Approximately how many years has your company been trading with firms in India?" A random sample of 44 responses to this question yielded a mean of 10.455 years. Suppose the population standard deviation for this question is 7.7 years. Using this information, construct a 90% confidence interval for the mean number of years that a company has been trading in India for the population of companies trading with firms in India.

The z formulas presented in Section 8.1 are inappropriate for use when the population standard deviation is unknown (and is replaced by the sample standard deviation). Instead, another mechanism to handle such cases was developed by a British statistician, William S. Gosset.

Gosset was born in 1876 in Canterbury, England. He studied chemistry and mathematics and in 1899 went to work for the Guinness Brewery in Dublin, Ireland. Gosset was involved in quality control at the brewery, studying variables such as raw materials and temperature. Because of the circumstances of his experiments, Gosset conducted many studies where the population standard deviation was unavailable. He discovered that using the standard z test with a sample standard deviation produced inexact and incorrect distributions. This finding led to his development of the distribution of the sample standard deviation and the t test.

Gosset was a student and close personal friend of Karl Pearson (who established the discipline of mathematical statistics in the early 1900s). When Gosset's first work on the t test was published, he used the pen name "Student." As a result, the t test is sometimes referred to as the Student's t test. Gosset's contribution was significant because it led to more exact statistical tests, which some scholars say marked the beginning of the modern era in mathematical statistics.[1]

The t Distribution

Gosset developed the **t distribution** family, *which is used instead of the z distribution for performing inferential statistics on the population mean when the population standard deviation is unknown and the population is normally distributed.* The formula for the t statistic is:

$$t = \frac{\bar{x} - \mu}{\frac{s}{\sqrt{n}}}$$

This formula is essentially the same as the z formula, but the distribution table values are different. The t distribution values are contained in Table A.6.

The t distribution is actually a series of distributions because every sample size has a different distribution, thereby creating the potential for many t tables. To make these **t values** more manageable, only select key values are presented; each line in the table contains values from a different t distribution. An assumption underlying the use of the t statistic is that the population is normally distributed. If the population distribution is not normal or is unknown, nonparametric techniques (presented in Chapter 17) should be used.

Robustness

Most statistical techniques have one or more underlying assumptions. If a statistical technique is *relatively insensitive to minor violations in one or more of its underlying assumptions*, the technique is said to be **robust** to that assumption (which is a desirable property). The t statistic for estimating a population mean is relatively robust to the assumption that the population is normally distributed.

Some statistical techniques are not robust, and a statistician should exercise extreme caution to be certain that the assumptions underlying a technique are being met before using it or interpreting statistical output resulting from its use. A business analyst should always be aware of statistical assumptions and the robustness of techniques being used in an analysis.

Characteristics of the t Distribution

Figure 8.8 displays two t distributions superimposed on the standard normal distribution. Like the standard normal curve, t distributions are symmetric and unimodal.

---

[1] Adapted from Arthur L. Dudycha and Linda W. Dudycha, "Behavioral Statistics: An Historical Perspective," in *Statistical Issues: A Reader for the Behavioral Sciences*, Roger Kirk, ed. (Monterey, CA: Brooks/Cole, 1972).

FIGURE 8.8 Comparison of Two *t* Distributions to the Standard Normal Curve

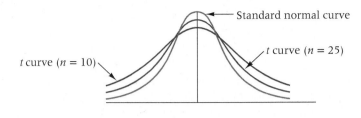

Standard normal curve

t curve (*n* = 25)

t curve (*n* = 10)

The *t* distributions are flatter in the middle and have more area in their tails than the standard normal distribution.

An examination of *t* distribution values reveals that the *t* distribution approaches the standard normal curve as *n* becomes large. The *t* distribution is the appropriate distribution to use any time the population variance or standard deviation is unknown, regardless of sample size, so long as it is known that the population of interest is normally distributed.

Reading the *t* Distribution Table

To find a value in the *t* distribution table requires knowing the degrees of freedom; each different value of degrees of freedom (df) is associated with a different *t* distribution. The *t* distribution shown in Table 8.2 is a compilation of many *t* distributions, with each line of the table having different degrees of freedom and containing *t* values for different *t* distributions. The degrees of freedom for the *t* statistic presented in this section are computed by $n - 1$. The term **degrees of freedom** refers to *the number of independent observations for a source of variation minus the number of independent parameters estimated in computing the variation.*[2] In this case, one independent parameter, the population mean, μ, is being estimated by $\bar{x}$ in computing *s*. Thus, the degrees of freedom formula is *n* independent observations minus one independent parameter being estimated ($n - 1$). Because the degrees of freedom are computed differently for various *t* formulas, a degrees of freedom formula is given along with each *t* formula in the text.

In Table A.6, the degrees of freedom are located in the left column. The *t* distribution table in this text does not use the area between the statistic and the mean, as does the *z* distribution (standard normal distribution). Instead, the *t* table uses the area in the tail of the distribution. The emphasis in the *t* table is on α, and each tail of the distribution contains $\alpha/2$ of the area under the curve when confidence intervals are constructed. For confidence intervals, the table *t* value is found in the column under the value of $\alpha/2$ and in the row of the degrees of freedom (df) value.

For example, if a 90% confidence interval is being computed, the total area in the two tails is 10%. Thus, α is 0.10 and $\alpha/2$ is 0.05, as indicated in **Figure 8.9**. The *t* distribution table shown in **Table 8.2** contains only six values of $\alpha/2$ (0.10, 0.05, 0.025, 0.01, 0.005, 0.001). The *t* value is located at the intersection of the df value and the selected $\alpha/2$ value. So, if the degrees of freedom for a given *t* statistic are 24 and the desired $\alpha/2$ value is 0.05, the *t* value is 1.711.

FIGURE 8.9 Distribution with α for 90% Confidence

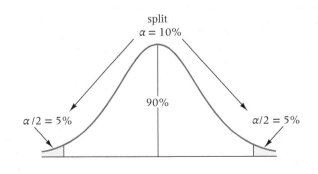

split
$\alpha = 10\%$

90%

$\alpha/2 = 5\%$

$\alpha/2 = 5\%$

[2] Roger E. Kirk, *Experimental Design: Procedures for the Behavioral Sciences* (Belmont, CA: Brooks/Cole Publishing Company, 1968).

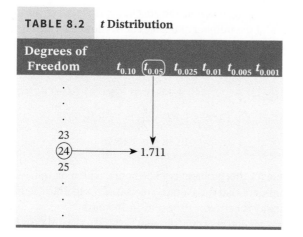

TABLE 8.2   *t* **Distribution**

Degrees of Freedom	$t_{0.10}$	$t_{0.05}$	$t_{0.025}$	$t_{0.01}$	$t_{0.005}$	$t_{0.001}$
.						
.						
.						
23						
24		1.711				
25						
.						
.						
.						

Confidence Intervals to Estimate the Population Mean Using the *t* Statistic

The *t* formula

$$t = \frac{\bar{x} - \mu}{\frac{s}{\sqrt{n}}}$$

can be manipulated algebraically to produce a formula for estimating the population mean when σ is unknown and the population is normally distributed. The results are the formulas given next.

> **Confidence Interval to Estimate μ: Population Standard Deviation Unknown and the Population Normally Distributed**
>
> $$\bar{x} \pm t_{\alpha/2,n-1}\frac{s}{\sqrt{n}}$$
>
> $$\bar{x} - t_{\alpha/2,n-1}\frac{s}{\sqrt{n}} \le \mu \le \bar{x} + t_{\alpha/2,n-1}\frac{s}{\sqrt{n}} \qquad (8.3)$$
>
> $$\mathrm{df} = n - 1$$

This formula can be used in a manner similar to the methods presented in Section 8.1 for constructing a confidence interval to estimate μ. For example, some companies allow their employees to accumulate extra working hours beyond their 40-hour week. These extra hours are sometimes referred to as *green* time, or *comp* time. Many managers work longer than the 8-hour workday preparing proposals, overseeing crucial tasks, and taking care of paperwork. Recognition of such overtime is important. Managers are often not paid extra for this work, but a record is kept of this time and occasionally the manager is allowed to use some of this comp time as extra leave or vacation time. Suppose an analyst wants to estimate the average amount of comp time accumulated per week for managers at a company. He randomly samples 18 managers, measures the amount of extra time they work during a specific week, and obtains the results shown (in hours).

6	21	17	20	7	0	8	16	29
3	8	12	11	9	21	25	15	16

He constructs a 90% confidence interval to estimate the average amount of extra time per week worked by a manager. He assumes that comp time is normally distributed in the population. The sample size is 18, so df = 17. A 90% level of confidence results in $\alpha/2 = 0.05$ area in each tail. The table *t* value is:

$$t_{0.05,17} = 1.740$$

The subscripts in the t value denote the area in the right tail of the t distribution (for confidence intervals $\alpha/2$) and the number of degrees of freedom. The sample mean is 13.56 hours, and the sample standard deviation is 7.8 hours. The confidence interval is computed from this information as:

$$\bar{x} \pm t_{\alpha/2,n-1}\frac{s}{\sqrt{n}}$$

$$13.56 \pm 1.740\frac{7.8}{\sqrt{18}} = 13.56 \pm 3.20$$

$$10.36 \leq \mu \leq 16.76$$

The point estimate for this problem is 13.56 hours, with a margin of error of ± 3.20 hours. The analyst is 90% confident that the average amount of comp time accumulated by a manager per week at this company is between 10.36 and 16.76 hours.

From these figures, managers could attempt to build a reward system for such extra work or evaluate the regular 40-hour week to determine how to use the normal work hours more effectively and thus reduce comp time.

DEMONSTRATION PROBLEM 8.3

The owner of a large equipment rental company wants to make a quick estimate of the average number of days a piece of ditch-digging equipment is rented out per person per time. The company has records of all rentals, but the amount of time required to conduct an audit of *all* accounts would be prohibitive. The owner decides to take a random sample of rental invoices. Fourteen different rentals of ditch-diggers are selected randomly from the files, yielding the following data. The owner uses these data to construct a 99% confidence interval to estimate the average number of days that a ditch-digger is rented, assuming that the number of days per rental is normally distributed in the population.

$$3 \quad 1 \quad 3 \quad 2 \quad 5 \quad 1 \quad 2 \quad 1 \quad 4 \quad 2 \quad 1 \quad 3 \quad 1 \quad 1$$

Solution Because $n = 14$, df $= 13$. The 99% level of confidence results in $\alpha/2 = 0.005$ area in each tail of the distribution. The table t value is:

$$t_{0.005,13} = 3.012$$

The sample mean is 2.14 and the sample standard deviation is 1.29. The confidence interval is:

$$\bar{x} \pm t_{\alpha/2,n-1}\frac{s}{\sqrt{n}}$$

$$2.14 \pm 3.012\frac{1.29}{\sqrt{14}} = 2.14 \pm 1.04$$

$$1.10 \leq \mu \leq 3.18$$

The point estimate of the average length of time per rental is 2.14 days, with a margin of error of ± 1.04. With a 99% level of confidence, the company's owner can estimate that the average length of time per rental is between 1.10 and 3.18 days. Combining this figure with variables such as frequency of rentals per year can help the owner estimate potential profit or loss per year for such a piece of equipment.

	A	B	C
1	Sample Mean	13.56	
2	Sample Standard Deviation	7.8	
3	Sample Size	18	
4	Alpha	0.1	
5	Calculated Margin of Error	3.20	=CONFIDENCE.T(B4,B2,B3)

FIGURE 8.10 **Excel Output for the Comp Time Example**

Using the Computer to Construct t Confidence Intervals for the Mean

Excel can be used to construct confidence intervals for μ using the t distribution. **Figure 8.10** displays the Excel output for the comp time problem. The Excel output calculates the margin of error using the sample mean, sample standard deviation, sample size, and significance level. The width of the confidence interval can then be calculated using the sample mean and margin of error.

Concept Check

1. When is it appropriate to use the confidence interval based on the *t* distribution for the population mean?
2. List two important properties of the *t* distribution.
3. What is the behaviour of t_α and $t_{\alpha/2}$ as the number of degrees of freedom describing a *t* distribution increases?

8.2 Problems

8.13 Suppose the following data are selected randomly from a population of normally distributed values.

40	51	43	48	44	57	54
39	42	48	45	39	43	

Construct a 95% confidence interval to estimate the population mean.

8.14 Assuming *x* is normally distributed, use the following information to compute a 90% confidence interval to estimate μ.

313	320	319	340	325	310
321	329	317	311	307	318

8.15 If a random sample of 41 items produces $\bar{x} = 128.4$ and $s = 20.6$, what is the 98% confidence interval for μ? Assume *x* is normally distributed for the population. What is the point estimate?

8.16 A random sample of 15 items is taken, producing a sample mean of 2.364 with a sample variance of 0.81. Assume *x* is normally distributed and construct a 90% confidence interval for the population mean.

8.17 Use the following data to construct a 99% confidence interval for μ. Assume *x* is normally distributed. What is the point estimate for μ?

16.4	17.1	17.0	15.6	16.2
14.8	16.0	15.6	17.3	17.4
15.6	15.7	17.2	16.6	16.0
15.3	15.4	16.0	15.8	17.2
14.6	15.5	14.9	16.7	16.3

8.18 According to Runzheimer International, the average cost of a domestic trip for business travellers in the financial industry is $1,250. Suppose another travel industry research company takes a random sample of 51 business travellers in the financial industry and determines that the sample average cost of a domestic trip is $1,192, with a sample standard deviation of $279. Construct a 98% confidence interval for the population mean from these sample data. Assume that the data are normally distributed in the population. Now go back and examine the $1,250 figure published by Runzheimer International. Does it fall into the confidence interval computed from the sample data? What does this tell you?

8.19 A valve manufacturer produces a butterfly valve composed of two semicircular plates on a common spindle that permits flow in one direction only. The semicircular plates are supplied by a vendor with specifications that the plates be 2.37 mm thick. A random sample of 20 such plates is taken. Electronic calipers are used to measure the thickness of each plate; the measurements are given here. Assuming that the thicknesses of such plates are normally distributed, use the data to construct a 95% level of confidence for the population mean thickness of these plates. What is the point estimate? How much is the error of the estimate?

2.4066	2.4579	2.6724	2.1228	2.3238
2.1328	2.0665	2.2738	2.2055	2.5267
2.5937	2.1994	2.5392	2.4359	2.2146
2.1933	2.4575	2.7956	2.3353	2.2699

8.20 Some fast-food chains offer a lower-priced combination meal in an effort to attract budget-conscious customers. One chain test-marketed a burger, fries, and drink combination for $4.71. The weekly sales volume for these meals was impressive. Suppose the chain wants to estimate the average amount its customers spent on a meal at their restaurant while this combination offer was in effect. An analyst gathers data from 28 randomly selected customers. The following data represent the sample meal totals.

$6.21 $8.40 $6.50 $7.39 $8.60 $11.65 $8.02 $7.20 $4.25 $10.64
6.28   6.57   6.26   6.80   8.46   12.87   7.67   8.86   6.73   7.08
8.47   7.49   8.19   8.82 10.62   7.83 11.42 12.10

Use these data to construct a 90% confidence interval to estimate the population mean value. Assume the amounts spent are normally distributed.

8.21 The marketing director of a large department store wants to estimate the average number of customers who enter the store every five minutes. She randomly selects five-minute intervals and counts the number of arrivals at the store. She obtains the figures 58, 32, 41, 47, 56, 80, 45, 29, 32, and 78. The analyst assumes the number of arrivals is normally distributed. Using these data, the analyst computes a 95% confidence interval to estimate the mean value for all five-minute intervals. What interval values does she get?

8.22 Runzheimer International publishes results of studies on overseas business travel costs. Suppose as part of one of these studies the following per diem travel accounts (in dollars) are obtained for 14 business travellers staying in Johannesburg, South Africa. Use these data to construct a 98% confidence interval to estimate the average per diem expense for business people travelling to Johannesburg. What is the point estimate? Assume per diem rates for any locale are approximately normally distributed.

$142.59 $148.48 $159.63 $171.93 $146.90 $168.87 $141.94
159.09   156.32   142.49   129.28   151.56   132.87   178.34

8.23 How much experience do supply-chain transportation managers have in their field? Suppose in an effort to estimate this, 41 supply-chain transportation managers are surveyed and asked how many years of managerial experience they have in transportation. Survey results (in years) are shown below. Use these data to construct a 99% confidence interval to estimate the mean number of years of experience in transportation. Assume that years of experience in transportation are normally distributed in the population.

5	8	10	21	20	25	14	6	19	3
1	9	11	2	3	13	2	4	9	4
5	4	21	7	6	3	28	17	32	2
25	8	13	17	27	7	3	15	4	16
6									

8.24 Cycle time in manufacturing can be viewed as the total time it takes to complete a product from the beginning of the production process. The concept of cycle time varies according to the industry and the product or service being offered. Suppose a boat manufacturing company wants to estimate the mean cycle time it takes to produce a 16-foot skiff. A random sample of such skiffs is taken, and the cycle times (in hours) are recorded for each skiff in the sample. The data are analyzed using Excel and the results are shown below in hours. What is the point estimate for cycle time? How large was the sample size? What is the level of confidence and what is the confidence interval? What is the margin of error of the confidence interval?

	A	B
1	**Hours of Cycle Time**	
2	Observations	26
3	Sample mean	25.4134
4	Sample standard deviation	5.3369
5	Margin of error	2.601

8.3 | Estimating the Population Proportion

LEARNING OBJECTIVE 8.3

Estimate a population proportion using the z statistic.

Business decision-makers and analysts often need to be able to estimate a population proportion. For example, what proportion of the market does our company control (market share)? What proportion of our products is defective? What proportion of customers will call customer service with complaints? What proportion of our customers is in the 20-to-40-year age group? What proportion of our workers speaks French as a first language? (See Thinking Critically About Statistics in Business Today 8.2)

Thinking Critically About Statistics in Business Today 8.2

Coffee Consumption in Canada

It has been reported that 81% of Canadians drink coffee occasionally and over 63% of Canadians over the age of 18 drink coffee on a daily basis. This makes coffee the number one beverage of choice for adult Canadians, other than water. Daily coffee consumption, however, varies across Canada, from a high of 70% in Quebec to a low of just over 53% in the Atlantic region. Around 60% of adults in Ontario, 67% in the Prairies, and 61% in British Columbia drink coffee on a daily basis.

Canadian coffee drinkers consume an average of 2.6 cups of coffee per day. Men and women are equally likely to be coffee consumers, with men drinking slightly more coffee than women. Nearly 51% of coffee is consumed at breakfast, 16% in the balance of the morning, 9% at lunch, 10% in the afternoon, 8% at dinner, and 7% in the evening.

Coffee is mostly consumed at home: 66%. Around 12% is consumed at work, 16% is consumed or purchased at eating establishments, and 5% is consumed in other places such as hospitals, schools, hockey rinks, and other institutions.

Around 79% of the coffee consumed at home is purchased at a grocery store or supermarket, with 7% being purchased at a gourmet/specialty coffee shop. The share of total coffee consumption accounted for by instant coffee is 17%. Around 9% of coffee consumers drink decaffeinated coffee on a regular basis.

How does Canadian consumption of coffee compare with that in other countries? The Canadian per-capita consumption of coffee is 4 kg, compared with 4.2 kg in the U.S., 5.56 kg in Europe in general, and 11.4 kg in Finland.

Because much of the information presented here was gleaned from surveys, virtually all of the percentages and means are sample statistics and not population parameters. Thus, what are presented as coffee population statistics are actually point estimates. Using the sample size and a level of confidence, confidence intervals can be constructed for the proportions. Confidence intervals for means can be constructed from these point estimates if the value of the standard deviation is known or can be calculated.

Things to Ponder

1. Canadian coffee drinkers consume an average of 2.6 cups of coffee per day. What might be some reasons why, on average, a Canadian consumes much less coffee than a Finnish person?

2. Note that the figures reported here are based on a 95% confidence interval with a ±4 percentage error, including both means and percentages. In what ways do the statistics in this report tie in to the information presented in this chapter?

Methods similar to those in Section 8.1 can be used to estimate the population proportion. The central limit theorem for sample proportions led to the following formula in Chapter 7:

$$z = \frac{\hat{p} - p}{\sqrt{\frac{p \cdot q}{n}}}$$

where $q = 1 - p$. Recall that this formula can be applied only when $n \cdot p$ and $n \cdot q$ are greater than 5.

Algebraically manipulating this formula to estimate p involves solving for p. However, p is in both the numerator and the denominator, which complicates the resulting formula. For this reason—for confidence interval purposes only and for large sample sizes—$\hat{p}$ is substituted for p in the denominator, yielding

$$z = \frac{\hat{p} - p}{\sqrt{\frac{\hat{p} \cdot \hat{q}}{n}}}$$

where $\hat{q} = 1 - \hat{p}$. Solving for p results in the confidence interval in the formula below.[3]

Confidence Interval to Estimate p

$$\hat{p} - z_{\alpha/2} \sqrt{\frac{\hat{p} \cdot \hat{q}}{n}} \leq p \leq \hat{p} + z_{\alpha/2} \sqrt{\frac{\hat{p} \cdot \hat{q}}{n}} \qquad (8.4)$$

where

$\hat{p}$ = sample proportion
$\hat{q} = 1 - \hat{p}$
p = population proportion
n = sample size

In this formula, $\hat{p}$ is the point estimate and $\pm z_{\alpha/2} \sqrt{\frac{\hat{p} \cdot \hat{q}}{n}}$ is the margin of error of the estimate. **Figure 8.11** underscores this structure.

As an example, a study of 87 randomly selected companies with a telemarketing operation revealed that 39% of the sampled companies used telemarketing to assist them in order processing. Using this information, how could an analyst estimate the *population* proportion of telemarketing companies that use their telemarketing operation to assist them in order processing?

The sample proportion, $\hat{p} = 0.39$, is the *point estimate* of the population proportion, p. For $n = 87$ and $\hat{p} = 0.39$, a 95% confidence interval can be computed to determine the

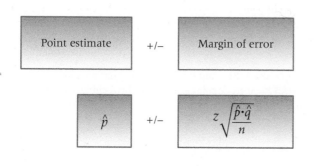

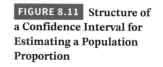

FIGURE 8.11 Structure of a Confidence Interval for Estimating a Population Proportion

---

[3] Because we are not using the true standard deviation of $\hat{p}$, the correct divisor of the standard error of $\hat{p}$ is $n - 1$. However, for large sample sizes, the effect is negligible. Although technically the minimal sample size for the techniques presented in this section is $n \cdot p$ and $n \cdot q$ greater than 5, in actual practice sample sizes of several hundred are more commonly used. As an example, for $\hat{p}$ and $\hat{q}$ of 0.50 and $n = 300$ the standard error of $\hat{p}$ is 0.02887 using n and 0.02892 using $n - 1$, a difference of only 0.00005.

interval estimation of p. The z value for 95% confidence is 1.96. The value of $\hat{q} = 1 - \hat{p} = 1 - 0.39 = 0.61$. The confidence interval estimate is

$$0.39 - 1.96\sqrt{\frac{(0.39)(0.61)}{87}} \le p \le 0.39 + 1.96\sqrt{\frac{(0.39)(0.61)}{87}}$$

$$0.39 - 0.10 \le p \le 0.39 + 0.10$$

$$0.29 \le p \le 0.49$$

This interval suggests that the population proportion of telemarketing firms that use their operation to assist order processing is somewhere between 0.29 and 0.49, based on the point estimate of 0.39 with a margin of error of ± 0.10. This result has a 95% level of confidence.

DEMONSTRATION PROBLEM 8.4

In a survey of 210 chief executives of fast-growing small companies, only 51% of the executives had a management succession plan in place. It was concluded that many companies do not worry about management succession unless it is an immediate problem. However, the unexpected exit of a corporate leader can disrupt and unfocus a company for long enough to cause it to lose its momentum.

Use the data given to compute a 92% confidence interval to estimate the proportion of *all* fast-growing small companies that have a management succession plan.

Solution The point estimate is the sample proportion given to be 0.51. It is estimated that 0.51, or 51%, of all fast-growing small companies have a management succession plan. Realizing that the point estimate might change with another sample selection, we calculate a confidence interval.

The value of n is 210, $\hat{p}$ is 0.51, and $\hat{q} = 1 - \hat{p} = 0.49$. Because the level of confidence is 92%, the value of $z_{0.04} = 1.75$. The confidence interval is computed as

$$0.51 - 1.75\sqrt{\frac{(0.51)(0.49)}{210}} \le p \le 0.51 + 1.75\sqrt{\frac{(0.51)(0.49)}{210}}$$

$$0.51 - 0.06 \le p \le 0.51 + 0.06$$

$$0.45 \le p \le 0.57$$

It is estimated with 92% confidence that the proportion of the population of fast-growing small companies that have a management succession plan is between 0.45 and 0.57.

DEMONSTRATION PROBLEM 8.5

A clothing company produces men's jeans. The jeans are made and sold with either a regular cut or a boot cut. In an effort to estimate the proportion of the men's jeans market in Kingston, Ontario, that consists of boot-cut jeans, the analyst takes a random sample of 212 jeans sales from the company's two Kingston retail outlets. Only 34 of the sales were for boot-cut jeans. Construct a 90% confidence interval to estimate the proportion of the population in Kingston who purchase boot-cut jeans.

Solution The sample size is 212, and the number purchasing boot-cut jeans is 34. The sample proportion is $\hat{p} = 34/212 = 0.16$. A point estimate for boot-cut jeans in the population is 0.16, or 16%. The z value for a 90% level of confidence is 1.645, and the value of $\hat{q} = 1 - \hat{p} = 1 - 0.16 = 0.84$. The confidence interval estimate is:

$$0.16 - 1.645\sqrt{\frac{(0.16)(0.84)}{212}} \le p \le 0.16 + 1.645\sqrt{\frac{(0.16)(0.84)}{212}}$$

$$0.16 - 0.04 \le p \le 0.16 + 0.04$$

$$0.12 \le p \le 0.20$$

The analyst estimates that the population proportion of boot-cut jeans purchases is between 0.12 and 0.20. The level of confidence in this result is 90%.

Concept Check

1. Provide a couple of business examples where the confidence interval of the population proportion might be useful.
2. Explain how the standard error of the population proportion behaves as the sample size n increases.

8.3 Problems

8.25 Use the information about each of the following samples to compute the confidence interval to estimate p.

    a. $n = 44$ and $\hat{p} = 0.51$; compute a 99% confidence interval.

    b. $n = 300$ and $\hat{p} = 0.82$; compute a 95% confidence interval.

    c. $n = 1{,}150$ and $\hat{p} = 0.48$; compute a 90% confidence interval.

    d. $n = 95$ and $\hat{p} = 0.32$; compute an 88% confidence interval.

8.26 Use the following sample information to calculate the confidence interval to estimate the population proportion. Let x be the number of items in the sample with the characteristic of interest.

    a. $n = 116$ and $x = 57$, with 99% confidence

    b. $n = 800$ and $x = 479$, with 97% confidence

    c. $n = 240$ and $x = 106$, with 85% confidence

    d. $n = 60$ and $x = 21$, with 90% confidence

8.27 Suppose a random sample of 85 items has been taken from a population and 40 of the items contain the characteristic of interest. Use this information to calculate a 90% confidence interval to estimate the proportion of the population that has the characteristic of interest. Calculate a 95% confidence interval. Calculate a 99% confidence interval. As the level of confidence changes and the other sample information stays constant, what happens to the confidence interval?

8.28 The Universal Music Group is the music industry leader worldwide in sales according to the company website. Suppose an analyst wants to determine what market share the company holds in Burnaby, B.C., by randomly selecting 1,003 people who purchased music last month. In addition, suppose 25.5% of the purchases made by these people were for music distributed by the Universal Music Group. Based on these data, construct a 99% confidence interval to estimate the proportion of the music sales market in Burnaby that is held by the Universal Music Group. Now suppose that the survey had been taken with 10,000 people. Recompute the confidence interval and compare your results with the first confidence interval. How did they differ? What might you conclude from this about sample size and confidence intervals?

8.29 According to the Stern Marketing Group, 9 out of 10 professional women say that financial planning is more important today than it was five years ago. Where do these women go for help in financial planning? Forty-seven percent use a financial advisor (broker, tax consultant, financial planner). Twenty-eight percent use written sources such as magazines, books, and websites. Suppose these figures were obtained by taking a sample of 560 professional women who said that financial planning is more important today than it was five years ago. Construct a 95% confidence interval for the proportion of professional women who use a financial advisor. Use the percentage given in this problem as the point estimate. Construct a 90% confidence interval for the proportion of professional women who use written sources. Use the percentage given in this problem as the point estimate.

8.30 What proportion of pizza restaurants that are primarily for walk-in business have a salad bar? Suppose that, in an effort to determine this figure, a random sample of 1,250 of these restaurants across Canada is called. If 997 of the restaurants sampled have a salad bar, what is the 98% confidence interval for the population proportion?

8.31 The highway department wants to estimate the proportion of vehicles on Ontario's Highway 401 between the hours of midnight and 5 A.M. that are 18-wheel tractor trailers. The estimate will be used to determine highway repair and construction considerations and in highway patrol planning. Suppose analysts for the highway department counted vehicles at different locations on the highway for several nights during this time period. Of the 3,481 vehicles counted, 927 were 18-wheelers.

    a. Determine the point estimate for the proportion of vehicles travelling Highway 401 during this time period that are 18-wheelers.

    b. Construct a 99% confidence interval for the proportion of vehicles on Highway 401 during this time period that are 18-wheelers.

8.32 What proportion of commercial airline pilots are more than 40 years of age? Suppose an analyst has access to a list of all pilots who are members of the Air Line Pilots Association. If this list is used as a frame for the study, she can randomly select a sample of pilots, contact them, and ascertain their ages. From 89 of these pilots so selected, she learns that 48 are more than 40 years of age. Construct an 85% confidence interval to estimate the population proportion of commercial airline pilots who are more than 40 years of age.

8.33 According to Runzheimer International, in a survey of relocation administrators, 63% of all workers who rejected relocation offers did so for family considerations. Suppose this figure was obtained by using a random sample of the files of 672 workers who had rejected relocation offers. Use this information to construct a 95% confidence interval to estimate the population proportion of workers who reject relocation offers for family considerations.

8.34 Suppose a survey of 275 executives is taken in an effort to determine what qualities are most important for an effective CEO to possess. The survey participants are offered several qualities as options, one of which is "communicator." Of the surveyed respondents, 121 select "communicator" as the most important quality for an effective CEO. Use these data to construct a 98% confidence interval to estimate the population proportion of executives who believe that "communicator" is the most important quality of an effective CEO.

<table>
<tr><td>**8.4**</td><td># Estimating the Population Variance</td></tr>
</table>

LEARNING OBJECTIVE 8.4

Use the chi-square distribution to estimate the population variance given the sample variance.

At times in statistical analysis, the analyst is more interested in the population variance than in the population mean or population proportion. For example, in the total quality movement, suppliers that want to earn world-class supplier status or even those that want to maintain customer contracts are often asked to show continual reduction of variation on supplied parts. Tests are conducted with samples in efforts to determine lot variation and to determine whether variability goals are being met.

Estimating the variance is important in many other instances in business. For example, variations between airplane altimeter readings need to be minimal. It is not enough just to know that, on average, a particular brand of altimeter produces the correct altitude. It is also important for the variation between instruments to be small. Thus, measuring the variation of altimeters is critical. Parts being used in engines must fit tightly on a consistent basis. A wide variability among parts can result in a part that is too large to fit into its slots or so small that it results in too much tolerance, which causes vibrations. How can variance be estimated?

You may recall from Chapter 3 that sample variance is computed by using the formula

$$s^2 = \frac{\Sigma(x_i - \bar{x})^2}{n - 1}$$

Because sample variances are typically used as estimators or estimations of the population variance, as they are here, a mathematical adjustment is made in the denominator by using $n - 1$ to make the sample variance an unbiased estimator of the population variance.

Suppose an analyst wants to estimate the population variance from the sample variance in a manner that is similar to the estimation of the population mean from a sample mean. The *relationship of the sample variance to the population variance* is captured by the **chi-square distribution** (χ^2). The ratio of the sample variance (s^2) multiplied by $n - 1$ to the population variance (σ^2) is approximately chi-square distributed, as shown in the formula below, if the population from which the values are drawn is normally distributed.

Caution: Use of the chi-square statistic to estimate the population variance is extremely sensitive to violations of the assumption that the population is normally distributed. For that reason, some analysts do not include this technique among their statistical repertoire. Although the technique is still rather widely presented as a mechanism for constructing confidence intervals to estimate a population variance, you should proceed with extreme caution and apply the technique only in cases where the population is known to be normally distributed. We can say that this technique lacks robustness.

Like the t distribution, the chi-square distribution varies by sample size and contains a df value. The number of degrees of freedom for the chi-square formula is $n - 1$.

χ^2 **Formula for Single Variance**

$$\chi^2 = \frac{(n - 1)s^2}{\sigma^2}$$ (8.5)

$$df = n - 1$$

The chi-square distribution is not symmetrical, and its shape will vary according to the degrees of freedom. **Figure 8.12** shows the shape of chi-square distributions for three different degrees of freedom.

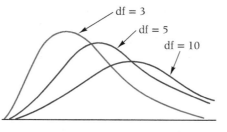

FIGURE 8.12   **Three Chi-Square Distributions**

The chi-square formula can be rearranged algebraically to produce a formula that can be used to construct confidence intervals for population variances. This new formula is shown below.

Confidence Interval to Estimate the Population Variance

$$\frac{(n-1)s^2}{\chi^2_{\alpha/2}} \leq \sigma^2 \leq \frac{(n-1)s^2}{\chi^2_{1-\alpha/2}}$$

$$df = n - 1$$

(8.6)

The value of alpha (α) is equal to 1 – (level of confidence expressed as a proportion). Thus, if we are constructing a 90% confidence interval, α is 10% of the area and is expressed in proportion form: $\alpha = 0.10$.

How can this formula be used to estimate the population variance from a sample variance? Suppose the diameters of eight purportedly 7 cm aluminum cylinders in a sample are measured, resulting in the following values:

6.91 cm	6.93 cm	7.01 cm	7.02 cm
7.05 cm	7.00 cm	6.98 cm	7.01 cm

In estimating a population variance from these values, the sample variance must be computed. This value is $s^2 = 0.0022125$. If a point estimate is all that is required, the point estimate is the sample variance, 0.0022125. However, realizing that the point estimate will probably change from sample to sample, we want to construct an interval estimate. To do this, we must know the degrees of freedom and the table values of the chi-squares. Because $n = 8$, the degrees of freedom are df $= n - 1 = 7$. What are the chi-square values necessary to complete the information needed in the formula? Assume the population of cylinder diameters is normally distributed.

Suppose we are constructing a 90% confidence interval. The value of α is $1 - 0.90 = 0.10$. It is the portion of the area under the chi-square curve that is outside the confidence interval. This outside area is needed because the chi-square table values given in Table A.8 are listed according to the area in the right tail of the distribution. In a 90% confidence interval, $\alpha/2$ or 0.05 of the area is in the right tail of the distribution and 0.05 is in the left tail of the distribution. The chi-square value for the 0.05 area in the right tail of the distribution can be obtained directly from the table by using the degrees of freedom, which in this case are 7. Thus, the right-side chi-square, $\chi^2_{0.05,7}$, is 14.0671. Because Table A.8 lists chi-square values for areas in the right tail, the chi-square value for the left tail must be obtained by determining how much area lies to the right of the left tail. If 0.05 is to the left of the confidence interval, then $1 - 0.05 = 0.95$ of the area is to the right of the left tail. This calculation is consistent with the $1 - \alpha/2$ expression used in the formula. Thus, the chi-square for the left tail is $\chi^2_{0.95,7} = 2.16735$. **Figure 8.13** shows the two table values of χ^2 on a chi-square distribution.

FIGURE 8.13 **Two Table Values of Chi-Square**

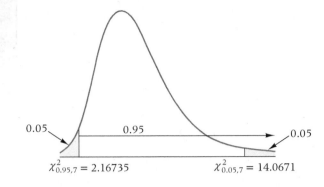

$$\chi^2_{0.95,7} = 2.16735 \qquad \chi^2_{0.05,7} = 14.0671$$

Incorporating these values into the formula, we can construct the 90% confidence interval to estimate the population variance of the 7 cm aluminum cylinders:

$$\frac{(n-1)s^2}{\chi^2_{\alpha/2}} \leq \sigma^2 \leq \frac{(n-1)s^2}{\chi^2_{1-\alpha/2}}$$

$$\frac{7(0.0022125)}{14.0671} \leq \sigma^2 \leq \frac{7(0.0022125)}{2.16735}$$

$$0.001101 \leq \sigma^2 \leq 0.007146$$

The confidence interval says that with 90% confidence, the population variance is somewhere between 0.001101 and 0.007146.

DEMONSTRATION PROBLEM 8.6

The U.S. Bureau of Labor Statistics publishes data on the hourly compensation costs for production workers in manufacturing for various countries. The latest figures published for Greece show that the average hourly wage for a production worker in manufacturing is $19.58. Suppose the business council of Greece wants to know how consistent this figure is. They randomly select 25 production workers in manufacturing from across the country and determine that the standard deviation of hourly wages for such workers is $1.12. Use this information to develop a 95% confidence interval to estimate the population variance for the hourly wages of production workers in manufacturing in Greece. Assume that the hourly wages for production workers across the country in manufacturing are normally distributed.

Solution By squaring the standard deviation, $s = 1.12$, we can obtain the sample variance, $s^2 = 1.2544$. This figure provides the point estimate of the population variance. Because the sample size, n, is 25, the degrees of freedom, $n - 1$, are 24. A 95% confidence interval means that α is $1 - 0.95 = 0.05$. This value is split to determine the area in each tail of the chi-square distribution: $\alpha/2 = 0.025$. The values of the chi-squares obtained from Table A.8 are:

$$\chi^2_{0.025,24} = 39.3641 \quad \text{and} \quad \chi^2_{0.975,24} = 12.40115$$

From this information, the confidence interval can be determined:

$$\frac{(n-1)s^2}{\chi^2_{\alpha/2}} \leq \sigma^2 \leq \frac{(n-1)s^2}{\chi^2_{1-\alpha/2}}$$

$$\frac{24(1.2544)}{39.3641} \leq \sigma^2 \leq \frac{24(1.2544)}{12.40115}$$

$$0.7648 \leq \sigma^2 \leq 2.4276$$

The business council can estimate with 95% confidence that the population variance of the hourly wages of production workers in manufacturing in Greece is between 0.7648 and 2.4276.

Concept Check

1. Why is it that some business analysts do not include the technique presented in this section for estimating the population variance among their statistical repertoire?

8.4 Problems

8.35 For each of the following sample results, construct the requested confidence interval. Assume the data come from normally distributed populations.

    a. $n = 12$, $\bar{x} = 28.4$, $s^2 = 44.9$; 99% confidence for σ^2

    b. $n = 7$, $\bar{x} = 4.37$, $s = 1.24$; 95% confidence for σ^2

    c. $n = 20$, $\bar{x} = 105$, $s = 32$; 90% confidence for σ^2

    d. $n = 17$, $s^2 = 18.56$; 80% confidence for σ^2

8.36 Use the following sample data to estimate the population variance. Produce a point estimate and a 98% confidence interval. Assume the data come from a normally distributed population.

27	40	32	41	45	29	33	39
30	28	36	32	42	40	38	46

8.37 According to Human Resources and Skills Development Canada, the average workweek in Canada was 36.5 hours. Suppose this figure was obtained from a random sample of 20 workers and that the standard deviation of the sample was 4.3 hours. Assume hours worked per week are normally distributed in the population. Use this sample information to develop a 98% confidence interval for the population variance of the number of hours worked per week for a worker. What is the point estimate?

8.38 A manufacturing plant produces steel rods. During one production run of 20,000 such rods, the specifications called for rods that were 46 cm in length and 3.8 cm in width. Fifteen of these rods making up a random sample were measured for length; the resulting measurements are shown here. Use these data to estimate the population variance of length for the rods. Assume rod length is normally distributed in the population. Construct a 99% confidence interval. Discuss the ramifications of the results.

44 cm	47 cm	43 cm	46 cm	46 cm
45 cm	43 cm	44 cm	47 cm	46 cm
48 cm	48 cm	43 cm	44 cm	45 cm

8.39 Suppose a random sample of 14 people 30 to 39 years of age produced the household incomes shown here. Use these data to determine a point estimate for the population variance of household incomes for people 30 to 39 years of age and construct a 95% confidence interval. Assume household income is normally distributed.

$37,500	$44,800
33,500	36,900
42,300	32,400
28,000	41,200
46,600	38,500
40,200	32,000
35,500	36,800

8.5 Estimating Sample Size

LEARNING OBJECTIVE 8.5

Determine the sample size needed in order to estimate the population mean and population proportion.

In most business research that uses sample statistics to make inferences about the population, being able to *estimate the size of sample necessary to accomplish the purposes of the study* is important. The need for this **sample-size estimation** is the same for the large corporation investing tens of thousands of dollars in a massive study of consumer preference and for students undertaking a small case study and wanting to send questionnaires to local business people. In either case, such things as level of confidence, sampling error, and width of estimation interval are closely tied to sample size. If the large corporation is undertaking a market study, should it sample 40 people or 4,000 people? The question is an important one. In most cases, because of cost considerations, business analysts do not want to sample any more units or individuals than necessary.

Determining Sample Size When Estimating μ

In research studies when μ is being estimated, the size of the sample can be determined by using the z formula for sample means and solving for n. Consider

$$z = \frac{\bar{x} - \mu}{\frac{\sigma}{\sqrt{n}}}$$

The difference between $\bar{x}$ and μ is the margin of error of estimation resulting from the sampling process. Let $E = \bar{x} - \mu$ be the margin of error of estimation. Substituting E into the preceding formula yields

$$z = \frac{E}{\frac{\sigma}{\sqrt{n}}}$$

Solving for n yields a formula that can be used to determine sample size.

Sample Size When Estimating μ

$$n = \frac{z_{\alpha/2}^2 \sigma^2}{E^2} = \left(\frac{z_{\alpha/2}\sigma}{E}\right)^2 \qquad\qquad (8.7)$$

Sometimes in estimating sample size, the population variance is known or can be determined from past studies. Other times, the population variance is unknown and must be estimated to determine the sample size. In such cases, it is acceptable to use the following estimate to represent σ:

$$\sigma \approx \frac{1}{4}(\text{range})$$

Using the formula for sample size, the business analyst can estimate the sample size needed to achieve the goals of the study before gathering data. For example, suppose an analyst wants to estimate the average monthly expenditure on bread by a family in Montreal. She wants to be 90% confident of her results. How much error is she willing to tolerate in the results? Suppose she wants the estimate to be within $1.00 of the actual figure, and the standard deviation of average monthly bread purchases is $4.00. What is the sample-size estimation for this problem? The value of z for a 90% level of confidence is 1.645. Using the formula with $E = \$1.00$, $\sigma = \$4.00$, and $z = 1.645$ gives

$$n = \frac{z_{\alpha/2}^2 \sigma^2}{E^2} = \frac{(1.645)(4)^2}{1^2} = 43.30$$

That is, at least $n = 43.3$ must be sampled randomly to attain a 90% level of confidence and produce an error within $1.00 for a standard deviation of $4.00. Sampling 43.3 units is impossible, so this result should be rounded up to $n = 44$ units.

In this approach to estimating sample size, we view the error of the estimate as the amount of difference between the statistic (in this case $\bar{x}$) and the parameter (in this case μ). The error could be in either direction; that is, the statistic could be over or under the parameter. Thus, the error, E, is actually $\pm E$ as we view it. So, when a problem states that the analyst wants to be within $1.00 of the actual monthly family expenditure for bread it means that the analyst is willing to allow a tolerance within $\pm\$1.00$ of the actual figure. Another name for this error is the **bounds** of the interval.

DEMONSTRATION PROBLEM 8.7

Suppose you want to estimate the average age of all Boeing 737-300 airplanes now in active domestic Canadian service. You want to be 95% confident, and you want your estimate to be within two years of the actual figure. The 737-300 was first placed in service about 28 years ago, but you believe that no active 737-300s in the Canadian domestic fleet are more than 20 years old. How large a sample should you take?

Solution Here, $E = 2$ years, the z value for 95% is 1.96, and σ is unknown, so it must be estimated by using $\sigma \approx (1/4)(\text{range})$. As the range of ages is 0 to 20 years, $\sigma = (1/4)(20) = 5$. Use the sample size formula:

$$n = \frac{z_{\alpha/2}^2 \sigma^2}{E^2} = \frac{(1.96)^2(5)^2}{2^2} = 24.01$$

Because you cannot sample 24.01 units, the required sample size is 25. If you randomly sample 25 airplanes, you have an opportunity to estimate the average age of active 737-300s within 2 years and be 95% confident of the results. If you want to be within one year for the estimate ($E = 1$), the sample-size estimate changes to

$$n = \frac{z_{\alpha/2}^2 \sigma^2}{E^2} = \frac{(1.96)^2(5)^2}{1^2} = 96.04$$

Note that cutting the error by a factor of 1/2 increases the required sample size by a factor of 4. The reason is the squaring factor in the formula. If you want to reduce the error to one half of what you used before, you must be willing to incur the cost of a sample that is four times larger, for the same level of confidence.

Note: Sample-size estimates for the population mean where σ is unknown using the t distribution are not shown here. Because a sample size must be known to determine the table value of t, which in turn is used to estimate the sample size, this procedure usually involves an iterative process.

Determining Sample Size When Estimating p

Determining the sample size required to estimate the population proportion, p, is also possible. The process begins with the z formula for sample proportions:

$$z = \frac{\hat{p} - p}{\sqrt{\frac{p \cdot q}{n}}}$$

where $q = 1 - p$.

As various samples are taken from the population, $\hat{p}$ will rarely equal the population proportion, p, resulting in an error of estimation. The difference between $\hat{p}$ and p is the margin of error of estimation, so $E = \hat{p} - p$:

$$z = \frac{E}{\sqrt{\frac{p \cdot q}{n}}}$$

Solving for n yields the formula for determining sample size.

Sample Size when Estimating p

$$n = \frac{z_{\alpha/2}^2 p \cdot q}{E^2} \tag{8.8}$$

where

  p = population proportion

  $q = 1 - p$

  E = error of estimation

  n = sample size

TABLE 8.3

$p \cdot q$ for Various Selected Values of p

p	$p \cdot q$
0.9	0.09
0.8	0.16
0.7	0.21
0.6	0.24
0.5	0.25
0.4	0.24
0.3	0.21
0.2	0.16
0.1	0.09

How can the value of n be determined prior to a study if the formula requires the value of p and the study is being done to estimate p? Although the actual value of p is not known prior to the study, similar studies might have generated a good approximation for p. If no previous value is available for use in estimating p, some possible p values, as shown in Table 8.3, might be considered.

Note that, as $p \cdot q$ is in the numerator of the sample-size formula, $p = 0.5$ will result in the largest sample sizes. Often *if p is unknown, analysts use 0.5 as an estimate of p* in the formula for sample size. This selection results in the largest sample size that could be determined from the formula for a given z value and a given error value.

DEMONSTRATION PROBLEM 8.8

Hewitt Associates conducted a national survey to determine the extent to which employers are promoting health and fitness among their employees. One of the questions asked was "Does your company offer on-site exercise classes?" Suppose it was estimated before the study that no more than 40% of the companies would answer yes. How large a sample would Hewitt Associates have to take in estimating the population proportion to ensure a 98% confidence interval in the results and to be within 0.03 of the true population proportion?

Solution   The value of E for this problem is 0.03. Because it is estimated that no more than 40% of the companies would say yes, $p = 0.40$ can be used. A 98% confidence interval results in a z value of 2.33. Inserting these values into the formula for sample size yields

$$n = \frac{(2.33)^2(0.40)(0.60)}{(0.03)^2} = 1{,}447.7$$

Hewitt Associates would have to sample 1,448 companies to be 98% confident in the results and maintain an error of 0.03.

DEMONSTRATION PROBLEM 8.9

Suppose that an analyst wants to estimate what proportion of refinery workers in Canada is contract workers. The analyst wants to be 99% confident of her results and be within 0.05 of the actual proportion. In addition, suppose that there have been no previous or similar studies to this, and therefore, the analyst has no idea what is the actual population proportion. How large a sample size should be taken?

Solution   The value of E for this problem is 0.05. The value of z for a 99% confidence interval is 2.575. Because no estimate of the population proportion is available, the analyst will use $p = 0.50$ and $q = 0.50$. Placing these values into the formula for sample size yields

$$n = \frac{(2.575)^2(0.50)(0.50)}{(0.05)^2} = 663.1$$

The analyst would have to sample at least 664 workers to attain a 99% level of confidence and produce an error no bigger than 0.05 if the population proportion is approximately 0.50.

Concept Check

1. When calculating the sample size for estimating the population mean or the population proportion, is there ever a need to take a preliminary sample? Why?

2. Should we always round up the calculated sample size n for both the population mean and the population proportion? Why or why not?

3. Why is $p = 0.5$ used to calculate the sample size when estimating the population proportion when an approximate value of the population proportion is unknown?

8.5 Problems

8.40 Determine the sample size necessary to estimate μ for the following information.

  a. $\sigma = 36$ and $E = 5$ at 95% confidence

  b. $\sigma = 4.13$ and $E = 1$ at 99% confidence

  c. Values range from 80 to 500, error is to be within 10, and the confidence level is 90%

  d. Values range from 50 to 108, error is to be within 3, and the confidence level is 88%

8.41 Determine the sample size necessary to estimate p for the following information.

  a. $E = 0.02$, p is approximately 0.40, and confidence level is 96%

  b. E is to be within 0.04, p is unknown, and confidence level is 95%

  c. E is to be within 5%, p is approximately 55%, and confidence level is 90%

  d. E is to be no more than 0.01, p is unknown, and the confidence level is 99%

8.42 A bank officer wants to determine the amount of the average total monthly deposits per customer at the bank. He believes an estimate of this average amount using a confidence interval is sufficient. How large a sample should he take to be within $200 of the actual average with 99% confidence? He assumes the standard deviation of total monthly deposits for all customers is about $1,000.

8.43 Suppose you have been following the share price of a particular airline for many years. You are interested in determining the average daily price of these shares in a 10-year period and you have access to the stock reports for these years. However, you do not want to average all the daily prices over 10 years because there are several thousand data points, so you decide to take a random sample of the daily prices and estimate the average. You want to be 90% confident of your results, you want the estimate to be within $2.00 of the true average, and you believe the standard deviation of the price of these shares is about $12.50 over this period of time. How large a sample should you take?

8.44 A group of investors wants to develop a chain of fast-food restaurants. In determining potential costs for each facility, they must consider, among other expenses, the average monthly electric bill. They decide to sample some fast-food restaurants currently operating to estimate the monthly cost of electricity. They want to be 90% confident of their results and want the error of the estimate to be no more than $100. They estimate that such bills range from $600 to $2,500. How large a sample should they take?

8.45 Suppose a production facility purchases a particular component part in large lots from a supplier. The production manager wants to estimate the proportion of defective parts received from this supplier. She believes the defective proportion is no more than 0.20 and wants to be within 0.02 of the true proportion of defective parts with a 90% level of confidence. How large a sample should she take?

8.46 What proportion of small manufacturing companies in the Greater Toronto Area has a 3D printer? You want to answer this question by conducting a random survey. How large a sample should you take if you want to be 95% confident of the results and you want the error of the confidence interval to be no more than 0.05?

8.47 What proportion of shoppers at a large appliance store actually makes a big-ticket purchase? To estimate this proportion within 10% and be 95% confident of the results, how large a sample should you take?

End-of-Chapter Review

Decision Dilemma Solved

Batteries and Bulbs: How Long Do They Last?

According to a study mentioned in the Decision Dilemma, the average battery life of a laptop computer is 10.44 hours. Assuming that this figure is not actually the population mean battery life but rather is a sample mean obtained from a sample of 60 tablet computers, we could use the sample mean, $\bar{x} = 10.44$, as a point estimate for the population mean. However, we realize that the 10.44 figure is merely a function of the particular 60 tablet computers that were selected for the study. A different sample of 60 tablet computers would likely produce a different sample mean. In order to account for this, we can compute a margin of error for this analysis, and combining it with the point estimate produce a confidence interval. Suppose the population standard deviation is 1.46 hours and that we want to be 98% confident of our results. To determine the value of z, divide the 98% confidence in half, $0.98/2 = 0.4900$. Table A.5 yields a z value of 2.33 for the area of 0.4900. Summarizing what we now know, $n = 60, \bar{x} = 10.44, \sigma = 1.46$, and $z = 2.33$. Entering these values into the formula for confidence interval to estimate μ: population standard deviation known yields

$$\bar{x} - z\frac{\sigma}{\sqrt{n}} \leq \mu \leq \bar{x} + z\frac{\sigma}{\sqrt{n}}$$

$$10.44 - 2.33\frac{1.46}{\sqrt{60}} \leq \mu \leq 10.44 - 2.33\frac{1.46}{\sqrt{60}}$$

$$10.44 - 0.44 \leq \mu \leq 10.44 - 0.44$$

$$10.00 \leq \mu \leq 10.88$$

We are 98% confident that the population mean battery life of a tablet computer is between 10.00 and 10.88 hours. The margin of error in this estimation is 0.44 hours.

One source in the Decision Dilemma says that the average life of an incandescent 60-watt bulb is 1.4 years based on a 3-hours-per-day usage (1,533 hours). It is highly unlikely that this figure is a population mean because in order to determine the population mean life of all incandescent 60-watt bulbs, company analysts would have to test all such bulbs, in which case they would be destroying all product (burning all bulbs until they quit giving light). Suppose, instead, the 1,533-hour average was computed from a sample of 41 light bulbs, in which case the 1,533-hour average life is a point estimate, not the actual population mean. Suppose also that the sample standard deviation for the 41 bulbs is 78 hours. Using these statistics, a 90% confidence interval for the average burn life for all such 60-watt incandescent bulbs can be computed.

Summarizing the sample information, $n = 41$, df = 40, $\bar{x} = 1,533$, and $s = 78$. The table t value is $t_{0.05,40} = 1.684$. From this information, we can construct the 90% confidence interval as:

$$\bar{x} - t\frac{s}{\sqrt{n}} \leq \mu \leq \bar{x} + t\frac{s}{\sqrt{n}}$$

$$1533 - 1.684\frac{78}{\sqrt{41}} \leq \mu \leq 1533 + 1.684\frac{78}{\sqrt{41}}$$

$$1533 - 20.5 \leq \mu \leq 1533 + 20.5$$

The point estimate number of hours of bulb life is 1,533 hours—the figure given in the chapter opener—with a margin of error of 20.5 hours. Combining these, we can construct the 90% confidence interval for the mean number of hours of burn of a 60-watt incandescent bulb as:

$$1512.5 \leq \mu \leq 1553.5$$

From this, analysts are 90% confident that the population mean life of a 60-watt incandescent bulb is between 1,512.5 hours and 1553.5 hours.

As presented in the Decision Dilemma, according to BatteryStuff.com, only 30% of car batteries make it to age four before dying. Suppose there were 280 car batteries in this survey. How could the results be used to estimate the percentage of all car batteries that make it to age four before dying?

Converting the 30% to a proportion of 0.30, we can construct a confidence interval to estimate the population proportion of car batteries that make it to age four before dying. The sample proportion, $\hat{p} = 0.30$, came from a sample of $n = 280$. Suppose we want the level of confidence to be 98%. To determine the value of z, divide the 98% confidence in half, $0.98/2 = 0.4900$. Table A.5 yields a z value of 2.33 for the area of 0.4900. In addition, we solve for $\hat{q}$ as $1 - \hat{p} = 1 - 0.3 = 0.7$. Entering these values into the formula for the Confidence Interval to Estimate p gives us

$$\hat{p} - z\sqrt{\frac{\hat{p} \cdot \hat{q}}{n}} \leq p \leq \hat{p} + z\sqrt{\frac{\hat{p} \cdot \hat{q}}{n}}$$

$$0.30 - 2.33\sqrt{\frac{(0.30)(0.70)}{280}} \leq p \leq 0.30 + 2.33\sqrt{\frac{(0.30)(0.70)}{280}}$$

$$0.30 - 0.06 \leq p \leq 0.30 + 0.06$$

$$0.24 \leq p \leq 0.36$$

From this, an analyst is 98% confident that if a study of all car batteries was undertaken, the actual population proportion of car batteries that make it to age four before dying would be between 0.24 and 0.36. Note that the final confidence interval is constructed from the point estimate, 0.3, and the margin of error, 0.06.

Also, according to Socket Survey, 70% of respondents said that they use LED bulbs in their home. Suppose there were 900 homes in this survey, how could the results be used to estimate the percentage for all homes?

As done previously, converting the 70% to a proportion of 0.70, we can construct a confidence interval to estimate the population proportion of homes that use LEDs. The sample proportion, $\hat{p} = 0.70$, came from a sample of $n = 900$. Suppose we want the level of confidence to be 99%. To determine the value of z, divide the 99% confidence in half, $0.99/2 = 0.4950$. Table A.5 yields a z value of 2.575 for the area of 0.4950 (interpolating between 0.4949 and 0.4951). In addition, we solve for $\hat{q}$ as $1 - \hat{p} = 1 - 0.7 = 0.3$. Entering these values into the formula for the Confidence Interval to Estimate p gives us

$$\hat{p} - z\sqrt{\frac{\hat{p} \cdot \hat{q}}{n}} \leq p \leq \hat{p} + z\sqrt{\frac{\hat{p} \cdot \hat{q}}{n}}$$

$$0.70 - 2.575\sqrt{\frac{(0.70)(0.30)}{900}} \leq p \leq 0.70 + 2.575\sqrt{\frac{(0.70)(0.30)}{900}}$$

$$0.70 - 0.04 \leq p \leq 0.70 + 0.04$$

$$0.66 \leq p \leq 0.74$$

From this, an analyst is 99% confident that if a study of all homes was undertaken, the actual population proportion of homes using LEDs would be between 0.66 and 0.74. Note that the final confidence interval is constructed from the point estimate, 0.7, and the margin of error, 0.04.

Key Considerations

Using sample statistics to estimate population parameters poses a couple of ethical concerns. Many survey reports and advertisers use point estimates as the values of the population parameter. Sometimes, no error value is stated, as would have been the case if a confidence interval had been computed. These point estimates are subject to change if another sample is taken. It is probably unethical to state as a conclusion that a point estimate is the population parameter without some sort of disclaimer or explanation about what a point estimate is.

The misapplication of t formulas when data are not normally distributed in the population is also of concern. Although some studies have shown that the t formula analyses are robust, an analyst should be careful not to violate the assumptions underlying the use of the t formulas. An even greater potential for misuse lies in using the chi-square for the estimation of a population variance, because this technique is highly sensitive to violations of the assumption that the data are normally distributed.

Why Statistics Is Relevant

The descriptive statistics presented in Chapter 3 are used to describe the basic features of the data under study in a manageable form. Together with the charts and graphs presented in Chapter 2, descriptive statistics form the basis of virtually every quantitative analysis of data.

The inferential statistics presented in this chapter, on the other hand, are used to reach conclusions that extend beyond the sample data, to make claims about the population that gave rise to the sample data that we collected, and to make inferences from our sample data to more general conditions.

For instance, Statistics Canada releases information on the unemployment rate every month. In order to generate this information, Statistics Canada samples households across Canada to determine the employment status of the members of those households. Extending beyond the sample results to generate unemployment figures that apply to different regions and to the entire country is an example of applying inferential statistics.

Chapters 8 to 11 present a variety of techniques to ensure that the inferences are sound and rational, even though they may not always be correct, since we are always dealing with the uncertainty of inferring from sample data.

Summary of Learning Objectives

Techniques for estimating population parameters from sample statistics are important tools in business analytics. Business analysts use techniques for estimating population means, techniques for estimating the population proportion and the population variance, and methodology for determining how large a sample to take.

LEARNING OBJECTIVE 8.1 Estimate the population mean with a known population standard deviation with the z statistic, correcting for a finite population if necessary.

At times in business research, a product is new or untested, or information about the population is unknown. In such cases, gathering data from a sample and making estimates about the population is useful and can be done with a point estimate or an interval estimate. A point estimate is the use of a statistic from the sample as an estimate for a parameter of the population. Because point estimates vary with each sample, it is usually best to construct an interval estimate. An interval estimate is a range of values computed from the sample within which the analyst believes with some confidence that the population parameter lies. Certain levels of confidence seem to be used more than others: 90%, 95%, 98%, and 99%. If the population standard deviation is known, the z statistic is used to estimate the population mean.

LEARNING OBJECTIVE 8.2 Estimate the population mean with an unknown population standard deviation using the t statistic and properties of the t distribution.

If the population standard deviation is unknown, the t distribution should be used instead of the z distribution. It is assumed when using the t distribution that the population from which the samples are drawn is normally distributed. However, the technique for estimating a population mean by using the t test is robust, which means it is relatively insensitive to minor violations of the assumption.

LEARNING OBJECTIVE 8.3 Estimate a population proportion using the z statistic.

Methods similar to those used to estimate a population mean when the population standard deviation is known can be used to estimate the population proportion.

LEARNING OBJECTIVE 8.4 Use the chi-square distribution to estimate the population variance given the sample variance.

The population variance can be estimated by using sample variance and the chi-square distribution. The chi-square technique for estimating the population variance is not robust; it is sensitive to violations of the assumption that the population is normally distributed. Therefore, extreme caution must be exercised in using this technique.

LEARNING OBJECTIVE 8.5 Determine the sample size needed in order to estimate the population mean and population proportion.

The formulas in Chapter 7 resulting from the central limit theorem can be manipulated to produce formulas for estimating sample size for large samples. Determining the sample size necessary to estimate a population mean, if the population standard deviation is unavailable, can be based on one fourth the range as an approximation of the population standard deviation. Determining sample size when estimating a population proportion requires the value of the population proportion. If the population proportion is unknown, the population proportion from a similar study can be used. If none is available, using a value of 0.50 will result in the largest sample-size estimation for the problem if other variables are held constant. Sample-size determination is used mostly to provide a ballpark figure to give analysts some guidance. Larger sample sizes usually result in greater costs.

Key Terms

bounds 8-24
chi-square distribution 8-20
degrees of freedom (df) 8-12
interval estimate
  (confidence interval) 8-4

lower bound of the
  confidence interval 8-6
margin of error of the interval 8-6
point estimate 8-4
robust 8-11

sample-size estimation 8-23
t distribution 8-11
t value 8-11
upper bound of the
  confidence interval 8-6

Formulas

(8.1) $100(1 - \alpha)\%$ confidence interval to estimate μ: population standard deviation known

$$\bar{x} - z_{\alpha/2}\frac{\sigma}{\sqrt{n}} \leq \mu \leq \bar{x} + z_{\alpha/2}\frac{\sigma}{\sqrt{n}}$$

(8.2) Confidence interval to estimate μ using the finite correction factor

$$\bar{x} - z_{\alpha/2}\frac{\sigma}{\sqrt{n}}\sqrt{\frac{N-n}{N-1}} \leq \mu \leq \bar{x} + z_{\alpha/2}\frac{\sigma}{\sqrt{n}}\sqrt{\frac{N-n}{N-1}}$$

(8.3) Confidence interval to estimate μ: population standard deviation unknown and the population normally distributed

$$\bar{x} - t_{\alpha/2,n-1}\frac{s}{\sqrt{n}} \leq \mu \leq \bar{x} + t_{\alpha/2,n-1}\frac{s}{\sqrt{n}}$$

$$df = n - 1$$

(8.4) Confidence interval to estimate p

$$\hat{p} - z_{\alpha/2}\sqrt{\frac{\hat{p}\cdot\hat{q}}{n}} \leq p \leq \hat{p} + z_{\alpha/2}\sqrt{\frac{\hat{p}\cdot\hat{q}}{n}}$$

(8.5) χ^2 formula for single variance

$$\chi^2 = \frac{(n-1)s^2}{\sigma^2}$$

$$df = n - 1$$

(8.6) Confidence interval to estimate the population variance

$$\frac{(n-1)s^2}{\chi^2_{\alpha/2}} \leq \sigma^2 \leq \frac{(n-1)s^2}{\chi^2_{1-\alpha/2}}$$

$$df = n - 1$$

(8.7) Sample size when estimating μ

$$n = \frac{z^2_{\alpha/2}\sigma^2}{E^2} = \left(\frac{z_{\alpha/2}\sigma}{E}\right)^2$$

(8.8) Sample size when estimating p

$$n = \frac{z^2_{\alpha/2}p\cdot q}{E^2}$$

Supplementary Problems

Calculating the Statistics

8.48 Use the following data to construct 80%, 94%, and 98% confidence intervals to estimate μ. Assume that σ is 7.75. State the point estimate.

44	37	49	30	56	48	53	42	51
38	39	45	47	52	59	50	46	34
39	46	27	35	52	51	46	45	58
51	37	45	52	51	54	39	48	

8.49 Video Construct 90%, 95%, and 99% confidence intervals to estimate μ from the following data. State the point estimate. Assume the data come from a normally distributed population.

12.3	11.6	11.9	12.8	12.5
11.4	12.0	11.7	11.8	12.3

8.50 Use the following information to compute the confidence interval for the population proportion.

a. $n = 715$ and $x = 329$, with 95% confidence

b. $n = 284$ and $\hat{p} = 0.71$, with 90% confidence

c. $n = 1,250$ and $\hat{p} = 0.48$, with 95% confidence

d. $n = 457$ and $x = 270$, with 98% confidence

8.51 Use the following data to construct 90% and 95% confidence intervals to estimate the population variance. Assume the data come from a normally distributed population.

212	229	217	216	223
219	208	214	232	219

8.52 Determine the sample size necessary under the following conditions.

a. To estimate μ with $\sigma = 44$, $E = 3$, and 95% confidence

b. To estimate μ with a range of values from 20 to 88 with $E = 2$ and 90% confidence

c. To estimate p with p unknown, $E = 0.04$, and 98% confidence

d. To estimate p with $E = 0.03$, 95% confidence, and p thought to be approximately 0.70

Testing Your Understanding

8.53 Video In planning both market opportunity and production levels, being able to estimate the size of a market can be important. Suppose a diaper manufacturer wants to know how many diapers

a one-month-old baby uses during a 24-hour period. To determine this usage, the manufacturer's analyst randomly selects 17 parents of one-month-olds and asks them to keep track of diaper usage for 24 hours. The results are shown. Construct a 99% confidence interval to estimate the average daily diaper usage of a one-month-old baby. Assume diaper usage is normally distributed.

12	8	11	9	13	14	10
10	9	13	11	8	11	15
10	7	12				

8.54 Suppose you want to estimate the proportion of cars that are sport utility vehicles (SUVs) being driven in Regina at rush hour by standing on the corner of Victoria Avenue and Albert Street and counting SUVs. You believe the figure is no higher than 0.40. If you want the error of the confidence interval to be no greater than 0.03, how many cars should you randomly sample? Use a 90% level of confidence.

8.55 Use the data in Problem 8.53 to construct a 99% confidence interval to estimate the population variance for the number of diapers used during a 24-hour period for one-month-olds. How could information about the population variance be used by a manufacturer or marketer in planning?

8.56 Companies often print their corporate policies for training purposes. What is the average length of a company's policy book? Suppose policy books are sampled from 45 medium-sized companies. The average number of pages in the sample books is 213, and the population standard deviation is 48. Use this information to construct a 98% confidence interval to estimate the mean number of pages for the population of policy books for medium-sized companies.

8.57 A random sample of small-business managers was given a leadership style questionnaire. The results were scaled so that each manager received a score for initiative. Suppose the following data are a random sample of these scores:

37	42	40	39	38	31	40
37	35	45	30	33	35	44
36	37	39	33	39	40	41
33	35	36	41	33	37	38
40	42	44	35	36	33	38
32	30	37	42			

Assuming σ is 3.891, use these data to construct a 90% confidence interval to estimate the average score on initiative for all small-business managers.

8.58 A national spa chain wants to estimate the number of times per year a woman has her nails done at one of their spas if she uses one at least once a year. The chain's analyst estimates that, of those women who use a spa at least once a year to get their nails done, the standard deviation of number of times of usage is approximately six. The national chain wants the estimate to be within one time of the actual mean value. How large a sample should the analyst take to obtain a 98% confidence level?

8.59 **Video** Is the environment a major issue with Canadians? To answer that question, an analyst conducts a survey of 1,255 randomly selected Canadians. Suppose 714 of the sampled people replied that the environment is a major issue. Construct a 95% confidence interval to estimate the proportion of Canadians who feel that the environment is a major issue. What is the point estimate of this proportion?

8.60 According to a survey by Topaz Enterprises, a travel auditing company, the average error by travel agents is $128. Suppose this figure was obtained from a random sample of 41 travel agents and the sample standard deviation is $21. What is the point estimate of the national average error for all travel agents? Compute a 98% confidence interval for the national average error based on these sample results. Assume the travel agent errors are normally distributed in the population. How wide is the interval? Interpret the interval.

8.61 A national survey on telemarketing was undertaken. One of the questions asked was "How long has your organization had a telemarketing operation?" Suppose the following data represent some of the answers received to this question (in years). Suppose further that only 300 telemarketing firms made up the population when this survey was taken. Use the following data to compute a 98% confidence interval to estimate the average number of years a telemarketing organization has had a telemarketing operation. The population standard deviation is 3.06.

5	5	6	3	6	7	5
5	6	8	4	9	6	4
10	5	10	11	5	14	7
5	9	6	7	3	4	3
7	5	9	3	6	8	16
12	11	5	4	3	6	5
8	3	5	9	7	13	4
6	5	8	3	5	8	7
11	5	14	4			

8.62 An entrepreneur wants to open an appliance repair shop. She would like to know about what the average home repair bill is, including the charge for the service call for appliance repair in the area. She wants the estimate to be within $20 of the actual figure. She believes the range of such bills is between $30 and $600. How large a sample should the entrepreneur take if she wants to be 95% confident of the results?

8.63 **Video** A national survey of insurance offices was taken, resulting in a random sample of 245 companies. Of these 245 companies, 189 responded that they were going to purchase new software for their offices in the next year. Construct a 90% confidence interval to estimate the population proportion of insurance offices that intend to purchase new software during the next year.

8.64 A national survey of companies included a question that asked whether the company had at least one bilingual telephone operator. The sample results of 90 companies follow. (Y denotes that the company does have at least one bilingual operator; N denotes that it does not.)

N	N	N	N	Y	N	Y	N	N
Y	N	N	N	Y	Y	N	N	N
N	N	Y	N	Y	N	Y	N	Y
Y	Y	N	Y	N	N	N	Y	N
N	Y	N	N	N	N	N	N	N
Y	N	Y	Y	N	N	Y	N	Y
N	N	Y	Y	N	N	N	N	N
Y	N	N	N	N	Y	N	N	N
Y	Y	Y	N	N	Y	N	N	N
N	N	N	Y	Y	N	N	Y	N

Use this information to estimate with 95% confidence the proportion of the population that does have at least one bilingual operator.

8.65 A movie theatre has had a poor accounting system. The manager has no idea how many large containers of popcorn are sold per movie showing. He knows that the amounts vary by day of the week and hour of the day. However, he wants to estimate the overall average per movie showing. To do so, he randomly selects 12 movie performances and counts the number of large containers of popcorn sold between 30 minutes before the movie showing and 15 minutes after the movie showing. The sample average is 43.7 containers, with a variance of 228. Construct a 95% confidence interval to estimate the mean number of large containers of popcorn sold during a movie showing. Assume the number of large containers of popcorn sold per movie is normally distributed in the population. Use this information to construct a 98% confidence interval to estimate the population variance.

8.66 According to a survey, the average cost of a fast-food meal (quarter-pound cheeseburger, large fries, medium soft drink, excluding taxes) in a certain city is $6.82. Suppose this figure was based on a sample of 27 different establishments and the standard deviation was $0.37. Construct a 95% confidence interval for the population mean cost for all fast-food meals in the city. Assume the costs of a fast-food meal in the city are normally distributed. Using the interval as a guide, is it likely that the population mean is really $6.50? Why or why not?

8.67 A survey of 77 commercial airline flights of under 2 hours resulted in a sample average late time for a flight of 2.48 minutes. The population standard deviation was 12 minutes. Construct a 95% confidence interval for the average time that a commercial flight of under 2 hours is late. What is the point estimate? What does the interval tell about whether the average flight is late?

8.68 A regional survey of 560 companies asked the vice president of operations how satisfied he or she was with the software support received from the company's computer staff. Suppose 33% of the 560 vice presidents said they were satisfied. Construct a 99% confidence interval for the proportion of the population of vice presidents who would have said they were satisfied with the software support if a census had been taken.

8.69 **Video** A research firm has been asked to determine the proportion of all restaurants in the province of Nova Scotia that serve alcoholic beverages. The firm wants to be 98% confident of its results but has no idea of what the actual proportion is. The firm would like to report an error of no more than 0.05. How large a sample should it take?

8.70 A national magazine marketing firm attempts to win subscribers with a mail campaign that involves a contest using magazine stickers. Often when people subscribe to magazines in this manner they sign up for multiple magazine subscriptions. Suppose the marketing firm wants to estimate the average number of subscriptions per customer of those who purchase at least one subscription. To do so, the marketing firm's analyst randomly selects 65 returned contest entries.

Twenty-seven contain subscription requests. Of the 27, the average number of subscriptions is 2.10, with a standard deviation of 0.86. The analyst uses this information to compute a 98% confidence interval to estimate μ and assumes that x is normally distributed. What does the analyst find?

8.71 **Video** A national survey showed that a certain brand of cold cuts was priced, on average, at $1.15 per 100 g. Suppose a national survey of 23 retail outlets was taken and the price per 100 g of these cold cuts was ascertained. If the following data represent these prices, what is a 90% confidence interval for the population variance of these prices? Assume prices are normally distributed in the population.

$1.14	$1.15	$1.16	$1.14	$1.17
1.14	1.13	1.16	1.15	1.13
1.11	1.14	1.16	1.15	1.14
1.15	1.12	1.15	1.15	1.17
1.15	1.14	1.14		

8.72 The price of a head of iceberg lettuce varies greatly with the season and the geographic location of a store. During February, an analyst contacts a random sample of 39 grocery stores across Canada and asks the produce manager of each to state the current price charged for a head of iceberg lettuce. Using the analyst's results that follow, construct a 99% confidence interval to estimate the mean price of a head of iceberg lettuce in February in Canada. Assume that σ is 0.205.

$1.59	$1.25	$1.65	$1.40	$0.89
1.19	1.50	1.49	1.30	1.39
1.29	1.60	0.99	1.29	1.19
1.20	1.50	1.49	1.29	1.35
1.10	0.89	1.10	1.39	1.39
1.50	1.50	1.55	1.20	1.15
0.99	1.00	1.30	1.25	1.10
1.00	1.55	1.29	1.39	

8.73 A study of 1,000 adult Canadians was undertaken in an effort to obtain information about Canadian shopping habits. One of the results of this survey was that 23% often buy items that are not on their shopping list but catch their eye. Use this study result to estimate with an 80% level of confidence the population proportion of Canadian shoppers who buy items that are not on their shopping list but catch their eye.

Interpreting the Output

8.74 A soft drink company produces a cola in a 355 ml can. Even though the machines are set to fill the cans with 355 ml, variation due to calibration, operator error, and other factors sometimes precludes the cans having the correct fill. To monitor the can fills, a quality team randomly selects some filled 355 ml cola cans and measures their fills in the lab. A 99% confidence interval for the population mean is constructed from the data. Shown here is the Excel output from this effort. Discuss the output.

	A	B
1	**Soft Drink**	
2	Count	510
3	Sample mean	354.373
4	Assumed standard deviation	1.5857
5	Margin of error	0.1809

8.75 A company has developed a new light bulb that seems to burn longer than most residential bulbs. To determine how long these bulbs burn, the company randomly selects a sample of the bulbs and burns them in the laboratory. The Excel output for a 90% confidence interval is shown here. Discuss the output.

	A	B
1	**Bulb Burn**	
2	Count	84
3	Sample mean	2198.217
4	Sample standard deviation	152.991
5	Margin of error	27.767

8.76 Suppose an analyst wants to estimate the average age of a person who is a first-time home buyer. A random sample of first-time home buyers is taken and their ages are ascertained. The Excel output for a 98% confidence interval is shown here. Study the output and explain its implications.

	A	B
1	**First-Time Home Buyer**	
2	Count	21
3	Sample mean	27.6300
4	Sample standard deviation	6.5400
5	Margin of error	3.320

Exploring the Databases with Business Analytics   *see* the databases on the Student Website and in *WileyPLUS*

1. The Financial Database contains financial data on 100 companies. Use this database as a sample and estimate Price per Share for all corporations from these data. Select several levels of confidence and compare the results.

2. Using the Financial Database with its sample of 100 companies, construct a 95% confidence interval to estimate the population proportion of companies that belong to industry type 4. State the point estimate and the error of the estimate. Change the level of confidence to 90%. What happens to the interval? Did the point estimate change?

Case

The Container Store

In the late 1970s, Kip Tindell (chairman and CEO), Garrett Boone (chairman emeritus), and John Mullen (architect) drew up plans

for a first-of-a-kind retail store specializing in storage solutions for both the home and the office. The vision that they created was realized when on July 1, 1978, the Container Store opened its doors

iStock.com/bopav

in a 1,600-square-foot retail space in Dallas. The store was stocked with products that were devoted to simplifying people's lives, such as commercial parts bins, wire drawers, mailboxes, milk crates, wire leaf burners, and many others. Some critics questioned whether a store selling "empty boxes" could survive. However, the concept took off, and in the past 40 years, the company has expanded coast to coast in the United States with stores in 90 locations. Now headquartered in Coppell, Texas, the Container Store has more than 4,000 employees and annual revenues of over $800 million. The company also maintains an e-commerce website and ships orders to customers in Canada and to international destinations.

Besides their innovative product mix, some of the keys to the success of the Container Store are the enthusiasm with which their employees work, the care that employees give to the customer, and employee knowledge of their products. For 19 straight years, the Container Store has made *Fortune* magazine's list of "100 Best Companies to Work For." Generally rated in the top 40 of this list each year, the company was number one for the first two years that it applied for consideration. The current president, Melissa Reiff, credits the company's devotion to recruiting and retaining a highly qualified workforce as one of the keys to its success. Company sources say that the Container Store offers more than 240 hours of formal training for full-time employees in the first year of employment with the company and that this compares to about 8 hours of such training with other companies in the industry. According to company sources, the Container Store believes that its employees are its number one stakeholder and "The Container Store is an absolutely exhilarating and inspiring place to shop and an equally exciting place to work."

In addition to innovative products and motivated employees, the Container Store has embraced a commitment to the environment. Chairman emeritus Garrett Boone says that it firmly believes that there is no conflict between economic prosperity and environmental stewardship. The Container Company is embracing sustainability as a key to its economic future. As part of this effort, it sells eco-friendly products, uses highly efficient HVAC units in its stores and warehouses, sponsors an employee purchase program for compact fluorescent lights, is switching from neon to LED lighting in all exterior signage, and offers an employee battery and light bulb recycling program.

Discussion

1. Among other things, the Container Store has grown and flourished because of strong customer relationships, which include listening to customer needs, selling storage products that meet customer needs, having salespeople who understand both customer needs and the products, and creating a store environment that is customer-friendly both in layout and in culture. Suppose

company management wants to formally measure customer satisfaction at least once a year and develops a brief survey that includes the following four questions. Suppose that the survey was administered to 115 customers with the following results. Use techniques presented in this chapter to analyze the data to estimate the population responses to these questions.

Question	Yes	No
1. Compared to most other stores that you shop in, is the Container Store more customer-friendly?	73	42
2. Most of the time, this store has the number and type of home or office storage solutions that I need.	81	34
3. The salespeople at this store appear to be particularly knowledgeable about their products.	88	27
4. Store hours are particularly convenient for me.	66	49

2. The Container Store is well known as a great company to work for. In addition, company management states that the employee is the number one stakeholder. Suppose in spite of its history as an employee-friendly company, management wants to measure employee satisfaction this year to determine if it is maintaining this culture. An analyst hired by the company randomly selects 21 employees and asks them to complete a satisfaction survey under the supervision of an independent testing organization. As part of this survey, employees are asked to respond to questions by providing a score from 0 to 50 along a continuous scale, where 0 denotes no satisfaction and 50 denotes the utmost satisfaction. Assume that the data are normally distributed in the population. The questions and the results of the survey are shown below. Analyze the results using techniques from this chapter. Discuss your findings.

Question	Mean	Standard Deviation
1. Are you treated fairly by the company as an employee?	42.4	5.2
2. Has the company given you the training that you need to do the job adequately?	44.9	3.1
3. Does management seriously consider your input in making decisions about the store?	38.7	7.5
4. Is your physical work environment acceptable?	35.6	9.2
5. Is the compensation for your work adequate and fair?	34.5	12.4
6. Overall do you feel that company management really cares about you as a person?	41.8	6.3

Sources: The Container Store websites, www.containerstore.com/welcome.htm, www.containerstore.com/careers/index.html, standfor.containerstore.com/; Wikipedia, s.v. "The Container Store," last modified August 6, 2019, en.wikipedia.org/wiki/The_Container_Store; Fortune 100 Best website, fortune.com/best-companies/2017/the-container-store; Jennifer Koch, "Thinking Outside the Box at The Container Store," *Workforce* magazine, February 28, 2001.

Big Data Case

In the Big Data Case for Chapter 8, we practise our confidence interval skills using the American Hospital Association database. Use this database to do the following:

1. Take a random sample of 40 of these hospitals using a systematic sample of every fiftieth hospital. Using the sample and assuming that the population standard deviation of beds is 150, construct a 95% confidence interval to estimate the mean Number of Beds for a hospital in the United States.

2. Take a different random sample of 30 of these hospitals using a simple random sample to construct a 90% confidence interval to estimate the average Census for hospitals. Assume that the population standard deviation of the Census is 110. Change the level of confidence to 99%. What happened to the interval? Did the point estimate change? Calculate the mean Census for the entire database. Did the mean Census value for the entire database fall in either one of your confidence intervals?

3. Using Excel, determine the sample proportion of the Hospital database under the variable "service" that is "general medical" (category 1). From this statistic, construct a 95% confidence interval to estimate the population proportion of hospitals that are "general medical." What is the point estimate? How much error is there in the interval?

Using the Computer

- Excel has some capability to construct confidence intervals to estimate a population mean using the z statistic when σ is known and using the t statistic when σ is unknown.

- To construct confidence intervals of a single population mean using the z statistic (σ is known), begin with the **Insert Function** (*fx*). To access the **Insert Function**, go to the **Formulas** tab on an Excel worksheet (top centre tab). The **Insert Function** is on the far left of the ribbon. In the **Insert Function** dialogue box at the top, there is a pulldown menu where it says **Or select a category**. From the pulldown menu associated with this command, select **Statistical**. Select **CONFIDENCE.NORM** from the **Insert Function's Statistical** menu. In the **CONFIDENCE.NORM** dialogue box, place the value of α (a number between 0 and 1), which equals $1 -$ level of confidence. (*Note:* level of confidence is given as a proportion and not as a percent.) For example, if the level of confidence is 95%, enter 0.05 as α. Insert the value of the population standard deviation in **Standard_dev**. Insert the size of the sample in **Size**. The output is the $\pm$ error of the confidence interval.

- To construct confidence intervals of a single population mean using the t statistic (σ is unknown), begin by selecting the **Data** tab on the Excel worksheet. From the **Analyze** panel at the right top of the **Data** tab worksheet, click on **Data Analysis**. If your Excel worksheet does not show the **Data Analysis** option, you can load it as an add-in as described in Chapter 2. From the **Data Analysis** menu, select **Descriptive Statistics**. In the **Descriptive Statistics** dialogue box, enter the location of the observations from the single sample in **Input Range**. Check **Labels** if you have a label for your data. Check **Summary Statistics**. Check **Confidence Level for Mean:** (required to get confidence interval output). If you want to change the level of confidence from the default value of 95%, enter it (in percent, between 0 and 100) in the box with the % sign beside it. The output is a single number that is the $\pm$ error portion of the confidence interval and is shown at the bottom of the **Descriptive Statistics** output as **Confidence Level**.

CHAPTER 9

Statistical Inference: Hypothesis Testing for Single Populations

LEARNING OBJECTIVES

The main objective of Chapter 9 is to help you learn how to test hypotheses on single populations, thereby enabling you to:

9.1 Develop both one- and two-tailed null and alternative hypotheses that can be tested in a business setting by examining the rejection and nonrejection regions in light of Type I and Type II errors.

9.2 Reach a statistical conclusion in hypothesis-testing problems about a population mean with a known population standard deviation using the z statistic.

9.3 Reach a statistical conclusion in hypothesis-testing problems about a population mean with an unknown population standard deviation using the t statistic.

9.4 Reach a statistical conclusion in hypothesis-testing problems about a population proportion using the z statistic.

9.5 Reach a statistical conclusion in hypothesis-testing problems about a population variance using the chi-square statistic.

9.6 Solve for possible Type II errors when failing to reject the null hypothesis.

Decision Dilemma

Business Referrals

Word-of-mouth information about products and services is exchanged on social media every day by millions of consumers, from the individual who stays at a hotel or eats at a restaurant and rates it on TripAdvisor to the social media influencers with millions following their posts on Instagram, Facebook, Twitter, and other platforms. A report issued by Roper Starch Worldwide states that influencers tend to be among the first to try new products. Over the past decade, it has become ever more important for businesses to understand the impact of such "referrals," because a positive review can potentially steer dozens of new customers to a business or product, and a negative comment can drive customers away.

According to eMarketer, social media influencer marketing "identifies and activates individuals who can sway the brand preferences, buying decisions, and loyalty of the broader population." A 2018 survey by the Association of National Advertisers (ANA) in the United States showed that 75 percent of national advertisers used

rido/123RF

influencer marketing, and 43 percent planned to increase their spending on it. An article from the Digital Marketing Institute claimed that 86% of women used social media to make purchasing decisions, and more than 50% were swayed by influencer posts; 57% of fashion and beauty companies used influencer marketing; and 60% of consumers were influenced by social media while shopping. A 2015 Minitel survey shows that 69% of Americans look online for recommendations before buying services or products. Forty-three percent seek advice when buying technology. When planning a vacation or a dinner out, 41% and 33%, respectively, seek advice and information from others.

However, studies show that most people still rely on recommendations from friends, family, and even store employees or other consumers over influencers. A July 2019 survey by Oracle shows that consumers from Gen Z (ages 18 to 24) to Baby Boomers (ages 55 to 75) are more likely to trust "Friends, family, colleagues" (93% to 86%) over "Influencers" (23% to 4%). And the Minitel survey shows that consumers consider independent review sites as the most useful (34%) and trustworthy (38%) when they're looking for information about products and services. Consumers see user review sites as useful (33%) but not as trustworthy (24%). And social media contacts are believed to be more trustworthy (31%) than useful (25%).

Managerial, Statistical, and Analytical Questions

1. Each of the figures enumerated in this Decision Dilemma was derived by studies conducted on samples and published as fact. If we wanted to challenge these figures by conducting surveys of our own, how would we go about testing these results? Are these studies dated now? Do they apply to all market segments (geographically, economically, etc.)? How could we determine whether these results apply to our market segment today?

2. The Roper Starch Worldwide study lists the mean number of recommendations made by influencers per year for different products or services, indicating that influencers make recommendations about office equipment an average of 5.8 times per year. How could we conduct our own tests to determine whether the same figure holds true for Canadians? If we randomly sampled some consumers and our mean figure did not match this figure, could we automatically conclude that their figure is not true? How much difference would we have to obtain to reject their claims? Is there a possibility that we could make an error in conducting such research?

3. Suppose you have theories regarding word-of-mouth advertising, business referrals, or influencers. How would you test the theories to determine whether they are true?

Sources: Association of National Advertisers, "Advertisers Love Influencer Marketing: ANA Study," press release, April 3, 2018, www. ana.net/content/show/id/48437; eMarketer, "Who Do US Internet Users Trust for Recommendations When Shopping?" July 30, 2019, www.emarketer.com/chart/229941/who-do-us-internet-users-trust-recommendations-shopping-of-respondents-by-generation-feb-2019; Emma Knightley, "20 Influencer Marketing Statistics That Will Surprise You," Digital Marketing Institute website, 2017, digitalmarketinginstitute.com/en-us/blog/20-influencer-marketing-statistics-that-will-surprise-you; Minitel, "Seven in 10 Americans Seek Out Opinions Before Making Purchases," June 3, 2015, www.mintel.com/press-centre/social-and-lifestyle/seven-in-10-americans-seek-out-opinions-before-making-purchases; Roper Starch Worldwide, *Influential Americans: Trendsetters of the New Millennium*, 4th ed. (New York: Roper Starch Worldwide, cosponsored by *The Atlantic Monthly*, 1995).

Introduction

A key statistical mechanism for decision-making is the hypothesis test. The concept of hypothesis testing lies at the heart of inferential statistics, and the use of statistics to prove or disprove claims hinges on the concept. With hypothesis testing, business analysts are able *to structure problems in such a way that they can use statistical evidence to test various theories about business phenomena*. Business applications of statistical hypothesis testing run the gamut from determining whether a production line process is out of control to providing conclusive evidence that a new management leadership approach is significantly more effective than an old one. With the ever-increasing quantities and sources of data, the field of business analytics holds great potential for generating new hypotheses that will need to be tested and validated.

Figure B.1 in Appendix B (Making Inferences About Population Parameters: A Brief Summary) displays a tree diagram taxonomy of inferential techniques organized by usage, number of samples, and type of statistic. While Chapter 8 contains the portion of these techniques that can be used for estimating a mean, a proportion, or a variance for a population with a single sample, Chapter 9 contains techniques used for testing hypotheses about a population mean, a population proportion, and a population variance using a single sample. The entire right side of the tree diagram taxonomy displays various hypothesis-testing techniques. The leftmost branch of this right side contains the Chapter 9 techniques (for single samples), and this branch is displayed in **Figure 9.1**. Note that at the bottom of each tree branch in Figure 9.1 the title of the statistical technique, along with its respective section number, is given for ease of identification and use. If a business analyst is testing a population mean and the population standard deviation is known, she will use the z test for μ contained in Section 9.2. If the population standard deviation is unknown and therefore the analyst is using the sample standard deviation, the appropriate technique is the t test for μ contained in Section 9.3. If the business analyst is testing a population proportion, she will use the z test for p presented in Section 9.4. If the analyst wants to test a population variance from a single sample, she will use the χ^2 test for σ^2 presented in Section 9.5. Section 9.6 contains techniques for solving for Type II errors.

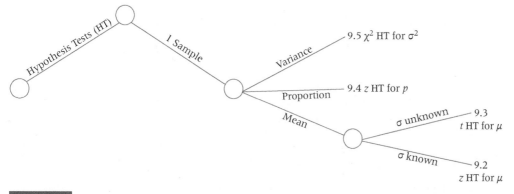

FIGURE 9.1   **Chapter 9 Branch of the Tree Diagram Taxonomy of Inferential Techniques**

9.1 | Introduction to Hypothesis Testing

LEARNING OBJECTIVE 9.1

Develop both one- and two-tailed null and alternative hypotheses that can be tested in a business setting by examining the rejection and nonrejection regions in light of Type I and Type II errors.

In the field of business, decision-makers are constantly attempting to find answers to questions such as the following:

- What container shape is most economical and reliable for shipping a product?
- Which management approach best motivates employees in the retail industry?
- How can the company's retirement investment financial portfolio be diversified for optimum performance?
- What is the best way to link client databases for fast retrieval of useful information?
- Which indicator best predicts the general state of the economy in the next six months?
- What is the most effective means of advertising in a business-to-business setting?

Business analysts are often called called on to provide insights and information to decision-makers to assist them in answering such questions. In searching for answers to questions and in attempting to find explanations for business phenomena, business analysts often develop hypotheses that can be studied and explored. Hypotheses are *tentative explanations of a principle operating in nature.*[1] In this text, we will explore various types of hypotheses, as well as methods of **hypothesis testing** and of interpreting the test results so that useful information can be brought to bear on the business decision-making process.

---

[1] Paraphrasing of definition published in *Merriam-Webster's Collegiate Dictionary*, 10th ed. (Springfield, MA: Merriam-Webster Inc.,1983).

Types of Hypotheses

Three types of hypotheses will be explored here:

1. *Research* hypotheses
2. *Statistical* hypotheses
3. *Substantive* hypotheses

Although much of the focus will be on testing statistical hypotheses, it is also important for business decision-makers to understand both research and substantive hypotheses.

Research Hypotheses

A **research hypothesis** is *a statement of what the analyst believes will be the outcome of an experiment or a study.* Before studies are undertaken, business analysts often have some idea or theory based on experience or previous work as to how the study will turn out. These ideas, theories, or notions established before an experiment or study is conducted are research hypotheses. Some examples of research hypotheses in business are:

- Older workers are more loyal to a company.
- Companies with more than $1 billion in assets spend a higher percentage of their annual budget on advertising than do companies with less than $1 billion in assets.
- The implementation of a Six Sigma quality approach in manufacturing will result in greater productivity.
- The price of scrap metal is a good indicator of the industrial production index six months later.
- Airline share prices are directly associated with the volume of OPEC oil production.

Virtually all inquisitive, thinking business people have similar research hypotheses concerning relationships, approaches, and techniques in business. Such hypotheses can lead decision-makers to new and better ways to accomplish business goals. However, to formally test research hypotheses, it is generally best to state them as statistical hypotheses.

Statistical Hypotheses

In order to scientifically test research hypotheses, a more formal hypothesis structure needs to be set up using **statistical hypotheses**. Suppose business analysts want to prove the research hypothesis that older workers are more loyal to a company. A loyalty survey instrument is either developed or obtained. If this instrument is administered to both older and younger workers, how much higher do older workers have to score on the loyalty instrument (assuming higher scores indicate more loyalty) than younger workers to prove the research hypothesis? What is the "proof threshold"? Instead of attempting to prove or disprove research hypotheses directly in this manner, business analysts convert their research hypotheses to statistical hypotheses and then test the statistical hypotheses using standard procedures.

All statistical hypotheses consist of two parts, a null hypothesis and an alternative hypothesis. These two parts are constructed to contain all possible outcomes of the experiment or study. Generally, the **null hypothesis** *states that the "null" condition exists; that is, there is nothing new happening, the old theory is still true, the old standard is correct, and the system is in control.* The **alternative hypothesis**, on the other hand, *states that the new theory is true, there are new standards, the system is out of control, and/or something is happening.* As an example, suppose flour packaged by a manufacturer is sold by mass, and a particular size of package is supposed to average 1 kg. Suppose the manufacturer wants to determine whether its packaging process is out of control as determined by the mass of the flour packages. The null hypothesis for this experiment is that the average mass of the flour packages is 1 kg (no problem). The alternative hypothesis is that the average is not 1 kg (process is out of control).

As an example, consider the flour package manufacturing example. The null hypothesis is that the average fill for the population of packages is 1 kg. Suppose a sample of 100 such packages is randomly selected, and a sample mean of 1.00025 kg is obtained. Because this mean is not 1 kg, should the business analyst decide to reject the null hypothesis? In the hypothesis-testing process, we are using sample statistics (in this case, the sample mean of 1.00025 kg) to make decisions about population parameters (in this case, the population mean of 1 kg). It makes sense that in taking random samples from a population with a mean of 1 kg, not all sample means will equal 1 kg. In fact, the central limit theorem (see Chapter 7) states that for large sample sizes, sample means are normally distributed around the population mean. Thus, even when the population mean is 1 kg, a sample mean might still be 1.00025 kg, 0.965 kg, or even 1.105 kg. However, suppose a sample mean of 1.25 kg is obtained for 100 packages. This sample mean may be so far from what is reasonable to expect for a population with a mean of 1 kg that the decision is made to reject the null hypothesis. This makes us want to know: when is the sample mean so far away from the population mean that the null hypothesis is rejected? The critical values established at Step 4 of the hypothesis-testing process are used to divide the means that lead to the rejection of the null hypothesis from those that do not. **Figure 9.3** displays a normal distribution of sample means around a population mean of 1 kg. Note the critical values in each end (tail) of the distribution. In each direction beyond the critical values lie the rejection regions. Any sample mean that falls in that region will lead the business analyst to reject the null hypothesis. Sample means that fall between the two critical values are close enough to the population mean that the business analyst will decide not to reject the null hypothesis. These means are in the nonrejection region.

FIGURE 9.3 **Rejection and Nonrejection Regions**

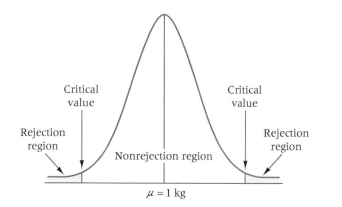

Type I and Type II Errors

Because the hypothesis-testing process uses sample statistics calculated from random data to reach conclusions about population parameters, it is possible to make an incorrect decision about the null hypothesis. In particular, two types of errors can be made in testing hypotheses: Type I errors and Type II errors.

A **Type I error** is committed by *rejecting a true null hypothesis*. With a Type I error, the null hypothesis is true, but the business analyst decides that it is not. As an example, suppose the flour package process is actually in control and is averaging 1 kg of flour per package. Suppose also that a business analyst randomly selects 100 packages, weighs the contents of each, and computes a sample mean. It is possible, by chance, to randomly select 100 of the more extreme packages (mostly heavy masses or mostly light masses), resulting in a mean that falls in the rejection region. The decision is to reject the null hypothesis even though the population mean is actually 1 kg. In this case, the business analyst has committed a Type I error.

The notion of a Type I error can be used outside the realm of statistical hypothesis testing in the business world. For example, if a manager fires an employee because some evidence indicates that she is stealing from the company when she really isn't stealing from the company, the manager has committed a Type I error. As another example, suppose a worker on the assembly line of a large manufacturer hears an unusual sound and decides to shut the line down (reject the null hypothesis). If the sound turns out not to be related to the assembly line and no problems are occurring with the assembly line, the worker has committed a Type I error. When products are in great demand and production capacity is tight, workers are sometimes strongly discouraged from making such Type I errors because the production downtime could be expensive. An analogous courtroom example of a Type I error is when an innocent person is sent to jail.

In Figure 9.3, the rejection regions represent the possibility of committing a Type I error. Means that fall beyond the critical values will be considered so extreme that the business analyst chooses to reject the null hypothesis. However, if the null hypothesis is true, any mean that falls in a rejection region will result in a decision that produces a Type I error. The *probability of committing a Type I error* is called **alpha** (α) or **level of significance**. Alpha equals the area under the curve that is in the rejection region beyond the critical value(s). The value of α is always set before the experiment or study is undertaken. As mentioned previously, common values of α are 0.05, 0.01, 0.10, and 0.001.

A **Type II error** is committed when a business analyst *fails to reject a false null hypothesis*. In this case, the null hypothesis is false, but a decision is made to not reject it. Suppose in the case of the flour problem that the packaging process is actually producing a population mean of 1.025 kg even though the null hypothesis is 1 kg. A sample of 100 packages yields a sample mean of 1.005 kg, which falls in the nonrejection region. The business decision-maker decides not to reject the null hypothesis. A Type II error has been committed. The packaging procedure is out of control and the hypothesis-testing process did not identify it.

Suppose in the business world an employee is stealing from the company. A manager sees some evidence that the stealing is occurring but lacks enough evidence to conclude that the employee is stealing from the company. The manager decides not to fire the employee for theft. The manager has committed a Type II error. Consider the manufacturing line with the noise. Suppose the worker decides not enough noise is heard to shut the line down, but in actuality one of the cords on the line is unravelling, creating a dangerous situation. The worker is committing a Type II error. Manufacturers can also protect themselves against Type II errors. In many cases, it is more costly to produce bad product (e.g., scrap/rework costs and loss of market share due to poor quality) than it is to make it right the first time. Manufacturers sometimes encourage workers to shut down the line if the quality of work is seemingly not what it should be (risking a Type I error) rather than allow poor-quality product to be shipped. In a court of law, a Type II error is committed when a guilty person is declared innocent.

The *probability of committing a Type II error* is **beta** (β). Unlike α, β is not usually stated at the beginning of the hypothesis-testing procedure. Actually, because β occurs only when the null hypothesis is not true, the computation of β varies with the many possible alternative parameters that might occur. For example, in the flour package problem, if the population mean is not 1 kg, then what is it? It could be 1.025, 0.95, or 1.05 kg. A value of β is associated with each of these alternative means. We will cover the method of calculating the probability of committing a Type II error later in the chapter.

How are α and β related? **Figure 9.4** shows the relationship between α, β, and another concept, power. In Figure 9.4, the "state of nature" is how things actually are (process is in control, etc.) and the "action" is the decision that the business analyst makes based on the sample statistic. Alpha can only be committed when the null hypothesis is rejected (row 2 of Figure 9.4) and β can only be committed when the null hypothesis is not rejected (row 1 of Figure 9.4). Thus, because the business analyst is the one who takes the "action" shown in Figure 9.4, the business analyst cannot commit both a Type I and a Type II error on the same hypothesis test (analyst's action is either in row 1 or row 2 but not both).

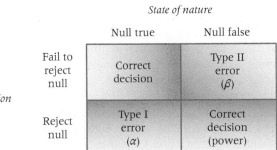

 FIGURE 9.4 Alpha, Beta, and Power

Generally speaking, α and β are inversely related. That is, if α is reduced, β is increased, and vice versa. In terms of the manufacturing assembly line, if management makes it harder for workers to shut down the assembly line (protect against Type I errors), then there is a greater chance that bad product will be made or that a serious problem with the line will arise (an increase in Type II errors). Legally, if the courts make it harder to send innocent people to jail, then they have made it easier to let guilty people go free. One way to reduce both errors simultaneously is to increase the sample size. If a larger sample is taken, it is more likely that it is representative of the population, which translates into a better chance that a business analyst will make a correct choice (and less chance of either a Type I or a Type II error). **Power**, which is equal to $1 - \beta$, is *the probability of a statistical test rejecting the null hypothesis when the null hypothesis is false*. More is said about the concept of power in Section 9.6.

Concept Check

1. The null hypothesis is denoted by _____, while the alternative hypothesis is denoted by _____.
2. Explain what rejection and nonrejection regions are and how they relate to hypothesis testing.
3. What is the relationship of α to the Type I error? What is the relationship of β to the Type II error? Explain.
4. Why is it possible for the null hypothesis to be rejected when it is in fact true?
5. Why is it possible to fail to reject the null hypothesis when it is in fact false?
6. What does $1 - \beta$ represent? Explain.
7. How are α and β related? Explain.

9.1 Problems

9.1. Read each of the following statements. Assuming that statistical hypotheses are set up to test them, classify each as a one-tailed or a two-tailed test.

a. Maritz Marketing Research reports that 42% of all adults seek advice from others in selecting a lawyer. A business analyst wants to test this claim.

b. A study reported by Roper Starch Worldwide states that, on average, an influential person makes 5.8 recommendations about office equipment per year. You believe that this figure is too high and you want to test your belief.

c. The results of a survey conducted by a purchasing unit revealed that the mean age of a purchasing manager is 46.2. This seems too young to you and you want to conduct a test to determine if the average age of a purchasing manager is older than 46.2.

d. According to a survey, the average family spends $3,465 annually on meals at home. A business analyst would like to conduct a survey of families in her province to determine if this figure is true for her province, but she does not have any idea whether the average might be higher or lower there.

9.2. In each of the following scenarios, tell if the analyst has committed a Type I error or a Type II error, or has made a correct decision.

a. An analyst is testing to determine if 0.31 of all families own more than one car. His null hypothesis is that the population proportion is 0.31. He randomly samples 600 families and obtains a sample proportion of 0.33 that own more than one car. Based on this sample data, his decision is to fail to reject the null hypothesis. The actual population proportion is 0.31.

b. Suppose it is generally known that the average price per square metre for a home in a particular suburb is $730. An analyst believes that due to the economy, the average may now be less than that. To test her belief, she takes a random sample of 45 homes in this community, resulting in a sample mean of $700 per square metre. The analyst's decision based on this sample information is to fail to reject the null hypothesis. The actual average price per square metre is now $680.

c. Suppose a utility analyst knows from past experience that the average water bill for a 200-square-metre home is $25 per month. The utility analyst wants to determine if this figure is still true today. Her null hypothesis is that the population mean is $25. To test this, she randomly samples 63 homes, resulting in a sample mean of $29. From this, she decides to reject the null hypothesis. The actual average is $27.

d. According to PR Newswire, 71% of all expectant mothers wish they had to go to only one source to get their baby information. Suppose you think that this figure is too high in your region of the country, so you conduct a test of 358 expectant mothers. In your study, only 66% of the expectant mothers wish they had to go to only one source to get their baby information. Based on this, your decision is to reject the null hypothesis. It turns out that in actuality, 71% of all expectant mothers in your region of the country wish they had to go to only one source to get their information.

9.2 | Testing Hypotheses About a Population Mean Using the *z* Statistic (*σ* Known)

LEARNING OBJECTIVE 9.2

Reach a statistical conclusion in hypothesis-testing problems about a population mean with a known population standard deviation using the *z* statistic.

One of the most basic hypothesis tests is a test about a population mean. A business analyst might be interested in testing to determine whether an established or accepted mean value for an industry is still true, or in testing a hypothesized mean value for a new theory or product. As an example, a computer products company sets up a telephone service to assist customers by providing technical support. The average wait time during weekday hours is 37 minutes. However, a recent hiring effort added technical consultants to the system; management believes that the average wait time has decreased, and they want to prove it. Other business scenarios resulting in hypothesis tests of a single mean might be as follows:

- A financial investment firm wants to determine whether the average hourly change in the Toronto Stock Exchange over a 10-year period is +0.25.
- A manufacturing company wants to determine whether the average thickness of a plastic bottle is 2.4 mm.
- A retail store wants to determine whether the average age of its customers is less than 40 years.

Formula 9.1 can be used to test hypotheses about a single population mean when *σ* is known if the sample size is large ($n \geq 30$) for any population and for small samples ($n < 30$) if *x* is known to be normally distributed in the population.

---

z Test for a Single Mean

$$z = \frac{\bar{x} - \mu}{\frac{\sigma}{\sqrt{n}}}$$

(9.1)

A survey of chartered professional accountants (CPAs) found that the average net income for sole proprietor CPAs is $74,914.[2] Because this survey is now more than 20 years old, an accounting analyst wants to test this figure by taking a random sample of 112 sole proprietor CPAs to determine whether the net income figure has changed. The analyst could use the eight steps of hypothesis testing to do so. Assume the population standard deviation of net incomes for sole proprietor CPAs is $14,530.

Step 1 At Step 1, the hypotheses must be established. Because the analyst is testing to determine whether the figure has changed, the alternative hypothesis is that the mean net income is not $74,914. The null hypothesis is that the mean still equals $74,914. These hypotheses follow.

$$H_0: \mu = \$74,914$$
$$H_a: \mu \neq \$74,914$$

Step 2 Step 2 is to determine the appropriate statistical test and sampling distribution. Because the population standard deviation is known ($14,530) and the analyst

---

[2] Adapted from Daniel J. Flaherty, Raymond A. Zimmerman, and Mary Ann Murray, "Benchmarking against the Best," *Journal of Accountancy* (July 1995): 85–88.

Solution

Step 1 Establish hypotheses. Because we are interested only in proving that the mean figure is lower in Canada, the test is one-tailed. The alternative hypothesis is that the population mean is lower than 4.30. The null hypothesis states the equality case.

$$H_0: \mu = 4.30$$
$$H_a: \mu < 4.30$$

Step 2 Determine the appropriate statistical test. The test statistic is:

$$z = \frac{\bar{x} - \mu}{\frac{\sigma}{\sqrt{n}}}$$

Step 3 Specify the Type I error rate:

$$\alpha = 0.05$$

Step 4 State the decision rule. Because this test is a one-tailed test, the critical z value is found by looking up $0.5000 - 0.0500 = 0.4500$ as the area in Table A.5. The critical value of the test statistic is $z_{0.05} = -1.645$. An observed test statistic must be less than -1.645 to reject the null hypothesis. The rejection region and critical value can be depicted as in the following diagram.

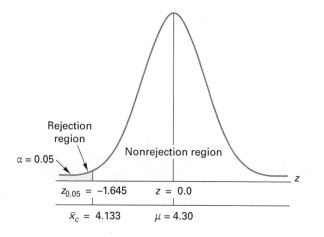

Step 5 Gather the sample data. The data are shown.

Step 6 Calculate the value of the test statistic:

$$\bar{x} = 4.156$$
$$\sigma = 0.574$$
$$z = \frac{4.156 - 4.30}{\frac{0.574}{\sqrt{32}}} = -1.42$$

Step 7 State the statistical conclusion. Because the observed test statistic is not less than the critical value and is not in the rejection region, the statistical conclusion is that the null hypothesis cannot be rejected. The same result is obtained using the p-value method. The observed test statistic is $z = -1.42$. From Table A.5, the probability of getting a z value at least this extreme when the null hypothesis is true is $0.5000 - 0.4222 = 0.0778$. Hence, the null hypothesis cannot be rejected at $\alpha = 0.05$ because the smallest value of α for which the null hypothesis can be rejected is 0.0778. Had α equalled 0.10, the decision would have been to reject the null hypothesis.

Step 8 Make a managerial decision. The test does not result in enough evidence to conclude that Canadian managers think it is less important to use customer service as a means of retaining customers than do managers in Scotland. Customer service is an important tool for retaining customers in both countries according to managers.

Using the critical value method: For what sample mean (or more extreme) value would the null hypothesis be rejected? This critical sample mean can be determined by using the critical z value associated with α, $z_{0.05} = -1.645$:

$$z_c = \frac{\bar{x}_c - \mu}{\frac{\sigma}{\sqrt{n}}}$$
$$-1.645 = \frac{\bar{x}_c - 4.30}{\frac{0.574}{\sqrt{32}}}$$
$$\bar{x}_c = 4.133$$

The decision rule is that a sample mean less than 4.133 would be necessary to reject the null hypothesis. Because the mean obtained from the sample data is 4.156, the analysts fail to reject the null hypothesis. The preceding diagram includes a scale with the critical sample mean and the rejection region for the critical value method.

Using the Computer to Test Hypotheses About a Population Mean Using the z Statistic

Excel can be used to test hypotheses about a single population mean using the z statistic. **Figure 9.9** contains output from Excel for Demonstration Problem 9.1. This p-value was calculated using Excel's Z.TEST function. Note that the Excel output contains only the right-tailed p-value of the z statistic. With a negative observed z for Demonstration Problem 9.1, the p-value was calculated by taking 1 minus Excel's answer. Due to rounding, the p-value reported here is slightly different from the one obtained in Demonstration Problem 9.1.

FIGURE 9.9 Excel Output for Demonstration Problem 9.1

	A	B
	Customer Service Problem	
1	Sample mean	4.15600
2	Standard error	0.10147
3	Standard deviation	0.57400
4	Observations	32
5	Hypothesized value of μ	4.30000
6	p-value	0.07829

Concept Check

1. Explain what a p-value is and how it is used in hypothesis testing.
2. Explain how a p-value relates to the rejection and nonrejection regions in hypothesis testing.

9.2 Problems

9.3 a. Use the data given to test the following hypotheses.

$$H_0: \mu = 25$$
$$H_a: \mu \neq 25$$

$\bar{x} = 28.1, n = 57, \sigma = 8.46, \alpha = 0.01$

b. Use the p-value to reach a statistical conclusion.

c. Using the critical value method, determine the critical sample mean values.

9.4 Use the data given to test the following hypotheses. Assume the data are normally distributed in the population.

$$H_0: \mu = 7.48$$
$$H_a: \mu < 7.48$$

$\bar{x} = 6.91, n = 24, \sigma = 1.21, \alpha = 0.01$

9.5 a. Use the data given to test the following hypotheses.

$$H_0: \mu = 1,200$$
$$H_a: \mu > 1,200$$

$\bar{x} = 1,215, n = 113, \sigma = 100, \alpha = 0.10$

b. Use the p-value to reach a statistical conclusion.

c. Solve for the critical value required to reject the null hypothesis.

9.6 Assume that for the city of Hamilton, Ontario, an environmental study reported that the average number of micrograms of suspended particles per cubic metre of air is 82. Suppose Hamilton officials have been working with businesses, commuters, and industries to reduce this figure. These city officials hire an environmental company to take random measures of air soot over a period of several weeks. The resulting data are shown below. Assume that the population standard deviation is 9.184. Use these data to determine whether the urban air soot in Hamilton is significantly lower than what the environmental study reported. Let $\alpha = 0.01$. If the null hypothesis is rejected, discuss the substantive hypothesis.

81.6	66.6	70.9	82.5	58.3	71.6	72.4
96.6	78.6	76.1	80.0	73.2	85.5	73.2
68.6	74.0	68.7	83.0	86.9	94.9	75.6
77.3	86.6	71.7	88.5	87.0	72.5	83.0
85.8	74.9	61.7	92.2			

9.7 Assume that the average weekly earnings of a production worker in 2010 were $424.20. Suppose a labour analyst wants to determine whether this figure is still accurate today. The analyst randomly selects 54 production workers from across Canada and obtains a representative earnings statement for one week from each. The resulting sample average is $432.69. Assuming a population standard deviation of $33.90 and a 5% level of significance, determine if there is sufficient evidence to claim that the mean weekly earnings of a production worker have changed.

9.8 According to a study several years ago by the Personal Communications Industry Association, the average mobile phone user earns $62,600 per year. Suppose an analyst believes that the average annual earnings of a mobile phone user are lower now and he sets up a study in an attempt to prove his theory. He randomly samples 18 mobile phone users and finds out that the average annual salary for this sample is $58,974, with a population standard deviation of $7,810. Use $\alpha = 0.01$ to test the analyst's theory. Assume salaries are normally distributed.

9.9 A manufacturing company produces valves in various sizes and shapes. One particular valve plate is supposed to have a tensile strength of 500 MPa (megapascals). The company tests a random sample of 42 such valve plates from a lot of 650 valve plates. The sample mean is a tensile strength of 506.11 MPa, and the population standard deviation is 28.03 MPa. Use $\alpha = 0.10$ and determine whether the lot of valve plates has an average tensile strength of 500 MPa.

9.10 A manufacturing firm has been averaging 18.2 orders per week for several years. However, during a recession, orders appeared to slow. Suppose the firm's production manager randomly samples 32 weeks and finds a sample mean of 15.6 orders. The population standard deviation is 2.3 orders. Determine whether the average number of orders is down by using $\alpha = 0.10$.

9.11 According to a report released by CIBC entitled "Women Entrepreneurs: Leading the Charge," the average age for Canadian businesswomen in a recent year was 41. In the report, there was some indication that analysts believed that this mean age will increase. Suppose now, several years later, business analysts want to determine if, indeed, the mean age of a Canadian businesswoman has increased. The

analysts randomly sample 97 Canadian businesswomen and ascertain that the sample mean age is 43.4. From past experience, it is known that the population standard deviation is 8.95. Determine if the mean age of a Canadian businesswoman has increased using a 1% level of significance. What is the *p*-value for this test? What is the decision? If the null hypothesis is rejected, is the result substantive?

9.12 Assume that the national average daily water usage in Canada for 2019 was 492 L per person. Suppose some analysts believe that more water is being used now and want to determine whether this is so. They randomly select a sample of Canadians and carefully keep track of the water used by each sample member for a day, then analyze the results by using a statistical computer software package. The output is given here. Assume $\alpha = 0.05$. How many people were sampled? What was the sample mean? Was this a one- or two-tailed test? What was the result of the study? What decision could be made about the null hypothesis from these results?

One-Sample z

Test of $\mu = 492$ vs. > 492
The assumed standard deviation = 101.72

n	Mean	SE Mean	95% Lower Bound	z	p
40	529.44	17.508	500.644	2.14	0.016

9.3 | Testing Hypotheses About a Population Mean Using the *t* Statistic (σ Unknown)

LEARNING OBJECTIVE 9.3

Reach a statistical conclusion in hypothesis-testing problems about a population mean with an unknown population standard deviation using the *t* statistic.

Very often when a business analyst is gathering data to test hypotheses about a single population mean, the value of the population standard deviation is unknown and the analyst must use the sample standard deviation as an estimate of it. In such cases, the *z* test cannot be used.

Chapter 8 presented the *t* distribution, which can be used to analyze hypotheses about a single population mean when σ is unknown if the population is normally distributed for the measurement being studied. In this section, we will examine the *t* test for a single population mean. In general, this *t* test is applicable whenever the analyst is drawing a single random sample to test the value of a population mean (μ), the population standard deviation is unknown, and the population is normally distributed for the measurement of interest. Recall from Chapter 8 that the assumption that the data will be normally distributed in the population is rather robust.

The formula for testing such hypotheses follows.

t Test for μ

$$t = \frac{\bar{x} - \mu}{\frac{s}{\sqrt{n}}}$$ (9.3)

$$df = n - 1$$

Table 9.2 highlights the differences between the *z* test and the *t* test for single means.

TABLE 9.2 z Test vs. t Test for a Single Mean

	z Test	t Test
Basic Formula:	$z = \dfrac{\bar{x} - \mu}{\frac{\sigma}{\sqrt{n}}}$	$t = \dfrac{\bar{x} - \mu}{\frac{s}{\sqrt{n}}}$
Degrees of Freedom (df):	Does not use degrees of freedom (df)	$df = n - 1$
Population Standard Deviation (σ):	Must know the population standard deviation, σ	Do not know σ. Uses sample standard deviation, s
Sample Size:	$n \geq 30$ always okay $n < 30$ okay only if population is normally distributed	Any size sample
Assumptions:	No assumptions unless $n < 30$. If $n < 30$, population must be normally distributed	Population must be normally distributed in all cases

The Maple Leaf Farmers' Production Company builds large harvesters. For a harvester to be properly balanced when operating, a 25 kg plate is installed on its side. The machine that produces these plates is set to yield plates that average 25 kg. The distribution of plates produced from the machine is normal. However, the shop supervisor is worried that the machine is out of adjustment and is producing plates that do not average 25 kg. To test this concern, he randomly selects 20 of the plates produced the day before and weighs them. Table 9.3 shows the masses obtained, along with the computed sample mean and sample standard deviation.

TABLE 9.3   **Masses in Kilograms of a Sample of 20 Plates**

22.6	22.2	23.2	27.4	24.5
27.0	26.6	28.1	26.9	24.9
26.2	25.3	23.1	24.2	26.1
25.8	30.4	28.6	23.5	23.6

$$\bar{x} = 25.51, s = 2.1933, n = 20$$

The test is to determine whether the machine is out of control, and the shop supervisor has not specified whether he believes the machine is producing plates that are too heavy or too light. Thus, a two-tailed test is appropriate. The following hypotheses are tested:

$$H_0: \mu = 25 \text{ kg}$$
$$H_a: \mu \neq 25 \text{ kg}$$

An α of 0.05 is used. Figure 9.10 shows the rejection regions.

FIGURE 9.10 Rejection Regions for the Machine Plate Example

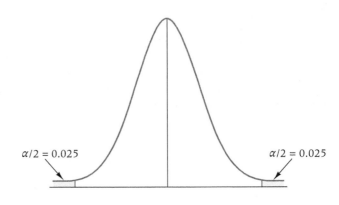

$\alpha/2 = 0.025$ $\alpha/2 = 0.025$

Step 8   Agri-business analysts can speculate about what it means to have larger farms. If the average size of a farm has increased from 315 ha to almost 335 ha, it may represent a substantive increase.

It could mean that small farms are not financially viable. It might mean that corporations are buying out small farms and that large company farms are on the increase. Such a trend might spark legislative movements to protect the small farm. Larger farm sizes might also affect commodity trading.

Using the Computer to Test Hypotheses About a Population Mean Using the *t* Test

We note that Excel does not have a one-sample *t* test function. However, by using the two-sample *t* test for means with unequal variances, the results for a one-sample test can be obtained. This is accomplished by inputting the sample data for the first sample and the value of the parameter being tested (in this case, $\mu = 315$) for each value of the second sample as many times as there are data points in the first sample. The output, in **Figure 9.13**, includes the observed *t* value (2.84) and both the table *t* values and *p*-values for one- and two-tailed tests. Because Demonstration Problem 9.2 was a one-tailed test, the *p*-value of 0.0048 is used.

	A	B
1	**t-Test: Two-Sample Assuming Unequal Variances**	
2		**Hectares**
3	Mean	333.57
4	Variance	986.53
5	Observations	23
6	df	22
7	t Stat	2.84
8	P (T<=t) one-tail	0.00482
9	t Critical one-tail	1.72
10	P (T<=t) two-tail	0.00964
11	t Critical two-tail	2.07

FIGURE 9.13   **Excel Output for Demonstration Problem 9.2**

Concept Check

1. Even if σ is unknown, what is the assumption about the probability distribution of the population for the measurement being studied?

2. Under what conditions should we use a *z* test or a *t* test when testing hypotheses about a population mean?

9.3 Problems

9.13 A random sample of size 20 is taken, resulting in a sample mean of 16.45 and a sample standard deviation of 3.59. Assume *x* is normally distributed and use this information and $\alpha = 0.05$ to test the following hypotheses:

$$H_0: \mu = 16$$
$$H_a: \mu \neq 16$$

9.14 A random sample of 51 items is taken, with $\bar{x} = 58.42$ and $s^2 = 25.68$. Use these data to test the following hypotheses, assuming you want to take only a 1% risk of committing a Type I error and that *x* is normally distributed:

$$H_0: \mu = 60$$
$$H_a: \mu < 60$$

9.15 The following data were gathered from a random sample of 11 items.

1,200	1,175	1,080	1,275	1,201	1,387
1,090	1,280	1,400	1,287	1,225	

Use these data and a 5% level of significance to test the following hypotheses, assuming that the data come from a normally distributed population:

$$H_0: \mu = 1,160$$
$$H_a: \mu > 1,160$$

9.16 The following data (in kilograms), which were selected randomly from a normally distributed population of values, represent measurements of a machine part that is supposed to weigh, on average, 8.3 kg.

8.1	8.4	8.3	8.2	8.5	8.6	8.4	8.3	8.4	8.2
8.8	8.2	8.2	8.3	8.1	8.3	8.4	8.5	8.5	8.7

Use these data and $\alpha = 0.01$ to test the hypothesis that the parts average 8.3 kg.

9.17 A hole-punch machine is set to punch a hole 1.84 cm in diameter in a strip of sheet metal in a manufacturing process. The strip of metal is then creased and sent on to the next phase of production, where a metal rod is slipped through the hole. It is important that the hole be punched to the specified diameter of 1.84 cm. To test punching accuracy, technicians have randomly sampled 12 punched holes and measured the diameters. The data (in centimetres) follow. Use an α of 0.10 to determine whether the holes being punched have an average diameter of 1.84 cm. Assume the punched holes are normally distributed in the population.

1.81	1.89	1.86	1.83
1.85	1.82	1.87	1.85
1.84	1.86	1.88	1.85

9.18 Suppose a study reports that the average price for 1 L of self-serve regular unleaded gas is $1.37. You believe that the figure is higher in your area of the country. You decide to test this claim for your part of Canada by randomly calling gas stations. Your random survey of 25 stations produces the following prices.

$1.40	$1.41	$1.37	$1.38	$1.44
1.38	1.39	1.38	1.38	1.39
1.37	1.34	1.40	1.34	1.43
1.36	1.39	1.36	1.33	1.43
1.38	1.36	1.36	1.34	1.35

Assume gas prices for a region are normally distributed. Do the data you obtained provide enough evidence to reject the claim? Use a 1% level of significance.

9.19 Suppose that in past years the average price per square metre for warehouses in Canada has been $347.46. A national real estate investor wants to determine whether that figure has changed now. The investor hires an analyst who randomly samples 49 warehouses that are for sale across Canada and finds that the mean price per square metre is $340.89, with a standard deviation of $13.89. Assume that prices of warehouse area are normally distributed in the population. If the analyst uses a 5% level of significance, what statistical conclusion can be reached? What are the hypotheses?

9.20 Major cities around the world compete with each other in an effort to attract new businesses. Some of the criteria that businesses use to judge cities as potential locations for their headquarters might include the labour pool; the environment, including work, government, and living; the tax structure; the availability of skilled/educated labour, housing, education, and medical care; and others. Suppose in a study done several years ago, the city of Calgary received a mean rating of 3.51 (on a scale of 1 to 5 and assuming an interval level of data) on housing, but that since that time, considerable residential building has occurred in the Calgary area such that city leaders feel the mean might now be higher. They hire a team of analysts to conduct a survey of businesses around the world to determine how businesses now rate the city on housing (and other variables). Sixty-one businesses take part in the new survey, and Calgary receives a mean response of 3.72 on housing with a sample standard deviation of 0.65. Assuming that such responses are normally distributed, use a 1% level of significance and these data to determine if the mean housing rating for the city of Calgary by businesses has significantly increased.

9.21 Based on population figures and other general information on the Canadian population, suppose it has been estimated that, on average, a family of four in Canada has about $1,135 annually in dental expenditures. Suppose further that a regional dental association wants to determine if this figure is accurate for its area of the country. To test this, 22 families of four are randomly selected from the population in that area of the country and a log is kept of the family's dental expenditures for one year. The resulting data are given below. Assuming that dental expenditures are normally distributed in the population, use the data and an α of 0.05 to test the dental association's hypothesis.

1,008	812	1,117	1,323	1,308	1,415
831	1,021	1,287	851	930	730
699	872	913	944	954	987
1,695	995	1,003	994		

9.22 According to data released by The World Bank, the mean PM10 (particulate matter) concentration for the city of Kabul, Afghanistan, in a recent year was 46. Suppose that because of efforts to improve air quality in Kabul, increases in modernization, and efforts to establish environmentally friendly businesses, city leaders believe rates of particulate matter in Kabul have decreased. To test this notion, they randomly sample 12 readings over a one-year period of time with the resulting readings shown below. Do these data present enough evidence to determine that PM10 readings are significantly less now in Kabul? Assume that particulate readings are normally distributed and that $\alpha = 0.01$.

31	44	35	53	57	47
32	40	31	38	53	45

9.23 According to a survey, the average commuting time for people who commute to a city with a population of 1 to 3 million is 19.0 minutes. Suppose an analyst lives in a city with a population of 2.4 million and wants to test this claim in her city. Assume that commuter times are normally distributed in the population. She takes a random sample of commuters and gathers data. The data are analyzed using Excel and the output is shown here. What are the hypotheses? What are the results of the study?

Excel Output

	A	B
1	Mean	19.534
2	Variance	16.813
3	Observations	26
4	df	25
5	t Stat	0.66
6	$P(T<=t)$ one-tail	0.256
7	t Critical one-tail	1.71
8	$P(T<=t)$ two-tail	0.513
9	t Critical two-tail	2.06

9.4 | Testing Hypotheses About a Proportion

LEARNING OBJECTIVE 9.4

Reach a statistical conclusion in hypothesis-testing problems about a population proportion using the z statistic.

Data analysis used in business decision-making often contains proportions to describe such aspects as market share, consumer makeup, quality defects, on-time delivery rate, and profitable stocks. Business surveys often produce information expressed in proportion form, such as 0.45 of all businesses offer flexible hours to employees or 0.88 of all businesses have websites. Business analysts conduct hypothesis tests about such proportions to determine whether they have changed in some way. (See Thinking Critically About Statistics in Business Today 9.1.) As an example, suppose a company held a 26% or 0.26 share of the market for several years. Due to a massive marketing effort and improved product quality, company officials believe that the market share has increased, and they want to prove it. Other examples of hypothesis testing about a single population proportion are as follows:

- A market analyst wants to determine whether the proportion of new car purchasers who are female has increased.

- A financial analyst wants to determine whether the proportion of companies that were profitable last year in the average investment officer's portfolio is 0.60.

- A quality manager for a large manufacturing firm wants to determine whether the proportion of defective items in a batch is less than 0.04.

Thinking Critically About Statistics in Business Today 9.1

Testing Hypotheses about Commuting

How do Canadians commute to work? Statistics Canada reported a few years ago that, when the job is within 5 km of the city centre, 24% of commuters took public transit. However, this falls quickly to 14% when the job is between 5 km and 10 km from the city centre. Public transit take-up rates were lower still for jobs farther than 10 km from downtown. Using the hypothesis-testing methodology presented in this chapter, analysts can test whether these proportions still hold true today as well as how these figures vary by region. For example, in Toronto it is possible that the proportion of commuters using public transportation when the job is within 5 km of the city centre is higher than 24%. In other parts of the country where public transportation is not as well established, the proportion of commuters using public transportation to city centres would be close to zero.

What is the average travel time of a commute to work in Canada? According to a recent study by Statistics Canada, the average Canadian spends nearly 12 full days a year getting to and from work. Commuters spent an average of 63 minutes a day making the round trip between their place of residence and their workplace. The longest commute is in the Greater Toronto Area, where commuters take an average of 79 minutes for a round trip. In fast-growing Calgary, the round trip takes an average of 66 minutes, 14 minutes longer than it did some 10 years ago. In contrast, Vancouver workers spend no more time on average getting to work than they did some 10 years earlier. It is possible to test any of these means using the hypothesis-testing techniques presented in this chapter to either validate the figures or determine whether the figures are no longer true.

Things to Ponder

1. Why do you think the public transit take-up rate drops dramatically from 24% for less than 5 km to 14% for 5 to 10 km commute distances measured from the city centre?

2. The mean commute time for workers in Canada is 63 minutes a day. Can you think of some reasons why Canadians might want to reduce this figure? What are some ways that this figure might be reduced?

3. It has been estimated that, for a comparable trip, the average travel time using a private vehicle is 24.1 minutes as compared to 44.8 minutes using public transportation. What advantages of public transportation over private vehicles might offset the nearly double commuter time?

Formula 9.4 for inferential analysis of a proportion was introduced in Section 7.3 of Chapter 7. Based on the central limit theorem, this formula makes possible the testing of hypotheses about the population proportion in a manner similar to that of the formula used to test sample means. Recall that $\hat{p}$ denotes a sample proportion and p denotes the population proportion. To validly use this test, the sample size must be large enough such that $n \cdot p \geq 5$ and $n \cdot q \geq 5$.

---

z Test of a Population Proportion

$$z = \frac{\hat{p} - p}{\sqrt{\frac{p \cdot q}{n}}} \qquad (9.4)$$

where

$\hat{p}$ = sample proportion

p = population proportion

$q = 1 - p$

A manufacturer believes exactly 8% of its products contain at least one minor flaw. Suppose a company analyst wants to test this belief. The null and alternative hypotheses are:

$$H_0: p = 0.08$$
$$H_a: p \neq 0.08$$

This test is two-tailed because the hypothesis being tested is whether the proportion of products with at least one minor flaw is 0.08. Alpha is selected to be 0.10. **Figure 9.14** shows the distribution, with the rejection regions and $z = 0.05$. Because α is divided for a two-tailed test, the table value for an area of $(1/2)(0.10) = 0.05$ is $z_{0.05} = \pm 1.645$.

FIGURE 9.14 **Distribution with Rejection Regions for Flawed-Product Example**

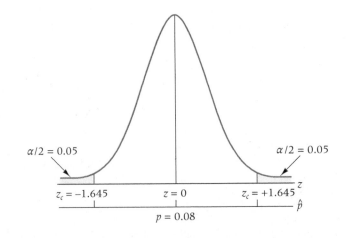

For the business analyst to reject the null hypothesis, the observed z value must be greater than 1.645 or less than −1.645. The business analyst randomly selects a sample of 200 products, inspects each item for flaws, and determines that 33 items have at least one minor flaw. Calculating the sample proportion gives:

$$\hat{p} = \frac{33}{200} = 0.165$$

The observed z value is calculated as:

$$z = \frac{\hat{p} - p}{\sqrt{\frac{p \cdot q}{n}}} = \frac{0.165 - 0.080}{\sqrt{\frac{(0.08)(0.92)}{200}}} = \frac{0.085}{0.0192} = 4.43$$

Note that the denominator of the z formula contains the population proportion. Although the business analyst does not actually know the population proportion, he is testing a population proportion value. Hence, he uses the hypothesized population value in the denominator of the formula as well as in the numerator. This method contrasts with the confidence interval formula, where the sample proportion is used in the denominator.

The observed value of z is in the rejection region (observed $z = 4.43 >$ table $z_{0.05} = +1.645$), so the business analyst rejects the null hypothesis. He concludes that the proportion of items with at least one minor flaw in the population from which the sample of 200 was drawn is not 0.08. With $\alpha = 0.10$, the risk of committing a Type I error in this example is 0.10.

The observed value of $z = 4.43$ is outside the range of most values in virtually all z tables. Thus, if the analyst were using the p-value to arrive at a decision about the null hypothesis, the probability would be approximately 0.0000, and he would reject the null hypothesis.

Suppose the analyst wanted to use the critical value method. He would enter the table value of $z_{0.05} = 1.645$ in the z formula for single-sample proportions, along with the hypothesized population proportion and n, and solve for the critical value of $\hat{p}$ denoted as $\hat{p}_c$. The result is:

$$z_{\alpha/2} = \frac{\hat{p}_c - p}{\sqrt{\frac{p \cdot q}{n}}}$$

$$\pm 1.645 = \frac{\hat{p}_c - 0.08}{\sqrt{\frac{(0.08)(0.92)}{200}}}$$

$$\hat{p}_c = 0.08 \pm 1.645 \sqrt{\frac{(0.08)(0.92)}{200}} = 0.08 \pm 0.032$$

$$= 0.048 \text{ and } 0.112$$

Using the critical value method, if the sample proportion is less than 0.048 or greater than 0.112, the decision will be to reject the null hypothesis. Since the sample proportion, $\hat{p}$, is 0.165, which is greater than 0.112, the decision here is to reject the null hypothesis. The proportion of products with at least one flaw is not 0.08. **Figure 9.15** shows these critical values, the observed value, and the rejection regions.

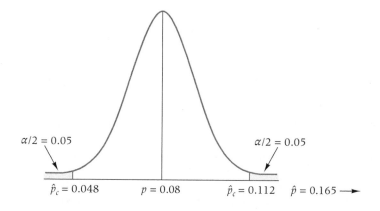

FIGURE 9.15 **Distribution Using Critical Value Method for the Flawed-Product Example**

$\alpha/2 = 0.05$ $\alpha/2 = 0.05$

$\hat{p}_c = 0.048$ $p = 0.08$ $\hat{p}_c = 0.112$ $\hat{p} = 0.165 \longrightarrow$

DEMONSTRATION PROBLEM 9.3

Assume that a survey of the morning beverage market shows that the primary breakfast beverage for 17% of Canadians is milk. A milk producer in Quebec, where milk is plentiful, believes the figure is higher for Quebec. To test this idea, he contacts a random sample of 550 Quebec residents and asks which primary beverage they consumed for breakfast that day. Suppose 115 replied that milk was the primary beverage. Using a level of significance of 0.05, test the idea that the milk figure is higher for Quebec.

Solution

Step 1   The milk producer's theory is that the proportion of Quebec residents who drink milk for breakfast is higher than the national proportion, which is the alternative hypothesis. The null hypothesis is that the proportion in Quebec does not differ from the national average. The hypotheses for this problem are:

$$H_0: p = 0.17$$
$$H_a: p > 0.17$$

Step 2 The test statistic is:

$$z = \frac{\hat{p} - p}{\sqrt{\frac{p \cdot q}{n}}}$$

Step 3 The Type I error rate is 0.05.

Step 4 This test is a one-tailed test, and the table value is $z_{0.05} = +1.645$. The sample results must yield an observed z value greater than 1.645 for the milk producer to reject the null hypothesis. The following diagram shows $z_{0.05}$ and the rejection region for this problem:

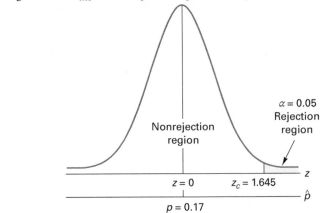

Step 5

$$n = 550$$
$$x = 115$$
$$\hat{p} = \frac{115}{550} = 0.209$$

Step 6

$$z = \frac{\hat{p} - p}{\sqrt{\frac{p \cdot q}{n}}} = \frac{0.209 - 0.17}{\sqrt{\frac{(0.17)(0.83)}{550}}} = \frac{0.039}{0.016} = 2.44$$

Step 7 Because $z = 2.44$ is beyond $z_{0.05} = 1.645$ in the rejection region, the milk producer rejects the null hypothesis. The probability of obtaining $z \geq 2.44$ by chance is 0.0073. Because this probability is less than $\alpha = 0.05$, the null hypothesis is also rejected with the p-value. On the basis of the random sample, the producer is ready to conclude that the proportion of Quebec residents who drink milk as the primary beverage for breakfast is higher than the national proportion.

Step 8 If the proportion of residents who drink milk for breakfast is higher in Quebec than in other parts of Canada, milk producers might have a market opportunity in Quebec that is not available in other parts of the country. Perhaps Quebec residents are being loyal to provincial products, in which case marketers of other Quebec products might be successful in appealing to residents to support their products. The fact that more milk is sold in Quebec might mean that if Quebec milk producers appealed to markets outside Quebec in the same way they do inside the province, they might increase their market share of the breakfast beverage market in other provinces. Is a proportion of almost 0.21 really a substantive increase over 0.17? Certainly in a market the size of Quebec an increase of almost 4 percentage points in the market share could be worth millions of dollars and would be substantive.

A critical proportion can be solved for by:

$$z_{0.05} = \frac{\hat{p}_c - p}{\sqrt{\frac{p \cdot q}{n}}}$$

$$1.645 = \frac{\hat{p}_c - 0.17}{\sqrt{\frac{(0.17)(0.83)}{550}}}$$

$$\hat{p}_c = 0.17 + 1.645\sqrt{\frac{(0.17)(0.83)}{550}} = 0.17 + 0.026 = 0.196$$

With the critical value method, a sample proportion greater than 0.196 must be obtained to reject the null hypothesis. The sample proportion for this problem is 0.209, so the null hypothesis is also rejected with the critical value method.

Concept Check

1. In Demonstration Problem 9.3, how were the population for p and the sample for $\hat{p}$ defined? What is the difference between p and $\hat{p}$?

9.4 Problems

9.24 Suppose you are testing H_0: $p = 0.45$ versus H_a: $p > 0.45$. A random sample of 310 people produces a value of $\hat{p} = 0.465$. Use $\alpha = 0.05$ to test these hypotheses.

9.25 Suppose you are testing H_0: $p = 0.63$ versus H_a: $p < 0.63$. For a random sample of 100 people, $x = 55$, where x denotes the number in the sample that have the characteristic of interest. Use a 0.01 level of significance to test these hypotheses.

9.26 Suppose you are testing H_0: $p = 0.29$ versus H_a: $p \neq 0.29$. A random sample of 740 items shows that 207 have this characteristic. With a 0.05 probability of committing a Type I error, test the hypothesis. For the p-value method, what is the probability of the observed z value for this problem? If you had used the critical value method, what would the two critical values be? How do the sample results compare with the critical values?

9.27 A survey of insurance consumers discovered that 48% of them always reread their insurance policies, 29% sometimes do, 16% rarely do, and 7% never do. Suppose a large insurance company invests considerable time and money in rewriting policies so that they will be more attractive and easy to read and understand. After using the new policies for a year, company managers want to determine whether rewriting the policies significantly changed the proportion of policyholders who always reread their insurance policy. They contact 380 of the company's insurance consumers who purchased a policy in the past year and ask them whether they always reread their insurance policies. One hundred and sixty-four respond that they do. Use a 1% level of significance to test the hypothesis.

9.28 A study by Hewitt Associates showed that 79% of companies offer employees flexible scheduling. Suppose an analyst believes that in accounting firms this figure is lower. The analyst randomly selects 415 accounting firms and through interviews determines that 303 of these firms have flexible scheduling. With a 1% level of significance, does the test show enough evidence to conclude that a significantly lower proportion of accounting firms offer employees flexible scheduling?

9.29 A survey was undertaken by Bruskin/Goldring Research for Quicken to determine how people plan to meet their financial goals in the next year. Respondents were allowed to select more than one way to meet their goals. Thirty-one percent said that they were using a financial planner to help them meet their goals. Twenty-four percent were using family/friends to help them meet their financial goals, followed by broker/accountant (19%), computer software (17%), and books (14%). Suppose another analyst takes a similar survey of 600 people to test these results. If 200 people respond that they are going to use a financial planner to help them meet their goals, is this proportion enough evidence to reject the 31% figure generated in the Bruskin/Goldring survey using $\alpha = 0.10$? If 158 respond that they are going to use family/friends to help them meet their financial goals, is this result enough evidence to declare that the proportion is significantly lower than Bruskin/Goldring's figure of 0.24 if $\alpha = 0.05$?

9.30 Multinational companies generally provide an allowance for personal entertainment for executives living overseas. Assume that 18% of Canadian-based multinational companies provide such an allowance. An analyst thinks that Canadian-based multinational companies are having a more difficult time recruiting executives to live overseas and that an increasing number of these companies are providing an allowance for personal entertainment to these executives to ease the burden of living away from home. To test this hypothesis, a study is conducted by contacting 376 multinational companies. Twenty-two percent of these surveyed companies are providing an allowance for personal entertainment to executives living overseas. Does the test show enough evidence to declare that a significantly higher proportion of multinational companies provide this allowance? Let $\alpha = 0.01$.

9.31 A large manufacturing company investigated the service it received from suppliers and discovered that, in the past, 32% of all materials shipments were received late. However, the company recently installed a just-in-time system in which suppliers are linked more closely to the manufacturing process. A random sample of 118 deliveries since the just-in-time system was installed reveals that 22 deliveries were late. Use this sample information to test whether the proportion of late deliveries was reduced significantly. Let $\alpha = 0.05$.

9.32 Where do CFOs get their money news? According to Robert Half International, 47% get their money news from newspapers, 15% get it from communication/colleagues, 12% get it from cable television, 11% from the Internet, 9% from magazines, 5% from Internet radio, and 1% don't know. Suppose an analyst wants to test these results. He randomly samples 67 CFOs and finds that 40 of them get their money news from newspapers. Does the test show enough evidence to reject the findings of Robert Half International? Use $\alpha = 0.05$.

9.5 | Testing Hypotheses About a Variance

LEARNING OBJECTIVE 9.5

Reach a statistical conclusion in hypothesis-testing problems about a population variance using the chi-square statistic.

At times an analyst needs to test hypotheses about a population variance. For example, in the area of statistical quality control, manufacturers try to produce equipment and parts that are consistent in measurement. Suppose a company produces industrial wire that is specified to be a particular thickness. Because of the production process, the thickness of the wire will vary slightly from one end to the other and from lot to lot and batch to batch. Even if the average thickness of the wire as measured from lot to lot is on specification, the variance of the measurements might be too great to be acceptable. In other words, on average the wire is the correct thickness, but some portions of the wire might be too thin and others unacceptably thick. By conducting hypothesis tests for the variance of the thickness measurements, the quality-control people can monitor for variations in the process that are too great.

The procedure for testing hypotheses about a population variance is similar to the techniques presented in Chapter 8 for estimating a population variance from the sample variance. Formula 9.5, used to conduct these tests, assumes a normally distributed population.

Formula for Testing Hypotheses about a Population Variance

$$\chi^2 = \frac{(n-1)s^2}{\sigma^2} \qquad (9.5)$$

$$df = n - 1$$

As an example, a manufacturing firm has been working diligently to implement a just-in-time inventory system for its production line. The final product requires the installation of a pneumatic tube at a particular station on the assembly line. With the just-in-time inventory system, the company's goal is to minimize the number of pneumatic tubes that are piled up at the station waiting to be installed. Ideally, the tubes should arrive just as the operator needs them. However, because of the supplier and the variables involved in getting the tubes to the line, most of the time there will be some buildup of tube inventory. The company expects that, on average, about 20 pneumatic tubes will be at the station. However, the production superintendent does not want the variance of this inventory to be greater than 4. On a given day, the number of pneumatic tubes piled up at the workstation is determined eight different times and the following numbers of tubes are recorded.

23   17   20   29   21   14   19   24

Using these sample data, we can determine whether the variance is greater than 4. The hypothesis test is one-tailed. Assume the number of tubes is normally distributed. The null hypothesis is that the variance is acceptable with no problems—the variance is equal to or less than 4. The alternative hypothesis is that the variance is greater than 4.

$$H_0: \sigma^2 = 4$$
$$H_a: \sigma^2 > 4$$

Suppose α is 0.05. Because the sample size is eight, the degrees of freedom for the critical table chi-square value are $8 - 1 = 7$. Using Table A.8, we find the critical chi-square value:

$$\chi^2_{0.05,7} = 14.0671$$

Because the alternative hypothesis is greater than 4, the rejection region is in the upper tail of the chi-square distribution. The sample variance is calculated from the sample data to be:

$$s^2 = 20.9821$$

The observed chi-square value is calculated as:

$$\chi^2 = \frac{(8-1)(20.9821)}{4} = 36.72$$

Because this observed chi-square value, $\chi^2 = 36.72$, is greater than the critical chi-square table value, $\chi^2_{0.05,7} = 14.0671$, the decision is to reject the null hypothesis. On the basis of this sample of eight data measurements, the population variance of inventory at this workstation is greater than 4. Company production personnel and managers might want to investigate further to determine whether they can find a cause for this unacceptable variance. **Figure 9.16** shows a chi-square distribution with the critical value, the rejection region, the nonrejection region, the value of α, and the observed chi-square value.

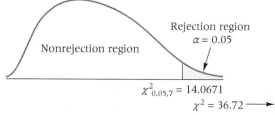

FIGURE 9.16 **Hypothesis Test Distribution for Pneumatic Tube Example**

Using Excel, the p-value of the observed chi-square, 36.72, is determined to be 0.0000053. Because this value is less than $\alpha = 0.05$, the conclusion is to reject the null hypothesis using the p-value. In fact, using this p-value, the null hypothesis could be rejected for:

$$\alpha = 0.00001$$

This null hypothesis can also be tested by the critical value method. Instead of solving for an observed value of chi-square, the critical chi-square value for α is inserted into Formula 9.5 along with the hypothesized value of σ^2 and the degrees of freedom $(n-1)$.

Solving for s^2 yields a critical sample variance value, s^2_c:

$$\chi^2_c = \frac{(n-1)s^2_c}{\sigma^2}$$

$$s^2_c = \frac{\chi^2_c \cdot \sigma^2}{n-1} = \frac{(14.0671)(4)}{7} = 8.038$$

The critical value of the sample variance is $s^2_c = 8.038$. Because the observed sample variance was actually 20.9821, which is larger than the critical variance, the null hypothesis is rejected.

DEMONSTRATION PROBLEM 9.4

A small business has 37 employees. Because of the uncertain demand for its product, the company usually pays overtime in any given week. The company assumes that about 50 total hours of overtime per week are required and that the variance on this figure is about 25. Company officials want to know whether the variance of overtime hours has changed. Given here is a sample of 16 weeks of overtime data (in hours per week). Assume hours of overtime are normally distributed. Use these data to test the null hypothesis that the variance of overtime data is 25. Let $\alpha = 0.10$.

57	56	52	44
46	53	44	44
48	51	55	48
63	53	51	50

Solution

Step 1 This test is a two-tailed test. The null and alternative hypotheses are:

$$H_0: \sigma^2 = 25$$
$$H_a: \sigma^2 \neq 25$$

Step 2 The test statistic is:

$$\chi^2 = \frac{(n-1)s^2}{\sigma^2}$$

Step 3 Because this test is two-tailed, $\alpha = 0.10$ must be split: $\alpha/2 = 0.05$.

Step 4 The degrees of freedom are $16 - 1 = 15$. The two critical chi-square values are:

$$\chi^2_{(1-0.05),15} = \chi^2_{0.95,15} = 7.26093$$
$$\chi^2_{0.05,15} = 24.9958$$

The decision rule is to reject the null hypothesis if the observed value of the test statistic is less than 7.26093 or greater than 24.9958.

Step 5 The data are as listed previously.

Step 6 The sample variance is:

$$s^2 = 28.06$$

The observed chi-square value is calculated as:

$$\chi^2 = \frac{(n-1)s^2}{\sigma^2} = \frac{(15)(28.06)}{25} = 16.84$$

Step 7 This observed chi-square value is in the nonrejection region because $\chi^2_{0.95,15} = 7.26094 < \chi^2_{observed} = 16.84 < \chi^2_{0.05,15} = 24.9958$. The company fails to reject the null hypothesis. There is insufficient evidence to state that the population variance is different from 25.

Step 8 This result indicates to the company managers that the variance of weekly overtime hours is about what they expected.

Concept Check

1. Are the conclusions from a hypothesis test about a variance useful and reliable if the population for the measurement being studied is not normally distributed?

9.5 Problems

9.33 Test each of the following hypotheses by using the given information. Assume the populations are normally distributed.

a. H_0: $\sigma^2 = 20$

   H_a: $\sigma^2 > 20$

   $\alpha = 0.05$, $n = 15$, $s^2 = 32$

b. H_0: $\sigma^2 = 8.5$

   H_a: $\sigma^2 \neq 8.5$

   $\alpha = 0.10$, $n = 22$, $s^2 = 17$

c. H_0: $\sigma^2 = 45$

   H_a: $\sigma^2 < 45$

   $\alpha = 0.01$, $n = 8$, $s^2 = 4.12$

d. H_0: $\sigma^2 = 5$

   H_a: $\sigma^2 \neq 5$

   $\alpha = 0.05$, $n = 11$, $s^2 = 1.2$

9.34 Previous experience shows the variance of a given process to be 14. Analysts are testing to determine whether this value has changed. They gather the following dozen measurements of the process. Use these data and $\alpha = 0.05$ to test the null hypothesis about the variance. Assume the measurements are normally distributed.

52	44	51	58	48	49
38	49	50	42	55	51

9.35 A manufacturing company produces bearings. One line of bearings is specified to be 1.64 cm in diameter. A major customer requires that the variance of the bearings be no more than 0.001 cm². The producer is required to test the bearings before they are shipped, so the diameters of 16 bearings are measured with a precise instrument, resulting in the following values. Assume bearing diameters are normally distributed. Use $\alpha = 0.01$ to test the data to determine whether the null hypothesis is to be rejected because of too high a variance.

1.69	1.62	1.63	1.70
1.66	1.63	1.65	1.71
1.64	1.69	1.57	1.64
1.59	1.66	1.63	1.65

9.36 A bank averages about \$100,000 in deposits per week. However, because of the way pay periods fall, seasonality, and erratic fluctuations in the local economy, deposits are subject to a wide variability. In the past, the variance for weekly deposits has been about 199,996,164. In terms that make more sense to managers, the standard deviation of weekly deposits has been \$14,142. Shown here are data from a random sample of 13 weekly deposits for a recent period. Assume weekly deposits are normally distributed. Use these data and $\alpha = 0.10$ to determine whether the variance for weekly deposits has changed.

in the study could be tested for Canada. The analyst would need to scientifically identify Canadian influencers in the population and randomly select a sample. A research mechanism could be set up whereby the number of referrals by each influencer could be recorded for a year and averaged, thereby producing a sample mean and a sample standard deviation. Using a selected value of α, the sample mean could be statistically tested against the hypothetical population mean (in this case, H_0: $\mu = 5.8$). The probability of falsely rejecting a true null would be α. If the null was actually false ($\mu \neq 5.8$), the probability (β) of failing to reject the false null hypothesis would depend upon what the true number of mean referrals on office equipment per year was for influencers.

If an analyst has theories on influencers, and these research theories can be stated as statistical hypotheses, the theory should be formulated as an alternative hypothesis, and the null hypothesis should be that the theory is not true. Samples are randomly selected. If the statistic of choice is a mean, a z test or a t test for a population mean should be used in the analysis, depending on whether the population standard deviation is known or unknown. In many studies, the sample standard deviation is used in the analysis instead of the unknown population standard deviation. In these cases, a t test should be used when the assumption that the population data are normally distributed can be made. If the statistic is a proportion, the z test for a population proportion is appropriate.

Key Considerations

The process of hypothesis testing encompasses several areas that could lead to inappropriate activity, beginning with the null and alternative hypotheses. In the hypothesis-testing approach, the preliminary assumption is that the null hypothesis is true. If an analyst has a new theory or idea that he is attempting to prove, it is somewhat inappropriate to express that theory or idea as the null hypothesis. In doing so, the analyst is assuming that what he is trying to prove is true and the burden of proof is on the data to reject this idea or theory. The analyst must take great care not to assume that what he or she is attempting to prove is true.

Hypothesis testing through random sampling opens up many possible inappropriate situations that can occur in sampling, such as identifying a frame that is favourable to the outcome the analyst is seeking or using nonrandom sampling techniques to test hypotheses. In addition, the analyst should be careful to use the proper test statistic for tests of a population mean, particularly when σ is unknown. If t tests are used, or in testing a population variance, the analyst should be careful to apply the techniques only when it can be shown with some confidence that the population is normally distributed. The chi-square test of a population variance has been shown to be extremely sensitive to the assumption that the population is normally distributed. The incorrect usage of this technique occurs when the analyst does not carefully check the population distribution shape for compliance with this assumption. Failure to do so can easily result in the reporting of spurious conclusions.

It can be inappropriate from the point of view of business decision-making to knowingly use the notion of statistical significance to claim business significance when the results are not substantive. Therefore, it may be unethical to intentionally attempt to mislead the business user by inappropriately using the word *significance*.

Why Statistics Is Relevant

Hypothesis testing is one of the most important tools for the application of statistics to business problems. The development of hypotheses forces the business analyst to clearly state the purpose of the research activity. This helps establish the focus and direction for the research effort. Moreover, the development of hypotheses requires the business analyst to have an operational definition of the variables of interest, thus determining what variables will be considered in the study, as well as what variables will not be considered.

It is important to keep in mind that the information given by hypothesis tests like the ones described in this chapter can also be obtained from confidence intervals like the ones described in Chapter 8. For instance, if the value of the parameter specified by the null hypothesis is contained in the 95% confidence interval, the null hypothesis cannot be rejected at the 0.05 level. If the value specified by the null hypothesis is not in the interval, the null hypothesis can be rejected at the 0.05 level. The relationship between hypothesis tests and confidence intervals will be further explored in Chapters 10 and 11.

Summary of Learning Objectives

Three types of hypotheses were presented in this chapter: research hypotheses, statistical hypotheses, and substantive hypotheses. Research hypotheses are statements of what the analyst believes will be the outcome of an experiment or study. In order to test hypotheses, business analysts formulate their research hypotheses into statistical hypotheses.

LEARNING OBJECTIVE 9.1 Develop both one- and two-tailed null and alternative hypotheses that can be tested in a business setting by examining the rejection and nonrejection regions in light of Type I and Type II errors.

All statistical hypotheses consist of two parts, a null hypothesis and an alternative hypothesis. The null and alternative hypotheses are structured so that either one or the other is true but not both. In testing hypotheses, the analyst assumes that the null hypothesis is true. By examining the sampled data, the analyst either rejects or does not reject the null hypothesis. If the sample data are significantly in opposition to the null hypothesis, the analyst rejects the null hypothesis and accepts the alternative hypothesis by default.

Hypothesis tests can be one-tailed or two-tailed. Two-tailed tests always utilize = and ≠ in the null and alternative hypotheses. These tests are nondirectional in that significant deviations from the hypothesized value that are either greater than or less than the value are in rejection regions. The one-tailed test is directional, and the alternative hypothesis contains < or > signs. In these tests, only one end or tail of the distribution contains a rejection region. In a one-tailed test, the analyst is interested only in deviations from the hypothesized value that are either greater than or less than the value but not both.

Not all statistically significant outcomes of studies are important business outcomes. A substantive result is when the outcome of a statistical study produces results that are important to the decision-maker.

When a business analyst reaches a decision about the null hypothesis, she either makes a correct decision or an error. If the null hypothesis is true, the analyst can make a Type I error by rejecting it. The probability of making a Type I error is alpha (α). Alpha is usually set by the analyst when establishing the hypotheses. Another expression sometimes used for the value of α is *level of significance*.

LEARNING OBJECTIVE 9.2 Reach a statistical conclusion in hypothesis-testing problems about a population mean with a known population standard deviation using the z statistic.

One of the most basic hypothesis tests is a test about a population mean. Here we test a hypothesis about a population mean assuming that the population standard deviation, σ, is known, and thus we use the z statistic. If the test for a population mean is being conducted with a known finite population, N, the population information can be incorporated into the hypothesis-testing formula. Other methods to reach a statistical conclusion in hypothesis-testing problems include the p-value method (where the p-value defines the smallest value of α for which the null hypothesis can be rejected) and the critical value method.

LEARNING OBJECTIVE 9.3 Reach a statistical conclusion in hypothesis-testing problems about a population mean with an unknown population standard deviation using the t statistic.

Very often when gathering data to test hypotheses about a population mean, the value of the population standard deviation, σ, is unknown and the analyst must use the sample standard deviation, s, as an estimate of it. In such cases, the z test cannot be used: we use instead the t statistic. In general, the t test is applicable whenever we draw a single random sample to test the value of a population mean, the population standard deviation, σ, is unknown, and the population is normally distributed for the measurement of interest.

LEARNING OBJECTIVE 9.4 Reach a statistical conclusion in hypothesis-testing problems about a population proportion using the z statistic.

Business data analysis often contains proportions to describe such aspects as market share, consumer makeup, quality defects, on-time delivery rate, and profitable stocks. Here we test a hypothesis about a population proportion using the z statistic. As with the population mean, other methods to reach a statistical conclusion in hypothesis-testing the population proportion include the p-value method and the critical value method.

LEARNING OBJECTIVE 9.5 Reach a statistical conclusion in hypothesis-testing problems about a population variance using the chi-square statistic.

At times an analyst needs to test hypotheses about a population variance, σ^2. The procedure for testing hypotheses about a population variance is similar to the techniques for estimating a population variance from the sample variance, and thus here we use the χ^2 statistic.

LEARNING OBJECTIVE 9.6 Solve for possible Type II errors when failing to reject the null hypothesis.

If the null hypothesis is false and the analyst fails to reject it, a Type II error is committed. Beta (β) is the probability of committing a Type II error. Type II errors must be computed from the hypothesized value of the parameter, α, and a specific alternative value of the parameter being examined. As many possible Type II errors exist in a problem as there are possible alternative statistical values.

If a null hypothesis is true and the analyst fails to reject it, no error is committed, and the analyst makes a correct decision. Similarly, if a null hypothesis is false and it is rejected, no error is committed. Power $(1 - \beta)$ is the probability of a statistical test rejecting the null hypothesis when the null hypothesis is false.

An operating characteristic (OC) curve is a graphical depiction of values of β that can occur as various values of the alternative values of the parameter are explored. This graph can be studied to determine what happens to β as one moves away from the value of the null hypothesis. A power curve is used in conjunction with an OC curve. The power curve is a graphical depiction of the values of power as alternative values of the parameter are examined. The analyst can view the increase in power as values of the parameter diverge from the value of the null hypothesis.

Key Terms

Formulas

(9.1) z test for a single mean

$$z = \frac{\bar{x} - \mu}{\frac{\sigma}{\sqrt{n}}}$$

(9.2) Formula to test hypotheses about μ with a finite population

$$z = \frac{\bar{x} - \mu}{\frac{\sigma}{\sqrt{n}} \sqrt{\frac{N-n}{N-1}}}$$

(9.3) t test for μ

$$t = \frac{\bar{x} - \mu}{\frac{s}{\sqrt{n}}}$$

$$df = n - 1$$

(9.4) z test of a population proportion

$$z = \frac{\hat{p} - p}{\sqrt{\frac{p \cdot q}{n}}}$$

(9.5) Formula for testing hypotheses about a population variance

$$\chi^2 = \frac{(n-1)s^2}{\sigma^2}$$

$$df = n - 1$$

Supplementary Problems

Calculating the Statistics

9.43 **Video** Use the information given and the eight-step approach to test the hypotheses. Let $\alpha = 0.01$.

$$H_0: \mu = 36$$
$$H_a: \mu \neq 36$$
$$n = 63, \bar{x} = 38.4, \sigma = 5.93$$

9.44 Use the information given and the eight-step approach to test the hypotheses. Let $\alpha = 0.05$. Assume the population is normally distributed.

$$H_0: \mu = 7.82$$
$$H_a: \mu < 7.82$$
$$n = 17, \bar{x} = 7.01, s = 1.69$$

9.45 **Video** For each of the following problems, test the hypotheses. Incorporate the eight-step approach.

a. $H_0: p = 0.28$

$H_a: p > 0.28$

$n = 783, x = 230, \alpha = 0.10$

b. $H_0: p = 0.61$

$H_a: p \neq 0.61$

$n = 401, \hat{p} = 0.56, \alpha = 0.05$

9.46 Test the following hypotheses by using the information given and the eight-step approach. Let α be 0.01. Assume the population is normally distributed.

$$H_0: \sigma^2 = 15.4$$
$$H_a: \sigma^2 > 15.4$$
$$n = 18, s^2 = 29.6$$

9.47 Solve for the value of β in each of the following problems.

a. $H_0: \mu = 130$

$H_a: \mu > 130$

$n = 75, \sigma = 12, \alpha = 0.01$

The alternative mean is actually 135.

b. $H_0: p = 0.44$

$H_a: p < 0.44$

$n = 1{,}095, \alpha = 0.05$

The alternative proportion is actually 0.42.

Testing Your Understanding

9.48 Assume that according to a survey, a majority of Canadian households have tried to cut long-distance phone bills. Of those who have tried to cut the bills, 32% have done so by switching long-distance companies. Suppose business analysts believe that this figure may be higher today. To test this theory, an analyst conducts another survey by randomly contacting 80 Canadian households that have tried to cut long-distance phone bills. If 39% of the contacted households say they have tried to cut their long-distance phone bills by switching long-distance companies, is this result enough evidence to state that a significantly higher proportion of Canadian households are trying to cut long-distance phone bills by switching companies? Let $\alpha = 0.01$.

9.49 According to Zero Population Growth, the average urban U.S. resident consumes 1.49 kg of food per day. Is this figure accurate for Canadian consumers? Suppose 64 Canadians are identified by a random procedure and their average consumption per day is 1.63 kg of food. Assume a population variance of 0.59 kg^2 of food per day. Use a 5% level of significance to determine whether the Zero Population Growth figure for urban U.S. residents is also true for Canadians on the basis of the sample data.

9.50 Brokers generally agree that bonds are a better investment during times of low interest rates than during times of high interest rates. A survey of executives during a time of low interest rates showed that 57% of them had some retirement funds invested in bonds. Assume this percentage is constant for bond market investment by executives with retirement funds. Suppose interest rates have risen lately and the proportion of executives with retirement investment money in the bond market may have dropped. To test this idea, an analyst randomly samples 210 executives who have retirement funds. Of these, 93 now have retirement funds invested in bonds. For $\alpha = 0.10$, does the test show enough evidence to declare that the proportion of executives with retirement fund investments in the bond market is significantly lower than 0.57?

9.51 Highway engineers in Alberta are painting white stripes on a highway. The stripes are supposed to be approximately 3 m long. However, because of the machine, the operator, and the motion of the vehicle carrying the equipment, considerable variation occurs among the stripe lengths. Engineers claim that the variance of stripes is not more than 0.41 m². Use the sample lengths given here from 12 measured stripes to test the variance claim. Assume stripe length is normally distributed. Let $\alpha = 0.05$.

Stripe Lengths in Metres

3.14	2.87	2.99	3.08
2.80	3.17	3.26	3.02
2.83	2.99	3.20	3.17

9.52 A computer manufacturer estimates that its line of laptop computers has, on average, 8.4 days of downtime per year. To test this claim, an analyst contacts seven companies that own one of these computers and is allowed to access company computer records. It is determined that, for the sample, the average number of downtime days is 5.6, with a sample standard deviation of 1.3 days. Assuming that number of downtime days is normally distributed, determine whether these laptop computers actually average 8.4 days of downtime in the entire population. Let $\alpha = 0.01$.

9.53 **Video** A life insurance salesperson claims the average worker in the city of Winnipeg has no more than $25,000 of personal life insurance. To test this claim, you randomly sample 100 workers in Winnipeg. You find that this sample of workers averages $26,650 of personal life insurance. The population standard deviation is $12,000.

a. Determine whether the test shows enough evidence to reject the null hypothesis posed by the salesperson. Assume the probability of committing a Type I error is 0.05.

b. Assuming that the actual average for this population is $30,000, what is the probability of committing a Type II error?

9.54 A financial analyst has been following the shares of a particular company for several months. The share price remained fairly stable during this time. In fact, the financial analyst claims that the variance of the share price did not exceed $4 for the entire period. Recently, the market has heated up, and the share price appears more volatile. To determine whether it is more volatile, a sample of closing share prices for eight days is randomly selected. The sample mean price is $36.25, with a sample standard deviation of $7.80. Using a level of significance of 0.10, determine whether the financial analyst's previous variance figure is now too low. Assume share prices are normally distributed.

9.55 A study of MBA graduates by Universum for The American Graduate Survey 1999 revealed that MBA graduates have several expectations of prospective employers beyond their base pay.

In particular, according to the study, 46% expect a performance-related bonus, 46% expect stock options, 42% expect a signing bonus, 28% expect profit sharing, 27% expect extra vacation/personal days, 25% expect tuition reimbursement, 24% expect health benefits, and 19% expect guaranteed annual bonuses. Suppose a study is conducted in an ensuing year to see whether these expectations have changed. If 125 MBA graduates are randomly selected and if 66 expect stock options, does this result provide enough evidence to declare that a significantly higher proportion of MBAs expect stock options? Let $\alpha = 0.05$. If the proportion is really 0.50, what is the probability of committing a Type II error?

9.56 Suppose the number of beds filled per day in a medium-sized hospital is normally distributed. A hospital administrator tells the board of directors that, on average, at least 185 beds are filled on any given day. One of the board members believes this figure is inflated, and she manages to secure a random sample of figures for 16 days. The data are shown here. Use $\alpha = 0.05$ and the sample data to test whether the hospital administrator's statement is false. Assume the number of filled beds per day is normally distributed in the population.

Number of Beds Occupied per Day

173	149	166	180
189	170	152	194
177	169	188	160
199	175	172	187

9.57 **Video** According to Gartner Inc., the largest share of the worldwide PC market is held by HP Inc. with 19.8%. Suppose that a market analyst believes that HP Inc. holds a higher share of the market in Ontario. To verify this theory, he randomly selects 428 people who purchased a personal computer in the last month in Ontario. Ninety of these purchases were HP Inc. computers. Using a 1% level of significance, test the market analyst's theory. If the market share is really 0.22 in Ontario, what is the probability of making a Type II error?

9.58 A national publication reported that a university student living away from home spends, on average, no more than $15 per month on laundry. You believe this figure is too low and want to disprove this claim. To conduct the test, you randomly select 17 university students and ask them to keep track of the amount of money they spend during a given month on laundry. The sample produces an average expenditure on laundry of $19.34, with a population standard deviation of $4.52. Use these sample data to conduct the hypothesis test. Assume you are willing to take a 10% risk of making a Type I error and that spending on laundry per month is normally distributed in the population.

9.59 A local company installs natural-gas barbecues. As part of the installation, a ditch is dug to lay a small natural-gas line from the barbecue to the main line. On average, the depth of these lines seems to run about 30 cm. The company claims that the depth does not vary by more than 103.2 cm² (the variance). To test this claim, an analyst randomly took 22 depth measurements at different locations. The sample average depth was 34 cm with a standard deviation of 15.2 cm. Is this enough evidence to reject the company's claim about the variance? Assume line depths are normally distributed. Let $\alpha = 0.05$.

9.60 A study of pollutants showed that certain industrial emissions should not exceed 2.5 parts per million. You believe a particular company may be exceeding this average. To test this supposition, you randomly take a sample of nine air tests. The sample average is 3.4 parts per million, with a sample standard deviation of 0.6. Does this result provide enough evidence for you to conclude that the company

Statistical Inferences About Two Populations

LEARNING OBJECTIVES

The focus of Chapter 10 is on testing hypotheses and constructing confidence intervals about parameters from two populations, thereby enabling you to:

10.1 Test hypotheses and develop confidence intervals about the difference in two means of independent samples with known population variances using the z statistic.

10.2 Test hypotheses and develop confidence intervals about the difference in two means of independent samples with unknown population variances using the t test.

10.3 Test hypotheses and develop confidence intervals about the difference in two dependent populations.

10.4 Test hypotheses and develop confidence intervals about the difference in two population proportions.

10.5 Test hypotheses about the difference in two population variances using the F distribution.

Decision Dilemma

L.L. Bean

L.L. Bean, with headquarters in Freeport, Maine, began as a one-man operation in 1912 selling hunting boots. It has evolved into the leading U.S. catalogue company and the largest supplier of outdoor gear in the world, with annual sales of US$1.44 billion. The company's founder, Leon Leonwood (L.L.) Bean, was an outdoorsman, hunter, and entrepreneur. As a result of one cold, wet hunting trip from which he returned with damp feet, he developed a new-style hunting boot with leather uppers and a rubber base. This hunting boot, called the Maine Hunting Shoe®, is credited with changing outdoor footwear forever. He sent a letter to other hunters and outdoorsmen from outside the state of Maine who had purchased a Maine hunting licence, offering them the new boot. He promised a money-back guarantee on sales, which is a mainstay of the company to this day. After some adjustments and restarts, sales of the boots took off and the company began.

Bean established his factory directly above the post office so that orders could be conveniently filled and shipped. Because he

John Greim/LightRocket/Getty Images

knew that hunters from out of state interested in seeing his operation might be passing through Freeport in the middle of the night on their way to hunting stands, he opened for business 24 hours a day—a policy that is still a distinctive feature of the flagship store today. In 1920, Bean opened a showroom adjacent to his factory, and by 1922, company sales had reached US$135,000 annually. As the company grew, other outdoor products were added. The company built its success, in part, on high-quality products offered at reasonable prices and on excellent customer service.

For the next 30 years, L.L. Bean increased sales through product innovation and word-of-mouth and print advertising. The company expanded its catalogue offerings, publishing several per year to offer products for different seasons. The company built its reputation on its Maine outdoor image, the appeal of its catalogues, and a postage-free policy on shipping. In 1954, L.L. Bean introduced its women's department. In the 1960s, with the founder's grandson, Leon A. Gorman, now at the helm, the company expanded both its target demographic group and its advertising budget along with implementing more competitive pricing. By 1975, annual sales had reached US$30 million, and by the end of the decade, L.L. Bean had built a distribution centre with over 27,000 square metres (300,000 square feet).

L.L. Bean achieved remarkable growth in the 1980s, in part due to several trends. The Bean label became affiliated with prep culture and clothing, the health and fitness boom sparked greater interest in the active lifestyle promoted by outdoor activities, and there was a surge in mail-order shopping. In the early 1990s, the company opened its first Japanese store, followed by 10 others by the end of the decade. Today, L.L. Bean employs over 5,000 people year-round and over 10,000 during the holiday season. In 2015, L.L. Bean produced 50 different catalogues distributed to over 170 countries. According to company sources, over 9.3-million customer contacts were received that year, with over 1.1-million orders shipped in the busiest week.

L.L. Bean has embraced mobile retailing. It is acknowledged as having the fastest-loading fashion retailer website and consistently takes, on average, 5 seconds to load. The most recent statistics available show that the average order size at L.L. Bean is $76.55, and the number of coupon clicks per month is about 6,454.

Managerial, Statistical, and Analytical Questions

1. Recent statistics have shown that L.L. Bean's e-commerce home page loaded, on average, in 5 seconds. Suppose the company did not have that figure broken down by daytime (between 8 A.M. and 5 P.M.) and nighttime (after 5 P.M. and before 8 A.M.) but held the theory that due to a slower volume at night, the home page might load faster then. To test this theory, a random sample of 37 uploads is taken during the daytime with a resultant mean time of 5.16 seconds. A second random sample of 45 uploads is taken at nighttime with a resulting mean time of 4.81 seconds. Previous studies indicate that the population standard deviation both during the daytime and at nighttime is 0.83 seconds. From this information, how would an analyst go about testing the proposed theory?

2. Is the average order size for women greater than the average order size for men? Suppose analysts at L.L. Bean want to test this hypothesis by taking a random sample of 44 orders from women and a random sample of 48 orders from men. Suppose that the sample mean for women is $80 with a sample standard deviation of $18. Suppose furthermore that the sample mean for men is $72 with a sample standard deviation of $16. How could we set up and carry out a hypothesis test to answer the question about order size using these data?

3. According to a survey conducted by comScore for UPS, about 41% of shoppers said that "receiving my product when expected" led them to recommend an online retailer. Suppose another analyst wanted to compare this result for L.L. Bean purchasers and a competitor's purchasers. Suppose a random sample of 310 L.L. Bean purchasers is obtained and they are asked this question, with a result that 136 agreed with this statement. Suppose a random sample of 195 competitor purchasers is obtained and they are asked this question, with a result that 72 agreed with this statement. If we wanted to use these data to determine if there is a significant difference between L.L. Bean purchasers and the competitor's purchasers on this issue, how would we go about doing it?

Sources: "L.L. Bean: Company Information," www.llbean.ca/company-info.html; "2016 L.L. Bean at a Glance," company fact sheet, www.llbean.ca/on/demandware.static/-/Library-Sites-LLBeanSharedLibrary/default/dw31fc0e1a/images/aboutLLBean/160428_company_fact_sheet.pdf; Bill Siwicki, "L.L. Bean Shows Other Mobile Retailers How to Speed Things Up," Internet Retailer, May 3, 2012, www.digitalcommerce360.com/2012/05/03/ll-bean-shows-other-mobile-retailers-how-speed-things/; Noa Shavit, "Website Speed Is the New Competitive Battleground for eCommerce," Insights@Moovweb, April 1, 2019, www.moovweb.com/site-speed-competitive-battleground-ecommerce/; "2013 UPS Pulse of the Online Shopper," comScore, thenewlogistics.ups.com/retail/comscore-survey/; "L.L. Bean Coupons," Coupon Cabin, September 28, 2012, www.couponcabin.com/coupons/ll-bean/; "L.L. Bean," *International Directory of Company Histories* at Encyclopedia.com, www.encyclopedia.com/topic/L.L._Bean.aspx.

Introduction

To this point, all discussion of confidence intervals and hypothesis tests has centred on single population parameters. That is, a single sample is randomly drawn from a population, and using data from that sample, a population mean, proportion, or variance is estimated or tested. In Chapter 8, we presented statistical techniques for constructing confidence intervals to estimate a population mean, a population proportion, or a population variance. In Chapter 9, we presented statistical techniques for testing hypotheses about a population mean, a population proportion, or a population variance. Often, it is of equal interest to make inferences about two populations. A retail analyst might want to compare per-person annual expenditures on shoes in 2021 with those in 2017 to determine whether a change has occurred over time. A market analyst might want to estimate or determine the proportion of market share of one company in two different regions.

In this chapter, we will consider several different techniques for analyzing data that come from two samples. One technique is used with proportions, one is used with variances, and the others are used with means. The techniques for analyzing means are separated into those using the z statistic and those using the t statistic. In four of the five techniques presented in this chapter, the two samples are assumed to be independent samples. The samples are independent because *the items or people sampled in each group are in no way related to those in the other group.* Any similarity between items or people in the two samples is coincidental and due to chance. One of the techniques presented in the chapter is for analyzing data from dependent, or related, samples in which items or persons in one sample are matched in some way with items or persons in the other sample. For four of the five techniques, we will examine both hypothesis tests and confidence intervals.

Figure B.1 in Appendix B (Making Inferences About Population Parameters: A Brief Summary) displays a tree diagram taxonomy of inferential techniques organized by usage, number of samples, and level of data. Chapter 10 contains techniques for constructing confidence intervals and testing hypotheses about the differences in two population means and two population proportions and, in addition, testing hypotheses about two population variances. In business analytics, we have many opportunities to compare two populations in a variety of ways using samples of each. The entire left side of the tree diagram taxonomy displays various confidence interval estimation techniques. The rightmost branch of this side contains Chapter 10 techniques and is displayed in **Figure 10.1**. The entire right side of the tree diagram taxonomy displays various hypothesis-testing techniques. The central branch of this contains Chapter 10 techniques (2 samples) for testing hypotheses, and this branch is displayed in **Figure 10.2**. Note that at the bottom of each tree branch in Figures 10.1 and 10.2, the title of the statistical technique, along with its respective section number in Chapter 10, is given for ease of identification and use. If a business analyst is constructing confidence intervals or testing hypotheses about the difference in two population means, and the population standard deviations or variances are known, then he will use the z test for $\mu_1 - \mu_2$ contained in Section 10.1. If the population standard deviations or variances are unknown, then the appropriate technique is the t test for $\mu_1 - \mu_2$ contained in Section 10.2. If a business analyst is constructing confidence intervals or testing hypotheses about the difference in two related populations, then she will use the t test presented

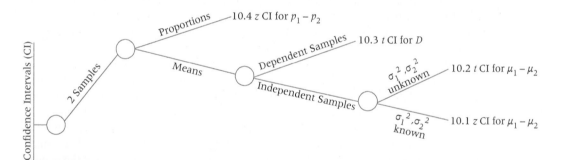

FIGURE 10.1 Branch of the Tree Diagram Taxonomy of Inferential Techniques: **Confidence Intervals**

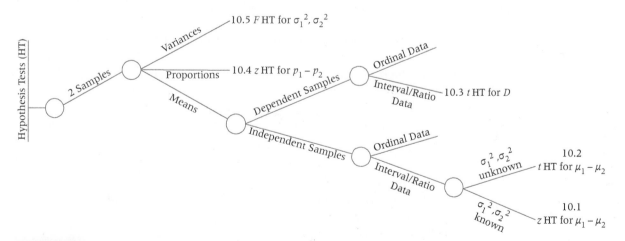

FIGURE 10.2 Branch of the Tree Diagram Taxonomy of Inferential Techniques: **Hypothesis Tests**

in Section 10.3. If a business analyst is constructing a confidence interval or testing a hypothesis about the difference in two population proportions, then he will use the z test for $p_1 - p_2$ presented in Section 10.4. If an analyst desires to test a hypothesis about two population variances, then she will use the F test presented in Section 10.5.

10.1 Hypothesis Testing and Confidence Intervals About the Difference in Two Means Using the z Statistic: Population Variances Known

LEARNING OBJECTIVE 10.1

Test hypotheses and develop confidence intervals about the difference in two means of independent samples with known population variances using the z statistic.

In some research designs, the sampling plan calls for selecting two **independent samples**, calculating the sample means, and using the difference in the two sample means to estimate or test the difference in the two population means. The object might be to determine whether the two samples come from the same population or, if they come from different populations, to determine the amount of difference in the populations. This type of analysis can be used to determine, for example, whether the effectiveness of two brands of toothpaste differs or whether two brands of tires wear differently. Business research might be conducted to study the difference in the productivity of men and women on an assembly line under certain conditions. An engineer might want to determine differences in the strength of aluminum produced under two different temperatures. Does the average cost of a two-bedroom, one-storey house differ between Kingston, Ontario, and Edmonton, Alberta? If so, how much is the difference? These and many other interesting questions can be researched by comparing the difference in two sample means.

How does an analyst analyze the difference in two samples by using sample means? The central limit theorem states that the difference in two sample means, $\bar{x}_1 - \bar{x}_2$, is normally distributed for large sample sizes (both n_1 and $n_2 \geq 30$), regardless of the shape of the populations. It can also be shown that:

$$\mu_{\bar{x}_1 - \bar{x}_2} = \mu_1 - \mu_2$$

$$\sigma_{\bar{x}_1 - \bar{x}_2} = \sqrt{\frac{\sigma_1^2}{n_1} + \frac{\sigma_2^2}{n_2}}$$

These expressions lead to a z formula for the difference in two sample means.

---

z Formula for the Difference in Two Sample Means (Independent Samples and Population Variances Known)

$$z = \frac{(\bar{x}_1 - \bar{x}_2) - (\mu_1 - \mu_2)}{\sqrt{\frac{\sigma_1^2}{n_1} + \frac{\sigma_2^2}{n_2}}} \tag{10.1}$$

where

μ_1 = the mean of population 1
μ_2 = the mean of population 2
n_1 = size of sample 1
n_2 = size of sample 2
σ_1^2 = the variance of population 1
σ_2^2 = the variance of population 2

This formula is the basis for statistical inferences about the difference in two means using two random independent samples.

Note: *If the populations are normally distributed on the measurement being studied and if the population variances are known, Formula 10.1 can be used for small sample sizes.*

Hypothesis Testing

In many instances, business analysts want to test the differences in the mean values of two populations. As an example, a consumer organization might want to test two brands of light bulbs to determine whether one burns longer than the other. A company planning to relocate might want to determine whether a significant difference separates the average price of a home in Kingston, Ontario, from house prices in Edmonton, Alberta. Formula 10.1 can be used to test the difference between two population means.

As a specific example, suppose we want to conduct a hypothesis test to determine whether the average annual salary of an advertising manager is different from the average annual salary of an auditing manager. Because we are testing to determine whether the means are different, it might seem logical that the null and alternative hypotheses would be:

$$H_0: \mu_1 = \mu_2$$
$$H_a: \mu_1 \neq \mu_2$$

where advertising managers are population 1 and auditing managers are population 2. However, analysts generally construct these hypotheses as:

$$H_0: \mu_1 - \mu_2 = \delta$$
$$H_a: \mu_1 - \mu_2 \neq \delta$$

This format not only allows the business analyst to test if the population means are equal, but also affords her the opportunity to hypothesize about a particular difference in the means (δ). Thus, δ is set equal to zero, resulting in the following hypotheses, which we will use for this problem and most others:

$$H_0: \mu_1 - \mu_2 = 0$$
$$H_a: \mu_1 - \mu_2 \neq 0$$

Note, however, that a business analyst could be interested in testing to determine if there is, for example, a difference of means equal to, say, 10, in which case $\delta = 10$.

A random sample of 32 advertising managers from across Canada is taken. The advertising managers are contacted by telephone and asked what their annual salary is. A similar random sample is taken of 34 auditing managers. The resulting salary data are listed in **Table 10.1**, along with the sample means, the population standard deviations, and the population variances.

In this problem, the business analyst is testing whether there is a difference in the average salary of an advertising manager and an auditing manager; therefore, the test is two-tailed. If the business analyst had hypothesized that one was paid more than the other, the test would have been one-tailed.

Suppose $\alpha = 0.05$. Because this test is two-tailed, each of the two rejection regions has an area of 0.025, leaving 0.475 of the area in the distribution between each critical value and the mean of the distribution. The associated critical table $z_{\alpha/2}$ value for this area is $z_{0.25} = \pm 1.96$. **Figure 10.3** shows the critical table *z* value along with the rejection regions.

Formula 10.1 and the data in Table 10.1 yield a *z* value to complete the hypothesis test:

$$z = \frac{(70.700 - 62.187) - 0}{\sqrt{\dfrac{264.164}{32} + \dfrac{166.409}{34}}} = 2.35$$

The observed value of 2.35 is greater than the critical value obtained from the *z* table, 1.96. The business analyst rejects the null hypothesis and can say that there is a significant difference between the average annual salary of an advertising manager and the average

TABLE 10.1	Salaries for Advertising Managers and Auditing Managers ($ thousands)		
Advertising Managers		**Auditing Managers**	
74.256	64.276	69.962	67.160
96.234	74.194	55.052	37.386
89.807	65.360	57.828	59.505
93.261	73.904	63.362	72.790
103.030	54.270	37.194	71.351
74.195	59.045	99.198	58.653
75.932	68.508	61.254	63.508
80.742	71.115	73.065	43.649
39.672	67.574	48.036	63.369
45.652	59.621	60.053	59.676
93.083	62.483	66.359	54.449
63.384	69.319	61.261	46.394
57.791	35.394	77.136	71.804
65.145	86.741	66.035	72.401
96.767	57.351	54.335	56.470
77.242		42.494	67.814
67.056		83.849	71.492

$n_1 = 32$ $n_2 = 34$
$\bar{x}_1 = 70.700$ $\bar{x}_2 = 62.187$
$\sigma_1 = 16.253$ $\sigma_2 = 12.900$
$\sigma_1^2 = 264.164$ $\sigma_2^2 = 166.409$

FIGURE 10.3 Critical Values and Rejection Regions for the Salary Example

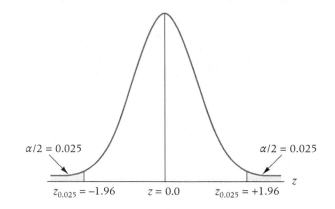

$\alpha/2 = 0.025$ $\alpha/2 = 0.025$

$z_{0.025} = -1.96$ $z = 0.0$ $z_{0.025} = +1.96$

annual salary of an auditing manager. The business analyst then examines the sample means (70.700 for advertising managers and 62.187 for auditing managers) and uses common sense to conclude that advertising managers earn more, on average, than do auditing managers. **Figure 10.4** shows the relationship between the observed z and $z_{\alpha/2}$.

This conclusion could have been reached by using the p-value. Looking up the probability of $z \geq 2.35$ in Table A.5, the z distribution table in Appendix A, yields an area of $0.5000 - 0.4906 = 0.0094$. This p-value (0.0094) is less than $\alpha/2 = 0.025$. The decision is to reject the null hypothesis.

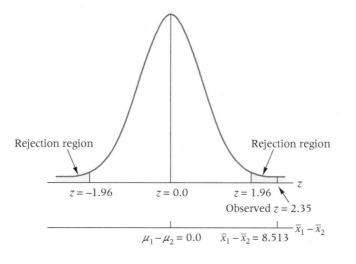

FIGURE 10.4 Location of Observed z Value for the Salary Example

DEMONSTRATION PROBLEM 10.1

A sample of 87 professional working women showed that the average amount paid annually into a retirement fund per person was $3,352. The population standard deviation is $1,100. A sample of 76 professional working men showed that the average amount paid annually into a retirement fund per person was $5,727, with a population standard deviation of $1,700. A women's group wants to prove that women do not pay as much per year as men into retirement funds. If they use $\alpha = 0.001$ and these sample data, will they be able to reject a null hypothesis that women annually pay the same as or more than men into retirement funds? Use the eight-step hypothesis-testing process.

Solution

Step 1 This test is one-tailed. Because the women's group wants to prove that women pay less than men into retirement funds annually, the alternative hypothesis should be $\mu_w - \mu_m < 0$, and the null hypothesis is that women pay the same as or more than men, $\mu_w - \mu_m = 0$.

Step 2 The test statistic is:

$$z = \frac{(\bar{x}_1 - \bar{x}_2) - (\mu_1 - \mu_2)}{\sqrt{\dfrac{\sigma_1^2}{n_1} + \dfrac{\sigma_2^2}{n_2}}}$$

Step 3 The level of significance has been specified as 0.001.

Step 4 By using this value of α, a critical $z_{0.001}$ of -3.08 can be determined. The decision rule is to reject the null hypothesis if the observed value of the test statistic, z, is less than -3.08.

Step 5 The sample data follow.

Women	Men
$\bar{x}_1 = \$3,352$	$\bar{x}_2 = \$5,727$
$\sigma_1 = \$1,100$	$\sigma_2 = \$1,700$
$n_1 = 87$	$n_2 = 76$

Step 6 Solving for z gives:

$$z = \frac{(3,352 - 5,727) - 0}{\sqrt{\dfrac{1,100^2}{87} + \dfrac{1,700^2}{76}}} = \frac{-2,375}{227.9} = -10.42$$

Step 7 The observed z value of -10.42 is deep in the rejection region, well past the table value of $z_{0.001} = -3.08$. Even with the small $\alpha = 0.001$, the null hypothesis is rejected.

Step 8 The evidence is substantial that women, on average, pay less than men into retirement funds annually. The following diagram displays these results.

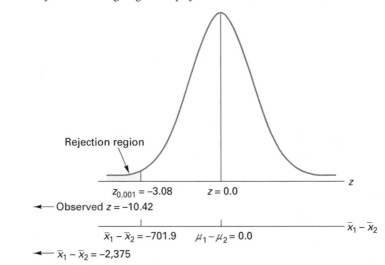

The probability of obtaining an observed z value of -10.42 by chance is virtually zero, because the value is beyond the limits of the z table. By the p-value, the null hypothesis is rejected because the probability is approximately 0.0000, or less than $\alpha = 0.001$.

If this problem were worked by the critical value method, what critical value of the difference in the two means would have to be surpassed to reject the null hypothesis for a table $z_{0.001}$ value of -3.08? The answer is:

$$\bar{x}_1 - \bar{x}_2 = (\mu_1 - \mu_2) - z_{0.001}\sqrt{\frac{\sigma_1^2}{n_1} + \frac{\sigma_2^2}{n_2}}$$
$$= 0 - 3.08(227.9) = -701.9$$

The difference in sample means would need to be at least 701.9 to reject the null hypothesis. The actual sample difference in this problem was $-2{,}375$ ($3{,}352 - 5{,}727$), which is considerably larger than the critical value of the difference. Thus, with the critical value method, the null hypothesis is also rejected.

Confidence Intervals

Sometimes being able to estimate the difference in the means of two populations is valuable. By how much do two populations differ in size or mass or age? By how much do two products differ in effectiveness? Do two different manufacturing or training methods produce different mean results? The answers to these questions are often difficult to obtain through census techniques. The alternative is to take a random sample from each of the two populations and study the difference in the sample means.

Algebraically, Formula 10.1 can be manipulated to produce a formula for constructing confidence intervals for the difference in two population means.

Confidence Interval to Estimate $\mu_1 - \mu_2$

$$(\bar{x}_1 - \bar{x}_2) - z_{\alpha/2}\sqrt{\frac{\sigma_1^2}{n_1} + \frac{\sigma_2^2}{n_2}} \le \mu_1 - \mu_2 \le (\bar{x}_1 - \bar{x}_2) + z_{\alpha/2}\sqrt{\frac{\sigma_1^2}{n_1} + \frac{\sigma_2^2}{n_2}} \qquad (10.2)$$

Suppose a study is conducted to estimate the difference between middle-income shoppers and low-income shoppers in terms of the average amount saved on grocery bills per week by using coupons. Random samples of 60 middle-income shoppers and 80 low-income shoppers are taken, and their purchases are monitored for one week. The average amounts saved with coupons, as well as sample sizes and population standard deviations, are in the table below.

Middle-Income Shoppers	Low-Income Shoppers
$n_1 = 60$	$n_2 = 80$
$\bar{x}_1 = \$5.84$	$\bar{x}_2 = \$2.67$
$\sigma_1 = \$1.41$	$\sigma_2 = \$0.54$

This information can be used to construct a 98% confidence interval to estimate the difference between the mean amount saved with coupons by middle-income shoppers and the mean amount saved with coupons by low-income shoppers.

The $z_{\alpha/2}$ value associated with a 98% level of confidence is 2.33. This value, the data shown, and Formula 10.2 can be used to determine the confidence interval.

$$(5.84 - 2.67) - 2.33\sqrt{\frac{1.41^2}{60} + \frac{0.54^2}{80}} \leq \mu_1 - \mu_2 \leq (5.84 - 2.67) + 2.33\sqrt{\frac{1.41^2}{60} + \frac{0.54^2}{80}}$$

$$3.17 - 0.45 \leq \mu_1 - \mu_2 \leq 3.17 + 0.45$$

$$2.72 \leq \mu_1 - \mu_2 \leq 3.62$$

There is a 98% level of confidence that the actual difference in the population mean coupon savings per week between middle-income and low-income shoppers is between $2.72 and $3.62. That is, the difference could be as little as $2.72 or as great as $3.62. The point estimate for the difference in mean savings is $3.17. Note that a zero difference in the population means of these two groups is unlikely, because zero is not in the 98% range.

DEMONSTRATION PROBLEM 10.2

A consumer test group wants to determine the difference in fuel efficiency of cars using regular unleaded gas and cars using premium unleaded gas. Analysts for the group divided a fleet of 100 cars of the same make in half and tested each car on one tank of gas. Fifty of the cars were filled with regular unleaded gas and 50 were filled with premium unleaded gas. The sample average for the regular gas group was 10.97 L/100 km, and the sample average for the premium gas group was 9.56 L/100 km. Assume that the population standard deviation of the regular unleaded gas population is 1.77 L/100 km, and that the population standard deviation of the premium unleaded gas population is 1.16 L/100 km. Construct a 95% confidence interval to estimate the difference in the mean fuel efficiency between the cars using regular gas and the cars using premium gas.

Solution   The $z_{\alpha/2}$ value for a 95% confidence interval is 1.96. The other sample information follows.

Regular	Premium
$n_1 = 50$	$n_2 = 50$
$\bar{x}_1 = 10.97$	$\bar{x}_2 = 9.56$
$\sigma_1 = 1.77$	$\sigma_2 = 1.16$

Based on this information, the confidence interval is

$$(10.97 - 9.56) - 1.96\sqrt{\frac{1.77^2}{50} + \frac{1.16^2}{50}} \leq \mu_1 - \mu_2 \leq (10.97 - 9.56) + 1.96\sqrt{\frac{1.77^2}{50} + \frac{1.16^2}{50}}$$

$$1.41 - 0.59 \leq \mu_1 - \mu_2 \leq 1.41 + 0.59$$

$$0.82 \leq \mu_1 - \mu_2 \leq 2.00$$

We are 95% confident that the actual difference in mean fuel efficiency between the two types of gas is between 0.82 L/100 km and 2.00 L/100 km. The point estimate is 1.41 L/100 km.

Designating one group as group 1 and another group as group 2 is an arbitrary decision. If the two groups in Demonstration Problem 10.2 were reversed, the confidence interval would be the same, but the signs would be reversed and the inequalities would be switched. Thus, the analyst must interpret the confidence interval in light of the sample information. For the confidence interval in Demonstration Problem 10.2, the population difference in mean fuel efficiency between regular and premium could be as much as 2.00 L/100 km. This result means that the premium gas could average 2.00 L/100 km less than regular gas. The other side of the interval shows that, on the basis of the sample information, the difference in favour of premium gas could be as little as 0.82 L/100 km.

If the confidence interval were being used to test the hypothesis that there is a difference in the average number of litres per 100 km between regular and premium gas, the interval would tell us to reject the null hypothesis because the interval does *not* contain zero. When both ends of a confidence interval have the same sign, zero is not in the interval. In Demonstration Problem 10.2, the interval signs are both positive. We are 95% confident that the true difference in population means is positive. Hence, we are 95% confident that there is a nonzero difference in means. For such a test, $\alpha = 1 - 0.95 = 0.05$. If the signs of the confidence interval for the difference of the sample means are different, the interval includes zero, and finding no significant difference in population means is possible.

Using the Computer to Test Hypotheses About the Difference in Two Population Means Using the z Test

Excel can test hypotheses about two population means using a z test. **Figure 10.5** shows Excel output for the advertising manager and auditing manager salary problem. For z tests, Excel requires knowledge of the population variances. The standard output includes the sample means and population variances, the sample sizes, the hypothesized mean difference (which here, as in most cases, is zero), the observed z value, and the p-values and critical table z values for both a one-tailed and a two-tailed test. Note that the p-value for this two-tailed test is 0.0189, which is less than $\alpha = 0.05$ and thus indicates that the decision should be to reject the null hypothesis.

FIGURE 10.5 Output for the Advertising Managers and Auditing Managers Salary Problem

	A	B	C
1	*z* Test: Two-Sample for Means		
2		Ad Mgr	Auditing Mgr
3	Mean	70.700	62.187
4	Known Variance	264.164	166.411
5	Observations	32	34
6	Hypothesized Mean Difference	0	
7	*z*	2.35	
8	*P(Z<=z)* one-tail	0.0094	
9	*z* Critical one-tail	1.64	
10	*P(Z<=z)* two-tail	0.0189	
11	*z* Critical two-tail	1.96	

Concept Check

1. The sampling plan calls for selecting two independent samples in order to use Formulas 10.1 and 10.2 to estimate the difference in two means. Explain in your own words what it means for the two samples to be independent.

2. Explain in your own words the relationship between a hypothesis test and a confidence interval about the difference in two means.

3. Are the conclusions from a hypothesis test and a confidence interval about the difference in two means useful and reliable if the populations for the measurements being studied are not normally distributed?

4. Explain the relationship between sample sizes and the width of the confidence interval for the difference in two population means.

10.1 Problems

10.1 a. Test the following hypotheses of the difference in population means by using the following data ($\alpha = 0.10$) and the eight-step process.

$$H_0: \mu_1 - \mu_2 = 0 \qquad H_a: \mu_1 - \mu_2 < 0$$

Sample 1	Sample 2
$\bar{x}_1 = 51.3$	$\bar{x}_2 = 53.2$
$\sigma_1^2 = 52$	$\sigma_2^2 = 60$
$n_1 = 31$	$n_2 = 32$

b. Use the critical value method to find the critical difference in the mean values required to reject the null hypothesis.

c. What is the p-value for this problem?

10.2 Use the following sample information to construct a 90% confidence interval for the difference in the two population means.

Sample 1	Sample 2
$n_1 = 32$	$n_2 = 31$
$\bar{x}_1 = 70.4$	$\bar{x}_2 = 68.7$
$\sigma_1 = 5.76$	$\sigma_2 = 6.1$

10.3 Examine the following data. Assume the variances for the two populations are 22.74 and 26.65, respectively.

a. Use the data to test the following hypotheses ($\alpha = 0.02$).

$$H_0: \mu_1 - \mu_2 = 0 \qquad H_a: \mu_1 - \mu_2 \neq 0$$

Sample 1						Sample 2					
90	88	80	88	83	94	78	85	82	81	75	76
88	87	91	81	83	88	90	80	76	83	88	77
81	84	84	87	87	93	77	75	79	86	90	75
88	90	91	88	84	83	82	83	88	80	80	74
89	95	97	95	93	97	80	90	74	89	84	79

b. Construct a 98% confidence interval to estimate the difference in population means using these data. How does your result validate the decision you reached in part (a)?

10.4 The Trade Show Bureau conducted a survey to determine why people go to trade shows. The respondents were asked to rate a series of reasons on a scale from 1 to 5, with 1 representing little importance and 5 representing great importance. One of the reasons suggested was general curiosity. The following responses for 50 people from the computers/electronics industry and 50 people from the food/beverage industry were recorded for general curiosity. Use these data and $\alpha = 0.01$ to determine whether there is a significant difference between people in these two industries on this question. Assume the variance for the computers/electronics population is 1.0188 and the variance for the food/beverage population is 0.9180.

Computers/Electronics					Food/Beverage				
1	2	1	3	2	3	3	2	4	3
0	3	3	2	1	4	5	2	4	3
3	3	1	2	2	3	2	3	2	3
3	2	2	2	2	4	3	3	3	3
1	2	3	2	1	2	4	2	3	3
1	1	3	3	2	2	4	4	4	4
2	1	4	1	4	3	5	3	3	2
2	3	0	1	0	2	0	2	2	5
3	3	2	2	3	4	3	3	2	3
2	1	0	2	3	4	3	3	3	2

10.5 Suppose you own a plumbing repair business and employ 15 plumbers. You are interested in estimating the difference in the average number of calls completed per day by two of the plumbers. A random sample of 40 days of plumber A's work results in a sample average of 5.3 calls. Historically, the variance for this plumber is known to be 1.99. A random sample of 37 days of plumber B's work results in a sample mean of 6.5 calls. Historically, the variance for this plumber is known to be 2.36. Use this information and a 95% level of confidence to estimate the difference in population mean daily efforts between plumber A and plumber B. Interpret the results. Is it possible that, for these populations of days, the average numbers of calls completed by plumber A and plumber B do not differ?

10.6 The Bureau of Labor Statistics in the U.S. shows that the average insurance cost to a company per employee per hour is $1.84 for managers and $1.99 for professional specialty workers. Suppose these figures were obtained from 35 managers and 41 professional specialty workers, and that their respective population standard deviations are $0.38 and $0.51. Calculate a 98% confidence interval to estimate the difference in the mean hourly company expenditures for insurance for these two groups. What is the value of the point estimate? Determine whether there is a significant difference in the hourly rates employers pay for insurance between managers and professional specialty workers. Use a 2% level of significance.

10.7 A company's auditor believes the per diem cost in Windsor, Ontario, rose significantly between 2011 and 2021. To test this belief, the auditor samples 51 business trips from the company's records for 2011; the sample average was $190 per day, with a population standard deviation of $18.50. The auditor selects a second random sample of 47 business trips from the company's records for 2021; the sample average was $198 per day, with a population standard deviation of $15.60. If he uses a risk of committing a Type I error of 0.01, does the auditor find that the per diem average expense in Windsor has gone up significantly?

10.8 Suppose a market analyst wants to determine the difference in the average price of 4 L of milk in Vancouver and Montreal. To do so, he takes a telephone survey of 31 randomly selected consumers in Vancouver. He first asks whether they have purchased 4 L of milk during the past two weeks. If they say no, he continues to select consumers until he selects $n = 31$ people who say yes. If they say yes, he asks them how much they paid for the milk. The analyst undertakes a similar survey in Montreal with 31 respondents. Using the resulting sample information that follows, compute a 99% confidence interval to estimate the difference in the mean price of 4 L of milk between the two cities. Assume the population variance for Vancouver is 0.12 and the population variance for Montreal is 0.06.

Vancouver			Montreal		
$3.77	$3.48	$3.59	$5.31	$5.69	$5.69
3.94	3.30	3.59	5.50	5.50	5.69
3.71	3.77	3.53	5.21	5.40	5.31
3.83	4.12	3.65	5.69	5.21	5.40
4.59	3.83	3.77	5.69	6.16	5.97
4.24	3.77	4.01	5.40	5.69	5.21
3.71	3.89	4.36	5.21	5.31	5.78
3.65	4.01	3.89	5.78	6.16	5.50
4.06	4.01	4.12	6.16	5.31	5.97
3.89	4.18	3.94	5.69	5.40	5.59
		4.01			5.78

10.9 Employee suggestions can provide useful and insightful ideas for management. Some companies solicit and receive employee suggestions more than others, and company culture influences the use of employee suggestions. Suppose a study is conducted to determine whether there is a significant difference in mean number of suggestions a month per employee between the Manan Corporation and the Prairie Corporation. The study shows that the average number of suggestions per month is 5.8 at Manan and 5.0 at Prairie. Suppose these figures were obtained from random samples of 36 and 45 employees, respectively. If the population standard deviations of suggestions per employee are 1.7 and 1.4 for Manan and Prairie, respectively, is there a significant difference in the population means? Use $\alpha = 0.05$.

10.10 Two processes in a manufacturing line are performed manually: operation A and operation B. A random sample of 50 different assemblies using operation A shows that the sample average time per assembly is 8.05 minutes, with a population standard deviation of 1.36 minutes. A random sample of 38 different assemblies using operation B shows that the sample average time per assembly is 7.26 minutes, with a population standard deviation of 1.06 minutes. For $\alpha = 0.10$, is there enough evidence in these samples to declare that operation A takes significantly longer to perform than operation B?

10.2 Hypothesis Testing and Confidence Intervals About the Difference in Two Means Using the *t* Statistic: Independent Samples with Population Variances Unknown

LEARNING OBJECTIVE 10.2

Test hypotheses and develop confidence intervals about the difference in two means of independent samples with unknown population variances using the *t* test.

The techniques presented in Section 10.1 are for use whenever the population variances are known. On many occasions, analysts test hypotheses or construct confidence intervals about the difference in two population means where the population variances are not known. If the population variances are not known, the *z* methodology is not appropriate. This section presents methodology for handling the situation when the population variances are unknown.

Hypothesis Testing

The hypothesis test presented in this section is a test that compares the means of two samples to determine whether there is a difference in the means of two populations from which the samples come. This technique is used whenever the population variances are unknown (and hence the sample variances must be used) and the samples are independent (not related in any way). *An assumption underlying this technique is that the measurement or characteristic being studied is normally distributed for both populations.* In Section 10.1, the difference in large sample means was analyzed by Formula 10.1:

$$z = \frac{(\bar{x}_1 - \bar{x}_2) - (\mu_1 - \mu_2)}{\sqrt{\dfrac{\sigma_1^2}{n_1} + \dfrac{\sigma_2^2}{n_2}}}$$

If $\sigma_1^2 = \sigma_2^2 = \sigma^2$, Formula 10.1 algebraically reduces to:

$$z = \frac{(\bar{x}_1 - \bar{x}_2) - (\mu_1 - \mu_2)}{\sigma \sqrt{\dfrac{1}{n_1} + \dfrac{1}{n_2}}}$$

If σ is unknown, it can be estimated by *pooling* the two sample variances and computing a pooled sample standard deviation:

$$\sigma \approx s_p = \sqrt{\frac{s_1^2(n_1 - 1) + s_2^2(n_2 - 1)}{n_1 + n_2 - 2}}$$

s_p^2 is the weighted average of the two sample variances, s_1^2 and s_2^2. Substituting this expression for σ and changing z to t produces a formula to test the difference in means.

---

t Formula to Test the Difference in Means Assuming σ_1^2 and σ_2^2 Are Equal

$$t = \frac{(\bar{x}_1 - \bar{x}_2) - (\mu_1 - \mu_2)}{\sqrt{\dfrac{s_1^2(n_1 - 1) + s_2^2(n_2 - 1)}{n_1 + n_2 - 2}} \sqrt{\dfrac{1}{n_1} + \dfrac{1}{n_2}}} \qquad (10.3)$$

$$df = n_1 + n_2 - 2$$

Formula 10.3 is constructed by assuming that the two population variances, σ_1^2 and σ_2^2, are equal. Thus, when using Formula 10.3 to test hypotheses about the difference in two means for small independent samples when the population variances are unknown, we must assume that the two samples come from populations in which the variances are essentially equal. (See Thinking Critically About Statistics in Business Today 10.1.)

Thinking Critically About Statistics in Business Today 10.1

Ethical Differences Between Men and Women

Until recently, there have been few studies comparing the ethics of men and women, but the topic is of growing interest. One study surveyed 164 managers of a large financial conglomerate to see if men and women made different ethical managerial decisions. A questionnaire was constructed using vignettes (brief, focused cases) to depict four ethical questions under two different scenarios. Vignettes dealt with (1) sale of an unsafe product, (2) bribery, (3) product misrepresentation, and (4) industrial espionage. These vignettes were to be considered under the scenarios of (a) enhancing the firm's profit position and (b) the individual's own economic gain. The questionnaire was structured to produce two scores for each respondent on each ethical question: the first score without regard to scenario and the second with regard to scenario. The null hypothesis that there is no significant difference in the mean ethical scores of men and women was tested for each question using a t test for independent samples.

The results were mixed. In considering the responses to the four vignettes without regard to either of the two scenarios, there was a significant difference between men and women on the sale of an unsafe product at ($\alpha = 0.01$). On this question, women scored significantly higher (more ethical) than men, indicating that women are less likely to sell an unsafe product. On the questions of product misrepresentation and industrial espionage, women scored significantly higher on both ($\alpha = 0.10$). There was no significant difference between men and women on the question of bribery.

The results were somewhat different when the two scenarios were considered (firm profit position and personal economic gain). On the question of selling an unsafe product, women were significantly more ethical ($\alpha = 0.01$) when considering enhancing the firm's profit position and significantly more ethical ($\alpha = 0.05$) when considering personal economic gain. On the question of bribery, there was no significant difference in the ethics scores of men and women in light of enhancing the firm's profit position but women were significantly more ethical ($\alpha = 0.10$) when considering personal economic gain. On the question of product misrepresentation, there was no significant difference between men and women when considering personal economic gain but women were significantly more ethical than men in light of enhancing the firm's profit position ($\alpha = 0.10$). On the question of industrial espionage, women were significantly more ethical than men ($\alpha = 0.10$)

in light of enhancing the firm's profit position, and women were also significantly more ethical than men ($\alpha = 0.01$) when considering personal gain.

Things to Ponder

1. This study used two-sample hypothesis testing in an effort to determine whether there is a difference between men and women on ethical management issues. Do you think the results here can assist decision-makers in assigning managers to various tasks that involve any of these four ethical questions?

2. Interesting studies have been carried out that question why women might be more ethical than men in some managerial situations and what might be done to foster stronger ethics among men. Do you think that these outcomes may change in time? Why or why not?

Sources: James J. Hoffman, "Are Women Really More Ethical Than Men? Maybe It Depends on the Situation," *Journal of Managerial Issues*, 10, no. 1 (Spring 1998): 60–73; Patricia W. Hatamyar and Kevin M. Simmons, "Are Women More Ethical Lawyers? An Empirical Study," Florida State University Law Review, 31 (2004): 785–857; Jessica A. Kennedy and Laura J. Kray, "Who Is Willing to Sacrifice Ethical Values for Money and Social Status? Gender Differences in Reactions to Ethical Compromises," *Social Psychological and Personality Science,* March 28, 2013.

At the Huang Manufacturing Company, an application of the test of the difference in small sample means arises. New employees are expected to attend a three-day seminar to learn about the company. At the end of the seminar, they are tested to measure their knowledge about the company. The traditional training method has been a lecture and a question-and-answer session. Management decided to experiment with a different training procedure, which processes new employees in two days by using online media and having no question-and-answer session. If this procedure works, it could save the company thousands of dollars over a period of several years. However, there is some concern about the effectiveness of the two-day method, and company managers would like to know whether there is any difference in the effectiveness of the two training methods.

To test the difference in the two methods, the managers randomly select one group of 15 newly hired employees to take the three-day seminar (method A) and a second group of 12 new employees for the two-day online-media method (method B). Table 10.2 shows the test scores of the two groups. Using $\alpha = 0.05$, the managers want to determine whether there is a significant difference in the mean scores of the two groups. They assume that the scores for this test are normally distributed and that the population variances are approximately equal.

TABLE 10.2 **Test Scores for New Employees After Training**

Training Method A					Training Method B			
56	50	52	44	52	59	54	55	65
47	47	53	45	48	52	57	64	53
42	51	42	43	44	53	56	53	57

Step 1   The hypotheses for this test follow.

$$H_0: \mu_1 - \mu_2 = 0$$
$$H_a: \mu_1 - \mu_2 \neq 0$$

Step 2   The statistical test to be used is Formula 10.3.

Step 3   The value of α is 0.05.

Step 4   Because the hypotheses are = and $\neq$, this test is two-tailed. The degrees of freedom are 25 ($15 + 12 - 2 = 25$) and α is 0.05. The t table requires an α value for one tail only, and, because it is a two-tailed test, α is split from 0.05 to 0.025 to obtain the table t value: $t_{0.025,25} = \pm 2.060$.

The null hypothesis will be rejected if the observed t value is less than -2.060 or greater than $+2.060$.

Step 5   The sample data are given in Table 10.2. From these data, we can calculate the sample statistics. The sample means and variances follow.

	Method A	Method B
	$\bar{x}_1 = 47.73$	$\bar{x}_2 = 56.5$
	$s_1^2 = 19.495$	$s_2^2 = 18.273$
	$n_1 = 15$	$n_2 = 12$

Step 6   The observed value of *t* is:

$$t = \frac{(47.73 - 56.50) - 0}{\sqrt{\dfrac{(19.495)(14) + (18.273)(11)}{15 + 12 - 2}}\sqrt{\dfrac{1}{15} + \dfrac{1}{12}}} = -5.20$$

Step 7   Because the observed value, $t = -5.20$, is less than the lower critical table value, $t = -2.06$, the observed value of *t* is in the rejection region. The null hypothesis is rejected. There is a significant difference in the mean scores of the two tests.

Step 8   **Figure 10.6** shows the critical areas and the observed *t* value. Note that the computed *t* value is -5.20, which is enough to cause the managers of the Huang Manufacturing Company to reject the null hypothesis. Their conclusion is that there is a significant difference in the effectiveness of the training methods. Upon examining the sample means, they realize that method B (the two-day online-media method) actually produced an average score that was more than eight points higher than that for the group trained with method A. Given that training method B scores are significantly higher and that the seminar is a day shorter than method A (thereby saving both time and money), it makes business sense to adopt method B as the standard training method.

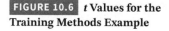

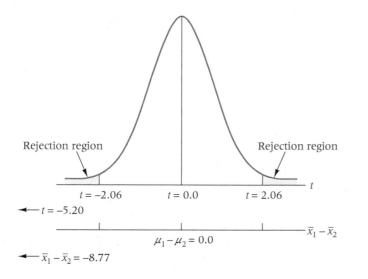

FIGURE 10.6 *t* Values for the Training Methods Example

In a test of this sort, which group is group 1 and which is group 2 is an arbitrary decision. If the two samples had been designated in reverse, the observed *t* value would have been $t = +5.20$ (same magnitude but different sign), and the decision would have been the same.

Note: If the equal variances assumption cannot be met, the following formula should be used.

***t* Formula to Test the Difference in Means**

$$t = \frac{(\bar{x}_1 - \bar{x}_2) - (\mu_1 - \mu_2)}{\sqrt{\dfrac{s_1^2}{n_1} + \dfrac{s_2^2}{n_2}}}$$

$$df = \frac{\left(\dfrac{s_1^2}{n_1} + \dfrac{s_2^2}{n_2}\right)^2}{\dfrac{\left(\dfrac{s_1^2}{n_1}\right)^2}{n_1 - 1} + \dfrac{\left(\dfrac{s_2^2}{n_2}\right)^2}{n_2 - 1}} \tag{10.4}$$

Because Formula 10.4 requires a more complex degrees-of-freedom component, it may be unattractive to some users. Many statistical computer software packages offer the user a choice of the "pooled" formula or the "unpooled" formula. The pooled formula in the computer packages is Formula 10.3, in which equal population variances are assumed. Excel refers to this as a t-Test: Two-Sample Assuming Equal Variances. The unpooled formula is Formula 10.4 and is used when population variances cannot be assumed to be equal. Excel refers to this as a t-Test: Two-Sample Assuming Unequal Variances. Again, in each of these formulas, the populations from which the two samples are drawn are assumed to be normally distributed for the phenomenon being measured.

Using the Computer to Test Hypotheses and Construct Confidence Intervals About the Difference in Two Population Means Using the t Test

Excel can analyze t tests for the difference in two means. **Figure 10.7** contains the Excel output for the Huang Manufacturing Company training methods example. Notice that the output contains the same sample means, the degrees of freedom (df $= 25$), the observed t value -5.20, and the p-value (0.000022 as two-tailed p). This p-value can be compared directly with $\alpha = 0.05$ for decision-making purposes (reject the null hypothesis).

FIGURE 10.7 **Excel Output for the Training Methods Example**

	A	B	C
1	t-Test: Two-Sample Assuming Equal Variances		
2		Method A	Method B
3	Mean	47.73	56.50
4	Variance	19.495	18.273
5	Observations	15	12
6	Pooled Variance	18.957	
7	Hypothesized Mean Difference	0	
8	df	25	
9	t Stat	−5.20	
10	$P(T<=t)$ one-tail	0.0000112	
11	t Critical one-tail	1.71	
12	$P(T<=t)$ two-tail	0.0000223	
13	t Critical two-tail	2.06	

Excel displays the sample variances and the pooled variance and prints out p-values for both a one-tailed test and a two-tailed test: the user must select the appropriate value for his or her test. Excel also prints out the critical t values for both one- and two-tailed tests. Notice that the critical t value for a two-tailed test (2.06) is the same as the critical t value obtained by using the t table (± 2.060).

DEMONSTRATION PROBLEM 10.3

Is there a difference in the way Chinese cultural values affect the purchasing strategies of industrial buyers in Taiwan and mainland China? Analysts at the National Chiao-Tung University in Taiwan attempted to determine whether there is a significant difference in the purchasing strategies of industrial buyers in Taiwan and mainland China based on the cultural dimension labelled "integration." Integration is being in harmony with one's self, family, and associates. For the study, 46 Taiwanese buyers and 26 mainland Chinese buyers were contacted and interviewed. Buyers were asked to respond to 35 items using a nine-point scale with possible answers ranging from no importance (1) to extreme importance (9). The resulting statistics for the two groups are shown in Step 5. Using $\alpha = 0.01$, determine whether there is a significant difference between buyers in Taiwan and buyers in mainland China on integration. Assume that integration scores are normally distributed in the population.

Solution

Step 1   If a two-tailed test is undertaken, the hypotheses and the table *t* value are as follows:

$$H_0: \mu_1 - \mu_2 = 0$$
$$H_a: \mu_1 - \mu_2 \neq 0$$

Step 2   The appropriate statistical test is Formula 10.3.

Step 3   The value of α is 0.01.

Step 4   The sample sizes are 46 and 26. Thus, there are 70 degrees of freedom. With this figure and $\alpha/2 = 0.005$, the critical table *t* value can be determined:

$$t_{0.005,70} = 2.648$$

Step 5   The sample data follow.

<table>
<tr><td colspan="2" align="center">**Integration**</td></tr>
<tr><td>**Taiwanese Buyers**</td><td>**Mainland Chinese Buyers**</td></tr>
<tr><td>$n_1 = 46$</td><td>$n_2 = 26$</td></tr>
<tr><td>$\bar{x}_1 = 5.42$</td><td>$\bar{x}_2 = 5.04$</td></tr>
<tr><td>$s_1^2 = 0.58^2 = 0.3364$</td><td>$s_2^2 = 0.49^2 = 0.2401$</td></tr>
<tr><td colspan="2" align="center">$df = n_1 + n_2 - 2 = 46 + 26 - 2 = 70$</td></tr>
</table>

Step 6   The observed *t* value is:

$$t = \frac{(5.42 - 5.04) - 0}{\sqrt{\dfrac{(0.3364)(45) + (0.2401)(25)}{46 + 26 - 2}} \sqrt{\dfrac{1}{46} + \dfrac{1}{26}}} = 2.82$$

Step 7   Because the observed value of $t = 2.82$ is greater than the critical table value of $t = 2.648$, the decision is to reject the null hypothesis.

Step 8   The Taiwan industrial buyers scored significantly higher than the mainland China industrial buyers on integration. Managers should keep in mind this cultural dimension when dealing with Taiwanese and mainland Chinese industrial buyers.

The following graph shows the critical *t* values, the rejection regions, the observed *t* value, and the difference in the raw means.

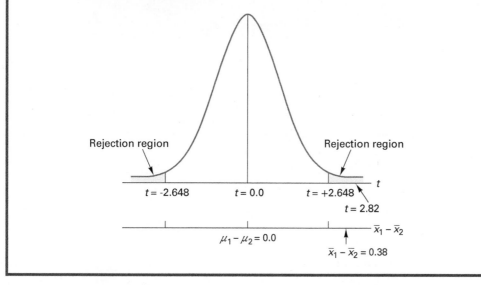

Confidence Intervals

Confidence interval formulas can be derived to estimate the difference in the population means for independent samples when the population variances are unknown. The focus in this section is only on confidence intervals when approximately equal population variances and normally distributed populations can be assumed.

Confidence Interval to Estimate $\mu_1 - \mu_2$ Assuming the Population Variances Are Unknown and Equal

$$(\bar{x}_1 - \bar{x}_2) - t\sqrt{\frac{s_1^2(n_1 - 1) + s_2^2(n_2 - 1)}{n_1 + n_2 - 2}}\sqrt{\frac{1}{n_1} + \frac{1}{n_2}} \leq \mu_1 - \mu_2 \leq$$

$$(\bar{x}_1 - \bar{x}_2) + t\sqrt{\frac{s_1^2(n_1 - 1) + s_2^2(n_2 - 1)}{n_1 + n_2 - 2}}\sqrt{\frac{1}{n_1} + \frac{1}{n_2}} \qquad (10.5)$$

$$df = n_1 + n_2 - 2$$

One group of analysts set out to determine whether there is a difference between "average Canadians" and those who are "phone survey respondents."[1] Their study was based on a well-known U.S. personality survey that attempted to assess the personality profile of both average Americans and phone survey respondents. Suppose the Canadian analysts sampled nine phone survey respondents and 10 average Canadians in this survey and obtained the results on one personality factor, conscientiousness, which are displayed in Table 10.3. Assume that conscientiousness scores are normally distributed in the population.

The table t value for a 99% level of confidence and 17 degrees of freedom is $t_{0.005,17} = 2.898$. The confidence interval is:

$$(37.09 - 34.99) \pm 2.898\sqrt{\frac{(1.727)^2(8) + (1.253)^2(9)}{9 + 10 - 2}}\sqrt{\frac{1}{9} + \frac{1}{10}}$$

$$= 2.10 \pm 1.99$$

$$0.11 \leq \mu_1 - \mu_2 \leq 4.09$$

TABLE 10.3	Conscientiousness Data on Phone Survey Respondents and Average Canadians	
Phone Survey Respondents		**Average Canadians**
35.38		35.03
37.06		33.90
37.74		34.56
36.97		36.24
37.84		34.59
37.50		34.95
40.75		33.30
35.31		34.73
35.30		34.79
		37.83
$n_1 = 9$		$n_2 = 10$
$\bar{x}_1 = 37.09$		$\bar{x}_2 = 34.99$
$s_1 = 1.727$		$s_2 = 1.253$
	$df = 9 + 10 - 2 = 17$	

---

[1] Data adapted from David Whitlark and Michael Geurts, "Phone Surveys: How Well Do Respondents Represent Average Americans?" *Marketing Research* (Fall 1998): 13–17. Note that the results on this portion of the actual study are about the same as those shown here except that in the actual study the sample sizes were in the 500–600 range.

The analysts are 99% confident that the true difference in population mean personality scores for conscientiousness between phone survey respondents and average Canadians is between 0.11 and 4.09. Zero is not in this interval, so they can conclude that there is a significant difference in the average scores of the two groups. Higher scores indicate more conscientiousness. Therefore, it is possible to conclude from Table 10.3 and this confidence interval that phone survey respondents are significantly more conscientious than average Canadians. These results indicate that analysts should be careful in using phone survey results to reach conclusions about average Canadians.

Figure 10.8 contains Excel output for this problem. Note that the Excel output includes the observed *t* value (3.06) for hypothesis testing. Because the *p*-value is 0.007, which is less than 0.01, the Excel hypothesis-testing information validates the conclusion reached that there is a significant difference in the scores of the two groups.

	A	B	C
1	*t*-Test: Two-Sample Assuming Equal Variances		
2		Survey Respondent	Average Canadian
3	Mean	37.09	34.99
4	Variance	2.98	1.57
5	Observations	9	10
6	Pooled Variance	2.2346	
7	Hypothesized Mean Difference	0	
8	df	17	
9	*t* State	3.061	
10	*P* (*T*<=*t*) one-tail	0.004	
11	*t* Critical one-tail	2.567	
12	*P* (*T*<=*t*) two-tail	0.007	
13	*t* Critical two-tail	2.898	

FIGURE 10.8 **Excel Output for the Phone Survey Respondent and Average Canadian Example**

DEMONSTRATION PROBLEM 10.4

A coffee manufacturer is interested in estimating the difference in the average daily coffee consumption of regular-coffee drinkers and decaffeinated-coffee drinkers. Its analyst randomly selects 13 regular-coffee drinkers and asks how many cups of coffee per day they drink. He randomly selects 15 decaffeinated-coffee drinkers and asks how many cups of coffee per day they drink. The average for the regular-coffee drinkers is 4.35 cups, with a standard deviation of 1.20 cups. The average for the decaffeinated-coffee drinkers is 6.84 cups, with a standard deviation of 1.42 cups. The analyst assumes, for each population, that the daily consumption is normally distributed. Construct a 95% confidence interval to estimate the difference in the averages of the two populations.

Solution   The table *t* value for this problem is $t_{0.025,26} = 2.056$. The confidence interval estimate is:

$$(4.35 - 6.84) \pm 2.056 \sqrt{\frac{(1.20)^2(12) + (1.42)^2(14)}{13 + 15 - 2}} \sqrt{\frac{1}{13} + \frac{1}{15}}$$
$$= -2.49 \pm 1.03$$
$$-3.52 \leq \mu_1 - \mu_2 \leq -1.46$$

The analyst is 95% confident that the difference in population average daily consumption of cups of coffee between regular- and decaffeinated-coffee drinkers is between 1.46 cups and 3.52 cups. The point estimate for the difference in population means is 2.49 cups, with an error of 1.03 cups.

Concept Check

1. Under what conditions should we use a z formula when dealing with the difference in two means? A t formula?

2. Are the conclusions from this section useful and reliable if the populations for the measurements being studied are not normally distributed?

3. What is the key difference between the t Formula 10.3 and the t Formula 10.4 to test the difference in means when population variances are unknown? Explain under what conditions each formula should be used.

4. Explain the relationship between sample sizes and the width of the confidence interval for the difference in two population means when population variances are unknown and equal.

10.2 Problems

10.11 Use the data given and the eight-step process to test the following hypotheses:

$$H_0: \mu_1 - \mu_2 = 0$$
$$H_a: \mu_1 - \mu_2 < 0$$

Sample 1	Sample 2
$n_1 = 8$	$n_2 = 11$
$\bar{x}_1 = 24.56$	$\bar{x}_2 = 26.42$
$s_1^2 = 12.4$	$s_2^2 = 15.8$

Use a 1% level of significance, and assume that x is normally distributed in the populations and the variances of the populations are approximately equal.

10.12 a. Use the following data and $\alpha = 0.10$ to test the stated hypotheses. Assume x is normally distributed in the populations and the variances of the populations are approximately equal.

$$H_0: \mu_1 - \mu_2 = 0$$
$$H_a: \mu_1 - \mu_2 \neq 0$$

Sample 1	Sample 2
$n_1 = 20$	$n_2 = 20$
$\bar{x}_1 = 118$	$\bar{x}_2 = 113$
$s_1 = 23.9$	$s_2 = 21.6$

b. Use these data to construct a 90% confidence interval to estimate $\mu_1 - \mu_2$.

10.13 Suppose that for years the mean of population 1 has been accepted to be the same as the mean of population 2, but now population 1 is believed to have a greater mean than population 2. Letting $\alpha = 0.05$ and assuming the populations have equal variances and x is approximately normally distributed, use the following data to test this belief.

Sample 1		Sample 2	
43.6	45.7	40.1	36.4
44.0	49.1	42.2	42.3
45.2	45.6	43.1	38.8
40.8	46.5	37.5	43.3
48.3	45.0	41.0	40.2

10.14 a. Suppose you want to determine whether the average values for populations 1 and 2 are different, and you randomly gather the following data.

	Sample 1						Sample 2				
2	10	7	8	2	5	10	12	8	7	9	11
9	1	8	0	2	8	9	8	9	10	11	10
11	2	4	5	3	9	11	10	7	8	10	10

Test your conjecture, using a probability of committing a Type I error of 0.01. Assume the population variances are the same and x is normally distributed in the populations.

b. Use these data to construct a 98% confidence interval for the difference in the two population means.

10.15 Suppose a real estate agent is interested in comparing the asking prices of condos in Montreal and Halifax. The agent conducts a small telephone survey in the two cities, asking the condo prices. A random sample of 21 listings in Montreal resulted in a sample average price of $328,000, with a standard deviation of $14,900. A random sample of 26 listings in Halifax resulted in a sample average price of $331,000, with a standard deviation of $13,700. The agent assumes condo prices are normally distributed and the variance in prices in the two cities is about the same. What would he obtain for a 90% confidence interval for the difference in mean condo prices between Montreal and Halifax? Test whether there is any difference in the mean prices of condos in the two cities for $\alpha = 0.10$.

10.16 According to an experiential education survey published at JobWeb.com, the average hourly wage of a university student working as a co-op student is $15.64 an hour and the average hourly wage of an intern is $15.44. Assume that such wages are normally distributed in the population and that the population variances are equal. Suppose these figures were actually obtained from the data in the following table. Use these data and $\alpha = 0.10$ to determine if there is a significant difference in the mean hourly wage of a university co-op student and the mean hourly wage of an intern. Using these same data, construct a 90% confidence interval to estimate the difference in the population mean hourly wages of co-op students and interns.

Co-op Students	Interns
$15.34	$15.10
14.75	14.45
15.88	16.21
16.92	14.91
16.84	13.80
17.37	16.02
14.05	16.25
15.41	15.89
16.74	13.99
14.55	16.48
15.25	15.75
14.64	16.42

10.17 Based on an indication that mean daily car rental rates may be higher for Toronto than for Montreal, a survey of eight car rental companies in Toronto is taken and the sample mean car rental rate is $47, with a standard deviation of $3. Further, suppose a survey of nine car rental companies in Montreal results in a sample mean of $44 and a standard deviation of $3. Use $\alpha = 0.05$ to determine whether the average daily car rental rates in Toronto are significantly higher than those in Montreal. Assume car rental rates are normally distributed and the population variances are equal.

10.18 What is the difference in average daily hotel room rates between Edmonton and Quebec City? Suppose we want to estimate this difference by taking hotel rate samples from each city and using a 98% confidence level. The data for such a study follow. Use these data to produce a point estimate for the mean difference in the hotel rates for the two cities. Assume the population variances are approximately equal and hotel rates in any given city are normally distributed.

Edmonton	Quebec City
$n_E = 22$	$n_Q = 20$
$\bar{x}_E = \$112$	$\bar{x}_Q = \$122$
$s_E = \$11$	$s_Q = \$12$

10.19 A study was conducted to compare the costs of supporting a family of four Canadians for a year in different foreign cities. The lifestyle of living in Canada on an annual income of $75,000 was the standard against which living in foreign cities was compared. A comparable living standard in Perth, Australia, and Mexico City was attained for about $64,000. Suppose an executive wants to determine whether there is any difference in the average annual cost of supporting her family of four in the manner to which they are accustomed in Perth and Mexico City. She uses the following data, randomly gathered from 11 families in each city, and an α of 0.01 to test this difference. She assumes the annual cost is normally distributed and the population variances are equal. What does the executive find?

Perth, Australia	Mexico City
$69,000	$64,000
64,500	64,000
67,500	66,000
64,500	64,900
66,700	62,000
68,000	60,500
65,000	62,500
69,000	63,000
71,000	64,500
68,500	63,500
67,500	62,400

Use the data from the table to construct a 95% confidence interval to estimate the difference in average annual costs between the two cities.

10.20 Some studies have shown that men spend more than women buying gifts and cards on Valentine's Day. Suppose an analyst wants to test this hypothesis by randomly sampling 9 men and 10 women. Each study participant is asked to keep a log beginning one month before Valentine's Day and record all purchases made for Valentine's Day during that one-month period. The resulting data are shown below. Use these data and a 1% level of significance to determine if, on average, men actually do spend significantly more than women on Valentine's Day. Assume that such spending is normally distributed in the population and that the population variances are equal.

Men	Women
$107.48	$125.98
143.61	45.53
90.19	56.35
125.53	80.62
70.79	46.37
83.00	44.34
129.63	75.21
154.22	68.48
93.80	85.84
	126.11

10.3 Statistical Inferences for Two Related Populations

LEARNING OBJECTIVE 10.3

Test hypotheses and develop confidence intervals about the difference in two dependent populations.

In the preceding section, hypotheses were tested and confidence intervals constructed about the difference in two population means when the samples are independent. In this section, a method is presented to analyze **dependent samples** or related samples. Some analysts refer to this test as the **matched-pairs test**. Others call it the *t* test for related measures or the **correlated *t* test**.

What are some types of situations in which the two samples being studied are related or dependent? Let's begin with the before-and-after study. Sometimes as an experimental control mechanism, the same person or object is measured both before and after a treatment. Certainly, the after measurement is *not* independent of the before measurement because the measurements are taken on the same person or object in both cases. **Table 10.4** gives data from a hypothetical study in which people were asked to rate a company before and after one week of viewing a 15-minute video about the company twice a day. The before scores are one sample and the after scores are a second sample, but each pair of scores is related because the two measurements apply to the same person. The before scores and the after scores are not likely to vary from each other as much as scores gathered from independent samples because individuals bring their biases about businesses and the company to the study. These individual biases affect both the before scores and the after scores in the same way because each pair of scores is measured on the same person.

TABLE 10.4	Rating of a Company (on a Scale from 0 to 50)	
Individual	**Before**	**After**
1	32	39
2	11	15
3	21	35
4	17	13
5	30	41
6	38	39
7	14	22

Other examples of related samples are studies in which twins, siblings, or spouses are matched and placed in two different groups. For example, a fashion merchandiser might be interested in comparing men's and women's perceptions of women's clothing. If the men and women selected for the study are spouses or siblings, a built-in relatedness to the measurements of the two groups in the study is likely. Their scores are more apt to be alike or related than those of randomly chosen independent groups of men and women because of similar backgrounds or tastes.

Hypothesis Testing

To ensure the use of the proper hypothesis-testing techniques, the analyst must determine whether the two samples being studied are dependent or independent. The approach to analyzing two *related* samples is different from the techniques used to analyze independent samples. Use of the techniques in Section 10.2 to analyze related group data can result in a loss of power and an increase in Type II errors.

The matched-pairs test for related samples requires that the two samples be the same size and that the individual related scores be matched. Formula 10.6 is used to test hypotheses about dependent populations.

---

t Formula to Test the Difference in Two Dependent Populations

$$t = \frac{\bar{d} - D}{\frac{s_d}{\sqrt{n}}} \qquad (10.6)$$

$$\text{df} = n - 1$$

where

n = number of pairs

d = sample difference in pairs

D = mean population difference

s_d = standard deviation of sample difference

$\bar{d}$ = mean sample difference

This t test for dependent measures uses the sample difference, d, between individual matched sample values as the basic measurement of analysis instead of individual sample values. Analysis of the d values effectively converts the problem from a two-sample problem to a single sample of differences, which is an adaptation of the single-sample means formula. This test utilizes the sample mean of differences, and the standard deviation of differences, s_d, which can be computed by using Formulas 10.7 and 10.8.

Formulas for $\bar{d}$ and s_d

$$\bar{d} = \frac{\sum d}{n}$$

$$s_d = \sqrt{\frac{\sum(d - \bar{d})^2}{n - 1}} = \sqrt{\frac{\sum d^2 - \frac{(\sum d)^2}{n}}{n - 1}} \qquad (10.7 \text{ and } 10.8)$$

An assumption for this test is that the differences of the two populations are normally distributed.

Analyzing data by this method involves calculating a t value with Formula 10.6 and comparing it with a critical t value obtained from the table. The critical t value is obtained from the t distribution table in the usual way, with the exception that, in the degrees of freedom ($n - 1$), n is the number of matched pairs of scores.

Suppose a stock market investor is interested in determining whether there is a significant difference in the price to earnings (P/E) ratio for companies from one year to the next. In an effort to study this question, the investor randomly samples nine companies listed on the Toronto Stock Exchange and records the P/E ratios for each of these companies at the end of year 1 and at the end of year 2. The data are shown in **Table 10.5**.

These data are related data because each P/E value for year 1 has a corresponding year 2 measurement on the same company. Because no prior information indicates whether P/E ratios have gone up or down, the hypothesis tested is two-tailed. Assume $\alpha = 0.01$. Assume that differences in P/E ratios are normally distributed in the population.

Step 1

$$H_0\!: D = 0$$
$$H_a\!: D \neq 0$$

Step 2 The appropriate statistical test is:

$$t = \frac{\bar{d} - D}{\frac{s_d}{\sqrt{n}}}$$

TABLE 10.5   **P/E Ratios for Nine Randomly Selected Companies**

Company	Year 1 P/E Ratio	Year 2 P/E Ratio
1	8.9	12.7
2	38.1	45.4
3	43.0	10.0
4	34.0	27.2
5	34.5	22.8
6	15.2	24.1
7	20.3	32.3
8	19.9	40.1
9	61.9	106.5

Step 3 $\alpha = 0.01$

Step 4   Because $\alpha = 0.01$ and this test is two-tailed, $\alpha/2 = 0.005$ is used to obtain the table t value. With nine pairs of data, $n = 9$ and df $= n - 1 = 8$. The table t value is $t_{0.005,8} = \pm 3.355$. If the observed test statistic is greater than 3.355 or less than -3.355, the null hypothesis will be rejected.

Step 5   The sample data are given in Table 10.5.

Step 6   Table 10.6 shows the calculations to obtain the observed value of the test statistic, which is $t = -0.70$.

TABLE 10.6   **Analysis of P/E Ratio Data**

Company	Year 1 P/E	Year 2 P/E	d
1	8.9	12.7	−3.8
2	38.1	45.4	−7.3
3	43.0	10.0	33.0
4	34.0	27.2	6.8
5	34.5	22.8	11.7
6	15.2	24.1	−8.9
7	20.3	32.3	−12.0
8	19.9	40.1	−20.2
9	61.9	106.5	−44.6

$\bar{d} = -5.033$ $s_d = 21.599$ $n = 9$

$$\text{Observed } t = \frac{-5.033 - 0}{\frac{21.599}{\sqrt{9}}} = -0.70$$

Step 7   Because the observed t value is greater than the critical table t value in the lower tail ($t = -0.70 > t = -3.355$), it is in the nonrejection region.

Step 8   There is not enough evidence from the data to declare a significant difference in the average P/E ratio between year 1 and year 2. The graph in **Figure 10.9** depicts the rejection regions, the critical values of t, and the observed value of t for this example.

Using the Computer to Make Statistical Inferences About Two Related Populations

Excel can be used to make statistical inferences about two related populations. **Figure 10.10** shows the Excel output for the P/E ratio problem. The Excel output contains the hypothesized

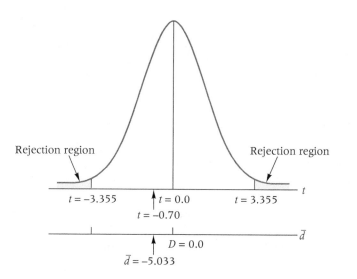

FIGURE 10.9 Graphical Depiction of P/E Ratio Analysis

	A	B	C
1	*t*-Test: Paired Two-Sample for Means		
2		Year 1 P/E	Year 2 P/E
3	Mean	30.644	35.678
4	Variance	268.135	837.544
5	Observations	9	9
6	Pearson Correlation	0.674	
7	Hypothesized Mean Difference	0	
8	df	8	
9	*t* Stat	−0.699	
10	*P* (*T*<=*t*) one-tail	0.252	
11	*t* Critical one-tail	2.896	
12	*P* (*T*<=*t*) two-tail	0.504	
13	*t* Critical two-tail	3.355	

FIGURE 10.10 Excel Output for the P/E Ratio Example

mean difference, the observed *t* value (−0.70), and the critical *t* values and their associated *p*-values for both a one-tailed and a two-tailed test. Because the *p*-value (0.504) is greater than the value of α (0.01), the decision is to fail to reject the null hypothesis.

DEMONSTRATION PROBLEM 10.5

Let us revisit the hypothetical study discussed earlier in the section in which consumers are asked to rate a company both before and after viewing a video on the company twice a day for a week. The data from Table 10.4 are displayed again here. Use an α of 0.05 to determine whether there is a significant increase in the ratings of the company after the one-week video treatment. Assume that differences in ratings are normally distributed in the population.

Individual	Before	After
1	32	39
2	11	15
3	21	35
4	17	13
5	30	41
6	38	39
7	14	22

Solution   Because the same individuals are being used in a before-and-after study, it is a related measures study. The desired effect is to increase ratings, which means the hypothesis test is one-tailed.

Step 1

$$H_0: D = 0$$
$$H_a: D < 0$$

Because the analysts want to prove that the ratings increase from before to after and because the difference is computed by subtracting the after ratings from the before ratings, the desired alternative hypothesis is $D < 0$.

Step 2 The appropriate test statistic is Formula 10.6.

Step 3 The Type I error rate is 0.05.

Step 4 The degrees of freedom are $n - 1 = 7 - 1 = 6$. For $\alpha = 0.05$, the table t value is $t_{0.05,6} = -1.943$. The decision rule is to reject the null hypothesis if the observed value is less than -1.943.

Step 5 The sample data and some calculations follow.

Individual	Before	After	d
1	32	39	−7
2	11	15	−4
3	21	35	−14
4	17	13	4
5	30	41	−11
6	38	39	−1
7	14	22	−8

$\bar{d} = -5.857$ $s_d = 6.0945$

Step 6 The observed t value is:

$$t = \frac{-5.857 - 0}{\frac{6.0945}{\sqrt{7}}} = -2.54$$

Computer analysis of this problem reveals that the p-value is 0.022.

Step 7 Because the observed value of -2.54 is less than the critical value of -1.943 and the p-value (0.022) is less than α (0.05), the decision is to reject the null hypothesis.

Step 8 There is enough evidence to conclude that, on average, the ratings have increased significantly. This result might be used by managers to support a decision to continue using the videos or to expand the use of such videos in an effort to increase public support for their company.

The following graph depicts the observed value, the rejection region, and the critical t value for the problem.

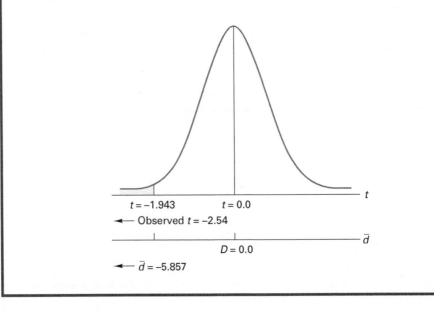

Confidence Intervals

Sometimes an analyst is interested in estimating the mean difference in two populations for related samples. A confidence interval for D, the mean population difference of two related samples, can be constructed by algebraically rearranging Formula 10.6, which was used to test hypotheses about D. Again the assumption is that the differences are normally distributed in the population.

Confidence Interval Formula to Estimate the Difference in Related Populations, D

$$\bar{d} - t\frac{s_d}{\sqrt{n}} \leq D \leq \bar{d} + t\frac{s_d}{\sqrt{n}}$$

$$df = n - 1$$

(10.9)

The following housing industry example demonstrates the application of Formula 10.9. The sale of new houses apparently fluctuates seasonally. Superimposed on the seasonality are economic and business cycles that also influence the sale of new houses. In certain parts of the country, new-house sales increase in the spring and early summer and drop off in the fall. Suppose a national real estate association wants to estimate the average difference in the number of new-house sales per company in Halifax between year 1 and year 2. To do so, the association randomly selects 18 real estate firms in the Halifax area and obtains their new-house sales figures for May of year 1 and May of year 2. The numbers of sales per company are shown in **Table 10.7**. Using these data, the association's analyst estimates the average difference in the number of sales per real estate company in Halifax for May of year 1 and May of year 2 and constructs a 99% confidence interval. The analyst assumes that differences in sales are normally distributed in the population.

TABLE 10.7 **Number of New-House Sales in Halifax**

Realtor	May of Year 1	May of Year 2
1	8	11
2	19	30
3	5	6
4	9	13
5	3	5
6	0	4
7	13	15
8	11	17
9	9	12
10	5	12
11	8	6
12	2	5
13	11	10
14	14	22
15	7	8
16	12	15
17	6	12
18	10	10

The number of pairs, n, is 18, and the degrees of freedom are 17. For a 99% level of confidence and these degrees of freedom, the table t value is $t_{0.005,17} = 2.898$. The values for $\bar{d}$ and s_d are shown in **Table 10.8**.

TABLE 10.8	Differences in Number of New-House Sales, Year 1–Year 2		
Realtor	**May of Year 1**	**May of Year 2**	**d**
1	8	11	−3
2	19	30	−11
3	5	6	−1
4	9	13	−4
5	3	5	−2
6	0	4	−4
7	13	15	−2
8	11	17	−6
9	9	12	−3
10	5	12	−7
11	8	6	2
12	2	5	−3
13	11	10	1
14	14	22	−8
15	7	8	−1
16	12	15	−3
17	6	12	−6
18	10	10	0
	$\bar{d} = -3.389$ and $s_d = 3.274$		

The point estimate of the difference is $\bar{d} = -3.39$. The 99% confidence interval is:

$$\bar{d} - t\frac{s_d}{\sqrt{n}} \le D \le \bar{d} + t\frac{s_d}{\sqrt{n}}$$

$$-3.389 - 2.898\frac{3.274}{\sqrt{18}} \le D \le -3.389 + 2.898\frac{3.274}{\sqrt{18}}$$

$$-3.389 - 2.236 \le D \le -3.389 + 2.236$$

$$-5.625 \le D \le -1.153$$

The analyst estimates with a 99% level of confidence that the average difference in new-house sales for a real estate company in Halifax between year 1 and year 2 in May is somewhere between −5.625 and −1.153 houses. Because year 2 sales were subtracted from year 1 sales, the minus signs indicate more sales in year 2 than in year 1. Note that both ends of the confidence interval contain negatives. This result means that the analyst can be 99% confident that zero difference is not the average difference. If the analyst were using this confidence interval to test the hypothesis that there is no significant mean difference in average new-house sales per company in Halifax between May of year 1 and May of year 2, the null hypothesis would be rejected for $\alpha = 0.01$. The point estimate for this example is −3.389 houses, with an error of 2.236 houses. **Figure 10.11** is the Excel computer output for the test.

distributions, we cannot merely place a minus sign on the upper-tail critical value and obtain the lower-tail critical value. (In addition, the F ratio is always positive—it is the ratio of two variances.) This dilemma can be solved by using Formula 10.14, which essentially states that the critical F value for the lower tail $(1 - \alpha)$ can be solved for by taking the inverse of the F value for the upper tail (α). The degrees-of-freedom numerator for the upper-tail critical value is the degrees-of-freedom denominator for the lower-tail critical value, and the degrees-of-freedom denominator for the upper-tail critical value is the degrees-of-freedom numerator for the lower-tail critical value.

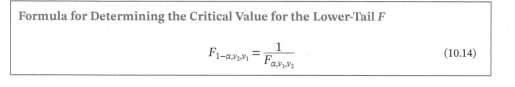

Formula for Determining the Critical Value for the Lower-Tail F

$$F_{1-\alpha,v_2,v_1} = \frac{1}{F_{\alpha,v_1,v_2}}$$ (10.14)

A hypothesis test can be conducted using two sample variances and Formula 10.13. The following example illustrates this process.

Suppose a machine produces metal sheets that are specified to be 22 mm thick. Because of the machine, the operator, the raw material, the manufacturing environment, and other factors, there is variability in the thickness. Two machines produce these sheets. Operators are concerned about the consistency of the two machines. To test consistency, they randomly sample 10 sheets produced by machine 1 and 12 sheets produced by machine 2. The thickness measurements of sheets from each machine are given in the table in Step 5. Assume sheet thickness is normally distributed in the population. How can we determine whether the variance from each sample comes from the same population variance (population variances are equal) or from different population variances (population variances are not equal)?

Step 1   Determine the null and alternative hypotheses. In this case, we are conducting a two-tailed test (variances are the same or not), and the following hypotheses are used:

$$H_0: \sigma_1^2 = \sigma_2^2$$
$$H_a: \sigma_1^2 \neq \sigma_2^2$$

Step 2   The appropriate statistical test is:

$$F = \frac{s_1^2}{s_2^2}$$

Step 3   Let $\alpha = 0.05$.

Step 4   Because we are conducting a two-tailed test, $\alpha/2 = 0.025$. Because $n_1 = 10$ and $n_2 = 12$, the degrees-of-freedom numerator for the upper-tail critical value is $v_1 = n_1 - 1 = 10 - 1 = 9$ and the degrees-of-freedom denominator for the upper-tail critical value is $v_2 = n_2 - 1 = 12 - 1 = 11$. The critical F value for the upper tail obtained from Table A.7 is:

$$F_{0.025,9,11} = 3.59$$

Table 10.9 is a copy of the F distribution for a one-tailed $\alpha = 0.025$ (which yields equivalent values for two-tailed $\alpha = 0.05$, where the upper tail contains 0.025 of the area). Locate $F_{0.025,9,11} = 3.59$ in the table. The lower-tail critical value can be calculated from the upper-tail value by using Formula 10.14:

$$F_{0.975,11,9} = \frac{1}{F_{0.025,9,11}} = \frac{1}{3.59} = 0.28$$

The decision rule is to reject the null hypothesis if the observed F value is greater than 3.59 or less than 0.28.

TABLE 10.9 A Portion of the *F* Distribution Table

Percentage Points of the *F* Distribution

$f(F)$

(curve with F_α marked, 0 at origin)

$\alpha = 0.025$

v_2 \ v_1	Numerator Degrees of Freedom								
	1	2	3	4	5	6	7	8	9
1	647.8	799.5	864.2	899.6	921.8	937.1	948.2	956.7	963.3
2	38.51	39.00	39.17	39.25	39.30	39.33	39.36	39.37	39.39
3	17.44	16.04	15.44	15.10	14.88	14.73	14.62	14.54	14.47
4	12.22	10.65	9.98	9.60	9.36	9.20	9.07	8.98	8.90
5	10.01	8.43	7.76	7.39	7.15	6.98	6.85	6.76	6.68
6	8.81	7.26	6.60	6.23	5.99	5.82	5.70	5.60	5.52
7	8.07	6.54	5.89	5.52	5.29	5.12	4.99	4.90	4.82
8	7.57	6.06	5.42	5.05	4.82	4.65	4.53	4.43	4.36
9	7.21	5.71	5.08	4.72	4.48	4.32	4.20	4.10	4.03
10	6.94	5.46	4.83	4.47	4.24	4.07	3.95	3.85	3.78
11	6.72	5.26	4.63	4.28	4.04	3.88	3.76	3.66	3.59
12	6.55	5.10	4.47	4.12	3.89	3.73	3.61	3.51	3.44
13	6.41	4.97	4.35	4.00	3.77	3.60	3.48	3.39	3.31
14	6.30	4.86	4.24	3.89	3.66	3.50	3.38	3.29	3.21
15	6.20	4.77	4.15	3.80	3.58	3.41	3.29	3.20	3.12
16	6.12	4.69	4.08	3.73	3.50	3.34	3.22	3.12	3.05
17	6.04	4.62	4.01	3.66	3.44	3.28	3.16	3.06	2.98
18	5.98	4.56	3.95	3.61	3.38	3.22	3.10	3.01	2.93
19	5.92	4.51	3.90	3.56	3.33	3.17	3.05	2.96	2.88
20	5.87	4.46	3.86	3.51	3.29	3.13	3.01	2.91	2.84
21	5.83	4.42	3.82	3.48	3.25	3.09	2.97	2.87	2.80
22	5.79	4.38	3.78	3.44	3.22	3.05	2.93	2.84	2.76
23	5.75	4.35	3.75	3.41	3.18	3.02	2.90	2.81	2.73
24	5.72	4.32	3.72	3.38	3.15	2.99	2.87	2.78	2.70
25	5.69	4.29	3.69	3.35	3.13	2.97	2.85	2.75	2.68
26	5.66	4.27	3.67	3.33	3.10	2.94	2.82	2.73	2.65
27	5.63	4.24	3.65	3.31	3.08	2.92	2.80	2.71	2.63
28	5.61	4.22	3.63	3.29	3.06	2.90	2.78	2.69	2.61
29	5.59	4.20	3.61	3.27	3.04	2.88	2.76	2.67	2.59
30	5.57	4.18	3.59	3.25	3.03	2.87	2.75	2.65	2.57
40	5.42	4.05	3.46	3.13	2.90	2.74	2.62	2.53	2.45
60	5.29	3.93	3.34	3.01	2.79	2.63	2.51	2.41	2.33
120	5.15	3.80	3.23	2.89	2.67	2.52	2.39	2.30	2.22
∞	5.02	3.69	3.12	2.79	2.57	2.41	2.29	2.19	2.11

$F_{0.025,9,11}$ (pointing to 3.59)

Denominator Degrees of Freedom

Step 5 Next we compute the sample variances. The data are shown here.

Machine 1		Machine 2	
22.3	21.9	22.0	21.7
21.8	22.4	22.1	21.9
22.3	22.5	21.8	22.0
21.6	22.2	21.9	22.1
21.8	21.6	22.2	21.9
		22.0	22.1
$s_1^2 = 0.11378$		$s_2^2 = 0.02023$	
$n_1 = 10$		$n_2 = 12$	

Step 6

$$F = \frac{s_1^2}{s_2^2} = \frac{0.11378}{0.02023} = 5.62$$

The ratio of sample variances is 5.62.

Step 7 The observed F value is 5.62, which is greater than the upper-tail critical value of 3.59. As **Figure 10.14** shows, this F value is in the rejection region. Thus, the decision is to reject the null hypothesis. The population variances are not equal.

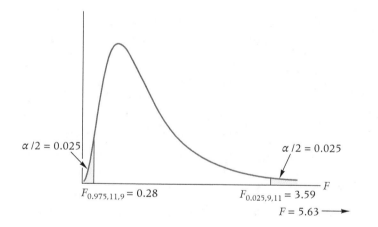

FIGURE 10.14 Graph of F Values and Rejection Region for the Sheet Metal Example

Step 8 An examination of the sample variances reveals that the variance from machine 1 measurements is greater than that from machine 2 measurements. The operators and process managers might want to examine machine 1 further; an adjustment may be needed or something else may be causing the seemingly greater variations on that machine.

Using the Computer to Test Hypotheses About Two Population Variances

Excel can directly test hypotheses about two population variances. **Figure 10.15** shows the Excel output for the sheet metal example. The Excel output contains the two sample means, the two sample variances, the observed F value, the p-value for a one-tailed test, and the critical F value for a one-tailed test. Because the sheet metal example is a two-tailed test, the Excel p-value must be doubled to 0.0094 in order to reach a decision, or we can just compare the p-value of 0.0047 with $\alpha/2 = 0.025$. Because this value is less than $\alpha = 0.05$, the decision is to reject the null hypothesis.

FIGURE 10.15 **Excel Output for the Sheet Metal Example**

	A	B	C
1	F-Test Two-Sample for Variances		
2		Machine 1	Machine 2
3	Mean	22.040	21.975
4	Variance	0.113778	0.02023
5	Observations	10	12
6	df	9	11
7	F	5.62	
8	P (F <= f) one-tail	0.0047	
9	F Critical one-tail	3.59	

DEMONSTRATION PROBLEM 10.7

Assume that a family of four in Moncton with $60,000 annual income spends more than $22,000 a year on basic goods and services. In contrast, a family of four in Saskatoon with the same annual income spends only $15,460 on the same items. Suppose we want to determine whether the variance of money spent per year on the basics by families across Canada is greater than the variance of money spent on the basics by families in Moncton—that is, whether the amounts spent by families of four in Moncton are more homogeneous than the amounts spent by such families nationally. Suppose a random sample of eight Moncton families produces the figures in the table below, which are given along with those reported from a random sample of seven families across Canada. Complete a hypothesis-testing procedure to determine whether the variance of values taken from across Canada can be shown to be greater than the variance of values obtained from families in Moncton. Let $\alpha = 0.01$. Assume the amount spent on the basics is normally distributed in the population.

Amount Spent on Basics by Family of Four with $60,000 Annual Income

Across Canada	Moncton
$18,500	$23,000
19,250	21,900
16,400	22,500
20,750	21,200
17,600	21,000
21,800	22,800
14,750	23,100
	21,300

Solution

Step 1 This is a one-tailed test with the following hypotheses:

$$H_0: \sigma_1^2 = \sigma_2^2$$
$$H_a: \sigma_1^2 > \sigma_2^2$$

Note that what we are trying to prove—that the variance for the Canadian population is greater than the variance for families in Moncton—is in the alternative hypothesis.

Step 2 The appropriate statistical test is:

$$F = \frac{s_1^2}{s_2^2}$$

Step 3 The level of significance is 0.01.

Step 4 This is a one-tailed test, so we will use the F distribution table in Table A.7 with $\alpha = 0.01$. The degrees of freedom for $n_1 = 7$ and $n_2 = 8$ are $v_1 = 6$ and $v_2 = 7$. The critical F value for the upper tail of the distribution is:

$$F_{0.01,6,7} = 7.19$$

The decision rule is to reject the null hypothesis if the observed value of F is greater than 7.19.

Step 5   The following sample variances are computed from the data:

$$s_1^2 = 5{,}961{,}428.6$$
$$n_1 = 7$$
$$s_2^2 = 737{,}142.9$$
$$n_2 = 8$$

Step 6   The observed F value can be determined by:

$$F = \frac{s_1^2}{s_2^2} = \frac{5{,}961{,}428.6}{737{,}142.9} = 8.09$$

Step 7   Because the observed value of $F = 8.09$ is greater than the table critical F_{α, v_1, v_2} value of 7.19, the decision is to reject the null hypothesis.

Step 8   The variance for families in Canada is greater than the variance for families in Moncton. Families in Moncton are more homogeneous in amount spent on basics than families across Canada. Marketing managers need to understand this homogeneity as they attempt to find niches in the Moncton population. Moncton may not contain as many subgroups as can be found across Canada. The task of locating market niches may be easier in Moncton than in the rest of the country because fewer possibilities are likely. The following graph shows the rejection region as well as the critical and calculated values of F.

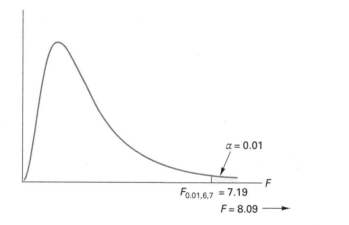

Note: Some authors recommend the use of this F test to determine whether the data being analyzed by a t test for two population means meet the assumption of equal population variances. However, some analysts suggest that for equal sample sizes, the t test is insensitive to the equal variance assumption, and therefore the F test is not needed in that situation. For unequal sample sizes, the F test of variances is "not generally capable of detecting assumption violations that lead to poor performance" with the t test.[2] This text does not present the application of the F test to determine whether variance assumptions for the t test have been met.

Concept Check

1. Is the F test of two population variances extremely sensitive to violations of the assumption that the populations are normally distributed? What is the key implication of this?

2. Explain why we cannot merely place a minus sign on the upper-tail critical value and obtain the lower-tail critical value when using the F distribution.

[2] Carol A. Markowski and Edward P. Markowski, "Conditions for the Effectiveness of a Preliminary Test of Variance," *The American Statistician* 44 (November 1990): 322–26.

10.5 Problems

10.39 Test the following hypotheses by using the given sample information and $\alpha = 0.01$. Assume the populations are normally distributed.

$$H_0: \sigma_1^2 = \sigma_2^2$$
$$H_a: \sigma_1^2 < \sigma_2^2$$
$$n_1 = 10, n_2 = 12, s_1^2 = 562, s_2^2 = 1{,}013$$

10.40 Test the following hypotheses by using the given sample information and $\alpha = 0.05$. Assume the populations are normally distributed.

$$H_0: \sigma_1^2 = \sigma_2^2$$
$$H_a: \sigma_1^2 \neq \sigma_2^2$$
$$n_1 = 5, n_2 = 19, s_1 = 4.68, s_2 = 2.78$$

10.41 Suppose the data shown here are the results of a survey to investigate gas prices. Ten service stations were selected randomly in each of two cities and the figures represent the prices of a litre of unleaded regular gas on a given day. Use the F test to determine whether there is a significant difference in the variances of the prices of unleaded regular gas between these two cities. Let $\alpha = 0.01$. Assume gas prices are normally distributed.

City 1			City 2		
$1.338	$1.295	$1.318	$1.299	$1.287	$1.342
1.326	1.322	1.318	1.334	1.349	1.314
1.322	1.318	1.278	1.322	1.322	1.318
1.303			1.310		

10.42 How long are resale houses on the market? Suppose that a survey reported that in Thunder Bay, resale houses are on the market an average of 112 days. Of course, the length of time varies by market. Suppose random samples of 13 houses in Thunder Bay and 11 houses in Moncton that are up for resale are traced. The data shown here represent the number of days each house was on the market before being sold. Use the given data and a 1% level of significance to determine whether the population variances for the number of days until resale are different in Thunder Bay than in Moncton. Assume the number of days that resale houses are on the market are normally distributed.

Thunder Bay		Moncton	
132	126	118	56
138	94	85	69
131	161	113	67
127	133	81	54
99	119	94	137
126	88	93	
134			

10.43 Suppose a recent study showed that the average annual amount spent by a Nova Scotia household on hotdog wieners was $23.84 compared with an average of $19.83 for Alberta households. Suppose a random sample of 12 Nova Scotia households showed that the standard deviation of these purchases was $7.52, whereas a random sample of 15 Alberta households resulted in a standard deviation of $6.08. Do these samples provide enough evidence to conclude that the variance of annual hotdog wiener purchases for Nova Scotia households is greater than the variance of annual hotdog wiener purchases for Alberta households? Let α be 0.05. Assume amounts spent per year on hotdog wieners are normally distributed. Suppose the data did show that the variance among Nova Scotia households is greater than that among Alberta households. What might this variance mean to decision-makers in the hotdog wiener industry?

10.44 Assume that the average age of a male public service worker is 43.6 years and that of a male worker in the private sector is 37.3 years. Is there any difference in the variation of ages of men in the public service and men in the private sector? Suppose a random sample of 15 male public service workers is taken and the variance of their ages is 91.5. Suppose also that a random sample of 15 male private-sector workers is taken and the variance of their ages is 67.3. Use these data and $\alpha = 0.01$ to answer the question. Assume ages are normally distributed.

End-of-Chapter Review

Decision Dilemma Solved

L.L. Bean

Various techniques presented in Chapter 10 can be used to analyze the L.L. Bean managerial and statistical questions and their associated data. Question 1 asks if, due to a smaller online volume at night, the home page might load faster then. To test this hypothesis, a random sample of 37 uploads is taken during the daytime with a resultant mean time of 5.16 seconds. A second random sample of 45 uploads is taken at nighttime with a resulting mean of 4.81 seconds. Previous studies indicate that the population standard deviation both during the daytime and at nighttime is 0.83 seconds. Because the business analyst is testing the difference in sample means taken from independent populations and the population standard deviations are known, the z

test featured in Section 10.1 is the appropriate test. A one-tailed test, with an α of 0.01, is set up because the business analyst is testing to determine if the upload time at night is faster. A z value of 1.90 is computed. Because this test statistic, $z = 1.90$, is less than the critical value of z (2.33) in the upper tail of the distribution, the statistical conclusion is to fail to reject the null hypothesis. There is not enough evidence to conclude that, on average, daytime uploads are slower than nighttime uploads.

Question 2 asks if the average order size for women is greater than the average order size for men. To test this hypothesis, a random sample of 44 orders from women and a random sample of 48 orders from men are taken, resulting in a sample mean for women of $80 with a sample standard deviation of $18, and a sample mean for men of $72 with a sample standard deviation of $16. Because the business analyst is testing the difference in sample means taken from independent populations and the sample standard deviations are given (population standard deviations are not known), the t test featured in Section 10.2 is the appropriate test. (Note that this test assumes that the population variances are equal.) A one-tailed test, with an α of 0.05, is set up because the business analyst is testing to determine if the average order size for women is greater than the average order size for men. A t value of 2.257 is computed. Because this test statistic, $t = 2.257$, is greater than the critical value of t (1.662) in the upper tail of the distribution, the statistical conclusion is to reject the null hypothesis. There is enough evidence to conclude that, on average, order sizes for women are greater than order sizes for men.

In question 3 of the Decision Dilemma, it is reported that about 41% of shoppers said that "receiving my product when expected" led them to recommend an online retailer. Suppose a business analyst wants to compare the proportion of L.L. Bean purchasers who agree with this statement with the proportion of a competitor's purchasers who agree with this statement. Suppose that a random sample of 310 L.L. Bean purchasers is obtained and each purchaser is asked this question, with a result that 136 agreed with this statement. Suppose a random sample of 195 competitor purchasers is obtained and each purchaser is asked this question, with a result that 72 agreed with this statement. If we want to use these data to determine if there is a significant difference between L.L. Bean purchasers and the competitor's purchasers on this issue, how would we go about doing it? Because the business analyst is testing the difference in sample proportions instead of means, the z test featured in Section 10.4 is the appropriate test. Since there is no idea as to which company might have a higher proportion of purchasers who agree with the statement, a two-tailed test is set up. Using an α of 0.05 and an $\alpha/2$ of 0.025 in each tail, critical z values of ± 1.96 are obtained. From the data given, an observed z of 1.56 is computed. Because this test statistic, $z = 1.56$, is less than the critical value of z (1.96) in the upper tail of the distribution, the statistical conclusion fails to reject the null hypothesis. There is not enough evidence to conclude that the proportion of L.L. Bean purchasers who agree with the statement is different from the proportion of the competitor's purchasers who agree with the statement.

Key Considerations

The statistical techniques presented in this chapter share some of the pitfalls of confidence interval methodology and hypothesis-testing techniques mentioned in preceding chapters. Included among these pitfalls are assumption violations. Remember, if small sample sizes are used in analyzing means, the z tests are valid only when the population is normally distributed and the population variances are known. If the population variances are unknown, a t test can be used if the population is normally distributed and if the population variances can be assumed to be equal. The z tests and confidence intervals for two population proportions also have a minimum sample size requirement that should be met. In addition, it is assumed that both populations are normally distributed when the F test is used for two population variances.

Use of the t test for two independent populations is not unethical when the populations are related, but it is likely to result in a loss of power. As with any hypothesis-testing procedure, in determining the null and alternative hypotheses, make certain you are not assuming true what you are trying to prove.

Why Statistics Is Relevant

A market segment is a group of people or organizations that have similar product and/or service needs. Marketing activities largely focus on the identification and description of market segments. Market segment analysis often involves the identification of segment differences and statistical questions about the business implications of those differences. The material presented in this chapter targets this type of analysis whenever geographic, demographic, behavioural, or other segmentation exists. In addition, the techniques presented in this chapter are especially important due to the crucial role of comparison in the analysis of variance and the design of experiments (Chapter 11).

Summary of Learning Objectives

Business research often requires the analysis of two populations. Three types of parameters can be compared: means, proportions, and variances. Except for the F test for population variances, all techniques presented contain both confidence intervals and hypothesis tests. In each case, the two populations are studied through the use of sample data randomly drawn from each population. The population means are analyzed by comparing two sample means.

LEARNING OBJECTIVE 10.1 Test hypotheses and develop confidence intervals about the difference in two means of independent samples with known population variances using the z statistic.

When sample sizes are large ($n \geq 30$) and population variances are known, a z test is used. When sample sizes are small, the population variances are known, and the populations are normally distributed, the z test is used to analyze the population means.

LEARNING OBJECTIVE 10.2 Test hypotheses and develop confidence intervals about the difference in two means of independent samples with unknown population variances using the t test.

If the population variances are unknown, and the populations are normally distributed, the t test of means for independent samples is used.

LEARNING OBJECTIVE 10.3 Test hypotheses and develop confidence intervals about the difference in two dependent populations.

For populations that are related on some measure, such as twins or before-and-after studies, a t test for dependent measures (matched pairs) is used. An assumption for this test is that the differences of the two populations are normally distributed.

LEARNING OBJECTIVE 10.4 Test hypotheses and develop confidence intervals about the difference in two population proportions.

The difference in two population proportions can be tested or estimated using a z test.

LEARNING OBJECTIVE 10.5 Test hypotheses about the difference in two population variances using the F distribution.

The population variances are analyzed by an F test when the assumption that the populations are normally distributed is met. The F value is a ratio of the two variances. The F distribution is a distribution of possible ratios of two sample variances taken from one population or from two populations containing the same variance.

Key Terms

correlated t test 10-22	F distribution 10-38	independent samples 10-4	t test for related measures 10-22
dependent samples 10-22	F value 10-38	matched-pairs test 10-22	

Formulas

(10.1) z formula for the difference in two sample means (independent samples and population variances known)

$$z = \frac{(\bar{x}_1 - \bar{x}_2) - (\mu_1 - \mu_2)}{\sqrt{\frac{\sigma_1^2}{n_1} + \frac{\sigma_2^2}{n_2}}}$$

(10.2) Confidence interval to estimate $\mu_1 - \mu_2$

$$(\bar{x}_1 - \bar{x}_2) - z_{\alpha/2}\sqrt{\frac{\sigma_1^2}{n_1} + \frac{\sigma_2^2}{n_2}} \leq \mu_1 - \mu_2 \leq (\bar{x}_1 - \bar{x}_2) + z_{\alpha/2}\sqrt{\frac{\sigma_1^2}{n_1} + \frac{\sigma_2^2}{n_2}}$$

(10.3) t formula to test the difference in means assuming σ_1^2 and σ_2^2 are equal

$$t = \frac{(\bar{x}_1 - \bar{x}_2) - (\mu_1 - \mu_2)}{\sqrt{\frac{s_1^2(n_1 - 1) + s_2^2(n_2 - 1)}{n_1 + n_2 - 2}}\sqrt{\frac{1}{n_1} + \frac{1}{n_2}}}$$

$$df = n_1 + n_2 - 2$$

(10.4) t formula to test the difference in means

$$t = \frac{(\bar{x}_1 - \bar{x}_2) - (\mu_1 - \mu_2)}{\sqrt{\frac{s_1^2}{n_1} + \frac{s_2^2}{n_2}}}$$

$$df = \frac{\left(\frac{s_1^2}{n_1} + \frac{s_2^2}{n_2}\right)^2}{\frac{\left(\frac{s_1^2}{n_1}\right)^2}{n_1 - 1} + \frac{\left(\frac{s_2^2}{n_2}\right)^2}{n_2 - 1}}$$

(10.5) Confidence interval to estimate $\mu_1 - \mu_2$ assuming the population variances are unknown and equal

$$(\bar{x}_1 - \bar{x}_2) - t\sqrt{\frac{s_1^2(n_1 - 1) + s_2^2(n_2 - 1)}{n_1 + n_2 - 2}}\sqrt{\frac{1}{n_1} + \frac{1}{n_2}} \le \mu_1 - \mu_2 \le$$

$$(\bar{x}_1 - \bar{x}_2) + t\sqrt{\frac{s_1^2(n_1 - 1) + s_2^2(n_2 - 1)}{n_1 + n_2 - 2}}\sqrt{\frac{1}{n_1} + \frac{1}{n_2}}$$

$$df = n_1 + n_2 - 2$$

(10.6) t formula to test the difference in two dependent populations

$$t = \frac{\bar{d} - D}{\frac{s_d}{\sqrt{n}}}$$

$$df = n - 1$$

(10.7 and 10.8) Formulas for $\bar{d}$ and s_d

$$\bar{d} = \frac{\sum d}{n}$$

$$s_d = \sqrt{\frac{\sum(d - \bar{d})^2}{n - 1}} = \sqrt{\frac{\sum d^2 - \frac{(\sum d)^2}{n}}{n - 1}}$$

(10.9) Confidence interval formula to estimate the difference in related populations, D

$$\bar{d} - t\frac{s_d}{\sqrt{n}} \le D \le \bar{d} + t\frac{s_d}{\sqrt{n}}$$

$$df = n - 1$$

(10.10) z formula for the difference in two population proportions

$$z = \frac{(\hat{p}_1 - \hat{p}_2) - (p_1 - p_2)}{\sqrt{\frac{p_1 \cdot q_1}{n_1} + \frac{p_2 \cdot q_2}{n_2}}}$$

(10.11) z formula to test the difference in population proportions

$$z = \frac{(\hat{p}_1 - \hat{p}_2) - (p_1 - p_2)}{\sqrt{(\bar{p} \cdot \bar{q})\left(\frac{1}{n_1} + \frac{1}{n_2}\right)}}$$

where $\bar{p} = \dfrac{x_1 + x_2}{n_1 + n_2} = \dfrac{n_1\hat{p}_1 + n_2\hat{p}_2}{n_1 + n_2}$ and $\bar{q} = 1 - \bar{p}$

(10.12) Confidence interval to estimate $p_1 - p_2$

$$(\hat{p}_1 - \hat{p}_2) - z\sqrt{\frac{\hat{p}_1 \cdot \hat{q}_1}{n_1} + \frac{\hat{p}_2 \cdot \hat{q}_2}{n_2}} \le p_1 - p_2$$

$$\le (\hat{p}_1 - \hat{p}_2) + z\sqrt{\frac{\hat{p}_1 \cdot \hat{q}_1}{n_1} + \frac{\hat{p}_2 \cdot \hat{q}_2}{n_2}}$$

(10.13) F test for two population variances

$$F = \frac{s_1^2}{s_2^2}$$

$$df_{numerator} = v_1 = n_1 - 1$$

$$df_{denominator} = v_2 = n_2 - 1$$

(10.14) Formula for determining the critical value for the lower-tail F

$$F_{1-\alpha,v_2,v_1} = \frac{1}{F_{\alpha,v_1,v_2}}$$

Supplementary Problems

Calculating the Statistics

10.45 **Video** Test the following hypotheses with the data given. Let $\alpha = 0.10$.

$$H_0: \mu_1 - \mu_2 = 0$$
$$H_a: \mu_1 - \mu_2 \ne 0$$

Sample 1	Sample 2
$\bar{x}_1 = 138.4$	$\bar{x}_2 = 142.5$
$\sigma_1 = 6.71$	$\sigma_2 = 8.92$
$n_1 = 48$	$n_2 = 39$

10.46 Use the following data to construct a 98% confidence interval to estimate the difference between μ_1 and μ_2.

Sample 1	Sample 2
$\bar{x}_1 = 34.9$	$\bar{x}_2 = 27.6$
$\sigma_1^2 = 2.97$	$\sigma_2^2 = 3.50$
$n_1 = 34$	$n_2 = 31$

10.47 **Video** The following data come from independent samples drawn from normally distributed populations. Use these data to test the following hypotheses. Let the Type I error rate be 0.05. Assume that the population variances are approximately equal.

$$H_0: \mu_1 - \mu_2 = 0$$
$$H_a: \mu_1 - \mu_2 > 0$$

Sample 1	Sample 2
$\bar{x}_1 = 2.06$	$\bar{x}_2 = 1.93$
$s_1^2 = 0.176$	$s_2^2 = 0.143$
$n_1 = 12$	$n_2 = 15$

10.48 Construct a 95% confidence interval to estimate $\mu_1 - \mu_2$ by using the following data. Assume the populations are normally distributed and the population variances are approximately equal.

Sample 1	Sample 2
$\bar{x}_1 = 74.6$	$\bar{x}_2 = 70.9$
$s_1^2 = 10.5$	$s_2^2 = 11.4$
$n_1 = 18$	$n_2 = 19$

10.49 **Video** The following data have been gathered from two related samples. The differences are assumed to be normally distributed in the population. Use these data and an α of 0.01 to test the following hypotheses.

$$H_0: D = 0$$

$$H_a: D < 0$$

$$n = 21, \quad \bar{d} = -1.16, \quad s_d = 1.01$$

10.50 Use the following data to construct a 99% confidence interval to estimate D. Assume the differences are normally distributed in the population.

Respondent	Before	After
1	47	63
2	33	35
3	38	36
4	50	56
5	39	44
6	27	29
7	35	32
8	46	54
9	41	47

10.51 **Video** Test the following hypotheses by using the given data and α equal to 0.05.

$$H_0: p_1 - p_2 = 0$$

$$H_a: p_1 - p_2 \neq 0$$

Sample 1	Sample 2
$n_1 = 783$	$n_2 = 896$
$x_1 = 345$	$x_2 = 421$

10.52 Use the following data to construct a 99% confidence interval to estimate $p_1 - p_2$.

Sample 1	Sample 2
$n_1 = 409$	$n_2 = 378$
$\hat{p}_1 = 0.71$	$\hat{p}_2 = 0.67$

10.53 Test the following hypotheses by using the given data. Let α equal 0.05.

$$H_0: \sigma_1^2 = \sigma_2^2$$

$$H_a: \sigma_1^2 \neq \sigma_2^2$$

$$n_1 = 8, \quad n_2 = 10, \quad s_1^2 = 46, \quad s_2^2 = 37$$

Testing Your Understanding

10.54 Suppose a large insurance company wants to estimate the difference between the average amount of term life insurance purchased per family and the average amount of whole life insurance purchased per family. To obtain an estimate, one of the company's actuaries randomly selects 27 families who have term life insurance only and 29 families who have whole life policies only. Each sample is taken from families in which the leading provider is younger than 45 years of age. Use the data obtained to construct a 95% confidence interval to estimate the difference in means for these two groups. Assume the amount of insurance is normally distributed.

Term	Whole Life
$\bar{x}_T = \$75,000$	$\bar{x}_W = \$45,000$
$s_T = \$22,000$	$s_W = \$15,500$
$n_T = 27$	$n_W = 29$

10.55 A study is conducted to estimate the average difference in bus ridership for a large city during the morning and afternoon rush hours. The transit authority's analyst randomly selects nine buses because of the variety of routes they represent. On a given day, the number of riders on each bus is counted at 7:45 A.M. and at 4:45 P.M., with the following results.

Bus	Morning	Afternoon
1	43	41
2	51	49
3	37	44
4	24	32
5	47	46
6	44	42
7	50	47
8	55	51
9	46	49

Use the data to compute a 90% confidence interval to estimate the population average difference. Assume ridership is normally distributed.

10.56 There are several methods people use to organize their lives by keeping track of appointments, meetings, and deadlines. Some of these include using a desk calendar, using informal notes of scrap paper, keeping dates "in your head," using a day planner, and keeping a formal "to do" list. Suppose a business analyst wants to test the hypothesis that a greater proportion of marketing managers keeps track of such obligations in their head than do accountants. To test this, a business analyst samples 400 marketing managers and 450 accountants. Of those sampled, 220 marketing managers keep track in their head while 216 of the accountants do so. Using a 1% level of significance, what does the business analyst find?

10.57 A study was conducted to compare the salaries of accounting clerks and data entry operators. One of the hypotheses to be tested is that the variability of salaries among accounting clerks is the same as the variability of salaries of data entry operators. To test this hypothesis, a random sample of 16 accounting clerks was taken, resulting in a sample mean salary of $36,400 and a sample standard deviation of $2,200. A random sample of 14 data entry operators was taken as well, resulting in a sample mean of $35,800 and a sample standard deviation of $2,050. Use these data and $\alpha = 0.05$ to determine whether the population variance of salaries is the same for accounting clerks as it is for data entry operators. Assume that salaries of data entry operators and accounting clerks are normally distributed in the population.

10.58 A study was conducted to develop a scale to measure stress in the workplace. Respondents were asked to rate 26 distinct work events. Each event was to be compared with the stress of the first week on the job, which was awarded an arbitrary score of 500. Sixty professional men and 41 professional women participated in the study. One of the stress events was "lack of support from the boss." The men's sample average rating of this event was 631 and the women's sample average rating was 848. Suppose the population standard deviations for both men and women were about 100. Construct a 95% confidence interval to estimate the difference in the population mean scores on this event for men and women.

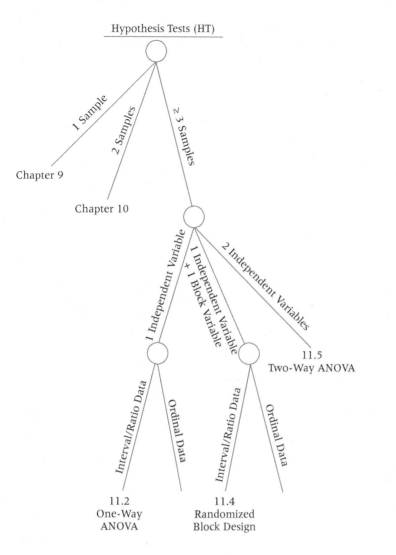

FIGURE 11.1 Branch of the Tree Diagram Taxonomy of Inferential Techniques

Introduction to Design of Experiments

LEARNING OBJECTIVE 11.1

Describe an experimental design and its elements, including independent variables—both treatment and classification—and dependent variables.

An **experimental design** is *a plan and a structure to test hypotheses in which the analyst either controls or manipulates one or more variables.* It contains independent and dependent variables. In an experimental design, an **independent variable** may be *either a treatment variable or a classification variable.* A **treatment variable** is *a variable the experimenter controls or modifies in the experiment.* A **classification variable** is *some characteristic of the experimental subject that was present prior to the experiment and is not a result of the experimenter's manipulations or control.* Independent variables are sometimes also referred to as **factors**. Tim Hortons executives might sanction an in-house study to compare daily sales volumes for a given-sized store in four different demographic settings: (1) inner-city stores (large city), (2) suburban stores (large city), (3) stores in a medium-sized city, and (4) stores in a small town. Managers might also decide to compare sales on the five different weekdays (Monday through Friday). In this study, the independent variables are store demographics and day of the week.

A finance analyst might conduct a study to determine whether there is a significant difference in application fees for home loans in the 10 provinces of Canada and might include three different types of lending organizations. In this study, the independent variables are provinces and types of lending organizations. Or suppose a manufacturing organization produces a valve that is specified to have an opening with a diameter of 6.37 cm. Quality controllers within the company might decide to test to determine how the openings for produced valves vary among four different machines on three different shifts. This experiment includes the independent variables of type of machine and work shift.

Whether an independent variable can be manipulated by the analyst depends on the concept being studied. Independent variables such as work shift, gender of employee, geographic region, type of machine, and quality of tire are classification variables with conditions that existed prior to the study. The business analyst cannot change the characteristic of the variable, so he or she studies the phenomenon being explored under several conditions of the various aspects of the variable. As an example, the valve experiment is conducted under the conditions of all three work shifts.

However, some independent variables can be manipulated by the analyst. For example, in the well-known Hawthorne studies of the Western Electric Company in the 1920s, the amount of light in production areas was varied to determine its effect on productivity. In theory, this independent variable could be manipulated by the analyst to allow any level of lighting. Other examples of independent variables that can be manipulated include the size of bonuses offered workers, temperature in the plant, number of hours of overtime, degree of encouragement by management, and many others. These are examples of treatment variables.

Each independent variable has two or more levels, or classifications. **Levels**, or **classifications**, of independent variables are *the subcategories of the independent variable used by the analyst in the experimental design.* For example, the different demographic settings listed for the Tim Hortons study are four levels, or classifications, of the independent variable Store Demographics: (1) inner-city store, (2) suburban store, (3) store in a medium-sized city, and (4) store in a small town. In the valve experiment, four levels or classifications of machines within the independent variable Machine Type are used: machine 1, machine 2, machine 3, and machine 4.

The other type of variable in an experimental design is a **dependent variable**. A dependent variable is *the response to the different levels of the independent variables.* It is the measurement taken under the conditions of the experimental design that reflect the effects of the independent variable(s). In the Tim Hortons study, the dependent variable is the dollar amount of daily total sales. For the study on loan application fees, the fee charged for a loan application is probably the dependent variable. In the valve experiment, the dependent variable is the size of the opening of the valve.

Experimental designs in this chapter are analyzed statistically by a group of techniques referred to as **analysis of variance**, or **ANOVA**. The analysis of variance concept begins with the notion that dependent variable responses (measurements, data) are not all the same in a given study. That is, dependent variable measures such as output, sales, length of stay, customer satisfaction, and product viscosity will often vary from item to item or observation to observation. Note the measurements for the openings of 24 valves randomly selected from an assembly line that are given in **Table 11.1**. The mean opening is 6.34 cm. Only one of the 24 valve opening measurements is actually the mean. Why do the valve openings vary?

TABLE 11.1	Valve Opening Measurements (in centimetres) for 24 Valves Produced on an Assembly Line			
6.26	6.19	6.33	6.26	6.50
6.19	6.44	6.22	6.54	6.23
6.29	6.40	6.23	6.29	6.58
6.27	6.38	6.58	6.31	6.34
6.21	6.19	6.36	6.56	

$\bar{x} = 6.34$

Total Sum of Squares of Deviation $= \text{SST} = \Sigma(x_i - \bar{x})^2 = 0.3915$

The total sum of squares of deviation of these valve openings around the mean is 0.3915 cm^2. Why is this value not zero? Using various types of experimental designs, we can explore some possible reasons for this variance with ANOVA techniques. As we explore each of the experimental designs and their associated analysis, note that the statistical technique is attempting to break down the total variance among the objects being studied into possible causes. In the case of the valve openings, this variance of measurements might be due to such variables as machine, operator, shift, supplier, and production conditions, among others.

Many different types of experimental designs are available to analysts. In this chapter, we will present and discuss three specific types of experimental designs: completely randomized design, randomized block design, and factorial experiments.

Concept Check

1. Explain in your own words the meaning of an experimental design.
2. Define the terms *treatment variable, classification variable, factor, level,* and *dependent variable.*

11.1 Problems

11.1 Some Toronto Stock Exchange analysts believe that 24-hour trading on the stock exchange is the wave of the future. As an initial test of this idea, assume that the Toronto Stock Exchange will open for two after-hours "crossing sections" and the results of these extra-hour sessions will be studied for one year.

  a. State an independent variable that could have been used for this study.

  b. List at least two levels, or classifications, for this variable.

  c. Give a dependent variable for this study.

11.2 WestJet Airlines is able to keep fares low in part because of relatively low maintenance costs on its airplanes. One of the main reasons for the low maintenance costs is that WestJet flies mainly one type of aircraft, the Boeing 737. However, WestJet flies three different versions of the 737. Suppose WestJet decides to conduct a study to determine whether there is a significant difference in the average annual maintenance costs for the three types of 737s used.

  a. State an independent variable for such a study.

  b. What are some of the levels or classifications that might be studied under this variable?

  c. Give a dependent variable for this study.

11.3 A large multinational banking company wants to determine whether there is a significant difference in the average dollar amounts purchased by users of different types of credit cards. Among the credit cards being studied are MasterCard, Visa, and American Express.

  a. If an experimental design were set up for such a study, what are some possible independent variables?

  b. List at least three levels, or classifications, for each independent variable.

  c. What are some possible dependent variables for this experiment?

11.4 Is there a difference in the family demographics of people who stay at hotels? Suppose a study is conducted in which three categories of hotels are used: economy hotels, modestly priced chain hotels, and exclusive hotels. One of the dependent variables studied might be the number of children in the family of the person staying in the hotel. Name three other dependent variables that might be used in this study.

11.2 The Completely Randomized Design (One-Way ANOVA)

LEARNING OBJECTIVE 11.2

Test a completely randomized design using a one-way analysis of variance.

One of the simplest experimental designs is the completely randomized design. In the **completely randomized design,** *subjects are assigned randomly to treatments.* The completely randomized design contains only one independent variable, with two or more treatment levels, or classifications. If only two treatment levels, or classifications, of the independent variable are present, the design is the same one used to test the difference in means of two independent populations presented in Chapter 10, which used the *t* test to analyze the data.

In this section, we will focus on completely randomized designs with three or more classification levels. Analysis of variance, or ANOVA, will be used to analyze the data that result from the treatments.

A completely randomized design could be structured for a tire-quality study in which tire quality is the independent variable and the treatment levels are low, medium, and high quality. The dependent variable might be the number of kilometres driven before the tread fails provincial inspection. A study of daily sales volumes for Tim Hortons stores could be undertaken by using a completely randomized design with demographic setting as the independent variable. The treatment levels, or classifications, would be inner-city stores, suburban stores, stores in medium-sized cities, and stores in small towns. The dependent variable would be sales dollars (see Thinking Critically About Statistics in Business Today 11.1).

Thinking Critically About Statistics in Business Today 11.1

Does Regional Ideology Affect a Firm's Definition of Success?

One analyst, G. C. Lodge, proposed that companies pursue different performance goals based on the ideology of their regional culture. L. Thurow went further by suggesting that such regional ideologies drive North American firms to be short-term profit maximizers, Japanese firms to be growth maximizers, and European firms to be a mix of the two.

Three other analysts, J. Katz, S. Werner, and L. Brouthers, decided to test these suggestions by studying 114 international banks from the U.S., the European Union (EU), and Japan listed in the Global 1,000. Specifically, there were 34 banks from the U.S., 45 banks from the EU, and 35 banks from Japan in the study. Financial and market data were gathered and averaged on each bank over a five-year period to limit the effect of single-year variations.

The banks were compared on general measures of success such as profitability, capitalization, growth, size, risk, and earnings distribution by specifically examining 11 measures. Eleven one-way ANOVA designs were computed, one for each dependent variable. These included return on equity, return on assets, yield, capitalization, assets, market value, growth, Tobin's Q, price-to-earnings ratio, payout ratio, and risk. The independent variable in each ANOVA was region, with three levels: U.S., EU, and Japan.

In all 11 ANOVAs, there was a significant difference between banks in the three regions ($\alpha = 0.01$), supporting the theme of different financial success goals for different regional cultures. Because of the overall significant difference attained in the ANOVAs, each ANOVA was followed by a Duncan's multiple range test (multiple comparison) to determine which, if any, of the pairs were significantly different. These comparisons revealed that U.S. and EU banks maintained significantly higher levels than

Japanese banks on return on equity, return on assets, and yield. This result underscores the notion that U.S. and EU banks have more of a short-term profit orientation than do Japanese banks. There was a significant difference between banks from each of the three regions in amount of capitalization. U.S. banks had the highest level of capitalization, followed by EU banks and then Japanese banks. This result may reflect the cultural attitude about how much capital is needed to ensure a sound economy, with U.S. banks maintaining higher levels of capital.

The study found that Japanese banks had significantly higher levels on growth, Tobin's Q, and price-to-earnings ratio than did the other two entities. This result confirms the hypothesis that Japanese firms are more interested in growth. In addition, Japanese banks had a significantly higher asset size and market value of equity than did U.S. banks. The analysts had hypothesized that EU banks would have a greater portfolio risk than U.S. or Japanese banks. They found that EU banks did have significantly higher risk and paid out significantly higher dividends than did either Japanese or U.S. banks.

Things to Ponder

1. If you represent a Canadian company wanting to do business in Japan, what are some points from this study that might guide you in your endeavour?

2. What did you learn about EU banks in this study that might set them apart from Canadian or U.S. banks?

Sources: Adapted from Jeffrey P. Katz, Steve Werner, and Lance Brouthers, "Does Winning Mean the Same Thing around the World? National Ideology and the Performance of Global Competitors," *Journal of Business Research* 44, no. 2 (February 1999); 117–26; George C. Lodge, *Comparative Business-Government Relations* (Englewood Cliffs, NJ: Prentice Hall, 1990); Lester Thurow, *Head to Head* (New York: William Morrow and Co., 1992).

As an example of a completely randomized design, suppose an analyst decides to analyze the effects of the machine operator on the valve opening measurements of valves produced in a manufacturing plant, like those shown in Table 11.1. The independent variable in this design is the machine operator. Suppose further that four different operators operate the machines. These four machine operators are the levels of treatment, or classification, of the independent variable. The dependent variable is the opening measurement of the valve.

Figure 11.2 shows the structure of this completely randomized design. Is there a significant difference in the mean valve openings of 24 valves produced by the four operators? **Table 11.2** contains the valve opening measurements for valves produced by each operator.

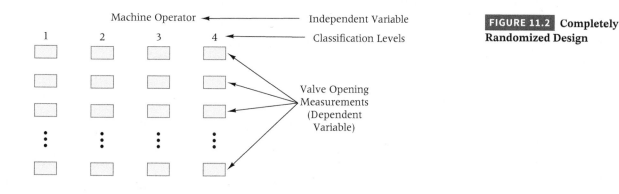

FIGURE 11.2 Completely Randomized Design

TABLE 11.2 Valve Opening Measurements by Operator

1	2	3	4
6.33	6.26	6.44	6.29
6.26	6.36	6.38	6.23
6.31	6.23	6.58	6.19
6.29	6.27	6.54	6.21
6.40	6.19	6.56	
	6.50	6.34	
	6.19	6.58	
	6.22		

One-Way Analysis of Variance

In the machine operator example, is it possible to analyze the four samples by using a t test for the difference in two sample means? These four samples would require $_4C_2 = 6$ individual t tests to accomplish the analysis of two groups at a time. Recall that if $\alpha = 0.05$ for a particular test, there is a 5% chance of rejecting a null hypothesis that is true (i.e., committing a Type I error). If enough tests are done, eventually one or more null hypotheses will be falsely rejected by chance. Hence, $\alpha = 0.05$ is valid only for one t test. In this problem, with six t tests, the error rate compounds, so when the analyst is finished with the problem there is a much greater than 0.05 chance of committing a Type I error. Fortunately, a technique has been developed that analyzes all the sample means at one time and thus precludes the buildup of error rate: analysis of variance (ANOVA). A completely randomized design is analyzed by a **one-way analysis of variance**.

In general, if k samples are being analyzed, the following hypotheses are being tested in a one-way ANOVA:

$$H_0: \mu_1 = \mu_2 = \mu_3 = \cdots = \mu_k$$

$$H_a: \text{At least one of the means is different from the others.}$$

The null hypothesis states that the population means for all treatment levels are equal. Because of the way the alternative hypothesis is stated, if even one of the population means is different from the others, the null hypothesis is rejected.

Testing these hypotheses by using one-way ANOVA is accomplished by partitioning the total variance of the data into the following two variances:

1. The variance resulting from the treatment (columns)
2. The error variance, or that portion of the total variance unexplained by the treatment

As part of this process, the total sum of squares of deviation of values around the mean can be divided into two additive and independent parts.

$$\text{SST} = \text{SSC} + \text{SSE}$$

$$\sum_{i=1}^{n_j}\sum_{j=1}^{C}(x_{ij}-\bar{x})^2 = \sum_{j=1}^{C}n_j(\bar{x}_j-\bar{x})^2 + \sum_{i=1}^{n_j}\sum_{j=1}^{C}(x_{ij}-\bar{x}_j)^2$$

where

SST = total sum of squares

SSC = sum of squares of column (treatment)

SSE = sum of squares of error

i = particular member of a treatment level

j = a treatment level

C = number of treatment levels

n_j = number of observations in a given treatment level

$\bar{x}$ = grand mean

$\bar{x}_j$ = mean of treatment group or level

x_{ij} = individual value

This relationship is shown in **Figure 11.3**. Observe that the total sum of squares of variation is partitioned into the sum of squares of treatment (columns) and the sum of squares of error.

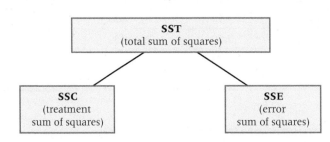

FIGURE 11.3 Partitioning Total Sum of Squares of Variation

The formulas used to accomplish one-way analysis of variance are developed from this relationship. The double summation sign indicates that the values are summed within a treatment level and across treatment levels. Basically, ANOVA compares the relative sizes of the *treatment* variation and the *error* variation (within-group variation). The error variation is unaccounted for and can be viewed at this point as due to individual differences within treatment groups. If a significant difference in treatments is present, the treatment variation should be large relative to the error variation.

Figure 11.4 displays the data from the machine operator example in terms of treatment level. Note the variation of values (*x*) *within* each treatment level. Now examine the variation

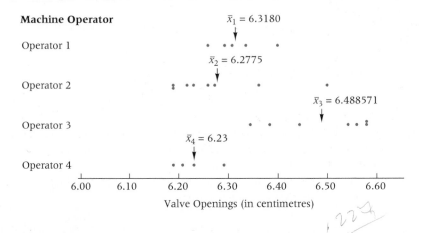

FIGURE 11.4 Location of Mean Valve Openings by Operator

between levels 1 through 4 (the difference in the machine operators). In particular, note that values for treatment level 3 seem to be located differently from those of levels 2 and 4. This difference is also underscored by the mean values for each treatment level:

$$\bar{x}_1 = 6.3180 \quad \bar{x}_2 = 6.2775 \quad \bar{x}_3 = 6.488571 \quad \bar{x}_4 = 6.23$$

Analysis of variance is used to determine statistically whether the variance between the treatment level means is greater than the variances within levels (error variance). Several important assumptions underlie analysis of variance:

1. Observations are drawn from normally distributed populations.
2. Observations represent random samples from the populations.
3. The variances of the populations are equal.

These assumptions are similar to those for using the t test for independent samples in Chapter 10. It is assumed that the populations are normally distributed and that the population variances are equal. These techniques should be used only with random samples.

An ANOVA is computed with the three sums of squares: total, treatment (columns), and error. Shown below are the formulas to compute a one-way ANOVA. SS represents sum of squares and MS represents mean square. SSC is the sum of squares of columns, which yields the sum of squares between treatments. It measures the variation between columns or between treatments, since the independent variable treatment levels are presented as columns. SSE is the sum of squares of error, which yields the variation within treatments (or columns). Some say that it is a measure of the individual differences unaccounted for by the treatments. SST is the total sum of squares and is a measure of all variation in the dependent variable. As shown previously, SST contains both SSC and SSE and can be partitioned into SSC and SSE. MSC and MSE are the mean squares of column and error. Mean square is an average and is computed by dividing the sum of squares by the degrees of freedom. Finally, the F value is determined by dividing the treatment variance (MSC) by the error variance (MSE). As discussed in Chapter 10, the F value is a ratio of two variances. In the ANOVA situation, the F **value** is *a ratio of the treatment variance to the error variance.*

Formulas for Computing a One-Way ANOVA

$$\text{SSC} = \sum_{j=1}^{C} n_j (\bar{x}_j - \bar{x})^2$$

$$\text{SSE} = \sum_{i=1}^{n_j} \sum_{j=1}^{C} (x_{ij} - \bar{x}_j)^2$$

$$\text{SST} = \sum_{i=1}^{n_j} \sum_{j=1}^{C} (x_{ij} - \bar{x})^2$$

$$\text{df}_C = C - 1$$

$$\text{df}_E = N - C$$

$$\text{df}_R = N - 1$$

$$\text{MSC} = \frac{\text{SSC}}{\text{df}_C}$$

$$\text{MSE} = \frac{\text{SSE}}{\text{df}_E}$$

$$F = \frac{\text{MSC}}{\text{MSE}}$$

(11.1)

where

i = a particular member of a treatment level
j = a treatment level
C = number of treatment levels
n_j = number of observations in a given treatment level
$\bar{x}$ = grand mean
$\bar{x}_j$ = column mean
x_{ij} = individual value

Performing these calculations for the machine operator example yields the following:

Machine Operator

1	2	3	4
6.33	6.26	6.44	6.29
6.26	6.36	6.38	6.23
6.31	6.23	6.58	6.19
6.29	6.27	6.54	6.21
6.40	6.19	6.56	
	6.50	6.34	
	6.19	6.58	
	6.22		

$$n_j: \quad n_1 = 5 \qquad n_2 = 8 \qquad n_3 = 7 \qquad n_4 = 4 \qquad N = 24$$

$$\bar{x}_j: \quad \bar{x}_1 = 6.318 \quad \bar{x}_2 = 6.2775 \quad \bar{x}_3 = 6.488571 \quad \bar{x}_4 = 6.230 \quad \bar{x} = 6.339583$$

$$\begin{aligned}
SSC = \sum_{j=1}^{C} n_j(\bar{x}_j - \bar{x})^2 &= [5(6.318 - 6.339583)^2 + 8(6.2775 - 6.339583)^2 \\
&\quad + 7(6.488571 - 6.339583)^2 + 4(6.230 - 6.339583)^2] \\
&= 0.00233 + 0.03083 + 0.15538 + 0.04803 \\
&= 0.23657
\end{aligned}$$

$$\begin{aligned}
SSE = \sum_{i=1}^{n_j}\sum_{j=1}^{C}(x_{ij} - \bar{x}_j)^2 &= [(6.33 - 6.318)^2 + (6.26 - 6.318)^2 + (6.31 - 6.318)^2 \\
&\quad + (6.29 - 6.318)^2 + (6.40 - 6.318)^2 + (6.26 - 6.2775)^2 \\
&\quad + (6.36 - 6.2775)^2 + \cdots + (6.19 - 6.230)^2 + (6.21 - 6.230)^2] \\
&= 0.15492
\end{aligned}$$

$$\begin{aligned}
SST = \sum_{i=1}^{n_j}\sum_{j=1}^{C}(x_{ij} - \bar{x})^2 &= [(6.33 - 6.339583)^2 + (6.26 - 6.339583)^2 \\
&\quad + (6.31 - 6.339583)^2 + \cdots + (6.19 - 6.339583)^2 \\
&\quad + (6.21 - 6.339583)^2] \\
&= 0.39150
\end{aligned}$$

$$df_C = C - 1 = 4 - 1 = 3$$

$$df_E = N - C = 24 - 4 = 20$$

$$df_T = N - 1 = 24 - 1 = 23$$

$$MSC = \frac{SSC}{df_C} = \frac{0.23657}{3} = 0.078857$$

$$MSE = \frac{SSE}{df_E} = \frac{0.15492}{20} = 0.007746$$

$$F = \frac{0.078857}{0.007746} = 10.18$$

From these computations, an analysis of variance chart can be constructed, as shown in **Table 11.3**. The observed F value is 10.18. It is compared with a critical value from the F table to determine whether there is a significant difference in treatment or classification.

TABLE 11.3 **ANOVA for the Machine Operator Example**

Source of Variance	df	SS	MS	F
Between	3	0.23657	0.078857	10.18
Error	20	0.15492	0.007746	
Total	23	0.39150		

Reading the *F* Distribution Table

The **F distribution** table is in Table A.7. Associated with every *F* value in the table are two unique df values: degrees of freedom in the numerator (df_C) and degrees of freedom in the denominator (df_E). To look up a value in the *F* distribution table, the analyst must know both degrees of freedom. Because each *F* distribution is determined by a unique pair of degrees of freedom, many *F* distributions are possible. Space constraints limit Table A.7 to *F* values for only $\alpha = 0.005, 0.01, 0.025, 0.05,$ and 0.10. However, statistical computer software packages for computing ANOVAs usually give a probability for the *F* value, which allows a hypothesis-testing decision for any α based on the *p*-value method.

In the one-way ANOVA, the df_C values are the treatment (column) degrees of freedom, $C - 1$. The df_E values are the error degrees of freedom, $N - C$. For the machine operator example, $df_C = 3$ and $df_E = 20$. $F_{0.05,3,20}$ from **Table 11.4** is 3.10. Table 11.4 contains a partial view of the *F* distribution table for $\alpha = 0.05$ with the critical *F* value

TABLE 11.4   A Partial *F* Distribution Table for $\alpha = 0.05$

		Numerator Degrees of Freedom							
	1	**2**	**3**	**4**	**5**	**6**	**7**	**8**	**9**
19	4.38	3.52	3.13	2.90	2.74	2.63	2.54	2.48	2.42
20	4.35	3.49	3.10	2.87	2.71	2.60	2.51	2.45	2.39
21	4.32	3.47	3.07	2.84	2.68	2.57	2.49	2.42	2.37

(Denominator Degrees of Freedom)

for the machine operator example. This value is the critical value of the *F* test. ANOVA tests are always one-tailed tests with the rejection region in the upper tail. The decision rule is to reject the null hypothesis if the observed *F* value is greater than the critical *F* value ($F_{0.05,3,20} = 3.10$). For the machine operator problem, the observed *F* value of 10.18 is larger than the critical *F* value of 3.10. The null hypothesis is rejected. Not all means are equal, so there is a significant difference in the mean valve opening measurements by machine operator. **Figure 11.5** is a graph of an *F* distribution showing the critical *F* value for this example and the rejection region. Note that the *F* distribution begins at zero and contains no negative values because the *F* value is the ratio of two variances, and variances are always positive.

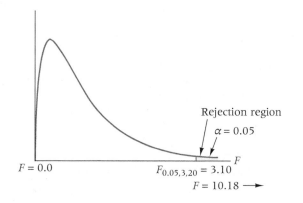

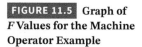

FIGURE 11.5 **Graph of *F* Values for the Machine Operator Example**

Using the Computer for One-Way ANOVA

Most analysts use the computer to analyze data with a one-way ANOVA. **Figure 11.6** shows the Excel output of the ANOVA computed for the machine operator example. The output includes the ANOVA table presented in Table 11.3. Excel ANOVA tables display the observed F value, mean squares, sum of squares, degrees of freedom, and a value of p. The value of p is the probability of an F value of 10.18 occurring by chance in an ANOVA with this structure (same degrees of freedom) even if there is no difference between means of the treatment levels. Using the p-value method of testing hypotheses presented in Chapter 9, we can easily see that because this p-value is only 0.000279, the null hypothesis would be rejected using $\alpha = 0.05$. Most computer output yields the value of p, so there is no need to look up a table value of F against which to compare the observed F value. The Excel output also includes the critical F value for this problem, $F_{0.05,3,20} = 3.10$.

FIGURE 11.6 **Excel Analysis of the Machine Operator Problem**

	A	B	C	D	E	F	G
1	ANOVA: Single Factor						
2							
3	SUMMARY						
4	*Groups*	*Count*	*Sum*	*Average*	*Variance*		
5	Operator 1	5	31.59	6.3180	0.0028		
6	Operator 2	8	50.22	6.2775	0.0111		
7	Operator 3	7	45.42	6.4886	0.0101		
8	Operator 4	4	24.92	6.2300	0.0019		
9							
10							
11	ANOVA						
12	*Source of Variation*	*SS*	*df*	*MS*	*F*	*P-value*	*F crit*
13	Between Groups	0.2366	3	0.0789	10.1810	0.0003	3.0984
14	Within Groups	0.1549	20	0.0077			
15							
16	Total	0.3915	23				

Comparison of F and t Values

Analysis of variance can be used to test hypotheses about the difference in two sample means from independent populations (Section 10.2).

The t test of independent samples is actually a special case of one-way ANOVA when there are only two treatment levels ($df_C = 1$). In this case, $F = t^2$. The t test is computationally simpler than ANOVA for two groups. However, some statistical computer software packages do not contain a t test. In these cases, the analyst can perform a one-way ANOVA and then either take the square root of the F value to obtain the value of t or use the generated probability with the p-value method to reach conclusions.

DEMONSTRATION PROBLEM 11.1

A company has three manufacturing plants, and company officials want to determine whether there is a difference in the average age of workers at the three locations. The following data are the ages of five randomly selected workers at each plant. Perform a one-way ANOVA to determine whether there is a significant difference in the mean ages of the workers at the three plants. Use $\alpha = 0.01$ and note that the sample sizes are equal.

Solution

Step 1 The hypotheses follow.

$$H_0: \mu_1 = \mu_2 = \mu_3$$
$$H_a: \text{At least one of the means is different from the others.}$$

Step 2 The appropriate test statistic is the F test calculated from ANOVA.

Step 3 The value of α is 0.01.

Step 4 The degrees of freedom for this problem are $3 - 1 = 2$ for the numerator and $15 - 3 = 12$ for the denominator. The critical F value is $F_{0.01,2,12} = 6.93$.

Because ANOVAs are always one-tailed with the rejection region in the upper tail, the decision rule is to reject the null hypothesis if the observed value of F is greater than 6.93.

Step 5

Plant (Employee Ages)

1	2	3
29	32	25
27	33	24
30	31	24
27	34	25
28	30	26

Step 6

$$n_j: \quad n_1 = 5 \quad n_2 = 5 \quad n_3 = 5 \quad N = 15$$
$$\bar{x}_j: \quad \bar{x}_1 = 28.2 \quad \bar{x}_2 = 32.0 \quad \bar{x}_3 = 24.8 \quad \bar{x} = 28.33$$

$$SSC = 5(28.2 - 28.33)^2 + 5(32.0 - 28.33)^2 + 5(24.8 - 28.33)^2 = 129.73$$

$$SSE = (29 - 28.2)^2 + (27 - 28.2)^2 + \cdots + (25 - 24.8)^2 + (26 - 24.8)^2 = 19.60$$

$$SST = (29 - 28.33)^2 + (27 - 28.33)^2 + \cdots + (25 - 28.33)^2 + (26 - 28.33)^2 = 149.33$$

$$df_C = 3 - 1 = 2$$
$$df_E = 15 - 3 = 12$$
$$df_T = 15 - 1 = 14$$

Source of Variance	SS	df	MS	F
Between	129.73	2	64.87	39.80
Error	19.60	12	1.63	
Total	149.33	14		

Step 7 The decision is to reject the null hypothesis because the observed F value of 39.80 is greater than the critical F value of 6.93.

Step 8 There is a significant difference in the mean ages of workers at the three plants. This difference can have hiring implications. Company leaders should understand that, because motivation, discipline, and experience may differ with age, the differences in ages may call for different managerial approaches in each plant.

The following chart displays the dispersion of the ages of workers from the three samples, along with the mean age for each plant sample. Note the difference in group means. The significant F value says that the difference between the mean ages is relatively greater than the differences of ages within each group.

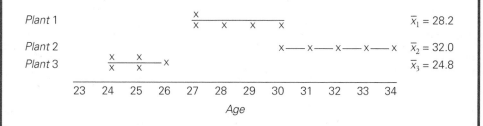

Following is the Excel output for this problem.

Excel Output

	A	B	C	D	E	F	G
1	ANOVA: Single Factor						
2							
3	SUMMARY						
4	*Groups*	*Count*	*Sum*	*Average*	*Variance*		
5	Plant 1	5	141	28.20	1.70		
6	Plant 2	5	160	32.00	2.50		
7	Plant 3	5	124	24.80	0.70		
8							
9							
10	ANOVA						
11	*Source of Variation*	*SS*	*df*	*MS*	*F*	*P-value*	*F crit*
12	Between Groups	129.73	2	64.87	39.71	0.00	6.93
13	Within Groups	19.60	12	1.63			
14							
15	Total	149.33	14				

Concept Check

1. Explain the difference between the *treatment* variation and the *error* variation.
2. What are the three assumptions that underlie analysis of variance?
3. How is the F value conceptually defined in the analysis of variance situation?

11.2 Problems

11.5 Compute a one-way ANOVA on the following data.

1	2	3
2	5	3
1	3	4
3	6	5
3	4	5
2	5	3
1		5

Determine the observed F value. Compare the observed F value with the critical F value and decide whether to reject the null hypothesis. Use $\alpha = 0.05$.

11.6 Compute a one-way ANOVA on the following data.

1	2	3	4	5
14	10	11	16	14
13	9	12	17	12
10	12	13	14	13
	9	12	16	13
	10		17	12
				14

Determine the observed F value. Compare the observed F value with the critical F value and decide whether to reject the null hypothesis. Use $\alpha = 0.01$.

11.7 Compute a one-way ANOVA on the following data.

1	2	3	4
113	120	132	122
121	127	130	118
117	125	129	125
110	129	135	125

Determine the observed F value. Compare it with the critical F value and decide whether to reject the null hypothesis. Use a 1% level of significance.

11.8 Compute a one-way ANOVA on the following data.

1	2
27	22
31	27
31	25
29	23
30	26
27	27
28	23

Determine the observed F value. Compare it with the critical F value and decide whether to reject the null hypothesis. Perform a t test for independent measures on the data. Compare the t and F values. Are the results different? Use $\alpha = 0.05$.

11.9 Suppose you are using a completely randomized design to study some phenomenon. There are five treatment levels and a total of 55 people in the study. Each treatment level has the same sample size. Complete the following ANOVA.

Source of Variance	SS	df	MS
Treatment	583.39		
Error	972.18		
Total	1,555.57		

11.10 Suppose you are using a completely randomized design to study some phenomenon. There are three treatment levels and a total of 17 people in the study. Complete the following ANOVA table. Use $\alpha = 0.05$ to find the critical F value and use the data to test the null hypothesis.

Source of Variance	SS	df	MS	F
Treatment	29.64			
Error	68.42			
Total				

11.11 A milk company has four machines that fill 4 L jugs with milk. The quality control manager is interested in determining whether the average fill for these machines is the same. The following data represent random samples of fill measure (in litres) for 19 jugs of milk filled by the different machines. Use $\alpha = 0.01$ to test the hypothesis. Discuss the business implications of your findings.

Machine 1	Machine 2	Machine 3	Machine 4
4.05	3.99	3.97	4.00
4.01	4.02	3.98	4.02
4.02	4.01	3.97	3.99
4.04	3.99	3.95	4.01
	4.00	4.00	
	4.00		

11.12 That the starting salaries of new accounting graduates would differ according to geographic regions of Canada seems logical. A random selection of accounting firms is taken from three provinces, and each is asked to state the starting salary for a new accounting graduate who is going to work in auditing. The data obtained follow. Use a one-way ANOVA to analyze these data. Note that the data can be restated to make the computations more reasonable (example: $42,500 = 4.25$). Use a 1% level of significance. Discuss the business implications of your findings.

Nova Scotia	Ontario	British Columbia
$40,500	$51,000	$45,500
41,500	49,500	43,500
40,000	49,000	45,000
41,000	48,000	46,500
41,500	49,500	46,000

11.13 A management consulting company presents a three-day seminar on project management to various clients. The seminar is basically the same each time it is given. However, sometimes it is presented to high-level managers, sometimes to mid-level managers, and sometimes to low-level managers. The seminar facilitators believe evaluations of the seminar may vary with the audience. Suppose the following data are some randomly selected evaluation scores from different levels of managers who attended the seminar. The ratings are on a scale from 1 to 10, with 10 being the highest. Use a one-way ANOVA to determine whether there is a significant difference in the evaluations according to manager level. Assume $\alpha = 0.05$. Discuss the business implications of your findings.

High Level	Mid-Level	Low Level
7	8	5
7	9	6
8	8	5
7	10	7
9	9	4
	10	8
	8	

11.14 Family transportation costs are usually higher than most people believe because those costs include car payments, insurance, fuel costs, repairs, parking, and public transportation. Twenty randomly selected families in four major cities are asked to use their records to estimate a monthly figure for transportation costs. Use the data obtained and ANOVA to test whether there is a significant difference in monthly transportation costs for families living in these cities. Assume that $\alpha = 0.05$. Discuss the business implications of your findings.

Edmonton	Toronto	Vancouver	Halifax
$650	$250	$850	$540
480	525	700	450
550	300	950	675
600	175	780	550
675	500	600	600

11.15 Shown here is the Excel output for a one-way ANOVA. Analyze the results. Include the number of treatment levels, the sample sizes, the F value, the overall statistical significance of the test, and the values of the means.

	A	B	C	D	E	F	G
1	ANOVA: Single Factor						
2							
3	SUMMARY						
4	*Groups*	*Count*	*Sum*	*Average*	*Variance*		
5	C1	18	4081.14	226.73	184.69		
6	C2	15	3581.85	238.79	88.55		
7	C3	21	4884.18	232.58	147.87		
8	C4	11	2638.02	239.82	20.96		
9							
10							
11	ANOVA						
12	*Source of Variation*	SS	df	MS	*F*	*P*-value	*F* crit
13	Between Groups	1701.00	3	567.00	2.95	0.04	2.7555
14	Within Groups	11728.00	61	192.00			
15							
16	Total	13429.00	64				

11.16 Business is very good for a chemical company. In fact, it is so good that workers are averaging more than 40 hours per week at each of the chemical company's five plants. However, management is not certain whether there is a difference between the five plants in the average number of hours worked per week per worker. Random samples of data are taken at each of the five plants. The data are analyzed using Excel. The results follow. Explain the design of the study and determine whether there is an overall significant difference between the means at $\alpha = 0.05$. Why or why not? What are the values of the means? What are the business implications of this study to the chemical company?

	A	B	C	D	E	F	G
1	ANOVA: Single Factor						
2							
3	SUMMARY						
4	*Groups*	*Count*	*Sum*	*Average*	*Variance*		
5	Plant 1	11	636.5577	57.87	63.5949		
6	Plant 2	12	601.7648	50.15	62.4813		
7	Plant 3	8	491.7352	61.47	47.4772		
	Plant 4	5	246.0172	49.20	65.6072		
	Plant 5	7	398.6368	56.95	140.3540		
8							
9							
10	ANOVA						
11	*Source of Variation*	SS	df	MS	F	*P*-value	*F* crit
12	Between Groups	900.0863	4	225.0216	3.10	0.026595	2.62
13	Within Groups	2760.136	38	72.63516			
14							
15	Total	3660.223	42				

| 11.3 |

Multiple Comparison Tests

LEARNING OBJECTIVE 11.3

Use multiple comparison techniques, including Tukey's honestly significant difference test and the Tukey-Kramer procedure, to test the difference in two treatment means when there is overall significant difference between treatments.

Analysis of variance techniques are particularly useful in testing hypotheses about the differences of means in multiple groups because ANOVA utilizes only one single overall test. The advantage of this approach is that the probability of committing a Type I error, α, is controlled. As noted in Section 11.2, if four groups are tested two at a time, it takes six t tests ($_4C_2$) to analyze hypotheses between all possible pairs. In general, if k groups are tested two at a time, $_kC_2 = k(k-1)/2$ paired comparisons are possible.

Suppose α for an experiment is 0.05. If two different pairs of comparisons are made in the experiment using α of 0.05 in each, there is a 0.95 probability of not making a Type I error in each comparison. This approach results in a 0.9025 probability of not making a Type I error in either comparison (0.95 × 0.95), and a 0.0975 probability of committing a Type I error in at least one comparison (1 − 0.9025). Thus, the probability of committing a Type I error for this experiment is not 0.05 but 0.0975. In an experiment where the means of four groups are being tested two at a time, six different tests are conducted. If each is analyzed using $\alpha = 0.05$, the probability that no Type I error will be committed in any of the six tests is 0.95 × 0.95 × 0.95 × 0.95 × 0.95 × 0.95 = 0.735 and the probability of committing at least one Type I error in the six tests is 1 − 0.735 = 0.265. If an ANOVA is computed on all groups simultaneously using $\alpha = 0.05$, the value of α is maintained in the experiment.

Sometimes the analyst is satisfied with conducting an overall test of differences in groups such as the one ANOVA provides. However, when it is determined that there is an overall difference in population means, it is often desirable to go back to the groups and determine from the data which pairs of means are significantly different. Such pairwise analyses can lead to the buildup of the Type I experimental error rate, as mentioned. Fortunately, several techniques, referred to as **multiple comparisons**, have been developed to handle this problem.

Multiple comparisons are to be used only when an overall significant difference between groups has been obtained by using the F value of the ANOVA. Some of these techniques protect more for Type I errors and others protect more for Type II errors. Some multiple comparison techniques require equal sample sizes. There seems to be some difference of opinion in the literature about which techniques are most appropriate. Here we will consider only a posteriori or post hoc pairwise comparisons.

A posteriori or **post hoc** pairwise comparisons are made *after the experiment when the analyst decides to test for any significant differences in the samples based on a significant overall F value.* In contrast, **a priori** comparisons are made when the analyst *determines before the experiment which comparisons are to be made.* The error rates for these two types of comparisons are different, as are the recommended techniques. In this text, we consider only pairwise (two-at-a-time) multiple comparisons. Other types of comparisons are possible but belong in a more advanced presentation. The two multiple comparison tests discussed here are Tukey's HSD test for designs with equal sample sizes and the Tukey-Kramer procedure for situations in which sample sizes are unequal.

Tukey's Honestly Significant Difference (HSD) Test: The Case of Equal Sample Sizes

Tukey's honestly significant difference (HSD) test, sometimes known as Tukey's T method, is *a popular test for pairwise a posteriori multiple comparisons.* This test, developed by John W. Tukey and presented in 1953, is somewhat limited by the fact that it requires equal sample sizes.

Tukey's HSD test takes into consideration the number of treatment levels, the value of the mean square error, and the sample size. Using these values and a table value, q, the HSD determines the critical difference necessary between the means of any two treatment levels for the means to be significantly different. Once the HSD is computed, the analyst can examine the absolute value of any or all differences between pairs of means from treatment levels to determine whether there is a significant difference. The formula to compute a Tukey's HSD test follows.

Tukey's HSD Test

$$\text{HSD} = q_{\alpha, C, N-C} \sqrt{\frac{\text{MSE}}{n}} \tag{11.2}$$

where

$\quad\quad$ MSE = mean square error

$\quad\quad\quad$ n = sample size

$\quad$ $q_{\alpha, C, N-C}$ = critical value of the studentized range distribution from Table A.10

In Demonstration Problem 11.1, an ANOVA test was used to determine that there was an overall significant difference in the mean ages of workers at the three different plants, as evidenced by the F value of 39.8. The sample data for this problem follow.

	Plant		
	1	**2**	**3**
	29	32	25
	27	33	24
	30	31	24
	27	34	25
	28	30	26
Group Means	28.2	32.0	24.8
n_j	5	5	5

Because the sample sizes are equal in this problem, Tukey's HSD test can be used to compute multiple comparison tests between groups 1 and 2, 2 and 3, and 1 and 3. To compute the HSD, the values of MSE, n, and q must be determined. From the solution presented in Demonstration Problem 11.1, the value of MSE is 1.63. The sample size, n_j, is 5. The value of q is obtained from Table A.10 by using

$$\text{Number of Populations} = \text{Number of Treatment Means} = C$$

along with $df_E = N - C$.

In this problem, the values used to look up q are:

$$C = 3$$
$$df_E = N - C = 12$$

Table A.10 has a q table for $\alpha = 0.05$ and one for $\alpha = 0.01$. In this problem, $\alpha = 0.01$. Shown in **Table 11.5** is a portion of Table A.10 for $\alpha = 0.01$.

TABLE 11.5 Some q Values of $\alpha = 0.01$

Degrees of Freedom	Number of Populations				
	2	3	4	5	...
1	90	135	164	186	
2	14	19	22.3	24.7	
3	8.26	10.6	12.2	13.3	
4	6.51	8.12	9.17	9.96	
.					
.					
.					
11	4.39	5.14	5.62	5.97	
12	4.32	5.04	5.50	5.84	

For this problem, $q_{0.01,3,12} = 5.04$. HSD is computed as

$$\text{HSD} = q_{\alpha,C,N-C}\sqrt{\frac{\text{MSE}}{n}} = 5.04\sqrt{\frac{1.63}{5}} = 2.88$$

Using this value of HSD, the business analyst can examine the differences between the means from any two groups of plants. Any of the pairs of means that differ by more than 2.88 are significantly different at $\alpha = 0.01$. Here are the differences for all three possible pairwise comparisons:

$$|\bar{x}_1 - \bar{x}_2| = |28.2 - 32.0| = 3.8$$
$$|\bar{x}_1 - \bar{x}_3| = |28.2 - 24.8| = 3.4$$
$$|\bar{x}_2 - \bar{x}_3| = |32.0 - 24.8| = 7.2$$

All three comparisons are greater than the value of HSD, which is 2.88. Thus, the mean ages between any and all pairs of plants are significantly different.

Using the Computer to Do Multiple Comparisons

To illustrate statistical calculations, this book mainly uses Excel, but Excel does not have a tool for performing Tukey's HSD test. Minitab, another widely used statistical software program, does contain this tool. **Table 11.6** shows the Minitab output for computing a Tukey's HSD test. The computer output contains the confidence intervals for the differences in pairwise means for pairs of treatment levels. If the confidence interval includes zero, there is no significant difference in the pair of means. (If the interval contains zero, there is a possibility of no difference in the means.) Note in Table 11.6 that all three pairs of confidence intervals contain the same sign throughout the interval. For example, the confidence interval for estimating the difference in means from 1 and 2 is $0.914 \leq \mu_1 - \mu_2 \leq 6.686$. This interval does not contain zero, so we are confident that there is more than a zero difference in the two means. The same holds true for levels 1 and 3 and levels 2 and 3.

TABLE 11.6 **Minitab Output for Tukey's HSD**

```
Tukey 99% Simultaneous Confidence Intervals
All Pairwise Comparisons among Levels of Plant

Individual confidence level = 99.62%

Plant = 1 subtracted from:

Plant   Lower   Center   Upper
2       0.914   3.800    6.686         -----+--------+-------+--------+-
3      -6.286  -3.400   -0.514             (---*---) (---*---)
                                       -----+--------+-------+--------+-
Plant = 2 subtracted from:                -6.0      0.0     6.0      12.0

Plant   Lower   Center   Upper
3     -10.086  -7.200   -4.314         -----+--------+-------+--------+-
                                       (---*---)
                                       -----+--------+-------+--------+-
                                          -6.0      0.0     6.0      12.0
```

DEMONSTRATION PROBLEM 11.2

A metal-manufacturing firm wants to test the tensile strength of a given metal under varying conditions of temperature. Suppose that in the design phase, the metal is processed under five different temperature conditions and that random samples with a sample size of five are taken under each temperature condition. The data follow.

Tensile Strength of Metal Produced under Five Different Temperature Settings

1	2	3	4	5
2.46	2.38	2.51	2.49	2.56
2.41	2.34	2.48	2.47	2.57
2.43	2.31	2.46	2.48	2.53
2.47	2.40	2.49	2.46	2.55
2.46	2.32	2.50	2.44	2.55

A one-way ANOVA is performed on these data using Minitab, with the resulting analysis shown here.

One-Way ANOVA: Tensile Strength versus Temp Setting

Source	df	SS	MS	F	p
Temp Setting	4	0.108024	0.027006	43.70	0.000
Error	20	0.012360	0.000618		
Total	24	0.120384			

Note from the ANOVA table that the F value of 43.70 is statistically significant at $\alpha = 0.01$. There is an overall difference in the population means of metal produced under the five temperature settings. Use the data to compute a Tukey's HSD to determine which of the five groups are significantly different from the others.

Solution From the ANOVA table, the value of MSE is 0.000618. The sample size, n_j, is 5. The number of treatment means, C, is 5 and the df_E is 20. With these values and $\alpha = 0.01$, the value of q can be obtained from Table A.10:

$$q_{0.01,5,20} = 5.29$$

HSD can be computed as:

$$\text{HSD} = q_{\alpha,C,N-C} \sqrt{\frac{\text{MSE}}{n}} = 5.29\sqrt{\frac{0.000618}{5}} = 0.0588$$

The treatment group means for this problem follow.

Group 1 = 2.446

Group 2 = 2.350

Group 3 = 2.488

Group 4 = 2.468

Group 5 = 2.552

Computing all pairwise differences between these means (in absolute values) produces the following data.

	Group				
	1	**2**	**3**	**4**	**5**
1	—	0.096	0.042	0.022	0.106
2	0.096	—	0.138	0.118	0.202
3	0.042	0.138	—	0.020	0.064
4	0.022	0.118	0.020	—	0.084
5	0.106	0.202	0.064	0.084	—

Comparing these differences with the value of HSD = 0.0588, we can determine that the differences between groups 1 and 2 (0.096), 1 and 5 (0.106), 2 and 3 (0.138), 2 and 4 (0.118), 2 and 5 (0.202), 3 and 5 (0.064), and 4 and 5 (0.084) are significant at $\alpha = 0.01$. Not only is there an overall significant difference in the treatment levels, as shown by the ANOVA results, but there is a significant difference in the tensile strength of metal between seven pairs of levels. By studying the magnitudes of the individual treatment levels' means, the steel-manufacturing firm can determine which temperatures result in the greatest tensile strength. The Minitab output for this Tukey's HSD is shown next. Note that the computer analysis shows significant differences between pairs 1 and 2, 1 and 5, 2 and 3, 2 and 4, 2 and 5, 3 and 5, and 4 and 5 because these confidence intervals do not contain zero. These results are consistent with the manual calculations.

```
Tukey 99% Simultaneous Confidence Intervals
All Pairwise Comparisons among Levels of Temp Setting

Individual confidence level = 99.87%


Temp Setting = 1 subtracted from:
Temp
Setting    Lower     Center     Upper     -----+---------+---------+---------+--
2        -0.15481   -0.09600   -0.03719        (---*--)
3        -0.01681    0.04200    0.10081                (---*--)
4        -0.03681    0.02200    0.08081              (---*--)
5         0.04719    0.10600    0.16481                   (---*--)
                                            -----+---------+---------+---------+--
                                              -0.15      0.00      0.15      0.30


Temp Setting = 2 subtracted from:
Temp
Setting    Lower     Center     Upper     -----+---------+---------+---------+--
3         0.07919    0.13800    0.19681                      (---*--)
4         0.05919    0.11800    0.17681                    (---*--)
5         0.14319    0.20200    0.26081                         (---*--)
                                            -----+---------+---------+---------+--
                                              -0.15      0.00      0.15      0.30


Temp Setting = 3 subtracted from:
Temp
Setting    Lower     Center     Upper     -----+---------+---------+---------+--
4        -0.07881   -0.02000    0.03881              (---*--)
5         0.00519    0.06400    0.12281                  (---*--)
                                            -----+---------+---------+---------+--
                                              -0.15      0.00      0.15      0.30


Temp Setting = 4 subtracted from:
Temp
Setting    Lower     Center     Upper     -----+---------+---------+---------+--
5         0.02519    0.08400    0.14281                  (---*--)
                                            -----+---------+---------+---------+--
                                              -0.15      0.00      0.15      0.30
```

Tukey-Kramer Procedure: The Case of Unequal Sample Sizes

Tukey's HSD was modified by C. Y. Kramer in the mid-1950s to handle situations in which the sample sizes are unequal. The *modified version of HSD is sometimes referred to as* the

Tukey-Kramer procedure. The formula for computing the significant differences with this procedure is similar to that for the equal sample sizes, with the exception that the mean square error is divided in half and weighted by the sum of the inverses of the sample sizes under the root sign.

***

Tukey-Kramer Formula

$$q_{\alpha,C,N-C}\sqrt{\frac{MSE}{2}\left(\frac{1}{n_r}+\frac{1}{n_s}\right)} \qquad (11.3)$$

where

MSE = mean square error

n_r = sample size for rth sample

n_s = sample size for sth sample

$q_{\alpha,C,N-C}$ = critical value of the studentized range distribution from Table A.10

***

As an example of the application of the Tukey-Kramer procedure, consider the machine operator example in Section 11.2. A one-way ANOVA was used to test for any difference in the mean valve opening measurements produced by four different machine operators. An overall F of 10.18 was computed, which was significant at $\alpha = 0.05$. Because the ANOVA hypothesis test is significant and the null hypothesis is rejected, this problem is a candidate for multiple comparisons. Because the sample sizes are not equal, Tukey's HSD cannot be used to determine which pairs are significantly different. However, the Tukey-Kramer procedure can be applied. Shown in **Table 11.7** are the means and sample sizes for the valve openings for valves produced by the four different operators.

The mean square error for this problem, MSE, is shown in Table 11.3 as 0.007746. The four operators in the problem represent the four levels of the independent variable. Thus, $C = 4$, $N = 24$, and $N - C = 20$. The value of α in the problem is 0.05. With this information, the value of $q_{\alpha,C,N-C}$ is obtained from Table A.10 as:

$$q_{0.05,4,20} = 3.96$$

The distance necessary for the difference in the means of two samples to be statistically significant must be computed by using the Tukey-Kramer procedure for each pair because the sample sizes differ. In this problem with $C = 4$, there are $C(C - 1)/2$ or six possible pairwise comparisons. The computations follow.

For operators 1 and 2:

$$3.96\sqrt{\frac{0.007746}{2}\left(\frac{1}{5}+\frac{1}{8}\right)} = 0.1405$$

The difference between the means of operator 1 and operator 2 is:

$$6.3180 - 6.2775 = 0.0405$$

Because this result is less than the critical difference of 0.1405, there is no significant difference between the average valve openings of valves produced by machine operators 1 and 2.

Table 11.8 reports the critical differences for each of the six pairwise comparisons as computed by using the Tukey-Kramer procedure, along with the absolute value of the actual distances between the means. Any actual distance between means that is greater than the critical distance is significant. As shown in the table, the means of three pairs of samples—operators 1 and 3, operators 2 and 3, and operators 3 and 4—are significantly different.

Table 11.9 shows the Minitab output for this problem. Minitab uses the Tukey-Kramer procedure for unequal values of n. As before with the HSD test, Minitab produces a confidence interval for the differences in means for pairs of treatment levels. If the confidence interval includes zero, there is no significant difference in the pairs of means. If the signs over the interval are the same (zero is not in the interval), there is a significant difference in the means. Note that the signs over the intervals for pairs (1, 3), (2, 3), and (3, 4) are the same, indicating a significant difference in the means of those three pairs. This conclusion agrees with the results determined through the calculations reported in Table 11.8.

TABLE 11.7

Means and Sample Sizes for the Valves Produced by Four Operators

Operator	Sample Size	Mean
1	5	6.3180
2	8	6.2775
3	7	6.4886
4	4	6.2300

TABLE 11.8	Results of Pairwise Comparisons for the Machine Operators Example Using the Tukey-Kramer Procedure		
Pair	**Critical Difference**		**Actual Difference**
1 and 2	0.1405		0.0405
1 and 3	0.1443		0.1706*
1 and 4	0.1653		0.0880
2 and 3	0.1275		0.2111*
2 and 4	0.1509		0.0475
3 and 4	0.1545		0.2586*

*Significant at $\alpha = 0.05$.

TABLE 11.9	Minitab Multiple Comparisons in the Machine Operator Example Using the Tukey-Kramer Procedure

```
Tukey 95% Simultaneous Confidence Intervals
All Pairwise Comparisons

Individual confidence level = 98.89%

Operator 1 subtracted from:

              Lower       Center      Upper
Operator 2   -0.18099    -0.04050    0.09999
Operator 3    0.02627     0.17057    0.31487
Operator 4   -0.25332    -0.08800    0.07732


             -----+-------+-------+-------+-
Operator 2               (----*----)
Operator 3                    (----*----)
Operator 4            (----*-----)
             -----+-------+-------+-------+-
                -0.25     0.00    0.25    0.50


Operator 2 subtracted from:
              Lower     Center      Upper
Operator 3    0.08353   0.21107    0.33862
Operator 4   -0.19841  -0.04750    0.10341


             -----+-------+-------+-------+-
Operator 3                  (---·*---)
Operator 4            (---·*---)
             -----+-------+-------+-------+-
                -0.25     0.00    0.25    0.50
Operator 3 subtracted from:

              Lower     Center      Upper
Operator 4   -0.41304  -0.25857   -0.10411


             -----+-------+-------+-------+-
Operator 4   (-----*----)
             -----+-------+-------+-------+-
                -0.25     0.00    0.25    0.50
```

In a randomized block design, the sum of squares is:

$$SST = SSC + SSR + SSE$$

where

SST = sum of squares total
SSC = sum of squares columns (treatment)
SSR = sum of squares rows (blocking)
SSE = sum of squares error

SST and SSC are the same for a given analysis whether a completely randomized design or a randomized block design is used. For this reason, the SSR (blocking effects) comes out of the SSE; that is, some of the error variation in the completely randomized design is accounted for in the blocking effects of the randomized block design, as shown in **Figure 11.7**. If the error term is reduced, it is possible that the value of F for treatment will increase (the denominator of the F value is decreased). However, if there is not sufficient difference between levels of the blocking variable, the use of a randomized block design can lead to a less powerful result than would a completely randomized design computed on the same problem. Thus, the analyst should seek out blocking variables that he or she believes are significant contributors to variation among measurements of the dependent variable. **Figure 11.8** shows the layout of a randomized block design.

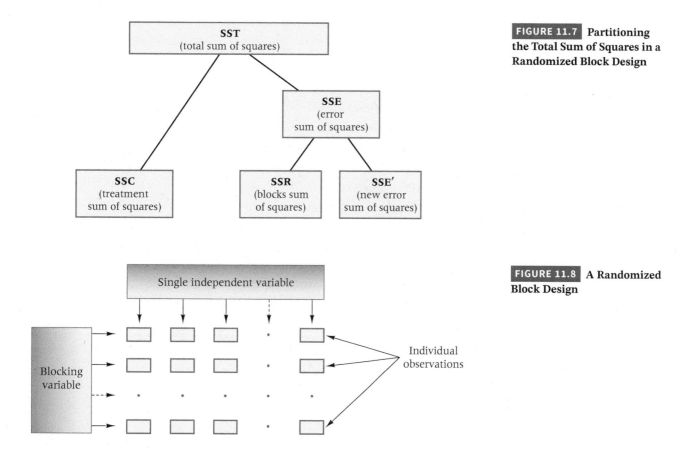

FIGURE 11.7 Partitioning the Total Sum of Squares in a Randomized Block Design

FIGURE 11.8 A Randomized Block Design

In each of the intersections of independent variable and blocking variable in Figure 11.8, one measurement is taken. In the randomized block design, one measurement is given for each treatment level under each blocking level.

The null and alternative hypotheses for the treatment effects in the randomized block design are:

$$H_0: \mu_1 = \mu_2 = \mu_3 = \cdots = \mu_C$$
$$H_a: \text{At least one of the treatment means is different from the others.}$$

For the blocking effects, the hypotheses are:

$$H_0: \mu_1. = \mu_2. = \mu_3. = \cdots = \mu_R.$$
$$H_a: \text{At least one of the blocking means is different from the others.}$$

Essentially, we are testing the null hypothesis that the population means of the treatment groups are equal. If the null hypothesis is rejected, at least one of the population means does not equal the others.

The formulas for computing a randomized block design follow.

Formulas for Computing a Randomized Block Design

$$SSC = n \sum_{j=1}^{C} (\bar{x}_j - \bar{x})^2$$

$$SSR = C \sum_{i=1}^{n} (\bar{x}_i - \bar{x})^2$$

$$SSE = \sum_{i=1}^{n} \sum_{j=1}^{C} (x_{ij} - \bar{x}_j - \bar{x}_i + \bar{x})^2$$

$$SST = \sum_{i=1}^{n} \sum_{j=1}^{C} (x_{ij} - \bar{x})^2 \qquad (11.4)$$

where

$i =$ block group (row)

$j =$ treatment level (column)

$C =$ number of treatment levels (columns)

$n =$ number of observations in each treatment level (number of blocks or rows)

$x_{ij} =$ individual observation

$\bar{x}_j =$ treatment (column) mean

$\bar{x}_i =$ block (row) mean

$\bar{x} =$ grand mean

$N =$ total number of observations

$$df_C = C - 1$$
$$df_R = n - 1$$
$$df_E = (C - 1)(n - 1) = N - n - C + 1$$
$$MSC = \frac{SSC}{C - 1}$$
$$MSR = \frac{SSR}{n - 1}$$
$$MSE = \frac{SSE}{N - n - C + 1}$$
$$F_{\text{treatments}} = \frac{MSC}{MSE}$$
$$F_{\text{blocks}} = \frac{MSR}{MSE}$$

The observed F value for treatments computed using the randomized block design formula is tested by comparing it with a critical F value, which is ascertained from Table A.7 by using α, df_C (treatment), and df_E (error). If the observed F value is greater than the table value, the null hypothesis is rejected for that α value. Such a result would indicate that not all population treatment means are equal. At this point, the business analyst can compute multiple comparisons if the null hypothesis has been rejected.

Some analysts also compute an F value for blocks even though the main emphasis in the experiment is on the treatments. The observed F value for blocks is compared with a critical F value determined from Table A.7 by using α, df_R (blocks), and df_E (error). If the F value for blocks is greater than the critical F value, the null hypothesis that all block population means are equal is rejected. This result tells the business analyst that including the blocking in the design was probably worthwhile and that a significant amount of variance was drawn off from the error term, thus increasing the power of the treatment test. In this text, we have omitted F_{blocks} from the normal presentation and problem solving. We leave the use of this F value to the discretion of the reader.

As an example of the application of the randomized block design, consider a tire company that developed a new tire. The company conducted tread wear tests on the tire to determine whether there was a significant difference in tread wear if the average speed at which the automobile was driven varied. The company set up an experiment in which the independent variable was speed of automobile. There were three treatment levels: slow speed (car was driven at 30 km/h), medium speed (car was driven at 65 km/h), and high speed (car was driven at 100 km/h).Company analysts realized that several possible variables could confound the study. One of these variables was supplier. The company used five suppliers to provide a major component of the rubber from which the tires were made. To control for this variable experimentally, the analysts used supplier as a blocking variable. Fifteen tires were randomly selected for the study, three from each supplier. Each of the three was assigned to be tested under a different speed condition. The data are given here, along with treatment and block totals. These figures represent tire wear in units of 10,000 km.

Supplier	Speed			Block Means $\bar{x}_i$
	Slow	Medium	Fast	
1	3.7	4.5	3.1	3.77
2	3.4	3.9	2.8	3.37
3	3.5	4.1	3.0	3.53
4	3.2	3.5	2.6	3.10
5	3.9	4.8	3.4	4.03
Treatment Means $\bar{x}_j$	3.54	4.16	2.98	$\bar{x} = 3.56$

To analyze this randomized block design using $\alpha = 0.01$, the computations are as follows.

$$C = 3$$
$$n = 5$$
$$N = 15$$

$$SSC = n \sum_{j=1}^{C} (\bar{x}_j - \bar{x})^2$$

$$= 5\left[(3.54 - 3.56)^2 + (4.16 - 3.56)^2 + (2.98 - 3.56)^2\right]$$

$$= 3.484$$

$$SSR = C \sum_{i=1}^{n} (\bar{x}_i - \bar{x})^2$$

$$= 3\left[(3.77 - 3.56)^2 + (3.37 - 3.56)^2 + (3.53 - 3.56)^2 + (3.10 - 3.56)^2\right.$$
$$\left. + (4.03 - 3.56)^2\right]$$

$$= 1.541$$

$$SSE = \sum_{i=1}^{n}\sum_{j=1}^{C}\left(x_{ij} - \bar{x}_j - \bar{x}_i + \bar{x}\right)^2$$

$$= (3.7 - 3.54 - 3.77 + 3.56)^2 + (3.4 - 3.54 - 3.37 + 3.56)^2$$

$$+ \cdots + (2.6 - 2.98 - 3.10 + 3.56)^2 + (3.4 - 2.98 - 4.03 + 3.56)^2$$

$$= 0.143$$

$$SST = \sum_{i=1}^{n}\sum_{j=1}^{C}(x_{ij} - \bar{x})^2$$

$$= (3.7 - 3.56)^2 + (3.4 - 3.56)^2 + \cdots + (2.6 - 3.56)^2 + (3.4 - 3.56)^2$$

$$= 5.176$$

$$MSC = \frac{SSC}{C - 1} = \frac{3.484}{2} = 1.742$$

$$MSR = \frac{SSR}{n - 1} = \frac{1.541}{4} = 0.3852$$

$$MSE = \frac{SSE}{N - n - C + 1} = \frac{0.143}{8} = 0.017875$$

$$F = \frac{MSC}{MSE} = \frac{1.742}{0.017875} = 97.45$$

Source of Variation	SS	df	MS	F
Treatment	3.484	2	1.742	97.45
Block	1.541	4	0.3852	
Error	0.143	8	0.017875	
Total	5.176	14		

For $\alpha = 0.01$, the critical F value is:

$$F_{0.01,2,8} = 8.65$$

Because the observed value of F for treatment (97.45) is greater than this critical F value, the null hypothesis is rejected. At least one of the population means of the treatment levels is not the same as the others; that is, there is a significant difference in tread wear for cars driven at different speeds. If this problem had been set up as a completely randomized design, the SSR would have been part of the SSE. The degrees of freedom for the blocking effects would have been combined with the degrees of freedom of error. Thus, the value of SSE would have been $1.541 + 0.143 = 1.684$, and df_E would have been $4 + 8 = 12$. These would then have been used to recompute $MSE = 1.684/12 = 0.1403$. The value of F for treatments would have been:

$$F = \frac{MSC}{MSE} = \frac{1.742}{0.1403} = 12.41$$

Thus, the F value for treatment with the blocking was 97.45 and *without* the blocking was 12.41. By using the random block design, a much larger observed F value was obtained.

Using the Computer to Analyze Randomized Block Designs

Excel can analyze a randomized block design. The computer output for the tire tread wear example is displayed in **Table 11.10**. Excel treats a randomized block design like a two-way ANOVA (Section 11.5) that has only one observation per cell. The Excel output includes sums, averages, and variances for each row and column. The Excel ANOVA table displays the observed F values for the treatment (columns) and the blocks (rows). An important inclusion in the Excel output is the p-value for each F, along with the critical F values.

TABLE 11.10   **Excel Output for the Tread Wear Example**

	A	B	C	D	E	F	G
1	ANOVA: Two-Factor Without Replication						
2							
3	SUMMARY	Count	Sum	Average	Variance		
4	Row 1	3	11.3000	3.7667	0.4933		
5	Row 2	3	10.1000	3.3667	0.3033		
6	Row 3	3	10.6000	3.5333	0.3033		
7	Row 4	3	9.3000	3.1000	0.2100		
8	Row 5	3	12.1000	4.0333	0.5033		
9							
10	Column 1	5	17.7000	3.5400	0.0730		
11	Column 2	5	20.8000	4.1600	0.2580		
12	Column 3	5	14.9000	2.9800	0.0920		
13							
14							
15	ANOVA						
16	Source of Variation	SS	df	MS	F	P-value	F crit
17	Rows	1.5493	4	0.3873	21.7196	0.0002	7.0061
18	Columns	3.4840	2	1.7420	97.6822	0.0000	8.6491
19	Error	0.1427	8	0.0178			
20							
21	Total	5.1760	14				

DEMONSTRATION PROBLEM 11.3

Suppose a national travel association studied the cost of premium unleaded gas in Canada during a recent summer. From experience, association directors believed there was a significant difference in the average cost of a litre of premium gas among urban areas in different parts of the country. To test this belief, they placed random calls to gas stations in five different cities. In addition, the analysts realized that the brand of gas might make a difference. They were mostly interested in the differences between cities, so they made city their treatment variable. To control for the fact that pricing varies with brand, the analysts included brand as a blocking variable and selected six different brands to participate. The analysts randomly telephoned one gas station for each brand in each city, resulting in 30 measurements (five cities and six brands). Each station operator was asked to report the current cost of a litre of premium unleaded gas at that station. The data are shown here. Test these data by using a randomized block design analysis to determine whether there is a significant difference in the average cost of premium unleaded gas by city. Let $\alpha = 0.01$.

			Geographic Region			
Brand	**Vancouver**	**Toronto**	**Calgary**	**Saskatoon**	**Montreal**	$\bar{x}_i$
A	$1.301	$1.275	$1.268	$1.245	$1.313	$1.280
B	1.286	1.279	1.283	1.256	1.290	1.279
C	1.290	1.279	1.286	1.260	1.294	1.282
D	1.298	1.294	1.275	1.238	1.294	1.280
E	1.298	1.275	1.271	1.271	1.305	1.284
F	1.290	1.286	1.283	1.271	1.309	1.288
$\bar{x}_j$	1.294	1.281	1.278	1.257	1.301	$\bar{x} = 1.282$

Solution

Step 1   The hypotheses follow.
For treatments:

$$H_0: \mu_{\cdot 1} = \mu_{\cdot 2} = \mu_{\cdot 3} = \mu_{\cdot 4} = \mu_{\cdot 5}$$
H_a: At least one of the treatment means is different from the others.

For blocks:

$$H_0: \mu_{1.} = \mu_{2.} = \mu_{3.} = \mu_{4.} = \mu_{5.}$$
$$H_a: \text{At least one of the blocking means is different from the others.}$$

Step 2 The appropriate statistical test is the F test in the ANOVA for randomized block designs.

Step 3 Let $\alpha = 0.01$.

Step 4 There are four degrees of freedom for the treatment ($C - 1 = 5 - 1 = 4$), five degrees of freedom for the blocks ($n - 1 = 6 - 1 = 5$), and 20 degrees of freedom for error [$(C - 1)(n - 1) = (4)(5) = 20$]. Using these, $\alpha = 0.01$, and Table A.7, we find the critical F values:

$$F_{0.01,4,20} = 4.43 \text{ for treatments}$$
$$F_{0.01,5,20} = 4.10 \text{ for blocks}$$

The decision rule is to reject the null hypothesis for treatments if the observed F value for treatments is greater than 4.43 and to reject the null hypothesis for blocking effects if the observed F value for blocks is greater than 4.10.

Step 5 The sample data including row and column means and the grand mean are given in the preceding table.

Step 6

$$SSC = n \sum_{j=1}^{C} (\bar{x}_j - \bar{x})^2$$
$$= 6\left[(1.294 - 1.282)^2 + (1.281 - 1.282)^2 + \cdots + (1.301 - 1.282)^2\right]$$
$$= 0.006822$$

$$SSR = C \sum_{i=1}^{n} (\bar{x}_i - \bar{x})^2$$
$$= 5\left[(1.280 - 1.282)^2 + (1.279 - 1.282)^2 + \cdots + (1.288 - 1.282)^2\right]$$
$$= 0.000285$$

$$SSE = \sum_{i=1}^{n} \sum_{j=1}^{C} (x_{ij} - \bar{x}_j - \bar{x}_i + \bar{x})^2$$
$$= (1.301 - 1.294 - 1.280 + 1.282)^2 + (1.286 - 1.294 - 1.279 + 1.282)^2 + \cdots$$
$$+ (1.305 - 1.301 - 1.284 + 1.282)^2 + (1.309 - 1.301 - 1.288 + 1.282)^2$$
$$= 0.001801$$

$$SST = \sum_{i=1}^{n} \sum_{j=1}^{C} (x_{ij} - \bar{x})^2$$
$$= (1.301 - 1.282)^2 + (1.286 - 1.282)^2 + \cdots + (1.305 - 1.282)^2$$
$$+ (1.309 - 1.282)^2$$
$$= 0.008908$$

$$MSC = \frac{SSC}{C - 1} = \frac{0.006822}{4} = 0.001706$$

$$MSR = \frac{SSR}{n - 1} = \frac{0.000285}{5} = 0.000057$$

$$MSE = \frac{SSE}{(C - 1)(n - 1)} = \frac{0.001801}{20} = 0.000090$$

$$F = \frac{MSC}{MSE} = \frac{0.001706}{0.000090} = 18.96$$

Source of Variance	SS	df	MS	F
Treatment	0.006822	4	0.001706	18.96
Block	0.000285	5	0.000057	
Error	0.001801	20	0.000090	
Total	0.008908	29		

Step 7   Because $F_{treat} = 18.96 > F_{0.01,4,20} = 4.43$, the null hypothesis is rejected for the treatment effects. There is a significant difference in the average price of a litre of premium unleaded gas in various cities.

A glance at the MSR reveals that there appears to be relatively little blocking variance. The result of determining an F value for the blocking effects is:

$$F = \frac{MSR}{MSE} = \frac{0.000057}{0.000090} = 0.63$$

The value of F for blocks is not significant at $\alpha = 0.01$ ($F_{0.01,5,20} = 4.10$). This result indicates that the blocking portion of the experimental design did not contribute significantly to the analysis. If the blocking effects (SSR) are added back into SSE and the df_R are included with df_E, the MSE becomes 0.000083 instead of 0.000090. Using the value 0.000083 in the denominator for the treatment F increases the observed treatment F value to 20.44. Thus, including nonsignificant blocking effects in the original analysis caused a loss of power.

Shown here is the Excel ANOVA table output for this problem.

	A	B	C	D	E	F	G
1	ANOVA						
2	Source of Variation	SS	df	MS	F	P-value	F crit
3	Rows	0.000285	5	0.000057	0.633004	0.676888	4.102685
4	Columns	0.006822	4	0.001706	18.940656	0.000001	4.430690
5	Error	0.001801	20	0.000090			
6							
7	Total	0.008908	29				

Step 8   The fact that there is a significant difference in the price of gas in different parts of the country can be useful information to decision-makers. For example, companies in the ground transportation business are greatly affected by increases in the cost of fuel. Knowledge of price differences in fuel can help these companies plan strategies and routes. Fuel price differences can sometimes be indications of cost-of-living differences or distribution problems, which can affect a company's relocation decision or cost-of-living increases given to employees who transfer to the higher-priced locations. Knowing that the price of gas varies around the country can generate interest among market analysts who might want to study why the differences are there and what drives them. This information can sometimes result in a better understanding of the marketplace.

Concept Check

1. Explain in your own words what a blocking variable is.
2. Consider Problem 11.12. Provide three examples of blocking variables that can be used for that particular experiment.

11.4 Problems

11.28 Use ANOVA to analyze the data from the randomized block design given here. Let $\alpha = 0.05$. State the null and alternative hypotheses and determine whether the null hypothesis is rejected.

		Treatment Level			
		1	2	3	4
	1	23	26	24	24
	2	31	35	32	33
Block	3	27	29	26	27
	4	21	28	27	22
	5	18	25	27	20

11.29 The following data were gathered from a randomized block design. Use $\alpha = 0.01$ to test for a significant difference in the treatment levels. Establish the hypotheses and reach a conclusion about the null hypothesis.

		Treatment Level		
		1	2	3
	1	1.28	1.29	1.29
Block	2	1.40	1.36	1.35
	3	1.15	1.13	1.19
	4	1.22	1.18	1.24

11.30 A randomized block design has a treatment variable with six levels and a blocking variable with 10 blocks. Using this information and $\alpha = 0.05$, complete the following table and reach a conclusion about the null hypothesis.

Source of Variance	SS	df	MS	F
Treatment	2,477.53			
Blocks	3,180.48			
Error	11,661.38			
Total				

11.31 A randomized block design has a treatment variable with four levels and a blocking variable with seven blocks. Using this information and $\alpha = 0.01$, complete the following table and reach a conclusion about the null hypothesis.

Source of Variance	SS	df	MS	F
Treatment	199.48			
Blocks	265.24			
Error	306.59			
Total				

11.32 Safety in motels and hotels is a growing concern among travellers. Suppose a survey was conducted by the National Motel and Hotel Association to determine Canadian travellers' perception of safety in various motel chains. The association chose four different national chains from the economy lodging sector and randomly selected 10 people who had stayed overnight in a motel in each of the four chains in the past two years. Each selected traveller was asked to rate each motel chain on a scale from 0 to 100 to indicate how safe he or she felt at that motel. A score of 0 indicates completely unsafe and a score of 100 indicates perfectly safe. The scores follow. Test this randomized block design to determine whether there is a significant difference in the safety ratings of the four motel chains. Use $\alpha = 0.05$.

Traveller	Motel 1	Motel 2	Motel 3	Motel 4
1	40	30	55	45
2	65	50	80	70
3	60	55	60	60
4	20	40	55	50
5	50	35	65	60
6	30	30	50	50
7	55	30	60	55
8	70	70	70	70
9	65	60	80	75
10	45	25	45	50

11.33 In recent years, the debate over the Canadian economy has been constant. The electorate seems somewhat divided as to whether the economy is in a recovery or not. Suppose a survey was undertaken to ascertain whether the perception of economic recovery in Nova Scotia differs according to political affiliation. People were selected for the survey from the Liberal party, the Conservative party, and the NDP. A 25-point scale was developed in which respondents gave a score of 25 if they felt the economy was definitely in complete recovery, a 0 if the economy was definitely not in a recovery, and

some value in between for more uncertain responses. To control for differences in socio-economic class, a blocking variable was maintained using five different socio-economic categories. The data are given here in the form of a randomized block design. Use $\alpha = 0.01$ to determine whether there is a significant difference in mean responses according to political affiliation.

	Political Affiliation		
Socio-Economic Class	Liberal	Conservative	NDP
Upper	11	5	8
Upper middle	15	9	8
Middle	19	14	15
Lower middle	16	12	10
Lower	9	8	7

11.34 As part of a manufacturing process, a plastic container is supposed to be filled with 46 ml of saltwater solution. The plant has three machines that fill the containers. Managers are concerned that the machines might not be filling the containers with the same amount of saltwater solution, so they set up a randomized block design to test this concern. A pool of five machine operators operates each of the three machines at different times. Company technicians randomly select five containers filled by each machine (one container for each of the five operators). The measurements are gathered and analyzed. The output from this analysis follows. What was the structure of the design? How many blocks were there? How many treatment classifications? Is there a statistical difference in the treatment means? Are the blocking effects significant? Discuss the implications of the output.

Two-Way ANOVA: Measurement versus Machine, Operator

Source	df	SS	MS	F	p
Machine	2	78.30	39.15	6.72	0.019
Operator	4	5.09	1.27	0.22	0.807
Error	8	46.66	5.83		
Total	14	130.06			

11.35 The comptroller of a company is interested in determining whether the average length of long-distance calls by managers varies according to type of telephone. A randomized block design experiment is set up in which a long-distance call by each of five managers is sampled for four different types of telephones: cellular, computer, regular, and cordless. The treatment is type of telephone and the blocks are the managers. The results of the analysis by Excel are shown here. Discuss the results and any implications they might have for the company.

ANOVA: Two-Factor without Replication

	A	B	C	D	E	F	G
1	ANOVA						
2							
3	*Source of Variation*	SS	df	MS	F	P-value	F crit
4	Managers	11.3346	4	2.8336	12.74	0.00028	3.26
5	Phone Type	10.6043	3	3.5348	15.89	0.00018	3.49
6	Error	2.6696	12	0.2225			
7	Total	24.6085	19				

11.5 | A Factorial Design (Two-Way ANOVA)

LEARNING OBJECTIVE 11.5

Test a factorial design using a two-way analysis of variance, noting the advantages and applications of such a design and accounting for possible interaction between two treatment variables.

Some experiments are designed so that *two or more treatments* (independent variables) *are explored simultaneously.* Such experimental designs are referred to as **factorial designs**. In factorial designs, *every level of each treatment is studied under the conditions of every level of all other treatments.* Factorial designs can be arranged such that three, four, or *n* treatments or independent variables are studied simultaneously in the same experiment. As an example, consider the valve opening data in Table 11.1. The mean valve opening for the 24 measurements is 6.34 cm. However, every valve but one in the sample measures something other than the mean. Why? Company management realizes that valves at this firm are made on different machines, by different operators, on different shifts, on different days, with raw materials from different suppliers. Business analysts who are interested in finding the sources of variation might decide to set up a factorial design that incorporates all five of these independent variables in one study. In this text, we explore the factorial designs with two treatments only.

Advantages of the Factorial Design

If two independent variables are analyzed by using a completely randomized design, the effects of each variable are explored separately (one per design). Thus, it takes two completely randomized designs to analyze the effects of the two independent variables. By using a factorial design, the business analyst can analyze both variables at the same time in one design, saving the time and effort of doing two different analyses and minimizing the experimentwise error rate.

Some business analysts use the factorial design as a way to control confounding or concomitant variables in a study. By building variables into the design, the analyst attempts to control for the effects of multiple variables in the experiment. With the completely randomized design, the variables are studied in isolation. With the factorial design, there is potential for increased power over the completely randomized design because the additional effects of the second variable are removed from the error sum of squares.

The analyst can explore the possibility of interaction between the two treatment variables in a two-factor factorial design if multiple measurements are taken under every combination of levels of the two treatments. Interaction will be discussed later.

Factorial designs with two treatments are similar to randomized block designs. However, whereas randomized block designs focus on one treatment variable and *control* for a blocking effect, a two-treatment factorial design focuses on the effects of both variables. Because the randomized block design contains only one measure for each (treatment-block) combination, interaction cannot be analyzed in randomized block designs.

Factorial Designs with Two Treatments

The structure of a two-treatment factorial design is featured in **Figure 11.9**. Note that there are two independent variables (two treatments) and that there is an intersection of each level of each treatment. These intersections are referred to as *cells*. One treatment is arbitrarily designated as the *row* treatment (forming the rows of the design), and the other treatment is designated as the *column* treatment (forming the columns of the design). Although it is

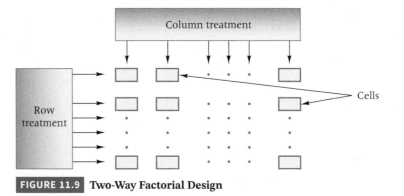

FIGURE 11.9 Two-Way Factorial Design

possible to analyze factorial designs with unequal numbers of items in the cells, the analysis of unequal cell designs is beyond the scope of this text. All factorial designs discussed here have cells of equal size.

Treatments (independent variables) of factorial designs must have at least two levels each. The simplest factorial design is a 2×2 factorial design, where each treatment has two levels. If such a factorial design were diagrammed in the manner of Figure 11.9, it would include two rows and two columns, forming four cells.

In this section, we study only factorial designs with $n > 1$ measurements for each combination of treatment levels (cells). This approach allows us to attempt to measure the interaction of the treatment variables. As with the completely randomized design and the randomized block design, a factorial design contains only *one* dependent variable.

Applications

Many applications of the factorial design are possible in business research. For example, the natural gas industry can design an experiment to study usage rates and how they are affected by temperature and precipitation. Theorizing that the outside temperature and type of precipitation make a difference in natural gas usage, industry analysts can gather usage measurements for a given community over a variety of temperature and precipitation conditions. At the same time, they can make an effort to determine whether certain types of precipitation, combined with certain temperature levels, affect usage rates differently than other combinations of temperature and precipitation (interaction effects).

Stock market analysts can select a company from an industry such as the construction industry and observe the behaviour of its shares under different conditions. A factorial design can be set up by using volume of the stock market and prime interest rate as two independent variables. For volume of the market, business analysts can select some days when the volume is up from the day before, some days when the volume is down from the day before, and some days when the volume is essentially the same as on the preceding day. These groups of days would constitute three levels of the independent variable, market volume. Business analysts can do the same thing with prime rate. Levels can be selected such that the prime rate is (1) up, (2) down, or (3) essentially the same. For the dependent variable, the analysts would measure how much the company's share price rises or falls on those randomly selected days (share price change). Using the factorial design, the business analyst can determine whether share price changes are different under various levels of market volume, whether share price changes are different under various levels of the prime interest rate, and whether share price changes react differently under various combinations of volume and prime rate (interaction effects).

Statistically Testing the Factorial Design

ANOVA is used to analyze data gathered from factorial designs. For factorial designs with two factors (independent variables), a **two-way analysis of variance** (two-way ANOVA) is used to test hypotheses statistically. The following hypotheses are tested by a two-way ANOVA.

Row effects: H_0: Row means are all equal.
                      H_a: At least one row mean is different from the others.

Column effects: H_0: Column means are all equal.
                      H_a: At least one column mean is different from the others.

Interaction effects: H_0: Interaction effects are zero.
                      H_a: An interaction effect is present.

Formulas for computing a two-way ANOVA are given in the box below. These formulas are computed in a manner similar to computations for the completely randomized design and the randomized block design. F values are determined for three effects:

1. Row effects

2. Column effects

3. Interaction effects

The row effects and the column effects are sometimes referred to as the main effects. Although F values are determined for these main effects, an F value is also computed for interaction effects. Using these observed F values, the analyst can make a decision about the null hypotheses for each effect.

Each of these observed F values is compared with a critical F value. The critical F value is determined by α, df_{num}, and df_{denom}. The degrees of freedom for the numerator (df_{num}) are determined by the effect being studied. If the observed F value is for columns, the degrees of freedom for the numerator are $C - 1$. If the observed F value is for rows, the degrees of freedom for the numerator are $R - 1$. If the observed F value is for interaction, the degrees of freedom for the numerator are $(R - 1)(C - 1)$. The number of degrees of freedom for the denominator of the table value for each of the three effects is the same: the error degrees of freedom, $RC(n - 1)$. The critical F values (critical F) for a two-way ANOVA follow.

Critical F Values for a Two-Way ANOVA

Row effects:	$F_{\alpha, R-1, RC(n-1)}$
Column effects:	$F_{\alpha, C-1, RC(n-1)}$
Interaction effects:	$F_{\alpha, (R-1)(C-1), RC(n-1)}$

Formulas for Computing a Two-Way ANOVA

$$SSR = nC\sum_{i=1}^{R}(\bar{x}_i - \bar{x})^2$$

$$SSC = nR\sum_{j=1}^{C}(\bar{x}_j - \bar{x})^2$$

$$SSI = n\sum_{i=1}^{R}\sum_{j=1}^{C}(\bar{x}_{ij} - \bar{x}_i - \bar{x}_j + \bar{x})^2$$

$$SSE = \sum_{i=1}^{R}\sum_{j=1}^{C}\sum_{k=1}^{n}(x_{ijk} - \bar{x}_{ij})^2$$

$$SST = \sum_{i=1}^{R}\sum_{j=1}^{C}\sum_{k=1}^{n}(x_{ijk} - \bar{x})^2 \qquad (11.5)$$

$$df_R = R - 1$$

$$df_C = C - 1$$

$$df_I = (R - 1)(C - 1)$$

$$df_E = RC(n - 1)$$

$$df_T = N - 1$$

$$MSR = \frac{SSR}{R - 1}$$

$$\text{MSC} = \frac{\text{SSC}}{C - 1}$$

$$\text{MSI} = \frac{\text{SSI}}{(R - 1)(C - 1)}$$

$$\text{MSE} = \frac{\text{SSE}}{RC(n - 1)}$$

$$F_R = \frac{\text{MSR}}{\text{MSE}}$$

$$F_C = \frac{\text{MSC}}{\text{MSE}}$$

$$F_I = \frac{\text{MSI}}{\text{MSE}}$$

where

$\quad n$ = number of observations per cell
$\quad C$ = number of column treatments
$\quad R$ = number of row treatments
$\quad i$ = row treatment level
$\quad j$ = column treatment level
$\quad k$ = cell member
$\quad x_{ijk}$ = individual observation
$\quad \bar{x}_{ij}$ = cell mean
$\quad \bar{x}_i$ = row mean
$\quad \bar{x}_j$ = column mean
$\quad \bar{x}$ = grand mean

Interaction

As noted before, along with testing the effects of the two treatments in a factorial design, it is possible to test for the interaction effects of the two treatments whenever multiple measures are taken in each cell of the design. **Interaction** occurs *when the effects of one treatment vary according to the levels of treatment of the other effect.* For example, in a study examining the impact of temperature and humidity on a manufacturing process, it is possible that temperature and humidity will interact in such a way that the effect of temperature on the process varies with the humidity. Low temperatures might not be a significant manufacturing factor when humidity is low but might be a factor when humidity is high. Similarly, high temperatures might be a factor with low humidity but not with high humidity.

As another example, suppose a business analyst is studying the amount of red meat consumed by families per month and is examining economic class and religion as two independent variables. Class and religion might interact in such a way that with certain religions, economic class does not matter in the consumption of red meat, but with other religions, class does make a difference.

In terms of the factorial design, interaction occurs when the pattern of cell means in one row (going across columns) varies from the pattern of cell means in other rows. This variation indicates that the differences in column effects depend on which row is being examined. Hence, an interaction of the rows and columns occurs. The same thing can happen when the pattern of cell means within a column is different from the pattern of cell means in other columns.

Interaction can be depicted graphically by plotting the cell means within each row (and can also be done by plotting the cell means within each column). The means within each row (or column) are then connected by a line. If the broken lines for the rows (or columns) are parallel, no interaction is indicated.

Figure 11.10 is a graph of the means for each cell in each row in a 2 × 3 (2 rows, 3 columns) factorial design with interaction. Note that the lines connecting the means in each row cross each other. In **Figure 11.11**, the lines converge, indicating the likely presence of some interaction. **Figure 11.12** depicts a 2 × 3 factorial design with no interaction.

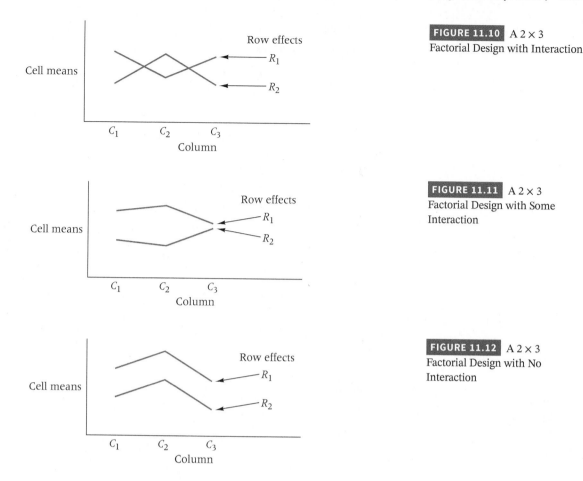

FIGURE 11.10 A 2×3 Factorial Design with Interaction

FIGURE 11.11 A 2×3 Factorial Design with Some Interaction

FIGURE 11.12 A 2×3 Factorial Design with No Interaction

When the interaction effects are significant, the main effects (row and column) are confounded and should not be analyzed in the usual manner. In this case, it is not possible to state unequivocally that the row effects or the column effects are significantly different because the difference in means of one main effect varies according to the level of the other main effect (interaction is present). Some specific procedures are recommended for examining main effects when significant interaction is present. However, these techniques are beyond the scope of material presented here. Hence, in this text, whenever interaction effects are present (F_{inter} is significant), the analyst should *not* attempt to interpret the main effects (F_{row} and F_{col}).

As an example of a factorial design, consider the fact that at the end of a financially successful fiscal year, CEOs must often decide whether to award a dividend to shareholders or to make a company investment. One factor in this decision might be whether attractive investment opportunities are available.[1] To determine whether this factor is important, business analysts randomly select 24 CEOs and ask them to rate how important "availability of profitable investment opportunities" is in deciding whether to pay dividends or invest. The CEOs are requested to respond to this item on a scale from 0 to 4, where 0 = no importance, 1 = slight importance, 2 = moderate importance, 3 = great importance, and 4 = maximum importance. The 0–4 response is the dependent variable in the experimental design.

The business analysts are concerned that where the company's shares are traded (New York Stock Exchange, Toronto Stock Exchange, and over the counter) might make a difference in the CEOs' response to the question. In addition, the business analysts believe that how shareholders are informed of dividends (annual reports versus presentations) might affect the outcome of the experiment. Thus, a two-way ANOVA is set up with "where the company's shares are traded" and "how shareholders are informed of dividends" as the two independent variables. The variable "how shareholders are informed of dividends" has two treatment levels, or classifications.

[1] H. Kent Baker, "Why Companies Pay No Dividends," *Akron Business and Economic Review* 20 (Summer 1989): 48–61.

1. Annual/quarterly reports
2. Presentations to analysts

The variable "where company shares are traded" has three treatment levels, or classifications.

1. New York Stock Exchange
2. Toronto Stock Exchange
3. Over the counter

This factorial design is a 2 × 3 design (2 rows, 3 columns) with four measurements (ratings) per cell, as shown in the following table.

		Where Company Shares Are Traded			
		New York Stock Exchange	Toronto Stock Exchange	Over the Counter	$\bar{x}_i =$
How Shareholders Are Informed of Dividends	Annual/Quarterly Reports	2 1 2 1 $\bar{x}_{11} = 1.5$	2 3 3 2 $\bar{x}_{12} = 2.5$	4 3 4 3 $\bar{x}_{13} = 3.5$	2.5
	Presentations to Analysts	2 3 1 2 $\bar{x}_{21} = 2.0$	3 3 2 4 $\bar{x}_{22} = 3.0$	4 4 3 4 $\bar{x}_{23} = 3.75$	2.9167
	$\bar{x}_j =$	1.75	2.75	3.625	
				$\bar{x} = 2.7083$	

These data are analyzed by using a two-way analysis of variance and $\alpha = 0.05$:

$$\text{SSR} = nC\sum_{i=1}^{R}(\bar{x}_i - \bar{x})^2$$
$$= 4(3)[(2.5 - 2.7083)^2 + (2.9167 - 2.7083)^2] = 1.0418$$

$$\text{SSC} = nR\sum_{j=1}^{C}(\bar{x}_j - \bar{x})$$
$$= 4(2)[(1.75 - 2.7083)^2 + (2.75 - 2.7083)^2 + (3.625 - 2.7083)^2] = 14.0833$$

$$\text{SSI} = \sum_{i=1}^{R}\sum_{j=1}^{C}(\bar{x}_{ij} - \bar{x}_i - \bar{x}_j + \bar{x})^2$$
$$= 4[(1.5 - 2.5 - 1.75 + 2.7083)^2 + (2.5 - 2.5 - 2.75 + 2.7083)^2$$
$$+ (3.5 - 2.5 - 3.625 + 2.7083)^2 + (2.0 - 2.9167 - 1.75 + 2.7083)^2$$
$$+ (3.0 - 2.9167 - 2.75 + 2.7083)^2 + (3.75 - 2.9167 - 3.625 + 2.7083)^2] = 0.0833$$

$$\text{SSE} = \sum_{i=1}^{R}\sum_{j=1}^{C}\sum_{k=1}^{n}(x_{ijk} - \bar{x}_{ij})^2$$
$$= (2 - 1.5)^2 + (1 - 1.5)^2 + \cdots + (3 - 3.75)^2 + (4 - 3.75)^2 = 7.7500$$

$$\text{SST} = \sum_{i=1}^{R}\sum_{j=1}^{C}\sum_{k=1}^{n}(x_{ijk} - \bar{x})^2$$
$$= (2 - 2.7083)^2 + (1 - 2.7083)^2 + \cdots + (3 - 2.7083)^2 + (4 - 2.7083)^2 = 22.9583$$

$$MSR = \frac{SSR}{R-1} = \frac{1.0418}{1} = 1.0418$$

$$MSC = \frac{SSC}{C-1} = \frac{14.0833}{2} = 7.0417$$

$$MSI = \frac{SSI}{(R-1)(C-1)} = \frac{0.0833}{2} = 0.0417$$

$$MSE = \frac{SSE}{RC(n-1)} = \frac{7.7500}{18} = 0.4306$$

$$F_R = \frac{MSR}{MSE} = \frac{1.0418}{0.4306} = 2.42$$

$$F_C = \frac{MSC}{MSE} = \frac{7.0417}{0.4306} = 16.35$$

$$F_I = \frac{MSI}{MSE} = \frac{0.0417}{0.4306} = 0.10$$

Source of Variation	SS	df	MS	F
Row	1.0418	1	1.0418	2.42
Column	14.0833	2	7.0417	16.35*
Interaction	0.0833	2	0.0417	0.10
Error	7.7500	18	0.4306	
Total	22.9583	23		

*Denotes significance at $\alpha = 0.01$.

The critical F value for the interaction effects at $\alpha = 0.05$ is:

$$F_{0.05,2,18} = 3.55$$

The observed F value for interaction effects is 0.10. Because this value is less than the critical F value (3.55), no significant interaction effects are evident. Because no significant interaction effects are present, it is possible to examine the main effects.

The critical F value of the row effects at $\alpha = 0.05$ is $F_{0.05,1,18} = 4.41$. The observed F value of 2.42 is less than the table value. Hence, no significant row effects are present.

The critical F value of the column effects at $\alpha = 0.05$ is $F_{0.05,2,18} = 3.55$. This value is coincidentally the same as the critical F value for interaction because in this problem the degrees of freedom are the same for interaction and column effects. The observed F value for columns (16.35) is greater than this critical value. Hence, a significant difference in column effects is evident at $\alpha = 0.05$.

A significant difference is noted in the CEOs' mean ratings of the item "availability of profitable investment opportunities" according to where the company's shares are traded. A cursory examination of the means for the three levels of the column effects (where shares are traded) reveals that the lowest mean rating was from CEOs whose companies traded shares on the New York Stock Exchange. The highest mean rating was from CEOs whose companies traded shares over the counter. Using multiple comparison techniques, the business analysts can statistically test for differences in the means of these three groups.

Because the sample sizes within each column are equal, Tukey's HSD test can be used to compute multiple comparisons. The value of MSE is 0.431 for this problem. In testing the column means with Tukey's HSD test, the value of n is the number of items in a column, which is eight. The number of treatments is $C = 3$ for columns and $N - C = 24 - 3 = 21$.

With these two values and $\alpha = 0.05$, a value for $q_{\alpha, C, N-C}$ can be determined from Table A.10:

$$q_{\alpha, C, N-C} = 3.58$$

From these values, the HSD can be computed:

$$HSD = q_{\alpha, C, N-C} \sqrt{\frac{MSE}{n}} = 3.58 \sqrt{\frac{0.431}{8}} = 0.831$$

The mean ratings for the three columns are:

$$\bar{x}_1 = 1.75, \bar{x}_2 = 2.75, \bar{x}_3 = 3.625$$

The absolute value of the differences between means are as follows:

$$|\bar{x}_1 - \bar{x}_2| = |1.75 - 2.75| = 1.00$$
$$|\bar{x}_1 - \bar{x}_3| = |1.75 - 3.625| = 1.875$$
$$|\bar{x}_2 - \bar{x}_3| = |2.75 - 3.625| = 0.875$$

All three differences are greater than 0.831 and are therefore significantly different at $\alpha = 0.05$ by the HSD test. Where a company's shares are traded makes a difference in the way a CEO responds to the question.

Using a Computer to Do a Two-Way ANOVA

A two-way ANOVA can be computed using Excel. The Excel output for two-way ANOVA with replications on the CEO dividend example is included in **Figure 11.13**. The Excel output contains cell, column, and row means along with observed F values for rows (sample), columns, and interaction. The Excel output also contains p-values and critical F values for each of these F's. Note that the output here is virtually identical to the findings obtained by the manual calculations.

	A	B	C	D	E	F	G
1	ANOVA: Two-Factor with Replication						
2							
3	SUMMARY	NYSE	TSE	OTC	Total		
4	A.Q. Reports						
5	Count	4	4	4	12		
6	Sum	6	10	14	30		
7	Average	1.5	2.5	3.5	2.5		
8	Variance	0.3333	0.3333	0.3333	1		
9							
10	Pres. to Analysts						
11	Count	4	4	4	12		
12	Sum	8	12	15	35		
13	Average	2	3	3.75	2.9167		
14	Variance	0.6667	0.6667	0.25	0.9924		
15							
16	Total						
17	Count	8	8	8			
18	Sum	14	22	29			
19	Average	1.75	2.75	3.6350			
20	Variance	0.5	0.5	0.2679			
21							
22	ANOVA						
23	Source of Variation	SS	df	MS	F	P-value	F crit
24	Sample	1.04167	1	1.04167	2.42	0.13725	4.41
25	Columns	14.0833	2	7.04167	16.35	8.9E-05	3.55
26	Interaction	0.08333	2	0.04167	0.10	0.90823	3.55
27	Within	7.75	18	0.43056			
28							
29	Total	22.9583	23				

FIGURE 11.13 Excel Output for the CEO Dividend Problem

DEMONSTRATION PROBLEM 11.4

Some theorists believe that training warehouse workers can reduce absenteeism.[2] Suppose an experimental design is structured to test this belief. Warehouses in which training sessions have been held for workers are selected for the study. The four types of warehouses are (1) general merchandise, (2) commodity, (3) bulk storage, and (4) cold storage. The training sessions are differentiated by length. Analysts identify three levels of training sessions according to the length of sessions: (1) 1–20 days, (2) 21–50 days, and (3) more than 50 days. Three warehouse workers are selected randomly for each particular combination of type of warehouse and session length. The workers are monitored for the next year to determine how many days they are absent. The resulting data are in the following 4 × 3 design (4 rows, 3 columns) structure. Using this information, calculate a two-way ANOVA to determine whether there are any significant differences in effects. Use $\alpha = 0.05$.

Solution

Step 1   The following hypotheses are being tested.
For row effects:

$H_0: \mu_{1.} = \mu_{2.} = \mu_{3.} = \mu_{4.}$
H_a: At least one of the row means is different from the others.

For column effects:

$H_0: \mu_1 = \mu_2 = \mu_3$
H_a: At least one of the column means is different from the others.

For interaction effects:

H_0: The interaction effects are zero.
H_a: There is an interaction effect.

Step 2   The two-way ANOVA with the F test is the appropriate statistical test.

Step 3 $\alpha = 0.05$

Step 4

$$df_{rows} = 4 - 1 = 3$$
$$df_{columns} = 3 - 1 = 2$$
$$df_{interaction} = (3)(2) = 6$$
$$df_{error} = (4)(3)(2) = 24$$

For row effects, $F_{0.05,3,24} = 3.01$; for column effects, $F_{0.05,2,24} = 3.40$; and for interaction effects, $F_{0.05,6,24} = 2.51$. For each of these effects, if any observed F value is greater than its associated critical F value, the respective null hypothesis will be rejected.

Step 5

Types of Warehouses		Length of Training Session (Days)			
		1–20	21–50	More than 50	$\bar{x}_r$
	General Merchandise	3 4.5 4	2 2.5 2	2.5 1 1.5	2.5556
	Commodity	5 4.5 4	1 3 2.5	0 1.5 2	2.6111
	Bulk Storage	2.5 3 3.5	1 3 1.5	3.5 3.5 4	2.8333
	Cold Storage	2 2 3	5 4.5 2.5	4 4.5 5	3.6111
	$\bar{x}_c$	3.4167	2.5417	2.75	

$$\bar{\bar{x}} = 2.9028$$

[2] Paul R. Murphy and Richard F. Poist, "Managing the Human Side of Public Warehousing: An Overview of Modern Practices," *Transportation Journal* 31 (Spring 1992): 54–63.

Step 6 The Excel (ANOVA table only) output for this problem follows:

	A	B	C	D	E	F	G
1	ANOVA						
2	Source of Variation	SS	df	MS	F	P-value	F crit
3	Sample	6.409722	3	2.136574	3.46	0.032205	3.01
4	Columns	5.013889	2	2.506944	4.06	0.030372	3.40
5	Interaction	33.15278	6	5.525463	8.94	0.000035	2.51
6	Within	14.83333	24	0.618056			
7							
8	Total	59.40972	35				

Step 7 Looking at the source of variation table, we must first examine the interaction effects. The observed F value for interaction is 8.94, which is greater than the critical F value. The interaction effects are statistically significant at $\alpha = 0.05$. The p-value for interaction shown in Excel is 0.000035. The interaction effects are significant at $\alpha = 0.0001$. The business analyst should not bother to examine the main effects because the significant interaction confounds the main effects.

Step 8 The significant interaction effects indicate that certain warehouse types in combination with certain lengths of training session result in different absenteeism rates than do other combinations of levels for these two variables. Using the cell means shown here, we can depict the interactions graphically.

		Length of Training Session (Days)		
		1–20	21–50	More than 50
Types of Warehouses	General Merchandise	3.8	2.2	1.7
	Commodity	4.5	2.2	1.2
	Bulk Storage	3.0	1.8	3.7
	Cold Storage	2.3	4.0	4.5

The following is a graph of the interaction.

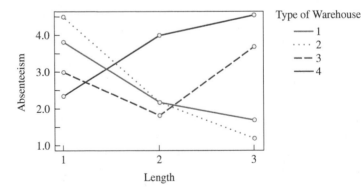

Note the intersecting and crossing lines, which indicate interaction. Under the short-length training sessions (1), cold storage workers had the lowest rate of absenteeism and workers at commodity warehouses had the highest. However, for medium-length sessions (2), cold storage workers had the highest rate of absenteeism and bulk storage had the lowest. For the longest training sessions (3), commodity warehouse workers had the lowest rate of absenteeism, even though these workers had the highest rate of absenteeism for short-length sessions. Thus, the rate of absenteeism for workers at a particular type of warehouse depended on length of session. There was an interaction between type of warehouse and length of session. This graph could be constructed with the row levels along the bottom axis instead of the column levels.

Tukey-Kramer procedure to determine which pairs, if any, are also significantly different. Let $\alpha = 0.05$.

Job Type

Bricklaying	Iron Working	Crane Operation
$19.25	$26.45	$16.20
17.80	21.10	23.30
20.50	16.40	22.90
24.33	22.86	19.50
19.81	25.55	27.00
22.29	18.50	22.95
21.20		25.52
		21.20

11.60 Why are mergers attractive to CEOs? One of the reasons might be the potential increase in market share that can come with the pooling of company markets. Suppose a random survey of CEOs is taken, and they are asked to respond on a scale from 1 to 5 (5 representing strongly agree) whether increase in market share is a good reason to consider merging their company with another. Suppose also that the data are as given here and that CEOs have been categorized by size of company and years they have been with their company. Use a two-way ANOVA to determine whether there are any significant differences in the responses to this question. Let $\alpha = 0.05$.

		Company Size ($ million per year in sales)			
		0–5	**6–20**	**21–100**	**>100**
		2	2	3	3
	0–2	3	1	4	4
		2	2	4	4
		2	3	5	3
Years with the Company	**3–5**	2	2	3	3
		1	3	2	3
		2	2	4	3
		3	3	4	4
	Over 5	2	2	3	2
		1	3	2	3
		1	1	3	2
		2	2	3	3

11.61 Are some office jobs viewed as having more status than others? Suppose a study is conducted in which eight unemployed people are interviewed. The people are asked to rate each of five positions on a scale from 1 to 10 to indicate the status of the position, with 10 denoting most status and 1 denoting least status. The resulting data are given below. Use $\alpha = 0.05$ to analyze the repeated measures randomized block design data.

		Job			
	Mail Clerk	**Typist**	**Recep-tionist**	**Secre-tary**	**Telephone Operator**
1	4	5	3	7	6
2	2	4	4	5	4
3	3	3	2	6	7
Respondent 4	4	4	4	5	4
5	3	5	1	3	5
6	3	4	2	7	7
7	2	2	2	4	4
8	3	4	3	6	6

Interpreting the Output

11.62 Analyze the following output. Describe the design of the experiment. Using $\alpha = 0.05$, determine whether there are any significant effects; if so, explain why. Discuss any other ramifications of the output.

```
One-way ANOVA: Dependent Variable versus Factor
Analysis of Variance
Source      df       SS      MS      F      p
Factor       3    876.6   292.2   3.01   0.045
Error       32   3107.5    97.1
Total       35   3984.1
                            Individual 95% CIs for
                            Mean  Based  on  Pooled
                            StDev
Level  N    Mean   StDev   -+----+----+----+--
C1     8   307.73   5.98   (----*----)
C2     7   313.20   9.71        (----*----)
C3    11   308.60   9.78     (----*----)
C4    10   319.74  12.18              (---*---)
                            -+----+----+----+--
Pooled StDev = 9.85      301.0 308.0 315.0 322.0
```

11.63 Following is Excel output for an ANOVA problem. Describe the experimental design. The given value of α was 0.05. Discuss the output in terms of significant findings.

ANOVA: Two-Factor without Replication

	A	B	C	D	E	F	G
1	ANOVA						
2	Source of Variation	SS	df	MS	F	P-value	F crit
3	Rows	48.278	5	9.656	3.16	0.057	3.33
4	Columns	10.111	2	5.056	1.65	0.239	4.10
5	Error	30.556	10	3.056			
6	Total	88.944	17				

11.64 Study the following output and graph. Discuss the meaning of the output.

Two-Way ANOVA: Dependent Variable versus Row Effects, Column Effects

Source	df	SS	MS	F	p
Row Effect	4	4.70	1.17	0.98	0.461
Col Effect	1	3.20	3.20	2.67	0.134
Interaction	4	22.30	5.57	4.65	0.022
Error	10	12.00	1.20		
Total	19	42.20			

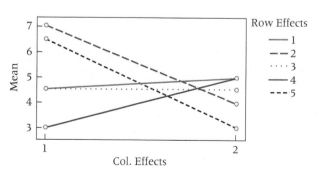

11.65 Interpret the following Excel output. Discuss the structure of the experimental design and any significant effects. α is 0.01.

ANOVA: Two-Factor with Replication

	A	B	C	D	E	F	G
1	ANOVA						
2	*Source of Variation*	SS	df	MS	F	P-value	F crit
3	Sample	2913.889	3	971.296	4.30	0.0146	3.01
4	Columns	240.389	2	120.194	0.53	0.5940	3.40
5	Interaction	1342.944	6	223.824	0.99	0.4533	2.51
6	Within	5419.333	24	225.806			
7	Total	9916.556	35				

11.66 Study the following output. Determine whether there are any significant effects and discuss the results. Assume that $\alpha = 0.05$. What kind of design was used and what was its size?

Two-Way Analysis of Variance

Source	df	SS	MS
Blocking	4	41.44	10.36
Treatment	4	143.93	35.98
Error	16	117.82	7.36
Total	24	303.19	

11.67 Discuss the following output.

```
One-Way Analysis of Variance
Source      df     SS      MS      F      p
Treatment    3   138.0    46.0    3.51   0.034
Error       20   262.2    13.1
Total       23   400.3
Individual 95% CIs For Mean Based on Pooled
StDev
Level  N   Mean    StDev ----+----+----+----+
1      6   53.778  5.470  (----*----)
2      6   54.665  1.840  (----*----)
3      6   59.911  3.845           (----*----)
4      6   57.293  2.088      (----*----)
                          ----+----+----+----+
Pooled StDev = 3.621      52.5 56.0 59.5 63.0

Tukey's pairwise comparisons
Family error rate = 0.0500
Individual error rate = 0.0111
Critical value = 3.96
Intervals for (column level mean) - (row level
mean)
          1        2        3
2     -6.741
       4.967
3    -11.987  -11.100
      -0.279    0.608
4     -9.369   -8.482   -3.236
       2.339    3.225    8.472
```

Exploring the Databases with Business Analytics

see the databases on the Student Website and in *WileyPLUS*

1. Do various financial indicators differ significantly according to type of company? Use a one-way ANOVA and the Financial Database to answer this question. Let Type of Industry be the independent variable with seven levels (as listed in Exploring the Databases in Chapter 1). Compute three one-way ANOVAs, one for each of the following dependent variables: Average Yield, Dividends per Share, and Average P/E Ratio. On each ANOVA, if there is a significant overall difference between Type of Industry, compute multiple comparisons to determine which pairs of industries, if any, are significantly different.

2. Use the Canadian Stock Market Database to determine whether there is any difference in stock market statistics for different weeks of the month. Use a one-way ANOVA with Composite Index as the dependent variable and Week of the Month as the independent variable with five levels. Compute a second ANOVA with I.T. Index as the dependent variable and Week of the Month as the independent variable. Is there a significant difference in Week of the Month on either of these variables? If there is, compute multiple comparisons to determine which weeks of the month, if any, are significantly different from the others.

3. The Canadian RRSP Contribution Database contains data on Total RRSP Contributors, Average Age of RRSP Contributors, and Total RRSP Contributions ($ × 1,000). Using the three territories (Yukon, Northwest Territories, Nunavut) as the independent variable, perform three different one-way ANOVAs—one for each of the three dependent variables (Total RRSP Contributors, Average Age of RRSP Contributors, and Total RRSP Contributions [$ × 1,000]). Did you find any significant differences by territory? If so, conduct an HSD test to determine which pairs of territories are significantly different.

Case

ASCO Valve Canada's RedHat Valve

With headquarters located in Brantford, Ontario, ASCO Valve Canada is one of Canada's top producers of solenoid valves. The company was founded in 1965, and since that time it has emerged as a successful industrial company that currently employs more than 75 people across Canada. ASCO offers an array of products to its customers ranging from valves that are used in the gas pipeline industry to valves that are used in medical procedures.

One of ASCO's goals was to develop a valve that could minimize the cost to customers, including cost of operations and the amount of power consumed. In 2005, ASCO achieved its goal by developing and introducing its RedHat valves. Today, these valves are well recognized and respected in many different countries due to their exceptional performance in difficult conditions. These valves are also energy efficient because they are able to use a mere 2 watts of power rather than the 17 watts of power that the typical solenoid valves use. This is an important cost benefit for any customer using valves because these new products can decrease the total cost of ownership by almost 14% over the installed life of the valve.

The RedHat valves have many advantages: for example, (1) better and more reliable functionality, (2) reduced usage of power, and (3) modular design. These advantages have allowed ASCO to provide customers with better-quality valves at reasonable prices, and to ensure fast delivery. ASCO made it clear that one of its objectives was to reduce lead times in order to satisfy customer demand. Within a short period of time, it accomplished this and can deliver products to its customers at a much faster rate.

Discussion

1. The RedHat valves are durable and reliable. They can operate with high air pressure of up to 2,200 psi (pounds per square inch). Suppose ASCO develops a new and stronger version of the RedHat valve. It wants to set up an experimental design to test the strength of the new valve, but it wants to conduct the tests under three different temperature conditions, 23°C, 49°C, and 68°C. In addition, suppose ASCO uses two different suppliers (supplier 1 and supplier 2) for the synthetic materials that are used to manufacture the valves. Some valves are made primarily of raw materials supplied by supplier 1, and some are made primarily of raw materials from supplier 2. Consequently, a 2 × 3 factorial design is appropriate for the experiment, with temperature and supplier as the independent variables and air pressure (measured in psi) as the dependent variable. An appropriate sampling frame has produced the data shown below. Analyze the data and discuss the business implications of the findings. If you were conducting the study, what conclusions would you report to the company?

	Temperature		
	23°C	**49°C**	**68°C**
Supplier 1	2257	2207	2201
	2479	2491	2173
	2361	2314	2192
Supplier 2	2215	2230	2229
	2308	2359	2088
	2511	2488	2287

2. It is estimated that these RedHat energy-efficient valves can save a great deal of power usage and lower the total cost of ownership by up to 14% over the installed life of the valve, therefore making the RedHat valves more attractive. ASCO does business

with pipeline companies globally. In an attempt to position itself as a market leader across the world, ASCO is keen on finding out whether the cost saved over the installed life of the valve is significantly different among the different countries in which it does business. Four countries, Canada, Spain, Japan, and the United States, are chosen for the study. Pipeline companies are selected from each country. The companies keep a log of valve power usage. A random sample of the data is shown below. Test whether there is a difference in relative cost savings in each of these countries. Justify your answer and prepare a short report to present to the management of ASCO in which your conclusions are explained, with support from the statistical test that you performed.

Canada	Spain	Japan	U.S.
12 %	9 %	14 %	13 %
14	10.5	14	12.5
11.5	11	13	14
10	14	13.5	11.5
14	8.5	12	14
13	12	12.5	13

3. As previously mentioned, ASCO has been able to reduce its lead time. Suppose ASCO's original lead time averaged 10 weeks and that the reduction is in the neighbourhood of 80%. As such, most lead times now average slightly below two weeks. ASCO is interested in knowing whether lead times differ significantly according to the type of RedHat valve it is manufacturing. To control the experiment, it will use as a blocking variable the day of the week the valve was ordered. One lead time was selected per valve per day of the week. The sample data are given below in weeks. Analyze the data and discuss your findings.

	Type of RedHat Valve		
	Two-Way	**Three-Way**	**Four-Way**
Monday	1.7	1.9	2.2
Tuesday	1.9	1.8	1.9
Wednesday	1.0	2.3	2.4
Thursday	1.4	1.5	1.8
Friday	2.1	2.0	2.5

Sources: Adapted from ASCO Valve Canada, www.ascovalve.ca; Frasers. com—Canada's Online Industrial Directory, "ASCO," www.frasers.com/public/extendedListingDetails.jsf?listingId=14701&cmoid=6; "ASCO Red Hat Next Generation Solenoid Valves," *The RHFS Pulse* 1, no. 1 (June 2007).

Big Data Case

Consider the American Hospital Association database of over 2,000 hospitals.

1. The hospital database contains data on hospitals from nine different geographic regions. Let this variable be the independent variable. Determine whether there is a significant difference in Number of Admissions for these geographic regions using a one-way ANOVA. Perform the same analysis using Number of Births as the dependent variable.

2. Ownership is a variable with six levels of classification denoting the form of ownership at each hospital (such as federal government or

for-profit). Use this variable as the independent variable to determine whether there is a significant difference in the Number of Outpatients at a hospital by form of ownership. Perform the same test using Personnel as the dependent variable.

3. In any of the ANOVAs, if there is an overall significance between treatments, conduct multiple comparison tests using the Tukey-Kramer procedure for unequal sample sizes.

Using the Computer

- Excel has the capability to perform a completely randomized design (one-way ANOVA), a randomized block design, and a two-way factorial design (two-way ANOVA).

- Each of the tests presented here in Excel is accessed through the **Data Analysis** feature.

- To conduct a one-way ANOVA, begin by selecting the **Data** tab on the Excel worksheet. From the **Analyze** panel at the right top of the **Data** ribbon, click on **Data Analysis**. If your Excel worksheet does not show the **Data Analysis** option, then you can load it as an add-in. From the **Data Analysis** menu, select **Anova: Single Factor**. Click and drag over the data and enter in **Input Range**. Check **Labels in the First Row** if you included labels in the data. Insert the value of α in **Alpha**.

- To conduct a randomized block design, load the treatment observations into columns. Data may be loaded either with or without labels. Select the **Data** tab on the Excel worksheet. From the **Analyze** panel at the right top of the **Data** ribbon, click on **Data Analysis**. If your Excel worksheet does not show the **Data Analysis** option, then you can load it as an add-in. From the **Data Analysis** menu, select **Anova: Two-Factor Without Replication**. Click and drag over the data and enter in **Input Range**. Check **Labels in the First Row** if you have included labels in the data. Insert the value of α in **Alpha**.

- To conduct a two-way ANOVA, load the treatment observations into columns. Excel is quite particular about how the data are entered for a two-way ANOVA. Data must be loaded in rows and columns as with most two-way designs. However, two-way ANOVA in Excel requires labels for both rows and columns; if labels are not supplied, Excel will incorrectly use some of the data for labels. Since cells will have multiple values, there need only be a label for each new row (cell). Select the **Data** tab on the Excel worksheet. From the **Analyze** panel at the top of the **Data** ribbon, click on **Data Analysis**. If your Excel worksheet does not show the **Data Analysis** option, then you can load it as an add-in. From the **Data Analysis** menu, select **Anova: Two-Factor With Replication**. Click and drag over the data and enter in **Input Range**. Enter the number of values per cell in **Rows per sample**. Insert the value of α in **Alpha**.

CHAPTER 12

Correlation and Simple Regression Analysis

LEARNING OBJECTIVES

The overall objective of this chapter is to give you an understanding of bivariate linear regression analysis, thereby enabling you to:

12.1 Calculate the Pearson product-moment correlation coefficient to determine if there is a correlation between two variables.

12.2 Explain what regression analysis is, and explain the concepts of independent and dependent variable.

12.3 Calculate the slope and *y*-intercept of the least squares equation of a regression line, and from those determine the equation of the regression line.

12.4 Calculate the residuals of a regression line, and from those determine the fit of the model, locate outliers, and test the assumptions of the regression model.

12.5 Calculate the standard error of the estimate using the sum of squares of error, and use the standard error of the estimate to determine the fit of the model.

12.6 Calculate the coefficient of determination to measure the fit for regression models, and relate it to the coefficient of correlation.

12.7 Use the *t* and *F* tests to test hypotheses for both the slope of the regression model and the overall regression model.

12.8 Calculate confidence intervals to estimate the conditional mean of the dependent variable and prediction intervals to estimate a single value of the dependent variable.

12.9 Determine the equation of the trend line to forecast outcomes for time periods in the future, using alternative coding for time periods if necessary.

12.10 Use a computer to develop a regression analysis, and interpret the output that is associated with it.

Decision Dilemma

Predicting International Hourly Wages by the Price of a Big Mac™

The McDonald's Corporation is the leading global food-service retailer, with more than 36,000 local restaurants serving nearly 69 million people in more than 100 countries each day. This global presence, in addition to its consistency in food offerings and restaurant operations, makes McDonald's a unique and attractive setting for economists to make salary and price comparisons around the world. Because the Big Mac™ hamburger is a standardized hamburger produced and sold in virtually every McDonald's around the world, *The Economist,* a weekly newsmagazine focusing on international politics and business news and opinion, was, as early as 1986, compiling information about Big Mac prices as an indicator of

iStock.com/sshaw75

exchange rates. Building on this idea, researchers Orley Ashenfelter and Stepán Jurajda proposed comparing wage rates across countries using the price of a Big Mac hamburger. Shown below are Big Mac prices and net hourly wage figures (in U.S. dollars) for 20 countries.

Country	Big Mac Price (US$)	Net Hourly Wage (US$)
Argentina	4.84	15.91
Australia	4.94	46.29
Brazil	6.16	11.65
Canada	5.00	36.56
Czech Republic	4.07	13.13
Denmark	5.48	51.67
Hungary	4.04	9.17
Israel	4.67	21.42
Japan	4.08	36.71
Mexico	2.74	6.48
New Zealand	4.41	23.38
Philippines	2.78	2.01
Poland	3.09	8.83
Singapore	3.65	22.60
South Korea	3.50	18.91
Sweden	7.64	49.12
Switzerland	8.06	60.40
Taiwan	2.60	9.34
United Kingdom	3.89	30.77
United States	4.07	35.53

Managerial, Statistical, and Analytical Questions

1. Is there a relationship between the price of a Big Mac and the net hourly wages of workers around the world? If so, how strong is the relationship?

2. Is it possible to develop a model to predict or determine the net hourly wage of a worker anywhere around the world by the price of a Big Mac hamburger in that country? If so, how good is the model?

3. If a model can be constructed to determine the net hourly wage of a worker anywhere around the world by the price of a Big Mac hamburger, what is the predicted net hourly wage of a worker in a country if the price of a Big Mac hamburger is $3.00?

Sources: McDonald's website, www.aboutmcdonalds.com/; Michael R. Pakko and Patricia S. Pollard, "Burgernomics: A Big Mac Guide to Purchasing Power Parity," research publication by the St. Louis Federal Reserve Bank, at research.stlouisfed.org/publications/review/03/11/pakko.pdf; Orley Ashenfelter and Stepán Jurajda, "Cross Country Comparisons of Wage Rates: The Big Mac Index," unpublished manuscript, Princeton University and CERGEEI/Charles University, October 2001; "Hourly Compensation Costs, U.S. Dollars" from the Bureau of Labor Statistics, U.S. Department of Labor, www.bls.gov/news.release/ichcc.t01.htm; D.H. and R.L.W., "The Big Mac Index," Economist.com, January 17, 2018, www.economist.com/comment/2186355.

Introduction

In business, the key to decision-making often lies in understanding the relationships between two or more variables. For example, a company in the distribution business may determine that there is a relationship between the price of crude oil and its own transportation costs. Financial experts, in studying the behaviour of the bond market, might find it useful to know if the interest rates on bonds are related to the prime interest rate set by the Bank of Canada. A marketing executive might want to know how strong the relationship is between advertising dollars and sales dollars for a product or a company.

In this chapter, we will study the concept of correlation and how it can be used to estimate the relationship between two variables. We will also explore simple regression analysis, through which mathematical models can be developed to predict one variable by another. We will examine tools for testing the strength and predictability of regression models and we will learn how to use regression analysis to develop forecasting trend lines. In addition, correlation and regression can be used to discover hidden relationships in the data and identify undiscovered patterns, making them useful techniques for descriptive analytics, data mining, and business analytics as a whole.

12.1 | Correlation

LEARNING OBJECTIVE 12.1

Calculate the Pearson product-moment correlation coefficient to determine if there is a correlation between two variables.

Correlation *is a measure of the degree of relatedness of variables.* It can help a business analyst determine, for example, whether the share prices of two airlines rise and fall in any related manner.

For a sample of pairs of data, correlation analysis can yield a numerical value that represents the degree of relatedness of the two share prices over time. In the transportation industry, is a correlation evident between the price of transportation and the mass of the object being shipped? If so, how strong is the correlation? In economics, how strong is the correlation between the producer price index and the unemployment rate? In retail sales, are sales related to population density, number of competitors, size of the store, amount of advertising, or other variables?

Several measures of correlation are available, the selection of which depends mostly on the level of data being analyzed. Ideally, analysts would like to solve for ρ, the population coefficient of correlation. However, because business analysts often deal with sample data, this section introduces a widely used sample **coefficient of correlation**, r. This measure is applicable only if both variables being analyzed have at least an interval level of data. Chapter 17 presents a correlation measure that can be used when the data are ordinal.

The statistic r is the **Pearson product-moment correlation coefficient**, named after Karl Pearson (1857–1936), an English statistician who developed several coefficients of correlation along with other significant statistical concepts. The term r is a *measure of the linear correlation of two variables*. It is a number that ranges from –1 to 0 to +1, representing the strength of the relationship between the variables. An r value of +1 denotes a perfect positive relationship between two sets of numbers. An r value of −1 denotes a perfect negative correlation, which indicates an inverse relationship between two variables: as one variable gets larger, the other gets smaller, and vice versa. An r value of 0 means no linear relationship is present between the two variables.

Pearson Product-Moment Correlation Coefficient

$$r = \frac{\Sigma(x - \bar{x})(y - \bar{y})}{\sqrt{\Sigma(x - \bar{x})^2 \Sigma(y - \bar{y})^2}} = \frac{\Sigma xy - \dfrac{\Sigma x \Sigma y}{n}}{\sqrt{\left[\Sigma x^2 - \dfrac{(\Sigma x)^2}{n}\right]\left[\Sigma y^2 - \dfrac{(\Sigma y)^2}{n}\right]}} \qquad (12.1)$$

Figure 12.1 depicts five different levels of correlation: (a) represents strong negative correlation, (b) represents moderate negative correlation, (c) represents moderate positive correlation, (d) represents strong positive correlation, and (e) contains no correlation (see Thinking Critically About Statistics in Business Today 12.1).

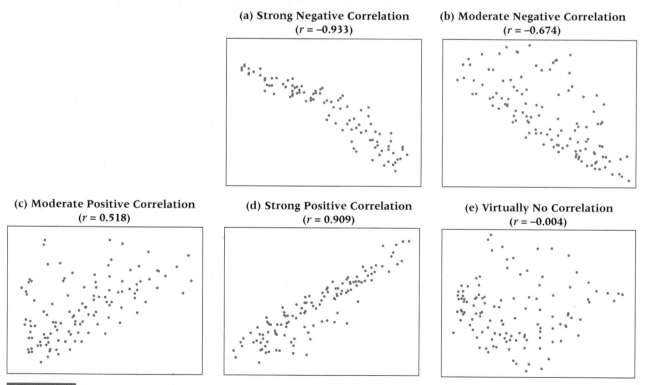

(a) Strong Negative Correlation
($r = -0.933$)

(b) Moderate Negative Correlation
($r = -0.674$)

(c) Moderate Positive Correlation
($r = 0.518$)

(d) Strong Positive Correlation
($r = 0.909$)

(e) Virtually No Correlation
($r = -0.004$)

FIGURE 12.1 **Five Correlations**

Thinking Critically About Statistics in Business Today 12.1

Are Facial Characteristics Correlated with CEO Traits?

Researchers from the Fuqua School of Business at Duke conducted a study using almost 2,000 participants in an effort to determine if facial characteristics are related to various CEO traits. In one experiment of the study, the researchers showed pictures of 138 CEOs to 230 study participants, who were asked to rate each CEO picture in terms of four attributes: competence, attractiveness, trustworthiness, and likeability. The results of the study showed that all four traits are positively correlated. That is, if a CEO (based on the picture) was rated as high on competence, he was also rated high on each of attractiveness, trustworthiness, and likeability. The largest correlation was between trustworthiness and likeability, and the smallest correlation was between trustworthiness and attractiveness. These ratings on each of the four traits were also analyzed to determine if there was a correlation with total sales of the CEO's firm and with CEO income. The results showed that there was a small positive correlation between CEO ratings on competence and company sales. There was also a small positive correlation between CEO ratings on competence and their income. In another experiment, 138 CEOs were rated on being "baby-faced." Analysis of the study data showed that there was a positive correlation between CEOs' baby-faced rating and likeability. That is, the more CEOs appeared to be baby-faced, the higher they were rated in likeability. However, there was a negative correlation between CEOs' baby-faced rating and competence.

Things to Ponder

1. Similar studies have been conducted in the area of political science to determine the electability of people running for office. What do you think is the real impact of studies like this in business?

2. The authors of the study suggest that baby-faced people tend to have large, round eyes, high eyebrows, and a small chin, thereby giving the impression of a baby. In this study, baby-faced CEOs were rated more highly on one attribute and low on another attribute. Based on these results, what advice would you give to a "baby-faced" business manager who aspires to be a CEO?

Source: Adapted from John R. Graham, Campbell R. Harvey, and Manju Puri, "A Corporate Beauty Contest," *Management Science* 63, 9 (2017): 3044–56.

What is the measure of correlation between the interest rate of federal funds and the commodities futures index? With data such as those shown in **Table 12.1**, which represent the values for interest rates of federal funds and commodities futures indexes for a sample of 12 days, a correlation coefficient, r, can be computed as shown in **Table 12.2**.

TABLE 12.1 Data for the Finance Example

Day	Interest Rate	Futures Index
1	7.43	221
2	7.48	222
3	8.00	226
4	7.75	225
5	7.60	224
6	7.63	223
7	7.68	223
8	7.67	226
9	7.59	226
10	8.07	235
11	8.03	233
12	8.00	241

Examination of the formula for computing a Pearson product-moment correlation coefficient reveals that the following values must be obtained to compute r: Σx, Σx^2, Σy, Σy^2, Σxy, and n. In correlation analysis, it does not matter which variable is designated x and which is designated y. For this example, the correlation coefficient is computed as shown in Table 12.2. The r value obtained ($r = 0.815$) represents a relatively strong positive relationship between interest rates and the commodities futures index over this 12-day period.

TABLE 12.2   **Computation of *r* for the Finance Example**

Day	Interest x	Futures Index y	x^2	y^2	xy
1	7.43	221	55.205	48,841	1,642.03
2	7.48	222	55.950	49,284	1,660.56
3	8.00	226	64.000	51,076	1,808.00
4	7.75	225	60.063	50,625	1,743.75
5	7.60	224	57.760	50,176	1,702.40
6	7.63	223	58.217	49,729	1,701.49
7	7.68	223	58.982	49,729	1,712.64
8	7.67	226	58.829	51,076	1,733.42
9	7.59	226	57.608	51,076	1,715.34
10	8.07	235	65.125	55,225	1,896.45
11	8.03	233	64.481	54,289	1,870.99
12	8.00	241	64.000	58,081	1,928.00
	$\Sigma x = 92.93$	$\Sigma y = 2{,}725$	$\Sigma x^2 = 720.220$	$\Sigma y^2 = 619{,}207$	$\Sigma xy = 21{,}115.07$

$$r = \frac{21{,}115.07 - \dfrac{(92.93)(2{,}725)}{12}}{\sqrt{\left[720.22 - \dfrac{92.93^2}{12}\right]\left[619{,}207 - \dfrac{2{,}725^2}{12}\right]}} = 0.815$$

Figure 12.2 shows Excel output for this problem.

	A	B	C
1		Interest Rate	Futures Index
2	Interest Rate	1	
3	Futures Index	0.815	1

FIGURE 12.2   **Excel Output for the Finance Example**

Concept Check

1. In statistics, the phrase "correlation does not imply causation" is used to emphasize that correlation between two variables does not automatically imply that one causes the other. Can you think of two variables (in the world of business or otherwise) that are correlated, yet one does not cause the other; that is, there is no cause-and-effect relationship between the variables?

12.1 Problems

12.1 Determine the value of the correlation coefficient, *r*, for the following data.

x	4	6	7	11	14	17	21
y	18	12	13	8	7	7	4

12.2 Determine the value of *r* for the following data.

x	158	296	87	110	436
y	349	510	301	322	550

12.3 In an effort to determine whether any correlation exists between the share prices of airlines, an analyst sampled six days of activity on the stock market. Using the following share prices of Air Canada and WestJet, compute the coefficient of correlation. Share prices have been rounded off to the nearest hundredth for ease of computation.

Air Canada	WestJet
25.12	17.10
27.22	17.53
31.68	20.65
33.36	20.58
32.79	19.54
36.21	18.52

12.4 The following data are the revenue and total CEO compensation for 25 large Canadian companies.

Company	Revenue ($ thousands)	Total Compensation ($ thousands)
1	673,304	3,638
2	4,486,900	3,667
3	16,252,000	7,469
4	3,060,642	4,824
5	614,300	1,445
6	16,218,000	11,105
7	929,274	3,874
8	1,312,315	4,952
9	6,942,200	5,568
10	1,551,324	2,255
11	2,275,362	5,855
12	2,198,300	2,143
13	22,823,000	1,236
14	4,658,800	2,110
15	5,134,000	3,108
16	2,479,421	0.001
17	3,310,000	2,853
18	4,741,019	6,778
19	2,350,162	2,527
20	2,007,200	6,338
21	4,001,000	10,038
22	1,705,456	2,000
23	6,245,000	5,348
24	12,048,000	7,687
25	32,050,999	9,973

Use the data to compute a correlation coefficient, r, to determine the correlation between company revenue and total CEO compensation.

12.5 The National Safety Council of the U.S. released the following data on the incidence rates for fatal or lost-worktime injuries per 100 employees for several industries in three recent years.

Industry	Year 1	Year 2	Year 3
Textile	0.46	0.48	0.69
Chemical	0.52	0.62	0.63
Communication	0.90	0.72	0.81
Machinery	1.50	1.74	2.10
Services	2.89	2.03	2.46
Nonferrous metals	1.80	1.92	2.00
Food	3.29	3.18	3.17
Government	5.73	4.43	4.00

Compute r for each pair of years and determine which years are most highly correlated.

12.2 | Introduction to Simple Regression Analysis

LEARNING OBJECTIVE 12.2

Explain what regression analysis is, and explain the concepts of independent and dependent variable.

Regression analysis is *the process of constructing a mathematical model or function that can be used to predict or determine one variable by another variable or other variables.* The most elementary regression model is called **simple regression** or **bivariate regression** and *involves two variables in which one variable is predicted by another variable.* In simple regression, *the variable to be predicted* is called the **dependent variable** and is designated as y. The *predictor* is called the **independent variable**, or *explanatory variable,* and is designated as x. In the simple regression analysis that is described here, only a straight-line relationship between two variables is examined. Nonlinear relationships and regression models with more than one independent variable can be explored by using multiple regression models, which are presented in Chapters 13 and 14.

Can the cost of flying a commercial airliner be predicted using regression analysis? If so, what variables are related to this cost? A few of the many variables that can potentially contribute are type of plane, distance, number of passengers, amount of luggage/freight, weather conditions, direction of destination, and perhaps even pilot skill. Suppose a study is conducted using only Boeing 737s travelling 800 km on comparable routes during the same season of the year. Can the number of passengers predict the cost of flying such routes? It seems logical that more passengers result in more mass and more baggage, which could, in turn, result in increased fuel consumption and other costs. Suppose the data displayed in **Table 12.3** are the costs and associated number of passengers for twelve 800 km commercial airline flights using Boeing 737s during the same season of the year. We will use these data to develop a regression model to predict cost by number of passengers.

Usually, the first step in simple regression analysis is to construct a **scatter plot** (or scatter diagram), discussed in Chapter 2. Graphing the data in this way yields preliminary information about the shape and spread of the data. **Figure 12.3** is an Excel scatter plot of the data in Table 12.3. **Figure 12.4** is a close-up view of the scatter plot. Try to imagine a line passing through the points. Is a linear fit possible? Would a curve fit the data better? The scatter plot gives some idea of how well a regression line fits the data. Later in the chapter, we present statistical techniques that can be used to determine more precisely how well a regression line fits the data.

TABLE 12.3

Airline Cost Data

Number of Passengers	Cost ($ thousands)
61	4.28
63	4.08
67	4.42
69	4.17
70	4.48
74	4.30
76	4.82
81	4.70
86	5.11
91	5.13
95	5.64
97	5.56

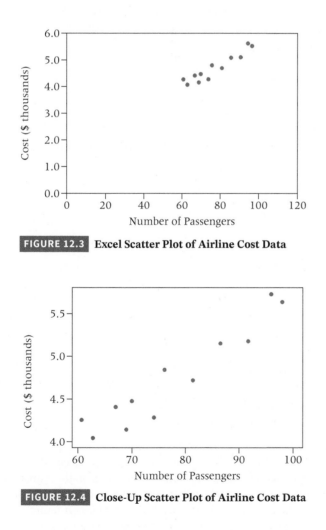

FIGURE 12.3 **Excel Scatter Plot of Airline Cost Data**

FIGURE 12.4 **Close-Up Scatter Plot of Airline Cost Data**

Concept Check

1. What is regression analysis?
2. You know the price and sales history of a product. You need to predict the effect of next year's price on sales. Do you think regression analysis is the right technique to use? Explain.

12.3 | Determining the Equation of the Regression Line

LEARNING OBJECTIVE 12.3

Calculate the slope and y-intercept of the least squares equation of a regression line, and from those determine the equation of the regression line.

The first step in determining the equation of the regression line that passes through the sample data is to establish the equation's form. Several different types of equations of lines are discussed in algebra, finite math, and analytic geometry courses. Recall that among these equations of a line are the two-point form, the point-slope form, and the slope-intercept form. In regression analysis, business analysts use the slope-intercept equation of a line. In math courses, the slope-intercept form of the equation of a line often takes the form:

$$y = mx + b$$

where

m = slope of the line
b = y-intercept of the line

In statistics, the slope-intercept form of the equation of the regression line through the population points is:

$$\hat{y} = \beta_0 + \beta_1 x$$

where

$\hat{y}$ = the predicted value of y
β_0 = the population y-intercept
β_1 = the population slope

For any specific dependent variable value, y_i,

$$y_i = \beta_0 + \beta_1 x_i + \in_i$$

where

x_i = the value of the independent variable for the ith value
y_i = the value of the dependent variable for the ith value
β_0 = the population y-intercept
β_1 = the population slope
$\in_i$ = the error of prediction for the ith value

Unless the points being fitted by the regression equation are in perfect alignment, the regression line will miss at least some of the points. In the preceding equation, $\in_i$ represents the error of the regression line in fitting these points. If a point is on the regression line, $\in_i = 0$.

These mathematical models can be either deterministic models or probabilistic models. **Deterministic models** are *mathematical models that produce an "exact" output for a given input.* For example, suppose the equation of a regression line is:

$$y = 1.68 + 2.40x$$

For a value of $x = 5$, the exact predicted value of y is:

$$y = 1.68 + 2.40(5) = 13.68$$

We recognize, however, that most of the time the values of y will not exactly equal the values yielded by the equation. Random error will occur in the prediction of the y values for values of x because it is likely that the variable x does not explain all the variability of the variable y. For example, suppose we are trying to predict the volume of sales (y) for a company through regression analysis by using the annual dollar amount of advertising (x) as the predictor. Although sales are often related to advertising, other factors related to sales are not accounted for by amount of advertising. Hence, a regression model to predict sales volume by amount of advertising probably involves some error. For this reason, in regression, we present the general model as a probabilistic model. A **probabilistic model** is *one that includes an error term that allows for the y values to vary for any given value of x.*

A deterministic regression model is:

$$y = \beta_0 + \beta_1 x$$

The probabilistic regression model is:

$$y_i = \beta_0 + \beta_1 x_i + \in$$

$\beta_0 + \beta_1 x$ is the deterministic portion of the probabilistic model, $\beta_0 + \beta_1 x_i + \in$. In a deterministic model, all points are assumed to be on the line and in all cases $\in$ is zero.

Virtually all regression analyses of business data involve sample data, not population data. As a result, β_0 and β_1 are unattainable and must be estimated by using the sample statistics b_0 and b_1. Hence, the equation of the regression line contains the sample y-intercept, b_0, and the sample slope, b_1.

Equation of the Simple Regression Line

$$\hat{y} = b_0 + b_1 x \qquad (12.2)$$

where

b_0 = the sample y-intercept

b_1 = the sample slope

To determine the equation of the regression line for a sample of data, the analyst must determine the values for b_0 and b_1. This process is sometimes referred to as least squares analysis. **Least squares analysis** is *a process whereby a regression model is developed by producing the minimum sum of the squared error values.* On the basis of this premise and calculus, a particular set of equations has been developed to produce components of the regression model.

Examine the regression line fit through the points in **Figure 12.5**. Observe that the line does not actually pass through any of the points. The vertical distance from each point to the line is the error of the prediction. In theory, an infinite number of lines could be constructed to pass through these points in some manner. The least squares regression line is the regression line that results in the smallest sum of errors squared.

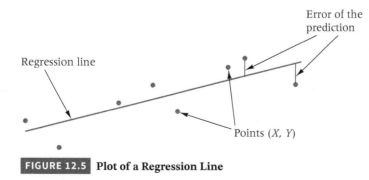

FIGURE 12.5 **Plot of a Regression Line**

Formula 12.2 is an equation for computing the value of the sample slope. Several versions of the equation are given to afford latitude in doing the computations.

Slope of the Regression Line

$$b_1 = \frac{\Sigma(x - \bar{x})(y - \bar{y})}{\Sigma(x - \bar{x})^2} = \frac{\Sigma xy - n\bar{x}\bar{y}}{\Sigma x^2 - n\bar{x}^2} = \frac{\Sigma xy - \dfrac{(\Sigma x)(\Sigma y)}{n}}{\Sigma x^2 - \dfrac{(\Sigma x)^2}{n}}$$

(12.3)

The expression in the numerator of Formula 12.2 appears frequently in this chapter and is denoted as SS_{xy}:

$$SS_{xy} = \Sigma(x - \bar{x})(y - \bar{y}) = \Sigma xy - \frac{(\Sigma x)(\Sigma y)}{n}$$

The expression in the denominator of Formula 12.2 also appears frequently in this chapter and is denoted as SS_{xx}:

$$SS_{xx} = \Sigma(x - \bar{x})^2 = \Sigma x^2 - \frac{(\Sigma x)^2}{n}$$

With these abbreviations, the equation for the slope can be expressed as in Formula 12.3.

Alternative Formula for Slope

$$b_1 = \frac{SS_{xy}}{SS_{xx}}$$

(12.4)

Formula 12.4 is used to compute the sample y-intercept. The slope must be computed before the y-intercept.

y-Intercept of the Regression Line

$$b_0 = \bar{y} - b_1\bar{x} = \frac{\Sigma y}{n} - b_1\frac{(\Sigma x)}{n}$$

(12.5)

Formulas 12.2, 12.3, and 12.4 show that the following data are needed from sample information to compute the slope and intercept: Σx, Σy, Σx^2, and Σxy, unless sample means are used. **Table 12.4** contains the results of solving for the slope and intercept and determining the equation of the regression line for the data in Table 12.3.

The least squares equation of the regression line for this problem is:

$$\hat{y} = 1.57 + 0.0407x$$

The slope of this regression line is 0.0407. Because the x values were recoded for ease of computation and are in $1,000 denominations, the slope is actually $40.70. One interpretation of the slope in this problem is that for every unit increase in x (every person added to the flight of the airplane), there is a $40.70 increase in the cost of the flight. The y-intercept is the point where the line crosses the y-axis (where x is zero). Sometimes in regression analysis, the y-intercept is meaningless in terms of the variables studied. However, in this problem, one interpretation of the y-intercept, which is 1.570 or $1,570, is that even if there were no passengers on the commercial flight, it would still cost $1,570. In other words, there are costs associated with a flight that carries no passengers.

Superimposing the line representing the least squares equation for this problem on the scatter plot indicates how well the regression line fits the data points, as shown in the Excel graph in **Figure 12.6**. The next several sections explore mathematical ways of testing how well the regression line fits the points.

TABLE 12.4	Solving for the Slope and the y-Intercept of the Regression Line for the Airline Cost Example		
Number of Passengers	**Cost ($ thousands)**		
x	*y*	x^2	*xy*
61	4.280	3,721	261.080
63	4.080	3,969	257.040
67	4.420	4,489	296.140
69	4.170	4,761	287.730
70	4.480	4,900	313.600
74	4.300	5,476	318.200
76	4.820	5,776	366.320
81	4.700	6,561	380.700
86	5.110	7,396	439.460
91	5.130	8,281	466.830
95	5.640	9,025	535.800
97	5.560	9,409	539.320

$\Sigma x = 930 \qquad \Sigma y = 56.690 \qquad \Sigma x^2 = 73,764 \qquad \Sigma xy = 4,462.220$

$$SS_{xy} = \Sigma xy - \frac{(\Sigma x)(\Sigma y)}{n} = 4,462.22 - \frac{(930)(56.69)}{12} = 68.745$$

$$SS_{xx} = \Sigma x^2 - \frac{(\Sigma x)^2}{n} = 73,764 - \frac{930^2}{12} = 1,689$$

$$b_1 = \frac{SS_{xy}}{SS_{xx}} = \frac{68.745}{1,689} = 0.0407$$

$$b_0 = \frac{\Sigma y}{n} - b_1 \frac{\Sigma x}{n} = \frac{56.69}{12} - (0.0407)\frac{930}{12} = 1.57$$

$$\hat{y} = 1.57 + 0.0407x$$

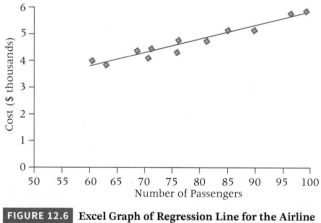

FIGURE 12.6 **Excel Graph of Regression Line for the Airline Cost Example**

DEMONSTRATION PROBLEM 12.1

A specialist in hospital administration stated that the number of full-time employees (FTEs) in a hospital can be estimated by counting the number of beds in the hospital (a common measure of hospital size). A health-care business analyst decided to develop a regression model in an attempt to predict the number of FTEs of a hospital by the number of beds. She surveyed 12 hospitals and obtained the following data. The data are presented in sequence, according to the number of beds.

Number of Beds	FTEs	Number of Beds	FTEs
23	69	50	138
29	95	54	178
29	102	64	156
35	118	66	184
42	126	76	176
46	125	78	225

Solution   The following graph is a scatter plot of these data. Note the linear appearance of the data.

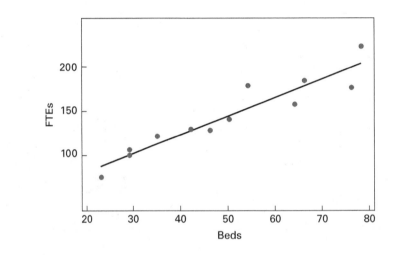

Next, the analyst determined the values of Σx, Σy, Σx^2, and Σxy.

Hospital	Number of Beds x	FTEs y	x^2	xy
1	23	69	529	1,587
2	29	95	841	2,755
3	29	102	841	2,958
4	35	118	1,225	4,130
5	42	126	1,764	5,292
6	46	125	2,116	5,750
7	50	138	2,500	6,900
8	54	178	2,916	9,612
9	64	156	4,096	9,984
10	66	184	4,356	12,144
11	76	176	5,776	13,376
12	78	225	6,084	17,550
	$\Sigma x = 592$	$\Sigma y = 1{,}692$	$\Sigma x^2 = 33{,}044$	$\Sigma xy = 92{,}038$

Using these values, the analyst solved for the sample slope (b_1) and the sample y intercept (b_0):

$$SS_{xy} = \Sigma xy - \frac{(\Sigma x)(\Sigma y)}{n} = 92{,}038 - \frac{(592)(1{,}692)}{12} = 8{,}566$$

$$SS_{xx} = \Sigma x^2 - \frac{(\Sigma x)^2}{n} = 33{,}044 - \frac{592^2}{12} = 3{,}838.667$$

$$b_1 = \frac{SS_{xy}}{SS_{xx}} = \frac{8{,}566}{3{,}838.667} = 2.232$$

$$b_0 = \frac{\Sigma y}{n} - b_1\frac{\Sigma x}{12} = \frac{1{,}692}{12} - (2.232)\frac{592}{12} = 30.888$$

The least squares equation of the regression line is:

$$\hat{y} = 30.888 + 2.232x$$

The slope of the line, $b_1 = 2.232$, means that for every unit increase of x (every bed), y (number of FTEs) is predicted to increase by 2.232. Even though the y-intercept helps the analyst sketch the graph of the line by being one of the points on the line (0, 30.888), it has limited usefulness in terms of this solution because $x = 0$ denotes a hospital with no beds. On the other hand, it could be interpreted that a hospital has to have at least 31 FTEs to open its doors even with no patients—a sort of "fixed cost" of personnel.

Concept Check

1. What does *slope* mean in regression analysis?
2. What does *intercept* mean in regression analysis?

12.3 Problems

12.6 Sketch a scatter plot from the following data, and determine the equation of the regression line.

x	12	21	28	8	20
y	17	15	22	19	24

12.7 Sketch a scatter plot from the following data, and determine the equation of the regression line.

x	140	119	103	91	65	29	24
y	25	29	46	70	88	112	128

12.8 A corporation owns several companies. The strategic planner for the corporation believes dollars spent on advertising can to some extent be a predictor of total sales dollars. As an aid in long-term planning, she gathers the following sales and advertising information from several of the companies for a particular year ($ millions).

Advertising	Sales
$12.5	$148
3.7	55
21.6	338
60.0	994
37.6	541
6.1	89
16.8	126
41.2	379

Develop the equation of the simple regression line to predict sales from advertising expenditures using these data.

12.9 Investment analysts generally believe the interest rate on bonds is inversely related to the prime interest rate for loans; that is, bonds perform well when lending rates are down and perform poorly when interest rates are up. Can the bond rate be predicted by the prime interest rate? Use the following data to construct a least squares regression line to predict bond rates by the prime interest rate.

Bond Rate	Prime Interest Rate
5%	16%
12	6
9	8
15	4
7	7

12.10 Is it possible to predict the annual number of business bankruptcies by the number of firm births (business starts)? The following table shows the number of business bankruptcies (1,000s) and the number of firm births (10,000s) for a six-year period. Use these data to develop the equation of the regression model to predict the number of business bankruptcies by the number of firm births. Discuss the meaning of the slope.

Business Bankruptcies (1,000s)	Firm Births (10,000s)
34.3	58.1
35.0	55.4
38.5	57.0
40.1	58.5
35.5	57.4
37.9	58.0

12.11 It appears that, over the past 50 years, the number of farms in Canada declined while the average size of farms (in hectares) increased. The following data show five-year interval data for Canadian farms. Use these data to develop the equation of a regression line to predict the average size of a farm by the number of farms. Discuss the slope and y-intercept of the model.

Year	Number (thousands of farms)	Total Area (millions of hectares)	Average Size (hectares)
1961	480.88	69.83	145
1966	430.50	70.46	164
1971	366.11	68.66	188
1976	338.55	68.43	202
1981	318.36	65.89	207
1986	293.09	67.83	231
1991	280.04	67.75	242
1996	276.55	68.05	246
2001	246.92	67.50	273
2006	229.37	67.59	295
2011	205.73	64.81	315
2016	193.49	64.23	332

Source: Adapted from Statistics Canada, Table 32-10-0152-01 "Number and Area of Farms and Farmland Area by Tenure, Historical Data", www150.statcan.gc.ca/t1/tbl1/en/tv.action?pid=3210015201.

12.12 Can the annual new orders for manufacturing be predicted by raw steel production? Shown here are the annual new orders for 10 years and the raw steel production for the same 10 years. Use these data to develop a regression model to predict annual new orders by raw steel production. Construct a scatter plot and draw the regression line through the points.

Raw Steel Production (100,000s of net tonnes)	New Orders (US$ trillions)
90.6	2.74
88.8	2.87
89.7	2.93
79.7	2.87
84.3	2.98
88.8	3.09
91.3	3.36
95.2	3.61
95.5	3.75
98.5	3.95

12.4 Residual Analysis

LEARNING OBJECTIVE 12.4

Calculate the residuals of a regression line, and from those determine the fit of the model, locate outliers, and test the assumptions of the regression, model.

How does a business analyst test a regression line to determine whether the line is a good fit for the data other than by observing the fitted line plot (i.e., the regression line fit through a scatter plot of the data)? One particularly popular approach is to use the *historical data* (x and y values used to construct the regression model) to test the model. With this approach, the values of the independent variable (x values) are inserted into the regression model and a predicted value ($\hat{y}$) is obtained for each x value. These predicted values ($\hat{y}$) are then compared with the actual y values to determine how much error the equation of the regression line produced. *Each difference between the actual y values and the predicted y values is the error of the regression line at a given point, $y - \hat{y}$, and is referred to as the* **residual**. It is the sum of squares of these residuals that is minimized to find the least squares line.

12.6 Problems

12.32 Compute r^2 for Problem 12.24 (Problem 12.6). Discuss the value of r^2 obtained.

12.33 Compute r^2 for Problem 12.25 (Problem 12.7). Discuss the value of r^2 obtained.

12.34 Compute r^2 for Problem 12.26 (Problem 12.8). Discuss the value of r^2 obtained.

12.35 Compute r^2 for Problem 12.27 (Problem 12.9). Discuss the value of r^2 obtained.

12.36 In Problem 12.10, you were asked to develop the equation of a regression model to predict the number of business bankruptcies by the number of firm births. For this regression model, solve for the coefficient of determination and comment on it.

12.37 The growth of a country's Gross Domestic Product (GDP) reflects the strength of the economy. Long-term interest rates, on the other hand, reflect the outlook for inflation in the future. It is said that economic growth often fuels inflation or inflationary expectations. Given here are the Canadian long-term interest rates and Canadian GDP growth rates (as percentages) for some recent years. Determine the equation of the regression line to predict the long-term interest rates from the GDP growth. Compute the standard error of the estimate for this model. Compute the value of r^2. Does GDP growth appear to be a good predictor of the long-term interest rate? Why or why not?

Year	Long-Term Interest Rates (%)	Real GDP Growth (%)
2002	5.29	2.8
2003	4.81	1.9
2004	4.58	3.1
2005	4.07	3.2
2006	4.21	2.6
2007	4.27	2.0
2008	3.61	1.2
2009	3.23	−2.7
2010	3.24	3.4
2011	2.78	3.0
2012	1.87	1.9
2013	2.26	2.0
2014	2.23	2.4

Source: Data from *OECD Factbook 2015–2016: Economic, Environmental and Social Statistics* (Paris: OECD Publishing, 2016).

12.7 | Hypothesis Tests for the Slope of the Regression Model and for the Overall Model

LEARNING OBJECTIVE 12.7

Use the *t* and *F* tests to test hypotheses for both the slope of the regression model and the overall regression model.

Testing the Slope

A hypothesis test can be conducted on the sample slope of the regression model to determine whether the population slope is significantly different from zero. This test is another way to determine how well a regression model fits the data. Suppose an analyst decides that it is not worth the effort to develop a linear regression model to predict y from x. An alternative approach might be to average the y values and use $\bar{y}$ as the predictor of y for all values of x. For the airline cost example, instead of using number of passengers as the predictor, the analyst would use the average value of airline cost, $\bar{y}$, as the predictor. In this case, the average value of y is:

$$\bar{y} = \frac{56.69}{12} = 4.7242, \text{ or } \$4,724.20$$

Using this result as a model to predict y, if the number of passengers is 61, 70, or 95—or any other number—the predicted value of y is still 4.7242. Essentially, this approach fits the line of $\bar{y} = 4.7242$ through the data, which is a horizontal line with a slope of zero. Would a regression analysis offer anything more than the $\bar{y}$ model? Using this nonregression model (the $\bar{y}$ model) as a worst case, the analyst can investigate the regression line to determine whether it adds a more significant amount of predictability of y than does the $\bar{y}$ model. Because the slope of the $\bar{y}$ line is zero, one way to determine whether the regression line adds significant predictability is to test the population slope of the regression line to find out whether the slope is different from zero. As the slope of the regression line diverges from zero, the regression model is adding predictability that the $\bar{y}$ line is not generating. For this reason, testing the slope of the regression line to determine whether the slope is different from zero is important. If the slope is not different from zero, the regression line is doing nothing more than the $\bar{y}$ line in predicting y.

How does the analyst go about testing the slope of the regression line? Why not just examine the observed sample slope? For example, the slope of the regression line for the airline cost data is 0.0407. This value is obviously not zero. The problem is that this slope is obtained from a sample of 12 data points, and if another sample were taken, it is likely that a different slope would be obtained. For this reason, the population slope is statistically tested using the sample slope. The question is: If all the pairs of data points for the population were available, would the slope of that regression line be different from zero? Here the sample slope, b_1, is used as evidence to test whether the population slope is different from zero. The hypotheses for this test follow.

$$H_0: \beta_1 = 0$$
$$H_a: \beta_1 \neq 0$$

Note that this test is two-tailed. The null hypothesis can be rejected if the slope is either negative or positive. A negative slope indicates an inverse relationship between x and y. That is, larger values of x are related to smaller values of y, and vice versa. Both negative and positive slopes can be different from zero. To determine whether there is a significant *positive* relationship between two variables, the hypotheses would be one-tailed, or:

$$H_0: \beta_1 = 0$$
$$H_a: \beta_1 > 0$$

To test for a significant negative relationship between two variables, the hypotheses would also be one-tailed, or:

$$H_0: \beta_1 = 0$$
$$H_a: \beta_1 < 0$$

In each case, testing the null hypothesis involves a t test of the slope.

---

t Test of Slope

$$t = \frac{b_1 - \beta_1}{s_b} \tag{12.9}$$

where

$$s_b = \frac{s_e}{\sqrt{SS_{xx}}}$$

$$s_e = \sqrt{\frac{SSE}{n-2}}$$

$$SS_{xx} = \Sigma x^2 - \frac{(\Sigma x)^2}{n}$$

$\beta_1 = $ the hypothesized slope

$df = n - 2$

The test of the slope of the regression line for the airline cost regression model for $\alpha = 0.05$ follows. The regression line derived for the data is:

$$\hat{y} = 1.57 + 0.0407x$$

The sample slope is $0.0407 = b_1$. The value of s_e is 0.1772, $\Sigma x = 930$, $\Sigma x^2 = 73,764$, and $n = 12$. The hypotheses are:

$$H_0: \beta_1 = 0$$
$$H_a: \beta_1 \neq 0$$

The $df = n - 2 = 12 - 2 = 10$. As this test is two-tailed, $\alpha/2 = 0.025$. The table t value is $t_{0.025,10} = \pm 2.228$. The observed t value for this sample slope is:

$$t = \frac{0.0407 - 0}{\dfrac{0.1772}{\sqrt{73,764 - \dfrac{930^2}{12}}}} = 9.43$$

As shown in **Figure 12.14**, the t value calculated from the sample slope falls in the rejection region and the p-value is 0.0000013. The null hypothesis that the population slope is zero is rejected. This linear regression model adds significantly more predictive information to the $\bar{y}$ model (no regression).

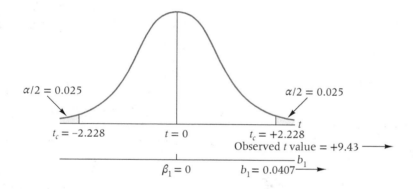

FIGURE 12.14 t Test of Slope from Airline Cost Example

It is desirable to reject the null hypothesis in testing the slope of the regression model. In rejecting the null hypothesis of a zero population slope, we are stating that the regression model adds something to the explanation of the variation of the dependent variable that the average value of the y model does not. Failure to reject the null hypothesis in this test causes the analyst to conclude that the regression model cannot predict the dependent variable, and the model, therefore, has little or no use.

DEMONSTRATION PROBLEM 12.5

Test the slope of the regression model developed in Demonstration Problem 12.1 to predict the number of FTEs in a hospital from the number of beds to determine whether there is a significant positive slope. Use $\alpha = 0.01$.

Solution The hypotheses for this problem are:

$$H_0: \beta_1 = 0$$
$$H_a: \beta_1 > 0$$

The level of significance is 0.01. With 12 pairs of data, $df = 10$. The critical table t value is $t_{0.01,10} = 2.764$. The regression line equation for this problem is:

$$\hat{y} = 30.888 + 2.232x$$

The sample slope, b_1, is 2.232, and $s_e = 15.65$, $\Sigma x = 592$, $\Sigma x^2 = 33{,}044$, and $n = 12$. The observed t value for the sample slope is:

$$t = \frac{2.232 - 0}{\dfrac{15.65}{\sqrt{33{,}044 - \dfrac{592^2}{12}}}} = 8.84$$

The observed t value (8.84) is in the rejection region because it is greater than the critical table t value of 2.764 and the p-value is 0.0000024. The null hypothesis is rejected. The population slope for this regression line is significantly different from zero in the positive direction. This regression model adds significant predictability over the y model.

Testing the Overall Model

It is common in regression analysis to compute an F test to determine the overall significance of the model. Most computer software packages include the F test and its associated ANOVA table as standard regression output. In multiple regression (Chapters 13 and 14), this test determines whether at least one of the regression coefficients (from multiple predictors) is different from zero. Simple regression provides only one predictor and only one regression coefficient to test. Because the regression coefficient is the slope of the regression line, the F test for overall significance tests the same thing as the t test in simple regression. The hypotheses being tested in simple regression by the F test for overall significance are:

$$H_0\colon \beta_1 = 0$$
$$H_a\colon \beta_1 \neq 0$$

In the case of simple regression analysis, $F = t^2$. Thus, for the airline cost example, the F value is:

$$F = t^2 = 9.43^2 = 88.92$$

The F value is computed directly by:

$$F = \frac{SS_{reg}/df_{reg}}{SS_{err}/df_{err}} = \frac{MS_{reg}}{MS_{err}}$$

where

$df_{reg} = k$
$df_{err} = n - k - 1$
 k = the number of independent variables

The values of the sum of squares (SS), degrees of freedom (df), and mean squares (MS) are obtained from the ANOVA table, which is produced with other regression statistics as standard output from statistical software packages. Shown here is the ANOVA table produced by Excel for the airline cost example.

ANOVA

	df	SS	MS	F
Regression	1	2.7980	2.7980	89.08
Residual	10	0.3141	0.0314	
Total	11	3.1121		

	Coefficients	Standard Error	t Stat	p-value
Intercept	1.5698	0.3381	4.6432	0.0009
Number of Passengers	0.0407	0.0043	9.4389	0.0000

The F value for the airline cost example is calculated from the ANOVA table information as:

$$F = \frac{2.7980/1}{0.3141/10} = \frac{2.7980}{0.03141} = 89.08$$

The difference between this value (89.08) and the value obtained by squaring the t statistic (88.92) is due to rounding error. The probability of obtaining an F value this large or larger by chance if there is no regression prediction in this model is 0.000 according to the ANOVA output (the p-value). This output value means it is highly unlikely that the population slope is zero and that there is no prediction due to regression from this model given the sample statistics obtained. Hence, it is highly likely that this regression model adds significant predictability of the dependent variable.

Note from the ANOVA table that the degrees of freedom due to regression are equal to 1. Simple regression models have only one independent variable; therefore, $k = 1$. The degrees of freedom error in simple regression analysis is always $n - k - 1 = n - 1 - 1 = n - 2$. With the degrees of freedom due to regression (1) as the numerator degrees of freedom and the degrees of freedom due to error $(n - 2)$ as the denominator degrees of freedom, Table A.7 can be used to obtain the critical F value $(F_{\alpha,1,n-2})$ to help make the hypothesis-testing decision about the overall regression model if the p-value of F is not given in the computer output. This critical F value is always found in the right tail of the distribution. In simple regression, the relationship between the critical t value to test the slope and the critical F value of overall significance is:

$$t^2_{\alpha/2,n-2} = F_{\alpha,1,n-2}$$

For the airline cost example with a two-tailed test and $\alpha = 0.05$, the critical value of $t_{0.025,10}$ is ± 2.228 and the critical value of $F_{0.05,1,10} = t^2_{0.025,10} = (\pm 2.228)^2 = 4.96$.

Concept Check

1. Why should you check the slope and the overall model before using the sample regression model you have developed?

12.7 Problems

12.38 Test the slope of the regression line determined in Problem 12.6. Use $\alpha = 0.05$.

12.39 Test the slope of the regression line determined in Problem 12.7. Use $\alpha = 0.01$.

12.40 Test the slope of the regression line determined in Problem 12.8. Use $\alpha = 0.10$.

12.41 Test the slope of the regression line determined in Problem 12.9. Use a 5% level of significance.

12.42 Test the slope of the regression line developed in Problem 12.10. Use a 5% level of significance.

12.43 Study the following ANOVA table, which was generated from a simple regression analysis. Discuss the F test of the overall model. Determine the value of t and test the slope of the regression line.

Analysis of Variance

Source	DF	SS	MS	F	p
Regression	1	116.65	116.65	8.26	0.021
Error	8	112.95	14.12		
Total	9	229.60			

12.8 | Estimation

LEARNING OBJECTIVE 12.8

Calculate confidence intervals to estimate the conditional mean of the dependent variable and prediction intervals to estimate a single value of the dependent variable.

One of the main uses of regression analysis is as a prediction tool. If the regression function is a good model, the business analyst can use the regression equation to determine values of the dependent variable from various values of the independent variable. For example, financial brokers would like to have a model with which they could predict the selling price of a stock on a certain day using a variable such as unemployment rate or producer price index. Marketing managers would like to have a site location model with which they could predict the sales volume of a new location using variables such as population density or number of competitors. The airline cost example presents a regression model that has the potential to predict the cost of flying an airplane by the number of passengers.

In simple regression analysis, a point estimate prediction of y can be made by substituting the associated value of x into the regression equation and solving for y. From the airline cost example, if the number of passengers is $x = 73$, the predicted cost of the airline flight can be computed by substituting the x value into the regression equation determined in Section 12.3:

$$\hat{y} = 1.57 + 0.0407x = 1.57 + 0.0407(73) = 4.5411$$

The point estimate of the predicted cost is 4.5411 or \$4,541.10.

Confidence Intervals to Estimate the Conditional Mean of y: $\mu_{y/x}$

Although a point estimate is often of interest to the analyst, the regression line is determined by a sample set of points; if a different sample is taken, a different line will result, yielding a different point estimate. Hence, computing a *confidence interval* for the estimation is often useful. Because for any value of x (independent variable) there can be many values of y (dependent variable), one type of **confidence interval** is *an estimate of the average value of y for a given x.* This average value of y is denoted $E(y_x)$—the expected value of y—and can be computed using Formula 12.6.

Confidence Interval to Estimate $E(y_x)$ for a Given Value of x

$$\hat{y} \pm t_{\alpha/2,n-2}s_e\sqrt{\frac{1}{n} + \frac{(x_0 - \bar{x})^2}{SS_{xx}}} \tag{12.10}$$

where

x_0 = a particular value of x

$$SS_{xx} = \Sigma x^2 - \frac{(\Sigma x)^2}{n}$$

The application of this formula can be illustrated with the construction of a 95% confidence interval to estimate the average value of y (airline cost) for the airline cost example when x (number of passengers) is 73. For a 95% confidence interval, $\alpha = 0.05$ and $\alpha/2 = 0.025$. The df $= n - 2 = 12 - 2 = 10$. The table t value is $t_{0.025,10} = 2.228$. Other needed values for this problem, which were solved for previously, are:

$$s_e = 0.1772 \qquad \Sigma x = 930 \qquad \bar{x} = 77.5 \qquad \Sigma x^2 = 73,764$$

For $x_0 = 73$, the value of $\hat{y}$ is 4.5411. The computed confidence interval for the average value of y, $E(y_{73})$, is:

$$4.5411 \pm (2.228)(0.1772)\sqrt{\frac{1}{12} + \frac{(73 - 77.5)^2}{73{,}764 - \frac{930^2}{12}}} = 4.5411 \pm 0.1219$$

$$4.4192 \leq E(y_{73}) \leq 4.6630$$

That is, with 95% confidence the average value of y for $x = 73$ is between 4.4192 and 4.6630.

Table 12.7 shows confidence intervals computed for the airline cost example for several values of x to estimate the average value of y. Note that as the x values get farther from the mean x value (77.5), the confidence intervals get wider; as the x values get closer to the mean, the confidence intervals narrow. The reason is that the numerator of the second term under the radical sign approaches zero as the value of x nears the mean and increases as x departs from the mean.

TABLE 12.7	Confidence Intervals to Estimate the Average Value of y for Some x Values in the Airline Cost Example	
x	**Confidence Interval**	
62	4.0934 ± 0.1875	3.9059 to 4.2809
68	4.3376 ± 0.1460	4.1916 to 4.4836
73	4.5411 ± 0.1219	4.4192 to 4.6630
85	5.0295 ± 0.1348	4.8947 to 5.1643
90	5.2330 ± 0.1656	5.0674 to 5.3986

Prediction Intervals to Estimate a Single Value of y

A second type of interval in regression estimation is a **prediction interval** to *estimate a single value of y for a given value of x.*

Prediction Interval to Estimate y for a Given Value of x

$$\hat{y} \pm t_{\alpha/2, n-2} s_e \sqrt{1 + \frac{1}{n} + \frac{(x_0 - \bar{x})^2}{SS_{xx}}} \qquad (12.11)$$

where

x_0 = a particular value of x

$$SS_{xx} = \Sigma x^2 - \frac{(\Sigma x)^2}{n}$$

Formula 12.7 is virtually the same as Formula 12.6, except for the additional value of 1 under the radical. This additional value widens the prediction interval to estimate a single value of y from the confidence interval to estimate the average value of y. This result seems logical because the average value of y is toward the middle of a group of y values. Thus, the confidence interval to estimate the average need not be as wide as the prediction interval produced by Formula 12.7, which takes into account all the y values for a given x.

A 95% prediction interval can be computed to estimate the single value of y for $x = 73$ from the airline cost example by using Formula 12.7. The same values used to construct the confidence interval to estimate the average value of y are used here:

$$t_{0.025, 10} = 2.228 \quad s_e = 0.1772 \quad \Sigma x = 930 \quad \bar{x} = 77.5 \quad \Sigma x^2 = 73{,}764$$

For $x_0 = 73$, the value of $\hat{y} = 4.5411$. The computed prediction interval for the single value of y is:

$$4.5411 \pm (2.228)(0.1772)\sqrt{1 + \frac{1}{12} + \frac{(73 - 77.5)^2}{73{,}764 - \frac{930^2}{12}}} = 4.5411 \pm 0.4132$$

$$4.1279 \leq y \leq 4.9543$$

Prediction intervals can be obtained by using the computer. Shown in **Figure 12.15** is the computer output for the airline cost example. The output displays the predicted value for $x = 73$ ($\hat{y} = 4.5411$), a 95% confidence interval for the average value of y for $x = 73$, and a 95% prediction interval for a single value of y for $x = 73$. Note that the resulting values are virtually the same as those calculated in this section.

FIGURE 12.15 **Prediction Intervals**

Fit	StDev Fit	95.0% CI	95.0% PI
4.5410	0.0547	(4.4191, 4.6629)	(4.1278, 4.9543)

Figure 12.16 displays confidence intervals for various values of x for the average y value and the prediction intervals for a single y value for the airline example. Note that the intervals flare out toward the ends as the values of x depart from the average x value. Note also that the intervals for a single y value are always wider than the intervals for the average y value for any given value of x.

FIGURE 12.16 **Intervals for Estimation**

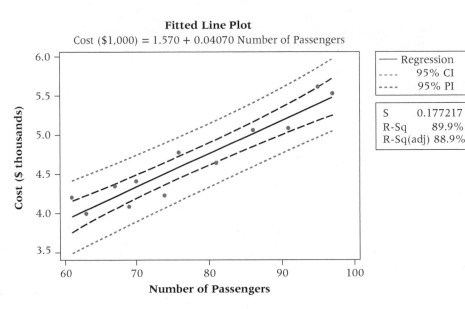

An examination of the prediction interval formula to estimate y for a given value of x explains why the intervals flare out:

$$\hat{y} \pm t_{\alpha/2,n-2} s_e \sqrt{1 + \frac{1}{n} + \frac{(x_0 - \bar{x})^2}{SS_{xx}}}$$

As we enter different values of x_0 from the regression analysis into the equation, the only thing that changes in the equation is $(x_0 - \bar{x})^2$. This expression increases as individual values of x_0 get farther from the mean, resulting in an increase in the width of the interval. The interval is narrower for values of x_0 nearer $\bar{x}$ and wider for values of x_0 farther from $\bar{x}$.

Caution: *A regression line is determined from a sample of points. The line, the* r^2, *the* s_e, *and the confidence intervals change for different sets of sample points. That is, the linear relationship developed for a set of points does not necessarily hold for values of* x *outside the domain of those used to establish the model. In the airline cost example, the domain of* x *values (number of passengers) varied from 61 to 97. The regression model developed from these points may not be valid for flights of say 40, 50, or 100 because the regression model was not constructed with* x *values of those magnitudes. However, decision-makers sometimes extrapolate regression results to values of* x *beyond the domain of those used to develop the formulas (often in time-series sales forecasting). Understanding the limitations of this use of regression analysis is essential.*

DEMONSTRATION PROBLEM 12.6

Construct a 95% confidence interval to estimate the average value of y (FTEs) for Demonstration Problem 12.1 when $x = 40$ beds. Then construct a 95% prediction interval to estimate the single value of y for $x = 40$ beds.

Solution For a 95% confidence interval, $\alpha = 0.05$, $n = 12$, and df = 10. The table t value is $t_{0.025,10} = 2.228$; $s_e = 15.65$, $\Sigma x = 592$, $\bar{x} = 49.33$, and $\Sigma x^2 = 33,044$. For $x_0 = 40$, $\hat{y} = 120.17$. The computed confidence interval for the average value of y is:

$$120.17 \pm (2.228)(15.65)\sqrt{\frac{1}{12} + \frac{(40 - 49.33)^2}{33,044 - \frac{592^2}{12}}} = 120.17 \pm 11.35$$

$$108.82 \le E(y_{40}) \le 131.52$$

With 95% confidence, the statement can be made that the average number of FTEs for a hospital with 40 beds is between 108.82 and 131.52.

The computed prediction interval for the single value of y is

$$120.17 \pm (2.228)(15.65)\sqrt{1 + \frac{1}{12} + \frac{(40 - 49.33)^2}{33,044 - \frac{592^2}{12}}} = 120.17 \pm 36.67$$

$$83.5 \le y \le 156.84$$

With 95% confidence, the statement can be made that a single number of FTEs for a hospital with 40 beds is between 83.5 and 156.84. Obviously this interval is much wider than the 95% confidence interval for the average value of y for $x = 40$.

The following graph depicts the 95% interval bands for both the average y value and the single y values for all 12 x values in this problem. Note once again the flaring out of the bands near the extreme values of x.

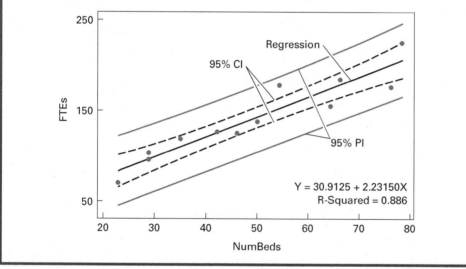

Concept Check

1. What is a confidence interval?

2. A regression equation gives the value of y given the value of x. Do we then need to construct a confidence interval around predicted values?

12.8 Problems

12.44 Construct a 95% confidence interval for the average value of y for Problem 12.6. Use $x = 25$.

12.45 Construct a 90% prediction interval for a single value of y for Problem 12.7 using $x = 100$. Construct a 90% prediction interval for a single value of y for Problem 12.7 using $x = 130$. Compare the results. Which prediction interval is greater? Why?

12.46 Construct a 98% confidence interval for the average value of y for Problem 12.8 using $x = 20$. Construct a 98% prediction interval for a single value of y for Problem 12.8 using $x = 20$. Which is wider? Why?

12.47 Construct a 99% confidence interval for the average bond rate in Problem 12.9 for a prime interest rate of 10%. Discuss the meaning of this confidence interval.

12.9 Using Regression to Develop a Forecasting Trend Line

LEARNING OBJECTIVE 12.9

Determine the equation of the trend line to forecast outcomes for time periods in the future, using alternative coding for time periods if necessary.

TABLE 12.8

Ten-Year Sales Data for Huntsville Chemical Company

Year	Sales ($ millions)
2010	7.84
2011	12.26
2012	13.11
2013	15.78
2014	21.29
2015	25.68
2016	23.80
2017	26.43
2018	29.16
2019	33.06

Business analysts often use historical data with measures taken over time in an effort to forecast what might happen in the future. A particular type of data that often lends itself well to this analysis is **time-series data**, which are defined as *data gathered on a particular characteristic over a period of time at regular intervals.* Some examples of time-series data are 10 years of weekly Toronto Stock Exchange averages, 12 months of daily oil production, or monthly consumption of coffee over a two-year period. To be useful to forecasters, time-series measurements need to be made at regular time intervals and arranged according to time of occurrence. As an example, consider the time-series sales data over a 10-year time period for the Huntsville Chemical Company shown in **Table 12.8**. Note that the measurements (sales) are taken over time and that the sales figures are given on a yearly basis. Time-series data can also be reported daily, weekly, monthly, quarterly, semi-annually, or for other defined time periods.

It is generally believed that time-series data contain any one or combination of four elements: trend, cyclicality, seasonality, and irregularity. While each of these four elements will be discussed in greater detail in Chapter 15, Time-Series Forecasting and Index Numbers, here we examine **trend** only and define it as *the long-term general direction of data.* Observing the scatter plot of the Huntsville Chemical Company's sales data shown in **Figure 12.17**, it is apparent that there is a positive trend in the data. That is, there appears to be a long-term upward general direction of sales over time. How can trend be expressed in mathematical terms? In the field of forecasting, it is common to attempt to fit a trend line through time-series data by determining the equation of the trend line and then using the equation of the trend line to predict future data points. How does one go about developing such a line?

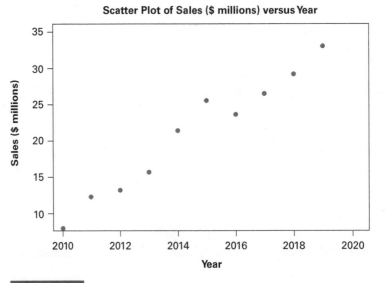

Scatter Plot of Sales ($ millions) versus Year

FIGURE 12.17 Scatter Plot of Huntsville Chemical Company Data

Regression Analysis: Sales versus Month

	Coefficients	Standard Error	t Stat	p-Value
Intercept	32,628.21	93.28	349.80	0.000
Month	−86.21	18.47	−4.67	0.003

The equation of the trend line is $\hat{y} = 32{,}628.21 - 86.21x$. A slope of −86.21 indicates that there is a downward trend in sales over this period of time at a rate of $86.21 (million) per month. The y-intercept of 32,628.21 represents what the trend line would estimate the sales to have been in period 0 or December of the previous year. The sales figure for October can be forecast by inserting $x = 10$ into this model and obtaining:

$$\hat{y}(10) = 32{,}628.21 - 86.21(10) = 31{,}766.11$$

Concept Check

1. How would you use regression analysis to predict future values? What type of data is used for this purpose?

12.9 Problems

12.48 Determine the equation of the trend line for the data shown below on Canadian balance of payments for exports of wheat over a five-year period provided by Statistics Canada. Using the trend line equation, forecast the value for the year 2021.

Year	Export—Balance of Payments (Unadjusted)—Wheat ($ millions)
2015	646.4
2016	546.4
2017	570.0
2018	592.4
2019	831.2

Source: Statistics Canada, Table 12-10-0120-01 "Historical (Real-Time) Releases of Merchandise Imports and Exports, Customs and Balance of Payments Basis for all Countries, by Seasonal Adjustment and North American Product Classification System (NAPCS) (× 1,000,000)."

12.49 Shown below are the long-term interest rates in Canada over a seven-month period according to the OECD. Use these data to construct a trend line and to forecast the long-term interest rate for June 2019.

		Long-Term Interest Rates
2018	Nov.	2.41
	Dec.	2.06
2019	Jan.	1.95
	Feb.	1.91
	Mar.	1.71
	Apr.	1.72
	May	1.67

12.50 Canada's new housing price index has been steadily increasing over the years. Given below are data for Canada's new housing price index between 2003 and 2018. Use these data to determine the equation of a trend line for new housing price indexes. Use the trend model you developed to forecast the new housing price index for 2019.

Year	New Housing Price Index
2003	66.5
2004	69.9
2005	74.1
2006	82.0
2007	87.1
2008	87.5
2009	86.7
2010	88.4
2011	90.7
2012	92.7
2013	93.9
2014	95.5
2015	97.0
2016 (Index base period)	100.0
2017	103.3
2018	103.3

Source: Statistics Canada, Table 18-10-0205-01 "New Housing Price Index, Monthly."

<table>
<tr><td>12.10</td><td></td></tr>
</table>

12.10 Interpreting the Output

LEARNING OBJECTIVE 12.10

Use a computer to develop a regression analysis, and interpret the output that is associated with it.

Most regression problems are analyzed by using a computer. In this section, computer output from Excel will be presented and discussed.

The Excel regression output is shown in **Figure 12.20** for Demonstration Problem 12.1. The regression equation is found under Coefficients at the bottom of ANOVA. The slope or coefficient of x is 2.2315 and the y-intercept is 30.9125. The standard error of the estimate for the hospital problem is given as the fourth statistic under Regression Statistics at the top of the output, Standard Error $= 15.6491$. The r^2 value is given as 0.886 on the second line. The t test for the slope is found under t Stat near the bottom of the ANOVA section in the "Number of beds" (x variable) row, $t = 8.83$. Adjacent to the t Stat is the p-value, which is the probability of the t statistic occurring by chance if the null hypothesis is true. For this slope, the probability shown is 0.000005. The ANOVA table is in the middle of the output with the F value having the same probability as the t statistic, 0.000005, and equalling t^2. The predicted values and the residuals are shown in the Residual Output section.

	A	B	C	D	E	F
1	SUMMARY OUTPUT					
2	Regression Statistics					
3	Multiple R	0.942				
4	R Square	0.886				
5	Adjusted R Square	0.875				
6	Standard Error	15.6491				
7	Observations	12				
8						
9	ANOVA					
10		df	SS	MS	F	Significance F
11	Regression	1	19115.0632	19115.0632	78.05	0.000005
12	Residual	10	2448.9368	244.8937		
13	Total	11	21564			
14						
15		Coefficients	Standard Error	t Stat	P-value	
16	Intercepts	30.9125	13.2542	2.33	0.041888	
17	Number of Beds	2.2315	0.2526	8.83	0.000005	
18						
19	RESIDUAL OUTPUT					
20	Observation	Predicted FTEs	Residuals			
21	1	82.237	−13.237			
22	2	95.626	−0.626			
23	3	95.626	6.374			
24	4	109.015	8.985			
25	5	124.636	1.364			
26	6	133.562	−8.562			
27	7	142.488	−4.488			
28	8	151.414	26.586			
29	9	173.729	−17.729			
30	10	178.192	5.808			
31	11	200.507	−24.507			
32	12	204.970	20.030			

FIGURE 12.20 **Excel Regression Output for Demonstration Problem 12.1**

End-of-Chapter Review

Decision Dilemma Solved

Predicting International Hourly Wages by the Price of a Big Mac™

In the Decision Dilemma, questions were raised about the relationship between the price of a Big Mac hamburger and net hourly wages around the world and whether a model could be developed to predict net hourly wages by the price of a Big Mac. Data were given for a sample of 20 countries. In exploring the possibility that there is a relationship between these two variables, a Pearson product-moment correlation coefficient, r, was computed to be 0.733. This r value indicates that there is a relatively high correlation between the two variables and that developing a regression model to predict one variable by the other has potential. Designating net hourly wages as the y or dependent variable and the price of a Big Mac as the x or predictor variable, the following regression output was obtained for these data using Excel.

Regression Statistics	
Multiple R	0.733
R Square	0.538
Adjusted R Square	0.512
Standard Error	11.8803
Observations	20

ANOVA

	df	SS	MS	F	Significance F
Regression	1	2957.87	2957.87	20.96	0.00023
Residual	18	2540.53	141.14		
Total	19	5498.40			

	Coefficients	Standard Error	t Stat	p-Value
Intercept	−12.444	8.703	−1.43	0.16987
Big Mac Price (US$)	8.458	1.848	4.58	0.00023

Taken from this output, the regression model is:

Net Hourly Wage = −12.444 + 8.458 (Price of Big Mac)

While the y-intercept has virtually no practical meaning in this analysis, the slope indicates that for every dollar increase in the price of a Big Mac, there is an incremental increase of $8.458 in net hourly wages for a country. It is worth underscoring here that just because there is a relationship between two variables, it does not mean there is a cause-and-effect relationship. That is, McDonald's cannot raise net hourly wages in a country just by increasing the cost of a Big Mac!

Using this regression model, the net hourly wage for a country with a $3.00 Big Mac can be predicted by substituting $x = 3$ into the model:

Net Hourly Wage = −12.444 + 8.458(3) = $12.93

That is, the model predicts that the net hourly wage for a country is $12.93 when the price of a Big Mac is $3.00.

How good a fit is the regression model to the data? Observe from the Excel output that the F value for testing the overall significance of the model (20.96) is highly significant with a p-value of 0.00023, and that the t statistic for testing to determine if the slope is significantly different from zero is 4.58 with a p-value of 0.00023. In simple regression, the t statistic is the square root of the F value, so these statistics relate essentially the same information—that there are significant regression effects in the model. The r^2 value is 53.8%, indicating that the model has moderate predictability. The standard error of the model, $s = 11.88$, indicates that if the error terms are approximately normally distributed, about 68% of the predicted net hourly wages would fall within ±$11.88.

Shown here is an Excel-produced line fit plot. Note from the plot that there generally appears to be a linear relationship between the variables but that many of the data points fall considerably away from the fitted regression line, indicating that the price of a Big Mac only partially accounts for net hourly wages.

Key Considerations

Regression analysis offers several opportunities for misleading interpretations. One way is to present a regression model in isolation from information about the fit of the model. That is, the regression model is represented as a valid tool for prediction without any regard for how well it actually fits the data. While it is true that least squares analysis can produce a line of best fit through virtually any set of points, it does not necessarily follow that the regression model is a good predictor of the dependent variable.

For example, sometimes business consultants sell regression models to companies as forecasting tools or market predictors without disclosing to the client that the r^2 value is very low, the slope of the regression line is not significant, the residuals are large, and the standard error of the estimate is large. This can be misleading and so the analyst should be cautious.

Another inappropriate use of simple regression analysis is stating or implying a cause-and-effect relationship between two variables just because they are highly correlated and produce a high r^2 in regression. The Decision Dilemma presents a good example of this with the regression analysis of the price of a Big Mac™ hamburger and the net hourly wages in a country. While the coefficient of determination is 53.8% and there appears to be a modest fit of the regression line to the data, that does not mean that increasing the price of a Big Mac in a given country will increase the country's net hourly wages. Often, two correlated variables are related to a third variable that drives the two of them but is not included in the regression analysis. In the Decision Dilemma example, both Big Mac prices and net hourly wages may be related to exchange rates or a country's economic condition.

Regression analysis is based on several assumptions, such as equal error variance, independent error terms, and error terms being normally distributed. Through the use of residual plots and other statistical techniques, a business analyst can test these assumptions. It is inappropriate to present a regression model as fact when the assumptions underlying it are being grossly violated, since this can mislead the user.

It is important to remember that since regression models are developed from sample data, when an x value is entered into a simple regression model, the resulting prediction is only a point estimate. While business people often use regression models as predicting tools, it should be kept in mind that the prediction value is an estimate, not a guaranteed outcome. By utilizing or at least pointing out confidence intervals and prediction intervals, such as those presented in Section 12.8, the business analyst places the predicted point estimate within the context of inferential estimation and thereby provides sufficient warning to the user.

Lastly, another issue we should be concerned about is using the regression model to predict values of the independent variable that are outside the domain of values used to develop the model. The airline cost model used in this chapter was built with between 61 and 97 passengers. A linear relationship appeared to be evident between flight costs and number of passengers over this domain. This model is not guaranteed to fit values outside the domain of 61 to 97 passengers, however. In fact, either a nonlinear relationship or no relationship may be present between flight costs and number of passengers if values from outside this domain are included in the model-building process. It is a mistake to make claims for a regression model outside the purview of the domain of values for which the model was developed.

Why Statistics Is Relevant

In a business context, you are constantly required to make decisions. To make effective decisions, you need to know how things work: Is the price of a product related to how many people would buy it? If you raise the salary of an employee, is he or she likely to stay with the company longer? Is customer satisfaction related to customer loyalty? Will inflation reduce your profit margin? Regression analysis can answer questions like these and provide input for making effective decisions.

Decision-makers also need to understand what is likely to happen in the future so they can plan for it. They need to predict such things as the effect of current investments on future sales and the effect of increased investments in machinery on future profitability. Regression analysis provides a method by which predictions can be carried out in a systematic manner.

A third reason why regression analysis is important is that sometimes decision-makers need to assess the effect of alternative scenarios. For example, a decision-maker may predict the sales next year to be $150 million, given an inflation rate of 3%. But what would happen if the inflation rate turned out to be 4%? Regression analysis can be used to understand the effect of alternative scenarios on business decisions.

Finally, with the increasing availability of large amounts of data such as transactional information and data culled from social media, data mining is being used progressively more and more by businesses. A huge part of data mining is grounded on regression-based techniques, and a proper use of these techniques is critical for modern businesses to thrive. Since huge amounts of data are available for all businesses, those that can extract reliable information out of data will have a sustainable competitive advantage.

Summary of Learning Objectives

LEARNING OBJECTIVE 12.1 Calculate the Pearson product-moment correlation coefficient to determine if there is a correlation between two variables.

Correlation is a measure that can be used to understand the existence and the strength of the relationship between two variables. The measure of correlation known as the correlation coefficient can range from –1.0 through 0 to +1.0. If the correlation coefficient is negative, as the value of one variable goes up (down), the value of the other variable goes down (up). If the correlation coefficient is positive, as the value of one variable goes up (down), the value of the other variable goes up (down) as well. A zero correlation indicates that the two variables under consideration are not related to each other.

LEARNING OBJECTIVE 12.2 Explain what regression analysis is, and explain the concepts of independent and dependent variable.

Regression is a mathematical model that can be used to predict the value of one variable given the value of other variables. Simple regression is bivariate (two variables) and linear (only a line fit is attempted). Simple regression analysis produces a model that attempts to predict a y variable, referred to as the dependent variable, by an x variable, referred to as the independent variable. The general form of the equation of the simple regression line is the slope-intercept equation of a line. The equation of the simple regression model consists of the slope of the line as the coefficient of x and the y-intercept value as the constant.

LEARNING OBJECTIVE 12.3 Calculate the slope and y-intercept of the least squares equation of a regression line, and from those determine the equation of the regression line.

The slope of the line (b_1) is an estimate of the effect of a one-unit increase in the independent variable on the dependent variable. For example, simple regression can answer the question of how much a consumer is likely to spend on clothing for each dollar increase in income.

LEARNING OBJECTIVE 12.4 Calculate the residuals of a regression line, and from those determine the fit of the model, locate outliers, and test the assumptions of the regression model.

After the equation of the line has been developed, several statistics are available that can be used to determine how well the line fits the data. Using the historical data values of x, predicted values of y (denoted as $\hat{y}$) can be calculated by inserting values of x into the regression equation. The predicted values can then be compared with the actual values of y to determine how well the regression equation fits the known data. The difference between a specific y value and its associated predicted $\hat{y}$ value is called the residual or error of prediction. Examination of the residuals can offer insight into the magnitude of the errors produced by a model. In addition, residual analysis can be used to help determine whether the assumptions underlying the regression analysis have been met. Specifically, graphs of the residuals can reveal (1) lack of linearity, (2) lack of homogeneity of error variance, and (3) independence of error terms. Geometrically, the residuals are the vertical distances from the y values to the regression line. Because the equation that yields the regression line is derived in such a way that the line is in the geometric middle of the points, the sum of the residuals is zero.

LEARNING OBJECTIVE 12.5 Calculate the standard error of the estimate using the sum of squares of error, and use the standard error of the estimate to determine the fit of the model.

The standard error of the estimate is the standard deviation of error of a model. A single value of error measurement called the standard error of the estimate, s_e, can be computed using the formula described. The value of s_e can be used as a single guide to the magnitude of the error produced by the regression model as opposed to examining all the residuals.

LEARNING OBJECTIVE 12.6 Calculate the coefficient of determination to measure the fit for regression models, and relate it to the coefficient of correlation.

The coefficient of determination is simply the square of the correlation coefficient. The coefficient of determination is the proportion of the total variance of the y variable accounted for or predicted by x. The coefficient of determination ranges from 0 to 1. The higher the r^2 value is, the stronger is the predictability of the model.

LEARNING OBJECTIVE 12.7 Use the t and F tests to test hypotheses for both the slope of the regression model and the overall regression model.

Testing to determine whether the slope of the regression line is different from zero is another way to judge the fit of the regression model to the data. If the population slope of the regression line is not different from zero, the regression model is not adding significant predictability to the dependent variable. A t statistic is used to test the significance of the slope. The overall significance of the regression model can be tested using an F statistic. In simple regression, because only one predictor is present, this test accomplishes the same thing as the t test of the slope, and $F = t^2$.

LEARNING OBJECTIVE 12.8 Calculate confidence intervals to estimate the conditional mean of the dependent variable and prediction intervals to estimate a single value of the dependent variable.

One of the most prevalent uses of a regression model is to predict the values of y for given values of x. Recognizing that the predicted value is often not the same as the actual value, a confidence interval has been developed to yield a range within which the mean y value for a given x should fall. A prediction interval for a single y value for a given x value is also specified. This second interval is wider because it allows for the wide diversity of individual values, whereas the confidence interval for the mean y value reflects only the range of average y values for a given x.

LEARNING OBJECTIVE 12.9 Determine the equation of the trend line to forecast outcomes for time periods in the future, using alternative coding for time periods if necessary.

Time-series data are data that are gathered over a period of time at regular intervals. Developing the equation of a forecasting trend line for time-series data is a special case of simple regression analysis where the time factor is the predictor variable. The time variable can be in units of years, months, weeks, quarters, and others.

LEARNING OBJECTIVE 12.10 Use a computer to develop a regression analysis, and interpret the output that is associated with it.

Most regression problems are analyzed by using a computer. Interpreting this output provides meaningful insight into how well the data fit the regression model, and whether the model is suitable to use for prediction.

Key Terms

Formulas

(12.1) Pearson product-moment correlation coefficient

$$r = \frac{\Sigma(x - \bar{x})(y - \bar{y})}{\sqrt{\Sigma(x - \bar{x})^2 \Sigma(y - \bar{y})^2}}$$

$$= \frac{\Sigma xy - \frac{\Sigma x \Sigma y}{n}}{\sqrt{\left[\Sigma x^2 - \frac{(\Sigma x)^2}{n}\right]\left[\Sigma y^2 - \frac{(\Sigma y)^2}{n}\right]}}$$

(12.2) Equation of the simple regression line

$$\hat{y} = b_0 + b_1 x$$

Sum of squares

$$SS_{xx} = \Sigma x^2 - \frac{(\Sigma x)^2}{n}$$

$$SS_{yy} = \Sigma y^2 - \frac{(\Sigma y)^2}{n}$$

$$SS_{xy} = \Sigma xy - \frac{(\Sigma x)(\Sigma y)}{n}$$

(12.3) Slope of the regression line

$$b_1 = \frac{\Sigma(x - \bar{x})(y - \bar{y})}{\Sigma(x - \bar{x})^2} = \frac{\Sigma xy - n\bar{x}\bar{y}}{\Sigma x^2 - n\bar{x}^2}$$

$$= \frac{\Sigma xy - \frac{(\Sigma x)(\Sigma y)}{n}}{\Sigma x^2 - \frac{(\Sigma x)^2}{n}}$$

(12.4) Alternative formula for slope

$$b_1 = \frac{SS_{xy}}{SS_{xx}}$$

(12.5) y-intercept of the regression line

$$b_0 = \bar{y} - b_1 \bar{x} = \frac{\Sigma y}{n} - b_1 \frac{(\Sigma x)}{n}$$

(12.6) Sum of squares of error

$$SSE = \Sigma(y - \hat{y})^2 = \Sigma y^2 - b_0 \Sigma y - b_1 \Sigma xy$$

(12.7) Standard error of the estimate

$$s_e = \sqrt{\frac{SSE}{n - 2}}$$

(12.8) Coefficient of determination

$$r^2 = 1 - \frac{SSE}{SS_{yy}} = 1 - \frac{SSE}{\Sigma y^2 - \frac{(\Sigma y)^2}{n}}$$

$$r^2 = \frac{b_1^2 SS_{xx}}{SS_{yy}}$$

(12.9) t test of slope

$$t = \frac{b_1 - \beta_1}{s_b}$$

$$s_b = \frac{s_e}{\sqrt{SS_{xx}}}$$

(12.10) Confidence interval to estimate $E(y_x)$ for a given value of x

$$\hat{y} \pm t_{\alpha/2, n-2} s_e \sqrt{\frac{1}{n} + \frac{(x_0 - \bar{x})^2}{SS_{xx}}}$$

(12.11) Prediction interval to estimate y for a given value of x

$$\hat{y} \pm t_{\alpha/2, n-2} s_e \sqrt{1 + \frac{1}{n} + \frac{(x_0 - \bar{x})^2}{SS_{xx}}}$$

Supplementary Problems

Calculating the Statistics

12.51 **Video** Determine the Pearson product-moment correlation coefficient for the following data.

x	1	10	9	6	5	3	2
y	8	4	4	5	7	7	9

12.52 Use the following data for parts (a) through (f).

x	5	7	3	16	12	9
y	8	9	11	27	15	13

a. Determine the equation of the least squares regression line to predict y by x.

b. Using the x values, solve for the predicted values of y and the residuals.

c. Solve for s_e.

d. Solve for r^2.

e. Test the slope of the regression line. Use $\alpha = 0.01$.

f. Comment on the results determined in parts (b) through (e), and make a statement about the fit of the line.

12.53 **Video** Use the following data for parts (a) through (g).

x	53	47	41	50	58	62	45	60
y	5	5	7	4	10	12	3	11

a. Determine the equation of the simple regression line to predict y from x.

b. Using the x values, solve for the predicted values of y and the residuals.

c. Solve for SSE.

d. Calculate the standard error of the estimate.

e. Determine the coefficient of determination.

f. Test the slope of the regression line. Assume $\alpha = 0.05$. What do you conclude about the slope?

g. Comment on parts (d) and (e).

12.54 If you were to develop a regression line to predict y by x, what value would the coefficient of determination have?

x	213	196	184	202	221	247
y	76	65	62	68	71	75

12.55 Determine the equation of the least squares regression line to predict y from the following data.

x	47	94	68	73	80	49	52	61
y	14	40	34	31	36	19	20	21

a. Construct a 95% confidence interval to estimate the mean y value for $x = 60$.

b. Construct a 95% prediction interval to estimate an individual y value for $x = 70$.

c. Interpret the results obtained in parts (a) and (b).

12.56 Determine the equation of the trend line through the following cost data. Use the equation of the line to forecast cost for year 7.

Year	Cost ($ millions)
1	56
2	54
3	49
4	46
5	45

Testing Your Understanding

12.57 **Video** A manager of a car dealership believes there is a relationship between the number of salespeople on duty and the number of cars sold. Suppose the following sample is used to develop a simple regression model to predict the number of cars sold by the number of salespeople. Solve for r^2 and explain what r^2 means in this problem.

Week	Number of Cars Sold	Number of Salespeople
1	79	6
2	64	6
3	49	4
4	23	2
5	52	3

12.58 The Chartered Professional Accountants of Canada reported that the average amount of planned spending on gifts for the holiday season in 2018 was $643. In the U.S., however, the average amount of planned spending on gifts for a recent holiday season was US$854, with 40% of those purchases being made from catalogues. Shown below are the average amounts of planned spending on gifts for the holiday season for 11 years along with the associated percentages to be made from catalogues. Develop a regression model to predict the amount of planned spending in a given year by the associated percentage to be made from catalogues for that year. Comment on the strength of the model and the output.

Year	Average Spending (US$)	Percentage Purchases to be Made from Catalogues
1	1,037	44
2	976	42
3	1,004	47
4	942	47
5	907	50
6	859	51
7	431	43
8	417	36
9	658	26
10	646	42
11	854	40

12.59 It seems logical that restaurant chains with more units (restaurants) would have greater sales. This assumption is mitigated, however, by several possibilities: some units may be more profitable than others, some units may be larger, some units may serve more meals, some units may serve more expensive meals, and so on. The data shown here were published by QSR 50. Perform a simple regression analysis to predict a restaurant chain's sales by its number of units. How strong is the relationship?

Chain	Sales ($ billions)	Number of Units (thousands)
McDonald's	37.48	15.0
Starbucks	13.17	13.9
Subway	10.80	25.9
Burger King	10.03	7.2
Taco Bell	9.79	6.4
Wendy's	9.29	5.8
Domino's Pizza	5.90	5.6
Pizza Hut	5.51	7.5
KFC	4.42	4.1
Dairy Queen	3.64	4.5

12.60 Shown here are the labour force figures (in millions) for the country of Bangladesh over a 10-year period published by the World Bank. Develop the equation of a trend line through these data and use the equation to predict the labour force of Bangladesh for the year 2021.

Year	Labour Force (millions)
2009	55.86
2010	56.81
2011	57.88
2012	58.96
2013	60.05
2014	61.16
2015	62.28
2016	63.39
2017	67.14
2018	68.37

12.61 How strong is the correlation between the inflation rate and the unemployment rate? The following data are given as pairs of inflation rates and unemployment rates for the month of May for 10 recent years.

Inflation Rate (%)	Unemployment Rate (%)
2.4	6.7
3.9	7.0
1.1	7.8
2.8	7.9
2.4	7.2
1.6	6.9
2.8	6.1
2.2	6.0
2.2	6.1
0.1	8.4

Compute the Pearson product-moment correlation coefficient to determine the strength of the correlation between these two variables. Comment on the strength and direction of the correlation.

12.62 The table below shows the gross domestic product at 2012 constant prices (in $ millions) of consumer durables and nondurables in Canada. Is there a linear relationship between the shipments of durables and nondurables? In other words, if we know the value of nondurables shipped in any one year, can we predict the value of durables during that year? (Hint: Make the value of nondurables the independent variable.) According to the model, if in any given year the nondurables shipment is $260,000 million, what would the predicted amount for durables shipment be for the same year? Construct a confidence interval for the average y value for $260,000 million. Use the t statistic to determine whether the slope is significantly different from zero. Use $\alpha = 0.05$.

Gross Domestic Product at 2012 Constant Prices ($ millions)

Year	Nondurable Goods	Durable Goods
2003	219,664	86,793
2004	224,188	89,100
2005	227,454	93,512
2006	231,389	100,148
2007	238,352	107,100
2008	242,055	112,799
2009	243,802	109,954
2010	247,783	115,751
2011	250,198	117,857
2012	251,358	121,511
2013	257,292	126,746
2014	261,794	133,312
2015	266,084	137,228
2016	270,475	142,302
2017	277,587	152,468
2018	282,154	154,293

Source: Data from Statistics Canada, Table 36-10-0369-01 "Gross Domestic Product, Expenditure-Based, at 2012 Constant Prices, Annual ($\times$ 1,000,000)."

12.63 **Video** People in the aerospace industry believe the cost of a space project is a function of the mass of the major object being sent into space. Use the following data to develop a regression model to predict the cost of a space project by the mass of the space object. Determine r^2 and s_e.

Mass (tonnes)	Cost (US$ millions)
1.721	$ 53.6
2.739	184.9
0.411	6.4
0.896	23.5
0.960	33.4
1.905	110.4
2.165	104.6

12.64 Canada's trade balance with the rest of the world has been steadily increasing over the past several years. It is well known that the U.S. is Canada's leading trade partner. Is there a predictable linear relationship between our total trade balance and our trade balance with the U.S.? Develop a regression model to predict the trade balance with the U.S. by our trade balance with the rest of the world. Comment on the strength of the model. Develop a time-series trend line for trade balance with the rest of the world by using the time periods given. Forecast total trade balance with the rest of the world for 2020 using this equation.

	Trade Balance ($ millions)	
Year	Rest of the World	U.S.
2010	2,290	4,991
2011	2,486	4,709
2012	2,776	4,641
2013	2,648	5,220
2014	3,068	5,041
2015	3,688	4,750
2016	4,111	4,321
2017	4,172	4,699
2018	3,669	4,777
2019	3,493	4,809

12.65 Is the amount of money spent by companies on advertising a function of the total sales of the company? Shown are sales income and advertising cost data for seven companies, published by *Advertising Age*.

Company	Advertising ($ millions)	Sales ($ billions)
Procter & Gamble	$4,898	$ 68.2
AT&T	3,345	63.1
General Motors	3,296	207.3
Verizon	2,822	93.2
Ford Motor	2,577	160.1
Walmart	1,073	351.1
HP Inc.	829	91.7

Water Use (millions of litres)	Temperature (degrees Celsius)
829	39
212	4
405	25
488	26
257	10
697	36
568	32
424	24

Use the data to develop a regression line to predict the amount of advertising by sales. Compute s_e and r^2. Assuming $\alpha = 0.05$, test the slope of the regression line. Comment on the strength of the regression model.

12.66 Can the consumption of water in a city be predicted by temperature? The following data represent a sample of a day's water consumption and the high temperature for that day.

Develop a least squares regression line to predict the amount of water used in a day in a city by the high temperature for that day. What would the predicted water usage be for a temperature of 38°? Evaluate the regression model by calculating s_e, by calculating r^2, and by testing the slope. Let $\alpha = 0.01$.

Interpreting the Output

12.67 Video Study the following Excel regression output for an analysis attempting to predict the number of union members by the size of the labour force for selected years over a 30-year period. Analyze the computer output. Discuss the strength of the model in terms of the proportion of variation accounted for, slope, and overall predictability. Using the equation of the regression line, attempt to predict the number of union members when the labour force is 100,000. Note that the model was developed with data already recorded in units of 1,000. Use the data in the model as is.

	A	B	C	D	E	F
1	SUMMARY OUTPUT					
2	Regression Statistics					
3	Multiple R	0.610				
4	R Square	0.372				
5	Adjusted R Square	0.320				
6	Standard Error	982.219				
7	Observations	14				
8						
9	ANOVA					
10		df	SS	MS	F	Significance F
11	Regression	1	6868285.79	6868286	7.12	0.0205
12	Residual	12	11577055.64	967455		
13	Total	13	18445341.43			
14						
15		Coefficients	Standard Error	t Stat	P-value	
16	Intercept	22348.97	1846.37	12.10	.000000044	
17	X Variable 1	−0.0524	0.02	−2.67	0.0205	
18						
19	RESIDUAL OUTPUT					
20	Observation	Predicted Y	Residuals			
21	1	19161.39	−1862.39			
22	2	18631.75	749.25			
23	3	18315.95	1295.05			
24	4	17602.12	2240.88			
25	5	17516.68	−176.68			
26	6	17394.71	−398.71			
27	7	17269.86	−294.86			
28	8	17144.07	−231.07			
29	9	17033.79	−31.79			
30	10	16925.13	34.87			
31	11	16902.86	−162.86			
32	12	16961.51	−393.51			
33	13	16914.23	−524.23			
34	14	16841.95	−243.95			

12.68 Study the following residual diagnostic graphs. Comment on any possible violations of regression assumptions.

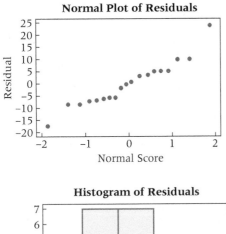

Normal Plot of Residuals

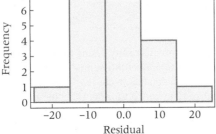

Histogram of Residuals

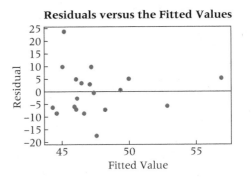

Residuals versus the Fitted Values

Exploring the Databases with Business Analytics   *see* the databases on the Student Website and in *WileyPLUS*

1. Develop a regression model from the Canadian RRSP Contribution Database to predict the RRSP annual contribution by the Average Age of RRSP Contributors for the province of Quebec. Discuss the model and its strength on the basis of statistics presented in this chapter. Now develop another regression model for the province of Ontario. Discuss the model and its strengths. Compare the two models. Does it make sense that age is a predictor of contribution? Why or why not?

2. Using the Financial Database, analyze the variables in columns D, E, F, G, H, J, and K by using a correlation matrix. These seven variables are capable of producing 21 pairs of correlations.

Which are most highly correlated? Select the variable that is most highly correlated with Average Price/Earnings (P/E) Ratio and use it as a predictor to develop a regression model to predict P/E ratio. How did the model do?

3. Use the Canadian Stock Market Database to develop a regression model to predict the Utility Index by the Composite Index. How well did the model perform? Did it perform as you expected? Why or why not? Construct a correlation matrix for the variables of this database (excluding Week of the Month) so that you can explore the stock market. Did you discover any apparent relationships between variables?

Case

Caterpillar, Inc.

Caterpillar, Inc., headquartered in Peoria, Illinois, is an American corporation with a worldwide dealer network that sells machinery, engines, financial products, and insurance. Caterpillar is the world's leading manufacturer of construction and mining equipment, diesel and natural gas engines, industrial gas turbines, and diesel-electric locomotives. Although it provides financial services through its Financial Products segment, Caterpillar primarily operates through its three product segments of Construction Industries, Resource Industries, and Energy & Transportation. Founded in 1925, the company presently has sales and revenues of $45.5 billion, total assets of $77 billion, and 98,400 employees. Caterpillar machinery are commonly recognized by the company's trademark "Caterpillar Yellow"

and its "CAT" logo. Some of its manufactured construction products include mini excavators, small-wheel loaders, backhoe loaders, multi-terrain loaders, and compact-wheel loaders. Other products include machinery for mining and quarrying applications, reciprocating engines and turbines in power systems, the remanufacturing of CAT engines and components, and a wide range of financial alternatives for customers and dealers of Caterpillar machinery and engines.

Caterpillar tractors have undertaken and completed many difficult tasks since the company's beginning. In the late 1920s, the Soviet Grain Trust purchased 2,050 Caterpillar machines for use on its large farm cooperatives. This sale helped to keep Caterpillar's factories busy during the Great Depression. In the 1930s, Caterpillar track-type tractors helped construct the Hoover Dam, worked on the Mississippi Levee construction project, helped construct the Golden Gate Bridge, and were used in the construction of the Chesapeake & Delaware Canal. During this time period, CATs were also used in construction projects around the world, in countries such as Palestine, Iraq, India, Canada, the Netherlands, and Belgium, and in the building of the Pan-American Highway. In World War II, Caterpillar built 51,000 track-type tractors for the U.S. military.

In the 1940s, Caterpillar tractors were used in the construction of the Alaska Highway; between 1944 and 1956, they were used to help construct 70,000 miles (over 110,000 kilometres) of highway in the United States. In the 1950s and '60s, usage of Caterpillar tractors around the world exploded, and they were used in such countries as Australia, Austria, Ceylon, France, Germany, Italy, Nigeria, Philippines, Rhodesia, Russia, Sweden, Switzerland, Uganda, and Venezuela, in a wide variety of projects. In addition, Caterpillar products were used to help construct the St. Lawrence Seaway between Canada and the United States. In the 1970s and '80s, Caterpillar equipment was used in numerous dam, power, and pipeline projects. Since then, Caterpillars have been used in the construction of several projects, such as Japan's Kansai International Airport, a marine airport approximately three miles offshore in Osaka Bay; the Chunnel between France and England; the "Big Dig" in Boston; Panama Canal expansion; and several Olympic Games sites.

Discussion

1. The United States Department of Agriculture (USDA), in conjunction with the Forest Service, publishes information to assist companies in estimating the cost of building a temporary road for such activities as a timber sale. Such roads are generally built for one or two seasons of use for limited traffic, and are designed with the goal of re-establishing vegetative cover on the roadway and adjacent disturbed area within 10 years after the termination of the contract, permit, or lease. The timber sale contract requires outsloping, removal of culverts and ditches, and building water bars or cross ditches after the road is no longer needed. As part of this estimation process, the company needs to estimate haul costs. The USDA publishes variable costs in dollars per cubic-yard-mile for hauling dirt according to the speed at which the vehicle can drive. Speeds are mainly determined by the road width, the sight distance, the grade, the curves, and the turnouts. Thus, on a steep, narrow, winding road, the speed is slow; on a flat, straight, wide road, the speed is faster. Shown below are data on speed, cost per cubic yard for a 12-cubic-yard end-dump vehicle, and cost per cubic yard for a 20-cubic-yard bottom-dump vehicle. Use these data and simple regression analysis to develop models for predicting the haul cost by speed for each of these two vehicles. Discuss the strength of the models. Based on the models, predict the haul cost for 35 miles per hour (mph) and for 45 mph for each of these vehicles.

Speed (mph)	Haul Cost 12-Cubic-Yard End-Dump Vehicle (US$ per cubic yd)	Haul Cost 20-Cubic-Yard Bottom-Dump Vehicle (US$ per cubic yd)
10	$2.46	$1.98
15	1.64	1.31
20	1.24	0.98
25	0.98	0.77
30	0.82	0.65
40	0.62	0.47
50	0.48	0.40

2. Shown here are Caterpillar's annual global sales and revenue streams for the years 2004 through 2018. By observing the data graphically and analyzing the data statistically using techniques and concepts from this chapter, share your insights and conclusions about Caterpillar's annual global sales and revenue streams over this period of time.

Year	Sales and Revenue Streams (US$ billions)
2004	30.31
2005	36.34
2006	41.52
2007	44.96
2008	51.32
2009	32.40
2010	42.59
2011	60.14
2012	65.88
2013	55.66
2014	55.18
2015	47.01
2016	38.54
2017	45.46
2018	54.72

Source: Adapted from www.cat.com.

Big Data Case

In the American Hospital Association database, there would seem to be several possible correlations between variables and potential for some simple regression analyses. Keeping this in mind, answer the following questions:

1. Using the entire database, develop a regression model to predict the number of Personnel by the Number of Births. Now develop a regression model to predict the number of Personnel by Number of Beds. Examine the regression output. Which model is stronger in predicting the number of Personnel? Using both techniques from the chapter and common sense, explain why.

Using the second regression model (with Number of Beds as the predictor), predict the number of Personnel in a hospital that has 110 beds. Construct a 95% confidence interval around this prediction for the average value of y.

2. Using the Small Hospitals Only sub-database, construct a correlation matrix employing all eight variables. Examining the correlation matrix, identify any correlations above 0.50, and explain in a sentence or two why you think each of these correlations makes sense in light of the two variables.

Using the Computer

- Excel has the capability of doing simple regression analysis. For a more inclusive analysis, use the **Data Analysis** tool. For a more "à la carte" approach, use Excel's **Insert Function**.

- To use the **Data Analysis** tool for a more inclusive analysis, begin by selecting the **Data** tab on the Excel worksheet. From the **Analyze** panel at the top right of the **Data** ribbon, click on **Data Analysis**. If your Excel worksheet does not show the **Data Analysis** option, you can load it as an add-in. From the **Data Analysis** menu, select **Regression**. In the **Regression** dialogue box, input the location of the y values in **Input Y Range**. Input the location of the x values in **Input X Range**. Check **Labels** if your selected data contains row headings. Check and input **Confidence Level**. To pass the line through the origin, check **Constant is Zero**. To print out the raw residuals, check **Residuals**. To print out residuals converted to z scores, check **Standardized Residuals**. For a plot of the residuals, check **Residual Plots**. For a plot of the line through the points, check **Line Fit Plots**. Standard output includes r, r^2, s_e, and an ANOVA table with the F test, the slope and intercept, t statistics with associated p-values, and any optionally requested output such as graphs or residuals.

- To use the **Insert Function (fx),** go to the **Formulas** tab on an Excel worksheet. The **Insert Function** is on the far left of the ribbon. In the **Insert Function** dialogue box at the top, there is a pulldown menu that says **Or select a category**. From the pulldown menu associated with this command, select **Statistical**. Select **INTERCEPT** from the **Insert Function's Statistical** menu to solve for the y-intercept, **RSQ** to solve for r^2, **SLOPE** to solve for the slope, and **STEYX** to solve for the standard error of the estimate.

A NOTE ON SOME COMPUTER OUTPUTS IN CHAPTERS 12–18

Please note that some of the exhibits in this and some subsequent chapters are produced using Minitab rather than Excel. Strictly speaking, they are to illustrate the points made in the text and are not necessary to follow the material presented. While there are many excellent add-ons to Excel that would perform complex analyses and graphics, the basic Excel program itself does not contain all the ready-made functionalities of dedicated statistical software.

Concept Check

1. Why is it important to test the multiple regression model once it is developed? What would you test it for?

13.2 Problems

13.7 Examine the results shown here for a multiple regression analysis. How many predictors were there in this model? Comment on the overall significance of the regression model. Discuss the t values of the variables and their significance.

	Coefficient	Standard Error	t	p
Constant	4.096	1.2884	3.24	0.006
X_1	−5.111	1.8700	2.73	0.011
X_2	2.662	2.0796	1.28	0.212
X_3	1.557	1.2811	1.22	0.235
X_4	1.141	1.4712	0.78	0.445
X_5	1.650	1.4994	1.10	0.281
X_6	−1.248	1.2735	0.98	0.336
X_7	0.436	0.3617	1.21	0.239
X_8	0.962	1.1896	0.81	0.426
X_9	1.289	1.9182	0.67	0.508

$s_e = 3.503$ R-sq = 40.8%   R-sq(adj.) = 20.3%

ANOVA	DF	SS	MS	F	p
Regression	9	219.746	24.416	1.99	0.0825
Residual	26	319.004	12.269		
Total	35	538.750			

13.8 Displayed here is another output for a multiple regression analysis. Study the ANOVA table and the t values and use these to discuss the strengths of the regression model and the predictors. Does this model appear to fit the data well? From the information here, what recommendations would you make about the predictor variables in the model?

	Coefficient	Standard Error	t	p
Constant	34.672	5.256	6.6	0
X_1	0.07629	0.02234	3.41	0.005
X_2	0.000259	0.001031	0.25	0.805
X_3	−1.1212	0.9955	−1.13	0.23

$s_e = 9.722$ R-sq = 51.5%   R-sq(adj) = 40.4%

ANOVA	DF	SS	MS	F	p
Regression	3	1306.99	435.66	4.61	0.021
Residual	13	1228.78	94.52		
Total	16	2535.77			

13.9 Using the data in Problem 13.5, develop a multiple regression model to predict per capita personal consumption by the consumption of paper, fish, and gasoline. Discuss the output and pay particular attention to the F test and the t tests.

13.10 Using the data from Problem 13.6, develop a multiple regression model to predict insider ownership from debt ratio and dividend payout. Comment on the strength of the model and the predictors by examining the ANOVA table and the t tests.

13.11 Develop a multiple regression model to predict y from x_1, x_2, and x_3 using the following data. Discuss the values of F and t.

y	x_1	x_2	x_3
5.3	44	11	401
3.6	24	40	219
5.1	46	13	394
4.9	38	18	362
7.0	61	3	453
6.4	58	5	468
5.2	47	14	386
4.6	36	24	357
2.9	19	52	206
4.0	31	29	301
3.8	24	37	243
3.8	27	36	228
4.8	36	21	342
5.4	50	11	421
5.8	55	9	445

13.12 Use the following data to develop a regression model to predict y from x_1 and x_2. Comment on the output. Develop a regression model to predict y from x_1 only. Compare the results of this model with those of the model using both predictors. What might you conclude by examining the output from both regression models?

y	x_1	x_2
28	12.6	134
43	11.4	126
45	11.5	143
49	11.1	152
57	10.4	143
68	9.6	147
74	9.8	128
81	8.4	119
82	8.8	130
86	8.9	135
101	8.1	141
112	7.6	123
114	7.8	121
119	7.4	129
124	6.4	135

13.13 Study the following Excel multiple regression output. How many predictors are in this model? How many observations? What is the equation of the regression line? Discuss the strength of the model in terms of F. Which predictors, if any, are significant? Why or why not? Comment on the overall effectiveness of the model.

	A	B	C	D	E	F
1	Summary Output					
2	Regression Statistics					
3	Multiple R	0.842				
4	R Square	0.710				
5	Adjusted R Square	0.630				
6	Standard Error	109.430				
7	Observations	15				
8						
9	ANOVA					
10		df	SS	MS	F	Significance F
11	Regression	3	321946.82	107315.6	8.96	0.0027
12	Residual	11	131723.20	11974.8		
13	Total	14	453670.02			
14						
15		Coefficients	Standard Error	t Stat	P-value	
16	Intercept	657.053	167.460	3.92	.0024	
17	X Variable 1	5.7103	1.792	3.19	.0087	
18	X Variable 2	-0.4169	0.322	-1.29	.2222	
19	X Variable 3	-3.4715	1.443	-2.41	.0349	

Residuals, Standard Error of the Estimate, and R^2

LEARNING OBJECTIVE 13.3

Calculate the residual, standard error of the estimate, coefficient of multiple determination, and adjusted coefficient of multiple determination of a regression model.

Three more statistical tools for examining the strength of a regression model are the residuals, the standard error of the estimate, and the coefficient of multiple determination. See Thinking Critically About Statistics in Business Today 13.1 for a discussion of how multiple regression analysis is used to assess robots in a manufacturing facility.

Thinking Critically About Statistics in Business Today 13.1

Using Regression Analysis to Help Select a Robot

Several factors contribute to the success of a manufacturing firm in the world markets. Some examples are creating more efficient plants, lowering labour costs, increasing the quality of products, improving the standards of supplier materials, and learning more about international markets. Basically, success boils down to producing a better product for less cost.

One way to achieve that goal is to improve the technology of manufacturing facilities. Many companies use robots in plants to increase productivity and reduce labour costs. The science of selecting and purchasing robots is imperfect and often involves considerable subjectivity.

Two researchers, Moutaz Khouja and David Booth, devised a way to use multiple regression to assist decision-makers in robot selection. After sorting through 20 of the more promising variables, they found that the most important variables related to robot performance are repeatability, accuracy, load capacity, and velocity. Accuracy is measured by the distance between where the robot goes on a single trial and the centre of all points to which it goes on repeated trials. Repeatability is the radius of the circle that just includes all points to which the robot goes on repeated trials. Repeatability is of most concern to decision-makers because it is hardest to correct. Accuracy can be viewed as bias and is easier to correct. Load capacity is the maximum mass that the robot can handle, and velocity is the maximum tip velocity of the robot arm.

Khouja and Booth used data gathered from 27 robots and regression analysis to develop a multiple regression model that attempts to predict repeatability of robots (the variable of most concern for decision-makers) by their velocity and load capacity. Using the resulting regression model and the residuals of the fit, they developed a ranking system for selecting robots that takes into account repeatability, load capacity, velocity, and cost.

Things to Ponder

1. How does this multiple regression method assist decision-makers in their robot selection process? Is the ranking system alone enough to make a sound decision? Why or why not?

2. Can you think of other similar applications of multiple regression in business?

Sources: Adapted from Moutaz Khouja and David E. Booth, "A Decision Model for the Robot Selection Problem Using Robust Regression," *Decision Sciences* 22, no. 3 (July/August 1991): 656–662 (*Decision Sciences* is published by the Decision Sciences Institute, located at Georgia State University); "The Seven Keys to World Class Manufacturing" (white paper by Infor, Alpharetta, GA, 2007); "The Robotics Industry Is Looking into a Bright Future," International Federation of Robotics news release, September 18, 2013.

Residuals

The **residual**, or error, of the regression model is *the difference between the y value and the predicted value, $\hat{y}$*:

$$\text{Residual} = y - \hat{y}$$

The residuals for a multiple regression model are solved for in the same manner as they are with simple regression. First, a predicted value, $\hat{y}$, is determined by entering the value for each independent variable for a given set of observations into the multiple regression equation and solving for $\hat{y}$. Next, the value of $y - \hat{y}$ is computed for each set of observations. Shown here are the calculations for the residuals of the first set of observations from Table 13.1. The predicted value of y for $x_1 = 1,605$ and $x_2 = 35$ is:

$$\hat{y} = 57.4 + 0.0177(1,605) - 0.666(35) = 62.50$$
$$\text{Actual value of } y = 63.0$$
$$\text{Residual} = y - \hat{y} = 63.0 - 62.50 = 0.50$$

All residuals for the real estate data and the regression model displayed in Table 13.1 and Figure 13.3 are displayed in **Table 13.2**.

An examination of the residuals in Table 13.2 can reveal some information about the fit of the real estate regression model. The business analyst can observe the residuals and decide whether the errors are small enough to support the accuracy of the model. The warehouse price figures are in units of $1,000. Two of the 23 residuals are more than 20.00, meaning that the model is more than $20,000 off in its prediction. On the other hand, two residuals are less than 1, meaning that the model is less than $1,000 off in its prediction.

Residuals are also helpful in locating outliers. **Outliers** are *data points that are apart, or far, from the mainstream of the other data.* They are sometimes data points that were mistakenly recorded or measured. Because every data point influences the regression model, outliers can exert an overly important influence on the model based on their distance from other points. In Table 13.2, the eighth residual listed is −27.699. This error indicates that the regression model was not nearly as successful in predicting warehouse price on this particular warehouse as it was with others (an error of more than $27,000). For whatever reason, this data point stands somewhat apart from other data points and may be considered an outlier.

Residuals are also useful in testing the assumptions underlying regression analysis. **Figure 13.4** displays the residuals for the real estate example. In the top right is a graph of the residuals. Notice that residual variance seems to increase in the right half of the plot, indicating potential heteroscedasticity. As discussed in Chapter 12, one of the assumptions underlying regression analysis is that the error terms have homoscedasticity or homogeneous variance. That assumption might be violated in this example. The normal plot of residuals is nearly a straight line, indicating that the assumption of normally distributed error terms has probably not been violated.

TABLE 13.2 Residuals for the Real Estate Regression Model

y	$\hat{y}$	$y - \hat{y}$
63.0	62.499	0.501
65.1	71.485	−6.385
69.9	71.568	−1.668
76.8	78.639	−1.839
73.9	74.097	−0.197
77.9	75.653	2.247
74.9	83.012	−8.112
78.0	105.699	−27.699
79.0	68.523	10.477
83.4	81.139	2.261
79.5	88.282	−8.782
83.9	91.335	−7.435
79.7	85.618	−5.918
84.5	95.391	−10.891
96.0	85.456	10.544
109.5	102.774	6.726
102.5	97.665	4.835
121.0	107.183	13.817
104.9	109.352	−4.452
128.0	111.230	16.770
129.0	105.061	23.939
117.9	134.415	−16.515
140.0	132.430	7.570

FIGURE 13.4 Residual Diagnosis for the Real Estate Example

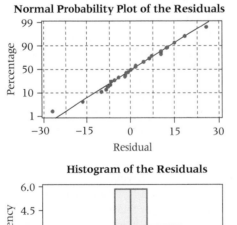

Normal Probability Plot of the Residuals

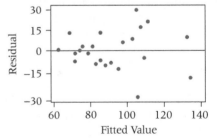

Residuals versus the Fitted Values

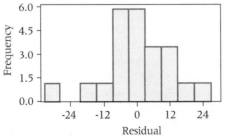

Histogram of the Residuals

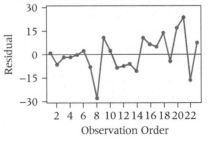

Residuals versus the Observation Order

3. The t ratios, which test the significance of the regression coefficients
4. The value of SSE
5. The value of s_e
6. The value of R^2
7. The value of adjusted R^2

From the data in the table, as shown under "Coefficients," the regression equation is $\hat{y} = 57.4 + 0.0177x_1 - 0.666x_2$.

	A	B	C	D	E	F
1	Summary Output					
2	Regression Statistics					
3	Multiple R	0.861				
4	R Square	0.741				
5	Adjusted R Square	0.715				
6	Standard Error	11.960				
7	Observations	23				
8						
9	ANOVA					
10		df	SS	MS	F	Significance F
11	Regression	2	8189.7	4094.9	28.63	0.000
12	Residual	20	2861.0	143.1		
13	Total	22	11050.7			
14						
15		Coefficients	Standard Error	t Stat	P-value	
16	Intercept	57.35	10.01	5.73	0.000	
17	Square Feet	0.017718	0.003146	5.63	0.000	
18	Age	-0.6663	0.228	-2.92	0.008	

Coefficient of determination
Adjusted R^2
Standard error of the estimate (s_e)
Analysis of variance (ANOVA) table
F test for the overall model
t test of regression coefficients and p-values

FIGURE 13.5 Annotated Version of the Excel Output of Regression for the Real Estate Example

DEMONSTRATION PROBLEM 13.2

Discuss the Excel multiple regression output for Demonstration Problem 13.1. Comment on the F test for the overall significance of the model, the t tests of the regression coefficients, and the values of s_e, R^2, and adjusted R^2.

Solution This regression analysis was done to predict the bank rate using the predictors unemployment rate and CPI. The equation of the regression model was presented in the solution of Demonstration Problem 13.1. Shown here is the complete multiple regression output of the data.

The value of F for this problem is 39.53, with a p-value of 0.0000, which is significant at $\alpha = 0.01$. On the basis of this information, the null hypothesis would be rejected for the overall test of significance. Both the regression coefficients are significantly different from zero, thus contributing to the predictability of the bank rate.

An examination of the t values supports this conclusion using an α of 0.01. The t value for unemployment rate is -4.58 with an associated p-value of 0.0006, and the t value of CPI is -8.10 with an associated p-value of 0.0000. Both p-values are highly significant.

The standard error of the estimate is $s_e = 0.646$, indicating that approximately 95% of the residuals are within $\pm 1.292 (2 \times 0.646)$. An examination of the Excel-produced residuals shows that actually 100% of the residuals fall in this interval. Financial analysts could examine the value of the standard error of the estimate to determine whether this model produces results with small enough error to suit their needs.

R^2 for this regression analysis is 0.868 or 86.8%; that is, 86.8% of the variation in the bank rate is accounted for by these two independent variables. Conversely, 13.2% of the variation is unaccounted for by this model. The value of the adjusted R^2 is 0.846, which is fairly close to the unadjusted R^2. We therefore conclude that the model provides a reasonable fit to the data.

By examining the values of F, t, s_e, R^2, and adjusted R^2, the business analyst can begin to understand whether the regression model provides any significant predictability for y.

	A	B	C	D	E	F	G	H	I
1	Summary Output								
2									
3	Regression Statistics								
4	Multiple R	0.93178593							
5	R Square	0.86822503							
6	Adjusted R Square	0.84626253							
7	Standard Error	0.64616563							
8	Observations	15							
9									
10	ANOVA								
11		df	SS	MS	F	Significance F			
12	Regression	2	33.011733	16.5058665	39.5321664	5.236E-06			
13	Residual	12	5.01036033	0.41753003					
14	Total	14	38.0220933						
15									
16		Coefficients	Standard Error	t Stat	P-value	Lower 95%	Upper 95%	Lower 95%	Upper 95%
17	Intercept	28.649562	2.94353949	9.73303131	4.7938E-07	22.2361404	35.0629837	22.2361404	35.0629837
18	Unemployment(%)	−1.1245498	0.24566969	−4.5774869	0.00063519	−1.6598181	−0.5892815	−1.6598181	−0.5892815
19	CPI	−0.163514	0.02017543	−8.1046102	3.2908E-06	−0.2074725	−0.1195555	−0.2074725	−0.1195555
20									
21									
22	Residual Output								
23									
24		Predicted							
25	Observation	Bank Rate	Residuals						
26	1	4.076	1.024						
27	2	4.651	0.269						
28	3	5.354	0.416						
29	4	4.465	−0.155						
30	5	3.639	−0.929						
31	6	3.392	−0.202						
32	7	3.580	−1.080						
33	8	3.752	−0.832						
34	9	3.987	0.323						
35	10	3.836	0.764						
36	11	3.413	−0.203						
37	12	0.741	−0.091						
38	13	0.751	0.099						
39	14	1.003	0.247						
40	15	0.900	0.350						
41									

Concept Check

1. What can we learn from the ANOVA table in a multiple regression analysis output?

13.4 Problems

13.22 Study the regression output that follows. How many predictors are there? What is the equation of the regression model? Using the key statistics discussed in this chapter, discuss the strength of the model and the predictors.

Regression Analysis: y versus x_1, x_2, x_3, x_4

Summary Output

Regression Statistics

R Square	0.802
Adjusted R Square	0.787
Standard Error	9.025
Observations	60

ANOVA	DF	SS	MS	F	p
Regression	4	18,088.5	4,522.1	55.52	0.000
Residual	55	4,479.7	81.4		
Total	59	22,568.2			

	Coefficient	Standard Error	t Stat	P-Value
Constant	−55.93	24.22	−2.31	0.025
x_1	0.01049	0.021	0.5	0.619
x_2	−0.1072	0.03503	−3.06	0.003
x_3	0.57922	0.07633	7.59	0.000
x_4	−0.8695	0.1498	−5.81	0.000

13.23 Study the Excel regression output that follows. How many predictors are there? What is the equation of the regression model? Using the key statistics discussed in this chapter, discuss the strength of the model and its predictors.

	A	B	C	D	E	F
1	Summary Output					
2	Regression Statistics					
3	Multiple R	0.814				
4	R Square	0.663				
5	Adjusted R Square	0.636				
6	Standard Error	51.761				
7	Observations	28				
8						
9	ANOVA					
10		df	SS	MS	F	Significance F
11	Regression	2	131567.0243	65783.5121	24.55	0.0000013
12	Residual	25	66979.6543	2679.1862		
13	Total	27	198546.6786			
14						
15		Coefficients	Standard Error	t Stat	P-value	
16	Intercept	203.3937	67.5177	3.01	0.0059	
17	x_1	1.1151	0.5278	2.11	0.0448	
18	x_2	−2.2115	0.5667	−3.90	0.0006	

13.5 Using Regression Analysis: Some Caveats

LEARNING OBJECTIVE 13.5

Understand the limitations and pitfalls of multiple regression analysis.

While regression analysis is easy to perform and easy to analyze, a host of problems can affect the results. Careless and casual use of the technique can result in conclusions that are incorrect and misleading. Fortunately, most such problems are well documented, and computer programs provide a number of diagnostics that would alert the analyst to their existence.

Influential Observations

Sometimes we get data points that are atypical, commonly known as *outliers*. These outliers affect the dependent variable in a way that is very different from other data points. These atypical observations can be so influential that they can actually change the regression line substantially. For instance, **Figure 13.6** shows the relationship between price and demand for a product for a group of buyers. It is clear from the figure that as the price goes up, the demand goes down.

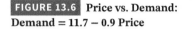
FIGURE 13.6 **Price vs. Demand:**
Demand = 11.7 − 0.9 Price

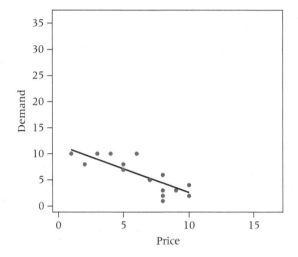

Suppose we find another buyer who buys the same product in large quantities at a very high price, as shown in **Figure 13.7**.

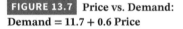
FIGURE 13.7 **Price vs. Demand:**
Demand = 11.7 + 0.6 Price

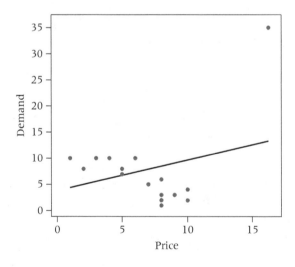

To accommodate this one single buyer, the regression equation changes. Now it looks as though the demand increases as the price goes up. When we find anomalous situations like this, removing the exceptional observation from the analysis would produce a different regression equation, which fits the remaining cases much better. The data point removed from the analysis is known as the influential observation since this observation "influences" the nature of the equation (for the worse).

The most common reasons for influential observations are: (1) atypical behaviour of some individuals in a sample and (2) mistakes in data entry. Since influential observations change the regression line such that it fits less well for the remaining observations, it is important

CHAPTER 14

Building Multiple Regression Models

LEARNING OBJECTIVES

This chapter presents several advanced topics in multiple regression analysis, enabling you to:

14.1 Generalize linear regression models as polynomial regression models using model transformation and Tukey's ladder of transformation, accounting for possible interaction among the independent variables.

14.2 Examine the role of indicator, or dummy, variables as predictors or independent variables in multiple regression analysis.

14.3 Use all possible regressions, stepwise regression, forward selection, and backward elimination search procedures to develop regression models that account for the most variation in the dependent variable and are parsimonious.

14.4 Recognize when multicollinearity is present, understanding general techniques for preventing and controlling it.

14.5 Explain when to use logistic regression, and interpret its results.

Decision Dilemma

Predicting CEO Salaries

Chief executive officers for large companies receive widely varying salaries for their work. What variables could contribute to the size of a CEO salary? Some possible company factors might include assets, sales, number of employees, type of industry, ownership structure, performance of the firm, and company location. Are any of these variables a determining factor in establishing a CEO salary? Do the personal characteristics of CEOs, such as age, experience, reputation, or academic degrees, matter in determining salary?

According to PayScale.com, skills that affect a CEO's salary can include team building, business strategy, strategic planning, and leadership. Generally, CEOs who have more years of relevant experience have higher salaries, although even those with less experience can enjoy high salaries. Surveys show that 45% of CEOs have 20 or more years of experience.

PayScale.com also reports that CEO pay varies with location. For example, pay rates for CEOs in Toronto average 23% more than the national average, in contrast to Winnipeg, where CEO salaries are 5% below the national average.

iStock.com/GBlakeley

The table contains data from 20 companies on four variables: (1) CEO salary in millions of dollars; (2) annual company revenue in billions of dollars; (3) number of company employees in thousands, and (4) type of company (manufacturing or not).

CEO Salary ($ millions)	Annual Company Revenue ($ billions)	Number of Employees (thousands)	Manufacturing Company (1 = Yes)
6.327	49.5	47.200	1
2.208	30.6	29.250	0
3.847	39.5	44.000	0
4.467	32.6	37.925	1
2.569	21.7	13.440	0
5.809	37.5	81.500	1
3.512	16.7	43.000	0
8.624	51.2	104.000	1
4.716	56.8	74.500	1
3.863	29.1	52.000	0
2.970	35.4	36.700	0
1.091	27.2	44.700	0
6.513	67.2	126.500	1
9.376	82.3	62.000	1
4.530	41.1	43.000	1
5.724	35.7	82.000	1
7.015	48.9	61.800	1
3.667	27.1	29.480	0
1.983	24.0	30.040	0
4.716	55.6	60.142	1

Managerial, Statistical, and Analytical Questions

1. Can a model be developed from these data and variables to predict CEO salaries?
2. If a model is developed, how can it be evaluated to determine how strong it is?
3. Is it possible to identify variables that appear to be related to CEO salary and determine which variables are more significant predictors?
4. Are some of the variables related to CEO salary but in a nonlinear manner?
5. Are some of the variables highly interrelated and redundant in their potential for determining CEO compensation?

Source: Adapted from CEO information adapted from PayScale.com at www.payscale.com/research/CA/Job=Chief_Executive_Officer_(CEO)/Salary.

Note: Data were created by Ken Black for illustrative purposes and do not necessarily reflect actual market conditions.

14.1 | Nonlinear Models: Mathematical Transformation

LEARNING OBJECTIVE 14.1

Generalize linear regression models as polynomial regression models using model transformation and Tukey's ladder of transformation, accounting for possible interaction among the independent variables.

The regression models presented thus far are based on the general linear regression model, which has the form:

General Linear Regression Model

$$y = \beta_0 + \beta_1 x_1 + \beta_2 x_2 + \cdots + \beta_k x_k + \varepsilon$$

where

β_0 = the regression constant

$\beta_1, \beta_2, \ldots, \beta_k$ are the partial regression coefficients for the k independent variables

$x_1, \ldots, x_k$ are the independent variables

k = the number of independent variables

In this general linear model, the parameters, β_i, are linear. This does not mean, however, that the dependent variable, y, is necessarily linearly related to the predictor variables. Scatter plots sometimes reveal a curvilinear relationship between x and y. Multiple regression response surfaces are not restricted to linear surfaces and may be curvilinear.

To this point, the variables, x_i, have represented different predictors. For example, in the real estate example presented in Chapter 13, the variables, x_1, x_2, represented two predictors: number of square feet in the warehouse and the age of the warehouse, respectively. Certainly, regression models can be developed for more than two predictors. For example, a marketing site location model could be developed in which sales, as the response variable, are predicted by population density, number of competitors, size of the store, and number of salespeople. Such a model could take the form:

$$y = \beta_0 + \beta_1 x_1 + \beta_2 x_2 + \beta_3 x_3 + \beta_4 x_4 + \varepsilon$$

This regression model has four x_i variables, each of which represents a different predictor.

The general linear model also applies to situations in which some x_i represent recoded data from a predictor variable already represented in the model by another independent variable. In some models, x_i represents variables that have undergone a mathematical transformation to allow the model to follow the form of the general linear model.

In this section, we explore some of these other models, including polynomial regression models, regression models with interaction, and models with transformed variables.

Polynomial Regression

Regression models in which the highest power of any predictor variable is 1 and in which there are no interaction terms—cross products $(x_i \cdot x_j)$—are referred to as *first-order models*. Simple regression models like those presented in Chapter 12 are *first-order models with one independent variable*. The general model for simple regression is:

$$y = \beta_0 + \beta_1 x_1 + \varepsilon$$

If a second independent variable is added, the model is referred to as a first-order model with two independent variables and appears as:

$$y = \beta_0 + \beta_1 x_1 + \beta_2 x_2 + \varepsilon$$

Polynomial regression models are regression models that are second- or higher-order models. They contain squared, cubed, or higher powers of the predictor variable(s) and contain response surfaces that are curvilinear. Yet, they are still special cases of the general linear model given in the General Linear Progression formula.

Consider a regression model with one independent variable where the model includes a second predictor, which is the independent variable squared. Such a model is referred to as a second-order model with one independent variable because the highest power among the predictors is 2, but there is still only one independent variable. This model takes the following form:

$$y = \beta_0 + \beta_1 x_1 + \beta_2 x_1^2 + \varepsilon$$

This model can be used to explore the possible fit of a quadratic model in predicting a dependent variable. A **quadratic regression model** is *a multiple regression model in which a variable and the square of that variable are the predictors*. How can this be a special case of the general linear model? Let x_2 of the general linear model be equal to x_1^2. Then, $y = \beta_0 + \beta_1 x_1 + \beta_2 x_1^2 + \varepsilon$ becomes $y = \beta_0 + \beta_1 x_1 + \beta_2 x_2 + \varepsilon$. What process does a business analyst go through to develop the regression constant and coefficients for a curvilinear model such as this one?

Multiple regression analysis assumes a linear fit of the regression coefficients and regression constant but not necessarily a linear relationship of the independent variable values (x). Hence, an analyst can often accomplish curvilinear regression by recoding the data before the multiple regression analysis is attempted (see Thinking Critically About Statistics in Business Today 14.1).

Thinking Critically About Statistics in Business Today 14.1

Predicting Export Intensity of Chinese Manufacturing Firms Using Multiple Regression Analysis

China is the world's top exporter of merchandise and is Canada's second-largest trading partner. What effects do external variables have on export performance? Researchers Hongxin Zhao and Shaoming Zou conducted a study of Chinese manufacturing firms and used multiple regression to determine whether both domestic market concentration and firm location are good predictors of a firm's export intensity. The study included 999 Chinese manufacturing firms that exported. The dependent variable was export intensity, defined to be the proportion of production output that is exported and computed by dividing the firm's export value by its production output value. The higher the proportion, the higher was the export intensity. Zhao and Zou used covariate techniques (beyond the scope of this text) to control for the fact that companies in the study varied by size, capital intensity, innovativeness, and industry. The independent variables were industry concentration and location. Industry concentration was computed as a ratio, with higher values indicating more concentration in the industry. The location variable was a composite index taking into account total freight volume, available modes of transportation, number of telephones, and size of geographic area.

The multiple regression model produced an R^2 of approximately 52%. Industry concentration was a statistically significant predictor at $\alpha = 0.01$, and the sign on the regression coefficient indicated that a negative relationship may exist between industry concentration and export intensity. This means that export intensity is lower in highly concentrated industries and higher in less concentrated industries. The researchers believe that in a more highly concentrated industry, the handful of firms dominating the industry will stifle the export competitiveness of firms. In the absence of dominating firms in a more fragmented setting, more competition and an increasing tendency to export are noted. The location variable was also a significant predictor at $\alpha = 0.01$. Firms located in coastal areas had higher export intensities than did those located in inland areas.

Things to Ponder

1. How would you modify this model to explicitly quantify the impact that total freight volume has on export intensity?
2. How could a new entrant to the Chinese manufacturing industry use this model in developing business strategies?
3. How could an importer of Chinese manufactured goods use this model in making import decisions?

Sources: Hongxin Zhao and Shaoming Zou, "The Impact of Industry Concentration and Firm Location on Export Propensity and Intensity: An Empirical Analysis of Chinese Manufacturing Firms," *Journal of International Marketing* 10, no. 1 (2002): 52–71; "Trade Profile: China," World Trade Organization, stat.wto.org/CountryProfile/WSDBCountryPFView.aspx?Country=CN&; "What Does Canada Trade with China?," CBC News online, July 12, 2012.

As an example, consider the data given in **Table 14.1**. This table contains sales volumes (in $ millions) for 13 manufacturing companies along with the number of manufacturer's representatives associated with each firm. A simple regression analysis to predict sales by the number of manufacturer's representatives results in the Excel output in **Figure 14.1**.

This regression output shows a regression model with an r^2 of 87.0%, a standard error of the estimate equal to 51.10, a significant overall F test for the model, and a significant t value for the predictor number of manufacturer's representatives.

Figure 14.2(a) is a scatter plot of the data in Table 14.1. Notice that the plot of number of representatives and sales is not a straight line and is an indication that the relationship between the two variables may be curvilinear. To explore the possibility that a quadratic relationship may exist between sales and number of representatives, the business analyst creates a second predictor variable, (number of manufacturer's representatives)^2, to use in the regression analysis to predict sales along with number of manufacturer's representatives, as

TABLE 14.1   **Sales Data for 13 Manufacturing Companies**

Manufacturer	Sales ($ millions)	Number of Manufacturer's Representatives
1	2.1	2
2	3.6	1
3	6.2	2
4	10.4	3
5	22.8	4
6	35.6	4
7	57.1	5
8	83.5	5
9	109.4	6
10	128.6	7
11	196.8	8
12	280.0	10
13	462.3	11

	A	B	C	D	E	F
1	SUMMARY OUTPUT					
2	Regression Statistics					
3	Multiple R	0.933				
4	R Square	0.870				
5	Adjusted R Square	0.858				
6	Standard Error	51.098				
7	Observations	13				
8						
9	ANOVA					
10		df	SS	MS	F	Significant F
11	Regression	1	192,395.416	192,395.416	73.69	0.0000033
12	Residual	11	28,721.452	2,611.041		
13	Total	12	221,116.868			
14						
15		Coefficients	Standard Error	t Stat	P-value	
16	Intercept	−107.029	28.7373	−3.72	0.0033561	
17	Reps	41.026	4.7794	8.58	0.0000033	

FIGURE 14.1 Excel Simple Regression Output for Manufacturing Example

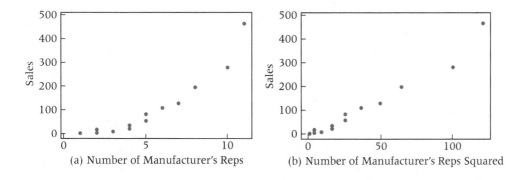

(a) Number of Manufacturer's Reps

(b) Number of Manufacturer's Reps Squared

FIGURE 14.2 Scatter Plots of Manufacturing Data

shown in Table 14.2. Thus, a variable can be created to explore second-order parabolic relationships by squaring the data from the independent variable of the linear model and entering it into the analysis. Figure 14.2(b) is a scatter plot of sales with (number of manufacturer's reps)^2. Note that this graph, with the squared term, more closely approaches a straight line than does the graph in Figure 14.2(a). By recoding the predictor variable, the analyst creates a potentially better regression fit.

TABLE 14.2 Display of Manufacturing Data with Newly Created Variable

Manufacturer	Sales ($ millions) y	Number of Manufacturer's Reps x_1	(Number of Manufacturer's Reps)^2 $x_2 = (x_1)^2$
1	2.1	2	4
2	3.6	1	1
3	6.2	2	4
4	10.4	3	9
5	22.8	4	16
6	35.6	4	16
7	57.1	5	25
8	83.5	5	25
9	109.4	6	36
10	128.6	7	49
11	196.8	8	64
12	280.0	10	100
13	462.3	11	121

With these data, a multiple regression model can be developed. **Figure 14.3** shows the Excel output for the regression analysis to predict sales by number of manufacturer's representatives and (number of manufacturer's representatives)^2.

FIGURE 14.3 Excel Output for Quadratic Model of Manufacturing Example

	A	B	C	D	E	F
1	SUMMARY OUTPUT					
2	Regression Statistics					
3	Multiple R	0.986				
4	R Square	0.973				
5	Adjusted R Square	0.967				
6	Standard Error	24.593				
7	Observations	13				
8						
9	ANOVA					
10		df	SS	MS	F	Significance F
11	Regression	2	215068.6001	107534.3	177.79	0.000000015
12	Residual	10	6048.3	604.8		
13	Total	12	221116.8677			
14						
15		Coefficients	Standard Error	t Stat	P-value	
16	Intercept	18.067	24.673	0.73	0.4808	
17	Reps	−15.723	9.550	−1.65	0.1307	
18	RepsSq	4.750	0.776	6.12	0.0001	

Examine the output in Figure 14.3 and compare it with the output in Figure 14.1 for the simple regression model. The R^2 for this model is 97.3%, which is an increase from the r^2 of 87.0% for the single linear predictor model. The standard error of the estimate for this model is 24.59, which is considerably lower than the 51.10 value obtained from the simple regression model. Remember, the sales figures were in millions of dollars. The quadratic model reduced the standard error of the estimate by 26.51($1,000,000), or $26,510,000. It appears that the quadratic model is a better model for predicting sales.

An examination of the t statistic for the squared term and its associated probability in Figure 14.3 shows that it is statistically significant at $\alpha = 0.001$ ($t = 6.12$ with a probability of 0.0001). If this t statistic were not significant, the analyst would most likely drop the squared term and revert to the first-order model (simple regression model).

Company	Sales ($ millions/year)	Advertising ($ millions/year)
1	2,580	1.2
2	11,942	2.6
3	9,845	2.2
4	27,800	3.2
5	18,926	2.9
6	4,800	1.5
7	14,550	2.7

One mathematical model that is a good candidate for fitting these data is an exponential model of the form:

$$y = \beta_0 \beta_1^x \varepsilon$$

This model can be transformed (by taking the log of each side) so that it is in the form of the general linear equation:

$$\log y = \log \beta_0 + x \log \beta_1 + \log \varepsilon$$

This transformed model requires a recoding of the y data through the use of logarithms. Notice that x is not recoded but that the regression constant, coefficient, and error are in logarithmic scale. If we let $y' = \log y$, $\beta_0' = \log \beta_0$, $\beta_1' = \log \beta_1$, and $\varepsilon' = \log \varepsilon$, the exponential model is in the form of the general linear model:

$$y' = \beta_0' + \beta_1' x + \varepsilon'$$

The process begins by taking the log of the y values. The data used to build the regression model and the Excel regression output for these data follow.

Log Sales (y)	Advertising (x)
3.4116	1.2
4.0771	2.6
3.9932	2.2
4.4440	3.2
4.2771	2.9
3.6812	1.5
4.1629	2.7

	A	B	C	D	E	F
1	SUMMARY OUTPUT					
2	Regression Statistics					
3	Multiple R	0.990				
4	R Square	0.980				
5	Adjusted R Square	0.977				
6	Standard Error	0.0543				
7	Observations	7				
8						
9	ANOVA					
10		df	SS	MS	F	Significance F
11	Regression	1	0.739215	0.739215	250.36	0.000018
12	Residual	5	0.014763	0.002953		
13	Total	6	0.753979			
14						
15		Coefficients	Standard Error	t Stat	P-value	
16	Intercept	2.9003	0.0729	39.80	0.00000019	
17	Advertising (x)	0.4751	0.0300	15.82	0.00001834	

A simple regression model (without the log recoding of the y variable) yields an R^2 of 87%, whereas the exponential model R^2 is 98%. The t statistic for advertising is 15.82 with a p-value of 0.00001834 in the exponential model and 5.77 with a p-value of 0.00219 in the simple regression model. Thus, the exponential model gives a better fit than does the simple regression model. An examination of (x^2, y) and (x^3, y) models reveals R^2 of 0.930 and 0.969, respectively, which are quite high but still not as good as the R^2 yielded by the exponential model.

The resulting equation of the exponential regression model is:

$$y = 2.9003 + 0.4751x$$

In using this regression equation to determine predicted values of y for x, remember that the resulting predicted y value is in logarithmic form, and the antilog of the predicted y must be taken to get the predicted y value in raw units. For example, to get the predicted y value (sales) for an advertising figure of 2.0 ($ millions), substitute $x = 2.0$ into the regression equation:

$$y = 2.9003 + 0.4751x = 2.9003 + 0.4751(2.0) = 3.8505$$

The log of sales is 3.8505. Taking the antilog of 3.8505 results in the predicted sales in raw units:

$$\text{antilog } (3.8505) = 7{,}087.61(\$ \text{ millions})$$

Thus, the exponential regression model predicts that $2.0 million of advertising will result in $7,087.61 million in sales.

Other ways can be used to transform mathematical models so that they can be treated like the general linear model. One example is an inverse model such as:

$$y = \frac{1}{\beta_0 + \beta_1 x_1 + \beta_2 x_2 + \varepsilon}$$

Such a model can be manipulated algebraically into the form:

$$\frac{1}{y} = \beta_0 + \beta_1 x_1 + \beta_2 x_2 + \varepsilon$$

Substituting $y' = 1/y$ into this equation results in an equation that is in the form of the general linear model:

$$y' = \beta_0 + \beta_1 x_1 + \beta_2 x_2 + \varepsilon$$

To use this "inverse" model, recode the data values for y by using $1/y$. The regression analysis is done on the $1/y$, x_1, and x_2 data. To get predicted values of y from this model, enter the raw values of x_1 and x_2. The resulting predicted value of y from the regression equation will be the inverse of the actual predicted y value.

DEMONSTRATION PROBLEM 14.1

In the aerospace and defence industry, some cost estimators have predicted the cost of new space projects by using mathematical models that take the form:

$$y = \beta_0 x^{\beta_1} \varepsilon$$

These cost estimators often use the weight of the object being sent into space as the predictor (x) and the cost of the object as the dependent variable (y). Quite often β_1 turns out to be a value between 0 and 1, resulting in the predicted value of y equalling some root of x.

Using the sample cost data given here, develop a cost regression model in the form just shown to determine the equation for the predicted value of y. Use this regression equation to predict the value of y for $x = 3,000$.

y ($ billions)	x (mass in tonnes)
1.2	450
9.0	20,200
4.5	9,060
3.2	3,500
13.0	75,600
0.6	175
1.8	800
2.7	2,100

Solution The equation:

$$y = \beta_0 x^{\beta_1} \varepsilon$$

is not in the form of the general linear model, but it can be transformed by using logarithms:

$$\log y = \log \beta_0 + \beta_1 \log x + \log \varepsilon$$

which takes on the general linear form:

$$y' = \beta_0' + \beta_1 x'$$

where

$y' = \log y$
$\beta_0' = \log \beta_0 + \log \varepsilon$
$x' = \log x$

This equation requires that both x and y be recoded by taking the logarithm of each.

log y	log x
0.0792	2.6532
0.9542	4.3054
0.6532	3.9571
0.5051	3.5441
1.1139	4.8785
−0.2218	2.2430
0.2553	2.9031
0.4314	3.3222

Using these data, the computer produces the following regression constant and coefficient:

$$b_0' = -1.25292 \quad b_1 = 0.49606$$

From these values, the equation of the predicted y value is determined to be:

$$\log \hat{y} = -1.25292 + 0.49606 \log x$$

If $x = 3,000$, $\log x = 3.47712$, and

$$\log \hat{y} = -1.25292 + 0.49606(3.47712) = 0.47194$$

then

$$\hat{y} = \text{antilog}(\log \hat{y}) = \text{antilog}(0.47194) = 2.9644$$

The predicted value of y is $2.9644 billion for $x = 3,000$ tonnes. Taking the antilog of $b_0' = -1.25292$ yields 0.055857. From this and $b_1 = 0.49606$, the model can be written in the original form:

$$y = (0.055857)x^{0.49606}$$

Substituting $x = 3,000$ into this formula also yields $2.9645 billion for the predicted value of y.

Concept Check

1. What are first-order models and how are they different from second-order models?
2. What is a quadratic model?
3. In what context would you use the ladder of transformation?
4. What is Tukey's four-quadrant approach? When is it useful?

14.1 Problems

14.1 Use the following data to develop a quadratic model to predict y from x. Develop a simple regression model from the data and compare the results of the two models. Does the quadratic model seem to provide any better predictability? Why or why not?

x	y	x	y
14	200	15	247
9	74	8	82
6	29	5	21
21	456	10	94
17	320		

14.2 Develop a multiple regression model of the form:

$$y = b_0 b_1^x \varepsilon$$

using the following data to predict y from x. From a scatter plot and Tukey's ladder of transformation, explore ways to recode the data and develop an alternative regression model. Compare the results.

y	x	y	x
2485	3.87	740	2.83
1790	3.22	4010	3.62
874	2.91	3629	3.52
2190	3.42	8010	3.92
3610	3.55	7047	3.86
2847	3.61	5680	3.75
1350	3.13	1740	3.19

14.3 The Publishers Information Bureau in New York City released magazine advertising expenditure data compiled by leading national advertisers. The data were organized by product type over several years. Shown here are data on total magazine advertising expenditures and household equipment and supplies advertising expenditures. Using these data, develop a regression model to predict total magazine advertising expenditures by household equipment and supplies advertising expenditures and by (household equipment and supplies advertising expenditures)^2. Compare this model to a regression model to predict total magazine advertising expenditures by only household equipment and supplies advertising expenditures. Construct a scatter plot of the data. Does the shape of the plot suggest some alternative models in light of Tukey's four-quadrant approach? If so, develop at least one other model and compare the model with the other two previously developed.

Total Magazine Advertising Expenditures ($ millions)	Household Equipment and Supplies Expenditures ($ millions)
1193	34
2846	65
4668	98
5120	93
5943	102
6644	103

14.4 Dun & Bradstreet reports, among other things, information about new business incorporations and number of business failures over the years. Shown here are data on business failures and current liabilities of the failing companies over several years. Use these data and the following model to predict current liabilities of the failing companies by the number of business failures:

$$y = b_0 b_1^x \varepsilon$$

Discuss the strength of the model. Now develop a different regression model by recoding x. Use Tukey's four-quadrant approach as a resource. Compare your models.

Rate of Business Failures (10,000s)	Current Liabilities of Failing Companies ($ millions)
44	1,888
43	4,380
42	4,635
61	6,955
88	15,611
110	16,073
107	29,269
115	36,937
120	44,724
102	34,724
98	39,126
65	44,261

14.5 Use the following data to develop a curvilinear model to predict y. Include both x_1 and x_2 in the model in addition to x_1^2 and x_2^2 and the interaction term $x_1 x_2$. Comment on the overall strength of the model and the significance of each predictor. Develop a regression model with the same independent variables as the first model but without the interaction variable. Compare this model with the model with interaction.

y	x_1	x_2
47.8	6	7.1
29.1	1	4.2
81.8	11	10.0
54.3	5	8.0
29.7	3	5.7
64.0	9	8.8
37.4	3	7.1
44.5	4	5.4

42.1	4	6.5
31.6	2	4.9
78.4	11	9.1
71.9	9	8.5
17.4	2	4.2
28.8	1	5.8
34.7	2	5.9
57.6	6	7.8
84.2	12	10.2
63.2	8	9.4
39.0	3	5.7
47.3	5	7.0

14.6 What follows is Excel output from a regression model to predict y using x_1, x_2, x_1^2, x_2^2, and the interaction term, x_1x_2. Comment on the overall strength of the model and the significance of each predictor. The data follow the Excel output. Develop a regression model with the same independent variables as the first model but without the interaction variable. Compare this model with the model with interaction.

	A	B	C	D	E	F
1	SUMMARY OUTPUT					
2	Regression Statistics					
3	Multiple R	0.954				
4	R Square	0.910				
5	Adjusted R Square	0.878				
6	Standard Error	7.544				
7	Observations	20				
8						
9	ANOVA					
10		df	SS	MS	F	Significance F
11	Regression	5	8089.275	1617.855	28.43	0.00000073
12	Residual	14	796.725	56.909		
13	Total	19	8886			
14						
15		Coefficients	Standard Error	t Stat	P-value	
16	Intercept	464.4433	503.0955	0.92	0.3716	
17	x_1	−10.5101	6.0074	−1.75	0.1021	
18	x_2	−1.2212	1.9791	−0.62	0.5471	
19	x_1^2	0.0357	0.0195	1.84	0.0876	
20	x_2^2	−0.0002	0.0021	−0.08	0.9394	
21	x_1x_2	0.0243	0.0107	2.28	0.0390	

y	x_1	x_2	y	x_1	x_2
34	120	190	45	96	245
56	105	240	34	79	288
78	108	238	23	66	312
90	110	250	89	88	315
23	78	255	76	80	320
34	98	230	56	73	335
45	89	266	43	69	335
67	92	270	23	75	250
78	95	272	45	63	372
65	85	288	56	74	360

Indicator (Dummy) Variables

LEARNING OBJECTIVE 14.2

Examine the role of indicator, or dummy, variables as predictors or independent variables in multiple regression analysis.

Some variables are referred to as **qualitative variables** (as opposed to *quantitative* variables) because qualitative variables do not yield quantifiable outcomes. Instead, *qualitative variables yield nominal- or ordinal-level information,* which is used more to categorize items. These variables have a role in multiple regression and are referred to as indicator, or dummy, variables. In this section, we will examine the role of **indicator** or **dummy variables** as predictors or independent variables in multiple regression analysis.

Indicator variables arise in many ways in business analytics. Questionnaire or personal interview demographic questions are prime candidates because they tend to generate qualitative measures on such items as gender, geographic region, occupation, marital status, level of education, economic class, political affiliation, religion, management/nonmanagement status, buying/ leasing a home, method of transportation, or type of broker. In one business study, business analysts were attempting to develop a multiple regression model to predict the distances shoppers drive to malls in the Greater Toronto Area. One independent variable was whether the mall was located near Highway 401. In a second study, a site location model for pizza restaurants included indicator variables for (1) whether the restaurant served beer and (2) whether the restaurant had a salad bar.

These indicator variables are qualitative in that no interval or ratio level measurement is assigned to a response. For example, if a mall is located near the 401, a score of 20 or 30 or 75 because of its location makes no sense. In terms of sex, what value would you assign to a man or a woman in a regression study? Yet these types of indicator, or dummy, variables are often useful in multiple regression studies and can be included if they are coded in the proper format.

Most analysts code indicator variables by using 0 or 1. For example, in the shopping mall study, malls located near the 401 could be assigned a 1, and all other malls would then be assigned a 0. The assignment of 0 or 1 is arbitrary, with the number merely holding a place for the category. For this reason, the coding is referred to as "dummy" coding; the number represents a category by holding a place and is not a measurement.

Many indicator, or dummy, variables are dichotomous, such as student/not a student, salad bar/no salad bar, employed/not employed, and lease/own. For these variables, a value of 1 is arbitrarily assigned to one category and a value of 0 is assigned to the other category. Some qualitative variables contain several categories, such as the variable "type of job" which might have the categories assembler, painter, and inspector. In this case, it is tempting to use a coding of 1, 2, and 3, respectively. However, that type of coding creates problems for multiple regression analysis. For one thing, the category inspector would receive a value that is three times that of painter. In addition, the values of 1, 2, and 3 indicate a hierarchy of job types: assembler < painter < inspector. The proper way to code such indicator variables is with the 0, 1 coding. Two separate independent variables should be used to code the three categories of type of job. The first variable is assembler, where a 1 is recorded if the person's job is assembler and a 0 is recorded if it is not. The second variable is painter, where a 1 is recorded if the person's job is painter and a 0 is recorded if it is not. A variable should not be assigned to inspector, because all workers in the study for whom a 1 was not recorded either for the assembler variable or the painter variable must be inspectors. Thus, coding the inspector variable would result in redundant information and is not necessary. This reasoning holds for all indicator variables with more than two categories. If an indicator variable has c categories, then $c - 1$ dummy variables must be created and inserted into the regression analysis in order to include the indicator variable in the multiple regression.[2]

---

[2] If c indicator variables are included in the analysis, no unique estimator of the regression coefficients can be found. J. Neter, M. H. Kuter, W. Wasserman, and C. Nachtsheim, *Applied Linear Regression Models*, 3rd ed. (Chicago: Richard D. Irwin, 1996).

An example of an indicator variable with more than two categories is the result of the following question taken from a typical questionnaire.

Your office is located in which region of the country?

_____ Atlantic _____ Quebec _____ Ontario _____ West

Suppose a business analyst is using a multiple regression analysis to predict the cost of doing business and believes geographic location of the office is a potential predictor. How does the analyst insert this qualitative variable into the analysis? Because $c = 4$ for this question, three dummy variables are inserted into the analysis. Table 14.4 shows one possible way this process works with 13 respondents. Note that rows 2, 7, and 11 contain all zeros, which indicate that those respondents have offices in the West. Thus, a fourth dummy variable for the West region is not necessary and, indeed, should not be included because the information contained in such a fourth variable is contained in the other three variables.

TABLE 14.4	Coding for the Indicator Variable of Geographic Location for Regression Analysis	
Atlantic x_1	Quebec x_2	Ontario x_3
1	0	0
0	0	0
1	0	0
0	0	1
0	1	0
0	1	0
0	0	0
0	0	1
1	0	0
1	0	0
0	0	0
0	1	0
0	0	1

A word of caution is in order. Because of degrees of freedom and interpretation considerations, it is important that a multiple regression analysis have enough observations to adequately handle the number of independent variables entered. Some analysts recommend as a guideline at least three observations per independent variable. If a qualitative variable has multiple categories, resulting in several dummy independent variables, and if several qualitative variables are being included in an analysis, the number of predictors can rather quickly exceed the limit of recommended number of variables per number of observations. Nevertheless, dummy variables can be useful and are a way in which nominal or ordinal information can be recoded and incorporated into a multiple regression model.

As an example, consider the issue of sex discrimination in the salary earnings of workers in some industries. In examining this issue, suppose a random sample of 15 workers is drawn from a pool of employed labourers in a particular industry and the workers' average monthly salaries are determined, along with their age and sex. The data are shown in Table 14.5. As sex can be only male or female, this variable is a dummy variable requiring 0, 1 coding.

TABLE 14.5 Data for the Monthly Salary Example

Monthly Salary ($ thousands)	Age (in decades)	Sex (1 = male, 0 = female)
2.548	3.2	1
2.629	3.8	1
2.011	2.7	0
2.229	3.4	0
2.746	3.6	1
2.528	4.1	1
2.018	3.8	0
2.190	3.4	0
2.551	3.3	1
1.985	3.2	0
2.610	3.5	1
2.432	2.9	1
2.215	3.3	0
1.990	2.8	0
2.585	3.5	1

Suppose we arbitrarily let 1 denote male and 0 denote female. **Figure 14.7** is the multiple regression model developed from the data of Table 14.5 to predict the dependent variable, monthly salary, by two independent variables, age and sex.

FIGURE 14.7 Regression Analysis for the Monthly Salary Example

	A	B	C	D	E	F
1	SUMMARY OUTPUT					
2	Regression Statistics					
3	Multiple R	0.943391				
4	R Square	0.889987				
5	Adjusted R Square	0.871652				
6	Standard Error	0.096792				
7	Observations	15				
8						
9	ANOVA					
10		df	SS	MS	F	Significance F
11	Regression	2	0.909488	0.454744	48.53914	1.77E-06
12	Residual	12	0.112423	0.009369		
13	Total	14	1.021912			
14						
15		Coefficients	Standard Error	t Stat	P-value	
16	Intercept	1.732061	0.235584	3.107425	0.009064	
17	Age (10 years)	0.11122	0.072083	1.542937	0.148796	
18	Sex (1= male, 0 = female)	0.458684	0.053458	8.58019	1.82E-06	

The Excel computer output in Figure 14.7 contains the regression equation (under Coefficients) for this model:

$$\text{Salary} = 1.732 + 0.111(\text{age}) + 0.459(\text{sex})$$

An examination of the t values reveals that the dummy variable "sex" has a regression coefficient that is significant at $\alpha = 0.001$ ($t = 8.58$, $p = 0.000$). The overall model is significant at $\alpha = 0.001$ ($F = 48.54$, $p = 0.000$). The standard error of the estimate, $s_e = 0.09679$, indicates that approximately 68% of the errors of prediction are within $\pm\$96.79$ ($0.09679 \times \$1,000$). The R^2 is relatively high at 89.0%, and the adjusted R^2 is 87.2%.

The t value for sex indicates that it is a significant predictor of monthly salary in this model. This significance is apparent when one looks at the effects of this dummy variable in another way. **Figure 14.8** shows the graph of the regression equation when sex = 1 (male) and the graph of the regression equation when sex = 0 (female). When sex = 1 (male), the regression equation becomes:

$$1.732 + 0.111(\text{age}) + 0.459(1) = 2.191 + 0.111(\text{age})$$

When sex = 0 (female), the regression equation becomes:

$$1.732 + 0.111(\text{Age}) + 0.459(0) = 1.732 + 0.111(\text{Age})$$

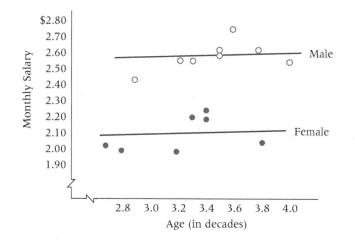

FIGURE 14.8 Regression Model for Male and Female

The full regression model (with both predictors) has a response surface that is a plane in a three-dimensional space. However, if a value of 1 is entered for sex into the full regression model, as just shown, the regression model is reduced to a line passing through the plane formed by monthly salary and age. If a value of 0 is entered for sex, as shown, the full regression model also reduces to a line passing through the plane formed by monthly salary and age. Figure 14.8 displays these two lines. Notice that the only difference in the two lines is the y-intercept. Observe the monthly salary with male sex, as depicted by ○, versus the monthly salary with female sex, depicted by ●. The difference in the y-intercepts of these two lines is 0.459, which is the value of the regression coefficient for sex. This intercept figure signifies that, on average, men earn \$459 per month more than women for this population.

Concept Check

1. What is an indicator or a dummy variable? Give three examples.
2. How would you code a dummy variable with three categories?

14.2 Problems

14.7 Analyze the following data by using a multiple regression computer software package to predict y using x_1 and x_2. Notice that x_2 is a dummy variable. Discuss the output from the regression analysis; in particular, comment on the predictability of the dummy variable.

y	x_1	x_2
16.8	27	1
13.2	16	0
14.7	13	0
15.4	11	1
11.1	17	0
16.2	19	1
14.9	24	1
13.3	21	0
17.8	16	1
17.1	23	1
14.3	18	0
13.9	16	0

14.8 Given here are the data from a dependent variable and two independent variables. The second independent variable is an indicator variable with several categories. Hence, this variable is represented by x_2, x_3, and x_4. How many categories are needed in total for this independent variable? Use a computer to perform a multiple regression analysis on this data to predict y from the x values. Discuss the output and pay particular attention to the dummy variables.

y	x_1	x_2	x_3	x_4
11	1.9	1	0	0
3	1.6	0	1	0
2	2.3	0	1	0
5	2.0	0	0	1
9	1.8	0	0	0
14	1.9	1	0	0
10	2.4	1	0	0
8	2.6	0	0	0
4	2.0	0	1	0
9	1.4	0	0	0
11	1.7	1	0	0
4	2.5	0	0	1
6	1.0	1	0	0
10	1.4	0	0	0
3	1.9	0	1	0
4	2.3	0	1	0
9	2.2	0	0	0
6	1.7	0	0	1

14.9 The output displayed here is the result of a multiple regression analysis with three independent variables. Variable x_1 is a dummy variable. Discuss the computer output and the role x_1 plays in this regression model.

```
The regression equation is
Y = 121 + 13.4 X₁ −0.632 X₂ + 1.42 X₃
Predictor       Coef      Stdev        T         p
Constant      121.31     11.56     10.50      .000
X₁             13.355     4.714      2.83      .014
X₂            -0.6322    0.2270     -2.79      .015
X₃             1.421     3.342       0.43      .678
S = 7.041 R-sq =79.5%        R-sq(adj) = 74.7%


Analysis of Variance
Source         df        SS       MS       F       p
Regression      3    2491.98   830.66   16.76    .000
Error          13     644.49    49.58
Total          16    3136.47
```

14.10 Given here is Excel output for a multiple regression model that was developed to predict y from two independent variables, x_1 and x_2. Variable x_2 is a dummy variable. Discuss the strength of the multiple regression model on the basis of the output. Focus on the contribution of the dummy variable. Plot x_1 and y with x_2 as 0, and then plot x_1 and y with x_2 as 1. Compare the two lines and discuss the differences.

	A	B	C	D	E	F
1	SUMMARY OUTPUT					
2	Regression Statistics					
3	Multiple R	0.623				
4	R Square	0.388				
5	Adjusted R Square	0.341				
6	Standard Error	11.744				
7	Observations	29				
8						
9	ANOVA					
10		df	SS	MS	F	Significance F
11	Regression	2	2270.11	1135.05	8.23	0.0017
12	Residual	26	3585.75	137.91		
13	Total	28	5855.86			
14						
15		Coefficients	Standard Error	t Stat	P-value	
16	Intercept	41.225	6.380	6.46	0.00000076	
17	x_1	1.081	1.353	0.80	0.4316	
18	x_2	−18.404	4.547	−4.05	0.0004	

14.11 A business analyst developed a multiple regression model to predict the average price of a meal at a restaurant in a western city. After exploring several variables that might affect the average price, the analyst decides the three most important variables that decide the price of a meal are (1) how long the restaurant is open (i.e., how many hours in a week), (2) how likely you are to be seated when you get to the restaurant, and (3) whether the restaurant is downtown or not. Use the following data and a computer to develop such a model. Comment on the output.

Price	Hours	Probability of Being Seated	Downtown[*]
$ 5.55	72	0.37	0
7.76	55	0.64	0
12.26	48	0.51	1
15.00	60	0.32	1
9.15	52	0.62	0
6.48	62	0.83	0
8.49	65	0.62	0
20.95	48	0.43	1
15.90	50	0.58	1
6.23	68	0.74	0
11.99	55	0.19	1
24.86	56	0.49	1
14.00	62	0.80	0
19.05	70	0.75	1

[*]0 = not located in downtown; 1 = located in downtown

14.12 A business analyst gathered 155 observations on four variables: job satisfaction, occupation, industry, and marital status. She wants to develop a multiple regression model to predict job satisfaction by the other three variables. All three predictor variables are qualitative variables with the following categories.

1. Occupation: accounting, management, marketing, finance
2. Industry: manufacturing, health care, transportation
3. Marital status: married, single

How many variables will be in the regression model? Delineate the number of predictors needed in each category and discuss the total number of predictors.

14.3 Model Building: Search Procedures

LEARNING OBJECTIVE 14.3

Use all possible regressions, stepwise regression, forward selection, and backward elimination search procedures to develop regression models that account for the most variation in the dependent variable and are parsimonious.

To this point in the chapter, we have explored various types of multiple regression models. We evaluated the strengths of regression models and learned more about the output from multiple regression computer packages. In this section, we examine procedures for developing several multiple regression model options to aid in the decision-making process.

Suppose a business analyst wants to develop a multiple regression model to predict the world production of crude oil. The analyst realizes that much of the world crude oil market is driven by variables related to usage and production in the U.S. The analyst decides to use as predictors the following five independent variables:

1. U.S. energy consumption
2. Gross U.S. nuclear electricity generation
3. U.S. coal production
4. Total U.S. dry gas (natural gas) production
5. Fuel rate of U.S.-owned automobiles

The analyst measured data for each of these variables for the year preceding each data point of world crude oil production, figuring that the world production is driven by the previous year's activities in the U.S. It would seem that, as the energy consumption of the U.S. increased, so would world production of crude oil. In addition, it makes sense that as nuclear electricity generation, coal production, dry gas production, and fuel rates increased, world crude oil production would decrease if energy consumption stayed approximately constant. Table 14.6 shows data for the five independent variables along with the dependent variable,

TABLE 14.6   Data for Multiple Regression Model to Predict Crude Oil Production

World Crude Oil Production (million barrels per day)	U.S. Energy Consumption (quadrillion BTUs generation per year)	U.S. Nuclear Electricity (billion kilowatt-hours)	U.S. Coal Gross Production (million short tons)	U.S. Total Dry Gas Production (trillion cubic feet)	U.S. Fuel Rate for Automobiles (miles per gallon)
55.7	74.3	83.5	598.6	21.7	13.4
55.7	72.5	114.0	610.0	20.7	13.6
52.8	70.5	172.5	654.6	19.2	14.0
57.3	74.4	191.1	684.9	19.1	13.8
59.7	76.3	250.9	697.2	19.2	14.1
60.2	78.1	276.4	670.2	19.1	14.3
62.7	78.9	255.2	781.1	19.7	14.6
59.6	76.0	251.1	829.7	19.4	16.0
56.1	74.0	272.7	823.8	19.2	16.5
53.5	70.8	282.8	838.1	17.8	16.9
53.3	70.5	293.7	782.1	16.1	17.1
54.5	74.1	327.6	895.9	17.5	17.4
54.0	74.0	383.7	883.6	16.5	17.5
56.2	74.3	414.0	890.3	16.1	17.4
56.7	76.9	455.3	918.8	16.6	18.0
58.7	80.2	527.0	950.3	17.1	18.8
59.9	81.4	529.4	980.7	17.3	19.0
60.6	81.3	576.9	1029.1	17.8	20.3
60.2	81.1	612.6	996.0	17.7	21.2
60.2	82.2	618.8	997.5	17.8	21.0
60.2	83.9	610.3	945.4	18.1	20.6
61.0	85.6	640.4	1033.5	18.8	20.8
62.3	87.2	673.4	1033.0	18.6	21.1
64.1	90.0	674.7	1063.9	18.8	21.2
66.3	90.6	628.6	1089.9	18.9	21.5
67.0	89.7	666.8	1109.8	18.9	21.6

world crude oil production. Using the data presented in Table 14.6, the analyst attempted to develop a multiple regression model using five different independent variables. The result of this process was the output in **Figure 14.9**. Examining the output, the analyst can reach some conclusions about that particular model and its variables.

	A	B	C	D	E	F
1	SUMMARY OUTPUT					
2	Regression Statistics					
3	Multiple R	0.959674				
4	R Square	0.920975				
5	Adjusted R Square	0.901218				
6	Standard Error	1.214705				
7	Observations	26				
8						
9	ANOVA					
10		df	SS	MS	F	Significance F
11	Regression	5	343.9264	68.78328	46.61668	2.41E–10
12	Residual	20	29.51015	1.475508		
13	Total	25	373.4365			
14						
15		Coefficients	Standard Error	t Stat	P-value	
16	Intercept	2.708474	8.90876	0.304024	0.76425	
17	EnCons	0.83567	0.180234	4.636595	0.000159	
18	NclrElec	−0.00654	0.009854	−0.66412	0.514197	
19	CoalProd	0.009815	0.007286	1.348422	0.192596	
20	DryGas	−0.14321	0.448408	−0.31938	0.752753	
21	FuelRate	−0.73414	0.548823	−1.33767	0.196018	

FIGURE 14.9 Excel Output of Regression for Crude Oil Production Example

The output contains an R^2 value of 92.1%, a standard error of the estimate of 1.215, and an overall significant F value of 46.62. Notice from Figure 14.9 that the t values indicate that the regression coefficients of four of the predictor variables—nuclear, coal, dry gas, and fuel rate—are not significant at $\alpha = 0.05$. If the analyst were to drop these four variables out of the regression analysis and rerun the model with the other predictor only, what would happen to the model? What if the analyst ran a regression model with only three predictors? How would these models compare with the full model with all five predictors? Are all the predictors necessary?

Developing regression models for business decision-making involves at least two considerations. The first is to develop a regression model that accounts for the most variation of the dependent variable—that is, develop models that maximize the explained proportion of the deviation of the y values. At the same time, the regression model should be as parsimonious (simple and economical) as possible. The more complicated a quantitative model becomes, the harder it is for managers to understand and implement the model. In addition, as more variables are included in a model, it becomes more expensive to gather historical data or update present data for the model. These two considerations (dependent variable explanation and parsimony of the model) are quite often in opposition to each other. Hence, the business analyst, as the model builder, often needs to explore many model options.

In the world crude oil production regression model, if three variables explain the deviation of world crude oil production nearly as well as five variables, the simpler model is more attractive. How might analysts conduct regression analysis so that they can examine several models and then choose the most attractive one? The answer is to use search procedures.

Search Procedures

Search procedures are *processes whereby more than one multiple regression model is developed for a given database, and the models are compared and sorted by different criteria,* depending on the given procedure. Virtually all search procedures are done on a computer. Several search procedures are discussed in this section, including all possible regressions, stepwise regression, forward selection, and backward elimination.

All Possible Regressions The **all possible regressions** search procedure *computes all possible linear multiple regression models from the data using all variables.* If a data set contains k independent variables, all possible regressions will determine $2^k - 1$ different models.

For the crude oil production example, the procedure of all possible regressions would produce $2^5 - 1 = 31$ different models from the $k = 5$ independent variables. With $k = 5$ predictors, the procedure produces all single-predictor models, all models with two predictors, all models with three predictors, all models with four predictors, and all models with five predictors, as shown in **Table 14.7**.

TABLE 14.7 **Predictors for All Possible Regressions with Five Independent Variables**

Single Predictor	Two Predictors	Three Predictors	Four Predictors	Five Predictors
x_1	x_1, x_2	x_1, x_2, x_3	x_1, x_2, x_3, x_4	x_1, x_2, x_3, x_4, x_5
x_2	x_1, x_3	x_1, x_2, x_4	x_1, x_2, x_3, x_5	
x_3	x_1, x_4	x_1, x_2, x_5	x_1, x_2, x_4, x_5	
x_4	x_1, x_5	x_1, x_3, x_4	x_1, x_3, x_4, x_5	
x_5	x_2, x_3	x_1, x_3, x_5	x_2, x_3, x_4, x_5	
	x_2, x_4	x_1, x_4, x_5		
	x_2, x_5	x_2, x_3, x_4		
	x_3, x_4	x_2, x_3, x_5		
	x_3, x_5	x_2, x_4, x_5		
	x_4, x_5	x_3, x_4, x_5		

The all possible regressions procedure enables the business analyst to examine every model. In theory, this method eliminates the chance that the business analyst will not consider some models, as can be the case with other search procedures. On the other hand, the search through all possible models can be tedious, time-consuming, inefficient, and even overwhelming.

Stepwise Regression Perhaps the most widely known and used of the search procedures is stepwise regression. **Stepwise regression** is *a step-by-step process that begins by developing a regression model with a single predictor variable and adds and deletes predictors one step at a time,* examining the fit of the model at each step until no more significant predictors remain outside the model.

Step 1 In Step 1 of a stepwise regression procedure, the k independent variables are examined one at a time by developing a simple regression model for each independent variable to predict the dependent variable. The model containing the largest absolute value of t for an independent variable is selected, and the independent variable associated with the model is selected as the "best" single predictor of y at the first step. Some computer software packages use an F value instead of a t value to make this determination. Most of these computer programs allow the analyst to predetermine critical values for t or F but they also contain a default value as an option. If the first independent variable selected at Step 1 is denoted x_1, the model appears in the form:

$$\hat{y} = b_0 + b_1 x_1$$

If, after examining all possible single-predictor models, it is concluded that none of the independent variables produces a t value that is significant at α, then the search procedure stops at Step 1 and recommends no model.

Step 2 In Step 2, the stepwise procedure examines all possible two-predictor regression models with x_1 as one of the independent variables in the model and determines which of the other $k - 1$ independent variables in conjunction with x_1 produces the highest absolute t value in the model. If this other variable selected from the remaining independent variables is denoted x_2 and is included in the model selected at Step 2 along with x_1, the model appears in the form:

$$\hat{y} = b_0 + b_1 x_1 + b_2 x_2$$

At this point, stepwise regression pauses and examines the t value of the regression coefficient for x_1. Occasionally, the regression coefficient for x_1 will become statistically nonsignificant when x_2 is entered into the model. In that case, stepwise regression will drop x_1 out of the model and go back and examine which of the other $k - 2$ independent variables, if any, will produce the largest significant absolute t value when that variable is included in the model along with x_2. If no other variables show significant t values, the procedure halts. It is worth noting that the regression coefficients are likely to change from step to step to account for the new predictor being added in the process. Thus, if x_1 stays in the model at Step 2, the value of b_1 at Step 1 will probably be different from the value of b_1 at Step 2.

Step 3   Step 3 begins with independent variables x_1 and x_2 (the variables that were finally selected at Step 2) in the model. At this step, a search is made to determine which of the $k - 2$ remaining independent variables in conjunction with x_1 and x_2 produces the largest significant absolute t value in the regression model. Let us denote the one that is selected as x_3. If no significant t values are acknowledged at this step, the process stops here and the model determined in Step 2 is the final model. At Step 3, the model appears in the form:

$$\hat{y} = b_0 + b_1 x_1 + b_2 x_2 + b_3 x_3$$

In a manner similar to Step 2, stepwise regression now goes back and examines the t values of the regression coefficients of x_1 and x_2 in this Step 3 model. If either or both of the t values are now nonsignificant, the variables are dropped out of the model and the process calls for a search through the remaining $k - 3$ independent variables to determine which, if any, in conjunction with x_3 produce the largest significant t values in this model. The stepwise regression process continues step by step until no significant independent variables remain that are not in the model.

In the crude oil production example, recall that Table 14.6 contained data that can be used to develop a regression model to predict world crude oil production from as many as five different independent variables. Figure 14.9 displayed the results of a multiple regression analysis to produce a model using all five predictors. Suppose the analyst were to use a stepwise regression search procedure on these data to find a regression model. Recall that the following independent variables were being considered:

1. U.S. energy consumption
2. U.S. nuclear generation
3. U.S. coal production
4. U.S. dry gas production
5. U.S. fuel rate

Step 1   Each of the independent variables is examined one at a time to determine the strength of each predictor in a simple regression model. The results are reported in Table 14.8.

Note that the independent variable energy consumption was selected as the predictor variable, x_1, in Step 1. An examination of Table 14.8 reveals that energy consumption produced the largest absolute t value (11.77) of the single predictors. By itself, energy consumption accounted for 85.2% of the variation of the y values (world crude oil production). The regression equation taken from the computer output for this model is:

$$y = 13.075 + 0.580 x_1$$

TABLE 14.8 Step 1: Results of Simple Regression Using Each Independent Variable to Predict Oil Production

Dependent Variable	Independent Variable	t Value	R^2
Oil production	Energy consumption	11.77	85.2%
Oil production	Nuclear	4.43	45.0
Oil production	Coal	3.91	38.9
Oil production	Dry gas	1.08	4.6
Oil production	Fuel rate	3.54	34.2

→ Variable selected to serve as x_1

where

y = world crude oil production

x_1 = U.S. energy consumption

Step 2 In Step 2, x_1 was retained initially in the model and a search was conducted among the four remaining independent variables to determine which of those variables in conjunction with x_1 produced the largest significant t value. **Table 14.9** reports the results of this search.

TABLE 14.9 Step 2: Regression Results with Two Predictors

Dependent Variable y	Independent Variable x_1	Independent Variable x_2	t Value of x_2	R^2
Oil production	Energy consumption	Nuclear	−3.60	90.6%
Oil production	Energy consumption	Coal	−2.44	88.3
Oil production	Energy consumption	Dry gas	2.23	87.9
Oil production	Energy consumption	Fuel rate	−3.75	90.8

→ Variables selected at Step 2

The information in Table 14.9 shows that the model selected in Step 2 includes the independent variables "energy consumption" and "fuel rate". Fuel rate has the largest absolute t value (−3.75), and it is significant at $\alpha = 0.05$. Other variables produced varying sizes of t values. The model produced at Step 2 has an R^2 of 90.8%. These two variables taken together account for almost 91% of the variation of world crude oil production in this sample.

From other computer information, it is ascertained that the t value for the x_1 variable in this model is 11.91, which is even higher than in Step 1. Therefore, x_1 will not be dropped from the model by the stepwise regression procedure. The Step 2 regression model from the computer output is:

$$y = 7.14 + 0.772x_1 - 0.517x_2$$

where

y = world crude oil production

x_1 = U.S. energy consumption

x_2 = U.S. fuel rate

Note that the regression coefficient for x_1 changed from 0.580 at Step 1 in the model to 0.772 at Step 2.

TABLE 14.11 Step 1: Backward Elimination, Full Model

Predictor	Coefficient	t Value	p
Energy consumption	0.8357	4.64	0.000
Nuclear	−0.00654	−0.66	0.514
Coal	0.00983	1.35	0.193
Dry gas	−0.1432	−0.32	0.753
Fuel rate	−0.7341	−1.34	0.196

Variable to be dropped from the model

Step 2 A second regression model is developed with $k - 1 = 4$ predictors. Dry gas has been eliminated from consideration. The results of this multiple regression analysis are presented in **Table 14.12**. The computer results in Table 14.12 indicate that the variable "nuclear" has the smallest absolute value of a nonsignificant t of the variables remaining in the model ($t = -0.64$, $p = 0.528$). In Step 3, this variable will be dropped from the model.

TABLE 14.12 Step 2: Backward Elimination, Four Predictors

Predictor	Coefficient	t Value	p
Energy consumption	0.7843	9.85	0.000
Nuclear	−0.004261	−0.64	0.528
Coal	0.010933	1.74	0.096
Fuel rate	−0.8253	−1.80	0.086

Variable to be dropped from the model

Step 3 A third regression model is developed with $k - 2 = 3$ predictors. Both "nuclear" and "dry gas" variables have been removed from the model. The results of this multiple regression analysis are reported in **Table 14.13**. The computer results in Table 14.13 indicate that the variable "coal" has the smallest absolute value of a nonsignificant t of the variables remaining in the model ($t = 1.71$, $p = 0.102$). In Step 4, this variable will be dropped from the model.

TABLE 14.13 Step 3: Backward Elimination, Three Predictors

Predictor	Coefficient	t Value	p
Energy consumption	0.75394	11.94	0.000
Coal	0.010479	1.71	0.102
Fuel rate	−1.0283	−3.14	0.005

Variable to be dropped from the model

Step 4 A fourth regression model is developed with $k - 3 = 2$ predictors. Nuclear, dry gas, and coal variables have been removed from the model. The results of this multiple regression analysis are reported in **Table 14.14**. Observe that all p-values are less than $\alpha = 0.05$, indicating that all t values are significant, so no additional independent variables need to be removed. The backward elimination process ends with two predictors in the model. The final model obtained from this backward elimination process on the crude oil production data is the same model as that obtained by using stepwise regression.

TABLE 14.14	Step 4: Backward Elimination, Two Predictors		
Predictor	**Coefficient**	**t Value**	**p**
Energy consumption	0.77201	11.91	0.000
Fuel rate	−0.5173	−3.75	0.001

All variables are significant at $\alpha = 0.05$.
No variables will be dropped from this model.
The process stops.

Concept Check

1. What does the term *search procedures* mean in regression analysis?
2. Name some commonly used search procedures in regression analysis and briefly describe them.

14.3 Problems

14.13 Use a stepwise regression procedure and the following data to develop a multiple regression model to predict y. Discuss the variables that enter at each step, commenting on their t values and on the value of R^2.

y	x_1	x_2	x_3		y	x_1	x_2	x_3
21	5	108	57		22	13	105	51
17	11	135	34		20	10	111	43
14	14	113	21		16	20	140	20
13	9	160	25		13	19	150	14
19	16	122	43		18	14	126	29
15	18	142	40		12	21	175	22
24	7	93	52		23	6	98	38
17	9	128	38		18	15	129	40

14.14 Given here are data for a dependent variable and four potential predictors. Use these data and a stepwise regression procedure to develop a multiple regression model to predict y. Examine the values of t and R^2 at each step and comment on those values. How many steps did the procedure use? Why do you think the process stopped?

y	x_1	x_2	x_3	x_4
101	2	77	1.2	42
127	4	72	1.7	26
98	9	69	2.4	47
79	5	53	2.6	65
118	3	88	2.9	37
114	1	53	2.7	28
110	3	82	2.8	29
94	2	61	2.6	22
96	8	60	2.4	48
73	6	64	2.1	42
108	2	76	1.8	34
124	5	74	2.2	11
82	6	50	1.5	61
89	9	57	1.6	53
76	1	72	2	72
109	3	74	2.8	36
123	2	99	2.6	17
125	6	81	2.5	48

14.15 The computer output given here is the result of a stepwise multiple regression analysis to predict a dependent variable by using six predictor variables. The number of observations was 108. Study the output and discuss the results. How many predictors ended up in the model? Which predictors, if any, did not enter the model?

```
STEPWISE REGRESSION OF Y ON 6 PREDICTORS,
WITH N = 108

STEP              1        2        3        4
CONSTANT       8.71     6.82     6.57     5.96
X3            -2.85    -4.92    -4.97    -5.00
T-VALUE        2.11     2.94     3.04     3.07
X1                      4.42     3.72     3.22
T-VALUE                 2.64     2.20     2.05
X2                               1.91     1.78
T-VALUE                          2.07     2.02
X6                                        1.56
T-VALUE                                   1.98
S              3.81     3.51     3.43     3.36
R-SQ          29.20    49.45    54.72    59.29
```

14.16 Study the output given here from a stepwise multiple regression analysis to predict y from four variables. Comment on the output at each step.

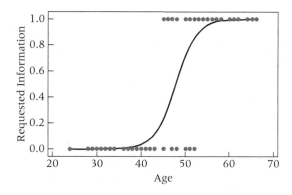

FIGURE 14.12 **Scatter Plot of Auto Club Data with Logistic Model**

where p is the probability that a club member fits into group 1 (returns the form). In general for multiple predictors, the logistic model is:

Logistic Model for Multiple Predictors

$$f(x) = p = \frac{e^{\beta_0 + \beta_1 x_1 + \cdots + \beta_k x_k}}{1 + e^{\beta_0 + \beta_1 x_1 + \cdots + \beta_k x_k}} \qquad (14.3)$$

For ease of computation in logistic regression, this expression is transformed into an odds ratio. Recall that the odds of an event occurring are computed by dividing the probability of the event occurring by the probability that the event will not occur. For example, if there is a 0.60 probability that it will rain, then there is a $1 - 0.60 = 0.40$ probability that it will not rain. The odds that it will rain are: $P(\text{rain}) \div P(\text{not rain})$ or $0.60 \div 0.40 = 1.50$. In transforming the logistic model, the function is converted to an odds ratio:

Odds Ratio

$$S = \frac{p}{1 - p} \qquad (14.4)$$

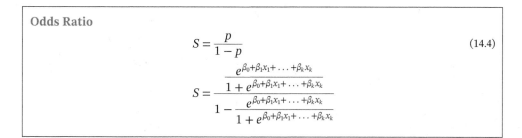

Rearranging and reducing this by algebra results in:

$$S = \text{Odds ratio} = e^{\beta_0 + \beta_1 x_1 + \cdots + \beta_k x_k}$$

The transformation is completed by taking the natural log of each side of the equation, resulting in:

Logit

$$\ln(S) = \ln(e^{\beta_0 + \beta_1 x_1 + \cdots + \beta_k x_k}) = \beta_0 + \beta_1 x_1 + \cdots + \beta_k x_k \qquad (14.5)$$

This log of the odds ratio is called the logit, and the transformed model is now linear in the β's. In logistic regression, for reasons mentioned before, least squares regression methodology is not used to develop the model; rather, a maximum likelihood method, which maximizes the probability of getting the observed results, is employed. Maximum likelihood estimation is an iterative process using the computer and is not described here. Minitab uses a maximum likelihood procedure to produce logistic regression results. We will now focus on interpreting the results of such an analysis.

Interpreting the Output

Figure 14.13 contains Minitab output from its binary logistic regression analysis of the auto club data. The model was developed in an attempt to predict by the age of the member whether an auto club member would send in a form asking for additional health insurance information.

FIGURE 14.13 Minitab Binary Logistic Regression Output for the Auto Club Example

```
Binary Logistic Regression: Requested Information versus Age

Method

Link function  Logit
Rows used       92


Response Information

Variable            Value  Count
Requested Infor.    1         36  (Event)
                    0         56
                    Total     92

Deviance Table

Source        DF  Adj Dev  Adj Mean  Chi-Square  P-Value
Regression     1    73.22   73.2197       73.22    0.000
  Age          1    73.22   73.2197       73.22    0.000
Error         90    49.94    0.5549
Total         91   123.16


Model Summary

Deviance   Deviance
   R-Sq   R-Sq(adj)      AIC
  59.45%      58.64%    53.94


Coefficients

Term        Coef   SE Coef       95% CI     Z-Value  P-Value   VIF
Constant  -20.41      4.52  (-29.27, -11.54)  -4.51    0.000
Age       0.4259    0.0948  (0.2401, 0.6118)   4.49    0.000  1.00


Odds Ratios for Continuous Predictors

      Odds Ratio         95% CI
Age       1.5310  (1.2714, 1.8437)


Regression Equation

 P(1)  =  exp(Y')/(1 + exp(Y'))

 Y'  = -20.41 + 0.4259 Age
```

Notice that in the Minitab summary of information, 36 of the 92 auto club members sent in the form (a little over 39%) and 56 of the members did not (almost 61%).

Found in the column Coef are the coefficients of the resulting logistic model: −20.41 for Constant and 0.4259 for Age.

Thus, the log of the odds ratio or logit equation is:

$$\ln(S) = -20.41 + 0.4259 \, (\text{Age})$$

Suppose we want to determine the probability that a 50-year-old auto club member will return the form. Inserting Age = 50 into the logit equation, $\ln(S) = -20.41 + 0.4259(\text{Age})$, results in a ln odds of $-20.7540 + 0.433680(50) = 0.885$.

Taking the antilog of this value results in the odds, S:

$$S = e^{0.885} = 2.423$$

The odds that a 50-year-old returns the form are 2.423 to 1. From this, we can compute the probability that a 50-year-old returns the form as:

$$\hat{p} = \frac{S}{S+1} = \frac{2.423}{2.423+1} = 0.7079$$

How can the probability that an auto club member will return the form be computed directly? The logistic model to predict the probability of returning the form is determined by:

$$\hat{p} = \frac{e^{-20.41+0.4259\,(\text{Age})}}{1+e^{-20.41+0.4259\,(\text{Age})}}$$

For the 50-year-old, the predicted probability is:

$$\hat{p} = \frac{e^{-20.41+0.4259(50)}}{1+e^{-20.41+0.4259(50)}} = \frac{e^{0.885}}{1+e^{0.885}} = \frac{2.423}{3.423} = 0.7079$$

The predicted probability that the 50-year-old returns the form is 0.7079. Using a probability of 0.50 as a cutoff between predicting a 0 or a 1, the 50-year-old would be classified as a 1 (a member who will return the form). The predicted probability that he/she will not return the form is $1 - 0.7079 = 0.2921$. Computing the odds from these probability values:

$$\text{Odds} = \frac{0.7079}{0.2921} = 2.423$$

This answer agrees with the odds calculated above using the odds ratio. In summary, with the logistic regression equation, one can calculate the probability, determine the $\log_e$ of the odds, and compute the odds of being in the 1 group.

In regression analysis, an F test is computed to determine if there is overall significance in the model. In multiple regression, this test determines whether at least one of the regression coefficients is different from zero. Logistic regression has an analogous test, the chi-square statistic. In Figure 14.13, the Minitab output for the auto club example problem shows a chi-square value of 73.22 with an associated p-value of 0.000. This result indicates that the logistic regression model has overall significance and there is at least one significant predictor variable.

Logistic regression can be run for models with more than one predictor. In these models, the chi-square statistic yields the same information as the single-predictor model. However, for multiple-predictor models, the degrees of freedom are equal to p, which equals the number of predictors in the model. Thus, if there are four predictors in the model, the degrees of freedom are 4. In the case of multiple predictors, a significant chi-square statistic indicates that at least one of the predictor variables is significant.

Testing Individual Predictor Variables

Determining the significance of individual predictor variables in logistic regression can be done by studying z values and their associated p-values. Minitab output contains the z value and its associated p-value for each predictor variable. Note in Figure 14.13 that the z value for Age is 4.49 with a p-value of 0.000. This indicates that age is a significant predictor in the model. With the single-predictor model, this information is similar to that gleaned from the test of the overall model. However, in models with multiple predictors, such z statistics and their associated p-values can help determine which variables are significant and are contributing to the model and which are not.[4]

---

[4] Alfred DeMaris, "A Tutorial in Logistic Regression," *Journal of Marriage and Family* 57, no. 4 (November 1995): 956–68; Joseph F. Hair Jr., William C. Black, Barry J. Babin, and Rolph E. Anderson, *Multivariate Data Analysis*, 7th ed. (Saddle River, NJ: Pearson, 2010); David W. Hosmer and Stanley Lemeshow, *Applied Logistic Regression*, 2nd ed. (New York: John Wiley & Sons, 2000); David G. Kleinbaum and Mitchel Klein, *Logistic Regression: A Self-Learning Text*, 2nd ed. (New York: Springer Science Productions, 2002); Fred C. Pampel, *Logistic Regression: A Primer* (Thousand Oaks, CA: Sage, 2000).

Concept Check

1. What kinds of situations call for the use of logistic regression?
2. List three ways in which logistic regression differs from multiple regression.
3. What is the main difference between simple linear regression and logistic regression?
4. What is an "odds ratio"?

14.5 Problems

14.23 In the following output, the variable "Service" is coded 0 for general medical hospitals and 1 for psychiatric hospitals. Shown below is Minitab output from a logistic regression attempt to predict capitalize Service by payroll expenditures. Study the output. What is the model? How good is the overall fit of the model? Comment on the strength of the predictor. Thinking about hospitals, does the model make sense to you? Use the model to estimate the probability that a hospital is a psychiatric hospital if the payroll expenditures are $80,000.

```
Variable            Value    Count
Service             1           32 (Event)
                    0          168
                    Total      200

Coefficients

Term      Coef       SE Coef     Z-Value  P-Value
Constant -0.932546   0.289749    -3.22    0.001
Payroll
Exp.     -0.000323   0.0000123    2.64    0.008

Regression Equation
P(1) = exp(Y')/(1 + exp(Y'))
Y' = -0.932546 - 0.0000323 Payroll Exp.
```

14.24 Shown below is Minitab output from a logistic regression attempt to predict if a family is from outside a metro area by annual food spending by household. Families residing in metro regions are coded as 0 and those residing outside metro regions as 1. Study the output. What is the model? Comment on the strength of the predictor. Thinking about households and metro areas, does the model make sense to you? Use the model to estimate the probability that a household is from outside a metro area if its annual food spending is $12,000.

```
Variable              Value    Count
Outside Metro Area    1           80 (Event)
                      0          120
                      Total      200

Coefficients

Term      Coef        SE Coef     Z-Value  P-Value
Constant  0.705987    0.451245    1.56     0.118
Annual Food
Spending  -0.0001257  0.0000489  -2.57     0.010

Regression Equation
P(1) = exp(Y')/(1 + exp(Y'))
Y' = 0.705987 - 0.0001257 Annual Food Spending
```

14.25 A logistic regression analysis was done in an attempt to predict the value of industrial shipments by the number of production workers. For the purposes of this analysis, Value of Industrial Shipments is coded 0 if the value is small and 1 if the value is large. The Minitab output is given below. Study the output. What is the model? Comment on the strength of the predictor. Use the model to estimate the probability that a selected company has a large value of industrial shipments if its number of production workers is 30.

```
Coefficients

Term       Coef       SE Coef    Z-Value P-Value
Constant  -3.07942   0.535638    -5.75   0.000
No. Prod.
Wkrs.      0.0544532 0.0096833   -5.62   0.000

Regression Equation
P(1) = exp(Y')/(1 + exp(Y'))
Y' = -3.07942 + 0.0544532 No. Prod. Wkrs.
```

14.26 Logistic regression analysis was used to develop a model to predict if a company was a North American company based on its Market Value. A variable was coded 1 if the company headquarters was located in North America, and coded 0 if the company headquarters was outside North America. The partial Minitab output is shown below. Using the regression equation, what is the probability that a company with a market value of 300 is a North American company? If the market value is 10, what is the probability that a company is a North American company?

```
Coefficients

Term           Coef     SE Coef Z-Value  P-Value
Constant      -1.1143   0.0646  -17.24   0.000
Market Value   0.00485  0.00104   4.67   0.000

Regression Equation
P(1) = exp(Y')/(1 + exp(Y'))
Y' = -1.1143 + 0.00485 Market Value ($ B)
```

End-of-Chapter Review

Decision Dilemma Solved

Predicting CEO Salaries

Models to predict CEO salaries can be developed using multiple regression and such predictor variables as age, years of experience, worth of company, and others. Search procedures such as stepwise regression can be used to sort out the more significant predictors of CEO salaries. In the Decision Dilemma, data was given for three possible predictors: Annual Revenue, Number of Employees, and nature of the company (manufacturing or not), along with corresponding data on CEO salaries.

Using these data and Minitab, a stepwise regression procedure was conducted on the Decision Dilemma data in an attempt to predict CEO salary by the three independent variables of Revenue, Employees, and Manufacturing (or not). An α of 0.10 was used as a cutoff for entry into the model. The result of the initial analysis is:

```
Candidate Terms: Employees, Revenue, Mgfr

                ----Step 1----      ----Step 2----
                Coef     P          Coef     P
Constant        0.462               1.109
Revenue         0.1041   0.000      0.0626   0.018
Mgfr                                1.878    0.026
S                        1.36412             1.20883
R-sq                     62.35%              72.08%
R-sq(adj)                60.26%              68.79%
R-sq(pred)               54.94%              60.19%
```

Company Revenue enters the model at Step 1, producing an R^2 of 62.35%. At Step 2, the qualitative variable, Manufacturing or Not, enters the model, joining Company Revenue, and the R^2 increases to 72.08%. No other variables enter into the stepwise process, and the regression equation is:

$$\text{CEO Salary} = 1.109 + 0.0626\,(\text{Revenue}) + 1.878\,(\text{Manufacturing})$$

In considering the possibility that there might be multicollinearity in these data, a modest correlation between Company Revenue and Number of Employees ($r = 0.63$) was observed. Because of this correlation, an interaction term was created for Company Revenue and Number of Employees. A second stepwise regression was then conducted using Minitab and including a new predictor variable, Interaction of Revenue and Employees, along with the three original predictors. The result of this new analysis is:

```
Candidate Terms: Employees, Revenue, Mgfr,
   Inter R&E

                ----Step 1----      ----Step 2----
                Coef     P          Coef     P
Constant        3.005               2.480
Inter R&E       0.000555 0.000      0.00369  0.001
Mgfr                                1.974    0.003
S                        1.30069             1.02161
R-sq                     65.77%              80.06%
R-sq(adj)                63.87%              77.71%
R-sq(pred)               53.36%              74.52%
```

Note that the interaction variable, Interaction of Revenue and Employees, enters the stepwise procedure at Step 1, producing an R^2 of 65.77%, which is higher than the R^2 for the first model (62.35%). At Step 2, the interaction variable is retained in the model and the Manufacturing variable enters the model. The resulting R^2 for the new model at Step 2 is 80.06%, which is considerably higher than the R^2 for the first analysis (72.08%). No other variables enter into this stepwise process, and the final regression equation is:

$$\text{CEO Salary} = 2.480 + 0.000369\,(\text{Interaction of Revenue and Employees}) + 1.974\,(\text{Manufacturing})$$

Key Considerations

Some business analysts misuse the results of search procedures by using the order in which variables come into a model (on stepwise and forward selection) to rank the variables in importance. They state that the variable entered at Step 1 is the most important predictor of y, the variable entering at Step 2 is second most important, and so on. In actuality, variables entering the analysis after Step 1 are being analyzed by how much of the unaccounted-for variation (residual variation) they are explaining, not how much they are related to y by themselves. A variable that comes into the model at the fourth step is the variable that most greatly accounts for the variation of the y values left over after the

first three variables have explained the rest. However, the fourth variable taken by itself might explain more variation of y than the second or third variable when seen as single predictors. In multiple regression, unlike in simple regression, the variance explained should be interpreted in the context of other variables involved in the regression equation.

Some people use the estimates of the regression coefficients (b) to compare the worth of the predictor variables; the larger the coefficient is, the greater its worth. However, the unstandardized regression b coefficients do not necessarily reflect the relative importance of the variables. Because different variables may have been measured in different units, regression coefficient weights are partly a function of the unit of measurement of the variable. Interpretation of multiple regression coefficients would also require that we have accounted for external distortions such as multicollinearity. Analysts who ignore these problems are at risk of presenting spurious results. Because of assumption violations, statisticians frown on the use of least squares multiple regression to develop regression models to predict dichotomous variables. The use of this methodology could be considered a form of unethical behaviour, especially by knowledgeable business analysts.

Why Statistics Is Relevant

Businesses are constantly affected by a multiplicity of variables. For example, what influences customer loyalty to our products? Is it our customer service, product quality, product pricing, or the product's wide availability? Once we can hypothesize what such variables might be, we can use multiple regression analysis to test our hypothesis. However, the relationships can be more complex. Some of them may be nonlinear: customers may be less price sensitive up to a certain point, but much more sensitive after that. They may reject poor-quality products but may also not assign value to products that exceed certain quality standards. Procedures described in this chapter show how to identify such complex relationships in order to make proper business decisions. In general, one would need more complex models (such as nonlinear regression, generalized linear models, and time-series analysis) to deal with large data situations.

Summary of Learning Objectives

LEARNING OBJECTIVE 14.1 Generalize linear regression models as polynomial regression models using model transformation and Tukey's ladder of transformation, accounting for possible interaction among the independent variables.

Even when the relationship between our independent variables and the dependent variable is nonlinear, we can use multiple regression analysis to analyze the data. One way to accommodate this issue is to recode the data and enter the variables into the analysis in the normal way. Other nonlinear regression models, such as exponential models, require that the entire model be transformed. Often the transformation involves the use of logarithms. In some cases, the resulting value of the regression model is in logarithmic form and the antilogarithm of the answer must be taken to determine the predicted value of y.

LEARNING OBJECTIVE 14.2 Examine the role of indicator, or dummy, variables as predictors or independent variables in multiple regression analysis.

Indicator, or dummy, variables are qualitative variables used to represent categorical data in the multiple regression model. These variables are coded as 0, 1 and are often used to represent nominal or ordinal classification data that the analyst wants to include in the regression analysis. If a qualitative variable contains more than two categories, it generates multiple dummy variables. In general, if a qualitative variable contains c categories, $c - 1$ dummy variables should be created.

LEARNING OBJECTIVE 14.3 Use all possible regressions, stepwise regression, forward selection, and backward elimination search procedures to develop regression models that account for the most variation in the dependent variable and are parsimonious.

You can build regression models in many ways. Search procedures are used to help sort through the independent variables as predictors in the examination of various possible models. Several search procedures are available, including all possible regressions, stepwise regression, forward selection, and backward elimination. The all possible regressions procedure computes every possible regression model for a set of data. The drawbacks of this procedure include the time and energy required to compute all possible regressions and the difficulty of deciding which models are most appropriate. The stepwise regression procedure involves selecting and adding one independent variable at a time to the regression process after beginning with a one-predictor model. Variables are added to the model at each step if they contain the most significant t value associated with the remaining variables. If no additional t value is statistically significant at any given step, the procedure stops. With stepwise regression, at each step the process examines the variables already in the model to determine whether their t values are still significant. If not, they are dropped from the model, and the process searches for other independent variables with large, significant t values to replace the variable(s) dropped. The forward selection procedure is the same as stepwise regression but does not drop variables out of the model once they have been included. The backward elimination procedure begins with a "full" model, a model that contains all the independent variables. The sample size must be large enough to justify a full model, which can be a limiting factor. Backward elimination drops out the least important predictors one at a time until only significant predictors are left in the regression model. The variable with the smallest absolute t value of the statistically nonsignificant t values is the independent variable that is dropped out of the model at each step.

LEARNING OBJECTIVE 14.4 Recognize when multicollinearity is present, understanding general techniques for preventing and controlling it.

One of the problems in using multiple regression is multicollinearity, or correlations among the predictor variables. This problem can cause overinflated estimates of the standard deviations of regression coefficients, misinterpretation of regression coefficients, undersized t values, and misleading signs on the regression coefficients. It can be lessened by using an intercorrelation matrix of independent variables to help recognize bivariate correlation, by using stepwise regression to sort the variables one at a time, or by using statistics such as a VIF.

LEARNING OBJECTIVE 14.5 Explain when to use logistic regression, and interpret its results.

For a variety of reasons, including assumption violations, statisticians do not recommend using least squares regression analysis to develop models to predict dichotomous dependent variables. A commonly used methodology for developing such models is logistic regression, which has some properties similar to multiple regression. However, logistic regression does not assume a linear relationship between the dependent and independent variables, and several of the assumptions underlying least squares regression need not be met. Sample size requirements for logistic regression are larger than for multiple regression, and it is recommended that there be at least 50 observations for each predictor variable in logistic regression.

Key Terms

all possible regressions 14-24	logistic regression 14-34	stepwise regression 14-24
backward elimination 14-28	multicollinearity 14-31	Tukey's four-quadrant approach 14-7
dummy variable 14-16	quadratic regression model 14-4	Tukey's ladder of transformations 14-7
forward selection 14-28	qualitative variable 14-16	variance inflation factor (VIF) 14-33
indicator variable 14-16	search procedures 14-23	

Formulas

(14.1) Variance inflation factor

$$\text{VIF} = \frac{1}{1 - R_i^2}$$

(14.2) General logistic model

$$f(x) = p = \frac{e^\mu}{1 + e^\mu}$$

(14.3) Logistic model for multiple predictors

$$f(x) = p = \frac{e^{\beta_0 + \beta_1 x_1 + \cdots + \beta_k x_k}}{1 + e^{\beta_0 + \beta_1 x_1 + \cdots + \beta_k x_k}}$$

(14.4) Odds ratio

$$S = \frac{p}{1 - p}$$

(14.5) Logit

$$\ln(S) = \ln(e^{\beta_0 + \beta_1 x_1 + \cdots + \beta_k x_k}) = \beta_0 + \beta_1 x_1 + \cdots + \beta_k x_k$$

Supplementary Problems

Calculating the Statistics

14.27 **Video** Given here are the data for a dependent variable, y, and independent variables. Use these data to develop a regression model to predict y. Discuss the output. Which variable is an indicator variable? Was it a significant predictor of y?

x_1	x_2	x_3	y
0	51	16.4	14
0	48	17.1	17
1	29	18.2	29
0	36	17.9	32

x_1	x_2	x_3	y
0	40	16.5	54
1	27	17.1	86
1	14	17.8	117
0	17	18.2	120
1	16	16.9	194
1	9	18	203
1	14	18.9	217
0	11	18.5	235

14.28 Use the following data and a stepwise regression analysis to predict y. In addition to the two independent variables given here, include three other predictors in your analysis: the square of each x as a predictor and an interaction predictor. Discuss the results of the process.

x_1	x_2	y	x_1	x_2	y
10	3	2002	5	12	1750
5	14	1747	6	8	1832
8	4	1980	5	18	1795
7	4	1902	7	4	1917
6	7	1842	8	5	1943
7	6	1883	6	9	1830
4	21	1697	5	12	1786
11	4	2021			

14.29 Video Use the x_1 values and the log of the x_1 values given here to predict the y values by using a stepwise regression procedure. Discuss the output. Were either or both of the predictors significant?

y	x_1	y	x_1
20.4	850	13.2	204
11.6	146	17.5	487
17.8	521	12.4	192
15.3	304	10.6	98
22.4	1029	19.8	703
21.9	910	17.4	394
16.4	242	19.4	647

Testing Your Understanding

14.30 Shown here are the volume trading figures for grain, oilseeds, and livestock products over a period of several years in the U.S. commodity futures exchanges. Use these data to develop a multiple regression model to predict grain futures volume of trading from oilseeds volume and livestock products volume. All figures are given in units of millions. Graph each of these predictors separately with the response variable and use Tukey's four-quadrant approach to explore possible recoding schemes for nonlinear relationships. Include any of these in the regression model. Comment on the results.

Grain	Oilseeds	Livestock
2.2	3.7	3.4
18.3	15.7	11.8
19.8	20.3	9.8
14.9	15.8	11
17.8	19.8	11.1
15.9	23.5	8.4
10.7	14.9	7.9
10.3	13.8	8.6
10.9	14.2	8.8
15.9	22.5	9.6
15.9	21.1	8.2

14.31 Shown here are the average prices per year for several minerals over a decade. Use these data and a stepwise regression procedure to produce a model to predict the average price of gold from the other variables. Comment on the results of the process.

Gold ($ per oz.)	Copper (¢ per lb.)	Silver ($ per oz.)	Aluminum (¢ per lb.)
161.1	64.2	4.4	39.8
308.0	93.3	11.1	61.0
613.0	101.3	20.6	71.6
460.0	84.2	10.5	76.0
376.0	72.8	8.0	76.0
424.0	76.5	11.4	77.8
361.0	66.8	8.1	81.0
318.0	67.0	6.1	81.0
368.0	66.1	5.5	81.0
448.0	82.5	7.0	72.3
438.0	120.5	6.5	110.1
382.6	130.9	5.5	87.8

14.32 Given below are the population, number of households, and average income for 10 Canadian cities. Use the data to develop a regression model to predict average income from population and number of households. Graph each of these predictors separately with the response variable and use Tukey's four-quadrant approach to explore possible recoding schemes for nonlinear relationships. Comment on the regression model and its strengths and weaknesses.

	Average Income ($)	Number of Families (thousands)	Population (thousands)
Toronto	109,480	2549	5928
Montreal	82,589	1904	4099
Vancouver	96,423	1141	2463
Calgary	140,919	617	1393
Ottawa-Gatineau	100,760	600	1324
Edmonton	121,620	593	1321
Winnipeg	89,975	352	778
Quebec City	81,261	387	800
Hamilton	97,211	327	748
London	83,246	230	494

14.33 This problem includes the consumer price index for a Canadian city over a period of 30 months. Also displayed are some of the major components of the index: beef, chicken, eggs, bread, and coffee. Use these data and a stepwise regression procedure to develop a model that attempts to predict the price index by the other five variables. Construct scatter plots of each of these variables with the price index. Examine the graphs in light of Tukey's four-quadrant approach. Develop any other appropriate predictor variables by recoding data, and include them in the analysis. Comment on the result of this analysis.

Month	Price Index	Beef	Chicken	Eggs	Bread	Coffee
1	117.8	119	138.5	127.9	163.9	127.2
2	118.1	119.6	135.2	131.5	167.6	129.5
3	119.4	123.6	134.3	131.5	169.7	133.8
4	119.8	124.8	137.1	134.2	173.9	134.7
5	120.6	126.4	137	136.3	174.7	136.7
6	119.8	128.1	136.8	136.5	175.8	138.9
7	120	127.3	139.1	140.3	174.7	141.1
8	120.3	127.4	139.1	141.6	175.9	143.2
9	120.6	128.2	141.2	142.2	178.1	144.4
10	120.8	128	138.4	142	181.2	143
11	120.9	128.4	139.7	142.9	181	144.1
12	120.2	130.4	140.3	145.8	179.5	141.4
13	120.7	133.2	143.8	145.5	180.2	144.2
14	121.2	132.8	142.9	146.1	179.7	144.8
15	121.7	133.6	141.8	147.1	180.1	144
16	122.2	132.7	143.1	146.1	180.9	145.4
17	122.1	135.5	146.6	147.3	176.7	142.9
18	121.6	137.1	141.3	147.3	177.2	145.5
19	121.5	136.6	145.1	147	178.5	146.4
20	121.8	137.2	145.2	150.4	177.8	143.9
21	122	136.2	144.5	150.4	178.8	146
22	122.2	135.4	146.1	151.4	180.9	143.2
23	121.9	137.3	143.5	155.2	180.6	144.7
24	121.2	137.2	145.3	153.7	181.5	143.5
25	121.3	136	147.6	153.9	182.2	144.3
26	122.7	140.1	144.6	153	185.6	145.1
27	122.9	138.3	145.9	153.6	186.9	146.5
28	122.7	139	147	153	187.8	143.1
29	123	139.1	145.4	154.4	185.7	144.6
30	123	139.5	144	154	184.8	143

14.34 Shown here are the unit production figures for three farm products for 10 years. Use these data and a stepwise regression analysis to predict corn production by the production of soybeans and wheat. Comment on the results.

Corn (million bushels)	Soybeans (million bushels)	Wheat (million bushels)
4152	1127	1352
6639	1798	2381
4175	1636	2420
7672	1861	2595
8876	2099	2424
8226	1940	2091
7131	1938	2108
4929	1549	1812
7525	1924	2037
7933	1922	2739

14.35 A Canadian supermarket carried out a survey among its customers to predict the factors that influenced the visit frequency to the store. Number of visits refers to the number of times a consumer visited the store in the past 30 days. All the remaining ratings are on a seven-point scale. For example, 7 on satisfaction means that the consumer is very satisfied with the supermarket while 1 means the customer is not at all satisfied with the supermarket. Use the data to develop a regression model to predict the number of visits to the supermarket on the basis of consumer ratings on the remaining variables. Discuss the results, highlighting both the significant and non-significant predictors.

Consumer ID	Number of Visits	Familiarity	Satisfaction	Proximity
1	8	7	7	6
2	2	2	3	3
3	3	3	4	3
4	3	3	7	5
5	7	7	7	7

(continued)

Consumer ID	Number of Visits	Familiarity	Satisfaction	Proximity
6	6	4	5	4
7	2	2	4	5
8	6	3	5	4
9	6	3	6	4
10	8	9	7	6
11	3	4	4	3
12	4	5	6	4
13	9	6	6	5
14	8	6	3	2
15	5	6	5	4
16	3	4	4	3
17	9	6	5	3
18	4	4	5	4
19	7	7	6	6
20	6	6	6	4
21	9	6	4	2
22	5	5	5	4
23	2	3	4	2
24	9	7	6	6
25	6	6	5	3
26	8	6	6	6
27	4	5	5	5
28	2	4	3	2
29	4	4	5	3
30	3	3	7	5

Interpreting the Output

14.36 A stepwise regression procedure was used to analyze a set of 20 observations taken on four predictor variables to predict a dependent variable. The results of this procedure are given next. Discuss the results.

```
STEPWISE REGRESSION OF Y ON 4
PREDICTORS, WITH N = 20
STEP               1        2
CONSTANT        152.2    124.5
X1              -50.6    -43.4
T-VALUE          7.42     6.13
X2                        1.36
T-VALUE                   2.13
S                15.2     13.9
R-SQ            75.39    80.59
```

14.37 [Video] Shown here are the data for y and three predictors, x_1, x_2, and x_3. A stepwise regression procedure has been done on these data; the results are also given. Comment on the outcome of the stepwise analysis in light of the data.

y	x_1	x_2	x_3
94	21	1	204
97	25	0	198
93	22	1	184
95	27	0	200
90	29	1	182
91	20	1	159
91	18	1	147
94	25	0	196
98	26	0	228
99	24	0	242
90	28	1	162
92	23	1	180
96	25	0	219

```
STEP              1         2         3
CONSTANT       74.81     82.18     87.89
X3             0.099     0.067     0.071
T-VALUE         6.90      3.65      5.22
X2                       -2.26     -2.71
T-VALUE                  -2.32     -3.71
X1                                 -0.256
T-VALUE                            -3.08
S               1.37      1.16      0.850
R-SQ           81.24     87.82     94.07
```

14.38 Shown here is output from two Excel regression analyses on the same problem. The first output was done on a "full" model. In the second output, the variable with the smallest absolute t value has been removed, and the regression has been rerun like the second step of a backward elimination process. Examine the two outputs. Explain what happened, what the results mean, and what might happen in a third step.

	A	B	C	D	E	F
1	FULL MODEL:					
2	Regression Statistics					
3	Multiple *R*	0.567				
4	*R* Square	0.321				
5	Adjusted *R* Square	0.208				
6	Standard Error	159.681				
7	Observations	29				
8						
9	ANOVA					
10		df	SS	MS	F	Significance F
11	Regression	4	289856.08	72464.02	2.84	0.046
12	Residual	24	611955.23	25498.13		
13	Total	28	901811.31			
14		Coefficients	Standard Error	t Stat	P-value	
15	Intercept	336.79	124.08	2.71	0.012	
16	x_1	1.65	1.78	0.93	0.363	
17	x_2	−5.63	13.47	−0.42	0.680	
18	x_3	0.26	1.68	0.16	0.878	
19	x_4	185.50	66.22	2.80	0.010	
20						
21	SECOND MODEL:					
22	Regression Statistics					
23	Multiple *R*	0.566				
24	*R* Square	0.321				
25	Adjusted *R* Square	0.239				
26	Standard Error	156.534				
27	Observations	29				
28						
29	ANOVA					
30		df	SS	MS	F	Significance F
31	Regression	3	289238.1	96412.7	3.93	0.020
32	Residual	25	612573.2	24502.9		
33	Total	28	901811.3			
34		Coefficients	Standard Error	t Stat	P-value	
35	Intercept	342.919	115.34	2.97	0.006	
36	x_1	1.834	1.31	1.40	0.174	
37	x_2	−5.749	13.18	−0.44	0.667	
38	x_4	181.220	59.05	3.07	0.005	

14.39 Shown here is Minitab output from a logistic regression analysis to develop a model to predict whether a shopper in a mall store would purchase something by the number of kilometres the shopper drives to get to the mall store. The original data were coded as 1 if the shopper purchases something and 0 if they do not. Study the output and determine the model. Discuss the strength or lack of strength of the model and the predictor. Use the output to compute the predicted probability that a person would purchase something if he/she drives 5 km to get to the store. Now calculate the probabilities for 4 km, 3 km, 2 km, and 1 km. What happens to the probability over these values?

```
Variable        Value           Count
Purchase        1               65   (Event)
                0               55
                Total          120

Coefficients

Term         Coef      SE Coef  Z-Value  P-Value
Constant     -3.94828  0.736737 -5.36    0.000
KM to Store   1.36988  0.255838  5.35    0.000
Regression Equation
P(1)  =   exp(Y')/(1 + exp(Y'))
Y' = -3.94828 + 1.36988 KM to Store
```

Exploring the Databases with Business Analytics

see the databases on the Student Website and in WileyPLUS

1. Develop a regression model using the Financial Database. Use Total Revenues, Average Yield, and Dividends per Share to predict Average P/E Ratio for a company. How strong is the model? Use stepwise regression to help sort out the variables. Several of these variables may be measuring similar things. Construct a correlation matrix to explore the possibility of multicollinearity among the predictors.

2. Use the Canadian Stock Market Database to develop a regression model to predict Composite Index from Week of the Month. Use the composite index for weeks 1, 2, and 3 to predict the composite index for week 4. You will need to treat Week of the Month as a qualitative variable with four subcategories (only use four since not every month has a fifth week). Drop out the least significant variable if it is not significant at $\alpha = 0.05$ and rerun the model. How much did R^2 drop? Continue this process until only significant predictors are left. Describe the final model.

Case

Ceapro Turns Oats into Beneficial Products

Ceapro is an Edmonton-based biotechnology company known for turning oats into beneficial products. Ceapro is the world's only commercial manufacturer of avenanthramides, a group of therapeutic molecules found exclusively in oats. Its clients use avenanthramides as ingredients in cosmetics and personal care products such as creams that help alleviate skin conditions resulting from eczema, chicken pox, and insect bites.

Scientists have recently discovered that avenanthramides could also be taken orally and may help reduce symptoms of diseases such as inflammatory bowel syndrome, atherosclerosis, colon cancer, and joint inflammation. Ceapro had long had a steady market for its avenanthramides for personal care products, with clients including Aveeno, Jergens, Coppertone, Dove, and Neutrogena, but realized that moving into the pharmaceutical area could open up potentially lucrative markets. However, it requires one tonne of oats to extract just a few spoonfuls of avenanthramides. In 2012, Ceapro entered into two agreements with Agriculture and Agri-Food Canada that will see the development of a new variety of oats with characteristics that should significantly increase the quantities and purity of avenanthramides, supplying Ceapro with enough oats to eventually produce pharmaceutical-grade avenanthramides. The company also sees the potential to use avenanthramides in "nutraceuticals"—foods that have therapeutic benefits.

In 2016, Ceapro opened a new bioprocessing extraction facility in Edmonton with state-of-the-art equipment to gear up for increased production. The company also expected to boost its profit margin as the new plant is more efficient. Three years later, in May 2019, Ceapro announced that both its plants had received Site Licences from Health Canada's Natural and Non-Prescription Health Products Directorate. These licences allow Ceapro to fabricate, package, label, release, and distribute biopharmaceutical products.

Ceapro also produces beta glucan, a by-product of oats, which helps reduce cholesterol, moderate blood sugar levels, and stimulate collagen synthesis. In 2018 the company began a long-term collaboration with the Montreal Heart Institute to carry out clinical research, starting with a study of beta glucan's ability to lower cholesterol.

The company signed a licence and distribution agreement in 2013 with German-based multinational Symrise, the leading provider of active ingredients in the cosmetic market. In 2017 Ceapro acquired Quebec-based company Juvente and launched a proprietary line of cosmeceutical products. Ceapro's annual sales have been over $10 million in the last few years, and President and CEO Gilles Gagnon has noted the company "has all the key components for success based on a very solid foundation, a highly competent team, a healthy balance sheet and a very strong technology and product portfolio with the potential to access key large markets."

Sources: Ceapro website, www.ceapro.com/; Leonard Zehr, "Ceapro Transitioning to Biopharmaceutical Company from Contract Manufacturer,"

BioTuesdays, May 7, 2019, biotuesdays.com/2019/05/07/2019-5-1-ceapro-transitioning-to-biopharmaceutical-company-from-contract-manufacturer/; "Ceapro Signs a License and Distribution Agreement with Symrise," company news release, May 9, 2013; "Ceapro Launched Proprietary Line of Cosmeceutical Products, JUVENTE," Nutraceutical Business Review, November 1, 2017, www.nutraceuticalbusinessreview.com/news/article_page/Ceapro_launched_proprietary_line_of_cosmeceutical_products_JUVENTE/135473; "Ceapro Inc. Reports Fourth Quarter and Full Year 2018 Results and Highlights," press release, April 11, 2019, www.ceapro.com/news/press-releases/detail/168/ceapro-inc-reports-fourth-quarter-and-full-year-2018

Discussion

1. With every business, it is important to evaluate what components are relevant to the size of a customer's purchase. Ceapro's management is interested in determining this information. Suppose its research team is able to obtain appropriate and relevant data on several customer companies. These data will allow Ceapro to analyze what variables may be predictors of the size of the purchase. The data that Ceapro collected from 15 companies include four variables: the total size of the purchase, the size of the purchasing company, the cost of delivery, and the number of similar products that the purchasing company has. Use the techniques learned in this chapter to obtain a multiple regression model to predict the size of the purchase on the basis of all or some of the other variables mentioned above. Determine the goodness of fit of the regression model, and determine which variables (if any) contribute significantly to the prediction of size of purchase.

Size of Purchase ($ thousands)	Company Size ($ millions sales)	Cost of Delivery ($)	Similar Products
26.3	26.3	200	3
87.9	108.1	710	4
11.8	39.7	180	2
33.7	15.3	1120	1
406.5	280.6	2130	1
175.4	98.1	1100	3
104.1	102.7	810	2
512.3	137.4	430	0
381.4	209.1	400	0
85.3	25.3	120	1
101.2	14.1	240	3
28.5	5.9	570	4
233.8	85.5	930	0
465.8	179.2	1980	1
307.2	133.4	770	2

2. Assume that Ceapro has been able to gather the following data for the past 10 years regarding average sales, average hours worked per week by full-time employees, and the number of

customers that purchase Ceapro's products. Analyze the average hours worked per week and the number of customers, and interpret how these two variables are relevant to the sales figures. In order to address this, construct scatter plots to analyze the possibility of a relationship between the sales and hours worked per week and the sales and the number of customers. Would it be possible to recode the data using Tukey's four-quadrant approach? If yes, use and explain the approach. The relationship between these variables may also be examined by using stepwise regression analysis; therefore, let the response variable be the sales figure and allow the predictors to be average number of hours worked per week, number of customers, and any new variables that have been developed through the recoding process. With all the information you have collected, you can now analyze the quadratic relationships, interaction, and any other relationships by using stepwise regression.

Average Sales ($ millions)	Hours Worked per Week	Number of Customers
16.4	45	56
16.1	41	51
15.7	42	55
13.8	39	53
12.3	41	38
9.2	40	26
9.9	44	42
10.1	37	59
12.6	33	70
13.8	38	188

3. Ceapro is doing well and is growing. However, there is always a risk of reverting back to being the financially unstable company it once was if it does not continue to invest in R&D and develop new products. Ceapro's sales have been healthy over the last few years; however, these sales may stall or decrease. What if, at this point, Ceapro still continues to hire employees? Below are the data indicating how these figures might look over a future 10-year period. By using the sales as the response variable and the number of employees as the predictor, graph the information and then use Tukey's four-quadrant approach to analyze the graph. Now, construct and explore a regression model in order to predict sales by using the number of employees. Analyze the information that you find and determine whether there is any need for concern or any need to contact top management to inform them of any critical issues.

Sales ($ millions)	Number of Employees
21.3	125
23.8	119
29.6	135
32.5	130
36.1	143
35.3	150
37.8	161
34.4	157
37.9	185
35.8	213

Big Data Case

Using the American Hospital Association database, explore the following analyses.

1. A little over 40% of the hospitals in this database had no births during the year for which the data were collected. Of the hospitals that did have births, the numbers varied from one birth to over 7,000. What variables might predict whether or not a hospital has births? In an effort to assist you in your search for answers to this question, a column (variable) entitled Births or Not has been added to the AHA database with a coding of 0 if there were not births at the hospital and a 1 if there was at least 1 birth at the hospital. Letting this column be a dependent variable, develop a logistic regression model to predict whether or not a hospital had at least one birth, using Beds as a predictor. Applying the resultant prediction equation, determine the probability that a hospital with 200 beds

had any births. Now, do the same for a hospital with 30 beds. What information might you be getting from this analysis? What conclusions might you make from the database about whether or not a hospital has births?

2. Using stepwise regression, develop a regression model to predict Personnel by Number of Beds, Number of Admissions, Census, Number of Outpatients, Number of Births, Total Expenditures, and Payroll Expenditures. Use an α of 0.10 as the cutoff for entering or removing a variable from the model. What did you find? How many steps did the process produce? How strong was the model?

What are the strongest predictors and what variables appear to add no significant predictability? Next, run a correlation matrix of the predictors in an effort to determine if there is multicollinearity. If you find that there is, how could you go about rectifying the situation?

Using the Computer

- Excel does not have model-building search procedure capability. However, Excel can perform multiple regression analysis. The commands are essentially the same as those for simple regression except that the x range of data may include several columns. Excel will determine the number of predictor variables from the number of columns entered in **Input X Range.**

- Begin by selecting the **Data** tab on the Excel worksheet. From the **Analyze** panel at the top right of the **Data** ribbon, click on **Data Analysis.** If your Excel worksheet does not show the **Data Analysis** option, you can load it as an add-in. From the **Data Analysis** menu, select **Regression.** In the **Regression** dialogue box, input the location of the y values in **Input Y**

Range. Input the location of the x values in **Input X Range.** Check **Labels** if your selected data contain row headings. Check and input **Confidence Level.** To pass the line through the origin, check **Constant is Zero.** To print out the raw residuals, check **Residuals.** To print out residuals converted to z scores, check **Standardized Residuals.** For a plot of the residuals, check **Residual Plots.** For a plot of the line through the points, check **Line Fit Plots.**

- Standard output includes R, R^2, and s_e; an ANOVA table with the F test, the slope and intercept, t-statistics, and associated p-values; and any optionally requested output such as graphs or residuals.

CHAPTER 15

Time-Series Forecasting and Index Numbers

LEARNING OBJECTIVES

This chapter discusses the general use of forecasting in business, several tools that are available for making business forecasts, the nature of time-series data, and the role of index numbers in business, thereby enabling you to:

15.1 Differentiate among various measurements of forecasting error, including mean absolute deviation and mean square error, in order to assess which forecasting method to use.

15.2 Describe smoothing techniques for forecasting models, including naive, simple average, moving average, weighted moving average, and exponential smoothing.

15.3 Determine trend in time-series data by using linear regression trend analysis, quadratic model trend analysis, and Holt's two-parameter exponential smoothing method.

15.4 Account for seasonal effects of time-series data by using decomposition and Winters' three-parameter exponential smoothing method.

15.5 Test for autocorrelation using the Durbin-Watson test, overcoming autocorrelation by adding independent variables and transforming variables, and taking advantage of autocorrelation with autoregression.

15.6 Differentiate among simple index numbers, unweighted aggregate price index numbers, weighted aggregate price index numbers, Laspeyres price index numbers, and Paasche price index numbers by defining and calculating each.

Decision Dilemma

Forecasting Air Pollution

For the past two decades, there has been heightened awareness of and increased concern over pollution in various forms in different countries around the world. One of the main areas of environmental concern is air pollution. Environment Canada regularly monitors the quality of air around the country. Some of the air pollutants monitored are carbon monoxide emissions, nitrogen oxide emissions, volatile organic compounds, sulphur dioxide emissions, particulate matter, fugitive dust, and lead emissions. Shown below are emission data for two of these air pollution variables, carbon monoxide and nitrogen oxides, over a 28-year period reported by the U.S. Environmental Protection Agency in millions of tonnes.

iStock.com/wolv

Year	Carbon Monoxide	Nitrogen Oxides
1991	147.13	25.18
1992	140.90	25.26
1993	135.90	25.36
1994	133.56	25.35
1995	126.78	24.96
1996	128.86	24.79
1997	117.91	24.71
1998	115.38	24.35
1999	114.54	22.85
2000	114.47	22.60
2001	106.26	21.55
2002	102.03	23.96
2003	99.59	22.65
2004	97.15	21.33
2005	88.55	20.36
2006	85.84	19.23
2007	83.13	18.10
2008	79.66	16.91
2009	72.75	15.77
2010	73.77	14.85
2011	73.76	14.52
2012	71.76	13.88
2013	69.76	13.24
2014	65.54	12.59
2015	64.46	11.84
2016	61.85	11.30
2017	60.00	10.77
2018	58.16	10.33

Managerial, Statistical, and Analytical Questions

1. Is it possible to forecast the emissions of carbon monoxide or nitrogen oxides for the years 2020, 2024, or even 2032 using these data?
2. What techniques best forecast the emissions of carbon monoxide or nitrogen oxides for future years from these data?

Sources: Average Annual Emissions, U.S. Environmental Protection Agency (EPA) at www.epa.gov/air-emissions-inventories/air-pollutant-emissions-trends-data; "About the Air Quality Health Index," Environment Canada, www.canada.ca/en/environment-climate-change/services/air-quality-health-index/about.html "Exposure to Air Pollution: A Major Public Concern" (Geneva: World Health Organization, 2012).

Introduction

Every day, forecasting is used in the decision-making process to help business people reach conclusions about buying, selling, producing, hiring, and many other actions. As an example, consider the following items:

- Market watchers predict a resurgence of stock values next year.
- Planners predict a crisis in fish stocks off the coast of Newfoundland.
- Future brightens for solar power.
- Energy minister sees rising demand for oil.
- CEO says difficult times won't be ending soon for the Canadian airline industry.
- Life insurance outlook fades.
- Increased competition from overseas businesses will result in significant layoffs in the Canadian software industry.

How are these and other conclusions reached? What forecasting techniques are used? Are the forecasts accurate? In this chapter, we discuss several forecasting techniques, how to measure the error of a forecast, and some of the problems that can occur in forecasting. In addition, this chapter will focus only on data that occur over time—that is, time-series data.

15.1 | Introduction to Forecasting

LEARNING OBJECTIVE 15.1

Differentiate among various measurements of forecasting error, including mean absolute deviation and mean square error, in order to assess which forecasting method to use.

Forecasting is *the art or science of predicting the future* to help business people make decisions about buying, selling, manufacturing, hiring, and a host of other business activities. Virtually all areas of business, including production, sales, employment, transportation, distribution, and inventory, produce and maintain time-series data.

Time-series data are *data gathered on a given characteristic over a period of time at regular intervals.* Time-series forecasting techniques attempt to account for changes over time by examining patterns, cycles, or trends, or using information about previous time periods to predict the outcome for a future time period. Time-series methods include naive methods, averaging, smoothing, regression trend analysis, and the decomposition of the possible time-series factors, all of which are discussed in subsequent sections.

Table 15.1 provides an example of time-series data containing the bond yield rates of three-month treasury bills for a 17-year period. Why does the average yield differ from year to year? Is it possible to use these time-series data to predict average yields for year 18 or ensuing years? Figure 15.1 is a graph of these data over time. A graphical depiction of time-series data can often give a clue about any trends, cycles, or relationships that might exist there. Does the graph in Figure 15.1 show that bond yields are decreasing? Will next year's yield rate be lower or is a cycle occurring in these data that will result in an increase? To answer such questions, it is sometimes helpful to determine which of the four components of time-series data exist in the data being studied.

TABLE 15.1
Bond Yields of Three-Month Treasury Bills

Year	Average Yield
1	14.03%
2	10.69
3	8.63
4	9.58
5	7.48
6	5.98
7	5.82
8	6.69
9	8.12
10	7.51
11	5.42
12	3.45
13	3.02
14	4.29
15	5.51
16	5.02
17	5.07

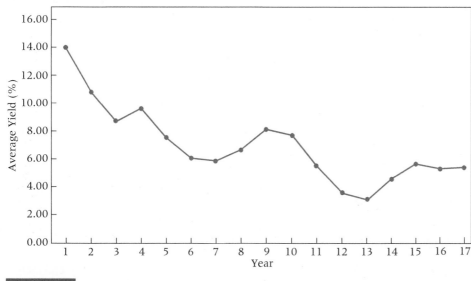

FIGURE 15.1 **Excel Graph of Bond Yield Time-Series Data**

Time-Series Components

It is generally believed that time-series data are composed of four elements: trends, cycles, seasonal effects, and irregular fluctuations. Not all time-series data have all these elements. Consider Figure 15.2, which shows the effects of these time-series elements on data over a period of 13 years.

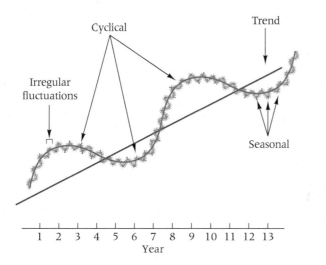

FIGURE 15.2 **Time-Series Effects**

The long-term general direction of data is referred to as **trend**. Notice that even though the data depicted in Figure 15.2 move through upward and downward periods, the general direction or trend is increasing (denoted in Figure 15.2 by the line). **Cycles** are *patterns of highs and lows through which data move over time periods usually of more than a year.* Notice that the data in Figure 15.2 seemingly move through two periods or cycles of highs and lows over a 13-year period. Time-series data that do not extend over a long period of time may not have enough "history" to show **cyclical effects**. **Seasonal effects**, on the other hand, are *shorter cycles, which usually occur in time periods of less than one year.* Often seasonal effects are measured by the month, but they may occur by quarter, or may be measured in as small a time frame as a week or even a day. Note the seasonal effects shown in Figure 15.2 as up and down cycles, many of which occur during a one-year period. **Irregular fluctuations** are *rapid changes or "blips" in the data, which occur in even shorter time frames than seasonal effects.* Irregular fluctuations can happen as often as day to day. They are subject to momentary change and are often unexplained. Note the irregular fluctuations in the data of Figure 15.2.

Observe again the bond yield data depicted in Figure 15.1. The general trend seems to move downward and contain two cycles. Each of the cycles traverses approximately five to eight years. It is possible, although not displayed here, that seasonal periods of highs and lows within each year result in seasonal bond yields. In addition, irregular daily fluctuations of bond yield rates may occur but are unexplainable.

Time-series data that contain no trend, cyclical effects, or seasonal effects are said to be **stationary**. Techniques used to forecast stationary data analyze only the irregular fluctuation effects.

The Measurement of Forecasting Error

In this chapter, several forecasting techniques will be introduced that typically produce different forecasts. How does a decision-maker know which forecasting technique is doing the best job of predicting the future? One way is to compare forecast values with actual values and determine the amount of **forecasting error** a technique produces. An examination of individual errors gives some insight into the accuracy of the forecasts. However, this process can be tedious, especially for large data sets, and often a single measurement of overall forecasting error is needed for the entire set of data under consideration. Any of several methods can be used to compute error in forecasting. The choice depends on the forecaster's objective, the forecaster's familiarity with the technique, and the method of error measurement used by the computer forecasting software. Several techniques can be used to measure overall error, including mean error (ME), mean absolute deviation (MAD), mean square error (MSE), mean percentage error (MPE), and mean absolute percentage error (MAPE). Here we will consider the mean absolute deviation (MAD) and the mean square error (MSE).

Error

The **error of an individual forecast** is *the difference between the actual value and the forecast of that value.*

Error of an Individual Forecast

$$e_t = X_t - F_t \qquad (15.1)$$

where
$\quad e_t$ = the error of the forecast
$\quad X_t$ = the actual value
$\quad F_t$ = the forecast value

Mean Absolute Deviation (MAD)

One measure of overall error in forecasting is the mean absolute deviation, MAD. The **mean absolute deviation (MAD)** is *the mean, or average, of the absolute values of the errors.*

Table 15.2 presents the nonfarm partnership tax returns in the U.S. over an 11-year period along with the forecast for each year and the error of the forecast. An examination of these data reveals that some of the forecast errors are positive and some are negative. In summing these errors in an attempt to compute an overall measure of error, the negative and positive values offset each other, resulting in an underestimation of the total error. The mean absolute deviation overcomes this problem by taking the absolute value of the error measurement, thereby analyzing the magnitude of the forecast errors without regard to direction.

TABLE 15.2   **Nonfarm Partnership Tax Returns**

Year	Actual	Forecast	Error
1	1402	—	—
2	1458	1402.0	56.0
3	1553	1441.2	111.8
4	1613	1519.5	93.5
5	1676	1585.0	91.0
6	1755	1648.7	106.3
7	1807	1723.1	83.9
8	1824	1781.8	42.2
9	1826	1811.3	14.7
10	1780	1821.6	−41.6
11	1759	1792.5	−33.5

Mean Absolute Deviation

$$\text{MAD} = \frac{\Sigma |e_i|}{\text{Number of Forecasts}} \tag{15.2}$$

The mean absolute error can be computed for the forecast errors in Table 15.2 as follows:

$$\text{MAD} = \frac{|56.0| + |111.8| + |93.5| + |91.0| + |106.3| + |83.9| + |42.2| + |14.7| + |-41.6| + |-33.5|}{10}$$

$$= 67.45$$

Mean Square Error (MSE)

The **mean square error (MSE)** is another way to circumvent the problem of the cancelling effects of positive and negative forecast errors. The MSE is *computed by squaring each error (thus creating a positive number) and averaging the squared errors.* The following formula states it more formally.

Mean Square Error

$$MSE = \frac{\sum e_i^2}{\text{Number of Forecasts}}$$ (15.3)

The mean square error can be computed for the errors shown in Table 15.2 as follows:

$$MSE = \left[\frac{56.0^2 + 111.8^2 + 93.5^2 + 91.0^2 + 106.3^2 + 83.9^2 + 42.2^2 + 14.7^2 + (-41.6)^2 + (-33.5)^2}{10} \right]$$
$$= 5,584.7$$

Selection of a particular mechanism for computing error is up to the forecaster. It is important to understand that different error techniques will yield different information. The business analyst should be informed enough about the various error measurement techniques to make an educated evaluation of the forecasting results.

Business Analytics, Predictive Analytics, and Forecasting

Forecasting's place in the era of big data and business analytics is substantial and important. However, because forecasting models have primarily been developed using historical time-series data that have often been recorded over years, many of the methods used have resulted in static models yielding information about long-term patterns for large populations. Of course, such forecasting modelling can be very helpful to decision-makers dealing with situations that require managerial action while taking into account the big picture.

In the business analytics scheme, forecasting is generally classified as a component of predictive analytics. Potentially, predictive analytics, paired with big data, can produce real-time forecasts that can be continuously updated. From a more narrow perspective, predictive analytics is used to predict the behaviour of individuals (rather than groups) on a short timeline (rather than long-term). In the past, traditional forecasting methodology has rarely, if ever, been used in this manner.

There are ways that traditional forecasting can contribute to business analytics. One of the issues in the era of big data is to sort out the signal from the noise. Many traditional forecasting techniques have been developed and used to smooth data and provide insights into a broader view, thereby reducing the impact of outliers and irregular fluctuations. In addition to smoothing techniques, the process of decomposition has great potential for taking long streams of data and removing superfluous information while highlighting trends, cycles, and seasons.

In the future, as a branch of predictive analytics, forecasting may well adapt itself in new ways to incorporate large influxes of real-time data to reach business conclusions about either individuals or populations.

Concept Check

1. What is a time series? Would you say that data collected at random intervals over a number of years may be called a time series? Why or why not?

2. What are the four components of time-series data? Do all time-series data have all four components?

3. Name two methods of measuring forecasting errors. Why do these methods avoid simply averaging positive and negative errors?

15.1 Problems

15.1 Use the forecast errors given here to compute MAD and MSE. Discuss the information yielded by each type of error measurement.

Period	e
1	2.3
2	1.6
3	−1.4
4	1.1
5	0.3
6	−0.9
7	−1.9
8	−2.1
9	0.7

15.2 Determine the error for each of the following forecasts. Compute MAD and MSE.

Period	Value	Forecast
1	202	—
2	191	202
3	173	192
4	169	181
5	171	174
6	175	172
7	182	174
8	196	179
9	204	189
10	219	198
11	227	211

15.3 Using the following data, determine the values of MAD and MSE. Which of these measurements of error seems to yield the best information about the forecasts? Why?

Period	Value	Forecast
1	19.4	16.6
2	23.6	19.1
3	24.0	22.0
4	26.8	24.8
5	29.2	25.9
6	35.5	28.6

15.4 Figures for hectares of tomatoes harvested over an 11-year period follow. With these data, forecasts have been made by using techniques presented later in this chapter. Compute MAD and MSE on these forecasts. Comment on the errors.

Year	Number of Hectares	Forecast
1	140,000	—
2	141,730	140,000
3	134,590	141,038
4	131,710	137,169
5	131,910	133,894
6	134,250	132,704
7	135,220	133,632
8	131,020	134,585
9	120,640	132,446
10	115,190	125,362
11	114,510	119,259

15.2 | Smoothing Techniques

LEARNING OBJECTIVE 15.2

Describe smoothing techniques for forecasting models, including naive, simple average, moving average, weighted moving average, and exponential smoothing.

Several techniques are available to forecast time-series data that are stationary, or that include no significant trend, cyclical effects, or seasonal effects. These techniques are often referred to as **smoothing techniques** because they *produce forecasts based on "smoothing out" the irregular fluctuation effects in the time-series data.* Three general categories of smoothing techniques are presented here: (1) naive forecasting models, (2) averaging models, and (3) exponential smoothing.

Naive Forecasting Models

Naive forecasting models are *simple models in which it is assumed that the more recent time periods of data represent the best predictions or forecasts for future outcomes.* Naive models do not take into account data trend, cyclical effects, or seasonality. For this reason, naive models seem to work better with data that are reported on a daily or weekly basis or in situations that show no trend or seasonality. The simplest of the naive forecasting methods is the model in which the forecast for a given time period is the value for the previous time period:

$$F_t = X_{t-1}$$

where

F_t = the forecast value for time period t

X_{t-1} = the value for time period $t - 1$

As an example, if 532 pairs of shoes were sold by a retailer last week, this naive forecasting model would predict that the retailer will sell 532 pairs of shoes this week. With this naive model, the actual sales for this week will be the forecast for next week.

Table 15.3 presents the average price of lettuce in Canada for a given year. **Figure 15.3** presents an Excel graph of the prices over the 12-month period. From these data, we can make a naive forecast of the price of lettuce for January of the next year by using the figure for December, which is 0.823.

TABLE 15.3

Average Price of Lettuce in Canada

Month	Average Price ($)
January	0.876
February	0.805
March	0.813
April	0.801
May	0.710
June	0.751
July	0.737
August	0.808
September	0.771
October	0.830
November	0.849
December	0.823

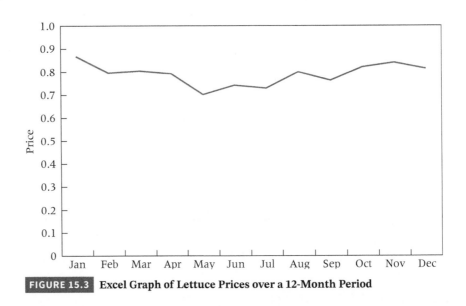

FIGURE 15.3 **Excel Graph of Lettuce Prices over a 12-Month Period**

Another version of the naive forecast might be to use the price in January of the previous year as the forecast for January of next year, because the business analyst may believe a relationship exists between lettuce prices and the month of the year. In this case, the naive forecast for next January from Table 15.3 is 0.876 (January of the previous year). The forecaster is free to be creative with the naive forecast model method and search for other relationships or rationales within the limits of the time-series data that would seemingly produce a valid forecast.

Averaging Models

Many naive model forecasts are based on the value of one time period. Often such forecasts become a function of irregular fluctuations of the data; as a result, the forecasts are "over-steered." Using averaging models, a forecaster enters information from several time periods into the forecast and "smooths" the data. **Averaging models** are computed by *averaging data from several time periods and using the average as the forecast for the next time period.*

Simple Averages

The most elementary of the averaging models is the **simple average model**. With this model, *the forecast for time period t is the average of the values for a given number of previous time periods,* as shown in the following equation:

$$F_t = \frac{X_{t-1} + X_{t-2} + X_{t-3} + \ldots + X_{t-n}}{n}$$

The data in **Table 15.4** provide the prices of natural gas futures in Canada for two years and five months. **Figure 15.4** displays a graph of these data.

A simple 12-month average could be used to forecast the price of natural gas for June of year 3 from the data in Table 15.4 by averaging the values for June of year 2 through May of year 3 (the preceding 12 months):

$$F_{\text{June, year 3}} = \frac{2.96 + 2.86 + 2.85 + 2.78 + 3.14 + 3.28 + 4.49 + 3.04 + 2.73 + 2.86 + 2.66 + 2.57}{12}$$
$$= 3.02$$

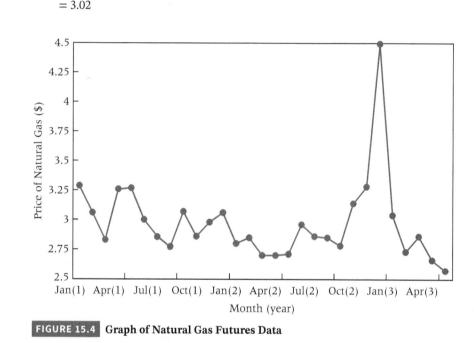

FIGURE 15.4 **Graph of Natural Gas Futures Data**

With this **simple average**, the forecast for year 3 June price of natural gas is $3.02. Note that none of the previous 12-month figures equal this value and that this average is not necessarily more closely related to values early in the period than to those late in the period. The use of the simple average over 12 months tends to smooth the variations, or fluctuations, that occur during this time.

Moving Averages

Suppose we were to attempt to forecast the price of natural gas for July of year 3 by using averages as the forecasting method. Would we still use the simple average for June of year 2 through May of year 3 as we did to forecast for June of year 3? Instead of using the same 12 months' average used to forecast June of year 3, it would seem to make sense to use the 12 months prior to July of year 3 (July of year 2 through June of year 3) to average for the new forecast. Suppose in June of year 3 the price of natural gas is $2.45. We could forecast July of year 3 with a new average that includes the same months used to forecast June of year 3, but without the value for June of year 2 and with the value of June of year 3 added:

$$F_{\text{July, Year 3}} = \frac{2.86 + 2.85 + 2.78 + 3.14 + 3.28 + 4.49 + 3.04 + 2.73 + 2.86 + 2.66 + 2.57 + 2.45}{12}$$
$$= 2.98$$

Computing an average of the values from July of year 2 through June of year 3 produces a moving average, which can be used to forecast the price of natural gas for July of year 3. In computing this moving average, the earliest of the previous 12 values, June of year 2, is dropped and the most recent value, June of year 3, is included.

TABLE 15.4

Prices of Natural Gas Futures ($)

Time Frame	Price of Natural Gas Futures ($)
January (year 1)	3.29
February	3.06
March	2.83
April	3.26
May	3.27
June	3.00
July	2.86
August	2.77
September	3.07
October	2.86
November	2.98
December	3.06
January (year 2)	2.80
February	2.85
March	2.70
April	2.70
May	2.71
June	2.96
July	2.86
August	2.85
September	2.78
October	3.14
November	3.28
December	4.49
January (year 3)	3.04
February	2.73
March	2.86
April	2.66
May	2.57

A **moving average** is *an average that is updated or recomputed for every new time period being considered.* The most recent information is utilized in each new moving average. This advantage is offset by the disadvantages that (1) it is difficult to choose the optimal length of time for which to compute the moving average and (2) moving averages do not usually adjust for such time-series effects as trend, cycles, or seasonality. To determine the optimal lengths for which to compute the moving averages, we would need to forecast with several different average lengths and compare the errors produced by them.

DEMONSTRATION PROBLEM 15.1

Shown here are shipments (in $ millions) for electric lighting and wiring equipment over a 12-month period. Use these data to compute a 4-month moving average for all available months.

Month	Shipments
January	1056
February	1345
March	1381
April	1191
May	1259
June	1361
July	1110
August	1334
September	1416
October	1282
November	1341
December	1382

Solution The first moving average is:

$$\text{4-Month Moving Average} = \frac{1{,}056 + 1{,}345 + 1{,}381 + 1{,}191}{4} = 1{,}243.25$$

This first 4-month moving average can be used to forecast the shipments in May. Because 1,259 shipments were actually made in May, the error of the forecast is:

$$\text{Error}_{\text{May}} = 1{,}259 - 1{,}243.25 = 15.75$$

Shown next, along with the monthly shipments, are the 4-month moving averages and the errors of forecast when using the 4-month moving averages to predict the next month's shipments. The first moving average is displayed beside the month of May because it is computed by using January, February, March, and April and because it is being used to forecast the shipments for May. The rest of the 4-month moving averages and errors of forecast are as shown.

4-Month Moving Forecast

Month	Shipments	Average	Error
January	1056	—	—
February	1345	—	—
March	1381	—	—
April	1191	—	—
May	1259	1243.25	15.75
June	1361	1294.00	67.00
July	1110	1298.00	−188.00
August	1334	1230.25	103.75
September	1416	1266.00	150.00
October	1282	1305.25	−23.25
November	1341	1285.50	55.50
December	1382	1343.25	38.75

The following graph shows the actual shipment values and the forecast shipment values based on the 4-month moving averages. Notice that the moving averages are "smoothed" in comparison with the individual data values. They appear to be less volatile and seem to be attempting to follow the general trend of the data.

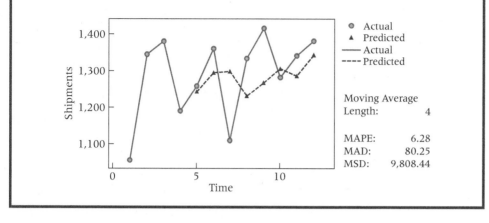

Weighted Moving Averages

A forecaster may want to place more weight on certain periods of time than on others. For example, a forecaster might believe that the previous month's value is three times as important in forecasting as other months. *A moving average in which some time periods are weighted differently than others* is called a **weighted moving average**.

As an example, suppose a 3-month weighted average is computed by weighting last month's value by 3, the value for the previous month by 2, and the value for the month before that by 1. This weighted average is computed as:

$$\bar{x}_{weighted} = \frac{3(M_{t-1}) + 2(M_{t-2}) + 1(M_{t-3})}{6}$$

where

M_{t-1} = last month's value
M_{t-2} = value for the previous month
M_{t-3} = value for the month before the previous month

Notice that the divisor is 6. With a weighted average, the divisor always equals the total number of weights. In this example, the value of M_{t-1} counts three times as much as the value for M_{t-3}.

DEMONSTRATION PROBLEM 15.2

Compute a 4-month weighted moving average for the electric lighting and wiring data from Demonstration Problem 15.1, using weights of 4 for last month's value, 2 for the previous month's value, and 1 for each of the values from the two months prior to that.

Solution   The first weighted average is:

$$\frac{4(1,191) + 2(1,381) + 1(1,345) + 1(1,056)}{8} = 1,240.875$$

This moving average is recomputed for each ensuing month. Displayed next are the monthly values, the weighted moving averages, and the forecast error for the data.

Month	Shipments	4-Month Weighted Moving Average Forecast	Error
January	1056	—	—
February	1345	—	—
March	1381	—	—
April	1191	—	—
May	1259	1240.9	18.1
June	1361	1268.0	93.0
July	1110	1316.8	−206.8
August	1334	1201.5	132.5
September	1416	1272.0	144.0
October	1282	1350.4	−68.4
November	1341	1300.5	40.5
December	1382	1334.8	47.2

Note that in this problem the errors obtained by using the 4-month weighted moving average were greater than most of the errors obtained by using an unweighted 4-month moving average, as shown here.

Forecast Error, Unweighted 4-Month Moving Average	Forecast Error, Weighted 4-Month Moving Average
—	—
—	—
—	—
—	—
15.8	18.1
67.0	93.0
−188.0	−206.8
103.8	132.5
150.0	144.0
−23.3	−68.4
55.5	40.5
38.8	47.2

Larger errors are not always associated with weighted moving averages. The forecaster can experiment with different weights in using the weighted moving average as a technique. Many possible weighting schemes can be used.

Exponential Smoothing

Another forecasting technique, **exponential smoothing**, is *used to weight data from previous time periods with exponentially decreasing importance in the forecast.* Exponential smoothing is accomplished by multiplying the actual value for the present time period, X_t, by a value between 0 and 1 (the exponential smoothing constant) referred to as α (not the same α used for a Type I error) and adding that result to the product of $(1 - \alpha)$ and the present time period's forecast, F_t. The following is a more formalized version.

Exponential Smoothing

$$F_{t+1} = \alpha \cdot X_t + (1 - \alpha) \cdot F_t \qquad (15.4)$$

where

F_{t+1} = the forecast for the next time period $(t + 1)$
F_t = the forecast for the present time period (t)
X_t = the actual value for the present time period
α = a value between 0 and 1 referred to as the exponential smoothing constant

---

Trend Analysis

LEARNING OBJECTIVE 15.3

Determine trend in time-series data by using linear regression trend analysis, quadratic model trend analysis, and Holt's two-parameter exponential smoothing method.

There are several ways to determine trend in time-series data, and one of the more prominent is regression analysis. In Section 12.9, we explored the use of simple regression analysis in determining the equation of a trend line. In time-series regression trend analysis, the response variable, Y, is the variable being forecast, and the independent variable, X, represents time.

Many possible trend fits can be explored with time-series data. In this section, we examine only the linear model and the quadratic model because they are the easiest to understand and simplest to compute. Because seasonal effects can confound trend analysis, it is assumed here that no seasonal effects occur in the data or they were removed prior to determining the trend (see Thinking Critically About Statistics in Business Today 15.1).

Thinking Critically About Statistics In Business Today 15.1

Can Scrap Metal Prices Forecast the Economy?

Economists are constantly on the lookout for valid indicators of a country's economy. Forecasters have sifted through oil indicators, the price of gold on the world markets, stock exchange averages, government-published indexes, and practically anything else that might seem related in some way to the state of the economy.

Would you believe that the price of scrap metal is a popular indicator of economic activity in the U.S.? Several well-known and experienced economic forecasters believe that the price of scrap metal is a good indicator of the industrial economy.

Scrap metal is leftover copper, steel, aluminum, and other metals. Scrap metal is a good indicator of industrial activity because as manufacturing increases, the demand for scrap metals increases, as does the price of scrap metal. Market analyst Donald Fine says that "scrap metal is the beginning of the production chain"; hence, an increasing demand for it is an indicator of increasing manufacturing production. Fine goes on to say that scrap metal is sometimes a better indicator of the future direction of the economy than many governmental statistics. In some cases, scrap metal correctly predicted no economic recovery when some government measures indicated that a recovery was under way.

Demand for steel and other metals in China, India, Turkey, the Middle East, and other emerging economies has helped drive up the price of scrap metal in the United States even when the U.S. economy has been somewhat stagnant. Perhaps the price of scrap metal in the United States has become more of a forecaster of the world economy than the U.S. economy.

In addition, because of an increased awareness of the need to protect the environment, there is a greater call for recycling, thereby resulting in a surge in the demand for, and the use of, scrap metal.

Things to Ponder

1. In the past, the U.S.-based scrap recycling industry has met about 40% of the global raw materials needs. If this is so, the scrap recycling industry is heavily involved in world industrial growth. Do you think that this source will continually replenish itself or eventually dry up? Why? What are some factors influencing your answer?
2. If U.S.-based scrap metal is reduced in the coming years, how might this impact world construction? Are there replacement sources? Where might such sources come from?

Sources: Anita Raghavan and David Wessel, "In Scraping Together Economic Data, Forecasters Turn to Scrap-Metal Prices," *The Wall Street Journal*, April 27, 1992, C1; Matt Phillips, "Beyond the Underwear Index: Four Other Odd Economic Indicators," *The Wall Street Journal* Market Beat blog, June 12, 2009, blogs.wsj.com/marketbeat/2009/06/12/beyond-the-underwear-index-four-other-odd-consumer-indicators/; "The Scrap-Metal Market: Nothing Glisters," *The Economist*, April 2, 2009; "Fast-Growing Global Economy Creates Expansion Opportunities for the Scrap Metal Industry," GLE Scrap Metal blog, glescrap.com/blog/fast-growing-global-economy-creates-expansion-opportunities-for-the-scrap-metal-industry/.

Linear Regression Trend Analysis

The data in **Table 15.5** represent 35 years of data on the average length of the workweek for manufacturing workers. A regression line can be fit to these data by using the time periods as the independent variable and length of workweek as the dependent variable. Because the

TABLE 15.5	Average Hours per Week in Manufacturing by Workers		
Time Period	**Hours**	**Time Period**	**Hours**
1	37.2	19	36.0
2	37.0	20	35.7
3	37.4	21	35.6
4	37.5	22	35.2
5	37.7	23	34.8
6	37.7	24	35.3
7	37.4	25	35.6
8	37.2	26	35.6
9	37.3	27	35.6
10	37.2	28	35.9
11	36.9	29	36.0
12	36.7	30	35.7
13	36.7	31	35.7
14	36.5	32	35.5
15	36.3	33	35.6
16	35.9	34	36.3
17	35.8	35	36.5
18	35.9		

Source: Data prepared by the U.S. Bureau of Labor Statistics, Office of Productivity and Technology.

time periods are consecutive, they can be renumbered from 1 to 35 and entered as X along with the time-series data (Y) into a regression analysis. The linear model explored in this example is:

$$Y_t = \beta_0 + \beta_1 X_t + \varepsilon_t$$

where
  Y_t = data value for period t
  X_t = tth time period

Figure 15.5 shows the Excel regression output for this example. By using the coefficients of the X variable and intercept, the equation of the trend line can be determined to be

$$\hat{Y} = 37.4161 - 0.0614 X_t$$

The slope indicates that for every unit increase in time period, X, a predicted decrease of 0.0614 occurs in the length of the average workweek in manufacturing. Because the workweek is measured in hours, the length of the average workweek decreases by an average of (0.0614) (60 minutes) = 3.7 minutes each year in manufacturing. The Y-intercept, 37.4161, indicates that in the year prior to the first period of these data the average workweek was 37.4161 hours.

The probability of the t ratio (0.00000003) indicates that a significant linear trend is present in the data. In addition, $R^2 = 0.611$ indicates considerable predictability in the model. Inserting the various period values (1, 2, 3, . . . , 35) into the preceding regression equation produces the predicted values of Y that are the trend. For example, for period 23 the predicted value is:

$$\hat{Y} = 37.4161 - 0.0614(23) = 36.0 \text{ hours}$$

	A	B	C	D	E	F
1	SUMMARY OUTPUT					
2	Regression Statistics					
3	Multiple R	0.782				
4	R Square	0.611				
5	Adjusted R Square	0.600				
6	Standard Error	0.5090				
7	Observations	35				
8						
9	ANOVA					
10		df	SS	MS	F	Significance F
11	Regression	1	13.4467	13.4467	51.91	0.000000029
12	Residual	33	8.5487	0.2591		
13	Total	34	21.9954			
14						
15		Coefficients	Standard Error	t Stat	P-value	
16	Intercept	37.4161	0.1758	212.81	0.00000000	
17	Year	−0.0614	0.0085	−7.20	0.00000003	

FIGURE 15.5 Excel **Regression Output for the Manufacturing Workweek Using Linear Trend**

The model was developed with 35 periods (years). From this model, the average workweek in manufacturing for period 41 (the 41st year) can be forecast:

$$\hat{Y} = 37.4161 - 0.0614(41) = 34.9 \text{ hours}$$

Figure 15.6 presents an Excel scatter plot of the average workweek lengths over the 35 periods (years). In this Excel plot, the trend line has been fitted through the points. Observe the general downward trend of the data, but also note the somewhat cyclical nature of the points. Because of this pattern, a forecaster might want to determine whether a quadratic model is a better fit for trend.

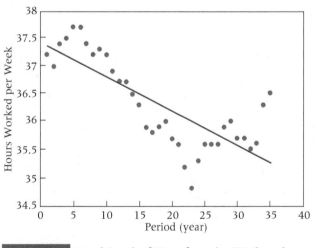

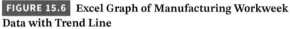

FIGURE 15.6 **Excel Graph of Manufacturing Workweek Data with Trend Line**

Regression Trend Analysis Using Quadratic Models

In addition to linear regression, forecasters can explore using quadratic regression models to predict data by using the time-series periods. The quadratic regression model is:

$$Y_t = \beta_0 + \beta_1 X_t + \beta_2 X_t^2 + \varepsilon_t$$

where
$\quad Y_t$ = the time-series data value for period t
$\quad X_t$ = the tth period
$\quad X_t^2$ = the square of the tth period

This model can be implemented in time-series trend analysis by using the time periods squared as an additional predictor. Thus, in the hours worked example, besides using $X_t = 1, 2, 3, 4, \ldots, 35$ as a predictor, we would use $X_t^2 = 1, 4, 9, 16, \ldots, 1{,}225$ as a predictor.

Table 15.6 provides the data needed to compute a quadratic regression trend model on the manufacturing workweek data. Note that the table includes the original data, the time periods, and the time periods squared.

TABLE 15.6 Data for Quadratic Fit of Manufacturing Workweek Example

Time Period	(TimePeriod)^2	Hours	Time Period	(Time Period)^2	Hours
1	1	37.2	19	361	36.0
2	4	37.0	20	400	35.7
3	9	37.4	21	441	35.6
4	16	37.5	22	484	35.2
5	25	37.7	23	529	34.8
6	36	37.7	24	576	35.3
7	49	37.4	25	625	35.6
8	64	37.2	26	676	35.6
9	81	37.3	27	729	35.6
10	100	37.2	28	784	35.9
11	121	36.9	29	841	36.0
12	144	36.7	30	900	35.7
13	169	36.7	31	961	35.7
14	196	36.5	32	1024	35.5
15	225	36.3	33	1089	35.6
16	256	35.9	34	1156	36.3
17	289	35.8	35	1225	36.5
18	324	35.9			

The Excel computer output for this quadratic trend regression analysis is shown in Figure 15.7. We see that the quadratic regression model produces an R^2 of 0.761 with both X_t and X_t^2 in the model. The linear model produced an R^2 of 0.611 with X_t alone. The quadratic regression seems to add some predictability to the trend model. Figure 15.8 displays an Excel scatter plot of the workweek data with a second-degree polynomial fit through the data.

FIGURE 15.7 Excel Regression Output for Manufacturing Workweek with Quadratic Trend

	A	B	C	D	E	F
1	SUMMARY OUTPUT					
2	Regression Statistics					
3	Multiple R	0.873				
4	R Square	0.761				
5	Adjusted R Square	0.747				
6	Standard Error	0.4049				
7	Observations	35				
8						
9	ANOVA					
10		df	SS	MS		F	Significance F
11	Regression	2	16.7483	8.3741		51.07	0.0000000001
12	Residual	32	5.2472	0.1640		
13	Total	34	21.9954			
14						
15		Coefficients	Standard Error	t Stat	P-Value	
16	Intercept	38.1644	0.2177	175.34	0.0000000	
17	Year	−0.1827	0.0279	−6.55	0.0000002	
18	YearSq	0.0034	0.0008	4.49	0.0000876	

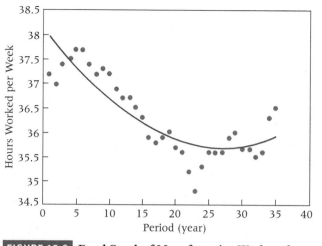

FIGURE 15.8 Excel Graph of Manufacturing Workweek with a Second-Degree Polynomial Fit

DEMONSTRATION PROBLEM 15.4

Following are data on the gross national per capita income of Canadians from the Organisation for Economic Co-operation and Development (OECD). Use regression analysis to fit a trend line through the data. Explore a quadratic regression trend also. Does either model do well? Compare the two models.

Year	Gross National Income per Capita
2007	38,963
2008	39,785
2009	38,226
2010	39,314
2011	40,876
2012	41,497
2013	43,538
2014	44,890
2015	43,987
2016	44,566
2017	46,305
2018	47,488

Solution Recode the time periods as 1 through 12 and let that be X. Run the regression analysis with Per Capita Income as Y, the dependent variable, and the time period as the independent variable. Now square all the X values, resulting in 1, 4, 9, . . ., 144 and let those formulate a second predictor (X^2). Run the regression analysis to predict the GNI per capita with both the time period variable (X) and the (time period)^2 variable. The results for each of these regression analyses follow.

Linear Trend Analysis

	A	B	C	D	E	F	G
1	SUMMARY OUTPUT						
2	*Regression Statistics*						
3	Multiple *R*	0.958064365					
4	*R* Square	0.917887327					
5	Adjusted *R* Square	0.90967606					
6	Standard Error	926.5165254					
7	Observations	12					
8							
9	ANOVA						
10		df	SS	MS	F	Significance F	
11	Regression	1	95958958.2	95958958	111.783881	9.51849E-07	
12	Residual	10	8584328.719	858432.9			
13	Total	11	104543286.9				
14							
15		Coefficients	Standard Error	*t* Stat	*P*-value	Lower 95%	Upper 95%
16	Intercept	37128.30303	570.2315027	65.11093	1.7778E-14	35857.74806	38398.858
17	Year	819.1713287	77.47920415	10.57279	9.5185E-07	646.5369037	991.805754

Quadratic Trend Analysis

	A	B	C	D	E	F	G
1	SUMMARY OUTPUT						
2	*Regression Statistics*						
3	Multiple *R*	0.963106363					
4	*R* Square	0.927573867					
5	Adjusted *R* Square	0.911479171					
6	Standard Error	917.2220131					
7	Observations	12					
8							
9	ANOVA						
10		df	SS	MS	F	Significance F	
11	Regression	2	96971620.92	48485810	57.6322694	7.40506E-06	
12	Residual	9	7571665.992	841296.2			
13	Total	11	104543286.9				
14							
15		Coefficients	Standard Error	*t* Stat	*P*-value	Lower 95%	Upper 95%
16	Intercept	37963.84091	947.9753833	40.04729	1.8783E-11	35819.37161	40108.3102
17	Year	461.0836663	335.2774353	1.37523	0.20232057	-297.3665855	1219.53392
18	Year Sq	27.5452048	25.10660917	1.09713	0.30107015	-29.24989098	84.3403006

A comparison of the models shows that the linear model accounts for 91.8% of the variability in Per Capita Income, and the quadratic model increases that predictability to 92.8%, a very marginal improvement at best. Even the standard errors of both models are approximately the same. When a more complex model (such as the quadratic model here) does not improve predictability by much, the simpler model should be preferred.

Holt's Two-Parameter Exponential Smoothing Method

The exponential smoothing technique presented in Section 15.2 (single or simple exponential smoothing) is appropriate to use in forecasting stationary time-series data but is ineffective in forecasting time-series data with a trend because the forecasts will lag behind the trend. However, another exponential smoothing technique, Holt's two-parameter exponential smoothing method, can be used for trend analysis. Holt's technique uses weights (β) to smooth the trend in a manner similar to the smoothing used in single exponential smoothing (α). Using these two weights and several equations, Holt's method is able to develop forecasts that include both a smoothing value and a trend value.

Concept Check

1. When you use linear regression to do trend analysis, what is the independent variable?
2. How do quadratic models differ from linear models in regression analysis?

15.3 Problems

15.10 Shown here are the figures for new manufacturers' orders over a 21-year period. Use a computer to develop a regression model to fit the trend effects for these data. Use a linear model and then try a quadratic model. How well does either model fit the data?

Year	Total Number of New Orders	Year	Total Number of New Orders
1	55,022	12	168,025
2	55,921	13	162,140
3	64,182	14	175,451
4	76,003	15	192,879
5	87,327	16	195,706
6	85,139	17	195,204
7	99,513	18	209,389
8	115,109	19	227,025
9	131,629	20	240,758
10	147,604	21	243,643
11	156,359		

15.11 The table below shows the Consumer Price Index (CPI) for food in Canada for the years 1998 to 2018. Using regression techniques discussed in this section, analyze the data for trend. Develop a scatter plot of the data and fit the trend line through the data. Discuss the strength of the model.

Year	CPI Food
1998	90.9
1999	92.0
2000	93.3
2001	97.4
2002	100.0
2003	101.7
2004	103.8
2005	106.4
2006	108.9
2007	111.8
2008	115.7
2009	121.4
2010	123.1
2011	127.7
2012	130.8
2013	132.4
2014	135.5
2015	140.5
2016	142.6
2017	142.7
2018	145.3

Source: Statistics Canada, Table 18-10-0005-01, "Consumer Price Index, annual average, not seasonally adjusted" (2002 = 100 unless otherwise noted).

15.12 Shown below is the part-time employment incidence (as a percentage of total employment) in Canada between 2008 and 2017, according to the Organisation for Economic Co-operation and Development (OECD). Plot the data, fit a trend line, and discuss the strength of the regression model. In addition, explore a quadratic trend and compare the results of the two models.

Year	Part-Time Employment (%)
2008	18.6
2009	19.3
2010	19.6
2011	19.3
2012	19.0
2013	19.1
2014	19.3
2015	18.9
2016	19.2
2017	19.1

Source: OECD, OECD Labour Force Statistics, 2018, doi.org/10.1787/oecd_lfs-2018-en (accessed on September 11, 2019).

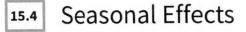

15.4 Seasonal Effects

LEARNING OBJECTIVE 15.4

Account for seasonal effects of time-series data by using decomposition and Winters' three-parameter exponential smoothing method.

Earlier in the chapter, we discussed the notion that time-series data consist of four elements: trend, cyclical effects, seasonality, and irregularity. In this section, we examine techniques for identifying seasonal effects. Seasonal effects are patterns of data behaviour that occur in periods of time of less than one year. How can we separate out the seasonal effects?

Decomposition

One of the main techniques for isolating the effects of seasonality is **decomposition**. The decomposition methodology presented here uses the multiplicative model as its basis. The multiplicative model is:

$$T \cdot C \cdot S \cdot I$$

where

T = trend
C = cycles
S = seasonal effects
I = irregular fluctuations

To illustrate the decomposition process, we will use the five-year quarterly time-series data on shipments of household appliances given in **Table 15.7**. **Figure 15.9** provides a graph of these data.

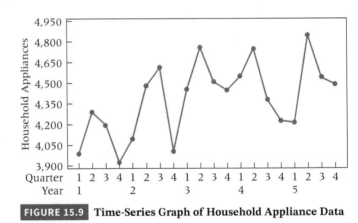

FIGURE 15.9 Time-Series Graph of Household Appliance Data

According to the multiplicative time-series model, $T \cdot C \cdot S \cdot I$, the data can contain the elements of trend, cycles, seasonal effects, and irregular fluctuations. The process of isolating the seasonal effects begins by determining $T \cdot C$ for each value and dividing the time-series data ($T \cdot C \cdot S \cdot I$) by $T \cdot C$. The result is:

$$\frac{T \cdot C \cdot S \cdot I}{T \cdot C} = S \cdot I$$

The resulting expression contains seasonal effects along with irregular fluctuations. After reducing the time-series data to the effects of SI (seasonal effects and irregular fluctuations), a method for eliminating the irregular fluctuations can be applied, leaving only the seasonal effects.

Suppose we start with time-series data that cover several years and are measured in quarterly increments. If we average the data over four quarters, we will have "damped" the seasonal effects of the data because the rise and fall of values during the quarterly periods will have been averaged out over the year.

TABLE 15.7

Shipments of Household Appliances

Year	Quarter	Shipments ($ millions)
1	1	4009
	2	4321
	3	4224
	4	3944
2	1	4123
	2	4522
	3	4657
	4	4030
3	1	4493
	2	4806
	3	4551
	4	4485
4	1	4595
	2	4799
	3	4417
	4	4258
5	1	4245
	2	4900
	3	4585
	4	4533

We begin by computing a 4-quarter moving average for quarter 1 through quarter 4 of year 1, using the data from Table 15.7.

$$\text{4-quarter average} = \frac{4{,}009 + 4{,}321 + 4{,}224 + 3{,}944}{4} = 4{,}124.5$$

The 4-quarter moving average for quarter 1 through quarter 4 of year 1 is 4,124.5 ($ millions) worth of shipments. Because the 4-quarter average is in the middle of the four quarters, it would be placed in the decomposition table between quarter 2 and quarter 3.

Quarter 1
Quarter 2
———— 4,124.5
Quarter 3
Quarter 4

To remove seasonal effects, we need to determine a value that is "centred" with each quarter. To find this value, instead of using a 4-quarter moving average, we use 4-quarter moving totals and then sum two consecutive moving totals. This 8-quarter total value is divided by 8 to produce a "centred" 4-quarter moving average that lines up across from a quarter. Using this method is analogous to computing two consecutive 4-quarter moving averages and averaging them, thus producing a value that falls in line with a quarter, in between the two averages. The results of using this procedure on the data from Table 15.7 are shown in Table 15.8 in column 5.

TABLE 15.8 Development of 4-Quarter Moving Averages for the Household Appliance Data

Quarter	Actual Values ($T{\cdot}C{\cdot}S{\cdot}I$)	4-Quarter Moving Total	4-Quarter Two-Year Moving Total	Ratios of Actual Centred Moving Average ($T{\cdot}C$)	Values to Moving Averages ($S{\cdot}I$)$\cdot$(100)
1 (year 1)	4009				
2	4321				
		16,498			
3	4224		33,110	4139	102.05
		16,612			
4	3944		33,425	4178	94.40
		16,813			
1 (year 2)	4123		34,059	4257	96.85
		17,246			
2	4522		34,578	4322	104.63
		17,332			
3	4657		35,034	4379	106.35
		17,702			
4	4030		35,688	4461	90.34
		17,986			
1 (year 3)	4493		35,866	4483	100.22
		17,880			
2	4806		36,215	4527	106.16
		18,335			
3	4551		36,772	4597	99.00
		18,437			
4	4485		36,867	4608	97.33
		18,430			
1 (year 4)	4595		36,726	4591	100.09
		18,296			
2	4799		36,365	4546	105.57
		18,069			
3	4417		35,788	4474	98.73
		17,719			
4	4258		35,539	4442	95.86
		17,820			
1 (year 5)	4245		35,808	4476	94.84
		17,988			
2	4900		36,251	4531	108.14
		18,263			
3	4585				
4	4533				

A 4-quarter moving total can be computed on these data starting with quarter 1 of year 1 through quarter 4 of year 1 as follows:

$$\text{First Moving Total} = 4{,}009 + 4{,}321 + 4{,}224 + 3{,}944 = 16{,}498$$

In Table 15.8, 16,498 is between quarter 2 and quarter 3 of year 1. The 4-month moving total for quarter 2 of year 1 through quarter 1 of year 2 is:

$$\text{Second Moving Total} = 4{,}321 + 4{,}224 + 3{,}944 + 4{,}123 = 16{,}612$$

In Table 15.8, this value is between quarter 3 and quarter 4 of year 1. The 8-quarter (two-year) moving total is computed for quarter 3 of year 1 as:

$$\text{8-Quarter Moving Total} = 16{,}498 + 16{,}612 = 33{,}110$$

Notice that in Table 15.8 this value is centred with quarter 3 of year 1 because it is between the two adjacent 4-quarter moving totals. Dividing this total by 8 produces the 4-quarter moving average for quarter 3 of year 1 shown in column 5 of Table 15.8:

$$\frac{33{,}110}{8} = 4{,}139$$

Column 3 contains the uncentred 4-quarter moving totals, column 4 contains the two-year centred moving totals, and column 5 contains the 4-quarter centred moving averages.

The 4-quarter centred moving averages shown in column 5 of Table 15.8 represent $T \cdot C$. Seasonal effects have been removed from the original data (actual values) by summing across the 4-quarter periods. Seasonal effects are removed when the data are summed across the time periods that include the seasonal periods, and the irregular effects are smoothed, leaving only trend and cycle.

Column 2 of Table 15.8 contains the original data (actual values), which include all effects ($T \cdot C \cdot S \cdot I$). Column 5 contains only the trend and cyclical effects, $T \cdot C$. If column 2 is divided by column 5, the result is $S \cdot I$, which is displayed in column 6 of Table 15.8.

The values in column 6, sometimes called ratios of actuals to moving average, have been multiplied by 100 to index the values. These values are thus seasonal indexes. An **index number** is *a ratio of a measure taken during one time frame to that same measure taken during another time frame, usually denoted as the time period*. Often the ratio is multiplied by 100 and expressed as a percentage. Index numbers will be discussed more fully in Section 15.6. Column 6 contains the effects of seasonality and irregular fluctuations. Now we must remove the irregular effects.

Table 15.9 contains the values from column 6 of Table 15.8 organized by quarter and year. Each quarter in these data has four seasonal indexes. Throwing out the high and low index for each quarter eliminates the extreme values. The remaining two indexes are averaged as follows for quarter 1:

Quarter 1: 96.85   100.22   100.09   94.84
Eliminate: 94.84 and 100.22
Average the Remaining Indexes:

$$\overline{X}_{\text{Q1 index}} = \frac{96.85 + 100.09}{2} = 98.47$$

TABLE 15.9 **Seasonal Indexes for the Household Appliance Data**

Quarter	Year 1	Year 2	Year 3	Year 4	Year 5
1	—	96.85	100.22	100.09	94.84
2	—	104.63	106.16	105.57	108.14
3	102.05	106.35	99.00	98.73	—
4	94.40	90.34	97.33	95.86	—

TABLE 15.10

Final Seasonal Indexes for the Household Appliance Data

Quarter	Index
1	98.47
2	105.87
3	100.53
4	95.13

Table 15.10 gives the final seasonal indexes for all the quarters of these data.

After the final adjusted seasonal indexes are determined, the original data can be **deseasonalized**. The deseasonalization of actual values is relatively common with data published by the government and other agencies. Data can be deseasonalized by dividing the actual values, which consist of $T \cdot C \cdot S \cdot I$, by the final adjusted seasonal effects:

$$\text{Deseasonalized Data} = \frac{T \cdot C \cdot S \cdot I}{S} = T \cdot C \cdot I$$

Because the seasonal effects are in terms of index numbers, the seasonal indexes must be divided by 100 before deseasonalization. Shown here are the computations for deseasonalizing the household appliance data from Table 15.7 for quarter 1 of year 1:

$$\text{Year 1 Quarter 1 Actual} = 4{,}009$$

$$\text{Year 1 Quarter 1 Seasonal Index} = 98.47$$

$$\text{Year 1 Quarter 1 Deseasonalized Value} = \frac{4{,}009}{0.9847} = 4{,}071.3$$

Table 15.11 gives the deseasonalized data for this example for all years. Figure 15.10 is a graph of the deseasonalized data.

TABLE 15.11 Deseasonalized Household Appliance Data

Year	Quarter	Shipments Actual Values $(T{\cdot}C{\cdot}S{\cdot}I)$	Seasonal Indexes S	Deseasonalized Data $T{\cdot}C{\cdot}I$
1	1	4009	98.47	4071
	2	4321	105.87	4081
	3	4224	100.53	4202
	4	3944	95.13	4146
2	1	4123	98.47	4187
	2	4522	105.87	4271
	3	4657	100.53	4632
	4	4030	95.13	4236
3	1	4493	98.47	4563
	2	4806	105.87	4540
	3	4551	100.53	4527
	4	4485	95.13	4715
4	1	4595	98.47	4666
	2	4799	105.87	4533
	3	4417	100.53	4394
	4	4258	95.13	4476
5	1	4245	98.47	4311
	2	4900	105.87	4628
	3	4585	100.53	4561
	4	4533	95.13	4765

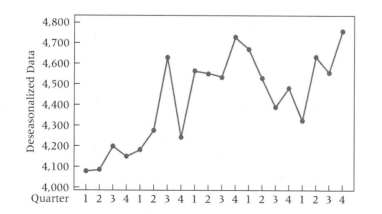

FIGURE 15.10 Graph of the Deseasonalized Household Appliance Data

Winters' Three-Parameter Exponential Smoothing Method

Holt's two-parameter exponential smoothing method can be extended to include seasonal analysis. This technique, referred to as Winters' method, not only smooths observations and trend but also smooths the seasonal effects. In addition to the single exponential smoothing weight of α and the trend weight of β, Winters' method introduces γ, a weight for seasonality. Using these three weights and several equations, Winters' method is able to develop forecasts that include a smoothing value for observations, a trend value, and a seasonal value.

Concept Check

1. What are seasonal effects?
2. What is the main technique used to isolate seasonality?

15.4 Problems

15.13 Given below are the monthly prices of orange juice for 24 months. Use these data to compute 12-month centred moving averages ($T \cdot C$). Using these computed values, determine the seasonal effects ($S \cdot I$).

		Orange Juice, 1L
2017	August	4.09
	September	4.02
	October	3.98
	November	4.04
	December	4.05
2018	January	4.02
	February	3.92
	March	3.99
	April	4.02
	May	4.09
	June	4.14
	July	4.12
	August	4.26
	September	4.02
	October	4.09
	November	4.20
	December	4.16
2019	January	4.30
	February	4.11
	March	4.13
	April	3.94
	May	4.17
	June	4.19
	July	4.19

Source: Statistics Canada, Table 18-10-0002-01, "Monthly average retail prices for food and other selected products."

15.14 The following table shows shipment data for paperboard containers and boxes. The shipment figures are given in millions of dollars. Use the data to analyze the effects of seasonality, trend, and cycle. Develop the trend model with a linear model only.

Month	Shipments	Month	Shipments
January (year 1)	$1891	January (year 3)	$2183
February	1986	February	2230
March	1987	March	2222
April	1987	April	2319
May	2000	May	2369
June	2082	June	2529
July	1878	July	2267
August	2074	August	2457
September	2086	September	2524
October	2045	October	2502
November	1945	November	2314
December	1861	December	2277
January (year 2)	$1936	January (year 4)	$2336
February	2104	February	2474
March	2126	March	2546
April	2131	April	2566
May	2163	May	2473
June	2346	June	2572
July	2109	July	2336
August	2211	August	2518
September	2268	September	2454
October	2285	October	2559
November	2107	November	2384
December	2077	December	2305

(continued)

Month	Shipments	Month	Shipments	Month	Shipments	Month	Shipments
January (year 5)	$2389	July	2304	January (year 6)	$2377	July	2341
February	2463	August	2511	February	2381	August	2491
March	2522	September	2494	March	2268	September	2452
April	2417	October	2530	April	2407	October	2561
May	2468	November	2381	May	2367	November	2377
June	2492	December	2211	June	2446	December	2277

15.5 | Autocorrelation and Autoregression

LEARNING OBJECTIVE 15.5

Test for autocorrelation using the Durbin-Watson test, overcoming autocorrelation by adding independent variables and transforming variables, and taking advantage of autocorrelation with autoregression.

Data values gathered over time are often correlated with values from past time periods. This characteristic can cause problems in the use of regression in forecasting and at the same time can open some opportunities. One of the problems that can occur in regressing data over time is autocorrelation.

Autocorrelation

Autocorrelation, or **serial correlation,** occurs in data *when the error terms of a regression forecasting model are correlated.* The likelihood of this occurring with business data increases over time, particularly with economic variables. Autocorrelation can be a problem in using regression analysis as the forecasting method because one of the assumptions underlying regression analysis is that the error terms are independent or random (not correlated). In most business analysis situations, the correlation of error terms is likely to occur as positive auto-correlation (positive errors are associated with positive errors of comparable magnitude and negative errors are associated with negative errors of comparable magnitude).

When autocorrelation occurs in a regression analysis, several possible problems might arise. First, the estimates of the regression coefficients no longer have the minimum variance property and may be inefficient. Second, the variance of the error terms may be greatly under-estimated by the mean square error value. Third, the true standard deviation of the estimated regression coefficient may be seriously underestimated. Fourth, the confidence intervals and tests using the t and F distributions are no longer strictly applicable.

First-order autocorrelation results from correlation between the error terms of adjacent time periods (as opposed to two or more previous periods). If first-order autocorrelation is present, the error for one time period, e_t, is a function of the error of the previous time period, e_{t-1}, as follows:

$$e_t = \rho e_{t-1} + v_t$$

The first-order autocorrelation coefficient, ρ, measures the correlation between the error terms. It is a value that lies between -1 and 0 and $+1$, as does the coefficient of correlation discussed in Chapter 12. v_t is a normally distributed independent error term. If positive auto-correlation is present, the value of ρ is between 0 and $+1$. If the value of ρ is 0, $e_t = v_t$, which means there is no autocorrelation and e_t is just a random, independent error term.

One way to test to determine whether autocorrelation is present in a time-series regression analysis is by using the **Durbin-Watson test** for autocorrelation. Shown next is the formula for computing a Durbin-Watson test for autocorrelation.

Durbin-Watson Test

$$D = \frac{\sum_{t=2}^{n}(e_t - e_{t-1})^2}{\sum_{t=1}^{n}e_t^2} \qquad (15.5)$$

where

n = the number of observations

Note from the formula that the Durbin-Watson test involves finding the difference between successive values of error $(e_t - e_{t-1})$. If errors are positively correlated, this difference will be smaller than with random or independent errors. Squaring this term eliminates the cancellation effects of positive and negative terms.

The null hypothesis for this test is that there is no autocorrelation. For a two-tailed test, the alternative hypothesis is that there is autocorrelation:

$$H_0: \rho = 0$$
$$H_a: \rho \neq 0$$

As mentioned before, most business forecasting autocorrelation is positive autocorrelation. In most cases, a one-tailed test is used:

$$H_0: \rho = 0$$
$$H_a: \rho > 0$$

In the Durbin-Watson test, D is the observed value of the Durbin-Watson statistic using the residuals from the regression analysis. A critical value for D can be obtained from the values of α, n, and k by using Table A.9 in the appendix, where α is the level of significance, n is the number of data items, and k is the number of predictors. Two Durbin-Watson tables are given in Appendix A. One table contains values for $\alpha = 0.01$ and the other for $\alpha = 0.05$. The Durbin-Watson tables include values for d_U and d_L. These values range from 0 to 4. If the observed value of D is above d_U, we fail to reject the null hypothesis and there is no significant autocorrelation. If the observed value of D is below d_L, the null hypothesis is rejected and there is autocorrelation. Sometimes the observed statistic, D, is between the values of d_U and d_L. In this case, the Durbin-Watson test is inconclusive.

As an example, consider **Table 15.12**, which contains crude oil production and natural gas withdrawal data for the U.S. over a 25-year time period published by the U.S. Energy Information Administration in its Annual Energy Review. A regression line can be fit through these data to determine whether the amount of natural gas withdrawals can be predicted by the amount of crude oil production. The resulting errors of prediction can be tested by the Durbin-Watson statistic for the presence of significant positive autocorrelation by using $\alpha = 0.05$. The hypotheses are:

$$H_0: \rho = 0$$
$$H_a: \rho > 0$$

The following regression equation was obtained:

Natural Gas Withdrawals = $22.7372 - 0.8507$(Crude Oil Production)

Using the values for crude oil production (X) from Table 15.12 and the regression equation shown here, predicted values of Y (natural gas withdrawals) can be computed. From the predicted values and the actual values, the errors of prediction for each time interval, e_t, can be calculated. **Table 15.13** shows the values of $\hat{Y}$, e_t, e_t^2, $(e_t - e_{t-1})$, and $(e_t - e_{t-1})^2$ for this example. Note that the first predicted value of Y is:

$$\hat{Y}_1 = 22.7372 - 0.8507(8.597) = 15.4237$$

The error for year 1 is:

$$\text{Actual}_1 - \text{Predicted}_1 = 17.573 - 15.4237 = 2.1493$$

	Crude Oil Production	Natural Gas Withdrawals from
Year	(1,000s of barrels)	Natural Gas Wells (1,000s of barrels)
1	8.597	17.573
2	8.572	17.337
3	8.649	15.809
4	8.688	14.153
5	8.879	15.513
6	8.971	14.535
7	8.680	14.154
8	8.349	14.807
9	8.140	15.467
10	7.613	15.709
11	7.355	16.054
12	7.417	16.018
13	7.171	16.165
14	6.847	16.691
15	6.662	17.351
16	6.560	17.282
17	6.465	17.737
18	6.452	17.844
19	6.252	17.729
20	5.881	17.590
21	5.822	17.726
22	5.801	18.129
23	5.746	17.795
24	5.681	17.819
25	5.430	17.739

TABLE 15.12 U.S. Crude Oil Production and Natural Gas Withdrawals over a 25-Year Time Period

The value of $e_t - e_{t-1}$ for year 1 and year 2 is computed by subtracting the error for year 1 from the error for year 2:

$$e_{\text{year 2}} - e_{\text{year 1}} = 1.8920 - 2.1493 = -0.2573$$

The Durbin-Watson statistic can now be computed:

$$D = \frac{\sum_{t=2}^{n}(e_t - e_{t-1})^2}{\sum_{t=1}^{n}e_t^2} = \frac{9.9589}{14.4897} = 0.6873$$

Because we used a simple linear regression, the value of k is 1. The sample size, n, is 25, and $\alpha = 0.05$. The critical values in Table A.9 are:

$$d_U = 1.45 \text{ and } d_L = 1.29$$

Because the computed D statistic, 0.6873, is less than the value of $d_L = 1.29$, the null hypothesis is rejected. A positive autocorrelation is present in this example.

TABLE 15.13	Predicted Values and Error Terms for the Crude Oil Production and Natural Gas Withdrawal Data				
Year	$\hat{Y}$	e_t	e_t^2	$e_t - e_{t-1}$	$(e_t - e_{t-1})^2$
1	15.4237	2.1493	4.6195	—	—
2	15.4450	1.8920	3.5797	−0.2573	0.0662
3	15.3795	0.4295	0.1845	−1.4625	2.1389
4	15.3463	−1.1933	1.4240	−1.6228	2.6335
5	15.1838	0.3292	0.1084	1.5225	2.3180
6	15.1056	−0.5706	0.3256	−0.8998	0.8096
7	15.3531	−1.1991	1.4378	−0.6285	0.3950
8	15.6347	−0.8277	0.6851	0.3714	0.1379
9	15.8125	−0.3455	0.1194	0.4822	0.2325
10	16.2608	−0.5518	0.3045	−0.2063	0.0426
11	16.4803	−0.4263	0.1817	0.1255	0.0158
12	16.4276	−0.4096	0.1678	0.0167	0.0003
13	16.6368	−0.4718	0.2226	−0.0622	0.0039
14	16.9125	−0.2215	0.0491	0.2503	0.0627
15	17.0698	0.2812	0.0791	0.5027	0.2527
16	17.1566	0.1254	0.0157	−0.1558	0.0243
17	17.2374	0.4996	0.2496	0.3742	0.1400
18	17.2485	0.5955	0.3546	0.0959	0.0092
19	17.4186	0.3104	0.0963	−0.2851	0.0813
20	17.7342	−0.1442	0.0208	−0.4546	0.2067
21	17.7844	−0.0584	0.0034	0.0858	0.0074
22	17.8023	0.3267	0.1067	0.3851	0.1483
23	17.8491	−0.0541	0.0029	−0.3808	0.1450
24	17.9044	−0.0854	0.0073	−0.0313	0.0010
25	18.1179	−0.3789	0.1436	−0.2935	0.0861
			$\Sigma e_t^2 = 14.4897$		$\Sigma(e_t - e_{t-1})^2 = 9.9589$

Ways to Overcome the Autocorrelation Problem

Several approaches to data analysis can be used when autocorrelation is present. One uses additional independent variables and another transforms the independent variable.

Addition of Independent Variables Often the reason autocorrelation occurs in regression analyses is that one or more important predictor variables have been left out of the analysis. For example, suppose an analyst develops a regression forecasting model that attempts to predict sales of new homes by sales of used homes over some period of time. Such a model might contain significant autocorrelation. The exclusion of the variable prime mortgage interest rate might be a factor driving the autocorrelation between the other two variables. Adding this variable to the regression model might significantly reduce the autocorrelation.

Transforming Variables When the inclusion of additional variables is not helpful in reducing autocorrelation to an acceptable level, transforming the data in the variables may help to solve the problem. One such method is the **first-differences approach**. With the first-differences approach, *each value of X is subtracted from each succeeding time period value of X;*

Table 15.16 displays all the index numbers for the data in Table 15.15, with 2000 as the base year, along with the raw data. A cursory glance at these index numbers reveals that the median income of Canadian families showed faster growth between 2000 and 2007, was quite static between 2008 and 2010, and resumed growth at a slower rate from 2011 to 2017. Because most people are easily able to understand the concept of 100%, it is likely that decision-makers can make quick judgements on the median family income of Canadians from one year relative to another by examining the index numbers over this period.

TABLE 15.16	Median Family Income in Canada: In Dollars and as an Index	
Year	Median Family Income ($)	Index
2000	50,800	100.0
2001	53,500	105.3
2002	55,000	108.3
2003	56,000	110.2
2004	58,100	114.4
2005	60,600	119.3
2006	63,600	125.2
2007	66,550	131.0
2008	68,860	135.6
2009	68,410	134.7
2010	69,860	137.5
2011	72,240	142.2
2012	74,540	146.7
2013	76,550	150.7
2014	78,870	155.3
2015	80,940	159.3
2016	82,110	161.6
2017	84,950	167.2

Unweighted Aggregate Price Index Numbers

The use of simple index numbers makes possible the conversion of prices, costs, quantities, and so on for different time periods into a number scale with the base year equalling 100%. One of the drawbacks of simple index numbers, however, is that each time period is represented by only one item or commodity. When multiple items are involved, multiple sets of index numbers are possible. Suppose a decision-maker is interested in combining or pooling the prices of several items, creating a "market basket" in order to compare the prices for several years. Fortunately, a technique does exist for combining several items and determining index numbers for the total (aggregate). Because this technique is used mostly in determining price indexes, the focus in this section is on developing aggregate price indexes. The formula for constructing the **unweighted aggregate price index number** follows.

Unweighted Aggregate Price Index Number

$$I_i = \frac{\sum P_i}{\sum P_0}(100) \qquad\qquad (15.7)$$

where

P_i = the price of an item in the year of interest (i)

P_0 = the price of an item in the base year (0)

I_i = the index number for the year of interest (i)

Suppose a business analyst wants to compare the cost of family food buying over the years. The analyst decides that instead of using a single food item to do this comparison, she will use a food basket that consists of five items: butter, eggs, bananas, potatoes, and sugar. She gathers price information on these five items for the years 2008, 2013, and 2018. The items and the prices are listed in **Table 15.17**.

TABLE 15.17 Prices for a Basket of Food Items

Item	2008	2013	2018
Butter, 454 g	4.25	4.39	4.76
Eggs, 1 dozen	2.57	3.25	3.13
Bananas, 1 kg	1.41	1.66	1.58
Potatoes, 4.54 kg	4.58	5.50	7.71
Sugar, white, 2 kg	2.41	3.04	2.64
Total	15.22	17.84	19.82

Source: Statistics Canada, CANSIM Table 326-0012, "Average retail prices for food and other selected items, annual (dollars)."

From the data in Table 15.17 and the formula, the unweighted aggregate price indexes for the years 2008, 2013, and 2018 can be computed by using 2008 as the base year. The first step is to add together, or aggregate, the prices for all the food basket items in a given year. These totals are shown in the last row of Table 15.17. The index numbers are constructed by using these totals (not individual item prices): $\Sigma P_{2008} = 15.22$, $\Sigma P_{2013} = 17.84$, and $\Sigma P_{2018} = 19.82$. From these figures, the unweighted aggregate price index for 2013 is computed as follows:

$$\text{For 2013: } I_{2013} = \frac{\Sigma P_{2013}}{\Sigma P_{2008}}(100) = \frac{17.84}{15.22}(100) = 117.2$$

Weighted Aggregate Price Index Numbers

A major drawback to unweighted aggregate price indexes is that they are *unweighted*—that is, equal weight is put on each item by assuming the market basket contains only one of each item. This assumption may or may not be true. For example, a household may consume 5 kg of bananas per year but 20 kg of sugar. In addition, unweighted aggregate index numbers depend on the units selected for various items. For example, if sugar is measured in 1 kg instead of 2 kg packages, the price of sugar used in determining the index numbers is considerably lower. A class of index numbers that can be used to avoid these problems is weighted aggregate price index numbers.

Weighted aggregate price index numbers are *computed by multiplying quantity weights and item prices in determining the market basket worth for a given year*. Sometimes when price and quantity are multiplied to construct index numbers, the index numbers are referred to as *value indexes*. Thus, weighted aggregate price index numbers are also value indexes.

Including quantities eliminates the problems caused by how many of each item are consumed per time period and the units of items. If 20 kg of sugar but only 5 kg of bananas are consumed, weighted aggregate price index numbers will reflect those weights. If the business analyst switches from 2 kg to 1 kg packages, the prices will change downward but the quantity will increase twofold.

In general, weighted aggregate price indexes are constructed by multiplying the price of each item by its quantity and then summing these products for the market basket over a given time period (often a year). The ratio of this sum for one time period of interest (year) to a base time period of interest (base year) is multiplied by 100. The following formula reflects a weighted aggregate price index computed by using quantity weights from each time period (year):

$$I_i = \frac{\Sigma P_i Q_i}{\Sigma P_0 Q_0}(100)$$

One of the problems with this formula is the implication that new and possibly different quantities apply for each time period. However, business analysts expend much time and money ascertaining the quantities used in a market basket. Redetermining quantity weights for each year is therefore often prohibitive for most organizations (even the government). Two particular types of weighted aggregate price indexes offer a solution to the problem of which quantity weights to use. The first and most widely used is the Laspeyres price index. The second and less widely used is the Paasche price index.

Laspeyres Price Index

The **Laspeyres price index** is *a weighted aggregate price index computed by using the quantities of the base period (year) for all other years*. The advantages of this technique are that the price indexes for all years can be compared, and new quantities do not have to be determined for each year. The formula for constructing the Laspeyres price index follows.

Laspeyres Price Index

$$I_L = \frac{\sum P_i Q_0}{\sum P_0 Q_0} (100) \qquad\qquad (15.8)$$

Notice that the formula requires the base period quantities (Q_0) in both the numerator and the denominator.

In Table 15.17, a food basket was presented in which aggregate price indexes were computed. This food basket consisted of butter, eggs, bananas, potatoes, and sugar. The prices of these items were combined (aggregated) for a given year and the price indexes were computed from these aggregate figures. The unweighted aggregate price indexes computed on these data gave all items equal importance. Suppose that the business analysts realize that applying equal weight to these five items is probably not a representative way to construct this food basket and consequently ascertain quantity weights on each food item for one year's consumption. **Table 15.18** lists these five items, their prices, and their quantity usage weights for the base year (2008). From these data, the business analysts can compute Laspeyres price indexes.

TABLE 15.18   **Food Basket Items with Quantity Weights**

		Price	
Item	**Quantity**	**2008**	**2018**
Butter, 454 g	12	4.25	4.76
Eggs, 1 dozen	45	2.57	3.13
Bananas, 1 kg	12	1.41	1.58
Potatoes, 4.54 kg	12	4.58	7.71
Sugar, white, 2 kg	18	2.41	2.64

The Laspeyres price index for 2018 with 2008 as the base year is calculated as follows:

$$\sum P_i Q_0 = \sum P_{2018} Q_{2008}$$
$$= \sum[(4.76)(12) + (3.13)(45) + (1.58)(12) + (7.71)(12) + (2.64)(18)] = 356.97$$
$$\sum P_0 Q_0 = \sum P_{2008} Q_{2018}$$
$$= \sum[(4.25)(12) + (2.57)(45) + (1.41)(12) + (4.58)(12) + (2.41)(18)] = 281.91$$
$$I_{2018} = \frac{\sum P_{2018}}{\sum P_{2008}} (100) = \frac{356.97}{281.91} (100) = 126.63$$

Paasche Price Index

The **Paasche price index** is *a weighted aggregate price index computed by using the quantities for the year of interest in computations for a given year*. The advantage of this technique is that it incorporates current quantity figures in the calculations. One disadvantage is that ascertaining quantity figures for each time period is expensive. The formula for computing Paasche price indexes follows.

Paasche Price Index

$$I_P = \frac{\sum P_i Q_i}{\sum P_0 Q_i}(100) \tag{15.9}$$

Suppose the yearly quantities for the basket of food items listed in Table 15.18 are determined. The result is the quantities and prices shown in **Table 15.19** for the years 2008 and 2018 that can be used to compute Paasche price index numbers.

TABLE 15.19 Food Basket Items with Yearly Quantity Weights for 2008 and 2018

Item	P_{2008}	Q_{2008}	P_{2018}	Q_{2018}
Butter, 454 g	4.25	12	4.76	13
Eggs, 1 dozen	2.57	45	3.13	50
Bananas, 1 kg	1.41	12	1.58	15
Potatoes, 4.54 kg	4.58	12	7.71	10
Sugar, white, 2 kg	2.41	18	2.64	10

The Paasche price index numbers can be determined for 2018 by using a base year of 2008 as follows:

For 2018

$$\sum P_i Q_i = \sum P_{2018} Q_{2018}$$
$$= \sum[(4.76)(13) + (3.13)(50) + (1.58)(15) + (7.71)(10) + (2.64)(10)] = 345.58$$
$$\sum P_0 Q_i = \sum P_{2008} Q_{2018}$$
$$= \sum[(4.25)(13) + (2.57)(50) + (1.41)(15) + (4.58)(10) + (2.41)(10)] = 274.80$$
$$I_{2018} = \frac{\sum P_{2018}}{\sum P_{2008}}(100) = \frac{345.58}{274.80}(100) = 125.76$$

DEMONSTRATION PROBLEM 15.5

The Reisman Pediatrics Clinic has been in business for 18 years. The office manager noticed that prices of clinic materials and office supplies fluctuate over time. To get a handle on the price trends for running the clinic, the office manager examined prices of six items the clinic uses as part of its operation. Shown here are the items, their prices, and the quantities for the years 2019 and 2020. Use these data to develop unweighted aggregate price indexes for 2020 with a base year of 2019. Compute the Laspeyres price index for the year 2020 using 2019 as the base year. Compute the Paasche index number for 2020 using 2019 as the base year.

15.36 Given below are data on the number of business establishments (millions) and the self-employment rate (%). Develop a regression model to predict the self-employment rate by the number of business establishments. Use this model to predict the self-employment rate for a year in which there are 7.0 (million) business establishments. Discuss the strength of the regression model. Use these data and the regression model to compute a Durbin-Watson test to determine whether significant autocorrelation is present. Let α be 0.05.

Number of Establishments (millions)	Self-Employment Rate (%)
4.54317	8.1
4.58651	8.0
4.63396	8.1
5.30679	8.2
5.51772	8.2
5.70149	8.0
5.80697	7.9
5.93706	8.0
6.01637	8.2
6.10692	8.1
6.17556	8.0
6.20086	8.1
6.31930	7.8
6.40123	8.0
6.50907	8.1
6.61272	7.9
6.73848	7.8
6.89487	7.7
6.94182	7.5
7.00844	7.2
7.07005	6.9

15.37 Shown here are the Canadian total monthly consumer price index (CPI) values for July 2016 through June 2019. Use the data to answer the following questions.

a. Compute the 4-month moving average to forecast the CPI from November 2016 to June 2019.

b. Compute the 4-month weighted moving average to forecast the CPI from November 2017 to June 2019. Weight the most recent year by 4, the next most recent year by 3, the next year by 2, and the last year of the four by 1.

c. Determine the errors for parts (a) and (b). Compute MSE for parts (a) and (b). Compare the MSE values and comment on the effectiveness of the moving average versus the weighted moving average for these data.

	Month	CPI
2016	July	128.9
	August	128.7
	September	128.8
	October	129.1
	November	128.6
	December	128.4
2017	January	129.5
	February	129.7
	March	129.9
	April	130.4
	May	130.5
	June	130.4

	Month	CPI
	July	130.4
	August	130.5
	September	130.8
	October	130.9
	November	131.3
	December	130.8
2018	January	131.7
	February	132.5
	March	132.9
	April	133.3
	May	133.4
	June	133.6
	July	134.3
	August	134.2
	September	133.7
	October	134.1
	November	133.5
	December	133.4
2019	January	133.6
	February	134.5
	March	135.4
	April	136
	May	136.6
	June	136.3

Source: Statistics Canada, Table 18-10-0004-01, "Consumer Price Index, monthly, not seasonally adjusted" (2002 = 100).

15.38 In the *Survey of Current Business,* the U.S. Department of Commerce publishes data on farm commodity prices. Given are the cotton prices from November of year 1 through February of year 4. The prices are indexes with a base of 100 from the year 1910. Use these data to develop autoregression models for a 1-month lag and a 4-month lag. Compare the results of these two models. Which model seems to yield better predictions? Why?

Time Period	Cotton Prices
November (year 1)	552
December	519
January (year 2)	505
February	512
March	541
April	549
May	552
June	526
July	531
August	545
September	549
October	570
November	576
December	568
January (year 3)	571
February	573
March	582
April	587
May	592
June	570
July	560
August	565
September	547

Time Period	Cotton Prices
October	529
November	514
December	469
January (year 4)	436
February	419

15.39 The U.S. Department of Commerce publishes data on industrial machinery and equipment. Shown here are the shipments (in US$ billions) of industrial machinery and equipment from the first quarter of year 1 through the fourth quarter of year 6. Use these data to determine the seasonal indexes for the data through time-series decomposition methods. Use the 4-quarter centred moving average in the computations.

Time Period	Industrial Machinery and Equipment Shipments
1st quarter (year 1)	$54.019
2nd quarter	56.495
3rd quarter	50.169
4th quarter	52.891
1st quarter (year 2)	51.915
2nd quarter	55.101
3rd quarter	53.419
4th quarter	57.236
1st quarter (year 3)	57.063
2nd quarter	62.488
3rd quarter	60.373
4th quarter	63.334
1st quarter (year 4)	$62.723
2nd quarter	68.380
3rd quarter	63.256
4th quarter	66.446
1st quarter (year 5)	65.445
2nd quarter	68.011
3rd quarter	63.245
4th quarter	66.872
1st quarter (year 6)	59.714
2nd quarter	63.590
3rd quarter	58.088
4th quarter	61.443

15.40 Use the seasonal indexes computed to deseasonalize the data in Problem 15.39.

15.41 Use both a linear and a quadratic model to explore trends in the deseasonalized data from Problem 15.40. Which model seems to produce a better fit for the data?

15.42 The OECD publishes data on inflows of foreign direct investments in different countries, including Canada, for which data are given below. Use these data to develop an autoregression model with a 1-period lag. Discuss the strength of the model.

Year	US$ millions
2007	116,809
2008	61,520
2009	22,733
2010	28,399
2011	39,667
2012	43,118

Year	US$ millions
2013	69,371
2014	59,008
2015	43,853
2016	35,992
2017	24,826
2018	42,231

Source: OECD, FDI flows (indicator), 2019, doi: 10.1787/99f6e393-en (accessed on September 12, 2019).

15.43 The data shown here, from the OECD, show the inflows and outflows of foreign direct investments in Canada. Use these data to develop a regression model to forecast the foreign inflows by foreign outflows. Conduct a Durbin-Watson test on the data and the regression model to determine whether significant autocorrelation is present. Let $\alpha = .01$.

Year	Inflows US$ millions	Outflows US$ millions
2005	25,693	27,540
2006	60,298	46,215
2007	116,809	64,621
2008	61,520	79,236
2009	22,733	39,660
2010	28,399	34,721
2011	39,667	52,144
2012	43,118	55,875
2013	69,371	57,364
2014	59,008	60,273
2015	43,853	67,467
2016	35,992	69,948
2017	24,826	79,802
2018	42,231	49,593

Source: OECD, FDI flows (indicator), 2019, doi: 10.1787/99f6e393-en (accessed on September 12, 2019).

15.44 The purchasing-power value figures for the minimum wage in dollars for the years 1 through 18 are shown here. Use these data and exponential smoothing to develop forecasts for the years 2 through 18. Try $\alpha = 0.1$, 0.5, and 0.8, and compare the results using MAD. Discuss your findings. Select the value of α that worked best and use your exponential smoothing results to predict the figure for year 19.

Year	Purchasing Power	Year	Purchasing Power
1	$6.04	10	$4.34
2	5.92	11	4.67
3	5.57	12	5.01
4	5.40	13	4.86
5	5.17	14	4.72
6	5.00	15	4.60
7	4.91	16	4.48
8	4.73	17	4.86
9	4.55	18	5.15

Interpreting the Output

15.45 Shown below is the Excel output for a regression analysis to predict the number of business bankruptcy filings over a 16-year period by the number of consumer bankruptcy filings. How strong is the model? Note the residuals. Compute a Durbin-Watson statistic from the data and discuss the presence of autocorrelation in this model.

	A	B	C	D	E	F
1	SUMMARY OUTPUT					
2	Regression Statistics					
3	Multiple R	0.529				
4	R Square	0.280				
5	Adjusted R Square	0.228				
6	Standard Error	8179.84				
7	Observations	16				
8						
9	ANOVA					
10		df	SS	MS	F	Significance F
11	Regression	1	364069877.4	364069877.4	5.44	0.0351
12	Residual	14	936737379.6	66909812.8		
13	Total	15	1300807257			
14						
15		Coefficients	Standard Error	t Stat	P-value	
16	Intercept	75532.43621	4980.08791	15.17	0.0000	
17	Consumer Bankruptcies	–0.01574	0.00675	–2.33	0.0351	
18						
19	RESIDUAL OUTPUT					
20	Observation	Predicted Bus. Bankruptcies		Residuals		
21	1	70638.58		–1338.6		
22	2	71024.28		–8588.3		
23	3	71054.61		–7050.6		
24	4	70161.99		1115.0		
25	5	68462.72		12772.3		
26	6	67733.25		14712.8		
27	7	66882.45		–3029.4		
28	8	65834.05		–2599.1		
29	9	64230.61		622.4		
30	10	61801.70		9747.3		
31	11	61354.16		9288.8		
32	12	62738.76		–434.8		
33	13	63249.36		–10875.4		
34	14	61767.01		–9808.0		
35	15	57826.69		–4277.7		
36	16	54283.80		–256.8		

Exploring the Databases with Business Analytics   *see* the databases on the Student Website and in *WileyPLUS*

1. Use the Agri-Business Canada Database and the variable "Wheat, total" to forecast Wheat for period 145 by using the following techniques.

   a. 5-month moving average

   b. Simple exponential smoothing with $\alpha = 0.6$

   c. Time-series linear trend model

   d. Decomposition

2. Use decomposition on Canola in the Agri-Business Canada Database to determine the seasonal indexes. These data actually represent 13 years of 12-month data. Do the seasonal indexes indicate the presence of some seasonal effects? Run an autoregression model to predict Canola by a 1-month lag and another by a 12-month lag. Compare the two models. Because crops are somewhat seasonal, is the 12-month lag model significant?

3. Use the Energy Resource Database to forecast year 36 of North American Hydro energy production by using simple exponential smoothing. Let $\alpha = 0.20$ and $\alpha = 0.80$. Compare the forecast with the actual figure. Which of the two models produces the forecast with the least error? Repeat the same test using the European data set. Is there any difference between North America and Europe in energy production through Hydro?

4. Use the International Labour Database to develop a regression model to predict the unemployment rate for Germany by the unemployment rate for Italy. Test for autocorrelation and discuss its presence or absence in this regression analysis.

Case

Dofasco Changes Its Style

Dofasco Inc. was founded in 1912 in Hamilton, Ontario, by Clifton W. Sherman. Dofasco provides steel to various industries, including the automotive and pipe industries, and today is considered one of Canada's leading steel makers. Originally, its strategy was based on producing as much steel as it could in order to be able to grow as much and as fast as possible. Financially, Dofasco was doing very well. However, in the late 1980s, things took an unexpected turn and Dofasco was left in a difficult position. The demand for steel was decreasing, competition was getting fiercer, and costs (operational and capital) were continuously increasing, negatively affecting Dofasco's sales and profitability. Between 1990 and 1992, Dofasco reported a total net loss of $900 million. The executives of the company understood that it had to take charge and restructure its operations if it were to survive this financial crisis. Dofasco's first order of business in restructuring the company was to sell off some of its assets, which included many of its divisions. It then went even further and cut its labour force from 13,000 to 7,000 employees. The final step that Dofasco took in its restructuring process was to enter into joint ventures, allowing it to work with companies from different countries. These actions allowed Dofasco to begin its slow climb to the top once again.

Dofasco realized that it was extremely important during the restructuring process to focus on its core: its employees. Dofasco made it its mission to engage the employees by recognizing their needs and opinions. This change in organizational setting and human resources represented a significant shift of strategy. Human capital was now becoming Dofasco's most valuable resource, hence opening the road to financial recovery. Dofasco realized that its workforce was hard-working and motivated and ready to take on challenging work. Dofasco therefore accommodated these needs and provided employees with resources and encouragement to have a more hands-on approach with their customers. The new responsibilities gave employees the ability to get involved in everyday decisions and allowed them to work in teams and cross-functional groups, providing them with a broader view of the overall company process. This made the employees an integral part of the company and made them understand that they were vital to the success of the business.

Dofasco believed that empowering employees was one effective way of improving the company, but it also realized that the employees needed to be healthy and safe in order to be more productive. Therefore, in its restructuring process, Dofasco also began health initiatives such as offering information sessions on how to sleep better, weekly Weight Watchers meetings, CPR and first aid demonstrations, yoga and workout sessions, and sessions on how to deal with stress.

After its restructuring program in the early 1990s, Dofasco made major strides and successfully managed to overcome its financial crisis. The results of fiscal year 2000 showed the degree of success of the change in business strategy, as sales and net profit reached $3.2 billion and $188 million, respectively. Dofasco now operates as a subsidiary of Luxembourg-based ArcelorMittal, the world's largest steel producer by volume. In 2012, ArcelorMittal had worldwide sales of more than $84.2 billion.

Discussion

1. Dofasco realized that the most effective way to improve its business and increase its sales was through a restructuring process. After this process was implemented, Dofasco's productivity and sales figures began to improve, allowing the company to overcome the financial crisis that it was facing. Dofasco's impressive sales figures from January 1998 to December 2005 (in billions) are reported below. When analyzing these figures, are any trends apparent? Are there any signs that indicate that Dofasco's sales may be seasonally influenced? Use the sales figures to perform a decomposition analysis using 12-month seasonality. Following this analysis, determine the trend line and a graphical display using Excel. Take a close look at all this information and put together a brief analysis of Dofasco's sales. In this analysis, focus on any specific direction that Dofasco's sales may have been heading toward before its takeover by ArcelorMittal.

Month	1998	1999	2000	2001	2002	2003	2004	2005
January	142.1	166.7	178.6	229.3	267.3	432.5	382.0	432.9
February	112.5	175.2	202.7	253.0	315.4	456.1	405.7	443.8
March	102.7	175.2	229.6	267.8	369.1	456.1	432.4	496.3
April	154.9	205.3	277.4	341.8	430.2	483.9	456.3	531.2
May	213.1	239.7	319.2	356.7	458.1	532.7	496.2	559.9
June	230.6	280.5	329.1	405.1	570.2	623.8	583.9	645.2
July	214.8	292.0	369.4	445.0	546.9	659.4	608.8	675.4
August	191.8	318.6	354.1	432.1	482.0	521.4	559.6	658.6
September	175.3	202.2	243.5	329.6	432.7	509.0	507.0	610.5
October	140.4	178.4	211.9	329.6	407.5	482.1	497.3	582.5
November	140.4	164.9	216.3	305.7	392.8	458.2	442.7	522.9
December	150.8	177.9	201.9	291.9	407.6	430.9	421.6	481.7

2. It is very important to be able to analyze the cost of steel on a per-unit basis. Assume that the company's financial team was able to calculate this cost for each year between 2009 and 2022. The result of these calculations is shown here. By using information learned in this chapter, such as smoothing techniques, moving averages, and trend analysis, forecast the per-unit labour costs for each year. How would you compute the error of the forecasts and determine which forecasting method is the most effective in reducing error?

Year	Per-Unit Labour Cost	Year	Per-Unit Labour Cost
2009	$81.25	2016	$58.44
2010	84.11	2017	59.67
2011	86.72	2018	56.71
2012	62.86	2019	57.83
2013	65.49	2020	56.12
2014	60.56	2021	56.99
2015	61.38	2022	56.12

Sources: Gordon DiGiacomo, "Case Study: Dofasco's Healthy Lifestyle Program," Canadian Labour and Business Centre, March 2002; Dofasco Inc., on the Funding Universe website, www.fundinguniverse.com/company-histories/Dofasco-Inc-Company-History.html; "Press Release Regarding Dofasco," Mittal news release, December 26, 2006; "ArcelorMittal Annual Review 2012," annualreview2012.arcelormittal.com.

Big Data Case

In order to more fully apply techniques from Chapter 15 to data, we will access more than one time-series database for the Big Data Case.

1. Open the Energy Resource Database. Attempt to determine if there is either a linear or quadratic trend for each of the following European energy supplies. Did either fit the data well? Which one and why?

   a. Solar, Wind, Tide, and Wave

   b. Nuclear

   c. Natural Gas

2. Open the Canadian Stock Market Database. Examine the data representing the Health Index and the Gold Index. Explore the data using decomposition methods to determine if there are any trends, cyclical effects, or seasonal effects in the data.

3. Examine the Flaxseed data in the Agri-Business Canada Database. Monthly weights of flaxseed seem to go up and down. Are there any cycles or seasonality in the data?

Using the Computer

- Excel has the capability to forecast using several of the techniques presented in this chapter. Two of the forecasting techniques are accessed using the **Data Analysis** tool, and two other forecasting techniques are accessed using the **Insert Function**.

- To use the **Data Analysis** tool, begin by selecting the **Data** tab on the Excel worksheet. From the **Analyze** panel at the top right of the **Data** ribbon, click on **Data Analysis**. If your Excel worksheet does not show the **Data Analysis** option, you can load it as an add-in.

- To do exponential smoothing, select **Exponential Smoothing** from the **Data Analysis** menu. In the dialogue box, input the location of the data to be smoothed in **Input Range**. Input the value of the damping factor in **Damping factor**. Excel will default to 0.3. Input the location of the upper left cell of the output table in the **Output Range** space. The output consists of forecast values of the data. If you check **Standard Errors**, a second column of output will be given with the standard errors.

- To compute moving averages, select **Moving Average** from the **Data Analysis** menu. In the dialogue box, input the location of the data for which the moving averages are to be computed in **Input Range**. Record how many values you want to include in computing the moving average in **Interval**. The default number is three values. Input the location of the upper left cell of the output table in **Output Range**. The output consists of the moving averages. If you check **Standard Errors**, a second column of output will be given with the standard errors.

- To use the **Insert Function** (f_x) to compute forecasts and/or to fit a trend line, go to the **Formulas** tab on an Excel worksheet (top centre tab). The **Insert Function** is on the far left of the ribbon. In the **Insert Function** dialogue box at the top, there is a pull-down menu where it says **Or select a category**. From the pull-down menu associated with this command, select **Statistical**.

- To compute forecasts using linear regression, select **FORECAST.LINEAR** from the **Insert Function**'s **Statistical** menu. In the first line of the **FORECAST.LINEAR** dialogue box, place the value of x for which you want a predicted value in **X**. An entry here is required. On the second line, place the location of the values to be used in the development of the regression model in **Known_y's**. On the third line, place the location of the x values to be used in the development of the regression model in **Known_x's**. The output consists of the predicted value.

- To fit a trend line to data, select **TREND** from the **Insert Function**'s **Statistical** menu. On the first line of the **TREND** dialogue box, place the location of the y values to be used in the development of the regression model in **Known_y's**. On the second line, place the location of the x values to be used in the development of the regression model in **Known_x's**. Note that the x values can consist of more than one column if you want to fit a polynomial curve. To accomplish this, place squared values of x, cubed values of x, and so on as desired in other columns, and include those columns in **Known_x's**. On the third line, place the values for which you want to return corresponding y values in **New_x's**. In the fourth line, place **TRUE in Const** if you want to get a value for the constant as usual (default option). Place **FALSE** if you want to set b_0 to zero.

CHAPTER 16

Analysis of Categorical Data

LEARNING OBJECTIVES

The overall objective of this chapter is to give you an understanding of two statistical techniques used to analyze categorical data, thereby enabling you to:

16.1 Use the chi-square goodness-of-fit test to analyze probabilities of multinomial distribution trials along a single dimension.

16.2 Use the chi-square test of independence to perform contingency analysis.

Decision Dilemma

Selecting Suppliers in the Electronics Industry

What criteria are used in the electronics industry to select a supplier? In years past, price was the dominant criterion of suppliers in many industries, and the supplier with the low bid often got the job. In more recent years, companies have been forced by global competition and a marked increase in quality to examine other aspects of potential suppliers.

John Pearson and Lisa Ellram investigated the techniques used by firms in the electronics industry to select suppliers to determine if there is a difference between small and large firms in supplier selection. They sent out a survey instrument with questions about criteria used to select and evaluate suppliers, the participation of various functional areas in the selection process, and the formality of methods used in the selection. Of the 210 survey responses received, 87 were from small companies and 123 were from large companies. The average sales were $33 million for the small companies and $583 million for the large companies.

Survey questions were worded in such a way as to generate frequencies. The respondents were given a series of supplier selection and evaluation criteria such as quality, cost, current technology, design capabilities, speed to market, manufacturing process, and location. They were asked to check off the criteria used in supplier selection and evaluation and to rank the criteria that they checked. As part of the analysis, the researchers recorded how many of each of the small- and large-company respondents ranked a criterion first, how many ranked it second, and how many ranked it third. The results are shown in the following table of raw numbers for the criteria of quality, cost, and current technology.

Chris Knapton/Science Source

	Company Size				Company Size	
Quality	Small	Large	Cost	Small	Large
1	48	70	1	8	14
2	17	27	2	29	36
3	7	6	3	26	37

Current Technology	Company Size	
	Small	Large
1	5	13
2	8	11
3	5	12

Sources: Adapted from John N. Pearson and Lisa M. Ellram, "Supplier Selection and Evaluation in Small Versus Large Electronics Firms," *Journal of Small Business Management* 33, no. 4 (October 1995): 53–65; Chin-Tsai Lin, Chie-Bein Chen, and Ying-Chan Ting, "An ERP Model for Supplier Selection in Electronics Industry," *Expert Systems with Applications* 38, iss. 3 (2011): 1760–65; S. Vinodh, Gopinath Rathod, and S.R. Devadasan, "Application of QFD for Supplier Selection in an Indian Electronics Switches Manufacturing Organisation," *International Journal of Indian Culture and Business Management* 4, no. 2 (2011): 181–98.

Managerial, Statistical, and Analytical Questions

1. Is there a difference between small and large companies in the ranking of criteria for the evaluation and selection of suppliers in the electronics industry?

2. The authors of the study used frequencies to measure the relative rankings of criteria. What is the appropriate statistical technique to analyze these data?

Introduction

In this chapter, we explore techniques for analyzing categorical data. **Categorical data** are *non-numerical data that can be summarized as frequency counts.* For example, it is determined that of the 790 people attending a convention, 240 are engineers, 160 are managers, 310 are sales reps, and 80 are information technologists. The variable is "position in company" with four categories: engineers, managers, sales reps, and information technologists. The data are not ratings or sales figures but rather frequency counts of how many of each position attended. Research questions producing this type of data are often analyzed using chi-square techniques. The chi-square distribution was introduced in Chapters 8 and 9. The techniques presented here for analyzing categorical data, the *chi-square goodness-of-fit test* and *the chi-square test of independence,* are an outgrowth of the binomial distribution and the inferential techniques for analyzing population proportions.

The present-day proliferation of data has given rise to large quantities of information holding potential to assist business decision-makers in making more informed decisions. As noted in Chapter 1, such big data comes in many forms and from many sources. Because of this, business analysts use data mining to convert raw data into forms that have both validity and value to businesses. The result of this process is data that can occur in any of the four levels of data measurement and can be labelled as either metric or nonmetric data. This chapter, along with Chapter 17, focuses on the analysis of nonmetric data (nominal or ordinal levels).

Specifically, both the chi-square goodness-of-fit test and the chi-square test of independence deal with frequency counts and categories that are either nominal or ordinal in level. Accordingly, there is potential, in the era of big data and business analytics, for these techniques to increase in prominence.

16.1 | Chi-Square Goodness-of-Fit Test

LEARNING OBJECTIVE 16.1

Use the chi-square goodness-of-fit test to analyze probabilities of multinomial distribution trials along a single dimension.

In Chapter 5, we studied the binomial distribution, in which only two possible outcomes could occur on a single trial in an experiment. An extension of the binomial distribution is a multinomial distribution in which more than two possible outcomes can occur in a single trial. The **chi-square goodness-of-fit test** is *used to analyze probabilities of multinomial distribution trials along a single dimension.* For example, if the variable being studied is economic class with three possible outcomes—lower income class, middle income class, and upper income class—the single dimension is economic class and the three possible outcomes are the three classes. On each trial, one and only one of the outcomes can occur. In other words, a family unit must be classified as lower income class, middle income class, or upper income class and cannot be in more than one class.

The chi-square goodness-of-fit test compares the *expected,* or theoretical, *frequencies* of categories from a population distribution with the *observed,* or actual, *frequencies* from a distribution to determine whether there is a difference between what was expected and what was observed. For example, airline industry officials might theorize that the ages of airline ticket purchasers are distributed in a particular way. To validate or reject this expected distribution, an actual sample of ticket purchaser ages can be gathered randomly, and the observed results can be compared with the expected results using the chi-square goodness-of-fit test. This test can also be used to determine whether the observed arrivals at teller windows at a bank are Poisson distributed, as might be expected. In the paper industry, manufacturers can use the chi-square goodness-of-fit test to determine whether the demand for paper follows a uniform distribution throughout the year.

Formula 16.1 is used to compute a chi-square goodness-of-fit test.

Chi-Square Goodness-of-Fit Test

$$\chi^2 = \sum \frac{(f_o - f_e)^2}{f_e}$$

$$df = k - 1 - c$$

(16.1)

where

f_o = frequency of observed values

f_e = frequency of expected values

k = number of categories

c = number of parameters being estimated from the sample data

---

This formula compares the frequency of observed values with the frequency of the expected values across the distribution. The test loses one degree of freedom because the total number of expected frequencies must equal the number of observed frequencies; that is, the observed total taken from the sample is used as the total for the expected frequencies. In addition, in some instances a population parameter, such as λ, μ, or σ, is estimated from the sample data to determine the frequency distribution of expected values. Each time this estimation occurs, an additional degree of freedom is lost. As a rule, if a uniform distribution is being used as the expected distribution or if an expected distribution of values is given, $k - 1$ degrees of freedom are used in the test. In testing to determine whether an observed distribution is Poisson, the degrees of freedom are $k - 2$ because an additional degree of freedom is lost in estimating λ.

Karl Pearson introduced the chi-square test in 1900. The **chi-square distribution** is *the sum of the squares of* k *independent random variables* and therefore can never be less than zero; it extends indefinitely in the positive direction. Actually the chi-square distributions constitute a family, with each distribution defined by the degrees of freedom (df) associated with it. For small df values, the chi-square distribution is skewed considerably to the right (positive values). As the degrees of freedom increase, the chi-square distribution begins to approach the normal curve. Table values for the chi-square distribution are given in Appendix A. Because of space limitations, chi-square values are listed only for certain probabilities.

How can the chi-square goodness-of-fit test be applied to business situations? Suppose that a large-scale benchmark study done by the hospitality industry has shown that across Canada, this is how consumers rate their hospitality experience.

Excellent	8%
Pretty good	47%
Only fair	34%
Poor	11%

Suppose a hotel manager wants to find out whether the hotel deviates significantly from this benchmark. To determine this, she interviews 207 randomly selected guests who stayed at the hotel in a given week. The response categories, as in the benchmark study, are excellent, pretty good, only fair, and poor. The observed responses from this study are given in **Table 16.1**. Now the manager can use a chi-square goodness-of-fit test and the eight-step approach to determine whether the observed frequencies of responses from this survey are the same as the frequencies that would be expected on the basis of the national survey.

TABLE 16.1

Results of a Local Survey of Consumer Satisfaction with the Hospitality Industry

Response	Frequency (f_o)
Excellent	21
Pretty good	109
Only fair	62
Poor	15

Step 1 The hypotheses for this example follow.

H_0: The observed distribution is the same as the expected distribution.

H_a: The observed distribution is not the same as the expected distribution.

Step 2 The statistical test being used is:

$$\chi^2 = \sum \frac{(f_o - f_e)^2}{f_e}$$

Step 3 Let $\alpha = 0.05$.

Step 4 Chi-square goodness-of-fit tests are one-tailed because a chi-square of zero indicates perfect agreement between distributions. Any deviation from zero difference occurs only in the positive direction because chi-square is determined by a sum of squared values and can never be negative. With four categories in this example (excellent, pretty good, only fair, and poor), $k = 4$. The degrees of freedom are $k - 1$ because the expected distribution is given: $k - 1 = 4 - 1 = 3$. For $\alpha = 0.05$ and df = 3, the critical chi-square value is:

$$\chi^2_{0.05,3} = 7.8147$$

After the data are analyzed, an observed chi-square greater than 7.8147 must be computed in order to reject the null hypothesis.

Step 5 The observed values gathered in the sample data from Table 16.1 sum to 207. Thus, $n = 207$. The expected proportions are given, but the expected frequencies must be calculated by multiplying the expected proportions by the sample total of the observed frequencies, as shown in **Table 16.2**.

TABLE 16.2	**Construction of Expected Values for Hospitality Study**	
Response	**Expected Proportion**	**Expected Frequency (f_e) (proportion × sample total)**
Excellent	0.08	(0.08)(207) = 16.56
Pretty good	0.47	(0.47)(207) = 97.29
Only fair	0.34	(0.34)(207) = 70.38
Poor	0.11	(0.11)(207) = 22.77
		207.00

Step 6 The chi-square goodness-of-fit can then be calculated, as shown in **Table 16.3**.

TABLE 16.3	**Calculation of Chi-Square for Hospitality Example**		
Response	f_o	f_e	$\dfrac{(f_o - f_e)^2}{f_e}$
Excellent	21	16.56	1.19
Pretty good	109	97.29	1.41
Only fair	62	70.38	1.00
Poor	15	22.77	2.65
	207	207.00	6.25

Step 7 Because the observed value of chi-square of 6.25 is not greater than the critical table value of 7.8147, the hotel manager will not reject the null hypothesis.

Step 8 The data gathered in the sample of 207 hotel customers indicate that the distribution of responses of hotel customers is not significantly different from the distribution of responses to the benchmark national survey.

The hotel manager may conclude that her customers do not appear to have attitudes different from those people who took the benchmark survey.

DEMONSTRATION PROBLEM 16.1

Dairies would like to know whether the sales of milk are distributed uniformly over a year so they can plan for milk production and storage. A uniform distribution means that the frequencies are the same in all categories. In this situation, the producers are attempting to determine whether the amounts of milk sold are the same for each month of the year. They ascertain the number of litres of milk sold by sampling one large supermarket each month during a year, obtaining the following data. Use $\alpha = 0.01$ to test whether the data fit a uniform distribution.

Month	Amount (L)	Month	Amount (L)
January	1,610	August	1,350
February	1,585	September	1,495
March	1,649	October	1,564
April	1,590	November	1,602
May	1,540	December	1,655
June	1,397	Total	18,447
July	1,410		

Solution

Step 1 The hypotheses follow.

H_0: The monthly figures for milk sales are uniformly distributed.

H_a: The monthly figures for milk sales are not uniformly distributed.

Step 2 The statistical test used is:

$$\chi^2 = \sum \frac{(f_o - f_e)^2}{f_e}$$

Step 3 Alpha is 0.01.

Step 4 There are 12 categories and a uniform distribution is the expected distribution, so the degrees of freedom are $k - 1 = 12 - 1 = 11$. For $\alpha = 0.01$, the critical value is $\chi^2_{0.01,11} = 24.725$. An observed chi-square value of more than 24.725 must be obtained to reject the null hypothesis.

Step 5 The data are given in the preceding table.

Step 6 The first step in calculating the test statistic is to determine the expected frequencies. The total for the expected frequencies must equal the total for the observed frequencies (18,447). If the frequencies are uniformly distributed, the same number of litres of milk is expected to be sold each month. The expected monthly figure is:

$$\frac{18,447}{12} = 1,537.25 \text{ L}$$

The following table shows the observed frequencies, the expected frequencies, and the chi-square calculations for this problem.

Month	f_o	f_e	$\frac{(f_o - f_e)^2}{f_e}$
January	1,610	1,537.25	3.44
February	1,585	1,537.25	1.48
March	1,649	1,537.25	8.12
April	1,590	1,537.25	1.81
May	1,540	1,537.25	0.00

Month	f_o	f_e	$\dfrac{(f_o - f_e)^2}{f_e}$
June	1,397	1,537.25	12.80
July	1,410	1,537.25	10.53
August	1,350	1,537.25	22.81
September	1,495	1,537.25	1.16
October	1,564	1,537.25	0.47
November	1,602	1,537.25	2.73
December	1,655	1,537.25	9.02
Total	18,447	18,447.00	$\chi^2 = 74.38$

Step 7 The observed χ^2 value of 74.38 is greater than the critical table value of $\chi^2_{0.01,11} = 24.725$, so the decision is to reject the null hypothesis. This problem provides enough evidence to indicate that the distribution of milk sales is not uniform.

Step 8 Because retail milk demand is not uniformly distributed, sales and production managers need to generate a production plan to cope with uneven demand. In times of heavy demand, more milk will need to be processed or on reserve; in times of less demand, provision for milk storage or for a reduction in the purchase of milk from dairy farmers will be necessary.

DEMONSTRATION PROBLEM 16.2

Chapter 5 indicated that, quite often in the business world, random arrivals are Poisson distributed. This distribution is characterized by an average arrival rate, λ, per some interval. Suppose a customer service representative (CSR) supervisor believes random arrivals at a local bank are Poisson distributed and sets out to test this hypothesis by gathering information. The following data represent a distribution of frequency of arrivals during one-minute intervals at the bank. Use $\alpha = 0.05$ and the eight-step approach to test these data in an effort to determine whether they are Poisson distributed.

Number of Arrivals	Observed Frequencies
0	7
1	18
2	25
3	17
4	12
≥ 5	5

Solution

Step 1 The hypotheses follow.

H_0: The frequency distribution is Poisson.

H_a: The frequency distribution is not Poisson.

Step 2 The appropriate statistical test for this problem is:

$$\chi^2 = \sum \frac{(f_o - f_e)^2}{f_e}$$

Step 3 Alpha is 0.05.

Step 4 The degrees of freedom are $k - 1 - 1 = 6 - 2 = 4$ because the expected distribution is Poisson. An extra degree of freedom is lost because the value of λ must be calculated by using the observed sample data. For $\alpha = 0.05$, the critical table value is $\chi^2_{0.05,4} = 9.4877$. The decision rule is to reject the null hypothesis if the observed chi-square is greater than 9.4877.

Step 5 To determine the expected frequencies, the supervisor must obtain the probability of each category of arrivals and then multiply each by the total of the observed frequencies. These probabilities are obtained by determining λ and then using the Poisson table. As it is the mean of a Poisson distribution, λ can be determined from the observed data by computing the mean of the data. In this case, the supervisor computes a weighted average by summing the product of the number of arrivals and the frequency of those arrivals and dividing that sum by the total number of observed frequencies.

Number of Arrivals	Observed Frequencies	Arrivals Observed
0	7	0
1	18	18
2	25	50
3	17	51
4	12	48
≥ 5	5	25
	84	192

$$\lambda = \frac{192}{84} = 2.3$$

With this value of λ and the Poisson distribution table in Appendix A, the supervisor can determine the probabilities of the number of arrivals in each category. The expected probabilities are determined from Table A.3 by looking up the values of $x = 0, 1, 2, 3$, and 4 in the column under $\lambda = 2.3$, shown in the following table as expected probabilities. The probability for $x \geq 5$ is determined by summing the probabilities for the values of $x = 5, 6, 7, 8$, and so on. Using these probabilities and the total of 84 from the observed data, the supervisor computes the expected frequencies by multiplying each expected probability by the total (84).

Arrivals	Expected Probabilities	Expected Frequencies
0	0.1003	8.42
1	0.2306	19.37
2	0.2652	22.28
3	0.2033	17.08
4	0.1169	9.82
≥ 5	0.0837	7.03
		84.00

Step 6   The supervisor uses these expected frequencies and the observed frequencies to compute the observed value of chi-square.

Arrivals	Observed Frequencies	Expected Frequencies	$\dfrac{(f_o - f_e)^2}{f_e}$
0	7	8.42	0.24
1	18	19.37	0.10
2	25	22.28	0.33
3	17	17.08	0.00
4	12	9.82	0.48
≥ 5	5	7.03	0.59
	84	84.00	$\chi^2 = 1.74$

Step 7   The observed value is not greater than the critical chi-square value of 9.4877, so the supervisor's decision is to not reject the null hypothesis; that is he fails to reject the hypothesis that the distribution of bank arrivals is Poisson.

Step 8   The supervisor can use the Poisson distribution as the basis for other types of analysis, such as queuing modelling.

Caution: *When the expected value of a category is small, a large chi-square value can be obtained erroneously, leading to a Type I error. To control for this potential error, the chi-square goodness-of-fit test should not be used when any of the expected frequencies is less than 5. If the observed data produce expected values of less than 5, combining adjacent categories (when meaningful) to create larger frequencies may be possible.*

Concept Check

1. A national drugstore chain would use the chi-square goodness-of-fit test for a particular product category to determine which of the following?

   a. Whether sales follow a uniform distribution throughout Canada.

   b. Whether observed sales revenues matched expected sales revenues.

   c. Whether merchandising managers can forecast what quantities to order for the holiday season.

2. Why should the goodness-of-fit test not be used when any of the expected frequencies is less than 5?

16.1 Problems

16.1 Use a chi-square goodness-of-fit test to determine whether the observed frequencies are distributed the same as the expected frequencies ($\alpha = 0.05$).

Category	f_o	f_e
1	53	68
2	37	42
3	32	33
4	28	22
5	18	10
6	15	8

16.2 Use the following data and $\alpha = 0.01$ to determine whether the observed frequencies represent a uniform distribution.

Category	f_o
1	19
2	17
3	14
4	18
5	19
6	21
7	18
8	18

16.3 Are the following data Poisson distributed? Use $\alpha = 0.05$ and the chi-square goodness-of-fit test to answer this question. What is your estimated λ?

Number of Arrivals	f_o
0	28
1	17
2	11
≥ 3	5

16.4 In one survey, successful female entrepreneurs were asked to state their personal definition of success in terms of several categories from which they could select. Thirty-nine percent responded that happiness was their definition of success, 12% said that sales/profit was their definition, 18% responded that helping others was their definition, and 31% responded that achievements/challenge was their definition. Suppose you wanted to determine whether male entrepreneurs felt the same way and took a random sample of men, resulting in the following data. Use the chi-square goodness-of-fit test to determine whether the observed frequency distribution of data for men is the same as the distribution for women. Let $\alpha = 0.05$.

Definition	f_o
Happiness	42
Sales/profit	95
Helping others	27
Achievements/challenge	63

16.5 The following percentages come from a national survey of the ages of recorded-music shoppers. A local survey produced the observed values. Does the evidence in the observed data indicate that we should reject the national survey distribution for local recorded-music shoppers? Use $\alpha = 0.01$.

Age	Percentage from National Survey	f_o
10–14	9	22
15–19	23	50
20–24	22	43
25–29	14	29
30–34	10	19
≥35	22	49

16.6 A 911 service keeps records of emergency telephone calls. A study of 150 five-minute time intervals resulted in the distribution of number of calls as follows. For example, during 18 of the five-minute intervals, no calls occurred. Use the chi-square goodness-of-fit test and $\alpha = 0.01$ to determine whether this distribution is Poisson.

Number of Calls (per 5-minute interval)	Frequency
0	18
1	28
2	47
3	21
4	16
5	11
6 or more	9

16.7 According to a recent survey, 40% of luxury car manufacturers, 12% of sports car makers, and 48% of economy auto manufacturers were planning to spend more on marketing in a certain year than in previous years. Suppose a business analyst conducts her own survey. She randomly selects 280 companies and determines that 96 luxury car manufacturers, 27 sports car manufacturers, and 157 economy car manufacturing companies do in fact plan to spend more on marketing next year. Use the chi-square goodness-of-fit test to determine if there is a significant difference between the distribution of car manufacturers in the survey and the distribution released by the analyst. Let $\alpha = 0.01$.

16.8 According to a report by the U.S. Environmental Protection Agency (EPA), containers and packaging generated about 30.3% of all municipal solid waste (MSW) in the country in a recent year. This was the largest category of such waste. The next highest group was nondurable goods, which accounted for 21.3% of waste. This was followed by durable goods at 19.6%, yard trimmings/other at 14.9%, and food scraps at 13.9%. Suppose last year, one large Midwestern U.S. city processed 300,000 tons of MSW broken down by categories as follows:

Category	MSW (1,000 tons)
Containers and packaging	86
Nondurable goods	74
Durable goods	70
Yard trimmings/other	41
Food scraps	29

Use the chi-square goodness-of-fit test to determine if there is a significant difference between the distribution of MSW in this Midwestern city and the distribution released by the EPA. Let $\alpha = 0.10$.

16.2 | Contingency Analysis: Chi-Square Test of Independence

LEARNING OBJECTIVE 16.2

Use the chi-square test of independence to perform contingency analysis.

The chi-square goodness-of-fit test is used to analyze the distribution of frequencies for categories of *one* variable, such as age or number of bank arrivals, to determine whether the distribution of these frequencies is the same as some hypothesized or expected distribution. However, the goodness-of-fit test cannot be used to analyze *two* variables simultaneously. A different chi-square test, the **chi-square test of independence**, can be *used to analyze the frequencies of two variables with multiple categories to determine whether the two variables are independent.* There are many cases in which this type of analysis is desirable. For example, a market analyst might want to determine whether the type of soft drink preferred by a consumer is independent of the consumer's age. An organizational behaviourist might want to know whether absenteeism is independent of job classification. Financial investors might want to determine whether the type of preferred stock investment is independent of the region where the investor resides (see Thinking Critically About Statistics in Business Today 16.1).

Thinking Critically About Statistics in Business Today 16.1

City Images of Cruise Destinations in the Taiwan Strait

A study was conducted by researchers Chiang-Chuan Lu and Ruey-Feng Chen in an effort to determine, in part, if there was a difference in cruise passengers' perceptions of the city images of the Taiwan Strait ports of Hong Kong, Shanghai, and Taipei. Researchers gathered data by administering questionnaires to cruise passengers over a four-year period. The participating passengers were about half men and half women, and over 50% had college degrees. Slightly over one-half of the respondents were from one of the port cities under study, and 72%, were from Malaysia, Singapore, China, or Taiwan.

One of the hypotheses being studied was if there is a difference between the images of the three cities—Hong Kong, Shanghai, and Taipei—held by passengers who resided in those three cities and the images held by passengers from other places. A chi-square test of independence was used to test this hypothesis. Shown here is a 2×2 contingency table with the raw number results:

	Perceived Difference in Three Port Cities	No Perceived Difference in Three Port Cities
Resident of One of the Three Port Cities	58	5
Not Resident of One of the Three Port Cities	37	25

The null hypothesis for this test is that perceived difference in the three port cities is independent of place of residence. An observed chi-square value of 17.97 is calculated from these data. Using $\alpha = 0.05$, df = 1, and a critical chi-square of 3.8415, the decision is to reject the null hypothesis. Perceived differences in the three port cities are not independent of place of residence. In fact, over 90% of residents of the three cities perceive that there are differences, but a little less than 60% of residents of other places perceive such differences.

Things to Ponder

1. Why do you think such a high percentage of residents of the three port cities perceive a difference between the three cities, but a much smaller percentage of passengers from outside the three cities do so?

2. How might this problem be examined using techniques given in Section 10.4 of the text? Compare the results using those techniques and the chi-square test of independence.

Source: Adapted from Chiang-Chuan Lu and Ruey-Feng Chen, "Differences in Tourism Image Among Cruise Passengers across the Taiwan Straits," *Global Journal of Business Research* 5 (2011): 95–108.

The chi-square test of independence can be used to analyze any level of data measurement, but it is particularly useful in analyzing nominal data. Suppose a business analyst is interested in determining whether geographic region is independent of type of financial investment. On a questionnaire, the following two questions might be used to measure geographic region and type of financial investment.

1. Where do you reside?
   A. A large town (or city)   B. A medium town   C. A small town   D. A rural area

2. Which type of financial investment are you most likely to make today?
   E. Stocks   F. Bonds   G. Treasury bills

The business analyst would *tally the frequencies of responses* to these two questions into a two-way table called a **contingency table** (see cross-tabulation in Chapter 2). Because the chi-square test of independence uses a contingency table, this test is sometimes referred to as **contingency analysis.**

Depicted in **Table 16.4** is a contingency table for these two variables. Variable 1, geographic type, uses four categories: A, B, C, and D. Variable 2, type of financial investment, uses three categories: E, F, and G. The observed frequency for each cell is denoted as o_{ij}, where i is the row and j is the column. Thus, o_{13} is the observed frequency for the cell in the first row and third column. The expected frequencies are denoted in a similar manner.

If the two variables are independent, they are not related. In a sense, the chi-square test of independence is a test of whether the variables are related. The null hypothesis for a chi-square test of independence is that the two variables are independent (not related). If the null hypothesis is rejected, the conclusion is that the two variables are not independent and are related.

Assume at the beginning that variable 1 and variable 2 are independent. The probability of the intersection of two of their respective categories, A and F, can be found by using the multiplicative law for independent events presented in Chapter 4:

$$P(A \cap F) = P(A) \cdot P(F)$$

TABLE 16.4 Contingency Table for the Investment Example

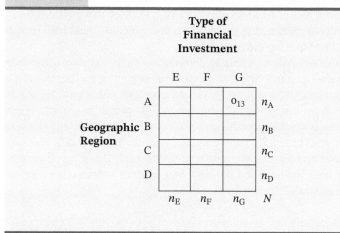

If A and F are independent, then:

$$P(A) = \frac{n_A}{N}, P(F) = \frac{n_F}{N}, \text{ and } P(A \cap F) = \frac{n_A}{N} \cdot \frac{n_F}{N}$$

If $P(A \cap F)$ is multiplied by the total number of frequencies, N, the expected frequency for the cell of A and F can be determined:

$$e_{AF} = \frac{n_A}{N} \cdot \frac{n_F}{N}(N) = \frac{n_A \cdot n_F}{N}$$

In general, if the two variables are independent, the expected frequency values of each cell can be determined by:

$$e_{ij} = \frac{n_i \cdot n_j}{N}$$

where:

i = the row
j = the column
n_i = the total of row i
n_j = the total of column j
N = the total of all frequencies

Using these expected frequency values and the observed frequency values, we can compute a chi-square test of independence to determine whether the variables are independent. Formula 16.2 is the formula for accomplishing this test.

Chi-Square Test of Independence

$$\chi^2 = \sum \sum \frac{(f_o - f_e)^2}{f_e}$$
$$\text{df} = (r - 1)(c - 1)$$

(16.2)

where:

r = number of rows
c = number of columns
f_o = frequency of observed values
f_e = frequency of expected values

The null hypothesis for a chi-square test of independence is that the two variables are independent. The alternative hypothesis is that the variables are not independent. This test is one-tailed. The degrees of freedom are $(r - 1)(c - 1)$. Note that Formula 16.2 is similar to Formula 16.1, with the exception that the values are summed across both rows and columns and the degrees of freedom are different.

Suppose a business analyst wants to determine whether type of gas preferred is independent of a person's income. She takes a random survey of gas purchasers, asking them one question about gas preference and a second question about income. The respondent is to check whether he or she prefers (1) regular gas, (2) premium gas, or (3) extra premium gas. The respondent is also to check his or her income bracket as being (1) less than $30,000, (2) $30,000 to $49,999, (3) $50,000 to $99,999, or (4) more than $100,000. The business analyst tallies the responses and obtains the results in Table 16.5. Using $\alpha = 0.01$, she can use the chi-square test of independence and the eight-step process to determine whether type of gas preferred is independent of income level.

TABLE 16.5 Contingency Table for the Gas Consumer Example

		Type of Gas			
		Regular	Premium	Extra Premium	
	Less than $30,000	85	16	6	107
Income	$30,000 to $49,999	102	27	13	142
	$50,000 to $99,999	36	22	15	73
	More than $100,000	15	23	25	63
		238	88	59	385

Step 1 The hypotheses follow.

H_0: Type of gas is independent of income.
H_a: Type of gas is not independent of income.

Step 2 The appropriate statistical test is:

$$\chi^2 = \sum\sum \frac{(f_o - f_e)^2}{f_e}$$

Step 3 Alpha is 0.01.

Step 4 Here, there are four rows ($r = 4$) and three columns ($c = 3$). The degrees of freedom are $(4 - 1)(3 - 1) = 6$. The critical value of chi-square for $\alpha = 0.01$ is $\chi^2_{0.01,6} = 16.8119$. The decision rule is to reject the null hypothesis if the observed chi-square is greater than 16.8119.

Step 5 The observed data appear in Table 16.5.

Step 6 To determine the observed value of chi-square, the analyst must first compute the expected frequencies. The expected values for this example are calculated as follows, with the first term in the subscript (and numerator) representing the row and the second term in the subscript (and numerator) representing the column:

$$e_{11} = \frac{(n_{1.})(n_{.1})}{N} = \frac{(107)(238)}{385} = 66.15 \quad e_{21} = \frac{(n_{2.})(n_{.1})}{N} = \frac{(142)(238)}{385} = 87.78$$

$$e_{12} = \frac{(n_{1.})(n_{.2})}{N} = \frac{(107)(88)}{385} = 24.46 \quad e_{22} = \frac{(n_{2.})(n_{.2})}{N} = \frac{(142)(88)}{385} = 32.46$$

$$e_{13} = \frac{(n_{1.})(n_{.3})}{N} = \frac{(107)(59)}{385} = 16.40 \quad e_{23} = \frac{(n_{2.})(n_{.3})}{N} = \frac{(142)(59)}{385} = 21.76$$

$$e_{31} = \frac{(n_{3.})(n_{.1})}{N} = \frac{(73)(238)}{385} = 45.13 \quad e_{41} = \frac{(n_{4.})(n_{.1})}{N} = \frac{(63)(238)}{385} = 38.95$$

$$e_{32} = \frac{(n_{3.})(n_{.2})}{N} = \frac{(73)(88)}{385} = 16.69 \qquad e_{42} = \frac{(n_{4.})(n_{.2})}{N} = \frac{(63)(88)}{385} = 14.40$$

$$e_{33} = \frac{(n_{3.})(n_{.3})}{N} = \frac{(73)(59)}{385} = 11.19 \qquad e_{43} = \frac{(n_{4.})(n_{.3})}{N} = \frac{(63)(59)}{385} = 9.65$$

The analyst then lists the expected frequencies in the cells of the contingency tables along with the observed frequencies. In this text, expected frequencies are enclosed in parentheses. Table 16.6 provides the contingency table for this example.

TABLE 16.6 Contingency Table of Observed and Expected Frequencies for Gas Consumer Example

		Type of Gas			
		Regular	Premium	Extra Premium	
Income	Less than $30,000	(66.15) 85	(24.46) 16	(16.40) 6	107
	$30,000 to $49,999	(87.78) 102	(32.46) 27	(21.76) 13	142
	$50,000 to $99,999	(45.13) 36	(16.69) 22	(11.19) 15	73
	More than $100,000	(38.95) 15	(14.40) 23	(9.65) 25	63
		238	88	59	385

Next, the analyst computes the chi-square value by summing $(f_o - f_e)^2/f_e$ for all cells:

$$\chi^2 = \frac{(85 - 66.15)^2}{66.15} + \frac{(16 - 24.46)^2}{24.46} + \frac{(6 - 16.40)^2}{16.40} + \frac{(102 - 87.78)^2}{87.78} + \frac{(27 - 32.46)^2}{32.46}$$
$$+ \frac{(13 - 21.76)^2}{21.76} + \frac{(36 - 45.13)^2}{45.13} + \frac{(22 - 16.69)^2}{16.69} + \frac{(15 - 11.19)^2}{11.19} + \frac{(15 - 38.95)^2}{38.95}$$
$$+ \frac{(23 - 14.40)^2}{14.40} + \frac{(25 - 9.65)^2}{9.65}$$
$$= 5.37 + 2.93 + 6.60 + 2.30 + 0.92 + 3.53 + 1.85 + 1.69 + 1.30 + 14.73 + 5.14 + 24.42$$
$$= 70.78$$

Step 7 The observed value of chi-square, 70.78, is greater than the critical value of chi-square, 16.8119, obtained from Table A.8. The business analyst's decision is to reject the null hypothesis; that is, type of gas preferred is not independent of income.

Step 8 Having established that conclusion, the business analyst can then examine the outcome to determine which people, by income brackets, tend to purchase which type of gas and use this information in market decisions.

DEMONSTRATION PROBLEM 16.3

Is the type of beverage ordered with lunch at a restaurant independent of the age of the consumer? A random poll of 320 lunch customers is taken, resulting in the following contingency table of observed values. Use $\alpha = 0.05$ and the eight-step process to determine whether the two variables are independent.

Preferred Beverage

	Coffee/Tea	Soft Drink	Water	
21–34	20	46	74	140
Age 35–55	35	25	50	110
>55	13	42	15	70
	68	113	139	320

Solution

Step 1   The hypotheses follow.

H_0: Type of beverage preferred is independent of age.

H_a: Type of beverage preferred is not independent of age.

Step 2   The appropriate statistical test is:

$$\chi^2 = \sum\sum\frac{(f_o - f_e)^2}{f_e}$$

Step 3   Alpha is 0.05.

Step 4   The degrees of freedom are $(3 - 1)(3 - 1) = 4$, and the critical value is $\chi^2_{0.05,4} = 9.4877$. The decision rule is to reject the null hypothesis if the observed value of chi-square is greater than 9.4877.

Step 5   The sample data were shown previously.

Step 6   The expected frequencies are the product of the row and column totals divided by the grand total. The contingency table, with expected frequencies, follows.

Preferred Beverage

	Coffee/Tea	Soft Drink	Water	
21–34	(29.75) 20	(49.44) 46	(60.81) 74	140
Age 35–55	(23.38) 35	(38.84) 25	(47.78) 50	110
>55	(14.88) 13	(24.72) 42	(30.41) 15	70
	68	113	139	320

For these values, the observed χ^2 is:

$$\chi^2 = \frac{(20 - 29.75)^2}{29.75} + \frac{(46 - 49.44)^2}{49.44} + \frac{(74 - 60.81)^2}{60.81} + \frac{(35 - 23.38)^2}{23.38} + \frac{(25 - 38.84)^2}{38.84}$$

$$+ \frac{(50 - 47.78)^2}{47.78} + \frac{(13 - 14.88)^2}{14.88} + \frac{(42 - 24.72)^2}{24.72} + \frac{(15 - 30.41)^2}{30.41}$$

$$= 3.20 + 0.24 + 2.86 + 5.78 + 4.93 + 0.10 + 0.24 + 12.08 + 7.81$$

$$= 37.24$$

Step 7   The observed value of chi-square, 37.24, is greater than the critical value, 9.4877, so the null hypothesis is rejected.

Step 8   The two variables—preferred beverage and age—are not independent. The type of beverage that a customer orders with lunch is related to or dependent on age. Examination of the categories reveals that younger people tend to prefer water and older people prefer soft drinks. Managers of eating establishments and marketers of beverage products can utilize such information in targeting their market and in providing appropriate products.

Caution: *As with the chi-square goodness-of-fit test, small expected frequencies can lead to inordinately large chi-square values with the chi-square test of independence. Hence, contingency tables should not be used with expected cell values of less than 5. One way to avoid small expected values is to collapse (combine) columns or rows whenever possible and whenever doing so makes sense.*

is the same as or different from the national figures, using $\alpha = 0.05$. What does she find?

16.23 Video Are the types of professional jobs held in the computing industry independent of the number of years a person has worked in the industry? Suppose 246 workers are interviewed. Use the results obtained to determine whether type of professional job held in the computer industry is independent of years worked in the industry. Let $\alpha = 0.01$.

Professional Position

Years		Manager	Programmer	Operator	Systems Analyst
	0–3	6	37	11	13
	4–8	28	16	23	24
	More than 8	47	10	12	19

16.24 A study found that the average workweek is getting longer for U.S. full-time workers. Forty-three percent of the responding workers in the survey cited "more work, more business" as the reason for this increase in workweek, 37% of the workers named insufficient number of workers to get the work done as the reason, and 5% of the workers blamed the use of technology that blurred the boundary between life and work. Additionally, 15% of the workers selected other reasons. Suppose you want to test these figures in Canada to determine whether Canadian workers feel the same way. A random sample of 315 Canadian full-time workers whose workweek has been getting longer is chosen. They are offered a selection of possible reasons for this increase and 120 pick "more work, more business," 114 select "insufficient number of workers," only 23 say "technology," and 58 cite "others." Use techniques presented in this chapter and an α of 0.10 to determine whether the U.S. figures hold true in Canada.

16.25 Is the number of children that a post-secondary student currently has independent of the type of college or university being attended? Suppose students were randomly selected from three types of colleges and universities and the data shown represent the results of a survey of those students. Use a chi-square test of independence to answer the question. Let $\alpha = 0.05$.

Type of College or University

Number of Children		Community College	Large University	Small University
	0	25	178	31
	1	49	141	12
	2	31	54	8
	3 or more	22	14	6

Interpreting the Output

16.26 A survey by Ipsos-Reid showed that given a $1,000 windfall, 36% of recipients would spend the money on home improvement, 24% on leisure travel/vacation, 15% on clothing, 15% on home entertainment or electronic products, and 10% on local entertainment including restaurants and movies. Suppose a business analyst believes that these

results would not be the same if the questions were posed to adults between 21 and 30 years of age. The analyst conducts a new survey, asking 200 adults between 21 and 30 years of age these same questions. A chi-square goodness-of-fit test is conducted to compare the results of the new survey with the one taken by Ipsos-Reid. The Excel results follow. The observed and expected values are for the categories as already listed and appear in the same order. Discuss the findings. How did the distribution of results from the new survey compare with the old? Discuss the business implications of this outcome.

21–30 Years of Age	General Population
Observed	Expected
36	72
64	48
42	30
38	30
20	20

The p-value for the chi-square goodness-of-fit test is 0.0000043. The observed chi-square for the goodness-of-fit test is 30.18.

16.27 Do men and women prefer the same colours of cars? That is, is gender independent of colour preference for cars? Suppose a study is undertaken to address this question. A random sample of men and women is asked which of five colours (silver, white, black, green, blue) they prefer in a car. The results of a chi-square test of independence are shown here. Discuss the test used, the hypotheses, the findings, and the business implications.

```
Chi-Square Test: Men, Women
─────────────────────────────────────────
Expected counts are printed below observed
counts.

Chi-square contributions are printed below
expected counts.
              Men        Women      Total
Silver        90         52         142
              85.20      56.80
              0.270      0.406
White         75         58         133
              79.80      53.20
              0.289      0.433
Black         63         30         93
              55.80      37.20
              0.929      1.394
Green         39         33         72
              43.20      28.80
              0.408      0.612
Blue          33         27         60
              36.00      24.00
              0.250      0.375
Total         300        200        500
─────────────────────────────────────────
Chi-Sq = 5.366, df = 4, P-Value = 0.252
```

1. The Financial Database contains companies in seven different types of industries. These seven are denoted by the variable Type. Use a chi-square goodness-of-fit test to determine whether the seven types of industries are uniformly distributed in this database.

2. In the Canadian RRSP Contribution Database, is the RRSP average annual contribution independent of province? The data given below are for the provinces from the Atlantic region of Canada. Use a chi-square test of independence to answer the question, $\alpha = 0.05$.

RRSP Contribution/ Atlantic Region	Newfoundland and Labrador	P.E.I.	Nova Scotia	New Brunswick	Total
Less than $2,100	1	6	2	5	14
$2,100 to $2,200	0	2	4	3	9
$2,200 to $2,300	5	1	4	2	12
$2,300 to $2,400	0	2	2	1	5
Over $2,400	6	1	0	1	8
Total	12	12	12	12	48

Case

Foot Locker in the Shoe Mix

Foot Locker, Inc., is the world's number one retailer of athletic footwear and apparel. Headquartered in New York City, the company has over 32,175 employees and 3,310 retail stores in 27 countries across North America, Europe, Asia, Australia, and New Zealand operating under such brand names as Foot Locker, Lady Foot Locker, Kids Foot Locker, Champs Sports, Footaction, Runners Point, Sidestep, and SIX:02. In addition, it operates direct-to-customer channels through Eastbay.com. The company intends to increase its share of the worldwide market by adding stores and by growing its Internet and catalogue business.

In recent years, Foot Locker officials have been rethinking the company's retail mix. Determining the shoe mix that will maximize profits is an important decision for Foot Locker. By the year 2002, in an effort to stock more lower-priced footwear, the company had reduced its inventory of sneakers priced at $120 or more by 50%.

Discussion

Suppose the data presented below represented the number of unit sales (US$ millions) for athletic footwear in the years 2000 and 2019. Use techniques presented in this chapter to analyze these data, and discuss the business implications for Foot Locker.

Price Category	2000	2019
Less than $30	$115	$126
$30–less than $40	38	40
$40–less than $50	37	35
$50–less than $60	30	27
$60–less than $70	22	20
$70–less than $85	21	20
$85–less than $100	11	11
$100 or more	17	18

Suppose Foot Locker strongly encourages its employees to make formal suggestions to improve the store, the product, and the working environment. Suppose a quality auditor keeps records of the suggestions, the people who submitted them, and the geographic region from which they come. A possible breakdown of the number of suggestions over a three-year period by employee gender and geographic location follows. Is there any relationship between the gender of the employee and the geographic location in terms of number of suggestions? If they are related, what does this relationship mean to the company? What business implications might there be for such an analysis?

		Gender	
		Male	Female
	U.S. West	29	43
	U.S. East	48	20
	Canada West	52	61
Location	Canada East	28	25
	Europe	78	32
	Australia and New Zealand	47	29

Sources: Adapted from Christopher Lawton and Maureen Tkacik, "Foot Locker Changes Mix of Sneakers," *The Wall Street Journal*, July 22, 2002, p. B3; Foot Locker, Inc., available at Source: www.footlocker-inc.com; "Venator Group, Inc. Announces Name Change to Foot Locker, Inc.," PR Newswire, November 1, 2001, p. 1; Foot Locker website, www.footlocker.com/.

Big Data Case

Drawing upon the American Hospital Association database (AHA), use techniques presented in Chapter 16 to address the following.

1. One of the variables included in this database is Region, which is coded as 1 through 9 representing nine regions of the United States. For example, 9 is the Pacific Region, which includes Alaska, California, Hawaii, Oregon, and Washington. Another variable is Control, which represents type of ownership of the hospital. Six categories of ownership are included in this database and are coded as 1 through 6.

An example is code 5, which is investor-owned for-profit. Is hospital Control independent of Region in this database?

2. Another variable in this AHA database is Service, which is essentially the type of hospital. In the database under Service, there are 15 different types of hospitals coded from 1 to 15. As an example, code 3 represents orthopedic hospitals. Using the database and techniques presented in this chapter, test to determine if Service (type of hospital) is independent of Region.

Using the Computer

- Excel can compute the chi-square goodness-of-fit test but not the chi-square test of independence.
- To compute the chi-square goodness-of-fit test, begin with **Insert Function (f_x)**. To access **Insert Function**, go to the **Formulas** tab on an Excel worksheet (top centre tab). The Insert Function tab is on the far left of the ribbon. In the **Insert Function** dialogue box at the top, there is a pull-down menu where it says **Or select a category**. From the pull-down menu associated with this command, select **Statistical**.

Select **CHISQ.TEST** from the **Insert Function's Statistical** menu. In the **CHISQ.TEST** dialogue box, place the location of the observed values in **Actual_range**. Place the location of the expected values in **Expected_range**. The output will consist of a *p*-value. To determine the observed chi-square from this *p*-value, go back to **Insert Function (f_x)** and select **Statistical**. Then, in the **CHISQ.INV** dialogue box, place the *p*-value in **Probability** and the degrees of freedom in **Deg_freedom**. The output is the chi-square value.

CHAPTER 17

Nonparametric Statistics

LEARNING OBJECTIVES

This chapter presents several nonparametric statistics that can be used to analyze data, thereby enabling you to:

17.1 Use both the small-sample and large-sample runs tests to determine whether the order of observations in a sample is random.

17.2 Use both the small-sample and large-sample cases of the Mann-Whitney U test to determine if there is a difference in two independent populations.

17.3 Use both the small-sample and large-sample cases of the Wilcoxon matched-pairs signed rank test to compare the differences in two related samples.

17.4 Use the Kruskal-Wallis test to determine whether samples come from the same or different populations.

17.5 Use the Friedman test to determine whether different treatment levels come from the same population when a blocking variable is available.

17.6 Use Spearman's rank correlation to analyze the degree of association of two variables.

Decision Dilemma

How Is the Doughnut Business Doing?

By investing $5,000, William Rosenberg founded the Industrial Luncheon Services company in 1946 to deliver meals and coffee break snacks to customers. Building on his success in this venture, Rosenberg opened his first coffee and doughnut shop, called the Open Kettle, in 1948. In 1950, Rosenberg changed the name of his shop to Dunkin' Donuts, and thus the first Dunkin' Donuts shop was established. The first Dunkin' Donuts franchise was awarded in 1955, and by 1963, there were 100 Dunkin' Donuts shops. In 1970, the first overseas Dunkin' Donuts shop was opened in Japan, and by 1979, there were 1,000 Dunkin' Donuts shops.

Today, there are over 11,000 Dunkin' Donuts worldwide in 32 countries. Despite the decline of the franchise in Canada, where the final three stores closed their doors in 2018, Dunkin' Donuts, renamed Dunkin' in 2019, is the world's largest coffee and baked goods chain, serving more than 3 million customers per day. Dunkin' sells 52 varieties of doughnuts and more than a dozen coffee beverages, as well as an array of bagels, breakfast

Richard Levine/Alamy Stock Photo

sandwiches, and other baked goods. Dunkin' is co-owned along with Baskin-Robbins by Dunkin' Brands Inc., based in Canton, Massachusetts.

Suppose analysts at Dunkin' are studying several manufacturing and marketing questions in an effort to improve the consistency of their products and understand their market. Manufacturing engineers want to ensure that the various machines produce a consistent doughnut size. In an effort to test this issue, four machines are selected for a study. Each machine is set to produce a doughnut that is supposed to be about 7.62 cm in diameter. A random sample of doughnuts is taken from each machine and the diameters of the doughnuts are measured. The result is the data shown as follows.

Machine 1	Machine 2	Machine 3	Machine 4
7.58	7.41	7.56	7.72
7.52	7.44	7.55	7.65
7.50	7.42	7.50	7.67
7.52	7.38	7.58	7.70
7.48	7.45	7.53	7.69
	7.40		7.71
			7.73

Suppose Dunkin' implements a national advertising campaign in the United States. Marketing analysts want to determine whether the campaign has increased the number of doughnuts sold at various outlets around the country. Ten stores are randomly selected and the number of doughnuts sold between 8 and 9 A.M. on a Tuesday is measured both before and after the campaign is implemented. The data follow.

Outlet	Before	After
1	301	374
2	198	187
3	278	332
4	205	212
5	249	243
6	410	478
7	360	386
8	124	141
9	253	251
10	190	264

Do bigger stores have greater sales? To test this hypothesis, suppose sales data were gathered from seven Dunkin' stores along with store size. These figures are used to rank the seven stores on each variable. The ranked data follow.

Store	Sales Rank	Size Rank
1	6	7
2	2	2
3	3	6
4	7	5
5	5	4
6	1	1
7	4	3

Managerial, Statistical, and Analytical Questions

1. The manufacturing analysts who are testing to determine whether there is a difference in the size of doughnuts by machine want to run a one-way ANOVA, but they have serious doubts that the ANOVA assumptions can be met by these data. Is it still possible to analyze the data using statistics?

2. The market analysts are uncertain that normal distribution assumptions underlying the matched-pairs t test can be met with the number of doughnuts data. How can the before-and-after data still be used to test the effectiveness of the advertisements?

3. If the sales and store size data are given as ranks, how do we compute a correlation to answer the research question about the relationship of sales and store size? The Pearson product-moment correlation coefficient requires at least interval-level data, and these data are given as ordinal level.

Sources: Adapted from information presented on the Dunkin' Donuts' website at www.dunkindonuts.com/en/about/about-us; Tim Forster, "Dunkin' Donuts Has Given up on Canada," Montreal Eater website, September 5, 2018, montreal.eater.com/2018/9/5/17823382/dunkin-donuts-closure-canada-lawsuit-tim-hortons; Wikipedia, s.v. "Dunkin' Donuts," last modified August 15, 2019, en.wikipedia.org/wiki/Dunkin%27_Donuts. Please note that the data used in the problem are fictional, were not supplied by Dunkin', and do not necessarily represent Dunkin's experience.

Introduction

Except for the chi-square analyses presented in Chapter 16, all statistical techniques presented in the text thus far have been parametric techniques. Parametric statistics are *statistical techniques based on assumptions about the population from which the sample data are selected.* For example, if a t statistic is being used to conduct a hypothesis test about a population mean, the assumption is that the data being analyzed are randomly selected from a *normally* distributed population. The name *parametric statistics* refers to the fact that an assumption (here, normally distributed data) is being made about the data used to test or estimate the parameter (in this case, the population mean). In addition, the use of parametric statistics requires quantitative measurements that yield interval- or ratio-level data.

For data that do not meet the assumptions made about the population, or when the level of data being measured is qualitative, nonparametric, or distribution-free, techniques are used.

Nonparametric statistics are *based on fewer assumptions about the population and the parameters than are parametric statistics.* They are sometimes referred to as *distribution-free* statistics because many of them can be used regardless of the shape of the population distribution. A variety of nonparametric statistics are available for use with nominal or ordinal data. Some require at least ordinal-level data, but others can be specifically targeted for use with nominal-level data.

Figure 17.1 contains a tree diagram that displays all of the nonparametric techniques presented in this chapter with the exception of Spearman's rank correlation, which is used to analyze the degree of association of two variables. As you peruse the tree diagram, you will see that it includes a test of randomness, the runs test; two tests of the differences of two populations, the Mann-Whitney U test and the Wilcoxon matched-pairs signed rank test; and two tests of the differences of three or more populations, the Kruskal-Wallis test and the Friedman test.

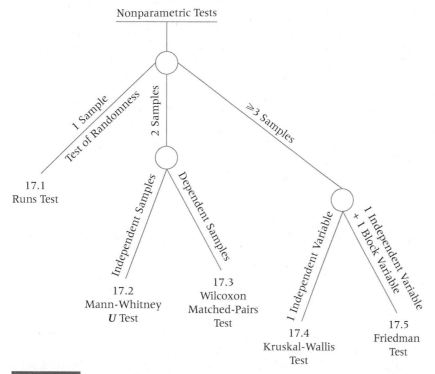

FIGURE 17.1   **Branch of the Tree Diagram Taxonomy of Inferential Techniques**

In this era of big data, as a result of an increase in both the volume and variety of data, there will likely be an upturn in the incidence of nonmetric data. Fortunately, business analysts have at their disposal a number of statistical techniques that specifically deal with nonmetric data. This chapter on nonparametric statistics presents some of the main techniques that are used to analyze nonmetric data (nominal or ordinal levels). Given a likely rise in the occurrence of nonmetric data, there is potential for nonparametric techniques to increase in prominence.

17.1   Runs Test

LEARNING OBJECTIVE 17.1

Use both the small-sample and large-sample runs tests to determine whether the order of observations in a sample is random.

The one-sample **runs test** is *a nonparametric test of randomness.* The runs test is *used to determine whether the order or sequence of observations in a sample is random.* The runs test examines the number of "runs" of each of two possible characteristics that sample items may have. A *run* is a succession of observations that have a particular one of the characteristics. For example, if a sample of people contains both men and women, one run could be a continuous succession of women. In tossing coins, the outcome of three heads in a row constitutes a run, as does a succession of seven tails.

Suppose an analyst takes a random sample of 15 people who arrive at a Canadian Tire store to shop. Eight of the people are women and seven are men. If these people arrive randomly at the store, it makes sense that the sequence of arrivals would have some mix of men and women, but probably not a perfect mix. That is, it seems unlikely (although possible) that the sequence of a random sample of such shoppers would be first eight women and then seven men. In such a case, there are two runs. Suppose, however, the sequence of shoppers is woman, man, woman, man, woman, and so on all the way through the sample. This would result in 15 runs. Each of these cases is possible, but neither is highly likely in a random scenario. In fact, if there are just two runs, it seems possible that a group of women came shopping together followed by a group of men who did likewise. In that case, the observations would not be random. Similarly, a pattern of woman-man all the way through may make the business analyst suspicious that what has been observed is not really individual random arrivals, but actually random arrivals of couples consisting of a man and a woman.

In a random sample, the number of runs is likely to be somewhere between these extremes. What number of runs is reasonable? The one-sample runs test takes into consideration the size of the sample, n; the number of observations in the sample having each characteristic, n_1, n_2 (man, woman for instance); and the number of runs in the sample, R, to reach conclusions about hypotheses of randomness. The following hypotheses are tested by the one-sample runs test:

H_0: The observations in the sample are randomly generated.
H_a: The observations in the sample are not randomly generated.

The one-sample runs test is conducted differently for small samples than it is for large samples. Each test is presented here. First, we consider the small-sample case.

Small-Sample Runs Test

If both n_1 and n_2 are less than or equal to 20, the small-sample runs test is appropriate. In the example of shoppers with $n_1 = 7$ men and $n_2 = 8$ women, the small-sample runs test could be used to test for randomness. The test is carried out by comparing the observed number of runs, R, to critical values of runs for the given values of n_1 and n_2. The critical values of R are given in Tables A.11 and A.12 in Appendix A for $\alpha = 0.05$. Table A.11 contains critical values of R for the lower tail of the distribution in which so few runs occur that the probability of that many runs or fewer occurring is less than 0.025 ($\alpha/2$). Table A.12 contains critical values of R for the upper tail of the distribution in which so many runs occur that the probability of that many runs or more occurring is less than 0.025 ($\alpha/2$). Any observed value of R that is less than or equal to the critical value of the lower tail (Table A.11) results in the rejection of the null hypothesis and the conclusion that the sample data are not random. Any observed value of R that is equal to or greater than the critical value in the upper tail (Table A.12) also results in the rejection of the null hypothesis and the conclusion that the sample data are not random.

As an example, suppose 26 cola drinkers are sampled randomly to determine whether they prefer regular cola or diet cola. The random sample contains 18 regular cola drinkers and 8 diet cola drinkers. Let C denote regular cola drinkers and D denote diet cola drinkers. Suppose the sequence of sampled cola drinkers is DCCCCCDCCDCCCCDCDCCCDDDCCC. Is this sequence of cola drinkers evidence that the sample is not random? Applying the eight-step process for testing a hypothesis to this problem results in the following analysis.

Step 1 The hypotheses tested follow.

H_0: The observations in the sample were generated randomly.

H_a: The observations in the sample were not generated randomly.

Step 2 Let n_1 denote the number of regular cola drinkers and n_2 denote the number of diet cola drinkers. Because $n_1 = 18$ and $n_2 = 8$, the small-sample runs test is the appropriate test.

Step 3 Alpha is 0.05.

Step 4 With $n_1 = 18$ and $n_2 = 8$, Table A.11 yields a critical value of 7 and Table A.12 yields a critical value of 17. If there are 7 or fewer runs or 17 or more runs, the decision rule is to reject the null hypothesis.

Step 5 The sample data are given as:

DCCCCCDCCDCCCCDCDCCCDDDCCC

Step 6 Tally the number of runs in this sample.

1	2	3	4	5	6	7	8	9	10	11	12
D	CCCCC	D	CC	D	CCCC	D	C	D	CCC	DDD	CCC

The number of runs, R, is 12.

Step 7 Because the value of R falls between the critical values of 7 and 17, the decision is to not reject the null hypothesis. Not enough evidence is provided to declare that the data are not random.

Step 8 The cola analyst can proceed with the study under the assumption that the sample represents randomly selected cola drinkers.

Excel cannot analyze data by using the runs test; however, Minitab can. **Figure 17.2** is the Minitab output for the cola example runs test. Notice that the output includes the number of runs, 12, and the significance level of the test. For this analysis, diet cola was coded as a 1 and regular cola as a 2. The Minitab runs test is a two-tailed test, and the reported significance of the test is equivalent to a p-value. Because the significance is 0.9710, the decision is to not reject the null hypothesis.

```
Runs Test: Cola
Runs above and below K = 1.69231
The observed number of runs = 12
The expected number of runs = 12.0769
18 observations above K; 8 below
* N Small, so following approximation may be invalid.
p-value = 0.971
```

FIGURE 17.2 **Output for the Cola Example**

Large-Sample Runs Test

Tables A.11 and A.12 do not contain critical values for n_1 and n_2 greater than 20. Fortunately, the sampling distribution of R is approximately normal with a mean and standard deviation shown in Formula 17.1. The test statistic is a z statistic, also described below.

Large-Sample Runs Test

$$\mu_R = \frac{2n_1 n_2}{n_1 + n_2} + 1$$

$$\sigma_R = \sqrt{\frac{2n_1 n_2 (2n_1 n_2 - n_1 - n_2)}{(n_1 + n_2)^2 (n_1 + n_2 - 1)}}$$

$$z = \frac{R - \mu_R}{\sigma_R} = \frac{R - \left(\frac{2n_1 n_2}{n_1 + n_2} + 1\right)}{\sqrt{\frac{2n_1 n_2 (2n_1 n_2 - n_1 - n_2)}{(n_1 + n_2)^2 (n_1 + n_2 - 1)}}}$$

(17.1)

where

$n_1 =$ number of observations exhibiting characteristic 1

$n_2 =$ number of observations exhibiting characteristic 2

$R =$ number of runs in the sample

The following hypotheses are being tested.

H_0: The observations in the sample were generated randomly.
H_a: The observations in the sample were not generated randomly.

The critical z values are obtained in the usual way by using α and Table A.5.

Consider the following manufacturing example. A machine occasionally produces parts that are flawed. When the machine is working in adjustment, flaws still occur but seem to happen randomly. A quality control person randomly selects 50 of the parts produced by the machine today and examines them one at a time in the order that they were made. The result is 40 parts with no flaws and 10 parts with flaws. The sequence of no flaws (denoted by N) and flaws (denoted by F) is shown below. Using an α of 0.05, the quality controller tests to determine whether the machine is producing randomly (the flaws are occurring randomly):

NNNFNNNNNNNFNNFFNNNNNNNFNNNNFNNNNNN

FFFFNNNNNNNNNNNN

Step 1 The hypotheses follow.

H_0: The observations in the sample were generated randomly.
H_a: The observations in the sample were not generated randomly.

Step 2 The appropriate statistical test is the large-sample runs test. The test statistic is:

$$z = \frac{R - \mu_R}{\sigma_R} = \frac{R - \left(\dfrac{2n_1 n_2}{n_1 + n_2} + 1\right)}{\sqrt{\dfrac{2n_1 n_2(2n_1 n_2 - n_1 - n_2)}{(n_1 + n_2)^2(n_1 + n_2 - 1)}}}$$

Step 3 The value of α is 0.05.

Step 4 This test is two-tailed. Too few or too many runs could indicate that the machine is not producing flaws randomly. With $\alpha = 0.05$ and $\alpha/2 = 0.025$, the critical values are $z_{0.025} = \pm1.96$. The decision rule is to reject the null hypothesis if the observed value of the test statistic is greater than 1.96 or less than -1.96.

Step 5 The preceding sequence provides the sample data. The value of n_1 is 40 and the value of n_2 is 10. The number of runs (R) is 13:

Step 6

$$\mu_R = \frac{2(40)(10)}{40 + 10} + 1 = 17$$

$$\sigma_R = \sqrt{\frac{2(40)(10)[2(40)(10) - 40 - 10]}{(40 + 10)^2(40 + 10 - 1)}} = 2.213$$

$$z = \frac{13 - 17}{2.213} = -1.81$$

Step 7 Because the observed value of the test statistic, $z = -1.81$, is greater than the lower-tail critical value, $z = -1.96$, the decision is to not reject the null hypothesis.

Step 8 There is no evidence that the machine is not producing flaws randomly. If the null hypothesis had been rejected, there might be concern that the machine is producing flaws systematically and thereby is in need of inspection or repair.

Figure 17.3 is the Minitab output for this example. The value of K is the average of the observations. The data were entered into Minitab with a nonflaw coded as a 0 and a flaw as a 1. The value $K = 0.20$ is merely the average of these coded values. In Minitab, a run is a sequence of observations above or below this mean, which effectively yields the same thing as the number of 0s in a row (nonflaws) or number of 1s in a row (flaws). The nonflaws and flaws could have been coded as any two different numbers and the same results would have been achieved. The output shows the number of runs as 13 (the same number obtained manually) and a test significance (p-value) equal to 0.071. The test statistic is not significant at $\alpha = 0.05$ because the p-value is greater than 0.05.

```
Runs Test For Flaws
Runs above and below K = 0.2
The observed number of runs = 13
The expected number of runs = 17
10 Observations above K; 40 below
* N is small, so the following approximation may be invalid.
p-value = 0.071
```

FIGURE 17.3 **Output for the Flawed Parts Example**

Concept Check

1. In your own words, describe the meaning of nonparametric statistics.
2. List two advantages and two disadvantages of nonparametric statistics.
3. State the null and the alternative hypotheses in a runs test.

17.1 Problems

17.1 Test the following sequence of observations by using the runs test and $\alpha = 0.05$ to determine whether the process produced random results.

XXXYXXYYYXYXYXYXXYYYYX

17.2 Test the following sequence of observations by using the runs test and $\alpha = 0.05$ to determine whether the process produced random results.

MMNNNNNMMMMMMNNNMMMMMNMM

NNNNNNNNNNNNNMMMMMMMMMMMM

17.3 A process produced good parts and defective parts. A sample of 60 parts was taken and inspected. Eight defective parts were found. The sequence of good and defective parts was analyzed by using Minitab. The output is given here. With a two-tailed test and $\alpha = 0.05$, what conclusions can be reached about the randomness of the sample?

```
Runs Test: Defects

Defects
K = 0.1333
The observed number of runs = 11
The expected number of runs = 14.8667
8 observations above K; 52 below
The test is significant at 0.0264.
```

17.4 Assume that a survey showed that 58% of all working Canadians are satisfied with their salary. Suppose an analyst randomly samples 27 Canadian workers and asks whether they are satisfied with their salary with the result that 15 say yes. The sequence of Yes and No responses is recorded and tested for randomness using Minitab. The output follows. Using an α of 0.05 and a two-tailed test, what could you conclude about the randomness of the sample?

```
Runs Test: Yes/No

Yes/No
K = 0.5556
The observed number of runs = 18
The expected number of runs = 14.3333
15 observations above K; 12 below
The test is significant at 0.1452.
Cannot reject at alpha = 0.05
```

17.5 An opinion poll by Roper Starch found that more than 70% of the women interviewed believe they have had more opportunity to succeed than their parents. Suppose an analyst in your province or territory conducts a similar poll and asks the same question with the result that of 64 women interviewed, 40 believe they have had more opportunity to succeed than their parents. The sequence of responses to this question is given below with Y denoting yes and N denoting no. Use the runs test and $\alpha = 0.05$ to test this sequence and determine whether the responses are random.

YYNYYNNYYYNNYNNYYYYYNYYYYYNNYYNNNYYY

NNYYYYNYNYYYNNNNYNNYYYYYYNNYYYY

17.6 A survey conducted by the Ethics Resource Center discovered that 35% of all workers say that co-workers have committed some kind of office theft. Suppose a survey is conducted in your large company to ask the same question of 13 randomly selected employees. The results are that five of the sample say co-workers have committed some kind of office theft and eight say they are not aware of such infractions. The sequence of responses follows (Y denotes yes and N denotes no). Use $\alpha = 0.05$ to determine whether this sequence represents a random sample.

NNNNYYYNNNNYY

17.2 | Mann-Whitney *U* Test

LEARNING OBJECTIVE 17.2

Use both the small-sample and large-sample cases of the Mann-Whitney *U* test to determine if there is a difference in two independent populations.

The **Mann-Whitney *U* test** is a *nonparametric counterpart of the* t *test used to compare the means of two independent populations.* This test was developed by Henry B. Mann and D. R. Whitney in 1947. Recall that the *t* test for independent samples presented in Chapter 10 can be used when data are at least interval in measurement and the populations are normally distributed. However, if the assumption of a normally distributed population is invalid or if the data are only ordinal in measurement, the *t* test should not be used. In such cases, the Mann-Whitney *U* test is an acceptable option for analyzing the data. The following assumptions underlie the use of the Mann-Whitney *U* test.

1. The samples are independent.
2. The level of data is at least ordinal.

The two-tailed hypotheses being tested with the Mann-Whitney *U* test are as follows:

H_0: The two populations are identical.
H_a: The two populations are not identical.

Computation of the *U* test begins by arbitrarily designating two samples as group 1 and group 2. The data from the two groups are combined into one group, with each data value retaining a group identifier of its original group. The pooled values are then ranked from 1 to *n*, with the smallest value being assigned a rank of 1. The sum of the ranks of values from group 1 is computed and designated as W_1 and the sum of the ranks of values from group 2 is designated as W_2 (see Thinking Critically About Statistics in Business Today 17.1).

Thinking Critically About Statistics in Business Today 17.1

Does an Iranian Auto Parts Manufacturer's Orientation Impact Innovation?

Two researchers, Ali Reza Maatoofi and Kayhan Tajeddini, studied Iranian auto parts manufacturers in an attempt to determine if there is any difference between companies whose strategic approach is more of a market orientation and companies whose strategic approach is more of an entrepreneurial orientation in the innovation of products. The researchers chose to study the auto parts industry because it is one of the most productive industries in Iran, and it has always had governmental support.

Market-oriented companies pay close attention to their customers, study their rivals, and try to understand factors that may affect customer needs and preferences. Such companies learn to adjust to the environment and look for competitive advantages. One could say that market-oriented companies are somewhat reactive to customer needs. Entrepreneurial-oriented companies, on the other hand, focus more on risky products and tend to be on the leading edge of new technological solutions. The approach of entrepreneurial-oriented companies is often exploratory and risky in nature. Some might argue that an entrepreneurial orientation is more likely than a market orientation to lead to behaviour that is congruent with an innovative product approach.

The researchers set out to determine if this assumption is true by studying 71 Iranian auto parts manufacturing firms. Based on a series of questions, they determined that 37 of these firms had more of a market orientation and 34 had more of an entrepreneurial orientation. They tested to determine if there was a significant difference between the two groups on five questions dealing with product innovation: (1) Is there a difference in the quality of products? (2) Is there a difference in marketing synergy? (3) Is there a difference in the expertise in offering new products? (4) Is there a difference in the amount of management support? (5) Is there a difference in the intensity of the competitive environment?

Because they were using a seven-point Likert scale producing only ordinal-level data, they decided to use the Mann-Whitney *U* test to compare the two types of firms on each question. Somewhat surprisingly, they found no significant difference between market-oriented firms and entrepreneurial-oriented firms on four of the five questions. The one question that resulted in a significant difference was "management support for innovation," where entrepreneurial-oriented firms scored significantly higher than market-oriented firms. There are many business research studies like this one where, because of the level of data, researchers choose to use nonparametric statistics such as those presented in this chapter to study the data.

Things to Ponder

1. Since the researchers failed to reject the null hypothesis of zero difference on four of the five questions, what might this say about a market-oriented culture and an entrepreneurial-oriented culture in terms of product innovation?

2. Consider two other industries different from auto manufacturing. Do you think the researchers might obtain different results from this study in either of those industries?

Source: Adapted from Ali Reza Maatoofi and Kayhan Tajeddini, "Effect of Market Orientation and Entrepreneurial Orientation on Innovation, Evidence from Auto Parts Manufacturing in Iran," *Journal of Management Research* 11, no. 1 (April 2011): 20–30.

The Mann-Whitney U test is implemented differently for small samples than for large samples. If both $n_1 \leq 10$ and $n_2 \leq 10$, the samples are considered small. If either n_1 or n_2 is greater than 10, the samples are considered large.

Small-Sample Case

With small samples, the next step is to calculate a U statistic for W_1 and for W_2. The test statistic is the smallest of these two U values. Both values do not need to be calculated; instead, one value of U can be calculated and the other can be found by using the transformation, U'.

Small-Sample Formulas for Mann-Whitney U Test

$$U_1 = n_1 n_2 + \frac{n_1(n_1 + 1)}{2} - W_1$$

$$U_2 = n_1 n_2 + \frac{n_2(n_2 + 1)}{2} - W_2 \qquad (17.2)$$

$$U' = n_1 n_2 - U$$

Table A.13 contains p-values for U. To determine the p-value for a U from the table, let n_1 denote the size of the smaller sample and n_2 the size of the larger sample. Using the particular table in Table A.13 for n_1, n_2, locate the value of U in the left column. At the intersection of the U and n_1 is the p-value for a one-tailed test. For a two-tailed test, double the p-value shown in the table.

DEMONSTRATION PROBLEM 17.1

Is there a difference between health service workers and educational service workers in the amount of compensation employers pay them per hour? Suppose a random sample of seven health service workers is taken along with a random sample of eight educational service workers from different parts of the country. Each of their employers is interviewed and figures are obtained on the amount paid per hour for employee compensation for these workers. The data below indicate total compensation per hour. Use a Mann-Whitney U test and the eight-step process for testing a hypothesis to determine whether these two populations are different in employee compensation.

Health Service Worker	Educational Service Worker
$20.10	$26.19
19.80	23.88
22.36	25.50
18.75	21.64
21.90	24.85
22.96	25.30
20.75	24.12
	23.45

Solution

Step 1 The hypotheses are as follows.

H_0: The health service population is identical to the educational service population on employee compensation.

H_a: The health service population is not identical to the educational service population on employee compensation.

Step 2 Because we cannot be certain the populations are normally distributed, we choose a non-parametric alternative to the t test for independent populations: the small-sample Mann-Whitney U test.

Step 3 Let α be 0.05.

Step 4 If the final p-value from Table A.13 (after doubling for a two-tailed test here) is less than 0.05, the decision is to reject the null hypothesis.

Step 5 The sample data were already provided.

Step 6 We combine scores from the two groups and rank them from smallest to largest while retaining group identifier information.

Total Employee Compensation	Rank	Group
$18.75	1	H
19.80	2	H
20.10	3	H
20.75	4	H
21.64	5	E
21.90	6	H
22.36	7	H
22.96	8	H
23.45	9	E
23.88	10	E
24.12	11	E
24.85	12	E
25.30	13	E
25.50	14	E
26.19	15	E

$$W_1 = 1 + 2 + 3 + 4 + 6 + 7 + 8 = 31$$
$$W_2 = 5 + 9 + 10 + 11 + 12 + 13 + 14 + 15 = 89$$

$$U_1 = (7)(8) + \frac{(7)(8)}{2} - 31 = 53$$

$$U_2 = (7)(8) + \frac{(8)(9)}{2} - 89 = 3$$

Because U_2 is the smaller value of U, we use $U = 3$ as the test statistic for Table A.13. Because it is the smallest size, let $n_1 = 7$ and $n_2 = 8$.

Step 7 Table A.13 yields a p-value of 0.0011. Because this test is two-tailed, we double the table p-value, producing a final p-value of 0.0022. Because the p-value is less than $\alpha = 0.05$, the null hypothesis is rejected. The statistical conclusion is that the populations are not identical.

Step 8 An examination of the total compensation figures from the samples indicates that employers pay educational service workers more per hour than they pay health service workers.

As shown in **Figure 17.4**, Minitab can compute a Mann-Whitney U test. The output includes a p-value of 0.0046 for the two-tailed test for Demonstration Problem 17.1. The decision based on the computer output is to reject the null hypothesis, which is consistent with what we computed. The difference in p-values is due to rounding error in the table.

```
Mann-Whitney Test and CI: Health, Education
Health N = 7 Median = 20.750
Education N = 8 Median = 24.485
Point estimate for ETA1-ETA2 is -3.385
95.7 Percent CI for ETA1-ETA2 is (-5.370, -1.551)
W = 31.0
Test of ETA1 = ETA2  versus  ETA1 ≠ ETA2 is significant at 0.0046
```

FIGURE 17.4 **Output for Demonstration Problem 17.1**

Large-Sample Case

For large sample sizes, the value of U is approximately normally distributed. Using an average expected U value for groups of this size and a standard deviation of U's allows computation of a z score for the U value. The probability of yielding a z score of this magnitude, given no difference between the groups, is computed. A decision is then made whether to reject the null hypothesis. A z score can be calculated from U by the following formulas.

Large-Sample Formulas for Mann-Whitney U Test

$$\mu_U = \frac{n_1 n_2}{2}$$

$$\sigma_U = \sqrt{\frac{n_1 n_2(n_1 + n_2 + 1)}{12}} \tag{17.3}$$

$$z = \frac{U - \mu_U}{\sigma_U}$$

For example, the Mann-Whitney U test can be used to determine whether there is a difference in the average income of families who watch CBC television and families who do not watch CBC television. Suppose a sample of 14 families that have identified themselves as CBC television viewers and a sample of 13 families that have identified themselves as non-CBC television viewers are selected randomly.

Step 1 The hypotheses for this example are as follows.

H_0: The incomes of CBC and non-CBC viewers are identical.
H_a: The incomes of CBC and non-CBC viewers are not identical.

Step 2 Use the Mann-Whitney U test for large samples.

Step 3 Let $\alpha = 0.05$.

Step 4 Because this test is two-tailed with $\alpha = 0.05$, the critical values are $z_{0.025} = \pm 1.96$. If the test statistic is greater than 1.96 or less than -1.96, the decision is to reject the null hypothesis.

Step 5 The average annual reported income for each family in the two samples is given in **Table 17.1**.

Step 6 The first step in computing a Mann-Whitney U test is to combine these two columns of data into one group and rank the data from lowest to highest, while maintaining the identification of each original group. **Table 17.2** shows the results of this step.

Note that in the case of a tie, the ranks associated with the tie are averaged across the values that tie. For example, two incomes of $43,500 appear in the sample. These incomes represent ranks 19 and 20. Each value is therefore awarded a ranking of 19.5, or the average of 19 and 20.

TABLE 17.1

Income of CBC and Non-CBC Viewers

CBC	Non-CBC
$24,500	$41,000
39,400	32,500
36,800	33,000
43,000	21,000
57,960	40,500
32,000	32,400
61,000	16,000
34,000	21,500
43,500	39,500
55,000	27,600
39,000	43,500
62,500	51,900
61,400	27,800
53,000	
$n_1 = 14$	$n_2 = 13$

		TABLE 17.2	Ranks of Incomes from Combined Groups of CBC and Non-CBC Viewers		
Income	**Rank**	**Group**	**Income**	**Rank**	**Group**
$16,000	1	Non-CBC	$39,500	15	Non-CBC
21,000	2	Non-CBC	40,500	16	Non-CBC
21,500	3	Non-CBC	41,000	17	Non-CBC
24,500	4	CBC	43,000	18	CBC
27,600	5	Non-CBC	43,500	19.5	CBC
27,800	6	Non-CBC	43,500	19.5	Non-CBC
32,000	7	CBC	51,900	21	Non-CBC
32,400	8	Non-CBC	53,000	22	CBC
32,500	9	Non-CBC	55,000	23	CBC
33,000	10	Non-CBC	57,960	24	CBC
34,000	11	CBC	61,000	25	CBC
36,800	12	CBC	61,400	26	CBC
39,000	13	CBC	62,500	27	CBC
39,400	14	CBC			

If CBC viewers are designated as group 1, W_1 can be computed by summing the ranks of all the incomes of CBC viewers in the sample:

$$W_1 = 4 + 7 + 11 + 12 + 13 + 14 + 18 + 19.5 + 22 + 23 + 24 + 25 + 26 + 27 = 245.5$$

Then, W_1 is used to compute the U value. Because $n_1 = 14$ and $n_2 = 13$, then:

$$U = n_1 n_2 + \frac{n_1(n_1 + 1)}{2} - W_1 = (14)(13) + \frac{(14)(15)}{2} - 245.5 = 41.5$$

Because $n_1, n_2 > 10$, U is approximately normally distributed, with a mean of:

$$\mu_U = \frac{n_1 n_2}{2} = \frac{(14)(13)}{2} = 91$$

and a standard deviation of:

$$\sigma_U = \sqrt{\frac{n_1 n_2 (n_1 + n_2 + 1)}{12}} = \sqrt{\frac{(14)(13)(28)}{12}} = 20.6$$

A z value can now be computed to determine the probability of the sample U value coming from the distribution with $\mu_U = 91$ and $\sigma_U = 20.6$ if there is no difference in the populations:

$$z = \frac{U - \mu_U}{\sigma_U} = \frac{41.5 - 91}{20.6} = \frac{-49.5}{20.6} = -2.40$$

Step 7 The observed value of z is -2.40, which is less than $z_{\alpha/2} = -1.96$, so the results are in the rejection region. That is, there is a difference between the income of a CBC viewer and that of a non-CBC viewer. Examination of the sample data confirms that, in general, the income of a CBC viewer is higher than that of a non-CBC viewer.

Step 8 The fact that CBC viewers have higher average income can affect the type of programming on CBC in terms of both trying to please present viewers and offering programs that might attract viewers of other income levels. In addition, advertising can be sold to appeal to viewers with higher incomes.

Assignment of CBC viewers to group 1 was arbitrary. If non-CBC viewers had been designated as group 1, the results would have been the same but the observed z value would have been positive.

Figure 17.8 displays the chi-square distribution for df = 3 along with the critical value, the observed value of the test statistic, and the rejection region. **Figure 17.9** is the Minitab output for the Friedman test. The computer output contains the value of χ_r^2, referred to as S, along with the p-value of 0.014, which informs the analyst that the null hypothesis is rejected at an α of 0.05. Additional information is given about the medians and the column sum totals of ranks.

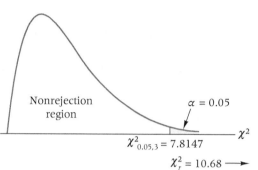

$$\chi_{0.05,3}^2 = 7.8147$$

$$\chi_r^2 = 10.68 \longrightarrow$$

FIGURE 17.8 **Distribution for Tensile Strength Example**

```
Friedman Test: Rank Versus Supplier Blocked by Day
S = 10.68   df = 3   p = 0.014

                            Sum
                Estimated    of
Supplier   N     Median    Ranks
1          5     62.125    14.0
2          5     61.375    13.0
3          5     56.875     5.0
4          5     64.125    18.0

Grand median = 61.125
```

FIGURE 17.9 **Output for the Tensile Strength Example**

DEMONSTRATION PROBLEM 17.5

A market research company wants to determine brand preference for refrigerators. Five companies contracted with the research company to have their products included in the study. As part of the study, the research company randomly selects 10 potential refrigerator buyers and shows them one of each of the five brands. Each survey participant is then asked to rank the refrigerator brands from 1 to 5. The results of these rankings are given in the table below. Use the Friedman test, $\alpha = 0.01$, and the eight-step process for testing a hypothesis to determine whether there are any significant differences between the rankings of these brands.

Solution

Step 1 The hypotheses are as follows.

H$_0$: The brand populations are equal.

H$_a$: At least one brand population yields larger values than at least one other brand population.

Step 2 The market analysts collected ranked data that are ordinal in level. The Friedman test is the appropriate test.

Step 3 Let $\alpha = 0.01$.

Step 4 Because the study uses five treatment levels (brands), $c = 5$ and df $= 5 - 1 = 4$. The critical value is $\chi_{0.01,4}^2 = 13.2767$. If the observed chi-square is greater than 13.2767, the decision is to reject the null hypothesis.

Step 5 The sample data follow.

Step 6 The ranks are totalled for each column, squared, and then summed across the column totals. The results are shown in the table.

Individual	Brand A	Brand B	Brand C	Brand D	Brand E
1	3	5	2	4	1
2	1	3	2	4	5
3	3	4	5	2	1
4	2	3	1	4	5
5	5	4	2	1	3
6	1	5	3	4	2
7	4	1	3	2	5
8	2	3	4	5	1
9	2	4	5	3	1
10	3	5	4	2	1
R_j	26	37	31	31	25
R_j^2	676	1,369	961	961	625

$$\Sigma R_j^2 = 4,592$$

The value of χ_r^2 is :

$$\chi_r^2 = \frac{12}{bc(c+1)} \sum_{j=1}^{c} R_j^2 - 3b(c+1) = \frac{12}{10(5)(5+1)}(4,592) - 3(10)(5+1) = 3.68$$

Step 7   Because the observed value of $\chi_r^2 = 3.68$ is not greater than the critical value, $\chi_{0.01,4}^2 = 13.2767$, the analysts fail to reject the null hypothesis.

Step 8   Potential refrigerator purchasers appear to have no significant brand preference. Marketing managers for the various companies might want to develop strategies for positively distinguishing their product from the others.

The chi-square distribution for four degrees of freedom, produced by Minitab, is shown with the observed test statistic and the critical value. In addition, Minitab output for the Friedman test is shown. Note that the p-value is 0.451, which underscores the decision not to reject the null hypothesis at $\alpha = 0.01$.

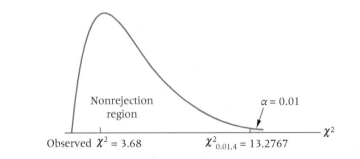

Friedman Output:

```
Friedman Test: Rank versus Brand Blocked by Individual
 S = 3.68    df = 4     p = 0.451
                       Estimated
 Brand        N         Median      Sum of Ranks
 1           10         2.300          26.0
 2           10         4.000          37.0
 3           10         3.000          31.0
 4           10         3.000          31.0
 5           10         1.700          25.0
 Grand median = 2.800
```

Concept Check

1. What is the parametric alternative to the Friedman test?
2. What are the key assumptions underlying the Friedman test?
3. State the null and alternative hypotheses of the Friedman test.

17.5 Problems

17.25 Use the following data to determine whether there are any differences between treatment levels. Let $\alpha = 0.05$.

		Treatment				
		1	**2**	**3**	**4**	**5**
	1	200	214	212	215	208
	2	198	211	214	217	206
Block	3	207	206	213	216	207
	4	213	210	215	219	204
	5	211	209	210	221	205

17.26 Use the Friedman test and $\alpha = 0.05$ to test the following data to determine whether there is a significant difference between treatment levels.

		Treatment					
		1	**2**	**3**	**4**	**5**	**6**
	1	29	32	31	38	35	33
	2	33	35	30	42	34	31
	3	26	34	32	39	36	35
	4	30	33	35	41	37	32
Block	5	33	31	32	35	37	36
	6	31	34	33	37	36	35
	7	26	32	35	43	36	34
	8	32	29	31	38	37	35
	9	30	31	34	41	39	35

17.27 An experiment is undertaken to study the effects of four different medical treatments on the recovery time for a medical disorder. Six physicians are involved in the study. One patient with the disorder is sampled for each physician under each treatment, resulting in 24 patients in the study. Recovery time in days is the observed measurement. The data are given here. Use the Friedman test and $\alpha = 0.01$ to determine whether there is a significant difference in recovery times for the four different medical treatments.

		Treatment			
		1	**2**	**3**	**4**
	1	3	7	5	4
	2	4	5	6	3
Physician	3	3	6	5	4
	4	3	6	7	4
	5	2	6	7	3
	6	4	5	7	3

17.28 Does the configuration of the workweek have any impact on productivity? This question is raised by an analyst who wants to compare the traditional five-day workweek with a four-day workweek and a workweek with three 12-hour days and one 4-hour day. The analyst conducts the experiment in a factory making small electronic parts. He selects 10 workers, who spend a month working under each type of workweek configuration. The analyst randomly selects one day from each of the three months (three workweek configurations) for each of the 10 workers. The observed measurement is the number of parts produced per day by each worker. Use the Friedman test and $\alpha = 0.05$ to determine whether there is a difference in productivity by workweek configuration.

		Workweek Configuration		
		Five Days	**Four Days**	**Three-and-a-Half Days**
	1	37	33	28
	2	44	38	36
	3	35	29	31
	4	41	40	36
Worker	5	38	39	35
	6	34	27	23
	7	43	38	39
	8	39	35	32
	9	41	38	37
	10	36	30	31

17.29 Shown here is Minitab output from a Friedman test. What is the size of the experimental design in terms of treatment levels and blocks? Discuss the outcome of the experiment in terms of any statistical conclusions.

Friedman Test

Friedman Test of Observations by Treatment
Blocked by Block

$S = 2.04$ $df = 3$ $p = 0.564$

Treatment	N	Estimated Median	Sum of Ranks
1	5	3.250	15.0
2	5	2.000	10.0
3	5	2.750	11.0
4	5	4.000	14.0

Grand median = 3.000

17.30 Shown here is Minitab output for a Friedman test. Discuss the experimental design and the outcome of the experiment.

Friedman Test

Friedman Test of Observations by Treatment
Blocked by Block

$S = 13.71$ $df = 4$ $p = 0.009$

Treatment	N	Estimated Median	Sum of Ranks
1	7	21.000	12.0
2	7	24.000	14.0
3	7	29.800	30.0
4	7	27.600	26.0
5	7	27.600	23.0

Grand median = 26.000

17.6 | Spearman's Rank Correlation

LEARNING OBJECTIVE 17.6

Use Spearman's rank correlation to analyze the degree of association of two variables.

In Chapter 12, the Pearson product-moment correlation coefficient, r, was presented and discussed as a technique to measure the amount or degree of association between two variables. The Pearson r requires at least interval level of measurement for the data. When only ordinal-level data or ranked data are available, **Spearman's rank correlation**, r_s, can be used to analyze the degree of association of two variables. Charles E. Spearman (1863–1945) developed this correlation coefficient.

The formula for calculating a Spearman's rank correlation is as follows.

Spearman's Rank Correlation

$$r_s = 1 - \frac{6\sum d^2}{n(n^2 - 1)} \qquad (17.7)$$

where

n = number of pairs being correlated

d = the difference in the ranks of each pair

The Spearman's rank correlation formula is derived from the Pearson product-moment formula and utilizes the ranks of the n pairs instead of the raw data. The value of d is the difference in the ranks of each pair.

The process begins by the assignment of ranks within each group. The difference in ranks between each group (d) is calculated by subtracting the rank of a member of one group from the rank of its associated member of the other group. The differences (d) are then squared and summed. The number of pairs in the groups is represented by n.

17.6 Problems

17.31 Compute a Spearman's rank correlation for the following variables to determine the degree of association between the two variables.

x	y
23	201
41	259
37	234
29	240
25	231
17	209
33	229
41	246
40	248
28	227
19	200

17.32 The following data are the ranks for values of the two variables x and y. Compute a Spearman's rank correlation to determine the degree of relation between the two variables.

x	y	x	y
4	6	3	2
5	8	1	3
8	7	2	1
11	10	9	11
10	9	6	4
7	5		

17.33 Compute a Spearman's rank correlation for the following data.

x	y	x	y
99	108	80	124
67	139	57	162
82	117	49	145
46	168	91	102

17.34 Over a period of a few months, is there a strong correlation between the value of the Canadian dollar (in US $) and the prime interest rate? The following data represent a sample of these quantities over a period of time. Compute a Spearman's rank correlation to determine the strength of the relationship between prime interest rates and the value of the dollar.

Dollar Value US $	Prime Rate (%)	Dollar Value US $	Prime Rate (%)
0.92	9.3	0.88	8.4
0.96	9.0	0.84	8.1
0.91	8.5	0.81	7.9
0.89	8.0	0.83	7.2
0.91	8.3		

17.35 Shown here are the percentages of consumer loans with payments that are 30 days or more overdue for both bank credit cards and home equity loans over a 14-year period according to the American Bankers Association. Compute a Spearman's rank correlation to determine the degree of association between these two variables.

Year	Bank Credit Card	Home Equity Loan
1	2.51%	2.07%
2	2.86	1.95
3	2.33	1.66
4	2.54	1.77
5	2.54	1.51
6	2.18	1.47
7	3.34	1.75
8	2.86	1.73
9	2.74	1.48
10	2.54	1.51
11	3.18	1.25
12	3.53	1.44
13	3.51	1.38
14	3.11	1.30

17.36 Shown here are the net tonnage figures for total pig iron and raw steel output as reported by the American Iron and Steel Institute over a 12-year period. Use these data to calculate a Spearman's rank correlation to determine the degree of association between production of pig iron and raw steel over this period. Was the association strong? Comment on the results.

Year	Total Pig Iron (net tons)	Raw Steel (Net Tons)
1	43,952,000	81,606,000
2	48,410,000	89,151,000
3	55,745,000	99,924,000
4	55,873,000	97,943,000
5	54,750,000	98,906,000
6	48,637,000	87,896,000
7	52,224,000	92,949,000
8	53,082,000	97,877,000
9	54,426,000	100,579,000
10	56,097,000	104,930,000
11	54,485,000	105,309,478
12	54,679,000	108,561,182

17.37 Is there a correlation between the number of companies listed on the New York Stock Exchange in a given year and the number of equity issues on the American Stock Exchange? Shown below are the values for these two variables over an 11-year period. Compute a Spearman's rank correlation to determine the degree of association between these two variables.

Year	Number of Companies on NYSE	Number of Equity Issues on AMEX
1	1774	1063
2	1885	1055
3	2088	943
4	2361	1005
5	2570	981
6	2675	936
7	2907	896
8	3047	893
9	3114	862
10	3025	769
11	2862	765

End-of-Chapter Review

Decision Dilemma Solved

How Is the Doughnut Business Doing?

The Dunkin' analysts' dilemma is that in each of the three studies presented, the assumptions underlying the use of parametric statistics are in question or have not been met. The distribution of the data is unknown, bringing into question the normal distribution assumption. Also, the level of data is only ordinal. For each study, a nonparametric technique presented in this chapter could appropriately be used to analyze the data.

The differences in doughnut sizes according to machine can be analyzed using the Kruskal-Wallis test. The independent variable is machine with four levels of classification. The dependent variable is size of doughnut in centimetres. The Kruskal-Wallis test is not based on any assumption about population shape. The following Minitab output is from a Kruskal-Wallis test on the machine data presented in the Decision Dilemma.

```
Kruskal-Wallis Test: Size versus Machine
Kruskal-Wallis Test on Size
Machine   N   Median   Average Rank      Z
   1      5   7.520     10.4          -0.60
   2      6   7.415      3.5          -3.57
   3      5   7.550     12.6           0.22
   4      7   7.700     20.0           3.74
Overall  23           12.0
H = 19.48  df = 3  p = 0.000
H = 19.51  df = 3  p = 0.000 (adjusted
                             for ties)
```

Because the H statistic (Minitab's equivalent to the K statistic) has a p-value of 0.000, there is a significant difference in the diameter of the doughnut according to machine at $\alpha = 0.001$. An examination of median values reveals that machine 4 is producing the largest doughnuts and machine 2 the smallest.

How well did the advertising work? One way to address this question is to perform a before-and-after test of the number of doughnuts sold. The nonparametric alternative to the matched-pairs t test is the Wilcoxon matched-pairs signed rank test. The analysis for these data is as follows.

Before	After	d	Rank
301	374	−73	−9
198	187	11	4
278	332	−54	−7
205	212	−7	−3
249	243	6	2
410	478	−68	−8
360	386	−26	−6
124	141	−17	−5
253	251	2	1
190	264	−74	−10

$T_+ = 4 + 2 + 1 = 7$

$T_- = 9 + 7 + 3 + 8 + 6 + 5 + 10 = 48$

observed $T = \min(T_+, T_-) = 7$

critical T for 0.025 and $n = 10$ is 8

Using a two-sided test and $\alpha = 0.05$, the critical T value is 8. Because the observed T is 7, the decision is to reject the null hypothesis. There is a significant difference between the before and after numbers of doughnuts sold. An observation of the ranks and raw data reveals that a majority of the stores experienced an increase in sales after the advertising campaign.

Do bigger stores have greater sales? Because the data are given as ranks, it is appropriate to use Spearman's rank correlation to determine the extent of the correlation between these two variables. Shown below are the calculations of a Spearman's rank correlation for this problem.

Sales	Size	d	d^2
6	7	−1	1
2	2	0	0
3	6	−3	9
7	5	2	4
5	4	1	1
1	1	0	0
4	3	1	1
			$\sum d^2 = 16$

$$r_s = 1 - \frac{6\sum d^2}{n(n^2-1)} = 1 - \frac{6(16)}{7(49-1)} = 0.714$$

There is a relatively strong correlation (0.714) between sales and size of store. It is not, however, a perfect correlation, which leaves room for other factors that may determine a store's sales such as location, attractiveness of store, population density, number of employees, management style, and others.

Key Considerations

The analyst should be aware of all assumptions underlying the usage of statistical techniques. Many parametric techniques have level-of-data requirements and assumptions about the distribution of the population or assumptions about the parameters. Inasmuch as these assumptions and requirements are not met, analysts set themselves up for misuse of statistical analysis. Spurious results can follow, and misguided conclusions can be reached. Nonparametric statistics can be used in many cases to avoid such pitfalls. In addition, some nonparametric statistics require at least ordinal-level data.

Why Statistics Is Relevant

Is income distributed normally in the population? Most likely not. Can we always verify the popular normality assumption for tests with small samples? Very often we cannot. These are examples of situations where nonparametric statistics are quite relevant. In general, nonparametric techniques allow us to work with data from small samples and/or on variables about which very little is known regarding their distribution. Recently, several successful applications of nonparametric techniques to market research have been reported. An example is corporate planning situations where a new product or service is being introduced and no (or little) prior data are available. Also, these techniques can be applied in situations in which an unprecedented event has occurred (such as airline or power deregulation), thus changing the way in which corporations do business.

Summary of Learning Objectives

Nonparametric statistics are a group of techniques that can be used for statistical analysis when the data are less than interval in measurement and/or when assumptions about population parameters, such as shape of the distribution, cannot be met. Nonparametric tests offer several advantages. Sometimes the nonparametric test is the only technique available, with no parametric alternative. Nonparametric tests can be used to analyze nominal- or ordinal-level data. Computations from nonparametric tests are usually simpler than those used with parametric tests. Probability statements obtained from most nonparametric tests are exact probabilities. Nonparametric techniques also have some disadvantages. They are wasteful of data whenever a parametric technique can be used. Nonparametric tests are not as widely available as parametric tests. For large sample sizes, the calculations of nonparametric statistics can be tedious.

Many of the parametric techniques presented in this text have corresponding nonparametric techniques. The six nonparametric statistical techniques presented here are the runs test, the Mann-Whitney U test, the Wilcoxon matched-pairs signed rank test, the Kruskal-Wallis test, the Friedman test, and Spearman's rank correlation.

LEARNING OBJECTIVE 17.1 Use both the small-sample and large-sample runs tests to determine whether the order of observations in a sample is random.

The runs test is a nonparametric test of randomness. It is used to determine whether the order of sequence of observations in a sample is random. A run is a succession of observations that have a particular characteristic. If data are truly random, neither a very high number of runs nor a very small number of runs is likely to be present.

LEARNING OBJECTIVE 17.2 Use both the small-sample and large-sample cases of the Mann-Whitney U test to determine if there is a difference in two independent populations.

The Mann-Whitney U test is a nonparametric version of the t test of the means from two independent samples. When the assumption of normally distributed data cannot be met or if the data are only ordinal in level of measurement, the Mann-Whitney U test can be used in place of the t test. The Mann-Whitney U test—like many nonparametric tests—works with the ranks of data rather than the raw data.

LEARNING OBJECTIVE 17.3 Use both the small-sample and large-sample cases of the Wilcoxon matched-pairs signed rank test to compare the differences in two related samples.

The Wilcoxon matched-pairs signed rank test is used as an alternative to the t test for related measures when assumptions cannot be met and/or if the data are ordinal in measurement. In contrast to the

Mann-Whitney U test, the Wilcoxon test is used when the data are related in some way. The Wilcoxon test is used to analyze the data by ranks of the differences of the raw data.

LEARNING OBJECTIVE 17.4 Use the Kruskal-Wallis test to determine whether samples come from the same or different populations.

The Kruskal-Wallis test is a nonparametric one-way ANOVA technique. It is particularly useful when the assumptions underlying the F test of the parametric one-way ANOVA cannot be met. The Kruskal-Wallis test is usually used when the analyst wants to determine whether three or more groups or samples are from the same or equivalent populations. This test is based on the assumption that the sample items are selected randomly and that the groups are independent. The raw data are converted to ranks and the Kruskal-Wallis test is used to analyze the ranks with the equivalent of a chi-square statistic.

LEARNING OBJECTIVE 17.5 Use the Friedman test to determine whether different treatment levels come from the same population when a blocking variable is available.

The Friedman test is a nonparametric alternative to the randomized block design. Friedman's test is computed by ranking the observations within each block and then summing the ranks for each treatment level. The resulting test statistic, χ_r^2, is approximately chi-square distributed.

LEARNING OBJECTIVE 17.6 Use Spearman's rank correlation to analyze the degree of association of two variables.

If two variables contain data that are ordinal in level of measurement, a Spearman's rank correlation can be used to determine the amount of relationship or association between the variables. Spearman's rank correlation coefficient is a nonparametric alternative to Pearson's product-moment correlation coefficient. Spearman's rank correlation coefficient is interpreted in a manner similar to the Pearson r.

Key Terms

Formulas

(17.1) Large-sample runs test

$$\mu_R = \frac{2n_1n_2}{n_1+n_2} + 1$$

$$\sigma_R = \sqrt{\frac{2n_1n_2(2n_1n_2-n_1-n_2)}{(n_1+n_2)^2(n_1+n_2-1)}}$$

$$z = \frac{R-\mu_R}{\sigma_R} = \frac{R-\left(\frac{2n_1n_2}{n_1+n_2}+1\right)}{\sqrt{\frac{2n_1n_2(2n_1n_2-n_1-n_2)}{(n_1+n_2)^2(n_1+n_2-1)}}}$$

(17.2) Mann-Whitney U test (small sample)

$$U_1 = n_1n_2 + \frac{n_1(n_1+1)}{2} - W_1$$

$$U_2 = n_1n_2 + \frac{n_2(n_2+1)}{2} - W_2$$

$$U' = n_1n_2 - U$$

(17.3) Mann-Whitney U test (large sample)

$$\mu_U = \frac{n_1 n_2}{2}$$

$$\sigma_U = \sqrt{\frac{n_1 n_2 (n_1 + n_2 + 1)}{12}}$$

$$z = \frac{U - \mu_U}{\sigma_U}$$

(17.4) Wilcoxon matched-pairs signed rank test

$$\mu_T = \frac{n(n + 1)}{4}$$

$$\sigma_T = \sqrt{\frac{n(n + 1)(2n + 1)}{24}}$$

$$z = \frac{T - \mu_T}{\sigma_T}$$

(17.5) Kruskal-Wallis test

$$K = \frac{12}{n(n + 1)}\left(\sum_{j=1}^{c} \frac{T_j^2}{n_j}\right) - 3(n + 1)$$

(17.6) Friedman Test

$$\chi_r^2 = \frac{12}{bc(c + 1)}\sum_{j=1}^{c} R_j^2 - 3b(c + 1)$$

(17.7) Spearman's rank correlation

$$r_s = 1 - \frac{6\sum d^2}{n(n^2 - 1)}$$

Supplementary Problems

Calculating the Statistics

17.38 Use the runs test to determine whether the sample is random. Let α be 0.05.

```
1  1  1  1  2  2  2  2  2  2  2  1  1  1  2  2  2
2  2  2  2  2  1  2  1  2  2  1  1  1  1  2  2  2
```

17.39 **Video** Use the Mann-Whitney U test and $\alpha = 0.01$ to determine whether there is a significant difference between the populations represented by the two samples given here.

Sample 1	Sample 2
573	547
532	566
544	551
565	538
540	557
548	560
536	557
523	547

17.40 Use the Wilcoxon matched-pairs signed rank test to determine whether there is a significant difference between the related populations represented by the matched pairs given here. Assume $\alpha = 0.05$.

Group 1	Group 2
5.6	6.4
1.3	1.5
4.7	4.6
3.8	4.3
2.4	2.1
5.5	6.0
5.1	5.2
4.6	4.5
3.7	4.5

17.41 **Video** Use the Kruskal-Wallis test and $\alpha = 0.01$ to determine whether the four groups come from different populations.

Group 1	Group 2	Group 3	Group 4
6	4	3	1
11	13	7	4
8	6	7	5
10	8	5	6
13	12	10	9
7	9	8	6
10	8	5	7

17.42 Use the Friedman test to determine whether the treatment groups come from different populations. Let α be 0.05.

Block	Group 1	Group 2	Group 3	Group 4
1	16	14	15	17
2	8	6	5	9
3	19	17	13	18
4	24	26	25	21
5	13	10	9	11
6	19	11	18	13
7	21	16	14	15

17.43 **Video** Compute a Spearman's rank correlation to determine the degree of association between the two variables.

Variable 1	Variable 2
101	87
129	89
133	84
147	79
156	70
179	64
183	67
190	71

Testing Your Understanding

17.44 Commercial fish raising is a growing industry in North America. What makes fish raised commercially grow faster and larger? Suppose that a fish industry study is conducted over the three summer months in an effort to determine whether the amount of water allotted per fish makes any difference in the speed with which the fish grow. The following data represent the amount of growth (in centimetres) of marked catfish in fish farms for different volumes of water per fish. Use $\alpha = 0.01$ to test whether there is a significant difference in fish growth by volume of allotted water.

4 L per Fish	20 L per Fish	40 L per Fish
2.8	7.4	7.9
3.6	6.4	6.1
4.3	6.6	7.6
3.3	5.6	5.8
4.8	5.3	7.4
3.6	5.1	4.8
5.3	6.9	

17.45 Manchester Partners International claims that 60% of the banking executives who lose their jobs stay in banking whereas 40% leave banking. Suppose 40 people who have lost their jobs as banking executives are contacted and asked whether they are still in banking. The results follow. Test to determine whether this sample appears to be random on the basis of the sequence of those who have left banking and those who have not. Let L denote "left banking" and S denote "stayed in banking." Let $\alpha = 0.05$.

S S L S L L S S S S S L S S L L L S S L

L L L S S L S S S S S S L L S L S S L S

17.46 Three machines produce the same part. Ten different machine operators work these machines. A quality team wants to determine whether the machines are producing parts that are significantly different from each other in mass. The team devises an experimental design in which a random part is selected from each of the 10 machine operators on each machine. The results follow.

Using an α of 0.05, test to determine whether there is a difference in machines.

Operator	Machine 1	Machine 2	Machine 3
1	231	229	234
2	233	232	231
3	229	233	230
4	232	235	231
5	235	228	232
6	234	237	231
7	236	233	230
8	230	229	227
9	228	230	229
10	237	238	234

17.47 In some firefighting organizations, you must serve as a firefighter for some period of time before you can become part of the emergency medical service arm of the organization. Does that mean EMS workers are older, on average, than traditional firefighters? Use the data shown and $\alpha = 0.05$ to test whether EMS workers are significantly older than firefighters. Assume the two groups are independent and you do not want to use a t test to analyze the data.

Firefighters	EMS Workers	Firefighters	EMS Workers
23	27	32	39
37	29	24	33
28	30	21	30
25	33	27	28
41	28		27
36	36		30

17.48 Automobile dealers usually advertise in the Yellow Pages. Sometimes they have to pay to be listed in the white pages, and some dealerships opt to save money by omitting that listing, assuming most people will use the Yellow Pages to find the telephone number. A two-year study is conducted with 20 car dealerships where in one year the dealer is listed in the white pages and the other year it is not. Ten of the dealerships are listed in the white pages the first year and the other 10 are listed there in the second year in an attempt to control for economic cycles. The following data represent the numbers of units sold per year. Is there a significant difference between the number of units sold when the dealership is listed in the white pages and the number sold when it is not listed? Assume all companies are continuously listed in the Yellow Pages, that the t test is not appropriate, and that $\alpha = 0.01$.

Dealer	With Listing	Without Listing
1	1180	1209
2	874	902
3	1071	862
4	668	503
5	889	974
6	724	675
7	880	821
8	482	567
9	796	602
10	1207	1097
11	968	962
12	1027	1045
13	1158	896
14	670	708
15	849	642
16	559	327
17	449	483
18	992	978
19	1046	973
20	852	841

17.49 Suppose you want to take a random sample of the Graduate Management Admission Test (GMAT) scores to determine whether there is any significant difference between the GMAT scores for the test given in March and the scores for the test given in June. You gather the following data from a sample of people who took each test. Use the Mann-Whitney U test to determine whether there is a significant difference in the two test results. Let $\alpha = 0.10$.

March	June
540	350
570	470
600	630
430	590
500	610
510	520
530	460
560	550
550	530
490	570

17.50 Does impulse buying really increase sales? A market analyst is curious to find out whether the location of packages of chewing gum in a grocery store really has anything to do with volume of gum sales. As a test, gum is moved to a different location in the store every Monday for four weeks (four locations). To control the experiment for type of gum, six different brands are moved around. Sales representatives keep track of how many packs of each type of gum are sold every Monday for the four weeks. The results follow. Test to determine whether there are any differences in the volume of gum sold at the various locations. Let $\alpha = 0.05$.

		Location			
		1	**2**	**3**	**4**
	A	176	58	111	120
	B	156	62	98	117
Brand	C	203	89	117	105
	D	183	73	118	113
	E	147	46	101	114
	F	190	83	113	115

17.51 Does perfume sell better in a box or without additional packaging? In a large store, an experiment is designed in which, for one month, all perfumes are sold packaged in a box and, during a second month, all perfumes are removed from the box and sold without packaging. Is there a significant difference in the number of units of perfume sold with and without the additional packaging? Let $\alpha = 0.05$.

Perfume	Box	No Box
1	185	170
2	109	112
3	92	90
4	105	87
5	60	51
6	45	49
7	25	11
8	58	40
9	161	165
10	108	82
11	89	94
12	123	139
13	34	21
14	68	55
15	59	60
16	78	52

17.52 Some people drink coffee to relieve stress on the job. Is there a correlation between the number of cups of coffee consumed on the job and perceived job stress? Suppose the data shown represent the number of cups of coffee consumed per week and a stress rating for the job on a scale of 0 to 100 for nine managers in the same industry. Determine the correlation between these two variables, assuming you do not want to use the Pearson product-moment correlation coefficient.

Cups of Coffee per Week	Job Stress
25	80
41	85
16	35
0	45
11	30
28	50
34	65
18	40
5	20

17.53 A Gallup/Air Transport Association survey showed that in a recent year, 52% of all air trips were for pleasure/personal and 48% were for business. Suppose the organization randomly samples 30 air travellers and asks them to state the purpose of their trip. The results are shown here, with B denoting business and P denoting personal. Test the sequence of these data to determine whether the data are random. Let $\alpha = 0.05$.

B P B P B B P B P P B P B P P

P B P B B P B P P B B P P B B

17.54 Does a statistics course improve a student's mathematics skills, as measured by a national test? Suppose a random sample of 13 students takes the same national mathematics examination just prior to enrolling in a statistics course and just after completing the course. Listed are the students' quantitative scores from both examinations. Use $\alpha = 0.01$ to determine whether the scores after the statistics course are significantly higher than the scores before.

Student	Before	After
1	430	465
2	485	475
3	520	535
4	360	410
5	440	425
6	500	505
7	425	450
8	470	480
9	515	520
10	430	430
11	450	460
12	495	500
13	540	530

17.55 Should male managers wear a tie during the workday to command respect and demonstrate professionalism? Suppose a measurement scale has been developed that generates a management professionalism score. A random sample of managers in a high-tech industry is selected for the study, some of whom wear ties at work and others of whom do not. One subordinate is selected randomly from each manager's department and asked to complete the scale on their boss's professionalism. Analyze the data taken from these independent groups to determine whether the managers with the ties received significantly higher professionalism scores. Let $\alpha = 0.05$.

With Tie	Without Tie
27	22
23	16
25	25
22	19
25	21
26	24
21	20
25	19
26	23
28	26
22	17

17.56 Many fast-food restaurants have soft drink dispensers with preset amounts, so that when the operator pushes a button for the desired drink, the cup is automatically filled. This method apparently saves time and seems to increase worker productivity. To test this conclusion, an analyst randomly selects 18 workers from the fast-food industry, 9 from a restaurant with automatic soft drink dispensers, and 9 from a comparable restaurant with manual soft drink dispensers. The samples are independent. During a comparable hour, the amount of sales rung up by the worker is recorded. Assume that $\alpha = 0.01$ and that a t test is not appropriate. Test whether workers with automatic dispensers are significantly more productive (higher sales per hour).

Automatic Dispenser	Manual Dispenser
$153	$105
128	118
143	129
110	114
152	125
168	117
144	106
137	92
118	126

17.57 A particular metal part can be produced at different temperatures (in degrees Celsius). All other variables being equal, a company would like to determine whether the strength of the metal part is significantly different for different temperatures. Given are the strengths of random samples of parts produced under different temperatures. Use $\alpha = 0.01$ and a nonparametric technique to determine whether there is a significant difference in the strength of the part for different temperatures.

5°	15°	20°	30°
216	228	219	218
215	224	220	216
218	225	221	217
216	222	223	221
219	226	224	218
214	225		217

17.58 Is there a strong correlation between the number of kilometres driven by a salesperson and sales volume achieved? Data were gathered from nine salespeople who worked territories of similar size

and potential. Determine the correlation coefficient for these data. Assume the data are ordinal in level of measurement.

Sales	Kilometres per Month
$150,000	1500
210,000	2100
285,000	3200
301,000	2400
335,000	2200
390,000	2500
400,000	3300
425,000	3100
440,000	3600

17.59 Workers in three different but comparable companies were asked to rate the use of quality control techniques in their firms on a 50-point scale. A score of 50 represents nearly perfect implementation of quality control techniques and 0 represents no implementation. Workers are divided into three independent groups. One group worked in a company that had required all its workers to attend a three-day seminar on quality control one year ago. A second group worked in a company in which each worker was part of a quality circle group that had been meeting at least once a month for a year. The third group of workers was employed by a company in which management had been actively involved in the quality control process for more than a year. Use $\alpha = 0.10$ to determine whether there is a significant difference between the three groups, as measured by the ratings.

Attended Three-Day Seminar	Quality Circles	Management Involved
9	27	16
11	38	21
17	25	18
10	40	28
22	31	29
15	19	20
6	35	31

17.60 The scores given are husband-wife scores on a marketing measure. Use the Wilcoxon matched-pairs signed rank test to determine whether the wives' scores are significantly higher on the marketing measure than the husbands'. Assume that $\alpha = 0.01$.

Husbands	Wives
27	35
22	29
28	30
19	20
28	27
29	31
18	22
21	19
25	29
18	28
20	21
24	22
23	33
25	38
22	34
16	31
23	36
30	31

Interpreting the Output

17.61 Study the following Minitab output. What is the purpose of this statistical test? What type of design was it? What was the result of the test?

```
Friedman Test of Observations by Treatment
Blocked by Block

S = 11.31    df = 3    p = 0.010

S = 12.16    df = 3    p = 0.007 (adjusted for
                                     ties)

                      Estimated    Sum of
 Treatment    N        Median      Ranks

     1        10       20.125       17.0
     2        10       25.875       33.0
     3        10       24.500       30.5
     4        10       22.500       19.5

 Grand median = 23.250
```

17.62 Examine the following Minitab output. Discuss the statistical test, its intent, and its outcome.

```
Runs Test

K = 1.4200

The observed number of runs = 28

The expected number of runs = 25.3600

21 observations above K; 29 below

The test is significant at 0.4387.

Cannot reject an alpha = 0.05
```

17.63 Study the following Minitab output. What is the purpose of this statistical test? What are the results of this analysis?

```
Mann-Whitney Confidence Interval and Test

C₁   N = 16    Median = 37.000
C₂   N = 16    Median = 46.500

Point estimate for ETA1 - ETA2 is -8.000.

95.2 Percent C.I. For ETA1 - ETA2 is (-13.999,
     -2.997).

W = 191.5

Test of ETA1 = ETA2 versus ETA1 ≅ ETA2 is
significant at 0.0067.

The test is significant at 0.0066 (adjusted
for ties).
```

17.64 Study the following Minitab output. What is the purpose of this statistical test? What were the hypotheses and what was the outcome? Discuss the results.

```
Kruskal-Wallis Test on Observations

                             Average
 Group    N     Median       Rank        Z

   1      5     35.00        14.8       0.82
   2      6     25.50         4.2      -3.33
   3      7     35.00        15.0       1.11
   4      6     35.00        16.0       1.40
 Overall  24                 12.5

H = 11.21   df = 3    p₅ 0.011
H = 11.28   df = 3    p₅ 0.010 (adjusted
                                 for ties)
```

Exploring the Databases with Business Analytics   *see* the databases on the Student Website and in *WileyPLUS*

1. Use a Kruskal-Wallis test to determine whether there is a significant difference in the Number of Tax Filers for the provinces of Quebec, Ontario, and Manitoba, at $\alpha = 0.05$? Data can be found in the Canadian RRSP Contribution Database.

2. Use the Canadian Stock Market Database and the Kruskal-Wallis test to determine whether there is a significant difference in Composite Index by week of the month.

Case

Schwinn

In 1895, Ignaz Schwinn and his partner, Adolph Arnold, incorporated Arnold, Schwinn & Company to produce bicycles. In the early years, with bicycle products such as the "Roadster," a single-speed bike that weighed 19 pounds (about 9 kg), Schwinn products appealed to people of all ages as a means of transportation. Because of the advent of the automobile in 1909, the use of bicycles as a means of transportation waned. In that same year, Schwinn developed manufacturing advances that allowed bicycles to be made more cheaply and sturdily. These advances opened a new market to the company as it manufactured and sold bicycles for children for the first time. Meanwhile, Ignaz Schwinn

bought out Arnold to become the sole owner of the company. Over the next 20 years, Schwinn bought out two motorcycle companies and developed mudguards as its major technological achievement. In the 1930s, Schwinn developed a series of quality, appearance, and technological breakthroughs including the balloon tire, which some say was the biggest innovation in mountain bike technology; the forewheel brake; the cantilever frame; and the spring fork. In 1946, built-in kickstands were added to its bikes. In the 1950s, Schwinn began an authorized dealer network and expanded its parts and accessory programs.

In the 1960s, Schwinn expanded into the fitness arena with in-home workout machines. In 1967, the company became the Schwinn Bicycle Company. The company introduced the Airdyne stationary bike in the late 1970s. In 1993, the company filed for bankruptcy, and in 1994 it was moved to Boulder, Colorado, to be nearer the mountain bike scene. In the next several years, Schwinn's mountain bike products won accolades and awards. In 2001, Pacific Cycle, the U.S.'s largest importer of quality bicycles, purchased Schwinn and united Schwinn bicycle lines with Pacific Cycle's other brands. Under new management in 2002, Schwinn bicycles began being featured, along with Pacific Cycle's other bikes, at mass retail outlets in North America. In 2004, Dorel Industries, Inc., a global consumer products company based in Montreal, purchased Pacific Cycle and made it a division of Dorel. Schwinn bicycles, now a part of the Dorel empire, are still made with quality for dependability and performance, and they continue to lead the industry in innovation.

Discussion

1. What is the age of the target market for Schwinn bikes? One theory is that in locales where mountain bikes are more popular, the mean age of customers is older than in locales where relatively little mountain biking is done. In an attempt to test this theory, a random sample of Colorado Springs customers is taken along with a random sample of customers in Alberta and British Columbia. The ages for these customers are given here. The customer is defined as "the person for whom the bike is primarily purchased." The shape of the population distribution of bicycle customer ages is unknown. Analyze the data and discuss the implications for Schwinn manufacturing and sales.

Colorado Springs	Alberta and BC
29	11
38	14
31	15
17	12
36	14
28	25
44	14
9	11
32	8
23	
35	

2. Suppose for a particular model of bike, the specified mass of a handlebar is 200 g and Schwinn uses three different suppliers of handlebars. Suppose Schwinn conducts a quality control study in which handlebars are randomly selected from each supplier and weighed. The results (in grams) are shown next. It is uncertain whether handlebar mass is normally distributed in the population. Analyze the data and discuss what the business implications are to Schwinn.

Supplier 1	Supplier 2	Supplier 3
200.76	197.38	192.63
202.63	207.24	199.68
198.03	201.56	203.07
201.24	194.53	195.18
202.88	197.21	189.11
194.62	198.94	
203.58		
205.41		

3. Quality technicians at Schwinn's manufacturing plant examine the finished products for paint flaws. Paint inspections are done on a production run of 75 bicycles. The inspection data are coded and the data analyzed using Minitab. If a bicycle's paint job contained no flaws, a 0 is recorded, and if it contained at least one flaw, the code used is a 1. Inspectors want to determine whether the flawed bikes occur in a random fashion or in a nonrandom pattern. Study the Minitab output. Determine whether the flaws occur randomly. Report on the proportion of flawed bikes and discuss the implications of these results to Schwinn's production management.

```
Runs Test: Paint Flaw

Paint Flaw
K = 0.2533
The observed number of runs = 29
The expected number of runs = 29.3733
19 observations above K; 56 below
The test is significant at 0.9083.
Cannot reject at alpha = 0.05
```

Sources: Schwinn website, www.schwinnbikes.com; Barbara Presley Noble, "No Hands: The Rise and Fall of the Schwinn Bicycle Company, an American Institution, by Judith Crown and Glenn Coleman," [book review], *Strategy + Business*, July 1, 1997; "Company News: Canadian Company Buys Maker of Schwinn Bikes," *New York Times*, January 14, 2004.

Big Data Case

Employing the American Hospital Association database, answer the following:

1. Use a Mann-Whitney U test to determine if there is a significant difference between children's hospitals and psychiatric hospitals (Service variables) on Personnel.

2. Use a Mann-Whitney U test to determine if there is a significant difference between children's hospitals and long-term acute care hospitals (Service variables) on Personnel.

3. Use a Mann-Whitney U test to determine if there is a significant difference between psychiatric hospitals and long-term acute care hospitals (Service variables) on Personnel.

Minitab

- Five of the nonparametric statistics presented in this chapter can be accessed using Minitab. For each nonparametric technique, select **Stat** from the menu bar. From the **Stat** pull-down menu, select **Nonparametrics**. From the **Nonparametrics** pull-down menu, select the appropriate nonparametric technique from **Runs Test**, **Mann-Whitney**, **Kruskal-Wallis**, **Friedman**, and **1-Sample Wilcoxon**.

- To begin a runs test, select **Runs Test** from the **Nonparametrics** pull-down menu. Supply the location of the column with the data in the **Variables** space: check either **Above and below the mean** or **Above and below**. Minitab will default to **Above and below the mean** and will use the mean of the numbers to determine when the runs stop. Select **Above and below** if you want to supply your own value.

- To begin a Mann-Whitney U test, select **Mann-Whitney** from the **Nonparametrics** pull-down menu. Place the column location of the data from the first sample in **First Sample**. Place the column location of the data from the second sample in **Second Sample**. Insert the level of confidence in **Confidence level**. In the slot beside **Alternative**, select the form of the alternative hypothesis. Choose from **not equal**, **less than**, and **greater than**.

- To begin a Kruskal-Wallis test, all observations from all treatment levels must be located in one column. Place the location of the column containing these observations in the space provided beside **Response**. Enter the treatment levels to match the observations in a second column. Place the location of the column containing these treatment levels in the space provided beside **Factor**.

- To begin a Friedman test, all observations must be located in one column. Place the location of the column containing these observations in the space provided beside **Response**. Enter the treatment levels to match the observations in a second column. Place the location of the column containing these treatment levels in the space provided beside **Treatment**. Enter the block levels to match the observations in a third column. Place the location of the column containing these block levels in the space provided beside **Blocks**. You can store residuals and fits by clicking on **Store residuals** and **Store fits**. You cannot store the fits without storing the residuals.

- There is no Wilcoxon matched-pairs signed rank test in Minitab. You must manipulate Minitab to perform this test. Either enter the data from the two related samples in two columns and use the calculator under **Calc** on the main menu bar to subtract the two columns, thereby creating a third column of differences, or enter the differences in a column to begin with. Select **1-sample Wilcoxon**. In the space provided next to **Variables**, enter the location of the column containing the differences. Place the level of confidence in the box beside **Confidence interval**. Minitab will default to 95%. It will also default to a hypothesis test of a 0.0 median. To test any other value, check **Test median** and enter the new test value for the median. In the slot beside **Alternative**, select the form of the alternative hypothesis. Choose from **not equal**, **less than**, and **greater than**.

CHAPTER 18

Statistical Quality Control

LEARNING OBJECTIVES

This chapter presents basic concepts in quality control, with a particular emphasis on statistical quality control techniques, thereby enabling you to:

18.1 Explain the meaning of quality in business, compare the approaches to quality improvement by various quality gurus and movements, and compare different approaches to controlling the quality of a product, including benchmarking, just-in-time inventory systems, Six Sigma, lean manufacturing, reengineering, poka-yoke, value-stream mapping, and Kaizen Event.

18.2 Compare various tools that identify, categorize, and solve problems in the quality improvement process, including flowcharts, Pareto analysis, cause-and-effect diagrams, control charts, check sheets, histograms, and scatter charts.

18.3 Measure variation among manufactured items using various control charts, including $\bar{x}$ charts, R charts, p charts, and c charts.

Decision Dilemma

Italy's Piaggio Makes a Comeback

Piaggio, founded in Genoa, Italy, in 1884 by a 20-year-old man named Rinaldo Piaggio, began as a luxury ship-fitting company. Expanding on its services and products, by the year 1900, the company was also producing rail carriages, luxury coaches, truck bodies, and trains. During World War I, Piaggio began producing airplanes and seaplanes and then expanded capacity by purchasing a new plant in Pisa in 1917 and taking over a small plant in Pontedera (in Tuscany) in 1921, making the Pontedera plant the company's centre for aeronautical production.

During World War II, the Pontedera plant was building state-of-the-art four-engine aircraft, but Allied planes destroyed the plant because of its military importance. With the Pontedera plant gone, the state of Italian roads a disaster, and the Italian economy in shambles, Enrico Piaggio (Rinaldo's son and then CEO) decided to focus the company's efforts on the personal mobility of the Italian people. Corradino D'Ascanio, Piaggio's ingenious aeronautical engineer, who had designed, constructed, and flown the first modern helicopter, was commissioned to design a simple, sturdy, economical vehicle for people to get around in that was both comfortable and elegant. Drawing from his aeronautical background, D'Ascanio, who did not like motorcycles, developed a completely new vehicle that had a front fork, like an airplane, allowing for easy wheel changing, and was housed in a unibody steel chassis. It was not noisy or uncomfortable like a motorcycle,

iStock.com/578foot

and the steel frame protected the rider from road dirt and debris. When Enrico Piaggio first saw the vehicle, he said, "Sembra una vespa!" ("It looks like a wasp!"), and, as a result, the vehicle became known as the Vespa.

By the end of 1949, 35,000 Vespas had been produced, and in 10 more years, over one million had been manufactured. Featured in such films as *Roman Holiday, The Talented Mr. Ripley,* and *Alfie,* the Vespa became popular around the world and known as a global symbol of Italy and Italian design. In 1959, the powerful Agnelli Family, owners of the car-maker Fiat SpA, took control of Piaggio, and the scooter maker flourished for the next two decades. However, during the latter half of the 20th century, revolving-door management and millions of euros wasted on ill-conceived expansion plans left the company with crushing debt and vulnerable to competition from companies in the Pacific Rim. Losing money and market share, Piaggio was caught up in a downward spiral of increasing debt, bad quality, and inability to meet market demand. As the 21st century arrived, the company's status looked bleak, until 2003, when Italian industrialist Roberto Colaninno bought the company. Implementing a series of strategic moves and quality initiatives, Colaninno turned around the fortunes of Piaggio, now the fourth-largest manufacturer of scooters and motorcycles in the world, producing more than 600,000 vehicles annually. In 2018, Piaggio had 6,515 employees and a revenue of €1.39 billion.

Managerial, Statistical, and Analytical Questions

1. Was the decline of Piaggio driven by poor quality? If so, how?
2. What quality initiatives did Colaninno implement at Piaggio that helped turn the company around?
3. Were company workers consulted about ways to improve the product and the process?

Sources: Barry Lillie, "History of an Icon: La Vespa," *Italy magazine*, August 4, 2014, www.italymagazine.com/featured-story/history-icon-la-vespa; Piaggio Vespa website, www.vespa.com/ca_EN; Gabriel Kahn, "Vespa's Builder Scoots Back to Profitability," *Wall Street Journal*, June 5, 2006, B1; Jonathan Glancey, "The Vespa: How a Motor Scooter Became Stylish," BBC Online, November 22, 2013; Roy Furchgott, "Vespa's Retention Value Keeps Scooting Forward," *Houston Chronicle*, December 28, 2018, B8; Piaggio Group website, www.piaggiogroup.com/it/investor/dati-finanziari/principali-dati-economici-finanziari-e-gestionali.

Introduction

In the past four decades, institutions around the world have invested millions of dollars in improving quality, and in some cases, corporate cultures have been changed through the implementation of new quality philosophies. Much has been written and spoken about quality, and a great deal of research has been conducted on the effectiveness of various quality approaches. In order to study and explore the myriad quality theories, approaches, tools, and concepts, it is important to first understand what quality is.

One major stumbling block to studying and implementing quality improvement methodologies is that quality means different things to different people. If you asked commuters whether their automobiles have quality, the response would vary according to each individual's perspective. One person's view of a quality automobile is one that goes 75,000 km without needing any major repair work. Other people perceive automobile quality as comfortable seats and extra electronic gadgetry. These people look for bells and whistles along with form-fitting, cushy seats in a quality car. Still other automobile commuters define automobile quality as the presence of numerous safety features.

In this chapter, we examine various definitions of quality and discuss some of the main concepts of quality and quality control. We explore some techniques for analyzing processes. In addition, we learn how to construct and interpret control charts.

18.1 | Introduction to Quality Control

LEARNING OBJECTIVE 18.1

Explain the meaning of quality in business, compare the approaches to quality improvement by various quality gurus and movements, and compare different approaches to controlling the quality of a product, including benchmarking, just-in-time inventory systems, Six Sigma, lean manufacturing, reengineering, poka-yoke, value-stream mapping, and Kaizen Event.

There are almost as many definitions of quality as there are people and products. However, one definition that captures the spirit of most quality efforts in the business world is that **quality** is *when a product delivers what is stipulated for it in its specifications*. From this point of view, quality is when the producer delivers what has been specified in the product description, as agreed upon by both buyer and seller. Philip B. Crosby, a well-known expert on quality, has said that "quality is conformance to requirements."[1] The product requirements must be met by the producer to ensure quality. This notion of quality is similar to the one based on specifications. Armand V. Feigenbaum, another well-known quality authority, says in his book *Total Quality Control* that "quality is a customer determination" as opposed to a management or designer determination.[2] He states that this determination is based on the customer's experience with the product or service and that it is always a moving target.

David A. Garvin, author of *Managing Quality,* argues that there are at least five types of quality: transcendent, product, user, manufacturing-based, and value.[3] **Transcendent quality** *implies that a product has an "innate excellence." It has "uncompromising standards and high achievement."* Garvin says that this definition offers little practical guidance to business people. **Product quality** *is measurable in the product.* Consumers perceive differences in products, *and quality products have more attributes.* For example, a personal computer with more memory has more quality. Tires with more tread have more quality.

User quality means that the *quality of a product is determined by the consumer* and is in the eye of the beholder. One problem with user-based quality is that because there are widely varying individual preferences, there can be a plethora of views of quality for a given product or service. **Manufacturing-based quality** has to do with engineering and manufacturing practices. Once specifications are determined, quality *is measured by the manufacturer's ability to target the requirements consistently with little variability.* Most manufacturing-based definitions of quality have to do with conformance to requirements. **Value quality** is defined in costs and prices. From a certain point of view, value quality *is based on cost-benefit analysis;* that is, by how much did the benefit of the good or service outweigh the cost? Did the customer get his or her money's worth?

What Is Quality Control?

How does a company know whether it is producing a quality product? One way is to practise quality control. **Quality control** (sometimes referred to as quality assurance) is *the collection of strategies, techniques, and actions taken by an organization to assure itself that it is producing a quality product.*

From this point of view, quality control begins with product planning and design, where attributes of the product or service are determined and specified, and continues through product production or service operation until feedback from the final consumer is looped back through the institution for product improvement. It is implied that all departments, workers, processes, and suppliers are in some way responsible for producing a quality product or service.

Quality control can be undertaken in two distinct ways: after-process control and in-process control. **After-process quality control** involves *inspecting the attributes of a finished product to determine whether the product is acceptable, is in need of rework, or is to be rejected and scrapped.* The after-process quality control method was the leading quality control technique for North American manufacturers for several decades until the 1980s. The after-process method emphasizes weeding out defective products before they reach the consumer. The problem with this method is that it does not generate information that can correct in-process problems or raw materials problems, nor does it generate much information about how to improve quality. Two main outcomes of the after-process methodology are (1) reporting the number of defects produced during a specific period of time and (2) screening defective products from consumers. Because North American companies dominated world markets in many areas for several decades during and after the World War II, their managers had little interest in changing from the after-process method.

However, as Japan, other Asian nations, and Western European countries began to compete strongly in the world market in the late 1970s and 1980s, North American companies

---

[1] Philip B. Crosby, *Quality Without Tears* (New York: McGraw-Hill, 1984).

[2] Armand V. Feigenbaum, *Total Quality Control*, 3rd ed. (New York: McGraw-Hill, 1991).

[3] David A. Garvin, *Managing Quality* (New York: The Free Press, 1988).

began to reexamine quality control methods. As a result, many North American companies, following the example of Japanese and European manufacturers, developed quality control programs based on in-process control. **In-process quality control** *techniques measure product attributes at various intervals throughout the manufacturing process in an effort to pinpoint problem areas.* This information enables quality control personnel in conjunction with production personnel to make corrections in operations as products are being made. This intervention in turn opens the door to opportunities for improving the process and the product.

Total Quality Management

W. Edwards Deming, who has been referred to as the father of the quality movement, advocated that the achievement of quality is an organic phenomenon that begins with top managers' commitment and extends all the way to suppliers on one side and consumers on the other. Deming believed that quality control is a long-term total company effort. The effort called for by Deming is **total quality management (TQM)**. TQM *involves all members of the organization—from the CEO to the line worker—in improving quality.* In addition, the goals and objectives of the organization come under the purview of quality control and can be measured in quality terms. Suppliers, raw materials, worker training, and opportunity for workers to make improvements are all part of TQM. The antithesis of TQM is when a company gives a quality control department total responsibility for improving product quality.

Deming presented a cause-and-effect explanation of the impact of TQM on a company. This idea has become known as the Deming chain reaction.[4] The chain reaction begins with improving quality. Improving quality will decrease costs because of less reworking, fewer mistakes, fewer delays and snags, and better use of machine time and materials. From the reduced costs comes an improvement in productivity because:

$$\text{Productivity} = \frac{\text{Output}}{\text{Input}}$$

A reduction of costs generates more output for less input and, hence, increases productivity. As productivity improves, a company is more able to capture the market with better quality and lower prices. This capability enables a company to stay in business and provide more jobs. As a note of caution, while Deming advocated that improved quality results in lower costs through efficiencies gained by streamlining and reducing waste, some managers have used it as an excuse to lay off workers in an effort to save money. It is likely that Deming would have argued that such cost-cutting actually reduces quality and productivity due to an increase in operational errors, errors of omission, and a lack of attention to detail by a reduced staff that is overworked and stressed.

Deming listed 14 points that, if followed, can lead to improved TQM:[5]

1. Create constancy of purpose for improvement of product and service.
2. Adopt the new philosophy.
3. Cease dependence on mass inspection.
4. End the practice of awarding business on price tag alone.
5. Improve constantly and forever every process for planning, production, and service.
6. Institute training.
7. Institute leadership.
8. Drive out fear.
9. Break down barriers between staff areas.
10. Eliminate slogans.
11. Eliminate numerical quotas.

[4] W. Edwards Deming, *Out of the Crisis* (Cambridge, MA: Massachusetts Institute of Technology Center for Advanced Engineering Study, 1986).

[5] Mary Walton, *The Deming Management Method* (New York: Perigee Books, 1986).

12. Remove barriers to pride of workmanship.

13. Institute a vigorous program of education and retraining.

14. Take action to accomplish the transformation.

The first point indicates the need to seek constant improvement in process, innovation, design, and technique. The second point suggests that, to truly make changes, a new, positive point of view must be taken; in other words, the viewpoint that poor quality is acceptable must be changed. The third point is a call for change from after-process inspection to in-process inspection. Deming pointed out that after-process inspection has nothing to do with improving the product or the service. The fourth point indicates that a company should be careful in awarding contracts to suppliers and vendors. Purchasers should look more for quality and reliability in a supplier than just for low price. Deming called for long-term supplier relationships in which the company and supplier agree on quality standards.

Point 5 conveys the message that quality is not a one-time activity. Management and labour should be constantly on the lookout for ways to improve the product. Institute training, the sixth point, implies that training is an essential element in TQM. Workers need to learn how to do their jobs correctly and to learn techniques that will result in higher quality. Point 7, institute leadership, is a call for a new management based on showing, doing, and supporting rather than ordering and punishing. The eighth point results in establishing a safe work environment, where workers feel free to share ideas and make suggestions without the threat of punitive measures. Point 9, breaking down barriers, emphasizes reducing competition and conflicts between departments and groups. It is a call for more of a team approach—the notion that we're all in this together.

Deming did not believe that slogans help affect quality products, as stated in point 10. Quality control is not a movement of slogans. Point 11 indicates that quotas do not help companies make quality products. In fact, pressure to make quotas can result in inefficiencies, errors, and lack of quality. Point 12 says that managers must find ways to make it easier for workers to produce quality products; faulty equipment and poor-quality supplies do not allow workers to take pride in what is produced. Point 13 calls for total re-education and training within a company about new methods and how to more effectively do one's job. Point 14 implies that rhetoric is not the answer; a call for action is necessary in order to institute change and promote higher quality.

Quality Gurus Some other important and well-known quality gurus are Joseph Juran, Philip Crosby, Armand Feigenbaum, Kaoru Ishikawa, and Genichi Taguchi. Juran was a contemporary of Deming's and, like Deming, assisted Japanese leaders in the 1950s in implementing quality concepts and tools so that they could produce products that would be attractive to world markets. Juran was particularly well-known for his "Juran Trilogy," which included quality planning, quality control, and quality improvement. Crosby, author of the popular book *Quality Is Free,* developed a zero-defects program to reduce defects in missile production in the U.S. in the late 1950s and early 1960s, and later established a Quality College. Crosby bases his approach to quality on four basic tenets that he refers to as absolutes: (1) Quality means conformance to requirements; (2) Defect prevention is the only acceptable approach; (3) Zero defects is the only performance standard; (4) The cost of quality is the only measurement of quality. Feigenbaum has been a worldwide leader in quality management for over half a century. He published his widely read text *Total Quality Control* in 1951 under the title *Quality Control: Principles, Practice, and Administration.* While Deming is often associated with TQM, it was Feigenbaum who actually coined the term *total quality control.* He originated the concept of *cost of quality* as a means of quantifying the benefits of a TQM approach, and he popularized the term *hidden factory,* which describes the part of plant capacity wasted due to poor quality. Ishikawa, a student of both Deming and Juran, is probably the most well-known figure in the Japanese quality movement. He has been credited with originating the concept of *quality circle* and championed what is now seen as Japan's company-wide approach to quality. Ishikawa emphasized data measurement and using statistical techniques in improving quality. He is known for developing the cause-and-effect or fishbone diagram, which is sometimes referred to as the Ishikawa diagram. Taguchi, an important figure in the Japanese quality movement, wrote a two-volume book on experimental design that has been widely used in quality improvement efforts. In the 1970s, Taguchi developed the concept of the *quality loss function* and refined a set of cost-saving quality improvement techniques that later became known as Taguchi methods.

Six Sigma

Currently, a popular approach to TQM is Six Sigma. Six Sigma is a quality movement, a methodology, and a measurement. As a quality movement, Six Sigma is a major player throughout the world in both the manufacturing and service industries. As a methodology, it is used to evaluate the capability of a process to perform defect-free, where a defect is defined as anything that results in customer dissatisfaction. Six Sigma is customer focused and has the potential to achieve exponential quality improvement through the reduction of variation in system processes. Under the Six Sigma methodology, quality improvement projects are carefully defined so that they can be successfully completed within a relatively short time frame. Financials are applied to each completed project so that management can estimate how much the project saves the institution. On each project, intense study is used to determine root cause. In the end, a metric known as a *sigma level* can be assigned to represent the level of quality that has been attained, and this is the measurement aspect of Six Sigma.

The Six Sigma approach to quality is said to have begun in 1987 with Bill Smith, a reliability engineer at Motorola.[6] However, Six Sigma took off as a significant quality movement in the mid-1990s when Jack Welch, CEO of General Electric, ". . . went nuts about Six Sigma and launched it," calling it the most ambitious task the company had ever taken on.[7] "Six Sigma has taken the corporate world by storm and represents the thrusts of numerous efforts in manufacturing and service organizations to improve products, services, and processes."[8] Six Sigma has been around for over 30 years and has shown a sustained impact on quality improvement within a variety of companies in many industries. Six Sigma is derived from a previous quality scheme in which a process was considered to be producing quality results if $\pm 3\sigma$ or 99.74% of the products or attributes were within specification. (Note: The standard normal distribution table, Table A.5, produces an area of 0.4987 for a z score of 3. Doubling that and converting to a percentage yields 99.74%, which is the portion of a normal distribution that falls within $\mu \pm 3\sigma$.) Six Sigma methodology requires that $\pm 6\sigma$ of the product be within specification. The goal of Six Sigma methodology is to have 99.99966% of the product or attributes be within specification, or no more than 0.00034% = 0.0000034 out of specification. This means that no more than 3.4 of the product or attributes per million can be defective. Essentially, it calls for the process to approach a defect-free status.

Why Six Sigma? Several reasons highlight the importance of adopting a Six Sigma philosophy. First, in some industries the three sigma philosophy is simply unacceptable. For example, the three sigma goal of having 99.74% of the product or attribute be in specification in the prescription drug industry implies that it is acceptable to have 0.26% incorrectly filled prescriptions, or 2,600 out of every million prescriptions filled. In the airline industry, the three sigma goal implies that it is acceptable to have 2,600 unsatisfactory landings by commercial aircraft out of every million landings. In contrast, a Six Sigma approach would require that there be no more than 3.4 incorrectly filled prescriptions or 3.4 unsatisfactory landings per million, with a goal of approaching zero.

A second reason for adopting a Six Sigma approach is that it forces companies that adopt it to work much harder and more quickly to discover and reduce sources of variation in processes. It raises the bar of the quality goals of a firm, causing the company to place even more emphasis on continuous quality improvement. A third reason is that Six Sigma dedication to quality may be required to attain world-class status and be a top competitor in the international market (see Thinking Critically About Statistics in Business Today 18.1).

Six Sigma contains a formalized problem-solving approach called the DMAIC process (Define, Measure, Analyze, Improve, and Control). At the beginning of each Six Sigma

---

[6] James R. Evans and William M. Lindsay, *The Management and Control of Quality*, 5th ed. (Cincinnati, OH: South-Western Publishing, 2002).

[7] Jack Welch, *Jack: Straight from the Gut* (New York: Warner Books, 2001), 329–30.

[8] James R. Evans and William M. Lindsay, *An Introduction to Six Sigma and Process Improvement* (Cincinnati, OH: Thomson South-Western Publishing, 2005), 4.

Thinking Critically About Statistics in Business Today 18.1

Six Sigma Focus at General Electric

General Electric's focus on quality began in the late 1980s with a movement called Work-Out®, which reduced company bureaucracy, opened its culture to new ideas, and helped create a learning environment that eventually led to Six Sigma. In the mid-1990s, GE established a goal of attaining Six Sigma quality by 2000. By 1999, GE had already invested more than $1 billion in its quality effort. Today at GE, Six Sigma defines the way it does business. GE continues to strive for greater quality by following a Six Sigma philosophy. In its push for Six Sigma status, GE engaged more than 5,000 employees in Six Sigma methodology in more than 25,000 completed projects.

GE's Six Sigma approach is data driven and customer focused. All of GE's employees are trained in the techniques, strategy, and statistical tools of Six Sigma. The focus of Six Sigma at GE is on reducing process variation and increasing process capability. The benefits delivered by this process include reduced cycle times, accelerated product designs, consistent efforts to eliminate variation, and increased probabilities of meeting customer requirements. The adoption of Six Sigma resulted in a culture in which quality thinking is embedded at every level in every operation throughout the company.

Why has GE pursued a Six Sigma philosophy? GE discovered that its customers were demanding better quality, and its employees thought they could be doing a better job. GE's competitors, such as Motorola, Texas Instruments, and Allied Signal, had proven that following a disciplined, rigorous approach to quality significantly improved customer service and resulted in greater productivity. Internal process defects had been limiting GE's ability to achieve growth objectives. With increased globalization and information access, GE believes that products and services continually change the way its customers do business, and the highly competitive worldwide marketplace leaves no room for error in designing, producing, and delivering products. Six Sigma provides the philosophy and approach needed to meet these goals.

GE points out the difference between three sigma and Six Sigma: With three sigma, there are 1.5 misspelled words per page in a book in a small library; with Six Sigma, there is 1 misspelled word in all the books in a small library. In a post office with three sigma, 20,000 articles of mail are lost per hour; with Six Sigma, only 7 are lost per hour. Imagine if Six Sigma could improve your golf score. If you played 100 rounds of golf per year, under a two sigma philosophy you would miss six putts per round. Under three sigma, you would miss one putt per round. Under Six Sigma, you would miss only one putt every 163 years!

Things to Ponder

1. Six Sigma is also used widely in the health-care industry. Go online and research how Six Sigma has improved patient satisfaction in a hospital.

Sources: Adapted from General Electric, "Making Customers Feel Six Sigma Quality," available on the GE website at www.ge.com/sixsigma/makingcustomers.html.

---

project, the project team carefully identifies the problem—not just the symptoms—at the Define stage. The scope of the project is limited so that it can be completed within four to six months. At the Measure stage, there is a heavy emphasis on metrics and measurement of current operating systems, along with identifying variables and targeting data collection. During the Analyze stage, the focus is on analyzing data and collected information in an effort to determine what is occurring and uncovering root causes of problems. At the fourth stage, Improve, the project team generates ideas for solving problems and improving performance. Lastly, at the fifth stage, Control, the focus is on putting into motion those tools, standards, and so on, that are needed to maintain the new quality that has been achieved through the Six Sigma project.

Another important aspect of Six Sigma as a methodology and a quality movement is the strong focus on the customer that is often referred to as critical to quality (CTQ). Maintaining a customer focus is vital to every stage of a Six Sigma project, keeping in mind that there are both internal and external customers. Six Sigma project team members work on things that are important to the customer and do not spend time on things that could be improved but are not important to the customer (not CTQ).

Under Six Sigma, most members of an organization are supposed to have at least some training in the methodology. Employees with minimal exposure to Six Sigma—perhaps only an introductory lecture—might be designated as "yellow belts" (named after the belt system in karate). Organizational members who have more extensive training and serve part-time on Six Sigma teams are designated as "green belts." Fully trained employees having over 150 hours of training in Six Sigma, usually including at least one Six Sigma project, are called "black belts." Black belts work full-time within an organization, usually directing several Six Sigma projects simultaneously. Master black belts are "experts" in Six Sigma. They have advanced training in statistical techniques and other Six Sigma tools and methods, and they work in the organization developing teams, training black belts, and providing technical direction.

Design for Six Sigma   Companies using Six Sigma discovered that some processes, outcomes, and services, often designed before the Six Sigma era, contained so many flaws and problems that even the in-depth root analysis of the Six Sigma methodology could not solve some quality issues, and thus a complete redesign was necessary. In fact, history has shown that most processes can only achieve about a 5.0 sigma status with quality improvement. To actually achieve 6.0 sigma status, organizations often need to *design* for 6.0 sigma; that is, because of constraints or limitations built in by its original design, there may be a ceiling on how much a process or operation can be improved. **Design for Six Sigma (DFSS)**, an offshoot of Six Sigma, is *a quality scheme that emphasizes designing the product or process right the first time,* thereby allowing organizations the opportunity to reach even higher sigma levels through Six Sigma.

Lean Manufacturing   **Lean manufacturing** is *a quality management philosophy that focuses on the reduction of waste and the elimination of unnecessary steps in an operation or process.* Whereas the tenets of lean manufacturing have existed in successful manufacturing circles for over a century, the Toyota Production System is generally credited with developing the notion of lean manufacturing as it exists today. Lean manufacturing requires a disciplined attitude for seeking out and eliminating waste in all areas of business, including supplier networks, customer relations, organization management, and design. Proponents of lean manufacturing claim it brings about an evaluation of the entire organization and restructures processes to reduce wasteful activities.

In particular, lean manufacturing focuses on seven types of waste: overproduction, waiting time, transportation, processing, inventory, motion, and scrap. Overproduction can include making more than is needed or making it earlier than is needed. Waiting includes products waiting for the next production step or people waiting for work to do. Transportation waste can include moving products farther than is minimally required, and inventory waste can include having more inventory than is minimally required at any point in the process, including end product. Processing waste is doing more work than the customer values or needs, and motion waste is people moving around unnecessarily or wasting motion in performing their production or operation functions.

Some advocates of lean manufacturing claim that even if a process or service is operating at a Six Sigma level, it does not necessarily follow that the process or service is lean. That is, the quality of the process or service can be quite high, but there can still be waste in the system. Some critics of Six Sigma say that just improving the quality does not necessarily reduce the time that it takes to perform the process. With this in mind, a newer approach to quality management has been developed by combining the investigative and variation reduction aspects of Six Sigma with the emphasis on increased efficiency of lean manufacturing, resulting in what some refer to as Lean Six Sigma.

Some Important Quality Concepts

Of the several widely used techniques in quality control, six in particular warrant discussion: benchmarking, just-in-time inventory systems, reengineering, poka-yoke, value-stream mapping, and Kaizen Event.

Benchmarking   One practice used by North American companies to improve quality is benchmarking. **Benchmarking** is *a method by which a company attempts to develop and establish TQM from product to process by examining and emulating the best practices and techniques used in its industry.* The ultimate objective of benchmarking is to use a positive, proactive process to make changes that will effect superior performance. The process of benchmarking involves studying competitors and learning from the best in the industry.

An American pioneer in what is called competitive benchmarking was Xerox. Xerox was struggling to hold on to its market share against foreign competition. At one point, other companies could sell a machine for what it cost Xerox to make a machine. Xerox set out to find out why. The company instituted a benchmarking process in which the internal workings and features of competing machines were studied in depth. Xerox attempted to emulate and learn from the best of these features in developing its own products. In time, benchmarking was so successful within the company that top managers included benchmarking as a major corporate effort.[9]

Just-in-Time Inventory Systems

Another technique used to improve quality control is the just-in-time system for inventory, which focuses on raw materials, subparts, and suppliers. Ideally, a **just-in-time (JIT) inventory system** means that *no extra raw materials or inventory of parts for production are stored.* Necessary supplies and parts needed for production arrive just in time. The advantage of this system is that holding costs, personnel, and space needed to manage inventory are reduced. Even within the production process, as subparts are assembled and merged, the JIT philosophy can be applied to smooth the process and eliminate bottlenecks.

A production facility is unlikely to become 100% JIT. One of the residual effects of installing a JIT system throughout the production process is that, as the inventory "fat" is trimmed from the production process, the pressure on the system to produce often discloses problems that previously went undetected. For example, one subpart being made on two machines may not be produced in enough quantity to supply the next step. Installation of the JIT system shows that this station is a bottleneck. The company might choose to add another machine to produce more subparts, change the production schedule, or develop another strategy. As the bottleneck is loosened and the problem is corrected, other areas of weakness may emerge. Thus, the residual effect of a JIT inventory system can be the opportunity for production and operations managers to work their way methodically through a maze of previously unidentified problems that would not normally be recognized.

A JIT inventory system typically changes the relationship between supplier and producer. Most companies using this system have fewer suppliers than they did before installing the system. The tendency is for manufacturers to give suppliers longer contracts under the JIT system. However, the suppliers are expected to produce raw materials and subparts to a specified quality and to deliver the goods as near to JIT as possible. JIT suppliers may even build production or warehouse facilities next to the producer's. In the JIT system, the suppliers become part of TQM.

JIT as a management philosophy has come to signify production with a minimum of waste by producing only the materials needed at a specified place and time. The goal of JIT is to minimize operations that don't add value and to reduce unneeded inventory in a production process or operation. In this sense, some view JIT, also known as "lean production," as the forerunner of what is now referred to as lean manufacturing. While some of the basic elements of JIT were used by Toyota in the 1950s, most historians give credit to Taiichi Ohno of Toyota for developing JIT in the 1970s, and Ohno is often referred to as the father of JIT.

There are several basic elements that underscore the JIT philosophy, including:

1. Levelling the loads on work centres to smooth the flow of goods or services.
2. Reducing or even eliminating setup times.
3. Reducing lot sizes.
4. Reducing lead times.
5. Conducting preventive maintenance on machines and equipment to ensure that they work perfectly when needed.
6. Having a flexible workforce.
7. Requiring supplier quality assurance and implementing a zero-defects quality program.
8. Improving, eliminating, or reducing anything that does not add value to the product.
9. Striving for simplicity.
10. Making workers responsible for the quality of their output.

By levelling loads at workstations throughout the process, bottlenecks are reduced or eliminated, and there is a greater chance that goods/services will flow smoothly through the process.

---

[9] Robert C. Camp, *Benchmarking* (Milwaukee, WI: Quality Press, ASQC, 1989).

Reengineering

Reengineering   A more radical approach to improving quality is reengineering. Whereas total quality approaches like Deming's 14 points call for continuous improvement, **reengineering** is *the complete redesigning of the core business process in a company.* It involves innovation and is often a complete departure from the company's usual way of doing business.

Reengineering is not a fine-tuning of the present process nor is it mere downsizing of a company. Reengineering starts with a blank sheet of paper and an idea about where the company would like to be in the future. Without considering the present limitations or constraints of the company, the reengineering process works backward from where the company wants to be in the future and then attempts to determine what it would take to get there. From this information, the company cuts or adds, reshapes, or redesigns itself to achieve the new goal. In other words, the reengineering approach involves determining what the company would be like if it could start from scratch and then redesigning the process to make it work that way.

Reengineering affects almost every functional area of the company, including information systems, financial reporting systems, the manufacturing environment, suppliers, shipping, and maintenance. Reengineering is usually painful and difficult for a company. Companies that have been most successful in implementing reengineering are those that faced big shifts in the nature of competition and required major changes to stay in business.

Some recommendations to consider in implementing reengineering in a company are to (1) get the strategy straight first, (2) lead from the top, (3) create a sense of urgency, (4) design from the outside in, (5) manage the firm's consultant, and (6) combine top-down and bottom-up initiatives. Getting the strategy straight is crucial because the strategy drives the changes. The company must determine what business it wants to be in and how to make money in it. The company's strategy determines its operations.

The focus of reengineering is outside the company; the process begins with the customer. Current operations may have some merit, but time is spent determining the need of the marketplace and how to meet that need.

A company need not necessarily reengineer its entire operation. A specific process, such as billing, production, or distribution, can be reengineered. For example, a mortgage loan company may completely rethink and restructure the process by which a loan applicant gets approved. In health care, a hospital might radically redesign its admissions procedure to significantly reduce admissions time and stress for both the patient and the admissions officer. An integral part of the reengineering effort is to question basic assumptions and traditions, rethink the way business has been done, and reinvent the process so that significant improvements can be made.

Poka-Yoke

Poka-Yoke   Another common quality concept that can be used in continuous improvement is **poka-yoke,** which means "mistake proofing." Poka-yoke, pronounced POH-kah YOH-kay and developed by Japanese industrial engineer Shigeo Shingo in the early 1960s, *uses devices, methods, or inspections in order to avoid machine error or simple human error.* There are two main types of poka-yokes: (1) prevention-based poka-yokes and (2) detection-based poka-yokes. Prevention-based poka-yokes are mechanisms that sense that an error is about to occur and send some sort of signal of the occurrence or halt the process. Detection poka-yokes identify when a defect has occurred and stop the process so that the defect is not built into the product or service and sent downstream.

In contrast to Deming, who believed that poor quality is generally not the fault of the worker (but rather the fault of equipment, training, materials, etc.), Shingo believed that "the causes of defects lie in worker errors, and defects are the results of neglecting those errors. It follows that mistakes will not turn into defects if worker errors are discovered and eliminated beforehand."[10] As an example, suppose a worker is assembling a device that contains two push buttons. A spring must be placed under each push button in order for it to work. If either spring is not put in place, the associated push button will not work, and an error has been committed. If the worker does an on-the-spot inspection by looking at the device or by testing it, then the cost of fixing the device (rework) is minimal, both in terms of the time to fix it and the time lost due to inspection. If, on the other hand, the error is not identified and the

---

[10] Shigeo Shingo, *Zero Quality Control: Source Inspection and the Poka-Yoke System* (University Park, IL: Productivity Press, 1986), 50.

device goes on down the assembly line and is incorporated as a part in a product, the cost of rework, scrap, repair, or warranty claim can become quite high. A simple poka-yoke solution might be that the worker first counts two springs out of the supply bin and places them both in a small dish before each assembly. If the worker is not paying attention, is daydreaming, or is forgetful, he or she merely needs to look at the dish to easily see if there is a leftover spring before sending the device on to the next station. Some other examples of poka-yoke include machines with limit switches connected to warning lights that go on if an operator improperly positions a part on a machine, computer programs displaying warning messages if a file is being closed but has not been saved, plugs on the back of a computer that have different sizes and/or shapes along with colour codes to prevent the connection of a plug into the wrong hole, electric hedge trimmers that force users to hold down two switches before the trimmers will work to make it harder for users to accidentally cut themselves, and a plate, which is only supposed to be screwed down in one position (orientation), that has screw holes in nonsymmetrical positions so that the holes only line up for mounting if the plate is in the proper position.

Shingo believed that most mistakes can be prevented if people make the effort to identify when and where errors happen and take corrective actions. Simple poka-yoke mechanisms, such as a device, a switch, a guide pin, a procedure, or a visual inspection, can go a long way in preventing errors that result in defects and thereby reduce productivity.

Value-Stream Mapping The value stream consists of all the activities needed to design and produce a given product or service from conception to finish, from order to delivery. **Value-stream mapping** is *a lean technique used to identify all activities required to produce such a product or service from start to finish.* Such mapping typically focuses on the flow of materials and information, thereby helping managers see and understand the entire process as goods or services flow through the value stream. It involves a single product stream that is analyzed for waste, reduction in cycle time, and/or improvement in quality. Some of the activities in the value stream add value from the point of view of the customer; others add no value but are necessary to the process; still others add no value and can be removed. Value-stream mapping is looking for these latter activities in particular. It is normally used to gain a more comprehensive view by displaying a wide range of information at a high level. It is often used to identify where to focus future projects, subprojects, and Kaizen Events.[11]

Kaizen Event The word *Kaizen* in Japanese means "change for the better." From a broad point of view, a **Kaizen Event** is *an action taken in manufacturing or business in which the intended goal is to improve an existing process.* Specifically, a Kaizen Event is a three- to five-day effort by a company using a cross-functional team of between 6 and 18 people to detect problems and waste. In these events, managers, process owners, operators, and quality leaders work together with Kaizen team members, who can come from such areas as engineering, marketing, maintenance, production, quality, and accounting. While it is important that the project stay within the scope of the participants, it is likewise important that the Kaizen team solicit input and buy-in from other affected parties. If the Kaizen is for a specific department, more team members are selected from that department. Usually, one Kaizen Event activity includes the mapping of the targeted process. Some possible outcomes of a Kaizen Event could be improved workflow, increased quality, a safer work environment, a reduction in non–value-added activities, saved floor space, and others.[12]

Quality and Business Analytics How do business analytics impact the quality movement? To some extent, we are still discovering the answers to this question. The overarching goal of business analytics is to help business people improve their decision-making

---

[11] Adapted from "Value-Stream Mapping," on the iSixSigma website, www.isixsigma.com/dictionary/value-stream-mapping/; Mike Rother and John Shook, *Learning to See: Value-Stream Mapping to Add Value and Eliminate Muda* (Brookline, MA: The Lean Enterprise Institute, 1999); Bill Wortman, et al., *The Certified Six Sigma Black Belt Primer* (Quality Council of Indiana, 2001), www.qualitycouncil1.com.

[12] Adapted from: "Kaizen Event," on the iSixSigma website, www.isixsigma.com/dictionary/kaizen-event/; Bill Wortman, et al., *The Certified Six Sigma Black Belt Primer* (Quality Council of Indiana, 2001), www.qualitycouncil1.com.

with insights gained from the analysis of usable valid data. This goal bears some similarity to the aims and objectives set out by the various quality approaches to business processes. For example, quality improvement investigators often search for root causes of quality issues. In doing so, they "dig down" into a problem or quality issue by examining available data at a deeper level and by searching for new sources of related data that might be pertinent. In this era of big data, there are more data sources available, sooner, in a variety of forms that might be used in deep root-cause analysis to improve quality. Specifically, in Six Sigma, the second phase of the DMAIC process is Measure. With the proliferation of data and data sources, there is potential for a more successful result at this phase of the improvement effort. The third step in the DMAIC process is Analyze, which is a major part of the business analytics movement.

In the age of business analytics, the speed and availability of big data will allow companies to expedite processes—for example, by eliminating paperwork—thereby reducing time and effort by both customers and employees. In the quality world, this is an application of Lean or Lean Six Sigma. Nevertheless, the quality movement may need to broaden its scope beyond improving processes to include company-wide and cross-organizational undertakings. Lastly, as a caution, quality analysts still have to be concerned about data quality, perhaps more than ever given the variety and abundance of available data.

Concept Check

1. What is the difference between manufacturing-based quality and value quality?
2. What are the two different ways in which quality control can be undertaken?
3. What is meant by "productivity"?
4. What do the following terms mean: Six Sigma, lean manufacturing, benchmarking, JIT, reengineering, poka-yoke, value-stream mapping, and Kaizen Event?

18.2 Process Analysis

LEARNING OBJECTIVE 18.2

Compare various tools that identify, categorize, and solve problems in the quality improvement process, including flowcharts, Pareto analysis, cause-and-effect diagrams, control charts, check sheets, histograms, and scatter charts.

Much of what happens in the business world involves processes. A **process** is *a series of actions, changes, or functions that bring about a result.* Processes usually involve the manufacturing, production, assembling, or development of some output from a given input. Generally, in a meaningful system, value is added to the input as part of the process. In the area of production, processes are often the main focus of decision-makers. Production processes abound in the chemical, steel, automotive, appliance, computer, furniture, and clothing manufacture industries, as well as many others. Production layouts vary, but it is not difficult to picture an assembly line with its raw materials, parts, and supplies being processed into a finished product that becomes worth more than the sum of the parts and materials that went into it. However, processes are not limited to the area of production. Virtually all other areas of business involve processes. The processing of a credit card from the moment it is used for a purchase, through the financial institution, and back to the user is one example. The hiring of new employees by a human resources department involves a process that might begin with a job description and end with the training of a new employee. Many different processes occur within health-care facilities. One process involves the flow of a patient from check-in at a hospital through an operation to recovery and release.

Meanwhile, the dietary and foods department prepares food and delivers it to various points in the hospital as part of another process.

Many tools have been developed over the years to assist managers and workers in identifying, categorizing, and solving problems in the continuous quality improvement process. Among these are the seven basic tools of quality developed by Kaoru Ishikawa in the 1960s. Ishikawa believed that 95% of all quality-related problems could be solved using these basic tools, which are sometimes referred to as the "seven old tools."[13] The seven basic tools are as follows:

1. Flowchart or process map
2. Pareto chart
3. Cause-and-effect diagram (Ishikawa or fishbone chart)
4. Control chart
5. Check sheet or checklist
6. Histogram
7. Scatter chart or scatter diagram

Flowcharts

One of the first activities that should take place in process analysis is the flowcharting of the process from beginning to end. A **flowchart** is *a schematic representation of all the activities and interactions that occur in a process.* It includes decision points, activities, input/output, start/stop, and a flow line. **Figure 18.1** displays some of the symbols used in flowcharting.

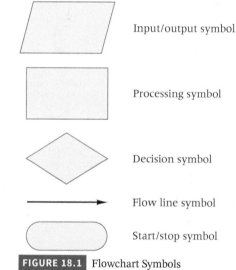

Input/output symbol

Processing symbol

Decision symbol

Flow line symbol

Start/stop symbol

FIGURE 18.1   Flowchart Symbols

The parallelogram represents input into the process or output from the process. In the case of the dietary/foods department at a hospital, the input includes uncooked food, utensils, plates, containers, and liquids. The output is the prepared meal delivered to the patient's room. The processing symbol is a rectangle that represents an activity. For the dietary/foods department, that activity could include cooking carrots or loading food carts. The decision symbol, a diamond, is used at points in the process where decisions are made that can result in different pathways. In some hospitals, the dietary/foods department supports a hospital cafeteria as well as patient meals. At some point in the process, the decision must be made as to whether the food is destined for a patient room or the cafeteria. The cafeteria food may follow a general menu, whereas patient food may have to be individualized for particular health conditions. The arrow is the flow line symbol designating to the flowchart user the sequence of activities of the process. The flow line in the hospital food example would follow the pathway of the food from raw ingredients (vegetables, meat, flour, etc.) to the delivered product in patient rooms or in the cafeteria. The elongated oval represents the starting and stopping points in the process.

Particularly in nonmanufacturing settings, it is common that no one maps out the complete flow of sequential stages of various processes in a business. For example, one NASA subcontractor was responsible for processing the paperwork for change items on space projects. Change requests would begin at NASA and be sent to the subcontractor's building. The requests would be processed there and returned to NASA in about 14 days. Exactly what happened to the paperwork during the two-week period? As part of a quality effort, NASA asked the contractor to study the process. No one had taken a hard look at where the paperwork went, how long it sat on various people's desks, and how many different people handled it. The contractor soon became involved in process analysis.

As an example, suppose we want to flowchart the process of obtaining a home improvement loan of $20,000 from a bank. The process begins with the customer entering the bank.

[13] Nancy R. Tague, *The Quality Toolbox*, 2nd ed. (Milwaukee, IL: ASQ Press, 2004), 15.

The flow takes the customer to a service representative, who poses a decision dilemma. For what purpose has the customer come to the bank? Is it to get information, to cash a cheque, to deposit money, to buy a money order, to get a loan, or to invest money? Because we are charting the loan process, we follow the flow line to the loan department. The customer arrives in the loan department and is met by another service representative, who asks what type and size of loan the person needs. For small personal loans, the customer is given a form to submit for loan consideration with no need to see a loan officer. For larger loans, such as the home improvement loan, the customer is given a form to fill out and is assigned to see a loan officer. Small personal loans are evaluated and the customer is given a response immediately. If the answer is yes, word of the decision is conveyed to a teller, who issues a cheque for the customer. For larger loans, the customer is interviewed by a loan officer, who then makes a decision. If the answer is yes, a contract is drawn up and signed. The customer is then sent to a teller, who has the cheque for the loan. **Figure 18.2** provides a possible flowchart for this scenario.

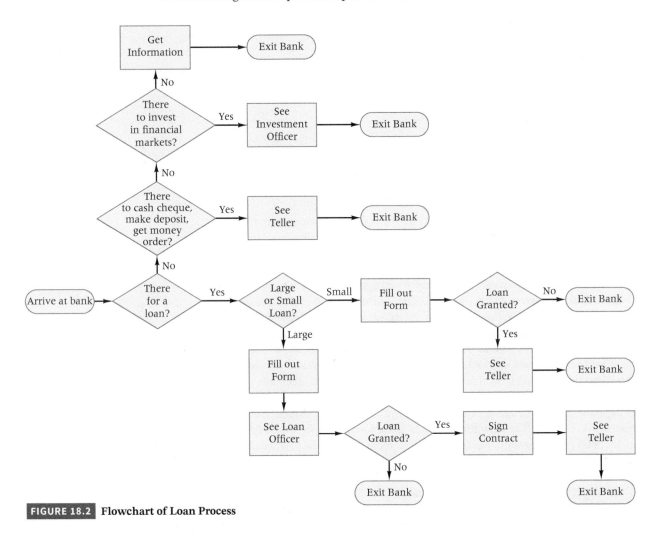

FIGURE 18.2 Flowchart of Loan Process

Pareto Analysis

Once the process has been mapped by such techniques as the flowchart, procedures for identifying bottlenecks and problem causes can begin. One technique for displaying problem causes is Pareto analysis. **Pareto analysis** is *a quantitative tallying of the number and types of defects that occur with a product or service.* Analysts use this tally to produce *a vertical bar chart that displays the most common types of defects, ranked in order of occurrence from left to right.* The bar chart is called a **Pareto chart**. Pareto charts are presented and explained in greater detail in Section 2.3 of Chapter 2. **Figure 18.3** contains a Minitab Pareto chart depicting various potential sources of medication error in a hospital. **Figure 18.4** redisplays Figure 2.9, which depicts the possible causes of electric motor problems.

Control charts are easy to use and understand. Often it is the line workers who record and plot product measurements on the charts. In more automated settings, sensors record chart values and send them to an information system, which compiles the charts. Control charts are used mainly to monitor product variation. The charts enable operators, technicians, and managers to see when a process gets out of control, which in turn improves quality and increases productivity.

Variation

If no variations occurred between manufactured items, control charts would be pointless. However, variation occurs for virtually any product or service. Variation can occur among units within a lot and can occur between lots. Among the reasons for product variation are differences in raw materials, differences in workers, differences in machines, changes in the environment, and wear and tear on machinery. Small variations can be caused by unnoticeable events, such as a passing truck that creates vibrations or dust that affects machine operation. Variations need to be measured, recorded, and studied so that out-of-control conditions can be identified and corrections can be made in the process.

Types of Control Charts

The two general types of control charts are (1) control charts for measurements and (2) control charts for attribute compliance. In this section, we discuss two types of control charts for measurements, $\bar{x}$ charts and R charts. We also discuss two types of control charts for attribute compliance, p charts and c charts.

Each control chart has a **centreline**, an **upper control limit (UCL)**, and a **lower control limit (LCL)**. Data are recorded on the control chart, and the chart is examined for disturbing patterns or for data points that indicate that a process is out of control. Once a process is determined to be out of control, measures can be taken to correct the problem causing the deviation.

$\bar{x}$ Charts   An $\bar{x}$ chart is *a graph of sample means computed for a series of small random samples over a period of time.* The means are average measurements of some product characteristic. For example, the measurement could be the volume of fluid in a litre container of rubbing alcohol, the thickness of a piece of sheet metal, or the size of a hole in a plastic part. These sample means are plotted on a graph that contains a centreline, the UCL, and the LCL.

$\bar{x}$ charts can be made from standards or without standards.[17] Companies sometimes have smoothed their process to the point where they have standard centrelines and control limits for a product. These standards are usually used when a company is producing products that have been made for some time and in situations where managers have little interest in monitoring the overall measure of location for the product. In this text, we will study only situations in which no standard is given. It is fairly common to compute $\bar{x}$ charts without existing standards—especially if a company is producing a new product, is closely monitoring proposed standards, or expects a change in the process. Many firms want to monitor the standards, so they recompute the standards for each chart. In the no-standards situation, the standards (such as mean and standard deviation) are estimated by using the sample data.

The centreline for an $\bar{x}$ chart is the average of the sample means, $\bar{\bar{x}}$. The $\bar{x}$ chart has a UCL that is three standard deviations of means above the centreline ($+3\sigma_{\bar{x}}$). The lower boundary of the $\bar{x}$ chart, or the LCL, is three standard deviations of means below the centreline ($-3\sigma_{\bar{x}}$). Recall the empirical rule presented in Chapter 3 stating that, if data are normally distributed, approximately 99.7% of all values will be within three standard deviations of the mean. Because the shape of the sampling distribution of $\bar{x}$ is normal for large sample sizes regardless of the population shape, the empirical rule applies. However, because small samples are often used, an approximation of the three standard deviations of means is used to determine the UCL and the LCL. This approximation can be made using either sample ranges or sample standard deviations. For small sample sizes ($n \leq 15$ is acceptable, but $n \leq 10$ is preferred), a weighted value of the average range is a good approximation of the three-standard-deviation distance to the UCL and the LCL. The range is easy to compute (difference of extreme values) and is

---

[17] Feigenbaum, *Total Quality Control.*

particularly useful when a wide array of nontechnical workers are involved in control chart computations. When sample sizes are larger, a weighted average of the sample standard deviations ($\bar{s}$) is a good estimate of the three standard deviations of means. The drawback of using the sample standard deviation is that it must always be computed, whereas the sample range can often be determined at a glance. Most control charts are constructed with small sample sizes; therefore, the range is more widely used in constructing control charts.

Table A.15 contains the weights applied to the average sample range or the average sample standard deviation to compute the UCL and the LCL. The value of A_2 is used for ranges and the value of A_3 is used for standard deviations. The following steps are used to produce an $\bar{x}$ chart.

1. Decide on the quality to be measured.
2. Determine a sample size, n.
3. Gather 20 to 30 samples.
4. Compute the sample average, $\bar{x}$, for each sample.
5. Compute the sample range, R, for each sample.
6. Determine the average sample mean for all samples, $\bar{\bar{x}}$, as:

$\bar{x}$ Chart Centreline

$$\bar{\bar{x}} = \frac{\Sigma \bar{x}}{k} \tag{18.1}$$

where k is the number of samples.

---

7. Determine the average sample range for all samples, $\bar{R}$, as:

$$\bar{R} = \frac{\Sigma R}{k}$$

or determine the average sample standard deviation for all samples, $\bar{s}$, as:

$$\bar{s} = \frac{\Sigma s}{k}$$

8. Using the size of the samples, n, determine the value of A_2 if using the range and A_3 if using standard deviations.
9. Construct the centreline, the UCL, and the LCL. For ranges:

$\bar{x}$ Chart Control Limits for Ranges

$$\text{Centerline} = \bar{\bar{x}}$$
$$\text{UCL} = \bar{\bar{x}} + A_2 \bar{R} \tag{18.2}$$
$$\text{LCL} = \bar{\bar{x}} - A_2 \bar{R}$$

For standard deviations:

$\bar{x}$ Chart Control Limits for Standard Deviations

$$\text{Centerline} = \bar{\bar{x}}$$
$$\text{UCL} = \bar{\bar{x}} + A_3 \bar{s} \tag{18.3}$$
$$\text{LCL} = \bar{\bar{x}} - A_3 \bar{s}$$

DEMONSTRATION PROBLEM 18.1

A manufacturing facility produces bearings. The diameter specified for the bearings is 5 mm. Every 10 minutes, six bearings are sampled and their diameters are measured and recorded. Twenty of these samples of six bearings are gathered. Use the resulting data and construct an $\bar{x}$ chart.

Sample 1	Sample 2	Sample 3	Sample 4	Sample 5
5.13	4.96	5.21	5.02	5.12
4.92	4.98	4.87	5.09	5.08
5.01	4.95	5.02	4.99	5.09
4.88	4.96	5.08	5.02	5.13
5.05	5.01	5.12	5.03	5.06
4.97	4.89	5.04	5.01	5.13

Sample 6	Sample 7	Sample 8	Sample 9	Sample 10
4.98	4.99	4.96	4.96	5.03
5.02	5.00	5.01	5.00	4.99
4.97	5.00	5.02	4.91	4.96
4.99	5.02	5.05	4.87	5.14
4.98	5.01	5.04	4.96	5.11
4.99	5.01	5.02	5.01	5.04

Sample 11	Sample 12	Sample 13	Sample 14	Sample 15
4.91	4.97	5.09	4.96	4.99
4.93	4.91	4.96	4.99	4.97
5.04	5.02	5.05	4.82	5.01
5.00	4.93	5.12	5.03	4.98
4.90	4.95	5.06	5.00	4.96
4.82	4.96	5.01	4.96	5.02

Sample 16	Sample 17	Sample 18	Sample 19	Sample 20
5.01	5.05	4.96	4.90	5.04
5.04	4.97	4.93	4.85	5.03
5.09	5.04	4.97	5.02	4.97
5.07	5.03	5.01	5.01	4.99
5.12	5.09	4.98	4.88	5.05
5.13	5.01	4.92	4.86	5.06

Solution   Compute the value of $\bar{x}$ for each sample and average these values, obtaining $\bar{\bar{x}}$.

$$\bar{\bar{x}} = \frac{\bar{x}_1 + \bar{x}_2 + \bar{x}_3 + \cdots + \bar{x}_{20}}{20}$$

$$= \frac{4.9933 + 4.9583 + 5.0566 + \cdots + 5.0233}{20}$$

$$= \frac{100.043}{20} = 5.002150 \text{ (the centreline)}$$

Compute the values of R and average them, obtaining $\bar{R}$:

$$\bar{R} = \frac{R_1 + R_2 + R_3 + \cdots + R_{20}}{20}$$

$$= \frac{0.25 + 0.12 + 0.34 + \cdots + 0.09}{20}$$

$$= \frac{2.72}{20} = 0.136$$

Determine the value of A_2 by using $n = 6$ (size of the sample) from Table A.15, giving $A_2 = 0.483$.

The UCL is:

$$\bar{\bar{x}} + A_2\bar{R} = 5.00215 + (0.483)(0.136) = 5.00215 + 0.06569 = 5.06784$$

The LCL is:

$$\bar{\bar{x}} - A_2\bar{R} = 5.00215 - (0.483)(0.136) = 5.00215 - 0.06569 = 4.93646$$

Using the standard deviation instead of the range, we have:

$$\bar{s} = \frac{\bar{s}_1 + \bar{s}_2 + \bar{s}_3 + \cdots + \bar{s}_{20}}{20}$$

$$= \frac{0.0905 + 0.0397 + 0.1136 + \cdots + 0.0356}{20}$$

$$= 0.0494$$

Next, determine the value of A_3 by using $n = 6$ (sample size) from Table A.15:

$$A_3 = 1.287$$

The UCL is:

$$\bar{\bar{x}} + A_3\bar{s} = 5.00215 + (1.287)(0.0494) = 5.00215 + 0.06358 = 5.06573$$

The LCL is:

$$\bar{\bar{x}} - A_3\bar{s} = 5.00215 - (1.287)(0.0494) = 5.00215 - 0.06358 = 4.93857$$

The following graph depicts the $\bar{x}$ control chart using the range (rather than the standard deviation) as the measure of dispersion to compute the LCL and the UCL. Observe that if the standard deviation is used instead of the range to compute the LCL and the UCL, because of the precision (or lack thereof) of this chart, there is little, if any, perceptible difference in the LCL and the UCL by the two methods.

Note that the sample means for samples 5 and 16 are above the UCL and the sample means for samples 11 and 19 are below the LCL. This result indicates that these four samples are out of control and alerts the production supervisor or worker to initiate further investigation of bearings produced during these periods. All other samples are within the control limits.

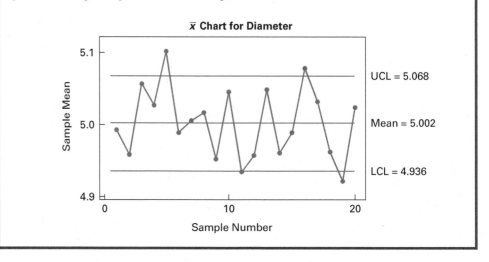

$\bar{x}$ Chart for Diameter

R **Charts** An *R* chart is *a plot of the sample ranges* and is often used in conjunction with an $\bar{x}$ chart. Whereas $\bar{x}$ charts are used to plot the location values, $\bar{x}$, for each sample, *R* charts are used to plot the variation of each sample as measured by the sample range. The centre-line of an *R* chart is the average range, $\bar{R}$. LCLs are determined by $D_3\bar{R}$, where D_3 is a weight applied to $\bar{R}$ reflecting sample size. The value of D_3 can be obtained from Table A.15. UCLs are determined by $D_4\bar{R}$, where D_4 is a value obtained from Table A.15, which also reflects sample size. The following steps lead to an *R* chart.

1. Decide on the quality to be measured.
2. Determine a sample size, n.
3. Gather 20 to 30 samples.
4. Compute the sample range, R, for each sample.

5. Determine the average sample range for all samples, $\bar{R}$, as:

$\bar{R}$ **Chart Centreline**

$$\bar{R} = \frac{\Sigma R}{k} \qquad\qquad (18.4)$$

where k is the number of samples.

---

6. Using the size of the samples, n, find the values of D_3 and D_4 in Table A.15.

7. Construct the centreline and control limits:

$\bar{R}$ **Chart Control Limits**

$$\text{Centreline} = \bar{R}$$
$$\text{UCL} = D_4\bar{R} \qquad\qquad (18.5)$$
$$\text{LCL} = D_3\bar{R}$$

DEMONSTRATION PROBLEM 18.2

Construct an R chart for the 20 samples of data in Demonstration Problem 18.1 on bearings.

Solution   Compute the sample ranges shown.

Sample	Range
1	0.25
2	0.12
3	0.34
4	0.10
5	0.07
6	0.05
7	0.03
8	0.09
9	0.14
10	0.18
11	0.22
12	0.11
13	0.16
14	0.21
15	0.06
16	0.12
17	0.12
18	0.09
19	0.17
20	0.09

Compute $\bar{R}$:

$$\bar{R} = \frac{0.25 + 0.12 + 0.34 + \cdots + 0.09}{20} = \frac{2.72}{20} = 0.136$$

For $n = 6$, $D_3 = 0$, and $D_4 = 2.004$ (from Table A.15):

$$\text{Centreline } \bar{R} = 0.136$$

$$\text{LCL} = D_3\bar{R} = (0)(0.136) = 0$$

$$\text{UCL} = D_4\bar{R} = (2.004)(0.136) = 0.2725$$

The resulting R chart for these data is shown next. Note that the range for sample 3 is out of control (beyond the UCL). The range of values in sample 3 appears to be unacceptable. Further investigation of the population from which this sample was drawn is warranted.

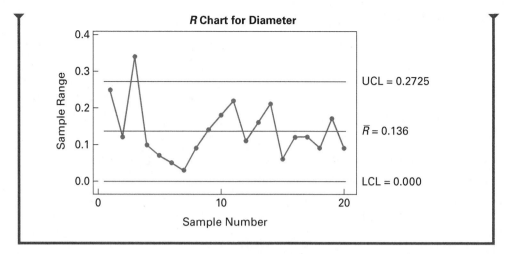

R Chart for Diameter

UCL = 0.2725

$\bar{R}$ = 0.136

LCL = 0.000

(Sample Range on y-axis, Sample Number on x-axis)

p Charts When product attributes are measurable, $\bar{x}$ charts and R charts can be formulated from the data. Sometimes, however, product inspection yields no measurement—only a yes-or-no type of conclusion based on whether the item complies with the specifications. For this type of data, no measure is available from which to average or determine the range. However, attribute compliance can be depicted graphically by a p chart. A **p chart** *graphs the proportion of sample items in noncompliance for multiple samples.*

For example, suppose a company producing electric motors samples 40 motors three times a week for a month. For each group of 40 motors, it determines the proportion of the sample group that does not comply with the specifications. It then plots these sample proportions, $\hat{p}$, on a p chart to identify trends or samples with unacceptably high proportions of nonconformance. Other p chart applications include determining whether a can of paint has been manufactured with acceptable texture, a pane of glass contains cracks, or a tire has a defective tread.

Like the $\bar{x}$ chart and the R chart, a p chart contains a centreline. The centreline is the average of the sample proportions. The UCL and the LCL are computed from the average of the sample proportions plus or minus three standard deviations of proportions. The following are the steps for constructing a p chart.

1. Decide on the quality to be measured.

2. Determine a sample size, n.

3. Gather 20 to 30 samples.

4. Compute the sample proportion:

$$\hat{p} = \frac{n_{\text{non}}}{n}$$

where
   n_{non} = the number of items in the sample in noncompliance
   n = the number of items in the sample

5. Compute the average proportion:

---

p Chart Centreline

$$\bar{p} = \frac{\Sigma\hat{p}}{k} \qquad (18.6)$$

where
   $\hat{p}$ = the sample proportion
   k = the number of samples

---

6. Determine the centreline, the UCL, and the LCL, when $\bar{q} = 1 - \bar{p}$:

---

p Chart Control Limits

$$\text{Centreline} = \bar{p}$$

$$\text{UCL} = \bar{p} + 3\sqrt{\frac{\bar{p}\cdot\bar{q}}{n}} \qquad (18.7)$$

$$\text{LCL} = \bar{p} - 3\sqrt{\frac{\bar{p}\cdot\bar{q}}{n}}$$

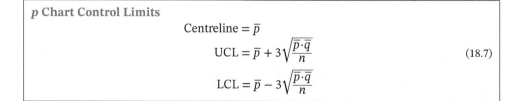

---

6. Determine the centreline, the UCL, and the LCL:

---

c **Chart Control Limits**

$$\text{Centreline} = \bar{c}$$
$$\text{UCL} = \bar{c} + 3\sqrt{\bar{c}}$$
$$\text{LCL} = \bar{c} - 3\sqrt{\bar{c}}$$

(18.9)

DEMONSTRATION PROBLEM 18.4

A manufacturer produces gauges to measure oil pressure. As part of the company's statistical process control, 25 gauges are randomly selected and tested for nonconformances. The results are shown here. Use these data to construct a *c* chart that displays the nonconformances per item.

Item Number	Number of Nonconformances	Item Number	Number of Nonconformances
1	2	14	2
2	0	15	1
3	3	16	4
4	1	17	0
5	2	18	2
6	5	19	3
7	3	20	2
8	2	21	1
9	0	22	3
10	0	23	2
11	4	24	0
12	3	25	3
13	2		

Solution   Determine the centreline, the UCL, and the LCL:

$$\text{Centreline} = \bar{c} = \frac{2 + 0 + 3 + \cdots + 3}{25} = \frac{50}{25} = 2.0$$

$$\text{UCL} = \bar{c} = 3\sqrt{\bar{c}} = 2.0 + 3\sqrt{2.0} = 2.0 + 4.2 = 6.243$$

$$\text{LCL} = \bar{c} - 3\sqrt{\bar{c}} = 2.0 - 3\sqrt{2.0} = 2.0 - 4.2 = -2.243$$

The LCL cannot be less than zero; thus, the LCL is 0. The graph of the control chart is shown next. Note that none of the points are beyond the control limits and that there is a healthy deviation of points both above and below the centreline. This chart indicates a process that is relatively in control, with an average of two nonconformances per item.

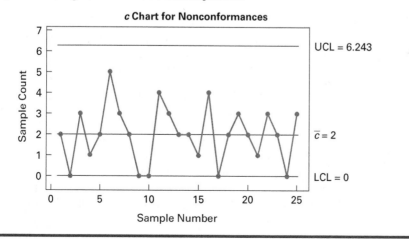

c **Chart for Nonconformances**

Interpreting Control Charts

How can control charts be used to monitor processes? When is a process out of control? An evaluation of the points plotted on a control chart examines several things. Obviously, one concern is points that are outside the control limits. Control chart outer limits (UCL and LCL) are established at three standard deviations above and below the centreline. The empirical rule discussed in Chapter 3 and the z table value for $z = 3$ indicate that approximately 99.7% of all values should be within three standard deviations of the mean of the statistic. Applying this rule to control charts suggests that fewer than 0.3% of all points should be beyond the UCL and the LCL by chance. Thus, one of the more elementary items a control chart observer looks for is points outside the LCL and the UCL. If the system is in control, virtually no data points should be outside these limits. Workers responsible for process control should investigate samples in which sample members are outside the LCL and the UCL. In the case of the c chart, items that are above the UCL line contain an inordinate number of nonconformances in relation to the average. The occurrence of points beyond the control limits calls for further investigation.

Several other criteria can be used to determine whether a control chart is plotting a process that is out of control. In general, there *should* be random fluctuation above and below the centreline within the UCL and the LCL. However, a process can be out of control if too many consecutive points are above or below the centreline. Eight or more consecutive points on one side of the centreline are considered too many. In addition, if 10 of 11 or 12 of 14 points are on the same side of the centre, the process may be out of control.[18]

Another criterion for process control operators to look for is trends in the control charts. At any point in the process, is a trend emerging in the data? As a guideline, if six or more points are increasing or decreasing, the process may be out of control.[19] Such a trend can indicate that points will eventually deviate increasingly from the centreline (the gap between the centreline and the points will increase).

Another concern with control charts is an overabundance of points in the outer one-third of the region between the centreline and the outer limits (LCL and UCL). By a rationalization similar to that imposed on the LCL and the UCL, the empirical rule and the table of z values show that approximately 95% of all points should be within two standard deviations of the centreline. With this in mind, fewer than 5% of the points should be in the outer one-third of the region between the centreline and the outer control limits (because 95% should be within two-thirds of the region). A rule to follow is that if two out of three consecutive points are in the outer one-third of the chart, a control problem may be present. Likewise, because approximately 68% of all values should be within one standard deviation of the mean (empirical rule, z table for $z = 1$), only 32% should be in the outer two-thirds of the control chart above and below the centreline. As a rule, if four out of five successive points are in the outer two-thirds of the control chart, the process should be investigated.[20]

Another consideration in evaluating control charts is the location of the centreline. With each successive batch of samples, it is important to observe whether the centreline is shifting away from specifications.

The following list provides a summary of the control chart abnormalities that should be of concern to a statistical process controller.

1. Points are above the UCL and/or below the LCL.

2. Eight or more consecutive points are above or below the centreline. Ten out of 11 points are above or below the centreline. Twelve out of 14 points are above or below the centreline.

3. A trend of six or more consecutive points (increasing or decreasing) is present.

4. Two out of three consecutive values are in the outer one-third.

5. Four out of five consecutive values are in the outer two-thirds.

6. The centreline shifts from chart to chart.

[18] James R. Evans and William M. Lindsay, *The Management and Control of Quality*, 4th ed. (Cincinnati, OH: South-Western College Publishing, 1999).

[19] Richard E. DeVor, Tsong-how Chang, and John W. Sutherland, *Statistical Quality Design and Control* (New York: Macmillan, 1992).

[20] Ibid.

Figure 18.7 contains several control charts, each of which has one of these types of problems. The chart in (a) contains points above and below the outer control limits. The one in (b) has eight consecutive points on one side of the centreline. The chart in (c) has seven consecutive increasing points. In (d), at least two out of three consecutive points are in the outer one-third of the control chart. In (e), at least four out of five consecutive points are in the outer two-thirds of the chart.

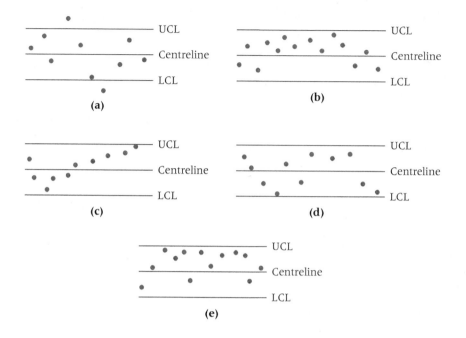

FIGURE 18.7 **Control Charts with Problems**

In investigating control chart abnormalities, several possible causes may be found. Some of them are listed here.[21]

1. Changes in the physical environment
2. Worker fatigue
3. Worn tools
4. Changes in operators or machines
5. Maintenance
6. Changes in worker skills
7. Changes in materials
8. Process modification

The statistical process control person should be aware that control chart abnormalities can also arise because of measurement errors or incorrect calculation of control limits. Judgement should be exercised so as not to overcontrol the process by readjusting to every oddity on a control chart.

Concept Check

1. What are control charts?
2. What is the difference between $\bar{x}$ charts, R charts, p charts, and c charts?

---

[21] Eugene L. Grant and Richard S. Leavenworth, *Statistical Quality Control*, 5th ed. (New York: McGraw-Hill, 1980).

18.3 Problems

18.4 A food-processing company makes potato chips, pretzels, and cheese chips. Although its products are packaged and sold by mass, the company has been taking sample bags of cheese chips and counting the number of chips in each bag. Shown here is the number of chips per bag for five samples of seven bags of chips. Use these data to construct an $\bar{x}$ chart and an R chart. Discuss the results.

Sample 1	Sample 2	Sample 3	Sample 4	Sample 5
25	22	30	32	25
23	21	23	26	23
29	24	22	27	29
31	25	26	28	27
26	23	28	25	27
28	26	27	25	26
27	29	21	31	24

18.5 A toy-manufacturing company has been given a large order for small plastic whistles that will be given away by a large fast-food hamburger chain with its kids' meal. Seven random samples of four whistles have been taken. The mass of each whistle has been ascertained in grams. The data are shown here. Use these data to construct an $\bar{x}$ chart and an R chart. What managerial decisions should be made on the basis of these findings?

Sample 1	Sample 2	Sample 3	Sample 4	Sample 5	Sample 6	Sample 7
4.1	3.6	4.0	4.6	3.9	5.1	4.6
5.2	4.3	4.8	4.8	3.8	4.7	4.4
3.9	3.9	5.1	4.7	4.6	4.8	4.0
5.0	4.6	5.3	4.7	4.9	4.3	4.5

18.6 A machine operator at a pencil-manufacturing facility gathered 10 different random samples of 100 pencils. The operator's inspection was to determine whether the pencils were in compliance or out of compliance with specifications. The results of this inspection are shown below. Use these data to construct a p chart. Comment on the results of this chart.

Sample	Size	Number out of Compliance
1	100	2
2	100	7
3	100	4
4	100	3
5	100	3
6	100	5
7	100	2
8	100	0
9	100	1
10	100	6

18.7 A large manufacturer makes valves. Currently it is producing a particular valve for use in industrial engines. As part of a quality control effort, the company engineers randomly sample seven groups of 40 valves and inspect them to determine whether they are in or out of compliance. Results are shown here. Use the information to construct a p chart. Comment on the chart.

Sample	Size	Number out of Compliance
1	40	1
2	40	0
3	40	1
4	40	3
5	40	2
6	40	5
7	40	2

18.8 A firm in Alberta manufactures light bulbs. Before the bulbs are released for shipment, a sample of bulbs is selected for inspection. Inspectors look for nonconformances such as scratches, weak or broken filaments, incorrectly bored turns, and insufficient outside contacts. A sample of 35 60-W bulbs has just been inspected, and the results are shown here. Use these data to construct a c chart. Discuss the findings.

Bulb Number	Number of Nonconformances	Bulb Number	Number of Nonconformances
1	0	19	2
2	1	20	0
3	0	21	0
4	0	22	1
5	3	23	0
6	0	24	0
7	1	25	0
8	0	26	2
9	0	27	0
10	0	28	0
11	2	29	1
12	0	30	0
13	0	31	0
14	2	32	0
15	0	33	0
16	1	34	3
17	3	35	0
18	0		

18.9 A soft drink bottling company just ran a long line of 355 mL soft drink cans filled with cola. A sample of 32 cans is selected by inspectors looking for nonconforming items. Among the things the inspectors look for are paint defects on the can, improper seal, incorrect volume, leaking contents, incorrect mixture of carbonation and syrup in the soft drink, and out-of-spec syrup mixture. The results of this inspection are given here. Construct a c chart from the data and comment on the results.

Can Number	Number of Nonconformances	Can Number	Number of Nonconformances
1	2	17	3
2	1	18	1
3	1	19	2
4	0	20	0
5	2	21	0
6	1	22	1
7	2	23	4
8	0	24	0
9	1	25	2
10	3	26	1
11	1	27	1
12	4	28	3
13	2	29	0
14	1	30	1
15	0	31	2
16	1	32	0

CHAPTER 19

Decision Analysis

LEARNING OBJECTIVES

This chapter describes how to use decision analysis to improve management decisions, thereby enabling you to:

19.1 Make decisions under certainty by constructing a decision table.

19.2 Make decisions under uncertainty using the maximax criterion, the maximin criterion, the Hurwicz criterion, and minimax regret.

19.3 Make decisions under risk by constructing decision trees, calculating expected monetary value and

expected value of perfect information, and analyzing utility.

19.4 Revise probabilities in light of sample information by using Bayesian analysis and calculating the expected value of sample information.

Decision Dilemma

Decision-Making at the CEO Level

CEOs face major challenges in today's business world. As the international marketplace evolves, competition often increases. Technology continues to improve products and process. The political and economic climates both internationally and domestically shift constantly. In the midst of such dynamics, CEOs make decisions about investments, products, resources, suppliers, financing, and so on. Decision-making may be the most important function of management. Successful companies are usually built around successful decisions. Even CEOs of successful companies feel the need to constantly improve the company's position.

In 2017, Ford Motor Company was the number one seller of cars, trucks, and SUVs in Canada, with 308,474 units sold. Its F-Series trucks were the most popular truck for the 52nd year in a row, and the best-selling vehicle overall for the eighth year. In the United States, Ford reported a profit of $7.6 billion for 2017, an increase of 65%. Yet in April 2018, Ford announced it was going to phase out all but two of its car models in North America and focus on trucks and SUVs.

Other CEOs have made tough decisions over the years. For example, in 2008, a Maple Leaf Foods plant in Toronto was confirmed as being involved in the outbreak of the food-borne illness caused by the bacterium *Listeria monocytogenes*. The CEO, Michael McCain, had to quickly decide how to handle the crisis and retain consumer confidence in Maple Leaf Foods products.

AP Images/John Raoux

In 2013, BlackBerry CEO Thorsten Heins decided not to launch the new operating system, BB10, on the PlayBook tablets, as he had previously promised, because the company's engineers couldn't get it to run smoothly on the device. "It was one of the toughest decisions I had to make because I knew I would break a commitment, but I also made a commitment to quality before that," Heins said.

CEOs of smaller companies also make tough decisions. The most critical decision-making period for a CEO is likely to be during growth phases. A study of 142 CEOs from small, private companies attempted to ascertain the types of decisions undertaken by top managers. Most of the companies in the study had experienced healthy growth in revenues over the four-year period preceding the study. CEOs in this study suggested that decisions made during growth phases are typically in the areas of expansion, personnel, finances, operations, and planning and control systems. According to respondents in the study, many of these decisions carry system-wide implications for the company, making the decisions critical.

CEOs responded that during a growth phase, decisions need to be made about how to handle new business. How is capacity to be expanded? Does the company build, lease, expand its present facility, relocate, automate, and so on? Risk is inevitably involved in undertaking most of these decisions. Will customer demand continue? Will competitors also increase capacity? How long will the increased demand continue? What is the lost opportunity if the company fails to meet customer demands?

According to the study, another critical area of decision-making is personnel. What is the long-term strategy of the company? Should significant layoffs be implemented in an effort to become "lean and mean"? Does the firm need to hire personnel? How does management discover and attract talented managers? How can substandard personnel be released? In the area of production, how does management align personnel with uneven product demand?

A third area of decision-making that the study participants considered important incorporated systems, business, and finance. How can the company make operations and procedures more efficient? How are cash flow problems handled? Under what conditions does the company obtain financial backing for capital development?

In the area of marketing, decisions need to be made about pricing, distribution, purchasing, and suppliers. Should the company market overseas? What about vertical integration? Should the company expand into new market segments or with new product lines?

The CEOs in the study enumerated decision choices that represent exciting and sometimes risky opportunities for growing firms. The success or failure of such decision-makers often lies in their ability to identify and choose optimal decision pathways for the company.

Managerial, Statistical, and Analytical Questions

1. In any given area of decision-making, what choices or options are available to the manager?

2. What occurrences in nature, the marketplace, or the business environment might affect the outcome or payoff for a given decision option?

3. What are some strategies that can be used to help decision-makers determine which option to choose?

4. If risk is involved, can probabilities of occurrence be assigned to various states of nature within each decision option?

5. What are the payoffs for various decision options?

6. Does the manager's propensity for risk enter into the final decision and, if so, how?

Sources: Derek McNaughton, "The 15 Top-Selling Vehicles in a Banner 2017 Sales Year For Canada," Driving website, January 10, 2018, driving.ca/ford/auto-news/news/313676; Alicja Siekierska, "Canadian Vehicle Sales Hit the Two Million Mark for First Time in 2017," *Financial Post*, January 3, 2018, business.financialpost.com/transportation/canadian-vehicle-sales-hit-the-two-million-mark-for-first-time-in-2017; Ian Thibodeau, "Ford Reports $7.6B Profit in 2017, up 65%," *Detroit News*, January 24, 2018, www.detroitnews.com/story/business/autos/ford/2018/01/24/ford-annual-earnings/109777880/; Matt Burns, "Ford to Stop Selling Every Car in North America But the Mustang and Focus Active," TechCrunch April 25, 2018, techcrunch.com/2018/04/25/ford-to-stop-selling-every-car-in-north-america-but-the-mustang-and-focus-active/; Tony Wilson, "The Best Legal Advice Is Often an Apology," *Globe and Mail*, February 1, 2011; Canadian Press, "Maple Leaf Recalls Meat Products after Outbreak," CTVNews.com, August 20, 2008; Simon Sage, "BlackBerry CEO on BB10 for PlayBook: 'It Was One of the Toughest Decisions I Had to Make'," Crackberry.com, July 10, 2013.

Introduction

The main focus of this text has been business decision-making. In this chapter, we discuss one last category of quantitative techniques for assisting managers in decision-making. These techniques, generally referred to as decision analysis, can be used in such diverse situations as determining whether and when to drill oil wells, deciding whether and how to expand capacity, deciding whether to automate a facility, and determining what types of investments to make.

In decision analysis, decision-making scenarios are divided into the following three categories:

1. Decision-making under certainty
2. Decision-making under uncertainty
3. Decision-making under risk

In this chapter, we discuss making decisions under each condition, as well as the concepts of utility and Bayesian statistics.

19.1   The Decision Table and Decision-Making Under Certainty

LEARNING OBJECTIVE 19.1

Make decisions under certainty by constructing a decision table.

Decision analysis is *particularly targeted at clarifying and enhancing the decision-making process.* Many decision analysis problems can be viewed as having three variables: decision alternatives, states of nature, and payoffs.

Decision alternatives are *the various choices or options available to the decision-maker in any given problem situation.* On most days, financial managers face the choices of whether to invest in blue chip stocks, bonds, commodities, guaranteed investment certificates (GICs), money markets, annuities, or other investments. Construction decision-makers must decide whether to concentrate on one building job today, spread out workers and equipment to several jobs, or not work today. In virtually every possible business scenario, decision alternatives are available. A good decision-maker identifies many options and effectively evaluates them.

States of nature are *the occurrences of nature that can happen after a decision is made, that can affect the outcome of the decision, and over which the decision-maker has little or no control.* These states of nature can literally be natural atmospheric and climatic conditions or they can be such things as the business climate, the political climate, the worker climate, or the condition of the marketplace, among many others. The financial investor faces such states of nature as the prime interest rate, the condition of the stock market, international monetary exchange rates, and so on. A construction company is faced with such states of nature as the weather, wildcat strikes, equipment failure, absenteeism, and supplier inability to deliver on time. States of nature are usually difficult to predict but are important to identify in the decision-making process.

The **payoffs** of a decision analysis problem are *the benefits or rewards that result from selecting a particular decision alternative.* Payoffs are usually given in terms of dollars. In the financial investment industry, for example, the payoffs can be small, modest, or large, or the investment can result in a loss. Most business decisions involve taking some chances with personal or company money in one form or another. Because for-profit businesses are looking for a return on the dollars invested, the payoffs are extremely important for a successful manager. The trick is to determine which decision alternative to choose in order to generate the greatest payoff. Suppose a CEO is examining various environmental decision alternatives. Positive payoffs could include increased market share, attracting and retaining quality employees, consumer appreciation, and governmental support. Negative payoffs might take the form of fines and penalties, lost market share, and lawsuit judgements.

Decision Table

The concepts of decision alternatives, states of nature, and payoffs can be examined jointly by using a **decision table**, or **payoff table**. **Table 19.1** shows the structure of a decision table. On the left side of the table are the various decision alternatives, denoted by d_i. Along the top row are the states of nature, denoted by s_j. In the middle of the table are the various payoffs for each decision alternative under each state of nature, denoted by $P_{i,j}$.

As an example of a decision table, consider the decision dilemma of the investor shown in **Table 19.2**. The investor is faced with the decision of where and how to invest $10,000 under several possible states of nature.

The investor is considering four decision alternatives:

1. Invest in the stock market
2. Invest in the bond market
3. Invest in GICs
4. Invest in a mixture of stocks and bonds

TABLE 19.1   Decision Table

		State of Nature				
		s_1	s_2	s_3	...	s_n
	d_1	$P_{1,1}$	$P_{1,2}$	$P_{1,3}$	...	$P_{1,n}$
	d_2	$P_{2,1}$	$P_{2,2}$	$P_{2,3}$	...	$P_{2,n}$
Decision Alternative	d_3	$P_{3,1}$	$P_{3,2}$	$P_{3,3}$	...	$P_{3,n}$
	.	.	.	.	.	.
	.	.	.	.	.	.
	.	.	.	.	.	.
	d_m	$P_{m,1}$	$P_{m,2}$	$P_{m,3}$	...	$P_{m,n}$

where
s_j = state of nature
d_i = decision alternative
$P_{i,j}$ = payoff for decision i under state j

TABLE 19.2   Yearly Payoffs on an Investment of $10,000

		State of the Economy		
		Stagnant	Slow Growth	Rapid Growth
Investment Decision Alternative	Stocks	−$500	$700	$2,200
	Bonds	−$100	$600	$900
	GICs	$300	$500	$750
	Mixture	−$200	$650	$1,300

Because the payoffs are in the future, the investor is unlikely to know ahead of time what the state of nature will be for the economy. However, the table delineates three possible states of the economy:

1. A stagnant economy
2. A slow-growth economy
3. A rapid-growth economy

The matrix in Table 19.2 lists the payoffs for each possible investment decision under each possible state of the economy. Notice that the largest payoff comes with a stock investment under a rapid-growth economic scenario, with a payoff of $2,200 per year on an investment of $10,000. The lowest payoff occurs for a stock investment during stagnant economic times, with an annual loss of $500 on the $10,000 investment.

Decision-Making Under Certainty

The most elementary of the decision-making scenarios is **decision-making under certainty**. In making decisions under certainty, *the states of nature are known*. The decision-maker needs merely to examine the payoffs under different decision alternatives and select the alternative with the largest payoff. In the preceding example involving the $10,000 investment, if it is known that the economy is going to be stagnant, the investor would select the decision alternative of GICs, yielding a payoff of $300. Indeed, each of the other three decision alternatives would result in a loss under stagnant economic conditions. If it is known that the economy is going to have slow growth, the investor would choose stocks as an investment, resulting in a $700 payoff. If the economy is certain to have rapid growth, the decision-maker should opt for stocks, resulting in a payoff of $2,200. Decision-making under certainty is almost the trivial case.

Concept Check

1. What is the meaning of the following terms: *decision alternatives, states of nature,* and *payoffs*?

19.2 | Decision-Making Under Uncertainty

LEARNING OBJECTIVE 19.2

Make decisions under uncertainty using the maximax criterion, the maximin criterion, the Hurwicz criterion, and minimax regret.

In making decisions under certainty, the decision-makers know for sure which state of nature will occur, and they base the decision on the optimal payoff available under that state. **Decision-making under uncertainty** occurs *when it is unknown which states of nature will occur and the probability of a state of nature occurring is also unknown.* Hence, decision-makers have virtually no information about which state of nature will occur, and they attempt to develop a strategy based on payoffs (see Thinking Critically About Statistics in Business Today 19.1).

Thinking Critically About Statistics in Business Today 19.1

The RadioShack Corporation Makes Decisions

In the 1960s, Charles Tandy founded and built a tight vertically integrated manufacturing and retailing company, the Tandy Corporation. RadioShack, a retail unit of the Tandy Corporation, has been one of the company's mainstays. However, RadioShack, along with the Tandy Corporation, has seen many changes over the years both because of decisions that management made and because of various states of nature that occurred.

In the early days, RadioShack was an outlet for Tandy products with a relatively narrow market niche. In the 1970s, the company made millions on the CB radio craze that hit the United States. In the early 1980s, RadioShack did well with an inexpensive personal computer. By the mid-1980s, the stores were becoming neglected, with much of the retailing profits being poured back into such unsuccessful manufacturing experiments as low-priced laptop computers and videodisc players.

In 1993, Tandy decided to sell its computer-making operations and re-emphasize retailing by bringing in a new president for RadioShack. The resulting series of decisions led to a significant positive turnaround for RadioShack. The company placed more emphasis on telephones and cut a deal with the Sprint Corporation to make Sprint its exclusive wireless provider. Sprint, in turn, provided millions of dollars to update RadioShack stores. In addition, RadioShack contracted to sell only Compaq computers and RCA audio and video equipment in its stores in exchange for these companies' investment in upgrading the retail outlet facilities. In 2000, RadioShack announced its alliance with Verizon Wireless, and the Tandy Corporation became the RadioShack Corporation.

Since then, RadioShack Corporation has sold its Incredible Universe stores and its Computer City superstores. These moves left RadioShack with its RadioShack stores as its main presence in the retail arena.

The fast-paced and ever-changing electronics industry presented many decision alternatives to RadioShack. In the early years, the corporation decided to sell mostly Tandy products in RadioShack stores. Then the corporation opened a variety of types and sizes of retail stores, only to sell most of them later. At one point, Tandy invested heavily in manufacturing new items at the expense of retail operations, and then it sold its computer manufacturing operations and renewed its focus on retail. At some point, many retail chains had the decision alternatives of (1) carrying only national brands (other company's brands), (2) carrying only private brands (their own labels), or (3) carrying a mix of the two.

Some of the states of nature that occurred include the rise and fall of CB radios, the exponential growth in personal computers and wireless telephones, the development of the Internet as a market and as an outlet for goods and services, a strong U.S. economy, and a growing atmosphere of disgust felt by large electronics manufacturers for electronics superstores and their deeply discounted merchandise.

The payoffs from some of these decisions for the RadioShack Corporation have been substantial. Some decisions resulted in revenue losses, thereby generating still other decisions. The decision selections, the states of nature, and the resulting payoffs can make the difference between a highly successful company and one that fails.

In 2004, Circuit City bought and rebranded RadioShack locations in Canada as The Source by Circuit City. In 2009, Bell Canada acquired these stores after Circuit City filed for Chapter 11 bankruptcy. Bell Canada rebranded Canadian stores as The Source.

In the United States, RadioShack filed for Chapter 11 bankruptcy in February 2015. After filing for bankruptcy a second time in 2017, RadioShack opened up around 100 RadioShack "Express" stores in partnership with HobbyTown USA in mid-2018. By late 2018, RadioShack dealers had reopened 500 or so stores.

Things to Ponder

1. List three to five states of nature that a national retail chain would face when deciding whether to carry national or private labels, or a mix of both.
2. Discuss how your level of optimism (or pessimism) will impact your decision-making strategy.

Sources: RadioShack corporate website, www.radioshackcorporation. com; "RadioShack Corporation and Verizon Wireless Announce Strategic Alliance," Verizon news release, August 1, 2000; Amy Doan, "RadioShack Redecorates," *Forbes*, May 31, 2000; "RadioShack Signs Off in Canada," *Ottawa Citizen*, December 8, 2006; Dalvin Brown, "RadioShack Maps a Comeback with 100 'Express' Locations," *USA Today*, July 2, 2018, www.usatoday.com/story/money/2018/07/26/ radioshack-plans-open-100-express-locations/843010002/; Clint Carter, "RadioShack Is Now Selling in Unexpected Places. Will Anyone Buy?" *Entrepreneur*, November 27, 2018, www.entrepreneur.com/ article/322966; Claire Brownell, "As RadioShack Flounders in the U.S. New Owners Bring Life to the Source," *Financial Post*, June 12, 2014, business.financialpost.com/news/retail-marketing/as-radioshack-flounders-in-the-u-s-new-owners-bring-life-to-the-source.

Several different approaches can be taken to making decisions under uncertainty. Each uses a different decision criterion, depending on the decision-maker's outlook. Each of these approaches will be explained and demonstrated with a decision table. Included are the maximax criterion, maximin criterion, Hurwicz criterion, and minimax regret.

In Section 19.1, we discussed the decision dilemma of the financial investor who wants to invest $10,000 and is faced with four decision alternatives and three states of nature. The data for this problem were given in Table 19.2. In decision-making under certainty, we selected the optimal payoff under each state of the economy and then, on the basis of which state we were certain would occur, selected a decision alternative. Shown next are techniques to use when we are uncertain which state of nature will occur.

Maximax Criterion

The **maximax criterion** approach is an optimistic approach in which the decision-maker bases action on a notion that the best things will happen. The decision-maker *isolates the maximum payoff under each decision alternative and then selects the decision alternative that produces the highest of these maximum payoffs*. The name "maximax" means selecting the maximum overall payoff from the maximum payoffs of each decision alternative. Consider the $10,000 investment problem. The maximum payoff is $2,200 for stocks, $900 for bonds, $750 for GICs, and $1,300 for the mixture of investments. The maximax criterion approach requires that the decision-maker select the maximum payoff of these four.

		State of the Economy			
		Stagnant	Slow Growth	Rapid Growth	**Maximum**
Investment	Stocks	−$500	$700	$2,200	$2,200
Decision	Bonds	−$100	$600	$900	$900
Alternative	GICs	$300	$500	$750	$750
	Mixture	−$200	$650	$1,300	$1,300

maximum of {$2,200, $900, $750, $1,300} = $2,200

Because the maximax criterion results in $2,200 as the optimal payoff, the decision alternative selected is the stock alternative, which is associated with the $2,200.

Maximin Criterion

The **maximin criterion** approach to decision-making is a pessimistic approach. *The assumption is that the worst will happen and attempts must be made to minimize the damage.* The decision-maker starts by examining the payoffs under each decision alternative and selects the worst, or minimum, payoff that can occur under that decision. Then, the decision-maker *selects the maximum or best payoff of those minimums selected under each decision alternative.* Thus, the decision-maker has maximized the minimums. In the investment problem, the minimum payoffs are −$500 for stocks, −$100 for bonds, $300 for GICs, and −$200 for the mixture of investments. With the maximin criterion, the decision-maker examines the minimum payoffs for each decision alternative given in the last column and selects the maximum of those values.

Applying the formula to the problem, we obtain the revised probabilities shown in the following tables. Suppose the forecaster predicts no growth (F_1). The prior probabilities of the states of the economy are revised as shown in Table 19.7.

TABLE 19.7   **Revision Based on a Forecast of No Growth (F_1)**

State of Economy	Prior Probabilities	Conditional Probabilities	Joint Probabilities	Revised Probabilities
No growth (s_1)	$P(s_1) = 0.65$	$P(F_1 \mid s_1) = 0.80$	$P(F_1 \cap s_1) = 0.520$	$0.520/0.625 = 0.832$
Rapid growth (s_2)	$P(s_2) = 0.35$	$P(F_1 \mid s_2) = 0.30$	$P(F_1 \cap s_2) = 0.105$	$0.105/0.625 = 0.168$
			$P(F_1) = 0.625$	

$P(F_1)$ is computed as follows:

$$P(F_1) = P(F_1 \cap s_1) + P(F_1 \cap s_2) = 0.520 + 0.105 = 0.625$$

The revised probabilities are computed as follows:

$$P(s_1 \mid F_1) = \frac{P(F_1 \cap s_1)}{P(F_1)} = \frac{0.520}{0.625} = 0.832$$

$$P(s_2 \mid F_1) = \frac{P(F_1 \cap s_2)}{P(F_1)} = \frac{0.105}{0.625} = 0.168$$

The prior probabilities of the states of the economy are revised as shown in Table 19.8 for the case in which the forecaster predicts rapid growth (F_2). These revised probabilities

TABLE 19.8   **Revision Based on a Forecast of Rapid Growth (F_2)**

State of Economy	Prior Probabilities	Conditional Probabilities	Joint Probabilities	Revised Probabilities
No growth (s_1)	$P(s_1) = 0.65$	$P(F_2 \mid s_1) = 0.20$	$P(F_2 \cap s_1) = 0.130$	$0.130/0.375 = 0.347$
Rapid growth (s_2)	$P(s_2) = 0.35$	$P(F_2 \mid s_2) = 0.70$	$P(F_2 \cap s_2) = 0.245$	$0.245/0.375 = 0.653$
			$P(F_2) = 0.375$	

can be entered into a decision tree that depicts the option of buying information and getting a forecast, as shown in Figure 19.6. Notice that the first node is a decision node to buy the forecast. The next node is a state-of-nature node, where the forecaster will predict either a no-growth economy or a rapid-growth economy. It is a state of nature because the decision-maker has no control over what the forecast will be. As a matter of fact, the decision-maker has probably paid for this independent forecast. Once a forecast is made, the decision-maker is faced with the decision alternatives of investing in bonds or investing in stocks. At the end of each investment alternative branch is a state of the economy of either no growth or rapid growth. The four revised probabilities calculated in Tables 19.7 and 19.8 are assigned to these states of economy. The payoffs remain the same. The probability of the forecaster predicting no growth comes from the sum of the joint probabilities in Table 19.7. This value of $P(F_1) = 0.625$ is assigned a position on the first set of states of nature (forecast). The probability of the forecaster predicting rapid growth comes from summing the joint probabilities in Table 19.8. This value of $P(F_2) = 0.375$ is also assigned a position on the first set of states of nature (forecasts). The decision-maker can make a choice from this decision tree after the EMVs are calculated. In Figure 19.6, the payoffs are the same as in the decision table without information. However, the probabilities of no-growth and rapid-growth states have been revised. Multiplying the payoffs by these revised probabilities and summing them for each investment produces EMVs at the state-of-economy nodes. Moving back to the

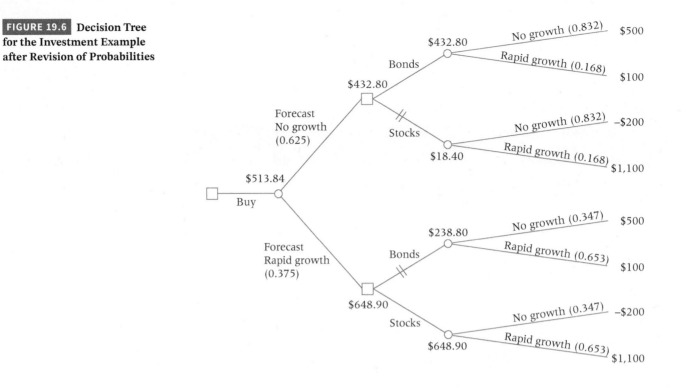

FIGURE 19.6 Decision Tree for the Investment Example after Revision of Probabilities

decision nodes preceding these values, the investor has the opportunity to invest in either bonds or stocks. The investor examines the EMVs and selects the investment with the highest value. For the decision limb in which the forecaster predicted no growth, the investor selects the bonds investment, which yields an EMV of $432.80 (as opposed to $18.40 from stocks). For the decision limb in which the forecaster predicted rapid growth, the investor selects the stocks investment, which yields an EMV of $648.90 (as opposed to $238.80 for bonds).

The investor is thus faced with the opportunity to earn an EMV of $432.80 if the forecaster predicts no growth or $648.90 if the forecaster predicts rapid growth. How often does the forecaster predict each of these states of the economy to happen? Using the sums of the joint probabilities from Tables 19.7 and 19.8, the decision-maker gets the probabilities of each of these forecasts:

$$P(F_1) = 0.625 \text{ (no growth)}$$
$$P(F_2) = 0.375 \text{ (rapid growth)}$$

Entering these probabilities into the decision tree at the first probability node with the forecasts of the states of the economy and multiplying them by the EMV of each state yields an overall EMV of the opportunity:

$$\text{EMV for Opportunity} = \$432.80(0.625) + \$648.90(0.375) = \$513.84$$

Expected Value of Sample Information

The preceding calculations for the investment example show that the EMV of the opportunity is $513.84 with sample information, but it is only $360 without sample information, as shown in Figure 19.5. Using the sample information appears to profit the decision-maker:

$$\text{Apparent Profit of Using Sample Information} = \$513.84 - \$360 = \$153.84$$

How much did this sample information cost? If the sample information is not free, less than $153.84 is gained by using it. How much is it worth to use sample information? Obviously, the decision-maker should not pay more than $153.84 for sample information because an expected $360 can be earned without the information. In general, the **expected value of sample information** is worth no more than *the difference between the EMV with the information and the EMV without the information.*

> **Expected Value of Sample Information**
>
> Expected Value of Sample Information = Expected Monetary Value with Information − Expected Monetary Value without Information

Suppose the decision-maker had to pay $100 for the forecaster's prediction. The EMV of the decision with information shown in Figure 19.6 is reduced from $513.84 to $413.84, which is still superior to the $360 EMV without sample information. **Figure 19.7** is the decision tree for the investment information with the options of buying the information or not buying the information included. The tree is constructed by combining the decision trees from Figures 19.5 and 19.6 and including the cost of buying information ($100) and the EMV with this purchased information ($413.84).

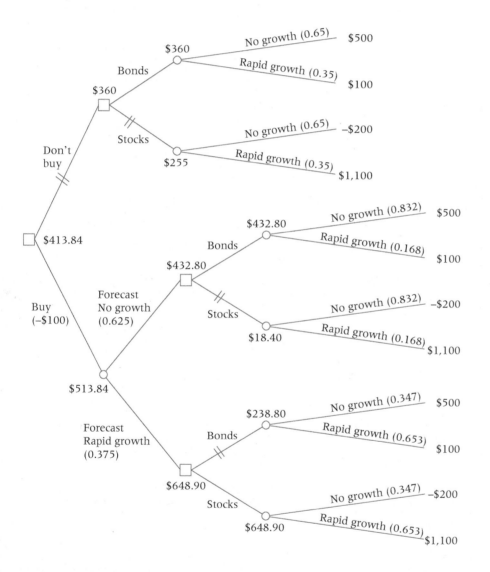

FIGURE 19.7 Decision Tree for the Investment Example— All Options Included

DEMONSTRATION PROBLEM 19.4

In Demonstration Problem 19.1, the decision-makers were faced with the opportunity to increase capacity to meet a possible increase in product demand. Here we have reduced the decision alternatives and states of nature and altered the payoffs and probabilities. Use the following decision table to create a decision tree that displays the decision alternatives, the payoffs, the probabilities, the states of demand, and the expected monetary payoffs. The decision-makers can buy information about the states of demand for $5 (recall that amounts are in $ millions). Incorporate this fact into your decision. Calculate the expected value of sampling information for this problem.

The decision alternatives are no expansion or build a new facility. The states of demand and prior probabilities are less demand (0.20), no change (0.30), or large increase (0.50).

		State of Demand		
		Less (0.20)	No Change (0.30)	Large Increase (0.50)
Decision	No Expansion	−$3	$2	$6
Alternative	New Facility	−$50	−$20	$65

The state-of-demand forecaster has historically not been accurate 100% of the time. For example, when the demand was less, the forecaster correctly predicted it 0.75 of the time. When there was no change in demand, the forecaster correctly predicted it 0.80 of the time. Sixty-five percent of the time the forecaster correctly predicted large increases when large increases occurred. Shown next are the probabilities that the forecaster will predict a particular state of demand under the actual states of demand.

		State of Demand		
		Less	No Change	Large Increase
	Less	0.75	0.10	0.05
Forecast	No Change	0.20	0.80	0.30
	Large Increase	0.05	0.10	0.65

Solution The following figure is the decision tree for this problem when no sample information is purchased.

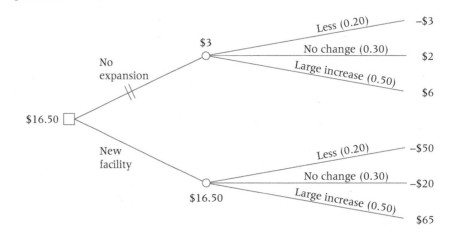

In light of sample information, the prior probabilities of the three states of demand can be revised. Shown here are the revisions for F_1 (forecast of less demand), F_2 (forecast of no change in demand), and F_3 (forecast of large increase in demand).

State of Demand	Prior Probability	Conditional Probability	Joint Probability	Revised Probability
For Forecast of Less Demand (F_1)				
Less (s_1)	0.20	$P(F_1\|s_1) = 0.75$	$P(F_1 \cap s_1) = 0.150$	$0.150/0.205 = 0.732$
No change (s_2)	0.30	$P(F_1\|s_2) = 0.10$	$P(F_1 \cap s_2) = 0.030$	$0.030/0.205 = 0.146$
Large increase (s_3)	0.50	$P(F_1\|s_3) = 0.05$	$P(F_1 \cap s_3) = 0.025$	$0.025/0.205 = 0.122$
			$P(F_1) = 0.205$	
For Forecast of No Change in Demand (F_2)				
Less (s_1)	0.20	$P(F_1\|s_1) = 0.20$	$P(F_1 \cap s_1) = 0.040$	$0.040/0.430 = 0.093$
No change (s_2)	0.30	$P(F_1\|s_2) = 0.80$	$P(F_1 \cap s_2) = 0.240$	$0.240/0.430 = 0.558$
Large increase (s_3)	0.50	$P(F_1\|s_3) = 0.30$	$P(F_1 \cap s_3) = 0.150$	$0.150/0.430 = 0.349$
			$P(F_1) = 0.430$	

For Forecast of Large Increase in Demand (F_3)

Less (s_1)	0.20	$P(F_1|s_1) = 0.05$	$P(F_1 \cap s_1) = 0.010$	$0.010/0.365 = 0.027$
No change (s_2)	0.30	$P(F_1|s_2) = 0.10$	$P(F_1 \cap s_2) = 0.030$	$0.030/0.365 = 0.082$
Large increase (s_3)	0.50	$P(F_1|s_3) = 0.65$	$P(F_1 \cap s_3) = 0.325$	$0.325/0.365 = 0.890$
			$P(F_1) = 0.365$	

From these revised probabilities and other information, the decision tree containing alternatives and states using sample information can be constructed. The following figure is the decision tree containing the sample information alternative *and* the portion of the tree for the alternative of no sampling information.

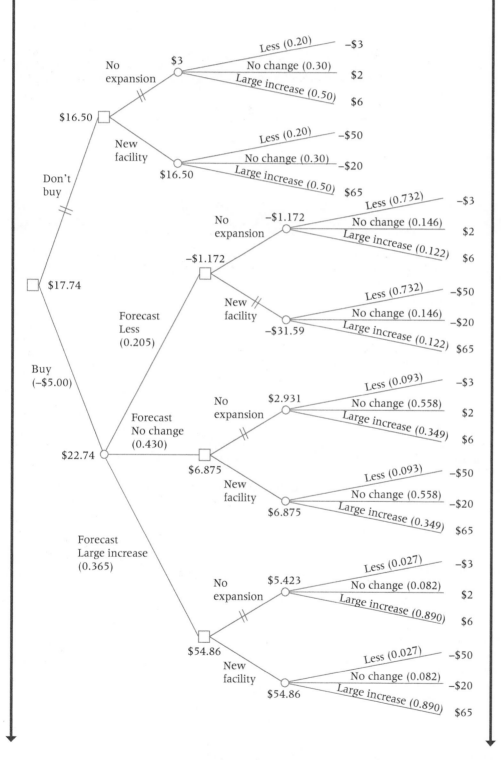

If the decision-makers calculate the EMV after buying the sample information, they will see that the value is $17.74. The final EMV with sample information is calculated as follows:

$$\text{EMV at Buy Node: } -\$1.172(0.205) + \$6.875(0.430) + \$54.86(0.365) = \$22.74$$

However, the sample information cost $5. Hence, the net EMV at the buy node is:

$$\$22.74 \text{ (EMV)} - \$5.00 \text{ (cost of information)} = \$17.74 \text{ (net EMV)}$$

The worth of the sample information (in $ millions) is:

$$\begin{aligned}\text{EMV of Sample Information} &= \text{EMV with Sample Information}\\&\quad - \text{EMV without Sample Information}\\&= \$22.74 - \$16.50 = \$6.24\end{aligned}$$

Concept Check

1. How does the expected value of sample information differ from the expected value of perfect information? Give an example of an instance where the expected value of sample information may be used.

19.4 Problems

19.12 Shown here is a decision table from a business situation. The decision-maker has an opportunity to purchase sample information in the form of a forecast. With the sample information, the prior probabilities can be revised. Also shown are the probabilities of forecasts from the sample information for each state of nature. Use this information to answer parts (a) through (d).

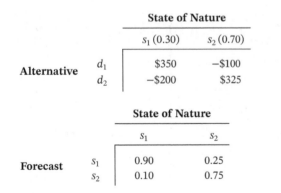

		State of Nature	
		s_1 (0.30)	s_2 (0.70)
Alternative	d_1	$350	-$100
	d_2	-$200	$325

		State of Nature	
		s_1	s_2
Forecast	s_1	0.90	0.25
	s_2	0.10	0.75

a. Compute the EMV of this decision without sample information.

b. Compute the EMV of this decision with sample information.

c. Use a decision tree to show the decision options in parts (a) and (b).

d. Calculate the EMV of the sample information.

19.13 a. A car rental agency faces the decision of buying a fleet of cars, all of which will be the same size. It can purchase a fleet of small cars, medium cars, or large cars. The smallest cars are the most fuel-efficient and the largest cars use the most fuel.

One of the problems for the decision-makers is that they do not know whether the price of fuel will increase or decrease in the near future. If the price increases, the small cars are likely to be most popular. If the price decreases, customers may demand the larger cars. Following is a decision table with these decision alternatives, the states of nature, the probabilities, and the payoffs. Use this information to determine the EMV for this problem.

		State of Nature	
		Fuel Decrease (0.60)	Fuel Increase (0.40)
Decision Alternative	Small Cars	-$225	$425
	Medium Cars	$125	-$150
	Large Cars	$350	-$400

b. The decision-makers have an opportunity to purchase a forecast of the world oil markets that has some validity in predicting gasoline prices. The following matrix gives the probabilities of these forecasts being correct for various states of nature. Use this information to revise the prior probabilities and recompute the EMV on the basis of sample information. What is the expected value of sample information for this problem? Should the agency decide to buy the forecast?

		State of Nature	
		Fuel Decrease	Fuel Increase
Forecast	Fuel Decrease	0.75	0.15
	Fuel Increase	0.25	0.85

19.14 a. A small group of investors is considering planting a tree farm. Their choices are (1) don't plant trees, (2) plant a small number of trees, or (3) plant a large number of trees. The investors are concerned about the demand for trees. If demand for trees declines, planting a large tree farm would probably result in a loss. However, if a large increase in the demand for trees occurs, not planting a tree farm could mean a large loss in revenue opportunity. They determine that three states of demand are possible: (1) demand declines, (2) demand remains the same as it is, and (3) demand increases. Use the following decision table to compute an EMV for this decision opportunity.

		State of Demand		
		Decline (0.20)	Same (0.30)	Increase (0.50)
Decision Alternative	Don't Plant	$20	$0	−$40
	Small Tree Farm	−$90	$10	$175
	Large Tree Farm	−$600	−$150	$800

b. Industry experts who believe they can forecast what will happen in the tree industry contact the investors. The following matrix shows the probabilities with which it is believed these experts can foretell tree demand. Use these probabilities to revise the prior probabilities of the states of nature and recompute the expected value of sample information. How much is this sample information worth?

		State of Demand		
		Decrease	Same	Increase
	Decrease	0.70	0.02	0.02
Forecast	Same	0.25	0.95	0.08
	Increase	0.05	0.03	0.90

19.15 a. Some oil speculators are interested in drilling an oil well. The rights to the land have been secured and they must decide whether to drill. The states of nature are that oil is present or that no oil is present. Their two decision alternatives are drill or don't drill. If they strike oil, the well will pay $1 million. If they have a dry hole, they will lose $100,000. If they don't drill, their payoffs are $0 when oil is present and $0 when it is not. The probability that oil is present is 0.11. Use this information to construct a decision table and compute an EMV for this problem.

b. The speculators have an opportunity to buy a geological survey, which sometimes helps in determining whether oil is present in the ground. When the geologists say there is oil in the ground, there actually is oil 0.20 of the time. When there is oil in the ground, 0.80 of the time the geologists say there is no oil. When there is no oil in the ground, 0.90 of the time the geologists say there is no oil. When there is no oil in the ground, 0.10 of the time the geologists say there is oil. Use this information to revise the prior probabilities of oil being present in the ground and compute the EMV based on sample information. What is the value of the sample information for this problem?

End-of-Chapter Review

Decision Dilemma Solved

Decision-Making at the CEO Level

The study of CEOs revealed that decision-making takes place in many different areas of business. No matter what the decision concerns, it is critical for the CEO or manager to identify the decision alternatives. Sometimes decision alternatives are not obvious and can be identified only after considerable examination and brainstorming. Many different alternatives are available to decision-makers in personnel, finance, operations, and so on. Alternatives can sometimes be obtained from worker suggestions and input. Others are identified through consultants or experts in particular fields. Occasionally, a creative and unobvious decision alternative is derived that proves to be the most successful choice.

Ford decided to focus on manufacturing trucks and SUVs, keeping only two car models in production. Other alternatives might have been to stop making cars altogether, keep more models in production, or make no change at all. At BlackBerry, Thorsten Heins made the decision not to develop the BB10 operating software for the PlayBook tablet. Heins had other options available, such as spending more time and money on development until all the bugs were worked out, or developing new PlayBook devices that would work with BB10. Maple Leaf Foods faced a crisis when cured meats manufactured in the Toronto plant

were found to be contaminated, which resulted in serious illnesses leading to some fatalities. The CEO chose to close the plant briefly in August 2008 and recalled several products.

CEOs need to identify as many states of nature that can occur under the decision alternatives as possible. What might happen to sales? Will product demand increase or decrease? What is the political climate for environmental or international monetary regulation? What will occur next in the business cycle? Will there be inflation? What will the competitors do? What new inventions or developments will occur? What is the investment climate? Identifying as many of these states as possible helps the decision-maker examine decision alternatives in light of those states and calculate payoffs accordingly.

Many different states of nature may arise that will affect the outcome of CEO decisions made in the 2010s. Ford may find that the demand for SUVs and trucks continues to grow, becomes more moderate, or stops completely as people turn to smaller vehicles or alternative forms of transportation. Another automotive manufacturer may develop a model that captures the attention of drivers. The North American economy might undergo a depression, a slowdown, constant growth, or even an accelerated rate of growth.

States of nature can affect a CEO's decision in other ways. The rate of growth and understanding of technology is uncertain in many ways. Ford plans to produce hybrid trucks and SUVs, as well as a fully electric SUV, taking on Toyota, the current leader in U.S. hybrid vehicle sales. But efficient, reliable technology must be developed. Will there be suppliers who can provide materials and parts? What about the raw materials used to manufacture these vehicles? Will there be an abundance, a shortage, or an adequate supply of raw materials? Will the price of raw materials fluctuate widely, increase, decrease, or remain constant?

The decision-maker should recognize whether he or she is a risk avoider or a risk taker. Does propensity for risk vary by situation? Should it? How do the board of directors and shareholders view risk? Will the employees respond to risk taking or avoidance?

Successful CEOs may well incorporate risk taking, risk avoidance, and expected value decision-making into their decisions. Perhaps the successful CEOs know when to take risks and when to pull back. In the case of Maple Leaf Foods, the CEO had to decide the extent of recall. Because consumer confidence is paramount where food products are concerned, Maple Leaf Foods broadened its recall to include a wide range of its products, including those sold under the Schneiders brand name and products supplied to McDonald's restaurants. Certainly, the decision by a successful company like Ford to refocus its product line is risk taking. BlackBerry's decision not to extend the BB10 operating system to the PlayBook risked alienating tablet owners.

If successful, the payoffs from these CEO decisions could be great. Ford's current sales figures may be dwarfed if its trucks and SUVs remain popular and its hybrid and electric versions catch on. On the other hand, the company could experience big losses or receive payoffs somewhere in between. The CEO of Maple Leaf Foods, Michael McCain, chose to go public and went on TV to reassure consumers, stating, "Tragically, our products have been linked to illness and loss of life. To those people who are ill, and to the families who have lost loved ones, I offer my deepest and sincerest sympathies." The CEO's decision not to leave crisis management entirely to PR agencies but to expand the product recall, face consumers head-on, and take responsibility may, at least in part, be the reason why consumer confidence returned very quickly to Maple Leaf products.

CEOs are not always able to visualize all decision alternatives. However, creative, inspired thinking along with the brainstorming of others and an extensive investigation of the facts and figures can result in the identification of most of the possibilities. States of nature are unknown and harder to discern. However, awareness, insight, understanding, and knowledge of economies, markets, governments, and competitors can greatly aid a decision-maker in considering possible states of nature that may affect the payoff of a decision along with the likelihood that such states of nature might occur. The payoffs for CEOs range from the loss of thousands of jobs including their own, loss of market share, and bankruptcy of the company, to worldwide growth, record stockholder dividends, and fame.

Key Considerations

Methodological considerations occasionally arise in decision analysis situations. The techniques presented in this chapter can aid the decision-maker in selecting from among decision alternatives in light of payoffs and expected values. Payoffs do not always reflect all costs. The decision-maker needs to decide whether to consider other factors not in the decision criteria in examining decision alternatives. For example, some decision alternatives are environmentally damaging in the form of ground, air, or water pollution. Other choices endanger the health and safety of workers. In the area of human resources, some decision alternatives include eliminating jobs and laying off workers. Should the issues involved in these decisions be factored into payoffs? For example, what effects would a layoff have on families and communities? Does a business have any social obligation toward its workers and its community that should be taken into consideration in payoffs? Does a decision alternative involve producing a product that is detrimental to a customer or a customer's family? States of nature are usually beyond the control of the decision-maker; therefore, it seems unlikely that methodological issues would be connected with a state of nature. However, obtaining sample or perfect information under which to make decisions about states of nature has the usual potential for methodological mistakes in sampling.

In many cases, payoffs other than the dollar values assigned to a decision alternative should be considered. In using decision analysis for optimal effectiveness, the decision-maker should attempt to factor into the payoffs the cost of pollution, safety features, human resource loss, and so on.

Why Statistics Is Relevant

Modern societies and businesses always operate under a great deal of uncertainty: What will the unemployment level be next year? Will the rate of inflation go up or down? How many beds will a hospital need to avoid turning away patients? How will my business be affected if the new product fails? Will the stock market go up? If we know the answer to these questions, we can plan for the future confidently (and make a lot of money in the stock market). But this is not the case. A decision-maker has to decide without having access to what may happen in the future.

Even though the decision-maker has no way of knowing the future, the decision has to be optimal in the sense that no matter what decision is taken, it is the one that is likely to decrease risk, increase the rewards, or both, given the level of uncertainty.

Decision theory provides a means of achieving these objectives. It does not eliminate risk but provides a means of assessing the consequences of different courses of action so decision-makers can achieve their objective of minimizing potential losses, maximizing potential gains, or optimizing both.

Summary of Learning Objectives

Decision analysis is a branch of quantitative management in which mathematical and statistical approaches are used to assist decision-makers in reaching judgements about alternative opportunities. Three types of decisions are (1) decisions made under certainty, (2) decisions made under uncertainty, and (3) decisions made with risk.

LEARNING OBJECTIVE 19.1 Make decisions under certainty by constructing a decision table.

Decision alternatives are the options open to decision-makers from which they can choose. States of nature are situations or conditions arising after the decision has been made, over which the decision-maker has no control. Payoffs are the gains or losses that the decision-maker will reap from various decision alternatives. These three aspects (decision alternatives, states of nature, and payoffs) can be displayed in a decision table or payoff table.

Decision-making under certainty is the easiest of the three types of decisions to make. In this case, the states of nature are known, and the decision-maker merely selects the decision alternative that yields the highest payoff.

LEARNING OBJECTIVE 19.2 Make decisions under uncertainty using the maximax criterion, the maximin criterion, the Hurwicz criterion, and minimax regret.

Decisions are made under uncertainty when the likelihoods of the states of nature occurring are unknown. Four approaches to making decisions under uncertainty are the *maximax* criterion, the *maximin* criterion, the *Hurwicz* criterion, and *minimax* regret.

The maximax criterion is an optimistic approach based on the notion that the best possible outcomes will occur. In this approach, the decision-maker selects the maximum possible payoff under each decision alternative and then selects the maximum of these. Thus, the decision-maker is selecting the maximum of the maximums. The maximin criterion is a pessimistic approach. The assumption is that the worst case will happen under each decision alternative. The decision-maker selects the minimum payoffs under each decision alternative and then picks the maximum of these as the best solution. Thus, the decision-maker is selecting the best of the worst cases, or the maximum of the minimums.

The Hurwicz criterion is an attempt to give decision-makers an alternative to maximax and maximin that is somewhere between an optimistic and a pessimistic approach. With this approach, decision-makers select a value called α between 0 and 1 to represent how optimistic they are. The maximum and minimum payoffs for each decision alternative are examined. The α weight is applied to the maximum payoff under each decision alternative and $1 - \alpha$ is applied to

the minimum payoff. These two weighted values are combined for each decision alternative, and the maximum of these weighted values is selected.

Minimax regret is calculated by examining opportunity loss. An opportunity loss table is constructed by subtracting each payoff from the maximum payoff under each state of nature. This step produces a lost opportunity under each state. The maximum lost opportunity from each decision alternative is determined from the opportunity table. The minimum of these values is selected, and the corresponding decision alternative is chosen. In this way, the decision-maker has reduced or minimized the regret, or lost opportunity.

LEARNING OBJECTIVE 19.3 Make decisions under risk by constructing decision trees, calculating expected monetary value and expected value of perfect information, and analyzing utility.

In decision-making with risk, the decision-maker has some prior knowledge of the probability of each occurrence of each state of nature. With these probabilities, a weighted payoff referred to as expected monetary value (EMV) can be calculated for each decision alternative. A person who makes decisions based on these EMVs is called an EMVer. The EMV is essentially the average payoff that would occur if the decision process were to be played out over a long period of time with the probabilities holding constant.

The expected value of perfect information can be determined by comparing the EMV if the states of nature are known to the EMV with no such information. The difference in the two is the expected value of perfect information.

Utility refers to a decision-maker's propensity to take risks. People who avoid risks are called risk avoiders. People who are prone to take risks are referred to as risk takers. People who use EMV generally fall between these two categories. Utility curves can be sketched to ascertain or depict a decision-maker's tendency toward risk.

LEARNING OBJECTIVE 19.4 Revise probabilities in light of sample information by using Bayesian analysis and calculating the expected value of sample information.

By using Bayes' theorem, the probabilities associated with the states of nature in decision-making under risk can be revised when new information is obtained. This information can be helpful to the decision-maker. However, it usually carries a cost. This cost can reduce the payoff of decision-making with sample information. The EMV with sample information can be compared with the EMV without it to determine the value of sample information.

Key Terms

Formula

(19.1) Bayes' rule

$$P(X_i \mid Y) = \frac{P(X_i) \cdot P(Y \mid X_i)}{P(X_1) \cdot P(Y \mid X_1) + P(X_2) \cdot P(Y \mid X_2) + \cdots + P(X_n) \cdot P(Y \mid X_n)}$$

Supplementary Problems

Calculating the Statistics

19.16 Use the following decision table to complete parts (a) through (d).

		State of Nature	
		s_1	s_2
	d_1	50	100
Decision	d_2	−75	200
Alternative	d_3	25	40
	d_4	75	10

a. Use the maximax criterion to determine which decision alternative to select.

b. Use the maximin criterion to determine which decision alternative to select.

c. Use the Hurwicz criterion to determine which decision alternative to select. Let $\alpha = 0.6$.

d. Compute an opportunity loss table from these data. Use this table and a minimax regret criterion to determine which decision alternative to select.

19.17 **Video** Use the following decision table to complete parts (a) through (c).

		State of Nature			
		s_1 (0.30)	s_2 (0.25)	s_3 (0.20)	s_4 (0.25)
Decision	d_1	400	250	300	100
Alternative	d_2	300	−100	600	200

a. Draw a decision tree to represent this decision table.

b. Compute the EMV for each decision and label the decision tree to indicate what the final decision would be.

c. Compute the expected payoff of perfect information. Compare this answer with the answer determined in part (b) and compute the value of perfect information.

19.18 Shown here is a decision table. A forecast can be purchased by the decision-maker. The forecaster is not correct 100% of the time. Also given is a table containing the probabilities of the forecaster being correct under different states of nature. Use the first table to compute the EMV of this decision without sample information. Use the second table to revise the prior probabilities of the various decision alternatives. From this and the first table, compute the EMV with sample information. Construct a decision tree to represent the options, the payoffs, and the expected monetary values. Calculate the value of sample information.

		State of Nature	
		s_1 (0.40)	s_2 (0.60)
Decision	d_1	$200	$150
Alternative	d_2	−$75	$450
	d_3	$175	$125

		State of Nature	
		s_1	s_2
Forecast	s_1	0.90	0.30
	s_2	0.10	0.70

Testing Your Understanding

19.19 **Video** Managers of a manufacturing firm decided to add picture frames to its list of production items. However, they have not decided how many to produce because they are uncertain about the level of demand. Shown here is a decision table that has been constructed to help the managers in their decision situation. Use this table to answer parts (a) through (c).

		State of Demand		
		Small	Moderate	Large
Decision Alternative (Produce)	Small Number	$200	$250	$300
	Modest Number	$100	$300	$600
	Large Number	−$300	$400	$2,000

a. Use maximax and maximin criteria to evaluate the decision alternatives.

b. Construct an opportunity loss table and use minimax regret to select a decision alternative.

c. Compare the results of the maximax, maximin, and minimax regret criteria in selecting decision alternatives.

19.20 Some companies use production learning curves to set pricing strategies. They price their product lower than the initial cost of making the product; after some period of time, the learning curve takes effect and the product can be produced for less than its selling price. In this way, the company can penetrate new markets with aggressive pricing strategies and still make a long-term profit.

A company is considering using the learning curve to set its price on a new product. There is some uncertainty as to how soon, if at all, the production operation will learn to make the product more quickly and efficiently. If the learning curve does not drop enough or the initial price is too low, the company will be operating at a loss on this product. If the product is priced too high, the sales volume might be too low to justify production. Shown here is a decision table that contains as its states of nature several possible learning-curve scenarios. The decision alternatives are three different pricing strategies.

a. Use this table and the Hurwicz criterion to make a decision about the pricing strategies with each given value of α.

		State of Nature		
		No Learning	Slow Learning	Fast Learning
Decision Alternative	Price Low	−$700	−$400	$1,200
	Price Medium	−$300	−$100	$550
	Price High	$100	$125	$150

   i. $\alpha = 0.10$

  ii. $\alpha = 0.50$

 iii. $\alpha = 0.80$

b. Compare and discuss the decision choices in part (a).

19.21 An entertainment company owns two amusement parks in British Columbia. It is faced with the decision of whether to open the parks in the winter. If it chooses to open the parks in the winter, it can leave the parks open during regular hours (as in the summer) or it can open only on the weekends. To some extent, the payoffs from opening the parks hinge on the type of weather that occurs during the winter season. Following are the payoffs for various decision options about opening the park for two different weather scenarios: mild weather and severe weather. Use the information to construct a decision tree. Determine the EMV and the value of perfect information.

		State of the Weather	
		Mild (0.75)	Severe (0.25)
Decision Alternative	Open Regular Hours	$2,000	−$2,500
	Open Weekends Only	$1,200	−$200
	Not Open at All	−$300	$100

19.22 A Canadian manufacturing company has decided to consider producing a particular model of one of its products just for sale in Germany. Because of the German requirements, the product must be made specifically for German consumption and cannot be sold in Canada. Company officials believe the market for the product is highly price sensitive. Because the product will be manufactured in Canada and exported to Germany, the biggest variable factor in being price competitive is the exchange rate between the two countries. If the Canadian dollar is strong, German consumers will have to pay more for the product in euros. If the Canadian dollar becomes weaker against the euro, Germans can buy more Canadian products for their money. The company officials are faced with decision alternatives of whether to produce the product. The states of the exchange rates are Canadian dollar weaker, Canadian dollar stays the same, and Canadian dollar stronger. The probabilities of these states occurring are 0.35, 0.25, and 0.40, respectively. Some negative payoffs will result from not producing the product because of sunk development and market research costs and because of lost market opportunity. If the product is not produced, the payoffs are −$700 when the dollar gets weaker, −$200 when the dollar remains about the same, and $150 when the dollar gets stronger. If the product is produced, the payoffs are $1,800 when the dollar gets weaker, $400 when the exchange rates stay about the same, and −$1,600 when the dollar gets stronger.

Use this information to construct a decision tree and a decision table for this decision-making situation. Use the probabilities to compute the EMVs of the decision alternatives. On the basis of this information, which decision should the company make? Compute the EMV of perfect information and the value of perfect information.

19.23 **a.** A small retailer began as a mom-and-pop operation selling crafts and consignment items. During the past two years, the store's volume grew significantly. The owners are trying to decide whether to purchase an automated checkout system. The store's present manual system is slow. They are concerned about lost business due to inability to ring up sales quickly. The automated system would also offer some accounting and inventory advantages. The problem is that the automated system carries a large fixed cost, and the owners feel that sales volume would have to grow to justify the cost.

The following decision table contains the decision alternatives for this situation, the possible states of future sales, prior probabilities of those states occurring, and the payoffs. Use this information to compute the expected monetary payoffs for the alternatives.

		State of Sales		
		Reduction (0.15)	Constant (0.35)	Increase (0.50)
Decision Alternative	Automate	−$40,000	−$15,000	$60,000
	Don't Automate	$5,000	$10,000	−$30,000

b. For a fee, the owners can purchase a sales forecast for the near future. The forecast is not always perfect. The probabilities of these forecasts being correct for particular states of sales are shown here. Use these probabilities to revise the prior state probabilities. Compute the EMV on the basis of sample information. Determine the value of the sample information.

		State of Sales		
		Reduction	Constant	Increase
	Reduction	0.60	0.10	0.05
Forecast	Constant	0.30	0.80	0.25
	Increase	0.10	0.10	0.70

19.24 a. A city is considering airport expansion. In particular, the mayor and city council are trying to decide whether to sell bonds to construct a new terminal. The problem is that at present demand for gates is not strong enough to warrant construction of a new terminal. However, a major airline is investigating several cities to determine which it will choose for its new headquarters. If this city is selected, the new terminal will easily pay for itself. The decision to build the terminal must be made by the city before the airline will say whether the city has been chosen. Shown here is a decision table for this dilemma. Use this information to compute EMVs for the alternatives and reach a conclusion.

		State of Nature	
		City Chosen (0.20)	City Not Chosen (0.80)
Decision Alternative	Build Terminal	$12,000	−$8,000
	Don't Build Terminal	−$1,000	$2,000

b. An airline industry expert indicates that she will sell the city decision-makers her best guess as to whether the city will be chosen. The probabilities of her being right or wrong are given. Use these probabilities to revise the prior probabilities of the city being chosen as the hub. Compute the EMV using the sample information and then determine the value of this sample information.

		State of Nature	
		City Chosen	City Not Chosen
Forecast	City Chosen	0.45	0.40
	City Not Chosen	0.55	0.60

Exploring the Databases with Business Analytics   *see the databases on the Student Website and in WileyPLUS*

1. Suppose you are the CEO of a financial company. You are considering expansion of the physical facility. What are some decision alternatives to consider? What are some states of nature that can occur in this decision-making environment (a publicly traded company)? What are some decisions that you might make in which you would consider decision alternatives? Name three arenas in which you would be making substantial strategic decisions (e.g., marketing, finance, production, and human resources). Delineate at least three decision alternatives in each of these arenas. Examine and discuss at least two states of nature that could occur under these decision alternatives in each arena.

Case

Fletcher-Terry: On the Cutting Edge

The Fletcher-Terry Company is a worldwide leader in the development of glass-cutting tools and accessories for professional glaziers, glass manufacturers, glass artisans, and professional framers. The company can trace its roots back to 1868. For many decades, Fletcher-Terry had much success making its traditional product lines of hand-held glass cutters and cutting wheels for the glass, glazing, and hardware markets. However, by the 1980s, Fletcher-Terry was facing a crisis. Its two largest customers, distributors of cutting devices, decided to introduce their own private-label cutters made overseas. By the end of 1982, Fletcher-Terry's sales of hand-held glass cutters were down 45%.

Fletcher-Terry responded by investing heavily in technology with the hope that automation would cut costs; however, the technology never worked. The company then decided to expand its line of offerings by creating private lines through imports, but the U.S. dollar weakened and any price advantage was lost. Eventually, Fletcher-Terry had to write off this line with a substantial loss.

Company managers realized that if they did not change the way they did business, the company would not survive. They began a signifi-

cant strategic planning process in which they set objectives and redefined the mission of the company. Among the new objectives were to increase market share where the company was already strong, penetrate new markets with new products, provide technological expertise for product development, promote greater employee involvement and growth, and achieve a sales growth rate twice that of the gross domestic product.

To accomplish these objectives, the company invested in plant and process improvements that reduced costs and improved quality. Markets were researched for both old and new products, and marketing efforts were launched to re-establish the company's products as being "the first choice of professionals." A participatory management system was implemented that encouraged risk taking and creativity among employees.

Following these initiatives, sales growth totalled 82.5% from 1987 to 1993. Fletcher-Terry expanded its offerings with bevel mat cutters, new fastener tools, and a variety of hand tools essential to professional picture framers, and graduated from being a manufacturer of relatively simple hand tools to being a manufacturer of mechanically complex equipment and tools. Because of its continuous pursuit of quality, the company earned the Ford Q-101 Quality Supplier Award. In 2001, Fletcher-Terry introduced its Framer-Solutions.com online business-to-business custom mat-cutting service especially designed for professional picture framers. In 2012, Fletcher-Terry purchased two picture-framing businesses from Illinois Tool Works, including Alfamacchine, which gives the company manufacturing facilities in Italy. Fletcher-Terry holds over 90 patents, including the "original" glass-cutting wheel, the first vertical glass-cutting machine, and the "wide-track" all-carbide cutting wheel. The mission of Fletcher-Terry is to develop innovative tools and equipment for the markets it serves worldwide and make customer satisfaction its number one priority.

Today, the Fletcher-Terry Company is known as the Fletcher Business Group and is a global brand and leading manufacturer of tabletop and wall-mounted/free-standing substrate cutters, points and drivers for picture framing, hand-held glass cutters and pliers, carbide scoring wheels, and pillar posts and inserts for the automated glass-processing industry.

Discussion

1. Fletcher-Terry managers have been involved in many decisions over the years. Of particular importance were the decisions made in the 1980s when the company was struggling to survive. Several states of nature took place in the late 1970s and 1980s over which managers had little or no control. Suppose the Fletcher-Terry management team wants to reflect on its decisions and the events that surrounded them, and asks you to make a brief report summarizing the situation. Delineate at least five decisions that Fletcher-Terry probably had to make during that troublesome time. Using your knowledge of the economic situation both in the U.S. and in the rest of the world in addition to information given in the case, present at least four states of nature during that time that had significant influence on the outcomes of the managers' decisions.

2. At one point, Fletcher-Terry decided to import its own private line of cutters. Suppose that before taking such action, the managers had the following information available. Construct a decision table and a decision tree by using this information. Explain any conclusions reached.

Suppose the decision for managers was to import or not import. If they imported, they had to worry about the purchasing value of the dollar overseas. If the value of the dollar went up, the company could profit by $350,000. If the dollar maintained its present position, the company would still profit by $275,000. However, if the value of the dollar decreased, the company would be worse off with an additional loss of $555,000. One business economic source reported that there was a 25% chance that the dollar would increase in value overseas, a 35% chance that it would remain constant, and a 40% chance that it would lose value overseas. If the company decided not to import its own private label, it would have a $22,700 loss no matter what the value of the dollar was overseas. Explain the possible outcomes of this analysis to the management team in terms of EMV, risk aversion, and risk taking. Bring common sense into the process and give your recommendations on what the company should do given the analysis. Keep in mind the company's situation and the fact that it had not yet tried any solution. Explain to company officials the expected value of perfect information for this decision.

Sources: Adapted from "Fletcher-Terry: On the Cutting Edge," Real-World Lessons for America's Small Businesses: Insights from the Blue Chip Enterprise Initiative. Published by *Nation's Business* magazine on behalf of Connecticut Mutual Life Insurance Company and the U.S. Chamber of Commerce in association with the Blue Chip Enterprise Initiative, 1994. See also Fletcher-Terry, available at www.fletcher-terry.com/; "Fletcher-Terry Acquires Global Leader in Picture Frame Assembly," company news release, July 31, 2012; "Fletcher-Terry Celebrates 140 Years," *Screen Printing* magazine online, October 2008, screenweb.com.

Big Data Case

Thinking about the American Hospital Association database, consider the following:

1. Suppose you are the CEO of a hospital and you are contemplating expansion of the physical facility. What are some decision alternatives to consider? What are some states of nature that can occur in this decision-making environment? How would you go about calculating the payoffs for such a decision?

2. According to the University of Minnesota, a patient's hospital experience can be improved by several hospital environmental factors such as reduction of noise; adaptable rooms for patient acuity; positive distractions such as gardens, landscapes, artwork, and aquariums; social spaces for families and friends; improved wayfinding such as signage; and others. However, major investment in such features can be costly and may not necessarily pay off in terms of increased revenue from additional patients. On the other hand, failure to implement such changes can result in a loss of patients, especially if there is a significant increase in competition. Shown here is a decision table for a hospital with possible choices of investing in such features along with possible payoffs ($ thousands). In addition, three states of nature are given concerning competition along with the probability that each would occur. Analyze this hospital's situation and make recommendations as to which courses of action the hospital administration should take considering that the hospital board and CEO might be risk takers, EMVs, or risk averse. Construct a decision tree and implement several of the techniques presented in the chapter in discussing and presenting your responses.

	No New Competition (30%)	Small Level of New Competition (25%)	Major New Competition (45%)
Significantly Upgrade	−5,000	−3,000	+4,000
Make Minor Changes	+500	+400	−1,000
Make No Changes	+2,000	+1,200	−3,000

Appendix A

Tables

TABLE A.1 **Random Numbers**

12651	61646	11769	75109	86996	97669	25757	32535	07122	76763
81769	74436	02630	72310	45049	18029	07469	42341	98173	79260
36737	98863	77240	76251	00654	64688	09343	70278	67331	98729
82861	54371	76610	94934	72748	44124	05610	53750	95938	01485
21325	15732	24127	37431	09723	63529	73977	95218	96074	42138
74146	47887	62463	23045	41490	07954	22597	60012	98866	90959
90759	64410	54179	66075	61051	75385	51378	08360	95946	95547
55683	98078	02238	91540	21219	17720	87817	41705	95785	12563
79686	17969	76061	83748	55920	83612	41540	86492	06447	60568
70333	00201	86201	69716	78185	62154	77930	67663	29529	75116
14042	53536	07779	04157	41172	36473	42123	43929	50533	33437
59911	08256	06596	48416	69770	68797	56080	14223	59199	30162
62368	62623	62742	14891	39247	52242	98832	69533	91174	57979
57529	97751	54976	48957	74599	08759	78494	52785	68526	64618
15469	90574	78033	66885	13936	42117	71831	22961	94225	31816
18625	23674	53850	32827	81647	80820	00420	63555	74489	80141
74626	68394	88562	70745	23701	45630	65891	58220	35442	60414
11119	16519	27384	90199	79210	76965	99546	30323	31664	22845
41101	17336	48951	53674	17880	45260	08575	49321	36191	17095
32123	91576	84221	78902	82010	30847	62329	63898	23268	74283
26091	68409	69704	82267	14751	13151	93115	01437	56945	89661
67680	79790	48462	59278	44185	29616	76531	19589	83139	28454
15184	19260	14073	07026	25264	08388	27182	22557	61501	67481
58010	45039	57181	10238	36874	28546	37444	80824	63981	39942
56425	53996	86245	32623	78858	08143	60377	42925	42815	11159
82630	84066	13592	60642	17904	99718	63432	88642	37858	25431
14927	40909	23900	48761	44860	92467	31742	87142	03607	32059
23740	22505	07489	85986	74420	21744	97711	36648	35620	97949
32990	97446	03711	63824	07953	85965	87089	11687	92414	67257
05310	24058	91946	78437	34365	82469	12430	84754	19354	72745
21839	39937	27534	88913	49055	19218	47712	67677	51889	70926
08833	42549	93981	94051	28382	83725	72643	64233	97252	17133
58336	11139	47479	00931	91560	95372	97642	33856	54825	55680
62032	91144	75478	47431	52726	30289	42411	91886	51818	78292
45171	30557	53116	04118	58301	24375	65609	85810	18620	49198
91611	62656	60128	35609	63698	78356	50682	22505	01692	36291
55472	63819	86314	49174	93582	73604	78614	78849	23096	72825
18573	09729	74091	53994	10970	86557	65661	41854	26037	53296
60866	02955	90288	82136	83644	94455	06560	78029	98768	71296
45043	55608	82767	60890	74646	79485	13619	98868	40857	19415
17831	09737	79473	75945	28394	79334	70577	38048	03607	06932
40137	03981	07585	18128	11178	32601	27994	05641	22600	86064
77776	31343	14576	97706	16039	47517	43300	59080	80392	63189
69605	44104	40103	95635	05635	81673	68657	09559	23510	95875
19916	52934	26499	09821	97331	80993	61299	36979	73599	35055
02606	58552	07678	56619	65325	30705	99582	53390	46357	13244
65183	73160	87131	35530	47946	09854	18080	02321	05809	04893
10740	98914	44916	11322	89717	88189	30143	52687	19420	60061
98642	89822	71691	51573	83666	61642	46683	33761	47542	23551
60139	25601	93663	25547	02654	94829	48672	28736	84994	13071

Adapted from *Million Random Digits With 100,000 Normal Deviates* by RAND Corporation. 1955 by RAND Corporation.

TABLE A.2   **Binomial Probability Distribution**

$n = 1$

x	Probability								
	.1	.2	.3	.4	.5	.6	.7	.8	.9
0	.900	.800	.700	.600	.500	.400	.300	.200	.100
1	.100	.200	.300	.400	.500	.600	.700	.800	.900

$n = 2$

x	Probability								
	.1	.2	.3	.4	.5	.6	.7	.8	.9
0	.810	.640	.490	.360	.250	.160	.090	.040	.010
1	.180	.320	.420	.480	.500	.480	.420	.320	.180
2	.010	.040	.090	.160	.250	.360	.490	.640	.810

$n = 3$

x	Probability								
	.1	.2	.3	.4	.5	.6	.7	.8	.9
0	.729	.512	.343	.216	.125	.064	.027	.008	.001
1	.243	.384	.441	.432	.375	.288	.189	.096	.027
2	.027	.096	.189	.288	.375	.432	.441	.384	.243
3	.001	.008	.027	.064	.125	.216	.343	.512	.729

$n = 4$

x	Probability								
	.1	.2	.3	.4	.5	.6	.7	.8	.9
0	.656	.410	.240	.130	.063	.026	.008	.002	.000
1	.292	.410	.412	.346	.250	.154	.076	.026	.004
2	.049	.154	.265	.346	.375	.346	.265	.154	.049
3	.004	.026	.076	.154	.250	.346	.412	.410	.292
4	.000	.002	.008	.026	.063	.130	.240	.410	.656

$n = 5$

x	Probability								
	.1	.2	.3	.4	.5	.6	.7	.8	.9
0	.590	.328	.168	.078	.031	.010	.002	.000	.000
1	.328	.410	.360	.259	.156	.077	.028	.006	.000
2	.073	.205	.309	.346	.313	.230	.132	.051	.008
3	.008	.051	.132	.230	.313	.346	.309	.205	.073
4	.000	.006	.028	.077	.156	.259	.360	.410	.328
5	.000	.000	.002	.010	.031	.078	.168	.328	.590

$n = 6$

x	Probability								
	.1	.2	.3	.4	.5	.6	.7	.8	.9
0	.531	.262	.118	.047	.016	.004	.001	.000	.000
1	.354	.393	.303	.187	.094	.037	.010	.002	.000
2	.098	.246	.324	.311	.234	.138	.060	.015	.001
3	.015	.082	.185	.276	.313	.276	.185	.082	.015
4	.001	.015	.060	.138	.234	.311	.324	.246	.098
5	.000	.002	.010	.037	.094	.187	.303	.393	.354
6	.000	.000	.001	.004	.016	.047	.118	.262	.531

(continued)

TABLE A.2 Binomial Probability Distribution (continued)

n = 7

Probability

x	.1	.2	.3	.4	.5	.6	.7	.8	.9
0	.478	.210	.082	.028	.008	.002	.000	.000	.000
1	.372	.367	.247	.131	.055	.017	.004	.000	.000
2	.124	.275	.318	.261	.164	.077	.025	.004	.000
3	.023	.115	.227	.290	.273	.194	.097	.029	.003
4	.003	.029	.097	.194	.273	.290	.227	.115	.023
5	.000	.004	.025	.077	.164	.261	.318	.275	.124
6	.000	.000	.004	.017	.055	.131	.247	.367	.372
7	.000	.000	.000	.002	.008	.028	.082	.210	.478

n = 8

Probability

x	.1	.2	.3	.4	.5	.6	.7	.8	.9
0	.430	.168	.058	.017	.004	.001	.000	.000	.000
1	.383	.336	.198	.090	.031	.008	.001	.000	.000
2	.149	.294	.296	.209	.109	.041	.010	.001	.000
3	.033	.147	.254	.279	.219	.124	.047	.009	.000
4	.005	.046	.136	.232	.273	.232	.136	.046	.005
5	.000	.009	.047	.124	.219	.279	.254	.147	.033
6	.000	.001	.010	.041	.109	.209	.296	.294	.149
7	.000	.000	.001	.008	.031	.090	.198	.336	.383
8	.000	.000	.000	.001	.004	.017	.058	.168	.430

n = 9

Probability

x	.1	.2	.3	.4	.5	.6	.7	.8	.9
0	.387	.134	.040	.010	.002	.000	.000	.000	.000
1	.387	.302	.156	.060	.018	.004	.000	.000	.000
2	.172	.302	.267	.161	.070	.021	.004	.000	.000
3	.045	.176	.267	.251	.164	.074	.021	.003	.000
4	.007	.066	.172	.251	.246	.167	.074	.017	.001
5	.001	.017	.074	.167	.246	.251	.172	.066	.007
6	.000	.003	.021	.074	.164	.251	.267	.176	.045
7	.000	.000	.004	.021	.070	.161	.267	.302	.172
8	.000	.000	.000	.004	.018	.060	.156	.302	.387
9	.000	.000	.000	.000	.002	.010	.040	.134	.387

n = 10

Probability

x	.1	.2	.3	.4	.5	.6	.7	.8	.9
0	.349	.107	.028	.006	.001	.000	.000	.000	.000
1	.387	.268	.121	.040	.010	.002	.000	.000	.000
2	.194	.302	.233	.121	.044	.011	.001	.000	.000
3	.057	.201	.267	.215	.117	.042	.009	.001	.000
4	.011	.088	.200	.251	.205	.111	.037	.006	.000
5	.001	.026	.103	.201	.246	.201	.103	.026	.001
6	.000	.006	.037	.111	.205	.251	.200	.088	.011
7	.000	.001	.009	.042	.117	.215	.267	.201	.057
8	.000	.000	.001	.011	.044	.121	.233	.302	.194
9	.000	.000	.000	.002	.010	.040	.121	.268	.387
10	.000	.000	.000	.000	.001	.006	.028	.107	.349

				$n = 11$					
				Probability					
x	.1	.2	.3	.4	.5	.6	.7	.8	.9
0	.314	.086	.020	.004	.000	.000	.000	.000	.000
1	.384	.236	.093	.027	.005	.001	.000	.000	.000
2	.213	.295	.200	.089	.027	.005	.001	.000	.000
3	.071	.221	.257	.177	.081	.023	.004	.000	.000
4	.016	.111	.220	.236	.161	.070	.017	.002	.000
5	.002	.039	.132	.221	.226	.147	.057	.010	.000
6	.000	.010	.057	.147	.226	.221	.132	.039	.002
7	.000	.002	.017	.070	.161	.236	.220	.111	.016
8	.000	.000	.004	.023	.081	.177	.257	.221	.071
9	.000	.000	.001	.005	.027	.089	.200	.295	.213
10	.000	.000	.000	.001	.005	.027	.093	.236	.384
11	.000	.000	.000	.000	.000	.004	.020	.086	.314

				$n = 12$					
				Probability					
x	.1	.2	.3	.4	.5	.6	.7	.8	.9
0	.282	.069	.014	.002	.000	.000	.000	.000	.000
1	.377	.206	.071	.017	.003	.000	.000	.000	.000
2	.230	.283	.168	.064	.016	.002	.000	.000	.000
3	.085	.236	.240	.142	.054	.012	.001	.000	.000
4	.021	.133	.231	.213	.121	.042	.008	.001	.000
5	.004	.053	.158	.227	.193	.101	.029	.003	.000
6	.000	.016	.079	.177	.226	.177	.079	.016	.000
7	.000	.003	.029	.101	.193	.227	.158	.053	.004
8	.000	.001	.008	.042	.121	.213	.231	.133	.021
9	.000	.000	.001	.012	.054	.142	.240	.236	.085
10	.000	.000	.000	.002	.016	.064	.168	.283	.230
11	.000	.000	.000	.000	.003	.017	.071	.206	.377
12	.000	.000	.000	.000	.000	.002	.014	.069	.282

				$n = 13$					
				Probability					
x	.1	.2	.3	.4	.5	.6	.7	.8	.9
0	.254	.055	.010	.001	.000	.000	.000	.000	.000
1	.367	.179	.054	.011	.002	.000	.000	.000	.000
2	.245	.268	.139	.045	.010	.001	.000	.000	.000
3	.100	.246	.218	.111	.035	.006	.001	.000	.000
4	.028	.154	.234	.184	.087	.024	.003	.000	.000
5	.006	.069	.180	.221	.157	.066	.014	.001	.000
6	.001	.023	.103	.197	.209	.131	.044	.006	.000
7	.000	.006	.044	.131	.209	.197	.103	.023	.001
8	.000	.001	.014	.066	.157	.221	.180	.069	.006
9	.000	.000	.003	.024	.087	.184	.234	.154	.028
10	.000	.000	.001	.006	.035	.111	.218	.246	.100
11	.000	.000	.000	.001	.010	.045	.139	.268	.245
12	.000	.000	.000	.000	.002	.011	.054	.179	.367
13	.000	.000	.000	.000	.000	.001	.010	.055	.254

(continued)

TABLE A.2 **Binomial Probability Distribution** (*continued*)

					$n = 14$				
					Probability				
x	.1	.2	.3	.4	.5	.6	.7	.8	.9
0	.229	.044	.007	.001	.000	.000	.000	.000	.000
1	.356	.154	.041	.007	.001	.000	.000	.000	.000
2	.257	.250	.113	.032	.006	.001	.000	.000	.000
3	.114	.250	.194	.085	.022	.003	.000	.000	.000
4	.035	.172	.229	.155	.061	.014	.001	.000	.000
5	.008	.086	.196	.207	.122	.041	.007	.000	.000
6	.001	.032	.126	.207	.183	.092	.023	.002	.000
7	.000	.009	.062	.157	.209	.157	.062	.009	.000
8	.000	.002	.023	.092	.183	.207	.126	.032	.001
9	.000	.000	.007	.041	.122	.207	.196	.086	.008
10	.000	.000	.001	.014	.061	.155	.229	.172	.035
11	.000	.000	.000	.003	.022	.085	.194	.250	.114
12	.000	.000	.000	.001	.006	.032	.113	.250	.257
13	.000	.000	.000	.000	.001	.007	.041	.154	.356
14	.000	.000	.000	.000	.000	.001	.007	.044	.229

					$n = 15$				
					Probability				
x	.1	.2	.3	.4	.5	.6	.7	.8	.9
0	.206	.035	.005	.000	.000	.000	.000	.000	.000
1	.343	.132	.031	.005	.000	.000	.000	.000	.000
2	.267	.231	.092	.022	.003	.000	.000	.000	.000
3	.129	.250	.170	.063	.014	.002	.000	.000	.000
4	.043	.188	.219	.127	.042	.007	.001	.000	.000
5	.010	.103	.206	.186	.092	.024	.003	.000	.000
6	.002	.043	.147	.207	.153	.061	.012	.001	.000
7	.000	.014	.081	.177	.196	.118	.035	.003	.000
8	.000	.003	.035	.118	.196	.177	.081	.014	.000
9	.000	.001	.012	.061	.153	.207	.147	.043	.002
10	.000	.000	.003	.024	.092	.186	.206	.103	.010
11	.000	.000	.001	.007	.042	.127	.219	.188	.043
12	.000	.000	.000	.002	.014	.063	.170	.250	.129
13	.000	.000	.000	.000	.003	.022	.092	.231	.267
14	.000	.000	.000	.000	.000	.005	.031	.132	.343
15	.000	.000	.000	.000	.000	.000	.005	.035	.206

				$n = 16$					
				Probability					
x	.1	.2	.3	.4	.5	.6	.7	.8	.9
0	.185	.028	.003	.000	.000	.000	.000	.000	.000
1	.329	.113	.023	.003	.000	.000	.000	.000	.000
2	.275	.211	.073	.015	.002	.000	.000	.000	.000
3	.142	.246	.146	.047	.009	.001	.000	.000	.000
4	.051	.200	.204	.101	.028	.004	.000	.000	.000
5	.014	.120	.210	.162	.067	.014	.001	.000	.000
6	.003	.055	.165	.198	.122	.039	.006	.000	.000
7	.000	.020	.101	.189	.175	.084	.019	.001	.000
8	.000	.006	.049	.142	.196	.142	.049	.006	.000
9	.000	.001	.019	.084	.175	.189	.101	.020	.000
10	.000	.000	.006	.039	.122	.198	.165	.055	.003
11	.000	.000	.001	.014	.067	.162	.210	.120	.014
12	.000	.000	.000	.004	.028	.101	.204	.200	.051
13	.000	.000	.000	.001	.009	.047	.146	.246	.142
14	.000	.000	.000	.000	.002	.015	.073	.211	.275
15	.000	.000	.000	.000	.000	.003	.023	.113	.329
16	.000	.000	.000	.000	.000	.000	.003	.028	.185

				$n = 17$					
				Probability					
x	.1	.2	.3	.4	.5	.6	.7	.8	.9
0	.167	.023	.002	.000	.000	.000	.000	.000	.000
1	.315	.096	.017	.002	.000	.000	.000	.000	.000
2	.280	.191	.058	.010	.001	.000	.000	.000	.000
3	.156	.239	.125	.034	.005	.000	.000	.000	.000
4	.060	.209	.187	.080	.018	.002	.000	.000	.000
5	.017	.136	.208	.138	.047	.008	.001	.000	.000
6	.004	.068	.178	.184	.094	.024	.003	.000	.000
7	.001	.027	.120	.193	.148	.057	.009	.000	.000
8	.000	.008	.064	.161	.185	.107	.028	.002	.000
9	.000	.002	.028	.107	.185	.161	.064	.008	.000
10	.000	.000	.009	.057	.148	.193	.120	.027	.001
11	.000	.000	.003	.024	.094	.184	.178	.068	.004
12	.000	.000	.001	.008	.047	.138	.208	.136	.017
13	.000	.000	.000	.002	.018	.080	.187	.209	.060
14	.000	.000	.000	.000	.005	.034	.125	.239	.156
15	.000	.000	.000	.000	.001	.010	.058	.191	.280
16	.000	.000	.000	.000	.000	.002	.017	.096	.315
17	.000	.000	.000	.000	.000	.000	.002	.023	.167

(*continued*)

TABLE A.2 **Binomial Probability Distribution** (*continued*)

					$n = 18$				
					Probability				
x	.1	.2	.3	.4	.5	.6	.7	.8	.9
0	.150	.018	.002	.000	.000	.000	.000	.000	.000
1	.300	.081	.013	.001	.000	.000	.000	.000	.000
2	.284	.172	.046	.007	.001	.000	.000	.000	.000
3	.168	.230	.105	.025	.003	.000	.000	.000	.000
4	.070	.215	.168	.061	.012	.001	.000	.000	.000
5	.022	.151	.202	.115	.033	.004	.000	.000	.000
6	.005	.082	.187	.166	.071	.015	.001	.000	.000
7	.001	.035	.138	.189	.121	.037	.005	.000	.000
8	.000	.012	.081	.173	.167	.077	.015	.001	.000
9	.000	.003	.039	.128	.185	.128	.039	.003	.000
10	.000	.001	.015	.077	.167	.173	.081	.012	.000
11	.000	.000	.005	.037	.121	.189	.138	.035	.001
12	.000	.000	.001	.015	.071	.166	.187	.082	.005
13	.000	.000	.000	.004	.033	.115	.202	.151	.022
14	.000	.000	.000	.001	.012	.061	.168	.215	.070
15	.000	.000	.000	.000	.003	.025	.105	.230	.168
16	.000	.000	.000	.000	.001	.007	.046	.172	.284
17	.000	.000	.000	.000	.000	.001	.013	.081	.300
18	.000	.000	.000	.000	.000	.000	.002	.018	.150

					$n = 19$				
					Probability				
x	.1	.2	.3	.4	.5	.6	.7	.8	.9
0	.135	.014	.001	.000	.000	.000	.000	.000	.000
1	.285	.068	.009	.001	.000	.000	.000	.000	.000
2	.285	.154	.036	.005	.000	.000	.000	.000	.000
3	.180	.218	.087	.017	.002	.000	.000	.000	.000
4	.080	.218	.149	.047	.007	.001	.000	.000	.000
5	.027	.164	.192	.093	.022	.002	.000	.000	.000
6	.007	.095	.192	.145	.052	.008	.001	.000	.000
7	.001	.044	.153	.180	.096	.024	.002	.000	.000
8	.000	.017	.098	.180	.144	.053	.008	.000	.000
9	.000	.005	.051	.146	.176	.098	.022	.001	.000
10	.000	.001	.022	.098	.176	.146	.051	.005	.000
11	.000	.000	.008	.053	.144	.180	.098	.017	.000
12	.000	.000	.002	.024	.096	.180	.153	.044	.001
13	.000	.000	.001	.008	.052	.145	.192	.095	.007
14	.000	.000	.000	.002	.022	.093	.192	.164	.027
15	.000	.000	.000	.001	.007	.047	.149	.218	.080
16	.000	.000	.000	.000	.002	.017	.087	.218	.180
17	.000	.000	.000	.000	.000	.005	.036	.154	.285
18	.000	.000	.000	.000	.000	.001	.009	.068	.285
19	.000	.000	.000	.000	.000	.000	.001	.014	.135

x	.1	.2	.3	.4	.5	.6	.7	.8	.9
				$n = 20$					
				Probability					
0	.122	.012	.001	.000	.000	.000	.000	.000	.000
1	.270	.058	.007	.000	.000	.000	.000	.000	.000
2	.285	.137	.028	.003	.000	.000	.000	.000	.000
3	.190	.205	.072	.012	.001	.000	.000	.000	.000
4	.090	.218	.130	.035	.005	.000	.000	.000	.000
5	.032	.175	.179	.075	.015	.001	.000	.000	.000
6	.009	.109	.192	.124	.037	.005	.000	.000	.000
7	.002	.055	.164	.166	.074	.015	.001	.000	.000
8	.000	.022	.114	.180	.120	.035	.004	.000	.000
9	.000	.007	.065	.160	.160	.071	.012	.000	.000
10	.000	.002	.031	.117	.176	.117	.031	.002	.000
11	.000	.000	.012	.071	.160	.160	.065	.007	.000
12	.000	.000	.004	.035	.120	.180	.114	.022	.000
13	.000	.000	.001	.015	.074	.166	.164	.055	.002
14	.000	.000	.000	.005	.037	.124	.192	.109	.009
15	.000	.000	.000	.001	.015	.075	.179	.175	.032
16	.000	.000	.000	.000	.005	.035	.130	.218	.090
17	.000	.000	.000	.000	.001	.012	.072	.205	.190
18	.000	.000	.000	.000	.000	.003	.028	.137	.285
19	.000	.000	.000	.000	.000	.000	.007	.058	.270
20	.000	.000	.000	.000	.000	.000	.001	.012	.122
				$n = 25$					
				Probability					
0	.072	.004	.000	.000	.000	.000	.000	.000	.000
1	.199	.024	.001	.000	.000	.000	.000	.000	.000
2	.266	.071	.007	.000	.000	.000	.000	.000	.000
3	.226	.136	.024	.002	.000	.000	.000	.000	.000
4	.138	.187	.057	.007	.000	.000	.000	.000	.000
5	.065	.196	.103	.020	.002	.000	.000	.000	.000
6	.024	.163	.147	.044	.005	.000	.000	.000	.000
7	.007	.111	.171	.080	.014	.001	.000	.000	.000
8	.002	.062	.165	.120	.032	.003	.000	.000	.000
9	.000	.029	.134	.151	.061	.009	.000	.000	.000
10	.000	.012	.092	.161	.097	.021	.001	.000	.000
11	.000	.004	.054	.147	.133	.043	.004	.000	.000
12	.000	.001	.027	.114	.155	.076	.011	.000	.000
13	.000	.000	.011	.076	.155	.114	.027	.001	.000
14	.000	.000	.004	.043	.133	.147	.054	.004	.000
15	.000	.000	.001	.021	.097	.161	.092	.012	.000
16	.000	.000	.000	.009	.061	.151	.134	.029	.000
17	.000	.000	.000	.003	.032	.120	.165	.062	.002
18	.000	.000	.000	.001	.014	.080	.171	.111	.007
19	.000	.000	.000	.000	.005	.044	.147	.163	.024
20	.000	.000	.000	.000	.002	.020	.103	.196	.065
21	.000	.000	.000	.000	.000	.007	.057	.187	.138
22	.000	.000	.000	.000	.000	.002	.024	.136	.226
23	.000	.000	.000	.000	.000	.000	.007	.071	.266
24	.000	.000	.000	.000	.000	.000	.001	.024	.199
25	.000	.000	.000	.000	.000	.000	.000	.004	.072

TABLE A.3 Poisson Probabilities

					λ				
x	.005	.01	.02	.03	.04	.05	.06	.07	.08	.09
0	.9950	.9900	.9802	.9704	.9608	.9512	.9418	.9324	.9231	.9139
1	.0050	.0099	.0196	.0291	.0384	.0476	.0565	.0653	.0738	.0823
2	.0000	.0000	.0002	.0004	.0008	.0012	.0017	.0023	.0030	.0037
3	.0000	.0000	.0000	.0000	.0000	.0000	.0000	.0001	.0001	.0001

x	.1	.2	.3	.4	.5	.6	.7	.8	.9	1.0
0	.9048	.8187	.7408	.6703	.6065	.5488	.4966	.4493	.4066	.3679
1	.0905	.1637	.2222	.2681	.3033	.3293	.3476	.3595	.3659	.3679
2	.0045	.0164	.0333	.0536	.0758	.0988	.1217	.1438	.1647	.1839
3	.0002	.0011	.0033	.0072	.0126	.0198	.0284	.0383	.0494	.0613
4	.0000	.0001	.0003	.0007	.0016	.0030	.0050	.0077	.0111	.0153
5	.0000	.0000	.0000	.0001	.0002	.0004	.0007	.0012	.0020	.0031
6	.0000	.0000	.0000	.0000	.0000	.0000	.0001	.0002	.0003	.0005
7	.0000	.0000	.0000	.0000	.0000	.0000	.0000	.0000	.0000	.0001

x	1.1	1.2	1.3	1.4	1.5	1.6	1.7	1.8	1.9	2.0
0	.3329	.3012	.2725	.2466	.2231	.2019	.1827	.1653	.1496	.1353
1	.3662	.3614	.3543	.3452	.3347	.3230	.3106	.2975	.2842	.2707
2	.2014	.2169	.2303	.2417	.2510	.2584	.2640	.2678	.2700	.2707
3	.0738	.0867	.0998	.1128	.1255	.1378	.1496	.1607	.1710	.1804
4	.0203	.0260	.0324	.0395	.0471	.0551	.0636	.0723	.0812	.0902
5	.0045	.0062	.0084	.0111	.0141	.0176	.0216	.0260	.0309	.0361
6	.0008	.0012	.0018	.0026	.0035	.0047	.0061	.0078	.0098	.0120
7	.0001	.0002	.0003	.0005	.0008	.0011	.0015	.0020	.0027	.0034
8	.0000	.0000	.0001	.0001	.0001	.0002	.0003	.0005	.0006	.0009
9	.0000	.0000	.0000	.0000	.0000	.0000	.0001	.0001	.0001	.0002

x	2.1	2.2	2.3	2.4	2.5	2.6	2.7	2.8	2.9	3.0
0	.1225	.1108	.1003	.0907	.0821	.0743	.0672	.0608	.0550	.0498
1	.2572	.2438	.2306	.2177	.2052	.1931	.1815	.1703	.1596	.1494
2	.2700	.2681	.2652	.2613	.2565	.2510	.2450	.2384	.2314	.2240
3	.1890	.1966	.2033	.2090	.2138	.2176	.2205	.2225	.2237	.2240
4	.0992	.1082	.1169	.1254	.1336	.1414	.1488	.1557	.1622	.1680
5	.0417	.0476	.0538	.0602	.0668	.0735	.0804	.0872	.0940	.1008
6	.0146	.0174	.0206	.0241	.0278	.0319	.0362	.0407	.0455	.0504
7	.0044	.0055	.0068	.0083	.0099	.0118	.0139	.0163	.0188	.0216
8	.0011	.0015	.0019	.0025	.0031	.0038	.0047	.0057	.0068	.0081
9	.0003	.0004	.0005	.0007	.0009	.0011	.0014	.0018	.0022	.0027
10	.0001	.0001	.0001	.0002	.0002	.0003	.0004	.0005	.0006	.0008
11	.0000	.0000	.0000	.0000	.0000	.0001	.0001	.0001	.0002	.0002
12	.0000	.0000	.0000	.0000	.0000	.0000	.0000	.0000	.0000	.0001

TABLE A.4   The e^{-x} Table

x	e^{-x}	x	e^{-x}	x	e^{-x}	x	e^{-x}
0.0	1.0000	3.0	0.0498	6.0	0.00248	9.0	0.00012
0.1	0.9048	3.1	0.0450	6.1	0.00224	9.1	0.00011
0.2	0.8187	3.2	0.0408	6.2	0.00203	9.2	0.00010
0.3	0.7408	3.3	0.0369	6.3	0.00184	9.3	0.00009
0.4	0.6703	3.4	0.0334	6.4	0.00166	9.4	0.00008
0.5	0.6065	3.5	0.0302	6.5	0.00150	9.5	0.00007
0.6	0.5488	3.6	0.0273	6.6	0.00136	9.6	0.00007
0.7	0.4966	3.7	0.0247	6.7	0.00123	9.7	0.00006
0.8	0.4493	3.8	0.0224	6.8	0.00111	9.8	0.00006
0.9	0.4066	3.9	0.0202	6.9	0.00101	9.9	0.00005
1.0	0.3679	4.0	0.0183	7.0	0.00091	10.0	0.00005
1.1	0.3329	4.1	0.0166	7.1	0.00083		
1.2	0.3012	4.2	0.0150	7.2	0.00075		
1.3	0.2725	4.3	0.0136	7.3	0.00068		
1.4	0.2466	4.4	0.0123	7.4	0.00061		
1.5	0.2231	4.5	0.0111	7.5	0.00055		
1.6	0.2019	4.6	0.0101	7.6	0.00050		
1.7	0.1827	4.7	0.0091	7.7	0.00045		
1.8	0.1653	4.8	0.0082	7.8	0.00041		
1.9	0.1496	4.9	0.0074	7.9	0.00037		
2.0	0.1353	5.0	0.0067	8.0	0.00034		
2.1	0.1225	5.1	0.0061	8.1	0.00030		
2.2	0.1108	5.2	0.0055	8.2	0.00027		
2.3	0.1003	5.3	0.0050	8.3	0.00025		
2.4	0.0907	5.4	0.0045	8.4	0.00022		
2.5	0.0821	5.5	0.0041	8.5	0.00020		
2.6	0.0743	5.6	0.0037	8.6	0.00018		
2.7	0.0672	5.7	0.0033	8.7	0.00017		
2.8	0.0608	5.8	0.0030	8.8	0.00015		
2.9	0.0550	5.9	0.0027	8.9	0.00014		

TABLE A.5 Areas of the Standard Normal Distribution

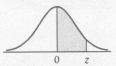

The entries in this table are the probabilities that a standard normal random variable is between 0 and z (the shaded area).

z	0.00	0.01	0.02	0.03	0.04	0.05	0.06	0.07	0.08	0.09
0.0	.0000	.0040	.0080	.0120	.0160	.0199	.0239	.0279	.0319	.0359
0.1	.0398	.0438	.0478	.0517	.0557	.0596	.0636	.0675	.0714	.0753
0.2	.0793	.0832	.0871	.0910	.0948	.0987	.1026	.1064	.1103	.1141
0.3	.1179	.1217	.1255	.1293	.1331	.1368	.1406	.1443	.1480	.1517
0.4	.1554	.1591	.1628	.1664	.1700	.1736	.1772	.1808	.1844	.1879
0.5	.1915	.1950	.1985	.2019	.2054	.2088	.2123	.2157	.2190	.2224
0.6	.2257	.2291	.2324	.2357	.2389	.2422	.2454	.2486	.2517	.2549
0.7	.2580	.2611	.2642	.2673	.2704	.2734	.2764	.2794	.2823	.2852
0.8	.2881	.2910	.2939	.2967	.2995	.3023	.3051	.3078	.3106	.3133
0.9	.3159	.3186	.3212	.3238	.3264	.3289	.3315	.3340	.3365	.3389
1.0	.3413	.3438	.3461	.3485	.3508	.3531	.3554	.3577	.3599	.3621
1.1	.3643	.3665	.3686	.3708	.3729	.3749	.3770	.3790	.3810	.3830
1.2	.3849	.3869	.3888	.3907	.3925	.3944	.3962	.3980	.3997	.4015
1.3	.4032	.4049	.4066	.4082	.4099	.4115	.4131	.4147	.4162	.4177
1.4	.4192	.4207	.4222	.4236	.4251	.4265	.4279	.4292	.4306	.4319
1.5	.4332	.4345	.4357	.4370	.4382	.4394	.4406	.4418	.4429	.4441
1.6	.4452	.4463	.4474	.4484	.4495	.4505	.4515	.4525	.4535	.4545
1.7	.4554	.4564	.4573	.4582	.4591	.4599	.4608	.4616	.4625	.4633
1.8	.4641	.4649	.4656	.4664	.4671	.4678	.4686	.4693	.4699	.4706
1.9	.4713	.4719	.4726	.4732	.4738	.4744	.4750	.4756	.4761	.4767
2.0	.4772	.4778	.4783	.4788	.4793	.4798	.4803	.4808	.4812	.4817
2.1	.4821	.4826	.4830	.4834	.4838	.4842	.4846	.4850	.4854	.4857
2.2	.4861	.4864	.4868	.4871	.4875	.4878	.4881	.4884	.4887	.4890
2.3	.4893	.4896	.4898	.4901	.4904	.4906	.4909	.4911	.4913	.4916
2.4	.4918	.4920	.4922	.4925	.4927	.4929	.4931	.4932	.4934	.4936
2.5	.4938	.4940	.4941	.4943	.4945	.4946	.4948	.4949	.4951	.4952
2.6	.4953	.4955	.4956	.4957	.4959	.4960	.4961	.4962	.4963	.4964
2.7	.4965	.4966	.4967	.4968	.4969	.4970	.4971	.4972	.4973	.4974
2.8	.4974	.4975	.4976	.4977	.4977	.4978	.4979	.4979	.4980	.4981
2.9	.4981	.4982	.4982	.4983	.4984	.4984	.4985	.4985	.4986	.4986
3.0	.4987	.4987	.4987	.4988	.4988	.4989	.4989	.4989	.4990	.4990
3.1	.4990	.4991	.4991	.4991	.4992	.4992	.4992	.4992	.4993	.4993
3.2	.4993	.4993	.4994	.4994	.4994	.4994	.4994	.4995	.4995	.4995
3.3	.4995	.4995	.4995	.4996	.4996	.4996	.4996	.4996	.4996	.4997
3.4	.4997	.4997	.4997	.4997	.4997	.4997	.4997	.4997	.4997	.4998
3.5	.4998									
4.0	.49997									
4.5	.499997									
5.0	.4999997									
6.0	.499999999									

TABLE A.6   **Critical Values from the *t* Distribution**

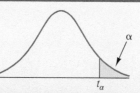

| Values of α for one-tailed test and $\alpha/2$ for two-tailed test |||||||
df	$t_{.100}$	$t_{.050}$	$t_{.025}$	$t_{.010}$	$t_{.005}$	$t_{.001}$
1	3.078	6.314	12.706	31.821	63.656	318.289
2	1.886	2.920	4.303	6.965	9.925	22.328
3	1.638	2.353	3.182	4.541	5.841	10.214
4	1.533	2.132	2.776	3.747	4.604	7.173
5	1.476	2.015	2.571	3.365	4.032	5.894
6	1.440	1.943	2.447	3.143	3.707	5.208
7	1.415	1.895	2.365	2.998	3.499	4.785
8	1.397	1.860	2.306	2.896	3.355	4.501
9	1.383	1.833	2.262	2.821	3.250	4.297
10	1.372	1.812	2.228	2.764	3.169	4.144
11	1.363	1.796	2.201	2.718	3.106	4.025
12	1.356	1.782	2.179	2.681	3.055	3.930
13	1.350	1.771	2.160	2.650	3.012	3.852
14	1.345	1.761	2.145	2.624	2.977	3.787
15	1.341	1.753	2.131	2.602	2.947	3.733
16	1.337	1.746	2.120	2.583	2.921	3.686
17	1.333	1.740	2.110	2.567	2.898	3.646
18	1.330	1.734	2.101	2.552	2.878	3.610
19	1.328	1.729	2.093	2.539	2.861	3.579
20	1.325	1.725	2.086	2.528	2.845	3.552
21	1.323	1.721	2.080	2.518	2.831	3.527
22	1.321	1.717	2.074	2.508	2.819	3.505
23	1.319	1.714	2.069	2.500	2.807	3.485
24	1.318	1.711	2.064	2.492	2.797	3.467
25	1.316	1.708	2.060	2.485	2.787	3.450
26	1.315	1.706	2.056	2.479	2.779	3.435
27	1.314	1.703	2.052	2.473	2.771	3.421
28	1.313	1.701	2.048	2.467	2.763	3.408
29	1.311	1.699	2.045	2.462	2.756	3.396
30	1.310	1.697	2.042	2.457	2.750	3.385
40	1.303	1.684	2.021	2.423	2.704	3.307
50	1.299	1.676	2.009	2.403	2.678	3.261
60	1.296	1.671	2.000	2.390	2.660	3.232
70	1.294	1.667	1.994	2.381	2.648	3.211
80	1.292	1.664	1.990	2.374	2.639	3.195
90	1.291	1.662	1.987	2.368	2.632	3.183
100	1.290	1.660	1.984	2.364	2.626	3.174
150	1.287	1.655	1.976	2.351	2.609	3.145
200	1.286	1.653	1.972	2.345	2.601	3.131
∞	1.282	1.645	1.960	2.326	2.576	3.090

TABLE A.7 Percentage Points of the *F* Distribution

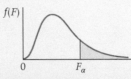

v_2 \ v_1	$\alpha = .10$ Numerator Degrees of Freedom								
	1	2	3	4	5	6	7	8	9
1	39.86	49.50	53.59	55.83	57.24	58.20	58.91	59.44	59.86
2	8.53	3.00	9.16	9.24	9.29	9.33	9.35	9.37	9.38
3	5.54	5.46	5.39	5.34	5.31	5.28	5.27	5.25	5.24
4	4.54	4.32	4.19	4.11	4.05	4.01	3.98	3.95	3.94
5	4.06	4.78	3.62	3.52	3.45	3.40	3.37	3.34	3.32
6	3.78	3.46	3.29	3.18	3.11	3.05	3.01	2.98	2.96
7	3.59	3.26	3.07	2.96	2.88	2.83	2.78	2.75	2.72
8	3.46	3.11	2.92	2.81	2.73	2.67	2.62	2.59	2.56
9	3.36	3.01	2.81	2.69	2.61	2.55	2.51	2.47	2.44
10	3.29	2.92	2.73	2.61	2.52	2.46	2.41	2.38	2.35
11	3.23	2.86	2.66	2.54	2.45	2.39	2.34	2.30	2.27
12	3.18	2.81	2.61	2.48	2.39	2.33	2.28	2.24	2.21
13	3.14	2.76	2.56	2.43	2.35	2.28	2.23	2.20	2.16
14	3.10	2.73	2.52	2.39	2.31	2.24	2.19	2.15	2.12
15	3.07	2.70	2.49	2.36	2.27	2.21	2.16	2.12	2.09
16	3.05	2.67	2.46	2.33	2.24	2.18	2.13	2.09	2.06
17	3.03	2.64	2.44	2.31	2.22	2.15	2.10	2.06	2.03
18	3.01	2.62	2.42	2.29	2.20	2.13	2.08	2.04	2.00
19	2.99	2.61	2.40	2.27	2.18	2.11	2.06	2.02	1.98
20	2.97	2.59	2.38	2.25	2.16	2.09	2.04	2.00	1.96
21	2.96	2.57	2.36	2.23	2.14	2.08	2.02	1.98	1.95
22	2.95	2.56	2.35	2.22	2.13	2.06	2.01	1.97	1.93
23	2.94	2.55	2.34	2.21	2.11	2.05	1.99	1.95	1.92
24	2.93	2.54	2.33	2.19	2.10	2.04	1.98	1.94	1.91
25	2.92	2.53	2.32	2.18	2.09	2.02	1.97	1.93	1.89
26	2.91	2.52	2.31	2.17	2.08	2.01	1.96	1.92	1.88
27	2.90	2.51	2.30	2.17	2.07	2.00	1.95	1.91	1.87
28	2.89	2.50	2.29	2.16	2.06	2.00	1.94	1.90	1.87
29	2.89	2.50	2.28	2.15	2.06	1.99	1.93	1.89	1.86
30	2.88	2.49	2.28	2.14	2.05	1.98	1.93	1.88	1.85
40	2.84	2.44	2.23	2.09	2.00	1.93	1.87	1.83	1.79
60	2.79	2.39	2.18	2.04	1.95	1.87	1.82	1.77	1.74
120	2.75	2.35	2.13	1.99	1.90	1.82	1.77	1.72	1.68
∞	2.71	2.30	2.08	1.94	1.85	1.77	1.72	1.67	1.63

Denominator Degrees of Freedom

10	12	15	20	24	30	40	60	120	∞	v_1 v_2
				$\alpha = .10$						
			Numerator Degrees of Freedom							
60.19	60.71	61.22	61.74	62.00	62.26	62.53	62.79	63.06	63.33	1
9.39	9.41	9.42	9.44	9.45	9.46	9.47	9.47	9.48	9.49	2
5.23	5.22	5.20	5.18	5.18	5.17	5.16	5.15	5.14	5.13	3
3.92	3.90	3.87	3.84	3.83	3.82	3.80	3.79	3.78	3.76	4
3.30	3.27	3.24	3.21	3.19	3.17	3.16	3.14	3.12	3.10	5
2.94	2.90	2.87	2.84	2.82	2.80	2.78	2.76	2.74	2.72	6
2.70	2.67	2.63	2.59	2.58	2.56	2.54	2.51	2.49	2.47	7
2.54	2.50	2.46	2.42	2.40	2.38	2.36	2.34	2.32	2.29	8
2.42	2.38	2.34	2.30	2.28	2.25	2.23	2.21	2.18	2.16	9
2.32	2.28	2.24	2.20	2.18	2.16	2.13	2.11	2.08	2.06	10
2.25	2.21	2.17	2.12	2.10	2.08	2.05	2.03	2.00	1.97	11
2.19	2.15	2.10	2.06	2.04	2.01	1.99	1.96	1.93	1.90	12
2.14	2.10	2.05	2.01	1.98	1.96	1.93	1.90	1.88	1.85	13
2.10	2.05	2.01	1.96	1.94	1.91	1.89	1.86	1.83	1.80	14
2.06	2.02	1.97	1.92	1.90	1.87	1.85	1.82	1.79	1.76	15
2.03	1.99	1.94	1.89	1.87	1.84	1.81	1.78	1.75	1.72	16
2.00	1.96	1.91	1.86	1.84	1.81	1.78	1.75	1.72	1.69	17
1.98	1.93	1.89	1.84	1.81	1.78	1.75	1.72	1.69	1.66	18
1.96	1.91	1.86	1.81	1.79	1.76	1.73	1.70	1.67	1.63	19
1.94	1.89	1.84	1.79	1.77	1.74	1.71	1.68	1.64	1.61	20
1.92	1.87	1.83	1.78	1.75	1.72	1.69	1.66	1.62	1.59	21
1.90	1.86	1.81	1.76	1.73	1.70	1.67	1.64	1.60	1.57	22
1.89	1.84	1.80	1.74	1.72	1.69	1.66	1.62	1.59	1.55	23
1.88	1.83	1.78	1.73	1.70	1.67	1.64	1.61	1.57	1.53	24
1.87	1.82	1.77	1.72	1.69	1.66	1.63	1.59	1.56	1.52	25
1.86	1.81	1.76	1.71	1.68	1.65	1.61	1.58	1.54	1.50	26
1.85	1.80	1.75	1.70	1.67	1.64	1.60	1.57	1.53	1.49	27
1.84	1.79	1.74	1.69	1.66	1.63	1.59	1.56	1.52	1.48	28
1.83	1.78	1.73	1.68	1.65	1.62	1.58	1.55	1.51	1.47	29
1.82	1.77	1.72	1.67	1.64	1.61	1.57	1.54	1.50	1.46	30
1.76	1.71	1.66	1.61	1.57	1.54	1.51	1.47	1.42	1.38	40
1.71	1.66	1.60	1.54	1.51	1.48	1.44	1.40	1.35	1.29	60
1.65	1.60	1.55	1.48	1.45	1.41	1.37	1.32	1.26	1.19	120
1.60	1.55	1.49	1.42	1.38	1.34	1.30	1.24	1.17	1.00	∞

Denominator Degrees of Freedom

(continued)

TABLE A.7   **Percentage Points of the *F* Distribution** (*continued*)

v_2 \ v_1	1	2	3	4	5	6	7	8	9
1	161.45	199.50	215.71	224.58	230.16	233.99	236.77	238.88	240.54
2	18.51	19.00	19.16	19.25	19.30	19.33	19.35	19.37	19.38
3	10.13	9.55	9.28	9.12	9.01	8.94	8.89	8.85	8.81
4	7.71	6.94	6.59	6.39	6.26	6.16	6.09	6.04	6.00
5	6.61	5.79	5.41	5.19	5.05	4.95	4.88	4.82	4.77
6	5.99	5.14	4.76	4.53	4.39	4.28	4.21	4.15	4.10
7	5.59	4.74	4.35	3.12	3.97	3.87	3.79	3.73	3.68
8	5.32	4.46	4.07	3.84	3.69	3.58	3.50	3.44	3.39
9	5.12	4.26	3.71	3.63	3.48	3.37	3.29	3.23	3.18
10	4.96	4.10	3.71	3.48	3.33	3.22	3.14	3.07	3.02
11	4.84	3.98	3.59	3.36	3.20	3.09	3.01	2.95	2.90
12	4.75	3.89	3.49	3.26	3.11	3.00	2.91	2.85	2.80
13	4.67	3.81	3.41	3.18	3.03	2.92	2.83	2.77	2.71
14	4.60	3.74	3.34	3.11	2.96	2.85	2.76	2.70	2.65
15	4.54	3.68	3.29	3.06	2.90	2.79	2.71	2.64	2.59
16	4.49	3.63	3.24	3.01	2.85	2.74	2.66	2.59	2.54
17	4.45	3.59	3.20	2.96	2.81	2.70	2.61	2.55	2.49
18	4.41	3.55	3.16	2.93	2.77	2.66	2.58	2.51	2.46
19	4.38	3.52	3.13	2.90	2.74	2.63	2.54	2.48	2.42
20	4.35	3.49	3.10	2.87	2.71	2.60	2.51	2.45	2.39
21	4.32	3.47	3.07	2.84	2.68	2.57	2.49	2.42	2.37
22	4.30	3.44	3.05	2.82	2.66	2.55	2.46	2.40	2.34
23	4.28	3.42	3.03	2.80	2.64	2.53	2.44	2.37	2.32
24	4.26	3.40	3.01	2.78	2.62	2.51	2.42	2.36	2.30
25	4.24	3.39	2.99	2.76	2.60	2.49	2.40	2.34	2.28
26	4.23	3.37	2.98	2.74	2.59	2.47	2.39	2.32	2.27
27	4.21	3.35	2.96	2.73	2.57	2.46	2.37	2.31	2.25
28	4.20	3.34	2.95	2.71	2.56	2.45	2.36	2.29	2.24
29	4.18	3.33	2.93	2.70	2.55	2.43	2.35	2.28	2.22
30	4.17	3.32	2.92	2.69	2.53	2.42	2.33	2.27	2.21
40	4.08	3.23	2.84	2.61	2.45	2.34	2.25	2.18	2.12
60	4.00	3.15	2.76	2.53	2.37	2.25	2.17	2.10	2.04
120	3.92	3.07	2.68	2.45	2.29	2.18	2.09	2.02	1.96
∞	3.84	3.00	2.60	2.37	2.21	2.10	2.01	1.94	1.88

$\alpha = .05$

Numerator Degrees of Freedom

Denominator Degrees of Freedom

$\alpha = .05$										v_1
Numerator Degrees of Freedom										v_2
10	12	15	20	24	30	40	60	120	∞	
241.88	243.90	245.90	248.00	249.10	250.10	251.10	252.20	253.30	254.30	1
19.40	19.41	19.43	19.45	19.45	19.46	19.47	19.48	19.49	19.50	2
8.79	8.74	8.70	8.66	8.64	8.62	8.59	8.57	8.55	8.53	3
5.96	5.91	5.86	5.80	5.77	5.75	5.72	5.69	5.66	5.63	4
4.74	4.68	4.62	4.56	4.53	4.50	4.46	4.43	4.40	4.36	5
4.06	4.00	3.94	3.87	3.84	3.81	3.77	3.74	3.70	3.67	6
3.64	3.57	3.51	3.44	3.41	3.38	3.34	3.30	3.27	3.23	7
3.35	3.28	3.22	3.15	3.12	3.08	3.04	3.01	2.97	2.93	8
3.14	3.07	3.01	2.94	2.90	2.86	2.83	2.79	2.75	2.71	9
2.98	2.91	2.85	2.77	2.74	2.70	2.66	2.62	2.58	2.54	10
2.85	2.79	2.72	2.65	2.61	2.57	2.53	2.49	2.45	2.40	11
2.75	2.69	2.62	2.54	2.51	2.47	2.43	2.38	2.34	2.30	12
2.67	2.60	2.53	2.46	2.42	2.38	2.34	2.30	2.25	2.21	13
2.60	2.53	2.46	2.39	2.35	2.31	2.27	2.22	2.18	2.13	14
2.54	2.48	2.40	2.33	2.29	2.25	2.20	2.16	2.11	2.07	15
2.49	2.42	2.35	2.28	2.24	2.19	2.15	2.11	2.06	2.01	16
2.45	2.38	2.31	2.23	2.19	2.15	2.10	2.06	2.01	1.96	17
2.41	2.34	2.27	2.19	2.15	2.11	2.06	2.02	1.97	1.92	18
2.38	2.31	2.23	2.16	2.11	2.07	2.03	1.98	1.93	1.88	19
2.35	2.28	2.20	2.12	2.08	2.04	1.99	1.95	1.90	1.84	20
2.32	2.25	2.18	2.10	2.05	2.01	1.96	1.92	1.87	1.81	21
2.30	2.23	2.15	2.07	2.03	1.98	1.94	1.89	1.84	1.78	22
2.27	2.20	2.13	2.05	2.01	1.96	1.91	1.86	1.81	1.76	23
2.25	2.18	2.11	2.03	1.98	1.94	1.89	1.84	1.79	1.73	24
2.24	2.16	2.09	2.01	1.96	1.92	1.87	1.82	1.77	1.71	25
2.22	2.15	2.07	1.99	1.95	1.90	1.85	1.80	1.75	1.69	26
2.20	2.13	2.06	1.97	1.93	1.88	1.84	1.79	1.73	1.67	27
2.19	2.12	2.04	1.96	1.91	1.87	1.82	1.77	1.71	1.65	28
2.18	2.10	2.03	1.94	1.90	1.85	1.81	1.75	1.70	1.64	29
2.16	2.09	2.01	1.93	1.89	1.84	1.79	1.74	1.68	1.62	30
2.08	2.00	1.92	1.84	1.79	1.74	1.69	1.64	1.58	1.51	40
1.99	1.92	1.84	1.75	1.70	1.65	1.59	1.53	1.47	1.39	60
1.91	1.83	1.75	1.66	1.61	1.55	1.50	1.43	1.35	1.25	120
1.83	1.75	1.67	1.57	1.52	1.46	1.39	1.32	1.22	1.00	∞

Denominator Degrees of Freedom

(continued)

TABLE A.7   Percentage Points of the *F* Distribution (*continued*)

v_2	v_1 $\alpha = .025$ Numerator Degrees of Freedom								
	1	**2**	**3**	**4**	**5**	**6**	**7**	**8**	**9**
1	647.79	799.48	864.15	899.60	921.83	937.11	948.20	956.64	963.28
2	38.51	39.00	39.17	39.25	39.30	39.33	39.36	39.37	39.39
3	17.44	16.04	15.44	15.10	14.88	14.73	14.62	14.54	14.47
4	12.22	10.65	9.98	9.60	9.36	9.20	9.07	8.98	8.90
5	10.01	8.43	7.76	7.39	7.15	6.98	6.85	6.76	6.68
6	8.81	7.26	6.60	6.23	5.99	5.82	5.70	7.60	5.52
7	8.07	6.54	5.89	5.52	5.29	5.12	4.99	4.90	4.82
8	7.57	6.06	5.42	5.05	4.82	4.65	4.53	4.43	4.36
9	7.21	5.71	5.08	4.72	4.48	4.32	4.20	4.10	4.03
10	6.94	5.46	4.83	4.47	4.24	4.07	3.95	3.85	3.78
11	6.72	5.26	4.63	4.28	4.04	3.88	3.76	3.66	3.59
12	6.55	5.10	4.47	4.12	3.89	3.73	3.61	3.51	3.44
13	6.41	4.97	4.35	4.00	3.77	3.60	3.48	3.39	3.31
14	6.30	4.86	4.24	3.89	3.66	3.50	3.38	3.29	3.21
15	6.20	4.77	4.15	3.80	3.58	3.41	3.29	3.20	3.12
16	6.12	4.69	4.08	3.73	3.50	3.34	3.22	3.12	3.05
17	6.04	4.62	4.01	3.66	3.44	3.28	3.16	3.06	2.98
18	5.98	4.56	3.95	3.61	3.38	3.22	3.10	3.01	2.93
19	5.92	4.51	3.90	3.56	3.33	3.17	3.05	2.96	2.88
20	5.87	4.46	3.86	3.51	3.29	3.13	3.01	2.91	2.84
21	5.83	4.42	3.82	3.48	3.25	3.09	2.97	2.87	2.80
22	5.79	4.38	3.78	3.44	3.22	3.05	2.93	2.84	2.76
23	5.75	4.35	3.75	3.41	3.18	3.02	2.90	2.81	2.73
24	5.72	4.32	3.72	3.38	3.15	2.99	2.87	2.78	2.70
25	5.69	4.29	3.69	3.35	3.13	2.97	2.85	2.75	2.68
26	5.66	4.27	3.67	3.33	3.10	2.94	2.82	2.73	2.65
27	5.63	4.24	3.65	3.31	3.08	2.92	2.80	2.71	2.63
28	5.61	4.22	3.63	3.29	3.06	2.90	2.78	2.69	2.61
29	5.59	4.20	3.61	3.27	3.04	2.88	2.76	2.67	2.59
30	5.57	4.18	3.59	3.25	3.03	2.87	2.75	2.65	2.57
40	5.42	4.05	3.46	3.13	2.90	2.74	2.62	2.53	2.45
60	5.29	3.93	3.34	3.01	2.79	2.63	2.51	2.41	2.33
120	5.15	3.80	3.23	2.89	2.67	2.52	2.39	2.30	2.22
∞	5.02	3.69	3.12	2.79	2.57	2.41	2.29	2.19	2.11

Denominator Degrees of Freedom

$\alpha = .025$										v_1
Numerator Degrees of Freedom										v_2
10	12	15	20	24	30	40	60	120	∞	
968.63	976.72	984.87	993.08	997.27	1001.40	1005.60	1009.79	1014.04	1018.00	1
39.40	39.41	39.43	39.45	39.46	39.46	39.47	39.48	39.49	39.50	2
14.42	14.34	14.25	14.17	14.12	14.08	14.04	13.99	13.95	13.90	3
8.84	8.75	8.66	8.56	8.51	8.46	8.41	8.36	8.31	8.26	4
6.62	6.52	6.43	6.33	6.28	6.23	6.18	6.12	6.07	6.02	5
5.46	5.37	5.27	5.17	5.12	5.07	5.01	4.96	4.90	4.85	6
4.76	4.67	4.57	4.47	4.41	4.36	4.31	4.25	4.20	4.14	7
4.30	4.20	4.10	4.00	3.95	3.89	3.84	3.78	3.73	3.67	8
3.96	3.87	3.77	3.67	3.61	3.56	3.51	3.45	3.39	3.33	9
3.72	3.62	3.52	3.42	3.37	3.31	3.26	3.20	3.14	3.08	10
3.53	3.43	3.33	3.23	3.17	3.12	3.06	3.00	2.94	2.88	11
3.37	3.28	3.18	3.07	3.02	2.96	2.91	2.85	2.79	2.72	12
3.25	3.15	3.05	2.95	2.89	2.84	2.78	2.72	2.66	2.60	13
3.15	3.05	2.95	2.84	2.79	2.73	2.67	2.61	2.55	2.49	14
3.06	2.96	2.86	2.76	2.70	2.64	2.59	2.52	2.46	2.40	15
2.99	2.89	2.79	2.68	2.63	2.57	2.51	2.45	2.38	2.32	16
2.92	2.82	2.72	2.62	2.56	2.50	2.44	2.38	2.32	2.25	17
2.87	2.77	2.67	2.56	2.50	2.44	2.38	2.32	2.26	2.19	18
2.82	2.72	2.62	2.51	2.45	2.39	2.33	2.27	2.20	2.13	19
2.77	2.68	2.57	2.46	2.41	2.35	2.29	2.22	2.16	2.09	20
2.73	2.64	2.53	2.42	2.37	2.31	2.25	2.18	2.11	2.04	21
2.70	2.60	2.50	2.39	2.33	2.27	2.21	2.14	2.08	2.00	22
2.67	2.57	2.47	2.36	2.30	2.24	2.18	2.11	2.04	1.97	23
2.64	2.54	2.44	2.33	2.27	2.21	2.15	2.08	2.01	1.94	24
2.61	2.51	2.41	2.30	2.24	2.18	2.12	2.05	1.98	1.91	25
2.59	2.49	2.39	2.28	2.22	2.16	2.09	2.03	1.95	1.88	26
2.57	2.47	2.36	2.25	2.19	2.13	2.07	2.00	1.93	1.85	27
2.55	2.45	2.34	2.23	2.17	2.11	2.05	1.98	1.91	1.83	28
2.53	2.43	2.32	2.21	2.15	2.09	2.03	1.96	1.89	1.81	29
2.51	2.41	2.31	2.20	2.14	2.07	2.01	1.94	1.87	1.79	30
2.39	2.29	2.18	2.07	2.01	1.94	1.88	1.80	1.72	1.64	40
2.27	2.17	2.06	1.94	1.88	1.82	1.74	1.67	1.58	1.48	60
2.16	2.05	1.94	1.82	1.76	1.69	1.61	1.53	1.43	1.31	120
2.05	1.94	1.83	1.71	1.64	1.57	1.48	1.39	1.27	1.00	∞

Denominator Degrees of Freedom

(*continued*)

TABLE A.7   **Percentage Points of the *F* Distribution** (*continued*)

v_2 \ v_1	$\alpha = .01$ Numerator Degrees of Freedom								
	1	2	3	4	5	6	7	8	9
1	4052.18	4999.34	5403.53	5624.26	5763.96	5858.95	5928.33	5980.95	6022.40
2	98.50	99.00	99.16	99.25	99.30	99.33	99.36	99.38	99.39
3	34.12	30.82	29.46	28.71	28.24	27.91	27.67	27.49	27.34
4	21.20	18.00	16.69	15.98	15.52	15.21	14.98	14.80	14.66
5	16.26	13.27	12.06	11.39	10.97	10.67	10.46	10.29	10.16
6	13.75	10.92	9.78	9.15	8.75	8.47	8.26	8.10	7.98
7	12.25	9.55	8.45	7.85	7.46	7.19	6.99	6.84	6.72
8	11.26	8.65	7.59	7.01	6.63	6.37	6.18	6.03	5.91
9	10.56	8.02	6.99	6.42	6.06	5.80	5.61	5.47	5.35
10	10.04	7.56	6.55	5.99	5.64	5.39	5.20	5.06	4.94
11	9.65	7.21	6.22	5.67	5.32	5.07	4.89	4.74	4.63
12	9.33	6.93	5.95	5.41	5.06	4.82	4.64	4.50	4.39
13	9.07	6.70	5.74	5.21	4.86	4.62	4.44	4.30	4.19
14	8.86	6.51	5.56	5.04	4.69	4.46	4.28	4.14	4.03
15	8.68	6.36	5.42	4.89	4.56	4.32	4.14	4.00	3.89
16	8.53	6.23	5.29	4.77	4.44	4.20	4.03	3.89	3.78
17	8.40	6.11	5.19	4.67	4.34	4.10	3.93	3.79	3.68
18	8.29	6.01	5.09	4.58	4.25	4.01	3.84	3.71	3.60
19	8.18	5.93	5.01	4.50	4.17	3.94	3.77	3.63	3.52
20	8.10	5.85	4.94	4.43	4.10	3.87	3.70	3.56	3.46
21	8.02	5.78	4.87	4.37	4.04	3.81	3.64	3.51	3.40
22	7.95	5.72	4.82	4.31	3.99	3.76	3.59	3.45	3.35
23	7.88	5.66	4.76	4.26	3.94	3.71	3.54	3.41	3.30
24	7.82	5.61	4.72	4.22	3.90	3.67	3.50	3.36	3.26
25	7.77	5.57	4.68	4.18	3.85	3.63	3.46	3.32	3.22
26	7.72	5.53	4.64	4.14	3.82	3.59	3.42	3.29	3.18
27	7.68	5.49	4.60	4.11	3.78	3.56	3.39	3.26	3.15
28	7.64	5.45	4.57	4.07	3.75	3.53	3.36	3.23	3.12
29	7.60	5.42	4.54	4.04	3.73	3.50	3.33	3.20	3.09
30	7.56	5.39	4.51	4.02	3.70	3.47	3.30	3.17	3.07
40	7.31	5.18	4.31	3.83	3.51	3.29	3.12	2.99	2.89
60	7.08	4.98	4.13	3.65	3.34	3.12	2.95	2.82	2.72
120	6.85	4.79	3.95	3.48	3.17	2.96	2.79	2.66	2.56
∞	6.63	4.61	3.78	3.32	3.02	2.80	2.64	2.51	2.41

Denominator Degrees of Freedom

$\alpha = .01$										v_1
Numerator Degrees of Freedom										v_2
10	12	15	20	24	30	40	60	120	∞	
6055.93	6106.68	6156.97	6208.66	6234.27	6260.35	6286.43	6312.97	6339.51	6366.00	1
99.40	99.42	99.43	99.45	99.46	99.47	99.48	99.48	99.49	99.50	2
27.23	27.05	26.87	26.69	26.60	26.50	26.41	26.32	26.22	26.13	3
14.55	14.37	14.20	14.02	13.93	13.84	13.75	13.65	13.56	13.46	4
10.05	9.89	9.72	9.55	9.47	9.38	9.29	9.20	9.11	9.02	5
7.87	7.72	7.56	7.40	7.31	7.23	7.14	7.06	6.97	6.88	6
6.62	6.47	6.31	6.16	6.07	5.99	5.91	5.82	5.74	5.65	7
5.81	5.67	5.52	5.36	5.28	5.20	5.12	5.03	4.95	4.86	8
5.26	5.11	4.96	4.81	4.73	4.65	4.57	4.48	4.40	4.31	9
4.85	4.71	4.56	4.41	4.33	4.25	4.17	4.08	4.00	3.91	10
4.54	4.40	4.25	4.10	4.02	3.94	3.86	3.78	3.69	3.60	11
4.30	4.16	4.01	3.86	3.78	3.70	3.62	3.54	3.45	3.36	12
4.10	3.96	3.82	3.66	3.59	3.51	3.43	3.34	3.25	3.17	13
3.94	3.80	3.66	3.51	3.43	3.35	3.27	3.18	3.09	3.00	14
3.80	3.67	3.52	3.37	3.29	3.21	3.13	3.05	2.96	2.87	15
3.69	3.55	3.41	3.26	3.18	3.10	3.02	2.93	2.84	2.75	16
3.59	3.46	3.31	3.16	3.08	3.00	2.92	2.83	2.75	2.65	17
3.51	3.37	3.23	3.08	3.00	2.92	2.84	2.75	2.66	2.57	18
3.43	3.30	3.15	3.00	2.92	2.84	2.76	2.67	2.58	2.49	19
3.37	3.23	3.09	2.94	2.86	2.78	2.69	2.61	2.52	2.42	20
3.31	3.17	3.03	2.88	2.80	2.72	2.64	2.55	2.46	2.36	21
3.26	3.12	2.98	2.83	2.75	2.67	2.58	2.50	2.40	2.31	22
3.21	3.07	2.93	2.78	2.70	2.62	2.54	2.45	2.35	2.26	23
3.17	3.03	2.89	2.74	2.66	2.58	2.49	2.40	2.31	2.21	24
3.13	2.99	2.85	2.70	2.62	2.54	2.45	2.36	2.27	2.17	25
3.09	2.96	2.81	2.66	2.58	2.50	2.42	2.33	2.23	2.13	26
3.06	2.93	2.78	2.63	2.55	2.47	2.38	2.29	2.20	2.10	27
3.03	2.90	2.75	2.60	2.52	2.44	2.35	2.26	2.17	2.06	28
3.00	2.87	2.73	2.57	2.49	2.41	2.33	2.23	2.14	2.03	29
2.98	2.84	2.70	2.55	2.47	2.39	2.30	2.21	2.11	2.01	30
2.80	2.66	2.52	2.37	2.29	2.20	2.11	2.02	1.92	1.80	40
2.63	2.50	2.35	2.20	2.12	2.03	1.94	1.84	1.73	1.60	60
2.47	2.34	2.19	2.03	1.95	1.86	1.76	1.66	1.53	1.38	120
2.32	2.18	2.04	1.88	1.79	1.70	1.59	1.47	1.32	1.00	∞

Denominator Degrees of Freedom

(*continued*)

TABLE A.7   Percentage Points of the *F* Distribution (*continued*)

v_2 \ v_1	$\alpha = .005$ Numerator Degrees of Freedom								
	1	2	3	4	5	6	7	8	9
1	16212.46	19997.36	21614.13	22500.75	23055.82	23439.53	23715.20	23923.81	24091.45
2	198.50	199.01	199.16	199.24	199.30	199.33	199.36	199.38	199.39
3	55.55	49.80	47.47	46.20	45.39	44.84	44.43	44.13	43.88
4	31.33	26.28	24.26	23.15	22.46	21.98	21.62	21.35	21.14
5	22.78	18.31	16.53	15.56	14.94	14.51	14.20	13.96	13.77
6	18.63	14.54	12.92	12.03	11.46	11.07	10.79	10.57	10.39
7	16.24	12.40	10.88	10.05	9.52	9.16	8.89	8.68	8.51
8	14.69	11.04	9.60	8.81	8.30	7.95	7.69	7.50	7.34
9	13.61	10.11	8.72	7.96	7.47	7.13	6.88	6.69	6.54
10	12.83	9.43	8.08	7.34	6.87	6.54	6.30	6.12	5.97
11	12.23	8.91	7.60	6.88	6.42	6.10	5.86	5.68	5.54
12	11.75	8.51	7.23	6.52	6.07	5.76	5.52	5.35	5.20
13	11.37	8.19	6.93	6.23	5.79	5.48	5.25	5.08	4.94
14	11.06	7.92	6.68	6.00	5.56	5.26	5.03	4.86	4.72
15	10.80	7.70	6.48	5.80	5.37	5.07	4.85	4.67	4.54
16	10.58	7.51	6.30	5.64	5.21	4.91	4.69	4.52	4.38
17	10.38	7.35	6.16	5.50	5.07	4.78	4.56	4.39	4.25
18	10.22	7.21	6.03	5.37	4.96	4.66	4.44	4.28	4.14
19	10.07	7.09	5.92	5.27	4.85	4.56	4.34	4.18	4.04
20	9.94	6.99	5.82	5.17	4.76	4.47	4.26	4.09	3.96
21	9.83	6.89	5.73	5.09	4.68	4.39	4.18	4.01	3.88
22	9.73	6.81	5.65	5.02	4.61	4.32	4.11	3.94	3.81
23	9.63	6.73	5.58	4.95	4.54	4.26	4.05	3.88	3.75
24	9.55	6.66	5.52	4.89	4.49	4.20	3.99	3.83	3.69
25	9.48	6.60	5.46	4.84	4.43	4.15	3.94	3.78	3.64
26	9.41	6.54	5.41	4.79	4.38	4.10	3.89	3.73	3.60
27	9.34	6.49	5.36	4.74	4.34	4.06	3.85	3.69	3.56
28	9.28	6.44	5.32	4.70	4.30	4.02	3.81	3.65	3.52
29	9.23	6.40	5.28	4.66	4.26	3.98	3.77	3.61	3.48
30	9.18	6.35	5.24	4.62	4.23	3.95	3.74	3.58	3.45
40	8.83	6.07	4.98	4.37	3.99	3.71	3.51	3.35	3.22
60	8.49	5.79	4.73	4.14	3.76	3.49	3.29	3.13	3.01
120	8.18	5.54	4.50	3.92	3.55	3.28	3.09	2.93	2.81
∞	7.88	5.30	4.28	3.72	3.35	3.09	2.90	2.74	2.62

Denominator Degrees of Freedom

α = .005										v_1
Numerator Degrees of Freedom										
10	**12**	**15**	**20**	**24**	**30**	**40**	**60**	**120**	**∞**	v_2
24221.84	24426.73	24631.62	24836.51	24937.09	25041.40	25145.71	25253.74	25358.05	25465.00	1
199.39	199.42	199.43	199.45	199.45	199.48	199.48	199.48	199.49	199.50	2
43.68	43.39	43.08	42.78	42.62	42.47	42.31	42.15	41.99	41.83	3
20.97	20.70	20.44	20.17	20.03	19.89	19.75	19.61	19.47	19.32	4
13.62	13.38	13.15	12.90	12.78	12.66	12.53	12.40	12.27	12.14	5
10.25	10.03	9.81	9.59	9.47	9.36	9.24	9.12	9.00	8.88	6
8.38	8.18	7.97	7.75	7.64	7.53	7.42	7.31	7.19	7.08	7
7.21	7.01	6.81	6.61	6.50	6.40	6.29	6.18	6.06	5.95	8
6.42	6.23	6.03	5.83	5.73	5.62	5.52	5.41	5.30	5.19	9
5.85	5.66	5.47	5.27	5.17	5.07	4.97	4.86	4.75	4.64	10
5.42	5.24	5.05	4.86	4.76	4.65	4.55	4.45	4.34	4.23	11
5.09	4.91	4.72	4.53	4.43	4.33	4.23	4.12	4.01	3.90	12
4.82	4.64	4.46	4.27	4.17	4.07	3.97	3.87	3.76	3.65	13
4.60	4.43	4.25	4.06	3.96	3.86	3.76	3.66	3.55	3.44	14
4.42	4.25	4.07	3.88	3.79	3.69	3.59	3.48	3.37	3.26	15
4.27	4.10	3.92	3.73	3.64	3.54	3.44	3.33	3.22	3.11	16
4.14	3.97	3.79	3.61	3.51	3.41	3.31	3.21	3.10	2.98	17
4.03	3.86	3.68	3.50	3.40	3.30	3.20	3.10	2.99	2.87	18
3.93	3.76	3.59	3.40	3.31	3.21	3.11	3.00	2.89	2.78	19
3.85	3.68	3.50	3.32	3.22	3.12	3.02	2.92	2.81	2.69	20
3.77	3.60	3.43	3.24	3.15	3.05	2.95	2.84	2.73	2.61	21
3.70	3.54	3.36	3.18	3.08	2.98	2.88	2.77	2.66	2.55	22
3.64	3.47	3.30	3.12	3.02	2.92	2.82	2.71	2.60	2.48	23
3.59	3.42	3.25	3.06	2.97	2.87	2.77	2.66	2.55	2.43	24
3.54	3.37	3.20	3.01	2.92	2.82	2.72	2.61	2.50	2.38	25
3.49	3.33	3.15	2.97	2.87	2.77	2.67	2.56	2.45	2.33	26
3.45	3.28	3.11	2.93	2.83	2.73	2.63	2.52	2.41	2.29	27
3.41	3.25	3.07	2.89	2.79	2.69	2.59	2.48	2.37	2.25	28
3.38	3.21	3.04	2.86	2.76	2.66	2.56	2.45	2.33	2.21	29
3.34	3.18	3.01	2.82	2.73	2.63	2.52	2.42	2.30	2.18	30
3.12	2.95	2.78	2.60	2.50	2.40	2.30	2.18	2.06	1.93	40
2.90	2.74	2.57	2.39	2.29	2.19	2.08	1.96	1.83	1.69	60
2.71	2.54	2.37	2.19	2.09	1.98	1.87	1.75	1.61	1.43	120
2.52	2.36	2.19	2.00	1.90	1.79	1.67	1.53	1.36	1.00	∞

Denominator Degrees of Freedom

TABLE A.8   The Chi-Square Table

Values of χ^2 for Selected Probabilities

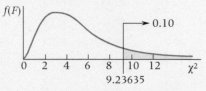

Example: df (Number of degrees of freedom) = 5, the tail above χ^2 = 9.23635 represents 0.10 or 10% of area under the curve.

Degrees of Freedom	Area in Upper Tail									
	.995	.99	.975	.95	.9	.1	.05	.025	.01	.005
1	0.0000393	0.0001571	0.0009821	0.0039322	0.0157907	2.7055	3.8415	5.0239	6.6349	7.8794
2	0.010025	0.020100	0.050636	0.102586	0.210721	4.6052	5.9915	7.3778	9.2104	10.5965
3	0.07172	0.11483	0.21579	0.35185	0.58438	6.2514	7.8147	9.3484	11.3449	12.8381
4	0.20698	0.29711	0.48442	0.71072	1.06362	7.7794	9.4877	11.1433	13.2767	14.8602
5	0.41175	0.55430	0.83121	1.14548	1.61031	9.2363	11.0705	12.8325	15.0863	16.7496
6	0.67573	0.87208	1.23734	1.63538	2.20413	10.6446	12.5916	14.4494	16.8119	18.5475
7	0.98925	1.23903	1.68986	2.16735	2.83311	12.0170	14.0671	16.0128	18.4753	20.2777
8	1.34440	1.64651	2.17972	2.73263	3.48954	13.3616	15.5073	17.5345	20.0902	21.9549
9	1.73491	2.08789	2.70039	3.32512	4.16816	14.6837	16.9190	19.0228	21.6660	23.5893
10	2.15585	2.55820	3.24696	3.94030	4.86518	15.9872	18.3070	20.4832	23.2093	25.1881
11	2.60320	3.05350	3.81574	4.57481	5.57779	17.2750	19.6752	21.9200	24.7250	26.7569
12	3.07379	3.57055	4.40378	5.22603	6.30380	18.5493	21.0261	23.3367	26.2170	28.2997
13	3.56504	4.10690	5.00874	5.89186	7.04150	19.8119	22.3620	24.7356	27.6882	29.8193
14	4.07466	4.66042	5.62872	6.57063	7.78954	21.0641	23.6848	26.1189	29.1412	31.3194
15	4.60087	5.22936	6.26212	7.26093	8.54675	22.3071	24.9958	27.4884	30.5780	32.8015
16	5.14216	5.81220	6.90766	7.96164	9.31224	23.5418	26.2962	28.8453	31.9999	34.2671
17	5.69727	6.40774	7.56418	8.67175	10.08518	24.7690	27.5871	30.1910	33.4087	35.7184
18	6.26477	7.01490	8.23074	9.39045	10.86494	25.9894	28.8693	31.5264	34.8052	37.1564
19	6.84392	7.63270	8.90651	10.11701	11.65091	27.2036	30.1435	32.8523	36.1908	38.5821
20	7.43381	8.26037	9.59077	10.85080	12.44260	28.4120	31.4104	34.1696	37.5663	39.9969
21	8.03360	8.89717	10.28291	11.59132	13.23960	29.6151	32.6706	35.4789	38.9322	41.4009
22	8.64268	9.54249	10.98233	12.33801	14.04149	30.8133	33.9245	36.7807	40.2894	42.7957
23	9.26038	10.19569	11.68853	13.09051	14.84795	32.0069	35.1725	38.0756	41.6383	44.1814
24	9.88620	10.85635	12.40115	13.84842	15.65868	33.1962	36.4150	39.3641	42.9798	45.5584
25	10.51965	11.52395	13.11971	14.61140	16.47341	34.3816	37.6525	40.6465	44.3140	46.9280
26	11.16022	12.19818	13.84388	15.37916	17.29188	35.5632	38.8851	41.9231	45.6416	48.2898
27	11.80765	12.87847	14.57337	16.15139	18.11389	36.7412	40.1133	43.1945	46.9628	49.6450
28	12.46128	13.56467	15.30785	16.92788	18.93924	37.9159	41.3372	44.4608	48.2782	50.9936
29	13.12107	14.25641	16.04705	17.70838	19.76774	39.0875	42.5569	45.7223	49.5878	52.3355
30	13.78668	14.95346	16.79076	18.49267	20.59924	40.2560	43.7730	46.9792	50.8922	53.6719
40	20.70658	22.16420	24.43306	26.50930	29.05052	51.8050	55.7585	59.3417	63.6908	66.7660
50	27.99082	29.70673	32.35738	34.76424	37.68864	63.1671	67.5048	71.4202	76.1538	79.4898
60	35.53440	37.48480	40.48171	43.18797	46.45888	74.3970	79.0820	83.2977	88.3794	91.9518
70	43.27531	45.44170	48.75754	51.73926	55.32894	85.5270	90.5313	95.0231	100.4251	104.2148
80	51.17193	53.53998	57.15315	60.39146	64.27784	96.5782	101.8795	106.6285	112.3288	116.3209
90	59.19633	61.75402	65.64659	69.12602	73.29108	107.5650	113.1452	118.1359	124.1162	128.2987
100	67.32753	70.06500	74.22188	77.92944	82.35813	118.4980	124.3221	129.5613	135.8069	140.1697

TABLE A.9   **Critical Values for the Durbin-Watson Test**

Entries in the table give the critical values for a one-tailed Durbin-Watson test for autocorrelation. For a two-tailed test, the level of significance is doubled.

	Significant Points of d_L and d_U: $\alpha = .05$ Number of Independent Variables									
k	1		2		3		4		5	
n	d_L	d_U	d_L	d_U	d_L	d_U	d_L	d_U	d_L	d_U
15	1.08	1.36	0.95	1.54	0.82	1.75	0.69	1.97	0.56	2.21
16	1.10	1.37	0.98	1.54	0.86	1.73	0.74	1.93	0.62	2.15
17	1.13	1.38	1.02	1.54	0.90	1.71	0.78	1.90	0.67	2.10
18	1.16	1.39	1.05	1.53	0.93	1.69	0.82	1.87	0.71	2.06
19	1.18	1.40	1.08	1.53	0.97	1.68	0.86	1.85	0.75	2.02
20	1.20	1.41	1.10	1.54	1.00	1.68	0.90	1.83	0.79	1.99
21	1.22	1.42	1.13	1.54	1.03	1.67	0.93	1.81	0.83	1.96
22	1.24	1.43	1.15	1.54	1.05	1.66	0.96	1.80	0.86	1.94
23	1.26	1.44	1.17	1.54	1.08	1.66	0.99	1.79	0.90	1.92
24	1.27	1.45	1.19	1.55	1.10	1.66	1.01	1.78	0.93	1.90
25	1.29	1.45	1.21	1.55	1.12	1.66	1.04	1.77	0.95	1.89
26	1.30	1.46	1.22	1.55	1.14	1.65	1.06	1.76	0.98	1.88
27	1.32	1.47	1.24	1.56	1.16	1.65	1.08	1.76	1.01	1.86
28	1.33	1.48	1.26	1.56	1.18	1.65	1.10	1.75	1.03	1.85
29	1.34	1.48	1.27	1.56	1.20	1.65	1.12	1.74	1.05	1.84
30	1.35	1.49	1.28	1.57	1.21	1.65	1.14	1.74	1.07	1.83
31	1.36	1.50	1.30	1.57	1.23	1.65	1.16	1.74	1.09	1.83
32	1.37	1.50	1.31	1.57	1.24	1.65	1.18	1.73	1.11	1.82
33	1.38	1.51	1.32	1.58	1.26	1.65	1.19	1.73	1.13	1.81
34	1.39	1.51	1.33	1.58	1.27	1.65	1.21	1.73	1.15	1.81
35	1.40	1.52	1.34	1.58	1.28	1.65	1.22	1.73	1.16	1.80
36	1.41	1.52	1.35	1.59	1.29	1.65	1.24	1.73	1.18	1.80
37	1.42	1.53	1.36	1.59	1.31	1.66	1.25	1.72	1.19	1.80
38	1.43	1.54	1.37	1.59	1.32	1.66	1.26	1.72	1.21	1.79
39	1.43	1.54	1.38	1.60	1.33	1.66	1.27	1.72	1.22	1.79
40	1.44	1.54	1.39	1.60	1.34	1.66	1.29	1.72	1.23	1.79
45	1.48	1.57	1.43	1.62	1.38	1.67	1.34	1.72	1.29	1.78
50	1.50	1.59	1.46	1.63	1.42	1.67	1.38	1.72	1.34	1.77
55	1.53	1.60	1.49	1.64	1.45	1.68	1.41	1.72	1.38	1.77
60	1.55	1.62	1.51	1.65	1.48	1.69	1.44	1.73	1.41	1.77
65	1.57	1.63	1.54	1.66	1.50	1.70	1.47	1.73	1.44	1.77
70	1.58	1.64	1.55	1.67	1.52	1.70	1.49	1.74	1.46	1.77
75	1.60	1.65	1.57	1.68	1.54	1.71	1.51	1.74	1.49	1.77
80	1.61	1.66	1.59	1.69	1.56	1.72	1.53	1.74	1.51	1.77
85	1.62	1.67	1.60	1.70	1.57	1.72	1.55	1.75	1.52	1.77
90	1.63	1.68	1.61	1.70	1.59	1.73	1.57	1.75	1.54	1.78
95	1.64	1.69	1.62	1.71	1.60	1.73	1.58	1.75	1.56	1.78
100	1.65	1.69	1.63	1.72	1.61	1.74	1.59	1.76	1.57	1.78

Adapted from J. Durbin and G. S. Watson, "Testing for Serial Correlation in Least Square Regression II," *Biometrika* 38 (1951): 159–78, Oxford University Press.

(*continued*)

TABLE A.9 **Critical Values for the Durbin-Watson Test** (*continued*)

	Significant Points of d_L and d_U: $\alpha = .01$ Number of Independent Variables									
k	**1**		**2**		**3**		**4**		**5**	
n	d_L	d_U	d_L	d_U	d_L	d_U	d_L	d_U	d_L	d_U
15	0.81	1.07	0.70	1.25	0.59	1.46	0.49	1.70	0.39	1.96
16	0.84	1.09	0.74	1.25	0.63	1.44	0.53	1.66	0.44	1.90
17	0.87	1.10	0.77	1.25	0.67	1.43	0.57	1.63	0.48	1.85
18	0.90	1.12	0.80	1.26	0.71	1.42	0.61	1.60	0.52	1.80
19	0.93	1.13	0.83	1.26	0.74	1.41	0.65	1.58	0.56	1.77
20	0.95	1.15	0.86	1.27	0.77	1.41	0.68	1.57	0.60	1.74
21	0.97	1.16	0.89	1.27	0.80	1.41	0.72	1.55	0.63	1.71
22	1.00	1.17	0.91	1.28	0.83	1.40	0.75	1.54	0.66	1.69
23	1.02	1.19	0.94	1.29	0.86	1.40	0.77	1.53	0.70	1.67
24	1.04	1.20	0.96	1.30	0.88	1.41	0.80	1.53	0.72	1.66
25	1.05	1.21	0.98	1.30	0.90	1.41	0.83	1.52	0.75	1.65
26	1.07	1.22	1.00	1.31	0.93	1.41	0.85	1.52	0.78	1.64
27	1.09	1.23	1.02	1.32	0.95	1.41	0.88	1.51	0.81	1.63
28	1.10	1.24	1.04	1.32	0.97	1.41	0.90	1.51	0.83	1.62
29	1.12	1.25	1.05	1.33	0.99	1.42	0.92	1.51	0.85	1.61
30	1.13	1.26	1.07	1.34	1.01	1.42	0.94	1.51	0.88	1.61
31	1.15	1.27	1.08	1.34	1.02	1.42	0.96	1.51	0.90	1.60
32	1.16	1.28	1.10	1.35	1.04	1.43	0.98	1.51	0.92	1.60
33	1.17	1.29	1.11	1.36	1.05	1.43	1.00	1.51	0.94	1.59
34	1.18	1.30	1.13	1.36	1.07	1.43	1.01	1.51	0.95	1.59
35	1.19	1.31	1.14	1.37	1.08	1.44	1.03	1.51	0.97	1.59
36	1.21	1.32	1.15	1.38	1.10	1.44	1.04	1.51	0.99	1.59
37	1.22	1.32	1.16	1.38	1.11	1.45	1.06	1.51	1.00	1.59
38	1.23	1.33	1.18	1.39	1.12	1.45	1.07	1.52	1.02	1.58
39	1.24	1.34	1.19	1.39	1.14	1.45	1.09	1.52	1.03	1.58
40	1.25	1.34	1.20	1.40	1.15	1.46	1.10	1.52	1.05	1.58
45	1.29	1.38	1.24	1.42	1.20	1.48	1.16	1.53	1.11	1.58
50	1.32	1.40	1.28	1.45	1.24	1.49	1.20	1.54	1.16	1.59
55	1.36	1.43	1.32	1.47	1.28	1.51	1.25	1.55	1.21	1.59
60	1.38	1.45	1.35	1.48	1.32	1.52	1.28	1.56	1.25	1.60
65	1.41	1.47	1.38	1.50	1.35	1.53	1.31	1.57	1.28	1.61
70	1.43	1.49	1.40	1.52	1.37	1.55	1.34	1.58	1.31	1.61
75	1.45	1.50	1.42	1.53	1.39	1.56	1.37	1.59	1.34	1.62
80	1.47	1.52	1.44	1.54	1.42	1.57	1.39	1.60	1.36	1.62
85	1.48	1.53	1.46	1.55	1.43	1.58	1.41	1.60	1.39	1.63
90	1.50	1.54	1.47	1.56	1.45	1.59	1.43	1.61	1.41	1.64
95	1.51	1.55	1.49	1.57	1.47	1.60	1.45	1.62	1.42	1.64
100	1.52	1.56	1.50	1.58	1.48	1.60	1.46	1.63	1.44	1.65

TABLE A.10   Critical Values of the Studentized Range (q) Distribution

Degrees of Freedom	$\alpha = .05$ Number of Populations																		
	2	3	4	5	6	7	8	9	10	11	12	13	14	15	16	17	18	19	20
1	18.0	27.0	32.8	37.1	40.4	43.1	45.4	47.4	49.1	50.6	52.0	53.2	54.3	55.4	56.3	57.2	58.0	58.8	59.6
2	6.08	8.33	9.80	10.9	11.7	12.4	13.0	13.5	14.0	14.4	14.7	15.1	15.4	15.7	15.9	16.1	16.4	16.6	16.8
3	4.50	5.91	6.82	7.50	8.04	8.48	8.85	9.18	9.46	9.72	9.95	10.2	10.3	10.5	10.7	10.8	11.0	11.1	11.2
4	3.93	5.04	5.76	6.29	6.71	7.05	7.35	7.60	7.83	8.03	8.21	8.37	8.52	8.66	8.79	8.91	9.03	9.13	9.23
5	3.64	4.60	5.22	5.67	6.03	6.33	6.58	6.80	6.99	7.17	7.32	7.47	7.60	7.72	7.83	7.93	8.03	8.12	8.21
6	3.46	4.34	4.90	5.30	5.63	5.90	6.12	6.32	6.49	6.65	6.79	6.92	7.03	7.14	7.24	7.34	7.43	7.51	7.59
7	3.34	4.16	4.68	5.06	5.36	5.61	5.82	6.00	6.16	6.30	6.43	6.55	6.66	6.76	6.85	6.94	7.02	7.10	7.17
8	3.26	4.04	4.53	4.89	5.17	5.40	5.60	5.77	5.92	6.05	6.18	6.29	6.39	6.48	6.57	6.65	6.73	6.80	6.87
9	3.20	3.95	4.41	4.76	5.02	5.24	5.43	5.59	5.74	5.87	5.98	6.09	6.19	6.28	6.36	6.44	6.51	6.58	6.64
10	3.15	3.88	4.33	4.65	4.91	5.12	5.30	5.46	5.60	5.72	5.83	5.93	6.03	6.11	6.19	6.27	6.34	6.40	6.47
11	3.11	3.82	4.26	4.57	4.82	5.03	5.20	5.35	5.49	5.61	5.71	5.81	5.90	5.98	6.06	6.13	6.20	6.27	6.33
12	3.08	3.77	4.20	4.51	4.75	4.95	5.12	5.27	5.39	5.51	5.61	5.71	5.80	5.88	5.95	6.02	6.09	6.15	6.21
13	3.06	3.73	4.15	4.45	4.69	4.88	5.05	5.19	5.32	5.43	5.53	5.63	5.71	5.79	5.86	5.93	5.99	6.05	6.11
14	3.03	3.70	4.11	4.41	4.64	4.83	4.99	5.13	5.25	5.36	5.46	5.55	5.64	5.71	5.79	5.85	5.91	5.97	6.03
15	3.01	3.67	4.08	4.37	4.59	4.78	4.94	5.08	5.20	5.31	5.40	5.49	5.57	5.65	5.72	5.78	5.85	5.90	5.96
16	3.00	3.65	4.05	4.33	4.56	4.74	4.90	5.03	5.15	5.26	5.35	5.44	5.52	5.59	5.66	5.73	5.79	5.84	5.90
17	2.98	3.63	4.02	4.30	4.52	4.70	4.86	4.99	5.11	5.21	5.31	5.39	5.47	5.54	5.61	5.67	5.73	5.79	5.84
18	2.97	3.61	4.00	4.28	4.49	4.67	4.82	4.96	5.07	5.17	5.27	5.35	5.43	5.50	5.57	5.63	5.69	5.74	5.79
19	2.96	3.59	3.98	4.25	4.47	4.65	4.79	4.92	5.04	5.14	5.23	5.31	5.39	5.46	5.53	5.59	5.65	5.70	5.75
20	2.95	3.58	3.96	4.23	4.45	4.62	4.77	4.90	5.01	5.11	5.20	5.28	5.36	5.43	5.49	5.55	5.61	5.66	5.71
24	2.92	3.53	3.90	4.17	4.37	4.54	4.68	4.81	4.92	5.01	5.10	5.18	5.25	5.32	5.38	5.44	5.49	5.55	5.59
30	2.89	3.49	3.85	4.10	4.30	4.46	4.60	4.72	4.82	4.92	5.00	5.08	5.15	5.21	5.27	5.33	5.38	5.43	5.47
40	2.86	3.44	3.79	4.04	4.23	4.39	4.52	4.63	4.73	4.82	4.90	4.98	5.04	5.11	5.16	5.22	5.27	5.31	5.36
60	2.83	3.40	3.74	3.98	4.16	4.31	4.44	4.55	4.65	4.73	4.81	4.88	4.94	5.00	5.06	5.11	5.15	5.20	5.24
120	2.80	3.36	3.68	3.92	4.10	4.24	4.36	4.47	4.56	4.64	4.71	4.78	4.84	4.90	4.95	5.00	5.04	5.09	5.13
∞	2.77	3.31	3.63	3.86	4.03	4.17	4.29	4.39	4.47	4.55	4.62	4.68	4.74	4.80	4.85	4.89	4.93	4.97	5.01

E. S. Pearson and H. O. Hartley, *Biometrika Tables for Statisticians,* vol. 1, 3rd edition, pp. 176–77. Copyright 1966, *Biometrika* Trustees.

(continued)

TABLE A.10 Critical Values of the Studentized Range (q) Distribution (continued)

	\multicolumn{19}{c}{$\alpha = .01$}
Degrees of Freedom	\multicolumn{19}{c}{Number of Populations}
	2	3	4	5	6	7	8	9	10	11	12	13	14	15	16	17	18	19	20
1	90.0	135.	164.	186.	202.	216.	227.	237.	246.	253.	260.	266.	272.	277.	282.	286.	290.	294.	298.
2	14.0	19.0	22.3	24.7	26.6	28.2	29.5	30.7	31.7	32.6	33.4	34.1	34.8	35.4	36.0	36.5	37.0	37.5	37.9
3	8.26	10.6	12.2	13.3	14.2	15.0	15.6	16.2	16.7	17.1	17.5	17.9	18.2	18.5	18.8	19.1	19.3	19.5	19.8
4	6.51	8.12	9.17	9.96	10.6	11.1	11.5	11.9	12.3	12.6	12.8	13.1	13.3	13.5	13.7	13.9	14.1	14.2	14.4
5	5.70	6.97	7.80	8.42	8.91	9.32	9.67	9.97	10.2	10.5	10.7	10.9	11.1	11.2	11.4	11.6	11.7	11.8	11.9
6	5.24	6.33	7.03	7.56	7.97	8.32	8.61	8.87	9.10	9.30	9.49	9.65	9.81	9.95	10.1	10.2	10.3	10.4	10.5
7	4.95	5.92	6.54	7.01	7.37	7.68	7.94	8.17	8.37	8.55	8.71	8.86	9.00	9.12	9.24	9.35	9.46	9.55	9.65
8	4.74	5.63	6.20	6.63	6.96	7.24	7.47	7.68	7.87	8.03	8.18	8.31	8.44	8.55	8.66	8.76	8.85	8.94	9.03
9	4.60	5.43	5.96	6.35	6.66	6.91	7.13	7.32	7.49	7.65	7.78	7.91	8.03	8.13	8.23	8.32	8.41	8.49	8.57
10	4.48	5.27	5.77	6.14	6.43	6.67	6.87	7.05	7.21	7.36	7.48	7.60	7.71	7.81	7.91	7.99	8.07	8.15	8.22
11	4.39	5.14	5.62	5.97	6.25	6.48	6.67	6.84	6.99	7.13	7.25	7.36	7.46	7.56	7.65	7.73	7.81	7.88	7.95
12	4.32	5.04	5.50	5.84	6.10	6.32	6.51	6.67	6.81	6.94	7.06	7.17	7.26	7.36	7.44	7.52	7.59	7.66	7.73
13	4.26	4.96	5.40	5.73	5.98	6.19	6.37	6.53	6.67	6.79	6.90	7.01	7.10	7.19	7.27	7.34	7.42	7.48	7.55
14	4.21	4.89	5.32	5.63	5.88	6.08	6.26	6.41	6.54	6.66	6.77	6.87	6.96	7.05	7.12	7.20	7.27	7.33	7.39
15	4.17	4.83	5.25	5.56	5.80	5.99	6.16	6.31	6.44	6.55	6.66	6.76	6.84	6.93	7.00	7.07	7.14	7.20	7.26
16	4.13	4.78	5.19	5.49	5.72	5.92	6.08	6.22	6.35	6.46	6.56	6.66	6.74	6.82	6.90	6.97	7.03	7.09	7.15
17	4.10	4.74	5.14	5.43	5.66	5.85	6.01	6.15	6.27	6.38	6.48	6.57	6.66	6.73	6.80	6.87	6.94	7.00	7.05
18	4.07	4.70	5.09	5.38	5.60	5.79	5.94	6.08	6.20	6.31	6.41	6.50	6.58	6.65	6.72	6.79	6.85	6.91	6.96
19	4.05	4.67	5.05	5.33	5.55	5.73	5.89	6.02	6.14	6.25	6.34	6.43	6.51	6.58	6.65	6.72	6.78	6.84	6.89
20	4.02	4.64	5.02	5.29	5.51	5.69	5.84	5.97	6.09	6.19	6.29	6.37	6.45	6.52	6.59	6.65	6.71	6.76	6.82
24	3.96	4.54	4.91	5.17	5.37	5.54	5.69	5.81	5.92	6.02	6.11	6.19	6.26	6.33	6.39	6.45	6.51	6.56	6.61
30	3.89	4.45	4.80	5.05	5.24	5.40	5.54	5.65	5.76	5.85	5.93	6.01	6.08	6.14	6.20	6.26	6.31	6.36	6.41
40	3.82	4.37	4.70	4.93	5.11	5.27	5.39	5.50	5.60	5.69	5.77	5.84	5.90	5.96	6.02	6.07	6.12	6.17	6.21
60	3.76	4.28	4.60	4.82	4.99	5.13	5.25	5.36	5.45	5.53	5.60	5.67	5.73	5.79	5.84	5.89	5.93	5.98	6.02
120	3.70	4.20	4.50	4.71	4.87	5.01	5.12	5.21	5.30	5.38	5.44	5.51	5.56	5.61	5.66	5.71	5.75	5.79	5.83
∞	3.64	4.12	4.40	4.60	4.76	4.88	4.99	5.08	5.16	5.23	5.29	5.35	5.40	5.45	5.49	5.54	5.57	5.61	5.65

TABLE A.11   Critical Values of R for the Runs Test: Lower Tail

n_1 \ n_2	2	3	4	5	6	7	8	9	10	11	12	13	14	15	16	17	18	19	20
													$\alpha = .025$						
2											2	2	2	2	2	2	2	2	2
3			2	2	2	2	2	2	2	2	2	2	2	3	3	3	3	3	3
4			2	2	2	3	3	3	3	3	3	3	3	3	4	4	4	4	4
5			2	2	3	3	3	3	3	4	4	4	4	4	4	4	5	5	5
6		2	2	3	3	3	3	4	4	4	4	5	5	5	5	5	5	6	6
7		2	2	3	3	3	4	4	5	5	5	5	5	6	6	6	6	6	6
8		2	3	3	3	4	4	5	5	5	6	6	6	6	6	7	7	7	7
9		2	3	3	4	4	5	5	5	6	6	6	7	7	7	7	8	8	8
10		2	3	3	4	5	5	5	6	6	7	7	7	7	8	8	8	8	9
11		2	3	4	4	5	5	6	6	7	7	7	8	8	8	9	9	9	9
12	2	2	3	4	4	5	6	6	7	7	7	8	8	8	9	9	9	10	10
13	2	2	3	4	5	5	6	6	7	7	8	8	9	9	9	10	10	10	10
14	2	2	3	4	5	5	6	7	7	8	8	9	9	9	10	10	10	11	11
15	2	3	3	4	5	6	6	7	7	8	8	9	9	10	10	11	11	11	12
16	2	3	4	4	5	6	6	7	8	8	9	9	10	10	11	11	11	12	12
17	2	3	4	4	5	6	7	7	8	9	9	10	10	11	11	11	12	12	13
18	2	3	4	5	5	6	7	8	8	9	9	10	10	11	11	12	12	13	13
19	2	3	4	5	6	6	7	8	8	9	10	10	11	11	12	12	13	13	13
20	2	3	4	5	6	6	7	8	9	9	10	10	11	12	12	13	13	13	14

Adapted from F. S. Swed and C. Eisenhart, "Tables for Testing Randomness of Grouping in a Sequence of Alternatives," *Annals of Mathematical Statistics* 14 (1943): 83–86.

TABLE A.12   Critical Values of R for the Runs Test: Upper Tail

n_1 \ n_2	2	3	4	5	6	7	8	9	10	11	12	13	14	15	16	17	18	19	20
													$\alpha = .025$						
2																			
3																			
4				9	9														
5			9	10	10	11	11												
6			9	10	11	12	12	13	13	13	13								
7			11	12	13	13	14	14	14	14	15	15	15						
8			11	12	13	14	14	15	15	16	16	16	16	17	17	17	17	17	17
9					13	14	14	15	16	16	16	17	17	18	18	18	18	18	18
10					13	14	15	16	16	17	17	18	18	18	19	19	19	20	20
11					13	14	15	16	17	17	18	19	19	19	20	20	20	21	21
12					13	14	16	16	17	18	19	19	20	20	21	21	21	22	22
13						15	16	17	18	19	19	20	20	21	21	22	22	23	23
14						15	16	17	18	19	20	20	21	22	22	23	23	23	24
15						15	16	18	18	19	20	21	22	22	23	23	24	24	25
16							17	18	19	20	21	21	22	23	23	24	25	25	25
17							17	18	19	20	21	22	23	23	24	25	25	26	26
18							17	18	19	20	21	22	23	24	25	25	26	26	27
19							17	18	20	21	22	23	23	24	25	26	26	27	27
20							17	18	20	21	22	23	24	25	25	26	27	27	28

TABLE A.13 p Values for Mann-Whitney U Statistic Small Samples ($n_1 \leq n_2$)

$n_2 = 3$ U_0	n_1 1	2	3		
0	.25	.10	.05		
1	.50	.20	.10		
2		.40	.20		
3		.60	.35		
4			.50		

$n_2 = 4$ U_0	n_1 1	2	3	4	
0	.2000	.0667	.0286	.0143	
1	.4000	.1333	.0571	.0286	
2	.6000	.2667	.1143	.0571	
3		.4000	.2000	.1000	
4		.6000	.3143	.1714	
5			.4286	.2429	
6			.5714	.3429	
7				.4429	
8				.5571	

$n_2 = 5$ U_0	n_1 1	2	3	4	5
0	.1667	.0476	.0179	.0079	.0040
1	.3333	.0952	.0357	.0159	.0079
2	.5000	.1905	.0714	.0317	.0159
3		.2857	.1250	.0556	.0278
4		.4286	.1964	.0952	.0476
5		.5714	.2857	.1429	.0754
6			.3929	.2063	.1111
7			.5000	.2778	.1548
8				.3651	.2103
9				.4524	.2738
10				.5476	.3452
11					.4206
12					.5000

Adapted from James E. Mendenhall and William Reinmuth, *Statistics for Management & Economics*, 5th edition. copyright 1986 South-Western, a part of Cengage Learning, Inc.

Answers to Selected Odd-Numbered Quantitative Problems

Chapter 1

1.7. a. ratio
b. ratio
c. ordinal
d. nominal
e. ordinal
f. ratio
g. nominal
h. ratio

1.9. a. 900 electric contractors
b. 35 contractors
c. average score for 35 participants
d. average score for all 900 electric contractors

Chapter 2

No answers given

Chapter 3

3.1. $\Sigma x = 333.6$
3.3. 39.4
3.5. 4
3.7. 107, 127, 145, 114, 127.5, 143.5
3.9. 3,024,149, 6,455,967.5, 2,337,237, 3,581,445, 6,793,714, 8,157,058
3.11. a. 8
b. 2.0408
c. 6.2041
d. 2.4908
e. 4
f. 0.69, −0.92, −0.11, 1.89, −1.32, −0.52, 0.29
3.13. a. 4.598
b. 4.598
3.15. 58,631.295, 242.139
3.17. a. .75
b. .84
c. .609
d. .902
3.19. a. 2.667
b. 11.06
c. 3.326
d. 5
e. −0.85
f. 37.65%
3.21. Between 113 and 137
Between 101 and 149
Between 89 and 161

3.23. 2.236
3.25. 95%, 2.5%, .15%, 16%
3.27. skewed right
3.29. 0.726; positively skewed
3.31. no mild or extreme outliers.
negatively skewed
3.33. Mean = 50.68
Std error = 1.187
Median = 51; mode = 44
Std dev = 11.86; Sample variance = 140.846
Kurtosis = −0.074; Skewness = −0.085
Range = 57
Min = 21; max = 78
Sum = 5,086; count = 100
3.35. 2.5, 2, 2, 7, 1, 3, 2
3.37. 6345.2, 5488.5, 4524, 6299.5, 10,441, 4485.5, 7741.5, 7769, 3256
3.39. a. 5.41, 4.1
b. 9.6, 2.9
c. 8.435, 2.904
d. 2.44, −0.04
e. 1.35
3.41. 10.78%, 6.43%
3.43. a. 392 to 446, 365 to 473, 338 to 500
b. 79.7%
c. −0.704
3.45. skewed right, median
3.47. 21.93, 18.14
3.49. High positive skewness to the right indicates a few advertisers in the Hispanic market who are spending extremely large numbers on advertising; data not normally distributed
3.51. Positive skewness; data not normally distributed since less than one standard deviation between the mean and minimum

Chapter 4

4.1. 15, .60
4.3. {4, 8, 10, 14, 16, 18, 20, 22, 26, 28, 30}
4.5. 20, combinations, .60
4.7. a. 38,760
b. 720
4.9. a. .7167
b. .5000
c. .6500
d. .5167
4.11. not solvable
4.13. a. .86
b. .31
c. .14

4.15. a. .2807
b. .0526
c. .0000
d. .0000
4.17. a. .0122
b. .0144
4.19. a. .44
b. .056
c. .054
d. .392
e. .498
f. .392
g. .498
4.21. a. .039
b. .571
c. .129
4.23. a. .2286
b. .2297
c. .3231
d. .0000
4.25. not independent
4.27. a. .4054
b. .3261
c. .4074
d. .32
4.29. a. .664
b. .906
c. .17
d. .530
e. .4087
4.31. .0538, .5161, .4301
4.33. .7941, .2059
4.35. a. .4211
b. .6316
c. .2105
d. .1250
e. .5263
f. .0000
g. .6667
h. .0000
4.37. a. .08974
b. .0000; A & B are mutually exclusive
c. .28205
d. .0000; mutually exclusive
e. .36364
f. .38095
g. .46154
h. .02513
4.39. a. .91
b. .09
c. .3462
d. .13
4.41. a. .032
b. .00629
c. .20
d. .0366
e. .7607
4.43. a. .20
b. .70
c. .05
d. .30
e. .45

4.45. a. .312
b. .572
c. .9176
d. .22
e. .9533
4.47. a. .21
b. .00; mutually exclusive
c. .00
d. .81
4.49. a. .42
b. .53
c. .0000
d. .5281
4.51. .3291, .0623
4.53. .11368, .12095, .13015, .63521

Chapter 5

5.1. 2.666, 1.8364, 1.3552
5.3. 0.956, 1.1305
5.5. a. .0036
b. .1147
c. .3822
d. .5838
5.7. a. 14, 2.05
b. 24.5, 3.99
c. 50, 5
5.9. a. .1356
b. .0032
c. .113
5.11. a. .585
b. .009
c. .013
5.13. a. .1032
b. .000
c. .0352
d. .348
5.15. a. .0538
b. .1539
c. .4142
d. .0672
e. .0244
f. .3702
5.17. a. 6.3, 2.51
b. 1.3, 1.14
c. 8.9, 2.98
d. 0.6, .775
5.19. 3.5
a. .0302
b. .1424
c. .0817
d. .42
e. .1009
5.21. a. .5488
b. .3293
c. .1220
d. .8913
e. .1912
5.23. a. .3012
b. .0000
c. .0336

5.25. a. .0104
b. .0000
c. .1653
d. .9636

5.27. a. .5091
b. .2937
c. .4167
d. .0014

5.29. a. .3756
b. .0002
c. .1486

5.31. a. .4286
b. .0714
c. .1143

5.33. .0474

5.35. a. .124
b. .849
c. .090
d. .000

5.37. a. .1607
b. .7626
c. .3504
d. .5429

5.39. .111, .017, 5, .180, .125, .000, .056, 8, 8

5.41. a. .2644
b. .0694
c. .0029
d. .7521

5.43. a. 3.52
b. .1098

5.45. a. .0687
b. .020
c. .1032
d. 2.28

5.47. .174

5.49. .5488, .0232, .3012

5.51. a. .0002
b. .0595
c. .2330

5.53. a. .0907
b. .0358
c. .1517
d. .8781

5.55. .0703

5.57. a. .2098
b. .0010
c. .2697

Chapter 6

6.1. a. 0.25
b. 220, 11.547
c. .250
d. .375
e. .625

6.3. 2.97, 0.098, .2941

6.5. 981.5, .000294, .2353, .0000, .2353

6.7. a. .7088
b. .0099
c. .5042
d. .1030
e. .6772
f. .1093

6.9. a. .0087
b. .6855
c. .2008
d. .0559

6.11. a. .9050
b. .0132
c. .1308
d. 17,293.23
e. $25,440

6.13. 2100, 2558

6.15. 22.98 minutes

6.17. a. $P(x \leq 16.5 \mid \mu = 21$ and $\sigma = 2.51)$
b. $P(10.5 \leq x \leq 20.5 \mid \mu = 12.5$ and $\sigma = 2.5)$
c. $P(21.5 \leq x \leq 22.5 \mid \mu = 24$ and $\sigma = 3.10)$
d. $P(x \geq 14.5 \mid \mu = 7.2$ and $\sigma = 1.99)$

6.19. a. .1170, .120
b. .4090, .415
c. .1985, .196
d. fails test

6.21. .0495

6.23. a. .1210
b. .7397
c. .0087
d. .0822

6.27. a. .0012
b. .8700
c. .0011
d. .9918

6.29. a. .0000
b. .0000
c. .0872
d. .41 minutes

6.31. 113, .01209, .8290

6.33. 15, 15, .1254

6.35. a. .1587
b. .0013
c. .6915
d. .9270
e. .0000

6.37. a. .0202
b. .9817
c. .1849
d. .4449

6.39. .0071

6.41. a. .0537
b. .0013
c. .1535

6.43. .5319, 41.5, .0213

6.45. a. .2119
b. .6284
c. .3617
d. .0028

6.47. a. .1251
b. .1131
c. .9913
d. .6115

6.49. a. .0009
b. .8790
c. .3458

6.51. a. .3594
b. .2887
c. .9761

6.53. $11,428.57

6.55. .5488, .2592, 1.67 months

6.57. 1940, 2018.75, 2269

6.59. .0401, .0132

Chapter 7

7.7. 825

7.13. a. .0548
  b. .7881
  c. .0082
  d. .8575
  e. .1664

7.15. 11.11

7.17. a. .9772
  b. .2385
  c. .1469
  d. .1230

7.19. .0000

7.21. a. .0268
  b. .00003
  c. .0000
  d. 11.78

7.23. a. .1492
  b. .9404
  c. .6985
  d. .1445
  e. .0000

7.25. .26

7.27. a. .9960
  b. .00003
  c. .1190

7.29. a. .1020
  b. .7568
  c. .7019

7.31. 55, 45, 90, 25, 35

7.37. a. .3156
  b. .00003
  c. .1736

7.41. a. .0021
  b. .9265
  c. .0281

7.43. a. .0025
  b. .0367
  c. .2181
  d. .1020
  e. .0005

7.45. a. .9564
  b. .0409
  c. .0023

7.49. .1461, .0000, .0000

7.51. .9394

Chapter 8

8.1. a. $24.11 \leq \mu \leq 25.89$
  b. $113.17 \leq \mu \leq 126.03$
  c. $3.136 \leq \mu \leq 3.702$
  d. $54.55 \leq \mu \leq 58.85$

8.3. $45.92 \leq \mu \leq 48.08$

8.5. 66, $62.75 \leq \mu \leq 69.25$

8.7. 5.3, $5.13 \leq \mu \leq 5.47$

8.9. $2.852 \leq \mu \leq 3.760$

8.11. 24.511, 1.497, $23.014 \leq \mu \leq 26.008$

8.13. $42.18 \leq \mu \leq 49.06$

8.15. $120.6 \leq \mu \leq 136.2$, 128.4

8.17. $15.631 \leq \mu \leq 16.545$, 16.088

8.19. $2.26886 \leq \mu \leq 2.45346$, 2.36116, .0923

8.21. $36.77 \leq \mu \leq 62.83$

8.23. $7.53 \leq \mu \leq 14.67$

8.25. a. $.316 \leq p \leq .704$
  b. $.777 \leq p \leq .863$
  c. $.456 \leq p \leq .504$
  d. $.246 \leq p \leq .394$

8.27. $.38 \leq p \leq .56$
  $.36 \leq p \leq .58$
  $.33 \leq p \leq .61$

8.29. $.4287 \leq p \leq .5113$
  $.2488 \leq p \leq .3112$

8.31. a. .266
  b. $.247 \leq p \leq .285$

8.33. $.5935 \leq p \leq .6665$

8.35. a. $18.46 \leq \sigma^2 \leq 189.73$
  b. $0.64 \leq \sigma^2 \leq 7.46$
  c. $645.45 \leq \sigma^2 \leq 1923.10$
  d. $12.61 \leq \sigma^2 \leq 31.89$

8.37. $9.71 \leq \sigma^2 \leq 46.03$, 18.49

8.39. 26,798,241.76, $14,084,038.51 \leq \sigma^2 \leq 69,553,848.45$

8.41. a. 2522
  b. 601
  c. 268
  d. 16,577

8.43. 106

8.45. 1,083

8.47. 97

8.49. 12.03, $11.78 \mu \leq 12.28$, $11.72 \leq \mu \leq 12.34$, $11.58 \leq \mu \leq 12.48$

8.51. $29.133 \leq \sigma^2 \leq 148.235$, $25.911 \leq \sigma^2 \leq 182.529$

8.53. $9.19 \leq \mu \leq 12.34$

8.55. $2.307 \leq \sigma^2 \leq 15.374$

8.57. $36.231 \leq \mu \leq 38.281$

8.59. $.542 \leq p \leq .596$, .569

8.61. $5.892 \leq \mu \leq 7.542$

8.63. $.726 \leq p \leq .814$

8.65. $34.11 \leq \mu \leq 53.29$, $101.44 \leq \sigma^2 \leq 821.35$

8.67. $-0.20 \leq \mu \leq 5.16$, 2.48

8.69. 543

8.71. $.00013 \leq \sigma^2 \leq .00037$

8.73. $.213 \leq p \leq .247$

Chapter 9

9.1. a. Two-tailed test
  b. One-tailed test
  c. One-tailed test
  d. Two-tailed test

9.3. a. $z = 2.77$, reject
  b. .0028, reject
  c. 22.115, 27.885

9.5. a. $z = 1.59$, reject
  b. .0559, reject
  c. 1212.04

9.7. $z = 1.84$, fail to reject

9.9. $z = 1.46$, fail to reject

9.11. $z = 2.64$, reject, .0041

9.13. $t = 0.56$, fail to reject

9.15. $t = 2.44$, reject

about the population and is particularly applicable to nominal- and ordinal-level data.

nonrandom sampling   Sampling in which not every unit of the population has the same probability of being selected into the sample.

nonrandom sampling techniques   Sampling techniques used to select elements from the population by any mechanism that does not involve a random selection process.

nonrejection region   Any portion of a distribution that is not in the rejection region. If the observed statistic falls in this region, the decision is to fail to reject the null hypothesis.

nonsampling errors   All errors other than sampling errors.

normal distribution   A widely known and much-used continuous distribution that fits the measurements of many human characteristics and many machine-produced items.

null hypothesis   The hypothesis that assumes the status quo—that the old theory, method, or standard is still true; the complement of the *alternative hypothesis.*

observed significance level   Another name for the p-*value* method of testing hypotheses.

observed value   A statistic computed from data gathered in an experiment that is used in the determination of whether or not to reject the null hypothesis.

ogive   A cumulative frequency polygon; plotted by graphing a dot at each class endpoint for the cumulative or decumulative frequency value and connecting the dots.

one-tailed test   A statistical test wherein the researcher is interested only in testing one side of the distribution.

one-way analysis of variance (ANOVA)   The process used to analyze a completely randomized experimental design. This process involves computing a ratio of the variance between treatment levels of the independent variable to the error variance. This ratio is an F value, which is then used to determine whether there are any significant differences between the means of the treatment levels.

operating characteristic (OC) curve   In hypothesis testing, a graph of Type II error probabilities for various possible values of an alternative hypothesis.

opportunity loss table   A decision table constructed by subtracting all payoffs for a given state of nature from the maximum payoff for that state of nature and doing this for all states of nature; displays the lost opportunities or regret that would occur for a given decision alternative if that particular state of nature occurred.

ordinal-level data   Next-higher level of data from nominal-level data; can be used to order or rank items, objects, or people.

outliers   Data points that lie apart from the rest of the points.

p chart   A quality control chart for attribute compliance that graphs the proportion of sample items in noncompliance with specifications for multiple samples.

p-value   A method of testing hypotheses in which there is no preset level of α. The probability of getting a test statistic at least as extreme as the observed test statistic is computed under the assumption that the null hypothesis is true. This probability is called the *p*-value, and it is the smallest value of α for which the null hypothesis can be rejected.

Paasche price index   A type of weighted aggregate price index in which the quantity values used in the calculations are from the year of interest.

parameter   A descriptive measure of the population.

parametric statistics   A class of statistical techniques that contains assumptions about the population and that is used only with interval- and ratio-level data.

Pareto analysis   A quantitative tallying of the number and types of defects that occur with a product or service, often recorded in a Pareto chart.

Pareto chart   A vertical bar chart in which the number and types of defects for a product or service are graphed in order of magnitude from greatest to least.

partial regression coefficient   The coefficient of an independent variable in a multiple regression model that represents the increase that will occur in the value of the dependent variable from a one-unit increase in the independent variable if all other variables are held constant.

payoff table   A matrix that displays the decision alternatives, the states of nature, and the payoffs for a particular decision-making problem. Also called a *decision table.*

payoffs   The benefits or rewards that result from selecting a particular decision alternative.

Pearson product-moment correlation coefficient   A measure of the linear correlation of two variables.

percentiles   Measures of central tendency that divide a group of data into 100 parts.

permutations   Distinct sequences of k objects that could be selected from a set of objects in which order matters.

pie chart   A circular depiction of data where the area of the whole pie represents 100% of the data being studied and slices represent a percentage breakdown of the sublevels.

platykurtic   A term to describe distributions that are flat and spread out.

point estimate   An estimate of a population parameter constructed from a statistic taken from a sample.

Poisson distribution   A discrete distribution that is constructed from the probability of occurrence of rare events over an interval; focuses only on the number of discrete occurrences over some interval or continuum.

poka-yoke   A quality concept (meaning "mistake proofing") that uses devices, methods, or inspections in order to avoid machine error or simple human error.

population   A collection of persons, objects, or items of interest.

post hoc   A term referring to after the experiment; pairwise comparisons made by the researcher *after* determining that there is a significant overall F value from ANOVA. Also called *a posteriori.*

power   The probability of rejecting a false null hypothesis.

power curve   A graph that plots the power values against various values of the alternative hypothesis.

prediction interval   A range of values used in regression analysis to estimate a single value of y for a given value of $x.$

predictive analytics   The second step in the analytics process, which finds relationships in data that are not readily apparent with descriptive analytics. It can find patterns or relationships that are extrapolated forward in time and can be used to make predictions about the future. Building and assessing algorithmic models aimed at making empirical rather than theoretical predictions, it can provide answers that move beyond using the historical data as the principal basis for decisions.

prescriptive analytics   Following descriptive and predictive analytics in an attempt to find the best course of action under certain circumstances, this is the final stage of business analytics. The goal of prescriptive analytics, which is still in its early stages of development, is to examine current trends and likely forecasts and use that information to make better decisions. It takes uncertainty into account, recommends ways to mitigate risks, and tries to see what the effect of future decisions will be in order to adjust the decisions before they are made. It involves using a set of mathematical techniques that computationally determine the optimal action of decision-making given a complex set of objectives, requirements, and constraints.

probabilistic model   A model that includes an error term that allows for various values of output to occur for a given value of input.

probability matrix   A two-dimensional table that displays the marginal and intersection probabilities of a given problem.

process   A series of actions, changes, or functions that bring about a result.

product quality   A view of quality in which quality is measurable in the product based on the fact that there are perceived differences in products and that quality products possess more attributes.

proportionate stratified random sampling A type of stratified random sampling in which the proportions of the items selected for the sample from the strata reflect the proportions of the strata in the population.

quadratic regression model A multiple regression model in which the predictors are a variable and the square of the variable.

qualitative variable Another name for a *dummy* or *indicator variable*; it represents whether or not a given item or person possesses a certain characteristic and is usually coded as 0 or 1.

quality What a product achieves when it delivers what is stipulated in its specifications.

quality control The collection of strategies, techniques, and actions taken by an organization to ensure the production of quality products.

quartiles Measures of central tendency that divide a group of data into four subgroups or parts.

quota sampling A nonrandom sampling technique in which the population is stratified on some characteristic and then elements selected for the sample are chosen by nonrandom processes.

R **chart** A plot of sample ranges used in quality control.

random sampling Sampling in which every unit of the population has the same probability of being selected for the sample.

random variable A variable that contains the outcomes of a chance experiment.

randomized block design An experimental design in which there is one independent variable of interest and a second variable, known as a blocking variable, that is used to control for confounding or concomitant variables.

range The difference between the largest and the smallest values in a set of numbers.

ratio-level data Highest level of data measurement; contains the same properties as interval-level data, with the additional property that zero has meaning and represents the absence of the phenomenon being measured.

rectangular distribution A relatively simple continuous distribution in which the same height is obtained over a range of values. Also called the *uniform distribution*.

reengineering A radical approach to total quality management in which the core business processes of a company are redesigned.

regression analysis The process of constructing a mathematical model or function that can be used to predict or determine one variable by any other variable.

rejection region The portion of a distribution in which a computed statistic lies that will result in the decision to reject the null hypothesis.

relative frequency The proportion of the total frequencies that fall into any given class interval in a frequency distribution.

relative frequency of occurrence method The method of assigning probability based on cumulated historical data.

repeated measures design A randomized block design in which each block level is an individual item or person, and that person or item is measured across all treatments.

research hypothesis A statement of what the researcher believes will be the outcome of an experiment or a study.

residual The difference between the actual *y* value and the *y* value predicted by the regression model; the error of the regression model in predicting each value of the dependent variable.

residual plot A type of graph in which the residuals for a particular regression model are plotted along with their associated values of *x*.

response plane A plane that is fit in a three-dimensional space and that represents the response surface defined by a multiple regression model with two independent first-order variables.

response surface The surface defined by a multiple regression model.

response variable The dependent variable in a multiple regression model; the variable that the researcher is trying to predict.

risk avoider A decision-maker who avoids risk whenever possible and is willing to drop out of a game when given the chance even when the payoff is less than the expected monetary value.

risk taker A decision-maker who enjoys taking risks and will not drop out of a game unless the payoff is more than the expected monetary value.

robust A term that describes a statistical technique that is relatively insensitive to minor violations in one or more of its underlying assumptions.

runs test A nonparametric test of randomness used to determine whether the order or sequence of observations in a sample is random.

sample A portion of the whole.

sample proportion The quotient of the frequency at which a given characteristic occurs in a sample and the number of items in the sample.

sample-size estimation An estimate of the size of sample necessary to fulfill the requirements of a particular level of confidence and to be within a specified amount of error.

sample space A complete roster or listing of all elementary events for an experiment.

sampling error Error that occurs when the sample is not representative of the population.

scatter plot (chart) A plot or graph of the pairs of data from a simple regression analysis.

search procedures Processes whereby more than one multiple regression model is developed for a given database, and the models are compared and sorted by different criteria, depending on the given procedure.

seasonal effects Patterns of data behaviour that occur in periods of time of less than one year, often measured by the month.

serial correlation A problem that arises in regression analysis when the error terms of a regression model are correlated due to time-series data. Also called *autocorrelation*.

set notation The use of braces to group numbers that have some specified characteristic.

simple average The arithmetic mean or average for the values of a given number of time periods of data.

simple average model A forecasting averaging model in which the forecast for the next time period is the average of values for a given number of previous time periods.

simple index number A number determined by computing the ratio of a quantity, price, or cost for a particular year of interest to the quantity, price, or cost of a base year, expressed as a percentage.

simple random sampling The most elementary of the random sampling techniques; involves numbering each item in the population and using a list or roster of random numbers to select items for the sample.

simple regression Bivariate, linear regression.

Six Sigma A total quality management approach that measures the capability of a process to perform defect-free work, where a defect is defined as anything that results in customer dissatisfaction.

skewness The lack of symmetry of a distribution of values.

smoothing techniques Forecasting techniques that produce forecasts based on levelling out the irregular fluctuation effects in time-series data.

snowball sampling A nonrandom sampling technique in which survey subjects who fit a desired profile are selected based on referral from other survey respondents who also fit the desired profile.

Spearman's rank correlation A measure of the correlation of two variables; used when only ordinal-level or ranked data are available.

standard deviation The square root of the variance.

standard error of the estimate (s_e) A standard deviation of the error of a regression model.

standard error of the mean The standard deviation of the distribution of sample means.

standard error of the proportion The standard deviation of the distribution of sample proportions.

standardized normal distribution *z* distribution; a distribution of *z* scores produced for values from a normal distribution with a mean of 0 and a standard deviation of 1.

states of nature The occurrences of nature that can happen after a decision has been made that can affect the outcome of the decision and over which the decision-maker has little or no control.

stationary A term to describe time-series data that contain no trend, cyclical, or seasonal effects.

statistic A descriptive measure of a sample.

statistical hypothesis A formal hypothesis structure set up with a null and an alternative hypothesis to scientifically test research hypotheses.

statistics A science dealing with the collection, analysis, interpretation, and presentation of numerical data.

stem-and-leaf plot A plot of numbers constructed by separating each number into two groups, a stem and a leaf. The leftmost digits are the stems and the rightmost digits are the leaves.

stepwise regression A step-by-step multiple regression search procedure that begins by developing a regression model with a single predictor variable and adds and deletes predictors one step at a time, examining the fit of the model at each step until there are no more significant predictors remaining outside the model.

stratified random sampling A type of random sampling in which the population is divided into various non-overlapping strata and then items are randomly selected into the sample from each stratum.

subjective method A method of assigning probabilities based on the intuition or reasoning of the person determining the probability.

substantive result What occurs when the outcome of a statistical study produces results that are important to the decision-maker.

sum of squares of error (SSE) The sum of the residuals squared for a regression model.

sum of squares of x The sum of the squared deviations about the mean of a set of values.

systematic sampling A random sampling technique in which every kth item or person is selected from the population.

t distribution A distribution that describes the sample data in small samples when the standard deviation is unknown and the population is normally distributed.

t test for related measures A t test to test the differences in two related or matched samples; sometimes called the *matched-pairs test* or the *correlated* t *test*.

t value The computed value of t used to reach statistical conclusions regarding the null hypothesis in small-sample analysis.

time-series data Data gathered on a given characteristic over a period of time at regular intervals.

total quality management (TQM) A program that occurs when all members of an organization are involved in improving quality; all goals and objectives of the organization come under the purview of quality control and are measured in quality terms.

transcendent quality A view of quality that implies that a product has an innate excellence, uncompromising standards, and high achievement.

treatment variable The independent variable of an experimental design that the researcher either controls or modifies.

trend Long-run general direction of a business climate over a period of several years.

Tukey-Kramer procedure A modification of the Tukey HSD multiple comparison procedure; used when there are unequal sample sizes.

Tukey's four-quadrant approach A graphical method using the four quadrants for determining which expressions of Tukey's ladder of transformations to use.

Tukey's honestly significant difference (HSD) test In analysis of variance, a technique used for pairwise a posteriori multiple comparisons to determine if there are significant differences between the means of any pair of treatment levels in an experimental design. This test requires equal sample sizes and uses a q value along with the mean square error in its computation.

Tukey's ladder of transformations A process used for determining ways to recode data in multiple regression analysis to achieve potential improvement in the predictability of the model.

two-stage sampling Cluster sampling done in two stages: A first round of samples is taken and then a second round is taken from within the first samples.

two-tailed test A statistical test wherein the researcher is interested in testing both sides of the distribution.

two-way analysis of variance (ANOVA) The process used to statistically test the effects of variables in factorial designs with two independent variables.

Type I error An error committed by rejecting a true null hypothesis.

Type II error An error committed by failing to reject a false null hypothesis.

ungrouped data Raw data, or data that have not been summarized in any way.

uniform distribution A relatively simple continuous distribution in which the same height is obtained over a range of values. Also called the *rectangular distribution*.

union A new set of elements formed by combining the elements of two or more other sets.

union probability The probability of one event occurring or the other event occurring or both occurring.

unweighted aggregate price index number The ratio of the sum of the prices of a market basket of items for a particular year to the sum of the prices of those same items in a base year, expressed as a percentage.

upper bound of the confidence interval What results when the margin of error is added to the point estimate.

upper control limit (UCL) The top-end line of a control chart, usually situated approximately three standard deviations of the statistic above the centreline; data points above this line indicate quality control problems.

user quality A view of quality in which the quality of the product is determined by the user.

utility The degree of pleasure or displeasure a decision-maker has in being involved in the outcome selection process given the risks and opportunities available.

value quality A view of quality having to do with price and costs and whether the consumer got his or her money's worth.

value-stream mapping A lean technique used to identify all activities required to produce a product or service from start to finish.

variable A characteristic of any entity being studied that is capable of taking on different values.

variance The average of the squared deviations around the arithmetic mean for a set of numbers.

variance inflation factor (VIF) A statistic computed using the R^2 value of a regression model developed by predicting one independent variable of a regression analysis by other independent variables; used to determine whether there is multicollinearity among the variables.

variety Refers to the many different forms of data available from a wide diversity of data sources that can be structured or unstructured.

velocity Refers to the speed at which the data are available and at which the data can be processed.

veracity Has to do with the quality, correctness, and accuracy of data.

volume Has to do with the ever-increasing size of data and databases.

weighted aggregate price index number A price index computed by multiplying quantity weights and item prices and summing the products to determine a market basket's worth in a given year and then determining the ratio of the market basket's worth in the year of interest to the same value computed for a base year, expressed as a percentage.

weighted moving average A moving average in which different weights are applied to the data values from different time periods.

Wilcoxon matched-pairs signed rank test A nonparametric alternative to the t test for two related or dependent samples.

$\bar{x}$ **chart** A quality control chart for measurements that graphs the sample means computed for a series of small random samples over a period of time.

z **distribution** A distribution of z scores; a normal distribution with a mean of 0 and a standard deviation of 1.

z **score** The number of standard deviations a value (x) is above or below the mean of a set of numbers when the data are normally distributed.

Note: Page numbers followed by *f* indicate figures; those followed by *n* indicate footnotes; those followed by *t* indicate tables.